Aesthetics and the Philosophy of Art – The Analytic Tradition

An Anthology

Edited by

Peter Lamarque and Stein Haugom Olsen

Blackwell
Publishing

Editorial material and organization © 2004 by Blackwell Publishing Ltd

BLACKWELL PUBLISHING
350 Main Street, Malden, MA 02148-5020, USA
9600 Garsington Road, Oxford OX4 2DQ, UK
550 Swanston Street, Carlton, Victoria 3053, Australia

The right of Peter Lamarque and Stein Haugom Olsen to be identified as the Authors of the Editorial Material in this Work has been asserted in accordance with the UK Copyright, Designs, and Patents Act 1988.

First published 2004 by Blackwell Publishing Ltd

3   2005

Library of Congress Cataloging-in-Publication Data

Aesthetics and the philosophy of art : the analytic tradition : an anthology / edited by Peter Lamarque and Stein Haugom Olsen.
    p. cm. – (Blackwell philosophy anthologies ; 21)
Includes bibliographical references and index.
ISBN 1-4051-0581-X (hardcover : alk. paper) – ISBN 1-4051-0582-8 (pbk. : alk. paper)
    1. Aesthetics. 2. Art – Philosophy. I. Lamarque, Peter. II. Olsen, Stein Haugom, 1946– III. Series.
BH39.A296 2003
111'.85'09045 – dc21

2002155979

ISBN-13: 978-1-4051-0581-1 (hardcover : alk. paper) – ISBN-13: 978-1-4051-0582-8 (pbk. : alk. paper)

A catalogue record for this title is available from the British Library.

Set in 9/11 pt Ehrhardt
by SNP Best-set Typesetter Ltd., Hong Kong
Printed and bound in the United Kingdom
by TJ International, Padstow, Cornwall

The publisher's policy is to use permanent paper from mills that operate a sustainable forestry policy, and which has been manufactured from pulp processed using acid-free and elementary chlorine-free practices. Furthermore, the publisher ensures that the text paper and cover board used have met acceptable environmental accreditation standards.

For further information on
Blackwell Publishing, visit our website:
www.blackwellpublishing.com

Contents

Contents

Contents

Preface

This anthology has been a long time in the making and, inevitably for a project of this size, has gone through a number of transformations. Our difficulty has always been one of cutting back, worrying over what must be excluded in the interests of manageability. There is a wealth of first-rate material in the analytic tradition in aesthetics and it is painful to have to leave out so many articles that attain such eminently high standards. But we believe and hope that in the end we have got the balance right, conforming to the ends we state in the Introduction. We owe a great deal of gratitude to the advice we have received from many quarters. First of all, we must acknowledge our students from the different universities where we have taught aesthetics. It soon becomes apparent which articles on reading lists actually get read and engage interest. We have tried out most of the items here on our students and there is no more exacting judge than the undergraduate coming to a topic for the first time. We have sought the advice of teachers as well, many just informally in conversation, but we should mention Stephen Davies and Jerrold Levinson in particular for their detailed suggestions. There have also been anonymous readers for Blackwell whose advice has been invaluable (we have nearly always followed it). Above all we owe a debt of gratitude to the Blackwell team who have seen it through the long production process. Jeff Dean has shown remarkable forbearance, and his own background in aesthetics has been especially helpful to us, notably in some last-minute decisions on what to include and exclude. Nirit Simon also merits thanks for his patience and practical guidance, as do Valery Rose and Caroline Richards for copy-editing work and Joanne Cartwright for following up permissions requests. We hope the anthology proves useful to the different categories of readers we envisage for it. In the end the credit goes not to us as editors but to the authors whose work appears here and provides a model for how aesthetics should be done. Our thanks, of course, to them as well.

Peter Lamarque
Stein Haugom Olsen
York and Hong Kong, February 2003

Acknowledgments

The editors and publisher gratefully acknowledge the permission granted to reproduce the copyright material in this book:

1   Morris Weitz, "The Role of Theory in Aesthetics," *Journal of Aesthetics and Art Criticism* 15 (1956), pp. 27–35. Reprinted by permission of Blackwell Publishing Ltd.
2   J. O. Urmson, "What Makes a Situation Aesthetic?" *Proceedings of the Aristotelian Society*, suppl. vol. 31 (1957), pp. 75–92. Reprinted by courtesy of the Editor of the Aristotelian Society, © 1957.
3   Arthur C. Danto, "The Artworld," *The Journal of Philosophy* 61 (1964), pp. 571–84. Reprinted by courtesy of The Journal of Philosophy.
4   Jerrold Levinson, "Defining Art Historically," *British Journal of Aesthetics* 19 (1979), pp. 232–50. Reprinted by permission of Oxford University Press.
5   George Dickie, "The New Institutional Theory of Art," *Proceedings of the 8th International Wittgenstein Symposium* 10 (1983), pp. 57–64. Reprinted by permission of the author.
6   Monroe C. Beardsley, "An Aesthetic Definition of Art," in Hugh Curtler (ed.), *What is Art?* (New York: Haven Publications, 1983), pp. 15–29.
7   Stephen Davies, "Weitz's Anti-Essentialism," chapter 1 (edited by the author for this volume) from Stephen Davies, *Definitions of Art* (Ithaca, NY: Cornell University Press, 1991). © 1991 by Cornell University. Used by permission of the publisher, Cornell University Press.
8   Joseph Margolis, "The Ontological Peculiarity of Works of Art," *Journal of Aesthetics and Art Criticism* 36 (1977), pp. 45–50. Reprinted by permission of Blackwell Publishing Ltd.
9   Jerrold Levinson, "What a Musical Work Is," *Journal of Philosophy* 77: 1 (January 1980), pp. 5–28. Reprinted by permission of The Journal of Philosophy.
10 Peter Kivy, "Platonism in Music: A Kind of Defense," *Grazer Philosophische Studien* 19 (1983), pp. 109–29.
11 Gregory Currie, "Art Works as Action Types," chapter 3 (edited by the author for this volume) from Gregory Currie, *An Ontology of Art* (London: Macmillan, 1989), pp. 46–84.
12 Frank Sibley, "Aesthetic Concepts," in Joseph Margolis (ed.), *Philosophy Looks at the Arts:*

Contemporary Readings in Aesthetics, rev. edn (Philadelphia: Temple University Press, 1978), pp. 64–87; reprinted with "extensive minor revisions" from *Philosophical Review* 68 (1959), pp. 421–50. Public domain.

13 Kendall L. Walton, "Categories of Art," *Philosophical Review* 79 (1970), pp. 334–67. Public domain.

14 Philip Pettit, "The Possibility of Aesthetic Realism," in E. Schaper (ed.), *Pleasure, Preference and Value: Studies in Philosophical Aesthetics* (Cambridge: Cambridge University Press, 1983), pp. 17–38. © by Cambridge University Press.

15 Stein Haugom Olsen, "The 'Meaning' of a Literary Work," *New Literary History: A Journal of Theory and Interpretation* 14: 1 (1982), pp. 13–32. © by New Literary History, University of Virginia. Reprinted with permission of the Johns Hopkins University Press.

16 Monroe C. Beardsley, "Intentions and Interpretations: A Fallacy Revived," in Michael J. Wreen and Donald M. Callan (eds.), *The Aesthetic Point of View* (Ithaca, NY: Cornell University Press, 1982), pp. 188–207. © 1982 by Cornell University. Used by permission of the publisher, Cornell University Press.

17 Jerrold Levinson, "Intention and Interpretation in Literature," in Jerrold Levinson, *The Pleasures of Aesthetics: Philosophical Essays* (Ithaca, NY: Cornell University Press, 1996), pp. 175–213.

18 Robert Stecker, "The Constructivist's Dilemma," *Journal of Aesthetics and Art Criticism* 55: 1 (Winter 1997), pp. 43–51. Reprinted by permission of Blackwell Publishing Ltd.

19 P. F. Strawson, "Aesthetic Appraisal and Works of Art," in P. F. Strawson, *Freedom and Resentment* (London: Methuen, 1974), pp. 178–88. Reprinted by permission of Thomson Publishing Services.

20 Frank Sibley, "Particularity, Art and Evaluation," *Proceedings of the Aristotelian Society*, suppl. vol. 42 (1974), pp. 1–21. Reprinted by courtesy of the Editor of the Aristotelian Society, © 1974.

21 Anthony Savile, chapter 1 from Anthony Savile, *The Test of Time* (Oxford: Oxford University Press, 1982), pp. 3–20. Reprinted by permission of Oxford University Press.

22 Malcolm Budd, chapter 1 from Malcolm Budd, *Values of Art* (London: Penguin, 1995), pp. 1–16; 38–43. © by Penguin. Reproduced by permission of Penguin Books Ltd.

23 Peter Lamarque, "Tragedy and Moral Value," from Peter Lamarque, *Fictional Points of View* (Ithaca, NY: Cornell University Press, 1996), pp. 135–48; originally, in a slightly shorter version, in *Australasian Journal of Philosophy* 73 (1995), pp. 239–49. Reprinted by permission of Oxford University Press.

24 Berys Gaut, "The Ethical Criticism of Art" in Jerrold Levinson (ed.), *Aesthetics and Ethics* (Cambridge: Cambridge University Press, 1998), pp. 182–203. © by Cambridge University Press.

25 Colin Radford, "How Can We Be Moved by the Fate of Anna Karenina?" *Proceedings of the Aristotelian Society*, suppl. vol. 69 (1975), pp. 67–80. Reprinted by courtesy of the Editor of the Aristotelian Society, © 1975.

26 Kendall L. Walton, "Fearing Fictions," *Journal of Philosophy* 75: 1 (January 1978), pp. 5–27. Reprinted by permission of The Journal of Philosophy.

27 John Searle, "The Logical Status of Fictional Discourse," from John Searle, *Expression and Meaning* (Cambridge: Cambridge University Press, 1979), pp. 58–75.

28 Peter Lamarque, "How Can We Fear and Pity Fictions?" *British Journal of Aesthetics* 21: 4 (Autumn 1981), pp. 291–304. Reprinted by permission of Oxford University Press.

29 Jerome Stolnitz, "On the Cognitive Triviality of Art," *British Journal of Aesthetics* 32: 3 (July 1992), pp. 191–200. Reprinted by permission of Oxford University Press.

30 Kendall L. Walton, "Are Representations Symbols?" *The Monist*, 58: 2 (1974), pp. 236–54. © 1974 by The Monist: An International Quarterly Journal of General Philosophical Inquiry, Peru, Illinois 61354, USA. Reprinted by permission.

31 Roger Scruton, "Photography and Representation," from Roger Scruton, *The Aesthetic Understanding: Essays in the Philosophy of Art and Culture* (London: Methuen, 1983), pp. 102–26. Reissued 1998 by St. Augustine's Press, South Bend, Ind. (pp. 119–33 their volume) and reproduced here by permission of St. Augustine's Press.

32 Jack W. Meiland, "Originals, Copies, and Aesthetic Value," in Denis Dutton (ed.), *The*

Forger's Art (Berkeley, CA: University of California Press, 1983), pp. 115–30.

33 Malcolm Budd, "How Pictures Look," in D. Knowles and J. Skorupski (eds.), *Virtue and Taste* (Oxford: Blackwell, 1993), pp. 154–75. Reprinted by permission of Blackwell Publishing Ltd.

34 Richard Wollheim, "On Pictorial Representation," *Journal of Aesthetics and Art Criticism* 56: 3 (Summer 1998), pp. 217–26. Reprinted by permission of Blackwell Publishing Ltd.

35 Jenefer M. Robinson, "Style and Personality in the Literary Work," *Philosophical Review* 94: 2 (April 1985), pp. 227–47. © 1985 by Cornell University. Reprinted by permission of the publisher and the author.

36 Stein Haugom Olsen, "Literary Aesthetics and Literary Practice," from Stein Haugom Olsen, *The End of Literary Theory* (Cambridge: Cambridge University Press, 1987), pp. 1–19. © by Cambridge University Press.

37 Peter Lamarque, "The Death of the Author: An Analytical Autopsy," *British Journal of Aesthetics* 40: 4 (1990), pp. 319–31. Reprinted by permission of Oxford University Press.

38 Roger Scruton, "Understanding Music," in Roger Scruton, *The Aesthetic Understanding* (London: Methuen, 1983), pp. 77–100. Reissued 1998 by St. Augustine's Press, South Bend, Ind. (pp. 88–115 their volume) and reproduced here by permission of St. Augustine Press.

39 Peter Kivy, "The Profundity of Music," in Peter Kivy, *Music Alone: Philosophical Reflections on the Purely Musical Experience* (Ithaca, NY: Cornell University Press, 1990). Used by permission of the publisher, Cornell University Press.

40 Jenefer M. Robinson, "The Expression and Arousal of Emotion in Music," *Journal of Aesthetics and Art Criticism* 52: 1 (Winter 1994), pp. 13–22. Reprinted by permission of Blackwell Publishing Ltd.

41 Noël Carroll, "The Power of Movies," *Daedalus*, 114: 4 (Fall 1985), pp. 79–103. Reprinted by permission of *Daedalus*, Journal of the American Academy of Arts and Sciences, from the issue entitled "The Moving Image."

42 Bruce Baugh, "Prolegomena to Any Aesthetics of Rock Music," *Journal of Aesthetics and Art Criticism* 51: 1 (Winter 1993), pp. 23–29. Reprinted by permission of Blackwell Publishing Ltd.

43 Stephen Davies, "Rock versus Classical Music," *Journal of Aesthetics and Art Criticism* 57: 2 (Spring 1999), pp. 193–204. Reprinted by permission of Blackwell Publishing Ltd.

44 R. W. Hepburn, "Contemporary Aesthetics and the Neglect of Natural Beauty," in Bernard Williams and Alan Montefiore (eds.), *British Analytical Philosophy* (London: Routledge & Kegan Paul, 1966), pp. 285–310. Reprinted by permission of the publisher, Routledge.

45 Allen Carlson, "Appreciation and the Natural Environment," *Journal of Aesthetics and Art Criticism* 37 (1979), pp. 267–76. Reprinted by permission of Blackwell Publishing Ltd.

46 Malcolm Budd, "The Aesthetic Appreciation of Nature," *British Journal of Aesthetics* 36 (1996), pp. 207–22. Reprinted by permission of Oxford University Press.

Every effort has been made to trace copyright holders and to obtain their permission for the use of copyright material. The publisher apologizes for any errors or omissions in the above list and would be grateful if notified of any corrections that should be incorporated in future reprints or editions of this book.

General Introduction

This anthology has a number of clearly statable aims:

- to present in a single volume some of the key texts from the analytic tradition in aesthetics and philosophy of art;
- to display the development of this tradition from its beginnings in the 1950s to the present day;
- to illustrate the broad range of topics and problems addressed by analytic aestheticians, from general issues of a theoretical nature to more specific issues relating to particular art forms;
- to provide a valuable reference resource for teaching and research purposes.

In selecting articles for inclusion we have tried to strike a balance on many fronts: between "classic" contributions and more recent developments, between topics, between art forms, between the needs of undergraduate teaching and the needs of a scholarly archive, between the desire for comprehensive coverage and the constraints of manageability. We hope the volume will act as something of a showcase for the considerable achievements of analytic aesthetics over the past 50 years. But above all, we have sought to put together a selection which will be of practical usefulness for those working in the field, at all levels.

Why "analytic"? This volume is a companion to Blackwell's *Continental Aesthetics – Romanticism to Postmodernism: An Anthology*, edited by Richard Kearney and David Rasmussen, and, we believe, nicely complements it, in showing the distinctive treatment of sometimes not dissimilar topics by those working in the Anglophone tradition and

from the perspective of analytic philosophy. Together the two volumes give an excellent overview of the full range of philosophical thinking about the arts in the twentieth century. It has often been remarked how inappropriate are the designations "Continental" and "analytic" in marking different approaches to philosophy. For one thing, the former is a geographical indicator, the latter a methodological one, so they are already incommensurate. But, more strikingly, many leading figures in analytic philosophy – Gottlob Frege, Ludwig Wittgenstein, Friedrich Waismann, Moritz Schlick and other members of the Vienna Circle – came from Continental Europe, and currently in Germany, France, Spain, Scandinavia, and Italy, there is extensive interest in analytical philosophical methods. However, these two volumes on aesthetics do show a pronounced difference in methodology and it is worth reflecting on the characteristics distinctive of the analytic tradition.

Clearly the idea of "analysis" is central to analytic philosophy. But the aims and methods of analysis differ markedly in the various incarnations of the analytic school. In the early years of the twentieth century, under the direct influence of Frege, Russell, and Wittgenstein (as author of *Tractatus Logico-Philosophicus*), the logical analysis of propositions was paramount, with the aim of displaying their "logical form," as distinct from their surface grammatical form. Russell's Theory of Descriptions was held to be paradigmatic in this regard. Superficially his theory might seem like a mere paraphrasing of sentences containing definite descriptions into a logical notation; in fact it had profound repercussions for traditional problems in philosophy, notably the problem of nonexistence, the relations between meaning and truth, and the manner in which false propositions relate to the world. Analytic aestheticians were to draw heavily on Russell's achievement in analyzing fictionality (see Part VI). The uncovering of logical forms developed into a more general program in philosophy: the use of logic to "regiment" language, in W. V. O. Quine's terms, into a "canonical notation," with the aim of eliminating vagaries in common usage and delivering a streamlined vehicle for science. An even grander ambition lay behind this species of analysis, encouraged by early ideas in Russell and Wittgenstein, namely that logical analysis could reveal the vacuity of much traditional philosophy. The high point of this ambition came with the Logical Positivists' sweeping denunciation of metaphysics as meaningless.

But analytic philosophy did not restrict itself to the logical analysis of propositions. Specific, problematic, concepts were also subject to analysis. Sometimes this took the form of seeking definitions for troublesome terms: "knowledge," "freedom," "truth," "good," "existence," and – later on – "art." Arguably this was an extension of an approach originating with Socrates, but the emphasis on "necessary and sufficient conditions" for the true application of a concept was a peculiarly modern – and "analytic" – phenomenon. However, not all analytic philosophers took definition to be the aim of conceptual analysis. Some, the Ordinary Language Philosophers from Oxford in the 1940s and 1950s, preferred the analogy with geography proposed by Gilbert Ryle, seeing their task as "mapping out" concepts or finding their "logical geography." Ryle's *Concept of Mind* (1949) was paradigmatic in this regard, owing much to the later work of Wittgenstein.

By the late 1960s the optimistic thought that logical analysis or the study of ordinary usage could alone solve – or dissolve – the major issues in philosophy, sweeping away centuries of metaphysical confusion, was being questioned. The interest in language and logic became focused into a relatively new form of inquiry, also traceable to Frege, namely "philosophy of language," which sought a clearer understanding of such concepts as meaning, truth, reference, and indeed language itself, but without any programmatic ambition toward solving all philosophical problems. By the 1970s few philosophers styled themselves as "linguistic philosophers" or "ordinary language philosophers," yet significantly the term "analytic

philosophy" grew in popularity. The Fregean tradition continued to inform philosophy of language but the original linguistic turn lost its "revolutionary" edge and settled down merely into a style of philosophizing.

Analytic philosophy now became distinctive for its methodology and its theoretical presuppositions. Characteristic of the analytic methodology are:

- the prominent application of logic and conceptual analysis;
- the commitment to rational methods of argument;
- the emphasis on objectivity and truth;
- the predilection for spare, literal prose, eschewing overly rhetorical or figurative language;
- the felt need to define terms and offer explicit formulation of theses;
- the quasi-scientific dialectical method of hypothesis/counter-example/modification;
- the tendency to tackle narrowly defined problems, often working within on-going debates.

Notable among presuppositions, although not universally held, are:

- the treatment of scientific discourse as paradigmatic;
- a tendency toward ontological "parsimony," realism about science, and physicalism about mind;
- the belief that philosophical problems are in some sense timeless or universal, at least not merely constructs of history and culture.

It is perhaps the latter presupposition that distinguishes the analytic tradition most obviously from the "Continental." Analytic philosophers tend not to historicize their debates; there is little reference to the historical development of problems or the history of ideas and a widespread skepticism about the value of historically contextualized study of earlier philosophers. A consequence is that analytic philosophers have little interest in the social, political, or ideological underpinnings of their work and tend to treat the problems they address as timeless, ahistorical, and solvable, if at all, by appeal to logic rather than to observations about external cultural factors.

Analytic philosophy came relatively late to aesthetics. It was not until the 1940s and 1950s that philosophers trained in analytic methods turned their attention to issues in aesthetics and these were mostly philosophers who had established their reputations in different areas of the subject. Typical in this regard was the highly influential anthology, *Aesthetics and Language*, edited by William Elton, in 1954, which collected papers published in the preceding decade from prestigious journals like *Mind*, *Proceedings of the Aristotelian Society*, and *The Philosophical Quarterly*, with contributors of the caliber of Gilbert Ryle, Stuart Hampshire, O. K. Bouwsma, John Passmore, and Arnold Isenberg. The editor was frank about the missionary purpose of the collection: "to diagnose and clarify some aesthetic confusions, which it holds to be mainly linguistic in origin" and "to provide philosophers and their students with a number of pieces that may serve as models of analytical procedures in aesthetics." It had many targets associated with less enlightened times: "obfuscatory jargon," the "pitfalls of generality," the "predisposition to essentialism," "misleading analogies" (e.g. between the aesthetic and the moral), and "irrefutable and non-empirical" theories.

The idea that the analytic philosopher, approaching aesthetics, must bring about an entirely fresh start, is well illustrated by the opening paragraph of J. O. Urmson's paper "What Makes a Situation Aesthetic?" (Part I):

> Philosophers have hoed over the plot of aesthetics often enough, but the plants that they have raised thereby are pitifully weak and straggling objects. The time has therefore not yet come for tidying up some corner of the plot; it needs digging over afresh in the hope that some sturdier and more durable produce may arise, even if its health be rather rude. I therefore make no excuse for reopening what seems to me to be the central problem of aesthetics.

Analytic contributions to aesthetics, however, soon took off and Frank Sibley saw no need, in his classic paper "Aesthetic Concepts" from 1959 (Part III), to keep disparaging earlier efforts. In fact, in 1958 the analytic school of aesthetics came of age with the publication of Monroe C. Beardsley's *Aesthetics: Problems in the Philosophy of Criticism*, which provided a sustained treatment of a wide range of problems illustrated by examples from an equally wide range of art forms. By the 1980s and 1990s the felt need to apologize for, or be defensive

about, working in aesthetics had long subsided. Philosophers of the highest caliber – Nelson Goodman, Richard Wollheim, Arthur Danto, Kendall Walton, Martha Nussbaum, Roger Scruton – were not only writing in aesthetics but were introducing debates in the subject to philosophers from quite different areas.

In fact, to the extent that aesthetics has been integrated into the mainstream analytic tradition this is because of movement in two directions. The first is through the appearance of ostensibly aesthetic issues in debates on quite other kinds of topics, often by philosophers who have no deep concern with aesthetics for its own sake. Thus, for example, in recent times, John McDowell, Crispin Wright, and Philip Pettit, among others, have used aesthetic properties as a test case for realism; David Lewis has applied possible world semantics to fiction; Peter van Inwagen and Nathan Salmon have written on fictional objects and ontology; David Wiggins has defended subjectivism in relation to aesthetic judgment. Many similar examples could be given. Discussions of realism and anti-realism, supervenience, ontology, secondary qualities, and relativism will not infrequently allude to the aesthetic realm. But these as it were incidental incursions into aesthetics are not the only measure of the standing of aesthetics in the analytic community. Of more central concern, moving in the opposite direction, is the recharacterization of traditional questions within aesthetics in an idiom drawn from other branches of philosophy. Treating aesthetics as a special case for metaphysics, ontology, epistemology, theory of meaning, value theory, and social or political philosophy, has served, perhaps above all else, to entrench aesthetics – and aestheticians – in the analytic mainstream. Work of aestheticians has made an impact beyond aesthetics back to the very areas from where the original issues grew up. One thinks of Goodman on symbolism, Walton on make-believe, Sibley on aesthetic concepts, Danto on indiscernibles, Levinson on ontology, Margolis on interpretation, Scruton on aesthetic culture, Currie on fiction. These are efforts which could never be deemed marginal in philosophy.

We take up later, in the different sections of the anthology, the story of how analytic aesthetics developed in its own right. Let us end this introduction, though, with a few more observations of a general nature about its characteristic features.

First of all, as just noted, analytic aesthetics has tended to give priority to topics arising from concerns elsewhere in philosophy. The emphasis on logic and philosophy of language, for example, led inevitably to an interest in questions about meaning and truth in aesthetics. One notable aspect of this is the attention given to fictionality. We saw how work by Frege and Russell raised problems about nonexistence and reference in the context of seeking logical forms. It did not escape the notice of aestheticians that this had a bearing on fictional narratives of all kinds in the arts. Nelson Goodman and Kendall Walton, among others, sought to make sense of the idea that pictures, or literary works, might be "about" the nonexistent (see Walton's discussion in Part VII). When speech act theory developed in the 1960s, initially through J. L. Austin's work, later by John R. Searle and others, it too was soon applied to aesthetics. Searle's speech act analysis of fiction (Part VI) had considerable impact. When Monroe Beardsley returned to the question of intention and literary meaning (Part IV) later in life he also appealed to speech acts. Indeed the debate about intention – to a large extent initiated by Beardsley in his original attack on the Intentional Fallacy – is typical of the analytic tradition, drawing both on theories of meaning and philosophy of mind. The influence of Wittgenstein, especially his views on language, can be felt throughout the development of analytic aesthetics. Most obviously, it manifested itself in Morris Weitz's attack on the idea of finding a definition of art (Part I), but it also appears in the thought that there is a distinctive "practice" associated with the arts (Olsen, Part VIII), and perhaps also in the appeal to "games" to illuminate our interactions with art (Walton, Part VI). The recent revival of interest in metaphysics among analytic philosophers has led to a substantial amount of work on the ontology of art (Part II). Again the logical emphasis – exploring the categorizations of objects, properties, types, instances – is distinctive of the analytic approach and marks it off from ontological enquiries in the "Continental" tradition, notably that of Heidegger, even though the problems are ostensibly similar. Finally, among characteristic topics, is the discussion of aesthetic concepts, initiated by Sibley (Part III). The debate about aesthetic and nonaesthetic properties in the framework of realism versus antirealism in philosophy of language (Pettit, Part III) well illustrates how aesthetic issues have become assimilated into wider philosophical concerns.

Given the nature of analytic philosophy it is not surprising to find the kinds of topics just mentioned – meaning, reference, ontology, concepts, definition, fictionality, representation – but a notable aspect of recent work in analytic aesthetics has been the attention given to particular art forms: painting, literature, music, film, photography. We have acknowledged this development with sections on the different arts and the anthology contains contributions on all the arts just listed. In becoming more specialized in this way analytic aesthetics might be seen as falling into line with other meta-enquiries in philosophy. No competent researcher in philosophy of mind, for example, can now show the kind of ignorance of empirical psychology provocatively flaunted by Gilbert Ryle half a century ago. And philosophy of science is commonly divided into distinct specialties – philosophy of physics, philosophy of biology – just as ethics has a growing normative strand in medical or business ethics. It is a strength of current analytic aesthetics that it too focuses on the individual arts. For one thing, it brings aesthetics closer to actual critical practice and encourages links with subject specialists, in musicology, film studies, literary theory, and art history. For another, it puts salutary constraints on the grand designs of aesthetics, particularly attempts to develop overarching or all-embracing theories of the arts.

It is, however, worth signaling potential dangers too. One danger is that aesthetics becomes more culture-bound. When philosophers talk about music or film or literature it is usually a pretty narrow band of works that are taken as paradigmatic – inevitably these are works that the writers know. More often than not they are canonical works in the Western tradition. Generalizations about these works and their properties might not always carry over to works from different cultural traditions. Nevertheless, even if it were the case that discussion of particular arts had a relatively narrow frame of reference, there is benefit to be gained just to the extent that philosophers can shed light on an important canon of works. In fact, more characteristic of the analytic approach is a balance between proposing genuinely universal claims about a particular art form and illustrating those claims by reference to individual works. We have selected papers on particular art forms – including painting, music, literature, photography, film, and other popular arts – which seem especially effective in this regard. Roger Scruton's paper on "Understanding Music" (Part IX) is a good example. Scruton illustrates his discussion mostly with examples from Western music yet he is dealing with phenomena – tone, rhythm, movement, harmony – by no means restricted to the musical examples offered. Like all analytic philosophers, he is interested in those features which are central and characteristic, not merely local or contingent. His claim that musical understanding is a kind of "intentional understanding" is a claim not restricted to time or culture.

Analytic aesthetics has sometimes been identified with "philosophy of art" or even metacriticism (Beardsley's *Aesthetics* made the identification explicit). But not all work by analytic aestheticians concerns the aesthetics of art. We have included a section on the aesthetics of nature, including Ronald Hepburn's pioneering paper (Part XI) on the subject, to acknowledge this wider application. J. O. Urmson in "What Makes a Situation Aesthetic?" (Part I) also resists the restriction of the aesthetic to the artistic, as does Sibley (Part V). The idea that aesthetic descriptions apply to all kinds of objects, not only works of art, is as important as is the recognition of other cultural traditions when speaking of art.

We mentioned at the beginning one feature characteristic of analytic philosophy, the tendency to tackle narrowly defined problems. The complaint of William Elton was that aesthetics, prior to the advent of the analytic school, was overly ambitious, inclined to generality, and given to untestable theories. We will end with a word about the scope of these essays. Individually, they do tend to stick to the proposing and defense of specific, even

limited, theses. Such is the manner of the analytic enterprise. Indeed, it has long been thought a merit of this enterprise that it favors slow, meticulous work – finding strong arguments to support precise, clearly defined theses – over generalizations weakly or imprecisely defended. This can give the impression of pedantry and lack of ambition. It is, however, a false impression. Certainly debates by analytic aestheticians seem to move slowly, but that is because attention to detail is highly valued. There is a sense of community among contributors to these debates, however overtly critical analytic philosophers can seem of each other's work. Progress comes through criticism, often in the form of unexpected counterexamples to general theses. Jenefer Robinson's paper on "Expression and Arousal of Emotion in Music" (Part IX) nicely illustrates how a debate advances. She enters a dialogue with other contributors and defines her own position in relation to theirs. This is the familiar analytic mode. The cumulative effect of such debates is a sense of concentrated effort on carefully circumscribed ground.

When we stand back and survey all the microdebates two features stand out: the seriousness of purpose and the difficulty of the issues. However narrowly defined the topics of individual papers and however small the steps taken, there is no disputing the centrality and resonance of the underlying questions: What is the nature of art? What is the place of art in human life? How do meaning and truth and representation arise in the arts? What is the scope of the aesthetic? These essays make a substantial impact on such questions.

Further reading

Alperson, Philip (ed.) (1992). *The Philosophy of the Visual Arts*. New York: Oxford University Press.

Beardsley, Monroe C. (1981). *Aesthetics: Problems in the Philosophy of Criticism*, 2nd edn. Indianapolis: Hackett.

Cooper, David (ed.) (1992). *A Companion to Aesthetics*. Oxford: Blackwell.

Eaton, Marcia Muelder (1988). *Basic Issues in Aesthetics*. Belmont, CA: Wadsworth.

Elton, William (ed.) (1954). *Aesthetics and Language*. Oxford: Blackwell.

Goodman, Nelson (1976). *Languages of Art*, 2nd edn. Indianapolis: Hackett.

Graham, Gordon (1997). *Philosophy of the Arts: An Introduction to Aesthetics*. London: Routledge.

Kelly, Michael (ed.) (1998). *Encyclopedia of Aesthetics*, in 4 volumes, Oxford: Oxford University Press.

Margolis, Joseph (1980). *Art and Philosophy: Conceptual Issues in Aesthetics*. Atlantic Highlands, NJ: Humanities Press.

Neill, Alex and Ridley, Aaron (eds.) (1995). *Arguing About Art: Contemporary Philosophical Debates*. New York: McGraw-Hill, Inc.

Shusterman, Richard (ed.) (1989). *Analytic Aesthetics*. Oxford: Blackwell Publishers.

Townsend, Dabney (1997). *An Introduction to Aesthetics*. Oxford: Blackwell Publishers.

Wollheim, Richard (1980). *Art and Its Objects*, 2nd edn. Cambridge: Cambridge University Press.

Part I

Identifying Art

Introduction to Part I

The question "What is art?" is often thought to be absolutely fundamental to aesthetics. After all, so the argument goes, without an answer to that question there would be no determinate subject matter for aesthetics. Without knowing what art is we could not know what enquiry we are pursuing. Furthermore, on this line of thought, nothing short of a list of essential or defining properties of art – those properties both necessary and sufficient for something to be a work of art – will satisfy the need to identify art apart from other human endeavors.

The early part of the twentieth century saw numerous attempts to provide just such a defining essence of art. Significant form, intuition, the expression of emotion, organic unity, and other notions, were offered to this end. (Morris Weitz gives a brief survey of such theories below.) It is surely not coincidental that art theories proliferated in a period which also saw the proliferation of art movements. But analytic philosophers on entering the fray in the 1950s saw only muddle and confusion amid the array of competing conceptions. There was a palpable sense that what was needed was an entirely fresh start.

No paper better epitomized the revolutionary zeal of analytic philosophy, at least on the question of how to identify art, than Morris Weitz's "The Role of Theory in Aesthetics." Weitz thought that the whole enterprise of trying to find an essence of art was misconceived. And to the extent that aesthetic theory took the search for such an essence to be its primary goal then aesthetic theory itself must be abandoned. "Aesthetic theory – all of it – is wrong in principle in thinking that a correct theory is possible because it radically misconstrues the logic of the concept of art. Its main contention that

'art' is amenable to real or any kind of true definition is false. Its attempt to discover the necessary and sufficient properties of art is logically misbegotten." The expression "the logic of the concept of art" became the touchstone for the analytic approach. For Weitz, the concept of art is an "open concept" not amenable to necessary and sufficient conditions. Indeed the very possibility of creativity in art demands this openness. All that binds together the disparate products and activities we call "art" are loosely interlocking "family resemblances." Here Weitz's debt is to Wittgenstein and this was an early example of how Wittgenstein's views about language might be applied.

Weitz's paper became seminal in the analytic tradition. It focused attention on the very idea of trying to define art. However, as Stephen Davies shows in his important book *Definitions of Art*, from which we have excerpted the first chapter ("Weitz's Anti-Essentialism"), modified by the author, not all analytic philosophers agree with Weitz, either on his specific proposal that "art" is an "open concept" yielding only family resemblances, or on his skepticism about finding necessary and sufficient conditions for art. In fact, attempts to find an "essence" of art, captured by properties all and only works of art possess, have by no means diminished in the wake of Weitz's objections. Crucially, though, what has changed – and Davies attributes the change to the influence of Weitz – is the kind of properties that are sought as part of the essence of art. Rather than look for *intrinsic* properties of objects, including aesthetic or formal properties, attention has turned to *extrinsic* or *relational* properties, notably of a social, historical, or "institutional" nature.

The exploration of such relational properties as providing an essence of art is nowhere better exemplified than in the work of Danto, Dickie, and Levinson, even though their approaches are significantly different. Danto takes the first crucial step – remarkable in the history of aesthetics – by directing our attention to features of artworks that are *not perceptible*. In his often-quoted words (in "The Artworld" below): "To see something as art requires something the eye cannot descry – an atmosphere of artistic theory, a knowledge of the history of art: an artworld." To help us grasp this revolutionary insight he uses thought-experiments about what he calls "indiscernibles." In his later work *The Transfiguration of the Commonplace* (1981) the idea is finely honed but it figures strikingly also in "The Artworld," printed here, where he uses the example of Andy Warhol's Brillo Boxes. If Warhol's Brillo Boxes are indistinguishable in appearance from ordinary Brillo boxes, how could the former be art but not the latter? The stark answer Danto offers (an answer that gets more refined in later work) is that what makes all the difference is "a certain theory of art." The artworld at particular stages of its development *makes possible* certain kinds of works. Only against the background of pop art – with its theoretical presuppositions – do works like Brillo Boxes, or, in Danto's other example, Rauschenberg's bed (which from a certain perspective looks like a quite ordinary bed), become possible. For Danto, then, there is something essential to all art – contra Weitz – namely embeddedness in an "artworld" along with its supporting theories.

George Dickie, in his "institutional theory" of art, developed and formalized certain aspects of Danto's account. In direct opposition to Weitz, and going further than Danto, Dickie proposed a *definition* of art, employing the notion of an "artworld." In an early version, Dickie offered the following definition: "A work of art in the classificatory sense is (1) an artifact (2) a set of the aspects of which has had conferred upon it the status of candidate for appreciation by some person or persons acting on behalf of a certain social institution (the artworld)." This definition (from 1974) occasioned a great deal of debate, with each key term carefully scrutinized. In the light of what he conceded to be serious criticisms, Dickie proposed a modified version, as laid out in his essay, "The New Institutional Theory of Art," reproduced here. This version is simpler: "A work of art is an artifact of a kind created to be presented to an art-world public." The crucial feature of both versions is that what makes something an artwork is not what it looks (sounds, etc.) like or what materials it is made of, or any of its intrinsic qualities, but how it relates to a loosely characterized institution or set of practices. Without the institution of art there would be no artworks even if there were things that looked exactly like what we call artworks. Dickie is content to acknowledge a circularity in his definition ("art" and "artworld" are interdefinable) but insists that it is nonvicious circularity.

Levinson, in "Defining Art Historically," takes off from both Weitz and Dickie, agreeing with both on the lack of definitive intrinsic or exhibited properties, but siding with Dickie against Weitz on the possibility of a definition in terms of other kinds of properties. For Levinson, what makes something a work of art is its relation to previous works of art. Only an object that is intended to be regarded in the way that earlier art has been regarded can itself count as art. Although at first glance this might seem even more viciously circular than institutional theories, Levinson stoutly defends its noncircularity by appeal to an important distinction in the analytic philosopher's toolkit, between the *meaning* of a term, which is what the definition seeks, and the *extension* of a term (i.e. the set of objects to which the term applies), which is all that is presupposed in the definiens. We should look to the art historian, not the philosopher, to identify the set of previous artworks, but listing such works is not to give a definition. The latter is the task of the philosopher and there is no reason why the philosopher should not look to the art historian for the materials out of which the definition is fashioned.

Both J. O. Urmson and Monroe C. Beardsley, in the papers below, stress the idea of the *aesthetic*, which seems to play so minor a role in the accounts described so far. Urmson's paper, "What Makes a Situation Aesthetic?," is important in a number of respects. He insists that the aesthetic is not limited to the artistic; he seeks to dissociate aesthetic response from some particular class of objects or some particular characteristics of objects or some special kind of emotion; he emphasizes the importance of *reasons* for judgments in distinguishing the aesthetic from, for example, the moral or the economic; and he tentatively connects aesthetic appreciation with the perceptible properties of objects. In a low-key manner Urmson's paper can be seen as sketching in the parameters for a distinctively analytic approach to aesthetics.

Beardsley's outlook in "An Aesthetic Definition of Art," is not dissimilar to Urmson's. While agreeing that the aesthetic is not limited to the artistic, Beardsley believes that the artistic is essentially connected to the aesthetic. (Interestingly, a parenthetical remark toward the end of Urmson's paper suggests the same.) He boldly presents a definition of art in these terms: "An artwork is something produced with the intention of giving it the capacity to satisfy the aesthetic interest." As an analytic philosopher he carefully analyzes – and thus explains and justifies – each of the main terms in the definition. The definition is important, not least for presenting a clear contrast with institutional or historical theories. The emphasis is on the function or aim of art rather than on institutional endorsement or historical embeddedness. Beardsley is much less tolerant of avant-garde art – such as Duchamp's "readymades" – than either Danto or Dickie but his insistence on "aesthetic interest" does, controversially, make problematic those species of "conceptual art" which overtly repudiate the aim Beardsley identifies. It should probably be conceded, though, that Beardsley captures an intuition about the nature of art which still has widespread support, if not among philosophers then certainly among the general public.

Further reading

Carroll, Noël (ed.) (1999). *Theories of Art* (Madison, WI: University of Wisconsin Press).

Carroll, Noël (2001). *Beyond Aesthetics: Philosophical Essays*, Part II, where Carroll develops his own historical definition of art (Cambridge: Cambridge University Press).

Danto, A. C. (1981). *The Transfiguration of the Commonplace* (Cambridge, MA: Harvard University Press).

Davies, Stephen (1991). *Definitions of Art* (Ithaca, NY: Cornell University Press).

Dickie, George (1974). *Art and the Aesthetic: An Institutional Analysis* (Ithaca, NY: Cornell University Press).

Dickie, George (1984). *The Art Circle* (New York: Haven).

Levinson, Jerrold (1990). *Music, Art & Metaphysics: Essays in Philosophical Aesthetics*, Part 1 (Ithaca, NY: Cornell University Press).

Margolis, Joseph (1999). *What, After All, is a Work of Art?* (University Park, PA: Pennsylvania State University Press).

Stecker, Robert (1997). *Artworks: Definition, Meaning, Value* (University Park, PA: Pennsylvania State University Press).

Yanal, Robert J. (ed.) (1994). *Institutions of Art: Reconsiderations of George Dickie's Philosophy* (University Park, PA: Pennsylvania State University Press).

The Role of Theory in Aesthetics

Morris Weitz

Theory has been central in aesthetics and is still the preoccupation of the philosophy of art. Its main avowed concern remains the determination of the nature of art which can be formulated into a definition of it. It construes definition as the statement of the necessary and sufficient properties of what is being defined, where the statement purports to be a true or false claim about the essence of art, what characterizes and distinguishes it from everything else. Each of the great theories of art – Formalism, Voluntarism, Emotionalism, Intellectualism, Intuitionism, Organicism – converges on the attempt to state the defining properties of art. Each claims that it is the true theory because it has formulated correctly into a real definition the nature of art; and that the others are false because they have left out some necessary or sufficient property. Many theorists contend that their enterprise is no mere intellectual exercise but an absolute necessity for any understanding of art and our proper evaluation of it. Unless we know what art is, they say, what are its necessary and sufficient properties, we cannot begin to respond to it adequately or to say why one work is good or better than another. Aesthetic theory, thus, is important not only in itself but for the foundations of both appreciation and criticism. Philosophers, critics, and even artists who have written on art, agree that what is primary in aesthetics is a theory about the nature of art.

Morris Weitz, "The Role of Theory in Aesthetics," *Journal of Aesthetics and Art Criticism*, 15 (1956), pp. 27–35. Reprinted by permission of Blackwell Publishing Ltd.

Is aesthetic theory, in the sense of a true definition or set of necessary and sufficient properties of art, possible? If nothing else does, the history of aesthetics itself should give one enormous pause here. For, in spite of the many theories, we seem no nearer our goal today than we were in Plato's time. Each age, each art-movement, each philosophy of art, tries over and over again to establish the stated ideal only to be succeeded by a new or revised theory, rooted, at least in part, in the repudiation of preceding ones. Even today, almost everyone interested in aesthetic matters is still deeply wedded to the hope that the correct theory of art is forthcoming. We need only examine the numerous new books on art in which new definitions are proffered; or, in our own country especially, the basic textbooks and anthologies to recognize how strong the priority of a theory of art is.

In this essay I want to plead for the rejection of this problem. I want to show that theory – in the requisite classical sense – is *never* forthcoming in aesthetics, and that we would do much better as philosophers to supplant the question, "What is the nature of art?," by other questions, the answers to which will provide us with all the understanding of the arts there can be. I want to show that the inadequacies of the theories are not primarily occasioned by any legitimate difficulty such e.g., as the vast complexity of art, which might be corrected by further probing and research. Their basic inadequacies reside instead in a fundamental misconception of art. Aesthetic theory – all of it – is wrong in principle in thinking that a correct theory is possible because it radically misconstrues the logic of the concept of art. Its main contention that "art" is amenable to real or any kind of true definition is false. Its attempt to discover the necessary and sufficient properties of art is logically misbegotten for the very simple reason that such a set and, consequently, such a formula about it, is never forthcoming. Art, as the logic of the concept shows, has no set of necessary and sufficient properties, hence a theory of it is logically impossible and not merely factually difficult. Aesthetic theory tries to define what cannot be defined in its requisite sense. But in recommending the repudiation of aesthetic theory I shall not argue from this, as too many others have done, that its logical confusions render it meaningless or worthless. On the contrary, I wish to reassess its role and its contribution primarily in order to show that it is of the greatest importance to our understanding of the arts.

Let us now survey briefly some of the more famous extant aesthetic theories in order to see if they do incorporate correct and adequate statements about the nature of art. In each of these there is the assumption that it is the true enumeration of the defining properties of art, with the implication that previous theories have stressed wrong definitions. Thus, to begin with, consider a famous version of Formalist theory, that propounded by Bell and Fry. It is true that they speak mostly of painting in their writings but both assert that what they find in that art can be generalized for what is "art" in the others as well. The essence of painting, they maintain, are the plastic elements in relation. Its defining property is significant form, i.e., certain combinations of lines, colors, shapes, volumes – everything on the canvas except the representational elements – which evoke a unique response to such combinations. Painting is definable as plastic organization. The nature of art, what it *really* is, so their theory goes, is a unique combination of certain elements (the specifiable plastic ones) in their relations. Anything which is art is an instance of significant form; and anything which is not art has no such form.

To this the Emotionalist replies that the truly essential property of art has been left out. Tolstoy, Ducasse, or any of the advocates of this theory, find that the requisite defining property is not significant form but rather the expression of emotion in some sensuous public medium. Without projection of emotion into some piece of stone or words or sounds, etc., there can be no art. Art is really such embodiment. It is this that uniquely characterizes art, and any true, real definition of it, contained in some adequate theory of art, must so state it.

The Intuitionist disclaims both emotion and form as defining properties. In Croce's version, for example, art is identified not with some physical, public object but with a specific creative, cognitive and spiritual act. Art is really a first stage of knowledge in which certain human beings (artists) bring their images and intuitions into lyrical clarification or expression. As such, it is an awareness, non-conceptual in character, of the unique individuality of things; and since it exists below the level of conceptualization or action, it is without scientific or moral content. Croce singles out as the defining essence of art this first stage of spiritual life and advances its identification with art as a philosophically true theory or definition.

The Organicist says to all of this that art is really a class of organic wholes consisting of distinguishable, albeit inseparable, elements in their causally efficacious relations which are presented in some sensuous medium. In A. C. Bradley, in piecemeal versions of it in literary criticism, or in my own generalized adaptation of it in my *Philosophy of the Arts*, what is claimed is that anything which is a work of art is in its nature a unique complex of interrelated parts – in painting, for example, lines, colors, volumes, subjects, etc., all interacting upon one another on a paint surface of some sort. Certainly, at one time at least it seemed to me that this organic theory constituted the one true and real definition of art.

My final example is the most interesting of all, logically speaking. This is the Voluntarist theory of Parker. In his writings on art, Parker persistently calls into question the traditional simple-minded definitions of aesthetics. "The assumption underlying every philosophy of art is the existence of some common nature present in all the arts."[1] "All the so popular brief definitions of art – 'significant form,' 'expression,' 'intuition,' 'objectified pleasure' – are fallacious, either because, while true of art, they are also true of much that is not art, and hence fail to differentiate art from other things; or else because they neglect some essential aspect of art."[2] But instead of inveighing against the attempt at definition of art itself, Parker insists that what is needed is a complex definition rather than a simple one. "The definition of art must therefore be in terms of a complex of characteristics. Failure to recognize this has been the fault of all the well-known definitions."[3] His own version of Voluntarism is the theory that art is essentially three things: embodiment of wishes and desires imaginatively satisfied, language, which characterizes the public medium of art, and harmony, which unifies the language with the layers of imaginative projections. Thus, for Parker, it is a true definition to say of art that it is ". . . the provision of satisfaction through the imagination, social significance, and harmony. I am claiming that nothing except works of art possesses all three of these marks."[4]

Now, all of these sample theories are inadequate in many different ways. Each purports to be a complete statement about the defining features of all works of art and yet each of them leaves out something which the others take to be central. Some are circular, e.g., the Bell–Fry theory of art as significant form which is defined in part in terms of our response to significant form. Some of them, in their search for necessary and sufficient properties, emphasize too few properties, like (again) the Bell–Fry definition which leaves out subject-representation in painting, or the Croce theory which omits inclusion of the very important feature of the public, physical character, say, of architecture. Others are too general and cover objects that are not art as well as works of art. Organicism is surely such a view since it can be applied to *any* causal unity in the natural world as well as to art.[5] Still others rest on dubious principles, e.g., Parker's claim that art embodies imaginative satisfactions, rather than real ones; or Croce's assertion that there is non-conceptual knowledge. Consequently, even if art has one set of necessary and sufficient properties, none of the theories we have noted or, for that matter, no aesthetic theory yet proposed, has enumerated that set to the satisfaction of all concerned.

Then there is a different sort of difficulty. As real definitions, these theories are supposed to be factual reports on art. If they are, may we not ask, Are they empirical and open to verification or falsification? For example, what would confirm or disconfirm the theory that art is significant form or embodiment of emotion or creative synthesis of images? There does not even seem to be a hint of the kind of evidence which might be forthcoming to test these theories; and indeed one wonders if they are perhaps honorific definitions of "art," that is, proposed redefinitions in terms of some *chosen* conditions for applying the concept of art, and not true or false reports on the essential properties of art at all.

But all these criticisms of traditional aesthetic theories – that they are circular, incomplete, untestable, pseudo-factual, disguised proposals to change the meaning of concepts – have been made before. My intention is to go beyond these to make a much more fundamental criticism, namely, that aesthetic theory is a logically vain attempt to define what cannot be defined, to state the necessary and sufficient properties of that which has no necessary and sufficient properties, to conceive the concept of art as closed when its very use reveals and demands its openness.

The problem with which we must begin is not "What is art?," but "What sort of concept is 'art'?" Indeed, the root problem of philosophy itself is to explain the relation between the employment of certain kinds of concepts and the conditions under which they can be correctly applied. If I may paraphrase Wittgenstein, we must not ask, What is the nature of any philosophical x?, or even, according to the semanticist, What does "x" mean?, a transformation that leads to the disastrous interpretation of "art" as a name for some specifiable class of objects; but rather, What is the use or employment of "x"? What does "x" do in the language? This, I take it, is the initial question, the begin-all if not the end-all of any philosophical problem and solution. Thus, in aesthetics, our first problem is the elucidation of the actual employment of the concept of art, to give a logical description of the actual functioning of the concept, including a description of the conditions under which we correctly use it or its correlates.

My model in this type of logical description or philosophy derives from Wittgenstein. It is also he who, in his refutation of philosophical theorizing in the sense of constructing definitions of philosophical entities, has furnished contemporary aesthetics with a starting point for any future progress. In his new work, *Philosophical Investigations*,[6] Wittgenstein raises as an illustrative question, What is a game? The traditional philosophical, theoretical answer would be in terms of some exhaustive set of properties common to all games. To this Wittgenstein says, let us consider what we call "games": "I mean board-games, card-games, ball-games, Olympic games, and so on. What is common to them all? – Don't say: 'there *must* be something common, or they would not be called "games"' but *look and see* whether there is anything common to all. – For if you look at them you will not see something that is common to *all*, but similarities, relationships, and a whole series of them at that . . ."

Card games are like board games in some respects but not in others. Not all games are amusing, nor is there always winning or losing or competition. Some games resemble others in some respects – that is all. What we find are no necessary and sufficient properties, only "a complicated network of similarities overlapping and crisscrossing," such that we can say of games that they form a family with family resemblances and no common trait. If one asks what a game is, we pick out sample games, describe these, and add, "This and *similar things* are called 'games'." This is all we need to say and indeed all any of us knows about games. Knowing what a game is is not knowing some real definition or theory but being able to recognize and explain games and to decide which among imaginary and new examples would or would not be called "games."

The problem of the nature of art is like that of the nature of games, at least in these respects: If we actually look and see what it is that we call "art," we will also find no common properties – only strands of similarities. Knowing what art is is not apprehending some manifest or latent essence but being able to recognize, describe, and explain those things we call "art" in virtue of these similarities.

But the basic resemblance between these concepts is their open texture. In elucidating them, certain (paradigm) cases can be given, about which there can be no question as to their being correctly described as "art" or "game," but no exhaustive set of cases can be given. I can list some cases and some conditions under which I can apply correctly the concept of art but I cannot list all of them, for the all-important reason that unforeseeable or novel conditions are always forthcoming or envisageable.

A concept is open if its conditions of application are emendable and corrigible; i.e., if a situation or case can be imagined or secured which would call for some sort of *decision* on our part to extend the use of the concept to cover this, or to close the concept and invent a new one to deal with the new case and its new property. If necessary and sufficient conditions for the application of a concept can be stated, the concept is a closed one. But this can happen only in logic or mathematics where concepts are constructed and completely defined. It cannot occur with empirically-descriptive and normative concepts unless we arbitrarily close them by stipulating the ranges of their uses.

I can illustrate this open character of "art" best by examples drawn from its sub-concepts. Consider questions like "Is Dos Passos' *U.S.A.* a novel?," "Is V. Woolf's *To the Lighthouse* a novel?," "Is Joyce's *Finnegan's Wake* a novel?" On the traditional view, these are construed as factual problems to be answered yes or no in accordance with the presence or absence of defining properties. But certainly this is not how any of these questions is answered. Once it arises, as it has many times in the development of the novel from Richardson to Joyce (e.g., "Is Gide's *The School for Wives* a novel or a diary?"), what is at stake is no factual analysis concerning necessary and sufficient properties but a decision as to whether the work under examination is similar in certain respects to other works, already called "novels," and consequently warrants the extension of the concept to cover the new case. The new work is narrative, fictional, contains character delineation and dialogue but (say) it has no regular time-sequence in the plot or is interspersed with actual newspaper reports. It is like recognized novels, A, B, C . . . , in some respects but not like them in others. But then neither were B and C like A in some respects when it was decided to extend the concept applied to A to B and C. Because work N + 1 (the brand new work) is like A, B, C . . . N in certain respects – has strands of similarity to them – the concept is extended and a new phase of the novel engendered. "Is N 1 a novel?," then, is no factual, but rather a decision problem, where the verdict turns on whether or not we enlarge our set of conditions for applying the concept.

What is true of the novel is, I think, true of every sub-concept of art: "tragedy," "comedy," "painting," "opera," etc., of "art" itself. No "Is X a novel, painting, opera, work of art, etc.?" question allows of a definitive answer in the sense of a factual yes or no report. "Is this *collage* a painting or not?" does not rest on any set of necessary and sufficient properties of painting but on whether we decide – as we did! – to extend "painting" to cover this case.

"Art," itself, is an open concept. New conditions (cases) have constantly arisen and will undoubtedly constantly arise; new art forms, new movements will emerge, which will demand decisions on the part of those interested, usually professional critics, as to whether the concept should be extended or not. Aestheticians may lay down similarity conditions but never necessary and sufficient ones for the correct application of the concept. With "art" its conditions of application can never be exhaustively enumerated since new cases can always be envisaged or created by artists, or even nature, which would call for a decision on someone's part to extend or to close the old or to invent a new concept. (E.g., "It's not a sculpture, it's a mobile.")

What I am arguing, then, is that the very expansive, adventurous character of art, its ever-present changes and novel creations, makes it logically impossible to ensure any set of defining properties. We can, of course, choose to close the concept. But to do this with "art" or "tragedy" or "portraiture," etc., is ludicrous since it forecloses on the very conditions of creativity in the arts.

Of course there are legitimate and serviceable closed concepts in art. But these are always those whose boundaries of conditions have been drawn for a *special* purpose. Consider the difference, for example, between "tragedy" and "(extant) Greek tragedy." The first is open and must remain so to allow for the possibility of new conditions, e.g., a play in which the hero is not noble or fallen or in which there is no hero but other elements that are like those of plays we already call "tragedy." The second is closed. The plays it can be applied to, the conditions under which it can be correctly used are all in, once the boundary, "Greek," is drawn. Here the critic can work out a theory or real definition in which he lists the common properties at least of the extant Greek tragedies. Aristotle's definition, false as it is as a theory of all the plays of Aeschylus, Sophocles, and Euripides, since it does not cover some of them,[7] properly called "tragedies," can be interpreted as a real (albeit incorrect) definition of this closed concept; although it can also be, as it unfortunately has been, conceived as a purported real definition of "tragedy," in which case it suffers from the logical mistake of trying to define what cannot be defined – of trying to squeeze what is an open concept into an honorific formula for a closed concept.

What is supremely important, if the critic is not to become muddled, is to get absolutely clear about the way in which he conceives his concepts; otherwise he goes from the problem of trying to define "tragedy," etc., to an arbitrary closing of the concept in terms of certain preferred conditions or characteristics which he sums up in some linguistic recommendation that he mistakenly thinks is a real definition of the open concept. Thus, many critics and aestheticians ask, "What is tragedy?," choose a class of samples for which they may give a true account of its common properties, and then go on to construe this account of the chosen closed class as a true definition or theory of the whole open class of tragedy. This, I think, is the logical mechanism of most of the so-called theories of the sub-concepts of art: "tragedy," "comedy," "novel," etc. In effect, this whole procedure, subtly deceptive as it is, amounts to a transformation of correct criteria for *recognizing* members of certain legitimately closed classes of works of art into recommended criteria for *evaluating* any putative member of the class.

The primary task of aesthetics is not to seek a theory but to elucidate the concept of art. Specifically, it is to describe the conditions under which we employ the concept correctly. Definition, reconstruction, patterns of analysis are out of place here since they distort and add nothing to our understanding of art. What, then, is the logic of "X is a work of art"?

As we actually use the concept, "Art" is both descriptive (like "chair") and evaluative (like "good"); i.e., we sometimes say, "This is a work of art," to describe something and we sometimes say it to evaluate something. Neither use surprises anyone.

What, first, is the logic of "X is a work of art," when it is a descriptive utterance? What are the conditions under which we would be making such an utterance correctly? There are no necessary and sufficient conditions but there are the strands of similarity conditions, i.e., bundles of properties, none of which need be present but most of which are, when we describe things as works of art. I shall call these the "criteria of recognition" of works of art. All of these have served as the defining criteria of the individual traditional theories of art; so we are already familiar with them. Thus, mostly, when we describe something as a work of art, we do so under the conditions of there being present some sort of artifact, made by human skill, ingenuity, and imagination, which embodies in its sensuous, public medium – stone, wood, sounds, words, etc. – certain distinguishable elements and relations. Special theorists would add conditions like satisfaction of wishes, objectification or expression of emotion, some act of empathy, and so on; but these latter conditions seem to be quite adventitious, present to some but not to other spectators when things are described as works of art. "X is a work of art and contains *no* emotion, expression, act of empathy, satisfaction, etc.," is perfectly good sense and may frequently be true. "X is a work of art and . . . was made by no one," or . . . "exists only in the mind and not in any publicly observable thing," or . . . "was made by accident when he spilled the paint on the canvas," in each case of which a normal condition is denied, are also sensible and capable of being true in certain circumstances. None of the criteria of recognition is a defining one, either necessary or sufficient, because we can sometimes assert of something that it is a work of art and go on to deny any one of these conditions, even the one which has traditionally been taken to be basic, namely, that of being an artifact: Consider, "This piece of driftwood is a lovely piece of sculpture." Thus, to say of anything that it is a work of art is to commit oneself to the presence of *some* of these conditions. One would scarcely describe X as a work of art if X were not an artifact, or a collection of elements sensuously presented in a medium, or a product of human skill, and so on. If none of the conditions were present, if there were no criteria present for recognizing something as a work of art, we would not describe it as one. But, even so, no one of these or any collection of them is either necessary or sufficient.

The elucidation of the descriptive use of "Art" creates little difficulty. But the elucidation of the evaluative use does. For many, especially theorists, "This is a work of art" does more than describe; it also praises. Its conditions of utterance, therefore, include certain preferred properties or characteristics of art. I shall call these "criteria of evaluation." Consider a typical example of this evaluative use, the view according to which to say of something that it is a work of art is to imply that it is a *successful* harmonization of elements. Many of the honorific definitions of art and its sub-concepts are of this form. What is at stake here is that "Art" is construed as an evaluative term which is either identified with its criterion or justified in terms of it. "Art" is defined in terms of its evaluative property, e.g., successful harmonization. On such a view, to say "X is a work of art" is (1) to say something which is taken *to mean* "X is a successful harmonization" (e.g., "Art *is* significant form") or (2) to say something praise-worthy *on the basis* of its successful harmonization. Theorists are never clear whether it is (1) or (2) which is being put forward. Most of them, concerned as they are with this evaluative use, formulate (2), i.e., that feature of art that *makes* it art in the praise-sense, and then go on to state (1), i.e., the definition of "Art" in terms of

its art-making feature. And this is clearly to confuse the conditions under which we say something evaluatively with the meaning of what we say. "This is a work of art," said evaluatively, cannot mean "This is a successful harmonization of elements" – except by stipulation – but at most is said in virtue of the art-making property, which is taken as a (the) criterion of "Art," when "Art" is employed to assess. "This is a work of art," used evaluatively, serves to praise and not to affirm the reason why it is said.

The evaluative use of "Art," although distinct from the conditions of its use, relates in a very intimate way to these conditions. For, in every instance of "This is a work of art" (used to praise), what happens is that the criterion of evaluation (e.g., successful harmonization) for the employment of the concept of art is converted into a criterion of recognition. This is why, on its evaluative use, "This is a work of art" implies "This has P," where "P" is some chosen art-making property. Thus, if one chooses to employ "Art" evaluatively, as many do, so that "This is a work of art and not (aesthetically) good" makes no sense, he uses "Art" in such a way that he refuses to *call* anything a work of art unless it embodies his criterion of excellence.

There is nothing wrong with the evaluative use; in fact, there is good reason for using "Art" to praise. But what cannot be maintained is that theories of the evaluative use of "Art" are true and real definitions of the necessary and sufficient properties of art. Instead they are honorific definitions, pure and simple, in which "Art" has been redefined in terms of chosen criteria.

But what makes them – these honorific definitions – so supremely valuable is not their disguised linguistic recommendations; rather it is the *debates* over the reasons for changing the criteria of the concept of art which are built into the definitions. In each of the great theories of art, whether correctly understood as honorific definitions or incorrectly accepted as real definitions, what is of the utmost importance are the reasons proffered in the argument for the respective theory, that is, the reasons given for the chosen or preferred criterion of excellence and evaluation. It is this perennial debate over these criteria of evaluation which makes the history of aesthetic theory the important study it is. The value of each of the theories resides in its attempt to state and to justify certain criteria which are either neglected or distorted by previous theories. Look at the Bell–Fry theory again. Of course, "Art is significant form" cannot be accepted as a true, real definition of art; and most certainly it actually functions in their aesthetics as a redefinition of art in terms of the chosen condition of significant form. But what gives it its aesthetic importance is what lies behind the formula: in an age in which literary and representational elements have become paramount in painting, *return* to the plastic ones since these are indigenous to painting. Thus, the role of the theory is not to define anything but to use the definitional form, almost epigrammatically, to pin-point a crucial recommendation to turn our attention once again to the plastic elements in painting.

Once we, as philosophers, understand this distinction between the formula and what lies behind it, it behooves us to deal generously with the traditional theories of art; because incorporated in every one of them is a debate over and argument for emphasizing or centering upon some particular feature of art which has been neglected or per-

verted. If we take the aesthetic theories literally, as we have seen, they all fail; but if we reconstrue them, in terms of their function and point, as serious and argued-for recommendations to concentrate on certain criteria of excellence in art, we shall see that aesthetic theory is far from worthless. Indeed, it becomes as central as anything in aesthetics, in our understanding of art, for it teaches us what to look for and how to look at it in art. What is central and must be articulated in all the theories are their debates over the reasons for excellence in art – debates over emotional depth, profound truths, natural beauty, exactitude, freshness of treatment, and so on, as criteria of evaluation – the whole of which converges on the perennial problem of what makes a work of art good. To understand the role of aesthetic theory is not to conceive it as definition, logically doomed to failure, but to read it as summaries of seriously made recommendations to attend in certain ways to certain features of art.

Notes

1   D. Parker, "The Nature of Art," reprinted in E. Vivas and M. Krieger, *The Problems of Aesthetics* (New York, 1953), p. 90.
2   Ibid., pp. 93–4.
3   Ibid., p. 94.
4   Ibid., p. 104.
5   See M. Macdonald's review of my *Philosophy of the Arts*, *Mind*, Oct., 1951, pp. 561–64, for a brilliant discussion of this objection to the Organic theory.
6   L. Wittgenstein, *Philosophical Investigations* (Oxford, 1953), tr. by E. Anscombe; see esp. Part I, Sections 65–75. All quotations are from these sections.
7   See H. D. F. Kitto, *Greek Tragedy* (London, 1939), on this point.

2

What Makes a Situation Aesthetic?

J. O. Urmson

Philosophers have hoed over the plot of aesthetics often enough, but the plants that they have raised thereby are pitifully weak and straggling objects. The time has therefore not yet come for tidying up some corner of the plot; it needs digging over afresh in the hope that some sturdier and more durable produce may arise, even if its health be rather rude. I therefore make no excuse for reopening what seems to me to be the central problem of aesthetics: I hope that by a somewhat new approach I may succeed in making a contribution, if but a small one, towards its solution.

We may refer to a person as, in a given situation, getting an aesthetic thrill or aesthetic satisfaction from something, or of his finding something aesthetically tolerable, or aesthetically dissatisfying, or even aesthetically hateful. In a suitable context the adjective 'aesthetic' and the adverb 'aesthetically' may well be superfluous, but it is sometimes necessary to introduce one of these words in order to make it clear that when we refer, say, to a person's satisfaction we are not thinking of moral satisfaction, economic satisfaction, personal satisfaction, intellectual satisfaction, or any satisfaction other than aesthetic satisfaction. If we merely know that someone gained satisfaction from a play we do not know for sure that we are in the aesthetic field. Thus a play may give me moral satisfaction because I think it likely to have improving effects on the audience; economic satisfaction because it is

J. O. Urmson, "What Makes a Situation Aesthetic?" *Proceedings of the Aristotelian Society,* suppl. vol. 31 (1957), pp. 75–92. Reprinted by courtesy of the Editor of the Aristotelian Society © 1957.

playing to full houses and I am financing it; personal satisfaction because I wrote it and it is highly praised by the critics; intellectual satisfaction because it solves a number of difficult technical problems of the theatre very cleverly. But the question will still be open whether I found the play aesthetically satisfying. Though these various types of satisfaction are not mutually exclusive, it is clear that when we call a satisfaction aesthetic the purpose must be to mark it off from the other types.

The philosophical task to be tackled in this paper is therefore this: to make explicit what it is that distinguishes aesthetic thrills, satisfactions, toleration, disgust, etc., from thrills, satisfactions, etc., that would properly be called moral, intellectual, economic, etc. I put the question in this form because I think that it is tempting to consider the aesthetic as an isolated matter and within the field of the aesthetic to concentrate unduly upon the most sublime and intense of our experiences; but I am convinced that it is important to ensure that our account of the aesthetic should be as applicable to toleration as to our most significant experiences and should make it clear that in characterising a reaction or a judgment as aesthetic the point is to distinguish it from other reactions and judgments that are moral, economic, and so on. Only thus can we hope to bring out the full forces of the term 'aesthetic'.

This is not intended to be a problem especially about the appreciation of works of art. No doubt many of our most intense aesthetic satisfactions are derived from plays, poems, musical works, pictures and other works of art. But to me it seems obvious that we also derive aesthetic satisfaction from artifacts that are not primarily works of art, from scenery, from natural objects and even from formal logic; it is at least reasonable also to allow an aesthetic satisfaction to the connoisseur of wines and to the gourmet. I shall therefore assume that there is no special set of objects which are the sole and proper objects of aesthetic reactions and judgments, and which are never the objects of an economic, intellectual, moral, religious or personal reaction or judgment. We may judge a power-station aesthetically and find economic satisfaction in a work of art that we own. We may take it, then, that we are not exclusively concerned with the philosophy of art, and that whatever the criteria of the aesthetic may be they cannot be found by trying to delimit a special class of objects.

If the aesthetic cannot be identified by its being directed to a special class of objects, it might be more plausibly suggested that the criteria of the aesthetic are to be sought by looking for some special features of objects which are attended to when our reaction or judgment is aesthetic; beauty and ugliness have often been adduced as the features in question. Alternatively it has often been suggested that aesthetic reactions and judgments contain or refer to some unique constituent of the emotions of the observer, either a special 'aesthetic emotion' or an 'aesthetic tinge' of some other emotion. I think that most commonly theories elicited by our problem have been variations on one or other of these two themes, a variation on the first theme being called an objectivist theory and a variation on the second being called subjectivist. I propose to give some reasons in this paper for finding both these theories unsatisfactory as answers to our problem, even if neither is wholly false as a mere assertion; in their place, I shall suggest that the correct answer is to be given in terms of the explanation of the reaction or the grounds of the judgment. I shall make some tentative remarks about what sort of grounds for a judgment make that judgment aesthetic, but cannot even begin the systematic treatment of the subject.

Let us revert to an illustration already casually used, and suppose that we observe a man in the audience at a play who is obviously beaming with delight and satisfaction. If I now maintain that his delight is purely economic, what have I to do in order to establish this contention? If the question at issue were whether he was delighted or merely contented it would no doubt be necessary to ascer-

tain fairly accurately his emotional state; but if it be agreed that he is delighted and the only issue is whether his delight is properly to be called economic, it is surely clear that phenomenological study of his emotions is not necessary. If, however, we find him to be the impresario, and he agrees that the complete explanation of his delight is that there is a full house and the reaction of the audience indicates a long run, what more could possibly be needed to justify us in describing his delight as economic? It seems hard to dispute that in the case of economic delight, satisfaction, disappointment and the like the criterion of the reaction's being economic lies in the nature of the explanation of that reaction. Similarly it would be beyond dispute that a man's delight was wholly personal if it were conceded that its explanation was entirely the fact that his daughter was acquitting herself well in her first part as a leading lady; again his delight will be moral if wholly explained by the belief that the play will have a good effect on the conduct of the audience. It would, I suggest, be very surprising if the way of establishing that delight, satisfaction and other reactions were aesthetic turned out to be quite different from the way in which we establish them to be moral, personal, economic, intellectual etc. Nor would it be surprising merely as a novelty; it would be logically disturbing to find that one had suddenly to depart from a single *fundamentum divisionis*, which had sufficed for all the other types, when one came to the aesthetic.

We must now note a further point about the logical relation between the concepts of the moral, the aesthetic, the economic, the intellectual, and the personal, as applied to reactions, both because it is of some logical interest and because a misunderstanding of it has led to some silly theories. *Triangular*, *square* and *pentagonal*, as applied to surfaces, are clearly species of a single genus and as such are mutually exclusive; there is a single *fundamentum divisionis* which is the number of sides that the rectilinear surface has. The same applies, *mutatis mutandis*, to *bachelor*, *married* and *widowed* as applied to men. On the other hand *triangular*, *red* and *large* are three logically unconnected predicates of surfaces, and *bachelor*, *bald* and *wealthy* are similarly unconnected predicates of men. What then are we to say about the predicates *moral*, *economic* and *aesthetic* as applied to, say, satisfactions? Clearly they are not technically species of a genus for they are not mutually exclusive as are species of a single genus; I may be simultaneously satisfied by a single object aesthetically, morally and economically, just as well as a man may be simultaneously bald, wealthy and a widower. But on the other hand to ask whether a satisfaction is moral or aesthetic makes as good sense as to ask whether a surface is square or triangular, whereas only in a very odd context can one ask whether a man is bald or a widower; furthermore, if a satisfaction is wholly moral it is not at all aesthetic, whereas being wholly bald does not prevent a man from being a widower, Thus moral, aesthetic and economic satisfactions seem neither to be logically disconnected nor to be true species of a genus.

Aesthetic and moral satisfactions thus seem to be related as are business and sporting associates. A man may be both a business and a sporting associate, yet the point of calling a man a business associate is to distinguish his status from that of a sporting or other type of associate, as it does not distinguish him from, say, an associate first met at Yarmouth. In the same way, to call a satisfaction aesthetic has the point of distinguishing its status from that of being a moral or economic satisfaction, though a satisfaction may be both aesthetic and moral. It surely follows that the criteria for a reaction's being aesthetic cannot be wholly unrelated to the criteria for its being moral or economic – they must be connected in such a way that we can see how being wholly one excludes being also another and yet how a single reaction can be both moral and aesthetic.

If we find the criterion for distinguishing aesthetic from kindred reactions in the nature of the explanation of the reaction we can readily account for this logical situation. To say that a satisfaction is wholly aesthetic, for example, will be to say that the explanation or grounds of the satisfaction are wholly of one sort, which will necessitate that the satisfaction cannot rest also on moral grounds; on the other hand there is clearly nothing to prevent our satisfaction from being multiply-grounded and thus simultaneously aesthetic and moral, aesthetic and economic, and so on.

But if we were to accept different kinds of criteria of the aesthetic, the moral and the economic we should be in difficulties here. Thus if a philosopher were to hold (and some apparently do) that a moral judgment is one that asserts an object to have a certain character and an aesthetic judgment to be one that announces or expresses the special emotional state of the speaker he would be maintaining views which, however plausible when consistently adhered to in isolation, are poor bed-fellows. For one would expect a wholly moral judgment interpreted as ascribing a moral character, to deny implicitly the presence of a special aesthetic or special economic character; similarly a wholly aesthetic judgment, interpreted as expressing a special aesthetic emotion, should deny implicitly the presence of a special moral or economic emotion. Consistency is required here.

So much for the logical point of being clear on the relation between the aesthetic, the moral, the economic etc. Unclarity on the point can lead to other less philosophical confusions. Thus the belief that moral considerations are relevant to a thing's aesthetic rank seems to stem from an awareness that appreciation may be simultaneously based on aesthetic and moral considerations coupled with a blindness to the fact that to call an appreciation aesthetic has as part of its point the effect of ruling out the moral as irrelevant. At the opposite extreme those who rage at any moral comment on a work of art are so conscious that the moral is irrelevant to the aesthetic that they suppose some error in allowing one's general satisfaction to have both a moral and an aesthetic component.

I have illustrated sufficiently the dangers of considering aesthetic reactions and judgments in abstraction from moral, economic and other kindred reactions and judgments. Similarly we must not concentrate on aesthetic delight and neglect other aesthetic reactions. The view that delight is aesthetic when that emotion has some special aesthetic tinge is not unplausible in isolation; we can no doubt bring aesthetic disgust under the same theory easily enough. But what if I am asked for an aesthetic judgment on what seems to me a very ordinary building and I reply truthfully that I find it merely tolerable? Am I reporting an emotion of toleration which has an aesthetic tinge, or perhaps an absolute tinge with no emotion to be tinged? But if I be taken to report merely the absence of any emotion or tinge by what criterion can we say that I am making an aesthetic judgment at all? It is surely important that we should be able to distinguish an aesthetic judgment of toleration from merely refraining from any aesthetic judgment at all; to regard a thing with mere aesthetic toleration is quite different from not considering it in an aesthetic light at all.

Thus the view that what distinguishes the aesthetic reaction and judgment is the presence of a special emotion or a special emotional tinge has already proved unsatisfactory on two counts. First, we have seen that we require a similar type of criterion of the aesthetic, the moral, the intellectual and the economic reaction, whereas the emotional criterion is very unplausible in some of these cases. Secondly, we have seen that however plausible with regard to strong emotional reactions, the emotional view is most unplausible when we consider such cool aesthetic reactions as that of bare toleration. Even if these difficulties were overcome, it is perhaps worth noticing that on this view a single reaction which involved, say, simultaneous economic, moral, aesthetic and intellectual satisfaction might well be required to involve an emotion having a quite kaleidoscopic variety of tinges.

But apart from these more logical points it is surely clear that when we experience emotions that we should wish to call aesthetic they are often very different from each other. Thus Tovey (*Essays in Musical Analysis*, Vol. I, p. 200) speaks of a theme 'which gives Mozart's most inimitable sense of physical well-being' precisely because most of even the most delightful musical themes are so different in emotional effect. Or again, is it so clear that aesthetic emotions are different in kind from others? Tovey, we have seen, compares a Mozart theme to a quite non-aesthetic delight, and Housman can be adduced as a still more striking, since unwilling, witness. Enumerating three types of 'symptoms' of poetical delight in his lecture, *The Name and Nature of Poetry*, he says: 'One of these symptoms was described in connexion with another object by Eliphaz the Temanite: "A spirit passed before my face; the hair of my flesh stood up;"' another he describes by using Keats's words about his feelings for Fanny Brawne, "everything that reminds me of her goes through me like a spear"; the third, he says, 'consists in a constriction of the throat and a precipitation of water to the eyes', an experience which is surely common to many emotional situations, and not confined to the aesthetic.

The objection to the view that what distinguishes the aesthetic judgment or reaction from others is that it alone involves the recognition or awareness of beauty and ugliness, if offered as a solution to our problem, is rather different. As a minor objection it is worth pointing out that we should hesitate to call many things for which we have a great aesthetic admiration 'beautiful', that 'beautiful' is a relatively specialised word of aesthetic appraisal, though this will inevitably elicit the answer that here 'beauty' is being used with a wider meaning than is currently assigned to it. But granted that 'beauty' and 'ugliness' are being used

with a wide enough significance, the trouble with this answer to our problem is not that it is false but that it is futile. Of course if I admire a thing aesthetically I must be aware of its beauty, or of its charm, or of its prettiness or some other 'aesthetic characteristic'; this is true in the same way as it is platitudinously true that moral admiration must involve awareness of a thing's moral goodness or rectitude or of some other 'moral characteristic'. But the trouble is that we have no independent way of telling whether we are aware of beauty or ugliness on the one hand or rightness or wrongness on the other; to know this we must know whether our admiration is aesthetic or moral, or, more accurately, to try to discover whether our admiration is aesthetic or moral and to try to discover whether we are aware of beauty or rightness are not two distinct enquiries but a single enquiry described in two ways neither of which is more luminous than the other. To identify the aesthetic judgment by the aesthetic characters of which it involves awareness is therefore not helpful.

Let me now set out more generally and completely the view that I wish to urge. The terms 'good', 'bad' and 'indifferent' are, I take it, among the widest terms of appraisal that we possess, and we do appraise things on the basis of criteria, criteria to be formulated in terms of the 'natural' features of the things appraised. But usually we wish at any time to appraise a thing only from a restricted point of view. We may, for instance, wish to appraise a career from the restricted point of view of its worth as a means to earning a livelihood; to do so we restrict our attention to a special set of the criteria of a good career, all others being for the purpose irrelevant. I wish to suggest that the moral, the aesthetic, the economic, the intellectual, the religious and other special appraisals should all be understood as being appraisals distinguished by their concentration on some special sub-set of criteria of value. To say that something is good as a means is not to say that it is good in some special sense distinct from that of 'good as an end' but to appraise it from a special point of view; similarly to judge a thing aesthetically good or first-rate is not to call it good in a sense different from that in which we call a thing morally good, but to judge it in the light of a different sub-set of criteria. We may if we wish choose to invent a special meaning for 'beautiful' in which it becomes shorthand for 'good from the aesthetic point of view', but that is only a dubious convenience of no theoretical significance. The central task of the philosopher of aesthetics is, I take it, to clarify the principles on which we select the special set of criteria of value that are properly to be counted as relevant to aesthetic judgment or appraisal. We may recognise an aesthetic reaction by its being due to features of the thing contemplated that are relevant criteria of the aesthetic judgment, and the aesthetic judgment is one founded on a special sub-set of the criteria of value of a certain sort of thing.

It may justly be said that so far I have done little more than to assert this view dogmatically, though I should wish to claim that I have given it some *a priori* probability by showing that it is a view which will enable us to deal with some of the difficulties that other views cannot surmount. Certainly I have as yet done nothing to indicate on what principles the criteria of value relevant to the aesthetic judgment are selected.

This lacuna can only be properly filled by field-work, and then only filled completely by a full-scale work on aesthetics. By doing field-work I mean studying examples of people actually trying to decide whether a certain judgment is or is not aesthetic and observing how they most convincingly argue the matter. Unfortunately to do this on an elaborate scale in one paper of a symposium is hardly possible; I can but ask you to believe that this paper has been written only after a considerable amount of such work, and produce one or two examples of it to show more clearly what I have in mind.

In his more philosophical moments A. E. Housman tried to account for the peculiar nature of the aesthetic in terms of emotional, and even physical, reactions; but here is an example of what he has to say at a more literary and less philosophical level: 'Again, there existed in the last century a great body of Wordsworthians, as they were called. It is now much smaller; but true appreciation of Wordsworth's poetry has not diminished in proportion: I suspect that it has much increased. The Wordsworthians, as Matthew Arnold told them, were apt to praise their poet for the wrong things. They were most attracted by what may be called his philosophy; they accepted his belief in the morality of the universe and the tendency of events to good; they were even willing to entertain his conception of nature as a living and sentient and benignant being; a conception as purely mythological as the Dryads and the Naiads. To that thrilling utterance which pierces the heart and brings tears to the eyes of thousands who care nothing for his opinions and beliefs they were not noticeably sensitive; and however justly they admired the depth of his insight into human nature and the nobility of his moral ideas, these things, with which his poetry was in close and harmonious alliance, are distinct from poetry itself.'

It does not matter whether we agree with Housman about Wordsworth; but I do hope that all will agree that this is the right sort of way to set about showing that an appreciation is not aesthetic. Clearly Housman does not deny that what the nineteenth century admired in Wordsworth was admirable; but he says that if your admiration of Wordsworth is based on certain grounds (the philosophical truth and moral loftiness of the content of the poetry) it is not aesthetic admiration, whereas if it is based on what Housman calls the 'thrilling utterance', by which the surrounding paragraphs abundantly show him to mean the sound, rhythm and imagery of the words used, then it is aesthetic admiration. Whether Housman is right about Wordsworth or not, whether he has selected the most important criteria of poetical merit or not, this is the type of argument to be expected in a competent discussion; but to have argued the case by adducing the claim that Wordsworthians tended to concentrate rather on traits other than beauty would in fact have been to have restated the case rather than to have argued it. Moreover, if some Wordsworthian had maintained that Wordsworth's pantheism did bring tears to his eyes it would clearly have made no difference to the argument; it is concentration on the utterance, rather than having tears in your eyes, that makes you truly appreciative of the poetry.

Housman's *The Name and Nature of Poetry* is a mine of similar examples. Though he says in a theoretical moment: 'I am convinced that most readers, when they think that they are admiring poetry, are deceived by inability to analyse their sensations, and that they are really admiring, not the poetry of the passage before them, but something else in it, which they like better than poetry,' in fact all the concrete examples are in accordance with my theory and not his own. Thus the later seventeenth-century writers are said by Housman to have but rarely true poetic merit not on the basis of any analysis of sensations but because, for example, they aimed to startle by novelty and amuse by ingenuity whereas their verse is inharmonious.

If, then, Housman's practice is sound it vindicates my view and stultifies his; nor is the obvious fact that we would not rate highly poetry that did not move us relevant to the question how we are to distinguish a high aesthetic rating from another type of high rating. If field work and reflection in general vindicate my contention as do these examples from Housman I cannot see what else can be relevant; but I freely own that it is the cumulative weight of a large collection of examples from a variety of fields that is necessary, and these I have not supplied; nor could we ever attain a strict proof.

But all this being granted we are still only on the periphery of our subject and the most difficult question remains to be dealt with. It is comparatively easy to see that there must be general principles of selection of evaluative criteria which determine whether our evaluation is to be counted as aesthetic, moral, intellectual or of some other kind; nor is it at all difficult to give examples of what anyone, who is prepared to accept this way of looking at the matter, can easily recognise as being a criterion falling under one or another principle. It would be a very odd person who denied that the sound of the words of a poem was one of the criteria of the aesthetic merit of a poem, or who maintained that being scientifically accurate and up to date was another; similarly it is clear that the honesty of a policy is a criterion of its moral goodness whereas, even if honesty is the best policy, honesty is not a direct criterion of economic merit. But it is by no means so easy to formulate these general principles.

This difficulty is by no means peculiar to aesthetics. Part of the general view of which the aesthetic doctrine given here is a fragment is that what determines whether a judgment is moral is what reasons are relevant to it; but everyone knows the difficulty of answering the question what makes a judgment a moral judgment. (In my terminology Kant's answer would be that the reasons must refer to the rationality or otherwise of consistently acting in a certain way.) Certainly it would be over-optimistic to expect to find very precise principles; probably there will be some overlap of criteria between the various spheres of evaluation in anybody's practice; certainly there are some overt border-line disputes whether this or that criterion is relevant to, say, aesthetic evaluation.

I think, however, that there is one peculiar difficulty in trying to find the principle, however vague, that determines what sort of reasons are relevant to a judgment if it is to be counted as aesthetic.

When we think of giving reasons for an aesthetic judgment we tend at once to call to mind what we would give as reasons for our appreciation of some very complex works of art; rightly considering, for example, that the plays of Shakespeare are things intended especially for consideration from the aesthetic point of view (I believe that a work of art can most usefully be considered as an artifact primarily intended for aesthetic consideration), we tend to think that we can most usefully tackle our problem by examining what would be relevant to an appreciation of, say, *Hamlet*, merely leaving aside obvious irrelevancies like cost of production. But this is most unfortunate, because, dealing with things intended primarily for aesthetic appreciation, we are inclined to treat as relevant to aesthetic appreciation very much more than we would in the case of things not so officially dedicated to aesthetic purposes; for practical purposes it would be pedantic to do otherwise. Moreover it is obviously very difficult to get straight our grounds for appreciating anything so complex. I am inclined to think that if *Hamlet* were rewritten to give the essential plot and characterisation in the jargon of the professional psychologist there could still be a lot to admire that we at present mention in our aesthetic appreciations, but we would no longer regard it as aesthetic appreciation but rather as intellectual appreciation of psychological penetration and the like.

For these and other reasons, it seems to me hopeless to start an enquiry into the nature of aesthetic grounds by concentrating our attention on great and complex works of art. Among the other reasons is that in evaluating great works of art the reasons proximately given will almost inevitably already be at a high level of generality and themselves evaluative – we will refer to masterly style, subtle characterisation, inevitability of the action and so on. If we are to have any hope of success we must first set our sights less high and commence with the simplest cases of aesthetic appreciation; in this paper, at least, I shall try to look no further.

If we examine, then, some very simple cases of aesthetic evaluation it seems to me that the grounds given are frequently the way the object appraised looks (shape and colour), the way it sounds, smells, tastes or feels. I may value a rose bush because it is hardy, prolific, disease-resistant and the like, but if I value the rose aesthetically the most obvious relevant grounds will be the way it looks, both in colour and in shape, and the way it smells; the same grounds may be a basis for aesthetic dislike. Though I might, for example, attempt to describe the shape to make you understand what I see in it these grounds seem to me to be really basic; if I admire a rose because of its scent and you then ask me why I admire its scent I should not in a normal context know what you want. These grounds are also those that we should expect to be basic in aesthetics from an etymological point of view, and while one can prove nothing philosophically from etymologies, etymological support is not to be despised. Things, then, may have sensible qualities which affect us favourably or unfavourably with no ulterior grounds. Surely there is no need to illustrate further these most simple cases of aesthetic evaluation.

But there are some slightly more sophisticated cases which need closer inspection. I have in mind occasions when we admire a building not only for its colour and shape but because it looks strong or spacious, or admire a horse because it looks swift as well as for its gleaming coat. These looks are not sensible qualities in the simple way in which colour and shape are. It is clear that in this sort of context to look strong or spacious or swift is not to seem very likely to be strong or spacious or swift. I might condemn a building for looking top-heavy when I knew very well that it was built on principles and with materials which ensured effectively that it would not be top-heavy. It is no doubt a plausible speculation that if a building looks top-heavy in the sense relevant to aesthetics it would probably seem really to be top-heavy in the untutored eye; but if an architect, who knows technically that a building is not top-heavy, judges it to look top-heavy when he considers it aesthetically he is in no way estimating the chances of its being blown over.

We are now considering the facts which, exclusively emphasised, lead to the functional view of aesthetics. The element of truth in that view I take to be that if a thing looks to have a characteristic which is a desirable one from another point of view, its looking so is a proper ground of aesthetic appreciation. What makes the appreciation aesthetic is that it is concerned with a thing's looking somehow without concern for whether it really is like that; beauty we may say, to emphasise the point, is not even skin-deep.

We have, then, isolated two types of aesthetic criteria, both of which are cases of looking (sounding etc.) somehow; in the simpler type it is the sensible qualities, in the narrowest sense, that are relevant; in the slightly more complex type it is looking to possess some quality which is non-aesthetically desirable that matters. We like our motor-cars in attractive tones and we like them to look fast (which does not involve peering under the bonnet); we like, perhaps, the timbre of a bird's note and we like it also for its cheerful or nobly mournful character, but would not be pleased if it sounded irritable or querulous; the smell of a flower may be seductive in itself but it will be still better if it is, say, a clean smell. Both these elementary types of criteria go hand in hand and are constantly employed.

The most obvious criticism of these suggestions is not that they are wrong but that they are incapable of extension to the more complicated situations in which we appraise a work of art. I cannot try now to deal with this sort of objection in any full way. But I should like to make two small points. First, I would repeat my suggestion that we are inclined to allow in non-aesthetic criteria 'by courtesy' when we are evaluating a work of art, so that we may even include intellectual merit. Secondly, the fact that such things as intellectual understanding are essential to an aesthetic appreciation of a work of art does not in itself establish the criticism. If for example we enjoy listening to a fugue it is likely that a part of our appreciation will be intellectual; no doubt intellectual understanding of what is going on is also necessary to aesthetic appreciation; but the fact that I cannot enjoy the sound of a theme being continually employed, sometimes inverted or in augmentation or in diminution, unless I have the theoretical training to recognise this, does not prevent my aesthetic appreciation from being of the sound. I am still appreciating the way a thing sounds or looks even when my intellect must be employed if I am to be aware of the fact that the thing does look or sound this way.

There remain many difficulties; above all the notion of 'looking in a certain way', especially in such cases as when we say something looks strong or swift, needs more elaboration. But to carry out this task is beyond the scope of this paper. Apart from a short appendix, I shall now close with a brief summary, a summary of a paper which is intended to do no more than to distinguish the aesthetic judgment and reaction from others and perhaps to indicate the best way in which to proceed to the further problems of the philosophy of aesthetics.

J. O. Urmson

Summary

1. The problem raised is how an aesthetic judgment, reaction or evaluation is to be distinguished from others.
2. We should expect to find a criterion which allows us to distinguish the aesthetic, the moral, the economic, the intellectual and other evaluations by a single *fundamentum divisionis*.
3. All evaluations are made on the basis of criteria for the merit of the kind of thing in question.
4. An aesthetic evaluation is one which is made on the basis of a selection from the total body of relevant criteria of merit.
5. In at least the simpler cases of aesthetic evaluation the relevant criteria appear to be those which are concerned with the way the object in question looks or presents itself to the other senses.
6. It is impossible to distinguish the aesthetic by a special object, by a special characteristic attended to, or by a special emotion.

Appendix

It may appear to some that too little importance has been accorded to the emotions in this paper. To avoid misunderstanding I will mention one or two ways in which I recognise the importance of considering the emotions in aesthetics.

First, I recognise that we would be very little interested in the aesthetic aspect of things but for their emotional effect upon us.

Secondly, I acknowledge that if we experience an emotional thrill when we look at a picture or hear a piece of music we do not normally have to examine our grounds and reasons to know that we are reacting aesthetically in a favourable way. But I do want to maintain that it is the nature of the grounds that makes our appreciation aesthetic and that if on an examination of our grounds we find, as sometimes happens, that our reasons are appropriate rather to moral evaluation or are erotic, or what you will, we will, if we are honest, recognise that our reaction was not after all aesthetic. Of course we have trained ourselves to a great extent to approach pictures and music from the aesthetic angle so that we shall not in general be mistaken if we rely on an unanalysed impression.

Thirdly, there are a great number of terms that we use in aesthetic evaluation – *pleasant*, *moving*, *pretty*, *beautiful*, *impressive*, *admirable* and *exciting* among others. I do not know what makes one more appropriate than another in a given context; partly, perhaps, they are more or less laudatory, or are based on a still more restricted selection of criteria than a mere judgment of goodness or badness; but I suspect that the choice of word is at least in part determined by the precise character of the emotion experienced.

For these and other reasons I do not wish to belittle the importance of the emotions in the philosophy of aesthetics; but I do wish to deny most emphatically that the aesthetic field can be distinguished from others by an attempt to analyse the emotions involved therein: and that is all that the thesis of this paper requires.

References

Houseman, A. E., *The Name and Nature of Poetry* (Cambridge: Cambridge University Press, 1933).

Tovey, Donald Francis, *Essays in Musical Analysis*, vol. 1 (London: Oxford University Press, 1935).

3

The Artworld

Arthur C. Danto

> *Hamlet*: Do you see nothing there?
> *The Queen*: Nothing at all; yet all that is I
> see.
>
> ### Shakespeare, Hamlet, III.iv

Hamlet and Socrates, though in praise and depre-
cation respectively, spoke of art as a mirror held up
to nature. As with many disagreements in attitude,
this one has a factual basis. Socrates saw mirrors
as but reflecting what we can already see; so art,
insofar as mirrorlike, yields idle accurate duplica-
tions of the appearances of things, and is of no
cognitive benefit whatever. Hamlet, more acutely,
recognized a remarkable feature of reflecting surfaces, namely that they show us what we could not
otherwise perceive – our own face and form –
and so art, insofar as it is mirrorlike, reveals us
to ourselves, and is, even by socratic criteria, of
some cognitive utility after all. As a philosopher,
however, I find Socrates' discussion defective on
other, perhaps less profound grounds than these. If
a mirror-image of *o* is indeed an imitation of *o*,
then, if art is imitation, mirror-images are art. But
in fact mirroring objects no more is art than returning weapons to a madman is justice; and reference
to mirrorings would be just the sly sort of coun-
terinstance we would expect Socrates to bring
forward in rebuttal of the theory he instead uses
them to illustrate. If that theory requires us to class
these as art, it thereby shows its inadequacy: "is an
imitation" will not do as a sufficient condition for

Arthur C. Danto, "The Artworld," *The Journal of
Philosophy*, 61 (1964), pp. 571–84. Reprinted by
courtesy of The Journal of Philosophy.

"is art." Yet, perhaps because artists *were* engaged
in imitation, in Socrates' time and after, the insufficiency of the theory was not noticed until the
invention of photography. Once rejected as a sufficient condition, mimesis was quickly discarded as
even a necessary one; and since the achievement of
Kandinsky, mimetic features have been relegated to
the periphery of critical concern, so much so that
some works survive in spite of possessing those
virtues, excellence in which was once celebrated as
the essence of art, narrowly escaping demotion to
mere illustrations.

It is, of course, indispensable in socratic discussion that all participants be masters of the concept
up for analysis, since the aim is to match a real
defining expression to a term in active use, and the
test for adequacy presumably consists in showing
that the former analyzes and applies to all and only
those things of which the latter is true. The popular
disclaimer notwithstanding, then, Socrates' auditors purportedly knew what art was as well as what
they liked; and a theory of art, regarded here as a
real definition of 'Art', is accordingly not to be of
great use in helping men to recognize instances of
its application. Their antecedent ability to do this is
precisely what the adequacy of the theory is to be
tested against, the problem being only to make
explicit what they already know. It is *our* use of the
term that the theory allegedly means to capture, but
we are supposed able, in the words of a recent
writer, "to separate those objects which are works of
art from those which are not, because . . . we know
how correctly to use the word 'art' and to apply the
phrase 'work of art'." Theories, on this account, are
somewhat like mirror-images on Socrates' account,

showing forth what we already know, wordy reflections of the actual linguistic practice we are masters in.

But telling artworks from other things is not so simple a matter, even for native speakers, and these days one might not be aware he was on artistic terrain without an artistic theory to tell him so. And part of the reason for this lies in the fact that terrain is constituted artistic in virtue of artistic theories, so that one use of theories, in addition to helping us discriminate art from the rest, consists in making art possible. Glaucon and the others could hardly have known what was art and what not: otherwise they would never have been taken in by mirror-images.

I

Suppose one thinks of the discovery of a whole new class of artworks as something analogous to the discovery of a whole new class of facts anywhere, viz., as something for theoreticians to explain. In science, as elsewhere, we often accommodate new facts to old theories via auxiliary hypotheses, a pardonable enough conservatism when the theory in question is deemed too valuable to be jettisoned all at once. Now the Imitation Theory of Art (IT) is, if one but thinks it through, an exceedingly powerful theory, explaining a great many phenomena connected with the causation and evaluation of artworks, bringing a surprising unity into a complex domain. Moreover, it is a simple matter to shore it up against many purported counterinstances by such auxiliary hypotheses as that the artist who deviates from mimeticity is perverse, inept, or mad. Ineptitude, chicanery, or folly are, in fact, testable predications. Suppose, then, tests reveal that these hypotheses fail to hold, that the theory, now beyond repair, must be replaced. And a new theory is worked out, capturing what it can of the old theory's competence, together with the heretofore recalcitrant facts. One might, thinking along these lines, represent certain episodes in the history of art as not dissimilar to certain episodes in the history of science, where a conceptual revolution is being effected and where refusal to countenance certain facts, while in part due to prejudice, inertia, and self-interest, is due also to the fact that a well-established, or at least widely credited theory is being threatened in such a way that all coherence goes.

Some such episode transpired with the advent of post-impressionist paintings. In terms of the prevailing artistic theory (IT), it was impossible to accept these as art unless inept art: otherwise they could be discounted as hoaxes, self-advertisements, or the visual counterparts of madmen's ravings. So to get them accepted *as* art, on a footing with the *Transfiguration* (not to speak of a Landseer stag), required not so much a revolution in taste as a theoretical revision of rather considerable proportions, involving not only the artistic enfranchisement of these objects, but an emphasis upon newly significant features of accepted artworks, so that quite different accounts of their status as artworks would now have to be given. As a result of the new theory's acceptance, not only were post-impressionist paintings taken up as art, but numbers of objects (masks, weapons, etc.) were transferred from anthropological museums (and heterogeneous other places) to *musées des beaux arts*, though, as we would expect from the fact that a criterion for the acceptance of a new theory is that it account for whatever the older one did, nothing had to be transferred out of the *musée des beaux arts* – even if there were internal rearrangements as between storage rooms and exhibition space. Countless native speakers hung upon suburban mantelpieces innumerable replicas of paradigm cases for teaching the expression 'work of art' that would have sent their Edwardian forebears into linguistic apoplexy.

To be sure, I distort by speaking of a theory: historically, there were several, all, interestingly enough, more or less defined in terms of the IT. Art-historical complexities must yield before the exigencies of logical exposition, and I shall speak as though there were one replacing theory, partially compensating for historical falsity by choosing one which was actually enunciated. According to it, the artists in question were to be understood not as unsuccessfully imitating real forms but as successfully creating new ones, quite as real as the forms which the older art had been thought, in its best examples, to be creditably imitating. Art, after all, had long since been thought of as creative (Vasari says that God was the first artist), and the post-impressionists were to be explained as genuinely creative, aiming, in Roger Fry's words, "not at illusion but reality." This theory (RT) furnished a whole new mode of looking at painting, old and new. Indeed, one might almost interpret the crude drawing in Van Gogh and Cézanne, the dislocation of form from contour in Rouault and Dufy, the arbitrary use of color planes in Gauguin and the Fauves, as so many ways of drawing attention to the fact that these were *non-imitations*, specifically intended not to deceive. Logically, this would be roughly like printing "Not Legal Tender" across a brilliantly counterfeited dollar bill, the resulting object (counterfeit *cum* inscription) rendered incapable of deceiving anyone. It is not an illusory dollar bill, but then, just because it is non-illusory it does not automatically become a real dollar bill either. It rather occupies a freshly opened area between real objects and real facsimiles of real objects: it is a non-facsimile, if one requires a word, and a new contribution to the world. Thus, Van Gogh's *Potato Eaters*, as a consequence of certain unmistakable distortions, turns out to be a non-facsimile of real-life potato eaters; and inasmuch as these are not facsimiles of potato eaters, Van Gogh's picture, as a non-imitation, had as much right to be called a real object as did its putative subjects. By means of this theory (RT), artworks re-entered the thick of things from which socratic theory (IT) had sought to evict them: if no *more* real than what carpenters wrought, they were at least no *less* real. The Post-Impressionist won a victory in ontology.

It is in terms of RT that we must understand the artworks around us today. Thus Roy Lichtenstein paints comic-strip panels, though ten or twelve feet high. These are reasonably faithful projections onto a gigantesque scale of the homely frames from the daily tabloid, but it is precisely the scale that counts. A skilled engraver might incise *The Virgin and the Chancellor Rollin* on a pinhead, and it would be recognizable as such to the keen of sight, but an engraving of a Barnett Newman on a similar scale would be a blob, disappearing in the reduction. A *photograph* of a Lichtenstein is indiscernible from a photograph of a counterpart panel from *Steve Canyon*; but the photograph fails to capture the scale, and hence is as inaccurate a reproduction as a black-and-white engraving of Botticelli, scale being essential here as color there. Lichtensteins, then, are not imitations but *new entities*, as giant whelks would be. Jasper Johns, by contrast, paints objects with respect to which questions of scale are irrelevant. Yet his objects cannot be imitations, for they have the remarkable property that any intended copy of a member of this class of objects is automatically a member of the class itself, so that these objects are logically inimitable. Thus, a copy of a numeral just *is* that numeral: a painting of 3 is a 3 made of paint. Johns, in addition, paints targets, flags, and maps. Finally, in what I hope are not unwitting footnotes to Plato, two of our pioneers – Robert Rauschenberg and Claes Oldenburg – have made genuine beds.

Rauschenberg's bed hangs on a wall, and is streaked with some desultory housepaint. Oldenburg's bed is a rhomboid, narrower at one end than the other, with what one might speak of as a built-in perspective: ideal for small bedrooms. As beds, these sell at singularly inflated prices, but one *could* sleep in either of them: Rauschenberg has expressed the fear that someone might just climb into his bed and fall asleep. Imagine, now, a certain Testadura – a plain speaker and noted philistine – who is not aware that these are art, and who takes them to be reality simple and pure. He attributes the paintstreaks on Rauschenberg's bed to the slovenliness of the owner, and the bias in the Oldenburg bed to the ineptitude of the builder or the whimsy, perhaps, of whoever had it "custom-made." These would be mistakes, but mistakes of rather an odd kind, and not terribly different from that made by the stunned birds who pecked the sham grapes of Zeuxis. They mistook art for reality, and so has Testadura. But it was meant to *be* reality, according to RT. Can one have mistaken reality for reality? How shall we describe Testadura's error? What, after all, prevents Oldenburg's creation from being a misshapen bed? This is equivalent to asking what makes it art, and with this query we enter a domain of conceptual inquiry where native speakers are poor guides: *they are lost themselves.*

II

To mistake an artwork for a real object is no great feat when an artwork is the real object one mistakes it for. The problem is how to avoid such errors, or to remove them once they are made. The artwork is a bed, and not a bed-illusion; so there is nothing like the traumatic encounter against a flat surface that brought it home to the birds of Zeuxis that they had been duped. Except for the guard cautioning Testadura not to sleep on the artworks, he might never have discovered that this was an artwork and not a bed; and since, after all, one cannot discover that a bed is not a bed, how is Testadura to realize that he has made an error?

A certain sort of explanation is required, for the error here is a curiously philosophical one, rather like, if we may assume as correct some well-known views of P. F. Strawson, mistaking a person for a material body when the truth is that a person *is* a material body in the sense that a whole class of predicates, sensibly applicable to material bodies, are sensibly, and by appeal to no different criteria, applicable to persons. So you cannot *discover* that a person is not a material body.

We begin by explaining, perhaps, that the paintstreaks are not to be explained away, that they are *part* of the object, so the object is not a mere bed with – as it happens – streaks of paint spilled over it, but a complex object fabricated out of a bed and some paintstreaks: a paint-bed. Similarly, a person is not a material body with – as it happens – some thoughts superadded, but is a complex entity made up of a body and some conscious states: a conscious-body. Persons, like artworks, must then be taken as irreducible to *parts* of themselves, and are in that sense primitive. Or, more accurately, the paintstreaks are not part of the real object – the bed – which happens to be part of the artwork, but are, *like* the bed, part of the artwork as such. And this might be generalized into a rough characterization of artworks that happen to contain real objects as parts of themselves: not every part of an artwork *A* is part of a real object *R* when *R* is part of *A* and can, moreover, be detached from *A* and seen *merely* as *R*. The mistake thus far will have been to mistake *A* for *part* of itself, namely *R*, even though it would not be incorrect to say that *A* is *R*, that the artwork is a bed. It is the 'is' which requires clarification here.

There is an *is* that figures prominently in statements concerning artworks which is not the *is* of either identity or predication; nor is it the *is* of existence, of identification, or some special *is* made up to serve a philosophic end. Nevertheless, it is in common usage, and is readily mastered by children. It is the sense of *is* in accordance with which a child, shown a circle and a triangle and asked which is him and which his sister, will point to the triangle saying "That is me"; or, in response to my question, the person next to me points to the man in purple and says "That one is Lear"; or in the gallery I point, for my companion's benefit, to a spot in the painting before us and say "That white dab is Icarus." We do not mean, in these instances, that whatever is pointed to stands for, or represents, what it is said to be, for the *word* 'Icarus' stands for or represents Icarus: yet I would not in

the same sense of *is* point to the word and say "That is Icarus." The sentence "That *a* is *b*" is perfectly compatible with "That *a* is not *b*" when the first employs this sense of *is* and the second employs some other, though *a* and *b* are used nonambiguously throughout. Often, indeed, the truth of the first *requires* the truth of the second. The first, in fact, is incompatible with "That *a* is not *b*" only when the *is* is used nonambiguously throughout. For want of a word I shall designate this the *is* of *artistic identification*; in each case in which it is used, the *a* stands for some specific physical property of, or physical part of, an object; and, finally, it is a necessary condition for something to be an artwork that some part or property of it be designable by the subject of a sentence that employs this special *is*. It is an *is*, incidentally, which has near-relatives in marginal and mythical pronouncements. (Thus, one *is* Quetzalcoatl; those *are* the Pillars of Hercules.)

Let me illustrate. Two painters are asked to decorate the east and west walls of a science library with frescoes to be respectively called *Newton's First Law* and *Newton's Third Law*. These paintings, when finally unveiled, look, scale apart, as follows:

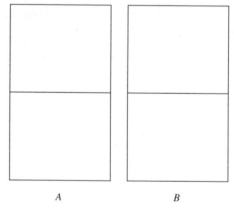

A   B

As objects I shall suppose the works to be indiscernible: a black, horizontal line on a white ground, equally large in each dimension and element. *B* explains his work as follows: a mass, pressing downward, is met by a mass pressing upward: the lower mass reacts equally and oppositely to the upper one. *A* explains his work as follows: the line through the space is the path of an isolated particle. The path goes from edge to edge, to give the sense of its *going beyond*. If it ended or began within the space, the line would be curved: and it is parallel to the top and bottom edges, for if it were closer to one than to another, there would have to be a force accounting for it, and this is inconsistent with its being the path of an *isolated* particle.

Much follows from these artistic identifications. To regard the middle line as an edge (mass meeting mass) imposes the need to identify the top and bottom half of the picture as rectangles, and as two distinct parts (not necessarily as two masses, for the line could be the edge of *one* mass jutting up – or down – into empty space). If it is an edge, we cannot thus take the entire area of the painting as a single space: it is rather composed of two forms, or one form and a non-form. We could take the entire area as a single space only by taking the middle horizontal as a *line* which is not an edge. But this almost requires a three-dimensional identification of the whole picture: the area can be a flat surface which the line is *above* (*Jet-flight*), or *below* (*Submarine-path*), or *on* (*Line*), or *in* (*Fissure*), or *through* (*Newton's First Law*) – though in this last case the area is not a flat surface but a transparent cross-section of absolute space. We could make all these prepositional qualifications clear by imagining perpendicular cross-sections to the picture plane. Then, depending upon the applicable prepositional clause, the area is (artistically) interrupted or not by the horizontal element. If we take the line as *through* space, the edges of the picture are not really the edges of the space: the space goes beyond the picture if the line itself does; and we are in the same space as the line is. As *B*, the edges of the picture can be *part* of the picture in case the masses go right to the edges, so that the edges of the picture are *their* edges. In that case, the vertices of the picture would be the vertices of the masses, except that the masses have four vertices more than the picture itself does: here four vertices would be part of the artwork which were not part of the real object. Again, the faces of the masses could be the face of the picture, and in looking at the picture, we are looking at these faces: but *space* has no face, and on the reading of *A* the work has to be read as faceless, and the face of the physical object would not be part of the artwork. Notice here how one artistic identification engenders another artistic identification, and how, consistently with a given identification, we are *required* to give others and *precluded* from still others: indeed, a given identification determines how many elements the work is to contain. These different identifications are incompatible with one another, or generally so, and each might be said to make a different artwork, even though each artwork contains the identical real object as part of itself – or at least parts of the identical real object as parts of itself. There are, of course, senseless identifications: no one could, I think, sensibly read the middle horizontal as *Love's Labour's Lost* or *The Ascendancy of St. Erasmus*. Finally, notice how acceptance of one identification rather than another is in effect to exchange one *world* for another. We could, indeed, enter a quite poetic world by identifying the upper area with a clear and cloudless sky, reflected in the still surface of the water below, whiteness kept from whiteness only by the unreal boundary of the horizon.

And now Testadura, having hovered in the wings throughout this discussion, protests that *all he sees is paint*: a white painted oblong with a black line painted across it. And how right he really is: that is all he sees or that anybody can, we aesthetes included. So, if he asks us to show him what there is further to see, to demonstrate through pointing that this is an artwork (*Sea and Sky*), we cannot comply, for he has overlooked nothing (and it would be absurd to suppose he had, that there was something tiny we could point to and he, peering closely, say "So it is! A work of art after all!"). We cannot help him until he has mastered the *is of artistic identification* and so *constitutes* it a work of art. If he cannot achieve this, he will never look upon artworks: he will be like a child who sees sticks as sticks.

But what about pure abstractions, say something that looks just like *A* but is entitled *No. 7*? The 10th Street abstractionist blankly insists that there is nothing here but white paint and black, and none of our literary identifications need apply. What then distinguishes him from Testadura, whose philistine utterances are indiscernible from his? And how can it be an artwork for him and not for Testadura, when they agree that there is nothing that does not meet the eye? The answer, unpopular as it is likely to be to purists of every variety, lies in the fact that this artist has returned to the physicality of paint through an atmosphere compounded of artistic theories and the history of recent and remote painting, elements of which he is trying to refine out of his own work; and as a consequence of this his work belongs in this atmosphere and is part of this history. He has achieved abstraction through rejection of artistic identifications, returning to the real world from which such identifications remove us (he thinks), somewhat in the mode of Ch'ing Yuan, who wrote:

Before I had studied Zen for thirty years, I saw mountains as mountains and waters as waters. When I arrived at a more intimate knowledge, I came to the point where I saw that mountains are not mountains, and waters are not waters. But now that I have got the very substance I am at rest. For it is just that I see mountains once again as mountains, and waters once again as waters.

His identification of what he has made is logically dependent upon the theories and history he rejects. The difference between his utterance and Testadura's "This is black paint and white paint and nothing more" lies in the fact that he is still using the *is* of artistic identification, so that his use of "That black paint is black paint" is not a tautology. Testadura is not at that stage. To see something as art requires something the eye cannot descry – an atmosphere of artistic theory, a knowledge of the history of art: an artworld.

III

Mr. Andy Warhol, the Pop artist, displays facsimiles of Brillo cartons, piled high, in neat stacks, as in the stockroom of the supermarket. They happen to be of wood, painted to look like cardboard, and why not? To paraphrase the critic of the *Times*, if one may make the facsimile of a human being out of bronze, why not the facsimile of a Brillo carton out of plywood? The cost of these boxes happens to be 2×10^3 that of their homely counterparts in real life – a differential hardly ascribable to their advantage in durability. In fact the Brillo people might, at some slight increase in cost, make their boxes out of plywood without these becoming artworks, and Warhol might make *his* out of cardboard without their ceasing to be art. So we may forget questions of intrinsic value, and ask why the Brillo people cannot manufacture art and why Warhol cannot *but* make artworks. Well, his are made by hand, to be sure. Which is like an insane reversal of Picasso's strategy in pasting the label from a bottle of Suze onto a drawing, saying as it were that the academic artist, concerned with exact imitation, must always fall short of the real thing: so why not just *use* the real thing? The Pop artist laboriously reproduces machine-made objects by hand, e.g., painting the labels on coffee cans (one can hear the familiar commendation "Entirely made by hand" falling painfully out of the guide's vocabulary when confronted by these objects). But the difference cannot consist in craft: a man who carved pebbles out of stones and carefully constructed a work called *Gravel Pile* might invoke the labor theory of value to account for the price he demands; but the question is, What makes it art? And why need Warhol *make* these things anyway? Why not just scrawl his signature across one? Or crush one up and display it as *Crushed Brillo Box* ("A protest against mechanization . . .") or simply display a Brillo carton as *Uncrushed Brillo Box* ("A bold affirmation of the plastic authenticity of industrial . . .")? Is this man a kind of Midas, turning whatever he touches into the gold of pure art? And the whole world consisting of latent artworks waiting, like the bread and wine of reality, to be transfigured, through some dark mystery, into the indiscernible flesh and blood of the sacrament? Never mind that the Brillo box may not be good, much less great art. The impressive thing is that it is art at all. But if it is, why are not the indiscernible Brillo boxes that are in the stockroom? Or *has* the whole distinction between art and reality broken down?

Suppose a man collects objects (ready-mades), including a Brillo carton; we praise the exhibit for variety, ingenuity, what you will. Next he exhibits nothing but Brillo cartons, and we criticize it as dull, repetitive, self-plagiarizing – or (more profoundly) claim that he is obsessed by regularity and repetition, as in *Marienbad*. Or he piles them high, leaving a narrow path; we treat our way through the smooth opaque stacks and find it an unsettling experience, and write it up as the closing in of consumer products, confining us as prisoners: or we say he is a modern pyramid builder. True, we don't say these things about the stockboy. But then a stockroom is not an art gallery, and we cannot readily separate the Brillo cartons from the gallery they are in, any more than we can separate the Rauschenberg bed from the paint upon it. Outside the gallery, they are pasteboard cartons. But then, scoured clean of paint, Rauschenberg's bed is a bed, just what it was before it was transformed into art. But then if we think this matter through, we discover that the artist has failed, really and of necessity, to produce a mere real object. He has produced an artwork, his use of real Brillo cartons being but an expansion of the resources available to artists, a contribution to *artists' materials*, as oil paint was, or *tuche*.

What in the end makes the difference between a Brillo box and a work of art consisting of a Brillo

Box is a certain theory of art. It is the theory that takes it up into the world of art, and keeps it from collapsing into the real object which it is (in a sense of *is* other than that of artistic identification). Of course, without the theory, one is unlikely to see it as art, and in order to see it as part of the Artworld, one must have mastered a good deal of artistic theory as well as a considerable amount of the history of recent New York painting. It could not have been art fifty years ago. But then there could not have been, everything being equal, flight insurance in the Middle Ages, or Etruscan typewriter erasers. The world has to be ready for certain things, the Artworld no less than the real one. It is the role of artistic theories, these days as always, to make the Artworld, and art, possible. It would, I should think, never have occurred to the painters of Lascaux that they were producing *art* on those walls. Not unless there were neolithic aestheticians.

IV

The Artworld stands to the real world in something like the relationship in which the City of God stands to the Earthly City. Certain objects, like certain individuals, enjoy a double citizenship, but there remains, the RT notwithstanding, a fundamental contrast between artworks and real objects. Perhaps this was already dimly sensed by the early framers of the IT who, inchoately realizing the nonreality of art, were perhaps limited only in supposing that the sole way objects had of being other than real is to be sham, so that artworks necessarily had to be imitations of real objects. This was too narrow. So Yeats saw in writing "Once out of nature I shall never take / My bodily form from any natural thing." It is but a matter of choice: and the Brillo box of the Artworld may be just the Brillo box of the real one, separated and united by the *is* of artistic identification. But I should like to say some final words about the theories that make artworks possible, and their relationship to one another. In so doing, I shall beg some of the hardest philosophical questions I know.

I shall now think of pairs of predicates related to each other as "opposites," conceding straight off the vagueness of this *démodé* term. Contradictory predicates are not opposites, since one of each of them must apply to every object in the universe, and neither of a pair of opposites need apply to some objects in the universe. An object must first be of a certain kind before either of a pair of oppo-

sites applies to it, and then at most and at least one of the opposites must apply to it. So opposites are not contraries, for contraries may both be false of some objects in the universe, but opposites cannot both be false; for of some objects, neither of a pair of opposites *sensibly* applies, unless the object is of the right sort. Then, if the object is of the required kind, the opposites behave as contradictories. If F and non-F are opposites, an object o must be of a certain kind K before either of these sensibly applies; but if o is a member of K, then o either is F or non-F, to the exclusion of the other. The class of pairs of opposites that sensibly apply to the $(ô)Ko$ I shall designate as the class of K-*relevant predicates*. And a necessary condition for an object to be of a kind K is that at least one pair of K-relevant opposites be sensibly applicable to it. But, in fact, if an object is of kind K, at least and at most one of each K-relevant pair of opposites applies to it.

I am now interested in the K-relevant predicates for the class K of artworks. And let F and non-F be an opposite pair of such predicates. Now it might happen that, throughout an entire period of time, every artwork is non-F. But since nothing thus far is both an artwork and F, it might never occur to anyone that non-F is an artistically relevant predicate. The non-F-ness of artworks goes unmarked. By contrast, all works up to a given time might be G, it never occurring to anyone until that time that something might both be an artwork and non-G; indeed, it might have been thought that G was a *defining trait* of artworks when in fact something might first have to be an artwork before G is sensibly predicable of it – in which case non-G might also be predicable of artworks, and G itself then could not have been a defining trait of this class.

Let G be 'is representational' and let F be 'is expressionist'. At a given time, these and their opposites are perhaps the only art-relevant predicates in critical use. Now letting '+' stand for a given predicate P and '−' for its opposite non-P, we may construct a style matrix more or less as follows:

F	G
+	+
+	−
−	+
−	−

The rows determine available styles, given the active critical vocabulary: representational expressionistic (e.g., Fauvism); representational nonexpressionistic (Ingres); nonrepresentational expressionistic (Abstract Expressionism); nonrepresentational nonexpressionist (hard-edge abstraction). Plainly, as we add art-relevant predicates, we increase the number of available styles at the rate of 2^n. It is, of course, not easy to see in advance which predicates are going to be added or replaced by their opposites, but suppose an artist determines that H shall henceforth be artistically relevant for his paintings. Then, in fact, both H and non-H become artistically relevant for *all* painting, and if his is the first and only painting that is H, every other painting in existence becomes non-H, and the entire community of paintings is enriched, together with a doubling of the available style opportunities. It is this retroactive enrichment of the entities in the Artworld that makes it possible to discuss Raphael and De Kooning together, or Lichtenstein and Michelangelo. The greater the variety of artistically relevant predicates, the more complex the individual members of the Artworld become; and the more one knows of the entire population of the Artworld, the richer one's experience with any of its members.

In this regard, notice that, if there are m artistically relevant predicates, there is always a bottom row with m minuses. This row is apt to be occupied by purists. Having scoured their canvasses clear of what they regard as inessential, they credit themselves with having distilled out the essence of art. But this is just their fallacy: exactly as many artistically relevant predicates stand true of their square monochromes as stand true of any member of the Artworld, and they can *exist* as artworks only insofar as "impure" paintings exist. Strictly speaking, a black square by Reinhardt is artistically as rich as Titian's *Sacred and Profane Love*. This explains how less is more.

Fashion, as it happens, favors certain rows of the style matrix: museums, connoisseurs, and others are makeweights in the Artworld. To insist, or seek to, that all artists become representational, perhaps to gain entry into a specially prestigious exhibition, cuts the available style matrix in half: there are then $2^n/2$ ways of satisfying the requirement, and museums then can exhibit all these "approaches" to the topic they have set. But this is a matter of almost purely sociological interest: one row in the matrix is as legitimate as another. An artistic breakthrough consists, I suppose, in adding the possibility of a column to the matrix. Artists then, with greater or less alacrity, occupy the positions thus opened up: this is a remarkable feature of contemporary art, and for those unfamiliar with the matrix, it is hard, and perhaps impossible, to recognize certain positions as occupied by artworks. Nor would these things be artworks without the theories and the histories of the Artworld.

Brillo boxes enter the Artworld with that same tonic incongruity the *commedia dell'arte* characters bring into *Ariadne auf Naxos*. Whatever is the artistically relevant predicate in virtue of which they gain their entry, the rest of the Artworld becomes that much the richer in having the opposite predicate available and applicable to its members. And, to return to the views of Hamlet with which we began this discussion, Brillo boxes may reveal us to ourselves as well as anything might: as a mirror held up to nature, they might serve to catch the conscience of our kings.

4

Defining Art Historically

Jerrold Levinson

The question of what makes something art is probably the most venerable in aesthetics. What is the artness of an artwork? Wherein does it reside? We would certainly like to know. We would certainly be interested to learn what ties together Dickens's *Oliver Twist*, Tallis's *Spem in alium*, Flavin's *Pink and Gold*, Balanchine's *Variations for a Door and a Sigh*, Wilson and Glass's *Einstein on the Beach*, the Parthenon, and countless other unknown and unsung objects under the common banner of art. After rejecting the many proposals made by philosophers from Plato to the present on grounds of narrowness, tendentiousness, inflexibility, vagueness, or circularity, one would appear to be left with no answer to the question at all, and perhaps a suspicion that it is unanswerable. Nevertheless, the question has been taken up in recent years and given a new sort of answer: the institutional theory of art, adumbrated by Arthur Danto and propounded explicitly by George Dickie. In short, the theory is that artworks are artworks because they occupy a certain place, which they must be given, in a certain institution, that of Art.[1]

I

In this essay I would like to begin to develop an alternative to the institutional theory of art, albeit one that is clearly inspired by it. What I will retain from that theory is the crucial idea that artwork-

Jerrold Levinson, "Defining Art Historically," *British Journal of Aesthetics*, 19 (1979), pp. 232–50. Reprinted by permission of Oxford University Press.

hood is not an intrinsic exhibited property of a thing, but rather a matter of being related in the right way to human activity and thought. However, I propose to construe this relation solely in terms of the *intention* of an *independent individual* (or individuals) – as opposed to an overt *act* (that of conferring the status of a candidate for appreciation) performed in an *institutional setting* constituted by many individuals – where the intention makes reference (either transparently or opaquely) to the *history of art* (what art has been) as opposed to that murky and somewhat exclusive institution, the *artworld*. The core of my proposal will be an account of what it is to regard-as-a-work-of-art, an account that gives this an essential historicity.[2] It is this which will do the work in my theory which the notion of artworld is supposed to do in the institutional theory. That art is necessarily backward-looking (though in some cases not consciously so) is a fact that the definition of art must recognize. To ignore it is to miss the only satisfying explanation of the unity of art across time and of its inherently continuous evolution – the manner in which art of a given moment must *involve*, as opposed to merely *follow*, that which has preceded it.

II

Before sketching my view in some detail, I want to remark on two major difficulties with the institutional theory. (I pass over the often-made charges that the theory is uninformative, and that the key notions of 'artworld' and 'conferral of status' are vague and artificial.)[3] The first problem is the implication that art making must involve a certain *cultural performance*, a ceremony or quasi ceremony, a kind of hand waving that draws into the fold. One must do something outwardly, and one must do it in relation to a certain social institution. On the contrary, I would urge that there can be private, isolated art that is constituted as art in the mind of the artist – and on no one's behalf but his or her own and that of *potential* experiencers of it. (I assume that *just that* is not enough to make the artworld, or else the notion becomes trivial and otiose.) Although in my scheme an art maker will *typically* have art and an existing society of art consumers in mind when producing an art object, this is not necessary. In no case *must* one invoke or accord with the shadowy infrastructure of the artworld to make what one makes into art. Consider the farmer's wife at a Nebraska country fair who sets an assemblage of egg shells and white glue down on the corner of a table for folks to look at. Isn't it possible that she has created art? Yet she and the artworld exist in perfect mutual oblivion. Consider a solitary Indian along the Amazon who steals off from his nonartistic tribe to arrange colored stones in a clearing, not outwardly investing them with special position in the world. Might not this also be art (and, note, before any future curator decides that it is)? The institutional theory comes close to conflating art and *self-conscious* art, art and *socially situated* art, art and *declared* art.

The second and main problem I find with the institutional theory is that the artworld must do all the work in specifying the *way* in which an object has to be presented or treated in order for it to be a work of art, whereas the notion of *appreciation* (the point of the enterprise) is not specified at all or only in the most general terms.[4] That is to say, we are not told enough about what the art maker must envisage must be done with his or her object by potential spectators. It seems, though, that some kind of specification of this must be essayed if making art is to be distinguished from making nonart. I believe the key to an adequate and revealing definition of art is to specify what the art object must be *intended for*, what sort of *regard* the spectator must be asked to extend to the object – rather than designate an *institution* on behalf of which some such request can be made. The trick, of course, is to do so without describing an intended way of regard given by fixed characteristics (e.g., with full attention, contemplatively, giving special notice to appearance, with emotional openness). It has been sufficiently shown that *that* sort of definition is doomed

to failure, given the impossibility of locating a single unitary aesthetic attitude or regard common to all the ways we approach and have approached works of art, and given the ways unthought of in which we will undoubtedly be approaching some works in the future. The definition I will offer does not hamstring the kinds of regard that may eventually be given to artworks, yet gives the art-making intention the content it sorely needs.

III

The above-mentioned content is to be found in the actual historical development of art. My idea is roughly this: a work of art is a thing intended for regard-as-a-work-of-art, regard in any of the ways works of art existing prior to it have been correctly regarded. In the absence of any identifiable 'aesthetic attitude', how else can 'regard-as-a-work-of-art' be understood? Obviously, in adopting this proposal we are not analyzing art completely in nonart terms. Rather, what we are doing is explicating what it is for an object to be art at a given time with reference to the body of past art taken as unproblematic. But what it is for a thing to be art at any time can eventually be exhibited in this manner, by starting with the present and working backward. New art is art because of this relation to past art, art of the recent past is art because of this relation to art of the not-so-recent past, art of the not-so-recent past is art because of this relation to art of the distant past . . . until one arrives presumably at the *ur*-arts of our tradition – those to which the mantle of *art* can be initially attached, but which are art *not* in virtue of any relation to preceding objects. (I will return to the *ur*-arts in section VII.) Before stating a more careful definition, let me further attempt to explain the motives for its introduction.

The concept of artwork is unlike that of other sorts of things that surround us – e.g., cars, chairs, persons. *Artwork* seems to lack antecedently defined limits in terms of intrinsic features, even flexible ones – as opposed to car, chair, person. There is no question of determining in all cases that something is art by weighing it against some archetype or other. The *only* clue one has is the particular, concrete, and multifarious population that art has acquired at any point (that is, assuming, as I do, the nebulousness and/or inessentiality of that institution, the artworld). It appears almost obvious, then, that for a prospective object to count as art must be for it to be related in some way to those objects that have already been decided or determined. For a thing to be art it must be linked by its creator to the repository of art existing at the time, as opposed to being aligned by him with some abstracted template of required characteristics. What I am saying is that currently the concept of art has no content beyond what art *has been*. It is this content that must figure in a successful definition.

Let me focus on the central case of art-aware art makers. In such cases making an artwork is a conscious act involving a conception of art. But what conception of art can all such art makers, existing at different times and places, have in common? It seems the only possibility is a conception of art tantamount to all or anything that has been art until now – a concrete conception not equivalent to any abstract principle or generalization drawn from a survey of art's past. Art-aware art makers are thus those who connect their creations to such a conception and, in so doing, make them art. If they do not do this – if their activities involve no reference whatsoever to the body of artworks preceding them – then I think we fail to understand in what sense they are consciously or knowingly producing art. Given the abandonment of special aesthetic attitudes and/or artistic purposes, some connection of some sort between current artworks and earlier ones must logically be demanded of the putative art maker. It looks as if there are three likely ways in which the connection might be established: (i) by making something that will be externally similar to previous artworks; (ii) by making something that is intended to afford the same kind of pleasure/experience that previous artworks have afforded; (iii) by making something that is intended for regard or treatment as previous artworks have been regarded or treated.

The first suggestion, while the simplest, clearly will not do. It is useless unless respects of similarity are indicated, since just about anything would be externally similar to some past artwork in some respect. But aside from that, artworks are just not to any great extent bound together by external similarity. For example, certain welded iron sculptures resemble portions of junkyards more closely than they do the sculptures that were their predecessors. External similarity to artworks is neither necessary nor sufficient for being an artwork. The second suggestion is more promising, but it fails too. There are two reasons for this: (1) the pleasures/experiences derived from art are not necessarily unique to art; (2) it is the *manner* in which artworks afford their pleasures/experiences, the *ways* in which one approaches or engages them *so that* they give those pleasures/experiences, which characterize them as art. To illustrate these points, imagine a drug that when ingested would provide a pleasure/experience akin to what one can have by listening intently to Beethoven's Quartet in C-sharp Minor, op. 131. Such a drug would not thereby be an artwork, although it would be a handy thing to have around. Furthermore, to focus on the pleasures derived from artworks is to emphasize the passive and resultant in the situation, as opposed to the active and causative – i.e., the way of taking the object. It is more reasonable to hold that an artist directing an object toward potential spectators is concerned intentionally with what is to be *done* with the object, as opposed to what might be *got* out of it, since spectators can only *directly* adjust themselves or behave with respect to the former. So I think we are left with the third suggestion as the only one around with which to build an account of what it is to be art.

IV

A definition that preserves my basic idea, but adds certain qualifications, is the following:

(I)   *X* is an artwork
     = df   *X* is an object that a person or persons, having the appropriate proprietary right over *X*, nonpassingly intends for regard-as-a-work-of-art, i.e. regard in any way (or ways) in which prior artworks are or were correctly (or standardly) regarded.

Several comments on this initial definition are in order. First, there is the phrase 'intends for.' This is to be understood as short for 'makes, appropriates or conceives for the purpose of,' so as to comprehend fashioned, found, and conceptual art. Second, there is the notion that the intent must be fairly stable ('nonpassing'), as opposed to merely transient. In other words, it is not enough to turn an object into art that one momentarily considers it for regard-as-a-work-of-art. Third, I have construed regard-as-a-work-of-art as equivalent to ways of regarding past art only in so far as they are or were *correct* (or *standard*) ways. If one omits this qualification, or appeals instead to *common* ways of regard, or even *rewarding* ways of regard, the definition will go awry. The following case illustrates this point.

Italian Renaissance portraits are presumably artworks. Suppose they come to be regarded in a new and unprecedented way – viz., they begin to be used as thermal insulation, and are found to be quite suitable for this. And suppose, through an amazing decline in taste or an unparalleled need for insulation, this manner of regard becomes the rule. If we omit 'correctly' from our definition, or replace it by 'commonly' or 'rewardingly,' then given the case as described, it follows from our definition that anything subsequently intended by its maker for use as insulation (e.g., a sheet of Fiberglas) would be an artwork. Why? Because Renaissance portraits are past artworks that are regarded, are commonly regarded, and are rewardingly regarded as insulation. This must be wrong. It can't be possible to turn all tomorrow's Fiberglas production into art simply through general misuse today of a certain class of portraits. To avoid this unwanted consequence, we *must* appeal to some notion of *correct* regarding for artworks.[5] Using Renaissance portraits as insulation is manifestly not a correct way of regarding them, no matter how widespread or satisfactory such a use might be. And so on our definition nothing can become art through intentional reference to such a prior way of regarding artworks.

Fourth, the definition includes a proprietary-right condition. What this amounts to is basically *ownership* – you cannot 'artify' what you do not own and thus have no right to dispose of. All your intentions will not avail in such a case, because another person's intention, that of the owner, has priority over yours. (Of course, if owners are not opposed to your intention, they can grant you permission to make their possessions into artworks.) One standardly attains the right in question by creating an object, but notice that this will not always suffice – for example, if the object is created under contract during working hours while in the employ of a metal tubing company. (On the other hand, neither is it necessary to create something in order to have the right to 'artify' it, as witnessed by found art.) It might be thought that the proprietary-right condition would rule out varieties of conceptual art, but this is not so. One must just avoid the mistake of taking the art object in such cases to be simply and solely what the artist has described or pointed to (e.g., Marilyn Monroe, the Empire State Building, a slice of the life of a family in Queens – things that the artist clearly has no proprietary right over), rather than a directed complex of the description and the object.

Given a proprietary-right condition, it is somewhat problematic whether curators, promoters, exhibitors can turn nonart objects of the past into art objects of the present as blithely as is usually allowed. Imagine an art museum having mounted for regard-as-a-work-of-art a strange ornate receptacle whose original purpose is unknown. The object comes from an ancient Mexican culture thought to have died out. However, a well-documented descendant of the tribe, armed with full knowledge of its customs and practices, appears and successfully demands the removal of the receptacle from public view (it is apparently a sacred ritual object, used for nocturnal royal baptisms, and not in any sense for appreciation). I maintain that the object in question does not just revert to being nonart – it never was art at all, because our present art establishment unknowingly lacked the right to make it such. This sort of case may be more prevalent than is generally imagined.

It will be useful to distinguish three kinds of intention which can realize the condition expressed in the definition: *intending for regard-as-a-work-of-art*. The first would be the *specific art-conscious* intention: intending for regard in the specific way or ways some particular past artworks (or class of artworks) have been correctly regarded. An example of this would be intending for regard in the way wire sculptures are to be regarded. The second is the *nonspecific art-conscious* intention: intending for regard in whatever ways any past artworks have been correctly regarded, having no particular ones in mind. The third is the *art-unconscious* intention: intending for regard in some specific way φ characterized in terms of intrinsic features, where φ is *in fact* a way in which some past artworks have been correctly regarded, though this fact is not known to the intender. An example of this might be intending for listening to with attention to timbre.

The first and second kinds realize *intending for regard-as-a-work-of-art* on a referentially *opaque* interpretation of that notion, whereas the third kind satisfies a *transparent* interpretation of it. Given the notion as readable in both modes, my definition thus allows (via the art-unconscious intention) for art makers ignorant of all artworks, all art activities, and all institutions of art. Such persons can be seen to make art if they intend their objects for regard in ways that *happen to be*, unbeknown to them, in the repertory of aesthetic regards established at that time. In such a case there is the requisite link to the prior history of art, but it is one such art makers are unaware of, though they have in fact forged it.

So cases of naïve activity can be cases of art making if they accord with the development of art at that point in the manner sketched. And I would insist that a theory must account for these cases. From where we stand such persons (e.g., the Amazon Indian mentioned before) are clearly making art – and it is not our recognition that makes it so.

V

The definition presented in the preceding section conveys in a fairly perspicuous fashion what I believe it now means for something to be an artwork. However, at the expense of some perspicuity but in the name of greater precision and flexibility, I offer a second definition that makes explicit the time-dependence of the status of 'artwork', clarifies the interpretation of 'prior artworks', and indicates more exactly what sort of definition of art I am giving.

(I_t) X is an artwork at t

= df X is an object of which it is true at t that some person or persons having the appropriate proprietary right over X, nonpassingly intends (or intended) X for regard-as-a-work-of-art – i.e., regard in any way (or ways) in which artworks existing prior to t are or were correctly (or standardly) regarded.

An object can be an artwork at one time and not another. This definition recognizes that an object may not be an artwork from the moment of its physical creation, but may only become an artwork at some *later* date. It also allows for an object that becomes an artwork even subsequent to its creator's intending it for a certain regard, and even subsequent to the death of its creator.[6]

The first sort of case is relatively common. Any piece of found art serves as an example. The snow shovel involved in Duchamp's *Snow Shovel*, or the bottle rack in his *Bottle Rack*, became works of art at a certain time owing to Duchamp's appropriating them with a certain intention, whereas they existed but were not works of art before that time. The same goes for driftwood mounted and displayed in someone's living room, or potsherds and door handles touched by curatorial intent in a museum of primitive art. Another kind of example would be a canvas that is undertaken and completed merely as a technical exercise but which after a few days' reflection is then viewed by its creator as for regarding-as-a-work-of-art. These things are art only *after* a certain intentional decision has taken place. Definition I_t makes this plain.

The second sort of case is less common, but I think a completely adequate definition of art must be capable of handling it. An example would be the following: A naïve or art-unaware creator makes an object Z at t, which he intends for a kind of treatment or regard that is not a correct way of regarding any artworks existing prior to t_1. However, it is a kind of treatment or regard that *will be* correct for certain artworks θ existing 200 years after t_1. I think we want to say that the naïve creator's work is art beginning around t_2 (= t_1 + 200) but not before. That is to say, Z becomes art 200 years after its intentioned creation, when the history of art, so to speak, catches up with what Z's creator was engaged in. It would be hard to deny at t_2 that Z was art; for, after all, it was created and intended for just the sort of treatment that θ's, which are recognized artworks at t_2, are correctly accorded. Z is art at t_2 because it was intended for a kind of regard which (unknown to its creator) turns out to be in the stock of standard regards for artworks at t_2. Z at t_2 can be seen as projected for a kind of appreciative activity which had become part of artistic tradition. However, before t_2 this cannot be seen. There is no plausible ground for considering Z to be art prior to t_2. Something cannot be art from the outset *just* in virtue of its future redemption by the evolution of art – only actual redemption will turn the trick then and there.

Definition I_t handles this case as desired. Z is an artwork at t_2 (and thereafter) because it is an object of which it is true at t_2 that someone rightfully and nonpassingly intended it (at t_1) for regard in a way in which some artworks existing prior to t_2 are correctly regarded. However, Z is *not*, according to I_t, an artwork at t_1.

So what sort of definition of art have we given? In short, a definition that explains what it is to be art at a given time in terms of what is art at previous times. To be art at t is to be intentionally related in the required way to something that is art prior to t. The present state of art shows us that certainly nothing more can be required. On the other hand, nothing less than this can be required if we are to locate a conception of art which will cover equally Donatello's *David* and Carl Andre's *Lever*, Mozart's *Jupiter* Symphony and Stockhausen's *Momente*, Shelley's "Ode to the West Wind" and John Berryman's *Dream Songs*. If there is now a univocal sense of 'art' in which all six items count as art, and count as such from the time of their creation, then I believe this sense is given (more or less) by definition I_t.

I can almost see readers shake their heads at this point and ask: But does this definition *really tell* me what art is? Doesn't it seem that I have to *know* what art is in order to use it? In fact, isn't the definition simply *circular*, in that it defines art in terms of art? This response is perfectly understandable, but it is nonetheless mistaken. True, there is something reflexive about the definition, in that it exhibits art as essentially referring to itself. But to eliminate this reflexiveness would be to eviscerate the term 'art' of the only universal content it now retains. If artworks at one time are essentially intentionally related to artworks at an earlier time, then on the assumption that definitions attempt to give essences, how could a definition of art fail to explicate artworks – to put it bluntly – in terms of artworks? Thus the *appearance* of circularity.

But, strictly speaking, I_t is *not* circular. What it does is define the *concept*: being art at a given time by reference to the *actual body of things* that are art prior to that time. True, one cannot tell what counts as art at t without its being granted what things count as art prior to t – but this is in fact just the way art itself works. Furthermore, and this also conforms to the reality of art, to the extent that it is unclear which objects *prior to* t are artworks, it will be equally unclear which objects *at* t count as art. True, one cannot use the definition to tell, all at once, what has, does, and will count as art at all times, but this is because the applicability of 'art' at any stage is always tied to its concrete, historical realization at that stage. That the definition is not circular if properly understood can be seen by reflecting that one doesn't have to know what 'artwork at t' *means* in order for I_t to *tell* you; one only has to grant that there is a set of things which

are artworks prior to t – *whatever* they are and *whatever* that (viz., 'artwork') might mean.

The last point suggests another way of expressing the analysis of art that I offer, a way I think that removes any lingering suspicion of circularity. Basically, what I have proposed is that the *meaning* of 'art now' involves the extension of 'art previously' – that the *meaning* of 'art at t' is to be given in terms of the *extension* of 'art prior to t'. Formulating a variant of I_t to make this explicit, we have:

(I_t') X is an artwork at t
    $=$ df X is an object of which it is true at t that some person or persons, having the appropriate proprietary right over X, nonpassingly intends (or intended) X for regard-as-a-work-of-art – i.e., regard in any way (or ways) in which objects in the extension of 'artwork' prior to t are or were correctly (or standardly) regarded.[7]

It is clear that the *meaning* of 'artwork' is not involved in the right-hand side of this definition, but only its past *extension* at some point. Thus, I maintain that I_t' or I_t captures our present concept of art – and without presupposing that concept in doing so.

VI

On the view I have presented, which makes art a necessarily backward-looking affair, one may wonder how the *revolutionary* aspect of art can be accommodated. Surely, one might say, if art is continually looking to the rear, how can it change or advance? Won't it always remain the same? To begin to answer this let me first distinguish revolutionary from merely new or original art. A new artwork is simply one nonidentical to any previously existing artwork. An original artwork is a new one significantly different in structural or aesthetic properties from any previously existing artwork. The production of original art could continue indefinitely without there being any additions to the stock of ways in which artworks are regarded. But by a revolutionary artwork I mean one for which any of the past ways of approaching art seems inadequate, inappropriate, pointless, or impossible; a revolutionary artwork appears to be ultimately calling for a kind of regard which is totally *unprecedented*. It is plainly only revolutionary art that poses any difficulty for my analysis.[8]

Art that is revolutionary because it demands or requires a new approach to yield up its fruits to spectators is not per se a problem. A problem only arises for artworks – e.g., Dadaist ones – which are *intended* as revolutionary by their artists, that is to say, intended for treatment in a manner completely distinct from what has gone before. (Whether all intentionally revolutionary art is thereby revolutionary *simpliciter* is a complicated question I will not go into here.) Two strategies suggest themselves for reconciling my proposal to this important and characteristic mode of art making. One is to maintain that although consciously revolutionary artists desire that eventually their objects will be dealt with in unprecedented ways, to make them *art* they must initially direct their audiences to take them (or try taking them) in some way that art *has* been taken – otherwise, what can we make of the claim that they have given us *art*, as opposed to something else? The art-making intention of consciously revolutionary artists may thus have to be a covertly disingenuous one, somewhat along these lines: 'My object is for regarding in any way artworks have been regarded in the past (but with the expectation that this will prove frustrating or unrewarding, thus prodding the spectator to adopt some other point of view – this being my ultimate intention).' The secondary intention embodies the true *aim* of such art, but the primary intention must be present to make it *art* at all.

A second strategy for dealing with this issue perhaps does less violence to the outward stance of the consciously revolutionary artist. This requires a liberalization of what regard-as-a-work-of-art amounts to. Instead of construing it as restricted to past correct ways of regarding artworks, broaden it to include completely unheralded types of regard so long as one is directed to adopt such regards in conscious opposition to those past correct ways. The liberalized version of regard-as-a-work-of-art then reads as follows: regard in any way (or ways) in which prior artworks are or were correctly (or standardly) regarded, or *in some other way in contrast to and against the* background of those ways. (Call this 'regard-as-a-work-of-art*'.) If this second strategy is adopted, one simply substitutes 'regard-as-a-work-of-art*' for 'regard-as-a-work-of-art' in I, I_t, and I_t' to get definitions adequate to revolutionary art. Whereas the idea of the first strategy was that self-aware revolutionary artists

must on one level intend the existing correct art regards, freeing them to intend on another level some entirely new regard, the present strategy does not insist that they should directly intend the existing ways at all, but only that they should project the new way *in relation* (albeit antagonistic relation) to its predecessors. If they fail to do even that, I think there are no grounds on which one could deny that they fail to make art. Of course it is open at that point for some other member of the art community, assuming they have the proprietary right, to appropriate the would-be artist's work at a later date with the right intention, and so bring it into the sphere of art. The point is, to get a revolutionary mode of activity to *be* art it is necessary that its creator (or the creator's subsequent proxy) should consciously nod in the direction of past artistic activity.

Which of the two strategies is ultimately preferable as a way of accommodating the historical definition of art to revolutionary art making is a question I will not attempt to settle here. However, for the sake of simplifying succeeding discussion, I will assume for the remainder of this essay the workability of the first strategy and tentatively adopt it. This means that definition I, I_t, I_t', properly understood, will be viewed as adequate to revolutionary (as well as evolutionary) art.

VII

The view presented so far suggests the following picture of art's evolution. Artworks are objects projected for regard, at least in part, in ways past artworks have been standardly regarded. These artworks, if at all original, will differ from those of the past more or less markedly, and will therefore optimally call for ways of regard (which the artist has usually envisaged) somewhat different from ones already in practice. But then *those* ways will become part of the tradition of art appreciation, allowing for newer works to be constituted as art by reference to *them*, and so on. There is thus a deeper continuity in the development of art than is generally noted. Artworks of a given period do more than *follow* their predecessors. They are even more than causally *descended* from them, more even than testimonies to the influence of style, medium, and subject matter. Rather, those predecessors are *necessarily involved* (via the ways in which they have been regarded) in the intentional structure which determines their successors as art. What art becomes depends conceptually, not just causally, on what art has been.

Definition I_t analyzes being art at a given time in terms of what is art prior to that time. The definition can be applied at the present time, and then at as many times back into the past as one chooses, until one at last reaches the origins of art[9] itself (i.e., the *ur*-arts). Having reached that terminus, however, we could then use it as the starting point of another kind of definition of art, one that begins with the hypothesized origins of art and yields serially all that has sprung from it up to the present. This would be a *recursive* definition and would reveal art as a recursive domain. Before giving one, let me tell a somewhat oversimplified tale.

The time predates the beginning of art. Certain societies are thriving in which various activities are going on. In some of these activities objects (including events) are produced and then treated in a certain manner. These activities can be identified retrospectively as the *ur*-arts of our tradition. At some point, new activities arise wherein objects of a different sort are produced which are intended for treatment as objects of some *ur*-art are. The new activity then becomes associated with that of the *ur*-art, under a wider category, that of *art*. At this stage, an activity of object making can only become art by relating itself to the purposes of some (or possibly more than one) *ur*-art; the objects of the activity can only be artworks by being thought of in connection with the ends toward which the objects of some *ur*-art were directed. Once a new activity and its objects are established as art, *further* activities and objects now enter the realm of art through intentional connection with *them*. Eventually one arrives at art as we find it today.[10] Let me state the definition suggested by this tale:

(II)   Initial Step: Objects of the *ur*-arts are artworks at t_0 (and thereafter).[11] Recursive Step: If X is an artwork prior to t, then Y is an artwork at t if it is true at t that some person or persons, having the appropriate proprietary right over Y, nonpassingly intends (or intended) Y for regard in any way (or ways) in which X is or was correctly regarded.

I believe this definition very nearly generates all and only those things that have been, are, or could be artworks, given the concept of art we presently have.[12] And yet, it is easy to understand how the definition might strike one as inoperative or incomplete. For recursion depends on the initial step, the

initial step speaks of the *ur*-arts – but one has not been told what the *ur*-arts *are*! I would be happy to supply their description if I knew what they were, but I don't. Nor does anyone. Is there, then, a way to save definition II from this charge of having merely programmatic status?

I think there is. Our explanation of the *idea* of an *ur*-art given earlier in this section can be turned to provide a method in principle for *actually identifying* the *ur*-arts. Basically, one just has to ask, of objects at points successively farther into the past, and until the questioning process terminates, "What makes this count as art?" More formally, and relying on definition I for simplicity of exposition, the procedure would be as follows: Begin with a group of related recent artworks, A. Then by I, A consists of objects that were *intended* for regard R, where R is the manner of regard *in fact* standardly accorded certain earlier artworks, A'. Now focus on A'. By I, A' consists of objects that were intended for regard R', R' being the regard in fact standardly given an even earlier set of artworks, A''. A, A', A'' . . . thus form a backward-reaching series of artworks whose principle of continuation should be clear. Eventually one arrives at a set of objects, A_0, which are such that objects succeeding them are intended for regard as A_0's are standardly regarded, but there are no objects X preceding A_0 such that A_0's were intended to be regarded as X's in fact standardly were. A_0 is then one set of *ur*-artworks. Of course to put this method into practice would be exceedingly difficult. It would require a great deal of knowledge of artists' intentions and actual appreciative practices of societies to perform successfully the backward trace on an initial sample. And one would have to do this for many such samples in order to unearth all the *ur*-arts of Western culture. However, *if* one did carry out this procedure for a wide, well-chosen variety of current paradigm artworks, one would have pretty good reason to be confident that all of the *ur*-arts had been ferreted out from their historical hiding places. At that point, if one liked, one could substitute for the place-holder '*ur*-arts' in II a specification in *intrinsic* terms of the activities that archaeological investigation had revealed to be *in fact* the roots of Western art. This would in effect 'complete' the recursive definition of art.

It is important to note that while the basic definition (I_t) is put forward as capturing the general concept of art which we now employ, the recursive definition aims only at displaying in a revealing way the *extension* of that concept. The basic definition explains the shared sense in which Donatello's *David* is art in 1420, Shelley's "Ode to the West Wind" is art in 1820, and Stockhausen's *Momente* is art in 1970. The recursive definition, though, does *not* explain the sense of 'artwork.' It would be implausible to maintain that our conception of artwork entails that all such things have ultimate ancestors of the sort that the *ur*-arts are. Surely the notion of *ur*-arts, whether characterized positionally or intrinsically, is not part of the content of a judgement that something is an artwork. What the recursive definition does, though, is to generate all artworks by a method that closely parallels and illuminates the actual historical process of the evolution of art.[13]

VIII

Having spelled out the theory I have to offer, in which the concrete history of art replaces the institutional network of art at center stage, I wish to remark further on certain issues over which my theory and the reigning institutional one differ. In particular, two issues that can be put in the form of questions: (1) Is art making in essence an *internal* (intention) or *external* (conferral) matter? (2) Need a person have a special *position* in the artworld to create certain sorts of artworks? I will consider these briefly in turn.

(1) Consider an object made by an artist, and intended for regard-as-a-work-of-art, but not offered, not placed, not mounted, not circumscribed, advertised, or sold – in short, not 'done with' in any way. Isn't this still an artwork? The institutionalist might argue that having the intention *just is* conferring a certain status, and no other 'action' is necessary. But if having the intention is always *thereby* conferring status, while any overt conferring must *anyway* include the requisite intention (or else it is mere sham, 'playing the artist'), then this seems to me tantamount to admitting that intention is really all that is essential to art making. This is not to say that art makers are very *likely* to *just* intend an object for regard-as-a-work-of-art. It is highly unlikely that they will fail to act so as to draw attention to their works. Artists naturally try to increase the chances of their works getting the regard they intend (both for their benefit and for ours).

On the other hand, the fear that taking everything outward away from the essentials of art making would mean a world pullulating with artworks of the unfashioned kind, generated at every turn of thought – that fear is groundless. It is relatively easy, natural, and common to summon the requisite nonpassing intention in connection with an object one has made, but difficult, unnatural, and rare to form such an intention in connection with an object one has not made – it takes a certain courage and occasionally perversity to convince oneself of the right or point of so appropriating what nature or another person has already fashioned. Only if one overlooks the fact that these intentions are not going to arise in many people will one suppose the need for an art maker to perform an action on behalf of the artworld, in order to account for the observation that not one person in a hundred has transformed his or her kitchen stove into a work of art.

(2) Arthur Danto gives an answer to question two in speaking of 'the making of artworks out of real things' – i.e., the appropriation/minimal-fashioning mode of art. "It is analytically true that artworks can only be *by* artists, so that an object, however much (or exactly) it may resemble an artwork is not *by* whoever is responsible for its existence, unless he is an artist. The mere object [e.g., a brass bushing] perhaps does not lie outside their [viz., non artists'] powers. But as an artwork it does."[14] If 'artist' in these remarks meant only 'person who at some time makes an artwork' then I would have no trouble agreeing that an artwork can be brought into being by nobody other than an artist. However, the context makes it clear that 'artist' means there something more like 'person with an established position in the artworld, one of whose main concerns is the making of artworks' (call this 'artist*'). Danto believes that tracing a 'real thing' to someone who is not an artist* defeats any claim it might have to be art. I cannot accept this. I do not believe the 'conventions of ascribing'[15] the predicate 'is art' are like that at all. The only reason I see why one would maintain they are is based on confusing *established* or *professional* art with *all* art. I am willing to admit that commanding a special position or having a certain background may be relevant to making brass bushings into *recognized* art, or making them into *significant* art, or into artworks that will affect the *development* of art – but *not* to making them into art *simpliciter*. The wittiest riposte of the season is presumably utterable *only* by a member of high society; art per se no more operates on this level than philosophy does.

Jerrold Levinson

IX

The concept of art has certainly changed over time. There is no doubt of that. It is thus worth emphasizing in this final section that my analysis is aimed just at capturing what the concept of art is *at present* – that is, what it *now* means for an object created *at any time* (past, present, or future) to count as art at that time, rather than what it meant at the time of the object's creation.[16] Claiming that the analysis indicates what it means, say, for something created in 1777 to be an artwork thus does not entail or require that the concept-of-art$_{1977}$ is identical with concept-of-art$_{1777}$. Presumably these two concepts would classify the field of objects into art and nonart somewhat differently. And calling Rembrandt's *The Night Watch* a work of art in 1777 undoubtedly meant something different from what is meant by calling it that in 1977. However, given my analysis of it, I think the only part of concept-of-art$_{1977}$ that could unarguably be held to have been *missing* from concept-of-art$_{1777}$ is the permissibility of objects as art which are unfashioned or only minimally fashioned by their creators.[17] Whereas concept-of-art$_{1977}$ associates *The Night Watch* with former stainless steel bars, coat racks, cardboard cartons, and goats' heads, concept-of-art$_{1777}$ served in part to differentiate *The Night Watch* from such things. This major conceptual changeover occurred, as we know, around 1920 as a result of the Dadaist movement.

I have already noted that the historical definition of art provides a powerful and direct explanation of the inherent unity and continuity of the development of art. In short, for something to be an artwork at any time is for it to be intentionally related to artworks that precede it – no more and no less. And the historical definition, if accepted, helps to dispel the lingering effects of the so-called 'intentional fallacy' understood as a claim about the irrelevance of artists' intentions to correct or full appreciation of their works. For if artists' intentions are recognized as central to the difference

between art and nonart, they are not so likely to be offhandedly declared irrelevant to an understanding of artworks once seen as so constituted. In particular, the historical definition indicates the overwhelming importance for appreciation of those past artworks/genres/ways of regard/modes of treatment which artists connect to their current productions through their art-making intentions.

The historical definition of art also casts a useful light on the fact that in art anything goes, but not everything works. The reason anything goes is that there are no clear limits to the sorts of things people may seriously intend us to regard-as-a-work-of-art. The reason not everything works is that regarding-something-as-a-work-of-art necessarily involves bringing the past of art to bear on what is being offered as art in the present. That the present object and past regards will mesh is not guaranteed.[18] The interaction of the two sometimes satisfies immediately, sometimes only after an interval. Sometimes we are shocked and unsettled, but recover and are illuminated. Sometimes we are forcibly impelled to adopt new modes of regard, leaving old ones aside. But sometimes we are simply bewildered, bored, bothered – or all three – and in a manner that is never transcended. In such cases we have artworks, all right, but such works don't work.

In conclusion, let me say that I do not mean to deny that there is a common practice of art, and a group of people bound together under that umbrella, nor do I deny that artworks need to be understood in relation to their cultural situation. What I do deny is that the institutions of art in a society are essential to art, and that an analysis of arthood must therefore involve them. The making of art is primary; the social frameworks and conventions that grow up around it are not. While the sociology of art is of great interest, the essence of art does not lie there but instead in art's relation to its contingent history. The theory I offer sketches in its main outlines what this relation is.

Notes

1 Dickie's definition of art runs as follows: "A work of art in the classificatory sense is (1) an artifact (2) a set of the aspects of which has had conferred upon it the status of candidate for appreciation by some person or persons acting on behalf of a certain social institution (the art-world)," *Art and the Aesthetics* (Ithaca: Cornell University Press, 1974), p. 34.

2 The suggestions that regarding-as-a-work-of-art may be a primary notion and that the nature of art must be located in its historical development can be found in Richard Wollheim's *Art and Its Objects* (New York: Harper & Row, 1971), sections 40 and 60–63, respectively. It is those remarks that first prompted me to work out the view I am trying to

present. I might add here that I use 'regard' in this essay as a broad term covering whatever is done in relation to an object so as to experience or interact with it.

3 For useful criticism of the institutional theory see R. Sclafani, "Art as a Social Institution: Dickie's New Definitions," *Journal of Aesthetics and Art Criticism*, 32 (1973); R. Sclafani, "Art Works, Art Theory, and the Artworld," *Theoria*, 39 (1973); T. Cohen, "The Possibility of Art: Remarks on a Proposal by Dickie," *Philosophical Review*, 82 (1973); A. Silvers, "The Artworld Discarded," *Journal of Aesthetics and Art Criticism*, 34 (1976); K. Walton, "Review: Dickie: *Art and the Aesthetic*," *Philosophical Review* (January 1977); M. Beardsley, "Is Art Essentially Institutional?" in *Culture and Art*, ed. L. Aagaard-Mogensen (Atlantic Highlands, N.J.: Humanities Press, 1976). I share many of the misgivings expressed by these authors.

4 Which even then may be subject to counterexamples, as well as being unilluminating in any case (cf. Cohen, "Possibility of Art"). Dickie's extremely general suggestion for the meaning of 'appreciation' is: "in experiencing the qualities of a thing one finds them worthy or valuable" (Dickie, *Art and the Aesthetic*, pp. 40–41).

5 The notion of correct regard for an artwork is a difficult one to make out, but surely relevant to it are the following considerations: (1) how the artist *intended* his work to be regarded; (2) what manner of regarding the work is *most* rewarding; (3) the kinds of regard *similar* objects have enjoyed; (4) what way of regarding the work is optimum for realizing the *ends* (e.g., certain pleasures, moods, awarenesses) which the artist envisaged in connection with appreciation; (5) what way of regarding the work makes for the most satisfying or coherent picture of its place in the *development* of art. (For an illuminating discussion of some of these factors, see Walton, "Categories of Art," *Philosophical Review*, 79 [1970].) Nothing in the present paper depends on the exact analysis of 'correct regard', however. To understand my account of art one only has to grant that *there are* correct ways of regarding past artworks, whatever that might amount to.

6 There are three times of importance that should be distinguished if we are to get clear on this issue. One is the time of physical creation of the object, t_p. A second is the time of intentioned-object creation, t_i – i.e., the time at which the brute object is structured or transformed by a certain intention concerning it. Every artwork is, strictly speaking, an intentioned object. A third is the time of art-becoming, t_a. In the typical or normal case of art production $t_p = t_i = t_a$; in the case of found art, t_p is earlier than t_i, and $t_i = t_a$; in the case of the naïve creator ahead of his time (discussed below), $t_p = t_i$, and t_a is later than t_i.

7 Note in this definition that when I speak of the extension of the term 'artwork' at a time t this means the extension of the term at t as it is understood *now* – i.e., in its current usage.

8 Most movements in art are revolutionary in a *weak* sense, in that they ask for or involve *some* specific new ways of taking art objects, but few such movements (perhaps none before Dadaism) deny the applicability of *all* past ways of taking art objects. For example, Impressionist paintings certainly are and were to be approached in specific ways (e.g., synoptic vision from a distance) which were not in practice for previous paintings (e.g., those of the Neo-classicists). But there clearly remained ways in common in which they were to be regarded. Thus, weakly revolutionary art does not challenge the historicity of the art-making intention.

9 That is, *art* as understood in present-day Western culture.

10 The story I tell here is consonant with a remark made in passing by Walton, "Review: Dickie," concerning the historical development of art. I should also emphasize that the story is told from the point of view of art as the production of artworks for appreciation by spectators, and not from the point of view of art as the release of psychic energy or the expression of artistic impulses by creators. As should be apparent, it is only the former idea of art that this essay is concerned to elucidate.

11 Let t_0 be the time roughly at which the *ur*-arts begin spawning non-*ur*-art artworks.

12 Wollheim, in section 60 of *Art and Its Objects*, mentions the possibility of a general *method* of identifying all works of art which would be recursive in form. He concludes that as a method of identification it would not work, the reason being the inability to formulate rules of transformation adequate to the concrete evolution of art in the distant and also the recent past. He has in mind rules that would operate on given structures or styles and spew out altered ones according with the direction taken by art at a given juncture. The problem is especially acute for the modern period: "whereas earlier changes in art affected only the more or less detailed properties of a work of art, e.g., painterly vs. linear, in the art of our day one work of art generates another by the supersession of its most general properties . . . e.g., hard-edge painting as the successor of abstract expressionism" (p. 126).

Granted that Wollheim is right about this, I think the possibility of a definition such as I propose is unaffected. The definition does not depend on rules of stylistic change but, rather, simply on the rule I have argued for as constraining the intention that makes something art. The definition, unlike Wollheim's projected method, does not of course generate all works of art in terms of their intrinsic observable features, but only in terms of certain external intentional relations they bear to other objects.

13 The recursive definition justifies perhaps more strongly than the basic definition my titular claim to be 'defining art historically.' Of course, I am not defining art simply as that which has a history; just about any activity has a history. But neither am I defining it simply as that activity whose historical source is the *ur*-arts. For some of the ultimate ancestors of art (viz., the *ur*-arts) may in fact also be ultimate ancestors of activities other than art. If that is so, does our recursive definition unwantedly generate those nonart activities as well as that of art? No, because in order to be art something must not only have an *ur*-art as ancestor but must also be descended from it in a particular fashion – namely, via intentional relations invoking previous standard regards. It is a good bet that even if there *are* other activities which have *ur*-arts as ultimate ancestors, they do not exhibit *that* principle of descent.

Now that we have concluded our discussion of the *ur*-arts as they figure in the recursive definition, it might be observed that objects of the *ur*-arts are artworks that do *not* conform to our basic definition of the meaning of 'artwork', namely, I_t (or I_t'). For there are no artworks and correct regards prior to the *ur*-arts. I_t (or I_t') thus strictly speaking only tell one what it means for any thing *apart from an ur-art object to* be an artwork. Objects of the *ur*-arts are, by contrast, simply stipulated to be artworks.

14 A. Danto, "Artworks and Real Things," *Theoria*, 39 (1973): 14.

15 Ibid., p. 12.

16 This is the distinction, difficult to grasp firmly, between: (i) what it *means at present* for something to *be art at the time of its creation*, and (ii) what it *meant at the time of its creation* for something to *be art at that time*.

17 On the other hand, it seems clear that there was much in the concept-of-art$_{1777}$ that is missing from the concept-of-art$_{1977}$. Concept-of-art$_{1777}$ was surely more restrictive than its 1977 counterpart; one could reasonably maintain that it included specification of structural features, technical requirements, purposes, ends, and even minimum aesthetic effectiveness. Thus, to get from concept-of-art$_{1777}$ to concept-of-art$_{1977}$ one must delete all such artistic specifications, while broadening the sphere of creation beyond that of fashioning; what is retained throughout is the common thread of reference by art at any time to the sort of treatment earlier art was accorded.

18 Thus it is clear that the historical theory of art leaves room for the sense of 'conceptual strain' accompanying some works of art (e.g., *Bottle Rack*) that Anita Silvers ("The Artworld Discarded") accuses the institutional theory of eliminating. The strain arises from the clash between the *nature* of the object and the *kinds of regard* typically accorded earlier artworks, which regards had to be invoked in making the object in question art.

5

The New Institutional Theory of Art

George Dickie

The version of the institutional theory that I worked out in 1974 in *Art and the Aesthetic*[1] was defective in several respects, but the institutional approach is, I think, still viable. By an institutional approach I mean the idea that works of art are art as the result of the position they occupy within an institutional framework or context. I have tried in a forthcoming book, *The Art Circle*, to work out a revised version of the theory. In this paper, I shall attempt to give a summary account of the new version of the institutional theory of art.

It should be made clear here at the beginning that the theory of art I am trying to work out is a classificatory one. Some theories of art have assumed that a work of art is necessarily a good thing, but this assumption would leave unaccounted for all the mediocre, bad, and worthless art. It is the wider class of objects which contain the worthless, the indifferent, the mediocre, the good, and the masterpieces about which I am concerned to theorize.

Traditional theories of art place works of art within simple and narrowly focused networks of relations. The imitation theory, for example, suspends the work of art in a three-place network between artist and subject matter, and the expression theory places the work of art in a two-place network of artist and work. The institutional theory attempts to place the work of art within a multi-placed network of greater complexity than

anything envisaged by the various traditional theories. The networks or contexts of the traditional theories are too "thin" to be sufficient. The institutional theory attemps to provide a context which is "thick" enough to do the job. The network of relations or context within which a theory places works of art I shall call "the framework" of that theory.

Despite my reservations about the traditional theories of art, they were, I believe, on the right track about the group of objects they focus on. All of the traditional theories assume that works of art are artifacts, although they differ about the nature of the artifacts. There is, then, a sense in which the institutional approach is a return to the traditional way of theorizing about art for it too maintains that works of art are artifacts. By the way, what is meant by "artifact" here is the ordinary dictionary definition: "an object made by man, especially with a view to subsequent use." Furthermore, although many are, an artifact need not be a physical object: for example, a poem is not a physical object, but it is, nevertheless, an artifact. Still further, things such as performances, for example, improvised dances, are also "made by man" and are, therefore, artifacts.

In the 1950s, first Paul Ziff and then Morris Weitz challenged the assumption of artifactuality, claiming that being an artifact is not a necessary condition of art. Although Ziff's and Weitz's views differ somewhat, they have in common the claim that there is no necessary condition for something's being art, not even artifactuality. Their common view can be called "the new conception of art." This new view conceives of the members of the class of works of art as having no common feature

George Dickie, "The New Institutional Theory of Art," *Proceedings of the 8th Wittgenstein Symposium*, 10 (1983), pp. 57–64. Reprinted by permission of the author.

of any theoretical significance. The members of the class are related only by means of similarities: work of art A resembles work of art B and work of art B resembles work of art C, but A does not have to resemble C. According to the new view, an object becomes a work of art by sufficiently resembling a prior-established work of art.

The new conception speaks of sufficient resemblance as the only way that a work of art can come into being. An examination of the new view reveals, however, that it entails that there must be another way than sufficient resemblance to a prior-established work of art for a work of art to come into being. That two ways of becoming art are required by the new conception of art can be shown in the following way. Suppose that work of art A had become art by sufficiently resembling prior-established work of art B. Work of art B would have had to become art by sufficiently resembling an earlier prior-established work of art, call it C. If resemblance to a prior-established work of art is the only way of becoming art, then the way back in time from work of art A to work of art B to work of art C generates an infinite regress of works of art receding into the past. If resemblance to a prior-established work of art were the only way of becoming art, there could be no first work of art and, consequently, there could not be any art at all. Some way of becoming art other than resemblance to a prior-established work is required for resemblance to a prior-established work to function as a way of becoming art. Works of art which become art by sufficiently resembling prior-established works may be called "similarity art." In order for there to be similarity art there must be at least one work of art which did not become art in virtue of its similarity to a prior-established work of art. Consequently, the new conception of art really requires two ways of becoming art: the similarity way and some nonsimilarity way. The new conception is an unacknowledged "double" theory of art.

What is the nature of the nonsimilarity art required by the new conception? Since neither Ziff nor Weitz was aware that their view requires nonsimilarity art, it is not surprising that they said nothing about it. The nature of nonsimilarity art will have to be inferred from the stated theory. First, nonsimilarity art is primary within the theory – there could not be similarity art unless there is first nonsimilarity art. Second, the class of works of art, according to the new conception, consists of two distinct subsets of which one (non-similarity art) is more basic than the other (similarity art). Finally, there is nothing in the new conception of art or outside of it which requires nonsimilarity art to be a one-time sort of thing the only function of which is to block the regress and get the art process going. Although nothing in the new conception entails that it is, the only plausible account of the nature of nonsimilarity art that I can think of is that it is art which is art as the result of someone's creating an artifact. This, of course, does not prove that nonsimilarity art is to be identified with what may be called "artifactual art," but artifactual art seems to be the only real contender. The new conception of art involves two distinct kinds of art – artifactual art and similarity – with the former being primary. Artifactual art is clearly not confined to the beginning of the art process, because such art is being created at the present and has been created throughout the history of art.

Ziff and Weitz demand that if one is to theorize about art, one must produce a theory which encompasses all members of the class of works of art. And according to their view, the members of the class have no common feature or features. Consequently, they claim that one cannot theorize about art in the traditional manner of discovering necessary and sufficient features. The closest they can come to theorizing about art is to say that there is a class of objects to which the terms "art" and "work of art" meaningfully apply and that this class cannot be theoretically characterized further.

The earlier examination of the new conception of art has shown that the class of objects to which the terms "art" and "work of art" meaningfully apply divides into two distinct subclasses of art. This division shows that the class can be theoretically characterized further. The first thing to be noted about the subclasses is that the two activities which generate the two subclasses are very different. Artifactual art is generated by the human activity of making. Similarity art is generated by the human activity of noticing similarities. The strikingly different activities which generate the two subclasses suggest that the two classes are not literally subclasses of a single class. The two classes seem more like a class picked out by the literal uses of a term and a derivative class picked out by the metaphorical uses of the same term. I will not, however, pursue this point here.

Even if one were to agree with Ziff and Weitz that artifactual art and similarity art are both literally art, why should this persuade philosophers to abandon their traditional concern with theorizing about what is in effect artifactual art? From Plato's time forward, philosophers of art have been concerned to theorize about the class of objects which is generated by a particular kind of human making. Philosophers have been interested in these objects precisely because they are human artifacts. The fact that there is another class of objects which is in some way derivative by means of similarities from the class of objects they have traditionally been interested in is not surprising and is no reason to divert philosophers of art from their traditional activity. That traditional activity is the attempt to describe correctly the nature of the making of artifactual art and, consequently, the nature of the objects made. Artifactuality is, in effect, a "built-in" characteristic of the interest of philosophers in works of art.

On the surface anyway, there is no mystery about the making of the great bulk of works of artifactual art; they are crafted in various traditional ways – painted, sculpted, and the like. (Later, I will attempt to go below the surface a bit.) There is, however, a puzzle about the artifactuality of some relatively recent works of art: Duchamp's readymades, found art, and the like. Some deny that such things are art because, they claim, they are not artifacts made by artists. It can, I think, be shown that they are the artifacts of artists. (In *Art and the Aesthetic* I claimed, I now think mistakenly, that artifactuality is *conferred* on things such as Duchamp's *Fountain* and found art, but I will not discuss this here.)

Typically an artifact is produced by altering some preexisting material: by joining two pieces of material, by cutting some material, by sharpening some material, and so on. This is typically done so that the altered material can be used to do something. When materials are so altered, one has clear cases which neatly fit the dictionary definition of "artifact" – "An object made by man, especially with a view to subsequent use." There are other cases which are less clear-cut. Suppose one picks up a piece of driftwood and without altering it in any way digs a hole or brandishes it at a threatening dog. The unaltered driftwood has been *made* into a digging tool or a weapon by the use to which it is put. These two cases do not conform to the nonnecessary clause of the definition "especially with a view to subsequent use" because they are pressed into service on the spot. There does seem to be a sense in which something is made in these cases, but what is it that has been made if the drift-

wood is unaltered? In the clear cases in which material is altered, a complex object is produced: the original material is for present purposes a simple object and its being altered produces the complex object – altered material. In the two less clear-cut cases, complex objects have also been made – the wood used as a digging tool and the wood used as a weapon. In neither of the two less clear-cut cases is the driftwood alone the artifact; the artifact in both cases is the driftwood manipulated and used in a certain way. The two cases in question are exactly like the sort of thing that anthropologists have in mind when they speak of unaltered stones found in conjunction with human or human-like fossils as artifacts. The anthropologists assume that the stones were used in some way. The anthropologists have in mind the same notion of a complex object made by the use of a simple (i.e., unaltered) object.

A piece of driftwood may be used in a similar way within the context of the artworld, i.e., picked up and displayed in the way that a painting or a sculpture is displayed. Such a piece of driftwood would be being used as an artistic medium and thereby would became part of the more complex object – the-driftwood-used-as-an-artistic-medium. This complex object would be an artifact of an artworld system. Duchamp's *Fountain* can be understood along the same lines. The urinal (the simple object) is being used as an artistic medium to make *Fountain* (the complex object) which is an artifact within the artworld – Duchamp's artifact. The driftwood would be being used and the urinal was used as artistic media in the way that pigments, marble, and the like are used to make more conventional works of art.

Thus far, I have talked of artifactuality as a necessary condition of art, but this discussion does not distinguish the institutional theory from the traditional theories, as the latter have assumed or implied that being an artifact is a necessary condition of art. In the last paragraph, however, I introduced without explanation the notion of the *artworld*, and it is now time to turn to a discussion of the artworld, for it is this notion which lies at the heart of the institutional theory.

Perhaps the best way to begin a discussion of the artworld is to quote the now-abandoned definition of "work of art" from the earlier version of the institutional theory. "A work of art in the classificatory sense is (1) an artifact (2) a set of the aspects of which has had conferred upon it the status of candidate for appreciation by some person or persons acting on behalf of a certain social institution (the artworld)."[2] Monroe Beardsley has observed that in the discussion which surrounds the definition in the earlier version of the theory I characterized the artworld as an "established practice" which is to say, an informal kind of activity. He then goes on to point out that the quoted definition makes use of such phrases as "conferred status" and "acting on behalf of." Such phrases typically have application within formal institutions such as states, corporations, universities, and the like. Beardsley correctly notes that it is a mistake to use the language of formal institutions to try to describe an informal institution as I conceive the artworld to be. Beardsley queries, ". . . does it make sense to speak of acting on behalf of a practice? Status-awarding authority can center in [a formal institution], but practices, as such, seem to lack the requisite source of authority."[3]

Accepting Beardsley's criticism, I have abandoned as too formal the notions of *status conferral* and *acting on behalf of* as well as those aspects of the earlier version which connect up with these notions. Being a work of art is a status all right, that is, it is the occupying of a position within the human activity of the artworld. Being a work of art is not, however, a status which is conferred but is rather a status which is achieved as the result of creating an artifact within or against the background of the artworld.

The claim is then that works of art are art as the result of the position or place they occupy within an established practice, namely, the artworld. There are two crucial questions about the claim. (1) Is the claim true and (2) if the claim is true, how is the artworld to be described?

The claim is a claim about the existence of a human institution, and the test of its truth is the same as for any other claim about human organization – the test of observation. "Seeing" the artworld and the works of art embedded in its structures, however, is not as easy as "seeing" some of the other human institutions which we are more accustomed to thinking about.

Arthur Danto has invented an argument which helps somewhat in "seeing" the structure in which works of art are embedded. (I must note, however, that what Danto himself "sees" with the use of his argument is quite different from what I "see," but I will not here attempt to rebut Danto's theory.) My version of Danto's argument runs as follows. Consider a painting and another object which looks exactly like it but which was produced accidently and is, therefore, not a work of art. Or consider *Fountain* and a urinal which is its twin but is not a work of art. Here are two pairs of objects with visually indistinguishable elements, but the first element in each pair is a work of art and the second element is not. The fact that the first element of each pair is a work of art and the second element is not although the elements of each pair are visually indistinguishable shows that the first object in each pair must be enmeshed in some sort of framework or network of relations in which the second element is not. It is the first element's being enmeshed in the framework which accounts for its being a work of art, and it is the second element's not being enmeshed in the framework which accounts for its not being a work of art. The framework in question is not, of course, visible to the eye in the way that the colors of the two objects are.

Some will argue that the *Fountain*/urinal pair does not show anything because *Fountain* is not a work of art. Fortunately, the other hypothetical pair is sufficient to get the argument off the ground. The *Fountain*/urinal pair, however, can also be shown to suffice even if *Fountain* is not a work of art. *Fountain* does not actually have to be a work of art to show the necessity of a context or framework. It is sufficient for the argument that at some time some person mistakenly thought *Fountain* to be a work of art. The framework within which *Fountain* apparently had a place would in this case explain the mistake. And, some persons have thought *Fountain* to be a work of art.

Danto's argument shows that works of art exist within a context or framework, but it does not reveal the nature of the elements which make up the framework. Moreover, many different frameworks are possible. Each of the traditional theories of art, for example, implies its own particular framework. For one example, Susanne Langer's view that "Art is the creation of forms symbolic of human feeling" implies a framework of artist (one who creates) and a specific kind of subject matter (human feeling). And as I noted at the beginning of the paper, the imitation theory and the expression theory each implies a particular framework. Langer's theory and the other traditional theories, however, fall easy prey to counterexamples, and, consequently, none of the frameworks they imply can be the right one. The reason that the traditional theories are easy prey for counterexamples is that the frameworks implied by the theories are too narrowly focused on the artist and various different of the more obvious characteristics which works of art may have rather than on *all* the framework elements which surround works of art. The result is that it is all too easy to find works of art which lack the properties seized upon by a particular traditional theory as universal and defining.

The frameworks of the traditional theories do lead in the right direction in one respect. Each of the traditional theories conceives of the making of art as a human practice, as an established way of behaving. The framework of each of these theories is conceived of, then, as a cultural phenomenon which persists through time and is repeatable. The persistence of a framework as a cultural practice is enough, I think, to make the traditional theories themselves quasi-institutional. That is to say, each of the traditional theories purports to describe an established cultural practice. In every one of the traditional theories, however, there is only one established role envisioned and that is the role of the artist or the maker of artifacts. And in every case, the artist is seen as the creator of an artifact with a property such as being representative, being symbolic, or being an expression. For the traditional theories the artist role is envisaged as simply that of producing representations, producing symbolic forms, producing expressions, or some such thing. It is this narrow conception of the artist role which is responsible for the ease with which counterexamples can be produced. Since the traditional theories are inadequate, there must be more to the artist role than the producing of any, or even all, of these kinds of things which the traditional theories envisage. What an artist understands and does when he creates a work of art far exceeds the simple understanding and doing entailed by the traditional theories.

Whenever art is created there is, then, an artist who creates it, but an artist always creates for a *public* of some sort. Consequently, the framework must include a role for a *public* to whom art is presented. Of course, for a variety of reasons many works of art are never in fact presented to any public. Some works just never reach their public although their makers intended for them to do so. Some works are withheld from their publics by their creators because they judge them to be in some way inferior and unworthy of presentation. The fact that artists withhold some of their works because they judge them unworthy of presentation shows that the works are things of a *kind* to be presented, otherwise, it would be pointless to judge them unworthy of presentation. Thus, even art not intended for public presentation presupposes a public, for not only is it possible to present it to a public (as sometimes happens), it is a thing of a type which has as a goal presentation to a public. The notion of a public hovers always in the background, even when a given artist refuses to present his work. In those cases in which works of art are withheld from a public, there is what might be called a "double intention" – there is an intention to create a thing of a kind which is presented, but there is also an intention not to actually present it.

But what is an artworld public? Such a public is not just a collection of people. The members of an artworld public are such because they know how to fulfill a role which requires knowledge and understanding similar in many respects to that required of an artist. There are as many different publics as there are different arts, and the knowledge required for one public is different from that required by another public. An example of one bit of knowledge required of the public of stage plays is the understanding of what it is for someone to act a part. Any given member of a public would have a great many such bits of information.

The artist and public roles are the minimum framework for the creation of art, and the two roles in relation may be called "the presentation group." The role of artist has two central aspects: first, a general aspect characteristic of all artists, namely, the awareness that what is created for presentation is art, and, second, the ability to use one or more of a wide variety of art techniques which enable one to create art of a particular kind. Likewise, the role of a public has two central aspects: first, a general aspect characteristic of all publics, namely, the awareness that what is presented to it is art and, second, the abilities and sensitivities which enable one to perceive and understand the particular kind of art with which one is presented.

In almost every actual society which has an institution of art-making, in addition to the roles of artist and public, there will be a number of supplementary artworld roles such as those of critic, art teacher, director, curator, conductor, and many more. The presentation group, i.e., the roles of artist and public in relation, however, constitutes the essential framework for art-making.

Among the more frequent criticisms of *Art and the Aesthetic* was that it failed to show that art-making is institutional because it failed to show that art-making is rule-governed. The underlying assumption of the criticism is that it is rule-governedness which distinguishes institutional practices such as, say, promising from noninstitutional ones such as, say, dog-walking. And it is true that *Art and the Aesthetic* did not bring out the rule-governedness of art-making and this requires correcting. There are rules implicit in the theory developed in the earlier book, but unfortunately I failed to make them explicit. There is no point in discussing the rules governing art-making implicit in the earlier theory, but those of the present revised theory can be stated. Earlier in this paper I argued that artifactuality is a necessary condition for being a work of art. This claim of necessity implies one rule of art-making: if one wishes to make a work of art, one must do so by creating an artifact. Also earlier in this paper I claimed that being a thing of a kind which is presented to an artworld public is a necessary condition for being a work of art. This claim of necessity implies another rule of art-making: if one wishes to create a work of art, one must do so by creating a thing of a kind which is presented to an artworld public. These two rules are jointly sufficient for making works of art.

The question naturally arises as to why the framework described as the institutional one is the correct essential framework rather than some other framework. The framework of the traditional theories are clearly inadequate, but their inadequacy does not prove the correctness of the framework of the present version of the institutional theory. Proving that a theory is true is notoriously difficult to do, although proving that a theory is false is sometimes easy to do. It can be said of the present version of the institutional theory that it is a conception of a framework in which works of art are clearly embedded and that no other plausible framework is in the offing. For lack of a more conclusive argument that the institutional theory's framework is the right one, I shall have to rely on the description of it I have given to function as an argument as to its rightness. If the description is correct, or approximately so, then it should evoke a "that's right" experience in the listener. In the remainder of the paper I shall, in effect, continue my description of the essential framework for the creation of art.

In *Art and the Aesthetic* I talked a great deal about conventions and how they are involved in the institution of art. In that book, I tried to distinguish between what I called "the primary convention" and other "secondary conventions" which are involved in the creation and presentation of art. One example of the so-called secondary conventions discussed there is the Western theatrical convention of concealing stagehands behind the scenery. This Western convention was there contrasted with that of classical Chinese theater in which the stagehand (called the property man) appears on stage during the action of the play and rearranges props and scenery. These two different theatrical solutions for the same task, namely, the employment of stagehands, brings out an essential feature of conventions. Any conventional way of doing something could have been done in a different way.

The failure to realize that things of the kind just discussed are conventions can result in confused theory. For example, it is another convention of Western theater that spectators do not participate in the action of a play. Certain aesthetic-attitude theorists failed to realize that this particular convention is a convention and concluded that the nonparticipation of spectators is a rule derived from aesthetic consciousness and that the rule must not be violated. Such theorists are horrified by Peter Pan's request for the members of the audience to applaud to save Tinkerbell's life. The request, however, merely amounts to the introduction of a new convention which small children, but not some aestheticians, catch on to right away.

There are innumerable conventions involved in the creation and presentation of art, but there is not, as I claimed in my earlier book, a *primary* convention to which all the other conventions are secondary. In effect, in *Art and the Aesthetic* I claimed that not only are there many conventions involved in the creation and presentation of art, but that at bottom the whole activity is completely conventional. But theater, painting, sculpting, and the like, are not ways of doing something which could be done in another way, and, therefore, they are not conventional. If, however, there is no *primary* convention, there is a primary *something* within which the innumerable conventions that there are have a place. What is primary is the understanding shared by all involved that they are engaged in an established activity or practice within which there is a variety of roles: artist roles, public roles, critic roles, director roles, curator roles, and so on. Our artworld consists of the totality of such roles with the roles of artist and public at its core. Described in a somewhat more structured way, the artworld consists of a set of individual artworld systems, each of which contains its own specific artist and public roles plus other roles. For example, painting is one artworld system, theater is another, and so on.

The institution of art, then, involves rules of very different kinds. There are conventional rules which derive from the various conventions employed in presenting and creating art. These rules are subject to change. There are more basic rules which govern the engaging in an activity, and these rules are not conventional. The artifact rule – if one wishes to make a work of art, one must do so by creating an artifact – is not a conventional rule; it states a condition for engaging in a certain kind of practice.

As I remarked earlier, the artifact rule and the other nonconventional rule are sufficient for the creating of art. And, as each rule is necessary, they can be used to formulate a definition of "work of art":

A work of art is an artifact of a kind created
to be presented to an artworld public.

This definition explicitly contains the terms "artworld" and "public," both of which have been discussed but not defined in this paper. The definition also involves the notions of *artist* and *artworld system*, both of which have been discussed but not definitionally characterized in this paper. I shall not attempt to define either "artist," "public," "artworld," or "artworld system" here, as I do in my book manuscript, but the definition of "work of art" given here and the definitions of these other four central terms provide the leanest possible description of the institutional theory of art.

To forestall an objection to the definition, let me acknowledge that there are artifacts which are created for presentation to the artworld publics which are not works of art: for example, playbills. Such things are, however, parasitic or secondary to works of art. Works of art are artifacts of a primary kind in this domain, and playbills and the like which are dependent on works of art are artifacts of a secondary kind within this domain. The word "artifact" in the definition should be understood to be referring to artifacts of primary kind.

The definition of "work of art" given in *Art and the Aesthetic* was, as I affirmed there, circular,

although not viciously so. The definition of "work of art" just given is also circular, although again not viciously so. In fact, the definitions of the five central terms constitute a logically circular set of terms.

There is an ideal of noncircular definition which assumes that the meaning of terms used in a definition ought not to lead back to the term originally defined, but rather ought to be or lead to terms which are more basic. The ideal of noncircular definition also assumes that we ought to be able to arrive at terms which are primitive in the sense that they can be known in some nondefinitional way, say, by direct sensory experience or by rational intuition. There may be some sets of definitions which satisfy this ideal, but the definitions of the five central terms of the institutional theory do not. Does this mean that the institutional theory involves a vicious circularity? The circularity of the definitions shows the interdependency of the central notions. These central notions are *inflected*, that is, they bend in on, presuppose, and support one another. What the definitions reveal is that artmaking involves an intricate, co-relative structure which cannot be described in the straight-forward, linear way envisaged by the ideal of noncircular definition. The inflected nature of art is reflected in the way we learn about art. This learning is sometimes approached through being taught how to be an artist – learning how to draw pictures which can be displayed, for example. This learning is sometimes approached through being taught how to be a member of an artworld public – learning how to look at pictures which are presented as the intentional products of artists. Both approaches teach us about artists, works, and publics all at the same time, for these notions are not independent of one another. I suspect that many areas within the cultural domain also have the same kind of inflected nature that the institution of art has. For example, the area which involves the notions of *law*, *legislature*, *executive*, and *judiciary*.

The ideal of noncircular definition holds also that sets of circular definitions cannot be informative. This may be true of some sets of definitions, but it is not, I think, true of the definitions of the institutional theory. For these definitions just mirror the mutually dependent items which constitute the art enterprise, and, thereby, inform us of its inflected nature.

George Dickie

Notes

1 G. Dickie, *Art and the Aesthetic* (Ithaca and London, 1974).

2 Ibid., p. 34.

3 M. Beardsley, "Is Art Essentially Institutional?", in *Culture and Art*, ed. Lars Aagaard-Mogensen (Atlantic Highlands, NJ, 1976), p. 202.

6

An Aesthetic Definition of Art

Monroe C. Beardsley

Like other questions of the same syntactic form, the question "What is art?" invites analysis of words and thoughts as well as the phenomena they refer to. But, being a philosophical question, it will not be satisfied by lexicography or psychology. I don't suppose that my task here is to inquire how various people commonly, or uncommonly, use the word "art" in English, or corresponding words in other languages, nor to canvas popular, or unpopular, opinion about what art is or ought to be. Taken philosophically, the question calls for decisions and proposals: What are the noteworthy features of the phenomena to which the word in question seems, however loosely, to call our attention? What are the significant distinctions that need to be marked for the purposes of theoretical understanding, and that the word "art" or one of its cognates ("artwork," "artistic," "artistry," etc.) is most apt and suitable for marking? How does art, defined in a comparatively clear, if somewhat unorthodox, way, differ from closely related things? Of course it will be a merit in any proposed definition of art if it matches reasonably well at least one fairly widespread use of the term, but it will not necessarily be a merit if the match is close, since philosophical reflection is expected to yield definitions and distinctions rather more valuable – to philosophy – than casual familiar ones.

I proclaim these assumptions or biasses at the start, to show my conception of my task – for which no further defense or apology will be forthcoming. What I will try to defend is a definition of art – actually, a rather old-fashioned one in essentials – that I have come to regard as best adapted to the requirements of a sound philosophy of art.

I

It should not be necessary to argue that we have need for a definition of art, but since this has been vigorously denied, some argument must be given. The point of a definition is, of course, to fix a meaning – to establish and stabilize it for some range of contexts – and thus mark out a class of things to be referred to by some group of people. One would think the philosopher of art could use a definition, since he should be curious to know what he is philosophizing about. Not that he can *begin* with an adequate definition – he only needs some uncontested examples of art, which are surely not hard to come by – but at some point he will want to say why these are examples of art, and how we are to tell what future things his philosophical conclusions are supposed to apply to. The critic of an art may be a similar case; it should be useful to him to have criteria for deciding what sorts of thing he is to criticize. The historian of an art – of dance, drama, architecture, or whatever – will surely have use for a definition to tell him what belongs in his history and what does not: Should the dance historian deal with parades and with cavorting bears? Should the architecture historian deal with igloos and Macdonald's eateries? If so, why? If not, why not? To answer such questions

Monroe C. Beardsley, "An Aesthetic Definition of Art," in Hugh Curtler (ed.), *What Is Art?* (New York: Haven Publications, 1983), pp. 15–29.

well requires a defensible definition. Even the practical legislator or administrator may have use for a definition, in deciding, for example, which imported objects to exempt from duties, or which allegedly artistic projects should be funded by the National Endowment for the Arts.

But we must especially note the needs of the anthropologist, and indeed as we move on we should keep in mind this broad cross-cultural perspective. Essential to our understanding of any culture is a grasp of the various forms of activity that it manifests, and of distinctions that are most significant to the members of the society that has that culture. When we observe someone carving wood or moving about in a circle with others, we must ask whether the activity is religious, political, economic, medical, etc. – or artistic. What function do the participants think of themselves as fulfilling, and how does it relate to other activities in which they engage? Even when the same act of carving or dancing in a ring has more than one character – it is both religious and artistic, say – we don't understand it unless we make this distinction and see that both descriptions apply. Distinction does not entail separation, and it is the distinction that is basic – though of course it may also be important to note that in one society these two forms of activity are always combined (the artists are the priests), while in another society they are kept apart and assigned to specialized persons. In a very few societies, horribly deprived or nearing destruction, we may be able to discern no activities to label "artistic," but there seems to be an ingredient or dimension of culture that runs across most societies, however varied, and whose nature we would like to articulate as well as we can. In other words, we want to define.

There are two definition questions that spring up when we take this anthropological point of view. We may, as I said, observe activities, and want to know which activities are artistic ones (allowing that they may also be political or pedagogical, etc.). We may notice certain objects that seem to engage the attention of many persons in the society from time to time, and want to know which of them, if any, are artworks (again allowing that they may also be sacred objects or economic objects, etc.). Here are two paired concepts, that of *artistic activity* and that of *artwork*; and already we are faced with one of the definitional decisions we must make. If we have an independent definition of "artwork," it is easy to define "artistic activity" as "activity that involves dealing with artworks." But it may turn out to be impossible, or inconvenient, to give a satisfactory definition of "artwork" without making reference to *some* form of artistic activity, either on the part of those who create artworks or those who receive them or both. We can hold off this problem for a moment.

If our definition of art must be designed to serve the varied purposes, both theoretical and practical, that I have reviewed, we obviously cannot accept some proposals that have been made in recent years and that still have adherents. It will not be wise to take as our basic notion that of an art as a skill of some kind. Of course this is a common use of the term, and has its value: we speak of the art of medicine, of salesmanship, of motorcycle maintenance, of cooking, of war. In a society in which various forms of activity, such as those just named, have been developed to a fairly high degree, they are done with art, artfully, in this broad sense. But when we want to distinguish the kind of activity that, in our society, results in oil paintings on museum walls, poems in books, sounds in concert halls, we are clearly after a narrower concept of art, rather remote perhaps from salesmanship, motorcycle maintenance, and war. It is this narrower concept that we must aim to capture in our definition – or at least *some* concept that will make a significant distinction and in so doing show us how to gather up into a single class a great many paintings, poems, and musical compositions and performances.

Nor will it help us, I think, to introduce the concept of *institution* at this point, even though this concept, when carefully delimited, is of great importance in the study of culture. First, it does not seem prudent to make noninstitutional artistic activities impossible by definition. Much of the artistic activity that we are familiar with in our society or observe in others is indeed institutionalized (for example, the Philadelphia Orchestra and New Directions Press). Some artistic activity occurs in the form of general practices (such as rural whittling and bluegrass musicmaking), without being, in a usefully strict sense, institutionalized at all. And it may be that still other artistic activities (such as amateur film-making and Sunday painting) should not even be called practices, though they may recur. At least, we should want our definitions to leave open the possibility of new forms of artistic activity appearing before they become encompassed by institutions. To define any form of activity in terms of the concept of institution, rather than the other way about, seems to be to invert logical order: how can we conceive of religious, political, artistic, and other institutions except in terms of the forms of activity that they sponsor and regularize? When, in studying an unfamiliar society, we try to identify the commercial institutions, say, we must surely begin by looking for sustained cooperative group *activities* (such as bartering and hoarding) that we acknowledge already to be economic in character.

Even more obviously, we cannot follow those who hold that in order to justify the current avant-garde we must allow that anything is art if anyone says it is. If being called "art" by someone is all it takes for something (say, an earthquake) to be an artwork, then when we say something is art we are saying no more than someone has applied this label to it. But of course our saying is also a performative, since in saying it is art we ourselves are applying the label to it; so the sentence "that is art" can never be *false*, no matter what it is said of or who says it. Sentences that become true merely by uttering them can be interesting if there are some rules to follow in uttering them, and hence some restrictions on when and by whom they can take effect. But sentences governed by no such rules have no point; on this proposal, the word "artwork" simply loses all content and becomes empty. No doubt there is sociological significance in the fact that there has been this effort in our society, in our age, to get us to cease to make any distinction between artistic and nonartistic activities, and between artworks and other things. This effort, I think, partly reflects a confused notion that if we allow a distinction we will encourage a separation; and it is partly a confused way of pleading for a far wider range of artistic activity than has ever before been recognized. But differences do not disappear just because we resolve to ignore them, and the avant-garde effort at erasure has no bearing on the philosophical task of finding out what differences are significant and deserve to be marked by appropriate terms.

II

Once we know what things are artworks in a particular society (and anything that is an artwork in some society is an artwork *tout court*), we can identify artistic activities by discovering which activities involve interaction with artworks. Artistic activities, so conceived, may be extremely varied, especially in a complex society, though we might want to draw some useful lines to separate interactions from more remote or indirect relationships. Thus editors of novels and dance coaches are plainly engaged in artistic activities, but typesetters of novels and doctors who strive to keep dancers in a state of physical repair are plainly not. Interesting as it might be to pause for a discussion of this distinction, and how to make it, we must stick to more central matters. And highly central are two artistic activities in particular, for they enable us to define "artwork," which can be used in turn to define the other artistic activities.

The first of these central activities is art-making or art-creating – what I shall call, very broadly, *art-production*. Again, tempting problems turn up, but we have to set them aside: they concern the concept of art-creation and the difference between making and creating. I use "production" generously, trying to slip around these puzzles: it includes making, altering, assembling, joining, arranging, and other distinguishable actions, including certain kinds of doing (as in dancing). What is produced, I think, is always something physical (an object or event) and perceptual, in that it has some properties that can be perceived. Often what is produced also has properties that are not perceptual or physical – such as meanings, messages, the capacity to evoke emotions or images, etc. Thus even an alleged work of conceptual art – one that is no more than a closed art gallery with a sign on it saying that the artwork being exhibited that week is just the closed art gallery itself – is a product in my sense (though whether it is an artwork is a question of the sort I expect my definition to clarify and help resolve). Since art-production is a species of production in general, if we are going to distinguish it from the rest, we shall need to specify a differentia. One plausible candidate for such a differentia, is *mode of production*. But this is barred to us, by the fact that the same process of production, as we said, may result in an object that is both an artwork and a religious object. Another plausible candidate is *intention*: that it is the presence of a certain kind of intention that makes production, art-production. This suggestion is immune to the counter-argument just given, for something can be produced with more than one intention – say, both an artistic and a religious intention. Another plausible candidate is *result*: that it is the achievement of a product of a certain kind that makes the production artistic. But this seems to lead to saying that production is artistic when it results in an artwork;

and I do not want to adopt this definition since I want to be able to define "artwork" (partly) in terms of its production.

Thus we seem to be beckoned toward adopting a definition of "art-production" that will make use of the concept of intention. But to characterize the specific type of intention needed we must turn to the second central artistic activity, which I have (for want of a better word) called *reception*. Reception comprises a variety of activities engaged in, in the presence of – or perhaps in response to reproductions or reports or memories of – sculpture, oral performances of literature, films, operas, etc. We view, listen to, contemplate, apprehend, watch, read, think about, peruse, and so forth. Sometimes in this receptive interaction we find that our experience (including all that we are aware of: perceptions, feelings, emotions, impulses, desires, beliefs, thoughts) is lifted in a certain way that is hard to describe and especially to summarize: it takes on a sense of freedom from concern about matters outside the thing received, an intense affect that is nevertheless detached from practical ends, the exhilarating sense of exercising powers of discovery, integration of the self and its experiences. When experience has some or all of these properties, I say it has an *aesthetic character*, or is, for short, aesthetic experience. Much more, of course, ought really to be said to fill out this mere sketch; and much more could be said, were room available. To say no more leaves, I am aware, a soft place in my definitional scheme, but if it proves to be the softest place, I shall have to be content.

When we voluntarily receive those things that are the result of art-production, we often do so with the intention of obtaining aesthetic experience – in other words, we have an *aesthetic interest* in those things. (We can have an aesthetic interest in other things as well – such as products of nature or technology.) I use the term "interest" in its fuller sense, which includes two ideas: (1) we *take* an interest in something, when approaching it and interacting with it, and we take an interest in the aesthetic character of the experience we hope to gain from it; but also (2) we *have* an interest in that experience, in the sense that it is *in our interest* to obtain it, since it is worthwhile. I do not defend this claim here, but I believe myself to be justified in making the assumption that aesthetic experience is desirable, has value, satisfies a genuine human interest.

We have now the makings of the definition I am after, and I propose that:

An artwork is something produced with the intention of giving it the capacity to satisfy the aesthetic interest.

Admirably terse, but therefore in need of exegesis, which I hope will guard it against misreading. It is an *aesthetic* definition of art, that is, a definition using the concept of the aesthetic, and though it is not the only possible aesthetic definition, it is the one I shall henceforth refer to.

To begin at the end, I have to assume that the concept of aesthetic interest is good enough for present purposes, even though it is defined in terms of aesthetic experience, which is the subject of lively and unabated controversy. It is important that the word "capacity" appears where it does: there are of course intimate cases of artistic activity in which the artist (i.e., artwork-producer) directly aims to provide aesthetic experience to some particular person or group of persons; but I say that it is enough if (as is more widely the case) he or she intends to fashion something that aesthetic experience *can* be obtained from. The artist may have no idea who, if anyone, will be able to obtain aesthetic experience from it, and maybe no one will (for example, if it is immediately destroyed). Appropriate interaction with the artwork may be extremely demanding or may depend on rare talents and extensive knowledge. The artist may be content to put his painting away or paint it over, once he is satisfied with what he has done – that is, believes that if someone with the requisite qualifications *were* to take an aesthetic interest in it, that interest would be satisfied to some degree. "Satisfaction," it should be noted, allows of degrees; it does not mean *complete* satisfaction.

The artist who works solely for his or her own enjoyment is an extreme case, no doubt; art-production is normally a social activity in which the producer and receiver are different persons. The impulse to make something capable of satisfying the aesthetic interest and to share it must be a very elementary one in very many societies, and must be present before there is a further desire to establish a continuing group (an institution) with an explicitly acknowledged group aim to foster artistic activity. In time there will emerge a tradition, a conviction that there are approved and disapproved ways, or better and worse ways, of carrying on the activity. But I can't see how tradition is essential to it, and I see no good reason to withhold the label "artwork" from art-production undertaken before or independently of a tradition. Artistic innovations involve rejection of at least some elements of a tradition, a striking out on one's own, but they must be counted within art as much as less adventurous works.

When I use the word "intention," I mean a combination of desire and belief: intending to produce a work capable of satisfying the aesthetic interest involves both (a) desiring to produce such a work and (b) believing that one will produce, or is in the process of producing, such a work. So normally the artist has a serious purpose: there is something he wants to do in producing what he produces; and he will have reason to believe that success is possible. If, for example, it is unlikely that a painter could believe that by closing the art gallery and placing a sign on it he would produce something capable of satisfying the aesthetic interest, then it is unlikely that in closing the art gallery and placing a sign on it he was producing an artwork. We must of course allow for far-out beliefs, however unreasonable; there are painters quite capable of believing that closing the art gallery and placing a sign on it might provide aesthetic experience to someone who came to the gallery, found the sign, and meditated on the symbolic significance of this higher order of art that is so self-effacing, so sublimely self-sacrificial that it denies itself its own existence (like Keats's unheard melodies that are sweeter than the heard ones). If this was indeed an intention the painter had in closing the gallery and placing the sign, then I am prepared to classify the closed and labeled gallery an artwork. There is, of course, no implication here about the degree of success; it is enough that something was intended. This places the painter's activity in a significant class of human activities, the artistic ones; it decides the kind of social enterprise he is engaged in, and it determines the primary (not the only) way in which his product is to be judged.

The example points up a problem in the application of this definition, though not, in my opinion, a fatal one. To identify the artistic activities and the artworks of a society we must make correct inferences about intentions. And intentions, being private, are difficult to know. But artistic activities are no different in this respect from all other significant activities of a society; if the anthropologist cannot understand what the observable behavior means to the people so behaving, what their desires and beliefs, purposes and motives, are, then he does not understand their culture. We must make use of available verbal tes-

timony, but inferences can legitimately reach beyond that. Once we discover that people in a given society have the *idea* of satisfying an aesthetic interest, and once we know at least some of their ways of satisfying this interest, we can reasonably infer the aesthetic intention (that is, the intention to produce something capable of satisfying the aesthetic interest) from properties of the product. A painting with a religious subject and evident power to move believers to religious devotion may also give evidence of extreme care in the composition, color harmony, subtle variations in light and texture; then we have a good reason to believe that *one* of the intentions with which the painter worked was the aesthetic one. The fact that a product belongs to a genre that already contains indubitable artworks also counts as evidence of aesthetic intention: hence, for example, some rather inferior statues of the Buddha sometimes find their way into art museums.

According to the definition I propose, and am defending, the aesthetic intention need not be the only one, or even the dominant one; it must have been present and at least to some degree effective – that is, it played a causal or explanatory role with respect to some features of the work. Again, even if we know that a Chinookan story, such as "Seal and Her Younger Brother Lived There," is told mainly to children to teach them a lesson (and so has primarily a pedagogical intention), the presence of aesthetically satisfying formal features and its successs in satisfying the aesthetic interest is enough to stamp it as a work of literary art. It is sometimes said that Paleolithic cave-drawings were not produced with any aesthetic intention at all, or aesthetically enjoyed, because they had a magical or religious function. One argument seems to be that no one in the culture could have had an aesthetic interest because the culture left no pure artworks (that is, works produced solely with an aesthetic intention). My view is that we know far too little about what was going on in the minds of Paleolithic people to be at all dogmatic about this, or to use their drawings as a counter-example to the aesthetic definition of art. Moreover – although this is a matter of interesting dispute, too – it seems highly probable to me that early human beings developed a capacity for aesthetic experience and a relish for it *before* they deliberately fashioned objects or actions for the purpose of providing aesthetic experience – just as they must have learned to use fire they found before they learned to make fires, and used found rocks as tools before they shaped rocks into better tools, and caves as housing before they built houses.

It is easy to point out vaguenesses in my definition; borderline cases can be found. This is true of most definitions, especially of cultural activities and objects. How pronounced must the aesthetic intention be? (It may be very subordinate to other intentions.) How much activity on the part of the artist is required in order to say that he is producing? (He may merely bring the snowflakes indoors and let them melt as they will.) How much of a sense of integration must an experience have to be aesthetic? (It may involve only a momentary pulling together of pleased attention to a particularly pregnant pothole.) There will inevitably be things we can cover by the definition if we are charitable but exclude if we want to be severe. Fuller explanation might tighten up the definition in some respects, but a rigorous line of demarcation is not to be expected – or even desired, perhaps, except by the legislator or administrator faced with practical decisions, and even he may have to decide some cases a bit arbitrarily, thinking mainly of precedents that will be set and untoward legal consequences to be avoided. Of course, if my definition is deemed hopelessly vague, so that it marks no useful distinction at all, it must be rejected; but surely, even as it stands, it clearly and decisively admits a large number of things and rules out a large number of other things. I would incline toward generosity and a welcoming attitude toward novelty – but I would look for evidence of some aesthetic intention, and I see no reason to twist my definition to make room for something like, say Edward T. Cone's one hundred metronomes running down with nobody silly enough to wait around for them – even if this "musical composition" is titled "Poème symphonique."

There will always be room for debate about such distinctions as that between producing art and kidding art – and perhaps the closed art gallery is a case in point. Kidding is a kind of message, and when done well certainly does not disqualify the kidding object from being itself an artwork; the enjoyment of wit can be an aesthetic experience. But common sense should not be abandoned along with philosophical acumen in these matters. The fuss that has been made about Duchamp's *Fountain* has long amazed me. It does not seem that in submitting that object to the art show and getting it more or less hidden from view, Duchamp or anyone else thought of it either as art or as having an aesthetic capacity. He did not establish a new meaning of "artwork," nor did he really inaugurate a tradition that led to the acceptance of plumbing figures (or other "readymades") as artworks today. If there was a point, it was surely to prove to the jury that even their tolerance had limits, and that they would *not* accept anything – at least gracefully. This small point was made effectively, but the episode doesn't seem to me to provide the slightest reason to regard the aesthetic definition as inadequate. Many objects exhibited today by the avant-garde evidently do make comments of some kind on art itself, but these objects may or may not be artworks. To classify them as artworks just because they make comments on art would be to classify a lot of dull and sometimes unintelligible magazine articles and newspaper reviews as artworks, and where is the advantage of that? To classify them as artworks just because they are exhibited is, to my mind, intellectually spineless, and results in classifying the exhibits at commercial expositions, science museums, stamp clubs and World's Fairs as artworks. Where is the advantage of that? To classify them as artworks just because they are called art by those who are called artists because they make things they call art is not to classify at all, but to think in circles. Perhaps these objects deserve a special name, but not the name of art. The distinction between objects that do and those that do not enter into artistic activities by reason of their connection with the aesthetic interest is still vital to preserve, and no other word than "art" is as suitable to make it.

III

It remains to consider some of the reasonable objections that may occur to the reader – partly to dispose (if I can) of the more obvious ones, thus encouraging potential critics of the aesthetic definition to concentrate on raising more surprising and far-reaching ones, and partly to suggest some guidelines for constructing alternative proposals to replace the definition with a better one. My method will be to consider briefly some propositions that may be suspected of being untoward consequences of the definition; some of them, I argue, do not really follow from it and the others are quite acceptable.

1. If we take artworks as I have characterized them, then it is possible for children, even quite young children, to create artworks. This conse-

quence is unacceptable to philosophers whose definitions assign to artworks an esssential dependence on institutions, traditions, or aesthetic theories, for we may suppose that seven-year-olds, say, when they draw pictures, write poems, or make up songs, do not yet participate in what is called the "artworld." But it seems to me invidious to deny children this capability, especially on rather a priori grounds. The basic social activity, as I see it, is one in which a person produces something that he or she finds aesthetically enjoyable and shares it with others who may be able to appreciate it. Once this concept arises, we can have artworks, however simple and crude they may be. This does not mean making pictures of Thanksgiving turkeys according to the directions of a teacher, and seeking commendation for doing the assignment right. But developmental psychologists who have studied the "artful scribbles" of children (notably Howard Gardner) discern a frequent ability to use pictorial symbol systems for aesthetic purposes.

2. The question arises whether, on the aesthetic definition, forgeries of artworks can themselves be artworks. My answer is that some are and some are not: it all depends on the effective presence of an aesthetic intention. To begin with one extreme, a mechanical reproduction of an artwork (such as a picture-postcard sold in an art-museum shop) should probably not be classified as an artwork, even though it may be capable of affording some aesthetic satisfaction. At the other extreme, we have free copies (such as a Reubens copy of a Titian) that are plainly painted with an aesthetic intention. But of course neither of these is a forgery, strictly speaking, because there is no intent to deceive, no misrepresentation of producership. Now we can imagine a person making an exact copy of a painting by Chirico for the purpose (that is, with the intention) of passing it off as a genuine Chirico; and we can imagine that his method of working is tediously atomistic: he uses instruments to make sure that each small area matches the original perfectly. In that case he might execute the forgery without any aesthetic intention at all. This is hard to believe; it is far more likely that he will paint with an eye to capturing the peculiar quality of the empty, lonely, ominous space in the Chirico in order to make sure the forgery is good enough as a painting to fool a connoisseur. In that case the forger is producing an artwork.

This conclusion will strike art historians as a reductio ad absurdum of the proposed definition, for they make no room in their history for forgeries.

I agree that forgeries do not belong to the history of art, any more than any other copies or reproductions, because they have no significance for the development of art. But I do not see why a careful copyist, though thoroughly unoriginal, cannot be producing an artwork; and I do not see how the addition of another intention (to deceive someone) makes the product less an artwork – especially since the very success of the deception may depend on the painter's having the intention to make his work as capable as the original one of satisfying the aesthetic interest.

3. It follows from my definition that once an artwork, always an artwork. Anyone who holds that something can become an artwork and cease to be an artwork will object to my definition, and be inclined to adopt an institutional definition. It is sometimes said that, for example, a spinning wheel or snow shovel may begin life as a nonartwork, tied down to its lowly function; that at some point the artworld (prodded by an enterprising museum curator or by a maverick painter like Duchamp) may open its arms to embrace it, placing it on display and thus converting it into an artwork; and that at a still later time this designation or status may be withdrawn, so that the spinning wheel or snow shovel reverts to its original state. If some versions of the institutional theory are right, and there is an implicit or explicit performative act by which nonart can be given art-status, then it seems the process should be reversible by a converse act, as marriages can be annulled, names changed, contracts declared void, cabinet appointments rescinded, votes overturned, priests defrocked, and so forth. But the notion of taking away an object's property of being art is prima facie puzzling, and this puzzlingness is accounted for on the aesthetic definition. Something that is not an artwork can of course be exhibited, can become the object of aesthetic interest, can fall from fashion as people lose aesthetic interest in it. But since what makes art, art is an intention with which it was produced, nothing can be art that was not art from the start, and nothing that is art can cease to be art. And this seems to me a more intelligible and less misleading way to talk than to say, for example, that the Victorian paintings now stored in the art-museum's basement have ceased to be art, just because they are no longer much admired.

4. If it is the intention that counts in art-production, does it follow that one cannot *fail* to produce an artwork, if one intends to? That might seem an unfortunate consequence of the proposed

definition, if it is a consequence. To straighten out the difficulty here requires some careful attention to certain features of actions and intentions. I do not say that the aesthetic intention is the intention to produce an artwork, but the intention to produce something capable of satisfying the aesthetic interest. To intend to produce an artwork is to intend to produce something produced with the intention of producing something capable of satisfying the aesthetic interest; and this second-order intention, though it does occur, is not the usual one, I think. Thus in a certain rather innocuous sense artworks are often produced unintentionally – that is, without the intention to produce an artwork. But of course an artwork cannot be produced without any intention, and in this sense there can be no unintentional artworks. Paint may be spilled and pottery cracked unintentionally, and the pattern of paint or of the cracks may be capable of satisfying the aesthetic interest; but that alone does not make an artwork.

One can fail in various ways in trying to produce an artwork: the work may not be as original as was hoped (the box of Kitty-Litter submitted to the avant-garde show turns out to be the second one submitted), or the work may not be the kind of work hoped for (the poem is not nearly as ironic as had been expected). But as far as I can see, the only way one can fail to produce an artwork after setting out to produce something capable of satisfying the aesthetic interest is by failing to make the physical object one tries to make (the clay is defective or the temperature of the kiln not right, so the pot falls apart), or to do the deed one tries to do (the dancer slips and falls instead of completing the pirouette). As long as *something* is produced with the aesthetic intention, an artwork is produced.

5.   It is a consequence of my aesthetic definition, then, that tawdry and negligible objects will be classified as artworks. In such a sorting there is no implication of worth or value. Admittedly, this insistence on preserving a value-neutral sense of "artwork," for the purposes sketched at the start of this essay, runs counter to a familiar use of "work of art" for artistic praise. But we need a term for the classification; indeed, without it we will not even be able to make sense of the evaluative expression "a good artwork." And there are other terms

to do the job of evaluating – indeed, a large number, because we call artworks not only "good" but many other things, both kind and unkind. Before the anthropologist could hope to discover which objects in a society are its "artworks" in the normative sense (that is, what I would call its good or great artworks), it seems that he or she will first have to gain some notion of the class of things in reference to which some of its members are judged superior or supreme. And the anthropologist (since he is not necessarily an art historian) may be as interested in the failed products of a society's artistic activities as in its successes – especially if he can come to understand the causes and the consequences of these failures. Moreover, when we take an anthropological interest in our own society, or others of a comparable level of civilization, we have to study a vast and highly significant phenomenon that is generally labeled "popular art." Part of my aim in providing a definition of art that has no built-in value-judgments ranking decorative designs, stories, dances, songs, etc. is to encompass the popular arts as well as those for which we lack a convenient label – I suppose because they have been thought of as the real thing: portraits in oil, epic poems, ballet, lieder, etc. To gather popular and "esoteric" artworks (using the latter term with some diffidence) in the same broad class is not, of course, to deny differences in value, but it is to invite study of continuities and degrees of accessibility, of complexity, of training in taste, of seriousness in affect, and so forth. I don't see any good reason for not regarding *Guys and Dolls* and *The Pirates of Penzance* as artworks, along with *Tannhäuser* and *The Marriage of Figaro*. When it comes to other sorts of product now much studied by scholars – bed-quilts, cigarstore Indians, Dixieland jazz, old Tarzan movies – it may strike some people that we have wandered to the edge of art, if not beyond. There will, of course, always be a question whether something was indeed produced with an aesthetic intention, but even when this intention was probably minimal and the skill to carry it out deficient, the social function served may be the same as that of clearly artistic activities, or closely related to it. So a broad definition of art that still retains its essential connection with the aesthetic interest has much to recommend it.

7

Weitz's Anti-Essentialism

Stephen Davies

Artists and philosophers have offered many characterizations of the distinctive nature of art. To mention just a few famous examples: for Plato art is imitation (or representation); for Wordsworth it is emotion recollected in tranquility, and for Tolstoy it is the expression of emotion; for Kant it is the interplay of forms, and for Clive Bell and Roger Fry it is significant form; Susanne Langer sees it as an iconic symbol of the forms of feelings.

Each of these theories seems plainly to fail as a definition. Either it does not distinguish artworks from other kinds of things – for example, tears are expressive of emotion but are not artworks – or it excludes from the realm of art pieces that indisputably are art – for example, at least some of Bach's fugues seem not to be expressive of emotion.

Of course, a proponent of one of these theories might stick by it in the face of all opposition, insisting that the theory can accommodate any alleged counter-instance. But in that case the defense saves the theory from falsity only at the cost of rendering it vacuous or meaningless. If nothing is to be accepted as falsifying the claim, for example, that all artworks have significant form, what now can be meant by the notion of significant form?

Morris Weitz argues in his famous paper, "The Role of Theory in Aesthetics" (1956), that the consistent failure of artists and aestheticians successfully to define art is no accident. Art is not

Stephen Davies, "Weitz's Anti-Essentialism," ch. 1 (edited by the editor for this volume) from Stephen Davies, *Definitions of Art* (Ithaca, NY: Cornell University Press, 1991) © 1991 by Cornell University. Used by permission of the publisher, Cornell University Press.

susceptible to definition, he claims. The reasons he gives for his conclusion are philosophical, but no doubt a general dismay at the state of contemporary art might have pointed to his conclusion. When it looks as if anything at all might become (or be declared) art, the idea that something is an artwork because it shares with others of its kind a common essence looks to be implausible.

Weitz's Argument

The quest for an essential definition of "artwork" is a quest for a nontrivial specification of the jointly necessary and sufficient condition for something's being art. Weitz claims not only that all past attempts to define art have failed but also that any attempt to provide an essential definition of art is doomed to failure for the reason that art has no essence. No property is jointly necessary and sufficient for something's being an artwork. If we "look and see," he says, we will observe that there is no property common to all and only artworks.

Weitz might have accepted that there are both some necessary and some sufficient properties for art; his point is that there are no *jointly* necessary and sufficient conditions for art. In fact, though, Weitz goes so far as to deny that there is any property common to all artworks. In other words, he denies that there is any necessary condition for something's being an artwork. He thinks the possession of artifactuality is a necessary condition for something's being an artwork, if any property is. But he also holds that something can be made into an artwork without its also being made into an artifact. A piece of driftwood can be removed from the beach and becomes an artwork (without being artifactualized) in being presented as such within an art gallery. He concludes: not even artifactuality is a necessary condition for art; so there is no necessary condition for something's being art.

Obviously if Weitz is right in this, he wins his case. If there is no necessary condition for something's being an artwork, it follows immediately that there can be no jointly necessary and sufficient condition for something's being an artwork, and hence, no essential definition of art.

Weitz does not rest his argument entirely upon empirical claims about what will be found when we "look and see," or about the legitimacy of "Driftwood art" and the like; he makes what he takes to be a telling conceptual point. A definition of art would foreclose on future creativity. If art has some immutable essence, then the art of the future could not, in its essential respects, challenge, alter, subvert, or depart from the art of the past. But the history of art is the history of such a process, of an exercise of revolutionary creativity that time and again has turned the prevailing conception of art on its head and back-to-front. So art could have no unalterable aspect and, hence, no essential definition. Were we to find some property common to all and only artworks (which in fact we do not), that property would be bound to be an incidental, nonessential property, for it might always be rejected or ignored in the art of the future. Indeed, such is the temperament of artists that the discovery of such a property would provoke a reaction against it!

The definitions of art offered in the past by philosophers are legislative rather than descriptive, Weitz says. Instead of characterizing the fixed essence of all artworks, each "definition" stipulates the range of properties regarded by its proponent as desirable in good art. What is no more than a recommendation in favor of some particular school is presented, instead, as a definition objectively applicable to all art.

How, though, are artworks grouped together as such in the absence of a defining property? Weitz adopts the idea of "family resemblance" introduced by Wittgenstein (1953). Just as the members of a family all resemble one another in some respect, though there is no single, pervasive respect in which each resembles every other, so too there are networks of similarity among artworks, despite the absence of a property common to all artworks. Just as the woven fibers of a rope can constitute a length of rope, though no single fiber runs through the full length of the rope, so too the complex web of resemblances among artworks groups them within a common, unified class. One piece is properly to be classed as an artwork along with other artworks by virtue of its sharing a family resemblance with them.

Although Weitz's paper was to become more widely cited than any other, he was not alone in pursuing the line of argument indicated above. W. B. Gallie (1956) argues that art has no essence and so is an essentially contested concept. John Passmore (1951) suggests that the dreariness of aesthetics follows from its futile pursuit of a definition. Paul Ziff (1953) is also an anti-essentialist who believes that artworks are classed as such in virtue of their resemblance to paradigm cases. William Kennick (1958) is another who dismisses the quest for a definition of art. He thinks artworks are grouped by resemblance and analogy.

Frequently anti-essentialist arguments are accompanied by the comment that, because we can make identifying references to art while lacking knowledge of its defining essence, a definition is unnecessary. Kennick (1958) makes the point by claiming that someone would know what to collect if asked to retrieve the artworks from a warehouse (= the world), but would be at a loss if told to bring from the warehouse all the items with "significant form" and the like.

It is true that, very commonly, we make identifying references to things without concerning ourselves with, or even knowing of, their defining essences, but the point is made by anti-essentialists in such a way as to suggest that they take it to reveal the total irrelevance, or even the impossibility, of one's providing an essential definition. It is a mistake, however, to think that such ability as we have in identifying artworks bears upon the possibility or otherwise of art's having a defining essence. And if it does have one, there is no reason to assume that the only interest a definition could have would lie in its making possible the identification of artworks as such, nor are there grounds to suppose that a definition must be applicable in this way.

Criticisms of Weitz's Argument

Many writers have challenged the specific claim that not even artifactuality is a necessary condition for something's being an artwork. Against Weitz's example they argue either that Driftwood art is not art at all, or that, one way or another, the piece of driftwood is artifactualized in the course of its attaining art status. Still, Weitz might be mistaken in insisting that artifactuality is not a necessary condition for something's being art without his being mistaken in his main claim: that art has no jointly necessary and sufficient conditions.

The explanatory power of the idea of family resemblance has been called into question (for instance, see Mandelbaum 1965). The very example from which the notion takes its name points up the problem. People are not grouped together in families by virtue of the ways in which they resemble each other. Typically they are grouped in families in terms of genetic relationships. (This is the common, but careless, way of putting the objection. Spouses, adopted children, in-laws, and so forth are not usually genetically related but are family members for all that. The objection could be put more carefully, however.) The recognition of a resemblance among family members presupposes, and does not explain, the basis for that membership.

More than this, in the absence of some way of specifying a restriction on the class within which resemblance is to be sought, or in the kinds and degrees of resemblances that are to be counted, resemblance is a notion that is useless as a basis for classification. Anything might resemble any other thing in some respect. (Germs resemble galaxies in that both are mentioned in this sentence, both have names beginning with "g," neither can be seen by the unaided eye in daytime, neither has the same weight as any emu, and so on.) If resemblance is to provide a basis for classification, there must be some restriction on the type and/or range and/or degree of resemblance that is relevant. Now, though, the specification of criteria of relevance for resemblances will lead unavoidably to an essential definition. We get something like this: an artwork is anything that resembles any paradigm artwork in not less than nineteen of the following fifty-two respects. . . . and a paradigm artwork is one that. . . .

George Dickie (1984) has produced a further objection on Weitz's appeal to family resemblance. He notes that family resemblance could never explain how the very first artwork qualified as an artwork. Even if most artworks are artworks in virtue of their similarity with earlier art, still there must be some original artworks that lack artistic predecessors. The explanation of the qualification of these early artworks for art status cannot rest on resemblance. A recursive definition in terms of resemblance (X is an artwork if it resembles the artworks of the past) is incomplete unless a different account of the art status of the earliest pieces is included (and the first artworks were artworks because . . .). So, at best, Weitz's appeal to family resemblance provides an incomplete explanation of how things become art.

One further difficulty with the claim that resemblance provides the basis for classifying items as artworks is posed by Marcel Duchamp's ready-mades, Driftwood art, and many instances of Conceptual art. Duchamp turned one urinal indistinguishable from others of its type into an artwork without thereby affecting the non-art status of those other urinals. If two urinals are alike in their appearance (and alike also in the causal history of their manufacture), how could the resemblance between artworks and one of these urinals explain how that urinal is an artwork without its showing the other urinal to be an artwork also? And again, one piece of driftwood resembles another piece of driftwood more closely than either resembles the vast majority of artworks, so how could resemblance explain how the one piece might be an artwork and the other not? (Of course one might challenge this objection by questioning the status as art of readymades, driftwood pieces, and the like, but that course is not open to Weitz since he accepts that pieces of driftwood actually can become artworks.)

Notice, however, that, if these criticisms are decisive, they show only that Weitz's positive account, his account of how we group artworks together, is mistaken. They do not show his main negative point to be in error; that is, they leave untouched the claim that artworks are not grouped together in terms of a common essence, since they have none.

Weitz exhorts us to look and see that art lacks an essence. Dickie (1980, 1984) has objected that Weitz is too liberal when he "looks and sees," in that Weitz accepts all uses of the word "artwork" as equally legitimate and so fails to distinguish the literal, classificatory use of the term from uses that are evaluative, metaphoric, ironic, and so on, as well as from those that simply are in error. Dickie's point is that we can hardly expect to find the essential core of art if, as well as considering the Mona Lisa as an artwork, we also count Aunt Flo's scones, my love's ear, and so on, as works of art. Further, Dickie notes that if just any use of the term "work of art" is to be accepted as legitimate, then conflicting judgments about what is and what is not art also will be equally legitimate, in which case the appearance of disagreement will be illusory because such judgments will amount to no more than expressions of personal taste.

Is Weitz guilty of the fault imputed to him? He may be, though I am not certain that he is. Anyway, Weitz's position does not rely for its plausibility on any such sleight of hand. It is arguable that not even art's paradigm instances share a common property. What intrinsic, perceptible feature is common to Shakespeare's *Hamlet*, a *Song without Words* by Mendelssohn, Donne's *Hymn to God the Father*, Picasso's *Guernica*, Austen's *Pride and Prejudice*, Michelangelo's *David*? It is not obvious that there is any perceptible, aesthetic property common to them all.

Weitz's main conceptual point is that an essential definition of art would determine the character of yet-to-be-made artworks in a way that would rule out art making as a creative activity. From this claim he concludes that it must be impossible to give an essential definition of art, since art making necessarily and inescapably is a creative activity.

A number of writers are unconvinced by the allegation of an incompatibility between creativity and the availability of necessary and sufficient conditions for art status (for instance, see Mandelbaum 1965; Brown 1969; Sclafani 1971), and rightly so, I think. After all, that it is made by a creative person might be a part of the essence of an artwork, might be something mentioned in its definition. How could such a definition foreclose on future creativity, since it does not tell artists what to do, although it insists that, whatever they do, they do it creatively? Moreover, why think of rules as restraints instead of as means facilitating one's actions, including one's creative actions? It is not chess I am playing if I do not play by the rules that map the limits of the game itself, and I can play creative, innovative, radical chess only within the framework of those rules.

There is a common view that dates back to Kant (and no doubt much further) according to which artists are geniuses unconstrained by rules and the artworks that result from their actions are valuable and interesting only insofar as they are unique and resistant to description in general terms. Now, if we see definitions as formulas or rules, it will be natural for us to share Weitz's conclusion that creativity precludes definability.

This argument (whether or not it be Weitz's) rests on several common (but mistaken) assump-

tions about the nature of creativity, of rules, and of the usefulness of definitions. The conception of the artist as genius and of creation as the unfettered expression of the intellect, emotions, or spirit is a peculiarly nineteenth-century, European one that sits ill with the character and the style of creation of such artists as J. S. Bach, who worked to order and with strict deadlines. Equally unacceptable is the view that an adequate definition must be usable as if it were a recipe. To return to the above example, how could a definition of artworks as the product of artists' creative efforts serve as a mere formula for the production of art?

Also misleading is the view that to follow a rule is to have the outcome of one's actions determined in advance and in a fashion that is independent of what people do and judge. Wittgenstein (1953) was the first to challenge this conception of rules and to emphasize not only that no rule determines its own interpretation, but also that what counts as following or applying a rule is determined in connection with patterns of communal behavior and judgment. The point is this: rule following is not necessarily mindless and often requires creativity in deciding how the rule is to be applied to new cases. To call us "rule followers" is misleading in implying that the rule has been there before us, so to speak – what we are is "rule appliers" or "rule interpreters." When we are seen in these terms, there is no reason to oppose the notions of creativity and of rule following.

A defender of Weitz might concede the previous argument and yet continue to hold that, in much if not all art, the norm is rule breaking rather than rule applying. Many artists of the past and yet more in the present set out deliberately to challenge the rules and conventions that seemed to govern their predecessors. Art often is reflexive in taking its own former self (its former practices and its former rules) as its present subject matter. In continually dissociating itself from itself, it transcends its past and the rules and conventions that typified that past.

This reply is unconvincing. If anything, it shows that the rules applied by artists in creating art can be changed, and not that there are no such rules. A change in first-order rules is perfectly consistent with the continuing application of second-order rules about how and to what degree first order rules might change, so change is not itself antithetical to rule application. Indeed, if what artists do is to be correctly understood as a new way of making art and not to be seen merely as a new way of indulging or amusing themselves, then some link with the past practice of art making must be preserved (Levinson 1979; Carroll 1988). If I create a new form of art, and not merely a new style of fruit picking, or paper folding, or house building, then there must be something about my fruit picking, paper folding, or house building – something about its intentional context, its consequences, its function, or whatever – which separates it from all non-art-making acts of fruit picking, paper folding, or house building and unites it with other acts of art creation. Artists cannot be so free that they leave all constraints behind them, because if they were, there would be no reason to think that what they are doing is creating new art, as distinct from creating mere new junk, mere new buildings, mere new pastimes, and so on.

Weitz concerns himself at first with openness with respect to the border between present and future art. Later (1973) he recognizes that openness might take many forms – suffice it to say that he recognizes the difficulty of tracing the borderline between present art and non-art, as well as between present art and future art. On the one hand, there are any number of controversial or otherwise "hard" cases where something alleged to be art is in most respects indiscriminable from non-artworks or seemingly is not worthy of the status of art – Duchamp's readymades, Driftwood art, Chimpanzee art, Minimal art, Conceptual art, Environmental art, and so forth. On the other hand, there are many pastimes and entertainments the products of which are not usually classed as artworks but which seem worthy of that appellation – musicals, break-dancing, joinery, finepoint sewing, pottery, scrimshaw, and so on. One way in which the concept of art might be open is in the absence of any clear border between what is and what is not to be classified as an artwork.

Even if we accept for the sake of the argument that there is no clear border between some artworks and some non-artworks, it is not obvious that the possibility of an essential definition of artwork has been ruled out. Two accounts of this type of openness are possible, and either is compatible with the giving of an essential definition. In the first type of case, the openness of the concept indicates an epistemic difficulty we have in deciding just where the boundary of the concept lies. In this view the concept does have a clear boundary, and so any given item really is or is not an artwork, but because we cannot be sure or cannot agree on where the boundary falls, we cannot always be certain what is

and what is not an artwork. In that event it will also be the case that we cannot be certain which of several plausible candidates is the correct, essential definition of artwork. But that we will then have a difficulty in demonstrating to everyone's satisfaction which is the correct definition does not show to be incoherent the notion that there is a correct definition. In the second type of case the borderline vagueness is ontological; it is characteristic of the way the concept is instantiated in the world and is not simply a reflection of the uncertain basis of our knowledge of the world. Cases are hard to determine precisely because there is at the borderline no definite, correct answer as to whether or not something is an artwork. But again, that a concept is indefinite in some respects is no bar to its being defined. An adequate, essential definition of the concept will record the limits of the area in which the application of the term is equivocal. If it is part of the essence of the concept that it is indefinite in some ways and/or at some places and/or at some times and/or under some conditions, then the dimensions of this indefiniteness will feature within an essential definition of the concept.

Weitz's instruction to look and see if artworks share a common, essential property indicates that he thinks an essential property (were there to be one) would be a property perceptible within each and every artwork – to put it crudely, that all and only artworks are red, for example. The same assumption is indicated by the conflict he postulates between creativity and definition, because these two most obviously would clash if the definition specified that the artwork, to qualify as an artwork, must possess a perceptible property, such as a particular type of form or content. These indications suggest that, in denying the possibility of an essential definition, Weitz is denying the possibility of an essential definition in terms of particular sorts of properties; that is, in terms of the perceptible properties intrinsic to artworks. Of course, he may be right in thinking that no internal, perceptible property is essential to something's being an artwork, while being mistaken in the claim that he actually makes – that no essential definition of art is possible.

The first commentator to put forth this powerful objection was Mandelbaum (1965). Instead of concluding (from the fact that there is no essential property perceptible within all and only artworks) that an essential definition of art is impossible, Mandelbaum points out that it would be as or more plausible to conclude that the essential property for art is some imperceptible property, such as a relational property between certain sorts of objects, practices, and people. Weitz cannot find an essential property for art only because he looks for that property in the wrong place. Mandelbaum does not go on to spell out a definition, but he does indicate the direction in which one is to be sought. He suggests that what all and only artworks might have in common is a particular function.

There is a reply to Mandelbaum's objection which, though it seems obvious, few people acknowledge. It is: if you "look and see," just as you will notice that there is no intrinsic property common to all and only artworks, equally you will find that there is no extrinsic property common to all and only artworks. There is no relational property the instantiation of which is essential to a thing's being an artwork. The shift of attention from perceptible to relational properties provides no guarantee that the difficulties that arise with respect to definitions citing the former will not recur with respect to definitions citing the latter.

This move is successful in staving off the immediate collapse of a Weitzian position, but as a long-term strategy it does not look to be promising. Weitz's claim that there is no property common to all and only artworks appears highly plausible when we confine our attention to the perceptible and/or intrinsic properties of artworks but is far less believable when extended to cover all the possible types of properties an artwork might have. For there are many properties that seem to be both important and common to a great many artworks, if not to them all – for example, that artworks are chosen, shaped, or created with certain sorts of purposes and effects in mind. Even if it is not self-evidently true that some relational property is essential to something's being art, it is by no means ridiculous to argue toward such a conclusion.

What was the effect of Weitz's paper, apart from its kindling an interest in the definition of art which he had hoped to scotch? Even if it did not convince everyone that definition is impossible, it did at least persuade many that artworks could not be defined in terms of their perceptible, intrinsic properties. In particular, the definition of "artwork" in terms of artworks being objects with certain aesthetic properties, such as beauty, seemed to be abandoned. Instead, those who pursue the definition of art turned their attention to the complex, extrinsic, relational properties possessed by artworks. They began to concern themselves with the historical and social context within which art is created, presented, interpreted, understood, and enjoyed and, in wider terms, with the function played by the production and consumption of art in our lives. This shift of focus was a radical departure from the preoccupations of traditional aesthetics, and a measure of responsibility for that most rewarding of reorientations belongs undoubtedly to Weitz.

References

Brown, Lee B. 1969. "Definitions and Art Theory," *The Journal of Aesthetics and Art Criticism*, 27, 409–15.

Carroll, Noël 1988. "Art, Practice, and Narrative," *The Monist*, 71, 140–56.

Dickie, George 1980. "Review of Weitz's *The Opening Mind*," *Journal of Philosophy*, 77, 54–6.

———1984. *The Art Circle: A Theory of Art* (New York: Haven).

Gallie, W. B. 1956. "Art as an Essentially Contested Concept," *The Philosophical Quarterly*, 6, 97–114.

Kennick, William, E. 1958. "Does Traditional Aesthetics Rest on a Mistake?" *Mind*, 67, 317–34.

Levinson, Jerrold 1979. "Defining Art Historically," *The British Journal of Aesthetics*, 19, 232–50.

Mandelbaum, Maurice 1965. "Family Resemblances and Generalizations Concerning the Arts," *The American Philosophical Quarterly* 2, 219–28.

Passmore, John 1951. "The Dreariness of Aesthetics," *Mind*, 60, 318–35.

Sclafani, Richard, J. 1971. "'Art', Wittgenstein, and Open-textured Concepts," *The Journal of Aesthetics and Art Criticism*, 29, 333–41.

Weitz, Morris 1956. "The Role of Theory in Aesthetics," *The Journal of Aesthetics and Art Criticism*, 15, 27–35.

———1973. "Wittgenstein's Aesthetics," in *Language and Aesthetics*, ed. Benjamin R. Tilghman (Kansas: University Press of Kansas), pp. 7–19.

Wittgenstein, Ludwig 1953. *Philosophical Investigations*, trans. G. E. M. Anscombe (Oxford: Blackwell).

Ziff, Paul 1951. "Art and the 'Object of Art,'" *Mind*, 60, 466–80.

———1953. "The Task of Defining a Work of Art," *Philosophical Review*, 62, 58–78.

Part II

Ontology of Art

Introduction to Part II

Among works of art are paintings, sculptures, prints, photographs, films, poems, novels, plays, buildings, ballets, symphonies, operas, and other more exotic species of multi-media productions, installations, and conceptual art. Is there any single ontological category to which all such items belong? Do they all share *au fond* the same "mode of existence," in virtue of being works of art?

On the face of it, it might seem impossible to find unity amidst such apparent diversity. Even the ways we talk about different kinds of works suggest the differences go deep. Of dance, music, and drama we speak of *performances* and we recognize that there could be strikingly different performances of the same work. Poems and novels have *copies* which allow us to read and enjoy them without ever seeing the original manuscript. Manuscripts, including musical scores, can be lost without the works being lost. Engraved prints and photographs have multiple *reproductions*, just as films can be reproduced and distributed. Yet paintings and carved (as opposed to cast) sculptures seem to be unique *physical objects*. Certainly they can be copied but to see a copy is not to see the real thing, which we call the *original*. Buildings seem sometimes to be unique objects – York Minster, the Taj Mahal – but sometimes they can have multiple instances, as in designs for housing estates.

One common move among philosophers seeking to bring order to this miscellany is to invoke a distinction from C. S. Peirce between *types* and *tokens*. This distinction is discussed at length by Joseph Margolis in "The Ontological Peculiarity of Works of Art." We might say that while individual works of music, drama, or dance are types, performances of those works are tokens, allowing there to be many tokens of the same single type. Similarly a copy of a novel or a distributed film would be classified as a token of a type. Those who employ this distinction often contrast those works that are types – of the kind mentioned – with works that are unique objects, such as paintings and non-cast sculptures. Such an account would be committed to a dualistic view of the arts, holding that works of art come in two fundamentally different kinds: those that are abstract entities, i.e. types, and those that are physical objects.

Many philosophers, though, are not content to settle for this dualism. They prefer to see all the arts as belonging to the same ontological category. One such view is to deny that any works of art are particular physical objects, not even paintings. Thus P. F. Strawson, in his paper "Aesthetic Appraisal and Works of Art," which we have included in Part V, argues that paintings are really types, not particulars, and the reason why we tend to treat them as unique particulars is the purely contingent one that we do not yet have the technology to make perfect reproductions of them. Once we have that technology we will cease to give any special priority to the "original." Gregory Currie, in "Art Works as Action Types," also denies that any works of art are physical objects. He agrees with Strawson that they are types, but of a rather special kind, namely, "action types." The action in question is that of discovering a certain structure – of sounds, words, colors, etc. – through a certain "heuristic path." The structure itself is not the work but the work is a combination of the structure and the particular means by which the artist came upon it.

Margolis also seeks a unified account of all works of art but, in contrast to Strawson and Currie, insists that all works are particulars; none is an abstract universal. All works are "tokens-of-a-type," they are "culturally emergent entities," "embodied" in physical objects although never identical to those objects. He compares works of art with persons at least to the extent that persons too are embodied in physical bodies but are not identical to their bodies. Michelangelo's *Pietà* is embodied in a block of marble but is not identical with that block, because the marble, *qua* marble, and the work do not share all the same properties.

In many respects musical works pose the greatest difficulty for ontology. It is far from straightforward how to give a precise account of what kind of entity a work of music is. There seem good reasons not to identify such works with relatively tractable entities like written scores, actual performances, sound waves, or even psychological states in the minds of composers or listeners. The thought that they must be *abstract* entities of a certain kind seems compelling. Jerrold Levinson, in his much discussed paper "What a Musical Work Is," brings the full weight of analytic philosophy to bear on the issue, arguing that a musical work cannot be merely a "sound-structure type" *tout court* for then no music would be *created* (pure abstract structures are timeless entities), and there would be no essential link between a work and the person who composed it or the historical context of composition. Instead, he suggests that musical works are sound-structure types of a highly complex kind, not timeless, and tied to the conditions of their origin. Currie raises some problems for Levinson's account, as does Peter Kivy in "Platonism in Music: A Kind of Defense." Kivy defends a more pure form of "Platonism" about musical works, accepting them as timeless universals, and arguing that from a musicological point of view there is no need to insist, with Levinson, that music is strictly created, rather than discovered. Kivy incidentally also criticizes Margolis for supposing that all artworks are particular.

These clusters of papers on the ontology of art are to some extent more technical than others in this anthology. The use of logical methods and logical terminology is more evident here than elsewhere. This perhaps should not be surprising given the already highly specialist nature of the enquiry itself. However, an appealing feature of all the discussions – most notably Levinson's – is that for all their technical sophistication points are nearly always illustrated by specific examples. Currie uses another device of the analytic philosopher, the thought-experiment. He asks us, for example, to suppose that a person on Twin Earth, otherwise identical to Beethoven, composed a work with an identical sound structure to one of Beethoven's. Would it be the same work? Our intuitions might not be clear but how we respond to such thought-experiments shows us something about the clarity – or unclarity – of the concepts we have.

Further reading

Danto, Arthur (1981). *The Transfiguration of the Commonplace* (Cambridge, MA: Harvard University Press).

Currie, Gregory (1989). *An Ontology of Art* (London: Macmillan).

Goodman, Nelson (1981). *Languages of Art*, 2nd edn. (Indianapolis: Hackett).

Lamarque, Peter (2002). "Work and Object," *Proceedings of the Aristotelian Society*, CII, pp. 141–62.

Margolis, Joseph (1980). *Art and Philosophy: Conceptual Issues in Philosophy* (Atlantic Highlands, NJ: Humanities Press).

Margolis, Joseph (1998). "Farewell to Danto and Goodman," *British Journal of Aesthetics*, 38, pp. 353–74.

Wollheim, Richard (1980). *Art and Its Objects*, 2nd edn. (Cambridge: Cambridge University Press).

Wolterstorff, Nicholas (1980). *Works and Worlds of Art* (Oxford: Clarendon Press).

8

The Ontological Peculiarity of Works of Art

Joseph Margolis

In the context of discussing the nature of artistic creativity, Jack Glickman offers the intriguing comment, "Particulars are made, types created."[1] The remark is a strategic one, but it is either false or misleading; and its recovery illuminates in a most economical way some of the complexities of the creative process and of the ontology of art. Glickman offers as an instance of the distinction he has in mind, the following: "If the chef created a new soup, he created a new kind of soup, a new recipe; he may not have made the soup [that is, some particular pot of soup]."[2] If, by "kind," Glickman means to signify a universal of some sort, then, since universals are not created (or destroyed), it could not be the case that the chef "created" a new soup, a new kind of soup.[3] It must be the case that the chef, in making a particular (new) soup, created (to use Glickman's idom) a kind of soup; otherwise, of course, that the chef created a new (kind of) soup may be evidenced by his having formulated a relevant recipe (which locution, in its own turn, shows the same ambiguity between type and token).

What is important, here, may not meet the eye at once. But if he can be said to create (to invent) a (new kind of) soup and if universals cannot be created or destroyed, then, in creating a kind of soup, a chef must be creating something other than a universal. The odd thing is that a kind of soup thus created is thought to be individuated among

Joseph Margolis, "The Ontological Peculiarity of Works of Art," *Journal of Aesthetics and Art Criticism*, 36 (1977). pp. 45–50. Reprinted by permission of Blackwell Publishing Ltd.

related creations; hence, it appears to be a particular of some sort. But it also seems to be an abstract entity if it is a particular at all. Hence, although it may be possible to admit abstract particulars in principle,[4] it is difficult to concede that what the chef created is an abstract particular *if* one may be said to have *tasted* what the chef created. The analogy with art is plain. If Picasso created a new kind of painting, in painting *Les Demoiselles d'Avignon*, it would appear that he could not have done so *by using oils*.

There is only one solution *if* we mean to speak in this way. It must be possible to instantiate particulars (of a certain kind or of certain kinds) as well as to instantiate universals or properties. I suggest that the term "type" – in all contexts in which the type/token ambiguity arises – signifies abstract particulars of a kind that can be instantiated. Let me offer a specimen instance. Printings properly pulled from Dürer's etching plate for *Melancholia I* are instances of *that* etching; but bona fide instances of *Melancholia I* need not have all their relevant properties in common, since later printings and printings that follow a touching up of the plate or printings that are themselves touched up may be genuine instances of *Melancholia I* and still differ markedly from one another – at least to the sensitive eye. Nothing, however, can instantiate a property without actually instantiating that property.[5] So to think of types as particulars (of a distinctive kind) accommodates the fact that we individuate works of art in unusual ways – performances of the same music, printings of the same etching, copies of the same novel – and that works of art may be created and destroyed. If, further, we grant that, in creating a new soup, a chef stirred the ingredients in his pot and that, in creating a new kind of painting, in painting *Les Demoiselles*, Picasso applied paint to canvas, we see that it is at least normally the case that one does not create a new kind of soup or a new kind of painting without (in Glickman's words) making a particular soup or a particular painting.

A great many questions intrude at this point. But we may bring this much at least to bear on an ingenious thesis of Glickman's. Glickman wishes to say that, though driftwood may be construed as a creation of "beach art," it remains true that driftwood was *made* by no one, is in fact a natural object, and hence that "the condition of artifactuality" so often claimed to be a necessary condition of being a work of art, is simply "superfluous."[6] "I see no conclusive conceptual block," says Glickman, "to allowing that the artwork [may] be a natural object."[7] Correspondingly, Duchamp's "ready-mades" are created out of artifacts, but the artist who created them did not actually make them. Glickman's thesis depends on the tenability of his distinction between making and creating; and as we have just seen, one does not, in the normal case at least, create a new kind of art (type) without making a particular work of that kind (that is, an instance of that particular, the type, not merely an instance of that kind, the universal). In other words, when an artist *creates* (allowing Glickman's terms) "beach art," a new kind of art, the artist *makes* a particular instance (or token) of a particular type – much as with wood sculpture, *this unique token of this driftwood composition*. He cannot create the universals that are newly instantiated since universals cannot be created. He can create a new type-particular, a particular of the kind "beach art", but he can do so only by making a token-particular of that type. What this shows is that we were unnecessarily tentative about the relation between types and tokens. We may credit an artist with having created a new type of art; but there are no types of art that are not instantiated by some token-instances or for which we lack a notation by reference to which (as in the performing arts) admissible token-instances of the particular type-work may be generated.

The reason for this strengthened conclusion has already been given. When an artist creates his work using the materials of his craft, the work he produces must have some perceptible physical properties at least; but it could not have such properties if the work were merely an abstract particu-

lar (or, of course, a universal). Hence, wherever an artist produces his work directly, even a new kind of work, he cannot be producing an abstract particular. Alternatively put, to credit an artist with having created a new *type* of art – a particular art-type – we must (normally) be thus crediting him in virtue of the particular (token) work he has made. In wood sculpture, the particular piece an artist makes is normally the unique instance of his work; in bronzes, it is more usually true that, as in Rodin's peculiarly industrious way, there are several or numerous tokens of the very same (type) sculpture. But though we may credit the artist with having created the type, the type does not exist except instantiated in its proper tokens. We may, by a kind of courtesy, say that an artist who has produced the cast for a set of bronzes has created an artwork-type; but the fact is: (i) he has *made* a particular cast, and (ii) the cast he's made is not the work *created*. Similar considerations apply to an artist's preparing a musical notation for the sonata he has created: (i) the artist makes a token instance of a type notation; and (ii) all admissible instances of his sonata are so identified by reference to the notation. The result is that, insofar as he creates a type, an artist must make a token. A chef's assistant may actually make the first pot of soup – of the soup the chef has created – but the actual soup exists only when the pot is made. Credit to the chef in virtue of his recipe is partly an assurance that his authorship is to be acknowledged in each and every pot of soup that is properly an instance of his creation, whether he makes it or not; and it is partly a device for individuating proper token instances of particular type objects. But only the token instances *of* a type actually exist and aesthetic interest in the type is given point only in virtue of one's aesthetic interest in actual or possible tokens – as in actual or contemplated performances of a particular sonata.

But if these distinctions be granted, then, normally, an artist makes a token of the type he has created. He could not create the type unless he made a proper token or, by the courtesy intended in notations and the like, he provided a schema *for* making proper tokens of a particular type. Hence, what is normally made, in the relevant sense, is a token of a type. It must be the case, then, that when Duchamp created his *Bottlerack*, although he did not make a bottlerack – that is, although he did not manufacture a bottlerack, although he did not first bring it about that an object instantiate being a bottlerack – nevertheless, *he did make a token of the Bottlerack*. Similarly, although driftwood is not a manufactured thing, when an artist creates (if an artist can create) a piece of "beach art," *he makes a token of that piece of "beach art."* He need not have made the driftwood. But that shows (i) that artifactuality is not superfluous, though it is indeed puzzling (when displaying otherwise untouched driftwood in accord with the developed sensibilities of a society can count as the creation of an artwork); and (ii) it is not the case (contrary to Glickman's claims) that a natural object can *be* a work of art or that a work can be created though *nothing* be made.

We may summarize the ontological peculiarities of the type/token distinction in the following way: (i) types and tokens are individuated as particulars; (ii) types and tokens are not separable and cannot exist separately from one another; (iii) types are instantiated by tokens and "token" is an ellipsis for "token-of-a-type"; (iv) types and tokens may be generated and destroyed in the sense that actual tokens of a novel type may be generated, the actual tokens of a given type may be destroyed, and whatever contingencies may be necessary to the generation of actual tokens may be destroyed or disabled; (v) types are actual abstract particulars in the sense only that a set of actual entities may be individuated as tokens of a particular type; (vi) it is incoherent to speak of comparing the properties of actual token- and type-particulars as opposed to comparing the properties of actual particular tokens-of-type; (vii) reference to types as particulars serves exclusively to facilitate reference to actual and possible tokens-of-a-type. These distinctions are sufficient to mark the type/token concept as different from the kind/instance concept and the set/member concept.

Here, a second ontological oddity must be conceded. The driftwood that is made by no one is not the (unique) token that is made of the "beach art" creation; and the artifact, the bottlerack, that Duchamp did not make is not identical with the (probably but not necessarily unique) token that Duchamp did make of the creation called *Bottlerack*. What Duchamp made was a token of *Bottlerack*; and what the manufacturer of bottleracks made was a particular bottlerack that served as the material out of which Duchamp created *Bottlerack* by making a (probably unique) instance of *Bottlerack*. For, consider that Duchamp made something when he created *Bottlerack* but he did not make a bottlerack; also, that no one made the

driftwood though someone (on the thesis) made a particular composition of art using the driftwood. If the bottlerack were said to be identical with Duchamp's *Bottlerack* (the token or the type), we should be contradicting ourselves; the same would be true of the driftwood case. Hence, in spite of appearances, there must be an ontological difference between tokens of artwork-types and such physical objects as bottleracks and driftwood that can serve as the materials out of which they are made.

My own suggestion is that (token) works of art are *embodied* in physical objects, not identical with them. I should argue, though this is not the place for it, that persons, similarly, are embodied in physical bodies but not identical with them.[8] The idea is that not only can one particular instantiate another particular in a certain way (tokens of types) but one particular can embody or be embodied in another particular with which it is (necessarily) not identical. The important point is that identity cannot work in the anomalous cases here considered (nor in the usual cases of art) and that what would otherwise be related by way of identity are, obviously, particulars. Furthermore, the embodiment relationship does not invite dualism though it does require a distinction among kinds of things and among the kinds of properties of things of such kinds. For example, a particular printing of Dürer's *Melancholia I* has the property of being a particular token of *Melancholia I* (the artwork type), but the physical paper and physical print do not, on any familiar view, have the property of being a token of a type. Only objects having such intentional properties as that of "being created" or, as with words, having meaning or the like can have the property of being a token of a type.[9]

What is meant in saying that one particular is embodied in another is: (i) that the two particulars are not identical; (ii) that the existence of the embodied particular presupposes the existence of the embodying particular; (iii) that the embodied particular possesses some of the properties of the embodying particular; (iv) that the embodied particular possesses properties that the embodying particular does not possess; (v) that the embodied particular possesses properties of a kind that the embodying particular cannot possess; (vi) that the individuation of the embodied particular presupposes the individuation of the embodying particular. The "is" of embodiment, then, like the "is" of identity and the "is" of composition[10] is a logically distinctive use. On a theory, for instance a theory about the nature of a work of art, a particular physical object will be taken to embody a particular object of another kind in such a way that a certain systematic relationship will hold between them. Thus, for instance, a sculptor will be said to make a particular sculpture by cutting a block of marble: Michelangelo's *Pietà* will exhibit certain of the physical properties of the marble and certain representational and purposive properties as well; it will also have the property of being a unique token of the creation *Pietà*. The reason for theorizing thus is, quite simply, that works of art are the products of culturally informed labor and that physical objects are not. So seen, they must possess properties that physical objects, *qua* physical objects, do not and cannot possess. Hence, an identity thesis leads to palpable contradictions. Furthermore, the conception of embodiment promises to facilitate a non-reductive account of the relationship between physical nature and human culture, without dualistic assumptions. What this suggests is that the so-called mind/body problem is essentially a special form of a more general culture/nature problem. But that is another story.

A work of art, then, is a particular. It cannot be a universal because it is created and can be destroyed; also, because it possesses physical and perceptual properties. But it is a peculiar sort of particular, unlike physical bodies, because (i) it can instantiate another particular; and (ii) it can be embodied in another particular. The suggestion here is that all and only culturally emergent or culturally produced entities exhibit these traits. So the ontological characteristics assigned are no more than the most generic characteristics of art: its distinctive nature remains unanalyzed. Nevertheless, we can discern an important difference between these two properties, as far as art is concerned. For, the first property, that of being able to instantiate another particular, has only to do with individuating works of art and whatever may, contingently, depend upon that; while the second property has to do with the ontologically dependent nature of actual works of art. This is the reason we may speak of type artworks as particulars. They are heuristically introduced for purposes of individuation, though they cannot exist except in the sense in which particular tokens of particular type artworks exist. So we can never properly *compare* the properties of a token work and a type work.[11] What we may compare are alternative tokens of the same type – different printings of the same etching or different performances of the same sonata. In

short, every work of art is a token-of-a-type; there are no tokens or types *tout court*. Again, this is not to say that there are no types or that an artist cannot create a new kind of painting. It is only to say that so speaking is an ellipsis for saying that a certain set of particulars are tokens of a type and that the artist is credited with so working with the properties of things, instantiated by the members of that set, that they are construed as tokens of a particular type.

So the dependencies of the two ontological traits mentioned are quite different. There are no types that are separable from tokens because there are no tokens except tokens-of-a-type. The very process for individuating tokens entails individuating types, that is, entails individuating different sets of particulars as the alternative tokens of this or that type. There is nothing left over to discuss. What may mislead is this: the concept of different tokens of the same type is intended, in the arts, to accommodate the fact that the aesthetically often decisive differences among tokens of the same type (alternative performances of a sonata, for instance) need not matter as far as the individuation of the (type) work is concerned.[12] But particular works of art cannot exist except as embodied in physical objects. This is simply another way of saying that works of art are culturally emergent entities; that is, that works of art exhibit properties that physical objects cannot exhibit, but do so in a way that does not depend on the presence of any substance other than what may be ascribed to purely physical objects. Broadly speaking, those properties are what may be characterized as functional or intentional properties and include design, expressiveness, symbolism, representation, meaning, style, and the like. Without prejudice to the nature of either art or persons, this way of viewing art suggests a very convenient linkup with the functional theory of mental traits.[13] Be that as it may, a reasonable theory of art could hold that when physical materials are worked in accord with a certain artistic craft then there emerges, culturally, an object embodied in the former that possesses a certain orderly array of functional properties of the kind just mentioned. Any object so produced may be treated as an artifact. Hence, works of art exist as fully as physical objects but the condition on which they do so depends on the independent existence of some physical object itself. Works of art, then, are culturally emergent entities, tokens-of-a-type that exist embodied in physical objects.

Notes

1 Jack Glickman, "Creativity in the Arts," in Lars Aagaard-Mogensen (ed.), *Culture and Art* (Nyborg and Atlantic Highlands, N.J., 1976), p. 140.

2 Loc. cit.

3 Difficulties of this sort undermine the thesis of Nicholas Wolterstorff's, namely, that works of art are in fact kinds. Cf. Nicholas Wolterstorff, "Toward an Ontology of Art Works," *Nous* IX (1975), 115–42. Also, Joseph Margolis, *Art and Philosophy* (Atlantic Highlands, N.J., 1977), Ch. 5.

4 Cf. Nelson Goodman, *The Structure of Appearance*, 2nd edn. (Indianapolis, 1966), on abstract individuals.

5 The subtleties of the type/token distinction are discussed at length in Margolis, loc. cit.

6 Op. cit., p. 144.

7 Ibid., p. 143.

8 A fuller account of the concept of embodiment with respect to art is given in *Art and Philosophy*, Ch. 1. I have tried to apply the notion to all cultural entities – that is, persons, works of art, artifacts, words and sentences, machines, institutionalized actions, and the like – in *Persons and Minds* (Dordrecht, 1978). Cf. also, "On the Ontology of Persons," *New Scholasticism*, X (1976), 73–84.

9 This is very close in spirit to Peirce's original distinction between types and tokens. Cf. *Collected Papers of Charles Sanders Peirce*, ed. Charles Hartshorne and Paul Weiss (Cambridge, 1939), IV, par. 537.

10 Cf. David Wiggins, *Identity and Spatio-Temporal Continuity* (Oxford, 1967).

11 This is one of the signal weaknesses of Wolterstorff's account, loc. cit. as well as of Richard Wollheim's account; cf. *Art and Its Objects* (New York, 1968).

12 This counts against Nelson Goodman's strictures on the individuation of artworks. Cf. *Languages of Art* (Indianapolis, 1968), and Joseph Margolis, "Numerical Identity and Reference in the Arts," *British Journal of Aesthetics*, X (1970), 138–46.

13 Cf. for instance Hilary Putnam, "Minds and Machines," in Sidney Hook (ed.) *Dimensions of Mind* (Englewood Cliffs, N.J., 1960); and Jerry Fodor, *Psychological Explanation* (New York, 1968).

9

What a Musical Work Is

Jerrold Levinson

What *exactly* did Beethoven compose? That is the question I will begin with. Well, for one, Beethoven composed a quintet for piano and winds (flute, oboe, clarinet, horn) in E-flat, Opus 16, in 1797. But what sort of thing is it, this quintet which was the outcome of Beethoven's creative activity? What does it consist in or of? Shall we say that Beethoven composed actual *sounds*? No, for sounds die out, but the quintet has endured. Did Beethoven compose a *score*? No, since many are familiar with Beethoven's composition who have had no contact with its score.[1]

Philosophers have long been puzzled about the identity or nature of the art object in nonphysical arts, e.g., music and literature. In these arts – unlike painting and sculpture – there is no particular physical "thing" that one can plausibly take to be the artwork itself. This puzzlement has sometimes led philosophers (e.g., Croce) to maintain that musical and literary works are purely mental – that they are in fact private intuitive experiences in the minds of composers and poets. But this does not seem likely, since experiences can be neither played nor read nor heard. More generally, the Crocean view puts the objectivity of musical and literary works in dire peril – they become inaccessible and unsharable. Fortunately, however, there is a way of accepting the nonphysicality of such works without undermining their objectivity.

Those familiar with recent reflection on the ontological question for works of art will know of

the widespread consensus that a musical work is in fact a variety of abstract object – to wit, a structural type or kind.[2] Instances of this type are to be found in the individual performances of the work. The type can be heard through its instances, and yet exists independently of its instances. I believe this to be basically correct. A piece of music is *some* sort of structural type, and as such is both nonphysical and publicly available. But *what* sort of type is it? I aim in this paper to say as precisely as I can what structural type it is that a musical work should be identified with.

The most natural and common proposal on this question is that a musical work is a *sound* structure – a structure, sequence, or pattern of sounds, pure and simple.[3] My first objective will be to show that this proposal is deeply unsatisfactory, that a musical work is more than just a sound structure *per se*. I will do this by developing three different objections to the sound-structure view. In the course of developing these objections, three requirements or desiderata for a more adequate view will emerge. The rightness – or at least plausibility – of those requirements will, I think, be apparent at that point. My second objective will then be to suggest a structural type that does satisfy the requirements, and thus can be identified with a musical work.[4]

At the outset, however, I should make clear that I am confining my inquiry to that paradigm of a musical work, the fully notated "classical" composition of Western culture, for example, Beethoven's Quintet for piano and winds in E-flat, Opus 16. So when I speak of a "musical work" in this paper it should be understood that I am speaking only of

Jerrold Levinson, "What a Musical Work Is," *Journal of Philosophy*, 77:1 (January 1980), pp. 5–28. Reprinted by permission of The Journal of Philosophy.

these paradigm musical works, and thus that all claims herein regarding musical works are to be construed with this implicit restriction.

I

The first objection to the view that musical works are sound structures is this. If musical works were sound structures, then musical works could not, properly speaking, be created by their composers. For sound structures are types of a pure sort which exist at all times. This is apparent from the fact that they – and the individual component sound types[5] that they comprise – can always have had instances.[6] A sound event conforming to the sound structure of Beethoven's Quintet, Opus 16 logically could have occurred in the Paleozoic era.[7] Less contentiously, perhaps, such an event surely could have taken place in 1760 – ten years before Beethoven was born. But if that sound structure was capable of being *instantiated* then, it clearly must have *existed* at that time. Beethoven's compositional activity was not necessary in order for a certain sound-structure type to exist. It was not necessary to the possibility of certain sound events occurring which would be instances of that structure. Sound structures *per se* are not created by being scored – they exist before any compositional activity. Sound structures predate their first instantiation or conception because they are possible of exemplification *before* that point.[8] So, if composers truly create their works – i.e., bring them into existence – then musical works cannot be sound structures.

We can also defend the pre-existence of pure sound structures (i.e., existence prior to any instantiation or conception) in a somewhat different manner. We need only remind ourselves that purely sound structures are in effect mathematical objects – they are *sequences* of sets of sonic elements. (Sonic elements are such as pitches, timbres, durations, etc.). Now if the pre-existence of simple sonic element types be granted – and I think it must be – it follows automatically that all sets and all sequences of sets of these elements also pre-exist. Therefore pure sound structures are pre-existent. But if pure sound structures pre-exist, then it is not open for them to be objects of creational activity. So again, if composers are truly creators, their works cannot be pure sound structures.[9]

But why should we insist that composers truly create their compositions? Why is this a reasonable requirement? This question needs to be answered. A defense of the desideratum of true creation follows.

The main reason for holding to it is that it is one of the most firmly entrenched of our beliefs concerning art. There is probably no idea more central to thought about art than that it is an activity in which participants create things – these things being artworks. The whole tradition of art assumes art is creative in the strict sense, that it is a godlike activity in which the artist brings into being what did not exist beforehand – much as a demiurge forms a world out of inchoate matter. The notion that artists truly *add* to the world, in company with cake-bakers, house-builders, law-makers, and theory-constructers, is surely a deep-rooted idea that merits preservation if at all possible. The suggestion that some artists, composers in particular, instead merely *discover* or *select* for attention entities they have no hand in creating is so contrary to this basic intuition regarding artists and their works that we have a strong prima facie reason to reject it if we can. If it is possible to align musical works with indisputably creatable artworks such as paintings and sculptures, then it seems we should do so.

A second, closely related reason to preserve true creation vis-à-vis musical works is that some of the status, significance, and value we attach to musical composition derives from our belief in this. If we conceive of Beethoven's Fifth Symphony as existing sempiternally, before Beethoven's compositional act, a small part of the glory that surrounds Beethoven's composition of the piece seems to be removed. There is a special glow that envelops composers, as well as other artists, because we think of them as true creators. We marvel at a great piece of music *in part* because we marvel that, had its composer not engaged in a certain activity, the piece would (almost surely) not now exist; but it does exist, and we are grateful to the composer for precisely that. Ecclesiastes was wrong – there *are* ever some things new under the sun, musical compositions being among the most splendid of them – and splendid, at least in part, in virtue of this absolute newness.

Shall we then accept the creatability requirement as suggested? Before we do so a last qualm should be addressed. It is open for someone to admit the importance of musical composition being characterized by true creation and yet waive the creatability of works themselves. Such a person will point to entities associated with the compositional process which composers unequivocally bring into existence – e.g., thoughts, scores, performances – and claim that true creation need be extended no further. Now it is certainly true that these entities are strictly created, and we may also accord composers some recognition of their creativity in regard to these things. But the fact of the matter remains that *works* are the main items, the center and aim of the whole enterprise, and that since musical works are not identical with scores, performances, or thoughts,[10] if those are the only things actually created, then much is lost. "Composers are true creators" acquires a hollow ring. Creation in music shrinks to an outer veneer with no inner core.

I propose then that a most adequate account of the musical work should satisfy the following requirement, that of *creatability*[11]:

(Cre) Musical works must be such that they do *not* exist prior to the composer's compositional activity, but are *brought into existence by* that activity.

II

The second objection to the view that musical works are sound structures is this. (1) If musical works were just sound structures, then, if two distinct composers determine the same sound structure, they necessarily compose the same musical work. (2) But distinct composers determining the same sound structure in fact inevitably produce different musical works.[12] Therefore, musical works cannot be sound structures *simpliciter*. The rest of this section is devoted to supporting and elucidating the second premise of this argument.

Composers who produce identical scores in the same notational system with the same conventions of interpretation will determine the same sound structure. But the musical works they thereby compose will generally not be the same. The reason for this is that certain attributes of musical works are dependent on more than the sound structures contained. In particular, the aesthetic and artistic attributes of a piece of music are partly a function of, and must be gauged with reference to, the total musico-historical context in which the composer is situated while composing his piece. Since the musico-historical contexts of composing individuals are invariably different, then even if their

works are identical in sound structure, they will differ widely in aesthetic and artistic attributes. But then, by Leibniz's law, the musical works themselves must be non-identical; if W_1 has any attribute that W_2 lacks, or *vice versa*, then $W_1 \neq W_2$.

I will not attempt to give a strict definition of musico-historical context, but will confine myself to pointing out a large part of what is involved in it. The total musico-historical context of a composer P at a time t can be said to include at least the following: (a) the whole of cultural, social, and political history prior to t,[13] (b) the whole of musical development up to t, (c) musical styles prevalent at t, (d) dominant musical influences at t, (e) musical activities of P's contemporaries at t, (f) P's apparent style at t, (g) P's musical repertoire[14] at t, (h) P's oeuvre at t, (i) musical influences operating on P at t. These factors contributing to the total musico-historical context might be conveniently divided into two groups, a–d and e–i. The former, which we could call the *general* musico-historical context, consists of factors relevant to anyone's composing at t; the latter, which we could call the *individual* musico-historical context, consists of factors relevant specifically to P's composing at t. In any event, all these factors operate to differentiate aesthetically or artistically musical works identical in sound structure, thus making it impossible to identify those works with their sound structures. I now provide several illustrations of this.[15]

(1) A work identical in sound structure with Schoenberg's *Pierrot Lunaire* (1912), but composed by Richard Strauss in 1897 would be aesthetically different from Schoenberg's work. Call it "Pierrot Lunaire*". As a Straussian work, *Pierrot Lunaire** would follow hard upon Brahms's *German Requiem*, would be contemporaneous with Debussy's *Nocturnes*, and would be taken as the next step in Strauss's development after *Also Sprach Zarathustra*. As such it would be more *bizarre*, more *upsetting*, more *anguished*, more *eerie* even than Schoenberg's work, since perceived against a musical tradition, a field of current styles, and an *oeuvre* with respect to which the musical characteristics of the sound structure involved in *Pierrot Lunaire* appear doubly extreme.[16]

(2) Mendelssohn's *Midsummer's Night Dream Overture* (1826) is admitted by all to be a highly *original* piece of music. Music of such elfin delicacy and feel for tone color had never before been written. But a score written in 1900 detailing the

very same sound structure as is found in Mendelssohn's piece would clearly result in a work that was surpassingly *unoriginal*.

(3) Brahms's Piano Sonata Opus 2 (1852), an early work, is strongly *Liszt-influenced*, as any perceptive listener can discern. However, a work identical with it in sound structure, but written by Beethoven, could hardly have had the property of being Liszt-influenced. And it would have had a visionary quality that Brahms's piece does not have.

(4) The symphonies of Johann Stamitz (1717–1757) are generally regarded as seminal works in the development of orchestral music. They employ many attention-getting devices novel for their time, one of which is known as the "Mannheim rocket" – essentially a loud ascending scale figure for unison strings. A symphony of Stamitz containing Mannheim rockets and the like is an *exciting* piece of music. But a piece written today which was identical in sound structure with one of Stamitz's symphonies, Mannheim rockets and all, would not be so much exciting as it would be exceedingly *funny*. Stamitz's symphony is to be heard in the context of Stamitz's earlier works, the persistence of late Baroque style, the contemporary activities of the young Mozart, and the Napoleonic wars. "Modern Stamitz"'s symphony would be heard in the context of "Modern Stamitz"'s earlier works (which are probably dodecaphonic), the existence of aleatory and electronic music, the musical enterprises both of Pierre Boulez and of Elton John, and the threat of nuclear annihilation.

(5) One of the passages in Bartok's *Concerto for Orchestra* (1943) satirizes Shostakovitch's *Seventh Symphony* ("Leningrad") of 1941, whose bombast was apparently not to Bartok's liking. A theme from that symphony is quoted and commented on musically in an unmistakable manner. But notice that if Bartok had written the very same score in *1939*, the work he would then have composed could not have had the same property of satirizing Shostakovitch's *Seventh Symphony*. Nor would the work that would have resulted from *Shostakovitch's* penning that score in 1943.

These examples should serve to convince the reader that there is always some aesthetic or artistic difference between structurally identical compositions in the offing in virtue of differing musico-historical contexts. Even small differences in musico-historical context – e.g., an extra work in P's *oeuvre*, a slight change in style dominant in P's milieu, some musical influence deleted from P's development as a composer – seem certain to induce some change in kind or degree in some aesthetic or artistic quality, however difficult it might be in such cases to pinpoint this change verbally.

For example, suppose there had been a composer (call him "Toenburg") in 1912 identical with Schoenberg in all musico-historical respects – e.g., birthdate, country, style, musical development, artistic intentions, etc., except that Toenburg had never written anything like *Verklarte Nacht* though he had in his *oeuvre* works structurally identical with everything else Schoenberg wrote before 1912. Now suppose simultaneously with Schoenberg he sketches the sound structure of *Pierrot Lunaire*. Toenburg has not produced the same musical work as Schoenberg, I maintain, if only because his work has a slightly different aesthetic/artistic content owing to the absence of a *Verklarte-Nacht*-ish piece in Toenburg's *oeuvre*. Schoenberg's *Pierrot Lunaire* is properly heard with reference to Schoenberg's *oeuvre* in 1912, and Toenberg's *Pierrot Lunaire* with reference to Toenburg's *oeuvre* in 1912. One thus hears something in Schoenberg's piece by virtue of resonance with *Verklarte Nacht* that is not present in Toenberg's piece – perhaps a stronger reminiscence of Expressionist sighs?

Before formulating a second requirement of adequacy, as suggested by the fatal problem that contextual differentiation poses for the equation of musical works with pure sound structures, I must confront an objection that may be lurking in the wings. The objection in short is that the aesthetic and artistic differences I have been discussing are not really an obstacle to equating works and sound structures, because these supposed differences between *works* due to compositional context really just boil down to facts about their *composers*, and are not attributes of works at all. The objection is understandable, but I find it rather unconvincing for several reasons which I will briefly detail.

(1) Artistic and aesthetic attributions made of musical works are as direct and undisguised as attributions typically made of composers. It seems to be as straightforwardly true that the Eroica symphony is noble, bold, original, revolutionary, influenced by Haydn, and reflective of Beethoven's thoughts about Napoleon, as it is that Beethoven had certain personal qualities, was a genius, changed the course of Western music, studied with Haydn, and at one point idolized Napoleon.

(2) Whereas we may admit some plausibility to reducing artistic attributions (e.g. "original", "influenced by Haydn") to attributes of persons, there is no plausibility in so reducing aesthetic attributions; it is absurd to maintain that "*W* is scintillating," for example, is just a way of saying "*W*'s composer is scintillating." (3) Finally, in the case of artistic attributions, not only do they appear as entrenched and legitimate as parallel attributions to composers, but, if anything, they often seem to be primary. Consider originality, for example, and imagine a composer and *oeuvre* that possess it. Surely the composer is original because *his works* are original; his works are not original because *he is*.

I thus propose a second requirement – that of *fine individuation* – to which any acceptable theory of the musical work should conform:

(Ind)   Musical works must be such that composers composing in different musico-historical contexts[17] who determine identical sound structures invariably compose distinct musical works.

III

The third objection to the view that musical works are sound structures is this. If musical works were simply sound structures, then they would not essentially involve any particular means of performance. But the paradigm musical works that we are investigating in this paper, e.g., Beethoven's Quintet Opus 16, clearly *do* involve quite specific means of performance, i.e., particular instruments, in an essential way. The instrumentation of musical works is an integral part of those works. So musical works cannot be simply sound structures *per se*. Arguments in defense of the claim that performance means are an essential component of musical works now follow.

(1)   Composers do not describe pure sound patterns in qualitative terms, leaving their means of production undiscussed. Rather, what they directly specify are means of production, through which a pure sound pattern is indirectly indicated. The score of Beethoven's Quintet, Opus 16, is not a recipe for providing an instance of a sound pattern *per se*, in whatever way you might like. Rather, it instructs one to produce an instance of a certain sound pattern through carrying out certain operations on certain instruments. When Beethoven writes a middle C for the oboe, he has done more

than require an oboe-like sound at a certain pitch – he has called for such a sound as emanating from that quaint reed we call an "oboe." The idea that composers of the last 300 years were generally engaged in composing pure sound patterns, to which they were usually kind enough to append suggestions as to how they might be realized, is highly implausible. Composers are familiar with tone colors only insofar as they are familiar with instruments that possess them. We do not find composers creating pure combinations of tone color, and then later searching about for instruments that can realize or approximate these aural canvases; it would obviously be pointless or at least frustrating to do so. Composers often call for complex sounds that they have never heard before and can scarcely imagine – e.g., the sound of two trombones and three piccolos intoning middle C while four saxophones and five xylophones intone the C-sharp a half-step above; it is obvious here that what is primarily composed is not a pure untethered sound but an instrumental combination.[18]

(2)   Scores are generally taken to be definitive of musical works, at least in conjunction with the conventions of notational interpretation assumed to be operative at the time of composition. It is hard to miss the fact that scores of musical works call for specific instruments in no uncertain terms. When we read in Beethoven's score the demand "clarinet" (rather, "Klarinett") we may wonder whether a clarinet of 1970 vintage and construction will do as well as one of 1800, but we have still been given a fairly definite idea of what sort of instrument is required. There is nothing in scores themselves that suggests that instrumental specifications are to be regarded as optional – any more than specifications of pitch, rhythm, or dynamics. Nor does the surrounding musical practice of the time encourage such a way of regarding them.[19] If we are not to abandon the principle that properly understood scores have a central role in determining the identity of musical works, then we must insist that the Quintet, Op. 16, without a clarinet is not the same piece – even if all sound-structural characteristics (including timbre) are preserved. To feel free to disregard as prominent an aspect of scores as performing means is to leave it open for someone to disregard any aspect of a score he does not wish to conform to – e.g., tempo, accidentals, accents, articulation, harmony – and claim that one nevertheless has the same work.[20] The only way it seems one could justify regarding performing-

means specifications as just optional features of scores is to simply *assume* that musical works are nothing but sound structures *per se*.

Consider a sound event aurally indistinguishable from a typical performance of Beethoven's Quintet Opus 16, but issuing from a versatile synthesizer, or perhaps a piano plus a set of newly designed wind instruments, two hundred in number, each capable of just two or three notes. If performance means were not an integral aspect of a musical work, then there would be no question that this sound event constitutes a performance of Beethoven's Quintet Opus 16. But there is indeed such a question. It makes perfect sense to deny that it is such a performance on the grounds that the sounds heard did not derive from a piano and four standard woodwinds. We can count something as a performance of Beethoven's Quintet Opus 16 only if it involves the participation of the instruments for which the piece was written – or better – of the instruments that were written into the piece.

(3)   To regard performing means as essential to musical works is to maintain that the sound structure of a work cannot be divorced from the instruments and voices through which that structure is fixed, and regarded as the work itself. The strongest reason why it cannot be so divorced is that the aesthetic content of a musical work is determined not only by its sound structure, and not only by its musico-historical context, but also in part by the actual means of production chosen for making that structure audible. The character of a musical composition, e.g., Beethoven's Quintet Opus 16 for piano and winds, is partly a function of how its sound structure relates to the potentialities of a certain instrument or set of instruments designated to produce that structure for audition. To assess that character correctly one must take cognizance not only of the qualitative nature of sounds heard but also of their source of origin. Musical compositions, by and large, have reasonably definite characters; that is to say, we can and do ascribe to them many fairly specific aesthetic qualities. But if prescribed performing forces were not intrinsic to musical compositions, then those compositions would not have the reasonably definite characters we clearly believe them to have. The determinateness of a work's aesthetic qualities is in peril if performing means are viewed as inessential so long as exact sound structure is preserved.

Consider a musical work W with specified performing means M which has some fairly specific aesthetic quality ϕ. The sound structure of W as produced by different performing means N, however, will invariably strike us either as not ϕ at all, or else as ϕ to a greater or lesser degree than before. Therefore, if means of sound production are not regarded as an integral part of musical works, then W cannot be said determinately to have the attribute ϕ. So if we wish to preserve a wide range of determinate aesthetic attributions, we must recognize performing means to be an essential component of musical works. I now provide two illustrations of this point.[21]

(a)   Beethoven's Hammerklavier Sonata is a sublime, craggy, and heaven-storming piece of music. The closing passages (marked by ascending chordal trills) are surely among the most imposing and awesome in all music. However, if we understand the very sounds of the Hammerklavier Sonata to originate from a full-range synthesizer, as opposed to a mere 88-key piano of metal, wood, and felt, it no longer seems so sublime, so craggy, so awesome. The aesthetic qualities of the Hammerklavier Sonata depend in part on the strain that its sound structure imposes on the sonic capabilities of the piano; if we are not hearing its sound structure *as* produced by a piano then we are not sensing this strain, and thus our assessment of aesthetic content is altered. The closing passages of the Hammerklavier are awesome in part because we seem to hear the piano bursting at the seams and its keyboard on the verge of exhaustion. On a 10-octave electronic synthesizer those passages do not have quite that quality, and a hearing of them with knowledge of source is an aesthetically different experience. The lesson here applies, I believe, to all musical works (of the paradigm sort). Their aesthetic attributes always depend, if not so dramatically, in part on the performing forces understood to belong to them.

(b)   Consider a baroque concerto for two violins, such as Bach's Concerto in D minor, BWV 1043. In such pieces one often finds a phrase (A) assigned to one violin, which is immediately followed by the *very same* phrase (B) assigned to the other violin. Now when one hears such passages *as* issuing from *two* violins (even if in a given performance there are no discernible differences between A and B in timbre or phrasing), a sense of question-and-answer, of relaxation and unhurriedness is communicated. But if one were to construe such passages as issuing from a *single* violin, that quality would be absent, and in its place the passages would assume a more emphatic, insistent, and repetitive cast.

(4) The dependence of aesthetic attributes on assumed or understood performing forces should now be apparent. The dependence of artistic attributes is even more plain. (a) Consider Paganini's Caprice Opus 1, No. 17. This piece surely deserves and receives the attribution "virtuosic." But if we did not conceive of the Caprice No. 17 as essentially for the violin, as inherently a *violin piece* (and not just a *violin-sounding piece*), then it would not merit that attribution. For, as executed by a computer or by some novel string instrument using nonviolinistic technique, its sound structure might not be particularly difficult to get through. (b) Imagine a piece written for violin to be played in such a way that certain passages sound more like a flute than they do like a violin. Such a piece would surely be accounted *unusual*, and to some degree, *original* as well. Understood as a piece for violin and occasional flute, however, it might have nothing unusual or original about it at all. Retaining the sound structure while setting actual performance means adrift completely dissolves part of the piece's artistic import. (c) According to one respected critic, Beethoven in the Quintet Opus 16 was interested in solving problems of balance between piano and winds – a nominally incompatible array of instruments – and succeeded in his own individual way.[22] It is not hard to agree with this assessment; thus, "solves the problem of balance between piano and winds" is an attribution true of Beethoven's Quintet. It is difficult to see how this would be so if the Quintet is purely a sound structure, if piano and winds are not strictly part of the piece at all.[23]

I thus propose a third requirement for any account of the musical work: *inclusion of performance means*:

(Per)   Musical works must be such that specific means of performance or sound production are integral to them.

IV

If musical works are not sound structures *simpliciter*, then what are they? The type that is a musical work must be capable of being created, must be individuated by context of composition, and must be inclusive of means of performance. The third desideratum is most easily met, and will be addressed first.

I propose that a musical work be taken to involve not only a pure sound structure, but also a structure of performing means. If the sound structure of a piece is basically a sequence of sounds qualitatively defined, then the performing-means structure is a parallel sequence of performing means specified for realizing the sounds at each point. Thus a musical work consists of at least two structures. It is a compound or conjunction of a sound structure and a performing-means structure. This compound is itself just a more complex structure; call it an "S/PM" structure, for short.[24] Beethoven's Opus 16 Quintet is at base an S/PM structure; the means of producing the sounds belonging to it are no more dispensable to its identity as a composition than the nature and order of those sounds themselves. This satisfies requirement (Per).

To satisfy the first and second requirements of adequacy we arrived at, it is necessary to realize that a musical work is not a structure of the *pure* sort at all, and thus not even an S/PM structure *simpliciter*. An S/PM structure is no more creatable or context-individuated than a sound structure is. I propose that we recognize a musical work to be a more complicated entity, namely this:

(MW)   S/PM structure-as-indicated-by-X-at-t

where X is a particular person – the composer – and t is the time of composition. For the paradigmatic pieces we are concerned with, the composer typically indicates (fixes, determines, selects) an S/PM structure by creating a score. The *piece* he thereby composes is the S/PM structure-as-indicated by him on that occasion.

An S/PM structure-as-indicated-by-X-at-t, unlike an S/PM structure *simpliciter*, does not pre-exist the activity of composition and is thus capable of being created. When a composer θ composes a piece of music, he indicates an S/PM structure ψ, but he does not bring ψ into being. However, through the act of indicating ψ, he does bring into being something that did not previously exist – namely, ψ-as-indicated-by-θ-at-t_1. Before the compositional act at t_1, no relation obtains between θ and ψ. Composition establishes the relation of indication between θ and ψ. As a result of the compositional act, I suggest, the world contains a new entity, ψ-as-indicated-by-θ-at-t_1. Let me call such entities *indicated structures*. And let me represent indicated structures by expressions of form "S/PM*x*t." It is important to realize that indicated structures are entities distinct from the pure structures *per se* from which they are derived. Thus, in particular, $\psi*\theta*t_1$ is *not* just the structure ψ with the accidental property of having been indicated by θ at $t_1 - \psi*\theta*t_1$ and ψ are strictly non-identical, though of course related. $\psi*\theta*t_1$, unlike ψ, can be and is created through θ's composing. Thus requirement (Cre) is satisfied.

Indicated structures also serve to satisfy our second requirement (Ind). If musical works are indicated structures of the sort we have suggested, then two such works, $\psi*\theta*t_1$ and $\alpha*\phi*t_2$ are identical iff (i) $\psi = \alpha$, (ii) $\theta = \phi$, and (iii) $t_1 = t_2$. But if musical works are necessarily distinct if composed either by different people or at different times, then it certainly follows that works composed in different musico-historical contexts will be distinct, since any difference of musico-historical context from one work to another can be traced to a difference of composer or time or both. Put otherwise, musico-historical context (as explained in section II) is a function of time and person; given a time and person, musico-historical context is fixed. So requirement (Ind) is satisfied. That it is satisfied by our proposal with something to spare is a matter I will return to in section V. I now endeavor to increase the reader's grasp of what indicated structures are.

Indicated structures are a different class of type from pure structures. Types of the latter class we may call *implicit* types, and those of the former class *initiated* types. *Implicit* types include all purely abstract structures that are not inconsistent, e.g., geometrical figures, family relationships, strings of words, series of moves in chess, ways of placing five balls in three bins, etc. By calling them "implicit types" I mean to suggest that their existence is implicitly granted when a general framework of possibilities is given. For example, given that there is space, there are all the possible configurations in space; given there is the game of chess, there are all the possible combinations of allowed moves. Sound structures *simpliciter* are clearly implicit types. Given that there are sounds of various kinds, then all possible patterns and sequences of those sounds must be granted existence immediately as well. For a sound structure, in company with all pure structures, is always capable of instantiation before the point at which it is noticed, recognized, mentioned, or singled out.

And thus its existence must predate that point. The same goes for a performance-means structure *simpliciter*. Given performing means (i.e., instruments) of various kinds, then all possible combinations and sequences of such means exist as well. The compound of these two, a sound/performance-means structure, thus of course also counts as an implicit type.

The other class of types, *initiated* types, are so called because they begin to exist only when they are initiated by an intentional human act of some kind. All those of interest can, I think, be construed as arising from an operation, like indication, performed upon a pure structure. Typically, this indication is effected by producing an exemplar of the structure involved, or a blueprint of it. In so indicating (or determining) the structure, the exemplar or blueprint inaugurates the type which is the *indicated* structure, the structure-as-indicated-by-x-at-t. All indicated structures are, perforce, initiated types.

Initiated types include such types as the Ford Thunderbird, the Lincoln penny, the hedgehog. The Ford Thunderbird is not simply a pure structure of metal, glass, and plastic. The pure structure that is embodied in the Thunderbird has existed *at least* since the invention of plastic (1870); there could certainly have been instances of it in 1900. But the Ford Thunderbird was created in 1957; so there could not have been instances of the Thunderbird in 1900. The Ford Thunderbird is an *initiated* type; it is a metal/glass/plastic structure-as-indicated (or determined) by the Ford Motor Company on such and such a date. It begins to exist as a result of an act of human indication or determination. The instances of this type are more than just instances of a pure structure – they are instances of an indicated structure. The Lincoln penny is similarly not a pure structure, an abstract pattern *tout court*, but a structure-as-indicated, a pattern-as-denominated-by-the-U.S. Government. Objects conforming to the pattern *tout court* but existing in 100 A.D. in Imperial Rome would not be instances of the Lincoln penny. Even the hedgehog is probably best understood, not as a pure biological structure, but rather as a biological structure-as-determined-or-fixed by natural terrestrial evolution at a particular point in history. The creatures we call "hedgehogs" possess a certain structure and stand in certain causal relations to some particular creatures which came into existence at a given past date. The biological structure of the hedgehog might have been instantiated in the Mesozoic era, or on Uranus, but nothing existing at that time, or at that place, could be an instance of the hedgehog as we understand it. Musical works, as I have suggested, are indicated structures too, and thus types that do not already exist but must instead be initiated. The same is true of poems, plays, and novels – each of these is an entity more individual and temporally bound than the pure verbal structure embodied in it.

The distinction between indicated structure and pure structure can perhaps be made clearer by analogy with the distinction between sentence and statement long enshrined in the philosophy of language.[25] These distinctions are motivated in similar ways. Statements were recognized partly in response to the need for entities individuated in some respects more finely than sentences, in order to provide bearers for the varying truth values that turned up in connection with a given sentence on different occasions.[26] Just so, indicated structures are recognized in response to the need for entities more finely individuated than pure structures, in order to provide bearers for various incompatible sets of aesthetic, artistic, cultural, semantic, and genetic properties. We allow that a given sentence can make different statements when uttered in different circumstances. Similarly, we realize that a given sound/performance-means structure yields different indicated structures, or musical works, when indicated in different musico-historical contexts.[27]

V

I have proposed that musical works be identified with rather specific indicated structures, in which a particular person and time figure ineliminably. The proposal MW was made, recall, in order to satisfy the creatability and individuation requirements. However, as I noted at that point, MW satisfies the individuation requirement with logical room to spare. Perhaps both requirements can be satisfied without invoking types that are quite so particularized? The obvious alternative is that a musical work is this sort of type:

(MW′)   S/PM structure-as-indicated-in
         musico-historical-context-C

Such types would be both creatable and sufficiently individuated. A type of this sort, like an MW type, comes into existence through some *actual* indication of an S/PM structure by a person at a time – a person who at that certain time is situated in a particular context. But the type's identity is not inherently tied to that of any individual as such. Thus, two composers composing simultaneously but independently in the same musico-historical context who determine the same S/PM structure create *distinct* MW types, but the *same* MW′ type.

Given these two proposals, then, which satisfy all our desiderata, do we have reason to prefer one or the other? I will discuss one consideration in favor of MW′, and three considerations in favor of MW.

(1)   On the MW′ proposal, it is at least logically possible for a musical work to have been composed by a person other than the person who actually composed it. If A is the actual composer of a musical work, ψ-as-indicated-in-C_1, then all we need imagine is that someone other than A was the person to first indicate the S/PM structure ψ in musico-historical context C_1. On the MW proposal, however, it becomes *logically impossible* for a work to have been composed by other than its actual composer. Could someone else have composed Beethoven's Quintet Opus 16, according to MW? For example, could Hummel have done so? No, because if ψ is the S/PM structure of the Quintet Opus 16, then all that Hummel might have composed is ψ-as-indicated-by-Hummel-in-1797, and not ψ-as-indicated-by-Beethoven-in-1797.[28] It must be admitted to be somewhat counterintuitive for a theory to make the composer of a work essential to that work.

(2)   We can turn this consequence upside-down, however. One might cite as a virtue of the MW proposal that it gives a composer *logical insurance* that his works are his very own, that no one else has or ever could compose a work identical to any of his. If A's musical work is an MW type, then even a fellow composer situated in an identical musico-historical context determining the same S/PM structure composes a distinct musical work. It seems to me this is a desirable consequence, from the point of view of preserving the uniqueness of compositional activity. Why should a composer have to fear, however abstractly, that his work is not exclusively his, any more than a painter painting a painting or a sculptor sculpting a sculpture need be troubled about whether his work is at least numerically distinct from anyone else's? Why not adopt a construal of "musical work" (and of "poem,"

"novel," "dance," etc.) which, while maintaining musical works as abstract types, guarantees this individuation by artist for them as well? Considerations (1) and (2) thus appear to fairly well cancel each other out.

(3) A more decisive reason, however, for ensuring by proposal MW that composers A and B who determine the same S/PM structure in the same musico-historical context yet compose distinct works W_1 and W_2, is that, although W_1 and W_2 do not, it seems, differ structurally or aesthetically or artistically at the time of composition t, differences of an artistic sort are almost certain to develop after t. So, unless we wish to embrace the awkwardness of saying that two musical works can be identical when composed, but non-identical at some later point, we have a strong incentive to adopt MW. W_1 and W_2 will almost certainly diverge artistically because of the gross improbability that A and B will continue to be subject to the exact same influences to the same degree and that A's and B's *oeuvres* will continue to appear identical after the composition of W_1 and W_2. If A's and B's artistic careers do exhibit these differences after t, then W_1 and W_2 will acquire somewhat different artistic significance, since W_1 will eventually be seen properly against A's total development, and W_2 against B's total development. W_1 may turn out to be *a seminal work*, whereas W_2 turns out to be *a false start*. Or W_1 may turn out to be *much more influential* than W_2, owing to the fact that A comes to be much better known than B. In any case, there will be *some* divergence in artistic attributions, if not always so marked, unless A and B remain artistic duplicates of one another throughout their lives (and thereafter). Since circumstances subsequent to a work's composition are not comprised in musico-historical context of composition, proposal MW' leaves us open for the awkwardness mentioned above. MW forestalls this problem completely.[29]

(4) A last consideration inclining us to MW comprises certain intuitions concerning what would count as a performance of what. It seems that, in order for a performance to be a performance *of W*, not only must it fit and be intended to fit the S/PM structure of A's work W; there must also be some *connection*, more or less direct, between the sound event produced and A's creative activity. Whether this is primarily an intentional or causal connection is a difficult question,[30] but, unless it is present, I think we are loath to say that A's work has been performed. Consider two com-

posers, Sterngrab and Grotesteen, who compose quartets with identical S/PM structures; suppose even that they share the same musico-historical context. Now imagine that the Aloysious Ensemble, who are great friends of Sterngrab, give the ill-attended première of Sterngrab's Quartet Opus 21. Clearly, the Aloysious have performed Sterngrab's Quartet Opus 21 – but have they also performed Grotesteen's Quartet Opus 21? I think not. Why? For several reasons: they don't know Grotesteen; they weren't using Grotesteen's scores; they didn't believe themselves to be presenting Grotesteen's work – in short, there was no connection between their performance and Grotesteen the creator. Grotesteen's creating his Opus 21 Quartet had nothing whatever to do with the sound event produced by the Aloysious Ensemble on the afore-mentioned occasion. Now, if Sterngrab's Quartet has performances that Grotesteen's does not, and *vice versa*, then, again by Leibniz's law, Sterngrab's and Grotesteen's quartets cannot be identical. On proposal MW', Sterngrab and Grotesteen have composed the same musical work; on proposal MW, their works are distinct. That MW squares with this intuition regarding identification of performances is thus one more point in its favor.

I therefore rest with the account of musical works represented by MW. In the next section I offer some remarks on performances and transcriptions in light of this account.

VI

(1) On my view, the following must all be distinguished: (a) instances of W; (b) instances of the sound structure of W; (c) instances of the S/PM structure of W; (d) performances of W. An *instance* of a musical work W is a sound event which conforms *completely* to the sound/performance-means structure of W and which exhibits the required connection[31] to the indicative activity wherein W's composer A creates W. An instance of W is typically produced, either directly or indirectly, from a score that can be causally traced and is intentionally related by the performer, to the act of creation of W by A. Thus, all instances of W are instances of W's sound structure, and instances of W's S/MP structure – but the reverse is not the case.

Instances are a subclass of the set of performances of a work. A *performance* of a musical work

W is a sound event which is *intended* to instantiate W – i.e., represents an attempt to exemplify W's S/PM structure in accordance with A's indication of it [32] – and which *succeeds to a reasonable degree.*[33] Since one cannot instantiate a musical work – an S/PM structure-as-indicated-by-X-at-t – without intending to, because instantiating *that* demands conscious guidance by instructions, memories, or the like which one regards as deriving from A's indicative act at t, it follows that the instances of W are all to be found among the performances of W. However, not all performances of W count as instances of W; many if not most attempts to exemplify S/PM structures fail by some margin. So these cannot count as instances of W, but they *are* performances – namely *incorrect* performances. (Of course, that they are strictly incorrect by no means entails that they are bad.) There are not, however, any incorrect *instances* of W; the *correct* performances of W are its instances, and no others.[34]

Finally, let me note that musical works as I understand them *can* be heard in or through their performances. One *hears* an S/PM structure-as-indicated-by-X-at-t whenever one hears an instance of that S/PM structure produced by performers who, roughly speaking, are guided by X's indication of the S/PM structure in question. And one *knows* precisely what musical work, i.e., structure-as-indicated, one is hearing if one knows what creative act is in effect the guiding source of the sound event being produced.

(2) On my view of what a musical work (of the paradigm sort) is, it follows immediately that a transcription of a musical work is a distinct musical work, whether it involves alteration of the sound structure (the normal case), or *even* of just the performance-means structure. It is a virtue of my view that it gives a clear answer to this question, which is often thought to be only arbitrarily decidable. If we want such pieces to have the definite aesthetic qualities we take them to have, instrumentation must be considered inseparable from them. Thus, we need not rely, in endorsing the distinctness position on transcriptions vis-à-vis original works, merely on the principle of fidelity to the composer's intended instrumentation. Rather we are also constrained by higher-order considerations of preserving the aesthetic integrity of such pieces.

In conclusion, let me stress some obvious consequences of accepting the theory of the musical work that I have proposed. First, composers would retain the status of creator in the strictest sense. Second, musical composition would be revealed as necessarily personalized. Third, musical composition could not fail to be seen as a historically rooted activity whose products must be understood with reference to their points of origin. Fourth, it would be recognized that the pure sound structure of a musical work, while graspable in isolation, does not exhaust the work structurally, and thus that the underlying means of performance must be taken into account as well if the work is to be correctly assessed.[35]

Notes

1 There are of course several other objections to these proposals, and to the Crocean proposal mentioned below. I do not mean to suggest that those I recall are clearly decisive by themselves.

2 See for example, C. L. Stevenson, "On 'What Is a Poem?'," *Philosophical Review*, LXVI, 3 (July 1957): 329–62; J. Margolis, *The Language of Art and Art Criticism* (Detroit: Wayne State University Press, 1965); R. Wollheim, *Art and Its Objects* (New York: Harper & Row, 1968).

3 It should be understood at the outset that sound structure includes not only pitches and rhythms, but also timbres, dynamics, accents – that is, all "purely aural" properties of sound.

4 The present paper owes a debt to two recent theories of the musical work: N. Wolterstorff, "Toward an Ontology of Artworks," *Noûs*, IX, 2 (May 1975): 115–42; and K. Walton, "The Presentation and Portrayal of Sound Patterns," *In Theory Only* (February 1977): 3–16. These writers are aware of some of the considerations that I adduce pointing to the complexity of a musical type. However, I believe they do not take them seriously enough, and thus are inclined to acquiesce in the view that musical works *are* or *may be* just sound structures. The present paper aims squarely to reject that view and to formulate one more adequate.

5 E.g., F-sharp minor triad, three-note French-dotted rhythmic figure, middle C of bassoon timbre, etc.

6 This point is made by Wolterstorff, *op. cit.*, p. 138.

7 Though of course lack of suitable production facilities made this impossible in some nonlogical sense.

8 I am aware that someone might hold that in saying that a certain novel sound instance is possible at t, all we are committed to is that the sound structure

of which it *would be* an instance might possibly *come into existence* at *t*, simultaneously with its first instance. But I do not think this a plausible view; in saying that a certain sound event could occur at *t* we are saying something stronger than that the structure it would exemplify might come into existence – we are saying that that structure is right then available.

9 Some who yet resist the idea that pure sound structures pre-exist compositional activity are possibly failing to distinguish between *structure* and *construction*. It is true that constructions need to have been constructed in order to exist; it does not follow that structures need to have been constructed – i.e., actually put together from parts – in order to exist. The Brooklyn Bridge is a construction, and embodies a structure. The Brooklyn Bridge did not exist before its construction. But the geometrical structure it embodies, which required and received no construction, has always existed.

Given that there will still be some who are attracted to the view that pure sound structures are in some way created by composers, presumably through mental activity, and that these are their works, I will take this occasion to point out briefly two untoward consequences of such a view. The first is that instances of pure sound structures can always have been sounded accidentally before any composer thinks them into existence by directing his attention on the realm of sounds. In which case we would then be countenancing compositions that have instances before those compositions begin to exist. The second is that a person who conceives or sketches a sound structure new to him has no (logical) assurance that he has in fact composed *anything*. For if composing is bringing sound structures into existence, one may fail to do so in writing a score, provided someone else has conceived the same structure earlier. Notice that this is not a matter of the latecomer having composed the *same* work as his predecessor, but rather – what he and we would surely find incredible – a matter of his having composed *no* work at all.

10 Though composers compose their works *by* writing scores, having thoughts, or, less typically, producing performances.

11 It would be well to note here that, even if one rejects the requirement of creatability, abandonment of the sound-structure view in favor of something like the view I eventually propose will be demanded by the second and third requirements developed. And those requirements strike me as being nonnegotiable.

12 Notice that if we assume that composing musical works is strictly creating them, it follows immediately that two composers cannot compose the very same musical work (no matter what sound structures they determine) unless they are either composing jointly or composing independently but simultaneously. This is just a consequence of the fact that the same thing cannot be created both at *t* and at a later time *t'*. (The same goes for a single composer on temporally separate occasions; if composing is creating, a composer cannot compose the same work twice.) I will not, however, in this section assume that composing is strict creation.

13 Cf. J. L. Borges, "Pierre Menard, Author of the Quixote," in *Labyrinths* (New York: New Directions, 1962), for a fictional demonstration of the dependence of artistic meaning on the historical context of creation.

14 Cf. Wollheim, op. cit., pp. 48–54, for a discussion of the dependence of a work's expression on the artistic repertoire of the artist. The notion of "repertoire" is roughly that of a set of alternative decisions or choices within which an artist appears to be operating in creating his works. Wollheim extracts this idea from E. K. Gombrich's discussions of artistic expression in *Art and Illusion* and *Meditations on a Hobby-Horse*.

15 The convincingness of these examples depends crucially on accepting something like the following principle: "Works of art *truly have* those attributes which they *appear* to have when *correctly* perceived or regarded." I cannot provide a defense of this principle here, but it has been well argued for by C. Stevenson, "Interpretation and Evaluation in Aesthetics," in W. E. Kennick, *Art and Philosophy* (New York: St. Martin's, 1964), and K. Walton, "Categories of Art," *Philosophical Review*, LXVI, 3 (July 1970): 334–67, among others.

16 It is a mistake to regard this illustration as concerned with what *Pierrot Lunaire* would have been like if *it* had been composed by Strauss. (I am not even sure what *that* supposition amounts to.) The illustration rather concerns a possible musical work that possesses the same sound structure as *Pierrot Lunaire*, but is composed by Strauss in 1897. This work would be distinct from *Pierrot Lunaire*, because aesthetically divergent. But if musical works were identified with sound structures it could *not* be distinct.

Another way of casting the argument using this example would be as follows. Consider a possible world *Q* in which both Schoenberg's *Pierrot Lunaire* and Strauss's *Pierrot Lunaire** exist, and call the sound structure they have in common "*K*." In *Q*, the works diverge aesthetically and hence are non-identical. Clearly, the works cannot both be identified with their common sound structure, but to so identify only one of them would be perfectly arbitrary. So in *Q*, *Pierrot Lunaire* ≠ *K*. But then in the actual world as well, *Pierrot Lunaire* ≠ *K*. why? Owing to the necessity that attaches to identity and difference. If two things are non-identical in any possible world, they are non-identical in every possible world in which they exist. Put otherwise, statements of identity and difference involving rigid designators are necessary. "Pierrot Lunaire" and "K" designate rigidly; they are proper names, not definite descriptions. Thus "Pierrot Lunaire $\neq K$" is necessarily true, since true in Q. Therefore, in the actual world, *Pierrot Lunaire $\neq K$*. The argument can be recast in this way, *mutatis mutandis*, for illustrations (2)–(5) as well.

17 This includes a single composer on separate occasions.

18 It is inevitable that someone will object at this point that certain composers, in certain periods, did not compose with definite instruments in mind and did not make specific instrumentation integral to their works. This may be true to some extent. But two points must be noted. First, I have set out to define the nature of the *paradigmatic* musical composition in Western culture, of which Beethoven's Quintet, Opus 16 is an example. It is enough for my purpose that most "classical" compositions, and effectively all from 1750 to the present, integrally involve quite definite means of performance. Second, even in a case such as J. S. Bach, where controversy has long existed as to exactly what performing forces Bach intended, called for, or would have allowed in such compositions as *The Well-Tempered Clavier* or the Brandenburg Concerto No. 2, it is clear there are still more restrictions as to performing forces which must be considered part of those compositions. Thus, *The Well-Tempered Clavier* may not be a work belonging solely to the harpsichord (as opposed to the clavichord or fortepiano), but it is clearly a work for *keyboard*, and a performance of its sound structure on five violins would just for that reason not be a performance of *it*. And although the performance component of the Brandenburg Concerto No. 2 may be indeterminate between a trumpet and a natural horn in that prominent instrumental part, it certainly excludes the alto saxophone. Finally, a composition such as Bach's *Art of the Fugue*, for which perhaps no means of sound production are either prescribed or proscribed, is in this context merely the exception that proves the rule.

19 This should not be confounded with the fact that many composers were ready and willing to adapt their works in response to exigencies – in short, to license transcriptions.

20 This is not to say that *everything* found in scores is constitutive of musical works. Some markings do not fix the identity of a work but are instead of the nature of advice, inspiration, helpful instruction, etc. However, the suggestion that instrumental specifications are of this sort is totally insupportable.

21 Cf. Walton, "Categories of Art," op. cit., pp. 349/50, for related examples.

22 James Lyons, liner notes, phonograph record *Nonesuch* 71054.

23 The best one could say would be that the Quintet achieved a satisfactory blending of piano-ish sounds and woodwind-ish sounds.

24 One could alternatively speak of a single structure which, construed rightly, entails both the required sounds and the required means of sound production. This would be a structure of *performed sounds*, as opposed to "pure" sounds. For example, one such *performed sound* would correspond to the following specification: "Middle C of half-note duration played on oboe." Clearly this implies both a certain sound qualitatively defined and a means of producing it.

The main reason I favor the S/PM formulation is that it is more transparent. It preserves some continuity with the sound-structure view which it supersedes, and displays more clearly than the performed-sound formulation that, although a musical work is *more* than a sound structure, it most definitely *includes* a sound structure.

25 This analogy was brought to my attention by Warren Ingber.

26 See, for example, J. L. Austin's "Truth," *Proceedings of the Aristotelian Society*, supp. vol. xxiv (1950):111–28.

27 The analogy might even be reversed, so as to illuminate the nature of statements. If musical works are structures-as-indicated . . . , then possibly statements just are: sentences-as-uttered . . .

28 I am assuming, of course, that Hummel could not possibly have *been* Beethoven. If he *could* have, then I suppose that, even on MW, Hummel might have composed Beethoven's Quintet.

29 I will take this opportunity to point out that although aesthetic and artistic attributes have played a large role in this paper, I have not insisted on them as *essential* to musical works, but only as relevant – in common with all other attributes – to *individuating* them. The argument has nowhere required as a premise that such attributes are essential attributes. It has assumed only that aesthetic/artistic attributes *truly belong* to works in a *reasonably determinate* fashion. As for what attributes *are* essential to musical works, given MW, it seems that certain structural and genetic attributes would have to be admitted: S/PM structure, composer, date of composition. But it is not obvious that aesthetic/artistic attributes will turn out to be essential, i.e., possessed by a work in all possible worlds it inhabits. Consider a possible world in which Schoenberg determines the S/PM structure of *Verklarte Nacht* during 1899 but in which Wagner had never existed. The resultant work might still be *Verklarte Nacht*, though some of its aesthetic/artistic attributes would be subtly different.

30 Quandaries arise when these considerations conflict, which I will not attempt to deal with here. For example, suppose the Aloysious Ensemble are actu-

ally reading copies of Grotesteen's score while believing themselves to be playing Sterngrab's score. Do they perform Sterngrab's Quartet, Grotesteen's Quartet, or both?

31 I will assume here that the required connection is primarily, if not wholly, intentional.

32 And thus an attempt to exemplify an S/PM-as-indicated-by-*X*-at-*t*.

33 What constitutes a "reasonable degree," and thus what differentiates poor or marginal performance from nonperformance, is for many compositions perhaps marked by the ability of an informed and sensitive listener to grasp, at least roughly, what S/PM structure is struggling to be presented. For example, even an especially informed and sensitive listener would grasp approximately nothing of the Hammerklavier Sonata from *my* attempt to present its structure, since my facility at the piano is next to nil – no performance (much less an instance) of the Hammerklavier Sonata can issue from me or my ilk.

34 Thus I am in opposition to Wolterstorff's suggestion, in "Toward an Ontology of Artworks," op. cit., that musical works be construed as norm-kinds, i.e., as having correct and incorrect, or proper and improper, or standard and defective instances. What we say about musical works can, I think, be more perspicuously interpreted in terms of the distinction between instance and performance. Further, con-struing instance as requiring full conformity to score (i.e., as an all-or-none proposition) has the virtue, as Nelson Goodman pointed out in *Languages of Art* (Indianapolis: Bobbs-Merrill, 1968), of assuring preservation of a work's identity from work to instance and from instance to work. But by also distinguishing between instance and performance (which Goodman does not do) one can sweeten the judgment, say, that Rubinstein's playing of the Chopin Ballade No. 3 with two mistakes is not an *instance* of the work, with the willing admission that it is surely a *performance* of it (and possibly a great one).

35 It is worth observing that, if the position developed in this paper is correct, it may have interesting implications not only for the identity of other sorts of art work (this I take to be obvious), but for the identity of abstract cultural objects of various sorts – e.g., scientific theories, speeches, laws, games. A physical theory, for example, can't be *simply* a set of sentences, propositions, or equations *if* it is in fact the possessor of properties such as brilliance, revolutionariness, derivativeness, immediate acceptance. For that very set of sentences, propositions, or equations might be found in another theory occurring fifty years earlier or later which lacked those properties.

10

Platonism in Music:
A Kind of Defense

Peter Kivy

The title of my paper is meant to suggest two things, obviously: that I offer here a defense of what I shall be calling musical "Platonism," and that I offer it in a far from confident tone. I have two reasons for wanting to defend it: first, because it offers a way to understand the relationship between musical works and their performances that, I believe, captures a great many of our intuitions and musical *façons de parler*; and, second, because I think some of the objections brought against the doctrine – those, in particular, that claim it is musically or aesthetically counterintuitive and contrary to the way we want to speak about music – are answerable. That I am neither confident, nor altogether happy, in defending this Platonism is because, like any other well-brought-up student of philosophy, at least in the Anglo-American tradition, I have a healthy skepticism with regard to Platonic metaphysics, and the multiplying of entities (particularly problematical ones) beyond need.

I should also say, at the outset, that I have no intention whatever of presenting any arguments in favor of Platonism in music; I shall confine myself solely to defending it against some objections, and assume that my readers know the arguments in its favor, and the details of the position, in its various forms. As a result, I shall be keeping the concept of musical Platonism, for the purposes of this paper, open, and distressingly ill-defined. I shall not, for instance, try to distinguish among such

Peter Kivy, "Platonism in Music: A Kind of Defense," *Grazer Philosophische Studien*, 19 (1983), pp. 109–29.

candidates for Platonic realism as universals, kinds, and types (assuming one wants to construe types Platonistically at all). The critics that I will be considering will always make it clear which form of the doctrine they are belaboring; and I leave it to the reader to determine what other of its forms the objection in question might touch.

In the first section of my paper I will be considering what I take to be three of the most important "traditional" objections to musical Platonism, in the second section two of the newer ones. (None of them, actually, is all that old.) That the "traditional" objections keep cropping up in the literature shows, I think, that they are far from impotent with age, and still deserve an answer. That new objections continue to arise certainly is an indication, if any were needed, of how problematical Platonism of any kind will always be.

I

(1) Let me begin with a criticism that has been advanced by, among others, Joseph Margolis, in *Art and Philosophy*. Margolis claims that a work of art "cannot be a universal because [in part] . . . it possesses physical and perceptual properties."[1] And with regard specifically to music, and to Nicholas Wolterstorff's claim that musical works are "kinds," he says later on, "The essential difficulty with Wolterstorff's proposal is that we wish to say that we *hear* the music . . . , that the music *sounds sweet* . . . ; in short, we wish to attribute certain properties to the work itself and, on Wolterstorff's view, we literally cannot," because, Margolis urges,

we cannot hear a kind nor can a kind (therefore) *sound* sweet.[2]

The obvious response to this is that to say "I hear the music" may be taken as short for, "I hear a performance of the music"; that, in other words, the performance might be the bearer of the properties that, Margolis insists, a universal or kind cannot be the bearer of. I mean here, of course, the performance taken to be the sound-occurrence, not the act of producing it, both of which can correctly be referred to in ordinary usage as the "performance."

The initial difficulty with this response is that there do seem to be properties of works that are heard properties of *them*, and cannot just be fobbed off on their performances. The unity of the *Goldberg Variations*, or the passion of Haydn's *Sturm und Drang* symphonies, are surely properties of those works themselves, whether or not they are properties of all (or any) of their performances. And, presumably, being *musical* unity and passion, they are audible properties.

The difficulty, however, may not be quite as heavy as it at first seems, if one does not forget what a Platonic construal of works and performances commits one to. It is said that there are statements one wants to make about works of music (as opposed to performances of those works) in which some heard property is predicated of the work; and since a universal or kind cannot possess heard properties, a universal or kind cannot be what we are referring to. But it should be noticed, in this regard, that when we say something like "The male lion has a mane," not in reference to a particular lion, we use the same locution; and we do feel we are making some sort of characterization of *the* lion, *as well as* of individual instances of it, without thinking that a "logical" entity can have a mane. When we say "The 49th Symphony of Haydn is passionate," we are, of course, saying that every properly formed instance – that is, performance – of it is passionate. But more: we are saying the work (kind or universal) is of such a nature as to be truly instantiated *only* by passionate performances. We are, then, saying something *about* the work (construed as a universal or kind): we are predicating passion of *it*, as of a universal or kind, even though we are not saying that it has the heard property of passion. This may be enough, it appears to me, to accommodate our intuition that when we say "The 49th Symphony of Haydn is passionate," we are not only saying something about correct performances of the work but something about the

work itself, even though passion is (in this instance) a heard property, and universals or kinds not heard, or, rather, are heard through their instances, i.e. performances. It would be odd, would it not, to be charged with a logical howler for saying "The male lion has a mane," on the grounds that species or natural kinds cannot grow hair.

To talk about "a performance *of* a work" sounds very much as if one were talking about two things: the performance and the work, one of which is standing in for the other, as in "a copy of the original." But a lion is not a stand-in for the kind: he is an *instance* of it. Similarly, to hear a performance of a symphony *is* to hear the symphony: *is* to hear the work, not a stand-in for it. The performance is an *instance* of the work, not a substitute for it; and to make a statement about the work is to make a statement about its instances. It seems to me that once one lets musical Platonism really sink in, psychologically, the gap between theory and intuition in this regard closes considerably. Not perhaps completely: but no matter what the theory, there will be a gap somewhere. So the question inevitably comes down to how wide a gap one will tolerate, and where. This is as good a place as any, and a more narrow gap than some.

(2) A second objection to musical Platonism, of more elaborate and searching a nature, can again be taken initially from Margolis, although I will go on, from there, to consider a more recent variation on the same theme. Margolis says that a work of art "cannot be a universal because [in part] it is created."[3] Later on, with specific reference to music, and, again, to Wolterstorff's views regarding it, he intimates that music cannot be a kind because "it is clear" that music is "actually invented," and, clearly, one cannot invent or create a kind.[4] I now want to spend a few minutes at the seemingly impossible task of convincing you that it would *not* be wildly counterintuitive to construe musical composition as a kind of "discovery" rather than as a kind of "creating" or "inventing."

Let me talk just a bit about "invention." The Wright brothers invented the airplane. I suppose that is a paradigm of invention, if anything is. But in order to do that, they had, as we now know, to discover certain aerodynamic principles first. (They were not, it turns out, merely a couple of lucky tinkerers.) Every invention is part discovery. Edison had to discover the right material for a filament, and that it burned more properly in a vacuum, in the process of *inventing* the thing we turn on and off at night. The reason we call the end product of the Wright brothers' and Edison's activities *inventions*, and the activities *inventing*, is that the thing they are remembered for is something we think of as not having existed before they started work, and existing after.

But just as invention is part discovery, discovery is part invention. Michelson discovered the speed of light (if you will permit me to use the word "discovery" in this regard). To do this, however, he had to invent what is now called the Michelson interferometer – no small scientific accomplishment, as Einstein noted in recognition of Michelson's genius. Gödel discovered the theorem which bears his name. But he had to invent Gödel numbering to do it. Of course in mathematics our strong inclination to Platonize makes it unclear whether we don't want to say instead that he discovered Gödel numbering rather than invented it. In any case, we think of the speed of light, or Gödel's theorem, or permutation groups, or what have you, as discovered rather than invented because, of course, although inventions may have made their discovery possible, *they* were there all along, and were not brought into being.

I mention this to make it clear, first, that if Mozart discovered his music rather than invented it, there was just as much complexity to his discovery, just as much give and take between discovery and invention, as there was to the discovery of the speed of light by Michelson, or the incompleteness theorem by Gödel, or permutation groups by Galois and Abel. So I am not necessarily suggesting that Mozart was not, in part, an inventor or creator as well as a discoverer. What I am suggesting is that it may be more plausible to think of his works as Platonic objects of some sort and, therefore, things that could not have been brought into being. But just as inventing is not all making, so discovery is not all finding: a discovery, of any great complexity and significance, is invention, or creation, as well.

But surely, you will insist, this is not enough; for wasn't Mozart a *creator* in the paradigmatic sense of that word? Wasn't he a *creative artist*? Isn't music one of the *creative* arts? In calling Mozart a discoverer, am I not taking more away from him than intuition will allow?

Well, in one sense of "creator," there never has been one at all except the Lord God Jehova himself. For even Plato's demiurge, a very creative fellow, from all accounts, didn't create *ex nihilo*. So if Mozart must have been a creator, he was a demiurge and not the Deity. But what distinguishes him from

any other sort of ordinary maker? Well, he was original. Or he made things that nobody else could make (if that doesn't come to the same thing). Or he made things of a certain kind better than almost anyone else has ever been able to do. But we can pack all of that just as well into Mozart the discoverer as Mozart the creator. The operative word here is not "creator" but "creative." Surely Mozart was creative if anyone was. He was as creative as, well, Galois, or Abel, or Michelson, or Gödel. Would you deny that *they* were creative? There are, after all, humdrum discoveries as well as creative ones. When Archimedes jumped out of the tub he had done more than just take a bath. It takes nothing away from Mozart's creativity, in the important sense (or senses) of the word, to think of Mozart as a discoverer rather than as an inventor or creator. His lustre remains untarnished. In the company of Newton, after all, one is hardly slumming.

But perhaps we have moved too quickly. There may be more to the question than has yet been uncovered: in particular, we are perhaps giving up more, it may be felt, in construing the composer as discoverer rather than creator, than intuition will allow. Recently, in defending the view that "A piece of music is *some* sort of structural type, . . ."[5] Jerrold Levinson has, nevertheless, made just this point, and insisted on what he calls the "requirement of *creatability*," to wit: "Musical works must be such that they do *not* exist prior to the composer's compositional activity, but are *brought into existence by* that activity."[6] His reason for insisting on this is worth going into. It is two-fold:

> The main reason for holding to it is that it is one of the most firmly entrenched of our beliefs concerning art. The whole tradition of art assumes art is creative in the strict sense, that it is a godlike activity in which the artist brings into being what did not exist beforehand – much as a demiurge forms a world out of inchoate matter . . .
>
> A second, closely related reason to preserve true creation vis-à-vis musical works is that some of the status, significance, and value we attach to musical composition derives from our belief in this . . . There is a special glow that envelops composers, as well as other artists, because we think of them as true creators.[7]

Levinson's first claim – that the artist as godlike creator is a firmly entrenched belief – is, to begin with, if not false, at least greatly exaggerated. In addition, even if it were true, without exaggeration, it would not be above being given up; for it is what it is supposed to *explain*, in my opinion, not its inherent plausibility of itself, that gives it what appeal it has – and what it is supposed to explain is in no need of that hypothesis at all.

First, as to its truth. As a matter of fact, the notion of the artist as godlike creator has a *history* – and not such a long one at that. Although suggested by Sir Philip Sidney in the *Apologie for Poetrie* (1595), it does not really come into its own until the end of the eighteenth century, partly through the influence on the Romantic movement, I imagine, of Kant's third *Critique*. It is, then, a gross exaggeration to suggest, as Levinson does, "that it is one of the most firmly entrenched of our beliefs concerning art." And it is just plain false that "The whole tradition of art assumes art is creative in the strict sense, that it is a godlike activity in which the artist brings into being what did not exist before . . . ." The "tradition of art" did without this assumption until barely two-hundred years ago, and managed to produce without it the *Iliad, Odyssey*, the Greek plays, Gothic cathedrals, Shakespeare, the Italian Renaissance, Bach, Handel, Haydn, Mozart, and a good deal more. Bach did not think he was God; Wagner did, with dire results.

But more, it is at least in part to explain *another* common belief that the Romantic movement gave birth to (or at least nurtured to maturation) the concept of the artist as godlike creator. That is the belief in the *originality* of the great artist – another belief, it must be remembered, that has not always been with us, and has itself a distinctly Romantic aroma. Be that as it may, it is, in part, to explain what makes a work of art *original*, that the notion of the artist as godlike creator is invoked. For what is the *original* but that which has never before existed, and is therefore unique? Then what but a *creation*, and who but a *creator*, can burgeon forth that which has never been before?

The playing off of these concepts against one another produced a hideous caricature of scientific discovery, already apparent in Kant's *Critique of Judgement*, and even more pronounced in Schopenhauer. For since, on the Romantic view, originality can only result from creation, and the scientist is a "mere" discoverer, the scientist, even of the stature of a Newton, can never deserve the epithet "creative," nor (therefore) "genius," the etymological connection between "genius" and "genesis" being too obvious to belabor here.

But once the Romantic circle connecting creation, genius, and originality exclusively together is broken, we can see that originality no more requires a godlike creator than does "creativity" itself, when understood in its full honorific sense. As Jack Glickman points out, "We say an activity such as painting, writing, or composing is creating if it achieves new and valuable results . . ."[8]; and to that list we can add scientific and mathematical discovery as well, thus giving them their rightful place as "creative" enterprises. It is the achieving of "new and valuable results" that warrants the epithet "creative," and it makes no matter whether that achieving is "inventing," "discovering," or "creating in the godlike way." An "original," "creative" discovery is not, in the literal sense, the bringing into being of what has never before existed, for then, of course, it would not be a "discovery" in the literal sense. It is the revealing, needless to say, of what has always been there, but which no one has yet had the genius and creative imagination to see; and it is all one whether the discovery is a scientific or a musical one.

One further word about Levinson's first argument for the *creatability* requirement. I venture to assert, without documentation, for the documentation would require a book, that the language of "discovery" is as pervasive, throughout history, in discussions of what artists do, as is the language of "godlike creativity." That in itself, if it is true, should lay to rest the claim that the concept of the artist as godlike creator is either essential to the Western tradition in art (I will say nothing of the non-Western, non-"original" traditions) or that it is one of our most firmly entrenched intuitions about the enterprise.

Moving on to Levinson's second argument, we see that it too, like the first, makes a factual claim, from which the *creatability* requirement is supposed to follow, or which, at least, is supposed to strongly suggest its acceptance. The factual claim is simply that we would value the composer and the composition less if the composer were "merely" a discoverer, not a creator, and the composition a pre-existent entity to be found out, rather than a creation that never before existed. This multiple fact urges upon us, on Levinson's view, that we preserve the *creatability* requirement.

Assume, for the nonce, that the factual claim is true. Is this a very strong reason for maintaining the *creatability* requirement? I hardly think so. It may be the case, for example, that an "instrumental" interpretation of scientific theories results in a lower estimate of scientists and their "creations" than a "realistic" interpretation would do. For, after all, on an "instrumental" account, scientists cease to be sages, and their theories cease to be revelatory of "the nature of things": rather, the former are now "merely" contrivers of artifacts for the use of man; the latter, those artifacts. Indeed, it is sometimes suggested that the transition from the medieval view of astronomy as merely "the saving of the appearances," to a more "realistic" interpretation of the enterprise, helped spur the astronomers on to the great accomplishments of the scientific revolution, just because it made their work seem more significant in their eyes. But it is difficult to imagine anyone arguing for the "realistic" interpretation on the grounds that, if it is accepted, science and scientists would get higher marks.

In any case, however, the factual assumption – and that, I think, is all it is, an unsubstantiated assumption – does not seem to me to be true. Or, at least, the waters are far more muddy than Levinson's rather artless claim makes them out to be. Composers, as a matter of historical fact, have tended to balk at the idea that they are mere makers or creators of artifacts, no matter how original those artifacts might be. If music were a mere created artifact, a kaleidoscope or arabesque in sound, to appropriate Eduard Hanslick's description, it would become, perhaps unjustly, lower in the estimation of most of its practitioners, as well as its audiences. The composer *wishes* to be known for just what Levinson seems to suggest would tarnish his reputation: he wishes to be known as a discoverer and purveyor of truths about the world, like almost everyone else in the Western tradition, obsessed, as it is, with knowledge and the acquisition thereof. Now, of course, the composer generally wishes to be known not merely for discovering sound structures but sound structures that are somehow revelatory of something beyond themselves: the metaphysical will, the emotive life, the harmony of the spheres, or what have you. But "discovery" as opposed to "godlike creation" is not what is at stake here. There is no advantage in being a "godlike creator," rather than a "mere discoverer," if what one creates are "mere" structures in sound, although I suspect that discovery may, even here, have the edge over creation, since, in a funny Platonic way, one is at least finding something out about "what there is," rather than merely actualiz-

ing the trivial. Where there *is* an *unqualified* advantage, as most musical thinkers in the past have seen it, is in being a "discoverer" through music of something beyond "mere" musical structure: something out there in the "real world." It is this wish to puff up the composer and his works that has led to most of the extravagant theories of music in the past, and in the present as well. And it hardly bears out the claim that to call the composer a "discoverer" is to rebuke him either in his eyes or in the eyes of his public. It is only a rebuke if what he is alleged to discover is mean in his eyes; but in that case it hardly is less a rebuke to say that what is mean in his eyes he has created rather than discovered. For I take it that to discover trash is not more ignoble a thing than to bring it into being where it was not.

Surely though, it will be objected, our whole picture of how composition goes on is completely out of phase with the notion of composition as discovery. And, anyway, is it really plausible to think of an "object" as complex and metaphysically unwieldy as a Mozart opera or Mahler symphony pre-existing its composition? In an incredibly short space of time, let me address these two objections at once.

You will all no doubt recall that dreadful relic of Victorianism, "The Lost Chord," poem by Adelaide Ann Procter, music by Sir Arthur Sullivan:

> Seated one day at the organ,
> I was weary and ill at ease,
> And my fingers wandered idly
> Over the noisy keys.
> I do not know what I was playing,
> Or what I was dreaming then;
> But I struck one chord of music,
> Like the sound of a great Amen.

Now surely this accidental discovery of a chord, in a fit of idle revery, hardly jibes with the realities of musical composition. Even a musician with the awesome mental equipment of a Mozart has to work at composing: he does not just fall into his discoveries. Discoveries in music, as elsewhere, are prepared for, even though there is an element of luck too. But what may not be so implausible in "The Lost Chord" is the notion that the chord was found, discovered, rather than invented or created; that that particular vertical arrangement of notes "existed," awaiting discovery, as did Kepler's laws, or permutation groups. Think of the *Tristan* chord. It seems to me quite plausible to regard it as a discovery of Wagner's rather than his invention, although, of course, the discovery of that chord required the labor of more than one lifetime. Nor does it stagger the metaphysical imagination to picture the *Tristan* chord – that particular relationship of four pitches – as pre-existing its discovery, in the manner of a Platonic object. But, after all, the *Tristan* chord is part of a larger relationship of pitches called *Tristan und Isolde*. And if you grant that that small but vital part pre-existed its composition, it seems to me you are on the slippery slope that must propel you into granting that the large composition of which it is a part also pre-existed its compositional discovery by Wagner. I am told, in a recent issue of *Science News*, that the existence of "the sporadic Group F_1" requires a proof exceeding 5,000 pages in length. If logical space, or Platonic heaven, has room for *that*, surely it can find a niche for Beethoven's Ninth, or an itty bitty Wagner opera.

(3) Closely related to the uncreatability of universals or kinds is, of course, their obvious indestructibility. I will close this section with a necessarily brief discussion of that, and again take my departure from Margolis. He says that a work of art "cannot be a universal because [in part] it . . . can be destroyed."[9] But when it comes to the particular case of music, he seems to waffle. He writes:

> Clearly, sculpture, architecture, painting, and etching *can* be destroyed . . . ; hence, they cannot be kinds. Music and literature cannot, in *this* sense, be destroyed, simply because their properly formed examples can be generated by reference to a notation *and* a notation is not a work of art. All the tokens of a notation may be destroyed, however, and the notation may cease to be remembered; in that sense, music and literature can be destroyed.[10]

It is not clear to me in *what* sense Margolis thinks music cannot be destroyed; whether, in fact, it might not be the sense in which I think it cannot. Clearly, I am committed to the view that the sense in which *The Art of the Fugue* or the *Tristan* chord cannot be destroyed is the sense in which permutation groups or that 5,000 page mathematical proof cannot be destroyed. Nor does it seem at all counterintuitive to me that that should indeed be the case. If you have already accepted the plausibility of the *Tristan* chord as a discovery rather than an invention, and hence as pre-existing its composition, you will already have prepared yourselves for the conclusion that it cannot be destroyed (although as we know from the *Phaedo* the pre-existence of souls does not of itself imply their immortality). But if the *Tristan* chord existed before it was thought of or notated, why should it cease to be when all notations, performances, and memories of it pass away? If it existed before anyone ever was aware of it, why should its existence be influenced by our ceasing to be aware of it? Once, I think, one is convinced that the pre-existence of a musical work holds no terrors, its immortality will seem equally if not more benign. So I will tarry no longer over the question, but go on, as I said I would at the outset, to discuss some more current objections to the Platonistic move in music.

II

(1) A recent criticism of the work-performance relation as the relation between type and token, advanced by R. A. Sharpe, is not without interest.[11] Sharpe points out, quite rightly, that "I can remove part of a token and replace it with part of another token and it remains a token of that type." For example:

> I could cut off part of a linen red flag and replace the missing part with the corresponding part of a plastic red flag of the same size. It is still a red flag, a token of that type.[12]

Suppose, now, that I try the same thing with two performances of the same musical work. The case, Sharpe argues, is not the same; for

> if I remove the last movement of Walter's *Das Lied [von der Erde]* and replace it with the last movement of Bernstein's my action does have aesthetic repercussions. For one thing we expect a conductor to present in performance a unified view of the work.[13]

If Sharpe's intention has been to establish by such examples that there is a logical disanalogy between the flag and the musical work, he has not, so far at least, accomplished that intention. Patching together a flag (token) from two separate flags (tokens) of the same type produces a flag (token) of the same type; but, it needs pointing out, a flag

Peter Kivy

(token) of rather poorer quality: half linen, half plastic, with an unsightly seam. Likewise, a performance which two conductors share is going to be, in all likelihood, a poor performance, with its own musical seams: but it does not, on that account, fail to be a genuine, recognizable token (performance) of the type (work). For certain purposes, of course, we don't much care if a token is well- or ill-formed: we can rally round a tattered flag as well as a spanking new one. Whereas it will seldom be a matter of indifference to us that a performance-token of *Das Lied von der Erde* is poor. But so far as I can see, as long as we recognize that tokens can be well- or ill-formed, good or bad products, symphonies and flags are logically on all fours.

But there is more to Sharpe's argument than this; and it emerges in his summation of his position.

> The general principle is, then, that a token remains a token of a type when one part is replaced by the corresponding part of another token. Whereas a copy of a poem survives this transplantation, two performances of a single piece of music may not necessarily survive the exchange of their parts. Substitution is only possible when the two performances are performances of the same interpretation. Otherwise it will leave us with merely two parts of two different performances juxtaposed rather than a single performance.[14]

The argument here seems to be this. If all performances were tokens, and all musical works types, then since I can always get a token of any given type by piecing together two (or more) parts of other tokens of the same type, I should always be able to get a performance of any given work by piecing together two (or more) parts of other performances of the same work. But the latter, on Sharpe's view, is not the case. For if the performance parts that are pieced together are too disparate – not performances of the same interpretation – then, Sharpe claims, the result of the patchwork is not *a* performance of the work but, rather, *two* performance parts. This, presumably, is the "aesthetic repercussion" spoken of earlier, that prevents performances being well-behaved tokens of types.

But this claim seems completely unfounded. Consider an occurrence (I will not beg the question from the start by calling it a performance) of *Tristan und Isolde*, the first act conducted by Leinsdorf, the second by Bernstein, and the third by Solti, each, we will assume, based on an entirely different reading of the score. What grounds are there for believing that this "occurrence" is not a "performance" of the work, but three different "performance parts?" No grounds at all, so far as I can see, just so long as one avoids slipping into an evaluative use of "performance," such that "performance" becomes "good performance," and being based on a single interpretation becomes a necessary condition of a good performance (I will assume that it is). As a matter of fact, I attended, some years ago, an "occurrence" of *Tristan und Isolde* at the Metropolitan Opera, which turned out to be very unusual indeed. As it happened, all three of the company's Tristans were sick. Each one, however, had enough to get through one act. And that was the expedient fixed upon. The soprano sang three Tristans under the table (the death of number three being particularly convincing). Now the point is that no one, after the "occurrence" was ever tempted to call it anything but "that extraordinary *performance* of *Tristan und Isolde*." No one referred to it as "performance parts," or anything of that kind. Nor, I think, would anyone have been tempted to do so if, because of the illness of the Met conductors, a different one were to have undertaken each act. Neither intuition nor linguistic usage seems to support Sharpe's contention that in such cases we would not have *a* performance but many performance parts. That being the case, why should we accept it? Merely to support Sharpe's theory? Not, clearly, if we have a prior commitment to the work–performance distinction as an instance of the type–token one.

Surely, neither Sharpe, nor anyone else, would want to argue that it is analytic to the notion of *a* performance, as used in musical contexts, that *a* performance must be the act of *one* person. Were that to be claimed, we could not, of course, have *a* performance of a symphony, an opera, or even a string quartet, except in a keyboard arrangement, since they are all co-operative ventures. Even less does it seem analytic to the notion of *a* performance that it be based on *one* or *one person*'s interpretation. The N.B.C. Symphony Orchestra, after the death of Toscanini, played for a number of years without a conductor at all. And although its performances might well have been criticized for lacking the unity or singleness of purpose that a conductor would have given them, there is surely nothing odd, logically or linguistically, in calling them "performances." No music critic, to my knowledge, ever called them anything else. Performances that produce an adequate number of the right notes, and fulfill an adequate number of the other requirements of a "correct" performance, may range in quality from great to terrible, unified to eclectic, but not from performance to non-performance or performance parts.

The conclusion, I think, must be that Sharpe has not succeeded in showing any logical disanalogy between the type–token distinction and the work–performance one. Just so long as one bears it in mind that at least some types can have both well-formed and badly-formed tokens, it will cause no problem to discover that performance parts can seldom be joined together without deleterious aesthetic repercussions; for there is a world of difference between an ill-formed token and no token at all. What Sharpe was obliged to show, to prove logical disanalogy, is that performance parts when not of the same interpretation cannot yield tokens – i.e. correct performances – at all. But all he has shown, I think, is that they cannot yield good performances – and from that only those with ass's ears would dissent.

(2) By far the most logically rigorous and thoroughgoing musical Platonism to be found is in Part Two of Nicholas Wolterstorff's *Works and Worlds of Art*. But, ironically, Wolterstorff is willing to accept as a consequence of his Platonism a conclusion about music that, I think, any musician or musical scholar must count as a serious objection – perhaps even a decisive one – to the whole doctrine. It is this consequence that I want to examine here with some care. I think it must be answered if musical Platonism is to stand.

The process of composition, on Wolterstorff's view, can be described as a process of *selection*. "The composer selects properties of sounds for the purpose of their serving as criteria for judging correctness of occurrence."[15] The end result of this selection process is, of course, works of music, which Wolterstorff construes as "norm-kinds," being, that is,

> kinds . . . such that it is possible for them to have improperly formed examples. The Lion is obviously a norm-kind. The kind: Red Thing, however, seems not to be. For there can be no such entity as an improperly red thing, a malformedly red thing.[16]

That works of music must be *norm*-kinds is required, of course, by the fact that they can have

improperly as well as properly formed examples: that is to say, "A symphony can have incorrect as well as correct performances."[17]

So far, nothing that Wolterstorff has said about the musical work, or its creation, is inconsistent with the views I have been expressing here: composition as "selection" does not seem to me to be incompatible with composition as "discovery," as selection would turn out to be, on my view, a matter of choosing what discovery to record in score and thus make public. But there follows from Wolterstorff's position, so he supposes, what he refers to as a "corollary" concerning the art of improvisation which, although it conflicts with nothing said so far in this paper, is profoundly contradictory of deeply entrenched musical intuitions that I share with many others. It is this supposed corollary that I want to examine and dispatch; for I believe that it is neither true, nor a genuine consequence of Wolterstorff's "Platonism," and would, indeed, if true, constitute a serious objection to it.

The "corollary" is "that to improvise is not to compose." Wolterstorff goes on:

> That corollary is clearly correct. Suppose that someone has improvised on the organ. And suppose that he then goes home and scores a work of such a sort that his improvisation, judged by the requirements for correctness specified in the score, is at all points correct. In spite of that, the composer did not compose his work *in* performing his improvisation. In all likelihood he did not, during his improvisation, finish selecting that particular set of requirements for correctness to be found in his score. Suppose, for example, that at a certain point in his improvisation he introduced a bit of rubato, with full consciousness of doing so. In so doing he has not yet decided whether to select rubato at that point as required for correctness of occurrence. One cannot uniquely extract a work from a performance.[18]

Let us look at a familiar historical case of improvisation. I think a bit of reflection on it will reveal how odd it would be to construe it as anything but composition. During his famous visit to Frederick the Great in Potsdam, which ultimately led to the composition of *The Musical Offering*, Johann Sebastian Bach was asked by the king to improvise a six-voiced *ricercare* (a kind of fugue) on a theme supplied by Frederick himself: the "royal theme." Finding Frederick's chromatic subject "unsuited" to the improvisation of so complex a composition, Bach improvised a three-voiced *ricercare* instead. Tradition has it that when he got back home to Leipzig, he wrote down, from memory, the improvised *ricercare* which we now know as part of *The Musical Offering*.

When did the composition of this *ricercare* take place? The obvious answer is: during Bach's visit to Potsdam, more exactly, as he was playing it for the king. Surely no musician would be tempted to say that he was composing it as he was writing it down. The composing was already done. Bach was merely (!) being his own copyist, recording in notation from his memory of what he had played: a prodigious feat, needless to say.

That this is the only intelligible way to look at Bach's improvisation, without ending up in absurdity, can be seen by altering the historical facts just a bit. Imagine, then, that Bach's great son, Karl Philipp Emanuel, who was undoubtedly present at his father's performance, was so taken by the piece that *he* wrote it down from memory and that Bach senior never did. Who, then, was the composer of the *ricercare*? Clearly not Karl Philipp Emanuel; and were he to claim he was, we would accuse him, quite rightly, of plagiarism. But if improvisation is not composition, then Johann Sebastian was not the composer either. There is no candidate, then, for composer of the *ricercare*; and we must conclude that it came into being without being composed at all.

Now there is nothing absurd about claiming that *some* music comes into being without being composed. Wolterstorff correctly observes that:

> There are works of indigenous folk music such that probably no one ever singled out the requisite properties in the requisite way for composing the work. The work just emerged from performances.[19]

But what is absurd, I think, is to claim that Johann Sebastian's *ricercare* is such a composer-less work. Surely three-voiced fugues are not the sorts of things that grow like "Greensleeves." And the one in question, improvised by Johann Sebastian, copied down by Karl Philipp Emanuel, owes its existence to the genius, originality, learning, and compositional choices of the former as much as do his other works. That its composition and first performance were the same act is something for us all

to wonder at, but not an occasion for metaphysical conclusions even worse than musical Platonism requires.

What exactly has driven Wolterstorff to insist that improvisation is not composition? It is that "One cannot," on Wolterstorff's view, "uniquely extract a work from a performance," and that because we cannot distinguish, merely in the performance or improvisation, without the authority of the score, apparently, what properties are requisite for a correct performance, and what merely requisite for a good one; for if, for example, the performer introduces "a bit of rubato" into his improvisation, we have no way of knowing, prior to his preparation of an autograph, whether the rubato is "required for correctness of occurrence," is merely a performance choice of the moment, or perhaps a recommendation, to be written into the score, for what the composer takes to be an optimal performance. That seems to be the substance of the argument.

The mistake, I think, lies in Wolterstorff's construal of musical scores as recipes for the realization of musical performances. It is not that this is wrong. Scores *can* be usefully seen as recipes for performances, and Wolterstorff is not the first to describe them as such. But if one *just* sees scores as recipes, one then comes to the conclusion, I think, as Wolterstorff has, that the conventions surrounding them only prescribe movement in one direction: from score to performance; cookbook to cookie. Such, however, is not the case, as a look at how students are taught to use scores – in what is called "ear training and dictation" – reveals. Every well-trained musician has learned to write down in score what he or she hears: to, in other words, take down musical dictation, just as a short-hand secretary learns to "take a letter." And were there not conventions for doing this, for, that is, going from sound to score, the task would not be possible.

Now the major goals of such exercises in dictation are, of course, to enable the musician to read scores and to "hear" music "in the head," and to enable him or her to realize in notation what is "heard in the head" or worked out at the keyboard. The skill of "taking dictation," having served its educational purpose, tends to fall into disuse. But the fact is that one *can* do it, at least within certain practical limits; and when scores were rare and difficult to obtain, it might well have been a useful skill, as well as a musical parlour trick. (A famous eight-voice *Miserere* by Allegri was revered as a sacred object in the Sistine Chapel; parts and scores were not permitted to be made or circulated, on pain of excommunication. The fourteen-year-old Mozart, however, acquired a score for himself by listening to the work once, committing it to memory on the spot, and writing it down afterwards.)

With this in mind, let us return to Bach's *ricercare*: the one, that is, improvised by Johann Sebastian, and written down by his son. Suppose that there is, in Sebastian's performance, a slackening of the tempo – a slight holding back – just before the entrance of the new triplet figure. Should Karl Philipp Emanuel write "poco rit." at this place, thus enshrining the ritard in his score? or should he not? The question is not, after all, an unanswerable one. As a matter of fact, such things were far more often than not left to the performer in those days, and were seldom indicated by composers in scores. Musical convention, then, would have dictated that that ritard was an artifact of performance, and not a property of the work. And had Johann Sebastian, in fact, also made a score of the improvisation, and written "poco rit." at the appropriate place, he would thereby have produced a different version of the work, since he was under the implicit discipline of the convention, during the improvisation, which made the ritard simply a performer's choice. (The same would apply to trills, and other ornaments.) In other words, the improvisation was a version of the work in which the ritard was not a requirement of correct performance; and musical convention gives us reasonable assurance of that. Philipp Emanuel's autograph scores that version of the work, on the authority of the reigning musical conventions. Sebastian's autograph, with "poco rit." in the appropriate place, becomes a different, and more definitive version of the same work. It is true that Karl Philipp Emanuel cannot be absolutely certain, when he hears the improvisation, that the ritard is an artifact of performance, and not a property of the work. But no more can we be absolutely certain about a great many things in scored musical works. There are conventions for interpreting them, without which they would be useless, and we helpless. But the conventions are no more iron-clad and beyond question than the one telling Karl Philipp Emanuel Bach that the ritard is not a part of the work.

What I think we can conclude from this is that in a loose sense of "uniquely," a score uniquely determines a correct performance, under a given set of implicit conventions for interpreting the score – conventions which may be quite different in different historical contexts – and a performance uniquely determines a score under a similar set of historically bound conventions for taking "musical dictation." In a logically strict sense of "uniquely," however, I doubt that a score uniquely determines a correct performance *or* that a performance uniquely determines a score. The "loose" interpretation has this very important point in its favor: it can accommodate the way musicians, musicologists, and, I think, the rest of us do in fact think about and talk about such things as composing improvisation, scores, performances, and the rest. It seems to me this point is decisive.

III

I have tried to defend a Platonic interpretation of the musical work against some new and some familiar objections. But, it might well be asked, why bother? Why Platonize music?

I cannot answer this question here and now; and, quite frankly, I do not know if I could ever answer it any better than it has already been by such elegant practitioners as Wollheim and Wolterstorff. But this much I can say. When I think of the mode of existence of Bach's *ricercare* before he had time to write it down, and after he had composed it, I tremble as Darwin did at the thought of the human eye. Where did that *ricercare* exist? In Bach's head. But what is the cash value of that? What mode of existence "in Bach's head" did that *ricercare* have?

One suggestion, that seems to be implied by something Margolis says, bothers me. In a passage previously quoted, he remarks, you will remember: "All the tokens of a notation may be destroyed, however, and the notation may cease to be remembered; in that sense music . . . may be destroyed." Does Margolis mean to suggest that when a piece of music is remembered or thought about, it is the *notation* that is remembered or thought about? Did the *notation* of Bach's *ricercare* exist "in his head"? That seems wrong to me, although I do not wish to deny that a composer *can* visualize notation "in his head." To remember the *ricercare* that way is to remember it the way the "memorist" might do in *The Thirty Nine Steps*. A person with what used to be called a "photographic memory," or "absolute recall," might, indeed, commit the score of a musical composition to memory, being, all the while, tone-deaf and completely ignorant of music, just as I could memorize a paragraph of Serbo-

Croatian, a language I neither speak, read, nor understand.

I do not think *that* is the way Bach remembered or thought about the *ricercare*. Rather, it "ran through his head," when he wanted to think about or remember it, much in the way a melody "runs through the heads" of lesser mortals like me. Might we then think of Bach's *ricercare* "running through his head" as a mental "performance" of the work? Perhaps that *is* the right way to think about it.[20] One is reminded, in this regard, of the statement attributed to Brahms, on his being invited out to attend a performance of *Don Giovanni* (I think it was). "Why should I bother?" he is supposed to have said, pointing to his score of the work; "I can have a better performance at home," meaning, of course, that all he needed to do to "hear" the music of *Don Giovanni* was to read his score. But if, at least when Bach was *conscious* of his *ricercare*, a "performance" of it was "running through his head," it makes perfect sense to ask: A performance (instance) of *what*? The work (kind or universal) of course; and before there was any notation of it. And here is where I feel impelled, wrongly perhaps, to take the Platonic plunge.

Margolis believes it no small advantage of his own way of thinking that it avoids "the extreme implausibility of platonizing with respect to art."[21] I hope I have succeeded in dispelling some of that apparent implausibility here. I am under no illusion that I have dispelled it all.

Notes

1 Joseph Margolis, *Art and Philosophy*, Atlantic Highlands, NJ: Humanities Press, 1980, p. 29.

2 Ibid., p. 75. See Nicholas Wolterstorff, "Toward an Ontology of Art Works," *Nous*, 9 (1975), and his more recent *Works and Worlds of Art*, Oxford: The Clarendon Press, 1980, of which more presently. Margolis is criticizing the earlier view; but the criticism can be directed with equal force at the later version.

3 Margolis, op. cit., p. 22.

4 Ibid., p. 75.

5 Jerrold Levinson, "What a Musical Work Is," *Journal of Philosophy*, 77 (1980), p. 6. [See this volume.]

6 Ibid., p. 9.

7 Ibid., pp. 8–9.

8 Jack Glickman, "Creativity in the Arts," *Culture and Art*, ed. Lars Aagaard-Mogensen, Atlantic Highlands, NJ: Humanities Press, 1976, p. 136.

9 Margolis, op. cit., p. 22.

10 Ibid., p. 75.

11 R. A. Sharpe, "Type, Token, Interpretation and Performance," *Mind*, 88 (1979). A criticism of Sharpe, along different lines, can be found in R. A. Dipert, "Types and Tokens: A Reply to Sharpe," *Mind*, 89 (1980), and Sharpe's reply in "Performing an Interpretation: A Reply," *Mind*, 91 (1982).

12 Sharpe, "Type, Token, Interpretation and Performance," p. 438.

13 Ibid.

14 Ibid., p. 439.

15 Wolterstorff, *Works and Worlds of Art*, p. 62.

16 Ibid., p. 56.

17 Ibid., p. 58.

18 Ibid., p. 64.

19 Ibid., p. 67.

20 We should not be misled, here, by a widely circulated, but undoubtedly spurious letter in which Mozart is made out to say that he imagines music atemporally, the whole before him in one instantaneous synoptic view. The feat is impossible – perhaps even *logically*, as some have claimed of God's supposed atemporal perception of temporal events.

21 Margolis, op. cit., p. 22.

11

Art Works as Action Types

Gregory Currie

1 Introduction

The aim of this chapter is to provide an argument for the hypothesis that art works are action types (ATH). It will be useful, however, if we begin by examining some alternative theories current in the literature and showing that they are deficient in various ways. This discussion will enable us to formulate a number of constraints on an ontology of art. It will then be shown that the ATH meets these constraints. In this way we do no more than build a provisional case for the ATH. There may be other theories that meet the constraints equally well. There may be constraints not considered here that the ATH does not meet. My aim is only to make the ATH seem a plausible hypothesis.

2 The Structural Account of the Work

Since the empiricist thinks that the aesthetic qualities of the work depend essentially only on how it looks, or how it sounds, or what sequence of words it contains, it seems natural for the empiricist to say simply that the work itself is a certain pattern of lines and colours, structure of sounds, or sequence of words. Thus a painting is a visual pattern, something that a particular physical object can instantiate by having that pattern painted on its surface; a musical work is a certain structure of sounds,

Gregory Currie, "Art Works as Action Types," chapter 3 (edited by the editor for this volume) from Gregory Currie, *An Ontology of Art* (London: Macmillan, 1989), pp. 46–84.

something that a certain performance can instantiate when the performers produce tokens of those sounds in the correct order; and a literary work is a sequence of words (i.e. a kind of structure), something that a certain physical object (e.g. bundle of pages) can instantiate when tokens of those words are inscribed on it. Any other view about what the work is would be ontologically inflationary from the empiricist's point of view, since it would invoke redundant structure, and empiricists are well known for their horror of ontological excess. The hypothesis that the work is a pattern or structure of the kind just described identifies the work with that thing which contains just enough structure to determine the work's aesthetic properties and no more. When we confront the pattern or structure we come into contact with all that we need in order to appreciate the work; therefore the work just is that pattern or structure. Let us call this view 'structuralism'. Structuralism, as I define it, is the natural ontology of the aesthetic empiricist.

... We must decide whether it is possible simultaneously to hold that a work is a pattern or structure in the sense of the previous paragraph, and that it has aesthetic properties not determined by (supervenient upon) that structure. In what follows I shall concentrate on musical and literary works, leaving the visual arts out of account until the end. In fact most of my examples will be from music.

Someone who attempts a combination of views such as I have just described is Richard Wollheim.[1] He treats literary and musical works as types. Wollheim does not give us much information about what he takes a type to be. But presumably his idea is that, just as a word type is a sequence of letter types, a literary work is a sequence of word types and hence ultimately a sequence of letter types (among which we include spaces and punctuation marks). So while the instances of the work are sequences of word tokens, the work is the corresponding sequences of word types. The natural extension of this to the musical case would be to say that the work is a sequence of sound types, these sound types being describable by expressions like 'B flat above middle C/semiquaver'. (Where the work involves more than one 'voice' we must treat it as a sequence of sequences. The term 'structure' is therefore most appropriate for musical works.) Thus types are structures in our sense, and a token of the work is simply a corresponding sequence of sound tokens; the work and its instances are structurally the same. A similar view (complicated somewhat by his nominalism) is that of Nelson Goodman: 'A literary work . . . is . . . the text or script itself' (1968, p. 209). Thus both Goodman and Wollheim think of the literary work as identified purely in terms of its word sequence.

Now neither of these authors has much sympathy with the empiricist aesthetic, and Wollheim certainly does not regard the work's aesthetic properties as supervenient upon its structure alone. Neither author confronts the issue raised here, though Goodman remarks at one point that in characterising the work itself we need not worry that we are not characterising all its properties (1968, pp. 209–10). This remark suggests the following treatment of the problem. In each possible world we identify the work in terms of its structure, for the work just is that structure. In different such worlds the work will have different histories of production, generated by the different activities of its composer (or author) and by differences in the surrounding art-historical context. Thus we make a distinction between properties that the work has essentially (properties it has in all possible worlds in which it exists) and properties that it has non-essentially (properties that it has in some worlds but not in others). The structure of the work will be an essential property, while its history will be inessential. Correspondingly, any aesthetic properties of the work that are (at least partly) a function of the work's history will be properties that the work has inessentially. Thus while this view admits, against the empiricist, that the work's aesthetic properties are partly a function

of its history, it retains an empiricist-minded regard for pure structure; the structure is essential, the history accidental. If there are any aesthetic properties determined by structure alone (I think that there are not) they will be essential properties of the work. Those that involve history as well will be accidental. Consistently with this view it may be said that it is an essential property of a work that it has a history that is relevant to the determination of its aesthetic properties. But what history it has will vary from world to world.

Our business is now to see whether this way of having an empiricist ontology without an empiricist's aesthetic is tenable. I shall argue that it is not, and I shall try to show that the position is susceptible to an objection that has been put by Jerrold Levinson.[2] Levinson has in fact two objections, one less significant in its consequences than the other, but it is worth stating both of them. I begin with the less significant one.

3 Musical Works and Performance Means

Levinson makes the point that the view of musical works as pure sound structures cannot be correct because considerations of performance means would thereby be left completely out of account. If someone produces by purely electronic means a pattern of sounds that conforms to the notes laid down in the score of Beethoven's Hammerklavier Sonata, has he thereby produced an instance of the work? Intuitions here may differ, but what is surely much clearer is that he has not produced a *correct* instance of it. It is an integral feature of the work that it is to be performed only in certain ways. A performance that violates the composer's directions as to how the sounds are to be produced is not a correct performance of it. But if works are pure sound structures then anything which is an instance of that structure must surely be equally an instance of the work. The purely structural view can be rescued from this objection by being modified in the following way. We do not any longer regard the work as a structure of pure sound-types, the elements of which are specified purely in terms of their sonic properties, but a structure of sounds-as-produced-by-certain-instruments. Thus the tokens of the type Middle-C-as-produced-by-a-violin are all notes produced by violins. This version of the work-as-type theory takes into account the fact that performance means is integral to the work. Let us call structures of sounds-as-produced-on-certain-instruments 'applied structures'. The structural view we shall consider from now on is the view that works are such applied structures.

4 An Objection to the Structural View

However, there is a more significant objection to be brought against the structural theory. Suppose it happens that two composers, working independently, produce identical scores. Have they produced the same work or distinct works? On the structural view they have presented us with recipes for performing tokens of the same type; they have composed the same work.

Levinson finds this consequence objectionable for two reasons. He finds it objectionable, first, because it makes the identification of works independent of their histories; and secondly because it fails to recognise that works are created rather than discovered by their composers. I think that Levinson's first objection is correct; his second not. Let us consider these objections in turn.

Levinson gives a number of examples of imaginary situations in which there are works that have the same sound structure or are correctly performable in the same way, but in which it seems we are confronted by different works because they have different histories of production. Here is one of the examples he gives.

> Brahms's Piano Sonata Opus 2 (1852), an early work, is strongly *Liszt-influenced*, as any perceptive listener can discern. However, a work identical with it in sound structure, but written by Beethoven, could hardly have the property of being *Liszt-influenced*. And it would have a visionary quality that Brahms's piece does not have. (1980, p. 12, italics in the original)

Thus the imaginary Beethoven sonata and the Brahms sonata are distinct works, even though they are the same from the structural point of view.

One objection to this example may quickly be disposed of. The objection is that cases like this do not concern properties of works, but rather properties of the composer's activity in producing the work. In that case they are examples of composers arriving in different ways at the same work. *Being Liszt-influenced* is not, on this view, a property of

the work, but rather a property of Brahms's compositional activity. To say this is certainly contrary to the practice of informed criticism in the arts, which emphasises features of the work such as originality of thematic invention or of orchestration. And critics clearly regard an understanding of such features as important for an understanding of the work itself. The point becomes more obvious if we consider a case more extreme even than Levinson's. Suppose, for instance, that Brahms had merely produced a slight variation on a work by Liszt. The resulting work would be very insignificant. But if Beethoven, uninfluenced by Liszt, had produced a work with the same sound structure he would surely have produced a much more important work.

While Levinson's example is, I think, a counter-example to the purely structural view as we have interpreted it (that is, as involving a distinction between essential structure and inessential history) we must resolve an ambiguity that lurks in the description of this and similar examples that Levinson gives. Is Levinson offering us a counterfactual situation (possible world) in which it is Beethoven *instead* of Brahms who composes Piano Sonata Opus 2, or a possible situation in which Beethoven composes a work with the same sound structure as Brahms's later work of which Brahms (and, we had better say, everybody else) was ignorant at the time when Brahms came around to composing his work? The difference I am pointing to is the difference between a world in which something happens *instead of* that which actually happens, and a world in which something happens *in addition to* what actually happens. If we interpret Levinson in the former way, we must treat his example from the point of view of *interworld* comparison of works; if the latter, it is an example that we must treat from the point of view of *intraworld* comparison between works. (Levinson's words, here and in other passages, suggest the former interpretation, but this is not the important point. The point is that the examples can be construed in these two different ways.[3])

Suppose that we interpret Levinson's examples in the first way. It is clear that the structuralist may respond by saying that the story as told is consistent with the idea that we are dealing with the same work in distinct possible worlds. He might say that all Levinson has established with an example like this is that works do not have their aesthetic properties essentially; that is, they do not have the same aesthetic properties in all the worlds in which they exist. And that has already been granted by the structuralist. Levinson has shown us that, while Brahms's Piano Sonata Opus 2 actually has the aesthetic quality of being Liszt-influenced, there are possible worlds in which it does not have that quality, and in some of these worlds the work has a visionary quality that it does not have in the actual world. So Levinson has given a counter-example to the claim that the aesthetic qualities of a work are (all) among its essential properties; he has not given a counter-example to the claim that the work's identity is independent of its history of production.

This response, whatever its merits, would have no force against the example if it were construed in the second way. On the second interpretation, we are to think of a world in which Beethoven composes a work (uninfluenced, of course, by Liszt); later Brahms composes a work with the same sound structure, under the influence of Liszt (but knowing nothing of this particular work by Beethoven). If we agree that properties like *being visionary*, and *being influenced by the work of Liszt* are properties of the work, rather than merely properties of the compositional activity of the composer – and the argument given above certainly suggests that they are – then we have a case which is undoubtedly a case of the composition of distinct works. One and the same work cannot be both visionary and non-visionary in the same world, for nothing can have a property and the negation of that property within a world. So we had better assume that Levinson's example is to be construed in this, second, way.

We now have a counter-example to the structuralist view of the work's identity. For on this view, two composers or authors who independently produce the same structure have produced the same work. But we have seen that there are possible cases where we want to say that distinct compositional acts result in distinct works with the same structure. And we have done this, moreover, without having to assume that a work has its aesthetic properties essentially. (We shall return to the question of essential properties in Section 17.)

5   Correct and Incorrect Instances of a Work

Before moving further towards our construction of a positive alternative to the structuralist view, I want to consider one other version of structuralism, because in doing so we shall make a distinction that will be important to us. We shall continue with our development of the argument in Section 7.

Nicholas Wolterstorff has offered an account of the nature of works that shares similarities with Wollheim's and Goodman's.[4] Wolterstorff's theory is best understood as a response to the following problem. Must every instance of a work be a correct instance of it? Let us concentrate here on the cases of literature and music. A correct instance of a novel is a copy that is correctly spelt; a correct performance of a sonata is one that conforms to all the requirements laid down in the score. Can something be said to be an instance of a novel if it is not correctly spelt? Can something be an instance of a sonata if it is not correctly performed? The tough-minded view that encourages a negative answer can hardly be right. Consider Jane Austen's original MS of *Emma*. Suppose, as is certainly possible, that it contains an error, in the sense that it contains a word not spelt according to the norms of spelling that prevailed at the time the work was written. Now there are two ways of interpreting the thesis that every instance of a work must be correctly spelt. On one interpretation being correctly spelt means being spelt in exactly the same way that the original was spelt. On that interpretation, every instance of *Emma* must contain exactly the same spelling mistake as the original – hardly a plausible view. On the other interpretation, being correctly spelt means conforming exactly to the rules of spelling prevailing at the time and in the place where the work was written. In that case Austen's MS would not itself be an instance of the work. Again, this is highly implausible. I conclude that we need a distinction between instances and correct instances of a work (the latter being a subclass of the former). I admit, however, that I can see no way in which *being an instance of* can be made a precise property. A copy that was so badly mis-spelt as to be unintelligible would, presumably, not count as an instance of the work it was intended to be an instance of. But we cannot say 'if the text has *n* or more deviations in spelling then it is not an instance of the relevant work', if for no other reason than that mistakes have to be weighted by context. Some spelling mistakes are more serious and confusing than others. *Being an instance of* is an ineluctably vague concept, but so are a lot of other concepts that we would find it hard to do without.

What we have said about the spelling of a literary work has an obvious analogy in the case of music. An instance of a musical work – a performance of it – is correct if it is played in accordance with the score, without deviation in pitch, intensity or means of performance from what the score allows. But clearly we want to say that there can be performances of a work that are genuinely instances of the work even though they are incorrect to some degree.

Nelson Goodman is an energetic defender of the view that strict conformity in spelling (or, in the case of music, strict conformity to the score) is a necessary condition for something being an instance of the work (he also thinks that it is a sufficient condition).[5] He recognises, indeed, that this hardly conforms to our ordinary ways of speaking about instances of works. He defends this discrepancy by saying that 'the exigencies that dictate our technical discourse need [not] govern our everyday speech. I am no more recommending that in ordinary discourse we refuse to say that a pianist who misses a note has performed a Chopin Polonaise than that we refuse to call a whale a fish, the earth spherical, or a grayish-pink human white' (1968, p. 187).

The analogy is misleading. We can all accept that while it is useful for certain purposes, or appropriate in certain conversational circumstances, to say that the earth is spherical, it is not really spherical. But consider again the case in which the MS of *Emma* contains a spelling error. Do we want to say that, while for certain purposes Austen's MS may be described as an instance of *Emma*, it is not really one? Or, to consider the alternative way of treating the case available to someone of Goodman's persuasion, do we want to say that, while my copy of *Emma* which does not contain the same spelling error may for some purposes be described as an instance of *Emma*, it is not really one? Neither alternative is palatable. While *being spherical* is a concept capable of precise definition which we may sometimes apply in a loose way, the concept *being an instance of*, as it applies to works of art like novels and sonatas, has a vagueness about it that can be removed only by doing violence to the concept itself. (This is not true, of course, of the concept *being a correct instance of*, which is precise.)

6 Works as Norm-Kinds

One account of the work which is intended to accommodate the possibility of incorrect instances of a work is Nicholas Wolterstorff's analysis of works as *norm-kinds*. He asks us to acknowledge a category of things which are kinds. For every property of the form *being an F* there is a kind F which things that have that property belong to. Now some kinds are normative in the sense that they can have both correct and incorrect instances. For something to be a tiger it must have all the essential properties of tigerhood, but it may lack some property necessary for being a properly formed tiger; suppose, for instance, that it has only three legs. *Tiger* is a (natural) norm kind and the Hammerklavier Sonata is a (non-natural) norm kind. Understood as norm-kinds works do not possess the properties that our usual talk attributes to them. Thus we say of the work that is Bartok's First String Quartet that it has a G sharp in its seventh measure. But on Wolterstorff's view this is not a property of the work, though it may be a property of some instances of the work and will be a property of any correct instance of it. When we say of a work that it has a G sharp in its seventh measure we mean, according to Wolterstorff, that it has the following property; *being such that something cannot be a correct instance of it without having a G sharp in its seventh measure*. Thus what the work-as-type version of structuralism explains as a type-token ambiguity, the work-as-norm-kind theory explains as the systematic suppression of an operator: 'being such that something cannot be a correct instance of the work without having property P.'[6]

This is a minimal account of Wolterstorff's theory. But we do not have to probe the resources of the theory very far in order to discover its fundamental flaw; the same flaw, indeed, that we discovered in the work-as-type version of structuralism. Suppose that two composers independently pick out the same norm kind by making the same properties normative within the kind. On Wolterstorff's view, they have both picked out the same musical work. Once we know how a work is properly to be played, then we know all there is to know about the identity of the work itself. Similarly, on the view that works are types, two composers who pick out the same sound structure will have picked out the same work. There is no room for the idea of distinct works with the same sound structure. How much of a deficiency in an account of works this consequence is has been pointed out in Section 4.

7 Works as Created

Levinson offers as an alternative to the structural view his own account of the nature of the work, an account that we shall have reason to reject. Before I describe his theory I shall present one further piece of motivation that he provides for it, for this will be important to us in Section 9.

Levinson has another objection to the structuralist view, based on his insistence that to compose (and he would presumably say, to write or paint) is to create. The artist with whom we associate a work is the person who, in virtue of his compositional activities, brings the work into being. But if we identify the work with a structure of sounds we must say that the work is something that exists eternally.[7] It is not clear to me that this is the only option open to someone who identifies the work with a sound structure. A rather complicated argument might be provoked by someone who claimed that certain abstract entities like sound structures are created. But we need not resolve that complex issue here, for the question reduces to something rather simpler. If your view is that composition is creation (or at least involves creation) then you must take the view that the same work cannot be composed on two different occasions (in the same possible world). For to create is to bring into being, and you cannot bring into being what already exists. Of course, one may want to argue that a work can be composed on distinct occasions if, sometime between the two, it is destroyed; in that case something is brought into being, destroyed, and then brought into being again. I am not sure that the idea employed here of numerically the same object being destroyed and then recreated again makes sense, but we will suppose that it does. So in order to find out what views about the ontology of art are inconsistent with the hypothesis that composition is creation we must find out what views allow a work to be composed on distinct occasions without intervening destruction.

Clearly the structuralist theory allows this. Two composers may independently present scores which specify the same structure of sound types (as relativised to instruments). And this would be the multiple composition of the same work. And Wolterstorff's theory also allows distinct composers independently to specify the same norm kind: to specify the same properties as normative within the work. And these things would be possible even if nothing happened between the first composition and the second to bring about a

destruction of the work. All that is required is that the second composer work in ignorance of the first. On views like these, then, to compose a work is not necessarily to create it. We return to the question of creation in Section 9.

8 Works as Indicated Structures

Levinson develops an account of works which builds a work's history into the conditions for its identity, and makes it the case that composition is creation. On his view a work is not merely an applied sound structure but a structure-as-indicated-by-C-at-t, where C is the composer and t is the time of composition.[8] The structure itself is admitted to be an eternally existing entity. The composer 'indicates' this structure S when he composes. But through the act of indicating, the composer brings something else into existence, namely, S-as-indicated-by-himself-at-t. Before t no relation obtained between C and S; composition establishes a relation of indication between them. As a result of the compositional act the world contains a new entity, S-as-indicated-by-C-at-t. This theory has the dual advantages, says Levinson, that it ensures that a work is created rather than discovered, and that works with the same sound structure composed in different situations by different people will be different works.[9]

In some ways Levinson's proposal is, I think, on the right lines. He is certainly right to think that the work is not simply a structure of abstract elements; its historical dimension must somehow be built into it. But his proposal as it stands is unacceptable. Note first that there are, on Levinson's account, two distinct things done by the composer. He discovers a certain pre-existent sound structure, and at the same time composes – that is creates – a musical work. What he discovers is S, what he composes is S-as-indicated-by-C-at-t; call it S'. But what exactly is S'? This is metaphysically obscure, to say the least. Columbus discovered America (let us suppose). In doing so, did he bring into being a new entity; America-as-discovered-by-Columbus? Fleming discovered penicillin; in the process of doing so did he bring into being penicillin-as-discovered-by-Fleming? What sort of entity would that be, if it is not simply identical with penicillin? If Levinson's arguments establish the existence of indicated structures in the arts, they seem to establish their existence in a number of other areas where they are not wanted. And in no sense do we have a grip on what these entities might be. It is hard to resist the conclusion that Levinson has merely postulated a kind of entity in order to solve his problem, without being able to tell us anything informative about that entity's nature.

However, it might be said that this objection concentrates on an inessential element in Levinson's theory. For the real content of Levinson's theory may be taken to be a claim about the identity conditions for works. We may in that case take him as telling us not what works are but when works are identical. And as Frege made clear for the case of numbers, telling us when things are identical does not amount to telling us what they are.[10] So we can leave the question of what works are in temporary obscurity and concentrate on Levinson's claim about their identity conditions. On this question we may take him to be saying that indicated structures involve three essential components; a structure, a person (composer) and a time (of composition). Indicated structures are the same if these three elements are the same. Given this, we might suppose ourselves able to generate a direct counter-example to Levinson's theory in the following way. Consider a case very like the one we quoted earlier from Levinson: Imagine that by 1852 Liszt had not written any piano music, or any music at all. In that case Brahms's Piano Opus 2 of 1852 would not be Liszt-influenced. It would be a more original work than it in fact is.

In this case we imagine a possible world in which the work retains its structure, composer and time of composition (and hence its identity) but in which it has an aesthetic property that it lacks in the actual world. But of course this is no counter-example to Levinson's proposal as long as he is willing to concede that works do not have (all) their aesthetic properties essentially; that they have aesthetic properties in some worlds that they do not have in others. But now we can see that it is much harder to find a direct counter-example to Levinson's theory than it was to find counter-examples to the structural view. For we cannot alter the example in such a way that we imagine the same work to be presented twice under different circumstances in the same world. Levinson rules this out by making time and authorship of composition integral to the work; two independently working composers who produce the same score do not compose the same work on Levinson's view. Perhaps if we worked hard enough with the idea of a brain-bisected, ambidextrous composer who wrote out the same score simultaneously with both hands, each half of his brain drawing on distinct musical ideas, we could generate a counter-example, but it would very likely be a rather lame one. I shall not try to construct such an example.

However, I think that we can still give some arguments against Levinson (in addition to the argument already given about metaphysical obscurity). Let us see how well his theory of work identification fits with our intuitions. Imagine two worlds, w_1 and w_2, which differ from the actual world in the following ways. In w_1 Beethoven composes a work that has exactly the same sound structure as his Hammerklavier Sonata except that at one place there is a note to be played slightly differently (fill out the example in such a way that the difference is as insignificant as any such difference can be). Otherwise, w_1 does not differ from the actual world in any significant musico–historical way. In w_2, however, there are rather larger divergencies from the actual world. In w_2 Beethoven composes in 1817 a work identical in sound structure to the Hammerklavier Sonata. But he does so in an exceedingly impoverished musico–historical setting. Suppose in fact that this composition is the first to be written since the time of Purcell, the art of composition having somehow been lost. This would surely be an astonishing achievement. Now it seems to me that, from an intuitive point of view, we are no more inclined to regard the work in w_1 as distinct from the Hammerklavier Sonata than we are to regard the work in w_2 as identical with it. But Levinson's identity conditions on works force us to say that in w_1 the work is not the Hammerklavier Sonata, and that in w_2 it is. Further, it seems clearly wrong to make the time of composition constitutive of the work. Surely at least some works might have been composed a few days (hours, minutes?) later or earlier than they in fact were. Levinson's theory makes this impossible. And it is far from clear that composer identity is integral to the work; imagine a possible world in which Beethoven and Schubert swap musical careers. Everything done musically by Beethoven in the actual world is done by Schubert in this world, and vice versa. Thus in this world all Beethoven's actual achievements are Schubert's, and vice versa. But surely we want to say of such a case that Beethoven composed all of Schubert's works and Schubert all of Beethoven's. Again, Levinson's theory precludes us from saying this.

An attempt to rescue something of Levinson's idea has been made by James Anderson.[11]

Anderson agrees that it is counter-intuitive to say that composer and time of composition are integral to the work's identity, but he wants to follow Levinson in ruling out the possibility of composers independently composing the same work in different musico-historical circumstances. The solution he comes up with is to define a work in such a way that, while the identity of its composer and the time of composition are left unspecified, it is stipulated that no work can be composed more than once in a given world. His definition looks like this:

$MW = S/PM$ as indicated by no more than one P per possible world at exactly one t per possible world,

where MW is a musical work, S/PM a 'sound/performance means structure' (an applied structure in our sense), and P and t are person and time variables respectively.

But this suggestion quickly comes to grief. For it has the consequence that in any world where composers come independently to the same sound structure, neither of them has composed a work. For something to be a work, it must be indicated only once in a given world. This would be violated in such an example. Thus, far from it being the case that this proposal sustains the intuition that distinct composers independently coming to the same sound structure in different musico-historical contexts present different works, it turns out that they do not present any works at all. If someone ignorant of musical history should tomorrow think up the sound structure of the Hammerklavier Sonata, it would then suddenly become true that Beethoven did not compose that work at all. But whether Beethoven composed that work surely cannot depend upon what happens later. This proposal is clearly no advance on Levinson's.

9   Are Works Created?

Levinson's identification of works with indicated structures is motivated, as we have seen, by a desire to endorse the view that a work is created by the artist associated with it. This motivation is certainly widely acknowledged; but is it correct? I shall argue that works of art are not created. I shall not, however, be arguing for the view that they are discovered. The relation of artist to work is different from both discovery and creation. We shall see why in Section 14.

We have agreed that, with reservations about destruction, a work cannot be created and then created again at a later time (in the same world, that is). In order to show that composition is not creation I shall produce an example where it seems intuitively clear that we do have such a case of multiple composition.

Our problem is to find a case where a work is composed on two different occasions. Now given what I have said about the dependence of the work's identity on its history of production, it looks as if it will be very difficult to find an example where independently produced works have exactly the same history of production. Surely two artists working independently will always be situated in musico-historical contexts that differ in some way or other. As Levinson says, 'even small differences in musico-historical context . . . seem certain to induce some change in kind or degree in some aesthetic or artistic quality, however difficult it might be to pinpoint this change verbally' (1980, p. 13). Thus Levinson's challenge is to construct a case where distinct artists working independently of each other are in exactly the same musico-historical situation.

Now talk of sameness of context or situation is subject to a type – token ambiguity. Two people may be in the same *type* of situation but not literally in the same (token) situation. I suggest that all we need here is a case of sameness of type of situation, as long as sameness is guaranteed in a very precise way. We need Hilary Putnam's idea of 'Twin Earth'.[12]

Imagine that there is, somewhere in the universe, a Twin Earth; a planet that is in every qualitative respect exactly like our own, except, of course, that it is inhabited by people different from us. By 'qualitatively the same' I mean that one cannot tell these planets apart by looking at what is going on in them. Each of us has a *doppelgänger* on the other planet who is physically indistinguishable from us, performs the same action (types) that we perform, thinks all the thoughts we think, experiences the same sensations. Our cultural and physical environments are the same, except for the identity of objects.[13] All the actions and achievements accomplished on Earth, including all the artistic ones, are duplicated on Twin Earth. In particular, Beethoven has a twin on Twin Earth. Everything that we would say about Beethoven's achievement in composing the Hammerklavier Sonata we would say about Twin Beethoven's achievement in producing a work with the same sound structure. Beethoven and Twin Beethoven solve the same musical problems in the same way, under the same influences and with the same degree of originality, coming up with that sound structure. There is no aesthetic feature of the one that is not an aesthetic feature of the other. Every judgement we would make about the one, *qua* art work, we would make about the other. Therefore, I claim, they each independently produce the same work.

Imagine also, to make the example a little more forceful, that while Twin Earth society develops in exactly the same way that Earth society develops (and independently of it), it develops somewhat later. In that case I think we ought to say that every work of art composed on Earth is composed somewhat later on Twin Earth. And in the time that elapses between the occurrence of composition on Earth and occurrence of composition on Twin Earth let us suppose that no work is destroyed. In that case we have a counter-example to the claim that composition is creation. For we have an example where works are composed on Earth and then later on Twin Earth.

Now someone who identifies composition with creation – let us call him the 'creationist' – may reply that the example can be described in such a way as to be consistent with his view. In the situation that I have described, Beethoven's Hammerklavier Sonata is first of all created on Earth by Beethoven, and then discovered on Twin Earth by Twin Beethoven. Works certainly are created, but once created they become part of the furniture of the universe and are available to be discovered. In the situation just described it would then look to the inhabitants of Twin Earth as if Twin Beethoven had composed the work but he would not in fact have done so. He would merely have discovered something already brought into existence.

But this reply is not a satisfactory one. Imagine a variation of our story. Everything that happens on Twin Earth happens slightly earlier than the corresponding events on Earth. In that case it would not be Beethoven who created the Hammerklavier Sonata but Twin Beethoven. But of course this possible situation might conceivably be the actual situation; there might be a Twin Earth somewhere in deep space. In that case the creationist cannot say definitely that Beethoven composed that work; on his own account the history of our culture is consistent with the possibility that he discovered it, in which case he would not have composed it. But this would be a very odd thing to say

of a situation in which Beethoven came to the sound structure of that sonata quite independently of anyone else. If he did come to that sound structure independently then surely, in the ordinary sense of 'compose', Beethoven did compose the work. To say that he might not have composed the work in that situation is to stipulate a new, technical, meaning for 'composition', not to explicate its ordinary meaning. It cannot be part of the concept of composition that composers create their works.

Of course the creationist could object to the example on the grounds that, since distinct composers are involved, distinct works must be involved too. But this is just to insist upon the point that composer identity is integral to work identity, it is not to argue for it. On the other hand, the position I advocate here seems well suited to an aesthetic based on the idea of artistic achievement. To appreciate the work is to appreciate the artist's achievement; if two artists achieve the same thing, why should we count their works as distinct?

At this point the creationist might issue a challenge of his own. If works are not, in fact, created, how is it that we all unreflectively think of them as created? Indeed, would it not be reasonable to argue in the following way? The overwhelming majority of us think that works are created. The best explanation of this convergence of opinion is that works are created and that we are aware of that fact.

Arguments like this deserve to be taken seriously, and I wish I could reply to this one by offering a better explanation of convergence than the one just canvassed. Unfortunately I cannot. However, this lack, deplorable though it may be, does not affect the dialectic of the present dispute. While I admit that I do not have a good explanation of why people should be so willing to believe something that I take to be wrong, the kind of creationist that I am arguing against here is in exactly the same position. Let us see why.

At this stage in the argument we have abandoned the view that works are structures (pure or applied). This view just gives the wrong results about the identity and diversity of works. And it is agreed by the remaining parties to the dispute that there can be cases of the multiple composition of works with the same sound structure. So it is agreed that the composer does not create the sound structure of his work. Those who think that he creates his work think that he creates something distinct from (though possibly involving) that sound structure. So the kind of creationist I am considering here agrees with me that, for example, Beethoven did not create the sound structure of the Hammerklavier Sonata. But that is exactly what is denied by pre-philosophical opinion, which identifies the work with the associated sound structure. Most people would say, I believe, that Beethoven created that very sound structure. (My own informal canvassing of opinion indicates this.) In that case, the creationist is in exactly the same position with respect to naive opinion that I am in, and cannot get any advantage from pointing out that I deviate from it.

10   Some Constraints on Theory

The purpose of the foregoing discussion has been partly to reveal the defects in extant theories about the nature of art works, and partly to lay the foundations for a better theory by suggesting a number of constraints that an acceptable theory must meet. We are now in a position to specify what these constraints are.

1.   What is partly constitutive of a given work is its pattern or structure. No theory of art works that made the structure extrinsic or incidental to the work itself could hope for acceptance. It is not just an accidental fact about *Emma* that it contains that particular word sequence. It is not just an accidental fact about the Hammerklavier Sonata that it contains that sound structure.
2.   The structure is, however, only partly constitutive of the work. Distinct works may possess the same structure. In cases like that, what differentiates the works is the circumstances in which the composer or author arrived at the structure. So we must find a way of capturing this idea of 'the circumstances in which the artist arrived at the pattern or structure' and try to build it into our account of the work itself.
3.   Our ontology of art must make it possible for cases of multiple composition, such as that described in our Twin Earth example, to occur. But it must not identify multiple composition with the independent presentation of the same structure. We must, in other words, find a middle way between the excesses of the structuralist view, which makes multiple composition too easy, and the creationist view, which makes it impossible.
4.   We want to avoid the inclusion of inessential elements as constitutive of the work. Our earlier discussion suggests that the composer's identity and the time of composition are such inessential elements.

Another constraint may be derived from the arguments of earlier chapters. We remarked in Section 1 that an ontology of art works should mesh with our preferred theory about the nature of appreciation. I hold that appreciation of the work is an appreciation of the artist's achievement. So we have

5.   Our account of the nature of art works must contribute to our understanding of the sense in which aesthetic appreciation is the appreciation of a certain kind of performance.

There is one further issue that an ontology of art works must decide, though the considerations at work here do not impose a compelling constraint on our theory one way or the other. Our first constraint tells us that a work's pattern or structure is intrinsic to it. We have not yet given a very precise formulation to this idea. We shall do so in the next section. And we must decide whether this intrinsicality of structure is consistent with an intuition to which I appealed in Section 8: that it makes sense to consider a work's structure as subject to variation (of some perhaps minimal kind) across possible worlds. We want to say, for instance, that 'The Hammerklavier Sonata might have had a different sound structure from the sound structure it does have.' I shall try to reconcile the intrinsicality of structure with the possibility of transworld variation of structure. The result will be presented in Section 17.

11   Works as Action Types

The hypothesis that most plausibly meets our constraints is, I suggest, the following: a work of art is an action type. We arrive at last at the ATH. To understand this proposal we shall have to take a brief excursion through the theory of action.

The type–token distinction has application to actions and other events. (I treat actions as a subclass of events.) There is a sense in which the same event can occur more than once. What we have in that case is many event tokens of the same event type. To add definiteness to our discussion I shall adopt the framework of one particular clear and serviceable theory of events; that due to Jaegwon Kim.[14] I think that Kim's theory is a good one, but there certainly are problems about it that I do not intend to discuss here. I hope that the things I am going to say about art works in the context of Kim's theory could be translated into the framework of some better theory of events, if there is one.

Kim takes an event token of the simplest kind to have three constitutive elements: an individual, a property and a time. Let us mark off expressions which designate events by putting a* at each end. Thus *John singing at time t* is an event which has as its constitutive individual John, its constitutive property x *is singing*, and its constitutive time t. An event can be something that occurs throughout an interval of time, e.g. *John singing between t_1 and t_2*. In that case the constitutive time is an interval rather than an instant. (In what follows I shall not distinguish between instants and intervals. To simplify the discussion further, I shall sometimes omit reference to time altogether.)

Events can also be relational. *Greg beating Alan at chess at time t* is an event with two constitutive objects, Greg and Alan, and a constitutive relation (two-place property), x *beats y at chess*. Now suppose I use a certain strategy S to beat Alan. Then *Greg beating Alan at chess using strategy S at time t* is an event which we can think of as having four constitutive elements; Greg, Alan and strategy S, and a three-place relation x *beats y at chess using strategy z*.

Turning to a more relevant case, consider the event which is Beethoven's composition of the Hammerklavier Sonata. Part of what this event involves is that Beethoven discovers a certain sound structure. Now there is, presumably, a story we can tell about the relevant circumstances of Beethoven's discovery. Telling that story informs us about the nature of Beethoven's achievement. If he cobbled the musical ideas together by acts of shameless plagiarism from several other composers, that achievement was not much. If he employed originality of melodic invention and boldness in harmonisation it was considerable. Let us introduce at this point the idea of a *heuristic path*.

Here I draw on the similarity between the assessment of a work of art and the appraisal of a scientific theory. I suggest that both kinds of appraisal are context relative. Theories that are empirically equivalent in the sense of having the same observational consequences may yet be differentially supported by the facts, because of the ways in which these theories are generated. To explain this idea some philosophers of science have found it useful to introduce the idea of a *heuristic*: a set of assumptions and directives about how to construct a theory. Scientific theories are not – at least not usually – devised by some immediate flash of insight. They are often painstakingly developed from simpler and less realistic pictures of the world that may have little empirical content, or from prior empirical theories that face anomalies of one kind or another. A heuristic helps to guide the scientist's progress towards his theory by providing him with a set of assumptions; assumptions about what metaphysical constraints the new theory must conform to, what kinds of analogical models may be appealed to, what mathematical techniques are appropriate. Guided by a strong heuristic, the scientist may proceed to construct his theory in relative independence from empirical facts. The fewer facts that are used in the construction of the theory (e.g. in the fixing of parameters) the more facts will count as potential confirmation for the theory when its empirical consequences are tested. On this view a theory is not just a set of postulates together with their consequences. It is the deductive closure of the postulates together with the heuristic. It is this dual structure that is corroborated by the evidence, and theories that are deductively equivalent can be differentially confirmed, according to the ways in which their heuristics differ.[15]

In speaking of a scientist's 'heuristic path' to a theory I mean the process whereby the theory was arrived at; the facts, methods and assumptions employed, including analogical models, mathematical techniques and metaphysical ideas. I do not mean, of course, that there is a uniform method for generating theories. And I do not deny that any such method must rely at some stage upon pure inspiration or invention on the scientist's part. Theory construction is not in any sense a mechanical procedure. But it is a process that is at least to some degree rational and rationally reconstructible.

I wish to take over the spirit of this idea for our analysis of art works, though it will undergo modification in the process. For our previous discussion has made it plain that appreciation of an art work is not merely the appreciation of a final product – a visual pattern, a word or sound sequence – but an appreciation of the artist's achievement in arriving at that pattern or structure. The critic's task in

Gregory Currie

helping us to appreciate the work is partly to help us to see or experience things in the pattern or sequence that we might otherwise miss. But it is more than this. It is to help us to understand, by means of historical and biographical research, the way in which the artist arrived at the final product. He must show us in what ways the artist drew on existing works for his inspiration, and how far that product was the result of an original conception. He must show us what problems the artist had to resolve in order to achieve his end result, and how he resolved them. His job, in other words, is to trace, as closely as he can, the artist's heuristic path to the final product.

When we specify a composer's heuristic path to a sound structure we specify the aesthetically relevant facts about his actions in coming to that sound structure. Thus in specifying Brahms's heuristic path to Piano Sonata Opus 2 we will specify, amongst other things, the influence of Liszt's composition on Brahms. This idea clearly has application to the other art forms. Thus in specifying an author's heuristic path to the word sequence that is his text we will specify the influences on him, the sources of his ideas, the conventions of genre to which he conformed.[16]

Clearly, the task of specifying the artist's heuristic path to a certain structure is a matter of rationally reconstructing the detailed history of this creative thought, in so far as the information available to us allows that to be done. Part of the difficulty of appreciating works from alien or lost cultures lies in the almost total absence of material upon which to base such a reconstruction. And even in the most favourable cases the work of reconstruction can hardly be done with the assurance of completeness. But what seems clear is that critics do regard it as an essential part of their task to understand, as completely as they can, the history of production of a work, and to distil from it an account of the artistic problems faced by the artist and the methods he used to overcome them; in short, the artist's heuristic path. And this is not merely a useful adjunct to critical activity, but an integral part of it. The heuristic path is constitutive of the work itself.

Now *Beethoven's composition of the Hammerklavier Sonata* can be seen to have amongst its constitutive elements three things: Beethoven, the sound structure of the work, and Beethoven's heuristic path to that sound structure. Adding to these things the three-place relation x discovers y via heuristic path z, and the time of composition t, we

have enough to specify the event in question. Let us now introduce some more useful notation.

Following Kim, let '[A, $\mathbf{P}$, t]' denote the event which is the object A having property $\mathbf{P}$ at time t (properties and relations will be denoted by bold letters). A relational event can be expressed as '[A, B, $\mathbf{R}$, t]'; the event *A bearing the relation $\mathbf{R}$ to B at time t*. We can then represent the event which is *Beethoven's composition of the Hammerklavier Sonata* as [B, S, H, $\mathbf{D}$, t] where B is Beethoven, S is the sound structure of the work, H Beethoven's heuristic path to S, $\mathbf{D}$ the (three-place) relation x discovers y via heuristic path z, and t the time of composition.

Now we can introduce the distinction between types and tokens in the following way. Suppose that John sings at time t_1 and Fred sings at time t_2. We have two tokens of the same event type, representable respectively as [J, S, t_1] and [F, S, t_2]. What these two events have in common after we subtract the identities of the constitutive objects and the times of occurrence is the type of which these events are both tokens. So let us denote such an event type in this way: [χ, S, τ], where the χ and the τ are variables that replace definite objects and times respectively. (Let us reserve τ for use as time variable.)

Now if we have a relational event like *Greg beating Alan at chess at t*, which we may represent as [G, A, $\mathbf{B}$, t], we can abstract from it the event type, victories at chess, of which there can be many tokens. We represent that type as '[χ, y, $\mathbf{B}$, τ]'. Now the same event token may be a token of many distinct types. *Greg beating Alan at chess* is also a token of the type chess victories by Greg, which we may represent as [G, y, $\mathbf{B}$, τ], and a token of the type chess defeats of Alan, which we may represent as [χ, A, $\mathbf{B}$, τ]. These last two event types have two constitutive elements. They are both partly constituted by the relation x beats y at chess ($\mathbf{B}$); and one is partly constituted by the object Greg, the other by the object Alan.

Now consider the musical event [B, S, H, $\mathbf{D}$, t]. This is an event token from which we can derive, by our process of abstraction, several distinct event types. Consider the type that we would represent as [χ, S, H, $\mathbf{D}$, τ]. This is the event type, discovering of S via heuristic path H. There can be many instances of this event type, one for each pair of choices of replacement for χ and τ. One instance of it is the act of discovery performed by Beethoven himself; this is an event that has actually occurred.

114

Another instance is Twin Beethoven's discovery on Twin Earth. This event token has not, I take it, actually occurred, because Twin Earth does not exist.

My proposal now is to identify Beethoven's Hammerklavier Sonata with the event type [χ, S, H, **D**, τ]. In general, an art work will be an action type with two 'open places' (one for a person, one for a time) and having three constitutive elements: a structure, a heuristic and the relation x *discovers* y *by means of* z. This last **D** is a constant element in all art works. It is the other two elements that serve to distinguish art works from one another. Consequently, it is these two things that I shall speak of as constitutive of the work, forgetting about **D**. Let us call these the work's 'identifying elements'.

Let us see that this proposal meets all our constraints. First of all, on the proposed identification it comes out true that the work has two identifying elements, a structure and a heuristic. Alter either of these things and you alter the identity of the work itself. The type contains all the information necessary to appreciate the work. Thus the proposal meets our first two constraints.

Secondly, the proposal makes it true that the work can be composed more than once in the same possible world. The work is composed by anyone who performs an action that instantiates the event type [χ, S, H, **D**, τ], as is the case in our hypothetical Twin Earth example. But it is not, on this view, composed by anyone simply in virtue of their having discovered the sound structure S; there will be many such discoverings that do not count as composings of that work, because the discovery was not via heuristic path H. Thus we make it possible for a work to be multiply composed, but we are not excessively liberal in what we will count as composition of the same work. Thus the proposal meets the third constraint. The proposal meets our fourth constraint, because the work is identified with a type that abstracts on the identity of the composer and on the time of composition. These things are not constitutive of the work.

Finally, our proposal meets the fifth constraint, because it makes clear exactly in what sense it is true that the appreciation of a work of art is an appreciation of the artist's performance. This turns out to be literally true. The work is the action type that the artist performs. In appreciating the work we are thereby appreciating the artist's performance.

12   A Question About Heuristics

Jerrold Levinson (in a personal communication) poses the following problem for my account. According to me, the heuristic of the work is determined by those factors that influence the artist in his selection of the work's structure. But this leaves out important artistic-cultural conditions that affect the aesthetic qualities of the work even though the artist was unaware of them. Thus it is an aesthetically relevant fact about Brahms's piano music that it bears certain similarities to Liszt's, whether or not Brahms was influenced by Liszt. Mere cultural proximity is enough; it does not need to be causal proximity as well. In introducing the idea of a work's heuristic I have certainly spoken of 'influences' on the artist; Levinson's point is that I may need a conception of heuristic wider than this. In fact, I have not attempted to provide necessary and sufficient conditions for the judgement that two artists have followed the same heuristic path. All I have done is to give the example of Twin Earth cases; cases like this are certainly cases of artists applying the same heuristic. Earth and Twin Earth are the same in every qualitative respect. *A fortiori*, they are alike in respect of influences on the artists, and also in respect of cultural proximities about which the artist knows nothing. So even if I follow Levinson in widening the concept of a heuristic to include factors unknown to the artist I should still be able to appeal to the same cases of heuristic identity. So my argument can certainly tolerate a more liberal concept of heuristic.

The question remains as to whether we should include in the heuristic of a work factors that the artist was unaware of. I think we should. The principle upon which I have based the argument of this book is that the appreciation of art works is the appreciation of a certain kind of achievement. Now it is relevant, as I have said, in finding out what someone's achievement is, to know what others have done. Thus – to consider an example from another area of human endeavour – our perception of Copernicus's achievement in advancing the heliocentric system of the world is affected by the knowledge that Arab astronomers had put forward a system similar in certain of its details two or three centuries before.[17] And this fact is relevant whether or not Copernicus knew of the Arab devices (this is disputed), though it might be said to be less relevant if he did not know of it than if he did.

This suggests, then, that we should be prepared, when describing the heuristic of a work, to include facts unknown to the artist if those facts are deemed relevant to an appreciation of his achievement. The heuristic tells us how that achievement came about, and in what relevant circumstances. I do not want to be more specific than this in my general characterisation of the notion of a heuristic. For there is much work to be done in deciding exactly what kinds of facts are relevant to an appreciation of the artist's achievement. About this there will be disagreement, and those who disagree on this score will disagree about how the heuristics of particular works ought to be characterised. I say only this: whatever you consider relevant in this way, you must regard as intrinsic to the work itself.

It may be said that if we take into account facts unknown to the artist, the domain of things that might be taken into account in the work's heuristic will expand intolerably. How can we rule out facts about the cultures of the distant planets? And what of future events? A work may have a great influence on future works, or it may have none. Describing the heuristic of the work starts to look like writing the history of the universe. But I think we do have a reason for ignoring these facts about the larger context of the work. They are facts that the artist could not have known about. The reason it may be relevant to say that a work of Brahms is similar to one of Liszt is that Brahms could have known about it even if he did not (just as Copernicus could have known about the work of his Arab predecessors). But we are not in touch with the distant planets, and no artist can know in advance what the influence of his work will be. It is information that is available in principle to the artist that is relevant to assessing his achievement. 'In principle' here is, of course, vague. But I think there will be wide agreement about how the idea is to be applied in particular cases.

13   Referential Properties

Works of art sometimes have what we might call referential properties. Goya's portrait of the Duke of Wellington depicts the Duke. Carravagio's *Martyrdom of St Peter* depicts the crucifixion of St Peter. In Tolstoy's *War and Peace* Napoleon is referred to by name. Tchaikovsky's 1812 Overture makes reference to the defeat of Napoleon in Russia. The ways in which painting, literature and music refer to real people and events are rather different; we have no well developed theory that explains the differences and similarities between these ways. Nevertheless, it seems intuitively clear that works of all these kinds (and others) do bear important relations to things in the real world.

The thought that they do so may prompt an objection to the theory here proposed. For, whatever the similarities between the work of Tolstoy and the work of his twin on Twin Earth, these works cannot have the same referential properties. Tolstoy refers to Napoleon, but Tolstoy's Twin is not referring to him; he refers instead to an inhabitant of Twin Earth that Twin Earthers call 'Napoleon' (Earthers and Twin Earthers are not using the same name when they utter 'Napoleon'; they are using two distinct but homophonic names). So their works have different referential properties. They cannot, therefore, be the same work. So one might argue.

Now we may agree that referential properties are properties of the work itself, or we may disagree. Suppose we agree. Then for works which do have referential properties we shall not be able to point to Twin Earth cases as cases of the multiple composition of such works. But this does nothing to rule out Twin Earth cases as cases of the multiple composition of works that have no referential properties – and some works surely do not make reference to any real thing (e.g. stories about imaginary societies in non-specifically located galaxies, abstract paintings and non-programmatic music). If these were the only kinds of cases I could appeal to they would still establish my case. For my claim is merely that multiple composition of the same work is not ruled out by general considerations about the nature of art works. Further, Twin Earth cases are merely one vivid kind of example of multiple composition. If they are not available to us in connection with works that have referential properties there may be other kinds of examples that we could consider – fantastical examples, no doubt, but not more fantastical than Twin Earth cases. Thus two authors, working independently of one another in the same community, might produce lexically identical works, having the same kinds of artistic intentions, influenced by the same literary tradition, making the same real-world references. If everything that we would say in describing the achievement of the one could be said of the other, I claim they would be producing the same work.

We might, on the other hand, disagree that referential properties are properties of the work, saying instead that they are rather aesthetically irrelevant aspects of the work's composition. In fact, this is the line I am inclined to adopt. I am inclined to say that it is not an aesthetically relevant feature of Tolstoy's *War and Peace* that Tolstoy refers to Napoleon with his use of the name 'Napoleon', though I concede that it is or may be an aesthetically relevant fact about the work that the author refers to a real person whose real characteristics bear certain relations to the activities of the character described in the book. But that, of course, does not distinguish Tolstoy's work from Twin Tolstoy's; for everything qualitative that one may say about the activities of Napoleon may be said about the activities of Twin Napoleon. But it would be a distraction from our present concern for me to argue for this here. If I am right in what I have said in the previous paragraph, it does not matter which way you jump.

14   Some Reflections on the Theory

An advantage of the theory I have proposed is that it is ontologically conservative. You do not have to believe in any more kinds of entities as a result of accepting my arguments than you did before you accepted them. I place art works in a familiar ontological category: action types. I do not postulate a new and ontologically obscure category of things, such as 'indicated structures' to solve the problem of what art works are. Of course the nature of action types is not pellucid, but at least they are something we already have reason to countenance. There are, of course, different ways of explicating action types; platonistic ways, nominalistic ways, etc. These are not questions that need concern us here. We can pass on questions about the ultimate nature of action types to the committee of philosophers working on the theory of actions and events.

We can now see that, while the artist does not create the work, he does not discover it either. The work is the action type that he performs in discovering the structure of the work. So rather than create or discover the work, the artist performs it. However, I shall use the expression 'enact' for what the artist does; to say that the artist performs the work, while true, invites a confusion with what, say, the orchestra does when it produces an instance of the work. These are two very different things. The orchestra instantiates the event type *playing of sound structure S*; the composer instantiates the

event type *discovering of S via H*. This lead us to another important point.

I have said that it is conventional to think of musical and literary works as types of which there can be many tokens, these tokens being copies or performances of the work. But now we see that this view cannot be right. On the theory presented here, the instances of the work do not bear the right relation to the work itself to count as tokens of it. A token of a type must exhaust the characteristics of the type. There cannot be essential features of the type that are not displayed by any correct token of it. But this is seen not to be the case when we consider the relation of the work to its instances. The work has important characteristics that one cannot know of by exposure simply to a correct copy or performance of it. To understand the heuristic which is partly constitutive of the work you must know some art history. And the history of a work is not evident from an inspection, however close, of an instance of it.

However, it is not difficult to see why people have been so inclined to assimilate the relation of work-to-instance to that of type-to-token. For the work is a type, and its instances are tokens. But the type of which the instances are tokens is not the work itself; it is the work's pattern or structure.

An objection to this proposal that might be made is that it does not square with our ordinary practice of appreciation. After all, it will be said, many people appreciate works when they know nothing about their histories. But appreciation is not an all or nothing affair. One does not have to know all the relevant facts about a work's history in order to get anything at all out of the work. And in the sense in which I speak of a work's history, all of us normally know something of the work's history; we know that it was produced by a human being rather than by a Martian, for instance, and this is certainly a relevant piece of knowledge – no less relevant, anyway, for being taken for granted. If we knew absolutely nothing about the historical background to a work then I think we would be in a position where we could not appreciate it at all; but that is certainly not the situation we are normally in. And just as people appreciate works to some extent on the basis of a very partial understanding of the work's history, so they appreciate the work on the basis of a very partial perception of its structure. The trained critic can pick out and retain detail from the sound structure of a musical work in a way that goes far beyond the capacity of the ordinary listener, who still may be said to appreciate the

Gregory Currie

work to some degree. So I do not think that there is, in fact, the asymmetry between the appreciation of structure and the appreciation of history that is presupposed by this objection.

In this essay I have not attempted to elaborate the theory by reference to detailed historical cases. But at this point I think that a general historical remark is in order. A good deal that has happened in the development of art during the twentieth century, particularly the visual arts, may be described as a revolt against traditional aesthetics. The development of thoroughly non-representational art is an obvious example. But we see also an attempt to refocus aesthetic attention, moving away from the purely visual properties of the work, and directing attention instead to the artist's activity. Notorious examples of this are Duchamp's *Fountain*, a urinal purchased and displayed by the artist, and Rauschenberg's *Erased De Kooning Drawing*, a surface from which a drawing by De Kooning has been carefully erased.[18] Considered from the point of view of their pictorial qualities, works such as these seem very impoverished. Their interest is located in the activity that leads to these objects being presented.

Many people find such works tedious and self-congratulatory. From one point of view they are both. But if we take seriously the hypothesis of this chapter, there is a more charitable way to understand them. They may be seen as attempts to direct our attention towards an important but neglected feature of the work; its heuristic. In these works the heuristic is much more important than the resulting pattern. They emphasise the fact that the pictorial properties of works radically underdetermine the work's heuristic. Simply by looking at *Fountain* we cannot tell whether it was carefully made by the artist or merely purchased from a plumbing suppliers. And a blank sheet of paper may never have had anything drawn on it. Perhaps the lesson that we should draw from works such as these is not that the traditionally prized aesthetic qualities of beauty and form are no longer relevant to art. It is rather that such qualities do not exhaust what is valuable in the work. Indeed, such qualities as beauty and significance of form cannot be identified in isolation from hypotheses about the nature of the artist's activity. What I take from these works is an affirmation of the view that the work itself is a kind of performance. And that is what I am arguing for here.

Note that we have provided a necessary but not a sufficient condition for something to be an art work. Someone might, for example, arrive at a certain word sequence via a certain heuristic and in doing so enact an action type that is not an art work. This will be the case if, for example, their text is that of a philosophy article or computer instruction manual. We may put the point in a way that again recalls Frege's discussion of the concept number. On the basis of the ATH, we can say the works *A* and *B* are identical just in case they have the same heuristic and the same pattern or structure. But we cannot appeal to this criterion in order to define the concept art work; we cannot say that art works are just those things that we identify and distinguish in this way. For there will be action types that are not art works, but for which this very criterion of identity is appropriate.

15 The Problem of Pictures

Our theory is that an art work is an action type, with two identifying elements: a structure and a heuristic. In literature the structure is a sequence of word types, in music a sequence of sound types. But what, then, of the visual arts? If a painting is to be regarded as a work of art amenable to our analysis we must decide what its constitutive elements are to be. There is no particular difficulty about the heuristic; just like any other kind of artist, the painter takes a certain path to the end result that he produces. Whatever that path is will determine the heuristic of his work. Is there something analogous to a structure that is the end result of the painter's activities? We may say that there is; what the painter arrives at is a certain visual pattern, something that is instantiated by the canvas that he paints. The painter's structure is a structure of coloured shapes, and in this sense two works of visual art can have the same structure without being the same work (as in Kendall Walton's example of *Guernica* and its imaginary look-alike (Walton 1970): these are works that differ from the point of view of their heuristics).

This suggestion brings us to a second hypothesis: the Instance Multiplicity Hypothesis (IMH). For if we take it that the work is constituted by a heuristic and an abstract visual pattern, then the artist's canvas, with paint distributed on its surface, cannot be constitutive of the work. It is merely an instance of it. And a moment's reflection will convince us that the artist's canvas could not be constitutive of the work. For if it were, Picasso and Twin Picasso on Twin Earth could not enact the same work, for their actions employ different canvases. The canvases of Picasso and of Twin Picasso are both instances of the work, so in our imagined situation there are two instances of that work. Paintings (and, by the same reasoning, sculptures) may have more than one instance.

Someone who regards painting and sculpture as singular arts (arts where the work is identical to a particular physical object) might react in one of two ways. They might simply reject the ATH; and perhaps it can be shown that there are reasons for doing that. They might, on the other hand, accept the ATH, claiming that it does not conflict with what people normally have in mind when they claim that painting is a singular art. Granted, they may say, that in the bizarre situation where Twin Earth exists, Picasso's *Guernica* and Twin Picasso's *Twin Guernica* are instances of the same work; that does not show that paintings are reproducible in the way that novels are. For the ATH does not entail that someone who produces a copy – even a 'perfect' copy – of *Guernica* has produced another instance of the work. It is this last claim that the dualist is really concerned to deny, and there certainly are cogent-sounding reasons for denying it.

If we are to decide this question properly, I think we must take a close look at the arguments that have been given for saying that painting is a singular art. (See Chapter 4 of the author's *An Ontology of Art*.)

16   Supervenience Again

In the light of the arguments here presented, what should we say about the supervenience of aesthetic properties? It may seem natural to say that aesthetic value supervenes on pictorial properties together with heuristic (generalising in the obvious way to the non-visual arts).

But such a supervenience claim reduces to a triviality. For suppose we say that if two works have the same pictorial properties and the same heuristic then they will have the same aesthetic value (providing also for the appropriate kind of necessitation here). Then we have said simply that if works are strictly identical they will have the same aesthetic value, and that is obviously true. I have claimed that works are identified in terms of their visual appearance and their heuristics; it is not possible for distinct works to be the same in both these respects. If a thesis of aesthetic supervenience is to be of interest it should (a) specify conditions the

co-exemplification of which ensures sameness of aesthetic value, and (b) specify conditions that numerically distinct works are capable of satisfying. But I do not know of any such thesis.

In saying this I do not mean, of course, to exclude the possibility that distinct works may have, on occasion, the same value. What I claim is that there is no way to specify in advance a sufficient condition for this. I suspect that the issue of supervenience in aesthetics may turn out to be something of a red herring.[19]

17   Transworld Identification of Works

I want to go back to the issue raised in Section 10 concerning the essential properties of art works. Could the Hammerklavier Sonata have had a sound structure different from the structure it in fact has? Could *Emma* have had a word sequence distinct from the word sequence it in fact has? Could either of these works have had histories distinct from their actual histories, to the extent that the heuristics of these works might themselves have been different? Intuitively we want positive answers to all these questions. At least we feel that a work's structure or history could have been slightly different from what it in fact is. But it seems that I am in no position to argue that this intuition is correct. On the contrary, it is a consequence of my theory that the work's structure and heuristic are its identifying elements; the things from which it gets its very identity; change either one, in however insignificant a way, and you change the work itself.

However, I shall argue that there is a way of making sense of our intuition within the framework of my theory. To understand how, we need to introduce some ideas from philosophical logic.

Following Kripke, let us introduce the distinction between rigid and non-rigid designators.[20] A designator is rigid if it designates the same thing in all possible worlds where it designates anything. Otherwise it is non-rigid. For instance, it seems intuitively correct to say that 'Ronald Reagan' denotes the same individual (Ronald Reagan) in all possible worlds in which it denotes anything, but that 'the President of the US' denotes different individuals in different worlds (and at different times in the same world). The first expression is rigid, the second non-rigid. Now I make the following claim: names of works of art, as those names usually function, are non-rigid. An expression like 'The Mona Lisa' does not denote the same thing in each possible world. Similarly for names of musical and literary works. How this comes about I shall now explain.

I have argued that the heuristic of an art work is integral to the identity of the work itself. Now it will readily be seen that in specifying the heuristic of a work we need to specify, among other things, the influence of other works of art on the artist. Thus the characterisation of many art works will involve reference to other works, and it is not clear that this can be done in a way that avoids circularity. (Suppose that two artists are simultaneously producing distinct canvases. The progress of the one may influence that of the other, and vice versa.) However, if we follow a suggestion of David Lewis, I think circularity can be avoided.[21] Lewis noted a similar problem in the causal theory of the mind: we characterise mental states by their causal roles. But part of the causal role of a given mental state may be its causal relations to other mental states. Again, circularity threatens. In order to solve the problem (and because he thinks that it is for other reasons correct to do so) Lewis introduced a general method for defining what he calls 'theoretical terms'; terms introduced via an antecedently understood vocabulary. Lewis suggests that we can define theoretical terms in the following way. We start off with a theory, T, that contains a number of such terms, $t_1, \ldots, t_n$. By replacing these terms with variables $x_1, \ldots, x_n$, and prefixing a string of existential quantifiers at the front of the resulting formula we obtain the 'Ramsey sentence' of T:

$$\exists x, \ldots, \exists x_n T[x_1, \ldots, x_n].$$

We can then define each theoretical term as follows:

$$t_1 = {}^1y_1 \exists y_2, \ldots, \exists y_n \forall x_1, \ldots, \forall x_n (T[x_1, \ldots, x_n]$$
$$\equiv y_1 = x_1 \& \ldots \& y_n = x_n).$$

And so on for each t_i.

The theoretical terms then refer to those things which make up the unique sequence that satisfies $t[x_1, \ldots, x_n]$. In any world where that formula is uniquely satisfied the theoretical terms refer. In a world where the formula is not uniquely satisfied because there is more than one sequence of things that satisfy it the theoretical terms do not refer. In a world where the formula is not uniquely satisfied because there is no sequence that satisfies it, the terms $t_1, \ldots, t_n$ may still be regarded as referring, as long as there is a unique sequence of things that comes close to satisfying $T[x_1, \ldots, x_n]$. If no

sequence comes close, then the terms do not refer in that world. Lewis then applies this method to the task of defining terms denoting mental states, developing thereby a causal theory of the mind.[22]

Now we can apply these ideas to our present problem in the following way. Let T be our global art-historical theory; the theory that tells us about all the art works there have ever been, exactly what their structures are, exactly what their heuristics are. This is a theory that art historians would like to have. What they have are rough approximations to it, but let us suppose, for the sake of simplicity, that they possess T. T contains names of art works, like 'Guernica', 'The Hammerklavier Sonata', 'Emma'. Some expressions that we use to refer to works, such as 'Beethoven's Fifth Symphony', seem to be descriptions rather than names in the ordinary sense. But I shall assume that expressions like the one last mentioned are used to pick out a work with a certain sound structure and heuristic, rather than whatever work it is that comes fifth in the chronological list of Beethoven's symphonies. If we replace all these names by variables bound by initial existential quantifiers we get a statement which might say that there is a work x, and a work y, and a work z, and x has sound structure S and y has sound structure R and z has sound structure U and x influenced y and y influenced z. This is the Ramsey sentence of an imaginary (and grossly oversimplified) musico-historical theory. The Ramsey sentence says that there are a number of things that occupy a number of musico-historical roles. The things which are musical works are then the things which occupy these roles.

Now our hypothesis, the ATH, may be interpreted as saying that the things which occupy these various roles are all action types. (Think of T as having our constraints 1–5 built in.) T specifies the art history of the actual world; let us call the class of worlds with the same art history as the actual world the class of T-worlds. (The T-worlds are the worlds in which T is true.) Now relative to the class of T-worlds, an expression like 'The Mona Lisa' will be rigid; it will denote the same action type in each T-world. This is easy to see. T specifies a structure and a heuristic for each work. In any world where T is true 'The Mona Lisa' will denote that action type with the structure and heuristic specified by T. But the class of action types which can be artworks – action types of the form $[x, S, H, D, \tau]$ – are uniquely identified in terms of a structure and a heuristic. Thus 'The Mona Lisa' denotes the same thing in each T-world. There will, on the other hand, be worlds in which 'The *Mona Lisa*' does not denote anything at all, because in those worlds there are either two equally good competitors for the role played by the *Mona Lisa* in our art history, or because there is nothing that comes close to playing that role. But – and this is the important point – there will be worlds in which 'The *Mona Lisa*' denotes something other than what it denotes in the actual world. These are amongst the worlds in which *T* turns out false, but not so badly false that we cannot identify a sequence of objects in that world as coming close to playing the art-historical roles played in the actual world by the art works we are familiar with.

Thus we might say that, while names of art works are non-rigid, because they do not denote the same things in each possible world, they are 'quasi-rigid'. In each possible world in which things go smoothly (in which *T* is true) they denote the same action type.[23] In some other worlds in which things don't go quite smoothly enough, they denote different action types. Thus there is a world in which 'The *Mona Lisa*' denotes an action type that has a structure or heuristic (or both) that deviates somewhat from the structure or heuristic possessed by the action type to which that expression refers in the actual world. How much deviation is possible is, on this view, globally determined. Consider something that looks a little bit different from the *Mona Lisa*. In one world, *w*, this thing might not be the referent of 'The *Mona Lisa*', because there are other respects in which *w* deviates too far from the actual world for us to be able to identify a sequence of action types capable of playing roles which are (overall) close to those specified in the actual world art history. On the other hand there will be a world *u* in which something that looks rather less like the *Mona Lisa* will be the referent of 'The *Mona Lisa*', because *u* is a world which in other respects comes very close to being a *T*-world.

This, I think, is the result we want. That is, our intuitive judgements of transworld identity for works are sensitive to global features of the counterfactual situation we are considering. Let *w* be a world in which only one art work is ever produced; one that looks rather like the *Mona Lisa*. Would it be the referent of 'The *Mona Lisa*'? It seems doubtful. But if we change our specification of *w* to make it more and more closely approximate the *T*-worlds, we get more confident about saying that this object is the referent of 'The *Mona Lisa*'.

Thus we see that the question 'Could the *Mona Lisa* have looked different from the way it does look?' is subject to a *de re/de dicto* ambiguity. If the question is 'Is there a possible world in which the thing which actually occupies the *Mona Lisa* role has a different look from the look it has in the actual world?', we have a *de re* construal. The answer then is no: that particular thing preserves its pictorial properties in all worlds where it exists at all. If the question is, on the other hand, 'Is there a possible world in which the thing occupying the *Mona Lisa* role in that world has a look different from the look of the thing which occupies the *Mona Lisa* role in the actual world?', we have a *de dicto* construal. The answer then is yes: the *Mona Lisa* role is occupied by different things in different worlds. These things do not all have the same pictorial properties. (More properly, these things (action types) do not all have the same identifying pattern.).

In summary, then, the theory I propose allows us to explain our intuition that certain modal claims like 'the *Mona Lisa* could have looked a bit different from the way it does look' are true. For on this theory there will be worlds in which the referent of 'The *Mona Lisa*' does look a little bit different from the way the actual looks. And this is not because the action types that I identify with works do not have their structures essentially – they do – but because names of art works are non-rigid.

This is merely a brief aside on the question of the semantics for art work denoting terms. There are considerable problems about developing this theory in detail. It is not appropriate that we should attempt to solve those problems here.

Notes

1 See Wollheim (1968) Sections 35–7.
2 See Levinson (1980).
3 In correspondence Levinson makes it clear that the second interpretation was intended.
4 See Wolterstorff (1980) pt 2.
5 See Goodman (1968) p. 115.
6 See Wolterstorff (1980), pp. 61–2.
7 See Levinson (1980), p. 7.
8 See ibid., p. 20.
9 See ibid., p. 14.

10   See Frege (1884), Section 66.

11   See Anderson (1982).

12   First introduced by Putnam (1975).

13   There must of course be other differences between Earth and Twin Earth. They have, for instance, different spatial locations. These differences would begin to show up if we had powerful telescopes, or started to travel through the universe. But assume that we never transcend our local environment.

14   See e.g. Kim (1976).

15   For a case study in the application of a heuristic in physical theory see Zahar (1972).

16   See e.g. Jocelyn Harris's study of the influence of Richardson on Jane Austen, Harris (1980).

17   See e.g. Kennedy and Roberts (1959) and Veselowsky (1973). The Persian and Damascene astronomers were working with a geocentric system. The similarities between their systems and that of Copernicus is a matter of certain technical devices for accommodating the eccentricities of the planets.

18   Duchamp wrote in 1917: 'Whether Mr Mutt [the work was signed "R. Mutt"] with his own hands made the fountain or not has no importance. He CHOSE it. He took an ordinary article of life, placed it so that its useful significance disappeared under the new title and point of view – created a new thought for that object' (see d'Harnoncourt and McShine (1973) p. 283). [Some remarks in this section are much too accommodating to the idea of conceptual art, and I believe it would be wrong to think that the theory here offered is especially friendly to art of this kind.]

19   The content of this section was suggested to me during correspondence with Crispin Wright. See his (1985).

20   See Kripke (1972).

21   See Lewis (1970).

22   See Lewis (1972).

23   Art work designators differ in this respect from designators of mental states. On the hypothesis of realisational plasticity, pain may designate some quite different state from the state it designates in the actual world, in another world where T ('folk psychology') is true. This is why I call art work designators 'quasi-rigid'. (They are still, of course, non-rigid in the proper sense.)

References

Anderson, J. (1982) 'Musical Identity', *Journal of Aesthetics and Art Criticism*, 40, pp. 285–91.

d'Harnoncourt, A. and McShine, K. (1973) *Marcel Duchamp* (New York: Museum of Modern Art).

Frege, G. (1884) *Foundations of Arithmetic*, 2nd edn (Oxford: Blackwell, 1980).

Goodman, N. (1968) *Languages of Art*, 2nd edn (Brighton: Harvester, 1980).

Harris, J. (1980) '"As if they had been Living Friends": *Sir Charles Grandison* into *Mansfield Park*', *Bulletin of Research in the Humanities*, 83, pp. 360–405.

Kennedy, E. and Roberts, V. (1959) 'The Planetary Theory of Ibn ash Shatir', *Isis*, 51, pp. 227–35.

Kim, J. (1976) 'Events as Property Exemplifications', in M. Brand and D. Walton (eds) *Action Theory* (Dordrecht: Reidel).

Kripke, S. (1972) *Naming and Necessity*, rev. and enlarged edn (Oxford: Blackwell, 1980).

Levinson, J. (1980) 'What a Musical Work is', *Journal of Philosophy*, 77, pp. 5–28. [See also this volume.]

Lewis, D. K. (1970) 'How to Define Theoretical Terms', *Journal of Philosophy*, 67, pp. 427–46.

Lewis, D. K. (1972) 'Psychophysical and Theoretical Identifications', *Australasian Journal of Philosophy*, 50, pp. 249–58.

Putnam, H. (1975) 'The Meaning of Meaning', in *Mind, Language and Reality, Philosophical Papers*, vol. 2 (London: Cambridge University Press).

Veselowsky, I. N. (1973) 'Copernicus and Nasi al-Din al Tusi', *Journal of the History of Astronomy*, 4, pp. 128–30.

Walton, K. L. (1970) 'Categories of Art', *Philosophical Review*, 79, pp. 334–67.

Wollheim, R. (1968) *Art and Its Objects*, 2nd edn (Cambridge: Cambridge University Press).

Wolterstorff, N. (1980) *Works and Worlds of Art* (Oxford: Clarendon Press).

Wright, C. J. G. (1985) Review of Blackburn *Spreading the Word*, *Mind*, 94, pp. 310–19.

Zahar, E. G. (1972) 'Why Did Einstein's Research Programme Supersede Lorentz's?' *British Journal for the Philosophy of Science*, 24, pp. 95–123 and 223–62.

Part III

Aesthetic Properties

Introduction to Part III

Frank Sibley's paper "Aesthetic Concepts" is of considerable importance in the analytic tradition. Not least, it offers a rigorous treatment of a topic – aesthetic description – all too often subject to vague or speculative theorizing. More than that, it presents and defends determinate, substantial theses on the topic with a thoroughness and attention to detail, which came to epitomize the potential of the new methodology in aesthetics. To a large extent it became a showpiece for analytic aesthetics and has been a constant point of reference ever since.

Sibley draws our attention to the diverse range of aesthetic characterizations applied to works of art. Among many other familiar aesthetic terms, he lists: *unified, balanced, integrated, lifeless, serene, somber, dynamic, powerful, vivid, delicate, moving, trite, sentimental, tragic*. The list is a striking reminder that aesthetics is concerned with concepts far more varied than just *beauty*, which dominated, and arguably distorted, debates in previous centuries. Sibley invites us to contrast such concepts with familiar nonaesthetic terms which are also applied to works of art (or parts of works): *circular, red, slow, monosyllabic, in sonnet form*. What interests Sibley are both the distinctness of these classes of terms and the relations between them. He thought that nonaesthetic properties of the latter kind could be "pointed out to anyone with normal eyesight, ears and intelligence" but that to discern aesthetic qualities "require[s] the exercise of taste, perceptiveness or sensitivity." It is possible to be fully apprised of a work's nonaesthetic properties but remain in ignorance of its aesthetic properties (failing the requisite "gestalt" or aesthetic receptivity). One role for the critic is to get people to *see* or *hear* or *notice* the aesthetic qualities in a work. While aesthetic qualities are always dependent on nonaesthetic ones, nevertheless no set of nonaesthetic properties is ever a *sufficient* condition for the presence of an aesthetic property. The latter are not condition- or rule-governed, although they are by no means arbitrarily or merely subjectively applicable.

Sibley's theses have been debated at length by analytic philosophers. One issue in particular that has been pursued – and in drawing on work in other areas of philosophy is characteristic of analytic aesthetics – is the precise nature of the dependence relation between the aesthetic and the nonaesthetic. Here the idea of *supervenience* is introduced, which in other contexts has been applied to the relation between, for example, values and facts or the mental and the physical. If we call aesthetic properties (of the kind listed by Sibley) A-properties and nonaesthetic properties B- (or "base") properties, then we can define "weak supervenience" as the claim that *there could be no difference in A-properties without a difference in B-properties*, and "strong supervenience" as: *if something has an A-property, then it has B-properties such that if anything, in any world, has just those B-properties then it has that A-property*. If there is a supervenience relation between the aesthetic and the nonaesthetic, then the question is what constitutes the B or base properties? If the base properties are restricted to intrinsic (physical or structural) properties of objects, which is perhaps what Sibley believed, then the thesis would have philosophical bite, particularly in its strong form (for one thing it would suggest close parallels between aesthetic properties and secondary qualities). However, that thesis is almost certainly false.

Arthur Danto's work on indiscernibles (see "The Artworld" in Part I) and Kendall Walton's on "categories of art" (see his paper in this section) offer powerful arguments, albeit of different kinds, to show that objects identical in physical composition and appearance could have different aesthetic properties, when, for example, the objects are located in different art-historical contexts or perceived as belonging to different categories. The trouble is if the supervenience base has to include relational properties, of a historical, cultural, or biographical kind, then the supervenience claim looks in danger not of falsity but of triviality (this is argued in Currie's paper in Part II).

Walton's "Categories of Art" is another paper of fundamental importance in the analytic tradition. In many ways it carries on the debate initiated by Sibley. Walton argues that we cannot identify aesthetic properties in a work of art simply from the nonaesthetic properties immediately perceived in a work, independently of other facts about the work, in particular what "category" it is assigned to. The very same object might have different aesthetic characteristics – and thus be perceived differently – relative to the artistic category it is placed in. We need to know in effect the *kind* of work it is before we can discern its aesthetic nature. Walton offers numerous compelling examples to establish the point. However, although Walton's thesis relativizes aesthetic properties to artistic categories, he is anxious to dispel the notion that it is a merely arbitrary matter how works are categorized. There is usually, he believes, a *correct* category within which to perceive a work, as determined by a number of criteria, including the intentions of the artist.

Philip Pettit's paper "The Possibility of Aesthetic Realism" brings to bear on this same cluster of problems a debate central to philosophy of language (in the analytic tradition): What is involved in construing different kinds of discourse in a realist or antirealist manner? In ethics, for example, we might ask whether the sentence "Killing is wrong" purports to state a fact (as the moral realist might claim) or whether it has at root some other function, for example to prescribe a course of action or express an emotion or commitment (as the antirealist might contend). Pettit seeks (a) to show what it would mean to construe aesthetic characterizations in a realist manner, and (b) to defend the appropriateness of doing so against a number of potential objections. Aesthetic characterizations, construed realistically, would have to conform to the logic of assertion, as genuine candidates for truth-values, and would have to be such that "the presentation of appropriate evidence leaves no distinctive room for the sincere reservation of assent." The difficulty is in squaring those conditions with the peculiar nature of aesthetic descriptions – their being "essentially perceptual" and "perceptually elusive." Pettit offers a subtle account of aesthetic perception, by no means stacking the argument in favor of realism. Toward the end he confronts some of the same issues faced by Walton in trying to avoid arbitrariness in how works are perceived. Works, he argues, must be correctly "positioned" and, like Walton, he offers constraints on this positioning.

Pettit's paper – like Sibley's and Walton's before it – gives a clear lead as to how discussion of aesthetic discourse might be assimilated into debates elsewhere in analytic philosophy. While that by no means guarantees consensus on matters of controversy, it ends the isolation of aesthetics and shows how new light can be shed on the problems by relocating them in a wider context.

Further Reading

Brady, E. and Levinson, J. (ed.) (2001). *Aesthetic Concepts: Essays After Sibley* (Oxford: Oxford University Press).

Cohen, Ted (1973). "Aesthetic/Non-Aesthetic and the Concept of Taste," *Theoria*, 39, pp. 113–52.

Fenner, David (1996). *The Aesthetic Attitude* (Atlantic Highlands, NJ: Humanities Press).

Goldman, Alan (1993). "Realism about Aesthetic Properties," *Journal of Aesthetics and Art Criticism*, 51, pp. 31–7.

Kivy, Peter (1973). *Speaking of Art* (The Hague: Martinus Nijhoff).

Meager, Ruby (1970). "Aesthetic Concepts," *British Journal of Aesthetics*, 10, pp. 303–22.

Sibley, Frank (2001). *Approaches to Aesthetics: Collected Papers on Philosophical Aesthetics*, ed. J. Benson, B. Redfern, and J. Roxbee Cox (Oxford: Oxford University Press).

Zangwill, Nick (2002). *The Metaphysics of Beauty*, (Ithaca, NY: Cornell University Press).

Zemach, Eddy (1996). *Real Beauty* (University Park: Pennsylvania State University Press).

12

Aesthetic Concepts

Frank Sibley

The remarks we make about works of art are of many kinds. For the purpose of this paper I wish to indicate two broad groups. I shall do this by examples. We say that a novel has a great number of characters and deals with life in a manufacturing town; that a painting uses pale colors, predominantly blues and greens, and has kneeling figures in the foreground; that the theme in a fugue is inverted at such a point and that there is a stretto at the close; that the action of a play takes place in the span of one day and that there is a reconciliation scene in the fifth act. Such remarks may be made by, and such features pointed out to, anyone with normal eyes, ears, and intelligence. On the other hand, we also say that a poem is tightly-knit or deeply moving; that a picture lacks balance, or has a certain serenity and repose, or that the grouping of the figures sets up an exciting tension; that the characters in a novel never really come to life, or that a certain episode strikes a false note. It would be neutral enough to say that the making of such judgments as these requires the exercise of taste, perceptiveness, or sensitivity, of aesthetic discrimination or appreciation; one would not say this of my first group. Accordingly, when a word or expression is such that taste or perceptiveness is required in order to apply it, I shall call it an *aesthetic* term or

Frank Sibley, "Aesthetic Concepts," in Joseph Margolis (ed.), *Philosophy Looks at the Arts: Contemporary Readings in Aesthetics*, revised edition (Philadelphia: Temple University Press), 1978, 64–87; reprinted with "extensive minor revisions" from *Philosophical Review*, 68 (1959), pp. 421–50. Public domain.

expression, and I shall, correspondingly, speak of *aesthetic* concepts or *taste* concepts.[1]

Aesthetic terms span a great range of types and could be grouped into various kinds of sub-species. But it is not my present purpose to attempt any such grouping; I am interested in what they all have in common. Their almost endless variety is adequately displayed in the following list: *unified, balanced, integrated, lifeless, serene, somber, dynamic, powerful, vivid, delicate, moving, trite, sentimental, tragic*. The list of course is not limited to adjectives; expressions in artistic contexts like *telling contrast, sets up a tension, conveys a sense of,* or *holds it together* are equally good illustrations. It includes terms used by both layman and critic alike, as well as some which are mainly the property of professional critics and specialists.

I have gone for my examples of aesthetic expressions in the first place to critical and evaluative discourse about works of art because it is there particularly that they abound. But now I wish to widen the topic; we employ terms the use of which requires an exercise of taste not only when discussing the arts but quite liberally throughout discourse in everyday life. The examples given above are expressions which, appearing in critical contexts, most usually, if not invariably, have an aesthetic use; outside critical discourse the majority of them more frequently have some other use unconnected with taste. But many expressions do double duty even in everyday discourse, sometimes being used as aesthetic expressions and sometimes not. Other words again, whether in artistic or daily discourse, function only or predominantly as aesthetic terms; of this kind are *graceful, delicate, dainty, handsome, comely, elegant, garish.* Finally, to make the contrast with all the preceding examples, there are many words which are seldom used as aesthetic terms at all: *red, noisy, brackish, clammy, square, docile, cured, evanescent, intelligent, faithful, derelict, tardy, freakish.*

Clearly, when we employ words as aesthetic terms we are often making and using metaphors, pressing into service words which do not primarily function in this manner. Certainly also, many words *have come* to be aesthetic terms by some kind of metaphorical transference. This is so with those like "dynamic," "melancholy," "balanced," "tightly-knit" which, except in artistic and critical writings, are not normally aesthetic terms. But the aesthetic vocabulary must not be thought wholly metaphorical. Many words, including the most common (*lovely, pretty, beautiful, dainty, graceful, elegant*), are certainly not being used metaphorically when employed as aesthetic terms, the very good reason being that this is their primary or only use, some of them having no current non-aesthetic use. And though expressions like "dynamic," "balanced," and so forth *have come* by a metaphorical shift to be aesthetic terms, their employment in criticism can scarcely be said to be more than quasi-metaphorical. Having entered the language of art description and criticism as metaphors they are now standard vocabulary in that language.[2]

The expressions I am calling aesthetic terms form no small segment of our discourse. Often, it is true, people with normal intelligence and good eyesight and hearing lack, at least in some measure, the sensitivity required to apply them; a man need not be stupid or have poor eyesight to fail to see that something is graceful. Thus taste or sensitivity is somewhat more rare than certain other human capacities; people who exhibit a sensitivity both wide-ranging and refined are a minority. It is over the application of aesthetic terms too that, notoriously, disputes and differences sometimes go helplessly unsettled. But almost everybody is able to exercise taste to some degree and in some matters. It is surprising therefore that aesthetic terms have been so largely neglected. They have received glancing treatment in the course of other aesthetic discussions; but as a broad category they have not received the direct attention they merit.

The foregoing has marked out the area I wish to discuss. One warning should perhaps be given. When I speak of taste in this paper, I shall not be dealing with questions which center upon expressions like "a matter of taste" (meaning, roughly, a matter of personal preference or liking). It is with an ability to *notice* or *see* or *tell* that things have certain qualities that I am concerned.

I

In order to support our application of an aesthetic term, we often refer to features the mention of which involves other aesthetic terms: "it has an extraordinary vitality because of its free and vigorous style of drawing," "graceful in the smooth flow of its lines," "dainty because of the delicacy and harmony of its coloring." It is as normal to do this as it is to justify one mental epithet by other epithets of the same general type, *intelligent* by *ingenious, inventive, acute,* and so on. But often when we apply aesthetic terms, we explain why by referring to features which do *not* depend for their recognition upon an exercise of taste: "delicate because of its pastel shades and curving lines," or "it lacks balance because one group of figures is so far off to the left and is so brightly illuminated." When no explanation of this latter kind is offered, it is legitimate to ask or search for one. Finding a satisfactory answer may sometimes be difficult, but one cannot ordinarily reject the question. When we cannot ourselves quite say what non-aesthetic features make something delicate or unbalanced or powerful or moving, the good critic often puts his finger on something which strikes us as the right explanation. In short, aesthetic terms always ultimately apply because of, and aesthetic qualities always ultimately depend upon, the presence of features which, like curving or angular lines, color contrasts, placing of masses, or speed of movement, are visible, audible, or otherwise discernible without any exercise of taste or sensibility. Whatever kind of dependence this is, and there are various relationships between aesthetic qualities and non-aesthetic features, what I want to make clear in this paper is that there are no non-aesthetic features which serve in *any* circumstances as logically *sufficient conditions* for applying aesthetic terms. Aesthetic or taste concepts are not in *this* respect condition-governed at all.

There is little temptation to suppose that aesthetic terms resemble words which, like "square," are applied in accordance with a set of necessary and sufficient conditions. For whereas each square is square in virtue of the *same* set of conditions, four equal sides and four right angles, aesthetic terms apply to widely varied objects; one thing is graceful because of these features, another because of those, and so on almost endlessly. In recent times philosophers have broken the spell of the strict necessary-and-sufficient model by showing that many everyday concepts are not of that type. Instead, they have described various other types of concepts which are governed only in a much looser way by conditions. However, since these newer models provide satisfactory accounts of many familiar concepts, it might plausibly be thought that aesthetic concepts are of some such kind and that they similarly are governed in some looser way by conditions. I want to argue that aesthetic concepts differ radically from any of these other concepts.

Amongst these concepts to which attention has recently been paid are those for which no *necessary-and-sufficient* conditions can be provided, but for which there are a number of relevant features, A, B, C, D, E, such that the presence of some groups or combinations of these features is *sufficient* for the application of the concept. The list of relevant features may be an open one; that is, given A, B, C, D, E, we may not wish to close off the possible relevance of other unlisted features beyond E. Examples of such concepts might be "dilatory," "discourteous," "possessive," "capricious," "prosperous," "intelligent" (but see below). If we begin a list of features relevant to "intelligent" with, for example, ability to grasp and follow various kinds of instructions, ability to master facts and marshall evidence, ability to solve mathematical or chess problems, we might go on adding to this list almost indefinitely.

However, with concepts of this sort, although decisions may have to be made and judgment exercised, it is always possible to extract and state, from cases which have *already* clearly been decided, the sets of features or conditions which were regarded as sufficient in those cases. These relevant features which I am calling conditions are, it should be noted, features which, though not sufficient *alone* and needing to be combined with other similar features, nevertheless carry some weight and can count only in one direction. Being a good chess player can count only *towards* and not *against* intelligence. Whereas mention of it may enter sensibly along with other remarks in expressions like "I say he is intelligent because . . . ," or "the reason I call him intelligent is that . . . ," it cannot be used to complete such negative expressions as "I say he is *un*intelligent because . . ." But what I want particularly to emphasize about features which function

as conditions for a term is that *some* group or set of them *is* sufficient fully to ensure or warrant the application of that term. An individual characterized by some of these features may not yet qualify to be called lazy or intelligent, and so on, beyond all question, but all that is needed is to add some further (indefinite) number of such characterizations and a point is reached where we have enough. There are individuals possessing a number of such features of whom one cannot deny, cannot but admit, that they are intelligent. We have left necessary-and-sufficient conditions behind, but we are still in the realm of sufficient conditions.

But aesthetic concepts are not condition-governed even in this way. There are no sufficient conditions, no non-aesthetic features such that the presence of some set or number of them will beyond question logically justify or warrant the application of an aesthetic term. It is impossible (barring certain limited exceptions, see below) to make any statements corresponding to those we can make for condition-governed words. We are able to say "If it is true he can do this, and that, and the other, then one just cannot deny that he is intelligent," or "if he does A, B, and C, I don't see how it can be denied that he is lazy," but we cannot make *any* general statement of the form "If the vase is pale pink, somewhat curving, lightly mottled, and so forth, it will be delicate, cannot but be delicate." Nor again can one say *any* such things here as "Being tall and thin is not enough *alone* to ensure that a vase is delicate, but if it is, for example, slightly curving and pale colored (and so forth) as well, it cannot be denied that it is." Things may be described to us in non-aesthetic terms as fully as we please but we are not thereby put in the position of having to admit (or being unable to deny) that they are delicate or graceful or garish or exquisitely balanced.[3]

No doubt there are some respects in which aesthetic terms *are* governed by conditions or rules. For instance, it may be impossible that a thing should be garish if all its colors are pale pastels, or flamboyant if all its lines are straight. There may be, that is, descriptions using only non-aesthetic terms which are incompatible with descriptions employing certain aesthetic terms. If I am told that a painting in the next room consists solely of one or two bars of very pale blue and very pale grey set at right angles on a pale fawn ground, I can be sure that it cannot be fiery or garish or gaudy or flamboyant. A description of this sort may make certain aesthetic terms *in*applicable or *in*appropriate; and

Frank Sibley

if from this description I inferred that the picture was, or even might be, fiery or gaudy or flamboyant, this might be taken as showing a failure to understand these words. I do not wish to deny therefore that taste concepts may be governed *negatively* by conditions.[4] What I am emphasizing is that they quite lack governing conditions of a sort many other concepts possess. Though on *seeing* the picture we might say, and rightly, that it is delicate or serene or restful or sickly or insipid, no *description* in non-aesthetic terms permits us to claim that these or any other aesthetic terms must undeniably apply to it.

I have said that if an object is characterized *solely* by certain sorts of features this may count decisively against the possibility of applying to it certain aesthetic terms. But of course the presence of *some* such features need not count decisively; other features may be enough to outweigh those which, on their own, would render the aesthetic term inapplicable. A painting might be garish even though much of its color is pale. These facts call attention to a further feature of taste concepts. One *can* find general features or descriptions which in some sense count in one direction only, only *for* or only *against* the application of certain aesthetic terms. Angularity, fatness, brightness, or intensity of color are typically *not* associated with delicacy or grace. Slimness, lightness, gentle curves, lack of intensity of color are associated with delicacy, but not with flamboyance, majesty, grandeur, splendor or garishness. This is shown by the naturalness of saying, for example, that someone is graceful *because* she's so light, but *in spite of* being quite angular or heavily built; and by the corresponding oddity of saying that something is graceful *because* it is so heavy or angular, or delicate *because* of its bright and intense coloring. This may therefore sound quite similar to what I have said already about conditions in discussing terms like "intelligent." There are nevertheless very significant differences. Although there is this sense in which slimness, lightness, lack of intensity of color, and so on, count only towards, not against, delicacy, these features, I shall say, at best count only *typically* or *characteristically* towards delicacy; they do not count towards in the same sense as condition-features count towards laziness or intelligence; that is, no group of them is ever logically sufficient.

One way of reinforcing this is to notice how features which are characteristically associated with one aesthetic term may also be similarly associated

with other and rather different aesthetic terms. "Graceful" and "delicate" may be on the one hand sharply contrasted with terms like "violent," "grand," "fiery," "garish," or "massive" which have characteristic non-aesthetic features quite unlike those for "delicate" and "graceful." But one the other hand "graceful" and "delicate" may also be contrasted with aesthetic terms which stand much closer to them, like "flaccid," "weakly," "washed out," "lanky," "anaemic," "wan," "insipid"; and the range of features characteristic of *these* qualities, pale color, slimness, lightness, lack of angularity and sharp contrast, is virtually identical with the range for "delicate" and "graceful." Similarly many of the features typically associated with "joyous," "fiery," "robust," or "dynamic" are identical with those associated with "garish," "strident," "turbulent," "gaudy," or "chaotic." Thus an object which is described very fully, but exclusively in terms of qualities characteristic of delicacy, may turn out on inspection to be not delicate at all, but anaemic or insipid. The failures of novices and the artistically inept prove that quite close similarity in point of line, color, or technique gives no assurance of gracefulness or delicacy. A failure and a success in the manner of Degas may be generally more alike, so far as their non-aesthetic features go, than either is like a successful Fragonard. But it is not necessary to go even this far to make my main point. A painting which has only the kind of features one would associate with vigor and energy but which even so fails to be vigorous and energetic *need* not have some other character, need not be instead, say, strident or chaotic. It may fail to have any particular character whatever. It may employ bright colors, and the like, without being particularly lively and vigorous at all; but one may feel unable to describe it as chaotic or strident or garish either. It is, rather, simply lacking in character (though of course this too is an aesthetic judgment; taste is exercised also in seeing that the painting has no character).

There are of course many features which do not in these ways characteristically count for (or against) particular aesthetic qualities. One poem has strength and power because of the regularity of its meter and rhyme; another is monotonous and lacks drive and strength because of its regular meter and rhyme. We do not feel the need to switch from "because of" to "in spite of." However, I have concentrated upon features which are characteristically associated with aesthetic qualities because, if a case could be made for the view that taste concepts are in any way governed by sufficient conditions, these would seem to be the most promising candidates for governing conditions. But to say that features are associated only *characteristically* with an aesthetic term *is* to say that they can never amount to sufficient conditions; no description however full, even in terms characteristic of gracefulness, puts it beyond question that something is graceful in the way a description may put it beyond question that someone is lazy or intelligent.

It is important to observe, however, that in this paper I am not merely claiming that no sufficient conditions can be stated for taste concepts. For if this were all, taste concepts might not be after all really different from one kind of concept recently discussed. They could be accommodated perhaps with those concepts which Professor H. L. A. Hart has called "defeasible"; it is a characteristic of defeasible concepts that we cannot state sufficient conditions for them because, for any sets we offer, there is always an (open) list of defeating conditions any of which might rule out the application of the concept. The most we can say schematically for a defeasible concept is that, for example, A, B, and C together are sufficient for the concept to apply *unless* some feature is present which overrides or voids them. But, I want to emphasize, the very fact that we *can* say this sort of thing shows that we are still to that extent in the realm of conditions.[5] The features governing defeasible concepts can ordinarily count only one way, *either* for *or* against. To take Hart's example, "offer" and "acceptance" can count only towards the existence of a valid contract, and fraudulent misrepresentation, duress, and lunacy can count only against. And even with defeasible concepts, if we are told that there are no voiding features present, we can know that some set of conditions or features, A, B, C, . . . , is enough, in this absence of voiding features, to ensure, for example, that there is a contract. The very notion of a defeasible concept seems to require that some group of features *would* be sufficient *in certain circumstances*, that is, in the absence of overriding or voiding features. In a certain way defeasible concepts lack sufficient conditions then, but they are still, in the sense described, condition-governed. My claim about taste concepts is stronger; that they are not, except negatively, governed by conditions at all. We could not conclude even in certain circumstances, e.g., if we were told of the absence of all "voiding" or uncharacteristic features (no angularities, and the like), that an object *must* certainly be graceful, no

matter how fully it was described to us as possessing features characteristic of gracefulness.

My arguments and illustrations so far have been rather simply schematic. Many concepts, including most of the examples I have used (*intelligent*, and so on, above), are much more thoroughly open and complex than my illustrations suggest. Not only may there be an open list of relevant conditions; it may be impossible to give precise rules telling how many features from the list are needed for a sufficient set or in which combinations; impossible similarly to give precise rules covering the extent or degree to which such features need to be present in those combinations. Indeed, we may have to abandon as futile any attempt to describe or formulate anything like a complete set of precise conditions or rules, and content ourselves with giving only some general account of the concept, making reference to samples or cases or precedents. We cannot fully master or employ these concepts therefore *simply* by being equipped with lists of conditions, readily applicable procedures or sets of rules, however complex. For to exhibit a mastery of one of these concepts we must be able to go ahead and apply the word correctly to new individual cases, at least to central ones; and each new case may be a uniquely different object, just as each intelligent child or student may differ from others in relevant features and exhibit a unique combination of kinds and degrees of achievement and ability. In dealing with these new cases mechanical rules and procedures would be useless; we have to exercise our judgment, guided by a complex set of examples and precedents. Here then there is a marked *superficial* similarity to aesthetic concepts. For in using aesthetic terms too we learn from samples and examples, not rules, and we have to apply them, likewise, without guidance by rules or readily applicable procedures, to new and unique instances. Neither kind of concept admits of a simply "mechanical" employment.

But this is *only* a superficial similarity. It is at least noteworthy that in applying words like "lazy" or "intelligent" to new and unique instances we say that we are required to exercise *judgment*; it would be indeed odd to say that we are exercising *taste*. In exercising judgment we are called upon to weigh the pros and cons against each other, and perhaps sometimes to decide whether a quite new feature is to be counted as weighing on one side or on the other. But this goes to show that, though we may learn from and rely upon samples and precedents rather than a set of stated conditions, we are not out of the realm of general conditions and guiding principles. These precedents necessarily embody, and are used by us to illustrate, a complex web of governing and relevant conditions which it is impossible to formulate completely. To profit by precedents we have to understand them; and we must argue consistently from case to case. This is the very function of precedents. Thus it is possible, even with these very loosely condition-governed concepts, to take clear or paradigm cases of X and to say "this is X because . . . ," and follow it up with an account of features which logically clinch the matter.

Nothing like this is possible with aesthetic terms. Examples undoubtedly play a crucial role in giving us a grasp of these concepts; but we do not and cannot derive from these examples conditions and principles, however complex, which will enable us, if we are consistent, to apply the terms even to some new cases. When, with a clear case of something which is in fact graceful or balanced or tightly-knit, someone tells me why it is, what features make it so, it is always possible for me to wonder whether, in spite of these features, it really is graceful, balanced, and so on. No such features logically clinch the matter.

The point I have argued may be reinforced in the following way. A man who failed to realize the nature of aesthetic concepts, or someone who, knowing he lacked sensitivity in aesthetic matters, did not want to reveal this lack might by assiduous application and shrewd observation provide himself with some rules and generalizations; and by inductive procedures and intelligent guessing, he might frequently say the right things. But he could have no great confidence or certainty; a slight change in an object might at any time unpredictably ruin his calculations, and he might as easily have been wrong as right. No matter how careful he has been about working out a set of consistent principles and conditions, he is only in a position to think that the object is very possibly delicate. With concepts like *lazy, intelligent,* or *contract,* someone who intelligently formulated rules that led him aright appreciably often *would* thereby show the beginning of a grasp of those concepts; but the person we are considering is not even beginning to show an awareness of what delicacy is. Though he sometimes says the right thing, he has not seen, but guessed, that the object is delicate. However intelligent he might be, we could easily tell him wrongly that something was delicate and "explain" why without his being able to detect the deception. (I am ignoring complications now about negative conditions.) But if we did the same with, say, "intelligent" he could at least often uncover some incompatibility or other which would need explaining. In a world of beings like himself he would have no use for concepts like delicacy. As it is, these concepts would play a quite different role in his life. He would, for himself, have no more reason to choose tasteful objects, pictures, and so on, than a deaf man would to avoid noisy places. He could not be praised for exercising taste; at best his ingenuity and intelligence might come in for mention. In "appraising" pictures, statuettes, poems, he would be doing something quite different from what other people do when they exercise taste.

At this point I want to notice in passing that there are times when it may look as if an aesthetic word could be applied according to a rule. These cases vary in type; I shall mention only one. One might say, in using "delicate" of glassware perhaps, that the thinner the glass, other things being equal, the more delicate it is. Similarly, with fabrics, furniture, and so on, there are perhaps times when the thinner or more smoothly finished or more highly polished something is, the more certainly some aesthetic term or other applies. On such occasions someone might formulate a rule and follow it in applying the word to a given range of articles. Now it may be that sometimes when this is so, the word being used is not really an aesthetic term at all; "delicate" applied to glass in this way may at times really mean no more than "thin" or "fragile." But this is certainly not always the case; people often *are* exercising taste even when they say that glass is very delicate because it is so thin, and know that it would be less so if thicker and more so if thinner. These instances where there appear to be rules are peripheral cases of the use of aesthetic terms. If someone did merely follow a rule we should not say he was exercising taste, and we should hesitate to admit that he had any real notion of delicacy until he satisfied us that he could discern it in other instances where no rule was available. In any event, these occasions when aesthetic words can be applied by rule are exceptional, not central or typical, and there is still no reason to think we are dealing with a logical entailment.[6]

It must not be thought that the impossibility of stating any conditions (other than negative) for the application of aesthetic terms results from an accidental poverty or lack of precision in language, or that it is simply a question of extreme complexity.

It is true that words like "pink," "bluish," "curving," "mottled" do not permit of anything like a specific naming of each and every varied shade, curve, mottling, and blending. But if we were to give special names much more liberally than either we or even the specialists do (and no doubt there are limits beyond which we could not go), or even if, instead of names, we were to use vast numbers of specimens and samples of particular shades, shapes, mottlings, lines, and configurations, it would still be impossible, and for the same reasons, to supply any conditions.

We do indeed, in talking about a work of art, concern ourselves with its individual and specific features. We say that it is delicate not simply because it is in pale colors but because of *those* pale colors, that it is graceful not because its outline curves slightly but because of *that* particular curve. We use expressions like "because of *its* pale coloring," "because of *the* flecks of bright blue," "because of *the* way the lines converge" where it is clear we are referring not to the presence of general features but to very specific and particular ones. But it is obvious that even with the help of precise names, or even samples and illustrations, of particular shades of color, contours and lines, any attempt to state conditions would be futile. After all, the very same feature, say a color or shape or line of a particular sort, which helps make one work may quite spoil another. "It would be quite delicate if it were not for that pale color there" may be said about the very color which is singled out in another picture as being largely responsible for its delicate quality. No doubt one way of putting this is to say that the features which make something delicate or graceful, and so on, are combined in a peculiar and unique way; that the aesthetic quality depends upon exactly this individual or unique combination of just these specific colors and shapes so that even a slight change might make all the difference. Nothing is to be achieved by trying to single out or separate features and generalizing about them.

I have now argued that in certain ways aesthetic concepts are not and cannot be condition- or rule-governed.[7] Not to be so governed is one of their essential characteristics. In arguing this I first claimed in a general way that no non-aesthetic features are possible candidates for conditions, and then considered more particularly both the "characteristic" *general* features associated with aesthetic terms and the individual or *specific* features found in particular objects. I have not attempted to examine what relationship these specific features of a work do bear to its aesthetic qualities. An examination of the locutions we use when we refer to them in the course of explaining or supporting our application of an aesthetic term reinforces with linguistic evidence the fact that we are certainly not offering them as explanatory or justifying *conditions*. When we are asked why we say a certain person is lazy or intelligent or courageous, we are being asked in virtue of what do we *call* him this; we reply with "because of the way he regularly leaves his work unfinished," or "because of the ease with which he handles such and such problems," and so on. But when we are asked to say why, in our opinion, a picture lacks balance or is somber in tone, or why a poem is moving or tightly organized, we are doing a different kind of thing. We may use similar locutions: "his verse has strength and variety *because of the way* he handles the meter and employs the caesura," or "it is nobly austere *because of* the lack of detail and the restricted palette." But we can also express what we want to by using quite other expressions: "it is the handling of meter and caesura which is *responsible for* its strength and variety," "its nobly austere quality is *due to* the lack of detail and the use of a restricted palette," "its lack of balance *results from* the highlighting of the figures on the left," "those minor chords *make it* extremely moving," "those converging lines *give it* an extraordinary unity." These are locutions we cannot switch to with "lazy" or "intelligent"; to say what *makes* him lazy, what is *responsible for* his laziness, what it is *due to*, is to broach another question entirely.

One after another, in recent discussions, writers have insisted that aesthetic judgments are not "mechanical": "Critics do not formulate general standards and apply these mechanically to all, or to classes of, works of art." "Technical points can be settled rapidly, by the application of rules," but aesthetic questions "cannot be settled by any mechanical method." Instead, these writers on aesthetics have emphasized that there is no "substitute for individual judgment" with its "spontaneity and speculation" and that "The final standard . . . [is] the judgment of personal taste."[8] What is surprising is that, though such things have been repeated again and again, no one seems to have said what is meant by "taste" or by the word "mechanical." There are many judgments besides those requiring taste which demand "spontaneity" and "individual judgment" and are not "mechanical." Without a detailed comparison we cannot see in what particular way *aesthetic* judgments are not "mechanical," or how they differ from those other judgments, nor can we begin to specify what taste is. This I have attempted. It is a characteristic and essential feature of judgments which employ an aesthetic term that they cannot be made by appealing, in the sense explained, to non-aesthetic conditions.[9] This, I believe, is a logical feature of aesthetic or taste judgments in general, though I have argued it here only as regards the more restricted range of judgments which employ aesthetic terms. It is part of what "taste" means.

II

A great deal of work remains to be done on aesthetic concepts. In the remainder of this paper I shall offer some further suggestions which may help towards an understanding of them.

The realization that aesthetic concepts are governed only negatively by conditions is likely to give rise to puzzlement over how we manage to apply the words in our aesthetic vocabulary. If we are not following rules and there are no conditions to appeal to, how are we to know when they are applicable? One very natural way to counter this question is to point out that some other sorts of concepts also are not condition-governed. We do not apply simple color words by following rules or in accordance with principles. We see that the book is red by looking, just as we tell that the tea is sweet by tasting it. So too, it might be said, we just see (or fail to see) that things are delicate, balanced, and the like. This kind of comparison between the exercise of taste and the use of the five senses is indeed familiar; our use of the word "taste" itself shows that the comparison is age-old and very natural. Yet whatever the similarities, there are great dissimilarities too. A careful comparison cannot be attempted here though it would be valuable; but certain differences stand out, and writers who have emphasized that aesthetic judgments are not "mechanical" have sometimes dwelt on and been puzzled by them.

In the first place, while our ability to discern aesthetic features is dependent upon our possession of good eyesight, hearing, and so on, people normally endowed with senses and understanding may nevertheless fail to discern them. "Those who listen to a concert, walk round a gallery, read a poem may have roughly similar sense perceptions, but some get a great deal more than others," Miss

Macdonald says; but she adds that she is "puzzled by this feature 'in the object' which can be seen only by a specially qualified observer" and asks, "What is this 'something more'?"[10]

It is this difference between aesthetic and perceptual qualities which in part leads to the view that "works of art are esoteric objects . . . not simple objects of sense perception."[11] But there is no good reason for calling an object esoteric simply because we discern aesthetic qualities in it. The *objects* to which we apply aesthetic words are of the most diverse kinds and by no means esoteric: people and buildings, flowers and gardens, vases and furniture, as well as poems and music. Nor does there seem any good reason for calling the *qualities* themselves esoteric. It is true that someone with perfect eyes or ears might miss them, but we do after all say we *observe* or *notice* them ("Did you notice how very graceful she was?," "Did you observe the exquisite balance in all his pictures?"). In fact, they are very familiar indeed. We learn while quite young to use many aesthetic words, though they are, as one might expect from their dependence upon our ability to see, hear, distinguish colors, and the like, not the earliest words we learn; and our mastery and sophistication in using them develop along with the rest of our vocabulary. They are not rarities; some ranges of them are in regular use in everyday discourse.

The second notable difference between the exercise of taste and the use of the five senses lies in the way we support those judgments in which aesthetic concepts are employed. Although we use these concepts without rules or conditions, we do defend or support our judgments, and convince others of their rightness, by talking; "disputation about art is not futile," as Miss Macdonald says, for critics do "attempt a certain kind of explanation of works of art with the object of establishing correct judgments."[12] Thus even though this disputation does not consist in "deductive or inductive inference" or "reasoning," its occurrence is enough to show how very different these judgments are from those of a simple perceptual sort.

Now the critic's talk, it is clear, frequently consists in mentioning or pointing out the features, including easily discernible non-aesthetic ones, upon which the aesthetic qualities depend. But the puzzling question remains how, by mentioning these features, the critic is thereby justifying or supporting his judgments. To this question a number of recent writers have given an answer. Stuart Hampshire, for example, says that "One engages in aesthetic discussion for the sake of what one might see on the way. . . . If one has been brought to see what there is to be seen in the object, the purpose of discussion is achieved. . . . The point is to bring people to see these features."[13] The critic's talk, that is, often serves to support his judgments in a special way; it helps us to *see* what he has seen, namely, the aesthetic qualities of the object. But even when it is agreed that this is one of the main things that critics do, puzzlement tends to break out again over *how* they do it. How is it that by talking about features of the work (largely non-aesthetic ones) we can manage to bring others to see what they had not seen? "What sort of endowment is this which *talking* can modify? . . . Discussion does not improve eyesight and hearing" (my italics).[14]

Yet of course we do succeed in applying aesthetic terms, and we frequently do succeed by talking (and pointing and gesturing in certain ways) in bringing others to see what we see. One begins to suspect that puzzlement over how we can possibly do this, and puzzlement over the "esoteric" character of aesthetic qualities too, arises from bearing in mind inappropriate philosophical models. When someone is unable to see that the book on the table is brown, we cannot get him to see that it is by talking; consequently it seems puzzling that we might get someone to see that the vase is graceful by talking. If we are to dispel this puzzlement and recognize aesthetic concepts and qualities for what they are, we must abandon unsuitable models and investigate how we actually employ these concepts. With so much interest in and agreement about *what* the critic does, one might expect descriptions of *how* he does it to have been given. But little has been said about this, and what has been said is unsatisfactory.

Miss Macdonald,[15] for example, subscribes to this view of the critic's task as presenting "what is not obvious to casual or uninstructed inspection," and she does ask the question "What sort of considerations are involved, *and how*, to justify a critical verdict?" (my italics). But she does not in fact go on to answer it. She addresses herself instead to the different, though related, question of the interpretation of art works. In complex works different critics claim, often justifiably, to discern different features; hence Miss Macdonald suggests that in critical discourse the critic is bringing us to see what he sees by offering new interpretations. But if the question is "what (the critic) does and how he does it," he cannot be represented either wholly

or even mainly as providing new interpretations. His task quite as often is simply to help us to appreciate qualities which other critics have regularly found in the works he discusses. To put the stress upon *new* interpretations is to leave untouched the question how, by talking, he can help us to see *either* the newly appreciated aesthetic qualities *or* the old. In any case, besides complex poems or plays which may bear many interpretations, there are also relatively simple ones. There are also vases, buildings, and furniture, not to mention faces, sunsets, and scenery, about which no questions of "interpretation" arise but about which we talk in similar ways and make similar judgments. So the "puzzling" questions remain: how do we support these judgments and how do we bring others to see what we see?

Hampshire,[16] who likewise believes that the critic brings us "to see what there is to be seen in the object," does give some account of how the critic does this. "The greatest service of the critic" is to point out, isolate, and place in a frame of attention the "particular features of the particular object which *make* it ugly or beautiful"; for it is "difficult to see and hear all that there is to see and hear," and simply a prejudice to suppose that while "things really do have colors and shapes . . . there do not exist literally and objectively, concordances of colors and perceived rhythms and balances of shapes." However, these "extraordinary qualities" which the critic "may have seen (in the wider sense of 'see')" are "qualities which are of no direct practical interest." Consequently, to bring us to see them the critic employs "an unnatural use of words in description"; "the common vocabulary, being created for practical purposes, obstructs any disinterested perception of things"; and so these qualities "are normally described metaphorically by some transference of terms from the common vocabulary."

Much of what Hampshire says is right. But there is also something quite wrong in the view that the "common" vocabulary "obstructs" our aesthetic purposes, that it is "unnatural" to take it over and use it metaphorically, and that the critic "is under the necessity of building . . . a vocabulary *in opposition to the main tendency of his language*" (my italics). First, while we do often coin new metaphors in order to describe aesthetic qualities, we are by no means always under the necessity of wresting the "common vocabulary" from its "natural" uses to serve our purposes. There does exist, as I observed earlier, a large and accepted vocabulary of aesthetic terms some of which, whatever their metaphorical origins, are now not metaphors at all, others of which are at most quasi-metaphorical. Second, this view that our use of metaphor and quasi-metaphor for aesthetic purposes is unnatural or a makeshift into which we are forced by a language designed for other purposes misrepresents fundamentally the character of aesthetic qualities and aesthetic language. There is nothing unnatural about using words like "forceful," "dynamic," or "tightly-knit" in criticism; they do their work perfectly and are exactly the words needed for the purposes they serve. We do not want or need to replace them by words which lack the metaphorical element. In using them to describe works of art, the very point is that we are noticing aesthetic qualities related to their literal or common meanings. If we possessed a quite different word from "dynamic," one we could use to point out an aesthetic quality unrelated to the common meaning of "dynamic," it could not be used to describe that quality which "dynamic" does serve to point out. Hampshire pictures "a colony of aesthetes, disengaged from practical needs and manipulations" and says that "descriptions of aesthetic qualities, which for us are metaphorical, might seem to them to have an altogether literal and familiar sense"; they might use "a more directly descriptive vocabulary." But if they had a new and "directly descriptive" vocabulary lacking the links with non-aesthetic properties and interests which our vocabulary possesses, they would have to remain silent about many of the aesthetic qualities we can describe; further, if they were more completely "disengaged from practical needs" and other non-aesthetic awarenesses and interests, they would perforce be blind to many aesthetic qualities we can appreciate. The links between aesthetic qualities and non-aesthetic ones are both obvious and vital. Aesthetic concepts, all of them, carry with them attachments and in one way or another are tethered to or parasitic upon non-aesthetic features. The fact that many aesthetic terms are metaphorical or quasi-metaphorical in no way means that common language is an ill-adapted tool with which we have to struggle. When someone writes as Hampshire does, one suspects again that critical language is being judged against other models. To use language which is frequently metaphorical might be strange for some *other* purpose or from the standpoint of doing something else, but for the purpose and from the standpoint of making aesthetic observations it is not. To say it is an unnatural use of language for doing *this* is to imply there is or could be for this purpose some other and "natural" use. But these *are* natural ways of talking about aesthetic matters.

To help understand what the critic does, then, how he supports his judgments and gets his audience to see what he sees, I shall attempt a brief description of the methods we use as critics.[17]

(1)   We may simply mention or point out non-aesthetic features: "Notice these flecks of color, that dark mass there, those lines." By merely drawing attention to those easily discernible features which make the painting luminous or warm or dynamic, we often succeed in bringing someone to see these aesthetic qualities. We get him to see B by mentioning something different, A. Sometimes in doing this we are drawing attention to features which may have gone unnoticed by an untrained or insufficiently attentive eye or ear: "Just listen for the repeated figure in the left hand," "Did you notice the figure of Icarus in the Breughel? It is very small." Sometimes they are features which have been seen or heard but of which the significance or purpose has been missed in any of a variety of ways: "Notice how much darker he has made the central figure, how much brighter these colors are than the adjacent ones," "Of course, you've observed the ploughman in the foreground; but had you considered how he, like everyone else in the picture, is going about his business without noticing the fall of Icarus?" In mentioning features which may be discerned by anyone with normal eyes, ears, and intelligence, we are singling out what may serve as a kind of key to grasping or seeing something else (and the key may not be the same for each person).

(2)   On the other hand we often simply mention the very qualities we want people to see. We point to a painting and say, "Notice how nervous and delicate the drawing is," or "See what energy and vitality it has." The use of the aesthetic term itself may do the trick; we say what the quality or character is, and people who had not seen it before see it.

(3)   Most often, there is a linking of remarks about aesthetic and non-aesthetic features: "Have you noticed this line and that, and the points of bright color here and there . . . don't they give it vitality, energy?"

(4)   We do, in addition, often make extensive and helpful use of similes and genuine metaphors: "It's as if there were small points of light burning," "as though he had thrown on the paint violently

and in anger," "the light shimmers, the lines dance, everything is air, lightness and gaiety," "his canvasses are fires, they crackle, burn, and blaze, even at their most subdued always restlessly flickering, but often bursting into flame, great pyrotechnic displays," and so on.

(5) We make use of contrasts, comparisons, and reminiscences: "Suppose he had made that a lighter yellow, moved it to the right, how flat it would have been," "Don't you think it has something of the quality of a Rembrandt?," "Hasn't it the same serenity, peace, and quality of light of those summer evenings in Norfolk?" We use what keys we have to the known sensitivity, susceptibilities, and experience of our audience.

Critics and commentators may range, in their methods, from one extreme to the other, from painstaking concentration on points of detail, line and color, vowels and rhymes, to more or less flowery and luxuriant metaphor. Even the enthusiastic biographical sketch decorated with suitable epithet and metaphor may serve. What is best depends on both the audience and the work under discussion. But this would not be a complete sketch unless certain other notes were added.

(6) Repetition and reiteration often play an important role. When we are in front of a canvas we may come back time and again to the same points, drawing attention to the same lines and shapes, repeating the same words, "swirling," "balance," "luminosity," or the same similes and metaphors, as if time and familiarity, looking harder, listening more carefully, paying closer attention may help. So again with variation; it often helps to talk round what we have said, to build up, supplement with more talk *of the same kind*. When someone misses the swirling quality, when one epithet or one metaphor does not work, we throw in related ones; we speak of its wild movement, how it twists and turns, writhes and whirls, as though, failing to score a direct hit, we may succeed with a barrage of near-synonyms.

(7) Finally, besides our verbal performances, the rest of our behavior is important. We accompany our talk with appropriate tones of voice, expression, nods, looks, and gestures. A critic may sometimes do more with a sweep of the arm than by talking. An appropriate gesture may make us see the violence in a painting or the character of a melodic line.

These ways of acting and talking are not significantly different whether we are dealing with a particular work, paragraph, or line, or speaking of an artist's work as a whole, or even drawing attention to a sunset or scenery. But even with the speaker doing all this, we may fail to see what he sees. There may be a point, though there need be no limit except that imposed by time and patience, at which he gives up and sets us (or himself) down as lacking in some way, defective in sensitivity. He may tell us to look or read again, or to read or look at other things and then come back again to this; he may suspect there are experiences in life we have missed. But these are the things he does. This is what succeeds if anything does; indeed it is all that can be done.

By realizing clearly that, whether we are dealing with art or scenery or people or natural objects, this is how we operate with aesthetic concepts, we may recognize this sphere of human activity for what it is. We operate with different kinds of concepts in different ways. If we want someone to agree that a color is red we may take it into a good light and ask him to look; if it is viridian we may fetch a color chart and make him compare; if we want him to agree that a figure is fourteen-sided we get him to count; and to bring him to agree that something is dilapidated or that someone is intelligent or lazy we may do other things, citing features, reasoning and arguing about them, weighing and balancing. These are the methods appropriate to these various concepts. But the ways we get someone to see aesthetic qualities are different; they are of the kind I have described. With each kind of concept we can describe what we do and how we do it. But the methods suited to these other concepts will not do for aesthetic ones, or vice versa. We cannot prove by argument or by assembling a sufficiency of conditions that something is graceful; but this is no more puzzling than our inability to prove, by using the methods, metaphors, and gestures of the art critic, that it will be mate in ten moves. The questions raised admit of no answer beyond the sort of description I have given. To go on to ask, with puzzlement, how it is that *when* we do these things people come to see, is like asking how is it that, when we take the book into a good light, our companion agrees with us that it is red. There is no place for this kind of question or puzzlement. Aesthetic concepts are as natural, as little esoteric, as any others. It is against the background of different and philosophically more familiar models that they seem queer or puzzling.

I have described how people justify aesthetic judgments and bring others to see aesthetic qualities in things. I shall end by showing that the methods I have outlined are the ones natural for and characteristic of taste concepts from the start. When someone tries to make me see that a painting is delicate or balanced, I have some understanding of these terms already and know in a sense what I am looking for. But if there is puzzlement over how, by talking, he can bring me to see these qualities in this picture, there should be a corresponding puzzlement over how I learned to use aesthetic terms and discern aesthetic qualities in the first place. We may ask, therefore, how we learn to do these things; and this is to inquire (1) what natural potentialities and tendencies people have and (2) how we develop and take advantage of these capacities in training and teaching. Now for the second of these, there is no doubt that our ability to notice and respond to aesthetic qualities is cultivated and developed by our contacts with parents and teachers from quite an early age. What is interesting for my present purpose is that, while we are being taught in the presence of examples what grace, delicacy, and so on are, the methods used, the language and behavior, are of a piece with those of the critic as I have already described them.

To pursue these two questions, consider first those words like "dynamic," "melancholy," "balanced," "taut," or "gay" the aesthetic use of which is quasi-metaphorical. It has already been emphasized that we could not use them thus without some experience of situations where they are used literally. The present inquiry is how we shift from literal to aesthetic uses of them. For this it is required that there be certain abilities and tendencies to link experiences, to regard certain things as similar, and to see, explore, and be interested in these similarities. It is a feature of human intelligence and sensitivity that we do spontaneously do these things and that the tendency can be encouraged and developed. It is no more baffling that we should employ aesthetic terms of this sort than that we should make metaphors at all. Easy and smooth transitions by which we shift to the use of these aesthetic terms are not hard to find. We suggest to children that simple pieces of music are hurrying or running or skipping or dawdling, from there we move to lively, gay, jolly, happy, smiling, or sad, and, as their experiences and vocabulary broaden, to solemn, dynamic, or melancholy. But the child also discovers for himself many of these parallels and takes interest or delight in them. He is likely on his own to skip, march, clap, or laugh with the music, and without this natural tendency our training would get nowhere. Insofar, however, as we do

take advantage of this tendency and help him by training, *we do just what the critic does.* We may merely need to persuade the child to pay attention, to look or listen; or we may simply *call* the music jolly. But we are also likely to use, as the critic does, reiteration, synonyms, parallels, contrasts, similes, metaphors, gestures, and other expressive behavior.

Of course the recognition of similarities and simple metaphorical extensions are not the only transitions to the aesthetic use of language. Others are made in different ways; for instance, by the kind of peripheral cases I mentioned earlier. When our admiration is for something as simple as the thinness of a glass or the smoothness of a fabric, it is not difficult to call attention to such things, evoke a similar delight, and introduce suitable aesthetic terms. These transitions are only the beginnings; it may often be questionable whether a term is yet being used aesthetically or not. Many of the terms I have mentioned may be used in ways which are not straightforwardly literal but of which we should hesitate to say that they demanded much yet by way of aesthetic sensitivity. We speak of warm and cool colors, and we may say of a brightly colored picture that at least it is gay and lively. When we have brought someone to make this sort of metaphorical extension of terms, he has made one of the transitional steps from which he may move on to uses which more obviously deserve to be called aesthetic and demand more aesthetic appreciation. When I said at the outset that aesthetic sensitivity was rarer than some other natural endowments, I was not denying that it varies in degree from the rudimentary to the refined. Most people learn easily to make the kinds of remarks I am now considering. But when someone can call bright canvasses gay and lively without being able to spot the one which is really vibrant, or can recognize the obvious outward vigor and energy of a student composition played *con fuoco* while failing to see that it lacks inner fire and drive, we do not regard his aesthetic sensitivity in these areas as particularly developed. However, once these transitions from common to aesthetic uses are begun in the more obvious cases, the domain of aesthetic concepts may broaden out, and they may become more subtle and even partly autonomous. The initial steps, however varied the metaphorical shifts and however varied the experiences upon which they are parasitic, are natural and easy.

Much the same is true when we turn to those words which have no standard non-aesthetic use, "lovely," "pretty," "dainty," "graceful," "elegant." We cannot say that these are learned by a metaphorical shift. But they still are linked to non-aesthetic features in many ways and the learning of them also is made possible by certain kinds of natural response, reaction, and ability. We learn them not so much by noticing similarities, but by our attention being caught and focussed in other ways. Certain phenomena which are outstanding or remarkable or unusual catch the eye or ear, seize our attention and interest, and move us to surprise, admiration, delight, fear, or distaste. Children begin by reacting in these ways to spectacular sunsets, woods in autumn, roses, dandelions, and other striking and colorful objects, and it is in these circumstances that we find ourselves introducing general aesthetic words to them, like "lovely," "pretty," and "ugly." It is not an accident that the first lessons in aesthetic appreciation consist in drawing the child's attention to roses rather than to grass; nor is it surprising that we remark to him on the autumn colors rather than on the subdued tints of winter. We all of us, not only children, pay aesthetic attention more readily and easily to such outstanding and easily noticeable things. We notice with pleasure early spring grass or the first snow, hills of notably marked and varied contours, scenery flecked with a great variety of color or dappled variously with sun and shadow. We are struck and impressed by great size or mass, as with mountains or cathedrals. We are similarly responsive to unusual precision or minuteness or remarkable feats of skill, as with complex and elaborate filigree, or intricate wood carving and fan-vaulting. It is at these times, taking advantage of these natural interests and admirations, that we first teach the simpler aesthetic words. People of moderate aesthetic sensitivity and sophistication continue to exhibit aesthetic interest mainly on such occasions and to use only the more general words ("pretty," "lovely," and the like). But these situations may serve as a beginning from which we extend our aesthetic interests to wider and less obvious fields, mastering as we go the more subtle and specific vocabulary of taste. The principles do not change; the basis for learning more specific terms like "graceful," "delicate," and "elegant" is also our interest in and admiration for various non-aesthetic natural properties ("She seems to move *effortlessly*, as if floating," "So very *thin* and *fragile*, as if a breeze might destroy it," "So *small* and yet so *intricate*," "So *economical* and *perfectly adapted*").[18] And even with these aesthetic terms which are not metaphorical themselves ("graceful," "delicate," "elegant"), we rely in the same way upon the critic's methods, including comparison, illustration, and metaphor, to teach or make clear what they mean.

I have wished to emphasize in the latter part of this paper the natural basis of responses of various kinds without which aesthetic terms could not be learned. I have also outlined what some of the features are to which we naturally respond: similarities of various sorts, notable colors, shapes, scents, size, intricacy, and much else besides. Even the non-metaphorical aesthetic terms have significant links with all kinds of natural features by which our interest, wonder, admiration, delight, or distaste is aroused. But in particular I have wanted to urge that it should not strike us as puzzling that the critic supports his judgments and brings us to see aesthetic qualities by pointing out key features and talking about them in the way he does. It is by the very same methods that people helped us develop our aesthetic sense and master its vocabulary from the beginning. If we responded to those methods then, it is not surprising that we respond to the critic's discourse now. It would be surprising if, by using this language and behavior, people could *not* sometimes bring us to see the aesthetic qualities of things; for this would prove us lacking in one characteristically human kind of awareness and activity.

Notes

1 I shall speak loosely of an "aesthetic term," even when, because the word sometimes has other uses, it would be more correct to speak of its *use* as an aesthetic term. I shall also speak of "non-aesthetic" words, concepts, features, and so on. None of the terms other writers use, "natural," "observable," "perceptual," "physical," "objective" (qualities), "neutral," "descriptive" (language), when they approach the distinction I am making, is really apt for my purpose.

2 A contrast will reinforce this. If a critic were to describe a passage of music as chattering, carbonated, or gritty, a painter's coloring as vitreous, farinaceous, or effervescent, or a writer's style as

glutinous, or abrasive, he *would* be using live metaphors rather than drawing on the more normal language of criticism. Words like "athletic," "vertiginous," "silken" may fall somewhere between.

3 In a paper ("Critical Communication") reprinted in *Aesthetics and Language*, ed. W. Elton (Oxford, 1954), pp. 131–146, Arnold Isenberg discusses certain problems about aesthetic concepts and qualities. Like others who approach these problems, he does not isolate them, as I do, from questions about verdicts on the *merits* of works of art, or from questions about *likings* and *preferences*. He says something parallel to my remarks above: "There is not in all the world's criticism a single purely descriptive statement concerning which one is prepared to say beforehand, 'if it is true, I shall *like* that work so much the better'" (p. 139, my italics). I should think *this* is highly questionable.

4 Isenberg (*op. cit.*, p. 132) makes a somewhat similar but mistaken point: "If we had been told that the colors of a certain painting are garish, it would be *astonishing* to find that they are *all* very pale and unsaturated" (my italics). But if we say "all" rather than "predominantly," then "astonishing" is the wrong word. The word that goes with "all" is "impossible"; "astonishing" might go with "predominantly."

5 H. L. A. Hart, "The Ascription of Responsibility and Rights," in *Logic and Language*, 1st ser., ed. A. G. N. Flew (Oxford, 1951). Hart indeed speaks of "conditions" throughout, see p. 148.

6 I cannot in the compass of this paper discuss the other types of apparent exceptions to my thesis. Cases where a man *lacking* in sensitivity might learn and follow a rule, as above, ought to be distinguished from cases where someone who *possesses* sensitivity might know, from a non-aesthetic description, that an aesthetic term applies. I have stated my thesis as though this latter kind of case never occurs because I have had my eye on the logical features of *typical* aesthetic judgments and have preferred to over-rather than understate my view. But with certain aesthetic terms, especially negative ones, there may perhaps be some rare genuine exceptions when a description enables us to visualize very fully, and when what is described belongs to certain restricted classes of things, say human faces or animal forms. Perhaps a description like "One eye red and rheumy, the other missing, a wart-covered nose, a twisted mouth, a greenish pallor" may justify in a strong sense ("must be," "cannot but be,") the judgments "ugly" or "hideous." If so, such cases are marginal, form a very small minority, and are uncharacteristic or atypical of aesthetic judgments in general. Usually when, on hearing a description, we say "it *must* be very beautiful (graceful, or the like)," we mean no more than "it surely must be, it's only remotely possible that it isn't." Different again are

situations, and these are very numerous, where we can move quite simply from "bright colors" to "gay," or from "reds and yellows" to "warm," but where we are as yet only on the borderline of anything that could be called an expression of taste or aesthetic sensibility. I have stressed the importance of this transitional and border area between non-aesthetic and obviously aesthetic judgments in Section II.

7 Helen Knight says (Elton, *op. cit.*, p. 152) that "piquant" (one of my "aesthetic" terms) "depends on" various features (a *retroussé* nose, a pointed chin, and the like), and that these features are *criteria* for it; this second claim is what I am denying. She also maintains that "good," when applied to works of art, depends on *criteria* like balance, solidity, depth, profundity (my aesthetic terms again; I should place piquancy in this list). I would deny this too, though I regard it as a different question and do not consider it in this paper. The two questions need separating: the relation of non-aesthetic features (*retroussé*, pointed) to aesthetic qualities, and the relation of aesthetic qualities to "aesthetically good" (verdicts). Most writings which touch on the nature of aesthetic concepts have this other (verdict) question mainly in mind. Mrs. Knight blurs this difference when she says, for example, "'piquant' is the same kind of word as 'good.'"

8 See articles by Margaret Macdonald and J. A. Passmore in Elton, *op. cit.*, pp. 118, 41, 40, 119.

9 As I indicated, above, I have dealt only with the relation of *non-aesthetic* to aesthetic features. Perhaps a description in *aesthetic* terms may occasionally suffice for applying another aesthetic term. Johnson's Dictionary gives "handsome" as "beautiful with dignity"; Shorter O. E. D. gives "pretty" as "beautiful in a slight, dainty, or diminutive way."

10 Macdonald in Elton, *op. cit.*, pp. 114, 119. See also pp. 120, 122.

11 Macdonald, *ibid.*, pp. 114, 120–123. She speaks of non-aesthetic properties here as "physical" or "observable" qualities, and distinguishes between "physical object" and "work of art."

12 *Ibid.*, 115–116; cf. also John Holloway, *Proceedings of the Aristotelian Society*, Supp. Vol. XXIII (1949), pp. 175–176.

13 Stuart Hampshire in Elton, *op. cit.*, p. 165. Cf. also remarks in Elton by Isenberg (pp. 142, 145), Passmore (p. 38), in *Philosophy and Psychoanalysis* by John Wisdom (Oxford, 1953), pp. 223–224, and in Holloway, *op. cit.*, p. 175.

14 Macdonald, *op. cit.*, pp. 119–120.

15 *Ibid.*, see pp. 127, 122, 125, 115. Other writers also place the stress on interpretation, cf. Holloway, *op. cit.*, p. 173ff.

16 *Op. cit.*, pp. 165–168.

17 Holloway, *op. cit.*, pp. 173–174, lists some of these very briefly.

18 It is worth noticing that most of the words which in current usage are primarily or exclusively aesthetic terms had earlier non-aesthetic uses and gained their present use by some kind of metaphorical shift. Without reposing too great weight on these etymological facts, it can be seen that their history reflects connections with the responses, interests, and natural features I have mentioned as underlying the learning and use of aesthetic terms. These transitions suggest both the dependence of aesthetic upon other interests, and what some of these interests are. Connected with liking, delight, affection, regard, estimation, or choice – *beautiful, graceful, delicate, lovely, exquisite, elegant, dainty*; with fear or repulsion – *ugly*; with what notably catches the eye or attention – *garish, splendid, gaudy*; with what attracts by notable rarity, precision, skill, ingenuity, elaboration – *dainty, nice, pretty, exquisite*; with adaptation to function, suitability to ease of handling – *handsome*.

13

Categories of Art

Kendall L. Walton

I Introduction

> False judgments enter art history if we judge
> from the impression which pictures of dif-
> ferent epochs, placed side by side, make on
> us. . . . They speak a different language.[1]

Paintings and sculptures are to be looked at;
sonatas and songs are to be heard. What is important about these works of art, as works of art, is
what can be seen or heard in them.[2] Inspired partly
by apparent commonplaces such as these, many
recent aesthetic theorists have attempted to purge
from criticism of works of art supposedly extraneous excursions into matters not (or not "directly")
available to inspection of the works, and to focus
attention on the works themselves. Circumstances
connected with a work's origin, in particular, are
frequently held to have no essential bearing on an
assessment of its aesthetic nature – for example,
who created the work, how, and when; the artist's
intentions and expectations concerning it, his
philosophical views, psychological state, and love
life; the artistic traditions and intellectual atmosphere of his society. Once produced (it is argued)
the work must stand or fall on its own; it must be
judged for what it is, regardless of how it came to
be as it is.

Arguments for the irrelevance of such historical
circumstances to aesthetic judgments about works
of art may, but need not, involve the claim that
these circumstances are not of "aesthetic" interest

Kendall L. Walton, "Categories of Art," *Philosophical Review*, 79 (1970), pp. 334–67. Public domain.

or importance, though obviously they are often
important in biographical, historical, psychological, or sociological researches. One might consider
an artist's action in producing a work to be aesthetically interesting, an "aesthetic object" in its
own right, while vehemently maintaining its irrelevance to an aesthetic investigation of the work.
Robert Rauschenberg once carefully obliterated a
drawing by de Kooning, titled the bare canvas
"Erased De Kooning Drawing", framed it, and
exhibited it.[3] His doing this might be taken as symbolic or expressive (of an attitude toward art, or
toward life in general, or whatever) in an "aesthetically" significant manner, perhaps somewhat as an
action of a character in a play might be, and yet
thought to have no bearing whatever on the aesthetic nature of the finished product. The issue I
am here concerned with is how far critical questions about works of art can be *separated* from
questions about their histories.[4]

One who wants to make this separation quite
sharp may regard the basic facts of art along the
following lines. Works of art are simply objects
with various properties, of which we are primarily
interested in perceptual ones – visual properties of
paintings, audible properties of music, and so
forth.[5] A work's perceptual properties include
"aesthetic" as well as "nonaesthetic" ones – the
sense of mystery and tension of a painting as well
as its dark coloring and diagonal composition; the
energy, exuberance, and coherence of a sonata, as
well as its meters, rhythms, pitches, timbres, and
so forth; the balance and serenity of a Gothic
cathedral as well as its dimensions, lines, and
symmetries.[6] Aesthetic properties are features or

characteristics of works of art just as much as non-aesthetic ones are.[7] They are *in* the works, to be seen, heard, or otherwise perceived there. Seeing a painting's sense of mystery or hearing a sonata's coherence might require looking or listening longer or harder than does perceiving colors and shapes, rhythms and pitches; it may even require special training or a special kind of sensitivity. But these qualities must be discoverable simply by examining the works themselves if they are discoverable at all. It is never even partly *in virtue of* the circumstances of a work's origin that it has a sense of mystery or is coherent or serene. Such circumstances sometimes provide hints concerning what to look for in a work, what we might reasonably expect to find by examining it. But these hints are always theoretically dispensable; a work's aesthetic properties must "in principle" be ascertainable without their help. Surely (it seems) a Rembrandt portrait does not have (or lack) a sense of mystery in virtue of the fact that Rembrandt intended it to have (or to lack) that quality, any more than a contractor's intention to make a roof leakproof makes it so; nor is the portrait mysterious in virtue of any other facts about what Rembrandt thought or how he went about painting the portrait or what his society happened to be like. Such circumstances are important to the result only in so far as they had an effect on the pattern of paint splotches that became attached to the canvas, and the canvas can be examined without in any way considering how the splotches got there. It would not matter in the least to the aesthetic properties of the portrait if the paint had been applied to the canvas not by Rembrandt at all, but by a chimpanzee or a cyclone in a paint shop.

The view sketched above can easily seem very persuasive. But the tendency of critics to discuss the histories of works of art in the course of justifying aesthetic judgments about them has been remarkably persistent. This is partly because hints derived from facts about a work's history, however dispensable they may be "in principle," are often crucially important in practice. (One might simply not think to listen for a recurring series of intervals in a piece of music, until he learns that the composer meant the work to be structured around it.) No doubt it is partly due also to genuine confusions on the part of critics. But I will argue that (some) facts about the origins of works of art have an *essential* role in criticism, that aesthetic judgments rest on them in an absolutely fundamental way. For this reason, and for another as well, the view that works

of art should be judged simply by what can be perceived in them is seriously misleading, though there is something right in the idea that what matters aesthetically about a painting or a sonata is just how it looks or sounds.

II   Standard, Variable, and Contra-Standard Properties

I will continue to call tension, mystery, energy, coherence, balance, serenity, sentimentality, pallidness, disunity, grotesqueness, and so forth, as well as colors and shapes, pitches and timbres *properties* of works of art, though "property" is to be construed broadly enough not to beg any important questions. I will also, following Sibley, call properties of the former sort "aesthetic" properties, but purely for reasons of convenience I will include in this category "representational" and "resemblance" properties, which Sibley excludes – for example, the property of representing or being a picture of Napoleon, that of depicting an old man (as) stooping over a fire, that of resembling, or merely suggesting, a human face, claws (the petals of Van Gogh's sunflowers), or (in music) footsteps or conversation. It is not essential for my purposes to delimit with any exactness the class of aesthetic properties (if indeed any such delimitation is possible), for I am more interested in discussing particular examples of such properties than in making generalizations about the class as a whole. It will be obvious, however, that what I say about the examples I deal with is also applicable to a great many other properties we would want to call aesthetic.

Sibley points out that a work's aesthetic properties depend on its nonaesthetic properties; the former are "emergent" or "*Gestalt*" properties based on the latter.[8] I take this to be true of all the examples of aesthetic properties we will be dealing with, including representational and resemblance ones. It is because of the configuration of colors and shapes on a painting, perhaps in particular its dark colors and diagonal composition, that it has a sense of mystery and tension, if it does. The colors and shapes of a portrait are responsible for its resembling an old man and (perhaps with its title) its depicting an old man. The coherence or unity of a piece of music (for example, Beethoven's *Fifth Symphony*) may be largely due to the frequent recurrence of a rhythmic motive, and the regular meter of a song plus the absence of harmonic modulation and of large intervals in the voice part may make it serene or peaceful.

Moreover, a work *seems* or *appears* to us to have certain aesthetic properties because we observe in it, or it appears to us to have, certain nonaesthetic features (though it may not be necessary to notice consciously all the relevant nonasthetic features). A painting depicting an old man may not look like an old man to someone who is color-blind, or when it is seen from an extreme angle or in bad lighting conditions so that its colors or shapes are distorted or obscured. Beethoven's *Fifth Symphony* performed in such a sloppy manner that many occurrences of the four-note rhythmic motive do not sound similar may seem incoherent or disunified.

I will argue, however, that a work's aesthetic properties depend not only on its nonaesthetic ones, but also on which of its nonaesthetic properties are "standard," which "variable," and which "contra-standard," in senses to be explained. I will approach this thesis by way of the psychological point that what aesthetic properties a work seems to us to have depends not only on what nonaesthetic features we perceive in it, but also on which of them are standard, which variable, and which contra-standard *for us* (in a sense also to be explained).

It is necessary to introduce first a distinction between standard, variable, and contra-standard properties relative to perceptually distinguishable categories of works of art. Such categories include media, genre, styles, forms, and so forth – for example, the categories of paintings, cubist paintings, Gothic architecture, classical sonatas, paintings in the style of Cézanne, and music in the style of late Beethoven – if they are interpreted in such a way that membership is determined solely by features that can be perceived in a work when it is experienced in the normal manner. Thus whether or not a piece of music was written in the eighteenth century is irrelevant to whether it belongs to the category of classical sonatas (interpreted in this way), and whether a work was produced by Cézanne or Beethoven has nothing essential to do with whether it is in the style of Cézanne or late Beethoven. The category of etchings as normally construed is not perceptually distinguishable in the requisite sense, for to be an etching is, I take it, simply to have been produced in a particular manner. But the category of *apparent* etchings, works which *look* like etchings from the quality of their lines, whether they are etchings or not, is perceptually distinguishable. A category will not count as "perceptually distinguishable" in my sense if in

order to determine perceptually whether something belongs to it, it is necessary (in some or all cases) to determine which categories it is correctly perceived in partly or wholly on the basis of nonperceptual considerations. (See Section IV below.) This prevents, for example, the category of serene things from being perceptually distinguishable in this sense.

A feature of a work of art is *standard* with respect to a (perceptually distinguishable) category just in case it is among those in virtue of which works in that category belong to that category – that is, just in case the lack of that feature would disqualify, or tend to disqualify, a work from that category. A feature is *variable* with respect to a category just in case it has nothing to do with works' belonging to that category; the possession or lack of the feature is irrelevant to whether a work qualifies for the category. Finally, a *contra-standard* feature with respect to a category is the absence of a standard feature with respect to that category – that is, a feature whose presence tends to *disqualify* works as members of the category. Needless to say, it will not be clear in *all* cases whether a feature of a work is standard, variable, or contra-standard relative to a given category, since the criteria for classifying works of art are far from precise. But clear examples are abundant. The flatness of a painting and the motionlessness of its markings are standard, and its particular shapes and colors are variable, relative to the category of painting. A protruding three-dimensional object or an electrically driven twitching of the canvas would be contra-standard relative to this category. The straight lines in stick-figure drawings and squarish shapes in cubist paintings are standard with respect to those categories respectively, though they are variable with respect to the categories of drawing and painting. The exposition–development–recapitulation form of a classical sonata is standard, and its thematic material is variable, relative to the category of sonatas.

In order to explain what I mean by features being standard, variable, or contra-standard *for a person on a particular occasion*, I must introduce the notion of perceiving a work in, or as belonging to, a certain (perceptually distinguishable) category.[9] To perceive a work in a certain category is to perceive the "*Gestalt*" of that category in the work. This needs some explanation. People familiar with Brahmsian music – that is, music in the style of Brahms (notably, works of Johannes Brahms) – or impressionist paintings can frequently recognize members of these categories by recognizing the Brahmsian or impressionist *Gestalt* qualities. Such recognition is dependent on perception of particular features that are standard relative to these categories, but it is not a matter of *inferring* from the presence of such features that a work is Brahmsian or impressionist. One may not notice many of the relevant features, and he may be very vague about which ones are relevant. If I recognize a work as Brahmsian by first noting its lush textures, its basically traditional harmonic and formal structure, its superimposition and alternation of duple and triple meters, and so forth, and recalling that these characteristics are typical of Brahmsian works, I have not recognized it by hearing the Brahmsian *Gestalt*. To do that is simply to recognize it by its Brahmsian *sound*, without necessarily paying attention to the features ("cues") responsible for it. Similarly, recognizing an impressionist painting by its impressionist *Gestalt*, is recognizing the impressionist *look* about it, which we are familiar with from other impressionist paintings; not applying a rule we have learned for recognizing it from its features.

To *perceive a Gestalt* quality in a work – that is, to perceive it in a certain category – is not, or not merely, to *recognize* that *Gestalt* quality. Recognition is a momentary occurrence, whereas perceiving a quality is a continuous state which may last for a short or long time. (For the same reason, seeing the ambiguous duck-rabbit figure as a duck is not, or not merely, recognizing a property of it.) We perceive the Brahmsian or impressionist *Gestalt* in a work when, and as long as, it *sounds* (*looks*) Brahmsian or impressionist to us. This involves perceiving (not necessarily being aware of) features standard relative to that category. But it is not *just* this, nor this plus the intellectual realization that these features make the work Brahmsian, or impressionist. These features are perceived combined into a single *Gestalt* quality.

We can of course perceive a work in several or many different categories at once. A Brahms sonata might be heard simultaneously as a piece of music, a sonata, a romantic work, and a Brahmsian work. Some pairs of categories, however, seem to be such that one cannot perceive a work as belonging to both at once, much as one cannot see the duck-rabbit both as a duck and as a rabbit simultaneously. One cannot see a photographic image simultaneously as a still photograph and as (part of) a film, nor can one see something both in the category of paintings and at the same time in the category (to be explained shortly) of *guernicas*.

It will be useful to point out some of the *causes* of our perceiving works in certain categories. (a) In which categories we perceive a work depends in part, of course, on what other works we are familiar with. The more works of a certain sort we have experienced, the more likely it is that we will perceive a particular work in that category. (b) What we have heard critics and others say about works we have experienced, how they have categorized them, and what resemblances they have pointed out to us is also important. If no one has ever explained to me what is distinctive about Schubert's style (as opposed to the styles of, say, Schumann, Mendelssohn, Beethoven, Brahms, Hugo Wolf), or even pointed out that there is such a distinctive style, I may never have learned to hear the Schubertian *Gestalt* quality, even if I have heard many of Schubert's works, and so I may not hear his works as Schubertian. (c) How we are introduced to the particular work in question may be involved. If a Cézanne painting is exhibited in a collection of French Impressionist works, or if before seeing it we are told that it is French Impressionist, we are more likely to see it as French Impressionist than if it is exhibited in a random collection and we are not told anything about it beforehand.

I will say that a feature of a work is standard for a particular person on a particular occasion when, and only when, it is standard relative to some category in which he perceives it, and is not contra-standard relative to any category in which he perceives it. A feature is variable for a person on an occasion just when it is variable relative to *all* of the categories in which he perceives it. And a feature is contra-standard for a person on an occasion just when it is contra-standard relative to *any* of the categories in which he perceives it.[10]

III   A Point about Perception

I turn now to my psychological thesis that what aesthetic properties a work seems to have, what aesthetic effect it has on us, how it strikes us aesthetically often depends (in part) on which of its features are standard, which variable, and which contra-standard for us. I offer a series of examples in support of this thesis.

(a)   Representational and resemblance properties provide perhaps the most obvious illustration of this thesis. Many works of art look like or resemble other objects – people, buildings, mountains, bowls of fruit, and so forth. Rembrandt's "Titus Reading" looks like a boy, and in particular like Rembrandt's son; Picasso's "Les Demoiselles d'Avignon" looks like five women, four standing and one sitting (though not *especially* like any particular women). A portrait may even be said to be a *perfect* likeness of the sitter, or to capture his image *exactly*.

An important consideration in determining whether a work *depicts* or *represents* a particular object, or an object of a certain sort (for example, Rembrandt's son, or simply *a* boy), in the sense of being a picture, sculpture, or whatever of it[11] is whether the work resembles that object, or objects of that kind. A significant degree of resemblance is, I suggest, a necessary condition in most contexts for such representation or depiction,[12] though the resemblance need not be obvious at first glance. If we are unable to see a similarity between a painting purportedly of a woman and women, I think we would have to suppose either that there is such a similarity which we have not yet discovered (as one might fail to see a face in a maze of lines), or that it simply is not a picture of a woman. Resemblance is of course not a *sufficient* condition for representation, since a portrait (containing only one figure) might resemble both the sitter and his twin brother equally but is not a portrait of both of them. (The title might determine which of them it depicts.)[13]

It takes only a touch of perversity, however, to find much of our talk about resemblances between works of art and other things preposterous. Paintings and people are *very* different sorts of things. Paintings are pieces of canvas supporting splotches of paint, while people are live, three-dimensional, flesh-and-blood animals. Moreover, except rarely and under special conditions of observation (probably including bad lighting) paintings and people *look* very different. Paintings look like pieces of canvas (or anyway flat surfaces) covered with paint and people look like flesh-and-blood animals. There is practically no danger of confusing them. How, then, can anyone seriously hold that a portrait resembles the sitter to any significant extent, let alone that it is a perfect likeness of him? Yet it remains true that many paintings strike us as resembling people, sometimes very much or even exactly – despite the fact that they look so very different!

To resolve this paradox we must recognize that the resemblances we perceive between, for example, portraits and people, those that are relevant in determining what works of art depict or represent, are resemblances of a somewhat special sort, tied up with the categories in which we perceive such works. The properties of a work which are standard for us are ordinarily irrelevant to what we take it to look like or resemble in the relevant sense, and hence to what we take it to depict or represent. The properties of a portrait which make it *so* different from, so easily distinguishable from, a person – such as its flatness and its *painted* look – are standard for us. Hence these properties just do not count with regard to what (or whom) it looks like. It is only the properties which are variable for us, the colors and shapes on the work's surface, that make it look to us like what it does. And these are the ones which are taken as relevant in determining what (if anything) the work represents.[14]

Other examples will reinforce this point. A marble bust of a Roman emperor seems to us to resemble a man with, say, an aquiline nose, a wrinkled brow, and an expression of grim determination, and we take it to represent a man with, or as having, those characteristics. But why don't we say that it resembles and represents a perpetually motionless man, of uniform (marble) color, who is severed at the chest? It is similar to such a man, it seems, and much more so than to a normally colored, mobile, and whole man. But we are not struck by the former similarity when we see the bust, obvious though it is on reflection. The bust's uniform color, motionlessness, and abrupt ending at the chest are standard properties relative to the category of busts, and since we see it as a bust they are standard for us. Similarly, black-and-white drawings do not look to us like colorless scenes and we do not take them to depict things as being colorless, nor do we regard stick-figure drawings as resembling and depicting only very thin people. A cubist work might look like a person with a cubical head to someone not familiar with the cubist style. But the standardness of such cubical shapes for people who see it as a cubist work prevents them from making that comparison.

The shapes of a painting or a still photograph of a high jumper in action are motionless, but these pictures do not look to us like a high jumper frozen in midair. Indeed, depending on features of the pictures which are variable for us (for example, the exact positions of the figures, swirling brush strokes in the painting, slight blurrings of the photographic image) the athlete may seem in a frenzy of activity; the pictures may convey a vivid sense of movement. But if static images exactly like those of the two pictures occur in a motion picture, and we see it as a motion picture, they probably would strike us as resembling a static athlete. This is because the immobility of the images is standard relative to the category of still pictures and variable relative to that of motion pictures. (Since we are so familiar with still pictures it might be difficult to see the static images as motion pictures for very long, rather than as [filmed] still pictures. But we could not help seeing them that way if we had no acquaintance at all with the medium of still pictures.) My point here is brought out by the tremendous aesthetic difference we are likely to experience between a film of a dancer moving *very* slowly and a still picture of him, even if "objectively" the two images are very nearly identical. We might well find the former studied, calm, deliberate, laborious, and the latter dynamic, energetic, flowing, or frenzied.

In general, then, what we regard a work as resembling, and as representing, depends on the properties of the work which are variable, and not on those which are standard for us.[15] The latter properties serve to determine what *kind* of a representation the work is, rather than what it represents or resembles. We take them for granted, as it were, in representations of that kind. This principle helps to explain also how clouds can look like elephants, how diatonic orchestral music can suggest a conversation or a person crying or laughing, and how a twelve-year-old boy can look like his middle-aged father.

We can now see how a portrait can be an *exact* likeness of the sitter, despite the huge differences between the two. The differences, in so far as they involve properties standard for us, simply do not count against likeness, and hence not against exact likeness. Similarly, a boy not only can resemble his father but can be his "spitting image," despite the boy's relative youthfulness. It is clear that the notions of resemblance and exact resemblance that we are concerned with are not even cousins of the notion of perceptual indistinguishability.

(b) The importance of the distinction between standard and variable properties is by no means limited to cases involving representation or resemblance. Imagine a society which does not have an established medium of painting, but does produce a kind of work of art called *guernicas*. Guernicas are like versions of Picasso's "Guernica" done in various bas-relief dimensions. All of them are surfaces with the colors and shapes of Picasso's "Guernica," but the surfaces are molded to protrude from the wall like relief maps of different kinds of terrain. Some *guernicas* have rolling surfaces, others are sharp and jagged, still others contain several relatively flat planes at various angles to each other, and so forth. Picasso's "Guernica" would be counted as a *guernica* in this society – a perfectly flat one – rather than as a painting. Its flatness is variable and the figures on its surface are standard relative to the category of *guernicas*. Thus the flatness, which is standard for us, would be variable for members of the other society (if they should come across "Guernica") and the figures on the surface, which are variable for us, would be standard for them. This would make for a profound difference between our aesthetic reaction to "Guernica" and theirs. It seems violent, dynamic, vital, disturbing to us. But I imagine it would strike them as cold, stark, lifeless, or serene and restful, or perhaps bland, dull, boring – but in any case *not* violent, dynamic, and vital. We do not pay attention to or take note of "Guernica"'s flatness; this is a feature we take for granted in paintings, as it were. But for the other society this is "Guernica"'s most striking and noteworthy characteristic – what is *expressive* about it. Conversely, "Guernica"'s color patches, which we find noteworthy and expressive, are insignificant to them.

It is important to notice that this difference in aesthetic response is not due *solely* to the fact that we are much more familiar with flat works of art than they are, and they are more familiar with "Guernica"'s colors and shapes. Someone equally familiar with paintings and *guernicas* might, I think, see Picasso's "Guernica" as a painting on some occasions, and as a *guernica* on others. On the former occasions it will probably look dynamic, violent, and so forth to him, and on the latter cold, serene, bland, or lifeless. Whether he sees the work in a museum of paintings or a museum of *guernicas*, or whether he has been told that it is a painting or a *guernica*, may influence how he sees it. But I think he might be able to shift at will from one way of seeing it to the other, somewhat as one shifts between seeing the duck-rabbit as a duck and seeing it as a rabbit.

This example and the previous ones might give the impression that in general only features of a work that are variable for us are aesthetically important – that these are the expressive, aesthetically active properties, as far as we are concerned, whereas features standard for us are aesthetically inert. But this notion is quite mistaken, as the following examples will demonstrate. Properties standard for us are not aesthetically lifeless, though the life that they have, the aesthetic effect they have on us, is typically very different from what it would be if they were variable for us.

(c) Because of the very fact that features standard for us do not seem striking or noteworthy, that they are somehow expected or taken for granted, they can contribute to a work a sense of order, inevitability, stability, correctness. This is perhaps most notably true of large-scale structural properties in the time arts. The exposition–development–recapitulation form (including the typical key and thematic relationships) of the first movements of classical sonatas, symphonies, and string quartets is standard with respect to the category of works in sonata-allegro form, and standard for listeners, including most of us, who hear them as belonging to that category. So proceeding along the lines of sonata-allegro form seems *right* to us; to our ears that is how sonatas are *supposed* to behave. We feel that we know where we are and where we are going throughout the work – more so, I suggest, than we would if we were not familiar with sonata-allegro form, if following the strictures of that form were variable rather than standard for us.[16] Properties standard for us do not always have this sort of unifying effect, however. The fact that a piano sonata contains only piano sounds, or uses the Western system of harmony throughout, does not make it seem unified to us. The reason, I think, is that these properties are *too* standard for us in a sense that needs explicating (cf. note 10). Nevertheless, sonata form is unifying partly because it is standard rather than variable for us.

(d) That a work (or part of it) has a certain determinate characteristic (for example, of size, speed, length, volume) is often variable relative to a particular category, when it is nevertheless standard for that category that the variable characteristic falls within a certain range. In such cases the aesthetic effect of the determinate variable property may be colored by the standard limits of the range. Hence these limits function as an aesthetic catalyst, even if not as an active ingredient.

Piano music is frequently marked *sostenuto*, *cantabile*, *legato*, or *lyrical*. But how can the pianist possibly carry out such instructions? Piano tones diminish in volume drastically immediately after the key is struck, becoming inaudible relatively promptly, and there is no way the player can prevent this. If a singer or violinist should produce sounds even approaching a piano's in suddenness

of demise, they would be nerve-wrackingly sharp and percussive – anything but *cantabile* or lyrical! Yet piano music *can* be *cantabile*, *legato*, or lyrical nevertheless; sometimes it is extraordinarily so (for example, a good performance of the *Adagio Cantabile* movement of Beethoven's *Pathétique* sonata). What makes this possible is the very fact that the drastic diminution of piano tones cannot be prevented, and hence never is. It is a standard feature for piano music. A pianist can, however, by a variety of devices, control a tone's rate of diminution and length within the limits dictated by the nature of the instrument.[17] Piano tones may thus be *more or less* sustained within these limits, and *how* sustained they are, how quickly or slowly they diminish and how long they last, within the range of possibilities, is variable for piano music. A piano passage that sounds lyrical or *cantabile* to us is one in which the individual tones are *relatively* sustained, given the capabilities of the instrument. Such a passage sounds lyrical only because piano music is limited as it is, and we hear it as piano music; that is, the limitations are standard properties for us. The character of the passage is determined not merely by the "absolute" nature of the sounds, but by that in relation to the standard property of what piano tones can be like.[18]

This principle helps to explain the lack of energy and brilliance that we sometimes find even in very fast passages of electronic music. The energy and brilliance of a fast violin or piano passage derives not merely from the absolute speed of the music (together with accents, rhythmic characteristics, and so forth), but from the fact that it is fast *for that particular medium*. In electronic music different pitches can succeed one another at any frequency up to and including that at which they are no longer separately distinguishable. Because of this it is difficult to make electronic music *sound* fast (energetic, violent). For when we have heard enough electronic music to be aware of the possibilities we do not feel that the speed of a passage approaches a limit, no matter how fast it is.[19]

There are also visual correlates of these musical examples. A small elephant, one which is smaller than most elephants with which we are familiar, might impress us as charming, cute, delicate, or puny. This is not simply because of its (absolute) size, but because it is small *for an elephant*. To people who are familiar not with our elephants but with a race of mini-elephants, the same animal may look massive, strong, dominant, threatening, lumbering, if it is large for a mini-elephant. The size of elephants is variable relative to the class of elephants, but it varies only within a certain (not precisely specifiable) range. It is a standard property of elephants that they do fall within this range. How an elephant's size affects us aesthetically depends, since we see it as an elephant, on whether it falls in the upper, middle, or lower part of the range.

(e) Properties standard for a certain category which do not derive from physical limitations of the medium can be regarded as results of more or less conventional "rules" for producing works in the given category (for example, the "rules" of sixteenth-century counterpoint, or those for twelve-tone music). These rules may combine to create a dilemma for the artist which, if he is talented, he may resolve ingeniously and gracefully. The result may be a work with an aesthetic character very different from what it would have had if it had not been for those rules. Suppose that the first movement of a sonata in G major modulates to C-sharp major by the end of the development section. A rule of sonata form decrees that it must return to G for the recapitulation. But the keys of G and C-sharp are as unrelated as any two keys can be; it is difficult to modulate smoothly and quickly from one to the other. Suppose also that while the sonata is in C-sharp there are signs that, given other rules of sonata form, indicate that the recapitulation is imminent (for example, motivichints of the return, an emotional climax, or a cadenza). Listeners who hear it as a work in sonata form are likely to have a distinct feeling of unease, tension, uncertainty, as the time for the recapitulation approaches. If the composer with a stroke of ingenuity accomplishes the necessary modulation quickly, efficiently, and naturally, this will give them a feeling of relief – one might say of deliverance. The movement to C-sharp (which may have seemed alien and brashly adventurous) will have proven to be quite appropriate, and the entire sequence will in retrospect have a sense of correctness and perfection about it. Our impression of it is likely, I think, to be very much like our impression of a "beautiful" or "elegant" proof in mathematics. (Indeed the composer's task in this example is not unlike that of producing such a proof.)

But suppose that the rule for sonatas were that the recapitulation must be *either* in the original key *or* in the key one half-step below it. Thus in the example above the recapitulation could have been in F-sharp major rather than G major. This possibility removes the sense of tension from the occurrence of C-sharp major in the development section, for a modulation from C-sharp to F-sharp is as easy as any modulation is (since C-sharp is the dominant of F-sharp). Of course, there would also be no special *release* of tension when the modulation to G is effected, there being no tension to be released. In fact, that modulation probably would be rather surprising, since the permissible modulation to F-sharp would be much more natural.

Thus the effect that the sonata has on us depends on which of its properties are dictated by "rules," which ones are standard relative to the category of sonatas and hence standard for us.

(f) I turn now to features which are contra-standard for us – that is, ones which have a tendency to disqualify a work from a category in which we nevertheless perceive it. We are likely to find such features shocking, or disconcerting, or startling, or upsetting, just because they are contra-standard for us. Their presence may be so obtrusive that they obscure the work's variable properties. Three-dimensional objects protruding from a canvas and movement in a sculpture are contra-standard relative to the categories of painting and (traditional) sculpture respectively. These features are contra-standard for us, and probably shocking, if despite them we perceive the works possessing them in the mentioned categories. The monochromatic paintings of Yves Klein are disturbing to us (at least at first) for this reason: we see them as paintings, though they contain the feature contra-standard for paintings of being one solid color. Notice that we find other similarly monochromatic surfaces – for example, walls of living rooms – not in the least disturbing, and indeed quite unnoteworthy.

If we are exposed frequently to works containing a certain kind of feature which is contra-standard for us, we ordinarily adjust our categories to accommodate it, making it contra-standard for us no longer. The first painting with a three-dimensional object glued to it was no doubt shocking. But now that the technique has become commonplace we are not shocked. This is because we no longer see these works as *paintings*, but rather as members of either (a) a new category – *collages* – in which case the offending feature has become standard rather than contra-standard for us, or (b) an expanded category which includes paintings both with and without attached objects, in which case that feature is variable for us.

But it is not just the rarity, unusualness, or unexpectedness of a feature that makes it shocking. If a work differs *too* significantly from the norms of a certain category we do not perceive it in that category and hence the difference is not contra-standard for us, even if we have not previously experienced works differing from that category in that way. A sculpture which is constantly and vigorously in motion would be so obviously and radically different from traditional sculptures that we probably would not perceive it as one even if it is the first moving sculpture we have come across. We would either perceive it as a *kinetic* sculpture, or simply remain confused. In contrast, a sculptured bust which is traditional in every respect except that one ear twitches slightly every thirty seconds would be perceived as an ordinary sculpture. So the twitching ear would be contra-standard for us and would be considerably more unsettling than the much greater movement of the other kinetic sculpture. Similarly, a very small colored area of an otherwise entirely black-and-white drawing would be very disconcerting. But if enough additional color is added to it we will see it as a colored rather than a black-and-white drawing, and the shock will vanish.

This point helps to explain a difference between the harmonic aberrations of Wagner's *Tristan and Isolde* on the one hand and on the other Debussy's *Pelléas et Mélisande* and *Feux* and Schoenberg's *Pierrot Lunaire* as well as his later twelve-tone works. The latter are not merely *more* aberrant, *less* tonal, than *Tristan*. They differ from traditional tonal music in such respects and to such an extent that they are not heard as tonal at all. *Tristan*, however, retains enough of the apparatus of tonality, despite its deviations, to be heard as a tonal work. For this reason its lesser deviations are often the more shocking.[20] *Tristan* plays on harmonic traditions by selectively following and flaunting them, while *Pierrot Lunaire* and the others simply ignore them.

Shock then arises from features that are not just rare or unique, but ones that are contra-standard relative to categories in which objects possessing them are perceived. But it must be emphasized that to be contra-standard relative to a certain category is not merely to be rare or unique *among things of that category*. The melodic line of Schubert's song, "*Im Walde*," is probably unique; it probably does not occur in any other songs, or other works of any sort. But it is not contra-standard relative to the category of songs, because it does not tend to dis-

qualify the work from that category. Nor is it contra-standard relative to any other category to which we hear the work as belonging. And clearly we do not find this melodic line at all upsetting. What is important is not the rarity of a feature, but its connection with the classification of the work. Features contra-standard for us are perceived as being misfits in a category which the work strikes us as belonging to, as doing *violence* to such a category, and being rare in a category is not the same thing as being a misfit in it.

It should be clear from the above examples that how a work affects us aesthetically – what aesthetic properties it seems to us to have and what ones we are inclined to attribute to it – depends in a variety of important ways on which of its features are standard, which variable, and which contra-standard for us. Moreover, this is obviously not an isolated or exceptional phenomenon, but a pervasive characteristic of aesthetic perception. I should emphasize that my purpose has not been to establish general principles about how each of the three sorts of properties affects us. How any particular feature affects us depends also on many variables I have not discussed. The important point is that in many cases whether a feature is standard, variable, or contra-standard for us has a great deal to do with what effect it has on us. We must now begin to assess the theoretical consequences of this.

IV Truth and Falsity

The fact that what aesthetic properties a thing seems to have may depend on what categories it is perceived in raises a question about how to determine what aesthetic properties it really does have. If "Guernica" appears dynamic when seen as a painting, and not dynamic when seen as a *guernica*, is it dynamic or not? Can one way of seeing it be ruled correct, and the other incorrect? One way of approaching this problem is to deny that the apparently conflicting aesthetic judgments of people who perceive a work in different categories actually do conflict.[21]

Judgments that works of art have certain aesthetic properties, it might be suggested, implicitly involve reference to some particular set of categories. Thus our claim that "Guernica" is dynamic really amounts to the claim that it is (as we might say) dynamic *as a painting*, or for people who see it as a painting. The judgment that it is not dynamic made by people who see it as a *guernica* amounts simply to the judgment that it is not dynamic *as a guernica*. Interpreted in these ways, the two judgments are of course quite compatible. Terms like "large" and "small" provide a convenient model for this interpretation. An elephant might be both small as an elephant and large as a mini-elephant, and hence it might be called truly either "large" or "small," depending on which category is implicitly referred to.

I think that aesthetic judgments are in *some* contexts amenable to such category-relative interpretations, especially aesthetic judgments about natural objects (clouds, mountains, sunsets) rather than works of art. (It will be evident that the alternative account suggested below is not readily applicable to most judgments about natural objects.) But most of our aesthetic judgments can be forced into this mold only at the cost of distorting them beyond recognition.

My main objection is that category-relative interpretations do not allow aesthetic judgments to be mistaken often enough. It would certainly be natural to consider a person who calls "Guernica" stark, cold, or dull, because he sees it as a *guernica*, to be *mistaken*: he misunderstands the work because he is looking at it in the wrong way. Similarly, one who asserts that a good performance of the *Adagio Cantabile* of Beethoven's *Pathétique* is percussive, or that a Roman bust looks like a unicolored, immobile man severed at the chest and depicts him as such, is simply wrong, even if his judgment is a result of his perceiving the work in different categories from those in which we perceive it. Moreover, we do not accord a status any more privileged to our own aesthetic judgments. We are likely to regard, for example, cubist paintings, serial music, or Chinese music as formless, incoherent, or disturbing on our first contact with these forms largely because, I suggest, we would not be perceiving the works as cubist paintings, serial music, or Chinese music. But after becoming familiar with these kinds of art we would probably *retract* our previous judgments, admit that they were mistaken. It would be quite inappropriate to protest that what we meant previously was merely that the works were formless or disturbing for the categories in which we then perceived them, while admitting that they are not for the categories of cubist paintings, or serial, or Chinese music. The conflict between apparently incompatible aesthetic judgments made while perceiving a work in different categories does not simply evaporate when the difference of categories is pointed out, as does the

conflict between the claims that an animal is large and that it is small, when it is made clear that the person making the first claim regarded it as a mini-elephant and the one making the second regarded it as an elephant. The latter judgments do not (necessarily) reflect a real disagreement about the size of the animal, but the former do reflect a real disagreement about the aesthetic nature of the work.

Thus it seems that, at least in some cases, it is *correct* to perceive a work in certain categories, and *incorrect* to perceive it in certain others; that is, our judgments of it when we perceive it in the former are likely to be true, and those we make when perceiving it in the latter false. This provides us with absolute senses of "standard," "variable," and "contra-standard": features of a work are standard, variable, or contra-standard absolutely just in case they are standard, variable, or contra-standard (respectively) for people who perceive the work correctly. (Thus an absolutely standard feature is standard relative to some category in which the work is correctly perceived and contra-standard relative to none, an absolutely variable feature is variable relative to all such categories, and an absolutely contra-standard feature is contra-standard relative to at least one such category.)

How is it to be determined in which categories a work is correctly perceived? There is certainly no very precise or well-defined procedure to be followed. Different criteria are emphasized by different people and in different situations. But there are several fairly definite considerations which typically figure in critical discussions and fit our intuitions reasonably well. I suggest that the following circumstances count toward its being correct to perceive a work, W, in a given category, C:

(i) The presence in W of a relatively large number of features standard with respect to C. The correct way of perceiving a work is likely to be that in which it has a minimum of contra-standard features for us. I take the relevance of this consideration to be obvious. It cannot be correct to perceive Rembrandt's *Titus Reading* as a kinetic sculpture, if this is possible, just because that work has too few of the features which make kinetic sculptures kinetic sculptures. But of course this does not get us very far, for "Guernica," for example, qualifies equally well on this count for being perceived as a painting and as a *guernica*.

(ii) The fact, if it is one, that W is better, or more interesting or pleasing aesthetically, or more worth experiencing when perceived in C than it is when perceived in alternative ways. The correct way of perceiving a work is likely to be the way in which it comes off best.

(iii)   The fact, if it is one, that the artist who produced W intended or expected it to be perceived in C, or thought of it as a C.

(iv)   The fact, if it is one, that C is well established in and recognized by the society in which W was produced. A category is well established in and recognized by a society if the members of the society are familiar with works in that category, consider a work's membership in it a fact worth mentioning, exhibit works of that category together, and so forth – that is, roughly if that category figures importantly in their way of classifying works of art. The categories of impressionist painting and Brahmsian music are well established and recognized in our society; those of *guernicas*, paintings with diagonal composition containing green crosses, and pieces of music containing between four and eight F-sharps and at least seventeen quarter notes every eight bars are not. The categories in which a work is correctly perceived, according to this condition, are generally the ones in which the artist's contemporaries did perceive or would have perceived it.

In certain cases I think the mechanical process by which a work was produced, or (for example, in architecture) the non-perceptible physical characteristics or internal structure of a work, is relevant. A work is probably correctly perceived as an apparent etching[22] rather than, say, an apparent woodcut or line drawing, if it was produced by the etching process. The strength of materials in a building, or the presence of steel girders inside wooden or plaster columns counts toward (not necessarily conclusively) the correctness of perceiving it in the category of buildings with visual characteristics typical of buildings constructed in that manner. Because of their limited applicability I will not discuss these considerations further here.

What can be said in support of the relevance of conditions (ii), (iii), and (iv)? In the examples mentioned above, the categories in which we consider a work correctly perceived seem to meet (to the best of our knowledge) each of these three conditions. I would suppose that "Guernica" is better seen as a painting than it would be seen as a *guernica* (though this would be hard to prove). In any case, Picasso certainly intended it to be seen as a painting rather than a *guernica*, and the category of paintings is, and that of *guernicas* is not, well established in his (that is, our) society. But this of course does not show that (ii), (iii), and (iv) *each* is rele-

vant. It tends to indicate only that one or other of them, or some combination, is relevant. The difficulty of assessing each of the three conditions individually is complicated by the fact that by and large they can be expected to coincide, to yield identical conclusions. Since an artist usually intends his works for his contemporaries he is likely to intend them to be perceived in categories established in and recognized by his society. Moreover, it is reasonable to expect works to come off better when perceived in the intended categories than when perceived in others. An artist tries to produce works which are well worth experiencing when perceived in the intended way and, unless we have reason to think he is totally incompetent, there is some presumption that he succeeded at least to some extent. But it is more or less a matter of chance whether the work comes off well when perceived in some unintended way. The convergence of the three conditions, however, at the same time diminishes the *practical* importance of justifying them individually, since in most cases we can decide how to judge particular works of art without doing so. But the theoretical question remains.

I will begin with (ii). If we are faced with a choice between two ways of perceiving a work, and the work is very much better perceived in one way than it is perceived in the other, I think that, at least in the absence of contrary considerations, we would be strongly inclined to settle on the former way of perceiving it as the *correct* way. The process of trying to determine what is in a work consists partly in casting around among otherwise plausible ways of perceiving it for one in which the work is good. We feel we are coming to a correct understanding of a work when we begin to like or enjoy it; we are finding what is really there when it seems to be worth experiencing.

But if (ii) is relevant, it is quite clearly not the *only* relevant consideration. Take any work of art we can agree is of fourth- or fifth- or tenth-rate quality. It is quite possible that if this work were perceived in some far-fetched set of categories that someone might dream up, it would appear to be first-rate, a masterpiece. Finding such *ad hoc* categories obviously would require talent and ingenuity on the order of that necessary to produce a masterpiece in the first place. But we can sketch how one might begin searching for them. (a) If the mediocre work suffers from some disturbingly prominent feature that distracts from whatever merits the work has, this feature might be toned down by choosing categories with respect to which it is standard, rather than variable or contra-standard. When the work is perceived in the new way the offending feature may be no more distracting than the flatness of a painting is to us. (b) If the work suffers from an overabundance of clichés it might be livened up by choosing categories with respect to which the clichés are variable or contra-standard rather than standard. (c) If it needs ingenuity we might devise a set of rules in terms of which the work finds itself in a dilemma and then ingeniously escapes from it, and build these rules into a set of categories. Surely, however, if there are categories waiting to be discovered which would transform a mediocre work into a masterpiece, it does not follow that the work really is a hitherto unrecognized masterpiece. The fact that when perceived in such categories it would appear exciting, ingenious, and so forth, rather than grating, cliché-ridden, pedestrian, does not make it so. It *cannot* be correct, I suggest, to perceive a work in categories which are totally foreign to the artist and his society, even if it comes across as a masterpiece in them.[23]

This brings us to the historical conditions (iii) and (iv). I see no way of avoiding the conclusion that one or the other of them at least is relevant in determining in what categories a work is correctly perceived. I consider both relevant, but will not argue here for the independent relevance of (iv). (iii) merits special attention in light of the recent prevalence of disputes about the importance of artists' intentions. To test the relevance of (iii) we must consider a case in which (iii) and (iv) diverge. One such instance occurred during the early days of the twelve-tone movement in music. Schoenberg no doubt intended even his earliest twelve-tone works to be heard as such. But his category was certainly not then well established or recognized in his society: virtually none of his contemporaries (except close associates such as Berg and Webern), even musically sophisticated ones, would have (of could have) heard these works in that category. But it seems to me that even the very first twelve-tone compositions are correctly heard as such, that the judgments one who hears them otherwise would make of them (for example, that they are chaotic, formless) are mistaken. I think this would be so even if Schoenberg had been working entirely alone, if *none* of his contemporaries had any inkling of the twelve-tone system. No doubt the first twelve-tone compositions are much better when heard in the category of twelve-tone works than when they are heard in any other

way people might be likely to hear them. But as we have seen this cannot *by itself* account for the correctness of hearing them in the former way. The only other feature of the situation which could be relevant, so far as I can see, is Schoenberg's intention.

The above example is unusual in that Schoenberg was extraordinarily self-conscious about what he was doing, having explicitly formulated rules – that is, specified standard properties – for twelve-tone composition. Artists are of course not often so self-conscious, even when producing revolutionary works of art. Their intentions as to which categories their works are to be perceived in are not nearly as clear as Schoenberg's were, and often they change their minds considerably during the process of creation. In such cases (as well as ones in which the artists' intentions are unknown) the question of what categories a work is correctly perceived in is, I think, left by default to condition (iv), together with (i) and (ii). But it seems to me that in almost all cases at least one of the historical conditions, (iii) and (iv), is of crucial importance.

My account of the rules governing decisions about what categories works are correctly perceived in leaves a lot undone. There are bound to be a large number of undecidable cases on my criteria. Artists' intentions are frequently unclear, variable, or undiscoverable. Many works belong to categories which are borderline cases of being well established in the artists' societies (perhaps, for example, the categories of rococo music – for instance, C. P. E. Bach – of music in the style of early Mozart, and of very thin metal sculptured figures of the kind that Giacometti made). Many works fall between well-established categories (for example, between impressionist and cubist paintings), possessing *some* of the standard features relative to each, and so neither clearly qualify nor clearly fail to qualify on the basis of condition (i) to be perceived in either. There is, in addition, the question of what relative weights to accord the various conditions when they conflict.

It would be a mistake, however, to try to tighten up much further the rules for deciding how works are correctly perceived. To do so would be simply to legislate gratuitously, since the intuitions and precedents we have to go on are highly variable and often confused. But it is important to notice just where these intuitions and precedents are inconclusive, for doing so will expose the sources of many critical disputes. One such dispute might well arise concerning Giacometti's thin metal sculptures. To a critic who sees them simply as sculptures, or sculptures of people, they look frail, emaciated, wispy, or wiry. But that is not how they would strike a critic who sees them in the category of thin metal sculptures of that sort (just as stick figures do not strike us as wispy or emaciated). He would be impressed not by the thinness of the sculptures, but by the expressive nature of the positions of their limbs, and so forth, and so no doubt would attribute very different aesthetic properties to them. Which of the two ways of seeing these works is correct is, I suspect, undecidable. It is not clear whether enough such works have been made and have been regarded sufficiently often as constituting a category for that category to be deemed well established in Giacometti's society. And I doubt whether any of the other conditions settle the issue conclusively. So perhaps the dispute between the two critics is essentially unresolvable. The most that we can do is to point out just what sort of a difference of perception underlies the dispute, and why it is unresolvable.

The occurrence of such impasses is by no means something to be regretted. Works may be fascinating precisely because of shifts between equally permissible ways of perceiving them. And the enormous richness of some works is due in part to the variety of permissible, and worthwhile, ways of perceiving them. But it should be emphasized that even when my criteria do not clearly specify a *single* set of categories in which a work is correctly perceived, there are bound to be possible ways of perceiving it (which we may or may not have thought of) that they definitely rule out.

The question posed at the outset of this section was how to determine what aesthetic properties a work has, given that which ones it seems to have depends on what categories it is perceived in, on which of its properties are standard, which variable, and which contra-standard for us. I have sketched in rough outline rules for deciding in what categories a work is *correctly* perceived (and hence which of its features are absolutely standard, variable, and contra-standard). The aesthetic properties it actually possesses are those that are to be found in it when it is perceived correctly.[24]

V Conclusion

I return now to the issues raised in Section I. (I will adopt for the remainder of this paper the simplifying assumption that there is only one correct way of perceiving any work. Nothing important depends on this.) If a work's aesthetic properties are those that are to be found in it when it is perceived correctly, and the correct way to perceive it is determined partly by historical facts about the artist's intention and/or his society, no examination of the work itself, however thorough, will by itself reveal those properties.[25] If we are confronted by a work about whose origins we know absolutely nothing (for example, one lifted from the dust at an as yet unexcavated archaeological site on Mars), we would simply not be in a position to judge it aesthetically. We could not possibly tell by staring at it, no matter how intently and intelligently, whether it is coherent, or serene, or dynamic, for by staring we cannot tell whether it is to be seen as a sculpture, a *guernica*, or some other exotic or mundane kind of work of art. (We could attribute aesthetic properties to it in the way we do to natural objects, which of course does not involve consideration of historical facts about artists or their societies. [Cf. p. 151] But to do this would not be to treat the object as a *work* of art.)

It should be emphasized that the relevant historical facts are not merely useful aids to aesthetic judgment; they do not simply provide hints concerning what might be found in the work. Rather they help to *determine* what aesthetic properties a work has; they, together with the work's nonaesthetic features, *make* it coherent, serene, or whatever. If the origin of a work which is coherent and serene had been different in crucial respects, the work would not have had these qualities; we would not merely have lacked a means for *discovering* them. And of two works which differ *only* in respect of their origins – that is, which are perceptually indistinguishable – one might be coherent or serene, and the other not. Thus, since artists' intentions are among the relevant historical considerations, the "intentional fallacy" is not a fallacy at all. I have of course made no claims about the relevance of artists' intentions as to the aesthetic properties that their works should have, and these intentions are among those most discussed in writings on aesthetics. I am willing to agree that whether an artist intended his work to be coherent or serene has nothing essential to do with whether it is coherent or serene. But this must not be allowed to seduce us into thinking that *no* intentions are relevant.

Aesthetic properties, then, are not to be found in works themselves in the straightforward way that colors and shapes or pitches and rhythms are. But

I do not mean to deny that we perceive aesthetic properties in works of art. I see the serenity of a painting, and hear the coherence of a sonata, despite the fact that the presence of these qualities in the works depends partly on circumstances of their origin, which I cannot (now) perceive. Jones's marital status is part of what makes him a bachelor, if he is one, and we cannot tell his marital status just by looking at him, though we can thus ascertain his sex. Hence, I suppose, his bachelorhood is not a property we can be said to perceive in him. But the aesthetic properties of a work do not depend on historical facts about it in anything like the way Jones's bachelorhood depends on his marital status. The point is not that the historical facts (or in what categories the work is correctly perceived, or which of its properties are absolutely standard, variable, and contra-standard) function as *grounds* in any ordinary sense for aesthetic judgments. By themselves they do not, in general, count either for or against the presence of any particular aesthetic property. And they are not part of a larger body of information (also including data about the work derived from an examination of it) from which conclusions about the work's aesthetic properties are to be deduced or inferred. We must learn to *perceive* the work in the correct categories, as determined in part by the historical facts, and judge it by what we then perceive in it. The historical facts help to determine whether a painting is, for example, serene *only* (as far as my arguments go) by affecting what way of perceiving the painting must reveal this quality if it is truly attributable to the work.

We must not, however, expect to judge a work simply by setting ourselves to perceive it correctly, once it is determined what the correct way of perceiving it is. For one cannot, in general, perceive a work in a given set of categories simply by setting himself to do it. I could not possibly, merely by an act of will, see "Guernica" as a *guernica* rather than a painting, or hear a succession of street sounds in any arbitrary category one might dream up, even if the category has been explained to me in detail. (Nor can I imagine except in a rather vague way what it would be like, for example, to see "Guernica" as a *guernica*.) One cannot merely decide to respond appropriately to a work – to be shocked or unnerved or surprised by its (absolutely) contra-standard features, to find its standard features familiar or mundane, and to react to its variable features in other ways – once he knows the correct categories. Perceiving a work in

a certain category or set of categories is a skill that must be acquired by training, and exposure to a great many other works of the category or categories in question is ordinarily, I believe, an essential part of this training. (But an effort of will may facilitate the training, and once the skill is acquired one may be able to decide at will whether or not to perceive it in that or those categories.) This has important consequences concerning how best to approach works of art of kinds that are new to us – contemporary works in new idioms, works from foreign cultures, or newly resurrected works from the ancient past. It is no use just immersing ourselves in a particular work, even with the knowledge of what categories it is correctly perceived in, for that alone will not enable us to perceive it in those categories. We must become familiar with a considerable variety of works of similar sorts.

When dealing with works of more familiar kinds it is not generally necessary to undertake deliberately the task of training ourselves to be able to perceive them in the correct categories (expect perhaps when those categories include relatively subtle ones). But this is almost always, I think, only because we have been trained unwittingly. Even the ability to see paintings as paintings had to be acquired, it seems to me, by repeated exposure to a great many paintings. The critic must thus go beyond the work before him in order to judge it aesthetically, not only to discover what the correct categories are, but also to be able to perceive it in them. The latter does not require consideration of historical facts, or consideration of facts at all, but it requires directing one's attention nonetheless to things other than the work in question.

Probably no one would deny that *some* sort of perceptual training is necessary, in many if not all instances, for apprehending a work's serenity or coherence, or other aesthetic properties. And of course it is not only *aesthetic* properties whose apprehension by the senses requires training. But the kind of training required in the aesthetic cases (and perhaps some others as well) has not been properly appreciated. In order to learn how to recognize gulls of various kinds, or the sex of chicks, or a certain person's handwriting, one must usually have gulls of those kinds, or chicks of the two sexes, or examples of that person's handwriting pointed out to him, practice recognizing them himself, and be corrected when he makes mistakes. But the training important for discovering the serenity or coherence of a work of art that I have been discussing is not of this sort (though this sort of training might be important as well). Acquiring the ability to perceive a serene or coherent work in the correct categories is not a matter of having had serene or coherent things pointed out to one, or having practiced recognizing them. What is important is not (or not merely) experience with other serene and coherent things, but experience with other things of the appropriate categories.

Much of the argument in this paper has been directed against the seemingly common-sense

notion that aesthetic judgments about works of art are to be based solely on what can be perceived in them, how they look or sound. That notion is seriously misleading, I claim, on two quite different counts. I do not deny that paintings and sonatas are to be judged solely on what can be seen or heard in them – when they are perceived correctly. But examining a work with the senses can by itself reveal neither how it is correct to perceive it, nor how to perceive it that way.

Notes

1. Heinrich Wölfflin, *Principles of Art History*, trans. by M. D. Hottinger (7th edn; New York, 1929), p. 228.
2. "[W]e should all agree, I think, . . . that any quality that cannot even in principle be heard in it [a musical composition] does not belong to it as music." Monroe Beardsley, *Aesthetics: Problems in the Philosophy of Criticism* (New York, 1958), pp. 31–32.
3. Cf. Calvin Tompkins, *The Bride and the Bachelors* (New York, 1965), pp. 210–211.
4. Monroe Beardsley argues for a relatively strict separation (*op. cit.*, pp. 17–34). Some of the strongest recent attempts to enforce this separation are to be found in discussions of the so-called "intentional fallacy," beginning with William Wimsatt and Beardsley, "The Intentional Fallacy," *Sewanee Review*, LIV (1946), which has been widely cited and reprinted. Despite the name of the "fallacy" these discussions are not limited to consideration of the relevance of artists' *intentions*.
5. The aesthetic properties of works of literature are not happily called "perceptual." For reasons connected with this it is sometimes awkward to treat literature together with the visual arts and music. (The notion of perceiving a work in a category, to be introduced shortly, is not straightforwardly applicable to literary works.) Hence in this paper I will concentrate on visual and musical works, though I believe that the central points I make concerning them hold, with suitable modifications, for novels, plays, and poems as well.
6. Frank Sibley distinguishes between "aesthetic" and "nonaesthetic" terms and concepts in "Aesthetic Concepts," *Philosophical Review*, LXVIII (1959).
7. Cf. Paul Ziff, "Art and the 'Object of Art,'" in Ziff, *Philosophic Turnings* (Ithaca, N.Y., 1966), pp. 12–16 (originally published in *Mind*, N.S. LX [1951]).
8. "Aesthetic and Nonaesthetic," *Philosophical Review*, LXXII (1965).
9. This is a very difficult notion to make precise, and I do not claim to have succeeded entirely. But the following comments seem to me to go in the right direction, and, together with the examples in the

next section, they should clarify it sufficiently for my present purposes.
10. In order to avoid excessive complexity and length, I am ignoring some considerations that might be important at a later stage of investigation. In particular, I think it would be important at some point to distinguish between different *degrees* or *levels* of standardness, variableness, and contra-standardness for a person; to speak, e.g., of features being *more* or *less* standard for him. At least two distinct sorts of grounds for such differences of degree should be recognized. (a) Distinctions between perceiving a work in a certain category to a greater and lesser extent should be allowed for, with corresponding differences of degree in the standardness for the perceiver of properties relative to that category. (b) A feature which is standard relative to more, and/or more specific, categories in which a person perceives the work should thereby count as more standard for him. Thus, if we see something as a painting and also as a French Impressionist painting, features standard relative to both categories are more standard for us than features standard relative only to the latter.
11. This excludes, e.g., the sense of "represent" in which a picture might represent justice or courage, and probably other senses as well.
12. This does not hold for the special case of photography. A photograph is a photograph of a woman no matter what it looks like, I take it, if a woman was in front of the lens when it was produced.
13. Nelson Goodman denies that resemblance is necessary for representation – and obviously not merely because of isolated or marginal examples of non-resembling representations (p. 5). I cannot treat his arguments here, but rather than reject *en masse* the common-sense beliefs that pictures do resemble significantly what they depict and that they depict what they do partly because of such resemblances, if Goodman advocates rejecting them, I prefer to recognize a sense of "resemblance" in which these beliefs are true. My disagreement with him is perhaps less sharp than it appears since, as will be

evident, I am quite willing to grant that the relevant resemblances are "conventional." Cf. Nelson Goodman, *Languages of Art* (Indianapolis, 1968), p. 39, n. 31.

14 The connection between features variable for us and what the work looks like is by no means a straightforward or simple one, however. It may involve "rules" which are more or less "conventional" (e.g., the "laws" of perspective). Cf. E. H. Gombrich, *Art and Illusion* (New York, 1960) and Nelson Goodman, *op cit.*

15 There is at least one group of exceptions to this. Obviously features of a work which are standard for us because they are standard relative to some *representational* category which we see it in – e.g., the category of nudes, still lifes, or landscapes – do help determine what the work looks like to us and what we take it to depict.

16 The presence of clichés in a work sometimes allows it to contain drastically disorderly elements without becoming chaotic or incoherent. Cf. Anton Ehrenzweig, *The Hidden Order of Art* (London, 1967), pp. 114–116.

17 The timing of the release of the key affects the tone's length. Use of the sustaining pedal can lessen slightly a tone's diminuendo by reinforcing its overtones with sympathetic vibrations from other strings. The rate of diminuendo is affected somewhat more drastically by the force with which the key is struck. The more forcefully it is struck the greater is the tone's relative diminuendo. (Obviously the rate of diminuendo cannot be controlled in this way independently of the tone's initial volume.) The successive tones of a melody can be made to overlap so that each tone's sharp attack is partially obscured by the lingering end of the preceding tone. A melodic tone may also be reinforced after it begins by sympathetic vibrations from harmonically related accompanying figures, contributed by the composer.

18 "[T]he musical media we know thus far derive their whole character and their usefulness as musical media precisely from their limitations." Roger Sessions, "Problems and Issues Facing the Composer Today," in Paul Henry Lang, *Problems of Modern Music* (New York, 1960), p. 31.

19 One way to make electronic music sound fast would be to make it sound like some traditional instrument, thereby trading on the limitations of that instrument.

20 Cf. William W. Austin, *Music in the 20th Century* (New York, 1966), pp. 205–206; and Eric Salzman, *Twentieth-Century Music: An Introduction* (Englewood Cliffs, N. J., 1967), pp. 5, 8, 19.

21 I am ruling out the view that the notions of truth and falsity are not applicable to aesthetic judgments, on the ground that it would force us to reject so much of our normal discourse and common-sense intuitions about art that theoretical aesthetics, conceived as attempting to understand the institution of art, would hardly have left a recognizable subject matter to investigate. (Cf. the quotation from Wölfflin, above.)

22 Cf. 144.

23 To say that it is incorrect (in my sense) to perceive a work in certain categories is not necessarily to claim that one *ought not* to perceive it that way. I heartily recommend perceiving mediocre works in categories that make perceiving them worthwhile whenever possible. The point is that one is not likely to *judge* the work correctly when he perceives it incorrectly.

24 This is a considerable oversimplification. If there are two equally correct ways of perceiving a work, and it appears to have a certain aesthetic property perceived in one but not the other of them, does it actually possess this property or not? There is no easy general answer. Probably in some such cases the question is undecidable. But I think we would sometimes be willing to say that a work is, e.g., touching or serene if it seems so when perceived in one correct way (or, more hesitantly, that there is "something very touching, or serene, about it"), while allowing that it does not seem so when perceived in another way which we do not want to rule incorrect. In some cases works have aesthetic properties (e.g., intriguing, subtle, alive, interesting, deep) which are not apparent on perceiving it in any single acceptable way, but which depend on the multiplicity of acceptable ways of perceiving it and relations between them. None of these complications relieves the critic of the responsibility for determining in what way or ways it is correct to perceive a work.

25 But this, plus a general knowledge of what sorts of works were produced when and by whom, might.

14

The Possibility of Aesthetic Realism

Philip Pettit

I

My concern in this essay is with aesthetic characterisations of works of art, in particular works of
pictorial art. I want to raise the question of whether
there is any general reason why such characterisations should not be taken in the realist's manner.
My personal belief is that there is not and I should
like to do something to bear this out: that is, to
establish the possibility of aesthetic realism. What
I shall do is to consider two objections that have
been brought against the realistic view and to
provide a sketch account of how the realist can
hope to evade these.

What are aesthetic characterisations of works of
art? In response I might simply say that they are
characterisations with which the objections that we
shall be considering engage; that would be to thrust
the onus of definition on to my opponent. It would
be unhelpful of me, however, to take such a short
line and I propose to make three comments which
may serve to focus the class of judgments that we
shall be discussing.

The first comment is that aesthetic characterisations of pictures are distinct from pictorial ones.
Pictorial characterisations are descriptions of the
colours displayed by pictures. Nelson Goodman
gives a convenient, though avowedly rough, account of them in the following passage.

Philip Pettit, "The Possibility of Aesthetic Realism,"
in E. Schaper (ed.), *Pleasure, Preference and Value:
Studies in Philosophical Aesthetics* (Cambridge:
Cambridge University Press, 1983), pp. 17–38. ©
by Cambridge University Press.

An elementary pictorial characterisation
states what colour a picture has at a given
place on its face. Other pictorial characterisations in effect combine many elementary
ones by conjunction, alternation, quantification, etc. Thus a pictorial characterisation
may name colours at several places, or state
that the colour at one place lies within a
certain range, or state that the colours at
two places are complementary, and so on.
Briefly, a pictorial characterisation says more
or less specifically what colours the picture
has at what places.[1]

My second comment on aesthetic characterisations is that they are ordinarily taken as relatively
primitive reports of experience rather than as
reports which have been rectified by background
information. The distinction in question arises
with pictorial characterisations as well as with aesthetic. Taken as primitive, 'It's red' is a report of
how something looks here and now; taken as rectified, it is a report of how it would look to a normal
eye under normal illumination. Aesthetic characterisations are taken as relatively primitive in so far
as the only rectification that is thought to be relevant to them is that which is already assumed for
pictorial reports.

In the last section of this essay we shall find ourselves forced to introduce a distinction between
primitive – that is, relatively primitive – aesthetic
characterisations – and characterisations that have
been submitted to a distinctive process of rectification. Until then, however, we shall go along with
the common assumption and treat them as primi-

tive reports of experience. Their primitiveness comes to this: that if a characterisation applies to one work, then it applies to any which, subject to rectification for colours, is observationally indistinguishable from that work; there is no possibility of an unobservable difference affecting how the works are respectively characterised.[2]

My third comment spells out something implied in the first two. If aesthetic characterisations are non-pictorial, and if they apply to any two works which are indistinguishable in pictorial profile, then this is to say that they are supervenient on pictorial characterisations. The indiscernibility of any two works with respect to their pictorial characterisations entails their aesthetic indiscernibility; equivalently, there cannot be an aesthetic difference between two works unless there is also a pictorial one.[3] Such supervenience on the pictorial – henceforth, I shall use the term 'pictorial supervenience' – comes to what Nelson Goodman describes as constancy relative to pictorial properties. 'A property is thus constant only if, although it may or may not remain constant where pictorial properties vary, it never varies where the pictorial properties remain constant. In other words, if it occurs anywhere, it also occurs whenever the pictorial properties remain the same.'[4]

The three comments which I have offered are designed to focus the class of aesthetic characterisations. They culminate in this third remark, that it is at least a necessary condition for such characterisations that they supervene on their pictorial counterparts. In conclusion, I should like to point out that the usual examples given of aesthetic characterisations do seem to meet this condition. For a list of examples we may turn to Roger Scruton, a writer who sponsors the objections which we shall later be considering. He writes as follows about the predicates used in the aesthetic characterisation of art, pictorial and non-pictorial.

Among these predicates we find a great variety. For example, there are predicates whose primary use is in aesthetic judgment, predicates like 'beautiful', 'graceful', 'elegant' and 'ugly'. These terms occur primarily in judgment of aesthetic value. Then there are descriptions referring to the formal or technical accomplishment of a work of art: 'balanced', 'well-made', 'economical', 'rough', 'undisciplined', and so on. Many aesthetic descriptions employ predicates that are normally used to describe the mental and emotional life of human beings. We describe works of art as sad, joyful, melancholy, agitated, erotic, sincere, vulgar, intelligent and mature . . . Aesthetic descriptions can also refer to the expressive features of works of art. Works of art are often said to express emotion, thought, attitude, character, in fact, anything that can be expressed at all . . . Closely connected with expression terms are the terms known philosophically as 'affective': terms that seem to be used to express or project particular human responses which they also indicate by name – examples include 'moving', 'exciting', 'evocative', 'nauseous', 'tedious', 'enjoyable' and 'adorable'. We must also include among aesthetic descriptions several kinds of comparison. For example, I may describe a writer's style as bloated or masculine, a colour as warm or cold, a piece of music as architectural . . . Finally there are various descriptions of a work of art in terms of what it represents, in terms of its truthfulness, or its overall character or genre (whether it is tragic, comic, ironical or what) which cannot easily be fitted into these classes, but which have an important role, despite this, in aesthetic judgment.[5]

Looking at the aesthetic characterisations of pictures towards which Scruton points, we must certainly judge the bulk of them to be pictorially supervenient. Three possible exceptions come to mind but none calls to be taken very seriously. The first is the characterisation of a work by reference to the motive of the artist, as sincere or whatever. Might not such a motive have differed while the work remained pictorially the same? In one sense it might, but not in the sense in which the characterisation which mentions it would really be of aesthetic interest. When we focus on such properties as the sincerity of a work of art we are interested usually in the sort of sincerity that shows through in the painting itself; thus were the work to differ in the sincerity it displays, it would also have to differ pictorially.

A second possible exception is the characterisation of a work by reference to that which it represents. Whether a picture represents this or that person, this or that scene, would seem to depend on factors other than its colour properties: in particular, it would seem to depend on the painter's intention. Thus any judgment of representational value must fail to be pictorially supervenient. Once again, however, it is not clear that such representational value is aesthetically interesting. What is of more direct aesthetic interest is the characterisation of a picture by reference to the sort of thing it represents: that is, as a child-picture, a landscape-picture, a Christ-picture, or whatever. Such a characterisation, unlike the judgment of particular representational value, must be expected to be pictorially supervenient.

The third possible exception to the pictorial supervenience thesis is the characterisation of a work of art as inventive or creative. Whether a picture has such a property would seem to depend as much on what other pictures are in existence as on the work itself; thus the characterisation of a picture by mention of it would not be pictorially supervenient. Here there is no accommodating response which I can immediately make but I hope to be able to describe one in section IV. In the meantime, it does not seem unreasonable to ask for charity towards the supervenience claim. That claim formulates a necessary condition on aesthetic characterisations and with respect to the utterances which it identifies, we now have to raise the realism versus non-realism issue.

II

What does it mean to regard aesthetic characterisations realistically? At a first level it means two things: that one believes that under their standard interpretation, under the interpretation which respects speakers' intentions, they come out as assertions; and further that one believes that the standard assertoric interpretation is unobjectionable. For the purposes at hand assertions may be taken as utterances which are capable of being true or false in a manner that distinguishes them from questions, commands and the like.[6] What exactly it is to be true or false is a question which we may for the moment ignore.

Under their standard interpretation, there is little doubt but that aesthetic characterisations generally come out as assertions. Under that interpretation they have the syntactical form of assertions and they have the distinctively assertoric mark of committing someone who utters them to a particular line of action, linguistic and non-linguistic: this, by contrast with non-assertoric utterances such as questions and commands.[7] There may be

some utterances which would pass as aesthetic characterisations and which do not count as assertions, but it seems that they must be less than typical. The obvious examples of non-assertoric aesthetic remarks – 'Think of the painting as a coloured canvas', 'Imagine the line of the shoulder raised' – will not do because they are not examples of characterisations of pictures.

One putative class of non-assertoric aesthetic characterisations which may be mentioned for illustrative purposes is that of metaphorical descriptions of pictures as sad or gay, heavy or light, or whatever. On one theory of metaphor such utterances are not assertions under their standard interpretation, or at least not assertions in the appropriate way. Taken literally, they are assertions, but taken with their proper metaphorical import they are distinguished by the non-assertoric intention to affect the hearer's way of seeing things; the intention is non-assertoric because the effect sought is not to be achieved just through changing the hearer's beliefs.[8] It would take us too far afield to consider this theory here, but, even if it is correct, it does not undermine the claim that generally aesthetic characterisations come out as assertions under their standard interpretation. I do not myself accept the theory, but I cannot set about defending my view here.

But if the standard interpretation casts aesthetic characterisations as assertions, is that interpretation unobjectionable? There may be objections forthcoming in respect of certain sub-classes: for example, it may be said that even if metaphorical characterisations are standardly taken as assertoric in the normal way, the cost of so construing them is for some reason unacceptable.[9] We may overlook such specific objections, on the assumption that they will leave us with some aesthetic characterisations still to discuss. The question is whether there is any general reason why the standard interpretation of such characterisations might be thought to be objectionable.

What may certainly be said is that the consideration which often leads anti-realists to seek out non-standard interpretations does not apply in the present case. The consideration is this: that with the body of apparent assertions under examination, the standard interpretation of them would wish us to ascribe truth-conditions to certain utterances when the relevant speakers have no way of telling whether or not the truth-conditions obtain. This consideration certainly applies to statements about other minds and about the distant past: with some such statements we shall have to admit that the relevant speakers have no evidence as to whether or not the truth-conditions realistically ascribed to the utterances actually obtain. With aesthetic characterisations, however, it seems to be irrelevant. Here there is no question of some of the utterances having to be regarded as verification-transcendent, if they are taken realistically; the characterisations are equally subject to the prospect of verification or equally resistant to it.[10]

Let us grant that, so far, the way seems to be open to us to regard at least some aesthetic characterisations realistically: that is, to believe that under their standard interpretation they come out as assertions, and to believe that that interpretation is unobjectionable. There is yet a second level, however, where it may be said that realism has also to establish certain claims. At this level, so it will be held, to regard aesthetic characterisations realistically again means two things: that one believes that under their standard interpretation they come out as assertions of a strict and genuine kind or, probably the same thought, have truth-value in the most substantial sense of that term; and further, that one believes that in this respect too the standard interpretation is unobjectionable.

It is possible to argue that it is unnecessary for the realist to enter debate at this second level. David Wiggins has urged that the notion of truth-value assumed in taking utterances as assertions is already as substantial as we should wish it to be.[11] In that case there is no useful distinction to be made between loose and strict assertions, between assertions which have truth-value in a merely formal sense and assertions which have it in a more substantial one. Although I am sympathetic, I do not propose to adopt Wiggins's strategy of argument. Rather I mean to be charitable to the opponent of aesthetic realism and to assume that he can reasonably hold at once that aesthetic characterisations are assertoric but not genuinely assertoric, capable of having truth-value but not capable of having it in the most substantial sense.[12]

Exercising such charity, I need to say that the realist holds at least some aesthetic characterisations not just to be assertions, but to be genuine assertions. And how may we define that class of utterances? Happily, we can help ourselves to a definition constructed in another context by Crispin Wright. According to this, genuine assertions are

statements communally associated with conditions of such a kind that one who is

sincerely unwilling to assent to such a statement when, by ordinary criteria, those conditions obtain, can make himself intelligible to us only by betraying a misunderstanding or some sort of misapprehension, or by professing some sort of sceptical attitude.[13]

The idea is that with a genuine assertion appropriate evidence leaves no room for discretion: someone presented with the evidence can sincerely fail to assent only through a failure of understanding or apprehension, or because of adopting some form of philosophical scepticism. By contrast the non-genuine assertion – the quasi-assertion, in Michael Dummett's phrase[14] – is an utterance with all the marks of an assertion except that the conditions with which it is communally associated leave room for discretion as to whether one should assent or not.

The most plausible threat to aesthetic realism comes at this second level of debate and the opponent whom I envisage in this paper takes his stand there. He says that the standard, or at least the proper, interpretation of aesthetic characterisations casts them as quasi-assertions, as assertions which have truth-value only in a weak sense. What might that sense be said to be? This, perhaps: that we can, and probably must, render them in an interpretative language using the formula, for any asserted sentence S, 'S is true if and only if p', where 'p' is a declarative sentence. Our opponent will wish to deny that such interpretability makes S-like utterances assertions in the genuine sense, for he will say that it may yet be the case, both for S and for 'p', that the appropriate evidence leaves room for the speaker's sincerely failing to assent. What may be required to motivate assent, he will say, is not only a belief that the circumstances associated with the assertion are realised but also a certain logically independent psychological response: say, an act of will or a visitation of feeling.

A denial of aesthetic realism on the lines just sketched can be found in Roger Scruton's *Art and Imagination*. Scruton takes his starting point from the following view about aesthetic characterisations: 'To understand such an aesthetic description involves realising that one can assert it or assent to it sincerely only if one has had a certain "experience", just as one can assert or assent to a normal description only if one has the appropriate belief.'[15] On the basis of this he constructs an alternative to realism which he describes as an affective theory.

The affective theory of aesthetic description argues that the acceptance condition of an aesthetic description may not be a belief but may rather be some other mental state which more effectively explains the point of aesthetic description. To agree to an aesthetic description is to 'see its point', and this 'seeing the point' is to be elucidated in terms of some response or experience that has yet to be described. Hence aesthetic descriptions need not have truth conditions in the strong sense, and to justify them may be to justify an experience and not a belief.[16]

From what we have already seen it will be clear that there are two possible forms for an affective theory such as Scruton's. The theory may be that the standard interpretation depicts aesthetic characterisations as non-genuine assertions or, in a revisionary spirit, that although the standard interpretation depicts them realistically, aesthetic characterisations ought properly to be taken as non-genuine assertions. From our point of view, it does not really matter which version of the theory is ascribed to the opposition. We shall be looking at two objections to realism and hoping to find a means of rebutting them. The objections might be invoked to support either form of the affective theory and it is no concern of ours to determine which of these is the more plausible.

III

So much for the delimitation of aesthetic characterisations and the definition of what it is to regard them realistically. We come now to the two objections mentioned: the objections which put in doubt the possibility of aesthetic realism. The objections each point to a problematic feature of aesthetic characterisations: the one is that the characterisations are essentially perceptual, the other that they are perceptually elusive. They are not the only objections imaginable but, among serious contenders, they are the most distinctively aesthetic ones; the others tend to be recast versions of objections more commonly raised against realism about secondary qualities or realism about values. I assume in what follows that such other objections are not overwhelming. The issue is whether there is any distinctive reason why aesthetic characterisations should not be taken realistically.

We may assume, as a matter of definition, that aesthetic characterisations are all essentially perceptual. What this means is that the putatively cognitive state one is in when, perceiving a work of art, one sincerely assents to a given aesthetic characterisation, is not a state to which one can have non-perceptual access. What I seem to know when, having seen a painting, I describe it as graceful or awkward, tightly or loosely organised, dreamy or erotic, inviting or distancing, is not something which you can know, or at least not something which you can know in the same sense, just through relying on my testimony. It may be that common parlance would allow you to say: 'I know that the picture is graceful and inviting; I have expert and reliable testimony on the matter.' The fact remains however that, phenomenologically, we must distinguish between the type of cognitive state I enjoy – we may assume for the moment that the state is properly cognitive – and that to which you have access. The difference is like that between someone who hears a joke, finds it funny and says that it is amusing and someone who says that it is amusing on the ground of having been told as much.

Aesthetic characterisations are essentially perceptual in the sense that perception is the only title to the sort of knowledge which perception yields – let us say, to the full knowledge – of the truths which they express. In this feature they contrast with pictorial characterisations, and sensory reports in general. The cognitive state of someone who sees and reports that an object is red is a type of state accessible to a companion who sees the object and fails to discern its colour, provided that the second person has good reason to trust the report of the first. Here, by contrast with the aesthetic case, one would find the following sort of remark quite reasonable: 'I don't have to look more closely; I know from my friend's testimony that it is red.' The remark signals the fact that the cognitive state of sincerely assenting on the basis of perception to the sentence 'The object is red' is one to which testimony may also give one access. Both perception and testimony may count as titles to the full knowledge of the truth which that sentence expresses.

The essentially perceptual nature of aesthetic characterisations is surprising in view of the contrast it marks with pictorial characterisations: one would have expected the two sorts of judgments to allow of the same titles to knowledge. It constitutes a difficulty for aesthetic realism because it is unclear how the realist is to explain the phenomenon. The affective theorist, on the other hand, can make ready sense of it. He will say that one is fully entitled to assent to an aesthetic characterisation only where one has had a certain non-cognitive experience in response to the work and that this naturally leads us to deny that there can be a non-perceptual title to full 'knowledge' of what the characterisation expresses. Just as one must be amused before one is fully entitled to describe a joke as funny – the opponent of realism will naturally take amusement as non-cognitive – so it will be said that one must be moved in some non-cognitive fashion, one must enjoy some appropriate non-cognitive flush, before one has a full title to endorse an aesthetic characterisation.

Roger Scruton sketches the affective theorist's explanation in the following passage:

> If ϕ is a visual property, say, then it is not true that I *have* to see ϕ for myself in order to know that an object possesses it: there are circumstances where the opinion of others can give me a logically conclusive reason for saying that ϕ is there, as indeed a blind man can have knowledge of colours. In aesthetics you have to see for yourself precisely because what you have to 'see' is not a property: your knowledge that an aesthetic feature is 'in' the object is given by the *same* criteria that show that you 'see' it. To see the sadness in the music and to know that the music is sad are one and the same thing. To agree in the judgement that the music is sad is not to agree in a belief, but in something more like a response or an experience; in a mental state that is – unlike belief – logically tied to the immediate circumstances of its arousal.[17]

The second problematic feature of aesthetic characterisations, and we may also take it as definitional, is that they are perceptually elusive. What this means is that visual scrutiny of a picture, necessary though it may be for aesthetic knowledge, is not always sufficient to guarantee it. One may look and look at a painting and fail to come to a position where one can sincerely assent to the aesthetic characterisations which are true of it. One may look and look and not see its elegance or economy or sadness, for example. This perceptual elusiveness is different from the lack of thoroughness that may affect any form of perception: the lack which may explain why one did not notice the blob

of yellow in the bottom left-hand corner of the canvas. Assuming a normal eye and normal illumination, pointing is sufficient to put such an oversight right, but there is no exercise which is guaranteed to bring the perceptually elusive into view.

The perceptual elusiveness of aesthetic characterisations can be dramatically illustrated by reference to the ambiguous *Gestalt*. Take the much discussed duck-rabbit drawing. The description of this as a duck-representation is a putative aesthetic characterisation of the drawing. Someone who sees the drawing as a rabbit, however, may not be able, even with herculean efforts at visual scrutiny, to come to a position where he can sincerely assert that it represents a duck. Although the characterisation is said to be determined by nothing more than what is seen, all that is seen is insufficient to produce recognition of its truth.

The perceptual elusiveness of aesthetic characterisations is surprising for the same reason as their essentially perceptual nature: it marks an unexpected contrast with pictorial characterisations. The phenomenon may be quoted as a difficulty for aesthetic realism because it is unclear how the realist can explain it. On the other hand, the affective theorist has an explanation ready to hand. He will say that assent to an aesthetic characterisation involves more than seeing that the picture has such and such a quality; it also involves having a certain sort of non-cognitive experience aroused by the picture. Saying this, he can explain the elusiveness in question by the fact that sometimes visual scrutiny of a work fails to arouse the appropriate experience, with the result that the person is not in a position in which he can sincerely assent to the characterisation.[18]

IV

The challenge for the aesthetic realist is clear. What has to be shown with aesthetic characterisations is that their being essentially perceptual and perceptually elusive can be explained consistently with a realistic construal: consistently with the view that they are genuine assertions and that the presentation of appropriate evidence leaves no distinctive room for the sincere reservation of assent. The problem, intuitively, is this. If aesthetic characterisations are held to direct us towards real properties of the works they characterise, how then do we account for the rather unusual nature of those properties? Short of making them out to be almost magical, how do we explain why the only general title to full knowledge of the properties is perception and why the most exact perception may yet fail to reveal their presence?

In order to see how such an explanation might go, let us consider the case with regular pictorial properties, i.e. properties of colour. The characterisation of something X as red is associated with an uncontentious, if analytically useless, conditional about how X looks to a normally equipped observer under normal conditions of illumination and the like. 'X is red', we can say, 'if and only if it is such that it looks red under standard presentation.' Granted the association with such a conditional, we can understand why the colour characterisation is neither essentially perceptual nor perceptually elusive. If the conditional tells us what it is for something to be red, then, given that the notion of standard presentation is appropriately determinate, we can see why the characterisation allows a testimonial title to knowledge and why it admits of ready perceptual adjudication.

Take first the issue of testimony. Given a sentence 'p', under what conditions might we want to endorse the following: person 1 knows that p but person 2, whom he informs of the fact, cannot be said to know in the same sense that p, even though person 2 has good reason to trust person 1? If person 1 has good evidence that p, so surely has person 2: he has good evidence of the good evidence which person 1 has. What then might make a difference? Presumably just this: that for some reason one can understand properly what is expressed by 'p' only if one has the non-testimonial relation to it enjoyed by person 1. In such a case, and it seems to be the only candidate, we might well wish to deny that person 2 knows that p, or at least that he knows that p in the same sense as person 1.

The claim can be borne out by illustration. Take the case where 'p' involves a demonstrative and where a non-testimonial relation to what 'p' describes is necessary for properly identifying the referent of the demonstrative. Suppose 'p' is 'He is fair-haired', that someone whom I trust asserts that sentence in my hearing, and that I am not in a position to see the person to whom he is referring. In such a case I could not be said to have access to the cognitive state enjoyed by my informant. I might be said to know that the assertion 'He is fair-haired', on the lips of my informant, expressed a truth, but knowledge that such an assertion is true may not involve knowledge of the truth expressed. I might be said to know that the person referred to is fair-haired, but knowledge of this kind, not involving a direct relationship with the person in question, is also less than my informant enjoys: it is knowledge *de dicto*, not *de re*.[19] Because testimony does not enable me fully to understand what is expressed by 'p', as this is asserted by my informant, so it does not give me a title to full knowledge of what is expressed by 'p'.

If the claim just presented is correct, then we can see why a colour characterisation, barring problems with demonstratives and the like, should allow a testimonial title to full knowledge. What is expressed by 'X is red' is given by the associated conditional and one can understand this properly even if one does not enjoy a non-testimonial relation to the fact reported. One knows what it is for something to look red, and one knows what standard presentation involves, even if one does not see the red object in question. Thus there is no reason why one should not be said to have knowledge that X is red, in the full and only sense of such knowledge, if one has been given testimony on the matter by someone whom one has good reason to trust.

It is less difficult to show why the colour characterisation should be, not only not essentially perceptual, but also not perceptually elusive. If what it is for something to be red is as the associated conditional says, then we must expect visual scrutiny to reveal the redness in every case. Only if standard presentation were a condition which was problematic in a certain manner could one have any other expectation. Were standard presentation a condition of which one could never be sure that it was fulfilled, for example, then we might reason that visual scrutiny would often fail to reveal the colour of the object scrutinised, even though all appears as normal. Granted that there are independent and relatively straightforward tests as to whether an object is standardly presented, there is no room for colour to be perceptually elusive. In any case where someone looks and fails to see, one must expect to be able to explain the failure by reference to independently checkable factors such as sensory impairment or an insufficiency of light.

Let us turn now from pictorial to aesthetic characterisations. Since these are also reports of experience, at least on a realistic construal, we must expect them to bear an association with parallel conditionals that say how the objects characterised look. Take 'X is sad' as an exemplar of aesthetic characterisation.[20] If we are realists we must expect such a characterisation to be linked with a condition which plays in relation to it the role which standard presentation plays in relation to 'X is red': we must look for a conditional of the form 'X is sad if and only if X is such that it looks sad under circumstance C'. Circumstance C, if it is to support realism, must ensure that not every work of art is sad and that any which is sad is not also at the same time, and in the same way, not sad: we shall return to this issue at the beginning of section v. It will include standard presentation and, in order to explain the difference between the pictorial and the aesthetic cases, some further condition. Thus we must look for a conditional of the form 'X is sad if and only if X is such that it looks sad under standard presentation and –'. The question is, how should the blank clause be filled?

Our discussion of colour characterisations may be of some help to us in dealing with this problem. It suggests two constraints which any filler must meet, if it is to enable us to explain the fact that aesthetic characterisations are essentially perceptual and perceptually elusive. If aesthetic characterisations are to be essentially perceptual, then the filler must describe a condition which can be fully understood only by someone who has a non-testimonial relation to the fact recorded in the characterisation: this, because we saw that the necessity of such a relation for understanding what is expressed by a proposition 'p' is the only likely explanation for why reliable testimony does not constitute a title for claiming full knowledge that p. If aesthetic characterisations are to be perceptually elusive on the other hand, then the filler must describe a condition which is appropriately problematic. The elusiveness could be explained if, for example, the condition were one of which one could never be sure that it had been brought about; in that case, one could explain someone's failure to see the fact recorded in a characterisation by the non-realisation, despite appearances, of the condition.

Where then do we turn for cues as to the nature of the required filler? One promising source is the ambiguous *Gestalt* such as the duck–rabbit, for here the condition that the filler describes must have a different value as the figure is differently seen. What is it that might be said to vary, in a manner consistent with realism, as the figure is seen now as a duck, now as a rabbit? With the particular duck–rabbit example it is not easy to say,

but there is another ambiguous *Gestalt* with which an answer readily suggests itself. The figure in question is the central one of the five in this display:

As the figure at the centre of the display shifts from being seen as a letter to being seen as numeral, what varies is the reference class in the background. Positioned in the row class the figure is seen as a letter, positioned in the column class it is seen as a numeral.

In this example, whether one sees the figure as a letter or a numeral depends on one's disposition to identify A and C on the one hand, 12 and 14 on the other, as relevant contrasts. But these contrasts might not have been visually presented or even visualised in fancy. Generalising, then, we can say that if such a figure looks like the second letter of the alphabet, that is because one knows that the other letters supply the relevant contrasts. This knowledge gives one the appropriate reference class and against the background which that class supplies, the figure looks like the letter B.

The generalisation suggests that for any property which an object can display in perception, the object displays that property only in so far as it is positioned in an appropriate class: that is, only in so far as the perceiver knows what the relevant contrasts are. The pictorial property of redness will be displayed only in so far as the bearer is positioned by reference to the colour paradigms or, allowing for denseness, the colour spectrum. The aesthetic property of sadness will be displayed only in so far as the bearer is positioned by reference to certain parallel contrasts.

There is a crucial difference, however, between the redness and the sadness case. Because the pictorial positioning is by reference to something given once and for all, that positioning can be taken as a further aspect, over and above normal sight and normal illumination, of standard presentation. The aesthetic positioning, on the other hand, is by reference to something which may change from case to case. It requires only normal information and memory to position an object appropriately for colour; it requires imagination to position it so that it displays a property like sadness. Henceforth we

Philip Pettit

shall ignore the positioning necessary for something like colour and reserve the term only for the
case where imagination is required. Notice that
imagination does not seem to be required for the
case where a figure appears as a letter or a numeral:
the class of letters or numerals by reference to
which the figure is positioned is normalised in the
same way as the class of colours.

The generalisation from our original example,
combined with this observation about the aesthetic
property of sadness, points us towards a general
hypothesis of the kind that we require. According
to the hypothesis, X is sad if and only if X is such
that it looks sad under standard presentation and
under suitable positioning. The positioning of the
work is determined by the reference class against
the background of which it is viewed. This class
is assumed to be available only on the basis of
imagination, not by the introduction of normalised
examples.

Leaving aside the complications of raised or
round surfaces, a picture can be seen as a mosaic of
equal square modules, each module being of just
less than perceptually distinguishable area. An elementary pictorial variation on a given picture is a
variation in which just one such module differs in
its pictorial properties. A compound pictorial variation, on the other hand, is a variation in which
more than one module is different. Among the
compound pictorial variations many, like elementary variations, will not differ discernibly from the
original, but some certainly will: these latter we
may refer to as the discernible variations on the
picture. It will be clear that for any picture the discernible variations will include all the pictures that
can be painted on the surface in question.

The hypothesis put forward is that every picture
on which an aesthetic characterisation is fixed is
seen against the background of a certain class of
discernible variations: for simplicity, we may ignore
the possibility that other sorts of items also play a
background role. These variations are made into a
reference class for the picture; they are used to
determine what we have called its positioning.
The reference class may be of any cardinality up
to that of the total class of discernible variations.
As the class changes in membership, the positioning changes, and as the positioning changes, the
property in question may come into, or go out of,
view.

Granted that a picture will have many aesthetic
properties, our hypothesis means that it will be
positioned at once in many different reference

classes. Each of these classes can be seen as a
dimension and the different dimensions may be
taken to describe a space within which the object is
seen when the appropriate properties are in view.
The concept of a multi-dimensional aesthetic
space offers a useful way of thinking about what
happens when a picture assumes an overall aesthetic character for an observer. The picture is
given coordinates, as it were, and fixed within an
appropriate system of reference.

How plausible is the hypothesis which we have
put forward? We cannot go into a full assessment
of the pros and cons here, but it may be useful to
note one respect in which it is intuitively a very
attractive idea. If we are offered a pictorial object
and are asked whether it sustains some aesthetic
characterisation, it is almost always in place to say
that the answer depends on what the object is compared with. Compared with one set of figures, O
may come out as a facial representation; compared
with another, it may not. Compared with one range
of alternatives, ⑩ may exemplify great regularity;
compared with another, it may depict the break-
down of form. These remarks are platitudes and
the attraction of our hypothesis is that it seems to
do nothing more than generalise such points as
they make.

Another way of bringing out the plausibility of
the hypothesis is this. Given a set of mutually
exclusive predicates F and G (or F, G and H: the
number does not matter), it is notorious how often
we agree on which member applies to any object,
even an object not normally described by either
term. We agree that Wednesday is fat and Tuesday
thin, that science is hard and art soft, even that
soup is pong and ice-cream ping. Such agreement
is forthcoming, and the examples make this clear,
only when it is obvious, for any object characterised, what objects are meant to contrast with it
in resisting application of the term in question.
Compared with Tuesday, Wednesday is fat; compared with art, science is hard; compared with ice-
cream, soup is pong. What our hypothesis does is
to extend the point to works of art, so far as those
works lend themselves to characterisation by
such sets of predicates as 'elegant–inelegant',
'economical–lavish', 'monumental–delicate', or
whatever: the sets may or may not be normally used
to describe pictures. The point is that pictures
display themselves as suitable subjects for a given
aesthetic characterisation, only so far as they are
cast in appropriate contrast: that is, only so far as
they are assigned to an appropriate reference class.

In connection with the plausibility of our hypothesis, what may also be mentioned is that it enables us to explain how a characterisation of a picture as inventive or creative can be cast as pictorially supervenient, and not as dependent on the other pictures in existence. We postponed the explanation from section I because we were not then in a position to describe it. The explanation is that the sort of creativity that is of aesthetic interest is the creativity which shows through in a picture when that picture is suitably positioned. Creativity is on a par with all of the other aesthetic properties: it is something which displays itself in perception, but only when the perceived object is situated within an appropriate reference class. (But see section V.)

Granted that our hypothesis is not implausible, the telling question is whether it would enable us to explain the two troublesome features of aesthetic characterisations. It offers us the following formula: 'X is sad if and only if X is such that it looks sad under standard presentation and under suitable positioning.' Does the condition described as suitable positioning meet the constraints formulated earlier? Is it fully understandable only from a non-testimonial point of view, so that the essentially perceptual feature of aesthetic characterisations is intelligible? Is it appropriately problematic, so that equally we can make sense of the fact that aesthetic characterisations are perceptually elusive?

To both questions, encouragingly, the answer must be 'yes'. Only someone looking at a picture and putting it imaginatively through various positionings can understand what that positioning is under which the picture looks sad. One fixes the positioning, one finds the appropriate reference class, only in so far as one succeeds in making the picture display the appearance of sadness. There is no access to the positioning parallel to the access which we have to standard presentation. Thus if I learn from a trustworthy and tested informant that the picture is sad, I may claim to know that the sentence 'The picture is sad' expresses a truth on his lips, but I still lack full knowledge of the truth expressed by the sentence. The reason is the same as in our earlier example with the demonstrative-involving report. What is expressed by the sentence is something which can be fully grasped only by someone who identifies the suitable positioning of the picture: that is, only by someone who has a non-testimonial relation to the fact in question.

As for our second question, it transpires that the condition described as suitable positioning is also appropriately problematic. There are tests for whether a picture is standardly presented, but not for whether it is suitably positioned. This means that we can never be sure, on grounds independent of what aesthetic characterisations are endorsed, whether or not a picture is suitably positioned for a given observer. Thus it is unsurprising that some observers will look and look at a picture and yet fail to come to a point where they can sincerely assent, on the basis of what they see, to an aesthetic characterisation which we find totally compelling.[21]

V

The preceding is a sketch-theory of aesthetic perception which indicates how a realist might respond to the two objections mentioned earlier. Rather than seek to elaborate the theory, I should like to try, in the remaining paragraphs, to buttress it against an obvious rejoinder. The opponent of aesthetic realism may argue that he can embrace our theory without embarrassment, and I must show why I think that he cannot.

We noted in the last section that the circumstance described as standard presentation plus suitable positioning, if it was to support realism, would have to ensure that not every work of art had an aesthetic property like sadness and that any which had did not, in the same way, have the property of not being sad. An opponent may now argue that this realistic constraint is not after all satisfied. He will say that for any work of art and for any aesthetic property there is likely to be a positioning, however bizarre, under which the work displays that property. Thus every work of art will have every aesthetic property and among the properties possessed by any work will be properties which are directly opposed to one another.

We may wish to cavil at the universality of our opponent's claims, but that would hardly be useful: even if the claims are only true of some works and some properties, they are still inimical to realism. They mean that we cannot generally take aesthetic characterisations as genuine assertions. The purveyor of troublesome characterisations may say that no characterisation rules out any other; in this case they cannot be regarded as assertions at all, not engaging with the notion of truth. Alternatively, and more plausibly, he may say that whether one defends one or another of a set of conflicting characterisations depends on how one positions the work. In this case they cannot be regarded realistically either, for someone appropriately placed may now be sincerely unwilling to assent to our aesthetic characterisation, even though he does not misunderstand, misapprehend, or maintain a philosophical scepticism. The factor which will explain such unwillingness is his positioning the work under characterisation in some deviant way. Deviant positioning is not an expression of scepticism and neither is it a product of misapprehension or misunderstanding. So at least it will be said.

The objection raised shows that aesthetic realism must be abandoned, if the positioning of a picture is taken to be unconstrained: if there is assumed to be no right or wrong way of positioning it. As against the objection, I wish to urge that there are at least two different sorts of constraints that must be acknowledged in the positional determination of a picture, and that where these are unsatisfied the positioning is incorrect. The recognition of such constraints, as we shall see, means a serious revision in our conception of aesthetic characterisations.

The first sort of constraints on aesthetic positioning are what might be described as holistic ones. These are the constraints on how we position a picture for one kind of aesthetic property which arise from the fact that we have positioned it in such and such a way for another. The reference classes for different kinds of properties, the different dimensions of aesthetic space, interact. If a picture is so positioned that it presents itself as a representation of a woman, for example, that naturally affects how it may be positioned with a view to displaying economy or lavishness, dreaminess or matter-of-factness, sadness or gaiety. This interactive influence means that for a given kind of property certain reference classes will be inappropriate, certain positionings wrong. The positioning for any one kind is bound by the constraint that it allows such positionings for other kinds of property that the picture presents itself as a coherent unity. A given positioning will be illegitimate if it means that we cannot make unified sense of the picture as a whole: that is, if it gives rise to a certain incoherence, or if it allows us only to make sense of part of the picture.

Holistic constraints may not be taken very seriously on their own, since the standards of what is a perceptual or aesthetic unity have been dramatically altered in modern painting. Among the lessons of the twentieth-century tradition we might number this: that not only is the duck-rabbit a unity when it is seen as a duck or as a rabbit, it is also a unity, although a different non-representational unity, when seen as a duck-rabbit. In order to salvage the force of our holistic constraints, we need to see that they do not operate alone but rather in combination with another set, a set which we may characterise as humanistic ones.

Humanistic constraints spring from the requirement, not that we see a work of art as a unity, but that we see it as something which it is intelligible that a human being should have produced. When we offer a positional account of a work of art, we necessarily suppose that the painter was moved by certain desires, and certain beliefs about how he might fulfil those desires: even if we invoke unconscious intentions and the like on his part, we must offer an account of the more mundane states of mind in which these are carried. That being so, we are obliged in putting forward our construal not to commit ourselves to the ascription of beliefs or desires which are unintelligible or which it is unintelligible that the painter, granted his milieu, should have had or should have acted upon.[22]

Humanistic constraints can be disregarded only at the cost of ignoring the human origin of pictures, or at a cost of ignoring the humanity of those with whom pictures originate. I assume that such a price is not worth paying. Together with holistic constraints they will have effects such as that of proscribing the construal of Egyptian pictographs as early cubist paintings, or the construal of pictures in the international Gothic style as paintings designed to dismantle perspective. If they seem to spoil sport in so undermining the cult of play, this may only be because art is not taken as a serious matter.

It may be said that if holistic and humanistic constraints are generally respected in the positioning, and consequently the aesthetic characterisation, of pictures, that is only a matter of changeable convention. It is certainly a matter of convention, just as it is a matter of convention that certain constraints define what is meant by standard presentation in ascertaining the colour of things. But might the convention change? Not, I would say, without a barely imaginable transformation in what is meant by artistic production and aesthetic appreciation.

Under our current and traditional conception of these matters, the artist and his ideal audience share a common knowledge in virtue of which each can expect the other to see a distinctive significance in certain painterly choices. Against such a background the artist seeks, and knows that he will be taken to seek, a certain unified effect in every picture he makes: in a sense, he speaks to his audience. This conception would be quite undermined if the holistic and humanistic constraints on aesthetic positioning were put aside. If it does not matter that a positioning makes only partial sense, or makes a sense that the artist could not have consciously or unconsciously sought, then the work of art might as well have been the product of chance. It ceases to be a challenge to enter into a perception sponsored by the artist and degenerates into an occasion for the play of whim and fancy.

The recognition that there are constraints of positioning forces us to recast what we have said in preceding sections about aesthetic characterisations of works of art. The sort of characterisation we have discussed satisfies the following schema: 'X is φ if and only if it is such that it looks φ under standard presentation and under suitable positioning.' The introduction of constraints of positioning forces us to recognise that our real interest is in a sub-species of this kind, namely the sort of characterisation which meets this more specific schema: "X is φ if and only if (1) it is such that it looks φ under standard presentation and under suitable positioning and (2) it is such that the positioning found suitable, assuming that there is one, is allowed by the appropriate constraints.' The difference between the two classes of judgment is that which we mentioned at the beginning of the paper: the one class is that of primitive aesthetic characterisations, the other that of aesthetic characterisations rectified by appropriate background information.

What appears in this section is that aesthetic realism can only be defended in the last resort for characterisations which are appropriately rectified. We may stave off the two objections considered by recourse to the idea of positioning, but that idea will underpin realism only if we introduce constraints and distinguish rectified from primitive characterisation. We should not be surprised at the result, for it parallels the case with characterisations of colour. The unrectified colour report would have to be taken as less than a genuine assertion, since something other than misapprehension, misunderstanding or scepticism would make intelligible a subject's sincere unwillingness to assent to an appropriate judgment: for example, his wearing

coloured contact lenses, his having been in bright sun, his being blinded by an intruding light, or whatever. We can construe colour reports realistically only because they are taken as rectified by the reference to standard presentation; this reference means that factors such as those just mentioned are recast as obstacles to apprehension.

This paper began with the discussion of primitive aesthetic characterisations because aesthetic characterisations are normally assumed to be such. The starting-point is also philosophically justified since rectified aesthetic characterisations can be defined only by reference to primitive. It must be noted, however, that rectified characterisations differ significantly from their primitive counterparts. The main differences spring from the fact that the characterisations depend on background as well as visual information. Thus they are not pictorially supervenient, for example: our background information will prevent us from characterising in the same way as the original a pictorial replica produced by some chance mechanism.[23] Furthermore, the realistic construal of rectified characterisations may be undermined by a non-realism in respect of the utterances, related to other minds and perhaps the distant past, which constitute relevant background information. If we defend aesthetic realism, we must assume that realism is appropriate in those other areas as well.

The theory sketched in the last section shows how one may hope to escape Scruton's objections and espouse aesthetic realism. The amendment constituted by the restriction to rectified aesthetic characterisations keeps open that hope. There is room for the endorsement of the following sort of remarks. In the sense in which it is usually assumed that the colours of a picture are there to be perceived, there to be more or less exactly characterised in pictorial description, so the aesthetic properties are there to be detected and characterised.[24] An aesthetic description of a picture may well fail to capture all that is there to be seen by the informed eye, but what it captures when it is a faithful record is something which properly belongs to the painting and something which is in principle accessible to all. Aesthetic characterisations, or at least those to which no special disqualification attaches, are both standardly and properly taken as assertoric, and as assertoric in the strictest and most genuine sense of that term.[25]

Notes

1 Nelson Goodman, *The Languages of Art*, Oxford University Press, 1969, p. 42. The account is rough; for example in ignoring the three-dimensional properties that a picture may have. Notice that if a painting changes shade of colour at some place it will alter in respect of the pictorial characterisations it sustains, though it may not invite a different colour name: this, because pictorial characterisations include comparisons with colour charts. The fact is important, since if pictorial characterisations were insensitive to such a change, they could not provide a base on which aesthetic characterisations supervene: see below.

2 My account of primitiveness draws on the account of observational predicates in Crispin Wright, 'Language-Mastery and the Sorites Paradox', in Gareth Evans and John McDowell (eds), *Truth and Meaning*, Oxford University Press, 1976, pp. 223–47.

3 For a useful account of supervenience see J. Kim, 'Supervenience and Nomological Incommensurables', *American Philosophical Quarterly*, Vol. 15, 1978, 149–58. Like Kim, I leave open the question of whether the necessity involved in supervenience is logical necessity or some weaker variety.

4 Goodman, p. 86.

5 Roger Scruton, *Art and Imagination*, Methuen, London, 1974, pp. 30–1.

6 Notice that not every characterisation must be said by the realist to be true or false; he may deny bivalence. See John McDowell, 'Truth Conditions, Bivalence, and Verificationism' in Evans and McDowell, pp. 42–66. Notice too that the following case is assumed not to arise: that of an utterance which is standardly taken as non-assertoric but which the realist wishes none the less to construe as an assertion. Notice finally that the reductivist who tries to fix the truth conditions of the assertions by reference to the truth conditions of certain other statements will be a non-realist only if he sees himself as combating the standard interpretation of the original assertions.

7 For a discussion of the latter point see Michael Dummett, *Frege: Philosophy of Language*, Duckworth, London, 1973, Chapter 10. An aspect of their having the syntactical form of assertions is that they pass the Geach test discussed by Dummett: the form of words in which an aesthetic characterisation is formulated can occur as the antecedent of a conditional. See Peter Geach, *Logic Matters*, Blackwell, Oxford, 1972, Chapter 8.

8 Such a view might be drawn from Donald Davidson, 'What Metaphors Mean', *Critical Inquiry*, Vol. 5, 1978, 31–47; reprinted in Mark Platts (ed.), *Reference, Truth and Reality*, Routledge and Kegan Paul, London, 1980, pp. 238–54.

9 It is also possible to read Davidson's position in this manner.

10 In this they are like the evaluations discussed in my paper 'Evaluative "Realism" and Interpretation', in Steven H. Holtzmann and Christopher M. Leich (eds), *Wittgenstein: To Follow a Rule*, Routledge and Kegan Paul, London, 1980, pp. 211–45.

11 David Wiggins, 'What Would be a Substantial Theory of Truth?' in Zak van Straaten (ed.), *Philosophical Subjects: Essays Presented to P. F. Strawson*, Oxford University Press, 1980, pp. 189–221.

12 In the paper mentioned in note 10 I do not consider the possibility of such a position with respect to evaluations.

13 Crispin Wright, *Wittgenstein on the Foundations of Mathematics*, Duckworth, London, 1980, p. 463.

14 See Dummett, Chapter 10. Wright's distinction is developed from Dummett's notion of the quasi-assertion, as he makes clear on p. 448.

15 Scruton, p. 49.

16 *Ibid.*, p. 55. For a denial of realism in respect of ethics which resembles the position characterised here for aesthetics see Simon Blackburn, 'Rule-Following and Moral Realism' in Holtzmann and Leich. Both Blackburn and Scruton indicate that they ascribe truth-value to the utterances which they discuss only in the weak sense that the utterances allow of interpretation by means of the formula described earlier. See Scruton, Chapter 5 for a lengthy discussion.

17 *Ibid.*, p. 54. I am grateful to John McDowell for drawing my attention to what I describe as the essentially perceptual nature of aesthetic characterisations. I should mention that, unlike Scruton, I would like to leave open the question of whether a congenitally blind person can have a non-perceptual access to knowledge of colours. Some of the data relevant to the question are presented in the next section.

18 Roger Scruton makes this point, among others (*ibid.*, Chapter 3). He later exempts representational characteristics from the affective thesis which he argues. 'Although the important facts about both representation and expression must be stated in terms of our reactions to works of art, the logic of these two notions is (or, in the case of expression, can be) a logic of description' (p. 205). However, it seems from Chapter 3 that he will have to treat the duck-rabbit case in the manner suggested.

19 See Tyler Burge, 'Belief *de re*', in *Journal of Philosophy*, Vol. 74, 1977, 338–62.

20 In taking 'X is sad' as an exemplar of aesthetic characterisations, I assume that its metaphorical character does not make it significantly distinctive. Unlike 'X is sad' other aesthetic characterisations, such as 'X expresses sadness', do not allow of a transformation exactly parallel to 'X is such that it

looks sad under a certain circumstance.' I also assume that this does not mean that 'X is sad' is significantly distinctive.

21 Notice that properties for which there is a normalised reference class will naturally fail to be essentially perceptual or perceptually elusive. This rules out colours as aesthetic properties and also properties such as that of being a certain letter or numeral. It may also be taken to rule out some apparently aesthetic qualities, such as that of being a landscape picture. One might argue that for such bland properties, there are often normalised reference classes.

22 As has often been noticed, holistic and humanistic constraints operate generally in the assignment of intentional characterisations to actions. See, for example, Graham Macdonald and Philip Pettit, *Semantics and Social Science*, Routledge and Kegan Paul, London, 1981.

23 It may be wondered whether there is room for a distinction between primitive and rectified aesthetic characterisation of such objects as natural scenes. I tend to think that there is. I assume that such characterisation presupposes positioning and I believe that one's general view of nature will supply constraints to distinguish reasonable positionings from wholly artificial ones. Artificial positionings encourage the quaint and the whimsical, reasonable positionings the genuinely revelatory.

24 The usual assumption may of course be questioned. It is often argued, for example, that colour ascriptions are improperly, if standardly, taken as genuine assertions. See, for instance, Bruce Aune, *Knowledge, Mind and Nature*, Ridgeview Publishing Co., Reseda, California, 1967, Chapter 7.

25 The clause about special disqualification is meant to cover such possibilities as that raised about metaphorical characterisations in section II.

Part IV

Intention and Interpretation

Introduction to Part IV

There are two competing conceptions of the nature of interpretation of artworks. On the first conception interpretation is seen as a retrieval by an audience or reader of the meaning or significance either embodied in the work itself or somehow placed there by the artist. This conception is grounded in the thought that interpretation essentially involves constraints: some interpretations of a work of art are obviously worse than other interpretations of the same work, and some alleged interpretations of a work of art do not appear to have anything to do with the work they claim to interpret and so cannot really be said to be interpretations of that work at all. Consequently there must be something in the work itself or in its relation to its origin that imposes constraints on any interpretation of the work. Let us reflect on this conception before turning to the second.

The central debate about the source of the constraints on an interpretation of a work of art conceptualizes the problem as a contest between intentionalism and anti-intentionalism, i.e. between the view that the artist's intention can be invoked as evidence in favor of or against an interpretation, and the view that only references to the work of art itself are admissible. The starting point of this debate was Monroe C. Beardsley and William K. Wimsatt's much anthologized article on "The Intentional Fallacy," which argued that biographical information about the author was irrelevant to the interpretation and evaluation of a work of literature. In "Intentions and Interpretations: A Fallacy Revived," reprinted here, Beardsley continues to defend the position of the irrelevance of information about the author, by employing a conceptual scheme borrowed from speech act theory. He distinguishes between two types of "saying," saying as the *performance* of an illocutionary act and saying as the *representation* of an illocutionary act, arguing that literary works must be understood as representations of the illocutionary acts occurring in them and as such are insulated from the actual intentions of, or actual biographical facts about, an author. In "Intention and Interpretation in Literature" Jerrold Levinson, while summarizing a number of the recent views that have been put forward on this question, develops a view that has recently been widely accepted. He argues against anti-intentionalism of the Wimsatt/Beardsley type, while at the same time also rejecting what he considers extreme forms of intentionalism ("actual intentionalism"). Levinson argues that one does indeed attribute intentions to an author but that these intentions are of two sorts. There are categorial intentions which are the actual intentions an author has in presenting his work as being of a certain type (e.g. as being a *literary* work). In this case, the artist's actual intention is decisive for categorizing a work as literature. Secondly, there are semantic intentions. In the case where a work is categorically intended as a work of literature, semantic intentions are hypothetically attributed to the author on the basis of "the work's internal structure and the relevant surrounding context of creation, in all its *legitimately* invoked specificity" (Levinson, this volume, p. 201). The really difficult question, though, which then arises, concerns the scope of the specific author-based contextual factors to which one can legitimately appeal. To this question, Levinson does not have a "principled answer," but it is where he believes that future discussion should focus.

Unfortunately, this is the point at which the contributions to this debate come to an abrupt halt.

On the second conception, interpretation is the construction of the meaning or significance of the work by an audience or reader, the meaning or significance originating in the process of interpretation itself. Such an interpretation consequently constructs the object it interprets since the meaning or significance which a work of art possesses will be a central property of that work. This conception of interpretation is responsive to the apparently undeniable empirical fact that there are, both among ordinary members of the audience and among critics, many competing interpretations of the same work of art without there being any apparent way of deciding which of these interpretations are correct. In "The Constructivist's Dilemma" Robert Stecker both summarizes and criticizes the constructivist position. If one adopts radical constructivism, i.e. the view that all interpretations construct the object they interpret, then one ends up in an infinite regress. If meaning is not found in a literary work but imputed, and if the interpretation that imputes the meaning is just one more text, the meaning of which needs to be constructed in interpretation, there is no end to this process. But "The buck has to stop somewhere; something has to *have* meaning rather than be given it" (Stecker, this volume p. 224). In the same way, Stecker argues, moderate constructivism, which holds that different interpretations can be interpretations of the same work but nevertheless change that work, faces a number of problems and leads to a number of paradoxes that make it ultimately untenable.

Theories of interpretation, no matter of what kind, tend to identify problems and formulate solutions using a semantic vocabulary. Interpretation aims at recovering "meaning" from, or imposing "meaning" on, the work of art. Though the term "meaning" has a broad use roughly synonymous with "intention" or "purpose," its use in debates about interpretation has encouraged theorists to construe the meaning of artworks analogously with the meaning of linguistic expressions such as metaphors, sentences, or utterances, or to see the work of art as a "text" to be interpreted in the way that texts are interpreted. There has been virtually no attempt to examine the usefulness of the concept of meaning for a theory of interpretation of artworks or to examine how far theoretical problems under discussion in the debate about interpretation are actually due to the employment of a semantic vocabulary. In "The 'Meaning' of a Literary Work" S. H. Olsen argues that the use of a semantic vocabulary is both inappropriate in the sense that its application to literary works and their constitutive elements is forced and that it imposes ways of thinking in literary aesthetics that are theoretically pernicious. That is, this vocabulary narrows the discussion of the role of biographical information in interpretation into a contest between intentionalist and anti-intentionalist explanations of "meaning." And it encourages a view of the literary work as an object of understanding rather than as an object of appreciation, thus blurring the important distinction between the literary mode of interpretation and other modes of interpretation which can also be used in the case of literary works. This is pernicious, Olsen argues, since a literary work is not merely a text and language that needs to be understood, but a work of art that invites appreciation.

Further reading

Barnes, Annette (1988). *On Interpretation* (Oxford: Blackwell).

Iseminger, Gary (ed.) (1992). *Intention & Interpretation* (Philadelphia, PA: Temple University Press).

Krausz, Michael (1993). *Rightness and Reasons: Interpretation in Cultural Practices* (Ithaca, NY: Cornell University Press).

Krausz, Michael (ed.) (2002). *Is There a Single Right Interpretation?* (University Park, PA: Pennsylvania State University Press).

Margolis, Joseph (1980). *Art and Philosophy: Conceptual Issues in Aesthetics* (Atlantic Highlands, NJ: Humanities Press).

Margolis, Joseph and Rockmore, Tom (eds.) (2000). *The Philosophy of Interpretation* (Oxford: Blackwell Publishers).

Newton-de Molina, David (ed.) (1976). *On Literary Intention: Critical Essays* (Edinburgh: University Press).

Stecker, Robert (1997). *Artworks: Definition, Meaning, Value* (University Park, PA: Pennsylvania State University Press).

Thom, Paul (2000). *Making Sense: a Theory of Interpretation* (Lanham, MD: Rowman & Littlefield).

Tollhurst, William (1979). "On what a Text Is and How It Means," *British Journal of Aesthetics*, 79, pp. 3–14.

15

The "Meaning" of a Literary Work

Stein Haugom Olsen

I

One of the major developments in literary theory
in the last half century has been the rise to theoretical prominence of the concept of meaning. The
concept of meaning has emerged as a tool not
merely in the literary analysis of words and sentences, but it has also come to be used with reference to literary works themselves. Locutions like
'the meaning of the poem', 'the meaning of the
work', 'poetic meaning', and 'literary meaning'
have appeared in the formulation of central problems in literary theory, and it has become a critical
commonplace that the literary work is a verbal
expression, a verbal construct or an utterance, and
that as such its peculiar nature is defined through
the special *way in which it means*. There are different theories about the way in which a literary work
means. The difference between the theories is in
their choice of analogy for the literary work and in
their choice of a semantic theory on which they can
draw for terms and conventions to use in an explanation of literary meaning. There are three main
types of theory about literary meaning: autonomy
theories, developed on the back of the practice of
the New Criticism; semiotic theories, developed
under the influence of the rising discipline of
theoretical linguistics; and intentionalist theories,
inspired by speech-act theory and Gricean analy-

Stein Haugom Olsen, "The 'Meaning' of a Literary
Work," *New Literary History: A Journal of Theory and
Interpretation*, 14: 1 (1982), pp. 13–32. © by New
Literary History, University of Virginia. Reprinted with
permission of The Johns Hopkins University Press.

ses of meaning. *Autonomy theories* adopt the
metaphor as the linguistic expression to which the
literary work is analogous. 'A metaphor', M. C.
Beardsley says, 'is a miniature poem, and the explication of a metaphor is a model of all explication.'[1]
Autonomy theories rely on a particular theory of
metaphor, commonly referred to as the *interaction
theory*, and the semantic vocabulary they employ is
inspired by this theory. 'In the simplest formulation,' says I. A. Richards in the passage where the
name of the theory originated, 'when we use a
metaphor we have two thoughts of different things
active together and supported by a single word, or
phrase, whose meaning is a resultant of their interaction.'[2] The interaction between the two terms
juxtaposed in the metaphorical expression is
usually explained by help of the concept of 'secondary meaning' or 'connotation'. One understands an expression like 'man is a wolf' by
identifying the connotations of the word *wolf*
which imply predicates logically applicable to man.
Juxtaposing in an expression two terms the combination of which constitutes a break with the
normal logic of language or thought forces the
receiver into this roundabout way of connecting
the two terms, and the result is a metaphorical
meaning for an apparently paradoxical or even non-
sensical expression. This illogical way of combining two terms creates an expression with an inner
tension which produces a new meaning. The literary work juxtaposes, in a similar way, expressions,
symbols, situations, and so forth with different,
often conflicting 'meanings', making use of exactly
the same semantic resources as metaphor – ambiguity, polysemy, connotations: 'The conclusion of

the poem is the working out of the various tensions – set up by whatever means – by propositions, metaphors, symbols. The unity is achieved by a dramatic process, not a logical; it represents an equilibrium of forces, not a formula.'[3]

The key concepts of *semiotic theories* are the concepts of *sign*, *system*, and *structure*. The meaning of a sign is determined by the totality of relationships into which it can enter with other signs of the system. The meaning of an expression of the system (that is, of a sequence of signs concatenated in accordance with the combinatorial conventions defining the system) is a function of the meaning of the signs making up the expression and the structural relations between them. Semiotic theories aim at defining minimal semantic units and formulating rules for combining them into expressions. In semiotic theories of literature the literary work is conceived of as a formal unit divisible into signs which have been combined in accordance with the conventions of the system which constitutes a text as a literary work. Such a theory 'tries to discover the conventions which make meaning possible. Here the goal is to develop a poetics which would stand to literature as linguistics stands to language. Just as the task of linguists is not to tell us what individual sentences mean but to explain according to what rules their elements combine and contrast to produce the meanings sentences have for speakers of a language, so the semiotician attempts to discover the nature of the codes which make literary communication possible.'[4] Semiotic theories are a miscellany, and there are divergences between different theories with regard to whether they consider a text closed (employing one particular code and thus yielding one determinate meaning), or open (as constituted by a number of codes which will yield a number of different meanings for the text); with regard to what they assume the system or code to be; what they regard the conventions of the system to be; and, indeed, with regard to how far they are willing to take the analogy, invoked by the critic quoted above, between the meaning of a text and the meaning of a *sentence*. In particular, recent semiotic theory has tended to fight shy of the sentence analogy and simply to rely on the general notions of sign, system, and structure without referring to the sentence to guide interpretation of these notions. However, if the semantic vocabulary employed by semiotic theories is to retain theoretical perspicuity, the sentence analogy must be insisted on. The only successful semiotic analysis of a social phenomenon has been the descriptions provided by structuralist linguistics of the sentence. In spite of all the successes claimed by the proponents of semiotics for semiotic analyses in the discipline of anthropology and in tackling isolated phenomena like 'the folktale',[5] these are not comparable to the case of linguistics. For only in connection with language do people have sufficiently strong intuitions about form and meaning for a *semantic* theory to make sense. Interpretation of other human actions, of habits, or of institutions does not in a comparable way involve such intuitions. Even where language is concerned, once one moves beyond the level of the sentence to larger slices of discourse, one is not only in uncharted but in virtually unchartable territory: beyond the sentence there are no intuitively clear borders, no intuitively recognizable formal units.

Intentionalist theories of literary meaning draw on what Strawson dubbed *communication-intention theories* of meaning[6] for their concepts and analogies, and they consequently take the utterance rather than any formally defined linguistic expression as the analogy for the literary work. In intentionalist theories the recognition of the meaning of a work is not a recognition of a meaning emerging from a pattern of juxtaposed meaningful elements, nor is it defined by a code or a number of codes governing a set of signs which constitutes the work. Instead, the meaning of a work is identified with the author's intention in producing it.[7] And one recognizes the author's intention in producing the work partly by recognizing his conventional means of expression, partly by recognizing the way in which he structures his work, but also partly by recognizing the assumptions peculiar to the author on which he builds when he produces the work, and by taking into account any piece of evidence found outside the text of the literary work which may be relevant in determining the author's intention in writing a sentence, a passage, or the whole work. Intentionalist theories recognize fully the role of structural and local semantic features in determining the meaning of a work, but their logical status is held to be that of evidence for the author's intention, and as such they are on the same logical level as any other evidence of his intentions.

II

The analogy between text or work on the one hand, and on the other the basic linguistic expressions of metaphor, sentence, and utterance, breaks down at two crucial points. First, it is natural to talk about the meaning of metaphors, sentences, and utterances, while it is distinctly odd to talk about the meaning of works or texts. A competent speaker of a language who meets a sentence or utterance in that language can say what the sentence or utterance means. He usually does this by providing a paraphrase or by filling in background knowledge if this is required. It is also possible to say what the meaning of a metaphor is, though the strategies called for in the explanation of the meaning of metaphors are different from those employed in interpreting literal expressions. However, asking about the meaning of texts in the same way as one asks about the meaning of sentences, metaphors, and utterances is pointless. For what would one expect as an answer to a question like, 'What is the meaning of *Macbeth*?' A class of students faced in their exam with such an essay question would surely be right to complain that they do not understand what sort of answer is required. One might perhaps argue that it makes sense to talk about '*analysing* the meaning of *Macbeth*', but this formulation too would have to be explained. Perhaps it means 'analysing *Macbeth*, paying special attention to the theme', or perhaps it means just 'interpreting *Macbeth*'. One might try to save the argument by admitting that analysing the meaning of *Macbeth* is no more than interpreting *Macbeth* and maintaining that the *meaning* of a literary work is *apprehended through interpretation*. However, this would do nothing to eliminate the oddity of talking about the meaning of a literary work. For the interpretation of a work is an interpretation of parts and passages, of characters, setting, symbols, structure, action, rhetorical features, and so forth. When a satisfactory interpretation of these different textual elements has been achieved, there is no further 'meaning' which an interpretation can reveal. Furthermore, if it is only half odd to talk about 'analysing the meaning of *Macbeth*', it is also half odd to talk about 'analysing the meaning of "Pass me the salt"'.

Second, literary works do not possess meaning-producing features analogous to those possessed by metaphors, sentences, and utterances. According to the interaction theory, the meaning of a metaphor is produced by the juxtaposition of two normally incompatible terms, each with its literal meaning, in one and the same expression. The explanation offered by the interaction theory of how the 'tension' created by this juxtaposition is 'resolved' and how the 'paradoxical' expression receives a 'metaphorical meaning' through the 'interaction' of the two juxtaposed terms is theoretically perspicuous and interesting (though one may believe it to be wrong). However, there is no analogous juxtaposition of meaningful but incompatible elements in a literary work of art. For the elements which can be understood as constituting a literary work, only a very few – for example, metaphors, symbols – can naturally be said to have meaning. It is as odd to talk about the meaning of characters, situations, actions, setting, rhymes, rhythm, stanza form, and so forth as it is to talk about the meaning of works. Furthermore, reading or analysing literary works, the reader meets a wide variety of elements serving a wide variety of functions, and these elements are interrelated in many different ways. To construe these diverse relationships and functions as a 'juxtaposition' of elements which 'interact' to create a 'tensive meaning' analogous to metaphorical meaning is to stretch the concepts of 'juxtaposition', 'interaction', and 'meaning' beyond the limits of their usefulness. Laertes and Hamlet are contrasted and this contrast serves to illuminate Hamlet's character. But to describe this contrast and its function in terms of 'juxtaposition', 'interaction', and 'meaning' would serve no purpose. Such a description would add nothing to the understanding of the contrast which one can achieve by exploring how the contrast helps to define Hamlet's character.

The sentence analogy has the same type of weakness as the metaphor analogy. For a competent speaker of a language it is intuitively clear what are the words of a sentence, what are the meanings of these words, what are the relationships between them (though one may have no name for these relationships), and what is the meaning of the sentence itself. This is the handle which language offers to the linguistician; turning it the right way he will open up a systematic syntactic and semantic description of the sentence, its parts, and their interrelationships. Literature offers no such handle. There are no clear intuitions about the correct way to segment a literary work into minimal semantic units, no intuitions about what could be the set of minimal semantic units from which the 'signs' presumably constituting a particular work are taken, no conventionally determined intuitions about what relationships the semantic units constituting a literary work can enter into. It is, of course, possible to describe the 'elements' of narrative, poetry, drama, and so forth as so many introductory books do. But no amount of theoretical sophistication can make this type of description analogous to a linguistic description, though there may be empirical generalizations about how certain types of elements are used by a group of authors, or (which is perhaps the same thing) about how certain elements function in a certain type of genre. To talk about the 'morphology of the folktale' or about 'Grammaire narrative' (heading in a bibliography in a collection of structuralist essays)[8] is to talk in metaphors which cannot be cashed in the valid coin of syntactic and semantic description.

Finally, the features which make an utterance meaningful are absent in the case of texts considered as wholes. Utterances are understood, according to the proponents of communication-intention theories, as expressions of utterer's intention. They must be interpreted as a part of a larger pattern of intentional actions which can be understood as a response to the circumstances in which the speaker finds himself. To understand an utterance, it is necessary to refer it back to the larger non-linguistic context of behaviour, circumstances and presuppositions into which it is introduced. Different types of texts, not merely literary works but also historical and philosophical treatises, are not, however, understood in this way. They are instead understood as having an interest and a relevance which is independent of the situation of utterance. In fact, in producing a philosophical or historical treatise or article, a literary work of some genre, and so forth, the author accepts certain notions of valid argument, of truth, of relevance, of 'seriousness', and so forth which replace the contextual frame provided by the occasion of utterance. These *genre conventions* define the mode of apprehension which a text requires if misunderstanding and, perhaps, unintelligibility are to be avoided. These conventions do not constitute a code which produces 'meaning', but they do constitute an institutional framework going beyond and superseding the contextual frame which the utterance must normally be referred back to.

III

If the literary work is not the type of entity to which one naturally ascribes meaning, and if the literary work does not have meaning-producing features of the type presumptively possessed by metaphors, sentences, and utterances, then one must seriously question whether the concept of the meaning of a literary work is a fruitful theoretical concept. One can recognize a useful role for this concept as a banner for those who were concerned to attack Romantic theories of literature as rapture or personalist theories of literature as the manifestation of a great soul. It was no doubt useful in reminding people that reading poetry and other literary works was not passive reception but active and cognitive reconstruction of thoughts, images, structures, rhetorical features, and so forth. However, beyond this function as a rhetorical instrument suited to fight certain theories and attitudes, the concept of the meaning of a literary work has little theoretical justification. In fact, it can be argued that this concept has done serious damage in literary aesthetics by distorting the formulation of basic problems and blocking important insights. The most important distortion which the concept of the meaning of a literary work introduces into the formulation of the basic problems of the field is the view it encourages of the apprehension of a work as a literary work of art as being independent of the recognition of its valuable qualities. Consider the following two responses to D. H. Lawrence's 'Piano':

Softly, in the dusk, a woman is singing
    to me;
Taking me back down the vista of years, till
    I see
A child sitting under the piano, in the boom
    of the tingling strings
And pressing the small, poised feet of a
    mother who smiles as she sings.

In spite of myself the insidious mastery
    of song
Betrays me back, till the heart of me weeps
    to belong
To the old Sunday evenings at home, with
    winter outside
And hymns in the cosy parlour, the tinkling
    piano our guide.

So now it is vain for the singer to burst
    into clamour
With the great black piano appassionato.
    The glamour
Of childish days is upon me, my manhood
    is cast
Down in the flood of remembrance, I weep
    like a child for the past.

After about 3 readings decide I don't like this. It makes me angry. . . . I feel myself responding to it and don't like responding. I think I feel hypnotised by the long boomy lines. But the noise when I stop myself being hypnotised seems disproportionate to what's being said. A lot of emotion is being stirred up about nothing much. The writer seems to love feeling sobby about his pure spotless childhood and to enjoy thinking of himself as a world-worn wretch. There's too much about 'insidiousness' and 'appassion-ato' for me. The whole comparison between childhood's Sunday evenings and passionate manhood etc. is cheap by which I mean (1) It is easy; (2) It is unfair both to childhood and manhood. I expect I am too irritated for this criticism to have value.

Re-read.

If not too lazy would throw the book into the corner.[9]

The 'vista of years' leads back to something sharply seen – a very specific situation that stands there in its own right; so that we might emend 'stating' into 'constating' in order to describe that effect as of prose statement (we are inclined to call it – but the situation is vividly realized) which marks the manner. The child is 'sitting under the piano, in the boom of the tingling strings' and 'pressing the small poised feet' of its mother – we note that 'poised', not only because of its particularity, but because the word seems to be significant in respect of an essential, though unobtrusive, quality of the poem. The main immediate point, however, is that in all this particularity we have something quite other than banal romantic generality: this is not the common currency of sentimental evocation or anything of the kind. The actuality of the remembered situation is unbeglamouring, becoming more so in the second stanza, with the 'hymns' and the 'tinkling piano'. Something is, we see, held and presented in this poem, and the presenting involves an *attitude towards*, an element of disinterested valuation. For all the swell of emotion the critical mind has its part in the whole; the constatation is at the same time in some measure a placing. That is, sensibility in the poem doesn't work in complete divorce from intelligence;

feeling is not divorced from thinking: however the key terms are to be defined, these propositions at any rate have a clear enough meaning in this context.[10]

The first response is well characterized by I. A. Richards' comment on it:

Here 'the long boomy lines' join hands neatly with the poet's 'pure spotless child-hood'. Both the movement and the material are introduced by the reader; they are not given in the poem, and they reflect only the reader's own private attempt at an analogous poem constructed on the basis of a remote and superficial awareness of this poem's apparent subject-matter. 'Insidious' and 'appassionato', the most evident hints that the poet is not doing, or attempting to do, what the reader is expecting, are dismissed without consideration. The poet 'as a world-worn wretch' and his 'passionate manhood' of which there is no hint, rather the reverse, in the poem, are occupying the reader's attention instead.[11]

The second passage, on the other hand, displays great sensibility both in its identification of the features of the poem which make it good poetry and in the description of their aesthetic function. The quoted paragraph is, in fact, just an extract from a fuller analysis of the poem, where the critic articulates his perception of the poem in some detail. This trained critic, unlike the untutored undergraduate, does not make up his own 'analogous poem' 'on the basis of a remote and superficial awareness of this poem's apparent subject-matter'. He keeps in close contact with the text and bases all the conclusions he draws on textual features which he identifies.

It would be incorrect to say that these two passages represent different levels of sophistication in the *understanding* of the poem. They must rather be considered as criteria for two qualitatively different pay-offs from the work. They express what one may call the reader's perception of the work of art, a perception which is a perception of value and which constitutes a *valuable experience*. They define different degrees of a type of value. The critic's description of the poem defines an experience which is richer than and superior to that of the untutored undergraduate: the critic shows a deeper *appreciation* of the poem than the undergraduate is capable of. For the undergraduate does not merely fail to understand, he fails to appreciate. He consequently fails to see why this is a worthwhile poem; his final reaction is a desire to 'throw the book into the corner'.[12]

Apprehension of meaning is a mode of understanding. One understands sentences and utterances, but one does not appreciate them as one would appreciate a good wine or a beautiful landscape. And this understanding is not an end in itself; it is directed outward from the sentence or utterance toward some aspect of the non-linguistic context of the linguistic expression. Employing the concept of the meaning of a literary work as a central theoretical concept, one runs the risk of blocking the insight that the reader's apprehension of a literary work is properly characterized and inquired into as appreciation rather than understanding. And this is in fact what happens in both semiotic theories and intentionalist theories of literary meaning:

> On voit clairement dans cette perspective pourquoi la poétique ne peut et même ne doit pas se poser comme tâche première l'explication du jugement esthétique. Celle-ci présuppose non seulement la connaissance de la structure de l'oeuvre, que la poétique doit faciliter, mais aussi une connaissance du lecteur et de ce qui détermine son jugement. Si cette deuxième partie de la tâche n'est pas irréalisable, si on trouve des moyens pour étudier ce qu'on appelle communément le 'goût' ou la 'sensibilité' d'une époque, que ce soit par une recherche des traditions qui les forment ou des aptitudes innées à tout individu, alors un passage sera établi entre poétique et esthétique, et la vieille question sur la beauté de l'oeuvre pourra être posée à nouveau.[13]

> *Meaning* is that which is represented by a text; it is what the author meant by his use of a particular sign sequence; it is what the signs represent. *Significance*, on the other hand, names a relationship between that meaning and a person, or a conception, or a situation, or indeed anything imaginable.[14]

Both the semiotician and the intentionalist conceive of meaning as being independent of aesthetic judgement or aesthetic enjoyment (which the intentionalist conceives of as belonging to the 'significance' of a work). Value and enjoyment are defined in these two types of theory by the external relations of the meaning or semantic properties of the work: it is value or enjoyment for an individual, a group, or a culture, and it resides in the relationship between the work and the individual, group, culture, and so forth. In these theories the reader's apprehension of a literary work is a matter of his *understanding* its meaning. This understanding is prior to any recognition of the value of a work. Value has to be 'explained' independently of apprehension. It is not at all seen in connection with the experience which is the apprehension of the work.

One may grant that there is a justifiable distinction between the type of judgement exercised in the apprehension of literary works and judgements about literary value: a value judgement is made only when it is called for by the circumstances. Apprehension can take place without a judgement of value being called for. However, the value judgement is wholly determined by the reader's apprehension of the work. For 'la structure de l'oeuvre' or its 'meaning' is recognized in an aesthetic judgement, that is to say in a judgement aimed at identifying the qualities which make the work a worthwhile object of appreciation: the critic who comments on Lawrence's 'Piano' judges that the point of the reference to 'hymns' and the 'tinkling piano' is to present the described situation as 'unbeglamouring'. He recognizes these words as a part of a vivid, unromantic, and particularized description of this situation. Furthermore, he judges that the function of the 'unbeglamouring' description of the situation which calls forth the speaker's emotional reaction and places that emotional reaction in perspective, provides a point of reference for an evaluation of the emotion. The 'meaning' or 'structure' which the critic sees in Lawrence's 'Piano' is set out in a series of interpretative descriptions which build up the poem as a good, 'hard' poem, free of sentimentality. On the other hand, those undergraduates whose reaction to the poem Richards quotes in *Practical Criticism* tend to see the poem simply as an indulgence in a gush of emotion and to criticize it for sentimentality because they fail to appreciate the aesthetically responsible handling of the described situation and the emotional reaction to it which the speaker of the poem has.

IV

The employment of the concept of 'the meaning of a literary work' also results in other distortions in the formulation of literary-aesthetic problems. If one accepts that this concept is central in the explanation of the apprehension of literary works, then one will be faced with a choice between two mutually exclusive explanations of literary apprehension. In the semantic theories on which theories of literary meaning draw, meaning is understood either as semantic properties of words or expressions, as determined by a code, or as utterer's intention. If one adopts the concept of meaning as semantic properties as a basis for the explanation of the meaning of a literary work, then one will have to give an account of the apprehension of literary works which discounts as having no role to play in literary apprehension all information which is not either a semantic property of the 'signs' employed or is information about how to combine these 'signs'. In particular, all the information which concerns the author's intentions, beliefs, attitudes, and so forth will be held to be of no relevance to the apprehension of a literary work. If one adopts the concept of meaning as utterer's intention, then one must give an account of the apprehension of a literary work which admits as relevant for this apprehension *all* the information which can be used as evidence for the author's intentions, beliefs, attitudes, and so forth.

The discussion of the problem concerning the nature of the facts on which apprehension of literary works rests has been bedevilled by this either/or approach dictated by the concept of the meaning of a literary work. This has been so despite the fact that a consistent anti-intentionalist position, as well as a consistent intentionalist position, has little superficial plausibility. It is indeed easy to show, if it is felt to be necessary, that interpreting a literary work is determining the author's intentions.[15] It takes a little more argument to show that the appreciation of literary works at least sometimes involves reference to facts other than those either in the work itself or those which constitute the conventions which the author may have made use of.

Consider, for example, Osvald's syphilis in *Ghosts*. Osvald has got his syphilis from his father; he himself is an innocent victim. But what kind of victim and a victim of what? There is very little information about syphilis in the play. Osvald refers to his disease as a sort of 'softness on the brain', as his 'inheritance', and as residing 'in here' (pointing to his forehead), ready to break out any moment and destroy his sanity and take his life. To make artistic sense of Osvald's disease, one must supplement these few facts with information brought in from outside the play: when Ibsen wrote *Ghosts*, Norwegian society was sexually restrictive and syphilis carried a moral stigma. It is most frequently contracted by those who have a number of sexual partners and are not too particular in their choice. Syphilis could be seen as the appropriate last stage of a life of dissipation which had been marred by sins other than fornication. It was believed to be heritable; the sperm itself was thought to be infected. Once the disease had entered a family, the family was doomed to degeneration, at least along the male line. Syphilis is thus the appropriate disease for Captain Alving to have contracted. In rough summary one may say that the theme of *Ghosts* is that the joy of life, which should properly express itself in human creativity and give meaning and dignity to human life, is suppressed by the conventions on which society rests and by the way in which society is organized. This society permits the joy of life no proper outlet. The repressive conventions of society distort the joy, and when it manifests itself it is in the debauchery and dissipation of a Captain Alving. The joy of life is corrupted by society and is turned into an evil force, the symbol of which is the syphilis, which destroys creativity, happiness, and human dignity. But Osvald's syphilis does not only function as the outward symbol of the distorted joy of life. It is also the actual, concrete evil force which destroys creativity, happiness, and human dignity; that is, it is a force with the same effects as repressive society. Thus in *Ghosts* the syphilis can also be construed as a symbol of the social order, which destroys the joy of life. The joy of life is natural in man, part of his biological inheritance; it is transferred from generation to generation, from Captain Alving to Osvald. However, syphilis too is heritable; once it is in the bloodstream it is transferred from father to son. The symbolic implication, of course, is that repressive and hypocritical society, too, is heritable, unavoidable. Once created, it gets into man's bloodstream, where in each generation it works insidiously, out of sight, distorting the joy of life which should give life meaning and dignity.

This attempt to make artistic sense of Osvald's disease involves a conception of syphilis which includes a number of aspects not referred to in the play. The reader does not build up this conception by free association. It is not open to him in his appreciation of *Ghosts* to make use of just any conception of syphilis which he may recognize himself or discover. If Ibsen's plays are still with us when syphilis is extinct and has been forgotten for centuries, the reader will need a footnote to understand the function of syphilis in *Ghosts*. This footnote would have to describe a conception which it would be reasonable to believe that Ibsen could have entertained, and not an accidentally chosen conception like, for instance, our own. The conception of syphilis current today is, of course, totally different from the nineteenth-century one. Syphilis is today easy to treat, rarely reaches its second and third stage, and is consequently no threat to sanity and life. Since our society is sexually emancipated, syphilis carries no moral stigma. And it is known not to be heritable. It is not transferred from the father through infected sperm but at birth through the eyes of the baby by an infected *mother*. This conception of syphilis would give us a wholly different play from that written by Ibsen.

It is equally easy to establish that there are cases where information about the author's attitudes, intentions, beliefs, and so forth is irrelevant in the appreciation of a certain aspect or element of a work. The example of Daniel Haakonsen's argument that the stranger in *Peer Gynt* is intended to be Lord Byron, is relevant here.[16] Now the problem posed by these two types of case – in which cases is reference to evidence of author's intentions, beliefs, attitudes, and so forth other than that provided by the work itself relevant in appreciation of a literary work? – cannot even be formulated as long as one employs the concept of the meaning of a literary work. A concept of literary meaning, to be theoretically perspicuous, must be construed as either utterer's communication-intention, to be determined with reference to all types of evidence for utterer's intention, or as semantic properties of 'signs'; either way it is a tool ill-suited to explain the logic of literary appreciation. To be able to tackle the question concerning when reference to external evidence is appropriate and when it is not, and questions similar to this, literary theory needs to break free of the concept of meaning and reject the analogy between the literary work and an utterance or a sentence. The assumption that it is a *deep* truth about literature that a literary work is a verbal expression must be abandoned.

V

A theory of literary meaning will aim at describing the types of fact which are the basis for inferences about the meaning of a literary work and at describing the nature of this type of inference. It will be concerned with *how* the literary work 'means'. A theory of literary meaning 'ne pourra être une science des contenus (sur lesquels seule la science historique la plus stricte peut avoir prise), mais une science des *conditions* du contenu, c'est-à-dire des formes: ce qui l'intéressera, ce seront les variations de sens engendrées, et, si l'on peut dire, *engendrables*, par les oeuvres: elle n'interprétera pas les symboles, mais seulement leur polyvalence; en un mot, son objet ne sera plus les sens pleins de l'oeuvre, mais au contraire le sens vide qui les supporte tous.'[17] This emphasis on form, on the special *way in which* the literary work means, is equally strong in autonomy theories as it is in semiotic theories: 'we can draw a line, even if a somewhat vague one, between discourse that has a good deal of secondary meaning and discourse that has not. We may now try out a definition: a literary work is a discourse in which an important part of the meaning is implicit. This is a Semantic Definition of "literature", since it defines "literature" in terms of meaning.'[18] Content or theme is excluded from any independent consideration. Content, indeed, is assumed to be a function of form. 'Complexity of form is sophistication of content':[19] 'Nevertheless our final view, implicit in our whole narrative and in whatever moments of argument we may have allowed ourselves, has been that "form" in fact embraces and penetrates "message" in a way that constitutes a deeper and more substantial meaning than either abstract message or separable ornament.'[20]

This concentration on *le sens vide* to the exclusion of *les sens pleins* constitutes a failure on the part of theories of literary meaning to deal with the 'human interest' question. The salient feature of the great works of the Western literary tradition, the fact that one is most likely to mention if asked what is their distinctive feature, is their concern with 'Mortal Questions', to borrow the title from a book by Thomas Nagel – questions concerned with 'mortal life: how to understand it and how to live it'.[21] The fact that literary works have themes with human interest is not incidental to their nature as literary works. The concept of a literary work used in Western culture for more than two thousand years includes the notion of theme with human interest. Plays, novels, poems, and so forth which do not aim at expressing such a theme are not considered literary works of art. Barbara Cartland is on the opposite side of the dividing line between art and non-art from Jane Austen because the novels of the latter can be appreciated as treatments of themes with human interest, while any theme one may find in Barbara Cartland is incidental: her concern is with intrigue and emotional arousal. Of course, there are other differences between Jane Austen and Barbara Cartland which could be characterized as 'formal', and, indeed, one may agree that Jane Austen's 'complexity of form is sophistication of content'. However, sophistication of content cannot be illuminatingly or even intelligibly characterized by a purely formal description. It is not clear what a formal description of a literary work would be, for, in so far as literature is concerned, a formal description depends on, or comes as a proper part of, a description of content.

Consider the *agon* between Teiresias and Oedipus in *King Oedipus*, where there are a number of superficial paradoxes and some far-reaching irony: the blind man who can see the truth, the seeing man who is blind to it; the frail and powerless man who pronounces the doom of the fit and powerful; the wisdom of man versus the revelation sent by the gods; the truth hidden from the protagonist and his fellows but known to the gods, their prophet, and the audience. These features of paradox and irony are apparently there, on the surface of the work, to be noticed by every reader who is trained to look for these types of features. It is, however, not immediately clear what the paradoxes and the irony amount to. It is not clear whether or not they can be developed and given detailed and precise descriptions. It is not clear whether they are paradoxes and ironies which are proper parts of the literary work or whether, from an artistic point of view, they are excrescences. So these superficial paradoxes and ironies present a problem of appreciation for the reader: he has to try to formulate descriptions of them which will reveal their full depth, and these descriptions will be an integral part of the explanation of the function served by these features in the literary work. The main paradox of 'seeing blindness/blind seeing' is stated by the blind Teiresias when he intimates that he can see under what conditions Oedipus lives, though Oedipus himself is blind to them:

> Listen – since you have taunted me with
> blindness!
> You have your sight, and yet you cannot see
> Where, nor with whom, you live, nor in
> what horror.[22]

One possible way of unpacking this paradox is to distinguish between human and divine insight. Oedipus is the most intelligent of men, a master of deduction and inference. This intellectual ability enables him to solve the riddle of the sphinx, and it is his faith in this intellectual ability which makes him so sure that he, if anybody, can discover Laius' murderer. However, the task of discovering Laius' murderer is radically different from the task of solving the riddle of the sphinx. The riddle of the sphinx – 'What being, with only one voice, has sometimes two feet, sometimes three, sometimes four, and is weakest when it has the most?' – requires the ability to observe and combine facts, and as Oedipus himself points out, nothing else is required. Oedipus solved this riddle 'thanks to his wit' (l. 389), 'knowing nothing' (l. 388). Observation and intellectual ability were all that was needed. The answer to the riddle constitutes a piece of general knowledge: knowledge of properties shared by all men, by all the individuals of a species. This type of knowledge is impersonal; it does not involve reference to the individual who possesses it.

Oedipus attacks the problem of discovering Laius' murderer as if it, too, was a case of observation and inference, of finding the necessary clues and building a hypothesis on the basis of these:

> *Oedipus.* Where was he murdered? In the
>   palace here?
>   Or in the country? Or was he abroad?
> *Creon.* He made a journey to consult
>   the god,
>   He said – and never came back
>   home again.
> *Oedipus.* But was there no report? no
>   fellow traveller
>   Whose knowledge might have helped
>   you in your search?
> *Creon.* All died, except one
>   terror-stricken man,
>   And he could tell us nothing – next
>   to nothing.
> *Oedipus.* And what was that? One thing
>   might lead to much,
>   If only we could find one ray of light.

> *Creon.* He said they met with brigands –
> not with one,
> But a whole company; they killed Laius.
> *Oedipus.* A brigand would not *dare* –
> unless perhaps
> Conspirators in Thebes had bribed
> the man.
>
> (ll. 112–25)

Oedipus is here trying to clarify the relevant facts; he expresses his belief that if they can unearth the relevant facts, then the problem will be solved ('One thing may lead to much'), and, upon hearing what Creon knows about the reports from the killing, he starts hypothesizing. However, to discover the truth about Laius' murderer, Oedipus needs to do more than find the right clues and interpret them. For not all knowledge is of the type which is needed to answer the riddle of the sphinx. Knowledge of those things which concern man most intimately – of the role of an individual in society, his relationship to other human beings and to the gods – is particular knowledge, knowledge about the single individual. This knowledge is not, however, knowledge of isolated and unrelated individuals; it is a knowledge of relationships, and, since every man is an individual among other individuals, the knowledge which one has of other individuals is dependent upon the knowledge one has of oneself. The individual is woven into a social and religious web which he observes from his individual point of view. To draw a conclusion about other individuals, it is important that one should hold the correct beliefs about one's own position. Self-knowledge provides the perspective which determines the perception of other people's position in this social and religious structure. If one fails in self-knowledge, then exact observation and sound inference will be of no help in reaching correct conclusions about other individuals. For the content of observation, the description under which one conceives of an individual, is determined by what one believes oneself to be. Oedipus signally lacks self-knowledge, and the perspective which his erroneous beliefs about himself provide him with prevents him from recognizing for what they are the individuals close to him, the society he lives in, and the role of the gods. When he meets Laius he does not see his father, the king. When he sees Iocasta he does not see his mother but his wife. When he sees his daughters he does not see his sisters. The gods appear impotent, maybe even non-existent, since their prophecy that Oedipus

should kill his father and marry his mother appears not to have come true. So observation and inference are inadequate in the attempt to discover Laius' murderer. To make that discovery Oedipus has to change his perspective, to change those presuppositions on which his recognition of the observed individuals is based. As long as Oedipus retains his old perspective, he is blind, he literally does not see who stands before him. Oedipus' intellectual ability is of only limited usefulness to him in bringing about the change of perspective, for this change involves a change of identity, a deep emotional crisis, and extreme suffering.

When, in his *agon* with Teiresias, Oedipus points out that he solved the riddle of the sphinx 'thanks to his wit', 'knowing nothing', he is at pains to contrast his way of solving problems with 'divination'. Divination or prophecy rests on the reading of signs and the interpretation of oracles. The knowledge it yields is revealed knowledge – a different mode of knowledge altogether from human knowledge based on observation and inference. Consequently, it cannot be judged by the same truth standards as human knowledge is judged by. A divine message has divine authority, and one must accept this authority to believe it. The divine insight revealed through divination is, then, blind in the sense that no appeal is made to observation or to the power of the human intellect to illuminate observation. This is the aesthetic reason why Teiresias is blind and why he, the blind representative of divine insight, confronts Oedipus, the superior human intellect. Since revealed knowledge is independent of observation and inference, it is free of the uncertainty which necessarily attaches to human knowledge. In particular, it does not suffer from the sort of perspectival distortion which lack of self-knowledge leads to.

The description of this paradox could be expanded in several directions, and the contrast between human and divine insight could be placed in a further context: there is in the play a fundamental conflict between a secular and a religious view of life, which is resolved when the prophecy of the Delphic oracle is recognized by all to have come true in spite of appearances to the contrary. A full appreciation of the play would require the reader to expand the description and place the paradox in some such larger context. However, the relatively limited description of the paradox given above has made the point that the paradox *as a formal feature* is not only recognized as aesthetically relevant by having its thematic contribution identified, but the very nature of the paradox itself is apprehended through an appreciation of how it contributes to the theme of the play. The formal feature, the paradox, is apprehended as a feature of content, and there is no independent way of apprehending this feature. In so far as literature is concerned, this is a general theoretical point: form can be identified only through the identification of content. There is thus no a priori reason to believe that the literary work has formal features which somehow have logical priority over features of content. On the contrary, both the logic of the concept of a literary work – the fact that one would hesitate to regard as a literary work of art a text which did not have a theme with human interest – and the fact that formal features are apprehended through the apprehension of content, point to the theoretical importance of content among the characteristic features of a literary work. The employment of the concept of the meaning of a literary work masks this fact, since a theory of meaning necessarily is a theory of *how* meaning is produced and not a theory of what meaning is characteristically produced.

VI

Literary theory is at the present moment in a situation where autonomy theories and semiotic theories are rapidly losing their influence. And for good reason. The formal semantics on which these theories rest is currently going through a crisis, and its explanatory power as a semantic theory is in doubt: it is becoming generally accepted that a mere formal analysis of meaning explains nothing. The decline of autonomy theories and semiotic theories offers the hope of a new departure in literary theory. It offers the hope that literary theory will now be able to break free from the semantic framework and the analogy between the literary work and basic linguistic expressions like metaphor, sentence and utterance. However, the new departure will not come automatically; an awareness of the weaknesses of the concept of the meaning of a literary work is essential to bring it about. For as structuralist semantics is being abandoned, speech-act theory and intentionalist theories of meaning are taking over. And these, too, find their way into literary theory. The representatives of the new intentionalist wave in literary theory make the same basic assumption as the proponents of the declining theories. 'This book is an attempt to provide and defend an analysis of our concept of the meaning of a literary work,' says P. D. Juhl in the Preface to his recent book, where he defends an intentionalist theory of literary meaning.[23] And in the Preface to a book with the title *Toward a Speech Act Theory of Literary Discourse*, the author says, 'The chief aim of this study is to suggest . . . that it is both possible and necessary to develop a unified theory of discourse which allows us to talk about literature in the same terms we use to talk about all the other things people do with language.'[24] This is why it is necessary, at this stage in the development of literary theory, to be aware that many of the difficulties of the declining theories are due to their use of the concept of the meaning of a literary work, and that these difficulties are unavoidable if the semantic framework, and with it the concept of meaning itself, is not rejected as a source of concepts, arguments, analogies, and insights for literary theory. The purpose of this essay has been to promote such an awareness.

Once the semantic framework has been rejected, the new departure could then come by turning to the sister discipline of literary theory, general aesthetics, for methods, concepts, and arguments. This would be a natural link-up and could prove fruitful for both literary theory and general aesthetics. For literature is not merely language: literature is art.

Notes

1 M. C. Beardsley, *Aesthetics: Problems in the Philosophy of Criticism* (New York 1958), p. 144.

2 I. A. Richards, *The Philosophy of Rhetoric* (New York 1965), p. 93.

3 Cleanth Brooks, *The Well Wrought Urn* (London, revised ed. 1968), p. 169.

4 Jonathan Culler, *The Pursuit of Signs* (London 1981), p. 37.

5 Propp, of course, is a favourite with semioticians with his *Morphology of the Folktale*, tr. Laurence Scott, rev. Louis A. Wagner (Austin, second ed. 1968).

6 P. F. Strawson, 'Meaning and Truth', *Logico-Linguistic Papers* (London 1971), pp. 171–2.

7 See A. J. Close, '*Don Quixote* and the "Intentionalist Fallacy"', *British Journal of Aesthetics*, 12 (1972),

rpt. in David Newton-De Molina ed., *On Literary Intention* (Edinburgh 1976); Skinner, 'Motives, Intentions and the Interpretation of Texts'; Juhl, *Interpretation: An Essay in the Philosophy of Literary Criticism* (Princeton 1980). E. D. Hirsch in *Validity in Interpretation* (New Haven 1967) presents an intentionalist theory with a different philosophical basis.

8   *Sémiotique narrative et textuelle*, ed. Claude Chabrol (Paris 1973), p. 209.

9   One of the responses to this poem presented by I. A. Richards in *Practical Criticism* (London 1929), p. 110. Richards' book, of course, is a mine of examples of failure of appreciation.

10   F. R. Leavis, *The Living Principle* (London 1975), pp. 76–7.

11   Richards, *Practical Criticism*, pp. 110–11.

12   The notion of 'appreciation' is developed in some detail in 'Criticism and Appreciation' in S. H. Olsen, *The End of Literary Theory* (Cambridge 1987).

13   Tzvetan Todorov, *Qu'est-ce que le structuralisme?* 2. *Poétique* (Paris 1968), p. 105.

14   Hirsch, *Validity in Interpretation*, p. 8.

15   Juhl marshals all the relevant arguments in his *Interpretation: An Essay in the Philosophy of Literary Criticism*. Juhl, however, overstates his case because he, too, views the literary work as having 'meaning'. See 'Text and Meaning' in *The End of Literary Theory*.

16   Daniel Haakonsen, *Henrik Ibsen's 'Peer Gynt'* (Oslo 1967), ch. 5, esp. pp. 100ff.

17   Roland Barthes, *Critique et vérité* (Paris 1966), p. 57.

18   Beardsley, *Aesthetics*, p. 126.

19   William K. Wimsatt, 'The Concrete Universal', *Papers of the Modern Language Association*, 62 (1947); rpt. in *The Verbal Icon* (London 1970), p. 82.

20   Cleanth Brooks and W. K. Wimsatt, Epilogue to *Literary Criticism: A Short History* (London 1957), p. 748.

21   Thomas Nagel, *Mortal Questions* (Cambridge 1979), p. ix. The question is dealt with in some detail in 'Thematic Concepts: Where Philosophy Meets Literature' in *The End of Literary Theory*.

22   *Sophocles: Three Tragedies*, tr. H. D. F. Kitto (Oxford 1967), ll. 403–5. Line references are to this translation.

23   Juhl, *Interpretation*, p. ix.

24   Mary Louise Pratt, *Toward a Speech Act Theory of Literary Discourse* (Bloomington 1977), p. vii.

16

Intentions and Interpretations: A Fallacy Revived

Monroe C. Beardsley

I

One of the greatest satisfactions of the philosopher is to expose the fallacy in what has hitherto been accepted as a conclusive argument; and I suppose this can be as selfless as any satisfaction in making a contribution to the general welfare. Equally satisfying, and equally altruistic, is to expose the fallacy in the fallacy – to demonstrate that it is not a fallacy after all, or not the sort of fallacy it was claimed to be. By this turn of the wheel, what was worth saving in the original argument gets rehabilitated, though it will never look quite the same.

An instance of this dialectical, or zigzag, pattern of philosophical progress – suitable for the climbing of steep slopes to truth – is the "intentional fallacy," articulated and named over thirty years ago as a kind of banner, or rallying cry, for those literary theorists who could no longer put up with the mishmash of philology, biography, moral admonition, textual exegesis, social history, and sheer burbling that largely made up what was thought of as literary criticism in academic circles, as well as in the wider world of letters. The rather youthful authors of this designedly subversive and unpleasantly provoking essay were out to insist on some distinctions and were convinced that various intellectual confusions

and invalid reasonings sprang from a failure to mark those distinctions. They were concerned with the logical relevance of information about the intentions of an author to the interpretation and the evaluation of his work. And they took the position that there is no such logical relevance.

Over the years, as these problems have been discussed by numerous other writers, it has turned out that the issues are a good deal more complicated and subtle than had been acknowledged. It has been argued that the anti-intentionalist position is unquestionably sound; it has been argued that the position is probably false or incoherent; and practically every plausible compromise has also been espoused. I have followed these developments with much interest, mainly from the sidelines. However, the recent publication of a lively collection of essays on the subject[1] has roused me to take another look at the issues, or some of them anyway. I shall not deal with the question of evaluation here, but stick to interpretation – which offers difficulties enough. I am still attacking intentionalism (by which I mean the view that interpretations of literature can be supported by appeal to knowledge of authors' intentions), but with concessions and qualifications that I owe to my critics (and thank them for) and, I hope, with help from some more recent work on language that I believe places the anti-intentionalist position in a clearer and more favorable light.

II

There have been complaints – some of them surely justifiable – about the slackness of the word

Monroe C. Beardsley, "Intentions and Interpretations: A Fallacy Revived," in Michael J. Wreen and Donald M. Callan (eds.), *The Aesthetic Point of View: Selected Essays* (Ithaca, NY: Cornell University Press, 1982), pp. 188–207. © 1982 by Cornell University. Used by permission of the publisher, Cornell University.

"intention" in the phrase "the author's intention." And even without complaints, the need for tightening the original use has been revealed by various objections that rest on taking the author's intention in a wrong way. Thus a certain amount of confusion has been caused by recurrent use of such expressions as "what the author meant" and "what the author intended." In the last analysis (on my view), it is only doings that can be intended; strictly speaking, one does not even intend states of affairs, rather one intends to bring about states of affairs.[2] What, then, does an author, in meaning something, actually intend to do?

I shall use the term "author" for anyone who intentionally produces a text: that is, a syntactically ordered sequence of words, spoken or written, in a natural language. To produce a text intentionally, on my view, is just to produce the text while wanting to do so and knowing that one is doing so. (This formula requires a little refinement, but is nearly correct, I believe.) A somnambulist, for example, may produce a text while unconscious; but he does not do so intentionally. When wide awake, however, one may produce a text and intend to *say* something in producing that text; and this is the way I shall understand "meaning something." More generally, the case in which I can truly be said to mean something is the case in which I intentionally perform an action of some kind and also intend to *say* something in performing that action. For example, I wave my hand to say good-bye. But I am concerned here only with the narrower case in which the action performed is that of producing a text – more precisely, a token (that is, an inscription or an utterance) of a text type. The author's intention in producing a text is his intention to say certain things in producing that text.

I use the word "say" in a convenient, though perhaps uncommonly broad, way, to include two very different kinds of speech act.

First, the word is to cover illocutionary actions in general. What the author intends to say may consist in giving unsolicited advice, protesting a rise in taxes, recommending for a job, authorizing the disbursement of company funds, or some such thing. Using another term, we might say he is voicing advice, or a report, or a request, or a threat. On my view of illocutionary actions, they are generated (in Alvin Goldman's sense of "act-generation") by text production under certain conditions, according to certain language conventions.

Thus, *if* Jones speaks in a serious tone to Smith, and Smith hears and understands Jones's words, and Jones owns a watch, and Jones believes that his watch has been stolen, *then* in saying the words "You stole my watch!" Jones is accusing Smith of theft. His act of producing the text, under those conditions, generates an act of accusing. These are the same action, on my view, but the action that is of the one kind becomes an action of the other kind when performed under the requisite conditions. I may not have stated here all of the requisite illocutionary-act-generating conditions, but I think I have. Perhaps some of those I have stated are not absolutely necessary. You may question whether Jones must believe his watch to have been stolen in order to accuse Smith of stealing it. But suppose this episode occurs on-stage, in a play: then Jones is not really accusing Smith, even though Jones has a watch, uses the right tone of voice, and secures what J. L. Austin called "uptake" (his text is heard and understood). The difference seems to be that in this case Jones does not really believe his watch is missing. On the other hand, of course, for the act of accusing to occur it is not necessary that Smith actually stole the watch; a false accusation is still an accusation.

Second, the word "say" is to cover the special case of refraining from illocutionary commitment in order to produce a fiction: this is the representation, rather than the performance, of an illocutionary action. Thus in Margaret Drabble's novel, *The Ice Age*, there is this passage: "'Never recommend your secretary to anyone,' said Len, still giving Maureen the eye, 'or they get stolen, didn't you know? We'll have her off you, if you don't keep an eye on her.'"[3] In writing the words between quotation marks, the author is not herself advising anyone, but she is representing an advising.

Verbal representation, or the representation of an illocutionary action, comes under the same general concept as pictorial representation (in the sense of depicting an acrobat or an anatomy lesson) and dramatic representation (playing a role on stage). In all these forms, the representer produces something that falls short of being the real thing, but provides certain features distinctive or characteristic of its kind, which thus refer (indefinitely) to something of that kind. Following in the wake of *Languages of Art*, there has been a great deal of dispute about pictorial representation, and I can't do justice at the moment to the many arguments that flourish. My own view, despite the powerful attacks of Nelson Goodman and his followers, is still that representation (in this sense of depiction, as I call it) involves *selective similarity*: the mime can represent himself as, say, climbing a ladder – without climbing and without actually having a ladder – but only by selecting certain movements that are characteristic of ladder climbing, rather than, say, riding a bicycle or milking a cow. So the draftsman can sketch a horse race, with perhaps an incredibly few lines, by selecting shapes and shape combinations that can be perceived as *telling* elements that would be present in an actual horse race.[4] And so a poet may write

> Milton! thou shouldst be living at this hour:
> England hath need of thee –

and by selecting words that could be used, under appropriate imaginable conditions, to perform an illocutionary action, he can represent an action of that sort – namely that of expressing a wish that the addressee were on hand to remedy the deplorable state of the nation. But of course the mime who mimes ladder climbing does not actually climb; the picture of a horse race is not a horse race; and Wordsworth, for all his passionate intensity, is not performing an illocutionary action in writing these words, since they are ostensibly addressed to a long-dead poet and could not be expected to secure uptake.

We must allow, of course, for a distinction between a *failure* to perform an illocutionary action and a *refraining* from one. One who fires a gun at another and misses is failing if he intended to hit, I suppose; but one who fires a gun knowing that it is loaded with blanks, while on location making a Western movie, is only representing a shooting. On the other hand, one who fires a gun in anger without knowing it is loaded with blanks might, under certain circumstances, try and fail to shoot someone, but *also* unintentionally represent a shooting. I claim that the term "represent" in pictorial contexts is not essentially tied to intention: a person might make marks on paper intending in doing so to depict a horse, but in fact depict a mule. So one might write certain words intending in doing so to make them a passage of praise, but for one reason or another they may turn out to represent a subtle insult.

In order to accommodate these and other distinctions, we must, I think, consider representation in any of its forms a kind of reference – but, as I suggested above, an indefinite reference, where what is represented is not this or that *X*, but *an X*. I don't have a full account of this form of reference, but I think it must involve at least two ele-ments, a form of synecdoche, or letting part stand for whole, and a transformation that might be called the "detachment of reference." The basic notion of reference is no doubt reference by persons: in using such-and-such symbols (words, pictures, gestures) someone refers to something. Much representational reference must be intentional in order to get a *practice* of representing going. One lets it be understood that the lines of a sketch are to be taken as a picture of a whole face, from which these few curves and angles have been culled; and the convention becomes accepted that an actor on the stage is not pouring poison in the porches of his brother's ear, but intends us to take his movements as a representation of an action of that kind. But once these representing practices are established, reference is detached from the referrer to the symbol; in a new sense the marks or gestures themselves are said to refer, and quite apart from any intentions. The part (if *indicative*, if selective enough) can be taken for the whole, as in synecdoche: so the firing of a blank cartridge on stage represents a shooting, and the writing of Wordsworth's apostrophe to Milton represents a wish expressing.

III

Sketchy as it is, this account of "saying," and the distinction between two sorts of saying, may serve to pin down adequately the issues over the intentionalist thesis about literary interpretation – that is, the thesis that facts about the author's intention, or facts tending to show that the author probably had such-and-such intentions, can give evidential support to the claim that a particular interpretation of a literary work is true or correct. To interpret a work is to declare what it says, in my broad sense. Of course it will make a great difference to the way we conceive of the interpreter's task whether the text to be interpreted is one whose production was the performance, or the representation, of an illocutionary action. On my view, lyric poems (for example) are representations, not performances – though this view is certainly debatable, and calls for a great deal more argument than I shall provide here.[5] When Wordsworth, in the sonnet I quoted earlier, goes on to say of England that

> she is a fen
> Of stagnant waters: altar, sword, and pen,
> Fireside, the heroic wealth of hall and
>   bower,

Have forfeited their ancient English dower
Of inward happiness,

it is tempting to say that in writing *these* words, Wordsworth was castigating England, or something of the sort. But my view is that in writing these words, Wordsworth was representing an illocutionary action of castigating England.

Of course to say that castigation is represented is not much of an interpretation, and would not be very helpful to a reader. It is the precise nuances of the illocutionary actions in the poem, the delicate shadings and subtle distinctions, that may call for comment. Why is England a "fen," not a "swamp"? What exactly is covered by "altar, sword, and pen," for example? What is the "heroic wealth of hall and bower"? What sort of happiness is "inward happiness," how is this a birthright of the English – and how could it have been forfeited? To answer such questions is to make plain what is being said, but not what is obviously or bluntly said.

Most intentionalists have not made, or at least featured, the distinction between performing and representing. And indeed I think that this omission has contributed to the plausibility of their view. For if we learned from letters, diaries, or the recollections of Wordsworth's friends that in 1802 he was distinctly alienated from the England of his day and believed, as he adds in the poem, that "we are selfish men," then it may seem that this information is evidence about the sorts of illocutionary actions he might *intend* to perform if he got to discussing the sorry state of things. Even here we should avoid the leap from what Wordsworth intended to what he actually did. The precise illocutionary contribution made by the metaphorical word "fen" is not affected by Wordsworth's intention, but is a function of its literal sense, its verbal context, and the conventions for grasping metaphorical senses. But if I am right in regarding this poem as a *representation* of an illocutionary action, the relevance of biographical information becomes even more remote. Even if Wordsworth in fact took a dim view of England in 1802, does that make it more likely that he would intend to *represent* a castigation? And, of course, even if we knew what Wordsworth *intended* to represent, we would still have to study the poem to see what he *did* represent.

The connections between saying and intending are, I think, often misunderstood; they are more complex than is generally realized. I disagree with those who have argued, along with Quentin Skinner, that "to know a writer's motives and intentions is to know the relationship in which he stands to what he has written. To know about intentions is to know such facts as whether the writer was joking or serious or ironic or in general what speech-act he was performing."[6] I agree that knowing whether a writer is serious is knowing something about his intention. The question of irony I shall come to shortly. As regards speech acts, if this means illocutionary actions, I differ. To know what illocutionary action was performed is to know what action the production of such a text generated by the appropriate conventions. I believe it is a misunderstanding of J. L. Austin's position to read him as holding "that an understanding of the illocutionary act being performed by an agent in issuing a given utterance will be equivalent to an understanding of that agent's primary *intentions* in issuing that particular utterance."[7]

Three comments seem to be called for.

First, we should note one necessary role that intention plays in illocutionary performance: to perform an illocutionary action in producing a certain text one must intend to produce that text: only intentional text production can generate illocutionary actions.

Unless George Washington intentionally produced the words of his Second Inaugural, his utterance of those words was not (among other things) a warning against foreign entanglements. But I don't think this principle applies to the *representation* of illocutionary actions, if we allow for the detachment of reference. Consider that once we establish the practice of depicting objects by line drawings and shading (that is, set up a system of representation), we can find pictures in clouds and window frost. Of course we cannot speak of an *act* of representing here, but we can say that in virtue of the existence of a system of representation, and in terms of that system, the marks made by nature depict a weasel or a mountain range.

So if, as I have suggested, a poem is (typically) a representation of an illocutionary action, it is not surprising that computer-generated poems, in which the selection of syntax and of lexis is random (within a range of choice), can also be said to represent illocutionary actions. Of course we might treat the programmer as a poet, despite his diminished role in the determination of the final product; but if we do not, we are left with a printout that has some analogy with clouds and window frost. And I see no objection to regarding even the verbal output of a myna bird as crude verbal depiction of illocutionary actions: the bird does not actually greet you or curse you but gives a pretty good imitation of it.

Second, the existence of a certain intention may be one of the requisite conditions for the performance of some illocutionary actions. It could be argued that an intention to assign moral or legal responsibility is a condition of performing an accusation; but I am inclined to say that this is really the same thing in different words, another way of (partially) describing what it is to accuse, not a *condition* of accusing. Perhaps one has to intend to deceive in order to lie, in the same way one has to intend to kill in order to commit murder – except, of course, in those jurisdictions where the legal definition of murder makes it include various kinds of homicide committed, even unintentionally or even by someone else, in the course of a felony.

Even if one must have a particular intention to *perform* a certain illocutionary action, it does not follow that one must have that intention to *represent* that action. This error in inference might seem too elementary to make, but even literary critics who hold, in general, that poems are fictions (and hence, I would say, representations) sometimes treat biographical facts about the author as relevant to the interpretation of his poem in a way that would make sense only if the poem were a performance rather than a representation.

Third, although most illocutionary actions can be performed intentionally – that is, with the intention of performing that action – that cannot be one of the *conditions* for performing the action. I will explain why.

There are illocutionary actions of a sort that are usually, but not always, performed intentionally. For example, suppose Jones believes that Smith has already laid a bet on Black Beauty in the third race at Liberty Bell, but conversationally passes on inside information that another horse in the same race, Bucephalus, is certain to lose. As a matter of fact, Smith has not yet laid his bet, and was inclined to back Bucephalus. Under the circumstances, we might say that Jones has unintentionally warned Smith against betting on Bucephalus. (If there had been no chance of Smith's betting on Bucephalus, Jones's remark would not have been a warning.) If you object to this analysis, I suppose you could argue that what happened here is that Jones unintentionally *alerted* Smith to his danger (a perlocutionary action) without warning him, though not without performing the illocutionary action of *reporting* Bucephalus' chances.

We cannot say that an illocutionary action is necessarily intentional (and hence that it is the intention that conclusively decides what sort of illocutionary action is being performed), because that would make intending to perform an action of a certain kind a requisite condition of performing it, and this would be circular and lead to conceptual confusion. You cannot intend to ride a horse, say, unless you understand what riding a horse consists in; so to ride a horse intentionally is not the same thing as to ride a horse. Even if in practice it turns out to be difficult, or empirically impossible, to ride a horse unintentionally, the distinction between riding a horse and riding it intentionally remains. I want to argue the same distinction for illocutionary actions: between performing the action and performing it intentionally – that is, with the intention to perform an act of that kind. (I do not mean to ride roughshod here over the distinctions among the three locutions I have used – say, accusing intentionally, accusing while intending to accuse, accusing with the intention to accuse – but I hold that each of these illocutionary actions connects with the others. And I distinguish them all from accusing.)

In any case, it is of course plain that *representing* an accusation cannot have as its condition an intention to accuse, and indeed these are somewhat at odds, for to take the representational stance is to renounce or withhold or suspend the illocutionary action. Yet strangely enough, this suspension is an extremely important and central feature of the process of poetic creation, which very often is a process in which real moral indignation, real grief, real affection, real religious devotion, real horror even, is made use of, is transformed into material for aesthetic representation and thus given a form that can long outlast the transient occasion of its birth.

IV

I turn now to consider some other pro-intention arguments that have been pressed in recent years, and see how they look in the light of my general principles.

One way of blowing up the importance of intention is to crowd under that label various considerations that really don't belong there. I give an example from an essay by Graham Hough:

> The intentionalists are right to maintain that
> the basic intentional act performed by the

author in writing must be correctly identified. They are right too in maintaining that this frequently requires a search for evidence outside the text. . . . Literary conventions, prevailing cultural assumptions, are not contained within the poem, but are necessary to its proper understanding. What could Lycidas mean to a reader who knew nothing of the long tradition of pastoral elegy? A good deal, no doubt, but half its significance would escape him, and some of its most prominent features would remain impenetrably obscure. . . . We need prior and external evidence about the poet's intentions.[8]

Let us agree at once that important parts of what *Lycidas* says depend on certain conditions external to it – literary traditions and conventions. To write the words of the poem was to say those things, among others, but only because the writing occurred against the background of those traditions and conventions. No doubt Milton was aware of them and knew what he was doing, but his knowledge on his part has no bearing on what he said in writing the words. Even if he had been ignorant of those traditions and conventions, he would still have been saying the same things – the "prominent features" Hough alludes to would still have been there. In just the same way, someone who enters a room and says, "The Phillies are leading," may be contradicting a previous speaker, though he is not aware of this, since he did not hear what the previous speaker said.

Another kind of example of how considerations get illegitimately listed under intention is provided by A. J. Close. He lists a number of statements about *Don Quixote*, of which he says:

> While I believe that all the above statements are at least arguably true, I maintain that (a), (b), (c), and (d) are either truisms or demonstrable truths. The fact is significant because it presupposes that one may state truths about the artist's intentions in doing what he does. Before this assertion the extreme forms of anti-intentionalism collapse.[9]

I don't know that anyone has ever been so "extreme" as to deny that "one may state truths about the artist's intention in doing what he does" – even those who doubted that we can *know* the

artist's intentions very specifically when they fail to be realized in the work. But consider the four examples he refers to as "truths about the artist's intentions":

> (a) *Don Quixote* is a work of comedy (genre-identification). (b) Cervantes often adapts rhetorical techniques of amplification and reduplication for ends of burlesque bathos (analysis of style). (c) Sancho Panza is an illiterate rustic simpleton (character-evaluation). (d) Sancho Panza's comic attributes are essentially those of the foolish funny servants – the *bobos* or *simples* – of sixteenth-century Spanish Drama (source-identification).[10]

Only one of these statements even mentions Cervantes, and that is not about his intentions but about his works. Granted that Cervantes intentionally made Sancho Panza an illiterate rustic simpleton; we do not need to know whether this making was intentional in order to know that Sancho Panza is an illiterate rustic simpleton.

Much more challenging – because more penetrating and more rigorously argued – is an essay by William E. Tolhurst, which defends a very persuasive theory of what the meaning of a literary text (its "utterance meaning") consists in. The essay has too much substance to be adequately considered in this context, and in part what it shows is that certain information about the circumstances or occasion of producing the text may be required to interpret it correctly (a thesis I do not contest). But its bearing on the problems of intention deserves to be acknowledged, as well as its force, even though with brief and inadequate comments.

> What we now argue is that utterance meaning [i.e., the meaning of a literary text] is best understood as the intention which a member of the intended audience would be most justified in attributing to the author based on the knowledge and attitudes which he possesses in virtue of being a member of the intended audience.[11]

This thesis is clearly and carefully guarded from potential confusions; it does not, for example, identify utterance meaning with "utterer's meaning" (i.e., what the author meant). Taken as a material equivalence, it is nearly acceptable, for in fact the meaning of a literary text will almost always be just the meaning that the intended audience would in fact be most justified by their characteristic qualities in attributing to the author. But as an *analysis* or *definition* of textual meaning I think it does not quite hold up. Imagine a would-be writer of children's stories who intends his book *Pinny the Who?* for an audience of eight-year-olds, but who woefully overestimates the range of their vocabulary. The actual meaning of this work may not correspond to the meaning that the intended audience would be most justified, in virtue of their skills and experience as eight-year-olds, in attributing to the author. Of course another audience could read the book aright; but the argument suggests to me that the reference to the "intended audience" does not belong here, and without it utterance (textual) meaning does not seem definable as most plausibly attributed utterer's meaning.

There has been much discussion of *allusiveness* in poetry, and a frequent intentionalist challenge: to recognize that, say, the words "Sweet Thames, run softly till I end my song" in *The Waste Land* as an allusion to Spenser's "Prothalamion" is to recognize Eliot's intention to allude to Spenser. Now there is no doubt that allusion in poetry is a form of reference; and I believe it is a form of the same synecdochic reference, from part to whole, that we have been talking about: the line occurs in Spenser's poem and is a distinctive, discriminative part of it, so it picks it out. Of course the possibility of allusion depends on the prior establishment of poetic quotation as a mode of reference, but given the general convention, there is again detachment of reference from the person to the vehicle or symbol itself. In his judicious discussion of these matters, Michael D. Wheeler quotes R. W. Stallman as proposing a distinction between "literary parallelisms" and "literary sources," including allusion; the distinction is that the latter are "conscious."[12] I don't deny the difference, but we need – and I think we have – a concept of allusion that does not require it. If we should, surprisingly, discover that Eliot never read or heard a line of Spenser, we would have to say that *Eliot* did not allude to "Prothalamion," but we could still *also* say that *The Waste Land* alludes to it.

Another recurrent argument for intentionalism is based on the so-called indeterminacy of poetry, and the supposed need to reduce it by appeal to the "will" of the author. This is a favorite theme of E. D. Hirsch, and I have discussed it elsewhere.[13] Here I only want to note its connection with what I have been proposing, and consider its relationship to illocutionary action theory. When the poet writes, "Gather ye Rose-buds while ye may," and we try to interpret this imperative, we can easily see in a general way what kind of illocutionary action is being represented. But can we be more specific? Is the speaker (the fictional utterer of the words) advising, or urging, or pleading, or commanding, or suggesting, or what? The very success of the poem may depend on getting the tone just right – and that means deciding precisely what sort of illocutionary action (or perhaps group of illocutionary actions) is represented. Especially if we wish to give an oral performance of the poem must we make up our minds about such matters.

Now if we are anti-intentionalists, all we can do is study the whole poem to find clues in the context of the first line; and I should think in this case that will tell us a great deal. According to E. D. Hirsch, it will never tell us enough – that is, there will always remain possible doubts as to whether the poem's opening action is, say, sage counsel or light-hearted teasing. At this point the two schools of interpreting part company. According to Hirsch, we must pursue the question beyond the reaches of the poem into the author's private life, so far as we can; when we find out what sort of person Robert Herrick was, we infer what sort of illocutionary action he would intend to perform, and conclude that this is what he did perform. (Hirsch treats poems as performances and performances as intended performances.) To my mind, it is more reasonable to conclude that our question is left undecided by the text, hence undecidable. The "indeterminacy" in the work cannot be replaced by the author's mental states. But of course oral performers are left free to present the poem in any way they wish, within the bounds set by the poem itself. That is why different oral performers can give quite different but equally satisfactory performances of the same work.

Some significant differences between the intentionalist and the anti-intentionalist perspectives are rather sharply brought out by a question about the explication of Yeats's "Leda and the Swan" (1924).

A shudder in the loins engenders there
The broken Wall, the burning roof and
    tower
And Agamemnon dead.

Suzanne S. Dean, in a term paper for a graduate seminar at Temple University, has argued that the word "tower" could be read as referring, *inter alia*, to the Tower, a card in the Tarot deck with readily connectable meanings. The argument for such a reading is that in earlier drafts of the poem Yeats capitalized "Tower." How should we reason in such a case – what is the proper interpretive inference from this evidence, if any? The intentionalist will say that the capital *T* makes the word refer to the Tarot card, shows that Yeats had such a reference in mind, and so permits us to conclude that "tower" in the final version carries this reference and the associated or consequent meanings. The anti-intentionalist will say that if the capital *T* was significant in the early draft, then the lowercase *t* is, by the same token, equally significant in the final draft. So whether Yeats intentionally changed the text from *T* to *t* or this happened by some accident, the change deleted the reference to the Tarot deck; and since there is no other warrant in the poem for such a reference, there is no justification for the intentionalist's reading.[14]

Another recurrent argument for intentionalism is based on the apparent possibility of private or idiosyncratic meanings: the poet who uses a word to which he is said to give a sense quite different from any of its standard senses, and whose contextual sense cannot be derived from any of its standard senses. Clear-cut cases are hard to find, even in Yeats. But suppose Yeats attached a wholly special meaning (as people are wont to say, though oddly) to one of his pet words, such as "gyre," and we know of this only because he wrote it in a letter or told it to a friend. Then it would seem that to interpret correctly a poem in which this word appears we must have recourse to Yeats's intention, and that appeal will be decisive.

Outside of poetry, the classic case, of course, is that of Humpty-Dumpty, and some years ago Keith Donnellan gave the right solution to that problem, in an exchange concerning reference.[15] I recast his proposal in terms of my own account of intention, but the substance is nearly the same. Humpty-Dumpty's own position is really inconsistent. His first claim is that when he said, "There's glory for you," he meant "There's a nice knock-down argument for you." This is the claim to be questioned in a moment. But, second, he admits that Alice could not know what he meant by "glory," as she complains, until he has provided a stipulative definition – which he proceeds to do. The illocutionary action in question is that of boasting that his argument for the superiority of unbirthdays to birthdays is a conclusive one. The

question is whether he can really intend to perform this action *in* producing the words "There's glory for you!" *before* giving a stipulative definition. Intending involves both wanting and believing: if you intend to go to a movie tonight, you desire to go and you believe you will go.[16] Now it may be possible for Humpty-Dumpty to *want* to boast in uttering those words, but it is not possible for him to *believe* that he *will* boast in uttering those words, because he knows that Alice has no way of assigning the novel sense to "glory," and therefore that he cannot secure the requisite uptake. And if he cannot intend to boast in uttering those words, he cannot boast intentionally in uttering them. So if to mean is to say intentionally, then Humpty-Dumpty cannot mean a nice knock-down argument by the word "glory," under the conditions given. As Donnellan says, if he had *begun* by offering the stipulation that in the ensuing conversation "glory" would be synonymous with "a nice knock-down argument," he would have made it mean what he wanted it to mean, because he would have provided conditions for securing uptake. But absent that stipulation, as lawyers say, he could not intend to do what he could not believe he would do.

V

This principle has a wider and more significant application to another recurrent thorn in the side of anti-intentionalism, namely the problem of irony. I should like to say something about this topic, which has been most interestingly discussed by three recent writers.

Although careless definers of literary theoretical terms still are wont to say that we have irony when we have a text of which the intended meaning is opposed to that expressed by words, in practice this crude description yields to a more defensible account. We look for tensions within the text – including those internal tensions that come about because of external conditions, for example, the political environment in which the text is produced. It is only because there exist texts designed to attract followers of various religious and quasi-religious sects, and these texts have the features they have, that it becomes possible to write an ironic invitation to join a sect. But then to say, with irony, that one should join a sect is (1) to perform the locutionary action of uttering such a sentence as "Drop what you're doing and give your all to the Reverend Moon," and (2) *in* performing this action, to perform the illocutionary action of urging people *not* to join the sect. The locutionary action (1) is performed *with* irony; the illocutionary action (2) is performed *through* irony.

The problem for the anti-intentionalist is said to be posed by the existence of texts that are ironic but are free of such inner tension, and hence can be recognized as ironic only by appeal to the author's intended meaning: how he intended the text to be read. Swift's *Modest Proposal* is the most familiar example, though there is growing and already wide agreement, I think, that it does not fully qualify – that it, so to speak, signals its ironic character. Another is the nineteenth-century Samuel Butler's book *The Fair Haven* (1873), an ostensible defense of Christianity designed to destroy its miraculous foundations. This book was first published anonymously and widely taken at face value.[17] E. D. Hirsch has discussed Defoe's tract *The Shortest Way with the Dissenters*, in which Defoe argued that dissenters deserved the worst that could be done to them; but Defoe was presumably trying to gain sympathy for them. Many took him seriously, and when he was discovered to be the dissenting author, he was jailed for the offense. This text, according to Hirsch, "clearly did *not* contain stylistic give-aways. . . . I cannot find a single stylistic barrier to a perfectly straightforward interpretation, and the historical evidence constitutes a prima facie case against any stylistician who claims to find such a linguistic barrier."[18]

Let us assume that Hirsch is right when he says there is nothing in the work to mark it as ironic. The question is, then, whether the tract *is* ironic. He concedes that the *only* ground for saying that it *is* ironic is that it was intended by Defoe to be ironic. I think this is no good ground, but I agree there is no other ground. Then was it intended to be ironic? According to my view, this would entail that Defoe intended to say that dissenters deserved better treatment and he intended to say this in writing a text containing sentences that would normally be used in saying that dissenters did *not* deserve better treatment. Now perhaps he *wanted* to do this; one can want the impossible. But he could not *believe* he was doing this; for if he took pains to exclude from the text (and title page) every hint of reservations about, or detachment of belief from, the ostensible attack on dissenters, he must know that he would not secure uptake from the reader. And thus he could not expect the illocutionary action of pleading for dissenters to be com-

pleted. Therefore the work was not intended to be ironic, and since there is, by hypothesis, no evidence in the work that it is ironic, there is no reason to believe that it is ironic. Consequently, it will not serve as an example of an ironic text whose irony requires to be discovered by appeal to evidence of what was intended.

Once we see that we must renounce the Hirschian path, we see that the definition of literary irony need make no reference to intention. Our task as interpreter is not to find out what was going on privately in the author's mind that he did not choose to reveal in his text, but to find out what is going on in the text to make it turn itself upside down or inside out and say the opposite of what it seems, on the surface, to say. Here I disagree with Göran Hermerén, who quotes a remark about Beckett's poem "Ooftisch": "We recognize the bitter irony that mimics cruelty partly in rage, partly in the certainty of understanding the case, partly to jolt the reader into awareness; and we can guess the mixture of personal pain and pugnacious courage in a pun like 'cough up your T. B.'"[19] Unlike Hermerén, I don't see that this depends on a distinction between what is said and what was intended, but only between levels or layers of what is said.

Jonathan Culler's comments are sound, I think, but need to be supplemented by the other side of the coin.

> Kierkegaard maintains that the true ironist does not wish to be understood, and though true ironists may be rare we can at least say that irony always offers the possibility of misunderstanding. No sentence is ironic *per se*. Sarcasm may contain internal inconsistencies which make its purport quite obvious and prevent it from being read except in one way, but for a sentence to be properly ironic it must be possible to imagine some group of readers taking it quite literally. Otherwise there is no contrast between apparent and assumed meaning and no space of ironic play.[20]

Kierkegaard's remark is characteristically paradoxical and self-defeating. Swift, Defoe, and Butler were "true ironists," if anyone ever was – and if they did not wish anyone to understand their real feelings, they were playing a most peculiar and incomprehensible game. Irony must offer the possibility of misunderstanding (yes, if all that means is that we can *imagine* someone missing the irony);

it also must offer the possibility of *understanding*, it seems to me, for if we and the author cannot imagine anyone taking it ironically, it can hardly have been intended as ironic, and there would be no reason at all to believe that it is.

In considering these fascinating examples, we must bear in mind that they are not works of fiction. They serve here as data for an a fortiori argument. The question about them is whether the author is actually performing the illocutionary actions of condemning, ridiculing, pleading, or whatever, and doing so through irony. And if *this* question is not to be settled by appeal to the author's intentions, how much less will that appeal decide what is being *represented* in works of fiction – as, for example, in the celebrated and not-to-be-forgotten case of A. E. Housman's poem on Queen Victoria's Golden Jubilee.[21] The irony representer certainly cannot rely on the existence of his masked attitudes (however displayed to actual friends and foes) to give his work the second layer of verbal action. His reliance must be on verbal signals that delineate someone mimicking a performance but refraining from it – and make it possible (even if difficult) for the reader to determine just what is done and what is withheld and what is said thereby.

Well, then – to turn back to the beginning briefly by way of conclusion – is there an intentional fallacy after all? (Is there really, we might ask, a naturalistic fallacy, a genetic fallacy, a fallacy of

misplaced concreteness, a fallacy of the suppressed correlative, a logocentric fallacy . . . ?) Perhaps the returns are not all in. I think we know enough to concede that the intentional fallacy is not as distinctly marked and bounded as, say, the post hoc, ergo propter hoc fallacy, or the fallacy of composition. But the term still points, sternly and unwaveringly, at a small cluster of errors in inference that center around the concept of the author's intention. The errors can be formulated as confusions: of illocutionary-act performance with illocutionary-act representation, of authorial meaning (what was intended to be said) with textual meaning (what was actually said), of the ostensible speaker of a poem with the biological author, of the subject of the poem with the occasion of its composition. One or more of these confusions seem to be implicated in the characteristic and central form of inference that the anti-intentionalist calls fallacious: from premises about the intentions of the author to conclusions about the meaning (that is, the saying content) of the work. Generally the argument has three stages, or two steps: from biographical data of various kinds to the probable intention, and from the probable intention to the proposed interpretation of the work. With the first step per se I have no quarrel, though its results are often rather unreliable and speculative; it is the second step whose logical legitimacy I still find very doubtful.

Notes

1 David Newton-De Molina, ed., *On Literary Intention* (Edinburgh, 1976). Wimsatt has also taken another, careful look at the problems in "Genesis: An Argument Resumed," in *Day of the Leopards: Essays in Defense of Poems* (New Haven, 1976).

2 See "Intending," in *Values and Morals*, ed. Alvin I. Goldman and Jaegwon Kim (Dordrecht, 1978).

3 *The Ice Age* (New York, 1977), p. 54.

4 See "*Languages of Art* and Art Criticism," *Erkenntnis* 12 (1978): 95–118.

5 See "Fiction as Representation," *Synthese* 46 (1981): 291–314.

6 "Motives, Intentions and the Interpretation of Texts," in *On Literary Intention*, ed. Newton-De Molina, p. 215.

7 Ibid., p. 216.

8 "An Eighth Type of Ambiguity," in *On Literary Intention*, ed. Newton-De Molina, p. 233. Hough holds that illocutionary actions are "intentional by definition" (p. 235). John Reichert argues in a similar

way in *Making Sense of Literature* (Chicago, 1977), chap. 3, esp. pp. 62–63. Like Reichert (p. 63), Mary Sirridge holds that "recourse to the author's motivations" (in her broad sense) "is *the right standard* for determining whether we are faced with irony, sympathy or simple illustration" (*British Journal of Aesthetics* 18 (1978): 150).

9 "Don Quixote and the 'Intentionalist Fallacy,'" in *On Literary Intention*, ed. Newton-De Molina, p. 185.

10 Ibid.

11 "On What a Text Is and How It Means," *British Journal of Aesthetics* 19 (1979): 11.

12 See "Biography, Literary Influence and Allusion as Aspects of Source Studies," *British Journal of Aesthetics* 17 (Spring 1977): 152.

13 See *The Possibility of Criticism* (Detroit, 1970), chap. 1.

14 For some discussion of Yeats's use of the Tower card in general, Suzanne Dean has referred me to

Thomas R. Henn, *The Lonely Tower* (London, 1950), pp. 124ff.

15 "Putting Humpty-Dumpty Together Again," *Philosophical Review* 77 (1968): 211–15.

16 See "Intending."

17 See the judicious discussion of this work by Ina Rae Hark, "Samuel Butler and the Gospel of No Gospel," in *Interspace and the Inward Sphere*, ed. Norman Anderson and Margene Weiss (Macomb, Ill., 1978). She brings out Butler's conflicting purposes that make the book work against itself. One conclusion: "Butler exercises much skillful irony outside the 'memoir' [which prefaces the main text], but he never gives it free enough rein to assure detection by those not in on the joke from the start" (p. 128). "Irony" here, I take it, refers to features of the work which would subtly but distinctly signal the reversal of assertion if they were not countered by opposing signals.

18 *The Aims of Interpretation* (Chicago, 1976), pp. 24–25.

19 "Intention and Interpretation in Literary Criticism," *New Literary History* 7 (1975–76): 74.

20 *Structuralist Poetics: Structuralism, Linguistics, and the Study of Literature* (Ithaca, 1975), p. 154.

21 My treatment of this example (in *Aesthetics: Problems in the Philosophy of Criticism* [New York, 1958], pp. 25–26) has been critically discussed by A. J. Ellis in "Intention and Interpretation in Literature," *British Journal of Aesthetics* 14 (1974): 322–23. Despite his confident statement that "there is no such thing" as the (ironic) meaning of this poem – "One might ask: Did Housman intend the lines to be ironical? . . . Or one might ask: How should we read them, how do they sound best? . . . But there is not some third question: Are the lines ironical?" – I still think there is a good question: Was Housman, in composing this poem, saying – or representing someone as saying – that Queen Victoria did not deserve all that adulation for building the Empire (this being said through irony, i.e., as opposed to the plain sense of the words)?

17

Intention and Interpretation in Literature

Jerrold Levinson

The issues surrounding the interpretation of literary texts and the relation of that activity to authors' intentions in writing such texts are of long standing and show little sign of being definitively settled anytime soon. Indeed, the debate over intentionalism in literature seems to have been given new life in recent years, thanks to the rise of pragmatist, neohistoricist, and autobiographical tendencies in literary studies as well as a concomitant counterreaction to the excesses of deconstructionist theory.

What I will do in this essay is spell out what I take to be the most defensible position on the central question in dispute between intentionalists and anti-intentionalists and, having done so, engage selectively with others who have written recently on the question, in light of the perspective I have arrived at.[1]

The view I defend concerning the interpretation and meaning of literary works is strictly neither intentionalism nor anti-intentionalism, as those are usually delineated, but what might be called *hypothetical* (or *constructive*) *intentionalism*.[2] Hypothetical intentionalism is logically and importantly different from *actual* intentionalism, which certainly has its adherents,[3] while also distinct from the sort of *anti*-intentionalism, relying on the meaning-generating force of conventions, which provided the theoretical underpinning for the New Criticism of the forties, fifties, and sixties.[4]

Jerrold Levinson, "Intention and Interpretation in Literature," in Jerrold Levinson, *The Pleasures of Aesthetics: Philosophical Essays* (Ithaca, NY: Cornell University Press, 1996), pp. 175–213.

I

When we ask ourselves what literary texts mean and how they embody such meaning as they have, I think there are only four models to choose from in answer. One is that such meaning is akin to word sequence (e.g., sentence) meaning *simpliciter*. Another is that it is akin to the utterer's (author's) meaning on a given occasion. A third assimilates it rather to the utterance meaning generated on a given occasion in specific circumstances.[5] A last model pictures it, most liberally, in terms of what might be called ludic meaning.[6]

Word sequence meaning, roughly, is "dictionary" meaning – the meaning (or usually, meanings) attachable to a sequence of words taken in the abstract by virtue of the operative syntactic and semantic (including connotative) rules of the specific, time-indexed, language in which those words are taken to occur. *Utterer's meaning* is the meaning an intentional agent (speaker, writer) has in mind or in view to convey by the use of a given verbal vehicle. *Utterance meaning*, on the other hand, is the meaning that such a vehicle ends up conveying in its context of utterance – a context that includes its being uttered by such-and-such agent. *Ludic meaning*, finally, comprises any meanings that can be attributed to either a brute text (a word-sequence-in-a-language) or a text-as-utterance, by virtue of interpretive play constrained by only the loosest requirements of plausibility, intelligibility, or interest.

It seems clear that literary meaning cannot be equated simply with untethered word sequence (or sentence) meaning, because it is crucial to the task of interpretation that the sentences of a literary text be presumed to issue from a single mind,[7] to have a purpose, and to be the vehicle of a specific act of communication, widely construed. We don't treat literary texts the way we would random collections of sentences, such as might be formed in the sands of a beach or spewed out by computer programs. The sentences that make up a literary work, on a primary level, are not merely a collection or assemblage but the body and substance of what we assume to be a unitary act of expression.

Equally clearly, though, literary meaning cannot be equated *tout court* with utterer's meaning, for that would dissolve the distinction between normal practical linguistic activity – where the paramount object is to communicate what the speaker or writer is thinking or wanting to say – and communication in a literary mode, where the text is held to have a certain amount of autonomy, to be something we interpret, to some extent, for its own sake, and thus not jettisonable in principle if we could just get, more directly, at what the author had in mind to tell us. When a poet vouchsafes us, in plain language, what some enigmatic poem of his might mean, we don't react by then discarding the poem in favor of the offered precis. In ordinary verbal intercourse, what a person meant takes precedence over, or overrides, what the person's language as uttered may end up meaning to a suitably grounded interlocutor; this seems not clearly so in the sphere of literary production. Finally, what I have labeled ludic meaning – which is related to what Arthur Danto posits as the object or outcome of "deep" interpretation[8] – is an inappropriate candidate for at least the fundamental meaning of literary texts, if only because it presupposes such in order to get off the ground.

This leaves just utterance meaning – the meaning a linguistic vehicle has in a given context of presentation or projection, a context that arguably includes, in addition to directly observable features of the act of utterance, something of the characteristics of the author who projects the text, something of the text's place in a surrounding oeuvre and culture, and possibly other elements as well. But what does such meaning amount to, for a typically complex work of literature? How do we get at it, and what are we aiming at in seeking it? To these questions William Tolhurst has given an instructive answer:

Utterance meaning is best understood as the intention which a member of the intended

audience would be most *justified in attributing* to the author based on the knowledge and attitudes which he possesses in virtue of being a member of the intended audience. Thus utterance meaning is to be construed as that *hypothesis* of utterer's meaning which is most justified on the basis of those beliefs and attitudes which one possesses qua intended hearer or intended reader.[9] . . .

In understanding an utterance one constructs a hypothesis as to the intention which that utterance is best viewed as fulfilling [my emphases].[10]

So utterance meaning is logically distinct from utterer's meaning, while at the same time necessarily related to it conceptually: we arrive at utterance meaning by *aiming at* utterer's meaning in the most comprehensive and informed manner we can muster as the utterance's intended recipients. *Actual* utterer's intention, then, is not what is determinative of the meaning of a literary offering or other linguistic discourse, but rather such intention as optimally *hypothesized*, given all the resources available to us in the work's internal structure and the relevant surrounding context of creation, in all its *legitimately* invoked specificity.[11] The core of utterance meaning can be conceived of analytically as our best appropriately informed projection of author's intended meaning from our positions as intended interpreters.

The compromise between intentionalism and anti-intentionalism suggested by Tolhurst's approach, then, is this: that the core of literary meaning, as with any piece of discourse publicly presented, is not the meaning (the many meanings) of the words and sentences taken in abstraction from the author, or precisely of necessity the meaning that the author actually intended to put across, but our best *hypothetical attribution* of such, formed from the position of intended audience. Of course it goes without saying that this latter will tend often (e.g., in successful cases) to coincide with actually intended meaning, but the principled distinction between them remains important, both for seeing clearly what we are about when we strive to pin down with some degree of definiteness the meanings – possibly manifold – of a work of literature, and for the light it casts on interpretive disputes in difficult cases.

This is a good point to remark how the idea of a best hypothetical attribution of intention to an author is itself best understood. I have in mind that this be done with a certain duality. Principally, a best attribution is one that is *epistemically* best – that has the most likelihood of being correct, given the total evidence available to one in the position of ideal reader. But secondarily, a best attribution of intention to an author might involve, in accord with a principle of charity, choosing a construal that makes the work *artistically* better, where there is room for choice, so long as plausibly ascribed to the author given the full context of writing. In other words, if we can make the author out to have created a cleverer or more striking or more imaginative work, without violating the image of his oeuvre underpinned by the total available textual and contextual evidence, we should perhaps do so. That is then our best projection of intent – "best" in two senses – as informed and sympathetic readers. This does not, however, license our viewing a work under an interpretation on which it comes off well artistically if such is not one we could on good grounds epistemically associate with or impute to the historical author as in the main understood by us.

Such is the view of literary meaning that guides my reflections throughout this essay. Before proceeding, though, we must address certain problems inherent in Tolhurst's formulation of the view and consider ways of meeting them.

II

The notion of a literary work's meaning, and thus of correct interpretations of it, is properly tied, as I have said, not to actual, even successfully realized, artist's intent but rather to our best construction, given the evidence of the work and appropriately possessed background information, of the artist's intent to mean such-and-such for his or her intended audience.[12] In short this is because literature-making, and art-making generally, is closely analogous to a speech act, that is, it is an act of attempted communication in a broad sense, one of an oblique sort. As such, its products – works of literature – should have the sort of meaning that the products or upshots of speech acts – utterances – centrally have, namely utterance meaning. And it can be further argued, as Tolhurst has done, that utterance meaning is capturable through the idea of the best contextually informed hypothesis of what a speaker/writer is attempting to communicate to his intended audience.

Tolhurst's proposal, however, has been criticized by Daniel Nathan, on a number of grounds.[13] I will first address those I regard as less troubling, and then proceed to the one that strikes me as more weighty. Nathan begins by criticizing Tolhurst for having too narrow a notion of word sequence meaning, one that abstracts unnecessarily from the "connotative characteristics of words."[14] This charge strikes me as unfounded. Tolhurst could allow all the general, languagewide, timebound connotations of words to be comprised in word sequence meaning and yet insist that the full meaning of an utterance in many cases is still determinately different from what the denotative and connotative meanings of the words involved will themselves underwrite, and is instead finally fixed by features of the individual, pragmatic context of utterance.

Nathan next holds that Tolhurst's examples, in particular his appeal to Swift's *A Modest Proposal*, depend essentially on ignoring the complete texts of which his extracts are a part. But surely the theoretical point that Tolhurst is after still holds – that there very well *could be* literary texts, which in their completeness justified either an ironic or literal reading leaving context of utterance aside, but which, given such context, we would judge as clearly either ironic or nonironic. Consider as an example the following, which serves also to illustrate the dependence of utterance meaning on activated context and its independence of speaker's actual meaning.

Emilia is a graduate student in history, whose advisor, Basil Bushwacker, is leaving to take a post at another university. As is well known among her friends, Emilia harbors ambivalent and resentful feelings toward her rather egoistic and unavailable mentor, though he, fortunately, is oblivious to this. She will, however, continue to require his support in external ways for the near future. After a farewell presentation in his honor prior to his departure, she writes him a short note, whose purpose is to assure his continued good will toward her in the coming years:

Dear Professor Bushwacker:

I was delighted to be present at your valedictory event last week; the tributes, although impressive, did not do you justice. We will all be immeasurably sad to lose you, and hope you will find many opportunities to visit the friends and colleagues you leave behind at Wunderwelt U.

Sincerely,
Emilia Edelweiss

The import of the preceding, as a letter sent or to be sent to Professor Bushwacker, is roughly one of appreciation, praise, and gentle entreaty. That is the gist of the utterance meaning of the text employed in that fashion – it is how Professor Bushwacker, or a similarly placed recipient of a letter from a seemingly respectful charge, would naturally take it. Label this Open Letter. On the other hand, as a text circulated or to be circulated among the student's circle of friends, with the knowledge they are privy to and rightly bring to bear, the phrases of the text acquire ironic content that they did not possess as part of a letter written openly to the salutee: the "tributes" do not do justice because insufficiently upbraiding, the "sadness" will be immeasurable because minuscule, and so on. The utterance meaning of this entity – label it Private Epistle – is quite different from that of Open Letter. It is largely one of blame, relief, and excoriation, for that is the authorial intention that would most naturally be projected on the words by Private Epistle's intended or appropriate audience. The texts – the complete texts – of both Open Letter and Private Epistle, however, are absolutely identical.[15]

I come now to Nathan's more worrisome charge. Tolhurst's proposal, he notes, is motivated by the desire to escape from strong intentionalism and its attendant problems, appealing instead only to a hypotheticized author's intention. But Tolhurst has failed to notice that his proposal is still anchored in the author's actual intentions, through that intention, namely, which picks out a certain class or kind of reader as charged with the justifiable projection of intended authorial meaning definitive of work meaning. This reference to author's intention, claims Nathan, is both pernicious and ineliminable. The reason is that

> Tolhurst allows cases where identifying the intended audience is not possible on public grounds, that is, the intended audience is different from the one the author is in fact addressing. . . . Further, given no limits to the narrowness of the intended audience, the author may be speaking a language the meaning of which is known only to himself and his family. . . . Tolhurst claims that the author is not in a privileged position vis-à-vis what he has written, that any member of that audience shares access to that meaning. But the determination of the intended audi-

ence is in principle a private matter, hence ultimately so is meaning.[16]

How should a hypothetical-intentionalist respond to this? I think there are two options. One is to try to show that an author's intentional identification of an intended *audience* is significantly different from, and less troubling than, an author's intentional determination of the *meaning* of his text, as endorsed by full-fledged intentionalists. The other is to abandon the notion of an intended audience in favor of that of an *appropriate* audience, where this is not up to authorial determination.

Taking the first tack, we may note that the content of an audience-identifying intention is at least less problematic than the content of a semantic intention, especially one as would govern a complex work of literature as a whole. Dostoyevsky's intended audience in writing *The Brothers Karamazov*, if we could ascertain it, would be something on this order: competent readers of Russian, practiced in narrative fiction, aware of Russian history, familiar with Russian religious traditions, and so on. But Dostoyevsky's comprehensive meaning intention for *The Brothers Karamazov* has as object something hardly even imaginable apart from the novel itself and an exhaustive interpretation of it. Given this great difference in level between the two, then, it might seem to represent some progress that an analysis would, if not wholly avoiding intentions whose accessibility is in question, at least substitute for one whose scope is rather mind-boggling another that is more down-to-earth, in the role of anchoring a work's otherwise indeterminate meaning.

Note next that the nature of the audience intentionally targeted by an author is not, after all, particularly opaque to us. Consider my partial sketch here of the audience at which *The Brothers Karamazov* was undoubtedly aimed. I consulted no oracle for it, nor did I study Dostoyevsky's diaries or the records left by his personal physician. Obviously I merely considered the novel itself, the demands of comprehension inherent in it, and the novel's context of creation (e.g., nineteenth-century Russia). This observation, however, shifts us toward the second option, that of an appropriate, as opposed to authorially intended, audience, in that it in effect invokes a hypothesization of the intended audience, that is, as that audience we would be most justified in assuming the author was aiming at – where "we" are now understood as just rational judgers possessed of all relevant contextual information. But if this is the pass to which we come, it might be better to simply drop reference to intended audiences, even reasonably hypothesizable intended audiences, and just speak of an audience that is an *appropriate* (or ideal) one for a given work, as judged by what it would appear to take to understand such a work properly. Let us pursue that idea.

I suggest we may be guided in identifying an appropriate audience for a given work, whose best projection of authorial intention will, as before, be constitutive of basic work meaning, by certain norms and conventions understood to define the sphere of literary production and reception.[17] Thus an appropriate reader, for anything presented in the framework of literature, might be profiled generally as one versed in and cognizant of the tradition out of which the work arises, acquainted with the rest of the author's oeuvre, and perhaps familiar as well with the author's public literary and intellectual identity or persona. These are ground rules, as it were, of the literary enterprise, of the implicit contract between writer and reader, and it is not clear that an author can unilaterally abrogate such an understanding in favor of a specified audience whose information or capacities are significantly at variance with those involved in the profile just sketched.

Thus the best response to Nathan's criticism of the residual actual intentionalism in Tolhurst's conception, as embodied in the idea of the author's intended audience, may be to excise that residue and rely instead on a notion of an appropriate reader, where the meaning of that is filled in both by what can be seen, from the work itself, as incontrovertibly required for textual understanding – for example, competence in the language, including dialects employed, knowledge of the references and allusions embedded in the text, and so on – and certain givens of the cultural "language game" in which writer and reader are bound, involving a presumption of shared knowledge of traditions, oeuvres, writerly identities, and the like.[18]

Finally, to emphasize the fact that the central meaning of a literary work should be thought of as akin to that of an utterance in a context, as opposed to either what a text means apart from its quite specific context of issuance, or what the author-utterer intends to convey, but to foreground more clearly its written condition and more formal mode of presentation, we could coin the term "literance" for what literary works are. Poems, novels, short stories

are literances – texts presented and projected in literary contexts, whose meaning, it is understood by both author and audience, will be a function of and constrained by – though in ways neither might clearly predict – the potentialities of the text per se together with the generative matrix provided by its issuing forth from individual A, with public persona B, at time C, against cultural background D, in light of predecessors E, in the shadow of contemporary events F, in relation to the remainder of A's artistic oeuvre G, and so on.

III

As an illustration of the hypothetical intentionalist position on interpretation I am advocating, consider Kafka's story "A Country Doctor." In this singular fiction the doctor of the title is awakened suddenly at night and summoned to the bedside of a boy suffering from a horrible wound, leaving his house servant at the mercy of his menacing groom. Though the boy is beyond help, the doctor is induced to attempt a curious cure, which involves getting into bed with the patient; the cure is, naturally, futile, and the doctor can scarcely extricate himself from the situation to return to what he fears are only the shambles of home and hearth he left behind just hours before. The relevant background information, or author-specific context of understanding, for an interpretation of this enigmatic narrative would surely include the following: that Kafka regularly worked at night; that Kafka thought of writing as "medicinal," "therapeutic," "a calling"; that Kafka did not separate his writing and his life; that Kafka was familiar with Freud's *The Interpretation of Dreams*; and Kafka's "A Hunger Artist," written five years after "A Country Doctor," about a man who starves himself publicly as both an artistic performance and an admission that ordinary food held no appeal for him.

Given that as background, and given the intrinsic matter of the text, one might readily come up with this interpretation: "A Country Doctor" is a stylized dream report. Its content is basically the conflict between ordinary, sensual life, as represented by the servant girl Rose and the doctor's comfortable home, and one's calling: to heal, edify, spiritually succor. The doctor is in effect an artist, as is, more transparently, the hunger artist of Kafka's later tale. He is caught betwixt and between, naked and disoriented, as was Kafka between his literary and his domestic duties and desires. And the sick boy is like the doctor's younger self – through art/Arzt one primarily tries to heal oneself, and only secondarily others.[19]

Thus our best informed-reader construction of what this specific writer, Kafka, was aiming to convey – was engaged in communicating – in writing "A Country Doctor," may be something like the preceding. It makes sense to attribute such a meaning or content to the author as he is available to us, his appropriate, contextually sensitized, readers.

Still, we might just find out – from Kafka's secret diary, say, or a close informant, or even advanced aliens who were scanning Kafka's thought processes at the time – that Kafka's immediate, explicit intent in writing "A Country Doctor" was in fact to critique rural medical practices, to lampoon their typical unpreparedness and lack of materials, and to expose the deep-seated ignorance of the Czech peasantry. The text could just barely support such a meaning, much as "my car ran out of gas" can perhaps just manage to be the vehicle of a meaning in mind involving cabooses and clouds of chlorine.[20] But this would not, I think, supplant the interpretation given earlier as to what the work, in a reader-accessible, Kafka-specific context, means. Our best construction, in the dual sense specified earlier, of what Kafka the writer is communicating in "A Country Doctor" would trump our discovery of what Kafka the person might oddly have been intending to mean, on the occasion of penning the story. Granted, the possibility of divergence between specific actual intent and best hypothesized intent given all appropriate reader data is fairly small, but is not therefore zero. And theoretically the difference is important for the philosophy of literary criticism.

IV

We must briefly confront yet another problem for any hypothetical intentionalist conception of literary meaning. Let us assume that the core meaning of a literary work is utterance meaning – that is, what a text says in an author-specific context of presentation to an appropriate, or suitably backgrounded, reader. Even if we agree that such meaning is given by a reader's best projection-in-context of what its author intended to mean, this still seems to leave aspects of utterance meaning – of what is said in a work – that go beyond that.

There are, it can be fairly held, unenvisaged and not plausibly envisageable implications, unforeseen and not plausibly foreseeable resonances, hidden significations, and the like, of a given text, which are yet properly comprised in literary meaning as just defined. These can seem part of what is conveyed literarily even while not reasonably attributable to the author as we have hypothesized him on the basis of our relevantly engaged background knowledge.

Three strategies suggest themselves for dealing with unintended meanings properly ascribed to a literary work, from the point of view of hypothetical intentionalism. A first strategy is straightforwardly to acknowledge them but to qualify them as secondary; primary literary meaning, it could be held, must still be in line with reasonably projectible intention, even though secondary meanings, ascribable to a work once it is centrally interpreted, need not conform to that standard of projectibility.

Without some indication of how secondary meanings might be distinguished from primary ones, such a strategy admittedly remains rather programmatic. But here are some suggestions to that end. Secondary meanings are secondary, we may submit, first, in that they cannot legitimately be assigned until primary literary meaning, discerned by the lights of plausibly hypothesized intentions to convey, has been assigned, at least provisionally; second, in that they must at least cohere with, and not undermine, primary meaning assigned by plausible intentional lights; and third, in that they cannot themselves figure as the core of an interpretation, where literary interpretations are understood as structured accounts of a work's import, the elements of such an account being ordered from most central to most peripheral.

A second strategy is to propose a broader notion of the author's intended meaning as hypothesizable by an appropriate reader, one that takes the existence of discoverable but unintended and not reasonably ascribable specific meanings in a literary utterance to be reasonably ascribable to the author as a class, or *collectively*, by virtue of his entry into the literary domain and implicit acceptance of a principle roughly licensing discerning of not-explicitly-intended-though-possible-for-the-author meanings[21] that directly emerge from or are implied by a text centrally interpreted in line with reasonably projected intent, even when such meanings are not *individually* ascribable to the author as likely to have been meant.

A third strategy, going beyond even a broadened notion of author's intended meaning, would be to appeal to what I have elsewhere called perspectives justified with respect to a given historically positioned work although not accessible to its author, and therefore not plausibly projectible by him. Such perspectives might be considered justified, and thus the aspects of the work they revealed part of its literary content, if they can be shown to be rooted, abstractly or embryonically, in the concerns of the historically constructable author.[22]

Because my main concern in this essay is primary or central literary meaning, and because I think hypothetical intentionalism gives the best account of that, I won't attempt here to settle definitively this issue of aptly-ascribed-to-work-yet-improbably-ascribable-to-author unintended meanings, but will assume that a treatment along one or another of the lines just sketched would ultimately be adequate.

V

Though I have distanced myself, following Tolhurst, from Hirschian intentionalism as an account of the meaning of literary works, I do nonetheless hold certain actual intentions to bear ineliminably, though indirectly, on such meaning, and on the appreciation and evaluation of works of art generally. Furthermore, these intentions are ones that remain extrinsic to the works themselves, in the last analysis, in the sense that they are not guaranteed to be implicit in, and extractable from, a work or its observable manner of production but reside instead in the stances and decisions of a work's maker, themselves perhaps embodied only in behavioral dispositions.

We need to distinguish two kinds of intentions relevant to the production and reception of art: *categorial* intentions, on the one hand, and *semantic* intentions, on the other. An author's intention to *mean* something in or by a text T (a semantic intention) is one thing, whereas an author's intention that T be *classified* or *taken* in some specific or general way (a categorial intention) is quite another. Categorial intentions involve the maker's framing and positioning of his product vis-à-vis his projected audience; they involve the maker's conception of what he has produced and what it is for, on a rather basic level; they govern not what a work is to mean but how it is to be fundamentally conceived or approached. The most general of cat-

egorial intentions of concern here would be the intention that something be regarded as literature (or as art) at all, which obviously enjoins certain modes of approach as opposed to others.

A modern writer might intend a text to project an attitude of reverence to nature, and yet, because of the writer's clumsiness or his mistaken beliefs about the plant kingdom, it not do so; his semantic intention would have failed. But if the writer intends his text *as a poem* – as opposed to a short story, a dramatic monologue, a piece of calligraphic visual art, or a mere diary entry – then that intention is of a different sort and of a different order, and virtually cannot fail – so long as the text in question at least allows of being taken, among other things, as a poem. And it is clear that whatever meaning the text-as-work ends up possessing, this will not be independent of whether it is properly construed as in one category or genre or medium rather than another, that is, whether it is to be read as a poem or scanned as a design or imagined as a passage to be acted, or treated – by averting our eyes – as a private confession with no envisioned relation to an audience whatsoever.[23] Semantic intentions, like that of our unfortunate writer, do *not* determine meaning, but categorial intentions, such as concern a literature maker's basic conception of what is made, *do* in general determine how a text is to be conceptualized and approached on a fundamental level and thus indirectly affect what it will resultingly say or express. Categorial intentions serve to orient a reader vis-à-vis a text at a very basic level, and without knowledge of them one is powerless even to begin to sort out its meanings, if any it has, by casting about for readings that could most reasonably be attributed to its contextually situated maker.

VI

Colin Lyas is one who has persuasively sketched a neo-Wittgensteinian account of literary intentions, according to which they, like intentions in other spheres, are embodied in and through the concrete acts and situations they govern and are inseparable from them.[24] But I think there is a real question whether such an account will do for all sorts of artistic intentions, and the categorial intentions toward texts or objects susceptible of being conceptually regarded in various ways invoked in the preceding are a case in point. It's just not clear that all artistic intentions are displayed in or through a work itself, or even the act of producing it. The strictures about embodiment that Lyas proposes seem to me to apply fairly vigorously to semantic intentions, but much less so to categorial ones; the former may not have embodiment in a work, or in the observable activity of its creation, but only, so to speak, in the vicinity of those.[25]

A categorial intention, unlike a semantic one, is literally part of *making* or *creating* the artwork in question. When a person finishes applying oils to a rectangular surface, or molding clay into a certain shape and firing it, or writing sentences consecutively in a notebook, or inscribing an index card with numbers and symbols, he hasn't yet made a painting, or a sculpture, or a poem, or a piece of conceptual art unless at some point in the process he decides and registers (at least to himself) that the first is a painting (not merely a hole-covering), the second a sculpture (not just a doorstop), the third a poem (not a grocery list), and the fourth a conceptual piece (not the mere doodle it appears to be). Because categorial intentions are inherently part of art-making, and because artists must be allowed to constitute their works as they wish, to make them whatever, within natural and logical limits, they want them to be, if not to make them mean, by fiat, whatever they want them to mean, categorial intentions must be recognized to have a status different from semantic ones.[26]

Contra Lyas, not all intentions relevant to appreciation of a work of literature can be effectively located internal to the work or its process of production. Those that relate to what the author is trying to communicate in writing a certain way perhaps can, by and large. But certainly not those that relate to how the text is to be taken as a whole, at a ground-floor level. Such intentions will generally reside outside the text per se or its observable conditions of genesis, because a given text, however produced, could be projected in several different ways – for example, as fiction or as nonfiction, as an instance of traditional (i.e., purely verbal) or concrete (i.e., partly graphic) poetry – by the same author, and the fact of such projection might be grounded only in the hypothetical behavior of the author, or in ancillary indications (e.g., writer's diaries, program notes, interviews) beyond the boundaries of the work and the action of creating it, properly speaking. A complete review of the artistic situation ineluctably brings one up against intentions that cannot be assumed to have received complete embodiment in public act, object, or circumstance.

Furthermore, even where semantic intentions are concerned, I think the intimacy that Lyas posits between them and the publicly determinable meaning of texts is somewhat in excess of what is warranted. Even if an intention to mean such-and-such by a text may be more nearly analyzed in terms of the observed product and circumstances than an intention that a text be conceptualized or taken in a certain manner, there is still, I think, an irreducible psychological remainder to such intention not always inherent in the text's outward face and full context of presentation. In discussing utterances – and by implication, literances – Lyas rightly observes that part of the meaning of such is constituted by the force, or illocutionary thrust, of what is uttered. Going on to observe that a given utterance does not end up having a particular force in virtue of facts about the speaker's will, Lyas notes that this might suggest that reference to intention is not required when we are dealing with questions about the force of an utterance. But despite appearances, this is, he claims, not so:

What is true is that whether or not an utterance has a clear force is not decided by asking the speaker what force he or she wanted it to have. For all that, force sometimes is made clear by the production of an utterance in a certain context. When it is made clear, then what is made clear is an intention on the part of the speaker to do something in speaking, for example, to give a warning threat, or promise. *Hence to refer to the force of an utterance is to refer to its speaker's intention* [my emphasis], even though what that force is need not be determined by asking the speaker what that intention was.[27]

The problem here is that utterer's meaning and utterance meaning are once again in danger of being collapsed into one another. When the force of an utterance is clear, from its lexical content, the context in which it issues, and any relevantly engaged information about the speaker as a public player in a given speech community, then that is an element of the utterance's meaning, and that, as we have seen, can be identified with the *most plausibly ascribed* intention to the utterer to do such-and-such in speaking. But this is still not the same as the speaker's *actual and concrete* intention, unless one is waxing verficationist, for this last may, even in such cases, reside in aspects of the situation outside of those public indications that fix utterance meaning, and force in particular. So even though I might grant that a speaker's or writer's semantic intentions are often transparently evident in the meaningful utterance or literance that results, this still seems to me a matter of inference, however natural and automatic. There is always some possibility of divergence; the inference is always defeasible. The most plausibly ascribable intention in context from an audience's point of view may turn out to be mistaken.[28] Utterance meaning, in brief, is never *constitutive* of utterer's meaning, however good a *guide* it is to it in most circumstances.

VII

Gary Iseminger, following Hirsch, has produced a clear and elegant argument that he has tentatively labeled "an intentional demonstration," that is, a demonstration that actual intentionalism in literary interpretation is correct.[29] His test case is the opening stanza of a poem by Gerard Manley Hopkins, "Henry Purcell," about the celebrated seventeenth-century English composer.[30] Two possible interpretive statements about Hopkins's poem are these: (1A) "Henry Purcell" expresses the wish that Henry Purcell shall have had good fortune, and (1B) "Henry Purcell" does not express the wish that Henry Purcell shall have had good fortune. Here, now, is Iseminger's demonstration:

1. The preceding stanza is compatible with both statement 1A and statement 1B about "Henry Purcell."
2. Exactly one of the two statements 1A and 1B is a true interpretive statement about "Henry Purcell."
3. If exactly one of two interpretive statements about a poem, each of which is compatible with its text, is true, then the true one is the one that conforms to the meaning intended by the author.
4. Therefore, of the two statements 1A and 1B, the true one is the one that conforms to the meaning intended by the author.[31]

Part of me would like to accede in this demonstration. For one, I concur with two of its three premises. For another, I share much of the argument's background motivation, particularly the desire to distinguish brute texts from literary works, and the conviction that what makes a text into a poem, and in part the poem that it is, is an intention resident outside that text as such.

Unfortunately, I have come not to believe in its conclusion, namely, the coincidence of literary meaning and authorially intended meaning. In my view, naturally, the culprit in this argument is the third premise, which holds that if just one of two opposed interpretations of that opening stanza, each of which is compatible with its brute text, that is, word sequence in English circa 1880, is true, then the true one is the one that conforms to the meaning intended by Hopkins. The justification for this, of course, is that if the stanza's – and by extension, the poem's – meaning is to be determinate, so as to at least license either a given interpretive statement or its negation with regard to it, then such determinacy can be reasonably supplied *only* by the lines meaning what the poet actually intended them to mean in writing them. And it is by identifying the poem in part with actually willed or intended meanings that the poem can be distinguished from the brute text, which is potentially ingredient in other, distinct poetic works.

It will be no surprise at this point why I find this brief for premise 3 insufficiently compelling. The determinacy in question, I maintain, can just as easily and reasonably come from an audience's best contextually informed hypothesis of authorial intention in a given passage, all things considered. So in the case at hand, in particular, if one takes into account Hopkins's unusual metrical and grammatical practices in other poems, his known religious views and sympathies (it is significant that, though born into the Anglican church, he converted to Catholicism in 1866 and subsequently entered the priesthood), his documented appreciation for Purcell's music, and the demands of coherence with the remainder of the poem, it turns out that the informed reader's best projection of what Hopkins was intending to convey in the opening stanza will make it determinately the case that the wish for past good fortune in spiritual matters, rather than anything exclusive of that, is what is expressed.[32] In addition to securing determinacy as represented by premise 2, such optimally hypothesized semantic intentions, together with concomitant actual categorial intentions, are more than enough to distinguish the poem from the text per se, and from other potential poems employing the same text, penned by poets other than Hopkins, or Hopkins himself at a different historical or cultural juncture, or even a more counterfactual Hopkins conjured up by altering aspects of the situation in which "Henry Purcell" was in fact indited.

Furthermore, not only is specific context-based hypothetical intentionalism equally as efficacious in underpinning minimal determinacy of meaning and in constituting a poem from a mere text, but it seems to me to have two signal advantages over actual intentionalism in this matter. One is that it preserves the intuitive difference between what ends up being *said* (or conveyed) in a complex discourse situation, whether literary or nonliterary, and what some agent was *trying* (or aiming) to say, that is, what someone – not some work – meant.[33] The second, closely related, is that it acknowledges the special interests, and attendant constraints, of the practice or activity of *literary* communication, according to which works – provided they are interpreted with maximal attention to relevant author-specific context, and thus really as the works of so-and-so – are ultimately more important than, and distinct from, the individuals who author them and those individuals' inner lives; works of literature thus retain, in the last analysis, a certain autonomy from the actual mental processes of their creators during composition, at least as far as resultant meaning is concerned. It is this small but crucial dimension of distinctness between agent's meaning and work's meaning – even when the latter is understood as roughly an optimal reader's best projection of the former from the text-in-full-context – which is obliterated by actual intentionalism but safeguarded by the hypothetical variety.

It is interesting to note that, in principle, different literary works turn out to be ambiguous on hypothetical intentionalism (HI) than on actual intentionalism (AI), though it is not obvious that more turn out ambiguous on the former than the latter. Cases where there is no optimally projectible intention for a given passage, but where a clear authorial intention exists (though beyond the reach of an individual in ideal reader position) will be ambiguous on HI but unambiguous on AI, whereas cases where a contextually informed ideal reader can arrive at a best attributable intention, though no such clear authorial intention exists or existed, will be ambiguous on AI but unambiguous on HI. Of special note would be cases where there are two divergent though equally defensible projections, all things considered, of authorial intent – that is, two "good" projections possible, which would indicate a work with an inherently dual, or disjunctive,

meaning. In such cases we see again that the meaning of a work according to HI can outstrip its meaning according to AI: let the author have in actuality only one of the two optimally projectible intentions just posited.

I now turn to the specific ontology that Iseminger recommends as part and parcel of the actual intentionalism he favors. This is an ontology, as already noted, to which I am broadly sympathetic, taking its raison d'être as it does from the obvious nonidentity between literary works and the brute texts out of which, in a sense, they are composed. My sympathy, however, does not run to complete agreement, for two reasons. One is that I think there are some unintuitive consequences of Iseminger's particular proposal. The other is that I have my own previously developed and similarly motivated ontological proposal for type artworks, which I think answers better to the critical and experiential data.

Iseminger offers the following, which he labels the Revised Identity Thesis: "A (typical) literary work is a textually embodied conceptual structure, whose conceptual component is (identical to) the structure – compatible with its text – which its author intended (meant) in composing it."[34]

In other words, seeing clearly that brute texts, that is, word sequences in a language, are not enough to individuate poems, that is, works of literature with specific meanings and qualities rooted in their authors' identities and life worlds, Iseminger arrives at the plausible suggestion that a poem is the sum or complex of the text and the specific literary content of which it is the vehicle, that is, a set of thoughts or ideas. A literary work is in effect an ordered pair of a text (verbal structure) and a meaning (conceptual structure). Though there are, in an abstract way, texts without authors, there are no literary works without authors, for only by being used to carry given meaning does a text become transformed into a work of literature.

My first qualm about this suggestion is perceptual. You can read a poem – that being a central mode of access to such – but can you read a conceptual structure, which constitutes part of the poem on Iseminger's proposal? Can you scan, recite, count the number of lines in, or grasp the rhyme scheme of a conceptual structure – even a textually embodied one? From being fundamentally a verbal object, a poem becomes on Iseminger's formula fundamentally a conceptual one – or at least as much a conceptual object as a verbal one. But we have just seen that this is a mistake. We must instead retain the idea that a poem is at base a structure of words, so that the fundamental activities proper to poems still make sense, while somehow acknowledging that the poem is not the brute text – the word sequence *simpliciter* – out of all connection to the particular author and act of writing. My own preference is to regard a poem as a *text-as-indicated-in-a-context*, which as a result *has* a certain meaning or conceptual content without *being* such, even in part.[35] It acquires this content through its being indicated or projected by an author A with artistically relevant characteristics R in literary context C, not necessarily through what the writer intends it to mean. What determines the content it has – rather than is – is again the best hypothesis of authorial meaning arrivable at by audiences fully cognizant of A, C, and R.

My principal objection to Iseminger's proposal is thus its distorting the basic kind of thing a poem is. Here, though, is another objection. On Iseminger's proposal, a given individual on a given day could write two poems, in the same genre, by writing down the same eight-line text twice, alternating inscriptions of each sentence, but thinking/intending different construals with each inscription, so yielding distinct conceptual structures. But this seems wildly implausible. If poems with identical texts are distinct, it must be differences in the context of generation, and thus appropriate later context of understanding, that differentiate them.[36] A difference in provenance or projection, not just fleeting authorial construal, must ground artistic difference among identical structures.

A person might be able to mean different things in ordinary discourse, by saying the same words over twice within the space of a few minutes, by virtue of his inner states during those utterings; but the nature of the literary "language game" does not, I would claim, allow for identical texts issuing from the same person at the same time to count as different in meaning – at least not by virtue of the writer's concurrent semantic intendings. It is instead by having a differential categorial intention, not by meaning or conceiving different things during penning, that the one text might just barely generate a different poem from the other. And for such subtly nuanced categorial intentions to be effective – even for the artist – the poet seemingly would have to avail himself of some internal individuating device, for example, different titles, or

different dates appended to the two texts, and so on.

One last objection, which cuts in the opposite direction from the preceding. On Iseminger's proposal two people with different literary identities and backgrounds would yet write the same poem if they produced the same text and had the same meaning in mind. But there are reasons to think there would be artistic differences between such poems (e.g. by virtue of different relations, resonances, with other works of their respective authors), thus confounding the supposition of their identity.[37]

VIII

This is a good juncture at which to observe that distinguishing between texts and literary works in the manner that I suggest pretty much douses, whereas that favored by Iseminger only fans the flames of, a worry that concerns a number of writers: that of the elusive identity of literary works, which seem to change as one goes from one interpretation of them to the next. For Michael Krausz, say, the literary work, or object-of-interpretation, varies as interpretations vary.[38] So regarding Wordsworth's familiar lyric "A slumber did my spirit seal" there is, according to Krausz, *F. W. Bateson's* "A slumber . . . ," and then there is *Cleanth Brooks's* "A slumber. . . ." These objects-of-interpretation, not being strictly identical to one another, have yet sufficient overlap for critical purposes, for example, comparison and mutual confrontation, which overlap is then labeled "unicity."

These, however, are unnecessary complications, a product both of constructivist metaphysical inclinations and the decision, shared with Iseminger, to see a literary work on the level of ontology as partly its meaning, or content under an interpretation. But this is to confuse a property or aspect of the thing with the thing itself. There is no difficulty whatsoever with saying that there is just one poem ("A slumber . . ." or "Henry Purcell"), though there are perhaps numerous interpretations or readings of it – so long as we recognize that the poem is not, of course, the brute text that it comprises but rather that text poetically projected in a specific context anchored to a particular person, time, and place. That anchoring, together with the text's complete orthography, is enough to fix a literary work's identity for all critical intents and purposes, and so there is no need to bring meanings, conceptual complexes, or interpretive guises into it. A poem as I suggest we ontologically construe it will, to be sure, *generate* meanings and conceptual structures under interpretation, correct or incorrect, multiple or singular; but the poem itself is not to be *identified*, even partially, with such meanings, concepts, thoughts, or views.

IX

A main thrust of Noël Carroll's engaging essay on the issues that concern us is to undercut opposition to intentionalism that derives from the belief that the context of literary discourse is significantly different from that of ordinary conversation, so that the intentionalism that is an exceedingly natural perspective in the latter case is not appropriate in the former.[39] I am in partial agreement with that thrust, since I would hold, with Carroll, that a more absolute disjunction between the two contexts than is warranted is a characteristic of a number of recent influential theories of literary meaning, such as Beardsleyan "New Criticism" and Barthesian "death-of-author-ism." But *contra* Carroll, I think there are residual differences between the contexts, and the rules and procedures of decipherment that hold sway in them.

One difference, it seems to me, between literary and conversational situations is that utterer's meaning is virtually all-important in the latter, whereas the meaning of the vehicle itself, if opposed to the former, counts for virtually nothing. I agree that when an author proffers a text as literature to a literary audience, just as when he or she speaks to others in the ordinary setting, the author is entering a public language game, a communicative arena, but I suggest that it is one with different aims and understandings from those that apply in normal, one-on-one, or even many-on-many, conversational settings. Although in informative discourse we rightly look for intended meaning first, foremost, and hindmost, in literary art we are licensed, if I am right, to consider what meanings the verbal text before us, viewed in context, *could* be being used to convey, and then to form, if we can, in accord with the practice of literary communication to which both author and reader have implicitly subscribed, our best hypothesis of what it is being used to convey, ultimately identifying that with the meaning of the work. What distin-

guishes our forming that hypothesis in regard to a literary work, as opposed to a piece of conversation, is that we do so for its own sake, the contextually embedded vehicle of meaning in literature being indispensable, not something to be bypassed in favor of more direct access to personal meaning when or if that is available.

So it seems to me that literary and practical linguistic communication are to be distinguished, at least in some respects. Carroll errs in denying or minimizing any difference in the operative conditions and criteria of the two. In this I am in agreement with Richard Shusterman, in his recent reflections on our topic.[40] But I am very far from anchoring the distinctness of literary and practical modes of communication, as Shusterman does, by ascribing historically unconstrained and reader-driven interpretability to the former. We may admit various types of literary interpretation, answering to interests other than those of truth, expression, and communication, while still holding it possible to locate among them what I have called basic interpretation, and to characterize in a fairly stable manner what that must orient itself toward. Only in relation to the results of basic, author-and-history respecting, interpretation, can such further modes of interpretation have a proper foothold and warrant. Shusterman claims that even if textual meaning (i.e., what I would call work meaning) is, as Knapp and Michaels insist, ineluctably intentional, there is no reason to think it must always be authors' intentions that are at issue.[41] Textual meaning is inseparable from intention, Shusterman allows, but perhaps reader's intentions are as relevant to determining, or contributing to, textual meaning as those of authors. This enfranchising of reader's intentions, purposes, or perspectives, unconstrained by the goal of hypothetically reconstructing best authorial intention, is a good illustration of the ludic model of interpretation, mentioned earlier, taken as paramount. By contrast, a virtue of hypothetical intentionalism stands out clearly, which is to mediate between a position, actual intentionalism, which gives just a little too much to authors as persons, and a ludic position such as that of Shusterman (or, more extremely, Rorty, Barthes, or Derrida), which gives altogether too much to readers, and threatens to undermine the motivations of authors for upholding their end of the implicit literary contract.[42] Lest I be misunderstood, let me remark that I regard ludic interpretation, about which I will have no more to say in this essay, as potentially an exciting and rewarding exercise in its own right, and a harmless one – so long as it does not displace the primary project of discerning fundamental, authorially anchored, if not authorially determined, literary meaning.

But to return to Carroll's essay, there is much I find congenial in it. Carroll rightly observes that having tentatively accepted the basic relevance of authorial intention, one can avoid being driven back into anti-intentionalism by the problem of aberrant authorial pronouncements, for these need not be taken at face value: the finished work will often make incredible certain stated intents. And Carroll generally agrees with Lyas, sensibly enough, that the intentions most relevant to literary or cinematic works are ones that are largely evident in the works themselves, including both successful and failed intentions, and that these should be conceived not after the fashion of private mental episodes but instead in neo–Wittgensteinian fashion, as fully embodied in behavior and the products thereof.

It is the next step in Carroll's brief that concerns me:

> Insofar as the intention is identified as the purposive structure of the work, this intention is the focus of our interest in and attention to the artwork . . . tracking the intention – the purposive structure of the work – is the very point of appreciation. . . . The more attractive, neo–Wittgensteinian view of intention not only makes authorial intention relevant to the interpretation of artworks, but implies that in interpreting an artwork, we are attempting to determine the author's intentions.[43]

I am inclined to concur with what is said here, but only if transposed into the key of hypothetical intentionalism, or if charitably taken as having a sense compatible with that already. The discernible purposive structure of the work can be identified with the author's intention, I would say, only if by this last one really means an optimal construction of authorial intention from the viewpoint of an ideal reader, imbued with the sorts of background information sketched earlier. For, Wittgenstein or no Wittgenstein, it is still possible for an author's semantic intentions in regard to a work, in whole or in part, not to be fully embodied in that work plus its ideal reader-accessible context of production.[44] And though it is true that "in interpreting

an artwork we are attempting to determine the author's intentions," the actual author's intentions function here mainly as a heuristic goal, and success in this attempt is to be measured not by correctly arriving at that actual intention which may still, despite Lyas's and Carroll's confident internalism, be grounded in matters external to the total literary context, but by the process of constructing, projecting, or hypothesizing a most plausible authorial intention, in light of both the text and the literature-germane circumstances of its issuance, having come satisfactorily to an end.

Perhaps Carroll's most striking example of a case of an artwork whose correct interpretation putatively requires us to advert to the author's actual intentions, even though we can, by ignoring such intentions, arrive at an interpretation that makes the work more rewarding aesthetically, concerns a grade B (or C) science-fiction movie of 1959, Edward Wood's *Plan 9 from Outer Space*. Carroll claims that Wood's film, which contains narrative incoherence and editing discontinuities, is not properly seen as "boldly and provocatively transgressing Hollywood codes" (as *Village Voice* film critic J. Hoberman has suggested) because Wood did *not* have the intentions in filmmaking that avant-gardists of the 1970's or 1980's had, with whom Wood is being ranged by this suggestion. I certainly agree with Carroll in rejecting Hoberman's interpretation as a correct one – as opposed to a practical recommendation for dealing with schlock most enjoyably – but am not convinced that Wood's *actual* semantic intentions need be called to account. For can't we say that such expressive intent as Hoberman ascribes to Wood is simply not our best *hypothesis* of such intent, given all appropriate internal and external evidence, such as Wood's solid track record of earlier hack films? Indeed, if we read him closely, this is precisely what Carroll does appear to say:

> All the evidence indicates that Edward Wood did not have the same intentions to subvert the Hollywood style of filmmaking that contemporary avant-gardists have. Indeed, given the venue Wood trafficked in, it seems the best hypothesis about his intentions is that he was attempting to imitate the Hollywood style of filmmaking in the cheapest way possible. Given what we know of Edward Wood and the B-film world in which he practiced his trade, it is

implausible to attribute to him the intention of attempting to subvert the Hollywood codes of filmmaking.[45]

Thus hypotheticized authorial (or, in this case, directorial) intent is perfectly adequate to handle the case of Wood's movie, that is, to avoid attributing avant-garde meaning and merit to it. Though we take aim at directorial intent, in our hypothetical construction of cinematic meaning, this doesn't entail that a director's actual semantic intent, whether plausibly hypothesizable or not, is determinant of such meaning.[46]

X

Carroll musters other considerations, however, which he labels "ontological," in arguing against Barthes's and Beardsley's extreme anti-intentionalisms. Barthes claims that when language is divorced from normal communicative purposes and narrated "intransitively," as in literature, the author and his intentions immediately become irrelevant, and the reader is instead freed "to explore the text in all its intertextual associations."[47] Carroll's reply to this is astutely skeptical:

> I am not sure that once language is used "intransitively," the author becomes irrelevant, since identifying such a use would appear to depend on fixing the author's *intention to work in certain genres or forms* [my emphasis], viz., those that function intransitively. That is, how will the interpreter know that the writing in question is of the right sort to be read in a writerly fashion without adverting to authorial intentions?[48]

This is exactly on the mark, but the point to note is that the real authorial intentions that it is crucial to get right here are categorial intentions, not semantic, that is, expressive or symbolic, ones.

In another observation in this vein Carroll says, in light of work in film, dance, and painting, as well as literature, that because in art we are often interested in doings, we must also be interested in intentions, for an action is the action it is only by virtue of the intention that informs it. But I would suggest that where the "doings" in question are semantic, for example, symbolic or expressive ones, as opposed to ones of creating, framing, projecting, it is open to us to ascribe such "doings" to the work

directly, and only indirectly to the artist, by virtue of his "doings" – his performance of actions – of that other sort. And that would mean that as far as art was concerned, our interest in what has been done would take us only so far as the actual categorial intentions of artists, allowing ideally hypothesizable semantic intentions sway in fixing what, if anything, has been meant.

This brings me, finally, to a suggestion Carroll makes in the course of his discussion of Beardsley's claim that literature always involves the *representation* of illocutionary actions – stating, questioning, relating, discoursing, haranguing – and never the actual performance of such – for example, by the author. After fairly observing that not all literature is, in the first instance, fictional, Carroll goes on to propose that there is no justification, even where it is literary fiction that is concerned, for universally positing an implied speaker or narrator distinct from the author, thus insulating the stating, questioning, and so on that often seems to be going on from the actual individual whose blood, sweat, and tears appear to have gone into the book. Carroll makes his strongest case for this in connection with what might be labeled essayistic or didactic novels, such as Tolstoy's *War and Peace*, Mann's *The Magic Mountain*, and Proust's *A la recherche du temps perdu*. Of the discursive portions of such novels, for instance, the discourse on whales in Melville's *Moby-Dick*, he says that, "though housed in fictions, where they undeniably perform a literary function, these are also essays whose authors produced them in order to make assertions. In interpreting these interludes, one needs to approach them as one would any other form of cognitive discourse."[49]

Though I recognize the motivation for wanting to connect the views expressed in literary works with the authors of those works, I think it cannot be done as easily as Carroll would like, even in the case of such quasi-essays. This is because the "nonfiction" parts of an essentially fictional work must, on pain of incoherence, first be attributed to an implied speaker or narrator of the sort Beardsley (following Wayne Booth) invokes. I will try to explain why. The narrator of a novel is fundamentally someone whom we agree to pretend is telling us about people and events that, of course, we know are fictions. That is to say, we know that, by and large, the people of the narrator's "world" do not really exist and the events of that "world" did not really happen. The narrator is, therefore, a particular sort of fictional character himself, who is in "contact" with things out of our ken and who "believes" in things we don't; he or she can't be taken to be a real individual expressing real beliefs. But the essayish portions of something like Melville's *Moby-Dick* or Mann's *The Magic Mountain* are understood to issue from the same persona, the same voice as is relating the narrative of fictional people and events: there are cross-references, allusions, similarities of style, explicit self-identifications, and so on. These essayish portions must, then, be the direct utterances of the fictional narrator of the novel's fictional occurrences. They cannot logically be unmediated pronouncements of the real person of the author – Thomas Mann, say – because Mann, unlike his narrator, is not someone who believes in Hans Castorp and Clavdia Chauchat and who reports that the two had an encounter at a Swiss sanatorium. This is not to deny that we are often entitled, by virtue of our more comprehensive grasp of the whole context of literary communication involved, to then infer, in given cases, that the author is virtually speaking, sometimes preaching, to readers in his own person via that of the narrator. But the narrator remains, in a traditional, non-self-deconstructive novel, as the immediate locus of all ostensibly direct pronouncements.

Making the narrative and essayistic portions out to have different sources, in *The Magic Mountain* or *Moby-Dick*, threatens the artistic integrity of these ambitious works – they become neither fiction nor nonfiction.[50] Only if the fictional premise is in place throughout, however transparently, is it possible to interpret such novels intelligibly and favorably; for without such an assumption the minimal unity of voice or narrational identity necessary to construe the texts as wholes disappears.

So this attempt to establish semantic intentionalism, at least for the essayistic portions of novels, seems to me not to go through in the way Carroll suggests. And if not here, one may rightly ask, then where?

XI

The position I favor is located somewhere in the logical space between that espoused by Carroll, in the essay just discussed, and that embraced by Daniel Nathan, in an essay I am about to discuss.[51] Where I disagree with Carroll is in insisting explicitly that the most defensible intentionalism is

of the hypothetical or constructive variety; we might consider this a "leftist" version of intentionalism. Where I will disagree with Nathan, on the other hand, is in suggesting that the most defensible anti-intentionalism – of which hypothetical intentionalism could be seen as a "far rightist" version – must acknowledge a readerly context of textual reception considerably broader, more replete than that which Nathan is prepared to contemplate.

Nathan grants that a literary text, to be properly interpreted, must be understood to be in a language in a relatively rich sense, one tied to the usage of a particular time and place, with all connotative and associative aspects intact.[52] When the language of the text is so understood, and when one takes care to consider the complete text involved, says Nathan, one is in an adequate position to assign to such a text its best sense, including whether it is ironical or metaphorical. In this way, he claims, is vindicated "the sufficiency of public conventions of usage to resolve questions of meaning."[53]

But I think it is clear that if this rather thin notion of a text's public context suffices in some cases to allow discrimination of its literary content, there are many cases in which it will not – many cases in which confining one's projection of work meaning to what can be grounded in the text and the specific public language in which it is written will not accord with what entrenched critical opinion or considered judgment would rather take this content to be. Nathan's notion of context is simply too narrow to do the job – the job of allowing a work's full content to emerge – because it is not an *author-specific* context. Two writers writing the same texts in the same public language of a given time and place may still end up saying different things, by virtue of their national identities, what they have done in the world, what circles they belong to, what their other works are like, and so on, all of which are relevantly brought to bear by potential readers and which then qualify, in subtle ways, what the full utterance is that each writer is making in employing the text in question – in literating it, so to speak, from out of who he or she is. Nathan relatedly fails to see that specific information about an author's other works, his general stance in civic life, and so on – and not just what is given in the text or its observable manner of presentation – can serve to modify or cancel what he labels "background default assumptions"[54] for construing some stretch of discourse in the usual public language fashion.

Consider something as simple and as timely as the judgment that a given newspaper column (or story, poem, etc.) is or is not racist (sexist, ageist, anti-Semitic, etc.). It seems we do not – and properly do not – form such judgments only from the language of the text itself and its current connotative resonances. Rather, nothing is more common than to consider the gender, vintage, and ethnic identity of the author, his or her public persona, his or her track record in previous writings or in the political sphere more generally, and any peculiar beliefs or trademark opinions that have become part of the author's known worldview. What is more, such writers *expect* readers to take this into account as a background frame for assessing the force and import of what is actually said. When William Buckley writes something, it means one thing; when Richard Cohen, or William Raspberry, or Judy Mann, or Dorothy Gilliam writes the very same "thing," and at roughly the same place and time, it can mean something else.[55] This is not to say one cannot express a view or attitude in print contrary to what might be expected for one or another of one's "identification groups" or even one's own specific past self, but this will require careful decisions as to how and what to write in order to accomplish that; at the least, an author who neglects to consider the background set of the informed reader in respect to where the author is publicly "coming from," as the current phrase has it, is sure not to communicate effectively what he or she wishes to. I should stress that though my illustration refers to journalistic writers of nonfiction, the moral clearly applies, if more indirectly, to writers of literary fiction.

The following, at least, are plausibly elements in relevant author-specific interpretive contexts: the author's ancillary theoretical pronouncements; the rest of the author's corpus; the work of those of the author's contemporaries of whom he was aware; the social movements or political developments of the time that had a demonstrable impact on the author; and the author's participation in or identification with artistic movements. The real issue, to my mind, is not whether *any* of this is relevant, as a New Critic might wonder – I think it incontestably is – but what the *limits* of relevant author-specific contextuality are.[56] How individualized a context can an author, in his own mind, be effectively writing out of, and how extensive a grasp of such context can an author – particularly a literary one – legitimately expect of even an ideal reader? I don't have a principled answer to this, but

it is where I believe future discussion should focus. Where Nathan and I would agree is that excluded from such context, at least, is any fact about the author's actual mental state or attitude during composition, in particular what I have called his semantic intentions for a text.

Nathan observes fairly that "the actual author must always intend . . . that [a work's] meaning be borne in a sufficiently public fashion that he need not personally accompany it to explain the meaning he placed there. Actual authors intend to create a work that can stand on its own, to send their work off complete, capable of being understood by its audience."[57] My response to this is a qualified affirmative: yes, but arguably only when such audiences bear in mind the author's specific nature, oeuvre, background, intellectual breeding ground, and so on. The work, if any good, will stand on its own, without the author on hand to explain regularly what he meant – but only if taken as the work of that specific author, with all that entails.

Literary meaning is generated out of knowledge shared between an author and his or her readers, but there is no reason to take it that the author must rely on communicating only on the basis of shared knowledge of the world and language generally, rather than the author's "own," more individualized, world and language, of which an ideal reader will apprise himself, to an appropriate extent. This needn't – and more, mustn't – require of the reader "inside" knowledge, so to speak, that which may be in the possession only of family members, private secretaries, and clairvoyants – as much as publicly accessible knowledge of the author's distinctive cultural identity and situation. For it is that, in part, which enables the creation and communication of aesthetic vehicles with richer, more finely nuanced contents than if we preclude any possibility of readers coming to authors with more than common knowledge of world and language in their interpretive kits. Why should authors be forced to present themselves on the literary stage as only Everymen, stripped of their individual identities and pasts behind a kind of critical "veil of ignorance"? Why should we accept only the more etiolated or generalized contents their writings will attain if we insist in taking them in that way?

XII

I have proposed that the ideal reader, in his or her attempt to construct a most plausible communicative intention for the author in relation to a given work, should take into account the intrinsic features of the text, the operative conventions and norms of the language and genre involved, and a number of author-specific though public contextual factors as well, but should stop short of the author's actual pronouncements of intent to mean or convey this or that. It has been objected that this cutoff of relevant evidence is arbitrary and thus should be abandoned, which would have the consequence, unfavorable to hypothetical intentionalism, that actual intentionalism and hypothetical intentionalism always converged in the hypotheses they generated as to what a literary work means.[58]

My response to this challenge is as follows. First, even if the hypotheses generated always did converge there would still be a theoretical difference as to why such hypotheses were to be identified with the work's meaning – in the one case, that this just was what the author meant, and in the other, that this was the best projection of what the author meant from an ideal reader's point of view – and I have tried to make the case for hypothetical intentionalism's correctness on this point.

Second, it is arguably one of the ground rules of the game of literary decipherment that literary works are not supposed to require authors to explain what they mean, and thus that direct authorial pronouncements of meaning can be set aside by the reader devoted to the central job of interpretation. The task of intuiting our way to an optimal construal of authorial intention for a text emerging from a rich author-specific public context is simply different from that of arriving at the truth about the author's intention with respect to a given text, from all the available evidence of no matter what sort – diaristic, journalistic, or electroencephalographic. Though as appreciators of literature we are entitled and expected to construe an author's offering against the background of the author's earlier work and the author's public identity as a writer, and in light of the author's explicit intentions for how a work is to be approached on the categorial plane (e.g. as a historical novel), we are, I think, implicitly enjoined from allowing an author's proclamations of meaning achieved to have an *evidential* role in the construction of a picture of what the author is most reasonably thought to have been trying to convey through that text offered in that context. Of course, such statements of intention may have a *suggestive* role in regard to such construction, but that is another matter.

But third, suppose one remains unconvinced that the practice of construing literature involves any such delimitation on what is to be taken into account in formulating hypotheses regarding what texts taken in context have been intended to convey, and thus that in such formulating notice is rightly taken of direct authorial pronouncements of meaning. Surely at least this much difference will remain between the interpretive task of a reader of literature and that of someone out to ascertain the real truth about authorial intention, by hook or by crook. Namely, that in the former task, an author's direct pronouncements will be given *minor* weight – a provisional status, easily discountable in favor of other factors in the total situation – whereas in the latter task such pronouncements, while perhaps not always determinative, will be given *major* weight, one at least equal to that accorded any more internal indications.

XIII

One literary phenomenon that might be thought to call absolutely for actual intentionalist treatment is that of *allusion*, whether from one work to another or from a work to some extraliterary matter. As it happens, Göran Hermerén has recently provided a detailed analysis of this phenomenon, in an essay devoted to the topic.[59] As Hermerén quite sensibly submits, to allude is to perform an action, and actions are performed by agents, so the existence and identity of an allusion, a sophisticated action of referring, would seem to be bound up with a concrete intention on some agent's part.[60] Thus if there are allusions in a work of literature, and if these are part of its meaning in a broad sense, then meaning will apparently depend directly, in part, on certain semantic intentions of the author.

The phenomenon of allusion clearly poses about the hardest case for any kind of thoroughgoing nonintentionalism regarding the meaning of literary works. Since hypothetical intentionalism is, from one angle, a species of nonintentionalism about work meaning, some accommodation with allusion, if possible, is in order.

I think if we distinguish between (a) allusion as a property of an author or an author's act in creating a work, and (b) allusion as a property of a work, then there is at least one sense of the latter that is not dependent on or tied to the former – that is, actual author's act of alluding – but only to a reasonably projected such act, whether or not realized in actuality. What I am suggesting is that work allusion, as opposed to artist allusion, *can* be understood to operate contextually – where the notion of context is a highly artist-specific one – and as not requiring an artist's will or knowledge to secure the reference involved.

The allusive reference of one work to another can be seen as independent, if not of the concrete context in which the work is generated and put forward, at least of the actual act of referring, if any there be, on the artist's part. And that is where the work is, taken in context, *most reasonably construed* to have been a vehicle of allusion on the creator's part.

Consider the case of a title that would be taken as a manifest allusion, given full knowledge of author and style, yet was not so intended or thought of by author. I think we might say the work alludes to this earlier thing even if the author was not alluding in so titling it, because that is a defensible projection of intent on the author by an appropriately informed audience. Clearly, in any event, such a work will be construed by the best-informed of auditors – in fact, particularly by them – as if the author were alluding, in the robust sense. So it seems not inapt to label this aspect of a work, which such readers would be responding to, its allusiveness.

Here is a concrete example. One section in Bruce Duffy's remarkable novel *The World as I Found It*,[61] about the lives, ideas, and interactions, romanticized to be sure, of Ludwig Wittgenstein, Bertrand Russell, and G. E. Moore, carries the heading "A Modest Proposal." The section deals with Russell's mental preparations for, and actual propositioning of, a beautiful young Belgian teacher who has just come to work at the school he has set up in the English countryside, and follows directly a section whose focus is the destructive antics of a misfit of a pupil recently deposited at the school, whom Russell and his wife are at wit's end to get rid of. Thus given such an internal context, and assuming in addition an Irish extraction for the author, it seems unavoidable that the heading in question be taken as an allusion to Swift's famous essay on the potato famine in Ireland and the naturalness of ameliorating it by consuming and hence doing away with excess children. As such, the heading neatly ties together the two sections in question, describing with a touch of litotes the substance of the section to which it is affixed, just as, in its allusive aspect, it makes explicit the sort of drastic solution to the problem of unwanted urchins that

it is hinted Russell in his extremity may have been driven to contemplate, if only idly.

The point to make now is that we would still insist on retaining the attribution of allusion or allusiveness, on some level, even if it were determined that Duffy himself was, improbably, ignorant of Swift's essay and had come up with his section heading only as a chiding label for Russell's rather immodest priapic ambitions – and thus that he, Duffy, was not literally alluding to Swift at all. And that is because we would still have every reason, as competent readers, to attribute such an intention and action to Duffy, given the internal evidence of his novel and the external evidence of his public position as an educated, twentieth-century Anglophone author.

Consider next, for variety's sake, a musical example. The first idea in the concluding *Galop* section of Khatchaturian's 1944 *Masquerade Suite* alludes, I submit, to the "Chicks in Their Shells" section of Mussorgsky's *Pictures at an Exhibition* in Ravel's 1922 orchestration. This is so, I claim, because the resemblance is striking – melodically, instrumentally, and expressively – and because Khatchaturian was trained and steeped in the tradition of Russian orchestral music, and so could be expected to be familiar with the Mussorgsky–Ravel *Pictures*. I would say that the attribution of allusiveness, and not just reminiscence, holds even if (a) Khatchaturian were to deny any explicit allusive intention, (b) Khatchaturian were truly not to recall ever hearing the Mussorgsky–Ravel *Pictures*, and even if, what would be yet more astonishing, (c) Khatchaturian had, by some happenstance, never had any encounter with the Mussorgsky–Ravel *Pictures* at all, thus blocking the suggestion of even an unacknowledged, unconscious allusive intention. Of course, in this last and most contentious case, we could not say that *Khatchaturian* was alluding to the Mussorgsky–Ravel *Pictures*, but we could, I think, rightly say that that section of *the piece*, as penned by a composer with Khatchaturian's profile and music-historical situatedness, was doing so. And this, to relate the case to our basic analysis, is because such an allusive intention would be one we were more than justified in hypothetically attributing to Khatchaturian, given the intrinsic character of the music and its full context of creation. The music ends up meaning that – being allusive of the Mussorgsky–Ravel *Pictures* – at one level that is independent of Khatchaturian's actual allusive intention or lack thereof.[62]

XIV

Those, such as hypothetical intentionalists, who maintain a strict logical distinction between what a text or work means and what an author means in writing it may still wonder whether what a passage of text means is also legitimately thought of as, *in some sense*, what the author meant. Does an author mean M if his or her text, knowingly projected, means M?

Because of a deep ambiguity in the notion of what an author means in penning a text, there is no simple answer. If the passage means M, and the passage occurs in a literary work knowingly projected by the author in conformity with the rules and conventions of the literary game, then presumably the author means M in the *broad*, or indirect, sense that he means *the text*, and the text means *M*, so by a sort of transitivity he ends up meaning M. Otherwise put, an author surely intends that the text he or she offers in the literary arena should have whatever meaning, interpreted in an appropriate and contextually sensitive way, it manages to have. But these admissions do not entail that the author will have meant M in the *narrow*, or direct, sense. The author doubtless acknowledges wanting the work to have the meanings it does, but does not necessarily want the work to mean *M*, where the content of M figures explicitly in thought. And in some cases an author might explicitly intend a meaning M1 and foresee but not intend a meaning M2; that is, the author recognizes M2 but does not purpose it. So in the broad sense, we might still say that the author meant M2 if his or her work means M2, though not in the narrow sense.

Throughout this essay one of my leading concerns has been the issue of the potential gap between (1) what an author intended to convey in writing his or her text and (2) an ideal reader's best construction or hypothesis of that intention, given ample knowledge of the author's and text's relevantly engaged diachronic and synchronic context. The gap narrows to zero if we take it that (2) in effect constitutes (1), just as warranted assertibility, according to some philosophers, is equivalent to or substitutable for truth. But I resist such a vanishing of the gap, because what we would most reasonably ascribe, even with all relevant knowledge as intended readers in hand, may not be what is the case, in matters of psychology and semantics.[63]

Even on a neo-Wittgensteinian view of intention, such as that favored by Lyas and Carroll, it is possible for actual intention, and best hypothetical intention from the point of view of an ideal reader, to diverge, even leaving such factors as authorial incompetence or misguidedness, usually invoked in this connection, to one side. In such cases as I have in mind an author's actual intention would be embedded in the world, but in aspects of the complete situation of the author's life and activity not open to an appropriate reader for the work and thus playing no proper part in the reader's imputation of a best semantic intention for the author in regard to the given text.

Thus, we arrive finally at neither intentionalism nor anti-intentionalism but at the form of non-intentionalism I call hypothetical intentionalism. Anti-intentionalism is right in thinking actual intention is not strictly determinative or criterial of a work's basic meaning, but intentionalism is right, first, insofar as our notion of the meaning of an artwork is one that makes essential reference to the artist's intentions, as plausibly projectible by an informed audience, and second, insofar as, in many cases ("successful ones"), artistic meaning and author's actual concrete intent happily coincide.

Knapp and Michaels have thrown down as a slogan that "there is no intentionless meaning."[64] I would concur, where literature is concerned, but not for the extreme intentionalist reasons they offer. Rather, it is because for something to be a literary work at all, rather than a set of meaningless shapes or even an abstract word sequence in a concrete language, is for it to be intended for a kind of reception whose character is given by the tradition and history of literating – for it to be created and conceived with such possible reception in mind. But the indissolubility of literature from categorial intentions of that kind does not entail that there is and can be no meaning in a literary work other than what the author in fact intended it to mean. We are in the last analysis entitled and empowered to rationally reconstruct an author as meaning, in a work, something different from what he or she did, in private and in truth, actually mean, so long as we have put ourselves in the best position for receiving the utterance of this particular historically and culturally embedded author.

Notes

1 The authors with whom I will engage were all contributors to a volume in which my essay originally appeared, *Intention and Interpretation*, ed. Gary Iseminger (Philadelphia: Temple University Press, 1992).

2 My view on these matters derives in large part from the theory of interpretation sketched by William Tolhurst in "On What a Text Is and How It Means," *British Journal of Aesthetics* 19 (1979): 3–14, though I suggest refinements to, and extensions of, what he there proposes. The view I favor is also akin to that found in Alexander Nehamas's "The Postulated Author: Critical Monism as a Regulative Ideal," *Critical Inquiry* 8 (1981): 133–49 – at least on one reading of that essay.

3 See E. D. Hirsch, *Validity in Interpretation* (New Haven: Yale University Press, 1967) and *The Aims of Interpretation* (Chicago: University of Chicago Press, 1976); P. D. Juhl, *Interpretation* (Princeton: Princeton University Press, 1980); and Mary Sirridge, "Artistic Intention and Critical Prerogative," *British Journal of Aesthetics* 18 (1978): 137–54. More recent defenses of actual intentionalism are Annette Barnes, *On Interpretation* (Oxford: Blackwell, 1988); Gary Iseminger, "An Intentional Demonstration?" in *Intention and Interpretation*, pp. 76–96; and Noël Carroll, "Art, Intention, and Conversation," in ibid., pp. 97–131. Another writer sympathetic to actual intentionalism is Robert Stecker; see his "The Role of Intention and Convention in Interpreting Artworks," *Southern Journal of Philosophy* 31 (1993): 471–90, and "Art Interpretation," *Journal of Aesthetics and Art Criticism* 52 (1994): 193–206. Finally, the crudest and most notorious recent defense of actual intentionalism is to be found in Stephen Knapp and Walter Benn Michaels, "Against Theory," in *Against Theory: Literary Studies and the New Pragmatism*, ed. W. J. T. Mitchell (Chicago: University of Chicago Press, 1985), and "Against Theory II: Hermeneutics and Deconstruction," *Critical Inquiry* 14 (1987).

4 See, most famously, W. K. Wimsatt and Monroe Beardsley, "The Intentional Fallacy," *Sewanee Review* 54 (1946). A later statement of Beardsley's position is *The Possibility of Criticism* (Detroit: Wayne State University Press, 1970). More recent defenses of anti-intentionalism, subtler in some respects than Beardsley's, are Stephen Davies, *Definitions of Art* (Ithaca: Cornell University Press, 1991), chap. 8; and Daniel Nathan, "Irony and the Artist's Intentions," *British Journal of Aesthetics* 23 (1982): 245–56, and "Irony, Metaphor, and the Problem of Intention," in *Intention and Interpretation*, pp. 183–202. Susan Feagin's "On Defining and Interpreting Art Intentionalistically," *British Journal of Aesthetics* 22 (1982): 65–77, gives support to the anti-intentionalist position, though without clearly endorsing it.

5 The distinction of word sequence meaning, utterer's meaning, and utterance meaning is clearly set out in Tolhurst's essay. It is also usefully reviewed in Jack Meiland's "The Meanings of a Text," *British Journal of Aesthetics* 21 (1981): 195–203.

6 From the Latin for "play" or "game."

7 Or several working together, as with co-authored works.

8 Arthur Danto, "Deep Interpretation," in *The Philosophical Disenfranchisement of Art* (New York: Columbia University Press, 1986), pp. 47–67.

9 Tolhurst, "On What a Text Is," p. 11. I have previously favorably invoked Tolhurst's ideas on literary interpretation in my "Artworks and the Future," in *Music, Art, and Metaphysics* (Ithaca: Cornell University Press, 1990).

10 Tolhurst, "On What a Text Is," p. 13.

11 As we shall see, this is really the crux of the issue as I conceive it: what is the scope of specific author-based contextual factors in the genesis of a literary work that are legitimately appealed to in constructing our best hypothesis of intended meaning? The answer to this, I suggest, lies somewhere between narrowing such scope, on the one hand, to nothing more than the language and century of composition, and widening it, on the other hand, so far as to encompass the expressed intentions of the author to mean such-and-such as recorded in external sources, e.g., private diaries, taped interviews. As players in the literary language game, readers are expected and entitled to take into account much more than the former, while stopping short of the latter. The question is where exactly, along this continuum, to stop.

12 Tying literary meaning to successfully realized authorial intent is central to Annette Barnes's account of interpretation in her book *On Interpretation* and is also endorsed by Robert Stecker in the essays cited in preceding notes. But I think such a strategy is problematic, because there is no way of cashing out what such success amounts to without an *independent* notion of what a work means or when it is being correctly understood. This is worth elaborating.

The basic flaw in the appeal to successfully realized intentions as a criterion of content in art is that no matter what the mode of artistic meaning – saying, expressing, symbolizing, representing – there must be an independent notion of what that consists in, in order for the intention to achieve that to be coherent and intelligible. If "W is M," where M is some kind of meaning or meaning property, be analyzed as "A intended W to have M, and A's intention was successfully realized, i.e., W has M," then clearly nothing has been explained: the analysandum recurs in the analysans. "W has M" must be given an explication that does not presuppose itself. The appeal to hypothetical or plausibly attributed intention accomplishes this, while the appeal to realized actual intention does not. On HI, to say A's intention to make W mean M was *successfully* realized is to say that A had that intention and that W does mean M, where this latter is cashed out not in terms of A's actual meaning intent but in terms of a meaning intention most reasonably ascribed to A by an informed reader or spectator. To explain W's having a semantic property S – e.g., its symbolizing such-and-such, its expressing so-and-so, or its satirizing this or that – in terms of W's creator having successfully realized his intention to S through W, or more transparently, to impart S to W, is to say nothing helpful, regardless of what S is. Rather, the analysis of such modes of artistic meaning must involve a perceiver effect or audience uptake condition. Without that, the idea of *successfully* realizing an intention to mean in one or another of these modes remains empty. The attempt to understand a work's meaning such-and-such primarily in terms of its creator's successfully realized intentions to mean is simply a nonstarter.

13 See his "Irony and the Author's Intentions."

14 Ibid., p. 248.

15 It is almost, but not quite, the case that the *utterance* meaning of Private Epistle is equatable with the *utterer*'s meaning of its predecessor, Open Letter. Although the student undoubtedly had the ironic content *in mind* while penning Open Letter, she does not intend to *convey* that to her aimed-at audience, that is, Professor Bushwacker.

16 "Irony and the Author's Intentions," p. 250.

17 The note of sympathy here with Stanley Fish's notion of interpretive communities is intended, but does not extend so far as to embrace the idea that it is the evolving consensus of such communities that fixes, through preferred strategies of interpretation, the meanings of works. Rather, such communities serve only to embody and exemplify the kinds of background assumptions and knowledge relevant to attempting to ascertain literary meanings generally.

18 The degree of knowledge, however, is not expected to be the same between authors and readers. Obviously, in most cases, an author will have a command of his own oeuvre, tradition, and public persona to a much higher degree than the average well-disposed appropriate reader.

19 The substance of this interpretation derives from Walter Sokel's *Franz Kafka* (New York: Columbia University Press, 1966) ("Arzt" is German for "doctor.")

20 I have here modified an example from Hirsch, *Validity in Interpretation*, p. 44. (In Hirsch's text the gas named is argon, but since argon, unlike chlorine,

is both invisible and odorless, that makes for an even more implausible construction of the given sentence.)

21 I mean by this phrase to exclude such as *anachronistic* meanings. An anachronistic meaning is not just one that is unlikely for an informed reader to attribute to a given author, but one that the author could not, in a strong sense, have meant. I mean to suggest also a further condition, namely that such meanings, though unintended, would not be ones that would clearly be repudiated by the author of a text whose primary meaning is such as we have justifiably projected in context.

22 Such a strategy was proposed in "Artworks and the Future" as a way of dealing with the possible Oedipal content of *Hamlet* from a Freudian perspective despite the impossibility of Shakespeare assuming any such point of view.

23 The idea behind this discussion, of course, can be traced at least to Northrop Frye's notion of "the radical of presentation." A later development of the importance of genre or kind classifications in understanding art is Kendall Walton's well-known "Categories of Art," *Philosophical Review* 79 (1970).

24 See his "Wittgensteinian Intentions," in *Intention and Interpretation*, pp. 132–51.

25 I grant that they must have embodiment somewhere in the total situation, but in some cases this may be only in an author's behavioral dispositions to respond to queries, or perhaps even only in the obtaining of certain states in the author's head.

26 Support for this view of categorial intentions can be found in remarks of Richard Wollheim on the work the artist does in creating a work of art, in his "Minimal Art," in *Minimal Art*, ed. G. Battcock (New York: Dutton, 1968), and in Timothy Binkley's "Piece: Contra Aesthetics," *Journal of Aesthetics and Art Criticism* 35 (1977): 265–77. See also my "Defining Art Historically" and "Refining Art Historically," in *Music, Art, and Metaphysics* (Ithaca: Cornell University Press, 1990).

27 "Wittgensteinian Intentions," p. 145.

28 And not, I might add, because the ghost-scanner has detected some private episode – an option that Wittgensteinians would scare one into thinking was the only alternative here.

29 See his "An Intentional Demonstration?" in *Intention and Interpretation*, pp. 76–96.

30 "Have fair fallen, O fair, fair have fallen, / so dear / To me, so arch-especial a spirit as heaves / in Henry Purcell, / An age is now since passed, since parted; / with the reversal / Of the outward sentence low lays him, / listed to a heresy, here."

31 Adapted, with some condensation, from Iseminger, "An Intentional Demonstration?" p. 77.

32 If there is, as in the present instance, a clear most-plausibly-ascribed-by-the-contextually-informed

authorial semantic intention, then the true interpretive claim is one that accords with that (e.g., 1A). If there isn't such, then the true interpretive claim is one that denies the preceding (or any univocal) ascription of content (e.g., 1B).

33 Iseminger seems to me to cloud these waters a bit when, in discussing the employment of a given sentence type to say varying things, he states that "where a given type can be used to say more than one thing, *which one . . . among the possibilities it is being used to say* [my emphasis] on a given occasion is a function of . . . the intention of the user" ("An Intentional Demonstration?" p. 17). The problem is that the phrase in italics is equivocal between "what is attempting to be said (by the speaker)" and "what ends up being said (by the speaker)," that is, between utterer's meaning and utterance meaning. The former is clearly a function of user's intention, but the latter may only be a function of intention reasonably projected on the user by a hearer sensitive to the relevant full context.

34 Iseminger, "An Intentional Demonstration?" p. 27.

35 For more on this conception, see "What a Musical Work Is," "Autographic and Allographic Art Revisited," and "Titles," in *Music, Art, and Metaphysics*.

36 Of course I have in mind here Borges's much-discussed "Pierre Menard, Author of the *Quixote*," in which the seventeenth-century Spaniard Cervantes and the nineteenth-century Frenchman Menard end up producing distinct literary works that are, however, identical in text.

37 See the essays cited in n. 35 for support of this point.

38 See Michael Krausz, "Intention and Interpretation: Hirsch and Margolis," in *Intention and Interpretation*, pp. 152–66.

39 See his "Art, Intention, and Conversation."

40 See "Interpreting with Pragmatist Intentions," in *Intention and Interpretation*, pp. 167–82, where the point is made in the course of a critique of Knapp and Michaels.

41 Ibid., pp. 169–70.

42 By contrast, one recent influential Continental view of interpretation, Jauss's Reception Theory, seems on my limited knowledge of it to aim at the kind of balance between author and reader that hypothetical intentionalism represents.

43 "Art, Intention, and Conversation," p. 101.

44 This is not, as I have cautioned earlier (n. 25), to deny that such intentions must be embodied somewhere in the physical situation of the author and his lived world, but only to insist that they may, in some unfortunate cases, be embodied in ways that are not open to discovery even by appropriate readers of the publicly available work.

45 "Art, Intention, and Conversation," pp. 119–20.

46 Carroll comes closest to displaying his intentionalism as really of the hypothetical type defended here in n. 46 of "Art, Intention, and Conversation," p. 130 – with which note I find nothing to disagree.

47 Ibid., p. 111.

48 Ibid.

49 Ibid., p. 107.

50 And not, I might add, in the less problematic way of the "New Journalism" narratives of Truman Capote, Norman Mailer, and Tom Wolfe.

51 "Irony, Metaphor, and the Problem of Intention."

52 Nathan also appeals to observable utterance features, e.g., gesture and tone of voice, for their role in giving sense to otherwise less determinate utterances; but there cannot be, on his account, anything analogous to this with written texts, whose conditions of actual emission are not part of the public face of literature but instead are closed to view in the author's study.

53 "Irony, Metaphor, and the Problem of Intention," p. 184.

54 E.g., widely known facts about the world, such as that alligators do not standardly wear shoes, which help to make a statement like "we sell alligator shoes" unambiguous in meaning. See ibid., p. 194.

55 These are columnists, some of them nationally syndicated, who appear regularly in the *Washington Post*. Their public identities, respectively and minimally, are: WASP male conservative; Jewish male liberal; black male moderate; white female liberal; black female liberal.

56 See n. 11.

57 Nathan, "Irony, Metaphor, and the Problem of Intention," p. 198.

58 This objection was advanced by Robert Stecker, in a paper delivered at the annual meeting of the American Society for Aesthetics, Santa Barbara, October 1993.

59 "Allusions and Intentions," in *Intention and Interpretation*, pp. 203–20.

60 I am leaving out many complexities and qualifications in Hermerén's review of the topic. Here, though, is a relatively concise statement of what Hermerén would apparently endorse: "To say that an artist or writer B alludes to another work of art X [of artist A] in one of his own works Y, is to say or imply that he intends those who look at Y to recall X and therefore creates Y with features reminiscent of X; and because Y has these features, beholders will . . . come to think of the earlier work; and furthermore, they will recognize that this is what artist B, among other things, wanted them to do." Ibid., p. 212.

61 Bruce Duffy, *The World as I Found It* (New York: Ticknor and Fields, 1987).

62 Perhaps I have somewhat exaggerated the degree of musical resemblance between the passages in ques-

tion, but the point I am trying to make is not materially affected. Imagine, if you will, an even greater resemblance between the passages than there actually is, but hold constant that this is merely accidental.

63 Once again, "all interpretation-relevant knowledge" can't go so far as to include the author's actual meaning intent, or else (2) always *would* coincide with (1).

64 See "Against Theory."

18

The Constructivist's Dilemma

Robert Stecker

Everyone believes that artworks and other artifacts are constructed, i.e., made. With regard to artwork, artists are standardly credited with the feat of construction. By a constructivist, I mean someone who holds the view that artworks are constructed not merely by the artists, but also by other people who interpret these objects.[1]

This claim requires initial clarification because constructivists do not claim that interpretations add chapters to novels, lines to poems, notes to scores, or paint to canvasses. Interpretations do not create, add to, or alter the *parts* of artworks, though that is what artists need to do to make artworks. Typically, constructivists make one of two claims. One is that interpretations alter the properties (features, aspects) of artworks. To the fussy, this would suggest that the constructivist claim is a misnomer because literal construction requires the addition or alteration of parts.[2] The alteration of properties is not enough to constitute construction; the passage of time alone alters the properties of objects without constructing them. I will ignore the fussy in what follows, assuming it would be accomplishment enough to show how interpretations alter the properties of artworks in interesting ways. The second claim made by some constructivists is that interpretation creates an(other) object that is the one that really gets interpreted.[3] This claim obviously needs further clarification since this object is not, straightforwardly, another painting, poem, or

Robert Stecker, "The Constructivist's Dilemma," *Journal of Aesthetics and Art Criticism*, 55: 1 (Winter 1997), pp. 43–51. Reprinted by permission of Blackwell Publishing Ltd.

musical piece. To the extent I am able, I will provide the clarification below (in sections I and IV).

Constructivism holds no allure for me. However, I have in the past regarded this as a matter of temperament rather than argument. Hence, I have equally regarded it as a matter to be left alone. I know of no convincing constructivist arguments, but my assumption has been that attempts at refuting constructivism would be equally futile. Constructivists and their enemies have too little in common to really engage.

I now think differently: that there are real objections to be put forward to constructivism. The purpose of what follows is to put forward such objections. I admit I may fail by importing too many anticonstructivist assumptions, but I have tried to guard against doing so.[4]

I. Radical Constructivism Quickly Rejected

A radical constructivist claims that every new interpretation creates a new work, even if each starts out from the same "text."[5] On this view, the only difference between an artist and a critic or an interpreter is that the artist creates a "text" that gets made into a work by being given an interpretation, while the critic or interpreter borrows a text. Although it is reasonable to make some distinction between text and work, the distinction used here in defining radical constructivism is intrinsically confused. It conceives of what we receive from an artist (if we ignore her interpretation of her text) as essentially blank until given an interpretation; as marks/sounds/movements yet to be given meaning. This is doubly wrong because no one takes what they receive from artists in this way (quite rightly), and, if they did, they would do no better with what they received from critics. Instead of receiving a text plus an interpretation, what they would get is a text plus another text, the second one being that which the critic produced in trying, vainly, to supply an interpretation. Suppose what is being interpreted is a poem and what does the interpreting is an essay. Both the poem and the essay are pieces of writing. If the text of the poem lacks a meaning to be *found* there, the text of the essay should be no less opaque. The same is true if the medium of the original text is paint rather than words. The buck has to stop somewhere; something has to *have* meaning rather than be given it, or the giving of meaning will not be possible.[6] The radical constructivist supplies no plausible candidate.

II.   A Dilemma for Moderate Constructivism

Far more attractive than radical constructivism is moderate constructivism. The moderate constructivist claims that we offer many competing interpretations of the same work, which can be identified apart from any single interpretation of it. However, interpretations do contribute to the construction of these works in virtue of the statements they make about them. I take this claim as equivalent to saying that interpretations change the works of which they are interpretations. As noted above, this in turn can only mean that they change the properties of those works.

If moderate constructivism essentially asserts that interpretations change their objects, it does not take a great deal of constructivist blood flowing in one's veins to find this view not merely more plausible than its radical cousin (which may not be saying much), but plausible – period. This is evidenced by the fact that many people would be inclined to accept the claim that interpretations change their objects.

There is a trivial version of moderate constructivism which may partly account for the inclination to accept this view (especially if the triviality of this version is not clearly recognized). When we give a new interpretation of a work, we are thinking of it in a new way and, in virtue of this, the work acquires the property of being thought of in this

new way. I take it that any constructivism worthy of the name would claim that interpretations change works in more robust ways than this. No doubt, few will be dissuaded from accepting moderate constructivism by becoming aware of this trivial version of it. No doubt, rather than giving up on constructivism, they will believe that there are more robust ways in which interpretations change their objects.

It is at this point that I will introduce the dilemma of constructivism as a more substantial reason to doubt that view. The dilemma goes like this: either interpretations make statements that are truth valued (true or false), or they do not. If they do, then when they are true, their objects already have the properties attributed to them, while if they are false, their objects do not have those properties and will not acquire them in virtue of such false ascription. What if interpretations lack truth value? I can change you by uttering certain things that lack truth value: if I say "walk," you might start walking, and that would be a fairly robust change in you. However, this does not carry over to artworks and other objects of interpretation. I cannot change an artwork by issuing a command, or by imagining something with regard to it. The best I can do is to bring about a change in myself or another human being by doing these things. An artwork might acquire new properties by my doing these things, but only of the trivial sort mentioned above. So it appears that on either supposition, interpretations do not change their objects.

III.   Can One Escape the Dilemma by Rejecting Bivalence?

Joseph Margolis offers an ingenious way out of this dilemma. Margolis claims that the alternatives the dilemma presents are not exhaustive. Hence, there is a way between its horns. Interpretive statements are properly understood, according to Margolis, as evaluable in a multivalent logic.[7] This means that they are not truth valueless, so we can reject the second horn of the dilemma. It also means that they lack bivalent truth values (in particular, the truth value *true*), so we can reject the first horn as well. Margolis believes that interpretive statements have *truth-like* values such as *plausible*, *reasonable*, or *apt*, as well as *false* (but not *true*).

Margolis is right at least in claiming that the existence of multivalent logics shows that the alternatives of the original dilemma are not exhaustive. However, this fact will help the constructivist only if two further claims can be established. First, it must be true that a bivalent logic is an inappropriate, and a multivalent logic is an appropriate, evaluative tool for interpretive statements. I have argued against this elsewhere,[8] but will, for the moment, accept it for the sake of argument. Second, the nature of interpretive statements – the purported fact that they have multiple truth-like values – has to help explain how interpretations can change their objects. Let us call the purported fact *Joe*. If *Joe* does not help to explain how interpretations can change their objects, we can remake our dilemma into a trilemma and be none the worse for wear.

It is not clear how *Joe* explains how interpretations can change their objects. Consider the interpretive question of whether Hamlet procrastinates. Before, we said that either an interpretation that says that he does is true, in which case *Hamlet* (the play) already has the property of representing Hamlet as procrastinating, or every interpretation which says this is false, in which case the play does not have the property. In either case the interpretation changes nothing except how people perceive or think about the play. Now we have to take into account a third possibility: that some interpretations that say that Hamlet procrastinates, though not true, are plausible, apt, or reasonable, which leaves it open that other interpretations which deny this are also plausible, apt, or reasonable. Does this show, or even suggest, that such interpretations change the play or what the play represents, or anything else that might be regarded as a property of the play other than the way people take it? It does not.

In fact, it seems to me, the present view *precludes* the possibility of an interpretation changing its object. The latter can occur only if the following is true: before an interpretation *i* is given for an object *o*, *o* does not have property *F*, but after *i* is given for *o*, *o* has *F*. *O* has *F* if and only if it is true that *o* has *F*. But it is never true that *o* has *F* on Margolis's proposal. Hence, on this view, no interpretation can change its object. The trilemma is in place. Further, if Margolis holds both *Joe* and the view that interpretations can change their objects, he holds a view that is true if and only if it is false.

I think Margolis might reply that I am trying to illegitimately impose a bivalent logic on cultural objects where the appropriate logic is a multivalent one. However, if we refrain from thinking in the way set out in the last paragraph, we seem equally precluded from concluding that an interpretation can change its object. All that we would be able to say is that it is plausible, apt, or reasonable to claim that interpretations can change their objects (e.g., that interpretation *i* changes *o*), where this claim can co-exist with the claim that it is plausible, apt, or reasonable that *i* does not change *o*. On this way of thinking about the matter, nothing is, or can be, settled about moderate constructivism.

IV.   Salience Imputation as Property Change

I now take up a somewhat different suggestion for defending the idea of interpretation-induced property change, one that has been offered by Michael Krausz.[9] Krausz's basic idea is that a given interpretation of an object makes certain features *F* salient, while a different interpretation makes other features *G* salient. So the property change that a given interpretation might bring about would be something like this: before interpretation *i* is given, the interpreted object *o* has *F* all right, but *F* does not have the property of being salient, while after *i* is given, *F* is salient. On this view, what interpretations change are second order properties, i.e., properties of properties.

An example or two might help us decide on the plausibility and significance of Krausz's proposal, as well as help us get a clearer idea of what it is. One example Krausz offers is that of an ambiguous figure like the duck/rabbit or the vase/faces. When one looks at a picture that can be seen either as a vase or as profiles of two faces facing each other, Krausz says that one interprets the picture by assigning salience to certain aspects of features (p. 68). An example of what Krausz has in mind would be taking this sharp angle as separating the forehead from the eyes and that one as representing the nose joining the mouth.

I have two questions about this example. The first, perhaps nit-picking, question is whether what is going on here is properly described as assigning salience to features (or aspects of features). I am unsure what Krausz means by salience, but to me, to assign salience is just to assign special significance, prominence, or importance to a feature – it is not to say what kind of significance we assign. All the features to which Krausz says we assign significance or prominence when we interpret (or see) the picture as two faces, we would equally assign significance or prominence to when interpreting (seeing) the picture as a vase. The converse of this, however, does not happen to be true. The top line of the picture has salience when we see it as representing the top of the vase, but it lacks salience if we see the picture as representing two faces. So, regarding the first question, my answer would be that some of what is going on when we interpret or see the picture in one way rather than another is a matter of assigning salience differentially; a good deal of what is going on is simply seeing the very same features as representing different things.

The second question is whether the creation of salience is best understood as property change. For that matter, is the fact that we can see or interpret the same features as representing different things best understood in terms of property change?

In answering this question (or these questions), we can note that the trivial sort of property change spoken of earlier certainly occurs. Before seeing or interpreting the picture, *I* did not take the line as representing this or that, and *I* did not give it special significance or importance. It was only upon my seeing or interpreting the picture that the line acquired the property of being so understood by me.

To decide whether any more interesting property change occurs, it is useful to consider what is asserted when we offer an interpretation or convey what we see. With regard to the ambiguous figures under discussion, which are not artworks, and whose origin in the study of psychology of perception is well enough known, what would or should be asserted is relatively straightforward, though still relative to the aim of interpretation. If the aim is to say what the picture represents, then what should be asserted is that it represents a vase *and* it represents two faces. The evidence one would give for this claim would be twofold: first, by noticing certain features and by taking them in certain ways (this angle can be taken as a forehead meeting the eyes or, alternatively, as a sharp corner of a vase), we can easily see the picture as both vase and faces; second, the figure was purposely made so that both vase and faces can be easily seen. The finding of certain features as salient, and the seeing of certain lines as representing this or that were simply the means by which we discovered the representational facts. No property change more interesting than the one already noted need occur when we see or interpret the features of the picture.

It might be that things are different with artworks such as paintings, since, with them, interpretive questions do not stop once we determine what is represented, and even determining that is a far more complex and debatable matter. In considering artworks in connection with Krausz's thesis that the assignment of salience to features brings about a significant change in the work, let us begin with an imaginary example in which this thesis is, I believe, as plausible as it could possibly be. Suppose that in a culture where the depiction of the human face and figure is prohibited, the art of painting has developed to omit depictions of these things. This culture has recently extended its domain to a land that has long loved the depiction of the human body and visage. The conquering culture introduces many examples of its art to exhibit its beauty and the nonnecessity of the human in art. Among these artworks is a new painting by one of their best artists: a row of vases, each a variation on a visual doppelgänger of the vase/faces. The inhabitants of the conquered land not only see faces everywhere in the painting, though none were intended, but a particular interpretation of it becomes dominant among these people, viz., that it is a subversive painting that purposely smuggles in faces among the vases. This interpretation actually becomes enshrined in art history, and becomes the standard way of seeing the painting.

Notice that this interpretation has radically and permanently changed the painting's reception; that is, the way it is perceived and thought about, its place in the cultural history of the conquered land. Has it changed the painting itself? Yes and no. Yes, in that the painting has acquired a significance never intended, which it did not have until after it received the interpretation in question. No, at least with regard to its representational properties. It was always true that the painting *could* be seen as representing faces, even if the artist did not realize this. It was never true, and the interpretation did not make it true, that the painting represented faces. It remains true that the interpretation that so changed the painting's reception and significance is a false interpretation precisely because it makes a false claim about what the painting represents.[10]

What this example illustrates is that when an interpretation changes the way we think about an object, those changes can be profound indeed. However, it does not illustrate any other kind of change that an interpretation brings about.

If we turn to actual interpretations of paintings or other artworks, and if we continue to assume that what these interpretations do is to give salience to pre-existing features, we get much the same result. Consider some interpretive claims made in four different interpretations (discussed by Krausz) of van Gogh's *The Potato Eaters*. H. P. Bremmer claims that the painting represents a close-knit family and this close-knittedness is paralleled, perhaps symbolized, by the placement of four mugs closely together. Albert Lubin, in a similar vein, claims that the glowing lights of the house speak of "warmth and happiness within," though he goes on to say that the painting is about mourning.[11] H. R. Graetz, on the other hand, sees lonely and isolated figures that represent van Gogh's relationship to his own family. The light symbolizes kindness, but as something longed for rather than possessed. Griselda Pollock sees the painting as the exploration of "otherness"; hence, she does not associate the painting with van Gogh and his family. An important aspect of the painting is the representation of peasants without the usual romantic clichés.

It is true that these interpretive claims suggest sometimes similar, sometimes quite different ways of thinking about (or seeing) van Gogh's painting, and one of the ways they do this is by giving special significance to certain features of the painting (e.g., the arrangement of the mugs, the lamplight, the "primitive faces" of the peasants). But of course, as Krausz recognizes (since he speaks of these as competing interpretations), one still has to decide whether the painting represents, symbolizes, or expresses the various things attributed to it in the proffered interpretations. The mere issuing of interpretive claims hardly settles which of these interpretations are true or acceptable. Such claims may indeed permanently alter the painting's reception, but as we have seen with our imaginary example, this still leaves these other questions open.

V. Objects-of-Interpretation

Krausz would object to the preceding discussion because it assumes that the representational, symbolic, and expressive properties that an interpretation assigns to a work either are already possessed by the work prior to interpretation or else they are incorrectly assigned. *Imputation*, as conceived of by Krausz, is supposed to be something different

from both discovery and false predication. It is supposed to be the partial creation of an object-of-interpretation. This, of course, is a constructivist view par excellence. If Krausz would charge the preceding discussion with begging a question, this supposition of Krausz's would be equally subject to the same charge.[12] Is there a way to pursue the issue further without begging questions?

I am not sure that there is such a way, but what I propose to do is this. I will examine Krausz's "imputational" conception of what is going on in (at least some) interpretations with an eye both to its internal coherence and to its consistency with what I take to be ordinary expectations about interpretation. Krausz insists, as does Margolis, that the "imputational" conception of interpretation comes off at least as well as a "realist" conception on both counts. I will argue otherwise.[13]

The imputationalist view holds that cultural entities are the class of their interpretations, and that there is no object-of-interpretation independent of interpretation as such. The object-of-interpretation has no structure independent of interpretation as such. (p. 93)

This is one characterization that Krausz offers of the imputationalist view. It is a puzzling characterization. Interpretations are normally supposed to have objects, to be about something. That is among the things I called "ordinary expectations" about interpretation. Krausz does not deny that interpretations have objects. He speaks of cultural entities (the things interpreted) and the class of *their* interpretations. What is puzzling is the relation that he claims holds between cultural entities and *their* interpretations. The relation is identity. Cultural entities are the class of their interpretations. This makes extremely elusive the object that seemed to be in hand. Consider again *The Potato Eaters*, which I take to be a cultural entity par excellence, and some interpretation of it, which I also take to be a cultural entity. Taken literally, the characterization of the imputationalist view says that *The Potato Eaters* is the class of its interpretations. This creates all kinds of puzzles, from oddities to paradoxes. One oddity concerns the sort of references one finds in a typical interpretation of *The Potato Eaters*. One will find references to *The Potato Eaters* as well as references to other interpretations. It is natural to partition these references, supposing them to refer to different types of things, but this turns out to be wrong if *The Potato Eaters* is just the class of its interpretations. Turning to the predicates commonly applied to *The Potato Eaters* and to the class of its interpretations, we cross over to paradox. For example, when Bremmer says that the close arrangement of mugs in *The Potato Eaters* parallels the close-knittedness of the family depicted in it, one would not have supposed he is saying that the close arrangement of mugs in a class of interpretations parallels the close-knittedness of the family depicted in that class. The second claim is nonsense; the first is not. Similarly, an interpreter of this painting may note that it is a property of the class of interpretations of it that some claim that the painting portrays a warm and close-knit family, while others do not claim this, but who would have thought that *The Potato Eaters* sometimes claims of itself that it portrays a warm and close-knit family while sometimes not claiming this of itself? *The Potato Eaters* was completed in 1885 and is composed of paint; the relevant class of interpretations has members not completed until 1963, 1972, 1974, and 1988, and is not composed of paint.

The idea that objects-of-interpretation are the class of their interpretations also generates an infinite regress. An interpretation of a painting is as much a cultural object as a painting. So, an interpretation of a painting is the class of its interpretations. That makes the painting the class of interpretations of the class of its interpretations. But an interpretation of an interpretation is a cultural object, so it is the class of its interpretations. That makes the painting the class of interpretations of the class of interpretations of the class of its interpretations ... The object-of-interpretation is elusive indeed on the present characterization of imputational interpretation.

We need a different characterization of imputational interpretation. At one point, Krausz suggests that the imputationalist is making claims about nominal rather than real existents. Of course, classes of interpretations are real existents, but perhaps the idea is that they are about a "nominal" rather than a real painting. This does not help, because if the sort of claims that an imputationalist is committed to are incoherent, making their object "nominal" does not make those claims more coherent: it just makes them less interesting. A nominal object is an *intentional* object, i.e., a way of thinking about a real object.[14] We knew all along that interpretations can change how we think.

Further, the object of thought has not been made any less elusive.

"Imputational interpretation involves selecting features from presented material with which to fashion an object-of-interpretation" (p. 94). This remark of Krausz's suggests a conception of imputational interpretation different from the one considered so far. *The Potato Eaters* (the painting) presents "material." The present claim is that an interpreter selects certain properties from that material, and thereby makes an object-of-interpretation. The interpreter goes on to make claims about this object-of-interpretation. These claims constitute the interpreter's imputational interpretation. This conception of imputational interpretation harks back to Krausz's remarks about salience. The selected properties are those that are salient for the interpreter. Thus Krausz sees each of the interpreters of *The Potato Eaters* as selecting properties from the painting which are salient from their point of view, and thereby imputing (i.e., creating) an object-of-interpretation. For example, Krausz says that

> Bremmer resists intentional features of the depicted figures and remarks about the formal parallel between the closely placed mugs and the unity of the family, [assigning] salience to those features. As such he imputes an object-of-interpretation about which his interpretation speaks. (p. 72)

On the present conception of imputational interpretation, imputation occurs in the first instance by the process of selection, which "imputes" or creates an object-of-interpretation. I believe that Krausz would say that there is also a second instance in which imputation occurs. This is because Krausz endorses the idea that some of what is said about the object-of-interpretation is not strictly true of it (the object being incomplete or indeterminate in some respects), but is completed by further properties being imputed to it in interpretation. It seems likely that there is not a sharp distinction between the "imputation" that selects presented features and thereby creates an (initial) object-of-interpretation, and the "imputation" that fills in this initially indeterminate object, but Krausz's language suggests some distinction, however fluid it may be.

The conceptions both of object-of-interpretation and of interpretation presented here are problematic, though they are not fraught with the obvious absurdities of thinking of the object-of-interpretation as the class of interpretations of the object. However, this is so at least in part because of the obscurity of the present conception.

Let us first look more closely at the new conception of objects-of-interpretation. Krausz recognizes the unacceptability of radical constructivism, and so is eager to avoid the view that every interpretation has its own unique object. Different interpretations of *The Potato Eaters* compete, and so must be about the same thing. Hence, the object-of-interpretation must be public or intersubjective, and shared by other interpretations. Yet we cannot just say that the object is the painting – the most obvious public object at hand – if we are to retain the idea that the object-of-interpretation is imputed by selecting salient features. In fact, that idea strongly tends toward the radical constructivist idea that there is a distinct object-of-interpretation for each interpretation. (Or it at least tends toward the idea that interpretations, all apparently of *The Potato Eaters*, have many different objects.) Krausz certainly tells us that each of the interpretations "of the painting" he considers make different features salient. For example, Bremmer's object-of-interpretation lacks intentional features while Graetz's and Lubin's objects-of-interpretation possess intentional features (though not the same ones). Ergo, they select different features imputing different objects-of-interpretation, or so it would seem.

Krausz hopes to solve this problem by using the notion of unicity (a term he borrows from Margolis[15]). The notion of unicity, as Krausz understands it, is that of *sufficient commonality*, i.e., *a* is unicitous with *b* if and only if *a* shares a sufficiently large number of properties with *b*. Proponents of unicity intentionally and unobjectionably leave unanswered the question of what is a sufficient number of properties, claiming that the answer can only be determined by critical (or other actual) practices, and even then allowing for some vagueness. We can live with vagueness and practice-dependence. The more serious problem for the notion of unicity is the question of whether it is an identity or a similarity relation. Unicity solves the problem (of moderate constructivism collapsing into radical constructivism) raised in the previous paragraph only if it is an identity relation, for even a radical constructivist could allow that different interpretations sometimes construct similar

objects. However, unicity looks for all the world like a similarity relation, for there is nothing in the definition of unicity (as Krausz sets it out) that implies that *a* and *b* are one and the same object.

So far I have pointed out that a (putative) pair of objects-of-interpretation can be unicitous, but merely similar rather than identical. Matters are actually worse, because the imputational notion of interpretation guarantees that the unicity relation is one of similarity rather than identity. Consider a (putative) pair of objects *a* and *b* and their respective interpretations *a'* and *b'*. The whole point of Krausz's talk of creating an object by selecting salient features from presented material is that *a* and *b* are different in some way or other. If there is absolutely no difference, there would be no need to talk about anything but a common object, e.g., van Gogh's painting. Similarly, if *a'* completes *a* in some way different from the way *b'* completes *b*, then again it follows that *a* is not *b* for, at a specific time *t*, the former would have a property lacking in the latter and vice versa.

Krausz sometimes tries to meet arguments like the one just given by claiming that many ordinary, coherent, identity claims would not make sense on the notion of strict identity used in the last paragraph. Thus Krausz claims that the notion of a self that develops over time cannot satisfy this notion of strict identity since it acquires very different properties in the course of development, but, in some sense, it is the very same self that undergoes these changes (see pp. 122–123). In making this and similar claims, Krausz makes an elementary blunder. The developments of the self of which he speaks are perfectly compatible with the strictest notion of identity, for that notion merely claims that self *a* is self *b* if and only if every property self *a* has at a time *t* is had by *b* at *t* and vice versa.[16] This allows one and the same self to have different properties at different times as it must if it develops or changes. Any notion of numerical identity which did not allow for identity through change would be clearly counterintuitive and unacceptable.

Unicity, as Krausz sets it out, is not a genuine identity relation, but it could be regarded as a fictional identity relation, i.e., we could suppose critics operating according to a fiction or pretense that sufficient similarity creates identity. This would leave these critics wide open to the radical constructivist onslaught because it actually justifies the claim that each interpretation creates its own object. We fail to recognize this only by pretending otherwise.

I conclude that the notion of unicity does not halt the slide to radical constructivism. Hence the Krauszian conception of objects-of-interpretation presently under consideration remains threatened by that problem.

Let us now turn to the complementary conception of interpretation. What I will claim here is that Krausz needs to think of interpretation in two distinct ways that do not cohere: as making claims (assertions, statements) about an object-of-interpretation, and as completing that object. Establishing this claim is the burden of what follows.

The claim has two parts: first, that Krausz needs to think of interpretation in the two ways just mentioned, and, second, that these two ways do not cohere. I take it that Krausz needs to think of interpretations as making claims, assertions, or statements because that is what interpretations typically do. We have seen this in all the interpretations we have considered so far: those of *The Potato Eaters*, those of the imaginary vase painting, and those of the ambiguous vase/faces. It may be that some interpretations do not make claims at all, but do something else.[17] However, this would be atypical. Further, I find no evidence that Krausz would deny that interpretations make claims about their objects. Margolis emphasizes this fact and takes it to be a condition of adequacy on an account of interpretation that it can accommodate the claim-making function of interpretations.

Both Krausz and Margolis believe that interpretations help to complete their objects. If they did not hold this view, they would not be constructivists. I suppose one might hold a more minimal version of constructivism according to which construction occurs only in creating (imputing) an object-of-interpretation, but not in interpreting that object. However, this is a less robust constructivism than either Krausz's or Margolis's.

Hence, Krausz thinks of interpretations, as does Margolis, in the two ways we have been discussing: as making claims and as completing objects. Further, they do not think of these as two distinct interpretive activities. It is in making claims about its object that an interpretation completes its object.

What is the problem with thinking of interpretation in both ways? The problem is to understand how making a claim about an object, even an object-of-interpretation, can give it a property claimed for it. Of course, making a claim about an object can change it in ways already discussed: it can get people to think of it as having the property in question, and in general, it can change the way people think about the object. These changes can be profound. But they do not add up to the object having the property claimed for it. If the claim is true, the object already has the property. If it is false, the object does not have the property. If it is neither true nor false, then what difference can be made by saying that the object has the property, or even by telling a plausible story according to which the object has the property? Before an interpretation is offered, an object may well be indeterminate with respect to a property, but if it is, then such saying or storytelling will not make it determinate, though it may get people to think of the object as determinate.[18]

We have now come full circle. The argument of the preceding paragraph is a variation on the dilemma of constructivism set out in section II. We have traced various attempts to avoid the dilemma of constructivism, and they have ultimately led us back to the dilemma, though we have noted various oddities, paradoxes, infinite regresses, and failures of coherence, among other problems, along the way. This suggests that the strategies we have considered to avoid the dilemma have failed.

Of course, there may be other strategies not considered here that would not fail. I would welcome seeing them and hereby extend the appropriate invitation. Know what I mean?[19]

Notes

1 This is a narrow construal of constructivism because it confines the constructing agency to interpretations. This paper does not attempt to rule out construction occurring in some other way. Although the authors I am mainly concerned with in this paper, Michael Krausz and Joseph Margolis, claim that interpretations (partly) construct their objects, they would also subscribe to the broader constructivism *not* under discussion here. There are other writers who are constructivists clearly enough, but are less clear about the agency of construction. One such, I find, is Graham McFee. McFee believes that

changes in the way artworks are understood bring about changes in their meaning. Since we arrive at our understanding of artworks by interpreting them, one would think it follows that interpretations change artworks. McFee might accept this, but his main examples of items bringing about alteration in artworks are to be found elsewhere, viz., in various events ranging from Picasso painting a series of works based on Velázquez's *Las Meninas*, to the invention of the submarine, to conceptual and theoretical change. Examples of conceptual/theoretical change are the discovery of the baroque as a stylistic category and the appearance of the psychoanalytic understanding of the mind.

See Graham McFee, "The Historicity of Art," *The Journal of Aesthetics and Art Criticism* 38 (1980): 302–324; "The Historical Character of Art: A Reappraisal," *The British Journal of Aesthetics* 32 (1992): 307–319; and "Back to the Future: A Reply to Sharpe," *The British Journal of Aesthetics* 35 (1995): 278–283. For a critique of the 1980 piece as well as other constructivist proposals, see Jerrold Levinson, "Artworks and the Future," in *Music, Art and Metaphysics* (Cornell University Press, 1990), pp. 179–214. McFee is also criticized in Sharpe's "Making the Past: McFee's Forward Retroactivism," *The British Journal of Aesthetics* 34 (1994): 170–173. McFee's 1992 piece replies to Levinson.

2 Found art, such as a readymade, illustrates the possibility of the creation of artworks without construction on the "fussy" reading of construction.

3 Some constructivists deny that this is "another" object because they doubt that things exist independently or prior to interpretations of them.

4 At various points, I may seem to make epistemic assumptions that a constructivist would question. Many constructivist projects are motivated by skepticism about our epistemic access to interpretation-independent objects. This skepticism sometimes directly argues that we lack access to such objects. Sometimes it is more indirect, claiming there are no such objects by arguing that we would lack access to them if they existed, and then invoking a verificationist criterion of what exists. A more moderate version of this line of thought adopts an agnosticism about such objects. I have argued against this sort of epistemic motivation for constructivism in "Fish's Argument for the Relativity of Interpretive Truth," *The Journal of Aesthetics and Art Criticism* 48 (1990): 221–230, and in "Pragmatism and Interpretation," *Poetics Today* 14 (1993): 181–191. Briefly, there are two problems with typical arguments concerning epistemic access. First, they would imply that we equally lack access to constructed entities conceived of as interpretations. For example, if we lack epistemic access to poems, interpretations of poems,

being put forward in the same linguistic medium, ought to fare no better. This problem is illustrated in the present paper in the criticism of radical constructivism in section I and in the infinite regress argument given in section IV. Second, as suggested by the first problem, the standard required in these arguments for epistemic access is confused or unreasonably high.

5 I do not know if anyone endorses this view. I argue below (section IV) that one conception of "object-of-interpretation" proposed by Michael Krausz may commit him to radical constructivism, though Krausz clearly does *not* endorse that view.

6 Richard Shusterman makes a similar point in "Beneath Interpretation: Against Hermeneutic Holism," *The Monist* 73 (1990): 181–203. Thus, Shusterman asks, "If we could never understand anything without interpreting it, how could we understand the interpretation itself?" (p. 196). He also foresees that such a view generates an infinite regress, as I argue in connection with a related position in section IV below.

The argument here might be misunderstood to suggest a conception of what interpretations are that I would not accept. I am not implying that interpretations are texts (any more than I think what is being interpreted is merely a text). The argument merely relies on the point that texts are the vehicle for expressing an object-of-interpretation, a work. If a text cannot bear a meaning other than by being given an interpretation, my point is that this is true for texts expressing interpretations as much as for texts expressing works.

Regarding what an interpretation is, I do not think one can give a uniform characterization. Most typically, critical interpretations are *statements* made for the purpose of better understanding and appreciating a work. For a fuller account, see my "Incompatible Interpretations," *The Journal of Aesthetics and Art Criticism* 50 (1992): 291–298; "Art Interpretations," *The Journal of Aesthetics and Art Criticism* 52 (1994): 193–206; or *Artworks: Meaning, Definition, Value* (Pennsylvania State University Press, 1997).

7 Margolis argues for this view in, among other places, *The Truth about Relativism* (Oxford: Basil Blackwell, 1991) and in "Plain Talk about Interpretation on a Relativistic Model," *The Journal of Aesthetics and Art Criticism* 53 (1995): 1–7.

8 In "Relativism about Interpretation," *The Journal of Aesthetics and Art Criticism* 53 (1995): 14–18. Also see Stephen Davies's "Relativism in Interpretation" in the same issue, pp. 8–13.

9 Michael Krausz, *Rightness and Reasons: Interpretation in Cultural Practices* (Cornell University Press, 1993). See especially chap. 3. Parenthetical page references in the remainder of this paper are to Krausz's book. It might be pointed out that on the

"larger" issue of whether we should accept multiple interpretations of the same work, Krausz and I are in agreement that we should.

10   It might be claimed that I am begging the question here by assuming that what a painting represents is fixed by the historical context in which it is produced, and more specifically, that a painting represents an *F* only if the artist intended viewers to see an *F* in the painting. Well, I am assuming this rather widely accepted view at this stage in the argument. This seems to me permitted by the issue at hand – whether interpretations change objects by making properties *they already possess* salient. I consider an alternative view in section v.

11   Lubin's interpretation, as set out by Krausz, seems to border on the incoherent, or at least the highly implausible. Not only is the happy family in mourning, but the faceless though clearly female figure in the foreground is said to represent Vincent's dead brother.

12   In the preceding discussion I was making the commonsense assumption that objects of interpretation are basically completed and independent of interpreters before the process of interpretation begins. Thus, *The Potato Eaters* was completed by van Gogh in 1885, and it is that painting that the four critics mentioned above are trying to understand. However, this commonsense assumption does not preclude property change after the painting is completed. The painting does change in all kinds of aesthetically significant as well as insignificant ways after completion. So I do not see that I beg any questions by making the commonsense assumption just mentioned.

13   Margolis's conception of imputation may not be the same as Krausz's. I focus on the latter because Krausz provides more examples of imputation purportedly in action.

14   In "Interpretation and Art Objects: Two Views," *The Monist* 73 (1990), Krausz suggests that objects-of-interpretation are best thought of as intentional objects, e.g., a "painting as seen in a certain way under specifiable historical circumstances" (p. 231).

15   It is not clear, however, that Krausz and Margolis use "unicity" in the same way. Margolis *may* use this term to denote a strict identity relation that an object, which lacks essential properties, still bears to itself. As I argue below, unicity for Krausz is not a strict identity relation.

16   Notice that this holds whether one thinks of identity as "absolute" (holding only for an object under any description) or "relative" (holding only for an object as described under a particular sortal expression).

17   Some suggestions here are that some interpretations are expressions of personal experience, prescriptions, or fictional extensions of works.

18   This point at least begins to address certain problems about the interpretation of works that are made to be performed, such as music and plays. Scores, understood in their historical context, indicate works, but underdetermine performances. Do not interpretations supply answers to questions that are not supplied by scores, thereby enabling a performance and completing the work? Interpretations, in one sense, do supply answers not supplied by scores, but they do not thereby complete the work if the work was truly indeterminate with respect to the question being answered by the interpretation. Interpretations in this sense indicate, or provide a rationale for, a way of performing a work *not* dictated by the work itself. Interpretations can also acceptably suggest that a performance should depart from the letter of the score for aesthetic reasons. A performance based on such an interpretation is still a performance of the work. It may be a strictly "incorrect" performance, but a perfectly acceptable one.

Part V

Values of Art

Introduction to Part V

Aesthetics and philosophy of art invite many questions about value:

- How are individual works to be evaluated?
- Are there any general principles of aesthetic evaluation?
- What degree of objectivity can value judgments in the arts attain?
- How do aesthetic values relate to other kinds of value, e.g. moral value?
- Are there aesthetic values that are not artistic values?
- Are there values that (all) works of art have *as* works of art?
- Are value judgments in the arts always historically situated or could there be genuinely universal artistic values?

Although it became fashionable in the 1970s and 1980s in certain cultural and intellectual circles either to try and sidestep all questions of value in the arts (notably in literary criticism) or to promote radical kinds of relativism, whereby values were deemed mere products of ideology, analytic philosophers have been reluctant to embrace either skepticism or relativism of this nature. It is a characteristic of the analytic approach, however, to focus attention either on value *terms* in aesthetics or on the kinds of *judgments* that critics make and the criteria for them.

Strawson and Sibley admirably illustrate this emphasis, in their papers below, each offering a careful examination of what it means to appraise an object aesthetically and what role there is for general criteria in so doing. Sibley proposes a subtle taxonomy of aesthetic terms – "intrinsically evalu-

ative," "descriptive merit-terms," "evaluation-added" – showing how evaluative and descriptive elements are often intertwined. Both Strawson and Sibley note the curious phenomenon in aesthetics whereby the very same feature (color configuration, musical harmony, poetic image) might positively contribute to the value of one work yet detract from the value of another. Sibley argues that we have to do more than point to the "particularity" of works to explain this and he criticizes Strawson's view that all the features relevant to the aesthetic appraisal of a work are also features that give the work its very identity. Sibley seeks to widen the discussion beyond works of art, arguing that the peculiarities of aesthetic value judgments occur in nonartistic contexts as well.

Malcolm Budd, in "Artistic Value," sets himself the ambitious task of identifying "the value of a work of art as a work of art," such value being common to all the arts. He finds it in the intrinsic value of the experience each work offers. That the value of art should be the value of an *experience* is not in itself surprising but Budd develops the idea well beyond its simple initial formulation. Thus he argues that the relevant experience is not a mere passive state but must be "imbued with an awareness of . . . the aesthetically relevant properties of the work" and might comprise such factors as "the invigoration of one's consciousness, or a refined awareness of human psychology or political or social structures, or moral insight, or an imaginative identification with a sympathetic form of life or point of view that is not one's own." Budd, however, resists identifying the value of art (as art) with instrumental values. The experience art affords is valued for its own sake but that does not imply the truth of formalism.

Budd also rejects the commonly made association of artistic value with a "message" or thought that might be communicated by art. He writes: "It is, of course, true that what a work of art communicates can be *integral* to its value as a work of art, for it may be integral to the experience the work offers. But it is the message *as communicated by the work*, the message *as realized in the experience of the work*, that determines the work's artistic value, not the message itself." A not dissimilar point of view is developed by Peter Lamarque in "Tragedy and Moral Value." He questions the notion that tragedies are valuable in virtue of conveying deep moral truths. The idea of the "moral content" of tragedy turns out not to be as straightforward as might be implied by the idea of moral truth. A work might offer a moral lesson, in the manner of Aesop's Fables, or be underpinned by a less explicit moral vision, but Lamarque argues that it is wrong to run together the literary and the moral so that literary value becomes subsumed under moral value. It is part of a wider argument which seeks to find autonomy in literary criticism, a distinctively *literary* – and by implication aesthetic – interest in works of art.

For Berys Gaut, however, in "The Ethical Criticism of Art," the aesthetic is not entirely distinct from the ethical. Gaut defends what he calls "ethicism": "the thesis that the ethical assessment of attitudes manifested by works of art is a legitimate aspect of the aesthetic evaluation of those works." So, for Gaut, if a work prescribes a moral attitude that is reprehensible, the work is for that reason weakened aesthetically. He argues for this view by reference to the idea of a "merited response." One example concerns comedy. A work that invites us to find amusement in heartless cruelty has not merited the response of humor: "the work's humor is flawed, and that is an aesthetic defect in it." Gaut's paper is a good example of a recent trend in analytic aesthetics linking aesthetics with ethics.

Finally, we have included the first chapter of Anthony Savile's important book *The Test of Time* (1982), which was one of the first in analytic aesthetics to give full-scale treatment to artistic value. In the extract here, Savile offers a characterization of the conditions under which a work of art could be said to have survived the test of time. Merely continuing in existence over a long period is not sufficient, Savile argues, and a work must command attention in its own right throughout the period and, more controversially, must do so under an appropriate interpretation. Savile resists the thought that works could survive time's test by being reinterpreted by successive generations. He develops his theory of interpretation in later chapters of the book. But here the general outline of his case is made for taking seriously the test of time as a criterion of value.

Further reading

Beardsmore, R. W. (1971). *Art and Morality* (London: Macmillan).

Budd, Malcolm (1995). *Values of Art* (London: Penguin Press).

Feagin, Susan L. (1996). *Reading with Feeling: The Aesthetics of Appreciation* (Ithaca, NY: Cornell University Press).

Goldman, Alan H. (1995). *Aesthetic Value* (Boulder, CO: Westview Press).

Levinson, Jerrold (ed.) (1998). *Aesthetics and Ethics* (Cambridge: Cambridge University Press).

Mothersill, Mary (1984). *Beauty Restored* (Oxford: Oxford University Press).

Ridley, Aaron (1995). *Music, Value and the Passions* (Ithaca, NY: Cornell University Press).

Savile, Anthony (1982). *The Test of Time* (Oxford: Oxford University Press).

Schaper, Eva (ed.) (1983). *Pleasure, Preference and Value* (Cambridge: Cambridge University Press).

Stecker, Robert (1997). *Artworks: Definition, Meaning, Value* (University Park, PA: Pennsylvania State University Press).

19

Aesthetic Appraisal and Works of Art

P. F. Strawson

We have the words, *assessment, appraisal, evaluation, criticism, judgment.* No doubt their senses are different. But I do not want now to distinguish between them. I want to consider instead one way in which we distinguish, within the application of each, between different *kinds* of assessment, appraisal or judgment. For some of these kinds we have special names: we speak of moral or logical or aesthetic appraisal, criticism or judgment. More often, perhaps, we speak of judging a thing from such-and-such a point of view, or by such-and-such standards, or of judging it as a so-and-so. Thus things may be judged by military or financial standards; from the soldier's, the plumber's or the economist's point of view; a thing may be judged as a piece of plumbing, as an investment, as a work of art or as a concert-hall. It is not redundant when we are assessing something, say an X, to precede our verdict with the phrase, 'as an X'; to say 'As an X, it is good, fair, bad'. It is not redundant, for there are many points of view from which anything can be assessed; and it is an important fact that we can sometimes make our point of view clear by using the ordinary classificatory name for a thing, by speaking of judging it as an X, where 'X' is that name.

Can anything clear and general be said which will distinguish, among these kinds of assessment, the aesthetic? We should note, first, that the word 'aesthetic' perhaps has normally a narrower use

P. F. Strawson, "Aesthetic Appraisal and Works of Art," in P. F. Strawson, *Freedom and Resentment* (London: Methuen, 1974), pp. 178–88. Reprinted by permission of Thomson Publishing Services.

than we at least half-wish to make of it in asking the question. It would be odd to say, 'He didn't really judge it as a painting; he judged it from a narrowly aesthetic point of view.' But it would not be odd to say, 'He judged it from a narrowly aesthetic point of view; he didn't really judge it *as a novel* at all.' In spite of this, we are inclined, or half-inclined, to think of our question as a question about a kind of assessment that includes judging a novel as a novel as well as judging a painting as a painting. If, on the other hand, someone said, 'He was judging it from a purely aesthetic point of view; he wasn't judging it as a game of football' (or 'as a contribution to the discussion' or 'as a piece of engineering'), then we should be less inclined to make reservations about the implied contrast. So we claim to be interested in a kind of assessment which certainly includes judging a painting as a painting, and perhaps includes judging a novel as a novel, but does not seem to include judging a game of football as a game of football, a contribution to a discussion as a contribution to a discussion or a piece of engineering as a piece of engineering. But though our kind of assessment does not seem to include these kinds, these kinds might be said by some to include our kind. And, whether this is said or not, we certainly want to say that the aesthetic is a kind of assessment which *can* be made of what is in fact a game of football, a contribution to a discussion or a piece of engineering. And the question then arises: is there such a kind of assessment? Or – since there *are* whatever kinds of things we like, and we can draw lines where we choose – can anything clear and general be said about the nature of this kind of assessment?

The reasons for answering 'No' seem very strong. For in what direction should we look for something clear and general? The traditional directions seem unpromising, the results of following them inspire a kind of disgust. Following one of these traditional directions consisted in asking: what is there common and peculiar to the objects of which we make a favourable assessment of the kind concerned? But we do not expect a helpful answer to this; for the items and kinds of items of which we may make an aesthetic assessment are nearly as diverse as the items and kinds of items there are. They are not quite as diverse as this. It would be very precious for anyone to say that he found predication or disjunction aesthetically admirable (though I have heard a logician say that he found quantification aesthetically admirable). But most of what we find or make, whether concrete like a lily-pond or abstract like a proof, can be so assessed.

Following another traditional direction of search consisted in asking: when we enjoy something of which we make a favourable assessment of the kind concerned, what is there special about our response to, our experience of, the thing? But the looking within, which this encourages, is, for good reasons, out of fashion. *Can* we detect a special experience which always accompanies this kind of enjoyment and no other? And, if we could, would *its* presence be what made it *this* kind of enjoyment?

A third and less debilitating line of enquiry might seem to exist: viz., in an examination of the kinds of language we typically use in articulating assessments of the kind concerned. And certainly there are plenty of questions about these uses of language: but the profitable ones seem more limited and departmental than the general question of the general distinction between aesthetic assessment and other kinds. In relation to this question, the apparently limitless elasticity and variety of the vocabulary of criticism are merely daunting.

So scepticism about the possibility of a clear and general answer to the general question is natural. And if challenged to explain why we nevertheless are here inclined to speak of one kind of assessment, the sceptic has a reasonable answer, which runs, or might run, like this. Many of the kinds of assessment we make are such that there is no particular relation between favourable assessment of a thing and *enjoyment* of that thing. But for some ways of praising, there is a very close, though not an invariable, connection between assessing something favourably and enjoying it. This is the case with what we call aesthetic appraisal and aesthetic enjoyments. Further, there are certain obvious analogies and contrasts between different kinds of enjoyment. One can enjoy a game, argument or dance one takes part in, and say at the end: 'That was a good game (argument, dance)'. One can also enjoy a game or a dance one watches or an argument one listens to or reads, and again say at the end, 'That was a good game (argument, dance)'. There is an analogy between the members of this second group of enjoyments and appraisals; and a contrast between the second group and the first. In general one can find a contrast between the enjoyment of what one reads, listens to, looks at or tastes on the one hand, and, on the other, the enjoyment of the activities of work, play and exercise in which one takes part; though the two kinds of enjoyment may be mixed. Suppose we call the former 'spectator-enjoyments' and the latter 'participant-enjoyments'. Then aesthetic enjoyments take their place among spectator-enjoyments. But they have no very *definite* place there. What happens, perhaps, is this. Certain spectator-enjoyments are easily discriminable by the fact that a certain single sense is appealed to; say, the eye or the ear. Suppose we regard these two as aesthetic enjoyments *par excellence*. Then, especially when we come to say what it is about the objects of our spectator-enjoyments that we enjoy, we find ourselves finding analogies between the objects of very different spectator-enjoyments. Not all objects of spectator-enjoyment are equally joined by these links of analogy to the objects of aesthetic enjoyment *par excellence*. Some (say, exhibitions of bear-baiting) are not joined at all; some (say, cheese, regarded as an object of taste) by very few links; some (say, mathematical proofs or philosophical arguments) by links of analogy which, though perhaps not weak, may seem insignificant in comparison with points of contrast; some, (say, poetry) by very strong links indeed. Objects not directly linked to the centre may be linked to it by other objects so linked. The existence of this network of analogy then generates the illusion that there is one definite and distinctive *kind* of enjoyment, and one definite and distinctive *kind* of appraisal, viz., the aesthetic. When we are said to be enjoying or admiring something from an aesthetic point of view, all this can in fact mean is that in saying what it is about the object of our spectator-enjoyment that we enjoy, we find ourselves on one of the indefinitely numerous, indefinitely extendable lines which make up this network of analogy. The attempt to find a more definite meaning than this, the attempt to describe the general nature or essence of aesthetic enjoyment or appraisal, must always be futile, must always end in promoting one impossibly stretched analogy to the status of a theory, or in fabricating a special experience, or in some other wearisome error.

Perhaps this scepticism is right. I am at least half-inclined to think that it is. But I am also half-inclined to think that it is not, half-inclined, that is to say, to favour a more positive account. I certainly do not claim that this account is original; only that it is, from time to time, worth reconsidering. For there seems to be a feature of aesthetic judgment, repeatedly but obscurely stressed by writers on the subject, which might contain the possibility of a general distinction; a distinction which does not relate to some special character of the objects of aesthetic enjoyment nor to some special experience of enjoying, but is, rather, a formal, or logical, distinction. The feature I have in mind was effectively stressed by Professor Hampshire in an article published some years ago.[1] He set in extreme contrast two classes of judgments: moral judgments of action and critical judgments of art. To the former, he said, general rules and principles are essential; to the latter, quite irrelevant. He meant, I think, that it is quite meaningless and empty to praise a man's character or express moral approval of one of his acts without having reasons of a certain sort – of such a sort that giving the reasons would involve mentioning, in terms not themselves evaluative, generally applicable criteria of excellence in men or rightness in acts; whereas judgment in aesthetic matters is not thus wedded to non-evaluative descriptions of general features of the thing judged. Of course, this does not mean that nothing can be said in amplification and support of an aesthetic 'This is good'. But either what is said in amplification and support is not non-evaluative, as when we amplify our judgment by the use of further evaluative words, such as 'masterly', 'brilliant', 'original', etc.; or it is not general, but consists essentially in drawing attention to particular features or parts of the object praised, and their relations to each other in the object. Typical sentences from Hampshire are: 'The canons of success and failure . . . are . . . internal to the work [of art] itself'; 'Virtue and good conduct are essentially repeatable and imitable, in a sense in which the work of art is not'; '[The] purpose [of the critic] is to lead people . . . to look at precisely this unique object, not to see the object as one of a kind, but as individual and unrepeatable.' Another writer on

aesthetics, Miss Macdonald, made similar assertions in an earlier article.[2] She said: 'Every work of art is unique and in the last resort, perhaps, can be judged by no standard but its own'; and again, 'Works of art are unique. Their performance cannot be repeated, even by the artist.'

The remarks I have quoted, and others like them by other writers who stress the individuality of the work of art, and the non-conceptual character of aesthetic appreciation, have this in common: that they seem true, but mysterious. One wants to ask *why* we can have no general principles of art in just the sense in which we have general principles in morals. Why are there no general descriptive criteria of excellence in the aesthetic sphere, such as there are not only in the sphere of moral behaviour but, it seems, in every other sphere in which we make assessments at all? One wants also to ask in what special sense the work of art is unique, individual, unrepeatable. Perhaps it is a tautology that there are no general descriptive criteria of aesthetic excellence, and, if so, this might provide just the logical distinction we want to make; but, if so, the tautology needs expanding a little. The two questions, 'Why are there no general descriptive criteria for aesthetic appraisal?' and 'In what sense is the work of art unique (individual, non-repeatable)?' are closely connected. We should remember that the general names we give to things allude to a kind of assessment; and the concepts 'work of art' and 'aesthetic assessment' are logically coupled and move together, in the sense that it would be self-contradictory to speak of judging something *as a work of art*, but not from the aesthetic point of view. So there is point in trying to clarify the notion of aesthetic appraisal *via* the notion of the work of art, even though things other than works of art may be objects of aesthetic appraisal.

First I must make a simple point about the logical status of works of art. Sometimes a distinction is made between, say, pictures and statues on the one hand, and literary and musical compositions on the other. The work of art in the first group of cases is sometimes said to be a concrete physical *particular*; while the work of art in the second group of cases is to be classified logically as a *type*, as something which, while not itself a particular physical phenomenon, can be embodied on different occasions in different particular physical phenomena. One and the same word can be spoken or written many times, one and the same flag (the Union Jack) can flutter simultaneously from many mast-heads. Individual literary or musical compositions are to be thought of as related to particular copies or renderings of them as the type-word and the type-flag are related to their particular embodiments in utterance or cloth. Now there is of course a genuine distinction between pictures and statues on the one hand and, at least, musical compositions on the other, a distinction which partly accounts for the form of this supposed further distinction; we might express it shortly by saying that pictures and statues are essentially such that the one original can be looked at again and again, while musical compositions are essentially such that they cannot be enjoyed again and again unless they are reproduced again and again. But this does not warrant distinguishing between the former as particulars and the latter as types. One is tempted, presumably, to make the distinction in this form by the merely contingent fact that we are, for all practical purposes, quite unable to make reproductions of pictures and statues which are completely indistinguishable, by direct sensory inspection, from the originals. If this practical limitation did not exist,[3] then the originals of paintings and works of sculpture, like the original manuscripts of poems, would not as such have any but a sentimental value, and, perhaps, a technical-historical interest as well; we should be able to speak of the same painting being seen by different people in different places at one time, in just the way in which we now speak of the same sonata being heard by different people at different times in one place. As far as the deeper logic is concerned, therefore, there is no reason for regarding the members of some classes of works of art as essentially particulars, rather than types. All works of art, certainly, are individuals; but all are equally types and not particulars.

Miss Macdonald, whom I quoted as saying 'Works of art are unique. Their performance cannot be repeated, even by the artist', goes on to amplify these remarks as follows: 'In this they seem to differ from certain other performances in which what is produced, though numerically different, may be qualitatively exactly similar. This is not a mysterious fact about work of art, but follows, I think, from the way in which we use the term "work of art".' Now if the statement that works of art cannot be both numerically different and qualitatively exactly similar is meant to elucidate the special sense in which the work of art is unique (and the sentence which follows suggests that it is), then it is plainly inadequate. For this remark, though it is true of works of art, is, to speak roughly, true of all types whatsoever and is indeed part of what may be said in elucidating the logical idea of a type. English sentences, electrical circuits, motor-cars, etc. all have this in common: that if we are speaking of the types, and not the particular instances of the types, then we cannot allow that there are numerically distinct but exactly similar sentences, circuits, cars, etc. So Miss Macdonald's explanation, if it is intended as such, of the special uniqueness of the work of art, will not do as it stands.

Perhaps, however, her explanation can be replaced by another which is more helpful, and may correspond more closely to her intentions than what she actually says. Suppose we were asked to consider two motor-car types or two wireless-set types, and to assess them from a certain point of view: say, from the point of view of performance, or from that of their suitability for a particular purpose. Suppose even that we were simply asked to assess them *as* motor-cars or *as* wireless-sets. We might make lists in non-evaluative terms of all and only the features of each which were relevant to this appraisal; and the two lists might be identical. An important consideration in appraising the wireless-sets might, for example, be high selectivity: but it would not matter in detail how the high selectivity was secured in each case, so long as no other relative advantage accrued to one of them from the difference in the detail of design. There may be qualitative differences between two types without there being any qualitative differences which are relevant to the kind of assessment actually being made, even when that assessment is of the kind alluded to by the ordinary classificatory name of the thing concerned. This may also be true of works of art, so long as they are *not* being assessed *as* works of art, i.e. from an aesthetic point of view. If what is wanted for a certain purpose is a picture of certain dimensions representing horses in a naturalistic manner, there may be several which answer equally well. In contrast with these examples, it seems a clear tautology that there could not be two different works of art which were indistinguishable in all the respects relevant to their *aesthetic* appraisal. (By a 'respect relevant to aesthetic appraisal' I must emphasize that I do not mean anything which has an evaluative name; but I do mean something on account of which evaluative names are applied.) But there could very well be two different type-arguments, type-motor-cars, type-sentences which resembled one another in all respects relevant respectively to their logical, mechanical or grammatical appraisal. To use a fashionable phrase, the *criterion of identity* of a work of art is the totality of features which are relevant to its aesthetic appraisal. So the work of art has not merely the qualitative uniqueness which any type logically possesses; it has a further kind of uniqueness when viewed as an object of a certain kind of appraisal, the kind which its name alludes to. Perhaps I could also express the point in this way: the only method of describing a work of art which is both entirely adequate for the purpose of aesthetic appraisal, and does not use evaluative language, is to say 'It goes like this' – and then reproduce it. And, of course, this is not a method of *describing* at all.

This perhaps answers, though still obscurely, the question 'In what sense is the work of art unique?'; and it goes a part, but only a part, of the way towards expanding the putative tautology that there can be no general descriptive criteria for aesthetic assessment. Certainly, it goes no more than a part of the way. For, it might be said, I have spoken of *respects* and *features* of works of art, on account of which evaluative names are applied; and even if the totality of aesthetically relevant features individuates a work of art, cannot individual respects or features, or sets of them, be shared by different works of art and hence provide a basis for general criteria? But to this I should reply that the words 'feature' and 'respect' are misleading here, just because they make us think of aesthetically relevant features as like shareable *properties* and *qualities*. There *is* a sense in which such features can be shared: it is illustrated by the fact that one poem can incorporate or quote a line from another, and by the fact that one poem or picture can be a *version* of another. But there are no aesthetic merit-conferring *properties*, with non-evaluative names. When you draw attention to some feature on account of which terms of aesthetic evaluation may be bestowed, you draw attention, not to a property which different individual works of art may share, but to a part or aspect of an individual work of art. There is ordinarily a distinction between individuals (whether types or particulars), and the properties directly on account of which we make assessments of the individuals; a distinction related, presumably, to the kinds of interest in objects which these assessments reveal. But this distinction seems to break down for the case of aesthetic assessment of the work of art. If this is true, then the impossibility of general descriptive criteria of aesthetic excellence follows as a consequence.

(At most, we could regard each individual work of art itself, as type, as a general rule for the production of its own particular instances.) But why it is true, if it is true, is hard to say. One might suggest, as above, that the ordinary distinction between individuals and their merit-conferring properties reflects certain features of those interests and aims which show themselves in *non*-aesthetic assessments; and that these features are simply absent from the kind of interest we display when we make aesthetic assessments – so different is the aesthetic attitude from other attitudes. To make this out in detail would, if it were possible, be hard. I do not propose to try. But a way to begin would, evidently, be to turn our question and ask, not: 'Why does the distinction between individuals and merit-conferring properties break down for the case of aesthetic appraisal of works of art?', but 'Why does the distinction play the role it does in our non-aesthetic assessments?' Why is the moralist concerned with shareable properties of different particular actions, the dietary adviser with shareable properties of different types of food, the writers of *Which?* with shareable properties of different type of motor-car or washing machine? These questions at least remind us that an aesthetic interest in an individual is not any kind of practical interest, not an interest in anything it can or should do, or that we can do with it, not even an interest in specific responses (say, excitement or stupefaction) which it will produce in us. (If it were this sort of interest, there could indeed be general rules and recipes.)

The suggestion is, then, that scepticism about the possibility of a general account of the nature of aesthetic appraisal is to be answered, if at all, by exploiting a justified scepticism about the possibility of general descriptive criteria for aesthetic appraisal. Thus the peculiarity of this way of assessing is that when we have a class of objects of which the name, 'works of art', marks them out as primarily to be assessed in this way, then there cannot be numerically distinct members of the class, or parts of these members, which yet share all the features relevant to this kind of assessment. Further it is suggested that what underlies this fact is the fact that, as far as works of art are concerned, the idea of an aesthetic merit-conferring *property* is a mistake, a misapplication of a distinction which does not apply at all in this sphere. This suggestion would be merely confirmed by the fact, if it is a fact, that the idea in question might have application in some cases of things other than works of art of which we may make aesthetic assessments. For instance, it seems that two motor-car types might be aesthetically indistinguishable (I do not mean just of *equal* merit, but identical in aesthetically relevant respects) and yet be numerically two, as containing, say, different mechanical features; and here we might perhaps think of their *appearance* as a shared property. The word 'property' is in order this time just because we individuate the objects not as works of art but as motor-car types.

Finally, it may help to make the central point a little clearer, if one contrasts what I have called aesthetically relevant *features* of works of art with different kinds of what can certainly be called shareable properties of works of art. First we have those characteristics whose names are not non-evaluative, but already incorporate an evaluative judgment. Thus different works of art can resemble one another in ways which we mark by such words as *witty*, *delicate*, *economical* and so on, into all the immense and largely figurative vocabulary of praise or dispraise. And works of course can share *these* qualities without quoting passages from one another or even belonging to the same form. Then we have technical properties: being contrapuntal, being written in hexameters, having consonant rhymes, and so on. But it is not on account of these features *as such* that aesthetically evaluative names are bestowed. Then there are names for the types of response the works tend to evoke: *stimulating*, *tranquilizing*, etc. (The behaviour of these words in this connection is, of course, distinctive: they are used not quite as a doctor uses them in talking about drugs.) Then there are names of, roughly, styles, again applied over different forms: baroque, classical, gothic. But to name the style is not to make an aesthetic evaluation, nor to supply a sufficient basis for evaluation of any individual exemplar of the style. So, then, the objects primarily of aesthetic assessment have plenty of shareable properties: there are plenty of ways in which we find general resemblances between them. But, in naming these, we do not name, in non-evaluative terms, those features directly on account of which we make aesthetic judgments of the individual bearers of those properties; for either these names of shareable general properties are themselves evaluative, or, if they are not, then, in applying them, we leave our listeners in the dark as to what evaluations to make of the individual works to which they are applied.

Notes

1 'Logic and Appreciation', *Aesthetics and Language*, ed. W. Elton, Oxford, Blackwell, 1954.
2 'Distinctive Features in Criticism of the Arts', *Proceedings of the Aristotelian Society*, supp. vol. XXIII, 1949.
3 There are comparable cases to which it does not apply. We should think of lithographs, etchings and bronzes as well as paintings and chiselled stone.

20

Particularity, Art and Evaluation

Frank Sibley

It has often been thought that aesthetic judgment, assessment and evaluation differ in some fundamental way from moral and other sorts of judgment, assessment and evaluation. The long tradition to this effect has been revived in recent years, when a number of philosophers have attempted to describe and account for the difference.

Amongst the differences people have claimed to discern, there seems to be, as Strawson says in an article not long ago ("Aesthetic Appraisal", *Oxford Review*, 1966), "a feature of aesthetic judgment, repeatedly but obscurely stressed by writers on the subject, which might contain the possibility of a general distinction", and one moreover that is "a formal, or logical, distinction". This has been variously described: for instance, that to moral and other assessments, general rules and principles are essential, but to aesthetic assessments irrelevant; that for many things, but not in aesthetic matters, there are general criteria of merit; and hence that, in supporting other assessments, but not aesthetic ones, reasons can be given which mention or employ these criteria. Strawson is half-inclined to scepticism over the matter, but also half-inclined to suppose there may be a genuine distinction to be made. I am somewhat less inclined to be sceptical, and I shall try in a way somewhat different from Strawson's to see what the difference might be if there is one.

F. N. Sibley, "Particularity, Art and Evaluation," *Proceedings of the Aristotelian Society*, suppl. vol. 48 (1974), pp. 1–21. Reprinted by courtesy of the Editor of the Aristotelian Society, © 1974.

As it stands, the claim about aesthetics is of course, as Strawson acknowledges, false. We have such general aesthetic merit-terms as 'handsome', 'elegant', 'graceful' and a host of others which function as criteria. (We use these both to support verdicts about works of art being good or fine, and also to support claims of aesthetic merit in people and natural phenomena where the general judgments of commendation supported by them may employ terms like 'splendid', 'marvellous', 'wonderful' etc. rather than, as often with art, 'good' or 'fine'.) Strawson however attempts a more careful statement. Although we may, he admits, support aesthetic verdicts by appeal to such general considerations, such general words as I have instanced are, he says, "not non-evaluative". He agrees with Hampshire that it is meaningless or empty to express moral approval without having reasons of a certain sort, and adds that "giving the reasons would involve mentioning, in terms *not themselves evaluative*, generally applicable criteria of excellence in men or rightness in acts" (my italics); but, he says, "judgment in aesthetic matters is not thus wedded to non-evaluative descriptions of general features of the thing judged". The situation is rather that if we examine those supporting *descriptive* remarks that we may make, we find them to be not general, but mentions of "particular features . . . of the object praised and their relations to each other in the object"; so he sets himself to explain "the putative tautology" that there are "no general descriptive criteria of excellence in the aesthetic sphere" as, by contrast, there are "not only in the sphere of moral behaviour but, it seems, in every other sphere in which we make assessments at all".

Assuming there may be some logical distinction, a contrast of particularity and generality, between aesthetic and other assessment, the writers I have in mind share a central strand of thought in their attempts to explain such a distinction. Most of those who stress the 'non-conceptual character of aesthetic appreciation' link it logically with 'the individuality of the work of art'; that is, they think it is connected with and explained by a certain feature, 'uniqueness', 'particularity', 'individuality' or 'non-repeatability' inherent in the concept of a work of art. Strawson, whose account is a more sophisticated version of a not dissimilar position, also holds "there is point in trying to clarify the notion of aesthetic appraisal *via* the notion of the work of art" and says that "the concepts 'work of art' and 'aesthetic assessment' are logically coupled and move together, in the sense that it would be self-contradictory to speak of judging something *as a work of art*, but not from the aesthetic point of view".

The doctrine I wish to question in this paper is the view, adumbrated by these writers, that any peculiarities there may be in aesthetic assessment are connected with logical features of the concept 'work of art.' I want to argue that the nature of aesthetic appraisal is precisely *not* to be clarified via the concept of a work of art, and that those many writers who have supposed this possible have been confusing two different issues. The adumbrated doctrine is, it seems, one that relies on the criterion of identity of a work of art, works of art being types, not particulars. According to this doctrine, with which I do not wish to quarrel, there cannot be two numerically different art-works which have identical properties or features, or at least, not identical qualities and features relevant to their aesthetic appraisal. Consequently, it is supposed, there cannot be, in Miss Macdonald's words ("Distinctive Features in Criticism of the Arts", *Arist. Soc. Suppl. Vol.* XXIII), two works which "though numerically different, may be qualitatively exactly similar". Miss Macdonald adds that this fact "follows from the way in which we use the term 'work of art'". From this it is supposed somehow to follow that two different works could not share or exhibit the same qualities or merits, and that general criteria in aesthetics are therefore out of place.

I am inclined to think these arguments largely misconceived because they consider aesthetic evaluation only with works of art in mind, which proves to be a red herring. I suggest instead that,

even though there may be philosophically interesting features of the concept 'work of art', any such peculiarities as lack of generality and a non-conceptual character which may characterize aesthetic assessment characterize the latter *independently*. They are typically present in aesthetic assessment as such *whatever* is being judged aesthetically, they do not result from the concept of a work of art, and they would remain in aesthetic judgment and assessment even if we did not have, as we conceivably might not, either any art-works or even the concept 'work of art'. To assess something as a work of art but not from the aesthetic point of view may be, as Strawson says, self-contradictory, but to assess something aesthetically but not as a work of art (as indeed Strawson certainly allows) is not.

I shall therefore suggest that if there are significant differences between aesthetic and other sorts of assessment, they result from certain features of aesthetic judgment as such, not from the concept of art. I shall aim partially to describe what these features might be, and how and why they come to be so. (However I shall not maintain that these features, which may characterize aesthetic assessment, are present in all aesthetic judgments, but only that they are present typically or in most cases of aesthetic judgment.)

Strawson's argument for the main issue involves certain claims about which I want to raise some questions. It is clear from his manner of describing the putative difference between aesthetic and other assessments that he thinks it intimately connected with an evaluative character possessed by aesthetic criteria. As I said, he does not claim that there are no general terms used in supporting aesthetic verdicts; but his claim is that all such general terms are evaluative, not descriptive. He says, e.g. "there are no aesthetic merit-conferring *properties*, with non-evaluative names", there is an "impossibility of general descriptive criteria of aesthetic excellence", and "either [the] names of shareable general properties are themselves evaluative, or, if not, then in applying them we leave our listeners in the dark as to what evaluations to make of the individual works to which they are applied". He certainly takes it however that works may "share these qualities", viz. "characteristics whose names are not non-evaluative". I want to question whether this is really the distinction between aesthetic and other sorts of assessment.

It seems to me that on this matter Strawson's view is unclear or false, at least as regards many aesthetic criteria. There seems, for example, no good reason to say that such criteria of merit as 'unified', 'balanced', 'evocative', 'moving', 'expressive' and 'dynamic' are not descriptive, or are somehow intrinsically evaluative rather than descriptive, or are names of qualities which have no non-evaluative names, whatever exactly that means. But to say what I have just said also raises questions as to the clarity of this evaluative-descriptive distinction of which Strawson avails himself throughout. For I find myself beset by a more radical difficulty than this first easy answer may imply. Despite, or perhaps because of, the sheer amount of writing, especially in ethics, in recent years, I find the notion 'evaluative' (and its correlate, 'descriptive') surrounded by murk and ambiguity, and I am not therefore sure how 'evaluative' should be taken in the present context. For example, should terms be called 'evaluative' when they are simply descriptive but happen to name qualities *valued* in a certain sphere? I will therefore attempt a brief and certainly inadequate conspectus of some of the things that might be meant by 'an evaluative term or expression' by sketching broadly some of the distinguishable things people might have in mind in calling a term evaluative (and hence not descriptive, or not simply or solely descriptive).

First, there may be terms the correct application of which to a thing indicates that the thing has some value without it thereby also being asserted that the thing has some particular or specified quality. It will no doubt be 'contextually implied' thereby that the thing has some qualities in virtue of which it is valued or disvalued but no indication is given of what these qualities may be. Perhaps, if we have such a kind of word in English (besides 'good', 'bad', 'mediocre' etc.), 'nice', 'nasty', 'obnoxious', 'valuable', 'effective', ineffectual', and 'worthless' might be examples.

Such terms as I have offered I will call *intrinsically* or *solely evaluative*: that is, with explainable exceptions in special contexts, they will be evaluative (pro or con) whatever the subject-matter they are applied to, and may be applied to any subject to which their application makes sense. The main point for our present purpose is that, though the thing in question merits these predicates, if it does, in virtue of some or other of its properties, applying the terms to it is not attributing any particular property and, when applied, gives little or no indication of what these properties might be; presumably therefore they may be called 'evaluative' but not 'descriptive' by anyone employing this

dichotomy. (I shall ignore the much-discussed question whether the evaluative or non-descriptive element is commendatory, expressive etc., and I shall assume that judgments applying these predicates are genuine judgments that can be true or false.)

Secondly I turn to what might be regarded as the extreme opposite of such expressions. A term may simply name a property, but a property which, vis-à-vis some sort of things, happens to constitute a merit in those things. 'Sharp' names such a property for razors, 'selective' for wireless sets, 'spherical' for tennis balls, and so on. I see no reason in this fact to suppose that such adjectives should be called 'evaluative' or 'not non-evaluative' rather than simply 'descriptive'; it is not a rule of their use that to apply them to anything, even these things, is to indicate some merit in (or to commend or express approval of) that thing. And, indeed, as applied to some things, the term need indicate no merit at all. I shall therefore assume that these terms are descriptive; I shall call them *descriptive merit-terms*, and whatever quality they name (e.g. sharpness in a razor), a *merit-quality* (of razors) to make clear that they are straightforward property terms. In general one does not need to know, with such a term, 'P', though one often will, that the property counts as a merit in something in order to be able to ascertain that the thing may correctly be called 'P'. This, I believe, is the situation with regard to very many merit-terms in all spheres, including many of those in aesthetics, and is true of many terms that might mistakenly be thought to be of some other type.

I come now to a possible third category of terms, over instances of which there might be dispute. These are terms which are supposed to have both a descriptive and an evaluative component: that is, when they are applied to something, not only is a property being attributed to it but an indication is being given that the speaker has a favourable or unfavourable attitude to that property. If there are such terms in the language, it would be a rule of their use that they are so used; they would be both descriptive, as indicating that a thing had a quality, P, and evaluative, in indicating that the speaker values or disvalues the quality P. But they would not therefore have become what I called intrinsically or solely evaluative terms above, since their correct application to things still entails that the thing has the property P. I will therefore call them *evaluation-added* property terms. That we have such terms in the language I shall not seriously question. Examples might be 'tasty' and 'insipid'. Both would seldom be used without, in the one case, a positive evaluative, in the other, a pejorative force. But the former also clearly means, descriptively, 'having a good deal of flavour', and the latter means 'having little flavour'. Other examples might be 'fragrant', 'noisome', 'cacophonous', 'brash', 'rancid' and so on.

Some philosophers seem to have supposed that merit-terms used in connexion with conduct are of this evaluation-added sort, words like 'courageous', 'honest' and 'considerate'. And if this is so, I see no reason why they should not have done the same with other merit-terms which apply to broad areas of human affairs in which we make evaluative judgments, for example, 'intelligent', 'perceptive', 'astute' and 'obtuse' with regard to mental endowment. About all these cases I am inclined to disagree. They seem to me all clear examples of descriptive terms which, it happens, are generally held to name properties which constitute merits or defects vis-à-vis certain spheres of assessment. In other words I see no better reason for denying that they are descriptive terms than I do in the case of 'sharp' or 'combustible'. One need not know initially that these qualities are held in esteem, though one doubtless usually will, in order to be able to attribute them correctly to things and people. However, for the sake of argument, I shall not deny that it may have come about in the language that some of these terms, correctly applicable only to things with a certain property, P, may have also come to obey a further rule, giving them a second, i.e. evaluation-added, use. If indeed it had become the case, as is sometimes suggested, that these terms have *only* the evaluation-added use, there would presumably be the possibility, if we were fastidious language users, of inventing a merely descriptive term, a name for the property P, and the words instanced above would then be the evaluation-added counterparts of 'P'. But I think no such heroic course is called for, first, because even if these terms do have an evaluation-added use, it seems to me to be secondary and that the terms 'honest', 'courageous', 'intelligent' etc. are available as plain *descriptive* terms, and secondly because if their main use were evaluation-added, it would presumably always be possible to make clear by the context and appropriate disclaimers that only the descriptive element is intended.

If we now turn to the general aesthetic merit-terms that are widely used, into which of the three categories roughly sketched above, if any, do they

fall? It might be held that some at least, the most general ones, 'beautiful', 'ugly', 'lovely', fall into the first, solely evaluative class and, attributing no property, merely imply some of a range of properties. And I shall not dispute this here, though, I am inclined not to think this is always so myself. Secondly, it seems to me that many of our terms fall fairly clearly into the descriptive category and could be applied by someone who did not value such qualities (though since they are widely valued, it would, as I said, be unlikely that a person using them would not either value these qualities himself or know that they were valued by others in a certain way). Such terms in aesthetics might include 'balanced', 'unified', 'evocative', 'vivid', 'funny', 'witty', 'dynamic', 'moving', and so on. These are descriptive, and indicate qualities generally valued in art and aesthetic matters: that is, they are descriptive merit-terms vis-à-vis art (and some of them are descriptive merit-terms vis-à-vis things other than art too).

But there are many other terms used as criteria in aesthetic assessment, and we therefore have to consider these too. It is about these that it might be claimed that some evaluative element is typically present. Examples are 'elegant', 'graceful', 'handsome', 'pretty', 'ungainly', 'garish', 'hideous', and so on. But clearly, of the categories I have suggested, they seem not to be of the intrinsically or solely evaluative type since they indicate the presence of a particular property. But it does seem possible that people would normally learn to use these words and know how to apply them only by also learning that they have an evaluative component and that speakers use them evaluatively vis-à-vis aesthetic matters. I am therefore prepared to admit that they may be in their basic or original use evaluation-added quality words. They seem to me in this respect not unlike 'tasty' or 'brash', and, though evaluative, give a clear enough idea of the quality to be found in things to which they are correctly applied. But even if this is so, I see no reason to suppose that, once we have come to recognize the property, P, which people generally value or admire, we cannot continue to use most of the terms in question, 'graceful', 'handsome', etc., in a neutral and purely descriptive way. This can and, I believe, does happen with the majority of aesthetic merit-terms, with the result that we have purely descriptive uses of many of these terms. That is, it can happen that a person can recognize that something is handsome or graceful, and is willing to call it so, without thereby making any positive evaluation or commendation. Such purely descriptive uses seem to me common in describing the particular aesthetic quality an object or an art-work has (though it is still recognized by those hearing the description that the work has a property which counts as a merit or defect vis-à-vis aesthetic evaluation). I therefore see no overriding case for denying that we have a use for many or most aesthetic terms which is not only partially, but is wholly, descriptive and where, as with 'sharp' or 'honest', a quality is named which happens to be one widely recognized as being of value in a certain sphere.

If I have given a remotely acceptable sketch of different kinds of 'evaluative' terms, it seems to me that, even if in both ethics and aesthetics, terms used as criteria of merit are sometimes used in the evaluation-added way, there are many that are also commonly used in a purely descriptive way, to attribute qualities which happen to be, vis-à-vis ethics or aesthetics, widely regarded as names of merit-qualities. And if this is so, no sufficient logical difference to distinguish between aesthetic and other realms of appraisal and assessment has yet been delineated. If so, the distinctive feature, an alleged form of 'particularity', present in aesthetic assessment, if there is such, still needs further investigation. So I turn to this now.

Where 'P' is a merit-term, it is generally the case, and perhaps nearly always is in aesthetics, that if X is P (say, graceful), something else is also true of X, this something else being that in virtue of which X is P, or which is responsible for X being P. If a woman is graceful, it is *because of* some properties she has, such that, if these later were changed in some ways, she could no longer truly be called graceful. But in a superficially similar way, if a man is courageous or honest, it is *because of* some facts about him or properties he has, such that, if these latter had been different in some way, he could not have been truly called courageous. Thus, X's merit *consists* in X's being P (graceful or courageous) and something else, Q, is, and ordinarily must be, *responsible for* X's being P, or having that merit. I shall call these respectively *merit-constituting* properties and *merit-responsible* properties. But if we ask about the nature of merit-responsible properties and the relationship indicated by the words 'because of' or 'responsible for' we often find, I believe (I hesitate to say always), significant differences between aesthetic instances and others. Perhaps it is in this area, rather than in a specially

evaluative character in aesthetic criteria, that differences should be sought.

Now the stress that writers on aesthetics place upon particularity seems to be a stress upon the alleged fact that that because of which 'P' is applicable to X is X's possession of some particular feature Q which it and *only it* can have. Such 'features', 'respects' or 'parts' are not to be confused, according to Strawson, with properties or qualities, which are shareable and hence general. Being individual they are not shareable, except in such ways as being for instance capable of being *incorporated in*, as a part of, another art-work. But it is here that there seems an unclarity.

A part of a work, it is true, is an individual, incapable of being shared, capable at best of being incorporated in another work. Parts are individual elements, not general features. But a part of a work has some characteristics or qualities, and these, being general and shareable, might be found also in, and so characterize, a part of another work, as for instance there are many parts with common qualities shared by Goya's *Maja Vestida* and *Maja Desnuda*. Indeed, if a part of feature of one work were identical with a part or feature of another work, being, say, of exactly the same colour, shape and arrangement, it would be because the parts or features shared identical qualities. This requires us to make a different distinction, not that between individual parts and properties, but between different types of properties and descriptions, namely, between particular properties and descriptions on the one hand and general or non-particular properties and descriptions on the other. And since there is clearly a possible ambiguity here about the word 'general', I shall use, instead of the terms 'particular' and 'general', the terms 'determinate' and 'determinable' in the sense in which, with respect to shape, 'square' is determinate and 'triangular' determinable. For whereas 'general' and 'particular' may be used to mean shareable and non-shareable respectively, in which case all properties, including determinate ones, are general, they may also be used to mean respectively 'determinable' and 'determinate', in which case only some properties would be general, though all are shareable. With this distinction, it may be said that, even if a part or feature of one work cannot be shared by another work, one work might have a part or feature qualitatively indistinguishable in all respects from part of another, both parts sharing the same determinate, not merely the same determinable properties.

Frank Sibley

I can now say what I want to, though what follows applies most directly to visual objects; slightly different but partially parallel things must be said about literature and music. When we apply a merit term, 'P', to a thing, X, we do so (as Strawson says) on account of some feature or part of X, and such parts or features are individuals and may be, as he says, unshareable. Nevertheless we do, of course, apply 'P' to 'X' because of the properties of the parts or features, and these properties, even if determinate, could be shared by parts or features of other works.

We may now be able to describe what I think may be the situation with much if not all aesthetic assessment. First it seems that, typically, when 'P', an *aesthetic* merit-predicate or evaluation-added predicate applies to a thing, X, it is normally because X or a part or feature of X has some *determinate* property (or complex of properties); and it is because of the fact that X or a part of X has this determinate character, not some merely *determinable* character, that X is P and therefore valued. More accurately, a thing is P (and valued for being so) in virtue of some *determinate* property, Q, because of which it possesses the (determinable) merit-property, P. A thing is graceful in virtue of being curved in exactly the way it is, not just in virtue of being curved. A slightly different curve might not be graceful, and so on. There is, it seems typically, no *determinable* description, 'Q', such that, if the description applies to the thing or part of it, the thing can be said to be P, even though having the *determinate* quality Q_1 is the reason for, or responsible for its being P. This may be where and how 'particularity' comes in. A line is not graceful because it is curved, but because of its particular curve, etc. Indeed it is a commonplace in aesthetics that the slightest change, of a word in a poem, a colour or line in a painting, or a note in a musical composition may give an entirely different aesthetic character to the whole or part. To say that 'general', as opposed to 'particular', explanations of the applicability of merit-terms is not possible may therefore often be to say that mention of merely determinable characteristics is no good. In many other spheres, especially those, like morality, often contrasted with the aesthetic, such a situation does not perhaps ordinarily obtain.

If this account is in the main correct, if in the aesthetic sphere the possession by X of determinable characteristics is not what is responsible for X being P (though something is), *it follows at once* that a thing cannot be judged to be P, or to have merit, by 'general descriptive criteria' if this means criteria mentioning determinable properties which are responsible for merit-qualities. To be assured that a thing, Y, has P, one has to be assured that it is *exactly* like X in respects relevant to P, and no criterion of the form "If a thing has the *determinable*, Q, it will be P" can be used. Yet if, on the other hand, 'general descriptive criteria' must mean criteria mentioning *determinate* qualities that are responsible for merit-qualities, we are at a loss how to proceed. With respect to colours and shapes for instance, the language contains such a (possibly ineradicable) paucity of words naming determinate properties; we might be able, uncharacteristically, to give a fully determinate description, say, of a Mondrian (two vertical black bars on a white ground, etc.) but we presumably could not for a Turner or a Pollock. And when we come to poems or music it is hard to see what a description of their determinate properties would be at all. Indeed the notion of a fully determinate description of a poem or a piece of music is a somewhat dubious one, amounting perhaps as Strawson says to no more than saying "It goes like this" – and then reproducing "or quoting or playing it", which, as he says, is not a description. But there is not after all much difference here with lines and colours; for a graceful line, we might equally be reduced to saying "it goes like this", and drawing it. So perhaps for present purposes we could allow as a determinate description of a line of poetry, anything which tied it down exactly; e.g. "it contains the words 'Of', 'Man's', 'first' 'disobedience', in that order", etc.

It is here, perhaps, that considerations about particularity, in the sense of *determinateness* (which is what, by many of their remarks, writers on this topic seem obscurely to have in mind) will take us. It is this apparent fact, namely, that a thing which is P (say, graceful) because of a determinate property Q_1, might fail to be P if it had instead a different determinate property Q_2, even where Q_1 and Q_2 are determinates of the same determinable (say, curved), which, I believe, is part of what aestheticians may have sought to express when they have said, e.g. that each thing must be judged by its own standards, that they cannot be judged by general criteria, that there are no rules for judging aesthetic excellence, etc. And this, if true, is about the relation between merit-terms or criteria and the sort of properties in virtue of which they are applied, and would presumably be so whether the correct account of aesthetic merit-terms, like 'P', is that they are descriptive merit-terms, or that they are evaluation-added ones. (I want to suggest only that this is a typical, not an invariable, feature of the relation between merit-responsible properties and merit-constituting properties in aesthetics. There may occasionally be cases of merit-responsible properties which are not determinate, in which case X is P simply because it has the determinable property Q. A possible example might be symmetrical (Q), which I take to be determinable, and in virtue of which a thing must be balanced (P). But if so, these are exceptional or peripheral cases, as is shown by the fact that a building or a picture might be balanced without being symmetrical, symmetricality being the limiting case into which balance shades off. We might call such terms as 'symmetrical', if there are a few such, terms for *determinable merit-responsible qualities*.) But, generally and typically, the qualities responsible for aesthetic merit-qualities are determinate. What of course may be the case is that, for instance, the applicability of the term P (graceful) may entail that the thing X has some determinable character (curving); but it does not entail that it has this or that determinate curve. Whether the determinate curve it has is one that makes it graceful is an open question to be decided by inspection.

It should be noticed that a general consequence of the foregoing would be that, if it were known that a thing, X, had a determinate characteristic, Q, and that Q was responsible for X having the aesthetic merit P, and if – as would be rare indeed – we had a name or description of the *determinate* characteristic Q, the general criterion, "Any thing which has the *determinate* (merit-responsible) character Q will have the merit P" *would* be available for use. But, given the resources of language and the almost total absence of determinate descriptions, such a criterion would rarely, if ever, be achieved, and, even if it were, it would be of little value since it would be usable only with other things, Y and Z, which had precisely the same determinate characteristic, Q. For instance, if one knew that the particular curve of the glass of a goblet gave it a graceful outline, one could safely say of identically shaped goblets, but only of those (whether of glass or silver), without inspection, that they would be graceful too. (It is to be noted that this principle, that even a slight difference in the merit-responsible qualities or features of an object may result in a very different aesthetic quality, is in no way tied to the notion of art-works. It applies to natural objects like trees or face-profiles and so on.

The fact therefore that, with art-works, the criterion of identity requires us to count two identical lines of poetry as one line (tokens of one type) has nothing to do with the matter of the absence of and virtual impossibility of stating determinate descriptive criteria of merit.)

I said that this may be where the question of particularity in aesthetics will take us in describing the typical character of aesthetic assessment. But there may be more that is characteristic of the aesthetic, and perhaps of equal importance, to describe. The all but abortive attempt to find general i.e. determinable merit-responsible qualities (as symmetrical was for balance) may bring us face to face with something equally fundamental about the conceptual character of aesthetic assessment. This is that the kind of responsibility relation that connects even determinate properties with the merit-predicate for whose correct application they are responsible is essentially non-conceptual and therefore different from the connexion in many other spheres of assessment.

For instance, in many spheres, including ethics, there is often a connexion of meaning perhaps approaching an entailment between some description of those features or properties (Q, R, etc.) responsible for the merit-term 'P' being applicable and the merit-term 'P' itself. This is why one can use the determinable descriptions 'Q', 'R', etc. to move with an assurance guaranteed conceptually from those descriptions to application of merit-terms and assertions of merit. Anyone who *understands the language involved* can see the relevance of the sort of description that appears in the citation, "he held several men at bay despite realizing the great danger to himself", etc. to 'courageous', or of "he always returns lost items, not his own, to their owner", etc. to "honest", and will understand the connexion. To fail to would be a failure of linguistic understanding. This may be typically the situation in ethics. But there are no or few such connexions of meaning between descriptions, even wholly determinate ones (on the rare occasions they may be possible) of those properties responsible for the applicability of an *aesthetic* merit-term and that term itself. No such conceptual connexion holds for instance between a description, even if determinate, given say in co-ordinates, of a particular curve and such a term as 'graceful', or between being the determinate British Standard Colour B.S.C. 8-090 (Columbine) and being delicate, let alone between *determinable* descriptions, say, of poetry or music ("it is strophic, monosyllabic, deals with unrequited love", etc.) and such terms as 'moving' or 'elegant'. Indeed, although, as I said, the notion of a fully determinate description of a poem, and perhaps of a piece of music is a dubious one, if we attempted to describe determinately a line of poetry by citing the words that occur in it and their order, there would be no conceptual connexion between the fact that the line went *like that* and its being, say, moving. Thus it seems to be that while in the aesthetic case, typically, a thing with such and such a determinate responsible property or character is, by having it, an instance of what is rightly described as 'graceful', 'moving' or 'elegant', in the moral case the *description* of the responsible property is a description of something which, *because it fits the description*, constitutes an instance of, say, courageousness. In the aesthetic case it is because of certain particular properties (Q) of X that X is P; in the moral case it is because a certain *description* of certain facts (Q) about X is appropriate that it *follows* (barring disclaimers in special contexts) that X is P. The one true application of 'P' is simply dependent on the fact that X *is* Q, the other on the fact that X is describable as 'Q' and upon the relation of the descriptions 'Q' to 'P'. This may be why it is said we have to read the poem, hear the music or see the picture (not merely have it described in non-merit and even determinate descriptive terms if that were possible), and then *judge* or *decide* whether an aesthetic merit-term applies to it or not, whereas we can often apply moral merit-terms on the basis of a description containing no moral merit-terms. This, then, may be a main difference, whatever may account for it, between ethics and other matters on the one hand and aesthetics on the other.

It might be worth noting a further contrast between aesthetic and certain other assessments which may be made. I have suggested that in aesthetics there would typically be lacking any conceptual connexion between the description (if one were possible) of the (usually determinate) merit-responsible characteristics and the merit-term. The aesthetic case is distinctive in another way and must be distinguished from other non-aesthetic cases where there is equally no conceptual or meaning connexion. This may be best exemplified by a contrast of examples. It may be the case that being easily visible, at varying distances and in varying light, is a merit vis-à-vis, say, motorway-workers' clothes. It may also be a contingent fact established by experience (not a connexion of

meaning between 'plain colour' and 'easily visible') that clothes which are plain colours are more easily visible than clothes that are speckled or flecked. Because of this contingent fact, being of one plain colour (Q) is a property responsible for the applicability of the merit-predicate 'P' in question ('easily visible'); it may even come to be treated as a criterion of merit. In such a case, however, the two facts about the clothing can be established or ascertained separately and independently; one might notice that certain clothing was more easily visible in certain lights or at some distance and discover later, when it was brought nearer, that it was of one plain colour. It need not be the case in such instances that, in discovering that the material has the merit of being more easily seen than others, one can at the same time see or be able to tell that it is monochromatic. That is, one property of it, which is a merit-property, for which another property is responsible, might conceivably be discovered without, in those circumstances, it being the case that one could simultaneously discern the other which is responsible for it. But in an aesthetic case, if a man were not in a position to see or discern that a line had such and such a curve, or a poem contained such and such a concatenation of words, or that B.S.C. 8-090 was of a certain shade, he could not conceivably tell that the line was, or pronounce it to be, graceful, or the poem moving, or the colour delicate. The two facts must be co-perceptual or co-discoverable. It is thus distinguishable from the visibility case. The perception of the merit, P, is not possible without the perception of X being Q. It is this particular way in which such aesthetic characteristics as being moving or being graceful are properties of a particular combination of words or of the particular curvature of a line that is distinctive. Just as a rich red is not just a rich colour and red, so too a line is not just curved in a certain way and graceful, nor are the words of a poem put together just so and also moving; the curvature is a graceful curvature, the combination of words a moving one. This is why one is able to decide the applicability of 'moving' or 'graceful' only in so far as one is at the same time able to discern the (responsible) properties which the lines or word-combination have; this is why they have to be co-discernible. One sees the grace *in* that particular curve, sees that that particular curve is a graceful one. And if one cannot clearly see or discern the determinate character or properties which are responsible for the merit-term 'P' being applicable, one cannot discern that 'P' applies. This is what, in aesthetics, tempts one, understandably but doubtless too inexactly, to think of these connexions as perceptual matters.

I return now briefly to the doctrine with which I began, that in the aesthetic sphere, unlike the moral, the reason there are no general descriptive criteria of merit results from the fact that, given the way we use the concept 'work of art', two or more works of art cannot be identical, identical ones being instances of a one art-work type; and hence that there is no place for general, i.e., shareable criteria of merit. There are, I believe, many objections to this view. I shall consider however only one, and one that applies, I believe, even to Strawson's more sophisticated version of the doctrine. He rejects the simple view that the absence in aesthetics of general non-evaluative criteria (and he must mean what I call merit-*responsible* as opposed to what I call merit-*constituting* characteristics, for he thinks the latter *are* evaluative and shareable) rests upon the fact that art-works are individuated by types, for so are wireless-sets, postage stamps and motor-cars. His supplementation of this view is that in so far as a work of art is being judged *aesthetically* (as works of art often, though not always, are), we are restricted to exactly that range of characteristics that make it the work it is and not another. He says that "when we have a class of objects of which the name 'works of art', marks them out as primarily to be assessed in this way" (i.e. aesthetically), "then there cannot be numerically distinct members of the class . . . which yet share all the features relevant to this kind of assessment". An art-work, considered as a type, is coextensive with the features relevant to its aesthetic appraisal. Everything that is relevant to its being this work, not another, is also relevant to its aesthetic character and value. Consequently, with works of art, all features relevant to their individuation as type-instances are also features relevant to their evaluation as works of art; whereas with cars or wireless-sets, merits might be identical but the objects be of different types. From this he concludes that one wireless-set (type), unlike an art-work (type), could be distinguished from another, yet both have, and so share, the same wireless merit-properties; and consequently that there logically is a place for general criteria of merit applicable to numerically different types of wireless-sets.

But if this were the explanation of the lack of general criteria in aesthetics, there would be the result, as Strawson seems to admit, that the same would be true of the *aesthetic* features of wireless-sets and other things which are *not* works of art. For if I understand him aright this would mean that whereas there logically *could not* be general non-evaluative aesthetic criteria of merit, shareable by more than one *work of art*, there *could* be such general aesthetic criteria available in judging things *other* than works of art. He says for example that "as far as works of art are concerned, the idea of an aesthetic merit-conferring *property*" (presumably with a "non-evaluative" name) is a mistake, but that "the idea in question might have application in some cases of things other than works of art of which we may make aesthetic assessments". For instance, two motor-car types might be "identical in aesthetically relevant respects and yet be numerically two" and that "here we might perhaps think of their *appearance* as a shared property".

Thus it seems that he thinks that it would be *only* in relation to works of art that aesthetic descriptive criteria would be, for logical reasons, unavailable. With other things there might be such descriptive aesthetic criteria. Yet Strawson has admitted that what I called merit-*constituting* properties (though he thinks the names of these properties, like 'delicate', 'graceful', 'economical', etc. are evaluative) are shareable by works of art and therefore presumably also by other things (whereas I have argued that most such aesthetic merit-constituting properties have, as names, merit-terms which are simply descriptive). So there is no difference *here* between judging works of art and things which are not; which leaves us with the question whether, with things *other* than works of art, but not with works of art, there are general descriptive criteria of merit available in merit-*responsible* descriptive terms. And if what I argued earlier is right, it seems that the situation here is the same for other things as it is for art. We cannot, and largely because we lack the ability to provide determinate descriptions, use any criterion that would guarantee that, say, the lines of a car were graceful. The most that could happen would be, as in my example of the goblets, that we could know that an object that shared the identical (descriptive) merit-responsible property would also be graceful. But the property in question, even if we could describe it, say by co-ordinates, would still have to be determinate, and so not applicable to even slightly different objects. All we get is some such statement as "Anything which is exactly like this in respects Q, R, etc. (a determinate description would follow here if one were possible) is graceful (or handsome, or balanced, or whatever)". It would therefore be virtually useless as a criterion of merit, even if it were attainable. And it is this unattainability of adequate determinate descriptions in our language that I have been at pains to stress. The uselessness in aesthetics of trying to give general criteria of merit in *determinable* merit-responsible terms or descriptions, and the virtual impossibility in our language of giving them in *determinate* merit-responsible terms or descriptions are the two main points I have wished to emphasize throughout. And this situation applies equally whether the criteria are to apply to works of art or to anything else. Thus, whatever 'particularity' and 'non-conceptual' character there is in the relationship of merit-responsible characteristics to the applicability of aesthetic merit-terms – features which distinguish aesthetic from moral and other sorts of assessment – these continue to exist in aesthetic evaluations even when the evaluations are not of works of art. They are not linked essentially to, or dependent upon, the concept of a work of art, and could exist without the existence of this concept.

I summarize what I have said about the particularity and non-conceptual character of aesthetic assessment: (1) There are criteria of merit in aesthetics in the sense that, if certain terms ('merit-terms') are applicable to a thing, it has thereby some aesthetic merit. But these terms are not significantly more 'evaluative' or less 'descriptive' than merit-terms to be found in many other spheres. (2) But there are at best few criteria of merit in aesthetics if this means that there are *determinable* descriptions of properties responsible for a merit-term being applicable which can serve as criteria or justifications for the application of a merit-term, whereas this is often the case in ethics and other spheres. This results from the fact that the properties responsible for an aesthetic merit-term being applicable are normally determinate. (3) Even if we could achieve *determinate* descriptions of those properties which are responsible for an aesthetic merit-term being applicable – and usually we cannot – they would be virtually useless because usable only with determinately identical things; nor would they be, as descriptions of merit-responsible features are in ethics, conceptually connected with the merit-terms in question. (4) Finally, I have suggested that, if there is a peculiarity, namely a certain sort of 'particularity' about aesthetic assessment, it concerns the nature of and relation between the neutrally descriptive properties of a thing and its possession of aesthetic merit-qualities, and does *not* therefore result, as many recent writers have thought, from the logical character of the concept 'work of art'. It is because writers on aesthetics have so constantly had their eyes on works of art, and have been bewitched by the criterion of identity for art-works being such that identical instances count as one work, that they have supposed this fact, which is in reality irrelevant, to be accountable for the 'particularity' present in aesthetic assessment. They are particularly prone to this because musical and literary creations form a large part of art and have no counterparts in nature. But if one thinks of natural objects (which are non-verbal and non-musical and do not therefore tempt us into this mistake), objects like faces, bodies, mountains, trees, swans, as well as *visual* artefacts like motor-cars, etc., one can see clearly that the features characteristic of aesthetic evaluation remain the same there, even though the criterion of identity of art-works is not involved.

21

The Test of Time

Anthony Savile

'His reforms in administration, judicial proceedings, financial and military organisation stood the test of time.' So speaks Rostovtzeff of the Emperor Diocletian.[1] But what exactly is meant by describing these reforms as having stood time's test? And what conclusions do we want to draw from their having done so? These two issues will occupy the present chapter.

I

The Premiss

Neither common parlance nor observation innocent of theory tells us more than a very little about what it might be for something to withstand time's test. We shall have to supplement that little dialectically, by choosing a description of the starting-point that looks as if it might justify kinds of inference we are inclined to base upon it. There will be nothing vicious about this procedure and there is no alternative to it. It leaves it entirely open whether such a derivation really can be effected. On the other hand it shows us a fair amount about what we must take ourselves to be talking about if the critical device I am concerned with is to be of any practical utility at all.

The first suggestion that comes to mind is that there is no more to passing the test than just surviving over a significant period. In their main lines

Anthony Savile, Chapter 1 from Anthony Savile, *The Test of Time* (Oxford: Oxford University Press, 1982), pp. 3–20. Reprinted by permission of Oxford University Press.

Diocletian's reforms dominated the civilized world for several centuries and formed the basis on which the empire rested. Yet a moment's thought makes it clear that mere survival cannot be sufficient, and a second moment's reflection that when considered in relation to the arts it may not even be necessary either. I take sufficiency first.

In the case of Diocletian matters might have stood thus, though in fact they did not. After its original introduction the administrative and military organization that he instituted might have come to determine the structure of the empire in a merely token way, much as the orders of precedence set out in Burke and Debrett give one only a token picture of the organization of English society today. In reality the empire might have been controlled by different factors altogether, and while Diocletian's reforms could still have enjoyed a lingering survival they would not then have merited Rostovtzeff's warm appraisal. We should not be able to say of them that they had stood time's test because we should not be able to conclude anything about their merits from such merely token persistence.

The same reflection will apply to art. Think of some long-lived carving, say one of the red granite crocodiles of the Ptolemaic period that inhabit the Capitoline museums. These stone beasts may well survive for centuries without attracting the notice of more than a few idle visitors, and their longevity will do absolutely nothing to secure them a place in the halls of artistic fame. So once again we shall not say they stand the test of time. Indeed, if the sheer physical persistence of an object were all that were relevant there would even be some reason to think that the longer a work of art survives the *less* worthy it is of our attention, and that would quite unfit our test for critical employment. For consider works which we associate with particular physical objects: painting, carved statues, drawings, and the like. The finer they are the more insistently we demand to see and touch them. Hence the greater their exposure to wear and tear, to accident and decay. The Limbourg brothers' *Très riches heures du Duc de Berry* exemplify this well. Exquisitely illuminated pages, they are in constant demand with the visiting public yet are extremely delicate. Were it not for the museum's discreet substitution of copies in their place, exposure to natural light would soon wreak havoc with their limpid colours. Only because this substitution is practised are they safe from a risk of destruction lesser works do not run. It follows that if survival alone were what mattered the verdict delivered by time would too often be in favour of the mediocre and the downright inferior and not of the genuinely great.

In the case of Diocletian's reforms it was obvious that what mattered was less unqualified survival than *effective* survival – that was what earned the historian's esteem. Correspondingly, in the arts what we care about is not survival *simpliciter* but effective survival's analogue, persistence of the work in our attention. This idea will receive some comment in a moment, but first we can reduce the theoretical importance of unqualified survival even further by making out that in the arts it is not even a necessary condition of a work's passing time's test, let alone a sufficient one.

Concentrating first on the autographic arts, by which I mean those whose individual works are constituted of matter, consider Leonardo's lost (probably destroyed) painting *Leda and the Swan*. Gone though the original canvas is we can still see Bugiardini's copy of it in the Borghese gallery, and while that is of little interest in its own right it does permit something of Leonardo's painting to survive. On its testimony, and on that of others – Raphael's drawing, the one in the Louvre, and the interpretation at Wilton – we can come to a tentative judgement of Leonardo's own work so that it may, despite its actual non-existence, still hold a place in our attention.

If another example is wanted imagine an exponent of auto-destructive art tracing his finest work upon the sands before the rising tide. The only record of his activity could well be photographic, and through this evidence we might reasonably aspire to sound judgement of his work. Maybe we

would do better to confront the original and savour its passage (if only we could), but without that experience we are not at a total loss. Once more the work may survive in our attention without itself surviving.

In the allographic arts, where the existence and survival of the individual work is not tied to the persistence of any particular physical object, the case is parallel. A musical composition or a work of literature is extant as long as there remains available to us a causally appropriate method of constructing a true performance of it or of giving it a true reading. Here the rejected idea of simple survival has to be construed in terms of such persisting availability – already a large step away from any naïve suggestion about physical persistence – but it is still arguable that the loss of all means of reconstructing true performance or reading need be no bar to the work's passing time's test. Suppose for instance that some major composition of J. S. Bach's had for some reason ceased to be available and was therefore no longer extant. We need not also suppose that the same holds true of some Busoni-like transcription of the work. Nor must we suppose it impossible for a good musicologist to get us to see what the original of Bach's would have been like even though he could not reconstruct from the transcription an accurate performance of the original. With his assistance, as with that of Bugiardini, the no longer extant work might still have some claim to survive in our attention.

Fanciful examples are of no importance in themselves, only for what they show. And that, I take it, is a confirmation of my assertion that the artistic analogue of the effective survival of Diocletian's reforms is the work of art's survival in our attention. That, I claim, is a necessary element in the passage of time's test, while survival strictly speaking is not, even though for the most part only those things that do survive in the stricter way survive time's test. None the less as far as logic goes that is just a contingent matter.

Survival of art in our attention is an opaque notion about which I shall not have much to say. Traditional discussion of it as bearing on aesthetics has repeatedly insisted that there are many reasons why a work of art may hold our attention and that only some of them have any close connection with the formation of reliable critical judgement. In particular our attention must be 'aesthetic', given to the work 'disinterestedly', and 'for its own sake,' not for some extraneous reason.

It is, however, far easier to know what such terms as these exclude than to give any positive and helpful characterization of them. They would rule out attention given to a work solely on account of its author's identity – say, to an obviously inferior Leonardo or to an unrecognized masterpiece by Winston Churchill; they would exclude vulgar curiosity about works which break price records in the sale-room; also such interest in the monstrance of Toledo Cathedral as is drummed up by the guides' revelation that its surmounting cross is made of the first gold Columbus sent back from the Indies. Only it is unclear what are the principles one relies on to extend the list. Perhaps the most satisfactory thing to say is that every ground of attention to an object should be let in, as contributing to its 'effective survival', that could pertinently bear on the formation of a critical estimation of it as the work of art it is. That at any rate is how I shall take this notion here, and I shall pause over the stipulation only long enough to make four parenthetical comments.

(a)   So glossed, the idea does not have the effect of allowing only those works of art to survive which are in fact correctly estimated or even enjoy high esteem. It is perfectly possible for our attention to be held for reasons which are relevant to the formation of critical estimation but for that estimate to be low or to be mistaken.

(b)   The proposal guides us better than the negatively inspired examples in fixing the proper extension of the expression 'survives in our attention'. If we were ambitious and aimed at capturing its intension in this way too, then we should need to be confident that our ideas of the aesthetic as it applies to nature could be developed on a base that restricts itself to the arts. I myself do not find that an unattractive prospect.

(c)   The suggestion also commits us to explaining what art itself is without reliance on an antecedently understood notion of the aesthetic. It is not evident that this is an impossibility. One might hope to introduce the two ideas simultaneously or else, more plausibly to my mind, proceed by first offering a recursive account of art and subsequently introducing the idea of the aesthetic on that base.[2] I shall have nothing to say about either project here.

(d)   It is a welcome consequence of fixing the notion of the aesthetic in this way that it avoids any suggestion of formalism. The connection between our aesthetic interest in something and its involvement with matters of moral, emotional, and cogni-

tive import may be as deep and inextricable as we like. This point is of much consequence.

To pass time's test, then, a work of art has to hold our attention for reasons that bear on its critical estimation as the work it is. To do this it must in particular hold our attention *under some interpretation*, and it seems clear that we have to say that the interpretation in point must be one that allows the work to be correctly perceived and understood. For supposing that we let in what we later come to recognize as a mistaken interpretation, since it could not found a justified estimation of the work the point of saying that under it the work had passed time's test would be nil. To the extent that we want survival *reliably* to underwrite evaluation we have to insist that the survival that counts must be under an interpretation that is appropriate to the work.

For the moment I shall attempt no greater precision than this. But it evidently gives rise to an issue that must occupy us deeply in due course. Can the interpretation that is allowed to be appropriate be one that varies over time? Shall we want to say, as many do, that at different times different ways of taking works of art may properly be recommended – perhaps as they accord better or worse with the cultural climate of the time – and consequently think that what survives for our purposes may have to take such changes into account? Or shall we say that proper interpretation is stable and liable to fade as time passes? The answers that we give to these questions are of the greatest importance, for not only do the alternative replies yield very different sets of works as withstanding time's test, they also force us to justify the inferences we hope to base on this premiss in different ways. Indeed it may turn out that on one of these alternatives justification of our critical practice is made impossible and has no worth. Such a consequence might itself have some weight in encouraging one choice here rather than another.

Description of the initial premiss cannot be left here. We know in advance that what survival must legitimize is an estimate of the surviving work as in some way exemplary; but, without further restrictions being imposed on what survival is, it will be easy to envisage situations in which a work of literature or music regularly attracts attention over a long period without our being in the least inclined to suppose it to be of high quality. This is far less bizarre than it sounds. Often we select a particular work for study because of the illumination it throws upon a different work, and we recognize that it is only by giving our attention (*aesthetic* attention) to the poorer piece that we come to form a just estimate of its successor's greatness. To take an example, we might agree with Auerbach that 'before Dante, vernacular literature – especially that of Christian inspiration – is on the whole rather naïve as far as questions of style are concerned, and that despite the influence of scholastic rhetoric'. But we also think that 'Dante, although he takes his material from the most living and sometimes from the humblest vernacular, has lost this naïve quality. He subdues every turn of expression to the gravity of his tone, and when he sings of the divine order of things, he solves his problem by using periodic articulations and devices of sentence structure which command gigantic masses of thought and concatenations of events; since antiquity nothing comparable had existed in literature.'[3] Now to make the truth of these sentences apparent to ourselves and others we may have to test what they say against early Christian vernacular literature, and then interesting though decidedly second-rate works may come to hold a place in our attention for their own sake which on their own they could scarcely justify.

To meet this difficulty we need only insist that the attention we give to the work that stands time's test be not only aesthetic attention but also be given to the work autonomously, in its own right, and not as a means to assist the evaluation and appreciation of other works. This clause has to be added because it cannot be assumed to be incorporated in the proper understanding of the aesthetic itself. For as we have just seen, the attention we give to the poorer work in learning to appreciate the greater must itself be acknowledged to be that; otherwise it could not serve its purpose. Hence even if some such phrase as 'disinterested' or 'for its own sake' should be useful to characterize that notion, we go further than this in requiring that the attention that the work receives be given to it in its own right as well.

One last preliminary matter calls for comment. I have spoken of survival without any attempt at quantifying it, and it would be natural to ask how much attention is going to be enough, and to inquire just whose attention is to count. To the former of these questions it ought to be apparent that there could be no determinate answer. Dr Johnson required the poet to have 'outlived his century, the term commonly fixed on as the test of literary merit'; Gustav Mahler apparently thought

that fifty years would do when claiming that within that time his turn would come; Gertrud Schönberg is rather less committal, saying simply that posterity would best judge her husband's work. ('When does posterity begin?', one might wonder.) The important things to note are that no one will be impressed by a critic's reference to the passage of time unless he sees the period during which the work has held our attention as of considerable length, and that the critic will be wise not to appeal to temporal considerations unless he thinks that his reader will be struck by them. There would, after all, be no point in making the claims we do in any other case. So it is perfectly legitimate to leave this point vague. The work must survive for a sufficient period. Nor should we forget that for the most part our interest in time's test is not one that imposes a yes/no answer to the question 'Does this work pass or fail?' What we are usually concerned about is not what happens at the margin, but how securely and how surely the work has survived. At the back of our minds we have a belief that there is a connection between the length of time over which the work has held our attention and the degree of confidence we have in our judgements of its merits, and this is one thing that has to be explained.

This thought makes it easier than it would otherwise be to say informatively who 'we' are whose attention to the work determines the matter. As before there need be no precise answer, but we know whose judgement, repeated or sustained over time, we find to be significant. Our confidence in inferences that are based on survival will be greater according as the work is widely appreciated over time by members of our common culture whom we recognize as artistically sensitive and concerned with correct perception and judgement in the arts. In particular we shall be impressed by the influence the work has had on later artists and critics whose work we think important, and by the place the work holds throughout the community in its picture of its own culture and its own traditions.

Practising critics may be disturbed by the simplicity and imprecision of these remarks. Such a reaction is not in point. In the first place no question is yet begged about the uniform accuracy of the perceptions that persons in this class make. For it is the task of later theory to explain how we get from the premiss that makes reference to this class of judgements to our conclusions. Secondly there is nothing in what I have said that denies that there may be much disagreement among members of the cultural core about the merits of any given work. Nothing said so far is incompatible with Schönberg's remark that 'I know after all, that the works which in every way arouse one's dislike are precisely those that the next generation will in every way like'[4] or with the common cynical view that the critic is often one whose responses to the arts are the bluntest. All that reference to a chosen class is meant to do is to point out that when we come to determine how well this work or that has stood the test we take into account the place that it holds in our culture, its degree of embeddedness, so to speak. Without reference to a core set of persons who give the culture its character, this notion of embeddedness would be empty.

The importance of the notion of degree of embeddedness that we attribute to the individual work will emerge later, especially when I discuss some corrupt forms of aesthetic judgement. For the moment we may note its use in helping us to determine how well this work or that has survived the rigours of time, and make appeal to it in our final formulation of what it is for art to do so. In passing, we may also find it useful in disqualifying such things as many of the better-known and perennially enjoyed children's stories, or Nahum Tate's sugary version of *King Lear*, which practically replaced Shakespeare's version of the play in public consciousness for the best part of 150 years. It is only if we have a way of dealing with such cases as these, which might otherwise appear to be good candidates for secure passage of the test, that there is any hope of providing it with adequate legitimization. And what could we use to avoid these dangers other than a structured view of a culture, one in which some opinions carry greater weight than others? If there is no alternative to making this move, then we must expect it to surface in a decently articulated version of our starting-point.

The final formulation I propose then, is this. A well-chosen autographic or allographic work of art securely survives the test of time if over a sufficiently long period it survives in our attention under an appropriate interpretation in a sufficiently embedded way.[5] This condition will only be satisfied if the attention that the work is given is of a kind that generates experience relevant to its critical appreciation and attracts the attention that is given to it in its own right. On the other hand, a work of either sort will fail the test if, being sufficiently available, it does not fulfil these criteria. Note that these two alternatives, secure passage

and sure failure, are not exhaustive. There are many works of art which for one reason or another are never even brought to the test. They are simply not available, being lost or destroyed, damaged or obscured. With them I shall not be concerned, nor for the most part shall I consider those works we think of as failures. Accounting for the store we set by success is taxing enough.

II

The Conclusions

In my introductory paragraphs I offered a rough and ready description of the way we are inclined to use the information that a poem or a painting 'lasts'. It helps us to sort out accurate from inaccurate estimates of disputed works, and to assess their stature. It assists us in buttressing our own assessment of works we believe are not adequately understood and appreciated, and to mitigate unfavourable criticism of them. That is a very general way of putting it, and what is intended under such heads can be more precisely put in terms of the conclusions we draw from a work's success or its failure by our test, or from the ways in which we compare one work against another in its success or failure.

Success. (1) Where a work of art has securely passed time's test we infer that it is a work of high quality. This vagueness in my formulation is deliberate. There is no one scale of quality with which we are concerned in our assessment of the arts, and native intuition about the conclusions we draw from the fact that a work has survived in our attention is not highly determinate. As before, precision can only come dialectically, with the development of theory. However, while the phrasing I have used in stating this first conclusion is pretty anodyne it is certainly not empty. To be told that a painting or a poem is of high quality or, as I shall sometimes say, is meritorious, is clearly to be told something interesting about it. In the sequel it is with the derivation of this conclusion that I shall primarily be concerned.

(2) Suppose a work of art that does pass time's test has at an early stage of its history been appreciated on the grounds that it displayed a particular aesthetic character, and that this is the reason traditionally advanced for thinking the work to be of merit. Then our inclination at a later time to appre-

ciate the work for these same reasons will confirm the earlier judgements of the work. It is an inference of this sort that we use when, in a dispute about a work's aesthetically interesting features we say, in despair of present agreement: 'time will tell'. For here we assume that the same judgement made at a later date will show that our present opinion is well founded and is as objectively assertible as matters in this area can be.

(3) Closely related to (2) is the way in which we also use the judgement of a later time to disconfirm earlier opinions, and not simply to confirm them. When first heard, Beethoven's late quartets were assailed as unstructured and cacophonous. Later judgements insisting on their internal order and melody, and appealing to these features to support our own estimate of their merit, serve to show that the early views were mistaken. They point to a failing in the contemporary listener, and not in the composition. It is just such an inference as this that Hume uses in claiming that the reputation of a bad poet or orator will never be durable (see *Essay on the Standard of Taste*), for the assumption is that over time it is the correct judgement that becomes established. In this he is right, though not quite for the reasons that he gives.

Failure. If we contrast success in passing time's test with its contrary, failure, rather than its contradictory, lack of success, our conclusions are strictly parallel to those I claim we can draw from success.

(4) What fails the test of time we think of as lacking in some important dimension. This, like (1), is deliberately vague, and for exactly the same reason. The importance of (4) for the moment is just to remind us that we should beware of thinking that we may make an inference from failure to the absence of all merit in the work that fails. Often enough we come across forgotten works that are highly accomplished in their way, but of which any claim to have been unfairly passed over would be ludicrous. So just as the first inference we made from success does not consist in attributing merit to a work in all dimensions, so failure does not comprehensively detract from it either.

(5) Earlier unfavourable criticism of a work may be confirmed by the failure of the work to pass time's test. The constancy with which particular criticisms are levelled against a piece of music or a poem may provide one with argument against the philistine objection that in these matters objectivity is not to be had. Failing the test is evidence, within the appropriate domain, that the work cannot but be seen in a certain dismal light.

(6) We may use failure as a corrective to earlier more favourable judgements. We may come to see our earlier enthusiasms as due to 'authority or prejudice', in Hume's phrase, and appeal to the effects of time to justify a change of view and protect it from any charge of caprice.

Comparisons. Two simple corollaries follow fairly naturally on these six points.

(7) If one work passes and another fails, and if there is any point to making comparisons between them – if they are not uninterestingly distant from one another – then we expect there to be a range of assessment within which it is informative to say that the first is a finer work than the second. It is sometimes suggested that such an inference is scarcely one of importance in aesthetics since that is above all the realm of non-practical choice, the realm in which we do not have to act. But this is misleading, since our preferences, and with them our choice of what we find it worthwhile giving our time to, cannot always be so easily divorced from our more nearly practical choices about the light in which we regard important aspects of the world.

(8) Finally, when we know that a work of art has not securely passed time's test, then in the absence of any special explanation of why it has not done so, such as having been lost or having been available only to a very restricted group of people, we have some good ground for thinking that it is unlikely to be as worthy of our attention as those works which do have the stamp of time's approval. Unless there are special reasons for not doing so, we should take non-passage of time's test as equivalent to failure, and in our reflections on it be guided by the inferences (4)–(7).

The effect of drawing these inferences is easily appreciable. First they enable us to test our critical opinions and assessments in a sure if not infallible way. Sure, because the inferences are supposed to be well-founded; but not infallible, because they are not conceived of as being other than defeasible in nature. Then also they have the effect of filtering out as accurately and definitively as may be the finer from the less fine, the greater from the less great, and in so doing reveal the true worth of the individual work. And they have, I claim, a large part to play in explaining why we think that the flow of time functions to secure some measure of objectivity in aesthetic judgement, an area in which it has often seemed notably difficult to come by.

If this line of thought is to impress as more than mere piety we shall have to meet sceptical challenges all along the way. We must rebut the Shavian contention that there is no more to be said on the subject than that 'one age's longing is another age's loathing' and that stabilities of taste occur only fortuitously. In particular the asymmetry of our preferring the later judgement over the earlier, on which appeal to 'the whirligig of time' rests, calls out for explanation and justification. Nevertheless it is heartening that the tradition of criticism in which we have all grown up places more stress on temporal considerations than we would expect if there were only a coincidental connection between value and survival. The very solidity of the tradition suggests that a preliminary readiness to take the verdicts of time seriously is not irrational. As Hume observed,

> to say that an event is derived from chance, cuts short all farther inquiry concerning it, and leaves the writer in the same state of ignorance with the rest of mankind. But when the event is supposed to proceed from certain and stable causes, he may then display his ingenuity in assigning these causes; and as a man of any subtlety can never be at a loss in this particular, he has thereby an opportunity of swelling his volumes and discovering his profound knowledge, in observing what escapes the vulgar and ignorant.[6]

III

My description in section I of what it is to pass time's test extended only to well-chosen standard examples of autographic and allographic art. It does not cover cases in which art of either sort survives the passage of time without itself surviving, as may happen when what receives our attention is a copy, or a colour print, or a plaster cast (as was the case with Bugiardini's *Leda*, or the imaginary photograph of the equally imaginary drawing by the Master of the Rising Tide). And such cases are not just fanciful possibilities to which our sense of intellectual neatness would like justifications of the inferences to extend. In an age when, as never before, sensitivity to the visual arts has come to depend so heavily on copies, colour prints and

mechanical forms of restoration, it would be rash to discuss the inferences without indicating how they might go beyond the standard cases, for we can reliably surmise that today, and progressively more so in the future, continued survival will often turn on the power of such intermediaries as these at least as much as on that of the originals themselves.

A convenient way of finding a place for the non-standard case is suggested by the way in which we tend to think about restoration. Our usual rather simplistic way of viewing a restored painting is to take it as a work whose visible surface has deteriorated and which we save from further deterioration by laying on more pigment. Much of the original often remains, and restoration ideally takes the form of making good a certain loss. Analogously in the case of a mosaic, a damaged pattern of tesserae is restored to its pristine material and sensuous consistency by replacement of the missing stones. In these normal cases it often happens that quite enough of the original remains for us to have no hesitation at all about saying that the restored work is the same one as that which was damaged. Yet not all cases are normal and we must beware of refusing ever to think of restoration in any other way, as we are reminded by Auguste Proste's comment of the fate of Metz Cathedral: 'On voulait réparer d'abord; on a été conduit ensuite à vouloir restaurer, et aujourd'hui on démolit ce qui restait du viel édifice pour le reconstruire entièrement.'[7]

Sometimes we cannot possibly say that restoration leaves us with the work that existed before the repairs were carried out, and this is not only true of buildings that we view as works of architecture, but may hold of paintings or mosaic and of sculpture and carving as well. Think say of Leonardo's *Last Supper* in S. Maria delle Grazie. Practically nothing of the original surface has survived the ravages of creeping damp, and what we now see is almost entirely by later hands, largely those of the nineteenth-century restorers Cavenaghi and Silvestri (with more now to come). Or consider the restored mosaics of Galla Placidia in Ravenna, or S. Apollinare in Classe, where now probably no single original tessera remains. In neither case can we happily say that enough of the original still exists for us to view it. This being so, we need to treat these cases differently from those common ones of good restoration where the original work is indeed the work we admire.

In these abnormal cases, even though we do not want to say that the original survives we must admit that the restorer's labours permit it to survive time's test. In this respect such restorations are surely assimilable to Leonardo's *Leda* which survives through Bugiardini's copy. If possible it would be convenient to assimilate these cases to the standard allographic ones where in attending to one thing (a performance or a reading) we attend to another (to the work itself).[8] Then we should only need: (a) to specify what is to count as attending to the original (as we attend say to Mozart's *Don Giovanni* by attending to a performance of it), and (b) to say what objects will count as intermediaries of the right sort (akin to specifying what will and what will not count as a performance of the opera). Let us then consider the first of these demands.

It is clearly not necessary that the object we attend to should be a work of art in the same genre as that which survives, for my examples have shown already that sometimes in these cases what we attend to need not be a work of art at all. This might be said of the plaster cast and of the photograph. Yet what counts is not absolutely anything that conveys information relevant to the formation of critical judgement of the original, for obviously we do not want to admit that the lost or destroyed works described by Vasari in his *Lives* survive time's test through his descriptions of them, or even that they might have done so in more florid and full Pateresque recreations. To let in photographs of paintings and rule out descriptions we might insist that we are only attending to the (autographic) original by attending to some distinct object which conveys its information about the former through the same sensory modality as that on which its master depends for its aesthetic effect.

Yet this provision is arguably overgenerous, for it would not exclude the following examples, any of which we might want to regard with suspicion: (i) Serlio's cut-away elevation of Bramante's *Tempietto*; (ii) Lord Burlington's and William Kent's reworking at Chiswick of Palladio's *Villa Capra*; (iii) interpretations of well-tried paintings as offered by Picasso in his version of *Las hilanderas* or by Degas's recreation in the Tours collection of Mantegna's Louvre *Crucifixion*; or (iv) (allographically) an English prose version of *Finnegans Wake*. Evidently further restrictions are needed.

One such narrowing of scope will be provided by insisting that there be sufficient structural affinity between master and mediating object. Thus it would always be a matter for discussion whether copy, or restoration, or photograph provided one with *enough* information of the right sort about the

original to make it a good candidate. Nothing need be said about this use of 'enough' beyond what has already been said on a similar score before. What we are concerned with is how well the original would survive in such conditions, and accuracy and repleteness of the mediating object would certainly be relevant to the truth of the matter in individual cases, however puzzling it may be to judge it.

Further, it may be quite conceivable that one object should convey enough accurate information about another within the permitted sensory mode, yet not be suitable to afford us access to the original. This could happen where the structural affinities between the two are purely fortuitous. Then I doubt whether we should allow that the latter might survive through the former, and hence we might want to restrict the field still further by insisting that the intermediary be made either in the intention of conveying to us sufficient structurally relevant information about the master work (as in the case of a copy), or that it actually do so in part because of the causal role the original plays in its production (as in the case of photographs or plaster casts).

So it looks as if some sort of assimilation of non-standard autographic art to standard allographic cases might be viable. We have a fairly clear suggestion as to what kind of objects will do as intermediaries, and have allowed ourselves to say that it is by attending to them that we may count ourselves as attending to the original. Furthermore, we do not have in these cases any special difficulty about how it is that through our attention to Bugiardini's *Leda* Leonardo's work survives while Bugiardini's does not. For in that case our attention is not given to the copy autonomously and that, it will be recalled, was made a condition of the standardly-chosen work's passing time's test in the first place. Here we might say we attend to the original autonomously by attending to the copy with an eye to a reconstruction of the original, while the copy has little interest for us in its own right. But where master work and mediating object are both of sufficient stature then perhaps both might be viewed autonomously. Then both would survive in our attention given to the copy – but that is not a result that is always forced on us.

Nevertheless I doubt whether this approach is ultimately sustainable. It assumes too easily that we should accept that we are attending to the original in attending to the copy or the thoroughgoing restoration. And to many it will be clear that this is not true, for surely it is not to Leonardo's work that I attend when I look at Bugiardini's, even when I do so with an eye to forming an estimate of the original that inspired it. Similarly it seems hard to accept that in Ravenna I attend to the original mosaics when I study their laborious and accurate reconstructions. So for those who, like me, are unable to swallow this assumption another route must be found that bypasses this difficulty.

What we need to do is to acknowledge that there may be two ways in which a work of art may pass time's test. The first applies to standardly chosen autographic and allographic art as set out in section I. These works pass the test by surviving autonomously in our attention under an appropriate interpretation in a sufficiently embedded way. Secondly, if an autographic work is non-standard it may still survive, despite loss or destruction, by standing in the right relationship to a different object which satisfies the following five conditions:

(i)   it must provide us with experience in the same sensory mode as the original;

(ii) it must provide us with sufficient structurally relevant information about the original to enable us to form a critical assessment of it;

(iii) it must be appropriately (intentionally or causally) related to the original through the history of its production;

(iv) it must receive such attention as generates autonomous interest in the original under its appropriately reconstructed interpretation;

(v)   through the satisfaction of condition (iv) it must enable our interest in the original to be sufficiently embedded in the sense previously explained.

While non-standard allographic survival is of far less importance than non-standard autographic survival we may note at least that a similar suggestion can be carried over to this sort of case too. My imaginary example of Bach's lost work could survive via the attention given to a series of performances of a different work (the transcription in my example) where the original's similarity of structure, suitably generated, is conveyed through the later work and to which we attend closely enough to say that we have an autonomous and sufficiently embedded interest in the original.

The disadvantage of the proposal, even when refined and purified further than this, lies in its sheer clumsiness. Maybe the only thing to say about that is that non-standard cases are, though important, non-standard, and that it is no surprise that some more cumbersome explanation is needed to account for their capacity to pass time's test than is demanded by their more straightforward fellows. What matters is that we should have a workable way of allowing them to do so.

Notes

1   M. Rostovtzeff, *Rome* (New York, 1960), 289.
2   As is proposed by R. A. Wollheim in *Art and Its Objects* (New York, 1968), §§ 60–1. The greatest difficulty would be to free the recursive account from any particular base, for we would not want to say that in the absence of those basal exemplars art could not have arisen.
3   E. Auerbach, *Mimesis* (New York, 1953), 174.
4   A. Schönberg, *Berliner Tagebuch* (Berlin, 1975).
5   Autographic and allographic art may here be treated on a par. We only need to remember that whereas standardly the direct object of our attention in the former case is the material object that constitutes the work, in allographic art our attention is given to the work via attention given to a range of other things (a series of performances, or readings, etc.). The formulation can remain the same in either case, only the ways in which it is satisfied will differ from art to art.
6   Hume, 'Of the Rise and Progress of the Arts and Sciences,' in *Essays Literary, Political and Moral*, (George Routledge, London, n.d.), 63.
7   Cit. E. Wind, *Art and Anarchy* (London, 1963), 86.
8   See n. 5 above.

22

Artistic Value

Malcolm Budd

> We all think that the quality of a work of art, or an artist, is proved if it seizes and deeply affects us. But *our own quality* of judgement and feeling would first have to be proved: which is not the case.
>
> **Nietzsche, Human, All Too Human, I, §161**

Artistic and Non-artistic Values

The central question in the philosophy of art is, What is the value of art? Philosophical reflection on art would be idle unless art were valuable to us, and the significance of any question that arises in philosophical reflection on art derives directly or ultimately from the light that its answer throws upon the value of art. But if this is so, What is the value of art? If we construe art as the totality of (actual or possible) works of art, the value of art is the sum of the individual values of these various works of art. What, then, is the value of a work of art?

However, it would be premature to attempt to answer this question as it stands, because its meaning is indeterminate. For whatever can be evaluated, can be evaluated from different points of view, and corresponding to the point of view from which it is assessed, the value attributed to it will be of a different kind. So a work of art can have many different kinds of value – a cognitive value, a social value, an educational value, a historical

Malcolm Budd, shortened version of Chapter 1 from Malcolm Budd, *Values of Art* (London: Penguin, 1995), pp. 1–16; 38–43. © by Penguin. Reproduced by permission of Penguin Books Ltd.

value, a sentimental value, a religious value, an economic value, a therapeutic value; it can possess as many kinds of value as there are points of view from which it can be evaluated. Now an artist is someone who practises an activity as an art. What an artist tries to do is to create a product with a distinctive kind of value. She attempts to make something that is valuable *as art*, or, more specifically, *as art of such-and-such a kind*. I shall call this value 'artistic value' or 'the value of a work of art *as a work of art*'. So artistic value is just the value referred to in such judgements as these: James Joyce's *Ulysses* is a better novel than D. H. Lawrence's *Kangaroo*, Grünewald's *Christ on the Cross with the Virgin, St John and Mary Magdalen* is a finer painting than Salvador Dali's *Christ of St John of the Cross*, and Beethoven's last piano sonata (Op. 111) is finer than his first (Op. 2, No. 1) – if not finer as a sonata, certainly finer music. Thus 'artistic value' signifies a value that has degrees: some works of art have more of it than others, some lack it entirely, and some have it to the same degree. The prime task of a theory of value in art is to elucidate the distinctive value of art – the value of a work of art as a work of art.

It will be as well to deal at once with an objection that is likely to be brought against this idea of the value of a work of art as a work of art. The objection is aimed at the implication that the value is unitary, and it exists in two related forms. The first maintains that it is necessary to give an irreducibly disjunctive account of value *across* the arts, because for each art form – music, painting, sculpture, architecture, literature, dance – there is a distinct kind of value: the value of a work of art of a particular art form *as* of that form is different for each art form. According to this version of the objection, there is the value of music as music, the value of painting as painting, the value of sculpture as sculpture, and so on, and there is no overarching value that unifies this set of values, which form a heterogeneous collection. The second version presses the point further by claiming that it is necessary to give an irreducibly disjunctive account of value *within* each art, since each art form admits works of art of different natures and aims and these various kinds of work have values specific to them. So within the art of music, there is the value of a song as a song, the value of a symphony as a symphony, and so on for the other musical genres; and within each of the other arts, there is a distinct kind of value for each artistic genre that falls within that art.

Now for either of these versions of the objection to assume a definite form, it would be necessary for it to indicate criteria for the identity and difference of the kinds of art to which it assigns distinct kinds of value; and if the second version is to stop short of assigning distinct kinds of value to each particular work of art, the individuating criteria it specifies must, without being arbitrary, allow different works to possess the same kind of value. But there is no need to pursue the issue, for neither form of the objection is persuasive, and each is open to same response. It is true that the features of a work of art that make it good as music are different from those that make a work good as literature, that what makes a painting a fine landscape is not what is responsible for the value of a painting of the Annunciation (its value *as* such a painting), and that there are different varieties of artistic value. But this shows only that artistic value can be realized in many different ways, not that it lacks an essence. So much for this blunt rejection of the idea of a work's artistic value.

Three linked issues immediately arise about artistic value: its individuation, its status and its epistemology. First, it is necessary to identify artistic value by answering the question, What is the value of a work of art *as* a work of art? Second, the status of the value must be elucidated. Is artistic value relative or absolute, subjective or intersubjective, a real property of works of art or a projection on to them of the responses they arouse in us? And a constraint on satisfactory solutions of the first two issues is that they should deliver the correct solution of the third, the epistemological issue. What is the fundamental procedure for finding out what the artistic value of a work of art is? Is it necessary to be acquainted with the work, and, if so, what explains the necessity?

It will quickly become clear that in answering the initial question I do not attempt, first to present a definition of a work of art or a philosophical theory of art or a statement of its supposed essence, then to derive from the definition a conception of artistic value, the value of a work of art *as such*, that is, as satisfying the definition. Given what has happened to the concept of art, especially in the twentieth century, it would be fruitless to proceed in this way: an account of artistic value cannot be extracted from the present concept of art. Instead, I specify a distinctive value – a value that works of art can possess, and which is possessed to a high degree by all great works of art; I then count an evaluation of a work of art as an evaluation of it *as art* in so far as the work is being evaluated with respect to the distinctive value I have specified. My answer to the question will demonstrate the unity of the concept of artistic value, or, more accurately, will give unity to it.

Intrinsic and Instrumental Values

A perspicuous elucidation of the concept of artistic value is possible in terms of what I shall call 'the experience a work of art offers'.[1] Although what is involved in understanding a work of art varies from art to art and also within each art, it is definitive of a work of art that it can be understood; and I mean by 'the experience a work of art offers' an experience of the work in which it is understood. So the experience a work offers is an experience of interacting with it in whatever way it demands if it is to be understood – reading it, looking at it, listening to it, performing it or in some other way appreciating it. For you to experience a work with (full) understanding your experience must be imbued with an awareness of (all) the aesthetically relevant properties of the work – the properties that ground the attribution of artistic value and that constitute the particular forms of value the work exemplifies. The experience a work of art offers is an experience *of* the work itself: it does not have a nature specifiable independently of the nature of the work. It is also not any person's actual experience, but a type, one that can be multiply instantiated, and more or less closely approximated to. It can be such that the order of its parts is fully determined by the nature of the work (as with music), or not so (as with painting and architecture).

My claim is that the value of a work of art as a work of art is intrinsic to the work in the sense that it is (determined by) the intrinsic value of the experience the work offers (so that if it offers more than one experience, it has more than one artistic value or an artistic value composed of these different artistic values). It should be remembered that the experience a work of art offers is an experience *of the work itself*, and the valuable qualities of a work are qualities *of the work*, not of the experience it offers. It is the nature of the work that endows the work with whatever artistic value it possesses; this nature is what is experienced in undergoing the experience the work offers; and the work's artistic value is the intrinsic value of this experience. So a work of art is valuable as art if it is such that the experience it offers is intrinsically valuable; and it is valuable to the degree that this experience is intrinsically valuable.

By the intrinsic value of an item I do not mean a value that depends solely on the intrinsic nature of the item – a value that depends solely on its internal properties (its qualities and inner relations) – as contrasted with an extrinsic value – a value that depends, wholly or in part, on its external properties (its relations to other things). My conception of intrinsic value opposes it, not to extrinsic value, but to instrumental value, and I do not assume that something's intrinsic value is dependent solely on its intrinsic nature.[2] By the instrumental value of a work of art I mean the value, from whatever point of view, of the actual effects of the experience of the work on people or the effects that would be produced if people were to experience the work. (I do not mean the *suitability* of the work, in virtue of its nature, to produce valuable or harmful effects on certain kinds of people as a result of their experience of the work.) My claim therefore implies that the instrumental value of a work of art, its beneficial or harmful, short- or long-term effects or influence, either on a given person or on people in general – where the effects are consequences of the experience and not elements or aspects of the experience itself – is not the value of the work of art *as* a work of art.

If a work possesses artistic value, this does not consist in the work's actually accomplishing some valuable end in the case of one, some or many of us, or in the fact that it would, if experienced with understanding, accomplish such an end. This is easy to see, for what is achieved by experiencing a work of art depends not only on the experience that its appreciation yields but also on the character, attitude and will of any person who experiences it. There is only a personal answer to the question whether the appreciation of a work of art kindles or dampens a desire to enhance the lives of other people, whether it is a stimulus to, or a safety-valve which prevents, immoral action, or whether it infects with, or inoculates against, a mood of despair, for example. The influence of a work of art is not like the operation of certain drugs which, independently of the subject's attitude, character and will, produce their distinctive effects regardless.

It counts in favour of the identification I propose that there is a conspicuous mismatch between our opinions about the artistic value of a work and our opinions about the instrumental value of the experience it offers. The instrumental value of the experience of a work of art is in fact many-headed and ill-defined, and it can be considered at an individual or a more general level. But at whatever level it is considered, there is unlikely to be a correspondence between the strength and nature of your opinion about the artistic value of a work and the strength and nature of your opinion about the instrumental value of its experience. The fact is that most of us, perhaps all of us, know very little about what the beneficial or harmful effects of the experience of a particular work of art, or particular kinds of work, on particular people or people in general, are or would be. Think of the difficulty of trying to establish the effects of the appreciation of a particular work of art, such as Titian's *Bacchus and Ariadne*, Defoe's *Robinson Crusoe* or Bruckner's Seventh Symphony.

But we do have a general knowledge of the kinds of relation that can hold between people's experience of a work of art and their later psychological condition and behaviour. We know that the gratification some people derive from works of art – even the finest works of art – leads them only to seek out the experience of more fine works of art; along other paths, their experience of art is sterile. Such people have an exceptional capacity to isolate or compartmentalize their appreciation of art. At bottom, they are unconcerned that the works of art they admire should affect their lives in any way that will be beneficial to themselves or others. Their approach to art is unreflectively or self-consciously 'aesthetic' or sentimental; the denial of this possibility is itself a form of sentimentalism.

The question whether an experience is worth undergoing for its own sake is not the same as the question whether the experience is in other ways beneficial to those who find the experience enjoyable, exciting or in some other way rewarding, even if in many cases the two questions may receive the same answer; and the evaluation of a work of art as a work of art must be based on an assessment of the intrinsic value, not the instrumental value, of the experience the work offers. It is vital to see that we can evaluate – we usually must evaluate – the character of the experience a work offers independently of any opinion about whether the experience will in fact have desirable or undesirable effects on the mind, character and behaviour of an individual or a group of people. The effects of the experience of a work of art on an individual (its individual instrumental value) or on people in general (its overall instrumental value) are certainly of great importance; but it is the character of the experience the work offers, in conjunction with the nature of those who undergo it, that determines what these effects are likely to be; and it is not these effects themselves, but the character of the experience, that determines the artistic value of the work.

There are two further considerations that should facilitate acceptance of my claim about artistic value. The first is that many of what are thought of as benefits of the experience of art are intrinsic to the experience, not merely products of it. The experience a work of art offers can involve the invigoration of one's consciousness, or a refined awareness of human psychology or political or social structures, or moral insight, or an imaginative identification with a sympathetic form of life or point of view that is not one's own; it can be beneficial in these and countless other ways. But since such benefits are aspects, not consequences, of the experience the work offers, the irrelevance of the actual effects of the experience to the work's artistic value does not imply the irrelevance of these kinds of benefits. On the contrary, such benefits contribute to making the experience intrinsically valuable and partly constitute the ways in which it is so.

The second consideration is that an experience can be *such as* to be conducive to a beneficial[3] effect on people – people who are concerned to profit from the work that affords the experience.[4] This is what Yvor Winters had in mind when thinking of poetry as a moral discipline:

Poetry, if pursued either by the poet or by the reader, in the manner which I have suggested, should offer a means of enriching one's awareness of human experience and so of rendering greater the possibility of intelligence in the course of future action; and it should offer likewise a means of inducing certain more or less constant habits of feeling, which should render greater the possibility of one's acting, in a future situation, in accordance with the findings of one's improved intelligence. It should, in other words, increase the intelligence and strengthen the moral temper; these effects should naturally be carried over into action, if, through constant discipline, they are made permanent acquisitions.[5]

Although the appreciation of poetry does not automatically result in improvements of the kind Winters indicates, the nature of fine poetry is such as to help to induce them in those who apply themselves in the manner he advocates.[6]

Aestheticism, Artist and Spectator

It would be a misunderstanding of my account of artistic value to object to the implied downgrading of the instrumental value of the experience of a work of art. For my identification of the artistic value of a work of art with the intrinsic value of the experience it offers carries no such implication. The identification of artistic value is not a matter of weighing one kind of value against another, but of discriminating the one from the other. I have made no claim about the difficult topic of the comparative ranking of different kinds of value. Measured by a certain yardstick (a moral yardstick, for example),[7] the value of a work of art as a work of art will not be the most important kind of value that a work of art can possess. But the issue of the identification of artistic value is, What is artistic value?, not, What is the worth of artistic value? The answer I have given to the constitutive question identifies the value of a work as a work of art with the intrinsic, not the instrumental, value of the experience it offers, and this implies nothing about the importance of artistic value relative to other kinds of value. Accordingly, my identification of artistic value is not equivalent to and does not imply a downgrading of the instrumental value of art.

There are two further misunderstandings to which my account of artistic value is liable. The first misconstrues it as an unacceptable form of aestheticism. The charge of aestheticism is likely to arise if it is thought that the identification of a work's artistic value with the intrinsic value of the experience the work offers is tantamount to the doctrine of 'Art for Art's Sake'. But this doctrine is strikingly equivocal: many different views have sought shelter under its banner, and the force of the charge varies accordingly. Here it will be sufficient to dissociate my account from four dogmas and one ethical stance, none of which it implies.

The first dogma is the existence of a specifically aesthetic emotion, which it is the artistic function of art to arouse. But it is clear that this does not follow from my claim about artistic value; and the emotion it posits is only a myth. The second is the irrelevance of a work's subject-matter to its artistic value. According to this doctrine, it does not matter what a work represents, only how it represents it. But not only is this doctrine not implied by the conception of a work's artistic value as the intrinsic value of the experience it offers, it is shown to be false in the examination of pictorial value I undertake in the second part of the book. The third dogma is the requirement that the spectator's response to a work of art should be disconnected from her attitude to the moral or other evaluative point of view that the work expresses. But it is not necessary to accept the theory of a work of art as a *sui generis* world, to be experienced and valued independently of whether it accords or conflicts with one's own beliefs and values, and only in terms of whether it creates a coherent and satisfying world of its own – the theory that was held up by adherents of the doctrine of 'Art for Art's Sake' against the demands for truth and morality in art – in order to restrict artistic value to the nature of the experience in which the work of art is understood, so as to exclude any further separable effect. It is not necessary to embrace the theory of a work of art as an autonomous world in order to maintain the thesis that the value of a work of art as a work of art is the intrinsic value of the experience it offers. The final dogma is the complete lack of determination of a work's artistic value by any values that are not specifically artistic or aesthetic values. But the claim that a work's artistic value is determined by the intrinsic, not the instrumental, value of the experience it offers does not imply that its artistic value is independent of any values it may possess that are not art-specific or specifically aesthetic. Values that are not specific to art or the aesthetic are not thereby essentially unrelated to artistic value. The truth is that artistic value does not exist in a watertight compartment impermeable by other values; on the contrary, other values can be determinants of artistic value, as when a novel's value is a function of its intelligence, wit, imagination, knowledge and understanding of human life.

The ethical stance that is not implied by my conception of artistic value assigns supreme importance to art in human life, claiming that life should be lived for art's sake, or that the highest form of life is devotion to art, or, rather differently, that, in Nietzsche's words, 'we have our highest dignity in our significance as works of art – for it is only as an *aesthetic phenomenon* that existence and the world are eternally *justified*'.[8] As with the comparative ranking of different values of art, so with the place of art in human life, no conclusions flow from the identification of artistic value with the intrinsic value of the experience a work of art offers.

The second misunderstanding I wish to protect my claim against represents it as being a spectator-oriented aesthetics that denies the true significance of the artist. Am I not placing the artistic value of a work in the experience of the spectator, neglecting both the value to the artist of the work she produces and the way in which the idea of the artist should occur in the spectator's appreciation of the artist's work? No. In the first place, it should be remembered that not only do 'artist' and 'spectator' refer to roles, rather than people, but that the role of the artist, properly understood, requires the artist, in the creation of her work, to adopt or bear in mind the role of the spectator. A so-called 'artist' who is unconcerned about the character of the experience her work offers is thereby unconcerned to endow her product with a distinctive kind of value – the one I have identified as the value of a work of art as a work of art. This consideration is reinforced by the fact that a work of art is intended to be understood *as* a work of art; the experience a work of art offers is one in which the work is understood; the meaning of a work of art – how it should be interpreted – is tied to the conception of the work under which the artist created it,[9] the style in which it is executed, the works of art to which it alludes and the view of the world and life out of which it arose; and the appreciation of a work of art is the appreciation of the artistry of the artist, which requires an appreciation of the artistic achievement the work represents,[10] so that experience of the work must be informed by an understanding of the aesthetically relevant facts about the work's history. Finally, it is a confusion to introduce the idea of the value to the artist herself of the work she produces and to complain that my account of artistic value neglects this. For a work never has a single value to the artist, and there are many values to the artist it might have that are irrelevant to its assessment as a valuable work of art. The objection would be sound only if a work has a value to the artist which is ignored in my account and which determines, wholly or in part, the value of the work as art. But this is not so. The fact is that the account of artistic value I have presented is neither spectator- nor artist-oriented, but assigns due weight to both roles.

Acquaintance

An elucidation of artistic value is correct only if it yields the right answer to the question, What is the fundamental procedure, the canonical method, for finding out what the artistic value of a work is? Clearly, the basic way of determining the value of a work of art requires you to experience the work with understanding – to undergo the experience the work offers. Although, contrary to what has sometimes been maintained, you can form a judgement on the merits of a work you are not acquainted with, this involves trust in the judgement of someone who is acquainted with it, an attempt to imagine what it would be like to experience it, or an extrapolation from the works with which you are acquainted.[11] Leaving these possibilities on one side, you can find out what the artistic value of a work is only by experiencing it in the relevant manner. This conclusion flows easily from the identification of artistic value with the intrinsic value of the experience a work offers. For what this identification requires you to find out is whether this experience is intrinsically valuable to undergo, and, if it is, to what degree and in what manner. The experience that a fine work of art offers must be such that it deserves to be found intrinsically rewarding. What could be a better way to find this out than to undergo the experience? As John Stuart Mill insisted, the only evidence for whether an experience is worth having for its own

sake is the verdict of those who are familiar with the experience. Of course, the satisfaction of the requirement that the work is experienced with understanding is a matter of degree, and you can misunderstand a work you think you understand. But these facts do not imply that you are never justified in taking yourself to experience a work with understanding. If you are justified, you are then in the best possible position to judge the intrinsic value of the experience. For whether you find it interesting, amusing, exciting, poignant or in any other way intrinsically rewarding is in general a matter that your experience declares to you. Admittedly, you may not endorse your first-order response to a work of art, and even if you do, the fact that *you* find the work intrinsically rewarding in some way does not imply that the experience it offers is intrinsically valuable. But all that is required for the implication to hold is that when you experience the response indicated by the term expressing the variety of intrinsic value, your response should be appropriate or justified, perhaps justified above all other responses. If you find the work intrinsically rewarding and you are right to do so, then the experience it offers is intrinsically valuable.[12] So the identification of artistic value with the intrinsic value of the experience the work offers yields a simple explanation of why acquaintance must play the fundamental role that has always been assigned to it in the determination of artistic value, without disallowing value judgements that are not immediately based on acquaintance with the work.

Art and Communication

I now need to refine the idea of assessing the intrinsic value of the experience offered by a work of art. In undergoing such an experience either you find it in some way rewarding or you do not. Given that you endorse your response, only if you find it in some way rewarding do you have reason to consider the experience intrinsically valuable. But the reward given by the experience can be related to the experience in two different ways. On the one hand, it can be such that in principle it is possible to obtain that reward without undergoing the experience of the work.[13] On the other hand, undergoing the experience of the work is partly constitutive of the reward. In a case of the first kind, it is not essential to the reward given by the experience that you should undergo the experience, just as it is not essential to the valued state of sleep that it should be induced in you in one way rather than another. If the experience is valuable to you only for this detachable reward, so that there is no conceptual constraint on the character of any experience that gives you exactly the same reward, you are not finding the work valuable as *a work of art*. You are valuing the work as you value a drug, for the effect it produces, the only difference from the artistic case being that there is a noticeable temporal gap between the effect caused by the drug and the ingestion of the drug. For you to find a work valuable as a work of art, what you find intrinsically rewarding in your experience of the work must not be something that could be present even if your experience lacked the character of the experience the work offers: your experience must not consist of two separable components, the intrinsically rewarding component being a mere effect of an intrinsically unrewarding component – the experience of the work itself.

This conclusion receives clarification and support from a consideration of the doctrine that art is essentially a form of communication.[14] An extreme version of this thesis conceives of the act of communication supposedly integral to the creation and appreciation of art as the transference of the artist's experience in a particularly strong sense – the sense in which a football player might be transferred from one team to another. This renders the idea incoherent: it makes no more sense to think of transferring an experience from one person to another than it does to think of transferring a goal scored in one match to another match. To obtain a coherent form of the doctrine it is necessary to understand the concept of communication in its usual sense, as in the conveyance of information from one person to another. Suppose I have received a letter from a friend in which she communicates her thoughts about the value of art. Here we can distinguish the vehicle of communication from the 'message' communicated. On the one hand, there is the sheet of paper with ink marks inscribed on its surface which has travelled from my friend to me. This is the means by which whatever is communicated to me is communicated to me. On the other hand, there is what is communicated – my friend's thoughts.[15] Now the vehicle is not identical with the message. There are many other ways in which the same message could have been communicated. If the message had been communicated by means of speech, semaphore or morse code, for example, a different vehicle would

have been used to communicate the same message. Rather than the inscribed sheet of paper, the vehicle would have been a sequence of sounds or positions of flags held in the hands or short and long flashes of light, say. This distinction between vehicle and message can be drawn in all cases of communication, no matter whether the message – what is communicated – is a thought, an emotion, an attitude or an experience.

The relevance of this distinction to the doctrine that art is essentially a form of communication emerges at once if this doctrine is understood as a thesis about the value of art, to the effect that when we value a work as a work of art: (i) it communicates something to us; (ii) we value it only because it communicates this to us; and (iii) we value it to the degree that we value what it communicates. In other words, the value of a work of art is the value of the thoughts, emotions or whatever else it communicates, so that a work of art that fails to communicate anything lacks artistic value, and the task of the artist is to create a vehicle adequate to convey a valuable message. But it is clear that this conception of the value of art misrepresents our attachment to works of art when we value them *as* works of art. For the distinction between vehicle and message intrinsic to the concept of communication means that for any message there are in principle many vehicles capable of communicating that message. So this conception of artistic value implies, first, that we must assign the same artistic value to anything else that communicates exactly the same message as the one communicated by a work we value, and, second, that from the point of view of our interest in art, for any work of art we must be indifferent between experiencing it or something else that communicates the same message (and so, according to this conception, possesses the same artistic value). Yet neither implication is correct. If our sole reason for valuing a work of art is that it communicates a particular message, so that the manner in which the message is communicated does not matter to us, our attachment to the work is wrongly described as our valuing it *as* a work of art. The moral is clear: the communication conception of artistic value misrepresents the importance of the experience of the work, crediting it only with an instrumental role in the production of what is valuable in the experience of art, rather than locating the reward in the experience itself.[16] It is, of course, true that what a work of art communicates can be *integral* to its value as a work of art, for it may be integral to the experience the work offers. But it is the message *as communicated by the work*, the message *as realized in the experience of the work*, that determines the work's artistic value, not the message itself. If you value Munch's *The Scream* as a work of art, and you value it because it conveys a sense of intense fright, it is the picture – the picture perceived as expressive of intense fear – that impresses you, not merely an impression of fear caused by it. Our attachment to the works we value as art is an attachment to the very experiences they offer, not to something detachable from them. To appreciate the value of a work of art it is necessary to undergo the experience it offers.

Intersubjectivity, Criticism, Understanding and Incommensurability

What kind of property is artistic value? In the first place, although it is not a genuinely absolute value, it is not relative in any disturbing way. For instance, it does not have the kind or degree of relativity that attaches to sentimental value, which is relative both to persons and times. Objects do not in themselves possess sentimental values, but are valued by some, but not other, people on account of what they remind them of: there is no one-place predicate 'is of sentimental value', only the three-place predicate 'is of sentimental value to P at time *t*'. In contrast with this, a sentence ascribing artistic value to a work does not indicate, explicitly or implicitly, a relation between a certain person or persons and the work. But artistic value resembles sentimental value in being a sentiment-dependent property. A sentiment-dependent property is one the idea of which has to be explicated in terms of an affective response to the object in which the value is found. If the artistic value of a work is the intrinsic value of the experience it offers, the idea of artistic value must be unpacked in terms of a person's finding it intrinsically rewarding to undergo the experience the work offers. Hence, given that the notion of a sentiment covers all the ways in which something can be found intrinsically rewarding, artistic value is a sentiment-dependent property.

But the fact that artistic value is a sentiment-dependent property does not imply that it is a 'merely' subjective property; for the instantiation of the property is independent of any individual's reaction to the work in which it is or is not instantiated. It is integral to our concept of artistic value

that nobody is immune to error about a work's artistic value: it does not follow from the fact that someone judge a work to have a certain artistic value that it does so, and the fact that I judge a work to have a certain artistic value does not imply that I thereby rule out the possibility that I might be mistaken. Artistic value is not a mere projection of a person's reaction to an object – as in the case of the niceness of smells and tastes. On the contrary, the concept of justifiability intrinsic to the concept of artistic value introduces the ideas of appropriateness and inappropriateness into our understanding of a person's response to a work of art, and renders the value intersubjective by admitting the possibility of well-founded approval or criticism of a person's assessment of the artistic value of a work. Intersubjectivity is not confined to judgements about the world as seen from no point of view, or from a point of view uncontaminated by anything that is specific to a particular manner of responding to the world, but equally covers response-based judgements of value conceived of as being justified.[17]

Artistic value is also an anthropocentric property. For there is nothing built into the conception of artistic value that extends the relevant range of people – the people for whom a judgement of artistic value holds good – beyond human beings to all rational subjects who perceive the world. Judgements of artistic value are thought of as valid only, at most, for those who possess a distinctively human sensibility, with distinctively human powers of perception, comprehension, and emotional response, and who flourish and are vulnerable to harm in distinctively human ways. (Contrast Kant, who attempted to show that a correct judgement of taste is based on a pleasure that is valid for all rational creatures with the same *perceptual* capacities as human beings, no matter how they might otherwise differ.) But the anthropocentricity of artistic value in no way detracts from its importance to us. Although the anthropocentricity of artistic value is a form of relativity, it is one that relativizes it to a kind of sensibility, not to an individual. In fact, artistic value can be thought of as anthropocentric in either of two ways. First, the experience a particular work of art offers might be one that only a subject with a distinctively human sensibility could undergo: it might call for responses which could be forthcoming only from such a sensibility.[18] Second, even if this is not so, there might be no good reason for a subject who lacks this human sensibility to value the experience as human beings do.

I have claimed that you attribute artistic value to a work in so far as and to the degree that you regard the experience it offers as being intrinsically valuable. For you to regard an experience as being intrinsically valuable is for you to consider it right or appropriate, merited or justified, to find it intrinsically rewarding. An experience merits such a response if there is good reason to find it intrinsically rewarding. My account of artistic value therefore has built into it a normative dimension, and this normative dimension houses reasons, not mere causes. The experience a work of art offers is intrinsically valuable if the work is such that it merits being found intrinsically rewarding to experience with understanding:[19] the response must be justifiable by reference to the nature of the work. Unless your response to a work is defensible by reference to features of the work that must be appreciated if the work is to be understood – features of the work that are open to others, that endow it with value, and that constitute good reasons for responding as you do – your response lacks any right to be thought of as indicative of the work's artistic value.

This is reflected in the distinctive practice, thoughts and feelings of those who evaluate works of art as art. For reflection on a work's artistic value has a twofold aim: to grasp the meaning of the work and so to appreciate it for what it is worth. This involves an attempt to characterize the work in such a manner as to warrant or mandate a certain kind of response. The primary concern of the art of criticism is the attempt to describe works of art in ways which justify our responses to them; it is the rational appreciation of works of art. The art of criticism tries to enforce agreement about the description of a work – a description under which the work must be experienced if it is to be appreciated. Criticism seeks to establish the correct understanding of a work, to articulate its distinctive merits and defects, and so to assess its artistic value. This involves encouraging a certain way of experiencing the work: criticism's claim is that the work should be experienced in accordance with the offered interpretation, which discloses the work's true aesthetic qualities. Now a work's artistic value is dependent on its aesthetic qualities, which in turn are dependent on its non-aesthetic features.[20] Accordingly, criticism, in its attempt to establish a work's artistic value, will draw attention to the aesthetic and also the non-aesthetic characteristics upon which its value depends. Since convincing criticism changes or refines your interpretation of

a work and what you are aware of in it, and since these are integral to the way you experience the work, a change of interpretation effects a change in your experience. Hence the similarity between aspect perception and the aesthetic experience of art and the appropriateness of the variety of resources available to criticism for the enhancement of appreciation.

Any work of art can be experienced in indefinitely many ways, but only an experience in which the work is understood is relevant to the work's artistic value. The possibility of lack of understanding carries with it the possibility of discounting a response to a work and the evaluation it implies. But it does not follow that there is only one possible evaluation of a work that is compatible with understanding it correctly and completely. In the first place, I have not claimed that there is only one understanding of a work that is both correct and complete.[21] If there is more than one such interpretation – my introductory definition of 'the experience a work of art offers' is formulated in such a way that it does not restrict admissible interpretations of a work to just one – then, since it is unlikely that evaluations based on different interpretations will coincide, there will be room for more than one evaluation that is not rendered null by lack of understanding. Secondly, even if there is only one correct and complete understanding of a work, it does not follow from the fact that lack of understanding undermines the authority of an evaluation that understanding guarantees its unique validity. Three additional premises are needed to reach this conclusion. The first is that the evaluation of works of art admits the concept of correctness. The second is that there is only one evaluation of a work that is not incorrect. The third is that correctness of understanding ensures correctness of evaluation. While the first of these is certainly consonant with our practice of evaluating works of art, the second is contentious and the third implausible.[22]

It should not be expected that the art of criticism, perfectly carried out, will always result in a single, definitive evaluation of a work. This would only be so if, for each pair of incompatible qualities, one being an aesthetic merit and the other a demerit, the following were true: if a particular work can be experienced as possessing one member of the pair and can also be experienced as possessing the other member of the pair, then for at least one of these qualities it must be incorrect to experience the work as possessing that quality –

that such a way of experiencing the work misunderstands it. But this is not always the case.[23] When it is not true, the work's nature and artistic value are indefinite, and the claim to universal assent or full intersubjective validity built into a judgement of the work's artistic value, based on experiencing the work as possessing one or the other of these incompatible qualities, cannot be vindicated: there is more than one evaluation of the work that is not incorrect. In such a case we must clip the wings of the aspiration to intersubjective validity of a judgement of artistic value and confine the demand for unanimous assent by relativizing the judgement to the work *as experienced as possessing one of the qualities.*

Indefiniteness also enters judgements of artistic value in another way. For an important feature of artistic value is its incommensurability. Although artistic value is a matter of degree, there is and can be no precise measure of the degree to which a work of art possesses it. Artistic value is not a measurable quantity. This implies that when one work is better than another, there is no precise amount by which it is better. It also implies that issues of comparative artistic value are sometimes indeterminate: in some (but not all) cases, it is neither true that one of the works is better than the other, nor that they are precisely equal in value. It is wrong to think that indeterminacy obtains when and only when the works being assessed belong to different arts. For indeterminacy can obtain within a single art and it can fail to obtain across arts. One reason

why artistic value is incommensurable is that there are different kinds of qualities that can endow a work with value and there is no common unit in terms of which their contributions to a work's artistic value can be measured.[24] This holds not only within particular art forms, but also within artistic genres; it also holds across different arts. Because incommensurability holds within each art, indeterminacy can obtain within a single art, and it is likely to do so: there will be some pairs of objects within that art for which the comparative ranking of their members is indeterminate. Indeterminacy also obtains across art forms, but not necessarily so: there are many pairs of objects taken from different arts for which the comparative ranking of their members is determinate. There is no problem about this, for the fact that artistic value is incommensurable, and that the substantive values of one art are not the same as those of another, does not imply that issues of comparative artistic value for works drawn from different arts must be indeterminate. Nor is there a problem about reconciling incommensurability with the existence of determinate comparative rankings within an art. In fact, incommensurability will be thought to threaten judgements of comparative artistic value only if incommensurability is thought, wrongly, to imply incomparability.

In sum: artistic value is intrinsic, sentiment-dependent, intersubjective, anthropocentric and incommensurable.

Notes

1 This idea is certainly as indefinite as the idea of a particular work of art, which in the case of the performing arts allows for different performances of the same work, and in the case of prints, etchings and engravings, for example, for different impressions of the same work, these different instances exhibiting aesthetically significant differences amongst them. Thus a musical work can be performed compatibly with the score, the performance traditions of the composer's musical culture, the composer's intention, and any other standard of correctness, in different ways – ways that endow the work, as so performed, with different aesthetic qualities. Although this limits the precision of the idea, it does not affect its primacy in an account of artistic value.

2 This assumption, in the case of representational works of art, would presuppose that certain questions about the representation, questions about the

relations between the content of the representation and reality, or between the response to the content (as represented) and the appropriate response to such a content in reality, are irrelevant to questions of artistic value. It would thus prejudge important issues in the philosophy of criticism – issues of truth and realism, for instance.

3 Contrariwise, the experience a work offers can be such as to be conducive to harmful effects, as when a work caters or panders to undesirable appetites or attitudes and by doing so not only provides satisfaction for them but is liable to encourage, strengthen or perpetuate them. But even in a case of this sort, it is the nature of the experience, not what influence it might actually have, that determines the artistic value of the work.

4 On a simpler level, an experience the nature of which involves a heightening of consciousness, our being more intensely alive than we normally are, is

liable to have a tonic effect or influence (something that outlasts the experience itself), so that we return from the world of art quickened and refreshed. But the experience of art may have a short-term devitalizing effect, as a result of emotional exhaustion, for example, as with a work as demanding as Wagner's *Tristan and Isolde*.

5 Yvor Winters, *In Defense of Reason* (London: Routledge & Kegan Paul, 1960), pp. 28–9. Compare Shelley's well-known statement in his 'A Defence of Poetry': 'A man, to be greatly good, must imagine intensely and comprehensively; he must put himself in the place of another and of many others; the pains and pleasures of his species must become his own. The great instrument of moral good is the imagination; and poetry administers to the effect by acting upon the cause.'

6 The crudity of Bentham's hedonistic conception of value and his understanding of human life is never more cruelly exposed than in his reflections on poetry (and the other arts). It is well known that he asserted that 'prejudice apart, the game of push-pin is of equal value with the arts and sciences of music and poetry. If the game of push-pin furnish more pleasure, it is more valuable than either.' (*Works*, II, p. 254, quoted in C. K. Ogden, *Jeremy Bentham 1832–1932* (London: Kegan Paul, Trench, Trubner, 1932), p. 66.) Less well known is his remark (quoted in Ogden, p. 87): 'Poetry: no more reason for teaching it than chess or cards.' In fact, Bentham believed that the immediate pleasure derived from poetry is more than offset by the ultimate pains which it is liable to give rise to by the 'misrepresentation' intrinsic to it, so that in the scales of the hedonic calculus it is outweighed by push-pin.

7 There are two ways in which art might be assessed by a moral (religious, social) yardstick. The first, exemplified by Tolstoy in *What is Art?*, is to define art in such a manner that a work's artistic value is determined by its contribution to morality (religion, society). The second, exemplified by Plato in his famous critique of art in the *Republic*, is to assign a work's artistic value no weight in comparison with the moral harm the work might do by encouraging socially undesirable attitudes and feelings in those who delight in the work.

8 Friedrich Nietzsche, *The Birth of Tragedy*, §5. Compare Nietzsche's later remark, 'As an aesthetic phenomenon existence is still *bearable* for us', and the wonderful continuation of the section in which it occurs (*The Gay Science*, §107). It should be remembered that in his later thought Nietzsche is recommending the adoption of both an aesthetic (spectatorial) and, especially, an artistic (creative) attitude, rather than (just) a moral attitude, *towards ourselves*.

9 See especially Kendall Walton, 'Categories of Art,' *The Philosophical Review*, Vol. LXXIX, 1970.

10 For an excellent defence of the view that to appreciate a work of art is to appreciate the artistic achievement it represents, see Gregory Currie, *An Ontology of Art* (Basingstoke/London: Macmillan, 1989).

11 It is a trivial truth that the only *access* to the value is through acquaintance with the work. But this does not imply that your judgement of a work is not properly a judgement of its artistic value unless you are acquainted with it.

12 Although standardly you will judge that a work possesses artistic value only if you find it intrinsically rewarding to experience, I have not argued, and it would be mistaken to do so, that you must find a work intrinsically rewarding if you are rightly to judge that it possesses artistic value. A fortiori, I have not argued that your judgement of a work's artistic value must reflect the nature and degree of your affective response to it. In fact, you can have good grounds for judging that a work you do not find intrinsically rewarding to experience offers an experience that is intrinsically valuable. Most of us are aware that we are not ideally sensitive aesthetic spectators, and that there are forms of art that leave us cold but which are found intrinsically rewarding by other people whose aesthetic sensitivity is not less than our own. Moreover, we can sometimes make fairly accurate discriminations of artistic value amongst works none of which interest us. So we can fail to appreciate works we properly judge to be valuable. This will generally be because when we interact with the work we do not undergo the experience the work offers. But there is also the possibility that although we undergo the right experience, we fail to find it rewarding, either at all or to the degree it merits.

13 'The experience of the work' must here be understood with a certain latitude in order to accommodate cases in which you value the experience of the work, although there are certain aspects of the work that displease you and that you regard as detracting from the work's merit, or there are aspects of the work that you are indifferent to and that you regard as not enhancing the work's value.

14 As it stands, the doctrine appears to require an artist to create a work of art with the intention of communicating something to a particular individual or group of people or with the hope that somebody will experience the work and understand its message. If the reference to an individual in this requirement is restricted to someone other than the artist, the requirement is often violated. But perhaps an adherent of the doctrine would allow the reference to include the artist and would claim that in creating a work of art the artist must assume the role of spectator and judge her product from the point of view of its suitability to communicate the message it contains.

15 My friend's letter may not only communicate her thoughts but give an impression of the process of her thinking them out. I ignore this complication.

16 The conclusion that the communication conception of artistic value fails to do justice to the experience of the work itself can be extended to cover the more general functional conception. Whatever function a work of art may perform, it is not the performance of this function that determines the value of a work of art as a work of art. The denial that the particular 'message' communicated by any valued work could be communicated by anything else, and the assertion that what a valued work communicates is *itself*, are closely related distortions of thought caused by the compulsion to use the model of communication but an unwillingness to accept the implications that flow from the notion. The motivation is to secure the indispensability of the experience of a work, but the strategy is misguided.

17 I have claimed that artistic value is an intersubjective value: it is built into the concept that a judgement of artistic value aspires to intersubjective validity. Note that scepticism about the possibility of vindicating this aspiration is not tantamount to rejection of the account of artistic value I have developed. All that such scepticism warrants is the claim that judgements of artistic value involve a mistaken or unfounded 'objectification'. Even if nothing were to make one affective response more appropriate than another, so that the concept of artistic value would lack any application, the status of artistic value would still be intersubjective. Conceptual analysis is one thing; the applicability of the concept another.

18 Consider humour. There is no reason to suppose that the capacity to find something funny is common to or even widespread amongst all rational agents. It might be specific to human beings. Even if it is not, different species might not find the same things funny, to the same degree.

19 A reductive analysis of the concept of the artistic value of a work in terms of its power to induce intrinsically rewarding experiences in subjects fails to do justice to the evaluative component of the concept, as do other dispositional accounts of value that omit reference to the idea of a merited response. The most sophisticated dispositional theory of aesthetic value is Anthony Savile's 'Beauty: A Neo-Kantian Account' in *Essays in Kant's Aesthetics*, eds. Ted Cohen and Paul Guyer (Chicago/London: University of Chicago Press, 1982). An outstanding attempt to articulate an account of aesthetic (and also moral) value that does justice both to its response-dependent nature and to its intersubjectivity and that also gives content to the implicit notion of merit or appropriateness is David Wiggins's 'A Sensible Subjectivism?' in his *Needs, Values, Truth* (Oxford: Blackwell, 1991).

20 For a penetrating account of the relation between aesthetic qualities and non-aesthetic features, see Frank Sibley, 'Aesthetic Concepts', *Philosophical Review*, 68, 1959, and 'Aesthetic and Non-Aesthetic', *Philosophical Review*, 74, 1965.

21 The claim that only one understanding of a work is both correct and complete is compatible with (i) a work's being intentionally ambiguous (so that its appreciation requires that it is experienced in ways that are concurrently incompatible), and (ii) a work's meaning being indeterminate (so that, without error, it can, within limits, be interpreted in more than one way). Given this, I believe there is no good reason to resist the claim. For an excellent defence of the uniqueness claim and an analysis of the idea of a work's canonical interpretation, see Anthony Savile, *The Test of Time* (Oxford: Clarendon Press, 1982), Ch. 4.

22 The notion of understanding a work of art, and so the idea of the experience a work of art offers, can be understood in more or less accommodating ways: so as to include, or so as to exclude, awareness of any feature of the work which requires the subject who experiences that feature in the work to respond favourably (or unfavourably) to its presence – as with beauty or insipidity, for example. It is only if the notion of understanding is given the wider, all-inclusive scope that it is plausible to believe that correctness of understanding ensures correctness of evaluation.

23 This has been emphasized by R. K. Elliott, especially in 'The Critic and the Lover of Art', *Linguistic Analysis and Phenomenology*, ed. Wolfe Mays and S. C. Brown (London: Macmillan, 1972).

24 Even if each of the qualities for which works of art are rightly valued as art were to be a quantity measurable in terms of a common unit, artistic value would not thereby be a commensurable value. For the artistic value of a work is not the sum of the valuable qualities it contains, as can most easily be seen from the consideration that qualities that are valuable in themselves can be combined together in an incongruous way – in such a manner that they do not support or enhance one another, but clash.

23

Tragedy and Moral Value

Peter Lamarque

The second order of the art [of drama] is that, where in dramatic representations . . . there is displayed a deep knowledge, not of individuals and their affairs alone, but of our whole species, of the world and of life. . . . But in my opinion the art of the dramatic poet has, besides all this, yet another and a higher end. The enigma of life should not barely be expressed but solved.

Carl Wilhelm Friedrich von Schlegel,
Lectures on the History of Literature

Real life is not tragic. Religion is not tragic. . . . Strictly speaking, tragedy belongs to literature. Tragedies are plays written by great poets.

***Iris Murdoch*, Metaphysics as a**
Guide to Morality

I

Philosophers have long been intrigued by tragedy. Aristotle sought to define and defend it, Hume wanted to account for the peculiar pleasures it affords, and Schopenhauer and Nietzsche were attracted by the view of life it implies. Those who study tragedy do so perforce from some perspective or other, with some particular interest in mind.

Peter Lamarque, "Tragedy and Moral Value," from Peter Lamarque, *Fictional Points of View* (Ithaca, NY: Cornell University Press, 1996), pp. 135–48; originally, in a slightly shorter version, in *Australasian Journal of Philosophy*, 73 (1995), pp. 239–49. Reprinted by permission of Oxford University Press.

The thought that tragic drama gives moral insight or teaches a moral lesson is one such familiar perspective. But it is one, I suggest, that we should treat with care if not suspicion.

The danger of the search for moral wisdom in the great works of tragedy is that it can become just another form of appropriation, in which one loses sight of what is truly distinctive about tragedy conceived as literature or art. No doubt there is something intrinsically uplifting or disturbing about the stories, however told, of Antigone or Agamemnon or King Lear such that reflection on these characters' more or less disastrous responses to a personal crisis can stir us to think again about our own moral precepts. But that seems to ignore the mode in which the stories are presented, the role of representation – of art itself – in what the stories have to tell. What needs exploring is the distinctive literary response to the works and how that might engage with moral content.

The focus for my discussion will be the question of why and how the representation of human suffering and disaster can have value and, specifically, moral value.[1] Clearly not any representation of human suffering is morally valuable; indeed, some representations are quite the opposite, being actually immoral, morally depraved, or morally exploitative. So how can we distinguish between those representations which, as it might be put, merit our sympathetic involvement and those which do not, being wantonly cruel or self-indulgent or voyeuristic or pornographic?

The representations that are valuable, we say, are works of art: they have some higher purpose, aesthetic or moral or both. Their mode of representation offers some special insight into the nature of human despair and human tragedy. But what does this claim amount to?

First, there is a constraint on subject matter: the suffering associated with tragic drama is of a distinctive kind. It is not just that someone suffers a disastrous reversal of fortune. Not just any piece of bad luck is tragic, nor is any unhappy ending. For one thing, circumstances must be largely outside the agents' control, for which they are not wholly culpable, and which bring about their downfall. But more than that, as Aristotle insists, the person who suffers in this way must be worthy of our respect, must have morally admirable qualities, such as to elicit pity and sympathy at his or her demise. It is wrong to think of the Aristotelian hamartia as a "fatal flaw" in the character, in a purely negative sense, for then the character would be somewhat less deserving of our sympathy. Rather, as Aristotle conceives it, hamartia is best thought of as a contingent by-product of otherwise admirable character traits – for example, the tendency of the courageous soldier to take especially unwise risks.[2] Inasmuch as we admire courage, it would be misleading to describe a risk-taking disposition as a "flaw" in the courageous soldier. Often hamartia involves not knowing or not acknowledging one's true identity either, as in the case of Oedipus, through a more or less excusable ignorance or, in the case of Phaedra in her fatal passion for Hippolytus, through some overwhelming emotion, not entirely within her control.

Nevertheless, the description of the tragic hero as morally admirable only compounds the problem of why the representation of such characters suffering reversals of fortune should have any moral or aesthetic value. Perhaps the most common line of thought which seeks to explain the moral seriousness of tragedy – which is part of a long tradition on the subject – is the notion that the dramatic portrayal of tragic events expresses, even epitomizes, metaphysical or religious views of the world which are of independent moral significance. It is part of Christian theology, for example, that suffering is the path to redemption, that all human suffering is prefigured in the story of Christ's Passion, that Christ died that man might be saved. Many tragic dramas – though not all – represent suffering and death as a kind of purging, a way of ushering in a new order, of laying a foundation for renewal and hope, even of resurrection. When Fortinbras enters at the end of *Hamlet*, he holds out the promise of a new order in the face of death and destruction.

Even in the non-Christian tradition, the value of tragedy is commonly seen to reside in a metaphysical picture of the world, albeit a bleaker, less consoling kind. Characteristically it is a metaphysics of a world governed by fate or natural law which is depicted as blindly indifferent to human suffering and to human conceptions of fairness and benevolence. Portraying humans in the grip of such metaphysically terrifying forces is seen as a salutary moral reminder of human frailty within an indifferent world – or simply as a revelation of cosmic justice that far transcends the narrow confines of human pity. The romantic metaphysicians of the nineteenth century – notably Hegel, Schopenhauer, and Nietzsche – all see the value of tragedy in the image it presents of human life overwhelmed by these uncontrollable, barely understood forces. Of the three, only Hegel manages to extract from tragedy any glimmer of optimism, seeing it as a reaffirmation of an absolute morality in the face of apparent moral conflict, even if the terrible price is the destruction of those who initiate the conflict (he takes Sophocles' *Antigone* as his paradigm). Schopenhauer presents an exactly opposite view; what tragedy offers – what makes it the "highest poetical achievement," is not any grand poetic justice but a stark confrontation with what he calls the "terrible side of life": "The unspeakable pain, the wretchedness and misery of mankind, the triumph of wickedness, the scornful mastery of chance, and the irretrievable fall of the just and the innocent are all here presented to us; and here is to be found a significant hint as to the nature of the world and of existence." The response it produces, he suggests, is one of "resignation, the giving up not merely of life, but of the whole will-to-live itself."[3] Nietzsche's position, though owing much to Schopenhauer, stands somewhere between the two – the source of tragedy, he claims, is not some remote external force but a conflict between two deeply rooted facets of humanity represented by the Apollonian rational order of phenomena, on the one hand, and the Dionysian irrational ecstatic order of things-in-themselves, on the other. The destruction of the Apollonian individuality of the hero in the Dionysian abyss serves to reaffirm the transitory and parochial nature of values in a valueless universe.[4]

Although my sketchy outline does scant justice to such religious and metaphysical conceptions of tragedy, I think they tell only part of the story at best. Because they apply only to particular tragedies within clearly defined traditions (in the case of the metaphysical view, principally to Greek tragedy and Sophoclean tragedy at that), they do not seem to answer in principle the question we have posed, which is far more general in nature, namely, What moral value *can* reside in depictions of human suffering, and what makes some but not all such representations morally valuable? It is not sufficient to locate this value in an independently stable metaphysical view of the place of man in nature even if there are characteristic themes in tragic drama which reinforce some such general vision. For what gets left out of the account is the specific means by which this vision, or these themes, are represented in literary works and the special achievement of this mode of presentation. The interesting question is not just what visions of human life underlie tragic drama but also what special contribution is made by the imaginative realization of such visions in works of literature. Here I believe that Aristotle is a better guide than the romantic metaphysicians, not least because he stresses the poetic character of tragedy (contrasting it, for example, with the narratives of history) and the peculiar range of responses that are appropriate to poetic mimesis, especially involving the emotions.

My own approach can be called humanistic in that I am inclined to suppose, like Aristotle, that the great tragic dramas retain an enduring human interest because they develop themes of a more or less universal nature; they have a "moral content," in a sense to be explained, that, while not necessarily offering moral solutions, engages imaginatively with some of the deepest concerns of human beings in their attempts and repeated failures at living a moral life. The interest of this conception lies, of course, less in its general formulation than in the way it is *worked out* and, specifically, the way it is located among other conceptions: that of literature, of moral content, of fiction, of the imagination. In this chapter I will take a few steps toward that further working out.

II

The humanistic view of tragedy has no commitment, as I would defend it, to the belief that tragedy (or any literature for that matter) inevitably heightens the moral sensibilities of its readers or brings them to lead morally better or more fulfill-

ing lives. Whether watching tragic drama or reading literature has such effects is a purely contingent and causal matter; and little empirical evidence exists for the morally beneficial effects of the study of literature (the same holds for the study of philosophy or social science). Sometimes Martha Nussbaum, for example, following in the footsteps of Matthew Arnold, F. R. Leavis, or even Nietzsche, seems to suggest a more essential link between literature and living a moral life.[5] But that is no part of my view. I do, however, hold that works of literature occupy an indispensable place in any literary culture and that all things being equal it is better to read the great works of literature than not. The reasons for this will partly emerge from a consideration of what might be meant by "moral content," as conceived in connection with a humanistic conception of literature.

Traditionally, we can identify two strands of thought about moral content in literature or in tragedy in particular. One is the idea of a *moral lesson* or moral principle derivable from a work; the other is the idea of a *moral vision* expressed in a work. The first idea, that of a moral lesson, can probably be traced back to the tradition of folktales or parables, whose purpose was to illuminate or teach a *moral* that gives meaning and interest to a narrative. It might be thought that this paradigm is too naïve or too remote from current conceptions of literature to merit much serious attention. But the idea of a moral lesson has more sophisticated formulations, and again, the interesting question is not whether moral lessons or principles can be drawn from great works of literature – for it is always easy enough to do so – but what status should be given to them or, as I shall put it, where they should be located within an adequate theory of literary appreciation. In some respects the generalizations about tragedy found in the work of Hegel, Schopenhauer, and Nietzsche – and unlike those of Aristotle, who is concerned with more formal features – can be thought of as statements of the moral lessons to be drawn from tragedy.

Consider, though, a much simpler example from George Orwell in his essay "Lear, Tolstoy, and the Fool," written in 1947. Orwell argues that *King Lear* has two morals, one explicitly stated, one merely implied:

> First of all, . . . there is the vulgar, common-sense moral drawn by the Fool: "Don't relinquish power, don't give away

your lands." But there is also another moral. Shakespeare never utters it in so many words, and it doesn't very much matter whether he was fully aware of it. It is contained in the story, which, after all, he made up, or altered to suit his purposes. It is: "Give away your lands if you want to, but don't expect to gain happiness by doing so. Probably you won't gain happiness. If you live for others, you must live *for others*, and not as a roundabout way of getting an advantage for yourself."[6]

Orwell is no doubt right that at one level such homespun lessons about what to expect if you give away your lands *can* be derived from *King Lear*. But the patent inadequacy of this account to explain either the literary interest of the play or its moral seriousness points up a general weakness of the moral lesson view of moral content. Perhaps the problem can be summarized like this: either the moral lesson is too close to the work, tied too specifically to the characters and incidents in the work, in which case it cannot function as an independent, generalizable moral principle, or the moral lesson is too detached, too loosely connected to the specifics of the work to be perceived as part of the literary content or meaning that the work expresses. The tension here is precisely between the *derivability* of the moral principle and its *independence* as a general moral truth.

It is important to see that the problem is not just that of how to formulate a moral lesson in some derived statement. For literary works all too often provide such statements themselves. The closing speech by the Chorus in the *Antigone* would be an obvious example: "Wisdom is the supreme part of happiness; and reverence towards the gods must be inviolate. Great words of prideful men are ever punished with great blows, and, in old age, teach the chastened to be wise."[7]

But to extract this moral homily from the play, independently of its specific literary function, would be utterly misleading. For the literary interest of the Chorus's words is much more subtle: although supposedly alluding to Creon as growing wise through suffering, they hint that they are referring to themselves as well. The Chorus's own stance with regard to Creon and Antigone shifts during the play – as the elders of Thebes, they have a vested interest in the power of the state, represented by Creon, yet in the light of Tiresias's warning, they come to fear for their city and to

blame Creon for undermining its stability. Many of the conflicts in the play are mirrored in the attitudes of the Chorus, a detailed account of which would need to explore the shifting dynamics of power and justice and fear and arrogance in the relations of the Chorus to the main protagonists. The moral lesson drawn by the Chorus reflects inward more than outward; it prompts us to think again about the kind of wisdom both they and Creon have acquired and the different forms that "chastening" has taken throughout the drama.[8]

When derived moral lessons are relativized in this way to interpretive frameworks (not least by the workings of irony), they come to acquire a status quite different from that of independent moral truths, that is, they acquire the status of thematic statements or descriptions. Here is Wilson Knight, in *The Wheel of Fire*, arguing that *King Lear* can be interpreted as what he calls "comedy of the grotesque": "Though love and music – twin sisters of salvation – temporarily may heal the racked consciousness of Lear, yet, so deeply planted in the facts of our life is this unknowing ridicule of destiny, that the uttermost tragedy of the incongruous ensues, and there is no hope save in the broken heart and limp body of death."[9]

Knight uses the concepts "ridicule of destiny" and "tragedy of the incongruous" not as components of a moral lesson which can be learned from the play and applied independently of it but as thematic concepts for an enhanced understanding of the play. Although he might appear to be making a generalizable comment about the role of ridicule and the comic in tragic situations, the interest of his analysis is grounded in what light it can shed on specific scenes in *King Lear*. It is a commonplace that moral concepts and moral propositions can appear in thematic descriptions, but it is not always recognized that moral content *as it figures in thematic statements* and moral content *as it figures in independent moral principles* are performing two radically different functions and are thus assessable in radically different ways.[10]

III

Let me turn next to moral content conceived as moral vision. Here the idea is that the moral value of tragedy lies in what it *shows* (to use Wittgensteinian terminology), not in what it *states* or *implies* propositionally. The metaphor of a picture or view or vision of the world is widely used in this context.

Thus Iris Murdoch writes, "The study of literature . . . is an education in how to picture and understand human situations."[11] It is Murdoch's view that great art helps us acquire a more detached, objective, and selfless perspective on the world which is always threatened by the essentially egocentric outlook of our ordinary lives. "The tragic poet breaks the egoistic illusory unity which is natural to art and is able to look at human evil with a just and steady eye."[12]

In a related strand of argument, the idea of moral vision in contrast to a moral lesson has been thought to embody an insight into ethics itself, as well as the connection between literature and ethics. This is notable in the Wittgensteinian school as represented, for example, by D. Z. Phillips and R. M. Beardsmore, who have both argued that the central task of ethics is not to formulate and apply general principles but rather to stress the particularity of moral situations and the idea that profound moral disagreements reside not in a difference of *beliefs* but in different ways of *looking* at the world.[13] The argument is then brought to bear on literature with a parallel drawn more or less explicitly between a moral agent on the one hand and a competent reader on the other. The idea is that the moral agent and the reader both confront complex moral situations, with both called on to adopt an imaginative perspective on those situations which should yield in the one case a moral judgment or appropriate action and in the other a moral insight or revised way of seeing. A competent reader might hope to learn from the literary work not by formulating a derived moral principle but by acquiring a new vision or perspective on the world.

A not dissimilar position is taken by Martha Nussbaum and Hilary Putnam as part of a general argument toward the assimilation of particular works of literature into moral philosophy as essential components of moral reasoning. Nussbaum states: "If the enterprise of moral philosophy is understood . . . as a pursuit of truth in all its forms, requiring a deep and sympathetic investigation of all major ethical alternatives and the comparison of each with our active sense of life, then moral philosophy requires such literary texts, and the experience of loving and attentive novel-reading, for its completion."[14] And according to Putnam: "Literature does not, or does not often, depict *solutions*. What especially the novel does is aid us in the imaginative re-creation of moral perplexities, in the widest sense. . . . If moral reasoning, at the

reflective level, is the conscious criticism of ways of life, then the sensitive appreciation in the imagination of predicaments and perplexities must be essential to sensitive moral reasoning. Novels and plays do not set moral knowledge before us, that is true. But they do (frequently) do something for us that must be done for us if we are to gain any moral knowledge."[15]

Again it seems beyond doubt that literary works – including perhaps par excellence works of tragedy – have the capacity to foster "sensitive appreciation in the imagination of predicaments and perplexities." And no doubt there is a moral aspect to this. But the danger with this whole line of thinking is that too much gets run together too fast. The imaginative and moral and literary dimensions blur into one another in a way that threatens to weaken such insights as we might hope to gain about the moral value of tragedy or the literary representation of suffering. But I do think we can build on the simple intuitions that govern both the "moral lesson" and "moral vision" views of moral content.

IV

First, we need to acknowledge at least a prima facie distinction between a *fictive* dimension, a *literary* dimension, and a *moral* dimension in works of tragedy. Explaining how these are distinct and also how they interrelate will be the basis of the account that follows. My suggestion is that these dimensions are not interchangeable, not coextensional, and not reducible one to the other but that if we want to find a general explanation of the moral values of tragedy, we need reference to all three.

The fictive dimension might seem problematic in relation to tragedy on the grounds that the subject matter of tragic drama was traditionally based on true stories – or at least stories assumed to be true – involving actual individuals, families, dynasties, emperors, or kings on whom misfortune had fallen. Even if that is right, however, though it is not part of a definition of tragedy, it is still appropriate to speak of a fictive dimension in the sense I intend. For the fictive dimension involves a mode of storytelling, not a kind of story told. Real events can be fictionalized by being represented in a certain way. Fictiveness in this sense is a mode of utterance, one that invites and elicits an imaginative response rather than a response grounded in belief and verification.[16] Fictive storytelling disengages standard conditions of assertion, it invites imaginative rather than belief-based involvement, it creates worlds and characters, and it encourages participation, not a concern for correspondence with the facts. The fictive dimension is value-neutral. There is no inherent value in the fictive mode, only instrumental values.

The literary dimension is different in several respects. For one thing it is not value-neutral. To identify a literary dimension in a work is to identify something of value in the work, some special interest that it promises, some expectation that it will reward a certain kind of attention. To appreciate a work for its literary values is to attend to its aesthetic qualities but especially to the way that it sustains and develops a humanly interesting content or theme.[17] We have already seen how such a theme might have a moral content, that is, how it might be expressed in a proposition apparently of the same form as a moral principle or injunction. Themes can take other forms as well. But a description of a theme with moral content is not functioning as a description of an independent moral principle but offers a way of identifying some central focus or unity in the work (it points inward, not outward). There is no implication that a work must sustain some one determinate theme. *King Lear* invites any number of interpretations, including what Jonathan Dollimore has called a "materialist reading" whereby the focus of the play is seen to be "power, property and inheritance": "The cherished norms of human kindness [are] shown to have no 'natural' sanction at all. A catastrophic redistribution of power and property . . . disclose[s] the awful truth that these two things are somehow prior to the laws of human kindness rather than vice versa."[18] This interpretation need not preclude that given by Knight, for example: both readings conform to the conventions of literary appreciation, both seeking to identify some thematic coherence that makes the play rewarding as a work of art.

The fictive and the literary dimensions can be explained in terms of a certain kind of attention given to a work: a certain perspective on the work, conventionally determined. The fictive dimension invites what might be called a fictive stance – that of imaginative involvement and cognitive distance – whereas the literary dimension invites a related, but distinct, literary response – the attempt to define a unifying aesthetic purpose in the work through thematic interpretation.

So it is, third, that a work can have a *moral dimen-sion*, not reducible to the other two, which facilitates some further moral appropriation of the work's content, either as a contribution to moral philosophy or as illustrative support for some broader metaphysical picture or just for clarifying one's own moral precepts. Thus when Dollimore goes on to say about *Lear*, "Human values are not antecedent to these material realities but are, on the contrary, informed by them,"[19] he is both talking about the play and making a statement about the nature of moral values as he sees them. Similarly, the moral vision theorists such as Murdoch or Phillips or Nussbaum (or even Schopenhauer and Nietzsche) appropriate the vision (moral content) of tragic drama into their own independent moral theories. Their mistake, I have suggested, is to suppose that the moral dimension is simply subsumed under the literary dimension, that there is a seamless transition from being literary critics to being moral philosophers; that in identifying a literary theme of a moral nature, they have ipso facto established a moral insight.

To bring out more precisely how the fictive, literary, and moral dimensions interrelate – and thus how it is that representations of suffering in tragedy can merit our moral interest and involvement – I will briefly bring in one further and final distinction: that between internal and external perspectives on imaginary worlds. This distinction is absolutely fundamental to understanding the values we attribute to fictional representations.

The internal perspective on an imaginary world is paradigmatically that of the fictive stance, namely, direct imaginative involvement with the subject of a work. Readers or viewers can project themselves into a fictional world and become, so it seems, participants or observers in that world. In contrast, the external perspective involves no imaginative projection; it focuses on the fictionality of the worlds depicted, on modes of representation, on literary devices and narrative structure, on theme and genre, on possible interpretations. Under the internal perspective, fictional characters are imagined to be fellow humans in real predicaments, objects of sympathy and concern, similar to ourselves in many respects; under the external perspective, they are viewed as fictional characters, linguistic or ideological constructs, whose nature and qualities are grounded in the descriptive modes by which they are presented.[20] The two perspectives nicely interact. Take our reaction to the death of Cordelia in *King Lear*: internally and imaginatively, viewers are dismayed by so futile and tragic a loss. Yet, from the external perspective, few would welcome Nahum Tate's rewriting of the play where Cordelia is saved. Cordelia's death, as we come to see, is essential to the tragic structure of the play. From the internal perspective, we might wish her spared; from the external perspective, we want the play just as it is.[21]

There are deeper connections still. Our imaginative response to, say, Lear and Cordelia is not just a response to them as persons in a tragic predicament but a response to them *as represented* in a dramatic context. As Flint Schier puts it, "Our reaction is necessarily governed by *how* they are represented, and the kind of emotion that it is appropriate to feel is determined by the quality of the representation."[22] Not all kinds of representation, even of ostensibly the same subject matter – for example, sentimental, sensational, melodramatic kinds – merit emotional involvement. The same point can be put like this: the external perspective, an awareness of modes of representation, dictates the kind of involvement appropriate from the internal perspective. If that is right, it follows that the responses of pity and fear which are so central to Aristotle's account of tragedy are not just vague and contingent reactions to characters conceived as real people but are also an integral part of an imaginative engagement with the tragedy's representational content; a failure to respond in that way is partly a failure of understanding. *Katharsis* can then be seen not merely as a clinical "purging" of the emotions but as a further kind of self-knowledge, one involving a clarification or "working through" of the emotions, revealing their proper objects.[23]

The distinction between internal and external perspectives can also help explain how literary tragedy differs from fantasy or horror. One difference in modes of imagining is this: sometimes we simply *find ourselves* in a certain state of mind, sometimes we adopt a state of mind because we recognize we are being invited to do so. Fantasy belongs with the former, art with the latter. In the case of works of art, we respond in a certain way to the fictive presentation at least partly because we recognize a reason for doing so, within the structure of the work. In contrast, the imaginings of fantasy are purely manipulative; attitudes and responses are the products of causes, and we adopt a point of view, as we might say, *in spite of ourselves.* We have only a minimal awareness of the representational modes in which the fantasy is embod-

ied. In fantasy, then, unlike in art, the internal perspective on an imaginary world overwhelms the external perspective.

What is valuable about artistic representation is the careful mediation of the two perspectives, the guidance of imaginative response by the very structures of representation itself. An appropriate response to the speech by the Chorus at the end of the *Antigone* is dictated by the function it is seen as serving in the structure of the play, that is, as more than just a moral homily offered for our edification. The matter is normative, for one who fails to respond has not only failed imaginatively but also in understanding.

Returning then to the moral content of tragedy, we can see different interlocking elements. Taken as a literary work, a tragic drama will invite an interpretation of its central themes, characterizable often, if not always, in moral terms. This interpretation will be specific to the work; it is a way of redescribing and unifying elements of the work's subject matter and must be sensitive to the modes in which that subject matter is presented. But tragedies are also dramatic productions that engage viewers imaginatively. Aristotle's emphasis on action rather than character, on dramatic form rather than narrative form, highlights the importance of first-person performance, not third-person narration, in tragedy: the direct presentation of the suffering hero, not just a report about him or her.[24] The dramatic presentation both elicits and controls a sympathetic and imaginative response that serves to make the moral themes more immediate. Only at this point is the further appropriation of the moral content of tragedy possible or valuable – be it in support of a Schopenhauerian pessimism or the cultural materialism of Jonathan Dollimore or in debates in moral philosophy. Generalizations on the theme of people of good character suffering terrible reversals of fortune can yield an important moral perspective on human life only in the light of a full assimilation of the sympathetic, imaginative response to the particularities of tragic drama, mediated by some overall conception of how the elements of the drama cohere within a thematic interpretation. Once again, what is further reinforced is the Murdochian-cum-Aristotelian view of the universal emerging from the particular in poetic art.

It is the interrelation between the moral and the literary which is of special interest; for one consequence of the account given – and surely a desirable consequence – is that a different kind of moral appropriation will be available under different thematic interpretations of a work. To take an extreme and trivial example: were *Othello* to be interpreted or performed as comedy, say, or as racialist propaganda, then the sympathetic engagement with the imaginary world dictated by its tragic elements would be diluted or made fun of and any corresponding moral insight would be lost or perverted. Only *under a certain description* does tragedy merit and reward a moral perspective.

The moral value of tragic drama is *constituted* by the fact that certain modes of representing tragic events afford controlled imaginative access to themes of human failure and disaster. This access is uniquely available to art in the way that it exploits and balances the tension between internal and external points of view. There is no simple answer to why we should want such access to human suffering. But, in general, surely no explanation is needed for why matters of such central human concern should be of enduring human interest.

Notes

1 The focus is not the same as that of Hume's "Of Tragedy," where Hume is concerned with "the unaccountable pleasure which the spectators of a well-written tragedy receive from sorrow, terror, anxiety," in *Essays: Moral, Political, and Literary* (Oxford, 1963), p. 221. No doubt *part* of the value of tragedy can be explained in terms of the pleasure it gives, but I suggest that the pleasure (properly defined) is as much a consequence of its moral value as an explanation of it. My account of moral value will, I hope, go some way toward shedding light on the appropriate kind of pleasure.

2 I have taken the point from Amélie Oksenberg Rorty, "The Psychology of Aristotelian Tragedy," in *Philosophy and the Arts*, Midwest Studies in Philosophy, ed. P. French, T. Uehling, and H. Wettstein, no. 16 (Minneapolis, 1991), pp. 61–3.

3 Arthur Schopenhauer, *The World as Will and Representation*, trans. E. F. J. Payne, vol. 1 (New York, 1958), p. 253.

4 For a succinct philosophical account of these metaphysical views, see Anthony Quinton, "Tragedy," *Proceedings of the Aristotelian Society* 34, suppl. vol. (1960): 145–64.

5 In *Love's Knowledge: Essays on Philosophy and Literature* (Oxford, 1990), Marthan Nussbaum writes, for example, "A novel, just because it is not our life, places us in a moral position that is favorable for perception" (p. 162), and "The universalizing tendency of the moral imagination is encouraged by the very activity of novel-reading itself" (p. 166).

6 Orwell, *The Collected Essays, Journalism, and Letters of George Orwell*, vol. 4, ed. Sonia Orwell and Ian Angus (London, 1968), p. 298.

7 Sir Richard C. Jebb, *The Tragedies of Sophocles* (1904; rpt., Cambridge, 1957), p. 172.

8 On the Chorus's role in *Antigone*, see R. W. B. Burton, *The Chorus in Sophocles' Tragedies* (Oxford, 1980), chap. 3.

9 G. Wilson Knight, *The Wheel of Fire* (London, 1972), p. 175.

10 For a detailed discussion, see Peter Lamarque and Stein Haugom Olsen, *Truth, Fiction, and Literature: A Philosophical Perspective* (Oxford, 1994), chap. 13.

11 Iris Murdoch, *The Sovereignty of Good* (London, 1970), p. 34.

12 Iris Murdoch, *Metaphysics as a Guide to Morals* (Harmondsworth, England, 1993), p. 117.

13 See, for example, D. Z. Phillips, *Through a Darkening Glass* (London, 1986), and R. M. Beardsmore, *Art and Morality* (London, 1971).

14 Nussbaum, *Love's Knowledge*, pp. 26–7.

15 Hilary Putnam, "Literature, Science, and Reflection," in *Meaning and the Moral Sciences* (London, 1978), pp. 86–7.

16 For more details of this account of fiction, see Lamarque and Olsen, *Truth, Fiction, and Literature*, pt. 1.

17 Again, for a fuller account, see ibid., pt. 3.

18 Jonathan Dollimore, "*King Lear* and Essentialist Humanism," in *Shakespearean Tragedy*, ed. John Drakakis (London, 1992), p. 201.

19 Ibid.

20 More on internal and external perspectives on fiction can be found in Lamarque and Olsen, *Truth, Fiction, and Literature*, chap. 6. There are also somewhat similar, though not identical, conceptions of internal and external ways of reflecting on characters proposed, for example, by Kendall Walton, Peter van Inwagen, and Frank Palmer. A rather different distinction is that between a first-order response to tragedy and a "metaresponse," that is, a response to the first-order response. This distinction has been used by Susan Feagin to account for the pleasures of tragedy. A metaresponse is not the same as the external perspective, for the latter is a way of contemplating a *work* (and its content), whereas the former is directed to a reader of the work. See Susan L. Feagin, "The Pleasures of Tragedy," *American Philosophical Quarterly* 20 (1983): 95–104; and Sally Markovitz, "Guilty Plea-

sures: Aesthetic Meta-Response and Fiction," *Journal of Aesthetics and Art Criticism* 50 (1992): 307–16.

21 Although in a different theoretical setting, the account is similar to that in Kendall L. Walton, *Mimesis as Make-Believe* (Cambridge, Mass., 1990), pp. 258–9.

22 Flint Schier, "Tragedy and the Community of Sentiment," in *Philosophy and Fiction: Essays in Liter-* *ary Aesthetics*, ed. Peter Lamarque (Aberdeen, 1983), p. 85.

23 The idea of "working through" emotions comes from Amélie Rorty, "Psychology of Aristotelian Tragedy," p. 66.

24 The importance of the dramatic and "first-person" nature of tragedy is emphasized by Ruby Meager in "Tragedy," *Proceedings of the Aristotelian Society* 34, suppl. vol. (1960): 165–86.

24

The Ethical Criticism of Art

Berys Gaut

Ethicism

This essay argues that the ethical criticism of art is a proper and legitimate aesthetic activity. More precisely, it defends a view I term *ethicism*. Ethicism is the thesis that the ethical assessment of attitudes manifested by works of art is a legitimate aspect of the aesthetic evaluation of those works, such that, if a work manifests ethically reprehensible attitudes, it is to that extent aesthetically defective, and if a work manifests ethically commendable attitudes, it is to that extent aesthetically meritorious.

This thesis needs elucidation. The ethicist principle is a pro tanto one: it holds that a work is aesthetically meritorious (or defective) *insofar as* it manifests ethically admirable (or reprehensible) attitudes. (The claim could also be put like this: manifesting ethically admirable attitudes *counts toward* the aesthetic merit of a work, and manifesting ethically reprehensible attitudes *counts against* its aesthetic merit.) The ethicist does not hold that manifesting ethically commendable attitudes is a necessary condition for a work to be aesthetically good: there can be good, even great, works of art that are ethically flawed. Examples include Wagner's Ring Cycle, which is marred by the anti-Semitism displayed in the portrayal of the *Nibelungen*; some of T. S. Eliot's poems, such as *Sweeney among the Nightingales*, which are similarly tainted

Berys Gaut, "The Ethical Criticism of Art," in Jerrold Levinson (ed.), *Aesthetics and Ethics* (Cambridge: Cambridge University Press, 1998), pp. 182–203. © by Cambridge University Press.

by anti-Semitism; and Leni Riefenstahl's striking propaganda film, *The Triumph of the Will*, deeply flawed by its craven adulation of Hitler. Nor does the ethicist thesis hold that manifesting ethically good attitudes is a sufficient condition for a work to be aesthetically good: there are works such as Harriet Beecher Stowe's *Uncle Tom's Cabin* which, though the ethical attitudes they display are admirable, are in many ways uninspired and disappointing. The ethicist can deny these necessity and sufficiency claims, because she holds that there are a plurality of aesthetic values, of which the ethical values of artworks are but a single kind.[1] So, for instance, a work of art may be judged to be aesthetically good *insofar as* it is beautiful, is formally unified and strongly expressive, but aesthetically bad *insofar as* it trivializes the issues with which it deals and manifests ethically reprehensible attitudes. We then need to make an *all-things-considered* judgment, balancing these aesthetic merits and demerits one against another to determine whether the work is, all things considered, good. And we should not suppose that there is any mechanically applicable weighing method that could determine the truth of such a judgment: overall judgments are plausibly ones that resist any form of codification in terms of mechanically applicable principles. These kinds of pro tanto and all-things-considered judgments are common in other evaluative domains, notably the moral domain.[2]

The notion of the aesthetic adopted here should be construed broadly. In the narrow sense of the term, aesthetic value properties are those that ground a certain kind of sensory or contemplative pleasure or displeasure. In this sense, beauty, elegance, gracefulness, and their contraries are aesthetic value properties. However, the sense adopted here is broader: I mean by "aesthetic value" the value of an object *qua* work of art, that is, its artistic value. This broader sense is required, since not all of the values of an object *qua* work of art are narrowly aesthetic. Besides a work's beauty, we may, for instance, aesthetically admire it for its cognitive insight (subject, as we shall see, to certain conditions), its articulated expression of joy, the fact that it is deeply moving, and so on. However, this broader sense of "aesthetic" does not mean that just any property of a work of art counts as aesthetic. Works of art have many other sorts of value properties that are not values of them *qua* works of art: they can have investment value, value as status symbols, and so forth.[3]

The notion of manifesting an attitude should be construed in terms of a work's displaying pro or con attitudes toward some state of affairs or things, which the work may do in many ways besides explicitly stating an opinion about them.[4] (Such attitudes can run the gamut from unmixed approval through neutrality to unmixed disapproval, and also include various complex and nuanced attitudes that display both approbatory and disapprobatory aspects, such as those revealed in jealous or conflicted attitudes.) What is relevant for ethicism are the attitudes *really* possessed by a work, not those it merely claims to possess; so the attitudes manifested may be correctly attributable only by subtle and informed critical judgment. A novel may state that it condemns the sexual activities it describes, but from the subtly lubricious and prying manner in which it dwells on them, it may be correct to attribute to it an attitude of titillation, not of moralistic disgust. Just as we can distinguish between the attitudes people really have and those they merely claim to have by looking at their behavior, so we can distinguish between real and claimed attitudes of works by looking at the detailed manner in which events are presented.

Ethicism does not entail the causal thesis that good art ethically improves people.[5] Since the ethicist principle is a pro tanto one, it allows for the existence of great but ethically flawed works; and even if all aesthetically good works were ethically sound, it would not follow that they improve people, any more than it follows that earnest ethical advice improves people, for they may be unmoved by even the most heartfelt exhortation. Much of the ethical discussion about art, particularly concerning the supposedly pernicious effects of some popular films and music genres, has been concerned with the question of whether such art morally corrupts. This is a version of the causal thesis and should be kept distinct from ethicism. Further, ethicism has nothing to say about the issue of censorship, nor does it give any grounds of support to either the friends or foes of artistic censorship. All that follows from ethicism is that if a work manifests morally bad attitudes it is to that extent aesthetically flawed, flawed as a work of art. The fact that a work of art is aesthetically flawed is not grounds for its censorship: if it were, the art museums of the world would suffer serious depletion.

Objections to Ethicism

1. Ethicism fails to distinguish sharply enough between ethical and aesthetic evaluation. There is an aesthetic attitude in terms of which we aesthetically evaluate works; this aesthetic attitude is distinct from the ethical attitude we may adopt toward works; and ethical assessment is never a concern of the aesthetic attitude. So the ethical criticism of works is irrelevant to their aesthetic value.

The existence of the aesthetic attitude has, of course, been much disputed.[6] But, even if we accept its existence, its adoption is compatible with ethicism. To see why, we need to specify in more detail what the aesthetic attitude is. There are two basic ways of doing this: the aesthetic attitude may be individuated by some feature intrinsic to it or by its formal objects.

Consider the case in which the attitude is individuated by its formal objects: these may be understood in narrow aesthetic fashion, as beauty and its subspecies, such as grace and elegance, or characterized more broadly by the criteria to which formalists appeal, such as Beardsley's unity, complexity, and intensity.[7] Since the presence of these properties arguably does not require, or suffice for, the presence of ethical properties, it may be held that ethical assessment is irrelevant to aesthetic evaluation.[8] Yet this objection is unconvincing, for the list of properties deployed is too narrow to embrace all those of aesthetic relevance. In the assessment of art, appeal is made to such properties as raw expressive power and deep cognitive insight as well as to beauty, elegance, and grace; and the relevance of these expressive and cognitive values explains how there can be great works, such as *Les Desmoiselles d'Avignon*, that are militantly ugly. So the narrow aesthetic view fails. In more sophisticated fashion, the formalist appeals to purely intrinsic properties of works as aesthetically relevant, an appeal motivated by a conception of the work of art as autonomous from its context. But that conception is flawed, for a work can be fully interpreted only by situating it within its generative context.[9] There is reason, then, to spurn the restricted diet of aesthetically relevant properties offered by the narrow aesthetic and formalist views, and as yet no reason to exclude ethical properties from a heartier menu.

The alternative is to individuate the aesthetic attitude by some feature intrinsic to it, and for the opponent of ethicism the most promising feature is the detachment or disengagement we purportedly display toward fictional events. Since it is logically impossible to intervene in such events, the will is detached, practical concerns are quiescent, an attitude of contemplation is adopted. Given the practical character of morality, it follows that ethical assessment plays no role in aesthetic attitude and therefore no role in aesthetic evaluation. But the step from the claim that the will is disengaged and therefore that ethical assessment has no role to play does not follow: there is similarly no possibility of altering historical events, and we are in this sense forced to have a detached or contemplative attitude toward them, but we still ethically assess historical characters and actions. If it is objected that we are ethically engaged in history because we hope to draw from it lessons for our current practice, the same may be said of the lessons we can draw from fiction, such as the psychological insights that Freud discovered there.

The point about ethics and the will deserves elaboration, for it will be relevant to the position defended later. On what might be termed the *purely practical* conception of ethics, the ethical assessment of a person's character is determined only by what he does and by the motives that determine his actions. Any feelings or thoughts that play no role in motivating actions are ethically irrelevant: thoughts, fantasies, and desires, however gruesome, inappropriate, or corrupt we would judge the actions they motivate to be, are not themselves ethically bad, unless they issue in actions that express these feelings and thoughts. So a person may be ethically good while having these feelings and thoughts, and his goodness may consist partly in his capacity to resist their influence on the will, for these feelings and thoughts may have arisen purely passively in him, and he is not to be held responsible for their occurrence.[10] This view, as has just been noted, speedily runs into problems in historical cases where the will cannot be engaged, yet where ethical assessment is still appropriate. But it can be shown to be flawed on other grounds too. Much of our ethical assessment is directed at what people feel, even though these feelings do not motivate their actions. Suppose that Joe is praised for some deserved achievement by his friends, but he later discovers that they are secretly deeply jealous and resentful of him. Their feelings have not motivated their actions, yet we would properly regard these people as less ethically good were we to discover this about them. They are flawed because of what they feel, not because of what they did or their motives for doing it. Also, that people feel deep sympathy for us, even though they are completely unable to help us in our distress, is something that we care about and that properly makes us think better of them. In fact, much of our vocabulary of ethical assessment is directed wholly or in part at the assessment of feelings: we criticize people for being crude, insensitive, callous, or uncaring; we praise them for being warm, friendly, and sensitive. So for the ethical assessment of character an *affective-practical* conception of assessment is correct, a conception which holds that not just actions and motives, but also feelings that do not motivate, are ethically significant. Virtue of character is "concerned with feelings and actions," as Aristotle correctly observes.[11] Such an affective-practical conception of ethical assessment allows the ethical assessment of the feelings that people have when they respond to fictions, even though they cannot act toward the fictional events described.

2. A more radical objection holds that ethical assessment has no place in the assessment of art. Works of art can at best manifest attitudes toward those fictional characters and situations they describe, and such attitudes are not ethically assessable, since they are directed toward merely imagined objects – such objects cannot be harmed or hurt in reality, for they do not exist. What is ethically assessable, in contrast, are attitudes directed toward real characters and situations, but works of art do not manifest attitudes toward such things, for they do not describe them. Hence, there is no place left for the ethical assessment of art.

Even at first blush, the objection is hyperbolic, since not all works of art are fictions: Riefenstahl's film is a documentary of the 1934 Nuremberg rally, and Hitler was not a fictional character. So, at best, the argument would apply only to a subclass of works of art. Second, attitudes directed toward only imagined states of affairs can in fact properly be ethically assessed. Consider a man whose sexual life consists entirely of rape fantasies, fantasies he has not about women he sees in real life, but about women he only imagines. Would we say that there is nothing to be said from an ethical point of view about the attitude he manifests in his imaginings about these fictional women? Clearly, what a person imagines and how he responds to those imaginings play an important part in the ethical assessment of his character. The mere fact that the women he imagines cannot be harmed does not bracket his inner life from ethical assessment, since what is at issue are the attitudes he manifests in his fantasy life. And nothing in our judgment about him requires us to assume that what is bad about his fantasies is that he may act on them – perhaps he is confined to prison for life. He stands ethically condemned for what and how he imagines, independently of how he acts or may act. (Here again, we return to the ethical importance of feelings, but see now that feelings toward merely imagined people can be ethically relevant too.) Further, the attitudes people (and works) manifest toward imagined scenarios have implications for their attitudes toward their real-life counterparts, for the attitudes are partly directed toward kinds, not just individuals.[12] When the rape fantasist imagines his fictional women, he is imagining them *as women*, that is, as beings of a kind that also has instances in the real world; and that he imagines them as women is, of course, essential to his imaginative project. Thus, by virtue of adopting such an attitude toward his imagined women, he implicitly adopts that attitude toward their real-life counterparts – and so reveals something of his attitude toward real-life women. Indeed, it is inevitable that, however apparently exotic the fictional world, the kinds shared between it and the real world will be vast, given the limits on the human imagination, the interests we have in fiction (which include exploring possibilities that reorder the actual world), and interpretive constraints, which involve drawing on background information about the real world in the interpretation of fictions. So the attitudes manifested toward fictional entities will have many implications for attitudes manifested toward real entities.

3. Ethical assessment is relevant to a work's aesthetic merit, but ethicism gives the connection the wrong valence: works can be good precisely *because* they violate our sense of moral rectitude.

Often the most fascinating characters in works are the evil ones, such as Satan in *Paradise Lost*. And recall the passage in *King Lear* in which blind Gloucester asks Lear, "Dost thou know me?" and Lear replies, "I remember thine eyes well enough. Dost thou squiny at me? / No, do thy worst, blind Cupid, I'll not love." As Lawrence Hyman writes, "The dramatic effect requires our moral disapproval," but Shakespeare manages to "transfigure that moral shock into aesthetic pleasure."[13]

It is important to distinguish between the evil or insensitive characters represented by a work and the attitude the work displays toward those characters. Only the latter is relevant to the ethicist thesis. Satan is indeed fascinating because evil, but the work represents him as such, showing the seductive power of evil, and does not approve of his actions. Milton was not a Satanist. And while the power of Lear's bad joke does rest on its hearty heartlessness, it is part of the point of *Lear* that the flamboyant insensitivity displayed by Lear in his derangement is of a piece with the gross egoism that leads to disaster, an egoism overcome only by grief and loss, and transmuted into a finer moral wisdom. Lear's attitude toward Gloucester is represented by the play, but not shared by it. It is true that some works, such as de Sade's *Juliette*, not merely represent evil, but also manifest approval toward that evil. If this work has indeed any serious aesthetic merit, it can in part be traced to the literary skill with which it represents the attitude of finding sexual torture erotically attractive; yet the ethicist can consistently and plausibly maintain that the novel's own espousal of this attitude is an aesthetic defect in it.

It may be objected that the novel's approbatory attitude toward evil is a reason why it is aesthetically good: evil arouses our curiosity, for the evil person may do and experience things we can scarcely imagine, let alone understand; and the novel's ability to satisfy this curiosity, to show us what it is like to engage in such actions, is a prime source of its aesthetic merit. Yet from the fact that we are fascinated by the attitudes manifested, we cannot conclude that our interest in them is aesthetic: our fascination with Adolf Hitler or Jeffrey Dahmer is not an aesthetic one, and our interest in de Sade's work may similarly stem from a curiosity about psychopathic states of mind. Suppose, however, that our interest in *Juliette* is aesthetic, perhaps because of the way that interest is inflected by a concern with the work's stylistic and rhetorical system. This still does not undermine ethicism.

For our interest here is in being able to imagine what it is like to have evil attitudes, and so in coming to understand them, and this is satisfied by the vivid *representation* of an evil attitude. But, again, representation of an attitude by a work does not require the work itself to share that attitude: works may manifest disapproval toward characters or narrators who are represented as evil. Moreover, if, as the objection holds, it is our curiosity that is aroused, we have a cognitive interest in not seeing evil approved of, for such approval implies that there is something good about an attitude we know to be bad.

Some Arguments for Ethicism

There are, of course, further objections and elaborations open to the opponent of ethicism, some of which will be touched on later, but enough has been said to give rational hope that they may be laid to rest. The question remains as to why ethicism should be endorsed. Part of the answer is to be sought in its congruence with our considered aesthetic judgments; we do decry works for their insensitivity, their moral crudity, their lack of integrity, their celebration of cruelty, their slimy salaciousness. But it is the mark of an interesting philosophical thesis that, while some find it obviously true, others find it obviously false; and ethicism is, fortunately and unfortunately, an interesting philosophical thesis. So it would be good to have an argument for its truth.

1. George Dickie has advanced a simple argument for the truth of ethicism. A work of art's moral vision is an (essential) part of that work; any statement about an (essential) part of a work of art is an aesthetic statement about that work; so a statement about a work of art's moral vision is an aesthetic statement about the work.[14]

However, it is not true that any statement about an essential part of a work is an aesthetic statement about it. For instance, it is essential to a poem that it be composed of the particular words that comprise it. So it is essential to it that it have in it the particular letters that it has. So, if it is true of a particular poem that it has in it exactly as many letter *e*'s as it has letter *c*'s, then that is an essential feature of the poem. But that is not an *aesthetic* statement about the work, since it standardly plays no role in our appreciation of it.[15] Likewise, consider a statue carved in limestone. It is essential to its being the particular statue which it is that it be

composed of the crushed shells of ancient sea creatures. But whereas the statue's texture and color are generally relevant to its aesthetic merits, the mere fact that it is composed of crushed shells is not. For, again, this fact standardly plays no role in our appreciation of it as a work of art. So a premise on which Dickie's argument rests is false.

2. Perhaps the most influential opponents of ethicism have been formalists.[16] However, David Pole not only has argued that ethicism is compatible with formalism, but has tried to derive ethicism from it. He holds that the immorality of a work is a formal defect in it, since it is a type of internal incoherence. For if a work of art presents a morally bad view, it will do so by distorting or glossing over something it presents. But then something is lacking within the work itself and so "some particular aspect [of the work] must jar with what – on the strength of the rest – we claim a right to demand." This jarring is an internal incoherence in the work and thus a defect that the formalist would acknowledge as such.[17]

If a work is morally corrupt, it follows that it distorts something and so jars with a truth about the world, but it does not follow that it has to jar with anything else in the work, for the work may be systematically immoral. *The Triumph of the Will*, for instance, is held together thematically by its offensive celebration of Nazism. So Pole's formalist derivation of ethicism fails.[18]

3. An approach glanced at by Hume and elaborated by Wayne Booth holds that literary assessment is akin to an act of befriending, for one assesses the implied author of a work as a suitable friend. A good friend may possess a variety of merits (being intelligent, good company, lively, etc.), and some of these are ethical: she is trustworthy, sensitive, kind, and so on. So assessing someone as a friend involves among other things assessing her ethical character, a character displayed in the case of the implied author in the literary work in which she is manifested.[19]

The approach has its merits, and captures the pro tanto structure of ethicism well, but it is ill-equipped to cope with some Hollywood films whose impersonality and industrial-style production may give the audience little sense of an implied author or authors, but whose ethical stance may elicit their aesthetic condemnation. And the approach also runs afoul of one of the objections considered earlier; for the implied author is a fictional construct, albeit one implicit in, rather than described by, the text. If fictional characters, such as Satan and Lear, can be interesting because of their moral failings, the corrupt fictional character of an author can similarly be interesting, and the aesthetic merit of her work be accordingly enhanced. Appeal to the characters of fictional beings will not ground ethicism.

4. More promising is an argument that may be extrapolated from views defended by Richard Eldridge and Martha Nussbaum. For Eldridge a person's moral self-understanding cannot completely be captured by general theories, but must be developed and sustained by an awareness of the relation of her story to the stories of others, an awareness that literature is peculiarly well placed to articulate and extend: "all we can do is to attempt to find ourselves in cases, in narratives of the development of persons."[20] For Nussbaum, too, morality is a matter of the appreciation of particular cases, and literature can refine our awareness of moral particularities in a way that eludes the flailing grasp of philosophy: "To show forth the force and truth of the Aristotelian claim that 'the decision rests with perception,' we need, then – either side by side with a philosophical 'outline' or inside it – texts which display to us the complexity, the indeterminacy, the sheer *difficulty* of moral choice."[21] This conception of literature as moral philosophy naturally suggests a cognitivist argument for ethicism: it is an aesthetic merit in a work that it gives insight into some state of affairs, and literature can yield insights into moral reality of a depth and precision that no other cultural form is well placed to match; so the moral insights delivered by literary works enhance their aesthetic worth.

There is much here that should be retained and accounted for in any successful defense of ethicism, and an attempt will be made to do so in what follows. Yet the argument rests on a radically particularist account of morality, which denies the existence of any general and informative moral principles. If that view be denied, as I believe it should,[22] the idea of literature as the culmination of moral philosophy is rendered less compelling. And even if the claims of literature were rendered more modest, we would still require an explanation of why the insights literature can provide are aesthetically relevant. Works of art can be interesting and informative as social documents, but the fact that much can be learned from them about the attitudes and circumstances of their time does not ipso facto make them aesthetically better: one can learn much about Victorian agricultural politics from

Tess, and on the subject of nineteenth-century whaling practices *Moby-Dick* is excruciatingly informative. Likewise, old photographs and films can have great value as documentary sources of their times, but these cognitive merits do not thereby improve these objects *qua* works of art. So the cognitivist approach must be supplemented in order to give an account of the conditions under which cognitive merits are aesthetically relevant.[23]

The Merited-Response Argument

Ethicism is a thesis about a work's manifestation of certain attitudes, but in what does this manifestation of attitudes consist? It is obvious that works prescribe the imagining of certain events: a horror film may prescribe imagining teenagers being assaulted by a monster; *Juliette* prescribes imagining that acts of sexual torture occur. Perhaps less obviously, works also prescribe certain responses to these fictional events: the loud, atonal music of the horror film prescribes us to react to the represented events with fear, *Juliette* invites the reader to find sexual torture erotically attractive, to be aroused by it, to be amused by the contortions described, to admire the intricacy of their implementation, and so forth.[24] The approbatory attitude that *Juliette* exhibits toward sexual torture, then, is manifested in the responses it prescribes its readers to have toward such torture. The attitudes of works are manifested in the responses they prescribe to their audiences.

It is important to construe this claim correctly to avoid an objection. Consider a novel that prescribes its readers to be amused at a character's undeserved suffering but that does so in order to show up the ease with which the reader can be seduced into callous responses. Then one response (amusement) is prescribed, but a very different attitude is manifested by the work (disapproval of the ease with which we can be morally seduced); hence, the manifestation of attitudes is wholly distinct from and independent of the prescription of responses. What this objection reveals is that prescriptions, like attitudes, come in a hierarchy, with higher-order prescriptions taking lower-order ones as their objects. Thus, my amusement at the character's suffering is prescribed, but there is a higher-order prescription that this amusement itself be regarded as callous and therefore is unmerited. So the complete set of prescriptions that a work makes must be examined in order to discover what attitudes it manifests: taking individual prescriptions out of context may mislead us about the work's attitudes. Here, as elsewhere, the application of the ethicist principle requires a grasp of interpretive subtleties and contextual factors. Talk of prescriptions from now on should be construed as involving the complete set of relevant prescriptions that a work makes toward fictional events.

The claim that works prescribe certain responses to the events described is widely applicable. *Jane Eyre*, for instance, prescribes the imagining of the course of a love affair between Jane and Rochester, and also prescribes us to admire Jane's fortitude, to want things to turn out well for her, to be moved by her plight, to be attracted to this relationship as an ideal of love, and so forth. Similar remarks apply to paintings, films, and other representational arts. Music without a text is also subject to ethical criticism if we can properly ascribe to the music a presented situation and a prescribed response to it. If Shostakovich's symphonies are a musical protest against the Stalinist regime, we can ethically assess them.

The notion of a response is to be understood broadly, covering a wide range of states directed at represented events and characters, including being pleased at something, feeling an emotion toward it, being amused about it, and desiring something with respect to it – wanting it to continue or stop, wanting to know what happens next. Such states are characteristically affective, some essentially so, such as pleasure and the emotions, while in the case of others, such as desires, there is no necessity that they be felt, although they generally are.

The responses are not simply imagined: we are prescribed by *Juliette* actually to find erotically attractive the fictional events, to be amused by them, to enjoy them, to admire this kind of activity. So the novel does not just present imagined events, it also presents a point of view on them, a perspective constituted in part by actual feelings, emotions, and desires that the reader is prescribed to have toward the merely imagined events. Given that the notion of a response covers such things as enjoyment and amusement, it is evident that some kinds of response are actual, not just imagined. Some philosophers have denied that we feel actual emotions toward fictional events, but there are, I believe, good reasons for holding this to be possible.[25]

Though a work may prescribe a response, it does not follow that it succeeds in making this response merited: horror fictions may be unfrightening, comedies unamusing, thrillers unthrilling. This is not just to say that fear, amusement, and thrills are not produced in the audience; for people may respond in a way that is inappropriate. Rather, the question is whether the prescribed response is merited, whether it is appropriate or inappropriate to respond in the way the work prescribes. If I am afraid of a harmless victim in a horror movie because of her passing resemblance to an old tormentor of mine, my fear is inappropriate. And my admiration for a character in a novel can be criticized for being based on a misunderstanding of what he did in the story. So prescribed responses are subject to evaluative criteria.

Some of these criteria are ethical ones. As noted earlier, responses outside the context of art are subject to ethical evaluation. I can criticize someone for taking pleasure in others' pain, for being amused by sadistic cruelty, for being angry at someone when she has done no wrong, for desiring the bad. The same is true when responses are directed at fictional events, for these responses are actual, not just imagined ones. If we actually enjoy or are amused by some exhibition of sadistic cruelty in a novel, that shows us in a bad light, reflects ill on our ethical character, and we can properly be criticized for responding in this fashion.

If a work prescribes a response that is unmerited, it has failed in an aim internal to it, and that is a defect. But not all defects in works of art are aesthetic ones. From the point of view of shipping them to art exhibitions, many of Tintoretto's paintings are very bad, since they are so large and fragile that they can be moved only at great risk. But that is not an aesthetic defect. Is the failure of a prescribed response to be merited an *aesthetic* defect (i.e., is it a defect in the work *qua* work of art)? That this is so is evidently true of many artistic genres: thrillers that do not merit the audience being thrilled, tragedies that do not merit fear and pity for their protagonists, comedies that are not amusing, melodramas that do not merit sadness and pity are all aesthetic failures in these respects. Works outside these genres, which similarly prescribe a range of responses, are likewise aesthetic failures if the responses are unmerited. And in general it is a bad work of art that leaves us bored and offers no enjoyment at all. We are also concerned not just with whether a response occurs, but with the quality of that response: humor may be crude, unimaginative, or flat, or may be revelatory, profound, or inspiring. And the aesthetic criticism of a work as being manipulative, sentimental, insensible, or crude is founded on a mismatch between the response the work prescribes the reader to feel and the response actually merited by the work's presentation of the fictional situation.

The aesthetic relevance of prescribed responses wins further support from noting that much of the value of art derives from its deployment of an affective mode of cognition – derives from the way works teach us, not by giving us merely intellectual knowledge, but by bringing that knowledge home to us. This teaching is not just about how the world is, but can reveal new conceptions of the world in the light of which we can experience our situation, can teach us new ideals, can impart new concepts and discriminatory skills – having read Dickens, we can recognize the Micawbers of the world. And the way knowledge is brought home to us is by making it vividly present, so disposing us to reorder our thoughts, feelings, and motivations in the light of it. We all know we will die, but it may take a great work of art to drive that point fully home, to make it vividly present. We may think of the universe as devoid of transcendent meaning, but it may take *Waiting for Godot* to make that thought concrete and real. We may believe in the value of love, but it may take *Jane Eyre* to render that ideal unforgettably alluring. On the cognitive-affective view of the value of art, whether prescribed responses are merited will be of aesthetic significance, since such responses constitute a cognitive-affective perspective on the events recounted. For such responses not merely are affective, but include a cognitive component, being directed toward some state of affairs or thing, and bringing it under evaluative concepts.[26] By prescribing us to be amused, to enjoy, to be aroused by scenes of sexual torture, *Juliette* aims to get us to approve of the imagined events, to think of them as in some way desirable, and so to endorse an evaluation about events of that kind.

These observations can be assembled into an argument for ethicism. A work's manifestation of an attitude is a matter of the work's prescribing certain responses toward the events described. If these responses are unmerited, because unethical, we have reason not to respond in the way prescribed. Our having reason not to respond in the way prescribed is a failure of the work. What responses the work prescribes is of aesthetic relevance. So the fact that we have reason not to respond in the way prescribed is an *aesthetic* failure of the work, that is to say, is an aesthetic defect. So

a work's manifestation of ethically bad attitudes is an aesthetic defect in it. Mutatis mutandis, a parallel argument shows that a work's manifestation of ethically commendable attitudes is an aesthetic merit in it, since we have reason to adopt a prescribed response that is ethically commendable. So ethicism is true.

To illustrate: a comedy presents certain events as funny (prescribes a humorous response to them), but if this involves being amused at heartless cruelty, we have reason not to be amused. Hence, the work's humor is flawed, and that is an aesthetic defect in it. If a work prescribes our enjoyment (as almost all art does to some extent), but if we are supposed to enjoy, say, gratuitous suffering, then we can properly refuse to enjoy it, and hence the work fails aesthetically. If a work seeks to get us to pity some characters, but they are unworthy of pity because of their vicious actions, we have reason not to pity them, and hence the work is aesthetically flawed. Conversely, if the comedy's humor is revelatory, emancipating us from the narrow bonds of prejudice, getting us to see a situation in a different and better moral light and respond accordingly, we have reason to adopt the response, and the work succeeds aesthetically in this respect. If the enjoyment it offers derives from this kind of revelatory humor, we have reason to enjoy the work. And if a work prescribes pity toward characters who suffer unfairly and through no fault of their own, we have reason to pity them, and the work succeeds aesthetically in this way. Similar remarks apply to the range of other responses prescribed by works, such as admiring characters, being angry on their behalf, wanting things for them, and so forth.

The merited-response argument for ethicism captures what is plausible in the last two of the arguments surveyed earlier, but sidesteps the pitfalls into which they stumble. If a work prescribes certain attitudes, these may be sufficiently patterned to justify crediting an implied author to it, and this explains why the befriending argument looks plausible. But the merited-response argument has the advantage of avoiding the problems that stem from taking the implied author as foundational in an argument for ethicism. And the cognitive argument is not so much rejected as incorporated into the current argument, which makes use of a cognitive-affective view of art. Art can teach us about what is ethically correct, but the aesthetic relevance of this teaching is guaranteed only when the work displays it in the responses it prescribes to story events. While tacking on to a novel a claim that a certain type of committed love is an ideal will not do much for its aesthetic worth, getting us to *feel* the attraction of that ideal as embodied in a particular relationship is the central and animating excellence of several novels, including *Jane Eyre*.

Objections to the Argument

1. The argument does not support ethicism. To say that a prescribed response is unmerited is to say that the work is emotionally unengaging; but then the work's failure is a result of the failure to engage, and not of its ethical corruption. Indeed, if, despite its ethical corruption, the work does emotionally engage, then its ethical badness is not an aesthetic defect.

The objection misconstrues the argument, even in respect of responses that are emotions. A work may engage an emotion even when it does not merit it (it may, for instance, manipulate us into feeling a sort of pity we know is merely sentimental), and only merited emotions are relevant to the argument. It is whether the emotion is merited that is important, and ethical merits are partly constitutive of whether the emotion is merited; hence, ethical values play a direct role in determining whether the work is aesthetically defective.

2. The argument is structurally unsound. Starting from a claim about ethical merit, ethicism ends up with a claim about aesthetic merit, so the argument commits a fallacy of equivocation in moving from an ethical reason to an aesthetic one, for there are no other resources available for making the transition.

There is no equivocation: the claim used to make the transition is that whether prescribed responses are merited is aesthetically relevant, and among the criteria that are relevant to determining whether they are merited are ethical ones. This is a substantive claim, and one that has been argued for by appeal to the language of art criticism and a supporting claim that art deploys an affective mode of cognition.

3. The aesthetic defects of a work cannot be reduced to a failure of prescribed responses: while some works clearly prescribe responses, other works need not, or may fail in respects in which no particular response is prescribed.

The point is correct, but the ethicist defense does not require that all aesthetic defects be failures of prescribed responses, for it is enough to establish its truth that some aesthetic defects are of this kind.

4. Works may prescribe responses that are not aesthetically relevant: a royal portrait may be designed to impart a sense of awe and respect toward the king depicted, and a religious work may aim at enhancing the viewer's sense of religious reverence, but such responses are aesthetically irrelevant. So ethicism rests on a false premise.

This is not so. A painting is not just (or even) a beautiful object: it aims to convey complex thoughts and feelings about its subject, providing an individual perspective on the object represented. Thus it is that a painting not only can be a representation, but can also embody a way of thinking in an affectively charged way about its subject, and this perspective on its subject is an important object of our aesthetic interest in the work. So if a painting does not succeed in meriting the responses prescribed, it fails on a dimension of aesthetic excellence.

5. Finally, the argument rests on a claim that real responses, not merely imagined ones, can be had toward fictions. Yet that claim has in respect of emotional responses been powerfully contested: some philosophers have argued that certain emotions cannot be really directed at fictional entities.[27] Thus, ethicism rests on a contentious claim, and its truth is hostage to the fortunes of this thesis.

The merited-response argument has indeed been framed by appeal to real emotions directed at fictions, both because I hold that such emotions can be had toward fictions and because the argument proceeds smoothly with this claim. But it is not in fact essential to the argument to appeal to fiction-directed real emotions. (The thesis that fiction-directed real emotions are possible I shall refer to as *emotional realism*, as opposed to *emotional irrealism*, which denies the possibility of such emotions.) There is a class of responses toward fictions – responses of pleasure and displeasure – that both sides to the dispute can agree to be real. It is evident that one can actually enjoy or be displeased by fictional events: one can actually enjoy Jane Eyre's (fictional) happiness at the end of the novel. Scarcely more contentious is the thought that there are many other fiction-directed responses that are real: I don't have to check to see whether a story is fictional or not in order to know whether I am really amused by it or only imagining that I am so. I don't have to know whether described events really occurred to know whether I am disgusted by them.[28] The battle between realists and irrealists is over the reality of those specific kinds of responses that are emotions, and indeed chiefly over the reality of pity and fear directed at fictions.

Ethicism can be fully defended by appeal to those responses the reality of which is relatively uncontentious. For these include pleasure and displeasure, which are pervasive in our responses to fictions, and, as we noted, a person can be ethically criticized for what she takes pleasure or displeasure in. Someone who actually enjoys imagined suffering can properly be condemned for this response. Hence, pleasure and displeasure felt toward fictions are the only kinds of responses the reality of which one needs to appeal to in order to defend ethicism successfully.

Further, the appeal to actual responses was made in order to avoid a possible objection that the audience's responses are only imagined, and the audience is not ethically at fault if it only imagines a response, as opposed to actually possessing it. But the claim that imagined responses are not ethically assessable can be denied in its full generality. Certain imagined responses, particularly when they are compulsive, vivid, or ones that in various ways fully engage their imaginers, may ground ethical criticism, for they too may be deeply expressive of the imaginer's moral character (for instance, the rape fantasist discussed earlier may be ethically criticized, even if he only imagines being aroused by the imagined scenarios). Hence, emotional irrealists can support ethicism on the grounds that people can be ethically condemned for some of their merely imagined responses.[29] Further, as we noted earlier, works that manifest certain attitudes toward fictional entities implicitly manifest the same attitudes toward real entities of that kind. Reading this in terms of prescribed imagined responses, the irrealist can hold that works prescribing an imagined response toward fictional entities implicitly prescribe the counterpart real response to real entities of that kind. Since no one denies that real emotional responses can be directed at real entities, the irrealist can hold that artworks are aesthetically flawed by virtue of the moral reprehensibility of the implied emotions directed at real states of affairs.[30] Thus, it is not essential to the success of the merited-response argument that emotional realism be true: emotional irrealists can and should sign up to it as well.

So the merited-response argument stands. And the truth of ethicism shows that the aesthetic and the ethical are intertwined. While those who have supposed them to form a unity have overstated their closeness, the two evaluative domains have proved to be more tightly and surprisingly interconnected than many had thought possible.

Notes

1 The view that the *only* aesthetic merits of works are ethical ones is known as *moralism* and is elegantly dispatched by R. W. Beardsmore, *Art and Morality* (London: Macmillan Press, 1971), chap. 2.

2 For a defense of this claim see my "Moral Pluralism," *Philosophical Papers* 22 (1993): 17–40, and my "Rag Bags, Disputes and Moral Pluralism," *Utilitas* 11 (1999): 37–8.

3 For my account of what a work of art is, see my "'Art' as a Cluster Concept," *Theories of Art*, ed. Noël Carroll (Madison: University of Wisconsin Press, 2000). It may be objected to this broader sense of "aesthetic" that it does not encompass the aesthetic properties of nature. Since we are here concerned only with artworks, this restriction would not matter for present purposes; but also note that the notion naturally extends to include aesthetic properties of nature, since nature may share some of the value properties that objects have *qua* artworks. These include narrow aesthetic properties and also various formal and metaphorically ascribed properties. (For a discussion of the latter and their significance, see my "Metaphor and the Understanding of Art," *Proceedings of the Aristotelian Society* 97 [1996–7]: 223–41.)

4 Evidently, talk of works manifesting attitudes is quite in order – we can, for instance, properly talk of *Small World* manifesting an attitude of wry amusement toward academic conferences. Talk of works manifesting attitudes is, I would argue, equivalent to talk of artists manifesting attitudes in works, though the sense of the terms needs careful specification, and the artist here is not to be understood as a mere fictional construct. (See Guy Sircello, "Expressive Properties of Art," in *Philosophy Looks at the Arts*, ed. Joseph Margolis, 3d ed. [Philadelphia: Temple University Press, 1987], for a suggestive discussion of the relation between what artists do and the properties their works possess.) However, given the fact that we can properly talk of works manifesting attitudes, investigation of this equivalence need not be pursued here.

5 Those who evince sympathy with this distinct causal claim include Kant, Matthew Arnold, Anthony Savile, and Anne Sheppard. Kant claims that the harmonious accord between cognitive faculties that

beauty produces in the man of good taste "at the same time promotes the sensibility of the mind for moral feeling." *Critique of Aesthetic Judgement*, trans. J. C. Meredith (Oxford: Oxford University Press, 1952), 39. See also Matthew Arnold, *Culture and Anarchy: an Essay in Political and Social Criticism*, 3d ed. (London: Smith, Elder, 1882), passim; Anthony Savile, *The Test of Time* (Oxford: Oxford University Press, 1982), chap. 5, sect. II; and Anne Sheppard, *Aesthetics* (Oxford: Oxford University Press, 1987), 151.

6   For the locus classicus of skepticism about the aesthetic attitude, see George Dickie, "The Myth of the Aesthetic Attitude," in *Philosophy Looks at the Arts*, ed. Margolis. As noted later, Dickie also uses an attack on the aesthetic attitude to argue for a variant of ethicism.

7   Monroe Beardsley, *Aesthetics*, 2d ed. (Indianapolis: Hackett, 1981), 462ff.

8   However, as will be seen later, some formalists, including David Pole, would deny this claim, and argue for the validity of ethical criticism.

9   See my "Interpreting the Arts: The Patchwork Theory," *Journal of Aesthetics and Art Criticism* 51 (1993): 597–609. For an extended critique of autonomism in reference to its implications for the ethical assessment of art, see Noël Carroll, "Moderate Moralism," *British Journal of Aesthetics* 36 (1996): 223–38.

10 This conception is Kantian in spirit, though Kant's own view differs from it in salient ways. His view is in one way narrower: it is only duty (not feelings) that can motivate actions that have genuine moral worth (or, on one reading of his position, feelings can operate only as primary motives of morally good action, while the secondary motive must be duty; see Marcia W. Baron, *Kantian Ethics Almost Without Apology* [Ithaca, N.Y.: Cornell University Press, 1996], chap. 4). In addition, Kant holds that actions are not directly assessable; only their maxims are.

11 Aristotle, *Nicomachean Ethics* 2.6 1106b16, trans. Terence Irwin (Indianapolis: Hackett, 1985).

12 Interpretive skill is needed, of course, to establish what the relevant properties of fictional characters are toward which attitudes are manifested. This can be a subtle matter; for instance, in some jokes a character being Irish is merely a conventional way of indicating stupidity and need not imply any derogatory attitudes toward Irish people. For a discussion of humor that is closely related to the issues discussed in this essay, see my "Just Joking: The Ethics and Aesthetics of Humor." *Philosophy and Literature* 22, 1 (1998): 51–68.

13 Lawrence Hyman, "Morality and Literature: The Necessary Conflict," *British Journal of Aesthetics* 24 (1984): 149–55, at 154–5.

14 George Dickie, "The Myth of the Aesthetic Attitude," in *Philosophy Looks at the Arts*, ed. Margolis,

113. In his *Evaluating Art* (Philadelphia: Temple University Press, 1988), chap. 7, Dickie also endorses the cognitivist derivation of ethicism that I discuss later. I place "essential" in parentheses, since Dickie makes the argument without explicitly using it, but appeals to it when giving the example of a novel; his argument is strengthened by appeal to the notion.

15 I do not mean to deny, of course, that in the case of certain poems this fact might play a role in the appreciation of the work. For instance, if a poet wished to demonstrate his skill by writing a poem containing exactly the same number of every letter of the alphabet, yet the resulting poem did not have this feature, this would reflect badly on his artistry. So in some unusual cases facts about the number of different letters in a poem might be aesthetically relevant. But Dickie's argument requires it to be *always* true that such facts are aesthetically relevant.

16 E.g., Monroe Beardsley, *Aesthetics*, 2d ed. (Indianapolis: Hackett, 1981). Though he attacks only moralism directly (564–7), it is clear from his remarks on page 457 that moral criteria play no part in the objective reasons that, he believes, exhaustively specify aesthetic evaluation.

17 David Pole, "Morality and the Assessment of Literature," in his *Aesthetics, Form and Emotion* (London: Duckworth, 1983), 49–70.

18 A parallel criticism is made by Dickie, "The Myth of the Aesthetic Attitude," 113.

19 Hume remarks, "We choose our favourite author as we do our friend" in his "Of the Standard of Taste," in *Critical Theory Since Plato* ed. Hazard Adams (San Diego, Calif.: Harcourt Brace Jovanovich, 1971), 321. See also Wayne Booth, *The Company We Keep: An Ethics of Fiction* (Berkeley: University of California Press, 1988), esp. chaps. 7 and 8.

20 Richard Eldridge, *On Moral Personhood: Philosophy, Literature, Criticism and Self-Knowledge* (Chicago: University of Chicago Press, 1989), 20.

21 Martha Nussbaum, "Flawed Crystals: James's *The Golden Bowl* and Literature as Moral Philosophy," *New Literary History* 15 (1983): 43.

22 See my "Moral Pluralism."

23 Richard W. Miller, "Truth in Beauty," *American Philosophical Quarterly* 16 (1979): 317–25, argues that truth is sometimes aesthetically relevant, since the "aesthetic goals of some works include the combination, in appropriate ways, of the true depiction of certain aspects of reality with other, exclusively and uncontroversially aesthetic virtues" (319). If there are ethical truths, this would yield a cognitivist defense of the relevance in certain conditions of the depiction of ethical truths to aesthetic worth. Miller's piece is important, since it seeks explicitly to meet the relevance problem, and his strategy shares some features with that advanced in the present essay though it differs in an important

respect in appealing directly to truth rather than to merited responses. But given his stress on the fact that it is not the truth of ideas per se that is aesthetically relevant, but their cognitive manner of expression, his approach appears to yield the result that if immoral views (such as Baudelaire's sexism) are well expressed in his poems, then their immorality does not constitute an aesthetic defect in the poem (322). Thus, the position yielded by Miller's argument is incompatible with ethicism and, given the argument for ethicism advanced later, is to be rejected as it stands.

24 The notion of prescribing imagined feelings is to be found in Kendall Walton, *Mimesis as Make-Believe: On the Foundations of the Representational Arts* (Cambridge, Mass.: Harvard University Press, 1990), chap. 7.2. The claim that actual feelings can be prescribed is defended by Richard Moran in "The Expression of Feeling in Imagination," *Philosophical Review* 103 (1994): 75–106. I am indebted at several points in this section to Moran's discussion.

25 For defenses of the view that real emotions can be felt toward events known to be merely imagined, see Noël Carroll, *The Philosophy of Horror or Paradoxes of the Heart* (New York: Routledge, 1990), 60–88, and Patricia Greenspan, *Emotions and Reasons: An Inquiry into Emotional Justification* (New York: Routledge, 1988), esp. part I.

26 For cognitive-evaluative views of responses, see Greenspan, *Emotions and Reasons*; Robert C. Roberts, "What an Emotion Is: A Sketch," *Philosophical Review* 97 (1988): 183–209; and Elijah Millgram, "Pleasure in Practical Reasoning," *Monist* 76 (1993): 394–415.

27 See, e.g., Walton, *Mimesis as Make-Believe*, 241–55; and Gregory Currie, *The Nature of Fiction* (Cambridge University Press, 1990), chap. 5.

28 Compare Carroll, *The Philosophy of Horror*.

29 A point I owe to Kendall Walton. See his "Morals in Fiction and Fictional Morality," *Proceedings of the Aristotelian Society*, suppl. vol. 68 (1994): 27–50, for an irrealist discussion of the ethical criticism of art.

30 I owe this point to Jerrold Levinson.

Part VI

Fictionality

Introduction to Part VI

Analytic philosophers have given a great deal of attention to problems related to fictionality. Indeed in the very early days of analytic philosophy – long before its application to aesthetics – an active debate about existence and nonexistence preoccupied the main protagonists. How could sentences containing nondenoting expressions, such as "the highest prime," "the present King of France," "phlogiston," or "Pegasus," be assigned meaning? If meaning is a species of denotation then such sentences should be meaningless and yet that couldn't be right because it would imply that the existence of such entities couldn't meaningfully be *denied*. The problem led Bertrand Russell to distinguish ordinary names from logical names and to argue that definite descriptions were not names at all. The resulting Theory of Descriptions was deemed the "paradigm of analysis."

Within aesthetics, three principal issues relating to fiction have arisen:

- How can fiction best be characterized? What is its "logic"?
- How are emotional responses to fiction best explained?
- How is fiction related to truth?

There have been numerous philosophical attempts to characterize fiction, some only remotely connected to aesthetics. Philosophers of language have sought to accommodate fictionality into a general account of meaning, offering theoretical explanations of fictional names, fictional reference, truth-valuation of fictional sentences, fictional entities, fiction and existence. Analytic aestheticians have often drawn on this work and it should be noted that an interest in fictionality is not confined to those working on the aesthetics of literature. Problems about fictionality arise wherever narrative occurs and all the representational arts, including film, dance, painting, opera, even sculpture, engage these problems.

One contribution from within philosophy of language, John Searle's "The Logical Status of Fictional Discourse," below, has been especially influential in attempts to characterize fiction. Searle distinguishes at the outset between fiction and literature, suggesting provocatively that "Whether or not a work is literature is for readers to decide, whether or not it is fictional is for the author to decide." But it is his application of speech act theory to fiction and his straightforward, intuitively plausible, account of fiction as "pretended illocutionary acts," which has prompted a minor industry drawing on the theory of speech acts to illuminate aspects of aesthetics.

It is the aesthetician Kendall Walton, though, to whom one would first turn for a comprehensive account of the logic of fiction applied to all representational arts. In his monumental book *Mimesis as Make-Believe* (1990) he seeks to show that to be fictional – in any context – is to be a "prop in a game of make-believe." One aspect of the theory, however, has arguably had the greatest impact, concerning psychological responses to fiction, in particular emotional responses. His paper "Fearing Fictions" has an enduring appeal, not only for its witty and engaging style but for producing a compelling argument for a view that few at first would be disposed to accept. In a nutshell, his view is that in watching horror movies, for example, audiences (in standard cases) are not *really* afraid of the movie monster, but it is only *make-believe* that they are afraid; they do not *really* pity the heroine, it is only *make-believe* that they do; and so on. What seems like real fear is only "quasi-fear," what seems like real pity is only "quasi-pity." Walton's reasoning is tight and persuasive; audiences do not normally believe they are in danger at horror films, nor are they disposed to take evasive action, yet these are conditions for genuine fear. A deeper explanation for Walton is that, as in all fictions, audiences are "playing a game of make-believe," in which they are protagonists. What occurs *within the game*, including emotional states, does not necessarily occur *in the real world*.

Underlying the examples Walton offers, philosophers have identified what is called a paradox of fiction, involving three intuitively plausible propositions:

(a) Readers or audiences often experience emotions such as fear, pity, desire, and admiration toward objects they know to be fictional, e.g. fictional characters.

(b) A necessary condition for experiencing emotions such as fear, pity, desire, etc. is that those experiencing them believe the objects of their emotions to exist.

(c) Readers or audiences who know that the objects are fictional do not believe that these objects exist.

As these three propositions are mutually inconsistent at least one must be false. Walton, as we have seen, rejects the first. Other philosophers, including Peter Lamarque, in "How Can We Fear and Pity Fictions?," question the second. Lamarque argues that belief recedes into the background in fictional contexts and vivid thoughts, in contrast to beliefs, are sufficient to stir the emotions. Colin Radford in his well-known paper "How Can We Be Moved by the Fate of Anna Karenina?," published before Walton's paper and before the paradox of fiction was characterized, takes a different tack in arguing that although it is very "natural" for us to be moved by the fate of fictional characters, it nonetheless involves "inconsistency and incoher-

ence." While it might not seem right that responding emotionally to fiction is irrational – it might even seem irrational in some cases not to do so – there undoubtedly remains an aura of paradox about this puzzling issue.

The third philosophical problem connected with fiction, which has also received considerable attention, is whether works of fiction can make any claim to truth or more general "cognitive values." The matter is important because it focuses on the values of the greatest narrative or representational arts. Ever since Plato banished the poets from his ideal state, one of the strongest indictments of art has been that it leads us away from rather than toward truth and knowledge. The indictment is both epistemic and moral. Art is not only epistemically frivolous, i.e. "made up" with no reference to what is true, but is also morally dangerous since it encourages those who traffic in art to produce and accept lies. There are two types of response to this indictment. One is to insist on the cognitive value of art, i.e. to insist that art is answerable to truth and does yield knowledge, for those who approach it rightly. The other response is to accept the cognitive triviality of art, and to insist that its value lies elsewhere.

In Part V there are papers dealing with the values of art, two of which directly debate the role of moral value and moral truth in the aims of art. In the current section we have included Jerome Stolnitz's polemical paper "On the Cognitive Triviality of Art," which makes the case against artistic truth. Stolnitz shows just how difficult it is to identify general (by implication significant) truths in works of fiction. The very details that make fictions compelling in the first place rapidly get lost when readers try to extract universal truths from them. And the universal truths that do emerge are nearly always, so Stolnitz claims, "distinctly banal." If Stolnitz is right then one must look elsewhere for the values of fiction. In fact both Searle and Walton in their papers suggest another avenue: the importance of the imagination in human life and, in Walton's case, the value of actually participating in (imaginative) games of make-believe.

Further reading

Crittenden, Charles (1991). *Unreality: The Metaphysics of Fictional Objects* (Ithaca, NY: Cornell University Press).

Currie, Gregory (1990). *The Nature of Fiction* (Cambridge: Cambridge University Press).

Hjort, Mette and Laver, Sue (eds.) (1997). *Emotion and the Arts* (Oxford: Oxford University Press).

Lamarque, Peter (1996). *Fictional Points of View* (Ithaca, NY: Cornell University Press).

Lamarque, Peter and Olsen, Stein Haugom (1994). *Truth, Fiction, and Literature: A Philosophical Perspective* (Oxford: Clarendon Press).

Thomasson, Amie (1999). *Fiction and Metaphysics* (Cambridge: Cambridge University Press).

Walton, Kendall L. (1990). *Mimesis as Make-Believe* (Cambridge, MA: Harvard University Press).

Wolterstorff, Nicholas (1980). *Works and Worlds of Art* (Oxford: Clarendon Press).

Yanal, R. J. (1999). *Paradoxes of Emotion and Fiction* (University Park, PA: Pennsylvania State University Press).

25

How Can We Be Moved by the Fate of Anna Karenina?

Colin Radford

What's Hecuba to him, or he to Hecuba,
That he should weep for her?
Shakespeare, Hamlet, II.ii

1.   That men feel concern for the fate of others, that they have some interest, and a warm and benevolent one in what happens to at least some other men, may be simply a brute fact about men, though a happy one. By this I mean that we can conceive that men might have been different in this respect, and so it is possible for us to be puzzled by the fact that they are not different. In a situation where men did not feel concern for others, children might be nurtured only because mothers could not stand the pain of not feeding them, or because it gave them pleasure to do this and to play with them, or because they were a source of pride. So that if a child died, a mother might have the kind of feeling the owner of a car has if his car is stolen and wrecked. He doesn't feel anything for the car, unless he is a sentimentalist, and yet he is sorry and depressed when it happens.

Of course there may be good biological reasons why men should have concern for each other, or at least some other men, but that is not to the point. The present point, a conceptual one, is that we can conceive that all men might have been as some men are, viz., devoid of any feeling for anyone but themselves, whereas we cannot conceive, e.g., that all men might be what some men are, chronic liars.

Colin Radford, "How Can We Be Moved by the Fate of Anna Karenina?" *Proceedings of the Aristotelian Society*, suppl. vol. 69 (1975), pp. 67–80. Reprinted by courtesy of the Editor of the Aristotelian Society, © 1975.

2.   So concern and related feelings are in this sense brute. But what are they? What is it to be moved by something's happening to someone?

Anything like a complete story here is a very long one, and in any case I have a particular interest. Suppose then that you read an account of the terrible sufferings of a group of people. If you are at all humane, you are unlikely to be unmoved by what you read. The account is likely to awaken or reawaken feelings of anger, horror, dismay or outrage and, if you are tender-hearted, you may well be moved to tears. You may even grieve.

But now suppose you discover that the account is false. If the account had caused you to grieve, you could not continue to grieve. If as the account sank in, you were told and believed that it was false this would make tears impossible, unless they were tears of rage. If you learned later that the account was false, you would feel that in being moved to tears you had been fooled, duped.

It would seem then that I can only be moved by someone's plight if I believe that something terrible has happened to him. If I do not believe that he has not and is not suffering or whatever, I cannot grieve or be moved to tears.

It is not only seeing a man's torment that torments us, it is also, as we say, the thought of his torment which torments, or upsets or moves us. But here thought implies belief. We have to believe in his torment to be tormented by it. When we say that the thought of his plight moves us to tears or grieves us, it is thinking of or contemplating suffering which we believe to be actual or likely that does it.

3.   The direction of my argument should now be fairly clear. Moving closer to its goal: suppose that you have a drink with a man who proceeds to tell you a harrowing story about his sister and you are harrowed. After enjoying your reaction he then tells you that he doesn't have a sister, that he has invented the story. In his case, unlike the previous one, we might say that the "heroine" of the account is fictitious. Nonetheless, and again, once you have been told this you can no longer feel harrowed. Indeed it is possible that you may be embarrassed by your reaction precisely because it so clearly indicates that you were taken in – and you may also feel embarrassed for the storyteller that he could behave in such a way. But the possibility of your being harrowed again seems to require that you believe that someone suffered.

Of course, if the man tells you in advance that he is going to tell you a story, you may reach for your hat, but you may stay and be moved. But this is too quick.

Moving closer still: an actor friend invites you to watch him simulate extreme pain, agony. He writhes about and moans. Knowing that he is only acting, could you be moved to tears? Surely not. Of course you may be embarrassed, and after some time you may even get faintly worried, "Is he really acting, or is he really in pain? Is he off his head?" But as long as you are convinced that he is only acting and is not really suffering, you cannot be moved by his suffering, and it seems unlikely as well as – as it were – unintelligible that you might be moved to tears by his portrayal of agony. It seems that you could only perhaps applaud it if it were realistic or convincing, and criticise if it were not.

But now suppose, horribly, that he acts or re-enacts the death agonies of a friend, or a Vietcong that he killed and tells you this. Then you might be horrified.

4.   If this account is correct, there is no problem about being moved by historical novels or plays, documentary films, etc. For these works depict and forcibly remind us of the real plight and of the real sufferings of real people, and it is for these persons that we feel.[1]

What seems unintelligible is how we could have a similar reaction to the fate of Anna Karenina, the plight of Madame Bovary or the death of Mercutio. Yet we do. We weep, we pity Anna Karenina, we blink hard when Mercutio is dying and absurdly wish that he had not been so impetuous.

5.   Or do we? If we are seized by this problem, it is tempting for us to argue that, since we cannot be anguished or moved by what happens to Anna Karenina, since we cannot pity Madame Bovary and since we cannot grieve at the marvellous Mercutio's death, we do not do so.

This is a tempting thesis especially because, having arrived at it, we have then to think more carefully about our reactions to and feelings about, e.g., the death of Mercutio, and these investigations reveal – how could they do otherwise? – that our response to Mercutio's death differs massively from our response to the untimely death of someone we know. As we watch Mercutio die the tears run down our cheeks, but as O.K. Bouwsma has pointed out,[2] the cigarettes and chocolates go in our mouths too, and we may mutter, if not to each other, then to ourselves, "How marvellous! How sublime!" and even "How moving!"

"Now", one might say,

> if one is *moved*, one surely cannot comment on this and in admiring tones? Surely being moved to tears is a massive response which tends to interfere with saying much, even to oneself? And surely the nature of the response is such that any comments made that do not advert to what gives rise to the feeling but to the person experiencing it tend to suggest that the response isn't really felt? Compare this with leaning over to a friend in a theatre and saying "I am completely absorbed (enchanted, spellbound) by this!"

But although we cannot truly grieve for Mercutio, we can be moved by his death, and are. If and when one says "How moving" in an admiring tone, one can be moved at the theatre. One's admiration is for the play or the performance, and one can admire or be impressed by this and avow this while being moved by it.

6.   So we cannot say that we do not feel for fictional characters, that we are not sometimes moved by what happens to them. We shed real tears for Mercutio. They are not crocodile tears, they are dragged from us and they are not the sort of tears that are produced by cigarette smoke in the theatre. There is a lump in our throats, and it's not the sort of lump that is produced by swallowing a fishbone. We are appalled when we realise what may happen, and are horrified when it does. Indeed, we may be so appalled at the prospect of what we think is going to happen to a character in a novel or a play

that some of us can't go on. We avert the impending tragedy in the only way we can, by closing the book, or leaving the theatre.

This may be an inadequate response, and we may also feel silly or shamefaced at our tears. But this is not because they are always inappropriate and sentimental, as, e.g., is giving one's dog a birthday party, but rather because we feel them to be unmanly. They may be excusable though still embarrassing on the occasion of a real death, but should be contained for anything less.

Of course we are not only moved by fictional tragedies but impressed and even delighted by them. But I have tried to explain this, and that we are other things does not seem to the point. What is worrying is that we are moved by the death of Mercutio and we weep while knowing that no one has really died, that no young man has been cut off in the flower of his youth.[3]

7. So if we can be and if some of us are indeed moved to tears at Mercutio's untimely death, feel pity for Anna Karenina and so on, how can this be explained? How can the seeming incongruity of our doing this be explained and explained away?

First Solution

When we read the book, or better when we watch the play and it works, we are "caught up" and respond and we "forget" or are no longer aware that we are only reading a book or watching a play. In particular, we forget that Anna Karenina, Madame Bovary, Mercutio, and so on are not real persons.

But this won't do. It turns adults into children. It is true that, e.g., when children are first taken to pantomimes they are unclear about what is going on. The young ones are genuinely and unambiguously terrified when the giant comes to kill Jack. The bolder ones shout "Look Out!" and even try to get on the stage to interfere.

But do we do this? Do we shout and try to get on the stage when, watching *Romeo and Juliet*, we see that Tybalt is going to kill Mercutio? We do not. Or if we do, this is extravagant and unnecessary for our being moved. If we really did think someone was really being slain, either a person called Mercutio or the actor playing that rôle, we would try to do something or think that we should. We would, if you like, be genuinely appalled.[4]

So we are not unaware that we are "only" watching a play involving fictional characters, and the problem remains.

Second Solution

Of course we don't ever forget that Mercutio is only a character in a play, but we "suspend our disbelief" in his reality. The theatre management and the producer connive at this. They dim the lights and try to find good actors. They, and we, frown on other members of the audience who draw attention to themselves and distract us by coughing, and if, during a scene, say a stage hand steals on, picks up a chair that should have been removed and sheepishly departs, our response is destroyed. The "illusion" is shattered.

All this is true but the paradox remains. When we watch a play we do not direct our thoughts to its only being a play. We don't continually remind ourselves of this – unless we are trying to reduce the effect of the work on us. Nonetheless, and as we have seen, we are never unaware that we are watching a play, and one about fictional characters even at the most exciting and moving moments. So the paradox is not solved by invoking "suspension of disbelief", though it occurs and is connived at.

Third Solution

It's just another brute fact about human beings that they can be moved by stories about fictional characters and events; i.e., human beings might not have been like this (and a lot of them are not. A lot of people do not read books or go to the theatre, and are bored if they do).

But our problem is that people *can* be moved by fictional suffering given their brute behaviour in other contexts where belief in the reality of the suffering described or witnessed is necessary for the response.

Fourth Solution

But this thesis about behaviour in non-fictional contexts is too strong. The paradox arises only because my examples are handpicked ones in which there is this requirement. But there are plenty of situations in which we can be moved to tears or feel a lump in the throat without thinking that anyone will, or that anyone is even likely to suffer or die an untimely death, or whatever.

But are there? A mother hears that one of her friend's children has been killed in a street accident. When her own children return from school she grabs them in relief and hugs them, almost with a kind of anger. (Is it because they have frightened her?) Their reaction is "What's wrong with you?" They won't get a coherent answer perhaps, but surely the explanation is obvious. The death of the friend's child "brings home", "makes real", and perhaps strengthens the mother's awareness of the likelihood of her own children being maimed or killed. We must try another case. A man's attention wanders from the paper he is reading in his study. He thinks of his sister and, with a jolt, realises that she will soon be flying to the States. Perhaps because he is terrified of flying he thinks of her flying and of her 'plane crashing and shudders. He imagines how this would affect their mother. She would be desolated, inconsolable. Tears prick his eyes. His wife enters and wants to know what's up. He looks upset. Our man is embarrassed but says truthfully, "I was thinking about Jean's flying to the States and, well, I thought how awful it would be if there were an accident – how awful it would be for my mother." Wife: "Don't be silly! How maudlin! And had you nearly reduced yourself to tears thinking about all this? Really, I don't know what's got into you, etc, etc."

In this case the man's response to his thoughts, his being appalled at the thought of his sister's crashing, *is* silly and maudlin, but it is intelligible and non-problematic. For it would be neither silly nor maudlin if flying were a more dangerous business than we are prone to think it is. Proof: change the example and suppose that the sister is seriously ill. She is not suffering yet, but she has cancer and her brother thinks about her dying and how her death will affect their mother. If that were the situation his wife would do well to offer comfort as well as advice.

So a man can be moved not only by what has happened to someone, by actual suffering and death, but by their prospect and the greater the probability of the awful thing's happening, the more likely are we to sympathise, i.e., to understand his response and even share it. The lesser the probability the more likely we are not to feel this way. And if what moves a man to tears is the contemplation of something that is most unlikely to happen, e.g., the shooting of his sister, the more likely are we to find his behaviour worrying and puzzling. However, we can explain his divergent behaviour, and in various ways. We can do this in terms of his having false beliefs. He thinks a 'plane crash or a shooting is more likely than it is, which itself needs and can have an explanation. Or his threshold for worry is lower than average, and again this is non-problematic, i.e., we understand what's going on. Or lastly, we may decide he gets some kind of pleasure from dwelling on such contingencies and appalling himself. Now this is, logically, puzzling, for how can a man get pleasure from pain? But if only because traces of masochism are present in many of us, we are more likely to find it simply offensive.

The point is that our man's behaviour is only more or less psychologically odd or morally worrying. There is no logical difficulty here, and the reason for this is that the suffering and anguish that he contemplates, however unlikely, is pain that some real person may really experience.

Testing this, let us suppose first that our man when asked "What's up?" says, "I was thinking how awful it would have been if Jean had been unable to have children – she wanted them so much." Wife: "But she's got them. Six!" Man: "Yes, I know, but suppose she hadn't?" "My God! Yes it would have been but it didn't happen. How can you sit there and weep over the dreadful thing that didn't happen, and now cannot happen." (She's getting philosophical. Sneeringly) "What are you doing? Grieving for her? Feeling sorry for her?" Man: "All right! But thinking about it, it was so vivid I could imagine just how it would have been." Wife: "You began to snivel!" Man: "Yes."

It is by making the man a sort of Walter Mitty, a man whose imagination is so powerful and vivid that, for a moment anyway, what he imagines seems real, that his tears are made intelligible, though of course not excusable.

So now suppose that the man thinks not of his sister but of a woman . . . that is, he makes up a story about a woman who flies to the States and is killed and whose mother grieves, and so on, and that this gives him a lump in his throat. It might appear that, if my thesis is correct, the man's response to the story he invents should be even more puzzling than his being moved by the thought of his sister's not having children. "Yet", one who was not seized by the philosophical problem might say, "this case is really not puzzling. After all he might be a writer who first gets some of his stories in this manner!"

But that is precisely why this example does not help. It is too close, too like what gives rise to the problem.[5]

Fifth Solution

A solution suggested by an earlier remark: if and when we weep for Anna Karenina, we weep for the pain and anguish that a real person might suffer and which real persons have suffered, and if her situation were not of that sort we should not be moved.

There is something in this, but not enough to make it a solution. For we do not really weep for the pain that a real person might suffer, and which real persons have suffered, when we weep for Anna Karenina, even if we should not be moved by her story if it were not of that sort. We weep for *her*. We are moved by what happens to her, by the situation she gets into, and which is a pitiful one, but we do not feel pity for her state or fate, or her history or her situation, or even for others, i.e., for real persons who might have or even have had such a history. We pity her, feel for her and our tears are shed for her. This thesis is even more compelling, perhaps, if we think about the death of Mercutio.

But all over again, how can we do this knowing that neither she nor Mercutio ever existed, that all their sufferings do not add one bit to the sufferings of the world?

Sixth Solution

Perhaps there really is no problem. In non-fictional situations it may be necessary that in order for a person to be moved, he must believe in the reality of what he sees or is told, or at least he must believe that such a thing may indeed happen to someone. But, as I concede, being moved when reading a novel or watching a play is not exactly like being moved by what one believes happens in real life and, indeed, it is very different. So there are two sorts of being moved and, perhaps, two senses of "being moved". There is being moved (Sense 1) in real life and "being moved" (Sense 2) by what happens to fictional characters. But since there are these two sorts and senses, it does not follow from the necessity of belief in the reality of the agony or whatever it is, for being moved (S. 1), that belief in its reality is, or ought to be necessary for "being moved" (S. 2). So I have not shown that there is a genuine problem, which perhaps explains why I can find no solution.

But although being moved by what one believes is really happening is not exactly the same as being moved by what one believes is happening to fictional characters, it is not wholly different. And it is what is common to being moved in either situation which makes problematic one of the differences, viz., the fact that belief is not necessary in the fictional situation. As for the hesitant claim that there is a different sense here, this clearly does not follow from the fact that being moved by what happens in real life is different from being moved in the theatre or cinema or when reading a novel, and I find it counterintuitive.[6] But even if the phrase did have different senses for the different cases, it would not follow that there was no problem. It may be that "being moved" (S. 2) is an incoherent notion so that we and our behaviour are incoherent, when we are "moved" (S. 2).

When, as we say, Mercutio's death moves us, it appears to do so in very much the same way as the unnecessary death of a young man moves us and for the same reason. We see the death as a waste, though of course it is really only a waste in the real case, and as a "tragedy", and we are, unambiguously – though problematically as I see it in the case of fiction – saddened by the death. As we watch the play and realise that Mercutio may die or, knowing the play, that he is about to die, we may nonetheless and in either case say to ourselves "Oh! No! Don't let it happen!" (It seems *absurd* to say this, especially when we know the play, and yet we do. This is part of what I see as the problem.) When he is run through we wince and gasp and catch our breath, and as he dies the more labile of us weep.

How would our behaviour differ if we believed that we were watching the death of a real young man, perhaps of the actor playing the part of Mercutio? First, seeing or fearing that the actor playing the part of Tybalt is bent on killing the other actor, we might try to intervene or, if we did not, we might reproach ourselves for not doing so. When he has been run through we might try to get help. But if we are convinced that we can do nothing, as we are when we watch the death of Mercutio or read about Anna, and if we thought that our watching was not improper, these irrelevant differences in our behaviour would disappear. Once again, we would say to ourselves – and, in this case also to each other since there is no question of aesthetic pleasure – "My God! How terrible!" And as the actor lay dying, perhaps delivering Mercutio's lines, either because he felt them to be appropriate or because, unaware that he was actually dying, he felt that the show must go on, we should again weep for the dying man and the pity of it. Secondly, but this is not irrelevant, our response to the real death is likely to be more massive, more intense and longer in duration for, after all, a real young man has been killed, and it will not be alloyed – or allayed – by aesthetic pleasure. But such differences do not destroy the similarity of the response and may even be said to require it.

So a similarity exists, and the essential similarity seems to be that we are saddened. But this is my difficulty. For we are saddened, but how can we be? What are we sad *about*? How can we feel genuinely and involuntarily sad, and weep, as we do, knowing as we do that no one has suffered or died?

To insist that there is this similarity between being moved and "being moved" is not to deny that there are other differences between them besides the necessary presence of belief in the one case and its puzzling absence in the other. Yet, as I have already indicated, some of the peculiar features of "being moved" add to the problem it presents. Not *any* difference between being moved and "being moved", over and above the difference in belief, has the effect of reducing the conceptual problem presented by the latter, as is suggested by this sixth solution. E.g., when we hope that Mercutio will not get killed, we may realise, knowing the play, that he must be killed, unless the play is altered or the performance is interrupted and we may not wish for that. So not only is our hope vain, for he must die and we know this,[7] but it exists alongside a wish that he will die. After the death, in retrospect, our behaviour differs. In the case of the real man, we should continue to be moved and to regret what happened. With Mercutio we are unlikely to do this and, in talking about his death later, we might only be moved to say "How moving it was!" For we are no longer at the performance or responding directly to it. We do not so much realise later as appropriately remind ourselves later that Mercutio is only a character and that, being a character, he will, as it were, be born again to die again at the next performance. Mercutio is not lost to us, when he dies, as the actor is when he dies.

Our response to Mercutio's death is, then, different from our response to the death of the actor. We do not entirely or simply hope that it will not happen, our response is partly aesthetic, the anguish at his death is not perhaps as intense, and

it tends not to survive the performance.

Perhaps we are and can be moved by the death of Mercutio only to the extent that, at the time of the performance, we are "caught up" in the play, and see the characters as persons, real persons, though to see them as real persons is not to believe that they are real persons. If we wholly believe, our response is indistinguishable from our response to the real thing, for we believe it to be the real thing. If we are always and fully aware that these are only actors mouthing rehearsed lines, we are not caught up in the play at all and can only respond to the beauty and tragedy of the poetry and not to the death of the character. The difficulty is, however – and it remains – that the belief, to say the least, is never complete. Or, better, even when we are caught up, we are still aware that we are watching a play and that Mercutio is "only" a character. We may become like children, but this is not necessary for our tears.

So the problem remains. The strength of our response may be proportionate to, *inter alia*, our "belief" in Mercutio. But we do not and need not at any time believe that he is a real person to weep for him. So that what is necessary in other contexts, *viz.*, belief, for being moved, is not necessary here and, all over again, how can we be saddened by and cry over Mercutio's death knowing as we do that when he dies no one really dies?

8. I am left with the conclusion that our being moved in certain ways by works of art, though very "natural" to us and in that way only too intelligible, involves us in inconsistency and so incoherence.

It may be some sort of comfort, as well as support for my thesis, to realise that there are other sorts of situation in which we are similarly inconsistent, i.e., in which, while knowing that something is or is not so, we spontaneously behave, or even may be unable to stop ourselves behaving, as if we believed the contrary. Thus, a tennis player who sees his shot going into the net will often give a little involuntary jump to lift it over. Because he knows that this can have no effect it is tempting to say that the jump is purely expressive. But almost anyone who has played tennis will know that this is not true. Or again, though men have increasingly come to think of death as a dreamless sleep, it was pointed out long ago – was it by Dr. Johnson or David Hume?[8] – that they still fear it. Some may say that this fear is not incoherent, for what appals such men is not their also thinking of death as an unpleasant state, but the prospect of their nonexistence. But how can this appal? There is, literally, nothing to fear. The incoherence of fearing the sleep of death for all that it will cause one to miss is even clearer. We do not participate in life when we are dead, but we are not then endlessly wishing to do so. Nonetheless, men fear the endless, dreamless sleep of death and fear it for all that they will miss.

Notes

1 Not for the performance which elicits this feeling or for the actor – for those we feel admiration, are impressed and so on. This may help to explain how we can enjoy tragedy. Besides the actor's skill and the producer's we also enjoy the skill of the writer. What is difficult is that we weep. This turns the usual problem upside down. People are more often puzzled about how we can enjoy a tragedy, not how it can harrow us, cf. Hume's essay, "Of Tragedy," in John W. Lenz (ed.) *Of the Standard of Taste and Other Essays* (Indianapolis: Bobbs-Merrill, 1965).

2 In "The Expression Theory of Art", collected in his *Philosophical Essays*, Lincoln: University of Nebraska Press (1965); cf. p. 29.

3 Though why that should worry us is another worry. There may be some who still feel that there really is no problem, so consider the following case. A man has a genre painting. It shows a young man being slain in battle (but it is not an historical picture, that is, of the death of some particular real young man who was killed in a particular battle). He says that he finds the picture moving and we understand, even if we do not agree. But then he says that, when he looks at the picture, he feels pity, sorrow, etc., for *the young man in the picture*. Surely this very odd response would be extremely puzzling? How *can* he feel sorry for the young man in the painting? But now suppose that the picture is a moving picture, i.e., a movie, and it tells a story. In this case we *do* say that we feel sorry for the young man in the film who is killed. But is there a difference between these two cases which not only explains but justifies our differing responses? Is it, perhaps, simply because most of us do respond in this way to films that we do not find our doing so puzzling?

4 Cf. "The delight of tragedy proceeds from our consciousness of fiction; if we thought murders and treasons real, they would please no more." Dr Johnson, *Preface to Shakespeare's Plays*, in Brian Vickers (ed.) Shakespeare: *The Critical Heritage* (London, 1974), Vol. 5, p. 71.

5 Incidentally, and to avoid misunderstanding, I do not have a monolithic view about aesthetic response. I am not saying, for example, that we must believe a story about Harold Wilson to find it *funny*. I am saying that, with the paradoxical exception of watching plays, films, etc., including those about Harold Wilson, we need to believe the story to weep for him, to feel pity for him.

6 Does "killed" have a different sense in "Nixon has been killed" and "Mercutio has been killed"?

7 Of course, seeing a clip from the newsreel of Kennedy's assassination may elicit the same response, "Don't let him get killed!", and here we do realise that our response is silly, is incompatible with our knowledge that he is dead and we are watching a film of his death. But there is in the theatre nothing analogous to actually witnessing Kennedy's death. The death of a character is always irrevocable, out of reach, and out of our control.

8 Either could have made such an observation, though Hume regarded death with phlegm, Johnson with honour. But in fact it was a contemporary, Miss Seward, "There is one mode of the fear of death which is certainly absurd; and that is the dread of annihilation, which is only a pleasing sleep without a dream." Boswell, *Life of Johnson*, for 1778.

26

Fearing Fictions

Kendall L. Walton

[T]he plot [of a tragedy] must be structured
. . . that the one who is hearing the events
unroll shudders with fear and feels pity at
what happens: which is what one would experience on hearing the plot of the Oedipus.

Aristotle, Poetics[1]

I

Charles is watching a horror movie about a terrible
green slime. He cringes in his seat as the slime
oozes slowly but relentlessly over the earth
destroying everything in its path. Soon a greasy
head emerges from the undulating mass, and two
beady eyes roll around, finally fixing on the camera.
The slime, picking up speed, oozes on a new course
straight toward the viewers. Charles emits a shriek
and clutches desperately at his chair. Afterwards,
still shaken, Charles confesses that he was "terrified" of the slime. *Was* he?

This question is part of the larger issue of how
"remote" fictional worlds are from the real world.
There is a definite barrier against *physical* interactions between fictional worlds and the real world.
Spectators at a play are prevented from rendering
aid to a heroine in distress. There is no way that
Charles can dam up the slime, or take a sample
for laboratory analysis.[2] But, as Charles's case
dramatically illustrates, this barrier appears to be
psychologically transparent. It would seem that
real people can, and frequently do, have psycho-

Kendall L. Walton, "Fearing Fictions," *Journal of
Philosophy*, 75: 1 (January 1978), pp. 5–27. Reprinted by permission of The Journal of Philosophy.

logical attitudes toward merely fictional entities,
despite the impossibility of physical intervention.
Readers or spectators detest Iago, worry about
Tom Sawyer and Becky lost in the cave, pity Willy
Loman, envy Superman – and Charles fears the
slime.

But I am skeptical. We do indeed get "caught
up" in stories; we often become "emotionally
involved" when we read novels or watch plays
or films. But to construe this involvement as
consisting of our having psychological attitudes
toward fictional entities is, I think, to tolerate
mystery and court confusion. I shall offer a different and, in my opinion, a much more illuminating account of it.

This issue is of fundamental importance. It is
crucially related to the basic question of why and
how fiction is important, why we find it valuable,
why we do not dismiss novels, films, and plays as
"mere fiction" and hence unworthy of serious
attention. My conclusions in this paper will lead
to some tentative suggestions about this basic
question.

II

Physical interaction is possible only with what
actually exists. That is why Charles cannot dam up
the slime, and why in general real people cannot
have physical contact with mere fictions. But the
nonexistence of the slime does not prevent Charles
from fearing it. One may fear a ghost or a burglar
even if there is none; one may be afraid of an earthquake that is destined never to occur.

But a person who fears a nonexistent burglar *believes* that there is, or at least might be, one. He believes that he is in danger, that there is a possibility of his being harmed by a burglar. It is *conceivable* that Charles should believe himself to be endangered by the green slime. He might take the film to be a live documentary, a news flash. If he does, naturally he is afraid.

But the situation I have in mind is the more usual and more interesting one in which Charles is not deceived in this straightforward way. Charles knows perfectly well that the slime is not real and that he is in no danger. Is he afraid even so? He says that he is afraid, and he is in a state which is undeniably similar, in some respects, to that of a person who is frightened of a pending real-world disaster. His muscles are tensed, he clutches his chair, his pulse quickens, his adrenalin flows. Let us call this physiological/psychological state "quasi-fear." Whether it is actual fear (or a component of actual fear) is the question at issue.

Charles's state is crucially different from that of a person with an ordinary case of fear. The fact that Charles is fully aware that the slime is fictional is, I think, good reason to deny that what he feels is fear. It seems a principle of common sense, one which ought not to be abandoned if there is any reasonable alternative, that fear[3] must be accompanied by, or must involve, a belief that one is in danger. Charles does not believe that he is in danger; so he is not afraid.

Charles might try to convince us that he was afraid by shuddering and declaring dramatically that he was "*really terrified*." This emphasizes the intensity of his experience. But we need not deny that he had an intense experience. The question is whether his experience, however intense, was one of fear of the slime. The fact that Charles, and others, call it "fear" is not conclusive, even if we grant that in doing so they express a truth. For we need to know whether the statement that Charles was afraid is to be taken literally or not.

More sophisticated defenders of the claim that Charles is afraid may argue that Charles *does* believe that the green slime is real and is a real threat to him. There are, to be sure, strong reasons for allowing that Charles realizes that the slime is only fictional and poses no danger. If he didn't we should expect him to flee the theater, call the police, warn his family. But perhaps it is *also* true that Charles believes, in some way or "on some level," that the slime is real and really threatens him. It has been said that in cases like this one "suspends one's disbelief," or that "part" of a person believes something which another part of him disbelieves, or that one finds oneself (almost?) believing something one nevertheless knows to be false. We must see what can be made of these notions.

One possibility is that Charles *half* believes that there is a real danger, and that he is, literally, at least half afraid. To half believe something is to be not quite sure that it is true, but also not quite sure that it is not true. But Charles has *no* doubts about whether he is in the presence of an actual slime. If he half believed, and were half afraid, we would expect him to have *some* inclination to act on his fear in the normal ways. Even a hesitant belief, a mere suspicion, that the slime is real would induce any normal person seriously to consider calling the police and warning his family. Charles gives no thought whatever to such courses of action. He is not *uncertain* whether the slime is real; he is perfectly sure that it is not.

Moreover, the fear symptoms that Charles does exhibit are not symptoms of a mere suspicion that the slime is real and a queasy feeling of half fear. They are symptoms of the certainty of grave and immediate danger, and sheer terror. Charles's heart pounds violently, he gasps for breath, he grasps the chair until his knuckles are white. This is not the behavior of a man who realizes basically that he is safe but suffers flickers of doubt. If it indicates fear at all, it indicates acute and overwhelming terror. Thus, to compromise on this issue, to say that Charles half believes he is in danger and is half afraid, is not a reasonable alternative.

One might claim that Charles believes he is in danger, but that this is not a hesitant or weak or half belief, but rather a belief of a special kind – a "gut" belief as opposed to an "intellectual" one. Compare a person who hates flying. He realizes, in one sense, that airplanes are (relatively) safe. He says, honestly, that they are, and can quote statistics to prove it. Nevertheless, he avoids traveling by air whenever possible. He is brilliant at devising excuses. And if he must board a plane he becomes nervous and upset. I grant that this person believes at a "gut" level that flying is dangerous, despite his "intellectual" belief to the contrary. I grant also that he is really afraid of flying.

But Charles is different. The air traveler performs *deliberate* actions that one would expect of someone who thinks flying is dangerous, or at least he is strongly inclined to perform such actions. If he does not actually decide against traveling by air he has a strong inclination to do so. But Charles does not have even an inclination to leave the theater or call the police. The only signs that he might really believe he is endangered are his more or less automatic, nondeliberate, reactions: his pulse rate, his sweaty palms, his knotted stomach, his spontaneous shriek.[4] This justifies us in treating the two cases differently.

Deliberate actions are done for reasons; they are done because of what the agent wants and what he thinks will bring about what he wants. There is a presumption that such actions are reasonable in light of the agent's beliefs and desires (however unreasonable the beliefs and desires may be). So we postulate beliefs or desires to make sense of them. People also have reasons for doing things that they are inclined to do but, for other reasons, refrain from doing. If the air traveler thinks that flying is dangerous, then, assuming that he wants to live, his actions or tendencies thereto are reasonable. Otherwise, they probably are not. So we legitimately infer that he does believe, at least on a "gut" level, that flying is dangerous. But we don't have to make the same kind of sense of Charles's automatic responses. One doesn't have reasons for things one doesn't *do*, like sweating, increasing one's pulse rate, knotting one's stomach (involuntarily). So there is no need to attribute beliefs (or desires) to Charles which will render these responses reasonable.[5] Thus, we can justifiably infer the air passenger's ("gut") belief in the danger of flying from his deliberate behavior or inclinations, and yet refuse to infer from Charles' automatic responses that he thinks he is in danger.

Someone might reply that at moments of special crisis during the movie – e.g., when the slime first spots Charles – Charles "loses hold of reality" and, *momentarily*, takes the slime to be real and really fears it. These moments are too short for Charles to think about doing anything; so (one might claim) it isn't surprising that his belief and fear are not accompanied by the normal inclinations to act.

This move is unconvincing. In the first place, Charles's quasi-fear responses are not merely momentary; he may have his heart in his throat throughout most of the movie, yet without experiencing the slightest inclination to flee or call the police. These long-term responses, and Charles's propensity to describe them afterwards in terms of "fear," need to be understood even if it is allowed that there are moments of real fear interspersed among them. Furthermore, however tempting the momentary-fear idea might be, comparable views of other psychological states are much less appealing. When we say that someone "pitied" Willy Loman or "admired" Superman, it is unlikely that we have in mind special moments during his experience of the work when he forgot, momentarily, that he was dealing with fiction and felt flashes of actual pity or admiration. The person's "sense of reality" may well have been robust and healthy throughout his experience of the work, uninterrupted by anything like the special moments of crisis Charles experiences during the horror movie. Moreover, it may be appropriate to say that someone "pities" Willy or "admires" Superman even when he is not watching the play or reading the cartoon. The momentary-*fear* theory, even if it were plausible, would not throw much light on cases in which we apparently have other psychological attitudes toward fictions.

Although Charles is not really afraid of the fictional slime depicted in the movie, the movie might nevertheless produce real fear in him. It might cause him to be afraid of something other than the slime it depicts. If Charles is a child, the movie may make him wonder whether there might not be real slimes or other exotic horrors *like* the one depicted in the movie, even if he fully realizes that the movie-slime itself is not real. Charles may well fear these suspected actual dangers; he might have nightmares about them for days afterwards. (*Jaws* caused a lot of people to fear sharks which they thought might really exist. But whether they were afraid of the fictional sharks in the movie is another question.)

If Charles is an older movie-goer with a heart condition, he may be afraid of the movie itself. Perhaps he knows that any excitement could trigger a heart attack, and fears that the movie will cause excitement, e.g., by depicting the slime as being especially aggressive or threatening. This is real fear. But it is fear of the depiction of the slime, not fear of the slime that is depicted.

Why is it so natural to describe Charles as afraid of the slime, if he is not, and how *is* his experience to be characterized? In what follows I shall develop a theory to answer these questions.

III

Propositions that are, as we say, "true in (the world of)" a novel or painting or film are *fictional*. Thus it is fictional that there is a society of tiny people called "Lilliputians." And in the example discussed above it is fictional that a terrible green slime is on the loose. Other fictional propositions are associated not with works of art but with games of make-believe, dreams, and imaginings. If it is "true in a game of make-believe" that Johnnie is a pirate, then fictionally Johnnie is a pirate. If someone dreams or imagines that he is a hero, then it is fictional that he is a hero.

Fictional truths[6] come in groups, and each of these groups constitutes a "fictional world." The fact that fictionally there was a society of tiny people and the fact that fictionally a man named "Gulliver" was a ship's physician belong to the same fictional world. The fact that fictionally a green slime is on the loose belongs to a different one. There is, roughly, a distinct fictional world corresponding to each novel, painting, film, game of make-believe, dream, or daydream.

All fictional truths are in one way or another man-made. But there are two importantly different ways of making them, and two corresponding kinds of fictional truths. One way to make a proposition fictional is simply to imagine that it is true. If it is fictional that a person is a hero because he imagines himself to be a hero, then this fictional truth is an *imaginary* one. Imagining is not always a deliberate, self-conscious act. We sometimes find ourselves imagining things more or less spontaneously, without having decided to do so. Thoughts pop into our heads unbidden. Dreams can be understood as simply very spontaneous imaginings.

Fictional truths of the second kind are established in a less direct manner. Participants in a game of mud pies may decide to recognize a principle to the effect that whenever there is a glob of mud in a certain orange crate, it is "true in the game of make-believe," i.e., it is fictional, that there is a pie in the oven. This fictional truth is a *make-believe* one. The principles in force in a given game of make-believe are, of course, just those principles which participants in the game recognize or accept, or understand to be in force.

It can be make-believe that there is a pie in the oven without anyone's imagining that there is. This will be so if there is a glob in the crate which no one knows about. (Later, after discovering the glob, a child might say, "There was a pie in the oven all along, but we didn't know it.") But propositions that are known to be make-believe are usually imaginary as well. When kids playing mud pies do know about a glob in the crate by virtue of which it is make-believe that a pie is in the oven, they imagine that there is a pie in the oven.

Principles of make-believe that are in force in a game need not have been formulated explicitly or deliberately adopted. When children agree to let globs of mud "be" pies they are in effect establishing a great many unstated principles linking make-believe properties of pies to properties of globs. It is implicitly understood that the size and shape of globs determine the make-believe size and shape of pies; it is understood, for example, that make-believedly a pie is one handspan across just in case that is the size of the appropriate glob. It is understood also that if Johnnie throws a glob at Mary then make-believedly Johnnie throws a pie at Mary. (It is *not* understood that if a glob is 40 per cent clay then make-believedly a pie is 40 per cent clay.)

It is not always easy to say whether or not someone does accept, implicitly, a given principle of make-believe. But we should notice that much of the plausibility of attributing to children implicit acceptance of a principle linking the make-believe size and shape of pies to the size and shape of globs rests on the dispositional fact that if the children should discover a glob to have a certain size or shape they would imagine, more or less automatically, that a pie has that size or shape. The children are disposed to imagine pies as having whatever size and shape properties they think the relevant globs have. In general, nondeliberate, spontaneous imagining, prompted in a systematic way by beliefs about the real world, is an important indication of implicit acceptance of principles of make-believe. I do not claim that a person disposed to imagine, nondeliberately, that p when be believes that q *necessarily* recognizes a principle of make-believe whereby if q then it is make-believe that p. It must be his understanding that whenever it is true that q, *whether he knows it or not*, it will be fictional that p. It may be difficult to ascertain whether this is his understanding, especially since his understanding may be entirely implicit. But the spontaneity of a person's imagining that p on learning that q strongly suggests that he thinks of p as having been fictional even before he realized that q.

A game of make-believe and its constituent principles need not be shared publicly. One might set up one's own personal game, adopting principles that no one else recognizes. And at least some of the principles constituting a personal game of make-believe may be implicit, principles which the person simply takes for granted.

Representational works of art generate make-believe truths. *Gulliver's Travels* generates the truth that make-believedly there is a society of six-inch-tall people. It is make-believe that a green slime is on the loose in virtue of the images on the screen of Charles's horror movie. These make-believe truths are generated because the relevant principles of make-believe are understood to be in force. But few such principles are ever formulated, and our recognition of most of them is implicit. Some probably seem so natural that we assume them to be in force almost automatically. Others we pick up easily through unreflective experience with the arts.[7]

IV

[The actor] on a stage plays at being another before a gathering of people who play at taking him for that other person.
Jorge Luis Borges[8]

Compare Charles with a child playing an ordinary game of make-believe with his father. The father, pretending to be a ferocious monster, cunningly stalks the child and, at a crucial moment, lunges viciously at him. The child flees, screaming, to the next room. The scream is more or less involuntary, and so is the flight. But the child has a delighted grin on his face even while he runs, and he unhesitatingly comes back for more. He is perfectly aware that his father is only "playing," that the whole thing is "just a game," and that only make-believedly is there a vicious monster after him. He is not really afraid.

The child obviously belongs to the fictional world of the game of make-believe. It is make-believe that the monster lunges, not into thin air, but at the child. Make-believedly the child is in grave and mortal danger. And when the child screams and runs, make-believedly he knows he is in danger and is afraid. The game is a sort of theatrical event in which the father is an actor portraying a monster and the child is an actor playing himself.

I propose to regard Charles similarly. When the slime raises its head, spies the camera, and begins oozing toward it, it is make-believe that Charles is threatened. And when as a result Charles gasps and grips his chair, make-believedly he is afraid. Charles is playing a game of make-believe in which he uses the images on the screen as props. He too is an actor impersonating himself. In this section I shall explain this proposal in detail. My main arguments for it will come later.

Charles differs in some important respects from an ordinary on-stage, self-portraying actor. One difference has to do with what makes it make-believe that Charles is afraid. Facts about Charles generate (_de re_) make-believe truths about him; in this respect he is like an actor portraying himself on stage. But the sorts of facts about Charles which do the generating are different. Make-believe truths about Charles are generated at least partly by what he thinks and feels, not just by how he acts. It is partly the fact that Charles is in a state of quasi-fear, the fact that he feels his heart pounding, his muscles tensed, etc., which makes it make-believe that he is afraid. It would not be appropriate to describe him as "afraid" if he were not in some such state.[9]

Charles's quasi-fear is not responsible, by itself, for the fact that make-believedly it is the _slime_ he fears, nor even for the fact that make-believedly he is afraid rather than angry or excited or merely upset. Here Charles's (actual) beliefs come into play. Charles believes (he knows) that make-believedly the green slime is bearing down on him and he is in danger of being destroyed by it. His quasi-fear results from this belief.[10] What makes it make-believe that Charles is afraid rather than angry or excited or upset is the fact that his quasi-fear is caused by the belief that make-believedly he is in danger. And his belief that make-believedly it is the slime that endangers him is what makes it make-believe that the slime is the object of his fear. In short, my suggestion is this: the fact that Charles is quasi-afraid as a result of realizing that make-believedly the slime threatens him generates the truth that make-believedly he is afraid of the slime.[11]

An on-stage actor, by contrast, generates make-believe truths solely by his acting, by his behavior. Whether it is make-believe that the character portrayed is afraid or not depends just on what the actor says and does and how he contorts his face, regardless of what he actually thinks or feels. It makes no difference whether his actual emotional state is anything like fear. This is just as true when the actor is playing himself as it is when he is portraying some other character. The actor may find that putting himself into a certain frame of mind makes it easier to act in the appropriate ways. Nevertheless, it is how he acts, not his state of mind, that determines whether make-believedly he is afraid.

This is how our conventions for theater work, and it is entirely reasonable that they should work

Kendall L. Walton

this way. Audiences cannot be expected to have a clear idea of an actor's personal thoughts and feelings while he is performing. That would require knowledge of his off-stage personality and of recent events that may have affected his mood (e.g., an argument with his director or his wife). Moreover, acting involves a certain amount of dissembling; actors hide some aspects of their mental states from the audience. If make-believe truths depended on actors' private thoughts and feelings, it would be awkward and unreasonably difficult for spectators to ascertain what is going on in the fictional world. It is not surprising that the make-believe truths for which actors on stage are responsible are understood to be generated by just what is visible from the galleries.

But Charles is not performing for an audience. It is not his job to get across to anyone else what make-believedly is true of himself. Probably no one but him much cares whether or not make-believedly he is afraid. So there is no reason why his actual state of mind should not have a role in generating make-believe truths about himself.

It is not so clear in the monster game what makes it make-believe that the child is afraid of a monster. The child *might* be performing for the benefit of an audience; he might be *showing* someone, an onlooker, or just his father, that make-believedly he is afraid. If so, perhaps he is like an on-stage actor. Perhaps we should regard his observable behavior as responsible for the fact that make-believedly he is afraid. But there is room for doubt here. The child experiences quasi-fear sensations as Charles does. And his audience probably has much surer access to his mental state than theater audiences have to those of actors. The audience may know him well, and the child does not try so hard or so skillfully to hide his actual mental state as actors do. It may be perfectly evident to the audience that the child has a case of quasi-fear, and also that this is a result of his realization that make-believedly a monster is after him. So it is not unreasonable to regard the child's mental state as helping to generate make-believe truths.

A more definite account of the situation is possible if the child is participating in the game solely for his own amusement, with no thought of an audience. In this case the child himself, at least, almost certainly understands his make-believe fear to depend on his mental state rather than (just) his behavior.[12] In fact, let us suppose that the child is an undemonstrative sort who does not scream or run or betray his "fear" in any other especially

overt way. His participation in the game is purely passive. Nevertheless the child does experience quasi-fear when make-believedly the monster attacks him, and he still would describe himself as being "afraid" (although he knows that there is no danger and that his "fear" isn't real). Certainly in this case it is (partly) his quasi-fear that generates the make-believe truth he expresses when he says he is "afraid."

My proposal is to construe Charles on the model of this undemonstrative child. Charles may, of course, exhibit his "fear" in certain observable ways. But his observable behavior is not meant to show anyone else that make-believedly he is afraid. It is likely to go unnoticed by others, and even Charles himself may be unaware of it. No one, least of all Charles, regards his observable behavior as generating the truth that make-believedly he is afraid.

V

It is clear enough now what makes it make-believe that Charles fears the slime, assuming that make-believedly he does fear the slime. But more needs to be said in support of my claim that this is a make-believe truth. What needs to be established is that the relevant principle of make-believe is accepted or recognized by someone, that someone understands it to be in force. I contend that Charles, at least, does so understand it.

It is clear that Charles imagines himself to be afraid of the slime (though he knows he is not). He thinks of himself as being afraid of it; he readily describes his experience as one of "fear" – once he has a chance to catch his breath. So it is at least imaginary (and hence fictional) that he fears the slime.

Charles's act of imagining himself afraid of the slime is hardly a deliberate or reflective act. It is triggered more or less automatically by his awareness of his quasi-fear sensations. He is simply disposed to think of himself as fearing the slime, without deciding to do so, when during the movie he feels his heart racing, his muscles tensed, and so forth. It is just such a disposition as this that goes with implicit recognition of a principle of make-believe. If a child is disposed to imagine a pie to be six inches across when he discovers that that is the size of a glob of mud, this makes it reasonable to regard him as recognizing a principle whereby the glob's being that size makes it make-believe that the

312

pie is also. Similarly, Charles's tendency to imagine himself afraid of the slime when he finds himself in the relevant mental state constitutes persuasive grounds for attributing to him acceptance of a principle whereby his experience makes it make-believe that he is afraid.[13]

Several further considerations will increase the plausibility of this conclusion. First, I have claimed only that Charles recognizes the principle of make-believe. There is no particular reason why anyone else should recognize it, since ordinarily only Charles is in a position to apply it and only he is interested in the make-believe truth that results. Others might know about it and realize how important it is to Charles. But even so the principle clearly is in important respects a personal one. It differs in this regard from the principles whereby an on-stage actor's behavior generates make-believe truths, and also from those whereby images on the movie screen generate make-believe truths about the activities of the green slime. *These* principles are fully public; they are clearly (even if implicitly) recognized by everyone watching the play or movie. Everyone in the audience applies them and is interested in the resulting make-believe truths.

This makes it reasonable to recognize two distinct games of make-believe connected with the horror movie – a public game and Charles's personal game – and two corresponding fictional worlds. The situation is analogous to that of an illustrated edition of a novel. Consider an edition of Dostoyevsky's *Crime and Punishment* which includes a drawing of Raskolnikov. The text of the novel, considered alone, establishes a fictional world comprising the make-believe truths that it generates, e.g., the truth that make-believedly a man named "Raskolnikov" killed an old lady. The illustration is normally understood not as establishing its own separate fictional world, but as combining with the novel to form a "larger" world. This larger world contains the make-believe truths generated by the text alone, plus those generated by the illustration (e.g., that make-believedly Raskolnikov has wavy hair and a receding chin), and also those generated by both together (e.g., that make-believedly a man with wavy hair killed an old lady). So we have two fictional worlds, one included within the other: the world of the novel and the world of the novel-plus-illustration.

Charles's state of mind supplements the movie he is watching in the way an illustration supplements what it illustrates. The movie considered alone establishes a fictional world consisting only of the make-believe truths that it generates (e.g., that make-believedly there is a green slime on the loose). But Charles recognizes, in addition, a larger world in which these make-believe truths are joined by truths generated by Charles's experience as he watches the movie, and also by truths generated by the images on the screen and Charles's experience together. It is only in this more inclusive world that make-believedly Charles fears the slime. (And it is the larger world that occupies Charles's attention when he is caught up in the movie.)

The analogy between Charles's case and the illustrated novel is not perfect. The novel-plus-illustration world is publicly recognized, whereas the fictional world established by the movie plus Charles's experience of it probably is not. Dolls provide an analogy which is better in this respect. Anyone who sees a doll of a certain sort will recognize that it generates the truth that make-believedly there is a blonde baby girl. The doll, regarded simply as a sculpture to be observed from a distance, generates make-believe truths such as this. But a child playing with the doll is playing a more personal game of make-believe, one in which she herself is a self-portraying actor and the doll serves as a prop. What she does with the doll generates make-believe truths, e.g., the truth that make-believedly she is dressing the baby for a trip to town. Similarly, Charles uses the screen images as props in a personal game of make-believe in which he himself is a character. He plays his own game with the images. The screen images, of course, do not lend themselves to being "dressed" or manipulated in all the ways that dolls do, and this limits the extent of Charles's participation in the game. But the relations and interactions between Charles and the images do generate a number of important make-believe truths: that make-believedly Charles notices the slime and stares apprehensively at it, that make-believedly it turns toward him and attacks, and that make-believedly he is scared out of his wits.[14]

One source of uneasiness about my claim that make-believedly Charles fears the slime may have been the impression that this can be so only if Charles belongs to the fictional world of the *movie*. (The movie itself doesn't depict Charles, nor does it make any reference to him, so he doesn't belong to the movie-world.) My two-worlds theory shows that this impression is mistaken and hence that the uneasiness based on it is out of place.

I have portrayed Charles so far as participating rather automatically in his game of make-believe. But he might easily slip into participating deliberately. The naturalness of his doing so gives added support to my claim that Charles does recognize a make-believe world that he and the slime share, even when his participation is not deliberate. Suppose that during the movie Charles exclaims, deliberately, to a companion or to himself, "Yikes, here it comes! Watch out!" How are we to understand this verbal action? Certainly Charles is not seriously asserting that a slime is coming and warning himself or his companion of it. Presumably he is asserting that it is *make-believe* that a slime is coming. But the indexical, "here," carries an implicit reference to the speaker. So Charles's exclamation shows that he takes it to be make-believe that the slime is headed toward *him*; it shows that he regards himself as coexisting with the slime in a make-believe world.

But this does not take us to the bottom of the matter. "Yikes!" and "Watch out!" are not assertions, and so not assertions of what make-believedly is the case. Moreover, if in saying, "Here it comes," Charles were merely making an assertion about what make-believedly is the case, he could well have made this explicit and exclaimed instead, "Make-believedly the slime is coming!" or "The slime is coming, in the fictional world!" But these variants lack the flavor of the original. Charles's exclamatory tone is absurdly out of place when the make-believe status of the danger is made explicit. Compare how ridiculous it would be for an actor playing Horatio in a performance of *Hamlet* to exclaim, when the ghost appears, "Look, my lord, it comes, in the fictional world of the play!"

The comparison is apt. For Charles is doing just what actors do, *pretending* to make an assertion. He is pretending to assert (seriously) that the slime is headed his way. (Pretending to assert this is not incompatible with actually asserting that make-believedly the slime is coming. Charles might be doing both at once.) In my terms, Charles understands his utterance of "Here it comes!" to generate the truth that make-believedly he asserts (seriously) that the slime is coming. He is playing along with the fiction of the movie, incorporating it into a game of make-believe of his own. This makes it obvious why it would not do to say, "Here it comes, in the fictional world!" Saying that is simply not (normally) how one would pretend to assert that a slime is (really) coming. The rest of

Charles's verbal behavior is now easily explainable as well. In saying "Yikes!" and "Watch out!" he is pretending to express amazement or terror and pretending to issue a (serious) warning; make-believedly he is doing these things.

We have now arrived at the solution to a pair of puzzles. Why is it that in everyday conversation we regularly omit phrases like "in the fictional world" and "in the novel," whereas we rarely omit other intensional operators such as "It is believed that," "Jones wished that," "Jones denies that"? Why do we so naturally say just "Tom and Becky were lost in a cave" rather than "In the novel Tom and Becky were lost in a cave," whereas it would be almost unheard of to shorten "Jones wishes that a golden mountain would appear on the horizon" to simply "A golden mountain will appear on the horizon" (even if the context makes it clear that Jones's wishes are the subject of conversation)?

The explanation lies in our habit of playing along with fictions, of make-believedly asserting, pretending to assert, what we know to be only make-believedly the case. We mustn't be too quick to assume that an utterance of "*p*" is merely an ellipsis for "Make-believedly *p*" (or for "In the novel *p*"). This assumption is wrong if the speaker make-believedly is asserting that *p*, rather than (or in addition to) asserting that make-believedly *p*. Charles's frantic, "Yikes, here it comes!" is an obvious case in point. A case only slightly less obvious is that of a person reading *The Adventures of Tom Sawyer* who remarks, gravely and with an expression of deep concern, that Tom and Becky are lost in a cave.

I do not suggest that the omission of "in the novel" is *never* a mere ellipsis. "Tom and Becky were lost in a cave" uttered by a critic analyzing the novel could easily have been expanded to "In the novel Tom and Becky were lost in a cave" without altering the character of the remark. The critic probably is not pretending to assert that Tom and Becky were (actually) lost in a cave. But our habit of dropping fictional operators persists even in sober criticism, and testifies to the ease with which we can be induced to play along, deliberately, with a work of fiction.

In German the indicative mood is used ordinarily only when the speaker is committed to the truth of the sentence or clause in question. But fictional statements constitute a striking exception to this generalization; the indicative is used in fictional statements even though the speaker is *not* committed to their truth. (One says, for example,

"Robinson Crusoe hat einen Schiffbruch überlebt," which is indicative, even though one is not claiming that there actually was a person named "Robinson Crusoe" who survived a shipwreck.) The explanation is that speakers are often pretending to express their commitment to the truth of sentences or clauses in fictional contexts. So naturally they use the indicative mood in these cases; they speak as they would if they were not pretending. And the habit of using the indicative persists even when there is little or no such pretense.

VI

The treatment of Charles's "fear of the slime" suggested above can serve as a model for understanding other psychological attitudes ostensibly directed toward fictional things. When it is said that someone pities Willy Loman, or worries about Tom and Becky, or detests Iago, or envies Superman, what is said is probably not literally true.[15] But the person is, actually, in a distinctive psychological (emotional?) state, even if that state is not pity or worry or hate or envy. And his being in this state is a result of his awareness of certain make-believe truths: that make-believedly Willy is an innocent victim of cruel circumstances, that make-believedly Tom and Becky might perish in the cave, that make-believedly Iago deceived Othello about Desdemona, that make-believedly Superman can do almost anything. The fact that the person's psychological state is as it is, and is caused by such beliefs, makes it make-believe that he pities Willy, worries about Tom and Becky, hates Iago, or envies Superman.

We have here a particularly intimate relation between the real world and fictional worlds. Insofar as make-believe truths are generated by a spectator's or reader's state of mind, he is no mere "external observer" of the fictional world. Ascertaining what make-believedly is true of himself is to a large extent a matter of introspection (or of whatever sort of "privileged access" one has to one's own beliefs and sensations). In fact, when Charles watches the horror movie, for example, introspection is involved in ascertaining not merely that make-believedly he is afraid of the slime, but also make-believe truths about the nature and progress of his fear. If it is make-believe that his fear is overwhelming, or that it is only momentary, this is so because his quasi-fear sensations are overwhelming, or are only momentary. Make-believedly his

fear grows more or less intense, or becomes almost unbearable, or finally subsides, etc., as his quasi-fear feelings change in these ways. So it is by attention to the nature of his own actual experience that Charles is aware of make-believe truths about the nature of his fear. He follows the progress of his make-believe fear by introspection, much as one who is literally afraid follows the progress of his actual fear.

It would not be too far wrong to say that Charles actually experiences his make-believe fear. I don't mean that there is a special kind of fear, make-believe fear, which Charles experiences. What he actually experiences, his quasi-fear feelings, are not feelings of fear. But it is true *of them* that *make-believedly* they are feelings of fear. They generate *de re* make-believe truths about themselves, and so belong to the fictional world just as Charles himself does. What Charles actually experiences is such that make-believedly it is (an experience of) fear.

Cases like that of Charles contrast strikingly with others in which an actual person belongs to a fictional world. Consider a performance of William Luce's play about Emily Dickinson, *The Belle of Amherst*, in which Julie Harris plays Emily Dickinson. Suppose that Emily Dickinson herself, with the help of a time machine or a fortuitous reincarnation, is in the audience. In order to discover make-believe truths about herself, including what make-believedly she thinks and feels, Dickinson must observe Julie Harris's actions, just as any spectator must. It is as though she is watching another person, despite the fact that that "person," the character, is herself. Dickinson has no special intimacy with make-believe truths about her own mental state.[16] The situation is basically the same if Dickinson should replace Julie Harris in the lead role and act the part herself. She still must judge from her external behavior, from what spectators could observe, whether or not it is make-believe that she is afraid or worried or whatever – and she might easily be mistaken about how she looks to spectators. It is still as though she considers herself "from the outside," from the perspective of another person.

This is clearly not true of Charles. It is not as though Charles were confronting another person, a fictional version of himself, but rather as though he himself actually fears the slime. (Nevertheless, he does not.) Make-believe facts about his fear, especially the fact that make-believedly it is his, are portrayed to Charles in an extraordinarily realistic manner. And make-believe facts about our pity for Willy, our dislike of Iago, and so forth, are similarly vivid to us. We and Charles feel ourselves to be part of fictional worlds, to be intimately involved with the slime, or Willy, or with whatever constituents of fictional worlds are, make-believedly, objects of our feelings and attitudes.

We see, now, how fictional worlds can seem to us almost as "real" as the real world is, even though we know perfectly well that they are not. We have begun to understand what happens when we get emotionally "involved" in a novel or play or film, when we are "caught up in the story."

The theory I have presented is designed to capture intuitions lying behind the traditional ideas that the normal or desired attitude toward fiction involves a "*suspension of disbelief,*" or a "*decrease of distance.*" These phrases are unfortunate. They strongly suggest that people do not (completely) disbelieve what they read in novels and see on the stage or screen, that, e.g., we somehow accept it as fact that a boy named "Huckleberry Finn" floated down the Mississippi River – at least while we are engrossed in the novel. The normal reader does not accept this as fact, nor should he. Our disbelief is "suspended" only in the sense that it is, in some ways, set aside or ignored. We don't believe that there was a Huck Finn, but what interests us is the fact that *make-believedly* there was one, and that make-believedly he floated down the Mississippi and did various other things. But this hardly accounts for the sense of "decreased distance" between us and fictions. It still has us peering down on fictional worlds from reality above, however fascinated we might be, for some mysterious reasons, by what we see.

On my theory we accomplish the "decrease of distance" not by promoting fictions to our level but by descending to theirs. (More accurately, we *extend* ourselves to their level, since we do not stop actually existing when it becomes fictional that we exist.) *Make-believedly* we do believe, we know, that Huck Finn floated down the Mississippi. And make-believedly we have various feelings and attitudes about him and his adventures. Rather than somehow fooling ourselves into thinking fictions are real, we become fictional. So we end up "on the same level" with fictions. And our presence there is accomplished in the extraordinarily realistic manner that I described. This enables us to comprehend our sense of closeness to fictions, without attributing to ourselves patently false beliefs.

We are now in a position to expect progress on the fundamental question of why and how fiction is important. Why don't we dismiss novels, plays, and films as "mere fiction" and hence unworthy of serious attention?

Much has been said about the value and importance of dreams, fantasy, and children's games of make-believe.[17] It has been suggested, variously, that such activities serve to clarify one's feelings, help one to work out conflicts, provide an outlet for the expression of repressed or socially unacceptable feelings, prepare one emotionally for possible future crises by providing "practice" in facing imaginary crises. It is natural to presume that our experience of representational works of art is valuable for similar reasons. But this presumption is not very plausible, I think, unless something like the theory I have presented is correct.

It is my impression that people are usually, perhaps always, characters in their own dreams and daydreams. We dream and fantasize about ourselves. Sometimes one's role in one's dream-world or fantasy-world is limited to that of observing other goings-on. But to have even this role *is* to belong to the fictional world. (We must distinguish between being, in one's dream, an observer of certain events, and merely "observing," having a dream about those events.) Similarly, children are nearly always characters in their games of make-believe. To play dolls or school, hobby horses or mud pies, is to be an actor portraying oneself.

I suggest that much of the value of dreaming, fantasizing, and making-believe depends crucially on one's thinking of oneself as belonging to a fictional world. It is chiefly by fictionally facing certain situations, engaging in certain activities, and having or expressing certain feelings, I think, that a dreamer, fantasizer, or game player comes to terms with his actual feelings – that he discovers them, learns to accept them, purges himself of them, or whatever exactly it is that he does.

If I am right about this, people can be expected to derive similar benefits from novels, plays, and films only if it is fictional that they themselves exist and participate (if only as observers) in the events portrayed in the works, i.e., only if my theory is on the right track.

I find encouragement for these speculations in the deliberate use of role-playing in educational simulation games, and as a therapeutic technique in certain kinds of psychotherapy (e.g., Gestalt therapy). A therapist may ask his patient to pretend that his mother is present, or that some inanimate object is his mother, and to "talk to her." He may then be asked to "be" the mother, and to say how he feels (when he "is" the mother), how he acts, what he looks like, etc. I will not venture an explanation of how such therapeutic techniques are effective, nor of why simulation games work. But whatever explanation is appropriate will, I suspect, go a long way toward explaining why we are as interested in works of fiction as we are, and clarifying what we get from them. The important place that novels, plays, and films have in our lives appears mysterious only on the supposition that we merely stand outside fictional worlds and look in, pressing our noses against an inviolable barrier. Once our presence within fictional worlds is recognized, suitable explanations seem within reach.

VII

A more immediate benefit of my theory is its capacity to handle puzzles. I conclude with the resolution of two more. First, consider a playgoer who finds happy endings asinine or dull, and hopes that the play he is watching will end tragically. He "wants the heroine to suffer a cruel fate," for only if she does, he thinks, will the play be worth watching. But at the same time he is caught up in the story and "sympathizes with the heroine"; he "wants her to escape." It is obvious that these two apparent desires may perfectly well coexist. Are we to say that the spectator is *torn* between opposite interests, that he wants the heroine to survive and also wants her not to? This does not ring true. Both of the playgoer's "conflicting desires" may be wholehearted. He may hope unreservedly that the work will end with disaster for the heroine, and he may, with equal singlemindedness, "want her to escape such an undeserved fate." Moreover, he may be entirely aware of both "desires," and yet feel no particular conflict between them.

My theory provides a neat explanation. It is merely make-believe that the spectator sympathizes with the heroine and wants her to escape. And he (really) wants it to be make-believe that she suffers a cruel end. He does not have conflicting desires. Nor, for that matter, is it make-believe that he does.

The second puzzle concerns why it is that works last as well as they do, how they can survive multiple readings or viewings without losing their effectiveness.[18]

Suspense of one kind or another is an important ingredient in our experience of most works: Will Jack, of *Jack and the Beanstalk*, succeed in ripping off the giant without being caught? Will Tom and Becky find their way out of the cave? Will Hamlet ever get around to avenging the murder of his father? What is in store for Julius Caesar on the Ides of March? Will Godot come?

But how can there be suspense if we already know how things will turn out? Why, for example, should Tom and Becky's plight concern or even interest a reader who knows, from reading the novel previously, that eventually they will escape from the cave? One might have supposed that, once we have experienced a work often enough to learn thoroughly the relevant features of the plot, it would lose its capacity to create suspense, and that future readings or viewings of it would lack the excitement of the first one. But this frequently is not what happens. *Some* works, to be sure, fade quickly from exposure, and familiarity does alter our experience in certain ways. But the power of many works is remarkably permanent, and the nature of their effectiveness remarkably consistent. In particular, suspense may remain a crucial element in our response to a work almost no matter how familiar we are with it. One may "worry" just as intensely about Tom and Becky while rereading *The Adventures of Tom Sawyer*, despite one's knowledge of the outcome, as would a person reading it for the first time. A child listening to *Jack and the Beanstalk* for the umpteenth time, long after she has memorized it word for word, may feel much the same excitement when the giant discovers Jack and goes after him, the same gripping suspense, that she felt when she first heard the story. Children, far from being bored by familiar stories, often beg to hear the same ones over and over again.

None of this is surprising on my theory. The child hearing *Jack and the Beanstalk* knows that make-believedly Jack will escape, but make-believedly she does *not* know that he will – until the reading of the passage describing his escape. She is engaged in her own game of make-believe during the reading, a game in which make-believedly she learns for the first time about Jack and the giant as she hears about them.[19] It is her make-believe uncertainty (the fact that make-believedly she is uncertain), not any actual uncertainty, that is responsible for the excitement and suspense that she feels. The point of hearing the story is not, or not merely, to learn about Jack's confrontation with the giant, but to play a game of make-believe. One cannot learn, each time one hears the story, what make-believedly Jack and the giant do, unless one always forgets in between times. But one can and does participate each time in a game of make-believe. The point of hearing *Jack and the Beanstalk* is to have the experience of being such that, *make-believedly*, one realizes with trepidation the danger Jack faces, waits breathlessly to see whether the giant will awake, feels sudden terror when he does awake, and finally learns with admiration and relief how Jack chops down the beanstalk, killing the giant.

Why play the same game over and over? In the first place, the game may not be exactly the same each time, even if the readings are the same. On one occasion it may be make-believe that the child is paralyzed by fear for Jack, overwhelmed by the gravity of the situation, and emotionally drained when Jack finally bests the giant. On another occasion it may be make-believe that the child is not very seriously concerned about Jack's safety and that her dominant feelings are admiration for Jack's exploits, the thrill of adventure, and a sense of exhilaration at the final outcome. But even if the game is much the same from reading to reading, one's emotional needs may require the therapy of several or many repetitions.

Notes

1 Chapter 14. Translated by Gerald F. Else (Ann Arbor: The University of Michigan Press, 1967).

2 I examine this barrier in a companion piece to the present paper, "How Remote Are Fictional Worlds from the Real World?," *Journal of Aesthetics and Art Criticism*, 37 (1978–9), pp. 11–23.

3 By "fear" I mean fear for oneself. Obviously a person can be afraid for someone else without believing that he himself is in danger. One must believe that the person for whom one fears is in danger.

4 Charles *might* scream *deliberately*. But insofar as he does, it is probably clear that he is only pretending to take the slime seriously. (See section v.)

5 Charles's responses are *caused* partly by a belief, though not the belief that he is in danger. (See section IV.) This belief is not a *reason* for responding as he does, and it doesn't make it "reasonable," in the relevant sense, to respond in those ways.

6 A "fictional truth" is the fact that a certain proposition is fictional.

7 I have developed the notion of make-believe truths and other ideas presented in this section more fully elsewhere, especially in "Pictures and Make-believe," *Philosophical Review*, LXXXI, 3 (July 1973): 283–319. Cf. also "Are Representations Symbols?," *The Monist*, LVIII, 2 (April 1974): 236–254. I should indicate that, in my view, there are no propositions "about" mere fictions, and hence none that are make-believe. It is make-believe not that Gulliver visited Lilliput, but that a man named "Gulliver" visited a place called "Lilliput." I shall occasionally ignore this point in the interest of simplicity, for example, when I write in section v as though the same slime resides in two different fictional worlds. Compare "How Remote Are Fictional Worlds from the Real World?," *op. cit.*, note 22.

8 From "Everything and Nothing," Borges, *Labyrinths: Selected Stories and Other Writings*, Donald A. Yates and James E. Irby, eds. (New York: New Directions, 1962), p. 248.

9 It is arguable that the purely physiological aspects of quasi-fear, such as the increase of adrenalin in the blood, which Charles could ascertain only by clinical tests, are not part of what makes it make-believe that he is afraid. Thus one might want to understand "quasi-fear" as referring only to the more psychological aspects of Charles's condition: the feelings or sensations that go with increased adrenalin, faster pulse rate, muscular tension, etc.

10 One can't help wondering why Charles's realization that make-believedly he is in danger produces quasi-fear in him, why it brings about a state similar to real fear, even though he knows he is not really in danger. This question is important, but we need not speculate about it here. For now we need only note that Charles's belief does result in quasi-fear, however this fact is to be explained.

11 This, I think, is at least approximately right. It is perhaps equally plausible, however, to say that the fact that Charles *believes* his quasi-fear to be caused by his realization that the slime endangers him is what makes it make-believe that his state is one of fear of the slime. There is no need to choose now between my suggestion and this variant.

12 Observers might, at the same time, understand his behavior alone to be responsible for his make-believe fear. The child and the observers might recognize somewhat different principles of make-believe.

13 These grounds are not conclusive. But the question of whether Charles accepts this principle is especially tricky, and there is reason to doubt that it can be settled conclusively. One would have to determine whether it is Charles's understanding that, if he were to have the quasi-fear sensations, etc., without realizing that he does and hence without

imagining that he is afraid, it would still be fictional that he is afraid. If so, the fictional truth depends not on his imagining but on his quasi-fear, etc. It is hard to decide whether this is Charles's understanding, mainly because it is hard to conceive of his being ignorant of his quasi-fear sensations, etc. But insofar as I can get a grip on the question I think that the answer is affirmative.

14 One important difference between dolls and the screen images is that the dolls generated *de re* make-believe truths about themselves and the images do not. The doll is such that make-believedly it is a baby that is being dressed for a trip to town. But a screen image is not such that make-believedly it (the image itself) is a green slime.

15 Assuming of course that the person realizes that he is dealing with a work of fiction. Even so, arguments are needed to show that such statements are not literally true, and I shall not provide them here. But it is plausible that pity, worry about, hate, and envy are such that one cannot have them without believing that their objects exist, just as one cannot fear something without believing that it threatens one. Yet even if one can, and does, envy a character, for example, it may *also* be make-believe that one does so, and this make-believe truth may be generated by facts of the sort my theory indicates.

16 I have in mind those make-believe truths about her mental state which are generated by what happens on stage. Dickinson is not only a character in the play, but also a spectator. In the latter capacity she is like Charles; her actual mental state generates make-believe truths about herself. Dickinson is in a curiously ambiguous position. But it is not an uncommon one; people frequently have dreams in which they watch themselves ("from the outside") doing things.

17 A good source concerning make-believe games is Jerome L. Singer, *et al.*, *The Child's World of Make-Believe* (New York: Academic Press, 1973).

18 David Lewis pointed out to me the relevance of my theory to this puzzle.

19 It is probably make-believe that someone (the narrator), whose word the child can trust, is giving her a serious report about a confrontation between a boy named "Jack" and a giant. Cf. my "Points of View in Narrative and Depictive Representation," *Noûs*, x, 1 (March 1976): 49–61.

27

The Logical Status of Fictional Discourse

John Searle

I

I believe that speaking or writing in a language consists in performing speech acts of a quite specific kind called "illocutionary acts." These include making statements, asking questions, giving orders, making promises, apologizing, thanking, and so on. I also believe that there is a systematic set of relationships between the meanings of the words and sentences we utter and the illocutionary acts we perform in the utterance of those words and sentences.[1]

Now for anybody who holds such a view the existence of fictional discourse poses a difficult problem. We might put the problem in the form of a paradox: how can it be both the case that words and other elements in a fictional story have their ordinary meanings and yet the rules that attach to those words and other elements and determine their meanings are not complied with: how can it be the case in "Little Red Riding Hood" both that "red" means red and yet that the rules correlating "red" with red are not in force? This is only a preliminary formulation of our question and we shall have to attack the question more vigorously before we can even get a careful formulation of it. Before doing that, however, it is necessary to make a few elementary distinctions.

The distinction between fiction and literature: Some works of fiction are literary works, some are not. Nowadays most works of literature are fictional, but by no means all works of literature are fictional. Most comic books and jokes are examples of fiction but not literature; *In Cold Blood* and *Armies of the Night* qualify as literature but are not fictional. Because most literary works are fictional it is possible to confuse a definition of fiction with a definition of literature, but the existence of examples of fiction which are not literature and of examples of literature which are not fictional is sufficient to demonstrate that this is a mistake. And even if there were no such examples, it would still be a mistake because the concept of literature is a different concept from that of fiction. Thus, for example, "the Bible as literature" indicates a theologically neutral attitude, but "the Bible as fiction" is tendentious.[2]

In what follows I shall attempt to analyze the concept of fiction but not the concept of literature. Actually, in the same sense in which I shall be analyzing fiction, I do not believe it is possible to give an analysis of literature, for three interconnected reasons.

First, there is no trait or set of traits which all works of literature have in common and which could constitute the necessary and sufficient conditions for being a work of literature. Literature, to use Wittgenstein's terminology, is a family-resemblance notion.

Secondly, I believe (though will not attempt to demonstrate here) that "literature" is the name of a set of attitudes we take toward a stretch of discourse, not a name of an internal property of the

John Searle, "The Logical Status of Fictional Discourse," from John Searle, *Expression and Meaning* (Cambridge: Cambridge University Press, 1979), pp. 58–75.

stretch of discourse, though why we take the attitudes we do will of course be at least in part a function of the properties of the discourse and not entirely arbitrary. Roughly speaking, whether or not a work is literature is for the readers to decide, whether or not it is fiction is for the author to decide.

Third, the literary is continuous with the nonliterary. Not only is there no sharp boundary, but there is not much of a boundary at all. Thus Thucydides and Gibbon wrote works of history which we may or may not treat as works of literature. The Sherlock Holmes stories of Conan Doyle are clearly works of fiction, but it is a matter of judgment whether they should be regarded as a part of English literature.

The distinction between fictional speech and figurative speech: It is clear that just as in fictional speech semantic rules are altered or suspended in some way we have yet to analyze, so in figurative speech semantic rules are altered or suspended in some way. But it is equally clear that what happens in fictional speech is quite different from and independent of figures of speech. A metaphor can occur as much in a work of nonfiction as in a work of fiction. Just to have some jargon to work with, let us say that metaphorical uses of expressions are "nonliteral" and fictional utterances are "nonserious." To avoid one obvious sort of misunderstanding, this jargon is not meant to imply that writing a fictional novel or poem is not a serious activity, but rather that, for example, if the author of a novel tells us that it is raining outside he isn't seriously committed to the view that it is at the time of writing actually raining outside. It is in this sense that fiction is nonserious. Some examples: If I now say, "I am writing an article about the concept of fiction," that remark is both serious and literal. If I say, "Hegel is a dead horse on the philosophical market," that remark is serious but nonliteral. If I say, beginning a story, "Once upon a time there lived in a faraway Kingdom a wise King who had a beautiful daughter . . ." that remark is literal but not serious.

The aim of this chapter is to explore the difference between fictional and serious utterances; it is not to explore the difference between figurative and literal utterances, which is another distinction quite independent of the first.

One last remark before we begin the analysis. Every subject matter has its catchphrases to enable us to stop thinking before we have got a solution to our problems. Just as sociologists and others who ponder social change find they can stop themselves from having to think by reciting phrases such as "the revolution of rising expectations," so it is easy to stop thinking about the logical status of fictional discourse if we repeat slogans like "the suspension of disbelief" or expressions like "mimesis." Such notions contain our problem but not its solution. In one sense I want to say precisely that what I do not suspend when I read a serious writer of non-serious illocutions such as Tolstoy or Thomas Mann is disbelief. My disbelief antennae are much more acute for Dostoevsky than they are for the *San Francisco Chronicle*. In another sense I do want to say that I "suspend disbelief," but our problem is to say exactly how and exactly why. Plato, according to one common misinterpretation, thought that fiction consisted of lies. Why would such a view be wrong?

II

Let us begin by comparing two passages chosen at random to illustrate the distinction between fiction and nonfiction. The first, nonfiction, is from the *New York Times* (December 15, 1972), written by Eileen Shanahan:

> Washington, Dec. 14 – A group of federal, state, and local government officials rejected today President Nixon's idea that the federal government provide the financial aid that would permit local governments to reduce property taxes.

The second is from a novel by Iris Murdoch entitled *The Red and the Green*, which begins,

> Ten more glorious days without horses! So thought Second Lieutenant Andrew Chase-White recently commissioned in the distinguished regiment of King Edward's Horse, as he pottered contentedly in a garden on the outskirts of Dublin on a sunny Sunday afternoon in April nineteen-sixteen.[3]

The first thing to notice about both passages is that, with the possible exception of the one word *pottered* in Miss Murdoch's novel, all of the occurrences of the words are quite literal. Both authors are speaking (writing) literally. What then are the differences? Let us begin by considering the passage from the *New York Times*. Miss Shanahan is making an assertion. An assertion is a type of illocutionary act that conforms to certain quite specific semantic and pragmatic rules. These are:

1. The essential rule: the maker of an assertion commits himself to the truth of the expressed proposition.
2. The preparatory rules: the speaker must be in a position to provide evidence or reasons for the truth of the expressed proposition.
3. The expressed proposition must not be obviously true to both the speaker and the hearer in the context of utterance.
4. The sincerity rule: the speaker commits himself to a belief in the truth of the expressed proposition.[4]

Notice that Miss Shanahan is held responsible for complying with all these rules. If she fails to comply with any of them, we shall say that her assertion is defective. If she fails to meet the conditions specified by the rules, we will say that what she said is false or mistaken or wrong, or that she didn't have enough evidence for what she said, or that it was pointless because we all knew it anyhow, or that she was lying because she didn't really believe it. Such are the ways that assertions can characteristically go wrong, when the speaker fails to live up to the standards set by the rules. The rules establish the internal canons of criticism of the utterance.

But now notice that none of these rules apply to the passage from Miss Murdoch. Her utterance is not a commitment to the truth of the proposition that on a sunny Sunday afternoon in April of nineteen-sixteen a recently commissioned lieutenant of an outfit called the King Edward's Horse named Andrew Chase-White pottered in his garden and thought that he was going to have ten more glorious days without horses. Such a proposition may or may not be true, but Miss Murdoch has no commitment whatever as regards its truth. Furthermore, as she is not committed to its truth, she is not committed to being able to provide evidence for its truth. Again, there may or may not be evidence for the truth of such a proposition, and she may or may not have evidence. But all of that is quite irrelevant to her speech act, which does not commit her to the possession of evidence. Again, since there is no commitment to the truth of the proposition there is no question as to whether we are or are not already apprised of its

truth, and she is not held to be insincere if in fact she does not believe for one moment that there actually was such a character thinking about horses that day in Dublin.

Now we come to the crux of our problem: Miss Shanahan is making an assertion, and assertions are defined by the constitutive rules of the activity of asserting; but what kind of illocutionary act can Miss Murdoch be performing? In particular, how can it be an assertion since it complies with none of the rules peculiar to assertions? If, as I have claimed, the meaning of the sentence uttered by Miss Murdoch is determined by the linguistic rules that attach to the elements of the sentence, and if those rules determine that the literal utterance of the sentence is an assertion, and if, as I have been insisting, she is making a literal utterance of the sentence, then surely it must be an assertion; but it can't be an assertion since it does not comply with those rules that are specific to and constitutive of assertions.

Let us begin by considering one wrong answer to our question, an answer which some authors have in fact proposed. According to this answer, Miss Murdoch or any other writer of novels is not performing the illocutionary act of making an assertion but the illocutionary act of telling a story or writing a novel. On this theory, newspaper accounts contain one class of illocutionary acts (statements, assertions, descriptions, explanations) and fictional literature contains another class of illocutionary acts (writing stories, novels, poems, plays, etc.). The writer or speaker of fiction has his own repertoire of illocutionary acts which are on all fours with, but in addition to, the standard illocutionary acts of asking questions, making requests, making promises, giving descriptions, and so on. I believe that this analysis is incorrect; I shall not devote a great deal of space to demonstrating that it is incorrect because I prefer to spend the space on presenting an alternative account, but by way of illustrating its incorrectness I want to mention a serious difficulty which anyone who wished to present such an account would face. In general the illocutionary act (or acts) performed in the utterance of the sentence is a function of the meaning of the sentence. We know, for example, that an utterance of the sentence "John can run the mile" is a performance of one kind of illocutionary act, and that an utterance of the sentence "Can John run the mile?" is a performance of another kind of illocutionary act, because we know that the indicative sentence form means something different from the interrogative sentence form. But now if the sentences in a work of fiction were used to perform some completely different speech acts from those determined by their literal meaning, they would have to have some other meaning. Anyone therefore who wishes to claim that fiction contains different illocutionary acts from nonfiction is committed to the view that words do not have their normal meanings in works of fiction. That view is at least *prima facie* an impossible view since if it were true it would be impossible for anyone to understand a work of fiction without learning a new set of meanings for all the words and other elements contained in the work of fiction, and since any sentence whatever can occur in a work of fiction, in order to have the ability to read any work of fiction, a speaker of the language would have to learn the language all over again, since every sentence in the language would have both a fictional and a nonfictional meaning. I can think of various ways that a defender of the view under consideration might meet these objections, but as they are all as unplausible as the original thesis that fiction contains some wholly new category of illocutionary acts, I shall not pursue them here.

Back to Miss Murdoch. If she is not performing the illocutionary act of writing a novel because there is no such illocutionary act, what exactly is she doing in the quoted passage? The answer seems to me obvious, though not easy to state precisely. She is pretending, one could say, to make an assertion, or acting as if she were making an assertion, or going through the motions of making an assertion, or imitating the making of an assertion. I place no great store by any of these verb phrases, but let us go to work on "pretend," as it is as good as any. When I say that Miss Murdoch is pretending to make an assertion, it is crucial to distinguish two quite different senses of "pretend." In one sense of "pretend," to pretend to be or to do something that one is not doing is to engage in a form of deception, but in the second sense of "pretend," to pretend to do or be something is to engage in a performance which is *as if* one were doing or being the thing and is without any intent to deceive. If I pretend to be Nixon in order to fool the Secret Service into letting me into the White House, I am pretending in the first sense; if I pretend to be Nixon as part of a game of charades, it is pretending in the second sense. Now in the fictional use of words, it is pretending in the second sense which is in question. Miss Murdoch is engaging in a nondeceptive pseudoperformance which constitutes pretending to recount to us a series of events. So

my first conclusion is this: the author of a work of fiction pretends to perform a series of illocutionary acts, normally of the assertive type.[5]

Now *pretend* is an intentional verb: that is, it is one of those verbs which contain the concept of intention built into it. One cannot truly be said to have pretended to do something unless one intended to pretend to do it. So our first conclusion leads immediately to our second conclusion: the identifying criterion for whether or not a text is a work of fiction must of necessity lie in the illocutionary intentions of the author. There is no textual property, syntactical or semantic, that will identify a text as a work of fiction. What makes it a work of fiction is, so to speak, the illocutionary stance that the author takes toward it, and that stance is a matter of the complex illocutionary intentions that the author has when he writes or otherwise composes it.

There used to be a school of literary critics who thought one should not consider the intentions of the author when examining a work of fiction. Perhaps there is some level of intention at which this extraordinary view is plausible; perhaps one should not consider an author's ulterior motives when analyzing his work, but at the most basic level it is absurd to suppose a critic can completely ignore the intentions of the author, since even so much as to identify a text as a novel, a poem, or even as a text is already to make a claim about the author's intentions.

So far I have pointed out that an author of fiction pretends to perform illocutionary acts which he is not in fact performing. But now the question forces itself upon us as to what makes this peculiar form of pretense possible. It is after all an odd, peculiar, and amazing fact about human language that it allows the possibility of fiction at all. Yet we all have no difficulty in recognizing and understanding works of fiction. How is such a thing possible?

In our discussion of Miss Shanahan's passage in the *New York Times*, we specified a set of rules, compliance with which makes her utterance a (sincere and nondefective) assertion. I find it useful to think of these rules as rules correlating words (or sentences) to the world. Think of them as vertical rules that establish connections between language and reality. Now what makes fiction possible, I suggest, is a set of extralinguistic, nonsemantic conventions that break the connection between words and the world established by the rules mentioned earlier. Think of the conventions of fictional discourse as a set of horizontal conventions that break the connections established by the vertical rules. They suspend the normal requirements established by these rules. Such horizontal conventions are not meaning rules; they are not part of the speaker's semantic competence. Accordingly, they do not alter or change the meanings of any of the words or other elements of the language. What they do rather is enable the speaker to use words with their literal meanings without undertaking the commitments that are normally required by those meanings. My third conclusion then is this: the pretended illocutions which constitute a work of fiction are made possible by the existence of a set of conventions which suspend the normal operation of the rules relating illocutionary acts and the world. In this sense, to use Wittgenstein's jargon, telling stories really is a separate language game; to be played it requires a separate set of conventions, though these conventions are not meaning rules; and the language game is not on all fours with illocutionary language games, but is parasitic on them.

This point will perhaps be clearer if we contrast fiction with lies. I think Wittgenstein was wrong when he said that lying is a language game that has to be learned like any other.[6] I think this is mistaken because lying consists in violating one of the regulative rules on the performance of speech acts, and any regulative rule at all contains within it the notion of a violation. Since the rule defines what constitutes a violation, it is not first necessary to learn to follow the rule and then learn a separate practice of breaking the rule. But in contrast, fiction is much more sophisticated than lying. To someone who did not understand the separate conventions of fiction, it would seem that fiction is merely lying. What distinguishes fiction from lies is the existence of a separate set of conventions which enables the author to go through the motions of making statements which he knows to be not true even though he has no intention to deceive.

We have discussed the question of what makes it possible for an author to use words literally and yet not be committed in accordance with the rules that attach to the literal meaning of those words. Any answer to that question forces the next question upon us: what are the mechanisms by which the author invokes the horizontal conventions – what procedures does he follow? If, as I have said, the author does not actually perform illocutionary acts but only pretends to, how is the pretense performed? It is a general feature of the concept of pretending that one can pretend to perform a higher order or complex action by *actually* per-forming lower order or less complex actions which are constitutive parts of the higher order or complex action. Thus, for example, one can pretend to hit someone by actually making the arm and fist movements that are characteristic of hitting someone. The hitting is pretended, but the movement of the arm and fist is real. Similarly, children pretend to drive a stationary car by actually sitting in the driver's seat, moving the steering wheel, pushing the gear shift lever, and so on. The same principle applies to the writing of fiction. The author pretends to perform illocutionary acts by way of actually uttering (writing) sentences. In the terminology of *Speech Acts*, the *illocutionary act* is pretended, but the *utterance act* is real. In Austin's terminology, the author pretends to perform *illocutionary acts* by way of actually performing *phonetic* and *phatic* acts. The utterance acts in fiction are indistinguishable from the utterance acts of serious discourse, and it is for that reason that there is no textual property that will identify a stretch of discourse as a work of fiction. It is the performance of the utterance act with the intention of invoking the horizontal conventions that constitutes the pretended performance of the illocutionary act.

The fourth conclusion of this section, then, is a development of the third: the pretended performances of illocutionary acts which constitute the writing of a work of fiction consist in actually performing utterance acts with the intention of invoking the horizontal conventions that suspend the normal illocutionary commitments of the utterances.

These points will be clearer if we consider two special cases of fiction, first-person narratives and theatrical plays. I have said that in the standard third-person narrative of the type exemplified by Miss Murdoch's novel, the author pretends to perform illocutionary acts. But now consider the following passage from Sherlock Holmes:

> It was in the year '95 that a combination of events, into which I need not enter, caused Mr. Sherlock Holmes and myself to spend some weeks in one of our great university towns, and it was during this time that the small but instructive adventure which I am about to relate befell us.[7]

In this passage Sir Arthur is not simply pretending to make assertions, but he is *pretending to be* John Watson, MD, retired officer of the Afghan campaign making assertions about his friend Sherlock Holmes. That is, in first-person narratives, the author often pretends to be someone else making assertions.

Dramatic texts provide us with an interesting special case of the thesis I have been arguing in this chapter. Here it is not so much the author who is doing the pretending but the characters in the actual performance. That is, the text of the play will consist of some pseudoassertions, but it will for the most part consist of a series of serious directions to the actors as to how they are to pretend to make assertions and to perform other actions. The actor pretends to be someone other than he actually is, and he pretends to perform the speech acts and other acts of that character. The playwright represents the actual and pretended actions and the speeches of the actors, but the playwright's performance in writing the text of the play is rather like writing a recipe for pretense than engaging in a form of pretense itself. A fictional story is a pretended representation of a state of affairs; but a play, that is, a play as performed, is not a pretended *representation* of a state of affairs but the pretended state of affairs itself, the actors pretend *to be* the characters. In that sense the author of the play is not in general pretending to make assertions; he is giving directions as to how to enact a pretense which the actors then follow. Consider the following passage from Galsworthy's *The Silver Box*:

> Act I, Scene I. The curtain rises on the Barthwicks' dining room, large, modern, and well furnished; the window curtains drawn. Electric light is burning. On the large round dining table is set out a tray with whiskey, a syphon, and a silver cigarette box. It is past midnight. A fumbling is heard outside the door. It is opened suddenly; Jack Barthwick seems to fall into the room . . .
>
> Jack: Hello! I've got home all ri—
> (*Defiantly*.)[8]

It is instructive to compare this passage with Miss Murdoch's. Murdoch, I have claimed, tells us a story; in order to do that, she pretends to make a series of assertions about people in Dublin in 1916. What we visualize when we read the passage is a man pottering about his garden thinking about horses. But when Galsworthy writes his play, he does not give us a series of pretended assertions about a play. He gives us a series of directions as to

how things are actually to happen on stage when the play is performed. When we read the passage from Galsworthy we visualize a stage, the curtain rises, the stage is furnished like a dining room, and so on. That is, it seems to me the illocutionary force of the text of a play is like the illocutionary force of a recipe for baking a cake. It is a set of instructions for how to do something, namely, how to perform the play. The element of pretense enters at the level of the performance: the actors pretend to be the members of the Barthwick family doing such-and-such things and having such-and-such feelings.

III

The analysis of the preceding section, if it is correct, should help us to solve some of the traditional puzzles about the ontology of a work of fiction. Suppose I say: "There never existed a Mrs. Sherlock Holmes because Holmes never got married, but there did exist a Mrs. Watson because Watson did get married, though Mrs. Watson died not long after their marriage." Is what I have said true or false, or lacking in truth value, or what? In order to answer we need to distinguish not only between serious discourse and fictional discourse, as I have been doing, but also to distinguish both of these from serious discourse about fiction. Taken as a piece of serious discourse, the above passage is certainly not true because none of these people (Watson, Holmes, Mrs. Watson) ever existed. But taken as a piece of discourse *about* fiction, the above statement is true because it accurately reports the marital histories of the two fictional characters Holmes and Watson. It is not itself a piece of fiction because I am not the author of the works of fiction in question. Holmes and Watson never existed at all, which is not of course to deny that they exist in fiction and can be talked about as such.

Taken as a statement about fiction, the above utterance conforms to the constitutive rules of statement-making. Notice, for example, that I can verify the above statement by reference to the works of Conan Doyle. But there is no question of Conan Doyle being able to verify what he says about Sherlock Holmes and Watson when he writes the stories, because he does not make any statements about them, he only pretends to. Because the author has created these fictional characters, we on the other hand can make true statements about them as fictional characters.

But how is it possible for an author to "create" fictional characters out of thin air, as it were? To answer this let us go back to the passage from Iris Murdoch. The second sentence begins, "So thought Second Lieutenant Andrew Chase-White." Now in this passage Murdoch uses a proper name, a paradigm referring expression. Just as in the whole sentence she pretends to make an assertion, in this passage she pretends to refer (another speech act). One of the conditions on the successful performance of the speech act of reference is that there must exist an object that the speaker is referring to. Thus by pretending to refer she pretends that there is an object to be referred to. To the extent that we share in the pretense, we will also pretend that there is a lieutenant named Andrew Chase-White living in Dublin in 1916. It is the pretended reference which creates the fictional character and the shared pretense which enables us to talk about the character in the manner of the passage about Sherlock Holmes quoted above. The logical structure of all this is complicated, but it is not opaque. By pretending to refer to (and recount the adventures of) a person, Miss Murdoch creates a fictional character. Notice that she does not really refer to a fictional character because there was no such antecedently existing character; rather, by pretending to refer to a person she creates a fictional person. Now once that fictional character has been created, we who are standing outside the fictional story can really refer to a fictional person. Notice that in the passage about Sherlock Holmes above, I really referred to a fictional character (i.e., my utterance satisfies the rules of reference). I did not *pretend* to refer to a real Sherlock Holmes; I *really referred* to the fictional Sherlock Holmes.

Another interesting feature of fictional reference is that normally not all of the references in a work of fiction will be pretended acts of referring; some will be real references as in the passage from Miss Murdoch where she refers to Dublin, or in Sherlock Holmes when Conan Doyle refers to London, or in the passage quoted when he makes a veiled reference to either Oxford or Cambridge but doesn't tell us which ("one of our great university towns"). Most fictional stories contain nonfictional elements: along with the pretended references to Sherlock Holmes and Watson, there are in Sherlock Holmes real references to London and Baker Street and Paddington Station; again, in *War and Peace*, the story of Pierre and Natasha is a fictional story about fictional characters, but the Russia of *War and Peace* is the real Russia, and the war against Napoleon is the real war against the real Napoleon. What is the test for what is fictional and what isn't? The answer is provided by our discussion of the differences between Miss Murdoch's novel and Miss Shanahan's article in the *New York Times*. The test for what the author is committed to is what counts as a mistake. If there never did exist a Nixon, Miss Shanahan (and the rest of us) are mistaken. But if there never did exist an Andrew Chase-White, Miss Murdoch is not mistaken. Again, if Sherlock Holmes and Watson go from Baker Street to Paddington Station by a route which is geographically impossible, we will know that Conan Doyle blundered even though he has not blundered if there never was a veteran of the Afghan campaign answering to the description of John Watson, MD. In part, certain fictional genres are defined by the nonfictional commitments involved in the work of fiction. The difference, say, between naturalistic novels, fairy stories, works of science fiction, and surrealistic stories is in part defined by the extent of the author's commitment to represent actual facts, either specific facts about places like London and Dublin and Russia or general facts about what it is possible for people to do and what the world is like. For example, if Billy Pilgrim makes a trip to the invisible planet Tralfamadore in a microsecond, we can accept that because it is consistent with the science fiction element of *Slaughterhouse Five*, but if we find a text where Sherlock Holmes does the same thing, we will know at the very least that that text is inconsistent with the corpus of the original nine volumes of the Sherlock Holmes stories.

Theorists of literature are prone to make vague remarks about how the author creates a fictional world, a world of the novel, or some such. I think we are now in a position to make sense of those remarks. By pretending to refer to people and to recount events about them, the author creates fictional characters and events. In the case of realistic or naturalistic fiction, the author will refer to real places and events intermingling these references with the fictional references, thus making it possible to treat the fictional story as an extension of our existing knowledge. The author will establish with the reader a set of understandings about how far the horizontal conventions of fiction break the vertical connections of serious speech. To the extent that the author is consistent with the conventions he has invoked or (in the case of revolutionary forms of literature) the conventions he has established, he will remain within the conventions. As far as the *possibility* of the ontology is concerned, anything goes: the author can create any character or event he likes. As far as the *acceptability* of the ontology is concerned, coherence is a crucial consideration. However, there is no universal criterion for coherence: what counts as coherence in a work of science fiction will not count as coherence in a work of naturalism. What counts as coherence will be in part a function of the contract between author and reader about the horizontal conventions.

Sometimes the author of a fictional story will insert utterances in the story which are not fictional and not part of the story. To take a famous example, Tolstoy begins *Anna Karenina* with the sentence "Happy families are all happy in the same way, unhappy families unhappy in their separate, different ways." That, I take it, is not a fictional but a serious utterance. It is a genuine assertion. It is part of the novel but not part of the fictional story. When Nabokov at the beginning of *Ada* deliberately misquotes Tolstoy, saying, "All happy families are more or less dissimilar; all unhappy ones more or less alike," he is indirectly contradicting (and poking fun at) Tolstoy. Both of these are genuine assertions, though Nabokov's is made by an ironic misquotation of Tolstoy. Such examples compel us to make a final distinction, that between a work of fiction and fictional discourse. A work of fiction need not consist entirely of, and in general will not consist entirely of, fictional discourse.

IV

The preceding analysis leaves one crucial question unanswered: why bother? That is, why do we attach such importance and effort to texts which contain largely pretended speech acts? The reader who has followed my argument this far will not be surprised to hear that I do not think there is any simple or even single answer to that question. Part of the answer would have to do with the crucial role, usually underestimated, that imagination plays in human life, and the equally crucial role that shared products of the imagination play in human social life. And one aspect of the role that such products play derives from the fact that serious (i.e. nonfictional) speech acts can be conveyed by fictional texts, even though the conveyed speech act is not represented in the text. Almost any important work of fiction conveys a "message" or "messages" which are conveyed *by* the text but are not *in* the text. Only in such children's stories as contain the concluding "and the moral of the story is ..." or in tiresomely didactic authors such as Tolstoy do we get an explicit representation of the serious speech acts which it is the point (or the main point) of the fictional text to convey. Literary critics have explained on an ad hoc and particularistic basis how the author conveys a serious speech act through the performance of the pretended speech acts which constitute the work of fiction, but there is as yet no general theory of the mechanisms by which such serious illocutionary intentions are conveyed by pretended illocutions.

Notes

1 For an attempt to work out a theory of these relationships, see J. R. Searle, *Speech Acts: An Essay in the Philosophy of Language* (Cambridge: Cambridge University Press, 1969), esp. Chapters 3–5.

2 There are other senses of "fiction" and "literature" which I will be discussing. In one sense "fiction" means falsehood, as in "The defendant's testimony was a tissue of fictions," and in one sense "literature" just means printed matter, as in "The literature on referential opacity is quite extensive."

3 Iris Murdoch, *The Red and the Green* (New York, 1965), p. 3. This and other examples of fiction used in this article were deliberately chosen at random, in the belief that theories of language should be able to deal with any text at all and not just with specially selected examples.

4 For a more thorough exposition of these and similar rules, see Searle (1969), Ch. 3.

5 The assertive class of illocutions includes statements, assertions, descriptions, characterizations, identifications, explanations, and numerous others. For an explanation of this and related notions see John Searle, "A Taxonomy of Illocutionary Acts," in Searle, *Expression and Meaning* (Cambridge: Cambridge University Press, 1979), pp. 1–29.

6 Ludwig Wittgenstein, *Philosophical Investigations*, trans. G. E. M. Anscombe (Oxford: Basil Blackwell, 1953), par. 249.

7 A. Conan Doyle, *The Complete Sherlock Holmes* (Garden City, NY, 1932), II, 596.

8 John Galsworthy, *Representative Plays* (New York, 1924), p. 3.

28

How Can We Fear and Pity Fictions?

Peter Lamarque

I

Desdemona lies innocent and helpless on the bed. Over her towers Othello who pronounces with solemn finality: 'Thou art to die.' The enormity and horror of what is about to happen fills us with anger and dismay. Desdemona pleads for her life. But, ''Tis too late.' Othello has resolved to act and, deaf to his wife's most pitiful pleas, he suffocates and kills her.

As we watch this tragedy unfold, can we truly be described as feeling fear and pity? Are we really *in awe* of Othello's violent jealousy and *moved* by Desdemona's innocent suffering? But how could we be when we know full well that what we are watching is just a play? Such questions have a long history[1] but recent discussion has thrown up a number of puzzling suggestions. It has been argued, for example, that our fear at horror films is only a 'quasi-fear' occurring as part of a 'game of make-believe' that we play with the images on the screen.[2] It has been argued, too, that although our fear and pity might be genuine and quite natural they nevertheless involve 'inconsistency' and 'incoherence'.[3] And different again, it has been argued, in contradiction to Aristotle, that what emotional responses we do have to fiction are not only quite dissimilar from 'real life emotions' but are in no way integral to a proper literary response.[4]

Peter Lamarque, "How Can We Fear and Pity Fictions?" *British Journal of Aesthetics*, 21: 4 (Autumn 1981), pp. 291–304. Reprinted by permission of Oxford University Press.

At the heart of the issue there seems to lie a paradox about beliefs. On the one hand, it is assumed that as reasonably sophisticated adults we are not *taken in* by fiction; that is, we do not believe or come to believe, when knowingly watching a fictional performance, that the depicted sufferings or dangers involve any real suffering or danger. No one is in fact murdered in the performance of *Othello*, just as no one is in fact jealous or innocent. And we know that. On the other hand, we respond often enough with a range of emotions, including fear and pity, that seem to be explicable only on the assumption that we do after all believe there to be real suffering or real danger. For how can we feel fear when we do not believe there to be any danger? How can we feel pity when we do not believe there to be any suffering?

This apparent tension between the beliefs we hold about the nature of fiction and the beliefs needed to explain our responses to fiction seems to threaten at least some common-sense intuitions.[5] But another intuition, I think, tells us that our beliefs about what is real or not fade into the background when we are watching a play. Belief and disbelief do not seem to do justice to the true nature of our attention. Why is this? I suggest that the best way to reconcile our intuitions and get a clearer perspective on the matter is to shift the focus of discussion away from beliefs to the fictions themselves and correspondingly from the emotions to the objects of the emotions. I hope that the paradox of beliefs will disappear when more basic issues on these lines have been sorted out. The central question I shall address is: What are we responding *to* when we fear Othello and pity Desdemona?

Kendall Walton has reminded us of the logical oddities of our relations with fictional characters.[6] For example, we can talk of them affecting us but not, in any straightforward way, of us affecting them. They seem to be able to induce in us sorrow, fear, contempt, delight and embarrassment. But we have no comeback with them. We cannot thank them, congratulate them or frighten them, or help, advise, rescue or warn them. There is a logical gap between us and them and those who think that fiction and reality are inextricably mixed should reflect on just how wide this gap is. Exploring the nature of the gap will be at the heart of this investigation.

Walton points out what looks like an asymmetry between physical and psychological interaction between the real world and fictional worlds. No *physical* interaction across worlds, in either direction, seems to be possible. Within their world, Othello can kill Desdemona and within ours I can kill you, but there is a logical barrier that prevents them from killing us and us from killing them. It looks as if the barrier against *psychological* interaction across worlds is more selective. Can we not be frightened, amused and angered by beings in a fictional world? That of course is the question at issue. Walton advises against accepting any cross-world interaction even in the one-way psychological cases where it seems to occur. His own ingenious suggestion is that when we appear to be psychologically affected by fictional characters this takes place not across worlds but *in a fictional world*. We are not *really* afraid or moved, but only *fictionally* so. The physical symptoms of our emotions, the clammy palms and prickly eyes, indicate merely a 'quasi' emotion in this world. For Walton, to interact in any way with a fictional character we must 'enter' a fictional world.

While I am sympathetic to much of what Walton proposes and heedful of his advice not to accept cross-world interaction if we can help it, I think there is a simpler and less paradoxical way out. Rather than having us enter fictional worlds, which involves problems about just which fictional worlds we can enter and whether we can ever enter the *right* worlds,[7] it seems more satisfactory to have the fictional characters enter our world. Against Walton, then, I will argue that it is *in the real world* that we psychologically interact with them. If this is right then we can, as our intuitions suggested, be really afraid and really moved.

II

How can fictional characters enter our world? What is it in our world that we respond to when we fear Othello and pity Desdemona? My suggestion, which I shall work out in detail, is that fictional characters enter our world in the mundane guise of descriptions (or strictly the senses of descriptions) and become the objects of our emotional responses as mental representations or, as I shall call them, thought-contents characterized by those descriptions. Simply put, the fear and pity we feel for fictions are in fact directed at thoughts in our minds.

First a word about thoughts. Adopting something like Descartes's distinction between the 'formal' reality of a thought and its 'objective' reality, I will distinguish, in my own terms, between thoughts as states of consciousness and thoughts as representations. As states of consciousness, thoughts are individual and unique; they are properties of a person at a time, probably properties of the brain. As representations, thoughts are types; they can be shared and repeated. As such, they are 'intentional' in that they are directed towards an object; they are *of* or *about* something. To avoid confusion in the context of a discussion of fiction it is preferable to talk of the *content* of a thought rather than its *object*. Two thoughts as representations are identical if and only if they have the same content. The content of a thought is identified under some description such that two thoughts have the same content if and only if they are identified under the same description. Identifying descriptions of thought-contents can be of two kinds, which I shall call 'propositional' and 'predicative'. The thought that-the-moon-is-made-of-green-cheese has a content identified under a propositional description, the thought a-piece-of-cheese is identified under a predicative description. By allowing both types of descriptions I intend to admit as thoughts everything we might consider as mental contents, including mental images, imaginings, fantasies, suppositions, and all that Descartes called 'ideas'. It is arguable that epistemologically we have privileged access to our thoughts only as representations, with regard to content-identifying descriptions, not as states of consciousness.[8]

It is important to notice the relations between a thought-content, as here conceived, and truth-value and belief. Strictly speaking, a thought-content, even if identified under a propositional description, is not assessable as true or false. Certainly the very same propositional content could be incorporated in a judgement or assertion and as such have a truth-value.[9] But as an identifying property of a thought the propositional description involves neither judgement nor assertion. For this reason it might be misleading to report the occurrence of a thought by the expression 'A thinks that p' for this would normally be taken to imply that A believes or is willing to affirm that p. In our required sense no such belief or willingness need be present. Having-a-thought-that-p means only being in a mental state characterized by the propositional description that-p. A thought-content is different from a belief. Belief is a psychological attitude held in relation to a propositional content. It is one among many attitudes, including disliking, rejecting, remembering and contemplating, that we might take to the contents of some of our thoughts. This distinction between thought and belief is important in what follows for the thought-contents derived from fictions do not have to be believed to be feared.

Thoughts as representations can be the proper objects of emotional responses such as fear and pity. What is it to be an object of fear? Not everything that we fear exists or is real; we might fear ghosts, Leprechauns or Martians. It is helpful to distinguish between being frightened *of* something and being frightened *by* something. 'A is frightened by X' normally implies the existence of X; it is X that in fact arouses the fear, though it might be unknown to A. 'A is frightened of ø' does not imply the existence of ø, though 'ø' would be one of the descriptions under which A identifies what he is frightened of. What we are frightened *by* I will call the 'real' object of our fear, what we are frightened *of* I will call the 'intentional' object.[10] It is my contention that the real objects of our fear in fictional cases are thoughts. We are frightened *by* thoughts, though we are not frightened *of* thoughts, except in special circumstances. There are parallels with the objects of pity. Our feelings of pity can have real and intentional objects. The real object of our pity, what we are moved *by*, is what arouses our emotion. As with fear, this too can be a thought. The intentional object of our pity will be the direct object of the verb 'pity' and will be identified under some intentional description. We do not pity thoughts: but thoughts can be pitiful and can fill us with pity.

The introduction of thoughts as the real objects of our responses to fiction arises out of our earlier

paradox of belief. It is not meant as a general explanation of intentional objects. Suppose we claim to be frightened of Martians and Martians do not exist. If we believe that they exist then it is no help to introduce *thoughts* of Martians as an attempt to eliminate intentional objects. For the belief itself has already landed us with such objects. But if we do not believe that Martians exist but still claim to find them frightening then the introduction of thoughts as an intermediary has genuine explanatory value. This value stems partly from the independence of thought and belief. We can be frightened by the thought of something without believing that there is anything real corresponding to the content of the thought. At most we must simply believe that the thought is frightening. And that belief raises no paradox in relation to our other beliefs about fiction.

There are further points to be made about being frightened by thoughts.

(1) The propensity of a thought to be frightening is likely to increase in relation to the level of reflection or imaginative involvement that is directed to it. There are two points here: thoughts can differ among themselves with respect to *vividness* and our reflection on thoughts can be graded with respect to *involvement*. Part of what I mean by involvement with a thought is the level of attention we give to it, which can be increased, for example, by bringing to mind accompanying mental images or by 'following through' its consequences. For this reason it is often not so much single thoughts that are frightening (though they might be disturbing or worrying) as thought-clusters. One has to be in the right 'frame of mind' to find a thought frightening and this is partly indicated by a tendency to develop thought-clusters.

(2) I can be frightened by a thought or thought-cluster at a time when I am in no actual danger and do not believe myself to be in danger. I am in no danger at the moment of being mauled by a lion. This is no doubt good reason for saying that it would be absurd and irrational for me at this moment to be afraid of being mauled by a lion. But it is not absurd or irrational, but natural and likely, that I might be frightened here and now by the thought of being mauled, should I bring to mind snarling teeth, thrashing of claws, searing pain, and so on.

(3) It need not be even remotely probable or likely that I will ever face the danger envisaged in a frightening thought, and I need not believe it to be probable. I might find the thought of being

stranded on a distant planet or being a monarch deposed in a military coup frightening without supposing that this will, or even could, happen to me.

(4) The fear associated with a frightening thought is a genuine, not a 'quasi' or fictional fear. This brings us back to Walton for whom, as we have seen, the fears associated with fictions are not real fears. Does anything argued by Walton count against thought-contents evoking real fears? He imagines Charles, who is like you and me watching a horror movie about a terrible green slime.[11] Charles shrieks and clutches his chair as the slime oozes relentlessly towards him, beady eyes rolling. First of all, Walton argues that *because Charles is fully aware that the slime is fictional* we cannot say that he is genuinely afraid. At best Charles is fictionally or make-believedly afraid. The argument here, though, does not affect the fear of a frightening thought; this fear is the real thing. We have seen in points (2) and (3) that we can be frightened by a thought regardless of whether we believe ourselves to be in any danger and regardless of whether we believe the content of the thought to be either true or probable. Walton's argument might establish that Charles is not and cannot be, given his beliefs, afraid *that the slime is threatening him* or *that he is in danger from the slime* but it does not show that he is not frightened. We need to distinguish between Charles's being frightened *by the slime* and his being frightened *by the thought of the slime*. The former presupposes the reality of the slime so it cannot be true; but neither the reality of the slime nor Charles's belief in its reality is presupposed by the latter. The thought of the slime, made vivid by the images on the screen, is a frightening thought for Charles and he is frightened.

The second part of Walton's argument to show that Charles is not genuinely afraid is that he does not manifest the behavioural evidence we would expect from someone who is genuinely afraid of the slime; he does not call the police or warn his friends. Indeed not, for he knows well enough that there is no real slime for the police to investigate. Nevertheless, there might be behavioural evidence that he is frightened by the thought of the slime. He might close his eyes, light a cigarette, and try to bring other things to mind. This surely is a common practice in audiences at horror films. It is a clue, I think, that we are on the right lines in identifying thoughts as the proper objects of our fear of fictions.

My conclusion at this stage of the argument is that mental representations or thought-contents can be the cause of emotions such as fear and pity quite independently of beliefs we might hold about being in personal danger or about the existence of real suffering or pain. This is the first step towards resolving our original paradox of belief.

III

What I must now argue is that when we fear Othello, or the slime, or pity Desdemona our fears and tears are directed at thought-contents. I must also show how these thought-contents are derived from the fictions and thus how the relevant thought-contents can be identified. In general, my claim here will be that the senses of fictional sentences determine and identify the thought-contents to which we react. A further claim will be that the contents of fictional sentences stand to truth and assertion in much the same relation as that of the contents of thoughts to truth and belief. I hope also that a clear understanding of the logic of fictional sentences will provide an explanation of the logical gap that exists between us and fictional worlds.

All that we know about the fictional worlds of novels and stories is derived ultimately from the contents of fictional sentences. What determines whether or not a sentence or description is fictional? We shall not find the defining characteristics among semantic or syntactic properties. The obvious candidates, literal falsity and the presence of non-referring names, are not sufficient, as non-fictional sentences can of course themselves be false and can also fail in reference. A sentence is fictional, I suggest, not in virtue of semantic features of its content but in virtue of pragmatic features of its use. And by 'use' here I mean what some philosophers have called the illocutionary force of its utterance. I will define a fictional use of a sentence in terms of a writer's illocutionary intentions and the conventions of story-telling.[12]

In normal, non-fictional, uses of sentences speakers and writers intend to perform illocutionary acts; that is, they intend to make assertions, give warnings, ask questions and so on. These illocutionary intentions will be satisfied in as much as the accompanying utterances conform to the social and linguistic conventions governing the intended acts. The writer of fiction, or the teller of a tale, has intentions that are parasitic on such illocutionary

Peter Lamarque

intentions. For in a fictional use of a sentence his intention is not to perform an illocutionary act but to *pretend* to perform an illocutionary act. Fiction is essentially a form of pretence, though pretence without intended deception, as in a charade or a child's game. A story-teller pretends to be reporting events that actually happened and the conversations of people who actually exist. That he is not doing so and yet does not intend to deceive is made possible by conventions of story-telling; story-telling is an established human practice.

I shall not develop this theory of fictional use here[13] but I shall draw from it certain consequences which are important for my argument. The theory rests on a distinction between the propositional content of a sentence and the illocutionary intentions with which it is used. Normal illocutionary intentions are suspended in fictional uses of sentences yet the content or sense of a sentence remains unchanged between fictional and non-fictional uses. This partly explains Frege's observation that our concern with fiction focuses on sense and away from truth-value and reference.[14] The writer of fiction does not assert facts, he pretends to assert facts; he does not describe events, he pretends to describe events; he does not refer to people, he pretends to refer to people. Furthermore, because he only pretends to make assertions in fact he makes neither true nor false assertions.

There is a parallel to be drawn between the propositional content of a fictional sentence and the content of a thought as previously described. As such neither is assessable as true or false and just as the latter is distinct from belief so the former is distinct from assertion. But of course the very same contents in other contexts could be asserted, could be assessed for truth-value and could be the object of belief. An analogy might be drawn from tennis. In a practice rally, or knock-up, before a game a player might run through some typical shots, like serves, volleys, half-volleys and so on. As far as the shots are concerned, the only difference between what the player does then and what he does in the game is that the practice shots cannot win or lose points. Likewise the contents of fictional sentences are not part of the assertion game. As with the contents of thoughts, they have no truth-value themselves yet have no intrinsic qualities which distinguish them from the contents of assertions or beliefs which do have truth-values. In a flight of fancy we might think of stories and fictions as a kind of imaginative and intellectual knock-up.

Fictional discourse is not distinguished from other discourse by sense but at least partly by intended reference. Where does that leave fictional characters? Do the names and descriptions in works of fiction make *no* reference? It is helpful to distinguish between reference *within a story* and reference *outside the story* in the real world. What could be more obvious than the observation that *within stories* names like 'Othello' and 'Desdemona', and even 'the slime', secure reference in a quite unexceptional way. One character's referring to another is no more (and no less) problematic than one character's killing another. We might call this *internal reference*. But from an external point of view what, in the world, do we refer to when we refer to a fictional character?

Consider the sentence 'Othello killed Desdemona'. This sentence has a fictional, non-assertive use as well as a non-fictional, assertive use. In circumstances which allow for the appropriate non-deceptive pretence, any speaker can use the sentence fictionally. To do so is in effect to *retell* the story (or part of it), continuing the pretence initiated by the creator of the fiction.[15] Using the conventions of story-telling, the speaker, like the original author before him, is pretending to assert that one person killed another. And like the author he is in fact asserting nothing true or false. He is not playing the assertion game. Similarly, he is not making any actual reference, only pretending to do so. This involves pretending that there are real people who are the objects of the reference. To ask, of such a fictional use, what the names refer to *in the world* would be as out of place as to ask what the score is in a practice rally at tennis.

There is, on the other hand, a non-fictional assertive use of this same sentence where it is used to describe a state of affairs which obtains *within a story*. Here we are not *telling someone a story*, as in the first use; we are *telling someone about a story*. As an assertion, and a candidate for a truth-value, the sentence must be taken as an ellipsis for a longer sentence of the form 'In Shakespeare's play, Othello killed Desdemona'. This sentence is true and can be the content of a genuine, not a pretended, assertion. Nor are the references merely pretended references. What, then, are the referents of the names 'Othello' and 'Desdemona' in this longer sentence?

Here we can appeal again to Frege. We can apply, I suggest, to these fictional contexts his observations about the behaviour of names and descriptions in contexts of the form 'A believes that –'. For prefixes like 'In Shakespeare's play', or Kendall Walton's more general idiom 'It is fictional that', share certain intentional features with 'A believes that'. For example, names and descriptions within the scope of these prefixes resist existential generalization. It does not follow from the fact that it is fictional that Superman can fly through walls that *there is* someone who can fly through walls. Frege suggests that in such contexts names and descriptions refer not to their customary referents but to their customary senses.

In spite of difficulties with Frege's terminology, and in spite of Quinean scepticism on the matter, this suggestion of a shift from reference to sense seems to contain important insights which we should not too readily abandon. It takes into account that a normal referential function is suspended in such contexts but suggests that the reference is not merely 'opaque' but rather has altered its direction; it acknowledges that some substitutions for the singular terms might still be permissible. This seems to point the way to a clearer understanding of external reference to fictions even though in the short run it introduces its own complications. The suggested shift of emphasis towards the *sense* of fictional names and away from their fictional references parallels our earlier emphasis on the sense of fictional sentences and away from their truth-values.

In application to our own case, the Fregean suggestion would be that when we truly assert 'In Shakespeare's play, Othello killed Desdemona' the names 'Othello' and 'Desdemona' refer only to their senses and not to any non-existent referents. That is to say, the reference of a fictional name in a non-fictional use is precisely its sense in a fictional use.

It is not without controversy to talk of the 'sense' of a name but, as the need is all the more pressing in fictional cases, let us at least loosely follow Frege and take the sense of a fictional name to be the 'mode of presentation' of its referent within a story. That is, the sense of the name will be given by those descriptions used in the fiction, or derivable from the fiction, which characterize and identify its internal reference. The sense of the name 'Desdemona', for example, is given by such descriptions as the following: the person who is named 'Desdemona' in Shakespeare's play *Othello*, who loses her handkerchief, who talks innocently to Cassio, who is killed by her jealous husband, and so on. Only the sense of these descriptions survives in the real world, not the reference. Stated baldly,

when Desdemona enters our world she enters not as a person, not as an individual, not even as an imaginary being, but as a complex set of descriptions with their customary senses.

Here, then, we have an explanation of the logical gap between our world and fictional worlds. Fictional, or internal, references are blocked as real-world references either in virtue of occurring as pretended references in fictional uses of sentences or in virtue of occurring within the scope of intensional prefixes such as 'In the play –' which transform fictional references into non-fictional references and thus into senses. Fictional characters as such can never cross these logical barriers. In the fictional world they exist as people, in the real world they exist only as the senses of descriptions. The word 'character' is a convenient, but endlessly confusing, device for talking of senses under the pretence of referring to people. 'Referring to a character' just means *either* pretending, through the conventions of storytelling, to refer to a person, *or* actually referring to descriptions found in, or derivable from, a fiction.[16]

IV

Now we have all the logical apparatus needed to show that when we fear and pity fictional characters our emotions are directed at real, albeit psychological, objects. We do not have to postulate either that the emotions are fictional or that they are directed irrationally at nothing at all. Nor do we have to postulate beliefs which we know to be false in order to explain the emotions. We have, on the one hand, the notion of a thought-content which can be the proper object of emotion. On the other hand, we have the propositional contents of fictional sentences in which, through the mediation of suspended illocutionary intentions or implicit intensional operators, the senses of the fictional names have replaced the fictional references. The final hurdle is to show what relations obtain between the thought-contents in our minds and the propositional contents of the fictions.

What thought-contents must we be responding to for us truly to be said to be fearing Othello or pitying Desdemona? Not any tears are tears for Desdemona, not any thoughts are thoughts about Othello. Strict criteria must be applied to identify the right thoughts and thus the right tears. It is beyond the scope of this paper to spell out these criteria in detail. I can only point to a few considerations which seem to be important.

In general there must be both a *causal* and a *content-based* connection between the thoughts in our minds and the sentences and descriptions in the fiction. A causal connection is needed to rule out the possibility of our responding to descriptions identifying properties which as it happens belong to a fictional character but which have come to our attention from a quite different, even non-fictional, source. Not even tears for the thought of an innocent wife killed by a jealous husband who happens to be a Moor of Venice are *ipso facto* tears for Desdemona. It seems to be a necessary condition that there be a causal route back from the thought to Shakespeare's play. That is, Shakespeare's play must have some explanatory role in accounting for the genesis of the thought.

A causal connection, though, is not sufficient. There must be a closer link as well connecting the senses of Shakespeare's sentences and the thoughts to which we respond. The paradigm connection would be one of *identity of content* where the very propositions or predicates expressed by Shakespeare also identify our thoughts, such that in grasping the sense of his sentences we directly acquire corresponding mental representations identified through his own propositional or predicative descriptions. Such a direct link would be sufficient to secure the appropriate thoughts but is not necessary. More often than not we acquire the relevant thoughts from a combination of our own descriptions and a suitable subset of an author's descriptions.

There are different ways of deviating from this paradigm content-based connection. First of all, suppose we have never read, or even heard, a word of Shakespeare's *Othello* and we come to learn of Desdemona's tragic plight only through a retelling of the story, or part of it, in summary or paraphrase, which perhaps involves none of the descriptions written by Shakespeare. Are our tears then tears for Desdemona? Much of course will depend on the retelling. I think we can say at least this: that if the descriptions are *logically* implied by some relevant descriptions in the play then the thoughts identified via these descriptions would qualify as thoughts *about Desdemona*.

However, we can go further than that, for much that we believe to be fictionally true about Desdemona will not be derived directly either from the sense of Shakespeare's sentences or from the sense of sentences logically implied by those

sentences. For we read fictional prose, or poetry, against an intellectual and imaginative background and much that we call understanding a fiction involves supplementing the sentences in the fiction with information drawn from this background. So the imaginative reconstruction that readers, or producers, put on the events and personalities leading up to Desdemona's death might issue in mental representations far different from those directly, or logically, related to the propositional contents of the fictional sentences. Yet these divergences might be licensed through looser forms of implication arising from conventions governing the reading of fiction. There is no denying a genuine indeterminacy in some of our claims to be responding to *particular* fictional characters and events. At these more distant reaches from the paradigm, no simple formula can settle the question whether our fear and pity are for Shakespeare's Othello and Desdemona or merely for some imaginative constructs of our own. But our concern here is only to show how these responses are possible. On the view proposed, the question now becomes whether we are responding to thoughts identifiable under descriptions *appropriately derived* from those offered in the play. The connection back to the original sentences must be maintained. I shall not attempt to specify criteria for the appropriate supplementation of fictions;[17] in practice, it is a matter that can call for acute critical sensitivity, as can the detailed unravelling of the senses of some fictional sentences. In general, though, we can say that we are responding to a fictional character if we are responding to thoughts, with the required causal history, which are identified through the descriptive or propositional content *either* of sentences in the fiction *or* of sentences logically derived from the fiction *or* of sentences supplementing the sentences of the fiction in appropriate ways.

It is worth noting that there is of course a higher-order supplementation of fiction in the form of literary interpretation. Literary interpretation is concerned with the aesthetic significance of the content of fictional sentences. It might be that the higher-order descriptions occurring in interpretations – as when we say, for example, that *Othello* is about Machiavellian sophistication and the destruction of innocence – could themselves give rise to thought-contents which in turn evince further emotions. Our responses at this level are important but should not be allowed to obscure our responses at a more basic and more particular level.[18]

V

My conclusion, then, is simple: when we respond emotionally to fictional characters we are responding to mental representations or thought-contents identifiable through descriptions derived in suitable ways from the propositional contents of fictional sentences. I think this conclusion, given the arguments leading up to it, affords explanations of a number of puzzling features of fictions. It shows, for example, how we can know something is fictional but still take it seriously without having to believe or even half-believe it. We can reflect on, and be moved by, a thought independently of accepting it as true. This in turn accounts for the intuition that belief and disbelief stay in the background when we are engaged with fiction. It explains any apparent dissimilarity between our emotional responses to fiction and 'real life emotions'. Although, indeed, we do not react to the killing of Desdemona as we would to a real killing before our eyes, we do react much as we would to the thought of a real killing. The thought and the emotion *are* real. Also, although it incorporates a *de dicto* account of fictional characters, it acknowledges the pull of *de re* accounts; fictions comprise sets of ideas, many having correlates in reality, and these ideas invite an imaginative supplementation and exploration. In connection with fictional characters this 'filling in' process is not unlike that of *coming to know another human being*. Further, it explains the logical asymmetry in our psychological interactions with fictional characters, why we can fear them but not rebuke them, admire them but not advise them; their transformation into mental representations determines these constraints.

We can push the conclusion a bit further and use it to explain why our responses to fictional characters are so closely bound up with our responses to the whole work in which they appear. The answer lies partly in the shift from reference to sense in fictional names. It is not just that *someone* is killed by a jealous husband that gives the emotive power to *Othello* but that the description of the killing is connected in a quite particular way with a great number of other descriptions in the play, including those of Desdemona. The cluster of descriptions that give sense to the name 'Desdemona' will tend to issue in just those clusters of thoughts which I earlier suggested can increase our involvement with a thought and thus the intensity of our response to it. I think, finally, this point opens up a whole new area of interest where we see the structural ordering of language in a literary work as determining the ordering of thoughts in a reader. Much of the value of literature, I suggest, both aesthetic and cognitive, lies in its power to create complex structures of thought in our minds.[19]

Notes

1 For an interesting discussion from the eighteenth century see Samuel Johnson, Preface to *The Plays of William Shakespeare* (1765) and William Kenrick, Review of Dr. Johnson's edition in *Monthly Review* Vol. 33 (1765). Both are reprinted in Brian Vickers, ed., *Shakespeare: The Critical Heritage* (London, 1979) Vol. 5, 1765–1774, see in particular pp. 70–1, 189f.

2 Kendall L. Walton, 'Fearing Fictions', *The Journal of Philosophy* Vol. 75 (1978) (hereafter: Walton, op. cit., I). [See also this volume.]

3 Colin Radford, 'How Can We Be Moved By the Fate of Anna Karenina?' *Proceedings of the Aristotelian Society* Suppl. Vol. 69 (1975) [See also this volume]; Colin Radford, 'Tears and Fiction: a Reply to Weston', *Philosophy* Vol. 52 (1977).

4 Stein Haugom Olsen, *The Structure of Literary Understanding* (Cambridge, 1978), Ch. 2.

5 Eva Shaper, in 'Fiction and the Suspension of Disbelief', *The British Journal of Aesthetics* Vol. 18 (1978), offers a detailed analysis of the relation between these two sets of beliefs and argues that, far from being contradictory, one set, when properly understood, can be seen to *presuppose* the other set. Some criticisms of this view appear in B. J. Rosebury, 'Fiction, Emotion and "Belief": A Reply to Eva Shaper', *The British Journal of Aesthetics* Vol. 19 (1979). The present discussion is meant more to supplement than to arbitrate this debate.

6 Kendall L. Walton, 'How Remote are Fictional Worlds from the Real World?' *The Journal of Aesthetics and Art Criticism* Vol. 37 (1978); also Walton op. cit., I.

7 See Robert Howell, 'Fictional Objects: How They Are And How They Aren't', *Poetics* Vol. 8 (1979), who raises difficulties for Walton's account along these lines.

8 For a discussion of related points, see Daniel Dennett. 'On the Absence of Phenomenology', in D. F. Gustafson & B. L. Tapscott. eds., *Body, Mind, and Method* (Dordrecht, 1979).

9 The notion of 'propositional content' here comes from J. R. Searle, *Speech Acts* (Cambridge, 1969), Ch. 2. 4; also see J. R. Searle, 'What is an Intentional State?' *Mind* Vol. 88 (1979).

10 The account of 'intentional object' here is similar to that in G. E. M. Anscombe, 'The Intentionality of Sensation: A Grammatical Feature', in R. J. Butler, ed., *Analytical Philosophy* (1965), 2nd series.

11 Walton, op. cit., I.

12 Here I follow J. R. Searle, 'The Logical Status of Fictional Discourse', *New Literary History* Vol. 6 (1975), reprinted in J. R. Searle, *Expression and Meaning* (Cambridge, 1979).

13 Apart from Searle, ibid., other similar speech act accounts can be found in: e.g., Richard M. Gale, 'The Fictive Use of Language', *Philosophy* Vol. 46 (1971); Richard Ohmann, 'Speech Acts and the Definition of Literature', *Philosophy and Rhetoric* Vol. 4 (1974); Marcia M. Eaton, 'Liars, Ranters and Dramatic Speakers', in B. J. Tilghman, ed., *Language and Aesthetics* (1973); M. C. Beardsley, 'The Concept of Literature', in F. Brady, J. Palmer & M. Price, *Literary Theory and Structure* (1973).

14 Gottlob Frege, 'On Sense and Reference', *Philosophical Writings of Gottlob Frege*, trans. and edited by P. Geach and M. Black (1952), p. 63.

15 What determines whether it is the *same* story as the original will depend on the *sense* of the names, as explained later in Section III.

16 For interesting discussions of the logic of fictional characters, see Marcia M. Eaton, 'On Being a Character', *The British Journal of Aesthetics* Vol. 16 (1976); D. E. B. Pollard, 'On Talk "About" Characters', *The British Journal of Aesthetics* Vol. 16 (1976).

17 A criterion based on procedures for counterfactual reasoning is offered by David Lewis in 'Truth in Fiction', *American Philosophical Quarterly* Vol. 15 (1978).

18 M. Weston, 'How Can We Be Moved By the Fate of Anna Karenina?' *Proceedings of the Aristotelian Society* Suppl. Vol. 69 (1975) [see also this volume] has been criticized in both C. Radford, 'Tears and Fiction: A Reply to Weston', *Philosophy* Vol. 52 (1977) and B. Paskins, 'On Being Moved by Anna Karenina and *Anna Karenina*', *Philosophy* Vol. 52 (1977) for trying to account for our responses at a thematic level. But the specificness of the responses looked for by Radford and Paskins is obtained on the present account.

19 The topic continues to generate considerable interest. Since writing and submitting this paper, four other articles, recently published on the same topic, have come to my attention: Jerry L. Guthrie, 'Self-Deception and Emotional Response to Fiction', *The British Journal of Aesthetics* Vol. 21, No. 1, (1981); David Novitz, 'Fiction, Imagination and Emotion', *The Journal of Aesthetics and Art Criticism* Vol. 38 (1980); H. O. Mounce, 'Art and Real Life', *Philosophy* Vol. 55 (1980); and Harold Skulsky, 'On Being Moved by Fiction', *The Journal of Aesthetics and Art Criticism* Vol. 39 (1980). Guthrie sees a close connection between the problem of self-deception and the problem of emotional response to fiction. He does not commit himself to any one solution to these problems but makes the interesting suggestion that we might view self-deception as an 'art form' where 'the self-deceiver becomes fictional'. The present article might provide a further context for exploring this suggestion, perhaps in terms of forming mental representations of oneself. Novitz and Mounce both agree that we can be genuinely moved by fiction. Novitz sees the explanation of this as rooted in the idea of 'imaginative response'; 'an imaginative response to fiction can generate beliefs about fictional events which are capable of moving us'. Mounce sees the solution rooted in a 'simple and obvious fact about human reaction' that 'like objects evoke like reactions'. Neither writer, though, takes the further step of explaining just what a fictional character is, such that it can become an object of emotion. Skulsky, on the other hand, who shares the intuition that there are genuine emotional responses to fiction, offers a detailed account of what it is to hold a belief about a fictional character or event; on his view, the belief to which we respond is a 'modal belief' about a set of possible worlds at which certain individual concepts are instantiated. Despite the difference of idiom, there is a great deal of common ground between Skulsky's view and that of the present article.

29

On the Cognitive Triviality of Art

Jerome Stolnitz

Already in Hesiod, the founding document of Western aesthetics, the poet is said to speak truths, and yet already here, for the first, not the last time, the cognitivist affirmation is qualified or warped, by the Muses previously telling the shepherd that they impart to him lies that only seem like truth.[1] Plato had his own use for 'lies' or 'fictions', but he did not hesitate to charge the poets with truths or truth-claims about the gods or how to wage warfare.[2] So far as one can characterize the vast, succeeding literature, the cognitivists have predominated against the sceptics, though we must always bear in mind their profound intra-mural differences over the nature of artistic truth, the vehicles of embodying and communicating such truths, and indeed the appropriate and therefore unorthodox meaning of 'truth'. Not only acknowledging but insisting upon these departures from a staple correspondence theory, they disparage Plato's obtuse literalism. Their celebrations of the distinctive nature of artistic truth have frequently been resonantly uplifting, though it will not be disputed that they have been almost as often manifestly vague and sometimes, one fears, quite gaseous.

Now, or any other time, is a good time to reconsider the issue. Further, should my argument for the cognitive triviality of fine art pass muster, it will go some way to explain why art's influence on social structure and historical change has been fairly

Jerome Stolnitz, "On the Cognitive Triviality of Art," *British Journal of Aesthetics*, 32: 3 (July 1992), pp. 191–200. Reprinted by permission of Oxford University Press.

inconsequential.[3] It may also afford a less hieratic defence of the currently popular view that the work of art has no reference beyond itself.

It is prudent to approach so volatile a concept as 'artistic truth' by identifying truths that are, by contrast, beyond dispute. Scientific truths, for one. We have a relatively clear and firm conception of how science arrives at its truths. It will be protested that the once unquestioned belief in 'scientific method' has recently been brought under fire and rejected. It continues to dominate the scientific community, however, and is still espoused by more traditionalist philosophers of science. In any event, both this conception and its challengers occupy positions of shared, partisan agreement within philosophy of science. But a 'method of artistic truth' is not matter for debate and hardly makes sense. Secondly, scientific truths, once arrived at, are truths about the great world. Evidence, in the face of recent philosophers of science, is to be found in those who have thought so and continue to think so – scientists, many other philosophers of science, and in those humans in all the continents who, because of its successes, like no other way of knowing, have turned to science to control their environments and improve their lives. Philosophers' theories have little force against the palpable reduction in infant mortality and increase in longevity. Do the arts give us truths about the great world? This question we take up presently. Short of that discussion, we can give clear instances of scientific truth, the inverse square law, for example. But art?

History, for all its ignorance, disagreements, biases and falsifications, has, unearthing documents, artefacts, and other evidence, attained undoubted truths about man's past, e.g., Caesar was assassinated in 44 BC.

A vast number of other truths about the great world have been gained by all human beings, not by any method, but simply by living and learning, e.g., Summer is warmer than Winter.

The models of science and history are relaxed even further if we turn to religious truths. Though talk of 'method' is again inappropriate, there are a number of putative ways of knowing, such as revelation and priestly authority. The second criterion is the rub, since there is weighty reason to doubt that religious beliefs are indisputably true of the great world. But though your materialist will deny the truth and may question the meaningfulness of 'Man is the creature of God', he will unhesitatingly accept that it is a recognizably religious truth-claim. The devout have sometimes thought to contend with such scepticism by abandoning 'truth' as unfitted to and even unworthy of their beliefs. The articles of faith are beyond 'truth', even beyond logical consistency, and though they are not amenable to the verification of scientific or historical truth, are more precious. They give 'wisdom'.

We may now be nearing a model more congenial to artistic truth. For where is it written, save in Philistia, that artistic truth must be subject to the same criteria as are satisfied by such prosaic truths as the inverse square law and the date of Caesar's assassination? This importunate demand will not be countenanced by those theorists who contend that the truths conveyed by art can be achieved in no other way. Artistic truths are truths broad and deep, too acute and suggestive, perhaps too tremulous, to be caught in the grosser nets of science, history, or garden variety experience, but no worse, indeed, all the better for that. But then they are also unlike religious truth-claims, being less doctrinaire, less parochial – freer. Did not Freud take more seriously the poets and novelists than virtually all of the academic psychology written up to his time?[4]

Thus urged, we go on to look for other reasons why artistic truth is *sui generis* and so to a linguistic oddity, or several such. Philosophers, critics, and others speak often enough of artistic truth. Considerably less often do they speak of artistic knowledge. How should there be truth without knowledge? We have scientific truth and scientific knowledge, historical truth and historical knowledge. Understandably, for once truth has been established as that and therefore accepted by a judging mind, it is knowledge. Why do we hear so little of artistic knowledge? In religion, there are, in part because of the uncertainties remarked a moment ago, recurrent references to the state of mind of the believer – *Credo quia impossibile*, 'I know that my Redeemer liveth', etc. There are, the phrase attests, religious believers; there are those who believe the findings of science and those who distrust them, those who accept history and those who think it 'bunk'. Whereas we have never heard of artistic believers. Why not? What would they believe, if they existed? There are also those who believe *in* science, in its capacity to yield more truths in future; so, similarly, those who believe in history and religion. Theorists aside, where are their counterparts in the arts? (There are certainly those who 'believe in' art in the sense of 'esteem highly' or 'take very seriously'.) Thus artistic truth moves still further away from religious truth as well as the other kinds of truth-*cum*-knowledge.

It is time now to consider some likely candidates for artistic truth. The Muses and their followers hold that truth is found in all the arts, including music, but novels and plays are in general closer than any of the others to the great world, the actualities of man in society. A comedy of manners, renowned for its deft psychological insights and thus propitious, gives us:

Stubborn pride and ignorant prejudice keep apart two attractive people living in Hertfordshire in Regency England.

This is, as far as it goes, a summary, reasonably accurate and thus true, of the story, of the fiction. So this is not what we want. Those who espouse artistic truth are not after the fiction. They will not, consequently, settle for other truths, of which there are a great many, about Elizabeth Bennet and Mr Darcy. They have much bigger game in mind – the truths that are, in some manner, created by the fiction – and so therefore do we. 'Lies like truth' might be fictions so plausible that the audience takes them to be truths. But neither are the cognitivists after *als ob* truths. Many of them have insisted that art brings to light, above all, human character – the hidden, unvoiced, perhaps, apart from art, the unknown impulses and affects that stir and move our inner and then outer beings. They will settle for nothing less than psychological truths about people in the great world, truths universal, more or less; nor, therefore, will we.

Hence: Stubborn pride and ignorant prejudice keep attractive people apart.

We are compelled to abandon the setting of the novel in order to arrive at psychological truth. Yet in abandoning Hertfordshire in Regency England, we give up the manners and morals that influenced the sayings and doings of the hero and heroine. A greater influence is that of their personal relationships to other characters – the feather-brained family members, the ne'er-do-well soldiers and priggish parsons. Their motivations and behaviour respond to and are thus largely shaped by these other people, fictional all, and to each other, of course, fictional too. These interactions are integral to the finely detailed delineation of their characters which is, the critics are as one in holding, a major ground of the novel's excellence. Finally, we abandon their individuality in all of its complexity and depth. My statement of the psychological truth to be gained from the novel is pitifully meagre by contrast. Necessarily, since the psychologies of Miss Bennet and Mr Darcy are fleshed out and specified within the fiction only. Once we divest ourselves of the diverse, singular forces at work in its psychological field, as we must, in getting from the fiction to the truth, the latter must seem, and is, distressingly impoverished.

Can this be all there is? From one of the world's great novels?

Think of the infinitely more detailed and determinate exfoliations of the psychologies of Miss Bennet and Mr Darcy that have been carried out by literary critics. Think, if you will, of the countless critiques of other novels and plays that have revealed the motivations and feelings of their characters with a subtlety and refinement to which a good deal of academic psychology hardly aspires. These critiques enthusiastically promise and would deliver the deepest truths of human nature. They presuppose and endorse artistic cognitivism. They become the subjects of vigorous study and lively debate within literary criticism. Then think, finally, that they do all this without so much as creating a ripple extra-murally, in professional psychology or anywhere else.

None the less, my formulation of this novel's truth may well be unduly skimpy and it is a mistake, for anyone, of any persuasion, to generalize from a single case. Let us therefore move to more stable ground, Greek tragedy, which, since Aristotle, a grandsire of cognitivism, has been put forth as stellar evidence of its soundness. Thus the familiar:

His *hybris* destroys the tragic hero.

Hybris is not best translated 'pride' but rather 'overweening arrogance'. There are knottier problems in deciding what the psychological truth-claim asserts exactly. We identify the tragic hero just by reading the tragedy. How shall we identify the tragic hero in a sense of 'tragic' that is not tied to the dramatic form? Possibly something like 'a great man in history, not wholly evil, who is suddenly brought low' will do. Alcibiades? Bismarck? Sir Winston? This raises the larger problem, endemic to all derivations of truth from literature, that of quantification. The initial statements refer to Miss Bennet and Mr Darcy, or Ajax and Creon. Do the statements of psychological truth refer to all or most or a few of the flesh-and-blood beings they designate? How can we know? The drama or novel will not tell us. Praises of its 'universality' must do more than beg the question or blur it. The difficulty is complicated in the instant case because *hybris*, to the Greeks, was inevitably destructive. Should we be sceptical of divine retribution, we would put it, '*Hybris* may destroy . . .'. All these tergiversations, tedious, but unavoidable and thus instructive, finally yield:

His *hybris* must destroy/may destroy a great man in history [some great men?] [all great men?] who . . . .

A messy statement, which is not its chief weakness. A biographer of Napoleon might use it, tidied up, as a classical tag, to add some tone to his prose. It would be little more than a tag. He explains the hero's downfall by the Continental System and the invasion of Russia. These might be taken to be acts of *hybris* or they might be described as strategic miscalculations or in yet other ways. Any more strict application of the literary model would be profoundly misleading. The compactness and lucidity of the Greek tragedies make out sharply the predominance of *hybris* in the behaviour of Ajax and Creon, and its consequences in their madness or misery. Was *hybris*, as in the dramas, the sole cause or the primary cause of Napoleon's downfall? Can we ever achieve, have we ever achieved, the same tightly knit, luminous concatenation of character, action, and consequence concerning a historical figure that the tragedy brilliantly achieves in the epiphanic two hours of its life, and its hero's? Given that his over-reaching contributed, in some measure, to Napoleon's downfall, did it play the same role as in the tragedies? The contingencies of the great world, the British bulldog, intestinal troubles, and Blücher's late arrival, leave behind the fictions and the inevitability of their unfolding. What remains of the truth(s) inferred from classical tragedy? We might as well settle for 'Pride goeth before a fall'. For such rewards, who needs great art?

Oedipus Tyrannus has been, since Aristotle, among the best evidence for those who think that tragedy teaches us about life. Now we are spared the tedium of formulating its truth because the play itself announces it. The Chorus, anguished by the calamities it has witnessed, would redeem some meaning from them:

'I will call no mortal happy . . . Till . . . all his hours have passed away'.[5] For life can suddenly afflict any man, even at times of his happy prosperity. (The author of an autobiography I happen to be reading learned early that 'unexpected things happen in life, one never knows what will happen'.[6]) There are numerous other truths gleaned from *Oedipus* by literary critics and scholars. A thoughtful and informed study of the play arrives briefly, at one point, at its universal truth:

> In Oedipus' extreme case we recognize our common case, in which action and understanding never entirely cohere. . . . Oedipus' fate opens our eyes to the gaps between being and doing and understanding.[7]

Oedipus certainly acted without understanding and came to realize it. So have we all, much of the time. It is less certain that those who have read the play – leave out those who have never heard of *Oedipus Tyrannus* – had not previously learned this truth, at the cost of their own less dramatic pain.

We have been trafficking in banalities but only so can the large sagacities dear to cognitivism be put to rest. The truths disclosed or suggested by art now resemble less religious truths. They come more and more to resemble garden variety truths. They are, indeed, in other respects, even flimsier.

There are contradictions within science, history, and religion – the nature of light, that Germany was solely responsible for the Great War, the Trinity. The contradictions are acknowledged. Then efforts are made to overcome them or else, in religion, they are, with some difficulty, absorbed by faith. The quotidian saws, 'Look before you leap' and 'He who hesitates is lost' might be thought, by some pedantic person, to contradict each other. Even he will not think that another well-known truth from *Oedipus*, Man can never control his fate, and

I am the master of my fate,
I am the captain of my soul,

contradict each other. The words are formal contradictories. The utterances are so distinct, so discrete, come from universes of discourse so unrelated to each other, that it would be silliness worse than pedantry to make the logical point. We may contrast the truths derived from works of literature. We never say that they are terms in a contradiction. How should there be truth without the possibility of contradiction?

The possibility of contradiction and the necessity of confirmation. There are organized bodies of evidence that confirm or go to confirm the inverse square law, the date of Caesar's assassination, that man is created by God. We could also adduce meteorological data to establish that Summer is warmer than Winter, though this is not how people gain this truth. They do so by living and learning. Art, uniquely, never confirms its truths. If we find that stubborn pride and ignorant prejudice sometimes keep attractive men and women apart, we find the evidence for this truth about the great world in the great world. The fiction does not and cannot provide the evidence. Mr and Mrs Darcy would doubtless be more than willing to confirm the truth but they are, alas, unable to do so.

Bleak House is the source of a truth more easily elicited and, because it is much less ambitious, much more exact than those we have previously considered: Estate litigation in the Court of Chancery in mid-nineteenth-century England moved very slowly.

This statement affirms that there was a Court of Chancery in London at the time of which the novel speaks. There was, but not because the novel says so. We have other, necessary and sufficient reasons. If we do not accept the existence of the Court of Chancery despite the novel's sometimes realistic description, we surely do not accept what the novel alleges about the pace of estate litigation despite its vivid, humorous, and touching account of Jarndyce and Jarndyce. The author knew this. From his Preface to the novel: '. . . everything set forth in these pages concerning the Court of Chancery is substantially true, and within the truth'. He points to cases of record which equal or exceed in notoriety that of Jarndyce and assures the reader that 'If I wanted other authorities for JARNDYCE and JARNDYCE, I could rain them on these pages'.[8]

By curious coincidence, it was in the same year, 1853, that Harriet Beecher Stowe did just the same thing. Beecher Stowe, indeed, went Dickens something better, since she devoted an entire book of several hundred pages to confirming documentation. Her novel's description of slavery, published a year earlier, had been found powerfully persuasive by a large audience, though other readers were incredulous. The fiction was not enough. The fiction had to be shown to be true, a constraint not peculiar to mid-nineteenth-century novels in English: 'It is *treated* as a reality [by the public] and therefore as a reality it may be proper that it should be defended'. Thus: *A Key to Uncle Tom's Cabin; presenting the original facts and documents upon which the story is founded. Together with corroborative statements verifying the truth of the work.*[9]

In both instances, the truth was knowable and known before the fictions appeared.

In science, history, and religion, confirmation of a statement also counts as evidence for other, logically related statements. Thus truths, notably in the cumulative advances of science, support and build on each other. Out of them and epistemic auxiliaries, theories are constructed. There are no theories, strictly, in garden variety cognition. Even there, however, truths attach themselves to other truths and make up crudely defined but substantial nodes of knowledge. That Summer is warmer than Winter is built up from small experiences and sustains a host of related beliefs concerning dress, festivals, and other behaviours appropriate to each. Art is unlike any of these kinds of knowing. The truth derived from one work of art never confirms that derived from another work of art, though the truths are related to or resemble one another, not even if they should be identical. They are truths about the great world. Yet who has ever said or thought that *Antigone* confirms *Ajax*, though they are both Greek tragedies, by the same dramatist? Hardy does not confirm *Oedipus* any more than *Invictus* refutes it. The very speculation is silly, though remarking that it is is, again, instructive.

Science, history, and religion deal with a certain sector or stratum of reality or, alternatively, reality viewed from a certain perspective. These studies are carried on by specialists, who are knowledgeable and possess unusual abilities of thought and research. Garden variety knowledge is made up chiefly of truths not reserved to any one field of study, e.g., Summer is warmer than Winter, parents

love their children. There are no specialists because almost anyone can learn these truths.

Art is quite extraordinary. It enters upon each of the above sectors of knowledge and any and all others besides. Its truths range from expansive pronouncements on man's fate to middle-sized assertions about the workings of pride in human nature to small-scale accounts of one period in the history of an English court. It is replete with epigrammatic observations hardly distinguishable from folk sayings. Like Terence's busybody, nothing human is alien to it, nor anything non-human either. It now falls out why there was, when we began, no trouble in finding clear cases of scientific, historical, religious, and garden variety truths, whereas no clear examples of artistic truth came to mind. None of its truths are peculiar to art. All are proper to some extra-artistic sphere of the great world. So considered, there are no artistic truths. Not one.

The metaphysicians and theologians have mulled over man's freedom from fate, the psychologists have studied pride along with other traits of character, the legal historians examine the cases to which Dickens only alludes in his Preface, the legal issues involved, and other cases as well. They have done so in elaborating complex theories of human destiny or human nature, or the centuries-long history of the Court, perhaps of the English judicial system. The metaphysician does not have to spend a good deal of his time, indeed most of his time, trying to find the cause of the plague on Thebes; there is no diverting dialogue of featherbrained family members or priggish parsons in the psychological studies, or any sub-plots or irrelevant though funny characters in the legal history.

Because novels and plays do spend most of their time on these other matters, the truths elicited from them are generally tangential, inchoate, vague, which may explain, in part, why they often seem to enjoy a weight of suggestiveness greater than they are entitled to. Such truths do not require specialists. The artist may chance to have first-hand knowledge – Dickens was a law reporter; most often, as Plato, an arch-cognitivist, complained, he does not. But it is not by virtue of such knowledge that he is an artist. And even when such knowledge shapes the work of art, it is not, we have seen, the work of art that confirms. We may see why, for all the talk of artistic truth, there has been fairly little talk of artistic knowledge.

The immediate exception to the foregoing conclusions would be knowledge of art itself, which is another sector of the great world. Art might speak authoritatively in dealing with art. There are, of course, distinctive truths *about* art. They are mostly amassed by art historians, musicologists, etc., who are not, it is sometimes deplored, themselves artists. A work of art may suggest truths or truth-claims concerning art. But these are assertions, once they have been disengaged, that fall within the philosophy or, perhaps more usually, the psychology or sociology of art. Then they are taken over, if they have not already been arrived at independently, by the specialists who, as before, specify, expand and, where possible, confirm them. There are also works of art, probably too many in recent decades, that insinuate or trumpet truths about themselves.

The remoteness of artistic truth even from garden variety knowledge is more apparent than ever. There are no specialists either in art or garden variety knowing because none are needed. In everyday cognition, however, experiences available to all support relatively well-founded truths. There, too, these truths merge into bodies of knowledge. So as one can believe and believe in science and other ways of knowing, one accepts the deliverances of ordinary experience and trusts to them in the future. 'That's just common sense', we say in knockdown tones; 'that's just art' bears a quite different intonation. There are no 'artistic believers' or people who 'believe in art'.

Finally, take the artistic truth that has as good a claim as any to be a breakthrough, a disclosure not previously known to science. The statement wrested from the novel is, once more, hopelessly unwieldy:

The criminal [some criminals?] [all criminals?] [criminals in St Petersburg?] [criminals who kill old moneylenders?] [criminals who kill old moneylenders and come under the influence of saintly prostitutes?] desires to be caught and punished.

It happens that the artist has formulated a more tractable statement in a letter sketching the prospective novel (the editor's brackets enclose Dostoevsky's additions to the letter): '[In addition] I hint at this thought in the novel, that [legal] punishment for a crime frightens a criminal much less than we think [the lawmakers in part] because the criminal himself [morally] demands it'.[10]

Twentieth-century psychologists acclaim Dostoevsky, particularly for his understanding of the criminal, as 'one of the greatest psychologists'.[11] His 'hint' has been taken up. It is therefore, of

necessity, placed within a psychological theory. Dostoevsky's reference to moral compunction is psychologized into the dominance of the superego over the ego. Raskolnikov is considered along with a number of psychoanalytic patients who have manifested 'the compulsion to confess'. Dostoevsky's 'a criminal' is replaced by a class of criminals.[12] A viable truth-claim, perhaps also a truth, is now established. Whereas the 'hint' occupies one sentence in the letter, as something of an afterthought ('in addition'). The letter consists of an extensive outline of the story of Raskolnikov: 'This is a psychological account of a crime. A young man expelled from the university . . .' and so on. Even so, it omits important elements of the plot, e.g., Sonia, that later appear in the finished work. Dostoevsky wrote a fiction. A supreme psychologist among novelists, he was a novelist, not a psychologist.

The proponents of artistic truth, justifiably reluctant to see it forced into the model of science or some other alien model, have typically insisted that it is *sui generis*. So it proves to be. Paradoxically, to start with, because there are no distinctively artistic truths. Generally, the truth is unvoiced. If so, it needs to be disentangled from the elements that enmesh it in the fiction. The uncertainty of their pertinence to the great world leads to a clumsy and ambiguous truth-claim. Only occasionally is the truth set out explicitly as a moral or *envoi*. In either case, the truth is one proper to some independent inquiry, usually psychology, and could probably have been arrived at otherwise. Only there is it developed systematically. In either case, there is no method of arriving at it in art and no confirmation or possibility of confirmation in art. Artistic truths, like the works of art that give rise to them, are discretely unrelated and therefore form no corpus either of belief or knowledge. Hence formal contradictions are tolerated effortlessly, if they are ever remarked. Only rarely does an artistic truth point to a genuine advance in knowledge. Artistic truths are, preponderantly, distinctly banal. Compared to science, above all, but also to history, religion, and garden variety knowing, artistic truth is a sport, stunted, hardly to be compared. These are the slight, dull, obvious realities which have been obscured by the grandiose pieties of cognitivism, the most lyrical, the very ecstasy of which is

'Beauty is truth, truth beauty' – that is all
Ye know on earth, and all ye need to know.

Notes

1 Hesiod, *Theogony*, lines 27–8.

2 Plato, *Republic*, 377a–e, 600a–d.

3 See Jerome Stolnitz, 'On the Historical Triviality of Art', *British Journal of Aesthetics*, 31 (1991), pp. 195–202.

4 See Peter Gay, *Freud* (New York, 1988), 159.

5 *Sophocles*, tr. Lewis Campbell (London, 1930), 128.

6 Felix Gilbert, *A European Past* (New York, 1988), 12.

7 Adrian Poole, *Tragedy* (New York, 1987), 91.

8 Charles Dickens, *Bleak House*, ed. George Ford and Sylvere Monod (New York, 1977), 3.

9 London, 1853. The foregoing quotation is from p. 1, italics in original.

10 Letter to M. N. Katkov, in Fyodor Dostoevsky, *The Notebooks for Crime and Punishment*, ed. Edward Wasiolek (Chicago, 1967), 172.

11 Theodor Reik, *The Compulsion to Confess* (New York, 1959), 275. See Sigmund Freud, *Character and Culture* (New York, 1963), ch. XXIV; Heinz Kohut, *Self Psychology and the Humanities* (New York, 1985), 41.

12 See Reik, op. cit., 258 ff., 309–12.

Part VII

Pictorial Art

Introduction to Part VII

In virtue of what does a picture *represent* some subject matter? How can pictures be *of* or *about* such subjects as the Duke of Wellington, a drunken man, a unicorn, or the climbing of Everest? A simple initial view has it that a picture represents in virtue of *resembling* its subject matter: the portrait *looks like* the Duke, and so forth. But it is hard to make this view precise. Resemblance cannot be sufficient for representation, for the Duke resembles the portrait as much as the portrait resembles the Duke but the Duke does not represent the portrait. Nor, arguably, is resemblance necessary, for a picture of a lamb might represent Christ without resembling Christ (except metaphorically). Simple observations of this kind have led philosophers to the thought that a representation is a *symbol* of some kind. Nelson Goodman, in *Languages of Art*, develops such a view, using the semantic notion of denotation as the model for pictorial representation. Kendall Walton, in the paper here ("Are Representations Symbols?"), follows up Goodman's proposal, spelling out in a perspicuous manner the fundamental elements of a symbolist view (particularly the relations between representation and "matching," a kind of resemblance), but also raises questions about it. While Walton endorses some of the "conventionalist" elements in Goodman's theory, he warns against too close an analogy between pictures and language. He also explores in detail what it might mean for a picture to represent a fictional character, such as Captain Ahab in *Moby Dick* or the unspecified Scholar in Paul Klee's painting. Walton's own preferred account of pictures in terms of games of make-believe is briefly introduced at the end of the paper and connects to his theory of fiction (in Section VI).

Roger Scruton, in "Photography and Representation," also criticizes the view that pictorial representation is directly analogous to linguistic representation, pointing out that "While there may be repertoires and conventions in painting there is nothing approaching grammar as we understand it." Nor is there need to learn a system of pictorial representation in the way one has to learn a language. Anyone can learn to "read" an unfamiliar system of pictorial representation by being shown a few examples of pictures using the system. However, in standard cases, according to Scruton, "understanding is not secured either by rules or by conventions but seems to be, on the contrary, a natural function of the normal eye." Various theories have been offered about how this function is served. Scruton, in his discussion of the difference between a photograph and a painting, suggests that a representational painting embodies thoughts about the objects that appear in the picture. This is the way, he argues, that paintings differ from photographs. Photographs do not represent, any more than mirrors do. They at best point (as does a finger) to the object in the photograph and it is the object not the photograph per se that holds our interest. The relationship between the photograph and the object depicted is a causal one and does not involve thought or intentionality (except in the pointing of the camera). There can be a photograph of a representation (i.e. of a scene in a stage play) but here the representation belongs to the object and not to the photograph.

Two other theories of representation are put forward in the articles by Budd and Wollheim respectively. Budd, in "How Pictures Look," tries to refurbish the resemblance theory, i.e. the theory that pictorial representation is based in the relation of similarity between the represented object and the representation. He does this by putting the relation of similarity into an intentional context: "to see a picture as a depiction of its subject is to *see it as* looking like it – looking like it in a specific manner I intend to define." Budd proceeds by introducing a notion of "visual field." A visual field is akin to, but not identical with, the "visual world," the world as we normally see it in three dimensions; the former differs from the latter in having the dimension of distance abstracted from it. A two-dimensional representational picture has as its object such a visual field. A representational painting is isomorphic in its structure with the visual field that is its object and this is how the relation of resemblance is constituted: "For a picture, the perception of this relation is . . . an experienced isomorphism of representations in the visual field."

Wollheim, partly in response to Budd's refurbishment of the resemblance theory, puts forward, in "On Pictorial Representation," an improved version of his theory of "seeing-in." Like Budd, he emphasizes that pictorial representation is a visual phenomenon. So a minimal requirement for a theory of pictorial representation is, according to Wollheim, that if a picture represents something "then there will be a visual experience of that picture that determines that it does so." This Wollheim calls the "appropriate experience" and he adds to this the requirement that if a "suitable" spectator looks at the picture, he will have this appropriate experience. Finally, this experience "will be, or include, a visual awareness of the thing represented." "Seeing-in" in Wollheim's theory is a special perceptual skill and is prior to representation "both logically and historically." Seeing-in is

the ability to look at a marked surface and be visually aware both of the marked surface and of something in front of or behind it. This is the perceptual basis for representation and furnishes "the appropriate experience." Thus we can see castles in the clouds and the man in the moon. Seeing-in, however, is not itself further grounded, for example, in resemblance.

As Wollheim points out in the introduction to his article, "Philosophical theories of representations abound." Those represented in this collection are central and much discussed theories, but there are a number of others, some of which are listed in note 2 of Budd's article. Readings presenting these theories are listed under Further Reading below.

Meiland's article, "Originals, Copies, and Aesthetic Value," exemplifies another area that has received considerable attention in analytic aesthetics: the issue of copies and forgeries. Here Meiland takes issue with a widely held view that knowledge of origin affects the way in which we see a picture, and thus evaluate it. He approaches the topic by arguing forcefully in support of what he calls "The Appearance Theory of Aesthetic Value." On this theory, an original has no aesthetic advantage over a copy in virtue of the fact that it is an original. This is a bolder step than Meiland seems to acknowledge since it cuts aesthetic judgment loose from the historical context in which the painting was produced. Quite apart from the question of value, it is arguable that *how* a picture is perceived aesthetically must always be relativized to other nonaesthetic facts about it (e.g. the *kind* of work it is taken to be). The discussion connects with debates about aesthetic properties (notably Walton and Pettit in Part III), and ontology (see Currie in Part II).

Further reading

Alperson, Philip (ed.) (1992). *The Philosophy of the Visual Arts* (New York: Oxford University Press).

Bryson, Norman, Holly, Michael Ann and Moxey, Keith (eds.) (1991). *Visual Theory: Painting and Interpretation* (Cambridge: Polity Press).

Goodman, Nelson (1976). *Languages of Art*, 2nd edn. (Indianapolis: Hackett).

Hopkins, Robert (1998). *Picture, Image and Experience* (Cambridge: Cambridge University Press).

Hyman, John (1989). *The Imitation of Nature* (Oxford: Blackwell).

Lopes, Dom (1996). *Understanding Pictures* (Oxford: Oxford University Press).

Novitz, David (1977). *Pictures and their Use in Communication* (The Hague: Martinus Nijhoff).

Peacocke, Christopher (1987). "Depiction," *Philosophical Review*, 96, pp. 383–410.

Schier, Flint (1986). *Deeper into Pictures* (Cambridge: Cambridge University Press).

Walton, Kendall (1990). *Mimesis as Make-Believe* (Cambridge, MA: Harvard University Press).

Wollheim, Richard (1980). *Art and Its Objects*, 2nd edn. (Cambridge: Cambridge University Press).

Wollheim, Richard (1988). *Painting as an Art* (London: Thames and Hudson).

30

Are Representations Symbols?

Kendall L. Walton

I

The representational arts seem friendly territory for "symbol" theories of aesthetics. Much of the initial resistance one may feel to the idea that a Mondrian composition or a Scarlatti sonata is a symbol evaporates when we switch to a portrait of Mozart, Michelangelo's *Pietá*, or Dickens's *A Tale of Two Cities*. These representational works have reference to things outside themselves. The portrait is a picture *of* Mozart; the *Pietá* is a sculpture *of* Christ and his Mother; *A Tale of Two Cities* is *about* London, Paris, and the French Revolution. It is natural enough to consider the relation between these works and what they are *of* or *about* a semantic one (reference, denotation, standing for, symbolizing). And if the representational is to be understood in terms of this semantic relation it is reasonable to hold that to be representational is to be a symbol of a certain kind.

But I shall argue that classifying even representations (representational works) as symbols is not nearly as appropriate as it appears to be, and that semiotic aestheticians ought to be much less comfortable with the representational arts than they are. No doubt *some* representations qualify unquestionably as symbols. What I challenge is the principle that any representation of whatever sort is a symbol, that to be representational at all is thereby

Kendall L. Walton, "Are Representations Symbols?" *The Monist*, 58: 2 (1974), pp. 236–54. © 1974 by The Monist: an International Quarterly Journal of General Philosophical Inquiry, Peru, Illinois 61354, USA. Reprinted by permission.

to be a symbol. Much of the discussion will focus on one species of representation, viz. depiction,[1] because the representational works which are least plausibly construed as symbols are depictions. Nevertheless many of the points made along the way will apply to representations of all kinds.

In *Languages of Art* Nelson Goodman seems simply to *assume* that representations, and depictions in particular, are symbols.[2] His discussion concerns mainly what *sort* of symbols they are, rather than whether they are symbols. And many who hold theories of depiction very different from Goodman's, including resemblance theories, would appear to agree that depictions are symbols – "iconic signs," "presentational symbols," "natural signs" – although this striking point of agreement is likely to be overlooked in the smoke of the battle.

The notion of a "symbol" is of course far from precise, and this may contribute to the casualness with which it is applied to representations. The principle that to be representational is to be a symbol might be taken as merely a *stipulation* about how to use "symbol." This appears to be Goodman's intention.[3] And to deny the principle outright would be to some extent arbitrary.

But "symbol" is not an entirely colorless term even for Goodman, and the principle is not innocuous. In calling representations "symbols" Goodman clearly means to suggest that they are importantly analogous to other symbols, e.g. linguistic ones, in particular that both have a fundamental "denotative" function. But, I shall argue, this analogy is largely an illusion, and calling representations "symbols" is likely to be highly misleading. I grant that representation like language is

Kendall L. Walton

"conventional" in important ways, and this argues for classifying them together. Nevertheless the common cavalier assimilation of representation to linguistic symbolization derives largely from, and is likely to engender, fundamental misconceptions about the nature of representation. Whether in the end it is deemed appropriate to consider representations symbols does not much matter. What is important is that we recognize and avoid those misconceptions.

II

To set the stage, I shall mark several crucial distinctions.

If a picture depicts, is a picture of, some actual existing object, I will say that it "*depicts$_q$*" that object. (Quantification over the thing depicted is allowable.) Thus Mozart's portrait depicts$_q$ Mozart. A representational work of any kind which is of or about some actual object *represents$_q$* what it is of or about. A poem or play about Mozart, like a picture or sculpture of him, represents$_q$ him.

Not every representation represents$_q$. Pictures "of witches" and stories "about fairies" do not represent$_q$ witches or fairies if there are none to be represented$_q$,[4] and they may well represent$_q$ nothing at all. They are however *witch-representations* or *fairy-representations*. Neither Paul Klee's painting, *Scholar*, nor Edgar Allan Poe's story *The Tell-Tale Heart* represents$_q$ any (actual) person, but both are man-representing works. In general if a work is "of" or "about" a *P*, in the sense in which that does not entail that there is a *P* which it is of or about, I will say that it is a *P*-representation. (It is, more specifically, a *P-depiction*, if it is a depiction.)[5]

A work may both represent$_q$ a *P* and be a *P*-representation: Mozart's portrait is a man-representation which represents$_q$ a man. But the independence of these two notions needs to be emphasized. A *P*-representation need not represent$_q$ a *P*, as we have seen. And neither must something which represents$_q$ a *P* be a *P*-representation. The Duke of Wellington is mentioned in *Languages of Art*, so a portrait of him represents$_q$ a man mentioned in *Languages of Art*. But (unless it somehow pictures the Duke *as* being mentioned in *Languages of Art*) it is not a man-mentioned-in-*Languages-of-Art*-representation.

A fat-man-representation which represents$_q$ a fat man can be said to correspond in this respect to what it represents$_q$, and it corresponds similarly to

any fat man. But a fat-man-representation and a fat man may fail in other ways to correspond; for example, the man may be poor, and the work a rich-man-representation (and not also a poor-man-representation). We need a notion of complete correspondence between a work and an object, or *matching*. A too hasty definition would be: A representation *R* matches an object *O* just in case for any property *P* such that *R* is a *P*-representation, *O* is *P*. Matisse's *Piano Lesson* is a boy-representation, a piano-representation, a human-head-representation, an action-of-playing-a-piano-representation, etc.[6] So to be matched by the picture something would have to be a boy, a piano, a human head, and an action! Plainly on this definition no ordinary representation, not even an absolutely perfectly faithful portrait, would match anything. A slightly more complicated definition is required, viz.:

R matches *O* if and only if ($\exists P$) (*R* is a *P*-representation and *O* is a *P*, and (*Q*) (If *R* is a *P*-which-is-a-*Q*-representation, *O* is a *Q*)).[7]

Piano Lesson is not a boy-who-is-a-piano-and-a-head-and-an-action-representation. Hence it can match a boy who is not also a piano, a head, and an action. Any boy it matches must *play* a piano, *have* a head, and *perform* an action, since it is a boy-who-is-playing-a-piano-and-has-a-head-and-is-performing-an-action-representation. And if it does match a boy it will match also the piano he is playing, his head, and his action of playing the piano.[8]

Intuitively, a *portrait* of someone matches him if, as we say colloquially, it "looks exactly like him in every detail." However, a novel or poem may match someone, but hardly looks like anyone. A man matched by a poem or a picture is one who, as one might say, *is* exactly like "the (or a) man *in* the poem or picture."

It is obvious that matching is not necessary for representing$_q$. Representing$_q$ without matching is simply *mis*representing. A glorifying portrait of Napoleon which pictures him as being taller and handsomer than he actually was represents$_q$ Napoleon but fails to match him. It is equally evident that matching is not sufficient for representing$_q$. Somewhere in the universe there might be a man, or even many men, whom *Scholar* just happens to match. But if so it does not follow that *Scholar* is a picture of, that it depicts$_q$, that man or any of those men. A portrait of Jones might perchance match Smith as well as, or instead of, Jones, yet it represents$_q$ Jones and not Smith. *Tom Sawyer* is not a novel about any boy there might happen to be who was and did precisely what "the boy in the novel" named *Tom Sawyer* was and did.

If what a work matches does not determine what it represents$_q$, what does? The answer probably varies with different kinds of representations, and there will be disagreement concerning any one kind. I shall merely offer several suggestions here, without attempting to settle the question.

(a) A work may represent$_q$ a certain object because, or partly because, the artist intended it to do so. (An *analysis* of representation$_q$ in terms of intended representation$_q$ would be sadly circular. I am not suggesting an analysis.)

(b) A work bears a causal relation, I suppose, to any object its maker intended it to represent$_q$. Perhaps other causal relations are relevant also. What a photograph represents$_q$ may be simply whatever reflected light into the camera and onto the lens, thus producing the image.[9] And it may be that who sat for a (painted) portrait is relevant to whom it represents$_q$, and that what or whom a novel represents$_q$ depends partly on what or whom the characters, setting, actions, are "modelled after."

(c) Titles and other conventional signs seem often to have important bearing on what a work represents$_q$. Whether a certain portrait depicts$_q$ John or his brother Frank may depend on whether it is titled "John" or "Frank." (But it is arguable that the artist's intention is what determines who is represented$_q$, and that the title simply serves as an indication of his intention.) A halo in a painting may help to make it represent$_q$ Christ or a saint. And a novel or play might represent$_q$ Warren Harding partly because one of the characters is named "Warren G. Harding."

(d) What *kind* of a representation something is, in Goodman's terms, i.e. for what values of P it is a P-representation, appears to have *some* relevance to what it represents$_q$. We have seen that whether a novel is a man-named-"Warren G. Harding"-representation may affect whether it represents$_q$ Harding. René Magritte's oil, *L'Annonciation*, a weight-lifter-holding-a-bone-in-one-hand-and-bar-bells-in-the-other-and-whose-head-is-one-of-the-bells-depiction, hardly depicts$_q$ the Annunciation, despite its title and even if Magritte intended it to (which is unlikely). It may be in some way "symbolic" of that event, or express a conception or attitude concerning it, but is not a picture of it. This suggests that a work must come reasonably close to matching something in order to represent$_q$ it; perhaps to represent$_q$ the Annunciation something must be at least a someone's-announcing-something-representation. But this does not alter the fact that a work need not match what it represents$_q$.

The above are no more than tentative suggestions. What matters for our purposes is that representing$_q$ is not matching and hence that *something* other than what a work matches helps to determine what, if anything, it represents$_q$.

III

Goodman claims that to depict an actual existing thing is to *denote* it, that for example a portrait of the Duke of Wellington denotes him. By "depicting something (actual)" I take Goodman to mean what I mean by "depicting$_q$."[10] It seems to me entirely appropriate to consider depicting$_q$ a semantic relation, and I have no objection to calling it "denotation." Further, I take not only depicting$_q$ but representing$_q$ in general to be a kind of denotation; stories and poems, as well as pictures, denote what they represent$_q$. And I shall assume that whatever denotes something automatically qualifies as a "symbol." So the Duke of Wellington's portrait and all representing$_q$ works are symbols.

What grounds are there for considering representations which do not represent$_q$ to be symbols? It would be obviously unreasonable to require that all symbols actually denote (or bear some semantic relation to something). The linguistic expressions "the wickedest witch," "the only person to climb Mt. Everest," "Lemuel Gulliver," and "Paul Henry O'Mallory," are all nondenoting symbols. Perhaps something is a symbol, whether or not it denotes, if it is assigned a denoting function or is in some way an element or constituent of a denoting scheme. Goodman apparently thinks that all depictions (and, no doubt, all representations) satisfy some such vague condition as this.

Although representation thus depends upon a relationship among symbols rather than upon their relationship to denotata, it nevertheless depends upon their *use* as denotative symbols. A dense set of elements does not constitute a representational scheme unless at least *ostensibly* provided with denotata. The rule correlating symbols with denotata may result in no assignment of any actual denotata to any symbol, so that the field of reference is null; but elements become representations only in conjunction with some such correlation actual or *in principle*.[11]

This is not very explicit. But if the denoting Goodman has in mind here is representing$_q$ (specifically depicting$_q$) it seems to me clearly mistaken. I shall argue that representation is not in any way to be understood in terms of depicting$_q$. To be representational is not thereby to belong to a representing$_q$ scheme. This casts serious doubt on the propriety of holding that to be representational is to be a symbol. (Later I shall consider whether representations are to be understood in terms of a semantic relation other than representing$_q$.)

It will be helpful to examine various sorts of nondenoting linguistic symbols. "The first person to climb Mt. Everest" denotes someone, but "the only person to climb Mt. Everest" does not.[12] The difference is simply that the world happens to contain someone who was first to climb Everest but not someone who was the only person to do so. The "rule correlating symbols with denotata" does not, I suppose, assign any denotatum to the latter expression. But it is not clear that there *is* a "rule" which applies to "Lemuel Gulliver" and "Paul Henry O'Mallory." (I assume that "Paul Henry O'Mallory" has never been used as anyone's name, not even in fiction.) It is not because denotata purportedly picked out for them happen not to exist that they fail to denote. (Cf. Sec. IV.) Of course "Lemuel Gulliver" and "Paul Henry O'Mallory" *would* have denoted whatever were so christened. But christening, it seems, is *establishing* a rule of correlation which did not previously exist. However, "Gulliver" at least is in one sense "ostensibly provided with" a denotatum. We pretend, imagine, make-believe that the words of Swift's novel constitute an account of the adventures of an actual person named "Gulliver."[13] No one has even pretended that "Paul Henry O'Mallory" denotes. But that expression is *denotative*: it is a member of a class of things – names – which are conventionally assigned denoting roles; it belongs to a repertory of potential denoters.

I take "the only climber of Everest," "Lemuel Gulliver," and "Paul Henry O'Mallory," though

nondenoting, to be constituents of a denoting scheme and to be properly called "symbols." Representational works of corresponding kinds similarly qualify as symbols. Suppose that an adventurer finds in Alaska what he claims to be footprints of a leopard, and produces a plaster cast of the prints accompanied by a leopard-depiction labelled "The leopard who made these prints."[14] If a leopard did produce the purported footprints, the sketch represents$_q$ it; otherwise it represents$_q$ nothing. The sketch thus corresponds to the symbol "the only climber of Everest"; whether it represents$_q$ depends on whether the world happens to contain something answering to the description in the title. An illustration of Gulliver in the novel is pretended to represent$_q$ someone, just as "Gulliver" is pretended to name someone. And *Scholar* might, I suppose, be classified as denotative along with "Paul Henry O'Mallory"; it is one of a class of things, representational pictures, which often are used to denote (in this case to represent). Thus the leopard-depiction, the illustration of Gulliver, perhaps *Scholar*, and other representations like these, are appropriately considered symbols.

But to be representational something need not be of any of these sorts. There could be a society of people (there might actually have been one) who make bison-depictions, man-depictions, etc., but not ones which depict$_q$ actual bison or men, and who have no provision for making anything represent$_q$ anything. They have no convention whereby attaching a title (or other sign) to something makes it represent$_q$, they never use anything as a "model" in producing a representation, and they do not know what representing$_q$ is and so cannot intend a work to represent$_q$. Drawing a bison is thought of as *creating, producing*, a (make-believe) bison, not as symbolizing or referring to an animal already in existence. (Children speak of drawing a giraffe as "making" a giraffe.) The possibility of a society of this kind seems to me almost too obvious to require mention.

A bison-depiction in such a society does not purport to represent$_q$ in the way the mentioned leopard-depiction does, nor is there any sort of pretense that it represents$_q$. It is not even denotative: it is not one of a kind of things used to represent$_q$. Yet there can be no question that it is *representational*. The notion of the representational thus is independent of that of representing$_q$. To be representational is not thereby to belong to a representing$_q$ scheme.

The failure to recognize this important point is due largely, I believe, to confusion between representing$_q$ and matching. But once representing$_q$ and matching are properly distinguished there is no excuse for supposing representation to presuppose or depend on the possibility of representing$_q$.

I have not claimed that *literary* representation is possible without provision for representing$_q$. It may be that literary works necessarily consist of linguistic expressions, symbols which (or some of which), used nonfictionally, have a denoting function. Thus fictional uses of language are said to be parasitic on nonfictional uses of language. But fictional uses of pictures are not similarly parasitic on nonfictional ones. Some pictures which depict$_q$ or purport to are used "nonfictionally" (e.g. drawings in advertisements). But for something to be a depiction no provision need be made either for depicting$_q$ or for using depictions nonfictionally. Pictorial representation and language are in this fundamental respect not comparable. Much confusion about the nature of depiction (and hence of representation) has resulted from forcing the analogy between them beyond the facts.

IV

Representing$_q$ as construed so far is a relation representations bear only to actual, real-world entities. But perhaps representations can denote *non*actual things in an analogous way, if our ontology is expanded to include them, and a natural extension of the notion of representing$_q$ might allow such things to be represented$_q$. Representation might then turn out to be understandable in terms of representing$_q$ after all; it may even be that all representations actually represent$_q$ (in the wider sense). If we but admit to our ontology the (nonactual) man *Scholar* is "of" and the murder *The Tell-Tale Heart* is "about," perhaps the picture and story will be seen to represent$_q$ (in the wider sense) these entities, and hence to qualify as symbols. I shall consider two main versions of this suggestion: that the objects such works represent$_q$ are possible ones existing in possible worlds, and that they are "fictional" ones existing in "fictional" worlds. Goodman of course will not welcome this line of argument, committed as he is to a spare ontology.

Whether any such nonactual entities should be recognized depends heavily on considerations lying far beyond the scope of this paper. For purposes of argument I shall recognize them. *Some* representations are easily regarded as representing$_q$ nonactual entities, given that there are such. But many are not. The relation between *Scholar* or *The Tell-Tale Heart* and any possible or fictional man or murder, I shall argue, is not at all analogous to the relation between (for example) a portrait of Mozart and Mozart, and no natural extension of the notion of representing$_q$ will cover it. Nor does representation presuppose even that provision be made for representing$_q$ nonactual things. The view that to be representational is to belong to a representing$_q$ scheme is no better off with an expanded ontology and an extended notion of representing$_q$.

I begin with possible entities. Does *Moby Dick* represent$_q$ a man, Captain Ahab, who resides in some possible world (or worlds)? If so, *which* resident of which world(s) is Ahab? One answer is that he is whoever, in some possible world, has an ivory leg, hunts a white whale, etc. But this seems to identify representing$_q$ with matching, and I see no reason to abandon the principle that they are distinct when representing$_q$ merely possible objects is envisioned.

But what it is to match a possible object is problematical. If a single thing can exist in more than one possible world and have different properties in each, a man who has an ivory leg and hunts a white whale in one world, might not have exactly those properties in some other world. *Moby Dick* may match someone as he is in one world, but not as he is in another.[15] To hold that representing$_q$ an object is matching it as it is in *some* possible world would be disastrous. There is a possible world in which Sir Francis Drake has an ivory leg and hunts a white whale, etc., i.e. *Moby Dick* matches him as he is in some world. But it certainly does not represent$_q$ him; it is not a novel about Sir Francis Drake. We can escape *this* disaster by taking what is represented$_q$ to be not simply a possible object, but an object-in-a-world. Representing$_q$ an actual object, O, as previously understood, is now expressed as representing$_q$ O-in-the-real-world. One might claim that although *Moby Dick* does not represent$_q$ Sir Francis Drake-in-the-real-world, if it matches Drake as he is in some other world, W, it represents$_q$ Drake-in-W. But thus to identify representing$_q$ O-in-W with matching O as it is in W would have the disastrous consequence that if there should happen to be an actual person whom *Moby Dick* matches as he is in the real world, *Moby Dick* represents$_q$ him-in-the-real-world. (A similar disaster ensues if representing$_q$ O-in-W is identified with matching O *and only* O as it is in W.)

It is worth noting that some representations do not match *anything* as it is in any possible world. So if matching a possible object as it is in some world is even a necessary condition of representing$_q$ it (or it-in-a-world), not all representations represent$_q$ possible objects. There is no reason why what "happens" in fiction must be logically consistent. M. C. Escher's print, *Waterfall*, shows water falling over a precipice and turning a waterwheel, then flowing through a trough constantly downhill and back to the *top* of the precipice where it again falls and turns the wheel. This is, I take it, a water-which-is-and-is-not-flowing-downhill-representation. So any possible water which the print matches as it is in some possible world must flow downhill and not downhill in that world. But there is no such possible water. (And anything other than water which the print matches as it is in some possible world would have to bear some relation in that world to water which is and is not flowing downhill.) Similarly, nothing prevents anyone from writing stories about such impossibilities as the largest round square, a donkey with two heads and no head, and (if it is an impossibility) time travel.[16]

We must reaffirm the distinctness of representing$_q$ from matching, and consider again whether representations represent$_q$ possible objects. The leopard-depiction mentioned earlier does. The marks which the Alaskan adventurer mistakenly took to be a leopard's footprints were, in some possible world, produced by a leopard. The sketch represents$_q$ that possible leopard (or it-in-that-world), I suppose, and it does so whether or not it matches the leopard as it is in that world.

But representations like *Scholar* and *Moby Dick* do not thus represent$_q$ possible objects. It is of course possible for them to represent$_q$; if *Scholar* had been titled instead "Anselm, the Scholar" it probably would have represented$_q$ St. Anselm, and in some possible worlds it may represent$_q$ someone who does not exist also in the real world. Just about anything possibly represents$_q$ just about anything. But our question is whether *Scholar* and similar works *actually* represent$_q$ possible objects, whether it is true *in the real world* that they represent$_q$ residents of possible worlds. A negative answer seems inescapable. Which *actual* object, if any, a work represents$_q$ seems to be determined by the artist's intention or a conventional sign or a causal relation between the object and the work. We would expect

some such feature to link a work with any merely possible object that it represents$_q$. And in fact the title of the leopard-depiction and its creator's intention both pick out a particular leopard in some possible worlds (though perhaps different ones in different worlds). But in the case of *Scholar* there is no such feature that does the job. Of the infinitely many possible objects in any given world which *Scholar could* represent$_q$, nothing makes it actually represent$_q$ any one of them rather than any other. (The title makes it a scholar-representation, but does not link it to any particular possible scholar.) Just as the name, "Paul Henry O'Mallory," has not been made to name anything, *Scholar* has not been made to represent$_q$ anything, neither anything possible nor anything actual.[17]

V

It is more tempting in some ways to connect representations with *fictional* worlds than with possible ones, to regard Ahab, for example, as a fictional rather than a possible man. If fictions are construed in one natural way, there is no problem of specifying which fictional entity Ahab is. Moreover, we can allow contradictions to be true in fictional worlds. Water might simultaneously flow downhill and not do so in some fictional world. (However, most fictional worlds are best understood to obey the same logical laws, and even the same laws of nature, that the real world does.) But it is no more plausible to claim that all representations represent$_q$ fictional things (if not real ones) than that they represent$_q$ possible things.

It seems reasonable to postulate a fictional world for each representational work. Ahab lives in the world of *Moby Dick*. A story world corresponds to *The Tell-Tale Heart* and a picture world to *Scholar*. (Occasionally a single fictional world will correspond to more than one work. Cf. the fifth paragraph hence.) And the existence of fictional worlds may be understood to depend on the existence of the corresponding representations. So to write a story or paint a picture is (usually) to bring into being a new story world or picture world. This makes the existence of fictional worlds, unlike that of possible ones, a contingent matter.

If we take representations to represent$_q$ fictional things we need not be embarrassed by the question of *which* things a given work represents$_q$ – it represents$_q$ the contents of the fictional world postulated to correspond to it. *Scholar*, for example, represents$_q$ whatever is "in the picture," i.e. in the fictional world corresponding to the painting.

What objects exist in a given fictional world and what properties they have depend on the nature of the corresponding representation. Daggoo would not have existed in the world of *Moby Dick* if the novel had been written without any mention of him, and the man in the world of *Scholar* is frowning because of the pattern of paint on the canvas. This suggests that for every value of *P* such that a work is a *P*-representation there is a *P* in the corresponding fictional world. But that would mean that a work must match the contents of its fictional world. Hence, if these contents are the fictional entities it "represents$_q$," matching a fictional object will be necessary for "representing$_q$" it, and "misrepresenting" one will be impossible. This makes "representing$_q$" a fictional object and representing$_q$ an actual one seriously disanalogous, and to call them both "representing$_q$" is unwarranted and misleading.

Of course we are not forced to stipulate that objects in fictional worlds have whatever properties they must have in order to be matched by the corresponding representations. One *might* decree that Ahab is a man in a world corresponding to *Moby Dick* who did not, or may not have, hunted a white whale, although the novel represents him as having done so. But this maneuver is ad hoc and pointless. What determines whether or not Ahab did hunt a white whale? What *are* his properties, if not the ones the novel represents him as having (assuming that it does represent$_q$ him)? We are faced with the choice of making some new and arbitrary stipulation about what Ahab was and did, or leaving this entirely indeterminate. Either way, he will hardly resemble fictional characters as they are ordinarily conceived. There is little to recommend postulating fictional entities which need not be matched by the corresponding representations, beyond a desire to rescue a beleaguered theory. And the theory is not worth saving if this is what it requires.

One final consideration should remove any remaining inclination to take *Scholar* or *Moby Dick* to represent$_q$ fictional objects. Since the fictional man whom *Scholar* supposedly represents$_q$ is to be identified as, simply, "the man in the picture," what is (supposedly) represented$_q$ does not depend on the artist's intention, the title, or a causal connection between the object and the work. *Scholar* would not have represented$_q$ any *other* fictional person instead if Klee had had a different inten-

tion, or had titled it differently, or its causal history had been different.[18]

Although many representations cannot plausibly be regarded as representing$_q$ fictional objects, some can. An illustration accompanying *Moby Dick* might represent$_q$ Ahab. Ahab owes his (fictional) existence to the novel, not to the illustration, and it is the novel that determines what he is and does. The picture *mis*represents him if it portrays him differently from how he is in the novel; it may depict him as being older, or fatter, than he is. Thus the picture need not match him. (But the novel neither misrepresents Ahab nor represents him correctly; it *makes* him as he is.) Further, that the picture depicts$_q$ Ahab rather than some other fictional person is determined in the usual way. It may have depicted$_q$ Daggoo or Starbuck instead if the artist had intended it to and had titled it appropriately.[19]

The ease with which the notion of representing$_q$ can be extended so that in special cases like this fictions are represented$_q$ merely underscores the absurdity of taking every representation to represent$_q$ something fictional (if not something actual). And representation does not presuppose that the possibility of representing$_q$ fictions be envisioned or provided for. A society might have no convention for making one representation "illustrate" another; a different fictional man is understood to correspond to every different man-representation.

I conclude that to be representational is not to belong to a representing$_q$ scheme, even if what can be represented$_q$ is understood to include either fictional or (merely) possible entities.

VI

Representing$_q$ is only one kind of semantic relation. I have argued that the representational is not to be understood in terms of representing$_q$, but we must consider whether it is to be understood in terms of some other semantic relation. Matching, in particular, though it is not representing$_q$, might be construable as a semantic relation. If so this will give new life to the view that representations are symbols.

The case for taking matching to be a semantic relation is most persuasive when representations are compared to linguistic predicates. In many instances this comparison is strikingly apt. A two-story-house-with-a-fireplace-and- . . . -depicting-picture labeled "1360 Maple Ave.," accompanying a real estate advertisement, represents$_q$ the house at that address, and represents it as having two stories, a fireplace, etc. The label is easily regarded as a subject expression, and the picture as a predicate used to attribute the complex property of being a two-story house with fireplace, etc., to the label's referent. Together the picture and label "express the proposition" that the house at 1360 Maple Ave. has two stories and a fireplace, etc. And the advertiser, in running the ad, *asserts* that this is so; he is guilty of false advertising if it is not. Representations which do not represent$_q$ anything probably cannot be said to "express propositions," and many which do are not vehicles of assertion. But of course predicates need not actually be used to make assertions or express propositions. So perhaps all representations, including ones which do not represent$_q$, are predicates.[20]

If representations are predicates they are related to what they match in the way linguistic predicates are related to what they truly apply to, and this relation is certainly a semantic one. A two-story-house-with-fireplace-and- . . . -representation, if it is a predicate, is *true of* two-story houses with fireplaces and . . . , as is "(is a) two-story house with fireplace and . . ."

But the plausibility of taking representations to be predicates seems to me to depend heavily on the fact that they *can* be used to express propositions, that provision is made for their representing$_q$ and attributing properties to what they represent$_q$. In a society which has no such provision it is by no means obvious that representations should be considered predicates.[21] It is arguable that "red" qualifies as a predicate only by virtue of its role in expressing propositions. Thus the view that to be representational is necessarily to be a predicate is hardly persuasive.

Not only might representations lack the normal function of predicates, there is another quite different function which they cannot lack; they serve as "props" in "games of make-believe." This claim is developed in "Pictures and Make-Believe," and I shall here merely sketch its outlines.

The statement "Ahab had an ivory leg," asserted in connection with *Moby Dick*, is to be taken in a certain nonliteral way. So understood it is true. In my terminology it is *make-believedly* true that Ahab had an ivory leg. And this is a make-believe truth because of, in virtue of, the sentences which occur in the novel. All representations engender make-believe truths similarly. It is make-believedly true

in virtue of any bison-depiction that something exists and is a bison. And in general R is a P-representation for society S just in case there is a game of make-believe in S such that it is make-believedly true in virtue of R that an object O exists and is a P. To be representational is to be a P-representation for some value of "P," i.e. to make it make-believedly true that something of some sort exists. (The reader is referred to "Pictures and Make-Believe" for the details and a defense of this theory.)[22]

The fundamental function of representation thus is not to *express* propositions, but rather to make them make-believedly true. This is a function which predicates do not have (although novels and poems containing them do). And the occasional use of representations as predicates is quite incidental to it.

Consider a convention whereby when a goal is scored in a basketball game an "announcer" indicates this fact by throwing a ball through a hoop himself and pointing to the player. His throwing the ball through the hoop is a predicate used to attribute a property to the player pointed to. But the similar action performed by the player, by which he *scores* a goal, is not a predicate. It is used not to express a proposition but to make one (literally) true, to give something a property rather than to attribute a property to it. The player's action is not *true of* any goal or goals, nor does it symbolize, refer to, stand for, or denote one; instead it brings one into existence. Representations, in their essential role, are comparable to an action of throwing a ball through a hoop whereby a goal is scored, not to one whereby a goal already scored is signalled.

VII

The case against the view that to be representational is to be a symbol or an element of a symbol scheme cannot be conclusive in the absence of a reasonably definite account of what sorts of things symbols or symbol schemes are. But the dangers of blithely accepting this view and assimilating representations to linguistic symbols, whether to predicates or to referring expressions, are apparent. To do so, at least without careful explanation and qualification, is to make fundamental misconceptions about the nature of representation all but inevitable.

Notes

1 Depiction comprises, roughly, representation by the "perceptual" arts, e.g. representational painting and sculpture. Cf. my "Pictures and Make-Believe," *Philosophical Review*, 82 (1973), pp. 283–319. Nelson Goodman, in *Languages of Art: An Approach to a Theory of Symbols* (Indianapolis: Bobbs-Merrill, 1968), usually uses "representation" as I use "depiction." Cf. p. 4n. (All references to Goodman in this paper will be to *Languages of Art*.)

2 More accurately, representations are for Goodman "marks" belonging to "symbol schemes." He does not claim that *all* works of art, including nonrepresentational ones, are marks. Cf. p. 210n.

3 "'Symbol' is used here as a very general and colorless term. It covers letters, words, texts, pictures, diagrams, maps, models, and more" (p. xi).

4 For now I am assuming, with Goodman, a lean ontology. Later I shall consider recognizing merely possible and other possibly nonactual entities, and allowing them to be "represented$_q$."

5 These expressions are borrowed from Goodman, and were used also in "Pictures and Make-Believe."

6 Goodman's account of "representation as" is clearly inadequate. (Cf. Goodman, pp. 28–29.) A portrait may be or contain a picture which as a whole both represents (i.e. represents$_q$, cf. the beginning of Sec. III, and note 10) Napoleon and is an action-of-standing-erect-representation, but it does not represent Napoleon as being an action.

7 Technically "P" and "Q" in this formula, when not part of a quantifier, should be understood as elliptical for "thing which has P" (or "thing-which-has-P") and "thing which has Q" (or "thing-which-has-Q"), where "P" and "Q" are variables ranging over properties (including relational ones). Nominalists are invited to rewrite this definition quantifying over predicates rather than properties. In the text "P" can be construed as replaceable by "man," "fat man," (or "fat-man") etc. It would be more awkward but equally correct to replace it by "thing which has the property of being a man," "thing which has the property of being a fat man," etc. (hyphenated where appropriate).

8 David Kaplan's notion of what a picture "resembles" seems close to what a picture "matches" in my sense, and he rightly separates that from what a picture is *of* (i.e. depicts$_q$). Cf. "Quantifying In," in *Words and Objections: Essays on the Work of W. V. Quine*, ed. Donald Davidson and Jaakko Hintikka (Dordrecht: Synthese Library Series, 1969), pp. 225–28. But "matching," as defined, is much clearer than "resembling," and it avoids commitment (real or apparent) to any resemblance theory of depiction. Moreover, it brings out a significant parallel between depiction and other kinds of representation.

9 Two senses of "represent$_q$" (or kinds of representing$_q$) may need to be distinguished. If someone photographs a model and titles the result "The Madonna," the picture represents$_q$ in one sense the model and in another the Madonna. Cf. Monroe Beardsley's distinction between "nominal and physical portrayal," *Aesthetics: Problems in the Philosophy of Criticism* (New York: Harcourt Brace, 1958), p. 227.

10 There is some evidence that this is not what he means. He claims that what a picture depicts depends only on its "pictorial properties," i.e. roughly "what colors the picture has at what places" (pp. 4–42). But it seems obvious that this is not true of what a picture depicts$_q$. Perhaps what a picture *matches* depends only on its pictorial properties (given the pictorial system and the nature of objects that might be matched), and Goodman may be confusing depicting$_q$ with matching. Goodman reinforces the impression that by "depicting" he means "matching" by assimilating "the relation between a picture and what it represents [depicts] . . . to the relation between a predicate and what it applies to" (p. 5). A picture's matching something does seem comparable to a predicate's applying to something, whereas depicting$_q$ seems more like the relation between a name and what it names. But the following considerations support my interpretation: (a) Goodman's examples of "depicting" (or "representing") generally are clear cases of depicting$_q$, but are not, or may well not be, instances of matching; (b) his usual ways of describing these cases would be quite inappropriate if the relation in question were matching – to match something is not thereby to make a picture *of* it, or to *depict* or represent it, in any ordinary sense of these expressions; (c) Goodman recognizes the possibility of *mis*representation, but he would have to deny it if representing were matching (cf. pp. 27ff.).

11 Goodman, pp. 227–28 (italics mine).

12 I am understanding these expressions as used "ascriptively" rather than "referentially," in Keith Donnellan's sense. Cf. "Reference and Definite Descriptions," *Philosophical Review*, 75 (1966), 281–304.

13 It is *make-believedly true*, in the technical sense introduced in "Pictures and Make-Believe," that Gulliver exists and that "Gulliver" denotes, and also that the illustration of Gulliver discussed below depicts$_q$ him.

14 The label is assumed to be used "ascriptively." Cf. note 12.

15 R matches O as it is in world W if and only if $(\exists P)$ (R is a P-representation, and O is a P in W, and (Q) (if R is a P-which-is-a-Q-representation, O is a Q in W)).

16 Deciding whether a given work is a thing-which-is-P-and-not-P-representation may take some care.

The occurrence in a novel of contradictory sentences is not sufficient. For the best interpretation might be simply that the narrator is confused, or a liar, i.e. the novel may be a thing-which-is-*described*-as-*P*-and-as-not-*P*-representation, rather than a thing-which-is-*P*-and-not-*P*-representation.

17 I am sympathetic to Saul Kripke's claim that neither Sherlock Holmes nor any unicorn possibly exists. Cf. "Naming and Necessity," in *Semantics of Natural Language*, ed. Donald Davidson and Gilbert Harmon (New York: Humanities Press, 1970), pp. 253–54, 763–64. But for my purposes it does not matter whether there are *any* possible unicorns; I contend here only that there is not a possible unicorn for every unicorn-representation.

18 This is too simple. A picture's title may determine properties of things in the corresponding fictional world, and if it determines their "essential" properties it determines *which* things are in that world. Whether a sketchy person-depiction is a black-man-depiction or a white-woman-depiction might depend on its title, and if a fictional person who is a black man could not have been a white woman instead, the identity of the person in the fictional world, whom the picture supposedly represents$_q$, depends on the title. But a work's title can affect what exists in the corresponding fictional world *only* by making the work a *P*-representation, where *P* is an essential property. By contrast, this is not the only way a title can affect which *actual* object is represented$_q$.

19 One *can* treat the picture independently of the novel, and postulate a fictional man matching it – whom it does not represent$_q$.

20 John G. Bennett suggests construing pictures in roughly this way. Cf. "Depiction and Convention," in *The Monist*, vol. 58, no. 2 (1974) pp. 255–268.

21 There is more than one way of using a predicate to express a proposition. "Red" can be used to express the propositions that there is something red, that not everything is red, that red is a color, etc., as well as to attribute redness to something. If representations can be used to express propositions of these other sorts it seems evident that they need not be so usable.

22 My theory disallows quantification over such dubious entities as fictional worlds and their contents, thus preserving a spare and pure ontology. What some consider (literally) true propositions about fictional objects become propositions which are only make-believedly true and are only make-believedly, not really, about anything. But the analysis of make-believe truth in "Pictures and Make-Believe" helps to explain the immense attractiveness of recognizing fictional worlds and objects. It analyzes away talk about fictions, while satisfying the intuitions behind it.

The desire to avoid distasteful ontological commitments has sometimes occasioned awkward but unnecessary squirming. Richard Cartwright claims that although there are neither dragons nor carnivorous cows, unreality can be predicated of the former but not of the latter. ("Negative Existentials," in *Philosophy and Ordinary Language*, ed. Charles Caton [Urbana: University of Illinois Press, 1963], pp. 55–66.) "The question whether something is real or not presupposes that the thing has some 'status' – imaginary, fictional, or whatever," he claims, and dragons have some such "status" but carnivorous cows do not (p. 65). Cartwright resists the idea that to have a "status" is to have *some* kind of *being*, and claims only that dragons can be *referred* to, as when they are said to lack fur. He thus swallows the paradox that one can refer to what is not. But on my theory we can avoid cluttering our ontology with dragons, insist that only what exists can be referred to, and still explain the difference between "dragons" and "carnivorous cows." It is make-believedly true that dragons exist, but not that carnivorous cows do. And one can make-believedly refer to dragons, although since there are none one cannot really do so any more than one can refer to carnivorous cows.

31

Photography and Representation

Roger Scruton

Critics and philosophers have occasionally been troubled by the question whether the cinema is an independent art form – independent, that is, of the theatre, from which it borrows so many conventions.[1] This question can be traced back to a more basic one, the question whether photography is capable of representing anything. I shall argue that it is not and that, insofar as there is representation in film, its origin is not photographic. A film is a photograph of a dramatic representation; it is not, because it cannot be, a photographic representation. It follows that if there is such a thing as a cinematic masterpiece it will be so because – like *Wild Strawberries* and *La règle du jeu* – it is in the first place a dramatic masterpiece.

It seems odd to say that photography is not a mode of representation. For a photograph has in common with a painting the property by which the painting represents the world, the property of sharing, in some sense, the appearance of its subject. Indeed, it is sometimes thought that since a photograph more effectively shares the appearance of its subject than a typical painting, photography is a better mode of representation. Photography might even be thought to have *replaced* painting as a mode of visual representation. Painters have felt that if the aim of painting is really to reproduce the appearances of things, then painting must give way to whatever means are available to reproduce an appearance more accurately. It has therefore been said that painting aims to record the appearances of things only so as to capture the experience of observing them (the *impression*) and that the accurate copying of appearances will normally be at variance with this aim. Here we have the seeds of expressionism and the origin of the view (a view which not only is mistaken but which has also proved disastrous for the history of modern art) that painting is somehow purer when it is abstract and closer to its essence as an art.

Let us first dismiss the word 'representation'. Of course this word can be applied to photography. We wish to know whether there is some feature, suitably called representation, common to painting and photography. And we wish to know whether that feature has in each case a comparable aesthetic value, so that we can speak not only of representation but also of representational art. (There is an important feature – sound – in common to music and to fountains, but only the first of these is properly described as an *art* of sound.)

1

In order to understand what I mean by saying that photography is not a representational art, it is important to separate painting and photography as much as possible, so as to discuss not actual painting and actual photography but an ideal form of each, an ideal which represents the essential differences between them. Ideal photography differs

Roger Scruton, "Photography and Representation," from Roger Scruton, *The Aesthetic Understanding: Essays in the Philosophy of Art and Culture* (London: Methuen, 1983), pp. 102–26. Reissued 1998 by St. Augustine's Press, South Bend, Ind. (pp. 119–43 their volume) and reproduced here by permission of St. Augustine's Press.

from actual photography as indeed ideal painting differs from actual painting. Actual photography is the result of the attempt by photographers to pollute the ideal of their craft with the aims and methods of painting.

By an 'ideal' I mean a logical ideal. The ideal of photography is not an ideal at which photography aims or ought to aim. On the contrary, it is a logical fiction, designed merely to capture what is distinctive in the photographic relation and in our interest in it. It will be clear from this discussion that there need be no such thing as an ideal photograph in my sense, and the reader should not be deterred if I begin by describing photography in terms that seem to be exaggerated or false.

The ideal painting stands in a certain 'intentional' relation to a subject.[2] In other words, if a painting represents a subject, it does not follow that the subject exists nor, if it does exist, that the painting represents the subject as it is. Moreover, if x is a painting of a man, it does not follow that there is some *particular* man of which x is the painting. Furthermore, the painting stands in this intentional relation to its subject because of a representational act, the artist's act, and in characterizing the relation between a painting and its subject we are also describing the artist's intention. The successful realization of that intention lies in the creation of an appearance, an appearance which in some way leads the spectator to recognize the subject.

The ideal photograph also stands in a certain relation to a subject: a photograph is a photograph *of* something. But the relation is here causal and not intentional.[3] In other words, if a photograph is a photograph of a subject, it follows that the subject exists, and if x is a photograph of a man, there is a particular man of whom x is the photograph. It also follows, though for different reasons, that the subject is, roughly, as it appears in the photograph. In characterizing the relation between the ideal photograph and its subject, one is characterizing not an intention but a causal process, and while there is, as a rule, an intentional act involved, this is not an essential part of the photographic relation. The ideal photograph also yields an appearance, but the appearance is not interesting as the realization of an intention but rather as a record of how an actual object looked.

Since the end point of the two processes is, or can be, so similar, it is tempting to think that the intentionality of the one relation and the causality of the other are quite irrelevant to the standing of the finished product. In both cases, it seems, the important part of representation lies in the fact that the spectator can see the subject *in* the picture. The appreciation of photographs and the appreciation of paintings both involve the exercise of the capacity to 'see as', in the quite special sense in which one may see x as y without believing or being tempted to believe that x is y.

2

Now, it would be a simple matter to define 'representation' so that 'x represents y' is true only if x expresses a thought about y, or if x is designed to remind one of y, or whatever, in which case a relation that was *merely* causal (a relation that was not characterized in terms of any thought, intention, or other mental act) would never be sufficient for representation. We need to be clear, however, why we should wish to define representation in one way rather than in another. What hangs on the decision? In particular, why should it matter that the relation between a painting and its subject is an intentional relation while the photographic relation is merely causal? I shall therefore begin by considering our experience of painting and the effect on that experience of the intentionality of the relation between a painting and its subject.

When I appreciate a painting as a representation, I see it as what it represents, but I do not take it for what it represents. Nor do I necessarily believe that what is represented in the painting exists nor, if it does exist, that it has the appearance of the object that I see *in* the painting. Suppose that a certain painting represents a warrior. I may in fact see it not as a warrior but as a god. Here three 'objects' of interest may be distinguished:

1 The intentional object of sight: a god (defined by my experience).
2 The represented object: a warrior (defined, to put it rather crudely, by the painter's intention).[4]
3 The material object of sight: the painting.[5]

The distinction between 1 and 2 is not as clear-cut as it might seem: it would become so only if we could separate the 'pure appearance' of the painting from the sense of intention with which it is endowed. We cannot do this, not only because we can never separate our experience of human activity from our understanding of intention but also because in the case of a picture we are dealing with an object that is manifestly the expression of thought. Hence we will look for clues as to how the painting is intended to be seen and – such being the nature of 'seeing as' – our sense of what is intended will determine our experience of what is there.

The 'inference' view of perception, the view that there are certain things that we *basically* see (sense-data, etc.) from which we then *infer* the existence of other things, is wrong both as a matter of philosophical psychology, since there is no criterion for distinguishing datum and inference, and as a matter of epistemology, since it is only if we sometimes have knowledge of the 'inferred' entities that we can have knowledge of the experience.[6] The point applies also to intention: we do not see the gestures and movements of another man and then infer from them the existence of intentions; rather, we see the gestures as intentional, and that is the correct description of what we see. But of course we cannot choose to see just what we will as a manifestation of intention. Our ability to see intention depends on our ability to interpret an activity as characteristically human, and here, in the case of representational art, it involves our understanding the dimensions and conventions of the medium. Art manifests the 'common knowledge' of a culture;[7] as E. H. Gombrich has made clear, to understand art is to be familiar with the constraints imposed by the medium and to be able to separate that which is due to the medium from that which is due to the man. Such facts lead us to speak of understanding or misunderstanding representational painting.

Although there is not space to discuss fully the concept of 'understanding' that is involved here, it is worth mentioning the following point: to understand a painting involves understanding thoughts. These thoughts are, in a sense, communicated by the painting. They underlie the painter's intention, and at the same time they inform our way of seeing the canvas. Such thoughts determine the perception of the man who sees with understanding, and it is at least partly in terms of our apprehension of thoughts that we must describe what we see in the picture. We see not only a man on a horse but a man of a certain character and bearing. And *what* we see is determined not by independent properties of the subject but by our understanding of the painting. It is the way the eyes are painted that gives that sense of authority, the particular lie of the arm that reveals the arrogant character, and so on. In other words, properties of the medium influence not only what is seen in the picture but also the way it is seen. Moreover, they present to us a vision that we attribute not to ourselves but to another man; we think of ourselves as sharing in the vision of the artist, and the omnipresence of intention changes our experience from something private into something shared. The picture presents us not merely with the perception of a man but with a thought about him, a thought embodied in perceptual form.[8] And here, just as in the case of language, thought has that character of objectivity and publicity upon which Frege commented.[9] It is precisely when we have the communication of thoughts about a subject that the concept of representation becomes applicable; and therefore literature and painting are representational in the same sense.

3

The ideal painting has no particular need for an identity of appearance with its subject. In order to present a visual account of the Duke of Wellington, it is not necessary for an artist to strive to present an exact copy of the Duke's appearance.[10] Indeed, it is tempting here to dispense with the notion of appearance altogether, to construe the painting as a conventional or even quasi-linguistic act which stands in a semantic relation – a relation of reference – to its subject, and which presents a visual appearance only as a means of fulfilling a referential function. Such a view would explain, perhaps better than all rival theories of representation, the role of intention in our understanding of art.[11]

I do not know how far those philosophers influenced by Gombrich's arguments – arguments emphasizing the place of convention in our understanding of visual art – would wish to take the analogy with language. I do not know, for example, whether a convention according to which colours were to be represented by their complements – a red object by a patch of green, a yellow object by a patch of blue – would be conceivable for such philosophers, conceivable, that is, as a mode of pictorial representation. It is undeniable, however, that such a painting would convey to someone who understood the convention as much information about its subject as another painting in which the colours copy the original. More bizarre conventions could also be imagined: a painting could be constructed entirely out of dashes and circles, arranged according to the grammar of a visual code. Given the right conventions, such a painting

Roger Scruton

would count, according to the reference theory, as an extremely faithful representation of its subject. It would be read as a kind of scrambled message which had to be decoded in order to permit an understanding of what it says.

However, we cannot treat the visual connection between a painting and its subject as an entirely accidental matter, accidental, that is, to any process of representation that the painting may display. For we cannot deny that representational painting interests us primarily because of the visual connection with its subject. We are interested in the visual relation between painting and subject because it is by means of this relation that the painting represents. The artist presents us with a way of seeing (and not just any way of thinking of) his subject. (Hence the revolutionary character of such painters as Caravaggio and de la Tour.) It is this visual relation which seems to require elucidation. We cannot explain pictorial representation independently of the visual aspect of paintings and still expect our explanation to cast light upon the problem of the visual relation between a picture and its subject-matter. And yet it is that relation which is understood by the appreciative spectator.

That objection is of course not conclusive. It also seems to assume that a semantic theory of art (a theory which sees representation in terms of reference) must necessarily also be a linguistic theory. Surely there could be relations of reference that do not reflect the conventions of language, even relations that need to be understood in essentially visual terms. Let us, then, consider what such a conception of reference might be like.

It is no accident that language has a grammar. The existence of grammar is a necessary part of language and part of the all-important connection between language and truth. But there is a further significance in grammar, at least as grammar is now conceived. For the contemporary logician, grammar is primarily a 'generative' function, a means of building complex sentences from the finite number of linguistic parts. Taken in conjunction with a theory of interpretation, a proper grammar will explain how speakers of a language understand an indefinite number of sentences on the basis of understanding only a finite number of words.[12] In this way we can show how the truth or falsehood of a sentence depends upon the reference of its parts, and the concept of reference in language becomes inextricably bound up with the idea that from the references of words we may derive the truth conditions of sentences. This 'generative

connection' between reference and truth is part of the intuitive understanding of reference which is common to all speakers of a language.

It is here, I think, that we find a striking difference between language and painting. While there may be repertoires and conventions in painting, there is nothing approaching grammar as we understand it. For one thing, the requirement of finitude is not obviously met. It is clearly true that we understand the representational meaning of, say, a Carpaccio through understanding the representational meaning of its parts. But the parts themselves are understood in *precisely the same way*; that is, they too have parts, each of which is potentially divisible into significant components, and so on ad infinitum. Moreover, there seems to be no way in which we can divide the painting into grammatically significant parts – no way in which we can provide a syntax which isolates those parts of the painting that have a particular semantic role. For in advance of seeing the painting, we have no rule which will decide the point, and thus the idea of syntactic or semantic rules becomes inapplicable. The means whereby we understand the total representation are identical with the means whereby we understand the parts. Understanding is not secured either by rules or by conventions but seems to be, on the contrary, a natural function of the normal eye. As we see the meaning of the painting, so do we see the meaning of its parts. This contrasts sharply with the case of reference in language, where we *construct* the meaning of the sentence from the reference of its parts, and where the parts themselves have reference in a way that its ultimately conventional.

There seems to be no justification, then, for thinking of representation in terms of reference. We could, however, insist that the relation of a painting to its subject is one of reference only by removing from 'reference' that feature which leads us to think that an account of reference is also an account of understanding. To speak of the connection between a word and a thing as one of reference is to show how we understand the word, for it is to show how the truth conditions of sentences containing the word are determined. If we speak of reference in describing paintings, therefore, we should not think that we thereby cast any light on the *understanding* of representation. What representation is, how we understand it, and how it affects us – those questions seem to remain as obscure as ever. The only thing that remains to support the invocation of reference is the fact that paintings may be true or false. It is that fact which we must now consider.

4

The fact that a painting may be true or false plays a vital role in visual appreciation. We could not explain realism, for example, either in painting or in literature, unless we invoked the concept of truth. Again we must emphasize information (and therefore the concept of reference) in our understanding of the painter's art; or at least we are obliged to find some feature of the painting that can be substituted for reference and which will show how the connection with truth is established.

Such a feature, as a matter of fact, has already been described: we may describe realism in terms of what we see *in* the painting. We therefore analyse truth not in terms of a relation between the painting and the world but in terms of a relation between what we see in the painting and the world. Goya's portrait of the Duke of Wellington is realistic because the figure we see in the painting resembles the Duke of Wellington.[13] The truth of the painting amounts to the truth of the viewer's perception; in other words, the 'intentional object of sight' corresponds to the nature of the subject. Those thoughts which animate our perception when we see the realistic painting with understanding are true thoughts.[14] Truth is not a property of the painting in the direct way in which it is the property of a sentence, and the possibility of predicating the truth of a painting does not open the way to a semantic theory of art any more than it opens the way to a semantic theory of, for example, clouds, or of any other phenomenon in which aspects may be seen.

Although distinctions may be made between true and false pictures, an aesthetic appreciation remains in one sense indifferent to the truth of its object. A person who has an aesthetic interest in the *Odyssey* is not concerned with the literal truth of the narrative. Certainly it is important to him that the *Odyssey* be lifelike, but the existence of Odysseus and the reality of the scenes described are matters of aesthetic indifference. Indeed, it is characteristic of aesthetic interest that most of its objects in representation are imaginary. For unless it were possible to represent imaginary things, representation could hardly be very important to us. It is important because it enables the presentation of scenes and characters toward which we have only contemplative attitudes: scenes and characters which, being unreal, allow our practical natures to remain unengaged.

If the concept of representation is to be of aesthetic importance, it must be possible to describe an aesthetic interest in representation. Only if there is such a thing as aesthetic interest which has representation as its object can there be representational art (as opposed to art that happens to be representational). It is commonly said that an aesthetic interest in something is an interest in it for its own sake: the object is not treated as a surrogate for another; it is *itself* the principal object of attention. It follows that an aesthetic interest in the representational properties of a picture must also involve a kind of interest in the picture and not merely in the thing represented.[15]

Now, *one* difference between an aesthetic interest in a picture, and an interest in the picture as a surrogate for its subject, lies in the kind of reason that might be given for the interest. (And to give the reasons for an interest is to give an account of its intentional object and therefore of the interest itself.) If I ask a man why he is looking at a picture, there are several kinds of reply that he might give. In one case his reasons will be reasons for an interest only in the things depicted: they will describe properties of the subject which make it interesting. Here the interest in the picture is derivative: it lies in the fact that the picture reveals properties of its subject. The picture is being treated as a means of access to the subject, and it is therefore dispensable to the extent that there is a better means to hand (say, the subject itself). With that case one may contrast two others. First, there is the case where the man's reasons refer only to properties of the picture – to pictorial properties, such as colour, shape, and line – and do not mention the subject. For such a man the picture has interest as an abstract composition, and its representational nature is wholly irrelevant to him. Second, there is the case where the reasons for the interest are reasons for an interest in the *picture* (in the way it looks) even though they make essential reference to the subject and can be understood as reasons only by someone who understands the reference to the subject. For example, the observer may refer to a particular gesture of a certain figure, and a particular way of painting that gesture, as revelatory of the subject's character (for example, the barmaid's hands on the counter in Manet's *Bar aux Folies-Bergère*). Clearly, that is a reason not only for an interest in the subject but also (and primarily) for an interest in the picture, since it gives a reason for an interest in something which can be understood only by looking at the picture. Such an interest leads naturally to another, to an interest in the use of the medium – in the way the painting presents its subject and therefore in the way in which the subject is seen by the painter. Here it could not be said that the painting is being treated as a surrogate for its subject: it is *itself* the object of interest and irreplaceable by the thing depicted. The interest is not in representation for the sake of its subject but in representation for its own sake. And it is such an interest that forms the core of the aesthetic experience of pictorial art, and which – if analysed more fully – would explain not only the value of that experience but also the nature and value of the art which is its object. We see at once that such an interest is not, and cannot be, an interest in the literal truth of the picture.

5

If I were to describe, then, *what I see* in a picture, I would be bound not merely to describe the visual properties of the subject but also to provide an interpretation of the subject, a way of seeing it. The description under which the subject is seen is given by the total thought in terms of which I understand the picture. In the case of portraiture, this interpretive thought need not be a thought about the momentary appearance of the subject: it need not be the thought 'He looked like that'. The thought may relate to the subject not as he appeared at any one moment but as he was or, rather, as the artist saw him to be. The appearance may be presented only because it embodies the reality, in which case it will be the reality that is understood (or misunderstood) by the spectator.

One of the most important differences between photography and portraiture as traditionally practised lies in the relation of each to time. It is characteristic of photography that, being understood in terms of a causal relation to its subject, it is thought of as revealing something momentary about its subject – how the subject looked at a particular moment. And that sense of the moment is seldom lost in photography, for reasons that will shortly be apparent. Portrait painting, however, aims to capture the sense of time and to re-present its subject as extended in time, even in the process of displaying a particular moment of its existence. Portraiture is not an art of the momen-

tary, and its aim is not merely to capture fleeting appearances. The aim of painting is to give insight, and the creation of an appearance is important mainly as the expression of thought. While a causal relation is a relation between events, there is no such narrow restriction on the subject-matter of a thought. This perhaps partially explains the frequently made comment that the true art of portraiture died with the advent of photography and that representational art, insofar as it still pursues an ideal of realism, is unable to capture, as the realist ought to capture, the sense of the passage of time.[16]

Of course a photographer can aim to capture that fleeting appearance which gives the most reliable indication of his subject's character. He may attempt to find in the momentary some *sign* of what is permanent. But there is a great difference between an image which is a sign of something permanent and an image which is an expression of it. To express the permanent is to give voice to a thought about its nature. To give a sign of the permanent is to create something from which its properties may be inferred. A man may remain silent when asked to defend his friend, and from that silence I infer his friend's guilt. Yet the man has certainly not expressed the thought that his friend is guilty. Similarly a photograph may give signs of what is permanent despite the fact that it is incapable of expressing it.

6

The ideal photograph, as I mentioned earlier, stands in a causal relation to its subject and 'represents' its subject by reproducing its appearance. In understanding something as an ideal photograph, we understand it as exemplifying this causal process, a process which originates in the subject 'represented' and which has as its end point the production of a copy of an appearance. By a 'copy' of an appearance I mean an object such that what is seen in it by a man with normal eyes and understanding (the intentional object of sight) resembles as nearly as possible what is seen when such a man observes the subject itself from a certain angle at a certain point in its history. A person studying an ideal photograph is given a very good idea of *how something looked*. The result is that, from studying a photograph he may come to know how something looked in the way that he might know it if he had actually seen it.

With an ideal photograph it is neither necessary nor even possible that the photographer's intention should enter as a serious factor in determining how the picture is seen. It is recognized at once for what it is – not as an interpretation of reality but as a presentation of how something looked. In some sense, looking at a photograph is a substitute for looking at the thing itself. Consider, for example, the most 'realistic' of all photographic media, the television. It seems scarcely more contentious to say that I saw someone on the television – that is, that in watching the television I saw *him* – than to say that I saw him in a mirror. Television is like a mirror: it does not so much destroy as embellish that elaborate causal chain which is the natural process of visual perception.

Of course it is not necessary to define the subject of a photograph in terms of this causal process, for the subject could be identified in some other way. But the fact remains that when we say that *x* is a photograph of *y* we *are* referring to this causal relation, and it is in terms of the causal relation that the subject of a photograph is normally understood. Let us at least say that the subject is so defined for my logical ideal of photography: that premise is all that my argument requires.

It follows, first, that the subject of the ideal photograph must exist; secondly, that it must appear roughly as it appears in the photograph; and thirdly, that its appearance in the photograph is its appearance at a particular moment of its existence.

The first of those features is an immediate consequence of the fact that the relation between a photograph and its subject is a causal relation. If *a* is the cause of *b*, then the existence of *b* is sufficient for the existence of *a*. The photograph lacks that quality of 'intentional inexistence' which is characteristic of painting. The ideal photograph, therefore, is incapable of representing anything unreal; if a photograph is a photograph of a man, then there is some particular man of whom it is a photograph.

Of course I may take a photograph of a draped nude and call it *Venus*, but insofar as this can be understood as an exercise in fiction, it should not be thought of as a photographic representation of Venus but rather as the photograph of a representation of Venus. In other words, the process of fictional representation occurs not in the photograph but in the subject: it is the *subject* which represents Venus; the photograph does no more than disseminate its visual character to other eyes. This is not to say that the model is (unknown to herself) acting

Venus. It is not she who is representing Venus but the photographer, who uses her in his representation. But the representational act, the act which embodies the representational thought, is completed before the photograph is ever taken. As we shall see, this fictional incompetence of photography is of great importance in our understanding of the cinema; but it also severely limits the aesthetic significance of 'representation' in photography. As we saw earlier, representation in art has a special significance precisely because of the possibility that we can understand it – in the sense of understanding its content – while being indifferent to, or unconcerned with, its literal truth. That is why fictional representation is not merely an important form of representational art but in fact the primary form of it, the form through which the aesthetic understanding finds its principal mode of expression.

One may wish to argue that my example is a special one, that there are other ways of creating fictional representations which are essentially photographic. In other words, it is not necessary for the photographer to create an independent representation in order for his photograph to be fictional. Suppose he were to take a photograph of a drunken tramp and label it *Silenus*. Would that not be a fictional photograph, comparable, indeed, to a painting of Silenus in which a drunken tramp was used as a model?

This example, which I owe to Richard Wollheim, is an interesting one, but it does not, I think, establish what it claims. Consider a parallel case: finding a drunken tramp in the street I point to him and say 'Silenus'. It is arguable that my gesture makes the tramp into a representation; but if it does, it is because I am inviting you to think of him in that way. I have expressed a representational thought: imagine this person as Silenus. And I have completed the thought by an act of ostension toward its dozing subject. The act of ostension might on some other occasion be accomplished by a camera (or a frame, or a mirror, or any other device which isolates what it shows).

The camera, then, is being used not to represent something but to point to it. The subject, once located, plays its own special part in an independent process of representation. The camera is not essential to that process: a gesturing finger would have served just as well. If the example shows that photographs can be representations, then it shows the same of fingers. To accept that conclusion is to fail to distinguish between what is accidental and what is essential in the expression of a representational thought. It is to open the way toward the theory that everything which plays a part in the expression of thought is itself a representation. Such a view does not account for the aesthetic significance of representations. It also, however, and far more seriously, implies that there is no distinction between representational and nonrepresentational art. The concept of representation that I am assuming makes such a distinction, and it makes it for very good reasons. I am not tempted by such dubious examples to abandon it. One might put the point by saying that a painting, like a sentence, is a *complete* expression of the thought which it contains. Painting is a sufficient vehicle of representational thought, and there may be no better way of expressing what a painting says. That is why representation can be thought of as an intrinsic property of a painting and not just as a property of some process of which the painting forms a part.

Consider also the second feature mentioned above: the subject of an ideal photograph must appear roughly as it appears in the photograph. By its very nature, photography can 'represent' only through resemblance. It is only because the photograph acts as a visual reminder of its subject that we are tempted to say that it represents its subject. If it were not for this resemblance, it would be impossible to see from the photograph how the subject appeared, except by means of scientific knowledge that would be irrelevant to any interest in the visual aspect of the photograph. Contrast here the case of an electron microscope, which punches out on a ticker tape a codified indication of a crystal's atomic structure. Is that a representation of the atomic structure? If it is, then why not say that any causal relation which enables us to infer the nature of the cause from the properties of its effect provides us with a representation of the cause in the effect? Such a concept of representation would be uninteresting indeed. It is impossible, therefore, that the ideal photograph should represent an object except by showing how it appeared at a certain moment in its history and still *represent* it in the way ideal photography represents anything. How indeed could we make sense of an ideal photograph representing its subject *as* other than it appeared? We could do so only if we could also say that a photograph sometimes represents its subject as it appears; that is, if we could say that representation here is 'representation as'. But consider this sentence: x is an ideal photograph of y as z. It seems that we have no means of filling out the

description 'z', no means, that is, of filling it out by reference only to the photographic process and not, say, to some independent act of representation that precedes or follows it. One might say that the medium in photography has lost all importance: it can present us with what we see, but it cannot tell us how to see it.

We *must* be aware of the three features mentioned above if we are to appreciate the characteristic effects of photography. In looking at an ideal photograph, we know that we are seeing something which actually occurred and seeing it as it appeared. Typically, therefore, our attitude toward photography will be one of curiosity, not curiosity about the photograph but rather about its subject. The photograph addresses itself to our desire for knowledge of the world, knowledge of how things look or seem. The photograph is a means to the end of seeing its subject; in painting, on the other hand, the subject is the means to the end of its own representation. The photograph is transparent to its subject, and if it holds our interest it does so because it acts as a surrogate for the thing which it shows. Thus if one finds a photograph beautiful, it is because one finds something beautiful in its subject. A painting may be beautiful, on the other hand, even when it represents an ugly thing.

7

Someone might accept the general difference I have indicated between an aesthetic interest and an attitude of curiosity, and accept too the implication that something is a representation only if it is capable of carrying a reference to its subject without merely standing as a surrogate for it. He still might argue, however, that it is possible to be interested in a photograph *as* a photograph and find it, and not just its subject, beautiful.

But what is it to be interested in a photograph as a photograph? Of course one might have a purely abstract aesthetic interest in a photograph – an interest in the photograph as a construction of lines and shapes (as one is intended to appreciate Man Ray's Rayogrammes, for example). One can have a purely abstract aesthetic interest in anything; photography is only a representational art if our interest in a photograph as a photographic 'representation' is a type of aesthetic interest.

Let us return to the previous discussion of representation in painting. It appears that there is a prima facie contradiction between saying that I am interested in a thing for its own sake and saying that I am interested in it as a representation of something else. In attempting to reconcile these two interests, it is necessary first to restrict the place of truth in aesthetic interest. Truth is aesthetically relevant only insofar as it may be construed as truth to the situation presented rather than 'truth to the facts'. From the point of view of aesthetic interest, it is always irrelevant that there should be a particular object which is the object represented or, if there is such an object, that it should exist as portrayed. That is not to say, of course, that an aesthetic interest does not require things to be in general roughly as they are shown; but that is another matter.

As I have already said, this conflicts with the typical way in which we are interested in photographs. Knowing what we know about photographs, it is at least natural that we should be interested in them both because they are true to the facts and because they tell us useful things about their subject-matter. It seems, therefore, that the emotional or 'aesthetic' qualities of a photograph tend to derive directly from the qualities of what it 'represents': if the photograph is sad, it is usually because its subject is sad; if the photograph is touching, it is because its subject is touching, and so on. It is worth reflecting on why there could not be a photograph of a martyrdom that was other than horrifying. One's curiosity here would be no different from one's curiosity in the act itself. Hence it would be as difficult (and perhaps also as corrupt) to have an aesthetic interest in the photograph as it would be in the real situation. By contrast, a painting of a martyrdom may be serene, as is Mantegna's great *Crucifixion* in the Louvre. The painting has emotional qualities in defiance of the qualities of its subject. In the case of a photograph – say of the victim of some accident – one's attitude is determined by the knowledge that this is how things are. One's attitude is made practical by the knowledge of the causal relation between photograph and object. This is not to deny that one might be interested in a photograph for its own sake and at the same time maintain a proper distance from its subject, even when it depicts a scene of agony or death. But the real question is, Can we have such an interest in a photograph without having the same interest in its subject? Can I have an aesthetic interest in the photograph of a dying soldier which is not also an aesthetic interest in the soldier's death? Or, rather, can I maintain that separation of interests and still be interested in the

'representational' aspect of the photograph? If we are distanced from the photograph only because we are distanced from its subject, then the important distinction that I wish to emphasize, between interest in the representation and interest in the subject, has still not been made. It seems necessary to show that photography *can* – by itself – create that sharp separation of interests which is everywhere apparent in serious painting. Consider too the photographs of old London. How is it possible to detach one's interest in their beauty from an interest in the beauty of London as it was? Regret is here the appropriate reaction to the photograph (as it is not – or at least not normally – an appropriate reaction to a Canaletto). 'That is how it looked!' is the central index of one's emotion.

Consider, then, the reasons that may be given in answer to the question, 'Why are you looking at that?' With a photograph, one mentions the features of the subject; with a painting, one mentions only the observable aspect captured in the picture. This essentially is what distinguishes an interest in a representation as a surrogate from an interest in a representation for its own sake. Suppose now that someone wishes to argue that it is *not* inevitable that we treat photographs, even ideal photographs, as I have described. Let us see what the consequences of such a position might be.

8

Imagine that we treat photographs as representations in just the same way that we treat paintings, so that their representational natures are themselves the objects of an aesthetic interest. What are the consequences if we study photography in such a way that it does not matter whether its subject actually existed or actually looked like the thing we see in the picture? Here we are interested not in the subject but in its manner of presentation. If there *can* be such an interest in a photograph, it suggests that a photograph may sometimes be the expression of a representational thought and not merely a simulacrum of its subject.

An interest in an object for its own sake, in the object as a whole, must encompass an interest in detail. For if there is nothing *for* which one contemplates an object, as has frequently been argued, there is no way of determining in advance of looking at it which features are, and which are not, relevant to one's interest.[17] It is for this reason that we cannot rest satisfied with nature but must have works of art as the objects of aesthetic judgment. Art provides a medium transparent to human intention, a medium for which the question, Why? can be asked of every observable feature, even if it may sometimes prove impossible to answer. Art is an expression of precisely the same rational impulses that find an outlet in aesthetic interest; it is therefore the only object which satisfies that interest completely.

The photographer, then, who aims for an aesthetically significant representation must also aim to control detail: 'detail' being here understood in the wide sense of 'any observable fact or feature'. But here lies a fresh difficulty. The causal process of which the photographer is a victim puts almost every detail outside of his control. Even if he does, say, intentionally arrange each fold of his subject's dress and meticulously construct, as studio photographers once used to do, the appropriate scenario, that would still hardly be relevant, since there seem to be few ways in which such intentions can be revealed in the photograph. For one thing, we lack all except the grossest features of style in photography; and yet it is style that persuades us that the question, Why this and not that? admits such fruitful exploration in the case of painting. Style enables us to answer that question by referring solely to aspects of the painting rather than to features which are aesthetically irrelevant, or in no way *manifest* in what is seen.[18] The search for meaning in a photograph is therefore curtailed or thwarted: there is no point in an interest in detail since there is nothing that detail can show. Detail, like the photograph itself, is transparent to its subject. If the photograph is interesting, it is only because what it portrays is interesting, and not because of the manner in which the portrayal is effected.

Let us assume, however, that the photographer could intentionally exert over his image just the kind of control that is exercised in the other representational arts. The question is, How far can this control be extended? Certainly there will be an infinite number of things that lie outside his control. Dust on a sleeve, freckles on a face, wrinkles on a hand: such minutiae will always depend initially upon the prior situation of the subject. When the photographer sees the photographic plate, he may still wish to assert his control, choosing just this colour here, just that number of wrinkles or that texture of skin. He can proceed to paint things out or in, to touch up, alter, or *pasticher* as he pleases. But of course he has now become a painter, precisely through taking representation seriously. The photograph has been reduced to a kind of frame around which he paints, a frame that imposes upon him largely unnecessary constraints.[19]

In other words, when the photographer strives towards representational art, he inevitably seems to move away from that ideal of photography which I have been describing toward the ideal of painting. This can be seen most clearly if we consider exactly what has to be the case if photography is to be a wholly representational art – if it is to manifest all those aspects of representation that distinguish it from mere copying and which endow it with its unique aesthetic appeal. No one could deny that from its origins photography has set itself artistic ideals and attempted to establish itself as a representational art. The culmination of the process – which can be seen in such photographs as Henry Peach Robinson's 'Autumn' – is to be found in the techniques of photo-montage used by the surrealists and futurists (and in particular, by such artists as László Moholy-Nagy and Hannah Höch). Here our interest in the result can be entirely indifferent to the existence and nature of the original subject. But that is precisely because the photographic figures have been so cut up and rearranged in the final product that it could not be said in any normal sense to be a *photograph* of its subject. Suppose that I were to take figures from a photograph of, say, Jane, Philip, and Paul, and having cut them out, I were to arrange them in montage, touching them up and adjusting them until the final result is to my mind satisfactory. It could very well be said that the final result represents, say, a lovers' quarrel; but it is not a photograph of one. It represents a quarrel because it stands in precisely the same intentional relation to a quarrel that a painting might have exhibited. Indeed, it is, to all intents and purposes, a painting, except that it happens to have employed photographic techniques in the derivation of its figures. Insofar as the figures can still be considered to be photographs, they are photographs of Jane, Philip, and Paul and not photographs of a lovers' quarrel. (Of course the fact of their *being* photographs might be aesthetically important. Some ironical comment, for example, may be intended in using figures cut from a medium of mass production.)

The history of the art of photography is the history of successive attempts to break the causal chain by which the photographer is imprisoned, to impose a human intention between subject and appearance, so that the subject can be both defined by that intention and seen in terms of it.[20] It is the history of an attempt to turn a mere simulacrum into the expression of a representational thought, an attempt to discover through techniques (from the combination print to the soft-focus lens) what was in fact already known.[21] Occasionally, it is true, photographers have attempted to create entirely fictional scenes through photography and have arranged their models and surroundings, as one might on the stage, in order to produce a narrative scene with a representational meaning. But, as I have argued, the resulting photograph would not be a representation. The process of representation was effected even before the photograph was taken. A photograph of a representation is no more a representation than a picture of a man is a man.

9

It might be felt that I have begged the question in allowing only one way in which photography may acquire representational meaning, a way which inevitably leads photography to subject itself to the aims of painting. One may argue that a photographer does not choose his subject at random, nor is he indifferent to the point of view from which he photographs it or to the composition in which it is set. The act of photography may be just as circumscribed by aesthetic intentions as the act of painting. A photograph will be designed to show its subject in a particular light and from a particular point of view, and by so doing it may reveal things about it that we do not normally observe and, perhaps, that we might not have observed but for the photograph. Such an enterprise leads to effects which are wholly proper to the art of photography, which therefore has its own peculiar way of showing the world. Why is that not enough to give to photography the status of a representational art?

I do not think that such an objection need cause me to revise my argument. For exactly the same might be said of a mirror. When I see someone in a mirror I see *him*, not his representation. This remains so even if the mirror is a distorting mirror and even if the mirror is placed where it is intentionally. This intention might even be similar to the intention in photography: to give a unique and remarkable view of an object, a view which reveals a 'truth' about it that might otherwise have gone unobserved. One could even imagine an art of mirrors, an art which involves holding a mirror aloft in such a way that what is seen in the mirror is rendered by that process interesting or beautiful.

This art of mirrors may, like the art of photography, sometimes involve representation. It may, for example, involve a representation of Venus or of Silenus in the manner of the two types of 'fictional' photographs considered earlier. But representation will not be a property of the *mirror*. It is impossible that I could, simply by holding a mirror before someone, make him into a representation of himself. For after all, whether I look at him or at the mirror, in either case it is *him* that I see. If the mirror is to become the expression of a representational thought, it too must be denatured; like the photomontage, it must be freed from the causal chain which links it to its subject. One can perhaps begin to see the truth in Oliver Wendell Holmes's description of the daguerreotype as a 'mirror with a memory'.[22] It was just such a mirror that led to the downfall of Lord Lambton.

It does not matter, therefore, how many aesthetic intentions underlie the act of photography. It does not matter that the subject, its environment, activity, or light are all consciously arranged. The real question is, What has to be done to make the resulting image into a representation? There are images which are representations (paintings) and images which are not (mirrors). To which class does the photograph belong? I have argued that it naturally belongs to the latter class. Photography can be *made* to belong to the former class by being made into the principal vehicle of the representational thought. But one must then so interfere with the relation between the photograph and its subject that it ceases to be a *photograph* of its subject. Is that not enough to show that it is not just my ideal of photography which fails to be a mode of representation, but also that representation can never be achieved through photography alone?

A final comparison: I mark out a certain spot from which a particular view of a street may be obtained. I then place a frame before that spot. I move the frame so that, from the chosen spot, only certain parts of the street are visible, others are cut off. I do this with all the skill available to me, so that what is seen in the frame is as pleasing as it might be: the buildings within the frame seem to harmonize, the ugly tower that dominates the street is cut off from view, the centre of the composition is the little lane between two classical façades which might otherwise have gone unnoticed, and so on. There I have described an activity which is as circumscribed by aesthetic intentions as anything within the experience of the normal photographer. But how could it be argued that what I see in the frame is not the street itself but a representation of it? The very suggestion is absurd.

10

Here one might object that representation is not, after all, an intrinsic property either of a painting or of a description. Representation is a relation; an object can be described as a representation only if one person uses it to represent something to another. On this view, there is no such thing as 'being a representation'; there is only 'having a representational use.' And if this were the case, my arguments would be in vain. Photographs are as much, and as little, representations as paintings, as gestures, as mirrors, as labels, and as anything else that can play its part in the process of communication.

The objection is more serious, and reflects a well-known dispute in the theory of meaning. Meaning, some say, is a property of a sentence; others, for instance, H. Paul Grice, argue that meaning is primarily a relation between utterance and speaker.[23] Now, even for Grice, there remains a distinction between utterances which are articulate and utterances which are not. Sentences are to be distinguished from nods of the head in that they participate in and exemplify a grammar, and through that grammar they can be understood independently of the context of their use. By being articulate, the sentence can stand alone as the principal expression of a thought. There arises a kind of interest in the sentence (and in its content) which is independent of any direct involvement in the act of communication. Meaning can be read *in* the sentence and need not be inferred from surrounding circumstances.

Similarly, painting, being fully articulate, can attract attention as the principal expression of a process of thought. It can be understood in isolation from the special circumstances of its creation, because each and every feature of a painting can be both the upshot of an intentional act and at the same time the creation of an intentional object. The interest in the intentional object becomes an interest in the thought which it conveys. A painter can fill his canvas with meaning in just the way that a writer may fill his prose. This is what makes painting and literature into representational arts: they are arts which can be appreciated as they are in themselves and at the same time understood in terms of a descriptive thought which they articulate.

In photography we may have the deliberate creation of an image. Moreover, I may use a photograph as a representation: I may use a photograph of Lenin as a representation of him, in the way that I might have used a clenched fist or a potato or a photograph of Hitler. The question is, What makes the image *itself* into the principal vehicle of representational thought? I wish to argue that an image can be deliberate without being properly articulate. The image becomes articulate when (a) the maker of the image can seriously address himself to the task of communicating thought through the image alone, and (b) when the spectator can see and understand the image in terms of the process of thought which it expresses. To satisfy (a) we require a painterly approach to detail; to satisfy (b) we must distract the spectator's attention from the causal relation which is the distinguishing feature of photography. Either way, the persistence of that relation – in other words, the persistence of the *photographic* image – can only hinder representation. It can contribute nothing to its achievement. This is perhaps what James Joyce meant when he wrote the following in his Paris notebooks of 1904:

> Question: Can a photograph be a work of art? Answer: A photograph is a disposition of sensible matter and may be so disposed for an aesthetic end, but it is not a human disposition of sensible matter. Therefore it is not a work of art.

If Joyce meant by 'work of art' what I mean by 'representation', then he was clearly getting at the same point. The property of representation, as I have characterized it, is the upshot of a complex pattern of intentional activity and the object of highly specialized responses. How can a photograph acquire that property? My answer is that it can do so only by changing in precisely those respects which distinguish photography from painting. For it is only if photography changes in those respects that the photographer can seriously address himself to the thoughts and responses of his spectators. It is only then, therefore, that the photograph becomes a proper *vehicle* of representational thought.

11

Photography is not representation; nor is it representation when used in the cinema. A film is a photograph of a dramatic representation, and whatever representational properties belong to it belong by virtue of the representation that is effected in the dramatic action, that is, by virtue of the words and activities of the actors in the film. *Ivan the Terrible* represents the life of Ivan, not because the camera was directed at *him*, but because it was directed at an actor who *played the part of* Ivan. Certainly the camera has its role in presenting the action, much as the apparatus of production has its role on the stage. It directs the audience's attention to this or that feature and creates, too, its own peculiar effects of atmosphere. Proper use of the camera may create an interest in situations that could not be portrayed on the stage. Hence photography permits the extension of dramatic representation into areas where previously it would not have been possible, just as music, which is not a representational art, enabled Wagner to create for the first time a theatrical representation of a cosmic theme.[24] (Consider, for example, the camera in Bergman's *Persona*, where it is used to create a dramatic situation between two characters, one of whom never speaks. Such mastery is perhaps rare, but it has existed as an ideal since the earliest days of cinema.) Nonetheless, the process of photography does not, because it cannot, *create* the representation. Thus documentary films are in no sense representations of their subject-matter. (Which is not to say that they cannot involve the realization of elaborate aesthetic ideas: it is hardly necessary to mention Leni Riefenstahl's film of the Berlin Olympics.) A cinematic record of an occurrence is not a representation of it, any more than a recording of a concert is a representation of its sound. As all must agree, representation in the cinema involves an *action*, in just the way that a play involves an action. The action is understood when the audience realizes that the figure photographed is attempting to portray adventures, actions, and feelings which are not his own, and yet which are nevertheless the proper subject-matter of aesthetic interest. It follows that the fundamental constraints which the cinema must obey as an art form – those constraints which are integral to its very nature as a representational art – are dramatic ones, involving the representation of character and action. ('Dramatic' here does not mean 'theatrical', but is applied in the sense which Henry James gave to it

when he spoke of the novel as a form of dramatic art.) To succeed as cinema, a film must have true characters, and it must be true to them; the director can no more sentimentalize with impunity than can the novelist or the playwright. The true source of the badness of most cinema lies, of course, in the fact that the gorgeous irrelevancies of photography obscure the sentimentality of the dramatic aim.

Photography, far from making dramatic representation more easy, in fact makes it more difficult. Indeed, the possibility of dramatic success in the cinema is a remote one, for with there are two reasons. The first, and somewhat shallow, reason is that the film director is photographing something which either is or purports to be a part of the actual world. It follows that he can only with the greatest difficulty convey to his audience an appropriate sense of detail. Typically the audience is given no criterion of relevance, no criterion which settles what must be attended to. Was the audience meant to notice the man on the street corner, the movement of the eyebrow, the colour of the macintosh, the make of the car? In every cinematographic image, countless such questions remain unanswered. There are various reasons for this. For one thing, a film is fixed with respect to all its details; although it is a dramatic representation, it cannot exist in more than one performance. Therefore features of interpretation cannot be separated from features of the action: there is no such distinction. It is only in understanding the representation as a whole that I come to see what I should be attending to. Furthermore, the cameraman operates under a permanent difficulty in making any visual comment on the action. The difficulty can be solved, but its solution is perforce crude in comparison with the simpler devices of the stage; crude because it must both create irrelevancies and at the same time persuade us to ignore them. (Consider, for example, the ritualized expressionism of *Der blaue Engel* or *The Cabinet of Doctor Caligari*. Even Fritz Lang's *Siegfried* contains reminiscences of this *commedia dell'arte* mannerism, whereby the actor attempts to divert the audience's attention from the infinite irrelevance of detail, toward the dramatic meaning of the whole. Of course more recent directors have emancipated themselves from the theatrical constraints of expressionism; as a result they have at least felt happy to ignore the problem, even if they could not solve it.)

In the theatre the situation is different. The necessary limitations of the stage and the conventions of stage performance, which derive from the fact that the play exists independently of its performance, provide a strong representational medium through which the dramatic action is filtered. Someone with a knowledge of the conventions will see at once what is relevant and what is not. Symbolism in the theatre is therefore clear and immediate, whereas on the screen it is too often vague, portentous, and psychologically remote. Consider, for example, *L'Eclisse*, where the camera, striving again and again to make a comment, succeeds only in inflating the importance of the material surroundings out of all proportion to the sentiments of the characters. The effect is to render the image all-engrossing, while at the same time impoverishing the psychology.

It is for this reason that what often passes for photographic comment in the cinema ought more properly to be described as photographic effect. The camera may create an atmosphere – it may be an instrument of expression – but it is unable to make any precise or cogent analysis of what it shows. Consider the techniques of montage, used to such effect by the Russians. Eisenstein argues that there is a precise parallel between the technique of montage and the sequential structure of verse.[25] For example, each image that Milton presents in the following passage corresponds to a precise and unambiguous shot:

> ... at last
> Farr in th'Horizon to the North appeer'd
> From skirt to skirt a fierie Region, stretch
> In battailous aspect, and neerer view
> Bristl'd with upright beams innumerable
> Of rigid Spears, and Helmets throng'd,
>   and Shields
> Various, with boastful Argument portraid,
> The banded Powers of *Satan* hasting on
> With furious expedition ...

(One may note the cinematographic device 'and neerer view' and the very Eisensteinian quality of the image that follows it.) The contention is that for each of Milton's images one may find a cinematic shot that somehow 'says the same thing'; the total montage would form a dramatic unity in precisely the same sense, and for the same reason, as Milton's lines. The director will be doing something analogous to the poet: he will be focusing attention on carefully chosen details with a view to creating a unified expression of the prevailing mood.

It should be noted, however, that each shot in the montage will also present infinitely many details that are *not* designed as objects of attention. The shot corresponding to 'Helmets throng'd' will capture that idea among others, but it will also say much more that is irrelevant. It will not be able to avoid showing the *kind* of helmet, for example, the material, size, and shape of it. By so concretizing the thought, the camera leaves nothing to the imagination. As a result the detail that really matters – the thronging of Satanic helmets – is in danger of being lost. It was for this reason that Eisenstein developed techniques of contrast and composition in order to control more effectively the attention of his audience. It is a testimony to his genius that the poetry of *Ivan the Terrible* has rarely been rediscovered by subsequent directors. Even in Eisenstein, however, comment comes primarily through drama rather than through image. The whole effort of photography lies in expression and effect. And interestingly enough the clearest examples of photographic comment in the cinema come when once again the causal relation between image and subject is replaced by an intentional one. Consider the following sequence from *The Battleship Potemkin*:

1 *Title*: 'And the rebel battleship answered the brutality of the tyrant with a shell upon the town.'
2 A slowly and deliberately turning gun-turret.
3 *Title*: 'Objective – the Odessa Theatre.'
4 Marble group at the top of the theatre building.
5 *Title*: 'On the general's headquarters.'
6 Shot from the gun.
7 Two very short shots of a marble figure of Cupid above the gates of the building.
8 A mighty explosion; the gates totter.
9 Three short shots: a stone lion asleep;
                        a stone lion with open
                                eyes;
                        a rampant stone lion.
10 New explosion, shattering the gates.[26]

Here we have one of Eisenstein's most striking visual metaphors. A stone lion rises to its feet and roars. This amazing image (impossible, incidentally, outside the limitations of the silent screen) acts as a powerful comment on the impotence of imperial splendour precisely because it startles us into a recognition of the underlying thought. But we know that this cannot be a photograph of a stone lion roaring. It is, rather, the intentional juxtaposition of unconnected images; it is the intention that we see and which determines our understanding of the sequence. It is of course lamentable that such art should have subjected itself to the inane mythmaking revealed in the titles to this script; that does not alter the fact that, if there is art here, it is an art which is essentially photographic.

The second and deeper point I wish to mention is extremely difficult to express in terms that would be acceptable to the contemporary analytical philosopher. I shall try not to be too deterred by that.[27] Photography, precisely because it does not represent but at best can only distort, remains inescapably wedded to the creation of illusions, to the creation of lifelike *semblances* of things in the world. Such an art, like the art of the waxworks, is an art that provides a ready gratification for fantasy, and in so doing defeats the aims of artistic expression. A dramatic art can be significant only if it is, at some level, realistic; but to be realistic it must first forbid expression to those habits of unseriousness and wish fulfilment that play such an important part in our lives. Unless it can do that, the greatest effects of drama – such as we observe in the tragedies of the Greeks, of Racine, and of Shakespeare – will be denied to it. Art is fundamentally serious; it cannot rest content with the gratification of fantasy, nor can it dwell on what fascinates us while avoiding altogether the question of its meaning. As Freud put it in another context, art provides the path from fantasy back to reality. By creating a representation of something unreal, it persuades us to consider again those aspects of reality which, in the urgency of everyday existence,

we have such strong motives for avoiding.[28] Convention in art, as Freud saw, is the great destroyer of fantasies. It prevents the ready *realization* of scenes that fascinate us, and substitutes for the creation of mere semblance the elaboration of reflective thought.

The cinema has been devoted from its outset to the creation of fantasies. It has created worlds so utterly like our own in their smallest details that we are lulled into an acceptance of their reality, and persuaded to overlook all that is banal, grotesque, or vulgar in the situations which they represent. The cinema has proved too persuasive at the level of mere realization and so has had little motive to explore the significance of its subject. It is entirely beguiling in its immediacy, so that even serious critics of literature can be duped into thinking that a film like *Sunset Boulevard* expresses an aesthetic idea, instead of simply preying on the stereotyped fantasies of its audience.

Moreover, the cinema, like the waxworks, provides us with a ready means of realizing situations which fascinate us. It can address itself to our fantasy directly, without depending upon any intermediate process of thought. This is surely what distinguishes the scenes of violence which are so popular in the cinema from the conventionalized death throes of the theatre. And surely it is this too which makes photography incapable of being an erotic art, in that it presents us with the object of lust rather than a symbol of it: it therefore gratifies the fantasy of desire long before it has succeeded in understanding or expressing the fact of it. The medium of photography, one might say, is inherently pornographic.

Notes

1 See for example, the discussions in Allardyce Nicoll, *Film and Theatre* (London, 1936; New York, 1972).

2 See Franz Clemens Brentano, *Psychology from an Empirical Standpoint*, ed. Linda McAlister (London and New York, 1973); Roderick M. Chisholm, *Perceiving* (London and Ithaca, NY, 1957), chapter 11; and G. E. M. Anscombe, 'The Intentionality of Sensation', in R. J. Butler (ed.), *Analytical Philosophy*, Second Series (Oxford, 1965).

3 I think that in this area nonextensionality (intensionality) and intentionality should be sharply distinguished, so that the claim is not affected by any argument to the effect that causal relations are nonextensional.

4 I pass over the problem here of selecting and describing the appropriate intention.

5 For the material/intentional distinction, I rely on Anscombe.

6 The most famous arguments for this conclusion occur in Kant's *Critique of Pure Reason* (in particular in the 'Transcendental Deduction') and in Wittgenstein's *Philosophical Investigations*, part I.

7 The importance of 'common knowledge', its complexity as a phenomenon, and its natural coexistence with conventions has been recognized in the philosophy of language; see especially the interesting discussion in David K. Lewis, *Convention: a*

Philosophical Study (Cambridge, Mass., 1969; Oxford, 1972).

8 I have discussed elsewhere what I mean by the 'embodiment' of thought in perception; see my *Art and Imagination* (London, 1974), chapters 7 and 8.

9 G. Frege, *Translations from the Philosophical Writings*, edited and translated by P. T. Geach and M. Black (Oxford, 1952; 3rd. edn. New Jersey, 1980), p. 79.

10 There is a problem here about 'identity of appearance' on which I touch again, sect. 8.

11 Nelson Goodman, the most important exponent of a semantic theory of art, manages to reconcile his approach with a view of photographs as representational; see his *Languages of Art* (Indianapolis, 1968; London, 1969), p. 9n.

12 I draw here on the now familiar arguments given by Donald Davidson in 'Truth and Meaning,' *Synthese*, vol. 17 (1967), pp. 304–23, which originate with Frege and which were given full mathematical elaboration in Alfred Tarski's theory of truth.

13 That is, provided the painting is independently *of* the Duke of Wellington.

14 See n. 8, above.

15 Hence the tradition in philosophy, which begins with Kant, according to which representation constitutes a threat to the autonomy of art.

16 I am thinking of recent exercises in 'photographic' realism by such painters as Ken Danby and Alex Colville. More traditional styles of realism have also emerged in open opposition to both the clinical lines of the photographic school and the contentless images of abstract expressionism. Witness here the paintings of David Inshaw and Robert Lowe.

17 See for example, Stuart Hampshire, 'Logic and Appreciation' in William Elton (ed.), *Aesthetics and Language* (Oxford, 1954; New Jersey, 1970).

18 See Richard Wollheim's interesting discussion 'Style now' in Bernard William Smith (ed.), *Concerning Contemporary Art* (Oxford and New York, 1975).

19 This argument is hinted at in B. Croce, *Estetica*, 10th edn (Bari, 1985), p. 20.

20 See for example, Aaron Scharf, *Creative Photography* (London, 1975) and Rudolf Arnheim, *Film as Art* (California, 1957; London, 1958).

21 See especially Henry Peach Robinson, *The Elements of a Pictorial Photograph* (London, 1896).

22 Holmes, quoted in Beaumont Newhall, *History of Photography* (New York, 1964; London, 1972), p. 22.

23 'Meaning', *Philosophical Review*, LXVI (1957), pp. 377–88.

24 See my 'Representation in Music', in *The Aesthetic Understanding* (London, 1983).

25 See Sergei Eisenstein, 'Word and Image', *The Film Sense* (London, 1943; New York, 1969).

26 Discussed by V. I. Pudovkin, *Writings*, trans. I. Montagu (London, 1954), p. 88.

27 The point is made at greater length, and more rigorously, in my 'Fantasy, Imagination and the Screen,' in *The Aesthetic Understanding*.

28 See *The Standard Edition of the Complete Psychological Works of Sigmund Freud*, ed. James Strachey, 24 vols. (London, 1953–74; New York, 1976), IX, p. 153; XI, p. 50; XII, p. 224; XIII, pp. 187–8; XIV, pp. 375–7; XX, p. 64.

32

Originals, Copies, and Aesthetic Value

Jack W. Meiland

In addressing the question of whether there could be any aesthetic difference between an original painting and a visually indistinguishable forgery, Nelson Goodman is careful to distinguish the matter of aesthetic *difference* from that of aesthetic *value*. Even if the original is aesthetically different from a copy, the copy may have greater aesthetic value than the original: "In our example, the original probably is much the better picture, since Rembrandt's paintings are in general much better than copies by unknown painters. But a copy of a Lastman by Rembrandt may well be better than the original."[1] Again, "Here, as earlier, we must be careful not to confuse genuineness with aesthetic merit. That the distinction between original and forgery is aesthetically important does not, we have seen, imply that the original is superior to the forgery . . ." (p. 119). But, although the questions of aesthetic difference and aesthetic value are distinct, they are logically related in a particular way. If there is no aesthetic difference between an original and a visually indistinguishable copy, then one would be forced to conclude that "the forgery is as good as the original" (p. 109). Goodman argues that the original and the copy can differ aesthetically, no matter how perfect the copy is. If Goodman is right about this, then it is an open question as to which – original or copy – is more valuable aesthetically. Yet it is commonly believed that originals are more valuable than copies. Forg-

Jack W. Meiland, "Originals, Copies and Aesthetic Value," in Denis Dutton (ed.), *The Forger's Art* (Berkeley, CA: University of California Press, 1983), pp. 115–30.

eries are usually removed from museum walls as soon as they are discovered to be forgeries. Originals are avidly sought by private collectors, while forgeries are not. All of this raises the question: What arguments can be given for the view that originals are aesthetically more valuable than copies?

I must first emphasize that we are here talking about *aesthetic* value. There is no doubt that an original Rembrandt is more valuable overall than a recent exact copy of it. For even if the original and the copy are identical in aesthetic value, the original has immense historical value in addition to its aesthetic value. It is simply a fact that we prize items from the past, and the longer they have survived, the greater value they have for us. This value – which is perhaps better termed "survival value" rather than historical value, since it attaches even to lowly items having no particular historical importance – is independent of aesthetic value. We treasure and exhibit in our museums even fragments of pottery and common utensils that have no aesthetic value at all, let alone historical value. Thus, survival value and historical value are distinguishable from aesthetic value. And the original Rembrandt, having greater survival and historical value than the copy, has greater *overall* value than the copy.

But does the original Rembrandt have greater *aesthetic* value than the copy? A theory which holds that the aesthetic value of a painting depends solely on the visual appearance of the painting – let us call this "The Appearance Theory of Aesthetic Value" – would imply that this copy, being visually indistinguishable from the original, is equal in aesthetic value to the original Rembrandt. The Appearance Theory holds that aesthetic value is independent of the nonvisual properties of a work of art, such as its historical properties. Is this position justified?

Leonard B. Meyer has argued forcefully against this position. Meyer gives at least two distinct arguments, but both are based on the principle that because "our fundamental beliefs influence our sensations, feelings, and perceptions, *what* we know literally changes our responses to a work of art. Thus, once we *know* that a work is a forgery, our whole set of attitudes and resulting responses is profoundly and necessarily altered."[2] We must pause immediately to ask what *type* of thesis Meyer is propounding here. This quoted passage makes Meyer's thesis sound like a psychological one; he seems to be reporting the alleged fact that once we know that a painting is a copy, we *do not* value it highly from an aesthetic point of view, that there is a factual psychological connection of this sort between our knowledge of the painting's origins and our aesthetic evaluation of the painting. In partial support of this, Meyer notices, as we have remarked, that when a painting is discovered to be a forgery it is removed from museum exhibition; he interprets this as evidence that the aesthetic value of a forgery – even of a perfect forgery – is judged by us to be low; the only remaining task, then, as Meyer sees it, is to explain why we judge the aesthetic value of a forgery in this way. His explanation takes the form of showing how our belief that this painting is a forgery interacts with our other beliefs so as to result in this low evaluation. Meyer is thus taking the rhetorical stance of explaining what he takes to be an undoubted fact. But he also tries to *justify* this low evaluation against those who make the normative claim that we ought to attribute a high aesthetic value to at least some copies. Meyer cites Clive Bell, who has suggested that an absolutely exact copy would be as moving as the original, and Emily Genauer, who has said that we should enjoy a work of art for what it is independently of its origin. Meyer says that our belief that a painting is a copy prevents us from ascribing high aesthetic value to it. He also believes that this is the way things *should* be. I will focus on the latter claim. *Should* copies be held to have lower aesthetic value than originals?

But before turning to this question and Meyer's arguments, I want to note in passing that Meyer might not be correct in holding that we *do* attribute

lower *aesthetic* value to copies. It is true that when a painting is discovered to be a copy, it is generally removed from museum walls. It is true that much lower prices are paid for copies and that museums find it terribly embarrassing to have paid hundreds of thousands of dollars for a work that turns out to be a copy. But we must not be hasty in drawing conclusions from these undoubted facts. As we have seen, there are several kinds of value that a work of art may have. That a discovered copy is removed from museum walls does show that people now judge that work to have less overall value than they formerly judged it to have. But because there are many kinds of value, this action does not show that people judge the work to have less *aesthetic* value than formerly.[3]

Meyer's first main argument is given in the following passage:

> Our willingness to become involved in aesthetic experience is partly a function of the relationship we feel with the artist's creative force. An original drawing, for instance, is more valuable than the finest reproduction, even one all but indistinguishable from it. This is true not merely in the economic sense that the original is scarce and hence costly. The original is also more valuable and more exciting aesthetically because our feeling of intimate contact with the magic power of the creative artist heightens awareness, sensitivity, and the disposition to respond. Once a work is known to be a forgery, that magic is gone. All that remains is a cultural aberration, less valuable than a reproduction. (*Music, the Arts, and Ideas*, p. 62)

This passage seems to be a psychological explanation of our low aesthetic appraisal of a copy rather than a philosophical justification of that appraisal. Can this be interpreted as a justification too? I think it can. For Meyer might be telling us that we are so constructed that we cannot do anything other than rate an original more highly. And if this were so, then it would be pointless to argue about whether we ought to rate exact copies as highly as originals since, as many writers on ethics have pointed out, "ought" implies "can." This is not exactly a justification in the usual sense of the claim that copies have less aesthetic value than originals, but this does seem to render argument about the issue otiose.

Nevertheless, when construed in this way, Meyer's argument is not conclusive. Notice that Meyer stresses the influence of beliefs on our aesthetic responses. If we believe that the work is a copy, we will rank it lower; if we believe that it is an original, we will rank it higher. But we might not believe anything one way or the other about its being an original or a copy. In such a case, this type of belief will have no influence on our aesthetic judgment, and this would be a way of obtaining a judgment on the purely aesthetic qualities of the work uncontaminated by "cultural beliefs." Thus, contrary to what Meyer's argument suggests, there are situations in which aesthetic judgment can be independent of cultural belief. So it still makes sense to argue about whether we ought to rate copies lower than originals.

Now let us interpret Meyer's argument as a justification in the ordinary sense – in particular, as a defense of the value of originality and hence of the greater value of an original work of art. Meyer says:

> To create is to discover something new – to reveal in a timely and timeless *aperçu* some aspect of the world or some relationship of which we were previously unaware and, by doing so, to change forever our experience of the world and of ourselves. [*Music, the Arts, and Ideas*, p. 58]

> The great artist "has dared to risk failure in order to reveal a new aspect of the universe to us." [*Music, the Arts, and Ideas*, p. 60]

The argument thus runs as follows:

1. Discoveries are valuable because they reveal new aspects of the world.
2. Each discovery can be made only once and is expressed only in the original work.
3. Consequently, copies of an original work cannot have the value that attaches to the original in virtue of the latter's expressing or embodying a discovery.

Meyer makes some telling points in support of this. For instance, he feels that the importance of originality explains why original creators are called "artists" while copyists and forgers are regarded as artisans. Yet there are data that are perhaps anomalous from Meyer's point of view. For example, if originality is so important, why do we go to museums to see the same works again and again?

Why are the works of great composers – works that are certainly not new to many in the audience – played repeatedly at concerts? Perhaps Meyer could argue that what makes these paintings and musical works great is that they reveal new aspects of the world *each time* a person sees or hears them. That would make these works *continuously* original and presumably help to preserve his thesis. But this type of originality is very different from the type Meyer describes. Meyer describes an original work as embodying a vision by the artist, whereas a continuously original work may embody no particular vision but instead generates new visions through interaction between itself and its audience. To put the point briefly, Meyer's view overemphasizes the value of originality in our appreciation of a work of art, since a work may continue to be highly valued for centuries after its vision has ceased to be new to us. Again, some works are highly valued by us even if they contain no new visions. For example, each of Degas's paintings of ballet dancers embodies the same general vision and yet each one is equally precious to us.

Many master painters learned to paint by copying the works of others. As Germain Bazin tells us of the Impressionists, "All, or almost all, from Delacroix and Theodore Rousseau, to Courbet, Degas, Renoir, and Matisse, formed their style by copying the old masterpieces in the Louvre which they found especially suited to their own temperament.... Delacroix, Courbet, Degas, Renoir only used these pictures as exercises in painting and copied them exactly."[4] It is instructive to vary this slightly by having Delacroix make, not an exact copy of, say, a Titian, but instead a copy that intentionally contains a small change, resulting in a better expression of Titian's vision. We do not have anything as serious and imposing as a new vision of the world as a result of Delacroix's change, only a small improvement in the old vision. Now, would you rather have Titian's original or Delacroix's almost-exact-but-slightly-improved copy? We might compare this situation with one in which you have your choice between one of Alexander Graham Bell's first telephones and a modern instrument. The improved version of the telephone is not original in the sense of being the first of its kind, but it does, as we might put it, express Bell's original vision and it is better than the original. We do not continue to use one of the first telephones in order to be closer to or to identify with "the magic power" of the creative inventor. Bell's early telephones are now mere curios, and yet surely they manifest originality and creativity. Some readers may think this comparison farfetched, since we are, after all, talking about art, not about machinery. Nevertheless, the comparison is perfectly valid from the standpoint of creativity and originality: the inventor has his vision – often a large-scale vision of how a certain aspect of our lives should be organized (in this case, communication). And Meyer clearly intends his thesis about originality to be a general thesis applicable to areas outside art too. Meyer says:

> For a great work of art or a great scientific discovery is great precisely because the creator has dared to choose beyond the limits and bounds of the normal, the accepted, and the obvious. In so doing, the creator – whether artist, scientist, scholar, or man of affairs – frees us from the determinism of the probable and the routine and makes significant changes in culture possible. [*Music, the Arts, and Ideas*, pp. 59–60]

Inventors "dare failure" and produce great changes in our culture too, but we do not revere their first and most original products as we do works of art. Nor do we so revere the manuscripts of the early quantum theorists, even though those manuscripts revealed a new aspect of the universe to us. We do not reread those manuscripts repeatedly in the way that we replay Mozart and Beethoven repeatedly. If originality is to play the role in aesthetic evaluation claimed by Meyer, it should do so too in other fields, but it does not and it should not.

If what a great work of art does is to present us with a new vision of the world, then an exact copy can perform exactly the same function. An exact copy expresses exactly the same vision of the world as the original does. In this sense the same work of art is present in both the original and the exact copy. The major difference seems to be that the original presents us with this vision for the first time. But suppose that the original had never been seen by anyone other than the painter himself, except for one person who made an exact copy; the original is destroyed, while the copy survives and is known to be a copy. It seems to me that the copy would be regarded as very, very valuable. My view can explain this: the copy embodies the very same work of art as did the original. Meyer's view can explain this too: the copy presents us with a new vision. But now let us change the case slightly: the

original artist himself makes the exact copy of one of his masterpieces; the original survives; the copy survives too and is known to be a copy and to be by the original artist. On Meyer's view, this copy would have little value. The original has presented us with the new vision already; and even though the copy is by the original artist, we cannot use this copy to identify with the magic power of the artist, since it is only a copy. And yet I would not be surprised (using Meyer's own criteria here) to find that copy hanging on museum walls, being revered, and fetching great prices.

I have been trying in various ways to throw doubt on the idea that originality significantly increases the *aesthetic* value of a great work. A work may acquire increased value through being original, but that value is not aesthetic value. In fact, it seems better to view the relation between originality value and aesthetic value in just the opposite way. Far from originality adding to the aesthetic value of a work (as distinct from adding to the *total* value of the work), the originality value depends upon that work first being valuable in other ways. No one cares about an original work of art that is a very bad work. Its originality matters only when it is very good.

We have been talking about creativity and originality. It should be noted that creativity is a property of the artist, while originality is a property of the work. And this should lead us to make a distinction between evaluating the creator on the one hand, and evaluating the creation on the other. This distinction is exceptionally important for the following reason. While the production of a particular work may not be terribly creative (as when a copy is made), nevertheless that work might itself express much originality. A copy of one of Goya's paintings expresses as much originality, relative to the time at which Goya worked, as the original painting does. Viewers would be just as struck by the originality of Goya's conception when viewing the copy as they would when viewing the original painting. Thus, we cannot infer from the lack of creativity on the part of the copyist that the copy does not express originality. In general, we cannot infer from the value of the productive act to the value of the product. The *act* of copying may be less valuable in itself than the *act* of creating the original painting, but it does not follow from this that the copy is less valuable than the original painting. Meyer focuses on creativity and emphasizes the distinction between artist and artisan. Maintaining a difference in value between artist and artisan, however, is quite compatible with maintaining that both original and copy have the same aesthetic value because they both express the same vision. We can see this principle operating in other areas too. The act of creating the first electric refrigerator was a creative and very valuable act, helping to cut down the incidence of illness due to spoiled food. Nevertheless, subsequent refrigerators are as valuable, if not more valuable, than the first refrigerator. Meyer makes many points to demonstrate the importance of the creative individual – for instance, our interest in the lives of artists, our "desire to know the name of the artist, composer, or writer who created the particular work we are enjoying" (*Music, the Arts, and Ideas*, p. 62). But even if these points do succeed in showing that creators perform more important and valuable acts than copyists do, it does not follow from this that copies have less aesthetic value than originals. I conclude from all this that Meyer's first argument – the argument from creativity and originality – does not show that copies have low aesthetic value.

But Meyer gives a second argument for believing that copies are less valuable aesthetically than originals, an argument which will lead us to discuss some very profound and subtle issues. Meyer says:

We invariably understand an event or an object, partly at least, by understanding how it came to be what it is and, if it is an event in the present, by imagining its implications for the future or, if it is an event in the past, by being aware of its implications as realized in history. . . . What a thing *is* – its significance – includes our knowledge and belief, whether these are correct or not, of how it came into being. . . . And just as we revise our opinion of the value of individuals depending on what they become – noting that this one succeeded beyond our expectation or that one failed to fulfill his promise – so too it is with works of art and artists. [*Music, the Arts, and Ideas*, pp. 63–64]

This is an argument to the effect that a work of art can be rightly judged only within a cultural and social context. Meyer gives the following illustration of this point:

Suppose, however, that our neo-Mozartian quartet, at first rejected as merely imitative of a past style, subsequently gave rise to new stylistic developments. Then, seen in retrospect as having been the beginning of a new movement, its implications would be different and, consequently, our understanding of its significance and value would be changed. It would no longer seem a bizarre anomaly. For it would now be judged not only in terms of its relationship to eighteenth-century music, but also in terms of its implications for twentieth-century music. [*Music, the Arts, and Ideas*, p. 65]

The idea here is that by knowing the relations of this quartet to later developments, we are able to determine whether this quartet was important in the development of music, and this knowledge may cause us to revise our opinion of the quartet's value.

Before going further, we must make explicit and emphasize a distinction Meyer's words suggest. What exactly is it about a work of art that depends, as Meyer thinks, on cultural and social context? Let us consider this question by talking about events in general, not just aesthetic events. Suppose that a gigantic political and social upheaval takes place in a certain country. The question immediately arises: How is this event to be understood? What is this event? Is it a revolution? If so, what kind of revolution is it? One way of finding out is to look at its consequences. If basic patterns of life and social organization are different after the event from what they were before, then we may decide to think of the event as a revolution. Now let us suppose that this event becomes an inspiration for revolutionaries in other countries due to their way of interpreting this event. What these revolutionaries do with this event as their inspiration may lead us to see characteristics in the event that we had not seen before. As a result, we come to think of this event – of its nature, of what it was – in a new way. I am suggesting that in some cases the external relations of a thing have a bearing on the nature of that thing. This bearing may be of one or two sorts: (1) the thing takes on brand-new properties by becoming, for example, "the event which inspired so-and-so"; (2) the thing is seen, in virtue of its external relations, to have properties which it had before but which it was not seen to have had before.

This distinction is extremely important. The cultural context of a work, action, or event bears on the evaluation of that work, action, or event in at least two distinguishable ways. First, that work, action, or event may have consequences. And if

Jack W. Meiland

those consequences are important or valuable, then the work, action, or event may take on greater importance or value in this way. Political and social revolutions that cause continental or worldwide changes provide clear-cut examples of this, but this phenomenon occurs in every area of life. For example, it sometimes happens that a mathematician will explore a new variety of mathematics and develop new mathematical techniques for their own sake, and then, years or decades later, a physicist will use these techniques to create an important physical theory. The physicist's use of these mathematical techniques, without which he would not have been able to construct his theory, gives the techniques new importance and value. This first way in which cultural context bears on evaluation must be sharply distinguished from the second way, which has been already described in the previous paragraph, namely the work, action, or event either taking on new properties or else being newly understood as a result of its consequences and other relationships. This second way also bears on evaluation. For if the work, action, or event either becomes different or is seen as different, it may well be differently evaluated too. A work which is initially regarded as "strange," "nonunderstandable," "chaotic," "not even art," and which may be generally ignored at the time of publication or exhibition may later come to be understood and to be seen as having a certain nature when we come to know its influence on other artists. And this often results in a reevaluation of the work. The distinction being made here can be put in the following way: The cultural and social consequences of a work of art may affect the value of that work in that (1) the *value* or *importance* of the consequences increases or decreases the *value* or *importance* of the work directly (a work may become more important by having important consequences); (2) the *nature* of the consequences changes the *nature* of the work or changes the way in which the nature of the work is *seen*; and this type of change leads to a reevaluation of the work itself.

Having made this distinction, let us focus on (1), that is, on the idea that the value of the consequences affects the value of the work of art. This idea does not seem to distinguish between originals and exact copies, however. Again imagine that the original masterpiece is accidentally destroyed after a perfect copy is made. Only the original artist and the copyist have seen the original. The copy is hung in museums and has enormous effects on subsequent art. Since it is the copy which has these

effects, the increase in aesthetic value accrues to the copy. So *in principle*, copies are in no worse position in this respect than are originals.

It may be objected that these consequences which add value are consequences of the original work acting through the medium of the copy. If we wish to talk that way, however, we must – in order to make that way of talking plausible – talk about the consequences being consequences of the work of art itself rather than of the original or the copy. After all, only people act through intermediaries; physical paintings do not act through intermediaries. We must say that the work of art, as manifested by the copy, influenced later painters. But to talk in this way is to admit that the work of art is present in the exact copy to the same extent that it is present in the original. And it follows from this that if what is aesthetically valuable is the work of art, then the copy is as valuable as the original.

A defender of Meyer's position can make a powerful reply at this point. The defender can say that in a situation in which the *original* has the valuable consequences, the original is more aesthetically valuable than the exact copy. This reply is powerful because it constitutes a strong attack on the Appearance Theory. The Appearance Theory maintains that only the appearance of the painting affects its aesthetic value. That is why the Appearance Theory holds that an exact copy is as aesthetically valuable as the original. The defender's reply does seem to show this view to be wrong. For if the original (but not the copy) has consequences which make it more aesthetically valuable than the original would otherwise be, then it seems to follow that aesthetic value does not depend solely on appearance. The case in which it is the *copy* (but not the original) which has the valuable aesthetic consequences shows that aesthetic value does not depend on *originality*. This does attack Meyer's idea that originality is a necessary condition of high aesthetic value. But to show that aesthetic value does not depend on originality is not to show that aesthetic value depends solely on appearance. And in fact the case in which the original (but not the copy) has valuable aesthetic consequences does seem to show that aesthetic value does not depend solely on appearance and thus helps to establish Meyer's basic contention that aesthetic value depends in part on cultural and social context.

This is a strong argument against the Appearance Theory of Aesthetic Value. But it rests on a crucially important assumption which must be examined: that if something has aesthetically valuable consequences, that thing, thereby, takes on additional aesthetic value. The general principle behind this assumption seems plausible on the surface and in application to other areas. For example, it seems plausible to say that if an item has economically valuable consequences, that item is itself economically valuable. But I believe that a closer look will lead us to modify this line of thinking. Suppose that an ordinary everyday item, which initially is strictly utilitarian and which, everyone agrees, has no aesthetic value – say, a soft drink bottle – inspires an artist to produce a painting incorporating an image of a soft drink bottle. Everyone agrees that this painting has aesthetic value, and in fact the painting begins a new school of painting which has a major impact on artistic work of a whole generation. Our general principle would urge that the soft drink bottle which inspired this development now has aesthetic value. I think that this is a mistake. The soft drink bottle has no more aesthetic value of the type in question now than it had before. What the soft drink bottle has acquired is aesthetic *significance* or *importance*. But significance and value are two different things. The situation here is complex because to say that something is important or significant is to evaluate that thing. But importance and what we might call "positive or negative value" are two different things. A thing can be important in a certain context and still have negative value. Those who say both that the rise of the Nazis was important and that it was deplorable are not contradicting themselves, and this shows that these are distinct evaluative dimensions.

Let us push this point a bit further by using an analogy from the realm of economic value. Suppose that an inventor, while traveling through Central America, happens across a makeshift waterwheel which a village uses to grind corn. This waterwheel is extremely inefficient, and in fact the energy used by the village in maintaining, overseeing, and repairing the wheel exceeds the energy produced by the wheel. But the inventor, stimulated by the village's need for an efficient way to grind corn, finds a way to adapt the unique mechanical principle embodied in this wheel and creates a waterwheel which can be constructed from inexpensive parts and which is tremendously efficient. We would all agree that there is a variety of economic value which the original wheel does not have, namely economic efficiency. But the original wheel certainly has economic importance because it stimulated the development of an eco-

nomically efficient wheel. Now consider a singing teacher who himself does not sing well but who can teach others to sing well, or a batting coach who cannot hit well but who can teach other people to be better hitters. The teacher has musical value; the coach has athletic value. But clearly the teacher and the coach have value of a different kind from that had by the great singer or the great hitter. There is in each of these cases a distinction to be made between primary value and derivative value. The singing teacher's ability to produce great singers is a valuable ability only because great singing is itself valuable. To revert to the economic example, the original waterwheel has economic value only in that it suggests a new principle which leads to a new type of waterwheel which itself has primary economic value (that is, productivity or economic efficiency). Importance and significance are values, but they are derivative or secondary values.

My point here is that we must distinguish between two different kinds of value, which I have termed "primary value" and "derivative value." This distinction can and must be made in all areas of value. The efficient waterwheel has primary economic value, while the old waterwheel derives its economic value from its relationship to the new waterwheel. The painting that incorporates the soft drink image has primary aesthetic value, while the actual soft drink bottle derives its aesthetic value from the painting. Now let us return to the objection to the Appearance Theory raised earlier. The objection is that aesthetic value does not stem solely from appearance, since a painting can have additional aesthetic value through having valuable aesthetic consequences (such as instigating a new school of painting). We can see, however, that the variety of aesthetic value which the painting possesses from this source is derivative value. For the painting would not have this additional aesthetic value if the later paintings which it instigated did not have primary aesthetic value. The painting has taken on only aesthetic importance or aesthetic significance in this way, not primary aesthetic value. Thus, if we restrict the Appearance Theory of Aesthetic Value to primary aesthetic value, this objection will have no force against the Theory.

We have seen that Meyer's arguments do not touch the Appearance Theory if that theory is restricted to primary aesthetic value. But we have also seen that with respect to derivative aesthetic value, exact copies are, in principle, in exactly the same position as originals. In principle, exact copies can have important consequences and can derive additional aesthetic value (derivative aesthetic value) from the value of those consequences. We have seen that exact copies can come to be different, or to be seen differently, in the light of their consequences, just as originals can. Thus, Meyer cannot reply by allowing the Appearance Theory to be correct about primary aesthetic value and then claim that originals are necessarily more valuable aesthetically because they necessarily have greater derivative aesthetic value. For originals and exact copies are not different in principle with respect to derivative aesthetic value either. There may be many situations in which an original has or would have greater total aesthetic value than an exact copy. Perhaps this would be so in the majority of cases. But there may also be situations in which an exact copy has at least as much aesthetic value – primary and derivative – as the original. And this should not be surprising, since an exact copy expresses exactly the same work of art as the original.

Notes

1 Nelson Goodman, *Languages of Art* (Indianapolis: Hackett, 1976), p. 109.
2 Leonard B. Meyer, *Music, the Arts, and Ideas* (Chicago: University of Chicago Press, 1967), p. 57.
3 Someone may object here by denying that there is a separate realm of experience called "aesthetic experience" and hence denying that there is a separate form of value called "aesthetic value." It should be noted that Meyer would not raise this objection. He tells us that the distinction, already made in classical Greek philosophy, between aesthetic experience and "other fields of philosophical inquiry" (religion, politics, science, and so on) is "necessary and justified" (Meyer, *Music, the Arts, and Ideas*, p. 54). Of course, we must be very careful about what Meyer subsumes under the rubric "aesthetic experience."
4 Germain Bazin, *French Impressionists in the Louvre* (New York: Harry N. Abrams, 1958), p. 10.

33

How Pictures Look

Malcolm Budd

I

Pictures are a distinct kind of representation: it is definitive of a picture that it represents what it depicts by depicting it, and depiction is a form of representation different from any other.[1] What distinguishes pictorial representation (depiction) from non-pictorial representation? An obvious and familiar idea is that a picture is a variety of iconic representation, representing its subject by means of the properties it shares with it. These properties are visual properties, so that the distinctive mark of a picture is that it represents its subject by virtue of looking like what it depicts. Now it is clear that this naive idea is inadequate as it stands. Perhaps its most important defect is that it operates with the concept of one thing's looking like another, and this is too loose a notion to bear much weight. It is, indeed, the vagueness of this concept that renders analyses of depiction based on it vulnerable to counter-example and at the same time allows them a further life when a different aspect of the concept is turned to face the objection. The resilience of the intuition that a picture looks like what it depicts is therefore partly due to the intuition's flexibility. The question is whether there is a stable form of the intuition upon which a correct theory of depiction can be founded. Is there a specific way a picture looks when it is seen as a depiction of its subject, and which is not shared with other kinds of repre-

Malcolm Budd, "How Pictures Look," in D. Knowles and J. Skorupski (eds.), *Virtue and Taste* (Oxford: Blackwell, 1993), pp. 154–75. Reprinted by permission of Blackwell Publishing.

sentation? Or are pictures distinguished from non-pictorial representations on some other ground?

But there is an ambiguity in the idea that a picture depicts something. When an item is said to be a picture of a woman, a landscape or any other kind of thing, there are two different ways in which the remark can be understood: it can be understood to license existential generalization or not to license it. If the remark is intended to license existential generalization, it follows from the fact that something is a picture of a woman that there is or was a woman of whom it is a picture; if the remark is understood otherwise, this conclusion does not follow (although it may in fact be true). The first concept of a picture can be called the relational sense and the second the non-relational sense. In the relational sense, a picture must stand in a certain relation to an actual thing, which it depicts; in the non-relational sense, this is not required. Now the fundamental concept in a theory of depiction is the concept of a picture in the non-relational sense. The reason this is so is not so much that, whereas every relational picture is at the same time a non-relational picture, the converse does not hold. The vital consideration is that what is constitutive of something's being a picture is its being a picture in the non-relational sense, and that this is what distinguishes pictorial representation from all other kinds of representation. The relations in which objects stand to relational pictures of them are not distinctive of, specific to, pictorial representation, as opposed to other kinds of representation. Relational pictures refer to what they depict; pictorial reference is not different in kind from other forms of reference; and, as with other forms of reference, it is the artist's intention or the causal role of the object in the production of the picture that determines reference. So an account of what is distinctive of depiction does not need to characterize the relation in which a relational picture stands to its subject. That is a task for a general theory of reference and representation. The primary task of a theory of depiction is the characterization of what it is to be a picture, that is, a picture in the non-relational sense. The question is whether the non-relational sense is rooted in the fact that a picture presents a distinctive visual appearance to the beholder.

If there is one thing that the most impressive recent philosophical theories of depiction are in agreement about it is precisely the rejection of the idea that depiction should be elucidated in term's of one thing's looking like another.[2] What I propose to do in this essay is to develop what seems to me the only viable form of this currently heretical idea by specifying the species of likeness perception it must invoke. If this version of the idea that a picture depicts its subject in virtue of looking like it is unacceptable, a theory of depiction cannot be founded on the relation *looking like*.

II

First, I want to arm myself against a brusque dismissal of the idea. Consider the following argument.[3] If one thing looks like another, then the second thing also looks like the first: *looking like* is a symmetrical relation. *Looking like* is also a reflexive relation: anything that has a look looks (exactly) like itself. But depiction is neither reflexive nor symmetrical: a picture does not depict itself, and a picture is not depicted by what it depicts. Moreover, there are many things that look like one another without any one of them being a picture of any other. Hence the concept of a picture cannot be analysed as the concept of an item that looks like another. Although this argument is both valid and sound, it inflicts no harm on the idea that it is of the essence of a picture that it looks like what it depicts, since it shows only that *looking like* is not fully constitutive of *depiction*, not that it is not a necessary condition of it.

It follows that if the intuition that a picture looks like what it depicts is to be turned into an analysis of the concept of depiction, it must be supplemented. The obvious supplement is a criterion of correctness determined by the history of produc-

tion of a picture: if the picture is drawn or painted it is designed, not only to look like what it depicts, but also with the intention that it should be seen to look like it (and, perhaps, that it should be recognized that this *is* the intention with which it has been designed); if it is a photograph, it must be a product of the interaction between the light-sensitive surface in the camera and a state of affairs of the kind depicted that transmitted light to the camera in the right way, and it is precisely the function of a camera to produce two-dimensional likenesses of the visible world it faces. Such a supplement renders the intuition proof against the dismissive argument.

But although a criterion of correctness must figure in a theory of depiction, the argument is in fact misdirected against the theory I propose. For the crucial concept is not the bare *looking like*, but a form of the more specific *seeing one thing as looking like another*: to see a picture as a depiction of its subject is to *see it as* looking like it – looking like it in a specific manner I intend to define. Since it is not true that if you see *a* as looking like *b* you thereby see *b* as looking like *a*, nor that whenever you see an object you see it as looking like itself, the fact that whereas the relation *looking like* is both symmetrical and reflexive *depiction* is neither, counts not at all against an account of depiction based on the perception of a likeness. So much for a swift rejection of the idea.

III

Now a picture is essentially a two-dimensional representation of a three-dimensional world, in the sense that the picture's depicted scene is visible in its two-dimensional marked surface. The crucial issue is the nature of the spectator's visual awareness of the picture-surface when he sees what a picture depicts. I shall assume that when the beholder sees a picture as a depiction of its subject he is visually aware of the presence and character of a marked surface in front of him.[4] The picture-surface does not look *to be* three-dimensional: it does not seem to the viewer that he is seeing a three-dimensional state of affairs. It follows, I believe, that the only relevant sense in which a picture, seen as a depiction of its subject, can look like its subject is with respect to the two-dimensional aspect of the subject's visual appearance. But what is this conception of the two-dimensional aspect of the visual appearance of a state of affairs?

IV

In elucidating this conception it will be helpful to make use of a distinction between my *visual world* and my *visual field*. The celebrated perceptual psychologist, James J. Gibson, made use of such a distinction in *The Perception of the Visual World* and other early works.[5] He there represents the distinction between visual field and visual world as a difference between two kinds of seeing or experience ('pictorial' and 'objective'), one of which involves the experience of a visual field, the other the experience of a visual world. The visual field, unlike the visual world, is defined by reference to what you are visually aware of when your eyes are fixated, so that the visual field has boundaries, roughly oval in shape, it changes when the eyes move from one fixation point to another, and it possesses a central-to-peripheral gradient of clarity, for example, whereas the visual world lacks boundaries, it is stable under eye movements, and it is everywhere clear and fully detailed. This is not how I shall understand the distinction between visual field and visual world. The distinction between visual field and visual world that I wish to draw is not based on any differences between, on the one hand, what I am aware of when my eyes are fixated and I adopt an unusual attitude to my visual experience and, on the other hand, what I am aware of when I look at the world in a normal manner. It is concerned only with how the world is represented as being no matter how I may be looking at the world, and what it proposes to do is to exploit a division within the class of so-called representational properties of my visual experience (intrinsic properties of my experience in virtue of which the world is represented to me as being a certain way). The division it highlights introduces a distinction between my visual field and my visual world that is quite different from the early Gibsonian conception, according to which the visual world is just the world (as we see it to be) and the visual field is never wholly depthless. I shall understand the distinction in such a way that my visual field is a proper part of my visual world and I shall extrude depth from the visual field and assign it a place only within the complete visual world.

My visual world at any time is the complete way the world is then represented to me by my visual experience. My visual field is a certain aspect of the way the world is represented to me by my visual experience. When I look at the world I see objects spread out in a three-dimensional space: this is how the world looks to me, this is how my visual experience represents it as being. Within my truncated cone of vision each part of any object I see is presented to me, clearly or indistinctly, as having a certain intrinsic character, as lying in a certain direction from me, and being at the same distance as, or nearer or further away than, other parts. All of this is included in my present visual world. If we abstract the apparent distance of anything I see we are left with my present visual field. So my visual field is just my visual world considered in abstraction from one of its three spatial dimensions, namely, distance outwards from my point of view.

This distinction between my visual world and my visual field can be illustrated in the following way. Suppose I am looking at a circular object which, as I can see, is tilted away from me. I see the object as being circular and as being tilted away from me. But if a characterization of how the world is presented to me by my visual experience is required to abstract from apparent distance from me, it must specify the appearance of the circular object without mentioning the fact that it seems to be tilted away from me, for this involves my seeing one part of it as being nearer to me than another part. It is clear in what terms such a description should be formulated. For when I look at the object I see the points along its rim as lying in certain directions and at various relative distances from me; if I am to observe the restriction imposed by the conception of my visual field I must omit any reference to outwards distance; and this leaves the apparent directions of the points along the rim as the form of the object in my visual field. Since these are directions in a two-dimensional space (up and down, right and left), if I were to indicate in which directions I see the points along its rim and were to keep my hand at the same distance in front of me, then, given the way the circular tilted object looks to me, my finger would trace an elliptical path: the angle apparently subtended at my eyes by diametrically opposed points on the rim varies in such a manner that it is greatest when the diameter is transverse to my line of sight and least when it lies along it. It is in this sense that the circular object, which I see *to be* circular, *looks* elliptical. It would be a misunderstanding of the distinction between visual field and world to conclude, as has frequently been done, that whereas my visual world contains a circular object, my visual field contains a different item, one that is elliptical. The distinction is between a complete and a partial account of how my visual experience represents the world as being, not between different items that I am visually aware of when I see the world, or when I attend to my experience in a certain manner. When I see the object I am *simultaneously* aware of the apparent directions and the apparent relative distances of the points along the rim, but whereas my visual world includes both factors my visual field includes only the first.

Consider two more examples. In the first, I am looking along railway tracks, which are parallel but, as they recede into the distance look to converge and meet; in the second, I am looking at two men of similar height, one of whom is at a much greater distance than the other and so looks smaller. Although the tracks look *to be* parallel and the men *to be* about the same height, the tracks look to converge and the more distant man looks smaller than the nearer. The sense in which the tracks look to converge is that the angle apparently subtended at my eyes by the width of the tracks gets less as they recede; the sense in which the more distant man looks smaller than the nearer is that the height of the first man apparently subtends a smaller angle than the height of the second. This is the sense in which, in the first case the representation of the tracks in my visual field can be said to consist of converging lines, and, in the second case the representation in my visual field of the more distant man can be said to occupy less space than that of the nearer. But it is important to remember that my visual field is not a two-dimensional *entity* that I see and a representation in my visual field is not an item that mediates my perceptual access to the world; a representation in my visual field is the manner in which the world is in some way visually represented to me in two of the three spatial dimensions.[6]

V

We are now in a position to return to the claim that the relevant sense in which a picture, seen as a depiction of its subject, looks like the subject it depicts is with respect to the two-dimensional aspect of the subject's visual appearance. This can be re-expressed in the following way: a picture looks like what it depicts only with respect to properties of the spectator's visual field, not those confined to his visual world.[7] So when you look at Poussin's *Echo and Narcissus* it is not so much your visual world, as your visual field that resembles the

one you would have if you were to see from a certain point of view a handsome youth enraptured by his reflection.

The plausibility of this line of thought emerges forcefully if we consider a schematic drawing of a cube (see figure). This schema of lines can be seen as depicting many different kinds of thing. Let us suppose you see it as a picture of, first, a cubical wire framework, and secondly a transparent cubical block. In both cases you are visually aware of the presence of an opaque surface marked with straight lines. Now if you were to be looking at a real, rather than a depicted wire framework from a similar point of view to the one from which it has been depicted in the figure, the representation of the wires in your visual field would be isomorphic with the representation of the drawn lines in your visual field when you look at the picture. Similarly, if you were to look at a transparent cubical block, the representation of the edges of the block in your visual field would have the same form as the representation of the drawn lines in your visual field. It is for this reason that the same arrangement of lines can so easily be seen as a picture of either kind of

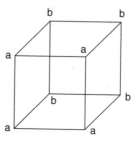

object. Moreover, whichever of these two kinds of object it is seen as a picture of, there is more than one way in which it can be seen: face *aaaa* can be seen either as lying in front of or as lying beneath face *bbbb*. The reason is similar: the visual field representations of different orientations of the same cubical wire framework, or the same transparent cubical block, match in two-dimensional structure. So when you look at the schematic drawing, no matter which of these kinds of picture you see it as being, your visual experience contains the same two components: a visual awareness of the lines as lying on the drawing surface and the same representation of the lines in your visual field.

It follows that this characterization of your experience fails to distinguish between your seeing the picture one way rather than another. But if we reflect on a case where you switch from seeing it one way to seeing it another way, it is clear what the distinguishing feature is. For the change in your way of seeing the picture cannot consist in the interpretation you are prepared to place on it, since you might already have been aware of the possibility of seeing it in different ways and have been prepared to interpret it accordingly. And it cannot consist in the fact that the representation of the lines in your visual field suddenly changes from being isomorphic with the visual field representation of one kind of thing to being isomorphic with that of another, since both before and after the change it is, as we have seen, isomorphic with them both. What happens when you switch from seeing the schematic cube as a picture of a wire framework to seeing it as a picture of a transparent block (or a wire framework orientated differently) is that *what you experience* your visual field representation as being isomorphic with changes: first, you see the structure of lines as being isomorphic with the visual field representation of a wire framework and then as being isomorphic with the visual field representation of a transparent block (or a differently orientated wire framework). So the change does not consist in your suddenly realizing that the lines are isomorphic with the visual field representation of a transparent block (or a wire framework with a different orientation) or that they can be seen as isomorphic with it. It is a matter of your *seeing* the lines as looking to be isomorphic with it.

If we now generalize this description of seeing a schematic drawing of a cube, we obtain the following account of pictorial perception. When you see a picture and see what it depicts, two things must be true of your visual experience. First, your experience must involve a visual awareness of the presence before you of a marked surface. Secondly, you must see the structure of the surface as being isomorphic with the structure of the visual field representation of the picture's subject when seen from a certain point of view, namely, that from which it has been depicted. So when you see what is pictured in the surface you see a relation between it and objects of the kind depicted, in a similar sense to that in which you hear a relation between one theme and another when you hear one as a variation of the other; and neither in the pictorial nor the musical case is the perception of this relation merely a matter of interpretation, rather than experience. For you to hear a musical passage as a variation on a certain theme you must experience

the structure of the music as being isomorphic with that of the theme (and understand the composer's intention to be to design his music so): this is what your hearing the relation with the theme consists in. For a picture, the perception of this relation is, according to the account I have developed, an experienced isomorphism of representations in the visual field. When you see what is pictured in the marked surface you *see* the structure of the surface as being isomorphic with that of the visual field of the state of affairs depicted (as you *hear* the resemblance between the music and the theme); and this is not just a matter of realizing that this is the case, but a visual experience, a state of consciousness possessing what Wittgenstein called 'genuine duration', a state with a sharp beginning and end which endures continuously from one time to the other. Furthermore, just as the idea of the theme is intrinsic to the description of your experience of the music when you hear it as a variation on the theme, and an awareness of how the theme goes a precondition of undergoing the experience, so the idea of the state of affairs depicted is intrinsic to the description of your experience of the picture surface when you see that state of affairs depicted in it, and an awareness of the look of that state of affairs a precondition of having the experience. For a perceived structural isomorphism with the visual field representation of a certain state of affairs is a perceived likeness with the visual field representation of that state of affairs *seen as* that state of affairs.

The significance of this last point can be brought out by considering a situation in which you are familiar with the look of one kind of thing, but have no idea what another kind of thing looks like. In fact, the two kinds of thing look just the same when seen from a certain point of view. Faced with a surface marked in such a way that the structure of its elements is isomorphic with that of the visual field representation of one or the other kinds of thing as seen from that point of view from which they look alike, the surface will look to you to be structurally isomorphic with the visual field representation of the familiar kind of thing, but not the unfamiliar kind – the surface will put you in mind only of the look *of the familiar object*.

The plausibility of this account of pictorial perception, and the importance of the idea of a *perceived* isomorphism of structure, is brought out by a consideration of Holbein's celebrated picture *The Ambassadors*. In the foreground of the picture there is a depiction of a skull, but the skull is represented anamorphically, so that if the picture is looked at from directly in front the depiction of the skull seems a strange yellow tilted smear, whereas seen from one side it assumes the form of a skull – the two men being transformed into blurs the more clearly the image of death enters the spectator's consciousness. Now the skull is represented anamorphically in the sense that its visual field form is grossly distorted when seen from the standard point of view that the spectator of a picture adopts: so much so that it is not seen as a distortion of the visual field of a skull seen normally. But although the depiction of the skull *is* isomorphic with the representation in the visual field of a skull in the sense that there is a one-to-one mapping between the points that compose the two, you *see* it *as* being structurally isomorphic only when you see it from the side and, accordingly, you see it as a depiction of a skull only from that unusual, oblique point of view, not when looking at it from straight on.

The plausibility of this account of pictorial perception is reinforced by recalling the scene in the second half of Goethe's *Elective Affinities*[8] where members of the assembled company provide entertainment by representing well-known pictures by posing in the appropriate costumes on a lighted stage: they compose tableaux vivants of tableaux morts. There are two ways in which, when the audience admires the resemblance between the staged composition and the picture it represents, the audience might see the tableau vivant. On the one hand, it might see it as looking like the scene the picture depicts; on the other, it might see it as looking like the picture. But if – and this is the interesting case – the audience sees it as looking like the picture, there is one important respect in which it will not look like the picture: it will not look as if it is a flat surface. To be struck by the tableau vivant's likeness specifically to the picture – to see it as a representation of the picture, rather than the scene the picture depicts – the audience must bracket off the perceived third dimension and see it as if it were a flat surface: the perceived resemblance excludes the third dimension. Now this is just the converse of what I have called pictorial seeing: in the one case, a flat surface is seen as a depiction of a three-dimensional scene; in the other, a three-dimensional scene is seen as a representation of a picture. If the account I have given of seeing a tableau vivant as a representation of a picture is along the right lines, so is my account of pictorial perception.

VI

But if this account is to provide the foundation of a theory of depiction it must be refined and developed. First, we must face up to the fact that for many, perhaps most, pictures the visual field representation of the picture-surface is strikingly unlike that of the state of affairs depicted. In itself this creates little difficulty for the proposed account. In the first place, an acknowledgement of the possible disparity between the two visual-field representations is already implicit in the account, since the isomorphism it highlights concerns the *relations* between the elements of the two visual fields, which is compatible with great differences between the corresponding elements. Secondly, an obvious replacement for the idea that the spectator sees the picture-surface as having a structure which is isomorphic with the structure of the relevant representation in the visual field will be the idea that he sees the one as being like the other. The account can therefore easily accommodate noticeable dissimilarities in the structure of visual field representations, since dissimilarities do not preclude a perceived resemblance.

But this response is uninformative about the pictorial significance of such perceived dissimilarities. There are two ways in which features of the visual field representation of the picture-surface can diverge from those of the state of affairs depicted and result in perceived differences. On the one hand, the visual field representation of the picture-surface can (and usually does) lack features possessed by the visual field representation of what is depicted; on the other hand, it can (and often does) possess additional features. How do such differences show up in what the spectator sees depicted?

It would be wrong to represent the absence of features, or the presence of additional features, in the representation in the visual field of the picture-surface as implying that the spectator sees what is depicted as lacking the absent features and as possessing the additional features. For this would overlook two distinctions, the distinction between something's not being depicted as possessing a certain feature and its being depicted as not possessing it, and the distinction between a perceived feature of the picture-surface that has pictorial significance and one that does not. To illustrate the first distinction: a black and white line drawing does not thereby depict its subject as lacking colour and a spectator who understands it does not see it as depicting a colourless state of affairs. The absence of colour in the picture is understood by the spectator, not as indicating a lack of colour in what is depicted, but only as not indicating any colour: the object, as depicted, has an indefinite appearance in the dimension of colour. The artist's intention is not to depict a black and white state of affairs, or a coloured state of affairs as being black and white; it is to depict only the spatial structure of a state of affairs and the comparative brightness of its parts, perhaps, not the colours of its constituent objects. To illustrate the second distinction: the individual lines or dots when cross-hatching or stipple is used to represent variations in tone lack pictorial significance and contribute to the depiction of light and shade only through the relative density of their combination with other lines or points. The spectator who understands these pictorial devices does not read their specific features into the objects depicted by means of them. As these examples show, to see the pictorial content of a picture it is often necessary to abstract from various details of the picture-surface, ignoring those aspects of the marks that are not representatives of depicted features of the depicted state of affairs. The fact of the matter is that, whereas every depicted feature of the object must have a perceptible feature of the picture which is representative of it, a perceptible feature of the picture need not be representative of any feature of the depicted object. The multiplicity of perceptible features of the picture can exceed the multiplicity of depicted features.[9]

It is important to recognize that perceived resemblances between representations in the visual field can involve very little of the detail of one or other of the representations, as the examples I have used to illustrate the second distinction show. Consider another example, Picasso's 1946 pencil drawing *Head of a Girl*. The looping, spiralling lines with which Picasso has drawn the girl's hair do not look much like the visual field representation of any girl's hair you are likely to see. But if we abstract from most of the details of any such visual field representation, retaining only the feature of curling surroundings of a face, there is sufficient left to found a perceived resemblance with the picture. Hence it is easy to see how there can be pictures that are abstract representations of their subjects or, more accurately, more abstract in their representation of some or all features of their subjects than other pictures. Schematic depictions of objects do not depict their objects' structure in detail and usually omit such features as the play of

light. Accordingly, they are seen as being like the visual field representations of their objects only with respect to the structural features they depict. The less the depicted detail of the visible structure of a state of affairs, the greater the abstract nature of the picture: the greater the level of abstraction, the less definite the nature of the subject *as depicted*.[10] Moreover, it should now be clear that the account of pictorial seeing in terms of an experienced isomorphism of structure does not need to be watered down by being reformulated as a perceived *similarity* of structure. For it is built into the requirement of isomorphism that its demands are limited: the perceived isomorphism of structure that is constitutive of pictorial seeing refers to structure *at a certain level of detail*, so that a perceived similarity (but not identity) of structure at one level just is a perceived isomorphism of structure at a higher level. The combination of this point with one I have previously made – perceived features of the picture-surface can lack pictorial significance – renders this account of pictorial seeing immune to what would otherwise be obvious counter-examples.

Nevertheless, the account is likely to be met with the objection that, if it applies at all, it applies only to certain styles of depiction, namely those that are fairly close relations of optical perspective. Now it is clear that the application of the theory is in fact unproblematic to pictures that are not designed to give a naturalistic effect of spatial recession, and even to pictures that are not constructed in accordance with a consistent mode of projection but depict some constituents of the depicted scene in plan and others in side elevation, say, as is often the case in Egyptian painting, or to pictures that are combinations of different views of a single thing or views from different points of view of parts of a single thing, as in Braque's *Pitcher and Violin*.[11] But, so it might be thought, there are kinds of projection, such as reverse perspective, which are not concerned to represent how things look from any point of view, and when we look at pictures that use such modes of projection we do not see their structures as being isomorphic with those of the visual field representations of the objects they depict. It would be a mistake, however, to object to the theory of pictorial seeing I have put forward on these grounds. For the objection relies on a failure to distinguish between seeing a picture as a depiction of an object which has a certain form and seeing a picture as a depiction of an object which is depicted as having that form. When we look at a picture in reverse perspective of an object of a certain kind (a table with a rectangular top, for example), we can see it as a depiction of such an object, if we understand the mode of projection; and the information conveyed to us about the object's structure can be the same as, or even greater than, that which we obtain from a picture in normal perspective. But in such a case we see the form of the object depicted as being distorted, and so can be said to see the picture as a distorted depiction of the object. (A picture that is in this sense a distorted depiction of an object of a certain kind is not an [undistorted] depiction of a misshapen object of that kind, even though a picture of one sort could look exactly like, and so be mistaken for, a picture of the other sort.) Of course, since distortion is a matter of degree and it can be applied to many aspects of the form of an object, a mode of projection that distorts an object's form may result not in a configuration that is seen as a distorted depiction of the object, but in one that is not seen as a depiction of it at all – as with Holbein's anamorphic representation of a skull.

This account of pictorial seeing applies as easily to pictures of mythical or fictional kinds as to pictures of actual kinds. For although you cannot see a winged horse, you know how something that looks like a horse with wings would look like, and can therefore perceive the resemblance the account requires. But a merely fictional kind is not the only type of non-existent object that can, so it might seem, be depicted. There are also pictures of 'impossible objects', such as the three-pronged tuning fork, which consists of two rectangular bars at one end and three cylindrical bars at the other. There are even pictures of 'impossible worlds', such as Escher's *Autre Monde*. In these cases, not only can you never see anything of the kind depicted, you cannot coherently imagine seeing something which has the look of that kind of thing, since there can be no such look. But the impossibility of visual field representations of impossible objects, or of possible objects that look how impossible objects supposedly look when their impossibility is apparent to the eye, does not count against the idea that pictorial seeing is founded on a perceived structural isomorphism of visual field representations, as is clear if we examine how we see depictions of impossible objects and worlds. The picture of the impossible tuning fork is designed in such a manner that if we direct our gaze at one end of the configuration of lines we see the structure of the lines as being isomorphic with that of the

visual field representation of two rectangular bars, whereas if we look at the other end the lines look to be structurally isomorphic with the visual field representation of three cylindrical bars. But if we allow our eyes to run back and forth along the lines, or take them in as a whole, we cannot impose on them a stable, consistent interpretation. The picture is just a tease, holding out to us with one hand what it withholds with the other, and we are looking at a picture of an impossible object only in the sense that the picture tempts us to see parts of it in ways which assign incompatible roles to the picture's elements. Escher's *Autre Monde*, which relies mainly on perspectival ambiguities, works in a similar fashion, and is not seen in its entirety as a depiction of a state of affairs, even an impossible one. Pictures of impossible objects or worlds are merely configurations which are composed of elements so designed that the spectator is strongly encouraged to see different sets of marks as depictions, but which resist integration when the spectator attempts to take in the complete configuration of marks and see it as a depiction of an object or scene. Hence they cause no trouble for an account of pictorial perception in terms of a perceived structural isomorphism.

It is important to realize that the idea of a perceived structural isomorphism is not restricted to the spatial structure of a visible state of affairs, that is, to spatial relations among its elements. It would be necessary to impose this restriction if the aim were to capture only what is barely essential to depiction; but it would be wrong to do so if the aim is to capture the full pictorial content of any depicted scene. Whereas a picture must be designed to depict spatial relations, it need not be designed to depict anything else. But if, as is usually so, it attempts more and aims to depict comparative brightness, perceived textures or colours, for example, then the perception of its pictorial content requires more than a perceived likeness with the spatial structure of the depicted state of affairs. When an artist depicts colour – when she depicts not merely a state of affairs composed of objects of kinds that are coloured in reality, but a state of affairs composed of objects that are depicted *as* coloured – the chromatic aspect of the visual field assumes a crucial role in the spectator's visual awareness of what the picture depicts. In such a case, the objects in the depicted state of affairs are seen as looking coloured according as their representatives in the picture-surface are seen as coloured, so that there is not only a perceived isomorphism of spatial relations but a correspondence of perceived colour: the spectator sees the picture not merely as a structural spatial isomorph but also as a chromatic icon.[12]

VII

A theory of depiction is incomplete without an account of naturalistic depiction, and it is a virtue of the theory I have developed that, as I shall show, it yields so easily a plausible account of naturalism. But the word 'naturalism', used to describe manners of depiction, is ambiguous, and a picture that is naturalistic in one sense may not be so in another. In the sense I am concerned with, a picture is naturalistic if, or to the extent that, the depicted state of affairs is depicted as it looks. So a naturalistic picture is one in which the subject's visual appearance is accurately depicted.

But this introduction of the idea of naturalistic depiction is not fully satisfactory: it must be improved by the acknowledgement of the relativity of the concept. For, in the first place, there is no such thing as *the* visual appearance of an object or scene. The appearance an object presents to the viewer is dependent upon the point of view from which it is seen, the manner in which it is illuminated, and the mental and visual apparatus of the viewer. It also depends on the nature and condition of the medium through which the object is seen, as is underlined by Hazlitt's comment that Turner's paintings had become 'representations not properly of the objects of Nature as of the medium through which they were seen'. Furthermore, an object's appearance is affected by how the viewer focuses his eyes, the distribution of his attention and the conscious or unconscious way in which he scans the environment; and since every artist sees the world he depicts, the manner in which he looks at the world will determine the appearance in his picture of the objects whose look he attempts to capture. It is characteristic of Cézanne's still-lifes to contain apparent distortions of the forms of the objects depicted, and the objects, as depicted, are normally seen by the spectator as distorted. But, as Anton Ehrenzweig has argued, Cézanne's so-called distortions:

make sense if they are experienced as part of the total (undifferentiated) visual field rather than a wandering pinpoint of precise focal vision. Peripheral vision that fills far

the greater part of the field of vision can easily distort the stable gestalt shapes of our ordinary awareness much in the way in which Cézanne made his apples bulge and his table tops topple, and fractured the edges of a table. Seen in this way Cézanne painted realistically.[13]

In addition to these reasons for admitting relativity, a picture can be naturalistic in its rendering of one aspect or feature of the world and not in another, and a picture that is overall more naturalistic than another can be less naturalistic in its treatment of some particular aspect of its subject matter. The use by Western artists of chiaroscuro and linear perspective to give the verisimilitude of solidity in natural objects and their recession in space makes their pictures *in these respects* more naturalistic depictions of the visible world than the works of, say, Japanese artists. Our judgements about the naturalism of pictures should be, therefore, not just comparative, but relative – relative to specific features of the world which are either not depicted or depicted more or less accurately.

Given this understanding of naturalism, what account should be given of the experience of seeing a picture as a naturalistic depiction? I have elucidated the experience of seeing what a picture depicts in terms of a perceived resemblance between the structures of two visual fields: the structure of the elements (drawn lines, for example) in one visual field is seen as looking like the structure of the elements (edges, say) in another visual field. Now the points of perceived resemblance between the one and the other can be more or less numerous. For a schematic picture they will be few, and for a more detailed picture many. If we consider some visible feature (colour, for example) that the state of affairs depicted possesses in reality, either some corresponding aspect of the representation in the visual field of the depiction is experienced as more or less closely resembling the representation of that feature in the relevant visual field of that state of affairs or not. If the spectator is aware of the appearance of that feature in the state of affairs, to the degree that there is an experienced match, to that degree the spectator experiences the picture as depicting that feature naturalistically. This account applies to all features of the representation of the state of affairs in the visual field, and this includes distance 'cues', such as aerial perspective. But it does not apply to represented distance itself, which belongs not to the visual field but to the visual world.

I believe that this is the point at which the idea of an imagined visual awareness of the third dimension should be introduced. A spectator experiences a picture that accurately depicts the spatial relations obtaining in a state of affairs as naturalistic in its depiction of distance not only to the degree that there is an experienced match of distance cues, but also (or alternatively) in so far as it encourages him to imagine the represented distances in the state of affairs depicted: the more vividly the spectator imagines the missing third dimension, the more intensely naturalistic he finds the picture's depiction of distance. The greater 'sense' of distance that some pictures give us arises from their strongly encouraging us to reverse in our imagination the activity of the artist, overcoming the loss of the third dimension intrinsic to a two-dimensional pictorial representation by its imagined reconstruction beyond (and perhaps in front of) the plane of the picture. The imaginative projection of the third dimension into the marks on the picture's surface, when strongly supported by the nature of the picture, makes the spectator's awareness of distance in the depicted state of affairs especially vivid and in that respect enhances the picture's naturalism.

VIII

A theory of depiction derives its support from its ability to explain salient facts about pictures and to make sense of pre-theoretical intuitions. The account I have developed accommodates the basic pre-theoretical intuition that a picture is designed to look like what it depicts by giving this intuition a definite form. The sense in which, for a spectator who sees a picture as a depiction of a certain state of affairs, the picture looks like what it depicts is that the spectator sees the structure of the picture as being isomorphic with that of the (appropriate) visual field of the state of affairs depicted: the picture must look like what it depicts, but only in respect of the perceived structure of the picture and the visual field structure of what is depicted. The power of the theory I have put forward is demonstrated by the ease with which it accounts for many of the most significant and distinctive features of pictorial representation:

1 The force of the consideration that a picture depicts its subject from a point of view is in no way weakened by the existence of pictures that combine depictions of an object, or parts of an object, from different points of view, as in Cubist works, nor by the existence of pictures that appear not to have a fixed point of view, as in certain of Cézanne's water-colours, or for which there is an indefiniteness in the location of the point of view with respect to the depicted world, as in a panoramic landscape by Ruisdael, nor, finally, by the existence of pictures for which the nature of the point of view is minimally determined, as in a typical schematic picture by a young child. The reason that depiction must always be from a point of view is that a picture is seen as depicting its subject only if it is seen as being isomorphic with the relevant visual field of that subject, and a visual field of that subject has to be a visual field of it *as seen from* a point of view.[14]

2 A spectator who has no idea what a certain state of affairs would look like (or, to cover fictional kinds, is supposed to look) cannot see a picture as a depiction of that state of affairs because the kind of seeing this requires involves a perceived isomorphism of structure between the picture and the visual field of the state of affairs depicted, something that is denied to a spectator who is unaware of the look of that state of affairs.[15]

3 This theory of pictorial perception easily explains what Richard Wollheim has called the fact of 'transfer'[16] – the fact that if I can recognize a picture in a certain style of one kind of thing (a cat, say), and I know what another kind of thing (a dog, say) looks like, I am thereby endowed with the ability to recognize a picture in that style of that other kind. For pictorial perception is founded on the capacity to see a surface as structurally isomorphic with a representation in the visual field, and the possession of this capacity for one kind of thing demands no more than for another kind. It also demands no less – an awareness of how the thing looks. Hence, if this requirement is satisfied, the capacity generalizes from one kind of thing to another.

4 The reason that pictorial perception must satisfy 'the requirement of localization'[17] – for each depicted part of a depicted object, if a spectator sees that part depicted there must be an answer to the question whereabouts in the picture he sees it depicted – is that seeing the structure of a surface as being isomorphic with the visual field structure

of a state of affairs requires seeing elements of the surface as being representatives of elements in the state of affairs depicted.

5 The (murky) intuition that depiction is based on a 'natural', rather than a purely 'conventional', relation can easily be preserved in the face of the obvious fact that, even given constancy of point of view and prevailing conditions, there are indefinitely many ways or styles of depicting any particular kind of thing. For a perceived structural isomorphism between each of the various members of a set and a certain state of affairs allows of differences in the representative elements of the structures of the members, differences in non-pictorial elements, differences in levels of abstraction at which the isomorphism is experienced, differences in the kind or number of features (colour, texture, play of light etc.) of the state of affairs which figure in the perceived resemblance, and, finally, for distortion of various aspects of the state of affairs.

6 The state of affairs depicted by a picture is often, as depicted, indefinite, so that it is neither depicted as possessing a particular visual feature nor depicted as not possessing it, and the spectator sees the picture accordingly. He is able to do this because the species of seeing that a picture demands does not require that for each visual feature of the state of affairs seen to be depicted some element of the picture must be seen as representative of it: it demands only a seen isomorphism of structure (at some level).

7 The naturalistic artist's attempt to 'copy' or produce a (two-dimensional) 'likeness' of the visible world – to be true to the world's visual appearance – receives its most unforced explanation by the account I have offered: within the limits of his medium, this is *exactly* what he tries to do. His work is a simulacrum of a visible state of affairs: it depicts a visual world state of affairs by being designed as a structural isomorph of a relevant visual field state of affairs.

8 Some pictures are much less easily recognizable as depictions of their subjects than are others: and parts or aspects of a depicted state of affairs can easily be overlooked and require careful scrutiny of the picture if they are to be discerned. Corresponding to this, in the first place, is the fact that a spectator may experience difficulty in seeing the structure of a picture as being isomorphic with that of the visual field of a state of affairs if much

detail of the picture-surface lacks pictorial significance (as in certain puzzle-pictures) or the depiction is sketchy, or the relevant visual field is that of the state of affairs as seen from an unusual point of view or in circumstances that distort its normal appearance. Secondly, the fact that an object in a scene can be overlooked is mirrored by the fact that characteristics of the picture-surface can go unnoticed, and the difficulty in discerning the nature of an object when looked at from a certain point of view is likely to be matched by the difficulty in seeing its depiction from that point of view as being isomorphic with its visual field representation from that point of view.

9 A perceived isomorphism of structure provides the appropriate foundation for the activity of imagining of one's seeing a picture that it is an instance of seeing face to face what is depicted – a mode of engagement with pictures that is familiar, although not mandatory. For the activity of imagined seeing must be disciplined if its content is not to diverge from that of the scene depicted, and the nature and specificity of what a spectator – who imagines of his seeing the picture-surface that it is an instance of seeing something else – imagines himself to be seeing is given by the respects in which the surface is perceived as structurally isomorphic with a visual field representation of a state of affairs, unless the spectator's imagination is not securely anchored in the pictorial content of the picture.

10 The fact that a picture looks like what it depicts (in the sense I have indicated) forms the necessary bridge between our interest in looking at pictures and our interest in looking at the world, and it explains a picture's ability to induce in us responses similar to those induced by what it depicts, as when a schematic depiction of a smiling face causes us to smile. In particular, the fact that our visual interest in the world around us is enhanced and transformed by the contemplation of appearances afforded by pictures, and that we naturally delight in seeing accurately depicted what we delight in looking at face to face, receives its most natural explanation from a theory of pictorial perception that, while doing justice to the spectator's visual awareness of a two-dimensional marked surface before him, links that awareness as firmly as possible with the appearance of the world when it is looked at directly.

Malcolm Budd

Notes

1 The *pictorial* content of a picture is what a picture depicts. What a picture represents on the basis of its pictorial content can exceed what it depicts, and what it represents may not be a state of affairs that could be seen, as when a picture represents a man dreaming a certain scene by depicting a bubble attached to his head within which the scene is visible. In what follows I am concerned to elucidate the perception of a picture's pictorial content, not any additional content the picture may have.

2 See Nelson Goodman's semiotic theory in his *Languages of Art* (Oxford University Press, London, 1969); Roger Scruton's seeing-as theory in his *Art and Imagination* (Methuen, London, 1974); Richard Wollheim's seeing-in theory in his *Art and its Objects*, 2nd edn (Cambridge University Press, Cambridge, 1980), supplementary essay V, 'Seeing-as, seeing-in, and pictorial representation', and his *Painting as an Art* (Thames and Hudson, London, 1987); Flint Schier's natural generativity theory in his *Deeper into Pictures* (Cambridge University Press, Cambridge, 1987); Christopher Peacocke's sensational property theory in his 'Depiction', *The Philosophical Review*, 46 (1987), pp. 383–410; and Kendall Walton's make-believe seeing theory in his *Mimesis as Make-Believe* (Harvard University Press, Cambridge, Mass. and London, 1990).

3 See Goodman, *Languages of Art*, ch. 1 s. 1.

4 This assumption would need to be reformulated if it were intended to cover all kinds of picture, e.g. projected pictures. When you see a projected picture *as a picture* – when you see it as a two-dimensional representation of a three-dimensional state of affairs – you may not be visually aware of the presence before you of an opaque surface, but you must be visually aware of seeing *a two-dimensional appearance* of a three-dimensional state of affairs. For my immediate purpose it is easier to operate with the assumption as it stands.

5 James J. Gibson, *The Perception of the Visual World* (Riverside Press, Cambridge, Mass. 1950), ch. 3. See also his *The Ecological Approach to Visual Perception* (Lawrence Erlbaum, Hillside, NJ and London, 1986), pp. 206–7, p. 286, where Gibson expresses regret at the title of his *The Perception of the Visual World*.

6 By 'my visual field representation' or 'a representation in my visual field' I mean the visual field representational *content* of my visual experience, not the experience itself: my visual field representation is *how* the world, with respect to its visual field properties, is represented to me by my visual experience.

7 Christopher Peacocke has also put forward a theory of depiction based upon experienced visual field similarity: see his 'Depiction' in *The Philosophical Review*. But his account differs from mine in three important ways. First, he construes the visual field in terms of *non-representational* (sensational) properties of visual experience, whereas my conception captures it in representational terms; see his *Sense and Content* (Clarendon Press, Oxford, 1983), ch. 1. (I believe the arguments for sensational properties are unconvincing.) Secondly, Peacocke's account represents experienced visual field *shape* similarity as being fundamental to pictorial perception, whereas mine is based on the more general idea of a perceived isomorphism of visual field *structure*. Thirdly, Peacocke's account of depiction does not involve the idea that a picture *looks like* what it depicts, whereas mine does. (This difference follows from our different understandings of the visual field.) This essay was completed in 1988. It was not until I read John Hyman's *The Imitation of Nature* (Basil Blackwell, Oxford, 1989) that I discovered that Rhys Carpenter in his *Greek Sculpture* (University of Chicago Press, Chicago and London, 1960) makes use of a distinction between visual field and visual world to elucidate the difference between pictures and sculptures. But, as Hyman points out, Carpenter mistakenly conceives of the visual field as the two-dimensional projection of the world onto the retina. Moreover, Carpenter appears to conceive of the perception of a picture as an experience that involves the illusion of seeing depth and distance.

8 Johann Wolfgang Goethe, *Wahlverwandschaften*, part II, ch. 5.

9 It is not always clear whether a perceived feature of the picture-surface possesses or lacks pictorial significance. Does Mondrian's stylized triangular and lozenge-shaped rendering of the nipples and navels in his triptych *Evolution* lack pictorial significance or depict the nipples and navels as so shaped?

10 A limiting case of abstraction in depiction would be a schematic picture intended to be seen as depicting a cube, but not any particular kind of cubical object (e.g. a cubical wire framework or a transparent cubical block). If you see the picture as intended, you see the structure of lines as being isomorphic with the structure of the visual field representation of a cube, but not, more specifically, a cubical object of a certain kind.

11 The extraction of pictorial content by pictorial perception should not be thought of in a simplistic way as an instantaneous occurrence. In the first place, even if each part of the depicted scene has been depicted from the same point of view, it is rarely the case that the full depicted scene can be recognized in a single look; on the contrary, it is usually necessary to scan the picture. Secondly, many pictures depict elements of their content from different points of view in such a manner that it is necessary to apply pictorial perception piecemeal, to one then

another part of the picture, in order to generate the right interpretation.

12 Conceiving of a picture as a structure of elements and of pictorial perception as requiring a perceived isomorphism of structure makes possible a unitary account of pictorial content and enables the limits of depiction to be drawn. The foundation of visual field representational content consists of (a) purely spatial relations, (b) variations in lightness and darkness, and (c) variations in hue. Structures of marks on a surface can depict these features in so far as aspects of the marks have the right logical multiplicity. So two-dimensional spatial relations can be depicted by the two-dimensional spatial relations of the marks, hue by the marks' colours, lightness and darkness by the relative densities of points or lines or by the degree of lightness or darkness of an area. Moreover, the fineness of the depicted detail is determined by the fineness of variations in the representative aspects: pictures in a medium that restricts the available variations in a representative aspect are thereby restricted in the subtlety with which they can depict the corresponding feature.

13 Anton Ehrenzweig, *The Hidden Order of Art* (Weidenfeld and Nicolson, London, 1968), p. 113.

14 What it is for a picture to depict its subject from a certain point of view is for the picture to be correctly seen as being structurally isomorphic with the visual field representation of that subject *as seen from* that point of view. The fact that a visual field representation of an object is always of the object as seen from a point of view is compatible with the existence of objects that look exactly the same from different points of view at equal distances, as in the case of a uniformly illuminated, uniformly coloured and textured spherical object.

15 The requirement is not that the viewer should be *familiar* with the look of the state of affairs, which would rule out the possibility of learning what a certain kind of thing looks like from a depiction of something of that kind. When an observer sees a depiction and learns from it what something of kind K (an ibex, say) looks like, what happens is that his prior knowledge of what a certain kind of thing (a powerful goat-like creature, with huge sweeping horns) looks like enables him to see the picture as a depiction of that kind of thing and he learns (from a title, say) that something of kind K looks like that. The fact that you *can* learn what a certain kind of thing looks like by seeing what a picture depicts is most naturally explained by the account of pictorial perception I have offered. Briefly: you learn what something of kind K looks like by seeing a picture as an L-depicting picture (in Nelson Goodman's sense) and by being informed that the picture is a K-depicting picture. This combination of factors generates the knowledge of how something of kind K looks only because to see a picture as an L-depicting picture is to see it as being structurally isomorphic with the [relevant] two-dimensional appearance of something of kind L, and in that sense to see it as looking like an L.

16 Wollheim, *Painting as an Art*, p. 77. Cf. Schier, *Deeper into Pictures*, p. 44.

17 See Wollheim, *Art and its Objects*, 2nd end, supplementary essay V, 'Seeing-as, seeing-in, and pictorial representation'.

34

On Pictorial Representation

Richard Wollheim

I

Philosophical theories of representation abound.

This tells us something; in fact, it tells us two things, two philosophical things, about representation. The first thing is that, when we set out to ascertain the extension of the concept representation, armed with the resources we should expect to be adequate – that is, such intuitions as we have, plus the careful consideration of examples – we encounter many hard cases. Are maps representations? Are traffic signs representations? The second thing is that these hard cases are totally resistant to stipulation. No-one (I find) will take it on trust from me that, say, *trompe-l'oeil* paintings are not representations, but that most abstract paintings are. The centrality of representation within the pictorial arts means that any answer that is not supported by a theory, moreover a theory that meshes at once with a general account of perception and with broad cultural practices, will not do.

Hence the abundance of theories of representation.

II

However, many such theories fall short of a certain minimal requirement, which has as its aim to safeguard our strongest intuition about representation,

Richard Wollheim, "On Pictorial Representation," *Journal of Aesthetics and Art Criticism*, 56: 3 (Summer 1998), pp. 217–26. Reprinted by permission of Blackwell Publishing.

this time about, not its extension, but its nature. And that is that pictorial representation is a perceptual, more narrowly a visual, phenomenon. Imperil the visual status of representation, and the visual status of the pictorial arts is in jeopardy. And for the duration of this lecture, I shall take what is nowadays called the "opticality" of pictorial art as given.

But how is the minimal requirement upon a theory of pictorial representation to be framed? I start with the following: (1) if a picture represents something, then there will be a visual experience of that picture that determines that it does so. This experience I call the "appropriate experience" of the picture, and (2), if a suitable spectator looks at the picture, he will, other things being equal, have the appropriate experience.

Some explanations:

A suitable spectator is a spectator who is suitably sensitive, suitably informed, and, if necessary, suitably prompted. The sensibility and information must include a recognitional skill for what is represented, and "other things being equal" means that, in addition to viewing conditions being good enough, the spectator must recruit all these qualifications to the task to hand. As to "suitably prompted," that is intended to forestall a possible oversight and to neutralize an all too common prejudice. What may be overlooked is that sometimes, even if a spectator has the relevant recognitional skills, he may not be suitably informed unless he is told, thing by thing, what the picture before him represents. Without this information, he will not have the appropriate experience. And the prejudice is to assume that, if, without this information, the spectator is unable to experience the picture appropriately, then, with this information, he will still not be able to. The information may affect what he says, but how could it affect what he sees?

Elsewhere I have argued that to dispel this prejudice we should recall those childhood days when we were given a line-drawing and asked to say what was in the foliage, and we said nothing, because, turn it this way, turn it that way, we saw nothing, and then we were prompted, we were shown the key, and we said "Boy," "Camel," "Fish," "Rabbit," "Deer," and what had changed was not just what we said. What had also changed was what we saw. Hence prompting, and the need for reference to it in even so skeletal a version of the minimal requirement.

What makes this version skeletal is that, though it insists that, for each representational picture, there *is* an appropriate experience, it says nothing about what this experience is like. Later we shall have to make good this deficiency. Meanwhile, are there any theories that fail the minimal requirement even in this version?

III

Suspicion falls first on the theory, or rather family of theories, that I have called Semiotic, which have in common that they ground representation in a system of rules or conventions that link the pictorial surface, or parts of it, with things in the world.

If, in our day, the most vociferous of these theories are those which model the rules of representation upon the rules of language, they are also the most vulnerable since, true to the analogy that inspires them, they hold that representational meaning depends upon pictorial structure. But, in the relevant, or combinatory, sense, pictures lack structure. There is no nontrivial way of segmenting pictures without remainder into parts that can be categorized functionally, or according to the contribution they make to the meaning of the whole.

Accordingly, what is specifically wrong with linguistically oriented Semiotic theories of representation can come to obscure what is essentially wrong with Semiotic theory. To bring this out I propose (1) to concentrate on the most plausible version of the Semiotic theory, which is one that not merely drops the commitment to pictorial structure, but insists that the rules of representation cannot be applied, either by artist or spectator,

without recognitional skills for the things represented, and (2) to consider whether such a theory meets the minimal requirement by seeing what it makes of the process by which representational meaning is assigned to pictures by a spectator. Of course, on the face of it, there is no smooth transition from what representational meaning is to how representational meaning is assigned, or vice versa. No theory of representation should neglect the fact that one of the best ways of finding out what a picture represents is by looking at the label. However, for any theory of representation, there is a way of assigning meaning to pictures that tracks how that theory says that pictures come by their meaning, and my current strategy is to see whether the way associated with the most plausible kind of Semiotic theory allows sufficient room for perception. Does it allow room for an appropriate experience?

The answer will turn out to be No. No, in that, though the most plausible Semiotic theory lets perception in at two distinct points in the process of assigning representational meaning to pictures, at a third, and what is the crucial, point it excludes perception.

Any Semiotic theory, linguistically oriented or plausible, lets perception in at point one: the spectator must be visually aware of the surface to which he then applies the rules of representation. Any plausible, as opposed to linguistically oriented, Semiotic theory lets perception in at point two: for the spectator must have the relevant recognitional skills if he is to apply the rules of representation. However, Semiotic theory of all kinds is debarred from finding any further need for perception. And that is because, from this point onwards, all the spectator has to do is to apply the rules to the surface, and the rules will take him, without any help from perception, to the thought of what is represented, which is his destination.

A way of putting the point is to say that, on any Semiotic theory, the grasp of representational meaning is fundamentally an interpretative, not a perceptual, activity. In consequence no appropriate experience is postulated, and it is thus that the Semiotic theory fails the minimal requirement.

IV

If it shows how wide of the mark Semiotic theory is that it fails the minimal requirement even in this skeletal version, this also suggests that, if further theories of representation are to be tested, the minimal requirement needs to be amplified. It will have to say, for every representation, what the appropriate experience is like.

At this point help comes from another strong intuition that we have, again about the nature of representation. For, if, before an otherwise suitable spectator, looking at a representation, can have the appropriate experience, he must have the relevant recognitional skills, the corollary is that, if he lacks these skills, he can, through looking at the representation and being suitably prompted, acquire them. Other things being equal, he will simultaneously have the appropriate experience and acquire the recognitional skill. It is thus that children acquire a very large number of their recognitional skills from looking at illustrated books. My daughter, on seeing her first elephant at age two, exclaimed, "Babar."

This being so, if we want to know what the appropriate experience is like, we have only to ask, Through what kind of experience do we gain a recognitional skill? and the answer to that question is surely this: We gain a recognitional skill through an experience in which we are visually aware of the thing, or the kind of thing, that we are thereby able to recognize. Arguably there could be degenerate cases in which we learn to recognize one thing on the basis of being shown something very like it and then getting ourselves to see the look-alike as the thing in question. But this method could as readily leave us with a merely inferential, as with a truly recognitional, skill. If all this is so, then we can fold this conclusion into our minimal requirement as clause three so that the whole thing now runs as follows: (1) if a picture represents something, there will be an experience of it, called the appropriate experience, that determines that it does so; (2) if a suitable spectator looks at the picture, he will, other things being equal, have this experience; and (3) this experience will be, or include, a visual awareness of the thing represented. I call this the amplified, as opposed to the skeletal, version of the minimal requirement.

Thus re-armed, I turn to the next theory on which suspicion falls, though it is also that on which common wisdom settles: that is, the Resemblance theory. It too is a family of theories, members of which may be divided up two ways.

The first way of dividing up such theories is between those which do not, versus those which do, insist that the resemblance, which holds, of course, between something pictorial and something extra-

pictorial, is experienced. However, what these latter theories insist upon is not that there is a resemblance between two such things, and that this resemblance is experienced. All that they ask for is that the two things are experienced as resembling, which is compatible with a very wide range of actual resemblance or actual dissimilarity. Clearly it is only the latter kind of Resemblance theory that will satisfy the minimal requirement, indeed, that will satisfy it even in its skeletal version. For it is only it that finds room for an appropriate experience.

Secondly, Resemblance theories may be divided up according to the terms between which the resemblance relation holds. (And, since, from now onwards, I shall confine myself to theories of experienced resemblance, and since experienced resemblance, unlike resemblance itself, is nonsymmetrical, I shall be able to talk about the right-hand, or resembled, term and the left-hand, or resembling, term.) Now, disagreements about the resembled term are, in effect, disagreements about the scope of representation, and I shall return to that topic later. As to disagreements about the resembling term, the crucial issue is whether it is, at any rate in the first instance, something on the pictorial surface or some part of the spectator's experience on looking at the pictorial surface.

Finally, and still on the issue of the resembling term, let us be on our guard against those versions of the Resemblance theory which rely upon generalizing remarks of a sort that we indisputably make in front of representational pictures, and which are of the form "That looks like a Saint Bernard," "That looks like Henry VIII." For note that, when we make such remarks, the demonstrative picks out, not some part of the pictorial surface, not some part of the spectator's experience, but the represented thing: the very breed of dog, the very royal person, that the picture represents. In other words, in each such remark, the resembling term is an artifact of, or has been brought into existence by, representation. In consequence, any generalization of such remarks will not be a theory that explains representation by reference to resemblance. It will be a theory within, not of, representation, which it presupposes.

It was received opinion that the Resemblance theory was dead, and then in the last few years two singularly subtle versions of it have appeared, raising second thoughts: one advanced categorically by Christopher Peacocke,[1] but renouncing the label, the other, coming from Malcolm Budd,[2] accepting the label, indeed, expressly looking to see the best that can be done under it, and hence advanced only hypothetically.

Both theories are theories of experienced resemblance, and both introduce the visual field of a spectator so as to obtain the left-hand or resembling term. However, the two theories conceive of the visual field somewhat differently. Peacocke conceives of it as having both representational and sensational properties – but only the sensational properties provide the resembling term in the case of pictorial representation. For Budd the visual field has only representational properties, and therefore these provide the resembling term. Indeed, for Budd my visual field is nothing but how the world, as I look out on it, is represented by vision, *with one proviso*: that we have abstracted away all properties involving distance, or outwardness. (Whether such an abstraction is possible, or whether the most that we can do in this direction is to conceive of the different things we see as represented to us as all equidistant from us, is an important matter, but not to be pursued here.) It follows from there being these differing conceptions of the visual field that, for Budd, when something in the visual field is experienced as resembling something else, something nonpictorial, so too is the corresponding part of the pictorial surface. But not so for Peacocke, who introduces another relation holding between the picture and what it represents, and this relation goes through, and is defined partly in terms of, experienced resemblance.

And just a word on what both theories take to be the resembled term. It is another visual field, a possible visual field: more precisely, it is that visual field which the spectator of the representation would have, were he, instead of looking at it, to look at what it represents. But, for any represented thing, there is a myriad of ways in which it can be seen, and to each of these ways there corresponds a different possible visual field. Accordingly, the second visual field, or the resembled term, fixes, not only what is represented, but how it is represented: that is to say, what properties it is represented as having. Take two of Monet's *Grainstacks* that represent the same two stacks. Evidently they represent them differently, or as having different properties, but how are we to account for these differences? On the present theory we are to do so by first taking the visual fields to which looking at these two pictures gives rise, and then asking of each, Which of the myriad visual fields to which

looking at two grainstacks in nature gives rise would a suitable spectator experience it as resembling? So, if one of these pictures represents a large grainstack, and it represents this as in full sunlight, it does so because the visual field generated by looking at it pairs itself off with the visual field that would arise when looking at a large grainstack and seeing it as in full sunlight.

The further details of both theories are more complex than I have need to take account of, but let me, at this stage, express a preference between the two theories. Peacocke's theory specifies that the experienced resemblance between the two visual fields is specifically in respect of shape. In doing so, it gratuitously comes down on one side rather than the other of Heinrich Wölfflin's famous distinction between the linear and the painterly modes of representation, between the art of stressed, and the art of unstressed, edges.[3] Peacocke's theory aligns itself with the linear mode. Budd professes to avoid this partiality by substituting experienced resemblance in structure for experienced resemblance in shape. If – and I repeat "if" – there is a real difference that correlates with this distinction, then Budd surely improves on Peacocke in substantive adequacy.

So now to the question whether the Resemblance theory thus refined can meet the minimal requirement. So long as the minimal requirement remains skeletal, the answer is Yes. The Resemblance theory clearly insists on an appropriate experience. What each picture represents is determined by some experienced resemblance. But amplify the minimal requirement along the lines suggested, and the answer is, just as surely, No. And that is because the experienced resemblance, which is between two visual fields, does not include a visual awareness of the second field, let alone of what the second field is of, or what the picture represents.[4] True: in order to experience the resemblance, we must have dispositionally a recognitional skill for what the second field is of, or what the picture represents. But it is no more required by the Resemblance theory than it is by the Semiotic theory that this skill is manifested in an actual or nondispositional awareness of the represented thing. And that, if I am right in characterizing the appropriate experience, is what is called for.

At the beginning of *Philosophical Investigations* II, xi,[5] pages which cast alternating beams of light and darkness on the topic of this lecture, Wittgenstein distinguishes between two situations in which I can experience or observe a resemblance. The first is this: Two faces confront me, and I observe a resemblance between them. The second is this: One face confronts me, and I observe its resemblance to another face, which is absent. Now, it is only if representations give rise to experienced resemblance of the first sort that a Resemblance theory could be constructed that satisfied the minimal requirement for a theory of representation. But it is only the second sort of experienced resemblance that it is plausible to think of in connection with representation.

At this point it might be objected that the amplification I have laid upon the minimal requirement, or that there must be a visual awareness of what is represented, is excessive, and that I have done this by reading too much into the conditions in which a recognitional skill is acquired.

I shall not follow this line of reasoning. Instead I shall turn to the theory of representation that I have long advocated, for this theory appears to meet the amplified requirement, and the question that I shall address is whether it does so at a cost in cogency or (some would add) intelligibility.

V

Central to this theory is a special perceptual skill, called "seeing-in," which we, and perhaps the members of some other species, possess.[6] Seeing-in is prior, both logically and historically, to representation. Logically, in that we can see things in surfaces that neither are nor are taken by us to be representations, say, a torso in a cloud, or a boy carrying a mysterious box in a stained, urban wall. And historically, in that doubtless our remote ancestors did such things before they thought of decorating the caves they lived in with images of the animals they hunted. However, once representation appears on the scene, it is seeing-in that furnishes, for each representation, its appropriate experience. For that is the experience of seeing in the pictorial surface that which the picture is of.

What is distinctive of seeing-in, and thus of my theory of representation, is the phenomenology of the experiences in which it manifests itself. Looking at a suitably marked surface, we are visually aware at once of the marked surface and of something in front of or behind something else. I call this feature of the phenomenology "twofoldness." Originally concerned to define my position in opposition to Gombrich's account,[7] which postulates two alternating perceptions, Now canvas,

Now nature, conceived of on the misleading analogy of Now duck, Now rabbit, I identified twofoldness with two simultaneous perceptions: one of the pictorial surface, the other of what it represents.

More recently I have reconceived twofoldness, and now I understand it in terms of a single experience with two aspects, which I call configurational and recognitional. Of these two aspects I have claimed that they are phenomenologically incommensurate with the experiences or perceptions – that is, of the surface, or of nature – from which they derive, and what I had in mind was something of this order: Sometimes we experience a pain in the knee. This is a complex experience, but it is not to be understood by seeing how one part of it compares with having a pain, but nowhere in particular, and how the other part compares with being aware of one's knee and where it is. What I never wanted to deny was that each aspect of seeing-in might be, through its phenomenology, functionally equivalent to the experience from which it derives. The fact that we can acquire recognitional skills through looking at representations, a point on whose theoretical significance I have always insisted, conclusively proves this to be so.

Criticism of my theory of representation has largely taken the form of asking for more: specifically, more about the phenomenology of seeing-in.[8]

On this request, some methodological remarks:

First, we must not respond to such a request as though there were a canonical mode of describing phenomenology so that we could, taking some experience, and proceeding region by region, finish up with a tolerably comprehensive account of what it is overall like.

Secondly, we must not expect from ourselves, or allow anyone else to do so, a description from which someone who had never had the experience could learn what it would be like to do so. In fact, the demand for such a description is implicitly a denial that the experience exists. For it implies that no-one will have had such an experience.

Thirdly, we must never lose sight of the philosophical point of phenomenological description. It is not to teach us the range of human experience. It is for us to see how some particular experience can, in virtue of what it is like, do what it does. It pursues phenomenology only to the point where function follows from it. In the case of seeing-in, we need to know how it can provide an appropriate experience for each and every representation, or how (the same thing) the scope of seeing-in can coincide with that of representation.

I shall pursue this last line of inquiry, but first I want to consider a proposal which many might find plausible. This is that, granted that seeing-in grounds representation, experienced resemblance grounds seeing-in. In other words, whenever we see something in a surface, this is in part because of a resemblance that we experience between it and the something else.

There are, I believe, three considerations that militate against such a view.

VI

The first consideration is this: The surface of any picture can contain elements that, though individually visible, make no contribution to what the picture represents. In Budd's phrase, they lack "pictorial significance." Consider, for instance, the punchmarks in a Gothic painting, or the dabs of complementary color, red, say, in a field of green, that Monet used to enhance vivacity.

Now, if seeing-in rested on experienced resemblance, we would need an antecedent way of filtering out such elements, otherwise we shall think of a picture as representing anything and everything that we can experience these elements as resembling. We shall think that Duccio represents the Madonna's halo as embroidered, or that Monet has scattered tiny scarlet blossoms through the reeds.

If, however, we retain seeing-in as prior, then we shall be encouraged to look at the picture, to see in it whatever we are inclined to, and it is only if we have reason to suspect what we have seen that we shall start to check the surface for elements that might have led us astray. However, since elements that are indubitably insignificant need not lead us astray, there is, so long as the priority of seeing-in is maintained, no necessity for an antecedent principle of exclusion. And this, as I see it, is fortunate, since none seems available.

The second consideration is this: If experienced resemblance is basic, then what we must be expected to do is to attend to each pictorially significant element that we can identify and be visually aware of it at least to this degree: that we experience it as resembling something or other. Perhaps additionally we need to experience it as having that property in respect of which the resemblance strikes us. And this is because, since, on this view, the only way in which anything can be represented in the picture is through some part of the picture being experienced as resembling it, neglect one pictorially significant element, and we shall lose some part of what the picture represents.

At this point the question arises whether a theory of experienced resemblance, like a linguistically oriented Semiotic theory, requires that pictures be capable of systematic segmentation. If the answer is No, which seems, on general grounds, more plausible, and pictorial elements can in principle swell so as to engulf both small groups of marks *and* the circumambient surface between them, a danger lurks. Consider, by way of example, "the small black circle" of which Roger Fry[9] made so much in his formalist onslaught upon Breughel's great *Procession to Calvary* – how are we to say for certain that we experience such elements as resembling something in the world that the picture represents, rather than as resembling a representation of those things? In other words, can we prevent the theory of experienced resemblance from declining into what I have called a theory within, as opposed to a theory of, representation?

By contrast, when seeing-in is given priority, all that is required is that we are visually aware of the surface, and how detailed this awareness must be is an open matter. And this is because there is no perceptible feature of the surface corresponding to every feature of what is represented. The representational content of a painting by Gainsborough or Turner is not constrained by what I have called "localization."

The third consideration against the priority of experienced resemblance is this: That this view requires us not only to be aware of what properties the pictorially significant elements have, but to infer from these properties how the corresponding object is represented, or (the same thing) what properties it is represented as having. But such inferences can be wild. Parmigianino's Madonna is not represented as having a long neck, nor did Ingres, who despised anatomy, show his odalisques – that is, the women themselves – with, as contemporary critics maintained, one vertebra too many.

A final observation: Those who find a place for experienced resemblance in an account of representation think it in their favor that such an account readily yields a criterion of naturalism in representation. If it does, I, on the contrary, see that as a mark against their account. For, once we start to survey the very different kinds of representation that we think of as naturalistic, it seems crude to believe that there is a single, let alone a simple, criterion, least of all one in which experienced resemblance plays a primary role, of naturalism, ahistorically conceived.

VII

I return to the question how the scope of seeing-in and the scope of representation can be identical, and I start by asking, What is the scope of representation?

The answer falls into two parts. The first part is ontological, and it gives us the various kinds of things that can be represented, or what I call the varieties of representation. The second part consists in an overarching constraint, and this is imposed by the limits of visibility. As Alberti put it, "The painter is concerned solely with representing what can be seen."

The varieties of representation are given by a cross-classification. Along one axis, we have representations of objects *versus* representations of events. Women (objects) can be represented, and so can battles (events). Along the other axis we have representations of particular objects or events *versus* representations of objects or events merely of a particular kind. So we can have a representation of Madame Moitessier (particular object), or a representation of a young woman behind a bar, perhaps a young woman of some specificity – but no particular young woman (object merely of a particular kind). Alternatively we can have a representation of the Battle of San Romano (particular event), or a representation of a cavalry skirmish – one fought at dusk, on level terrain, between sides evenly matched, muskets reinforcing sabers – but no particular skirmish (event merely of a particular kind). Representations that are of things merely of some particular kind, whether objects or events, are, I believe, best identified through their intrinsic failure to sustain answers to the question, Which object? Which event? or, Which woman? Which battle?

Nelson Goodman[10] has pointed to another variety of representation: that is, a representation of all things of a certain kind. These are to be found in dictionaries or manuals, but seldom in pictorial art.

However, in considering the scope of representation, I believe that the better starting-point is with the second part of the account: the *constraint* upon representation, or visibility. It gives us more

immediate insight into how the scope of representation and the scope of seeing-in coincide. And that is because of what this constraint asks for. Representation does not have to limit itself to what can be seen face-to-face: what it has to limit itself to is what can be seen in a marked surface.

But what is the difference? For is there anything that can be seen in a surface that cannot be seen face-to-face?

The answer is Yes, and we already know at least part of the reason. For we can see in pictures things merely of a particular kind, and these we cannot see face-to-face. We cannot see face-to face women and battles of which we may not ask, Which woman? Which battle?

But some might insist that, though we can see in pictures kinds of things that we cannot see face-to-face, we cannot see them as having *properties* that we cannot see, or cannot see things as having, face-to-face. It was in elaboration of this doctrine that Lessing famously denied that pictures can represent events unfolding in time; that is, that they can represent events *as* unfolding in time.

It is arguable that where Lessing was really at fault was in the limits he attributed to what can be seen face-to-face rather than in the limits that he consequentially imposed upon what can be represented. Without opening up this issue, let me simply point out that pictures can represent things as having properties that lie extremely close to the limits of face-to-face visibility, and leave it open on which side they actually lie. So pictures can represent a man as singing and a woman as listening to him; they can represent kings as seeing things that are not given to the human eye; they can represent a man as renouncing all earthly goods but one, and why; and they can represent a woman as hearing news the greatness, the terribleness, of which she struggles to take in.

VIII

If we now ask, How is this so? we are asking for a general account of what it is for something to be visible in a surface.

Consider the following experiment: I look at a picture that includes a classical landscape with ruins. And now imagine the following dialogue: "Can you see the columns?" "Yes." "Can you see the columns as coming from a temple?" "Yes." "Can you see the columns that come from the temple as having been thrown down?" "Yes." "Can you see them as having been thrown down some hundreds of years ago?" "Yes." "Can you see them as having been thrown down some hundreds of years ago by barbarians?" "Yes." "Can you see them as having been thrown down some hundreds of years ago by barbarians wearing the skins of wild asses?" (Pause.) "No."

At each exchange, what "Yes" means is that the prompt has made a difference to what has been seen in the scene, just as the "No" signifies that, for *at least this spectator here and now*, the limits of visibility in this surface have been reached. Now, let us assume that this spectator is the suitable spectator for this picture. In that case we can understand the "No" as a refusal on his part to be forced beyond the appropriate experience, hence a refusal to force upon the picture something that it does not represent.

What this thought-experiment primarily shows is the central phenomenological feature of seeing-in, which is its permeability to thought, whether the thought is directly caused by the marked surface or is partly prompted by another. And it is this feature that in turn accounts for the wide scope of seeing-in, wider, as we have seen, than that of seeing face-to-face. It is the permeability of seeing-in to thought that accounts for the wide range of things that can be represented and for the wide range of properties they can be represented as having.

However, two observations are called for.

The first is this: Just because it is true that, on looking at a picture, we can recruit a thought to our perception so that what we see in the picture changes, it does not follow from this that we have any way of indicating where the change occurs, or what it amounts to – apart, of course, from repeating the thought that has brought about the change. Secondly, in insisting that thought, conceptual thought, can bring about changes in what we see in a surface, I am not taking sides on the issue whether the experience of seeing-in has a conceptual or nonconceptual content. Tasting soup has a nonconceptual content, but, if we are prompted conceptually about what is in the soup, the soup can taste different.

IX

Another psychological phenomenon that is highly permeable by thought is imagination, and it is tempting to think that imagination, specifically in its more perceptual mode, or visualizing, grounds seeing-in.

A simple version of this proposal is that, when I see a face in a picture, I am led, by the marks on the surface, to imagine seeing a face. However, imagining seeing a face, which is now assigned the role of the appropriate experience, floats free of the representation. Though it determines what the picture represents, it and the seeing of the pictorial surface are only externally related.

A more complex, and a far superior, version of this proposal, which has been championed by Kendall Walton,[11] is this: I see the pictorial surface, I imagine seeing a face, and of my seeing the surface I imagine it to be an experience of seeing a face. Furthermore, the veridical experience of the surface and the imaginary experience of the face, both perceptual, form, in Walton's phrase, "a single experience": twofoldness again.

My difficulty with this second proposal is how to understand the core project, or imagining one perceptual experience to be another. For, if we succeed, in what way does the original experience retain its content? For, what is left of the experience of seeing the surface when I successfully imagine it to be some other experience? However, if I do continue to see the surface, or this experience retains its content, how have I succeeded in imagining it, the experience, to be an experience of seeing a face? And note two things: First, that imagining one experience to be another is something more experiential than simply imagining that one experience is the other. And, secondly, note that this problem arises exclusively where (1) what we imagine to be something different from what it is is something perceptual *and* (2) what we imagine it to be is also something perceptual. There is clearly no fundamental difficulty in my moving my hands and arms in a jerky and irregular fashion and imagining of it that I am conducting some great orchestra, nor, for that matter, in my looking hard at an old enemy and imagining of it that I am burning him up with my gaze. In the first case neither experience is perceptual: in the second case, only one is perceptual.

X

I too find a place for imagination in my account of representational meaning, but it is a place that is ancillary to seeing-in and is relevant only to certain paintings.[12] These are paintings in which the suitable spectator is offered a distinctive form of access through the presence in the represented space – though not in that part of it which is represented – of a figure, whom I call the Spectator in the Picture. The Spectator in the Picture has, amongst other things, a psychological repertoire: a repertoire of beliefs, desires, attitudes, responses. What then happens is that the suitable spectator, the suitable *external* spectator we might say, starts to identify with the internal spectator: that is, to imagine him, the internal spectator, centrally, or from the inside, interacting with the represented scene as the repertoire assigned to him allows or constrains him to. The net result will be that the external spectator will find himself in a residual state analogous to that of the internal spectator, and this state will in turn influence what he sees in the picture when he reverts from imagination to perception.

Take as examples of representations that contain a Spectator in the Picture some of Manet's single-figure compositions: say, *The Woman with a Parrot* or *The Street-Singer*. When I look at either of these paintings, I see in its surface a woman momentarily but intensely preoccupied. She is distracted by a secret. Then I recognize from a variety of cues the existence of a second figure, male perhaps or perhaps indeterminate as to sex, who stands in the represented space somewhere just this side of the picture plane. I then start centrally imagining this figure trying, trying hard, trying in vain, to make contact with the represented figure. The tedium, the frustration, the despair that I come to imagine, to imagine from the inside, the Spectator in the Picture's experiencing will trickle back into me and reinforce how I see the woman.

I recapitulate this account of the Spectator in the Picture, taken from *Painting as an Art* – though omitting all discussion of what evidence we might have, in the case of any given picture, for there being such an intervention – in order to emphasize the difference in role, and the division of labor, as I see it, between perception and imagination in our interaction with representational paintings. But, note, none of this is intelligible unless we acknowledge the existence of a form of imagination that contemporary philosophy has, implicitly at any rate, rejected. And that is centrally imagining someone other than oneself. Currently, imagination from the inside is treated as though it must be *de se*. If I imagine anyone from the inside it can only be myself, and, if I *seem to* imagine another, what I really imagine is either myself in another's shoes, which falls short of the project I am assuming, or

myself being another, which is incoherent. Much recent discussion of the role of imagination, or (as it is currently called) simulation, in grounding our knowledge of other minds is vitiated by this failure to recognize the scope of imagination.

XI

Let me, even at this late date, point to a surprising omission in this lecture: surprising, since the phenomenon not only figures large in many accounts of representation, but it is the keystone of my own account. There has been no mention of artist's intention: "intention" being the word that has come to mean those psychological factors in the artist which cause him to work as he does.

The most schematic way of fitting the artist's intention into the account that I have given is this: With any representational picture there is likely to be more than one thing that can be seen in it: there is more than one experience of seeing-in that it can cause. However, the experience of seeing-in that determines what it represents, or the appropriate experience, is the experience that tallies with the artist's intention. With omission of the artist's intention from the argument, I have had to put the point more obliquely in terms of the suitable spectator, who is identified as the spectator with suitable sensitivity and suitable information and suitably prompted. But it is the same point, for consider what "suitable" here means. It means the sensitivity, the information, the prompting, that are required if the spectator is to see the picture as the artist desires him to.

However, there has also been an advantage in putting the matter as I have had to: that is, in terms of what the suitable spectator sees rather than of the artist's intentions. For it has made it clear why, for some representations, there will be no appropriate experience. Such an experience will elude even the suitable spectator, and that is because the artist failed to make a work that can be experienced in a way that tallies with the intentions that he undoubtedly had. In such cases the work, we must conclude, represents nothing – though, of course, to put it like this obscures the fact that failure, failure to realize intention, is always a matter of degree. Balzac's Frenhofer apart, can it ever be total?

Representational meaning, indeed pictorial meaning in general, is, on my view, dependent, not on intention as such, but on fulfilled intention. And intention is fulfilled when the picture can cause, in a suitable spectator, an experience that tallies with the intention. And note that the spectator's knowledge of the artist's intention, however acquired, can legitimately mold what he sees in the picture. However, what this, or indeed any other, knowledge cannot legitimately do is to substitute itself for perception. If all the suitable spectator can do is to pick up on the artist's intention, and interpret the work accordingly, and there is no register of this in his experience of the picture, the conditions of representation have not been satisfied.

Notes

1 Christopher Peacocke, "Depiction," *The Philosophical Review* 96 (1987): 383–410.

2 Malcolm Budd, "How Pictures Look," in *Virtue and Taste*, eds. Dudley Knowles and John Skorupski (Oxford: Basil Blackwell, 1993), pp. 154–175.

3 Heinrich Wölfflin, *The Principles of Art History*, trans. M. D. Hottinger (New York: Holt, 1932).

4 Peacocke expressly makes this point when he contends that, in the case of the representation of, e.g., a castle, his theory demands that the concept castle enter the content of the appropriate experience in a more embedded fashion than it would if that experience were an experience as of something falling under that concept. He also says that, if the appropriate experience were an experience as of a castle, that would favor an illusionistic account of representation. "Depiction," p. 403. My thesis of twofoldness is intended to block that line of reasoning.

5 Ludwig Wittgenstein, *Philosophical Investigations*, ed. G. E. M. Anscombe (Oxford: Blackwell, 1953).

6 See Richard Wollheim, *Art and its Objects*, 2nd ed. (Cambridge: Cambridge University Press, 1980), supplementary essay V, "Seeing-as, seeing-in, and pictorial representation"; and *Painting as an Art* (Princeton University Press, 1987), lecture II.

7 E. H. Gombrich, *Art and Illusion* (London: Phaidon, 1960).

8 E.g., Malcolm Budd, "On Looking at a Picture," and Kendall L. Walton, "Seeing-In and Seeing Fictionally," both in *Psychoanalysis, Mind and Art: Perspectives on Richard Wollheim*, eds. Jim Hopkins and Anthony Savile (Oxford: Blackwell, 1992).

9 Roger Fry, *Transformations: Critical and Speculative Essays on Art* (London: Chatto and Windus, 1926), pp. 15–16. For a discussion of this passage, and of formalist criticism, see Richard Wollheim, *On Formalism and its Kinds* (Barcelona: Fundacio Antoni Tapies, 1995).

10 Nelson Goodman, *The Languages of Art* (Indianapolis: Hackett, 1969), chap. I.

11 Kendall L. Walton, *Mimesis as Make-Believe* (Cambridge, MA: Harvard University Press, 1990).

12 Wollheim, *Painting as an Art*, lecture III.

13 This lecture was originally delivered as the Gareth Evans Memorial Lecture at the University of Oxford, on November the 26th, 1996.

Literature

Introduction to Part VIII

Certain characteristics make literature more problematic as an art form than other arts. Since the medium of literature is language (which must be understood and construed) and not colors, physical matter (stone, bronze, steel, plaster), or sounds, which at least in some sense are directly accessible to perception, problems of interpretation and artistic intention become especially prominent in the appreciation of literature. And since literary works are always descriptive in some way and often have a strong narrative component, the question of how literary descriptions and narratives – at least those that are "made up" – relate to other modes of description and narrative (notably "fact-stating" modes), which they look like, becomes pressing in a way not found in the other arts. Finally, since literature always presents us with narrated and described human situations, it has a power to move us in special and immediate ways. This is the reason why Parts IV and VI seem heavily weighted toward literature. For these are the problems on which the analytic tradition in literary aesthetics has focused attention: problems of authorial intention, interpretation, and the nature of literary appreciation; the relationship between literature, fiction, and truth (knowledge); and the potential of literature to arouse emotion.

The three contributions in this section emphasize two main developments that do not come out clearly in Parts IV and VI. From being, in its early days (under the influence of Monroe C. Beardsley), anti-intentionalist and noncontextualist, literary aesthetics in the analytic tradition has more recently tended to be intentionalist and contextualist. The development has been toward the view not only that reference to authorial intention is conceptually built into the notion of a literary work, but that a proper appreciation of the work is ultimately dependent upon understanding it as the work of a particular author. Indeed, Jenefer Robinson, in "Style and Personality in the Literary Work," argues that features of style in the literary work can only be identified by help of the notion of an author's personality. An individual's style of behavior, according to Robinson, is constituted by the way that individual consistently performs a range of different types of actions. The manner in which these actions are performed expresses the personality of the agent and it is precisely this, the expression of personality, that counts as style. *Literary* style is "a way of performing 'artistic acts,' describing a setting, portraying character, manipulating plot and so on, and it is the writer's way of performing these acts which is expressive of all those standing traits, attitudes, qualities of mind and so on that together form her personality" (Robinson, in Chapter 35). However, Robinson makes the concession to the anti-intentionalists that the "personality" expressed through style may be that of an "implied author" rather than the real author.

One of the strongest reassertions of the reality of the author after the onslaught of the post-structuralists on that notion, is Peter Lamarque's "The Death of the Author: An Analytical Autopsy." Lamarque analyzes in detail what can possibly be meant by the claim that the author is "dead." As an empirical claim that the author is no longer referred to in criticism or by readers, Lamarque points out, the claim is false. As a logical claim about the nature of the literary work (that the literary text is authorless writing) it is incoherent.

It is part and parcel of the concept of writing that it is authored and has a purpose. It is "inevitably and properly conceived as purposive." Only by a process of abstraction could one come to look at writing as without origin and purpose, but this would then have to serve some further purpose which again needs to be specified and justified. The author, therefore, as a being with an individual history embedded in a cultural and social context that will be relevant to the understanding of his work, remains the anchor-point of the literary work.

An attempt to give an account of this contextual nature of the literary work is offered by Stein Haugom Olsen in "Literary Aesthetics and Literary Practice." Traditional theories of literature, he points out, are of two sorts, reductive and nonreductive. Reductive theories attempt to answer the question "What is Literature?" by identifying those textual features, be they relational or inherent, that are necessary and sufficient for classifying a text as a literary work. A nonreductive theory introduces a notion of "aesthetic feature" which, in a particular work, is supervenient on a "constellation" of textual features but not reducible to them. However, both reductive and nonreductive theories are atomistic: they explain the special nature of the literary work by reference to inherent or relational properties of the single work, and as a result there are serious objections to both kinds of theories. Olsen suggests that one needs to introduce a perspective where the focus of attention is moved away from the single literary work to the role that a literary work plays in an institutional practice and where the author and reader are also construed as *roles* defined institutionally and not as individuals. This is a concept of a practice which is not only a habit, a way of doing things, but a practice governed by certain conventions which those who participate in that institutional practice can be seen as following. These conventions and concepts create the possibility of taking up certain roles and determine how these roles must be performed. This notion of institution provides a conceptual scheme that is rich enough for a thick description of literature and the literary work, including a description of aesthetic appreciation and consequently also a description of artistic value. Though this could be called an "institutional theory of literature" it is far from the "institutional theory of art" developed by George Dickie (see Part I). The latter does not permit any characterization of appreciation and value: it merely discriminates between art and nonart. In Olsen's account the concept of "literary appreciation," made possible by the institutional framework of the literary practice, is central.

Further reading

Beardsley, Monroe C. (1958). *Aesthetics: Problems in the Philosophy of Criticism* (New York: Harcourt, Brace & World), Parts III, V, VIII, and IX.

Cascardi, Anthony J. (1987). *Literature and the Question of Philosophy* (Baltimore, MD: The Johns Hopkins University Press).

Lamarque, Peter (1996). *Fictional Points of View* (Ithaca, NY: Cornell University Press).

Lamarque, Peter and Olsen, Stein Haugom (1994). *Truth, Fiction, and Literature: A Philosophical Perspective* (Oxford: Oxford University Press).

Lang, Berel (ed.). (1979). *The Concept of Style* (Philadelphia, PA: University of Pennsylvania Press).

Livingston, Paisley (1988). *Literary Knowledge: Humanistic Inquiry and the Philosophy of Science* (Ithaca, NY: Cornell University Press).

New, Christopher (1999). *Philosophy of Literature: An Introduction* (London: Routledge).

Olsen, Stein Haugom (1978). *The Structure of Literary Understanding* (Cambridge: Cambridge University Press).

Olsen, Stein Haugom (1987). *The End of Literary Theory* (Cambridge: Cambridge University Press).

Skilleås, Ole Martin (2001). *Philosophy and Literature: An Introduction* (Edinburgh: Edinburgh University Press).

Weitz, Morris (1964). Hamlet *and the Philosophy of Literary Criticism* (Chicago: University of Chicago Press).

35

Style and Personality in the Literary Work

Jenefer M. Robinson

Introduction

In this paper I want to describe and defend a certain conception of literary style. If we look at literary style in the way I shall suggest, it will explain many of the problems that surround this elusive concept, such as why something can be an element of style in the work of one author and not in another, what the difference is between individual style and general style, and how style differs from "signature." The ordinary conception of style is that it consists of nothing but a set of verbal elements such as a certain kind of vocabulary, imagery, sentence structure and so on. On my conception, however, a literary style is rather a way of *doing* certain things, such as describing characters, commenting on the action and manipulating the plot. I shall claim that an author's way of doing these things is an expression of her personality, or, more accurately, of the personality she seems to have. The verbal elements of style gain their stylistic significance by contributing to the expression of this personality, and they cannot be identified as *stylistic* elements independently of the personality they help to express.

Many theorists and critics have written as if style were an expression of personality. A good recent example is an essay on the first paragraph of Henry

Jenefer M. Robinson, "Style and Personality in the Literary Work," *Philosophical Review*, 94:2 (April 1985), pp. 227–47. © 1985 by Cornell University. Reprinted by permission of the publisher and the author.

James' novel *The Ambassadors*, in which the writer, Ian Watt, claims that

> the most obvious and demonstrable features of James' prose style, its vocabulary and syntax, are direct reflections of his attitude to life and his conception of the novel . . .[1]

Watt lists some of the most notable elements in James' style: the preference for "non-transitive" verbs, the widespread use of abstract nouns, the prevalence of the word "that," the presence of "elegant variation" in the way in which something is referred to, and the predominance of negatives and near-negatives. Then Watt proceeds to show how these stylistic elements are expressive of James' *interest* in the abstract, his *preoccupation* with what is going on in the consciousness of his characters and his *attitude* of humorous compassion for them.

This essay is an attempt to explain and justify the assumption of Watt and others like him that style is essentially an expression of qualities of mind, attitudes, interests and personality traits which appear to be the author's own. My thesis is a thesis about what Richard Wollheim calls "individual style" and not about the style of periods or of groups of writers within a period.[2] I do not want to suggest that the unity of period or group styles, such as the Augustan style, can be explained in terms of the "personality" of a group or period. One other point should be mentioned. I believe that my remarks apply equally well to the non-literary arts, but for reasons of space I shall not attempt to justify this claim here.

I Style as the Expression of Personality

In this first section I shall argue that style is essentially a way of doing something and that it is expressive of personality. Further, I shall suggest that what count as the verbal elements of style are precisely those elements which contribute to the expression of personality.

Intuitively, my style of dress, work, speech, decision-making and so on is the mode or manner or way in which I dress, work, speak and make decisions. In short it is the way I *do* these things. In ordinary contexts, then, a style is always a way of *doing* something. No less intuitively, my style of dressing, working, speaking and making decisions is typically an *expression* of (some features of) my personality, character, mind or sensibility. Thus my vulgar way of dressing is likely to be an expression of my vulgar sensibility, my witty, intellectual way of speaking an expression of my witty, intellectual mind, and my uncompromisingly courageous way of making decisions an expression of my uncompromisingly courageous character.

In saying that a person's way of doing things is an *expression* of that person's traits of mind, character or personality, I am saying (1) that the person's way of doing things exhibits or manifests these traits, and (2) that it is these traits which cause the person to do things in the way they do. Thus these traits leave a matching imprint or trace upon the actions which express them. If my timid way of behaving at parties is an expression of my timid character, then (1) my behavior exhibits or manifests timidity – I behave in a manifestly timid fashion, blushing, refusing to talk to strangers, hiding in the washrooms, etc. – and (2) my timid behavior is caused by my timid character, i.e., it is not due to the fact that (say) I am pretending to be timid, imitating a timid person or acting the part of a timid person in a play, nor is it the result of secret arrogance and contempt for parties. In general, if a person's actions are an expression of her personality, then those actions have the character that they have – compassionate, timid, courageous or whatever – in virtue of the fact that they are caused by the corresponding trait of mind or character in that person, compassion, timidity or courage. In expression, as the word itself suggests, an "inner" state is expressed or forced out into "outer" behavior. An "inner" quality of mind, character or personality causes the "outer" behavior to be the way it is, and also leaves its

"trace" upon that behavior. A timid or compassionate character leaves a "trace" of timidity or compassion upon the actions which express it.[3]

Just as a person's style of dressing, working and speaking is the mode or manner or way in which she dresses, works and speaks, so an author's style of description, character delineation and treatment of a theme is the mode or manner or way in which she describes things, delineates character and treats her theme. In other words, it is her way of *doing* certain things, such as describing or characterizing a setting, delineating character, treating or presenting a theme, and commenting on the action. Moreover, the writer's way of describing, delineating, commenting and so on is typically an *expression* of (some features of) her personality, character, mind or sensibility. Thus James' humorous yet compassionate way of describing Strether's bewilderment expresses the writer's own humorous yet compassionate attitude. Jane Austen's ironic way of describing social pretension expresses her ironic attitude to social pretension.

Now, a style is not simply a way of doing something. We do not say that a person has a *style* of doing so-and-so unless that person does so-and-so in a relatively consistent fashion. Thus we say I have a vulgar and flamboyant *style* of dressing only if I consistently dress in a vulgar and flamboyant way. It may be, of course, that my way of dressing differs considerably from one day to the next: yesterday I wore a purple silk pyjama suit, today I am wearing a frilly scarlet mini-dress and tomorrow it will be leather dungarees and a transparent blouse. Despite these differences, however, we still say that I have a consistent way of dressing, because all my outfits are consistently vulgar and flamboyant. Moreover, my style of dressing is expressive of a particular feature of my personality, namely vulgarity and flamboyance. In an exactly similar way, we say that Jane Austen has a *style* of describing social pretension, because she consistently describes social pretension in an *ironic* way and the way she describes social pretension is expressive of a particular feature of her outlook, namely her irony.

So far I have talked only about a person's style of doing a particular thing, such as dressing. By contrast, when we say that a person has "a style," we normally mean that he or she has the same style of doing a number of different things. Thus when we accuse John of having a vulgar and flamboyant style, we may be referring to the vulgar and flamboyant way in which John not only dresses but also talks and entertains his dinner guests. Again, in characterizing Mary's style as generous, open, casual and easy-going, we may mean that Mary is generous, open, casual and easy-going in almost everything that she does. In this case Mary's style is expressive not of a single trait but of a number of traits which together "sum up" Mary's personality.

In just the same way, a person's literary style is their style of performing a wide range of (literary) activities. Thus, clearly, Jane Austen's style is not simply her style of doing any one thing, such as describing social pretension, but rather her style of doing a number of things, such as *describing*, *portraying* and *treating* her characters, theme and social setting, *commenting* on the action, *presenting* various points of view, and so on. In short, to borrow a concept from Guy Sircello, it is the way in which she performs the various "artistic acts"[4] which constitute the writing of a literary work. Now, a style of doing a wide range of things is just like a style of doing a particular thing in that it consistently expresses certain features of the mind, personality, etc., of the agent. We say that Mary has "a style" in virtue of the consistently generous, open, casual and easy-going way in which she does a number of different things. Similarly, a writer has a literary style in virtue of the fact that her style of performing a wide variety of artistic acts expresses the same qualities of (her) mind and temperament. For example, James' style of *treating* Strether, of *portraying* the difference between what Strether thinks of Waymarsh and what he thinks he thinks, of *emphasizing* the abstract and the timeless, of *commenting* on Strether's bewilderment and so on together constitute what we call "James' style." And this style owes its coherence to the fact that all these artistic acts express the same set of attitudes, interests and qualities of mind.

Of course, not every artistic act of a writer in a particular work expresses exactly the same qualities of mind, character or personality. In *Emma*, for example, Jane Austen portrays Mrs. Elton in a quite different way from Jane Fairfax. This is because Jane Austen's attitude to Mrs. Elton is quite different from her attitude to Jane Fairfax. In the one portrayal she expresses (among other things) her love of the ridiculous, and in the other she expresses (among other things) her compassion for suffering sensibility. But Jane Austen's way of portraying Mrs. Elton and her way of portraying Jane Fairfax, as well as her way of portraying the other characters in the novel, her way of describ-

ing their personal relationships, her way of developing the plot, and all the other innumerable artistic acts which go into writing the novel *Emma* together add up to the style in which *Emma* is written, a style which expresses all those attitudes that together form the personality of the author of *Emma*.

If a writer has an individual style, then the way she writes has a certain consistency: the same traits of mind, character and personality are expressed throughout her work. Now, at a particular point in a novel, the writer may seem to express anxiety about, anger at or contempt towards a particular character, event or idea, although the writer does not seem to be a chronically anxious, angry or contemptuous sort of person. However, such "occasional" properties should not be thought of as properties of style. Only those properties which are "standing" or long-term properties can be considered stylistic. Thus stylistic qualities are likely to be qualities of mind, moral qualities and deepseated character traits, rather than mood or emotional qualities such as "angry," "joyful," and "afraid." In the same way, we do not treat every angry, joyful or fearful action performed in real life as an expression of basic character or personality; it is only when someone consistently acts in a choleric or a cheerful way, that we infer to her essentially choleric or cheerful nature.

I have argued that a literary style is a way of performing "artistic acts," describing a setting, portraying character, manipulating plot and so on, and it is the writer's way of performing these acts which is expressive of all those standing traits, attitudes, qualities of mind and so on that together form her personality. What, then, is the relation between the performance of these acts and what have traditionally been thought of as the verbal elements of style, such as a certain vocabulary, imagery and sentence structure? When a writer describes a setting and portrays character, she uses words, and the kind of word she uses, the sort of sentence structure she forms and so on together constitute the elements of verbal style. If a writer manipulates his theme from the point of view of one whose main interest is in thought and the development of consciousness (James) or if she portrays her characters with a judicious mixture of irony and compassion (Austen), then he or she does so by using language in certain ways.

Obviously the presence of certain verbal elements does not *entail* that a particular personality is being expressed.[5] If, however, (on a reasonable interpretation) those verbal elements are being used by a writer to perform artistic acts in a particular way, then we can infer from the way the acts are performed to characteristics of the writer's mind, character and personality. For example, Henry James uses negatives, abstract nouns, etc., in order to describe Strether's state of consciousness, to comment on Strether's bewilderment and to characterize Strether's attitude to Waymarsh, and he thereby expresses qualities of his own mind and personality.

Moreover, negatives, abstract nouns, non-transitive verbs, elegant variation and so on are verbal elements which at first sight seem to have nothing in common. What links them all together, however, as elements of "James' style" is their use in the artistic acts James performs: they are all elements of his style because they all contribute to the expression of his personality and attitudes. For example, using these particular verbal elements, James thereby describes Strether's state of consciousness in a particular judicious, abstractive, expository way and thereby expresses his own "subjective and abstractive tendency,"[6] his interest in the relations between minds (Strether's, the narrator's, the reader's), his moral sensitivity and his cool and judicious intellect.

II   The Personality of the Implied Author

So far in this essay I have written as if the personality expressed by the style of a work were that of the writer herself. I have suggested that we infer from the way in which the writer performs the artistic acts in a work to the presence of personality traits and so on *in the writer* which cause her to perform those acts in the way that she does. But this is an oversimplification. What is more typically expressed by the style of a work is not the personality of the actual author, but of what, following Wayne Booth, we might call the "implied author,"[7] that is, the author as she seems to be from the evidence of the work. Thus however querulous and intolerant the actual Tolstoy may have been in real life, the implied author of *Anna Karenin* is full of compassionate understanding.

Because the way in which people act typically expresses features of their minds, attitudes and personalities, we are justified in making inferences from the way in which people perform actions to the presence in them of certain character or personality traits. If we see Mary constantly acting in a generous and compassionate way, then, barring any evidence to the contrary, it is reasonable to infer that Mary has a generous and compassionate nature which is responsible for her generous and compassionate actions.[8] The situation is more complicated, however, when we are considering acts performed by an author in the composition of a literary work. Although it may sometimes be legitimate to infer from the way these acts are performed to personality traits in the actual author, it is normally the case that the personality expressed by the style of a literary work is not that of the actual author but that of the implied author.

This might sound as if the author were trying to mislead us. After all if in real life it turns out that Mary's generous and compassionate actions are entirely due to her desire to impress John, then we might well accuse her of deceiving us – or at least John – about her true nature. She seems to be a generous and compassionate person but in fact is not. However, the situation is significantly different in the literary case. It is, after all, a commonplace convention of fiction-writing that the author more or less consciously "puts on" or "adopts" a persona to tell "her" story, but normally at any rate the author is not thereby trying to deceive us into believing that this assumed persona or personality is her own.[9] When we make inferences from the way the artistic acts in a work are performed to the personality of this implied author, the "person" who seems to be performing these acts, we are aware that the personality which leaves its "trace" on the way those acts are performed is a personality created and adopted by the author and which may be different from that of the author herself.[10] Thus, as Booth points out, even the implied author of *Emma* does not have all her qualities in common with the real Jane Austen. Both are wise, witty, unsentimental and so on, but the implied author of *Emma* has a moral perfection beyond the scope of the real Jane Austen.[11]

Some literary works deliberately exploit a number of different styles. A good example is James Joyce's *Ulysses*. In this case the style of at least some of the different episodes of the book should be identified with the style not of the implied author "James Joyce" but of the narrator of that episode. The personality expressed by the style of the Cyclops episode, for example, is not the personality which the author seems to have; the coarse and unpleasant personality expressed belongs only to the nameless narrator of the episode. Notice, however, that this kind of case is parasitic upon the normal case: it is because a style is normally an expression of the personality of the writer that we infer from the style of the Cyclops episode to the presence of a coarse and unpleasant person writing or narrating it.[12]

Does it make sense to talk about "the style" of *Ulysses*? In a way it does not, because *Ulysses* contains so many different styles (some of which are not even "individual" styles).[13] Nevertheless, we can identify an implied author of *Ulysses* and detect the way in which he appears to *manipulate* the narrative point of view, *treat* the *Ulysses* theme, *characterize* Molly Bloom, etc. The way these artistic acts are performed is part of *the style of Ulysses*. For example, the presence of many different narrators with different styles is itself a feature of *Joyce's* style and it is expressive of certain traits that Joyce seems to have, such as a boisterous creativity, a delight in the expressive capacities of language and an interest in the way reality can be viewed and reported from so many different points of view.[14]

One of the ways in which we identify "Joyce's style" is by looking at Joyce's *oeuvre* as a whole. Thus we may be inclined to see the style of the early Stephen episodes in *Ulysses* (as opposed to, say, the Cyclops episode) as in "Joyce's style" partly because they are in somewhat the same style as other works by Joyce, notably *A Portrait of the Artist*. The style of an *oeuvre*, just like the style of an individual work, is an expression of the personality of the implied author of that *oeuvre*. Just as we sometimes find a variety of styles in a single work (like *Ulysses*), so it is possible to find in a single *oeuvre* a variety of styles corresponding to radically different implied authors. But in the normal case the implied author of different works in a single *oeuvre* is recognizably the "same person." Of course no two works do or even can express exactly the same personality, but there will normally be striking similarities. Typically, the personality expressed by an author's style matures over time. Thus the implied author of Jane Austen's books becomes less acerbic in her wit, more compassionate and tender;[15] the implied author of Henry James' works becomes ever more complex, subtle and abstract in his thinking and moralizing. A style grows and matures with the personality it expresses.

III An Objection Considered

My thesis has been that the defining feature of a literary work which has an individual style is that the work is an expression of the personality of the implied author,[16] and that what links the diverse verbal elements of style together into a coherent whole is that they all contribute to the expression of this particular personality. One objection to this thesis is that there are many qualities of a work which *prima facie* are qualities of its style but which do not seem to express any qualities of mind or personality in the implied author. In particular, there are formal qualities (euphonious, Latinate, colloquial, ornate) and expressive qualities (dramatic, heroic, violent) which may be attributed to the style of a work but which are not (or need not be) qualities of the implied author's mind or personality.

In this section of the paper I shall argue that such formal and expressive qualities are not always qualities of the individual style of a work, and that when they are it is only because they contribute to the expression of qualities of mind, personality, etc. in the implied author. Among works which possess striking formal or expressive qualities (euphony, violence, etc.), I distinguish three sorts of case: (1) works which have such properties but lack style altogether, (2) works which have such properties and also belong to a general style category but which lack individual style, and (3) works which have such properties and which also possess individual style.

(1) Intuitively, there could be a piece of characterless prose which nevertheless happens to be *euphonious*, i.e., the words it contains make a pleasing musical sound. Imagine, for example, an incompetent Freshman English paper in which the ideas are unclearly expressed, the sentence structure confused and the choice of words unimaginative. No one reading the paper would attribute to it an individual style. Yet, quite by chance, the ill-chosen words are euphonious: l's, m's and n's predominate, there are only a few plosives or fricatives, and the vowel sounds fit together in a melodious way. To say that this work is in a "euphonious style," however, is at best misleading, since intuitively it is not in a style at all. The possession of just one striking formal quality, such as euphony, is not normally sufficient to endow a work with style. Indeed even a string of nonsense syllables may be euphonious, although presumably they cannot be

in a style. Hence euphony does not always contribute to individual style, just because it may be a quality of a work that lacks style altogether. On my view, of course, a euphonious work that lacks individual style is a euphonious work which fails to express any individual personality in the implied author.

(2) A more interesting situation arises when a work is in a "euphonious style" in the sense that it belongs to what Wollheim calls a "general" style category, although it does not possess *individual* style. General style categories, such as period or school styles, group together writers, painters or other artists who seem to the critic and historian to have important characteristics in common, for example, the Elizabethan pastoral lyric style or the style of the school of Donne (the Metaphysical style). To belong to a general category of literary style often involves obeying certain conventions and using certain techniques. Thus the style of Elizabethan pastoral love lyrics demands a certain stylized way of referring to the lover and the beloved, of describing their surroundings and so on. The imagery and the poetic forms employed all fall within a fairly narrow and predictable range. More importantly for my present argument, membership in a particular general style category often requires a work to have certain formal and expressive qualities. Thus the style of an Elizabethan pastoral love lyric is supposed to be charming and euphonious, the Metaphysical style colloquial and dramatic, and the Miltonic epic style (i.e., the style of works which imitate *Paradise Lost*) Latinate and heroic.

Now, intuitively, there is a distinction between merely belonging to a general style category and having a formed individual style. For example, although a poem must be (somewhat) colloquial and (somewhat) dramatic in order to count as a Metaphysical poem at all, it does not follow that every minor lyric by Carew or Suckling has an individual style. Indeed we may often be hard-pressed to distinguish between the lesser works of Carew and Suckling, just because they do lack "individuality." Similarly, many of the poems in the collection *England's Helicon* obey all the requirements of the Elizabethan pastoral lyric style and yet remain "characterless." They are charming and euphonious but they have an anonymous air about them: they do not seem to have been written by anyone in particular. In short, a work which belongs to a general style category may have certain striking formal or expressive qualities even though it lacks

individual style. An Elizabethan love lyric may be euphonious, a Metaphysical poem dramatic, a Miltonic epic Latinate without necessarily being in an individual style.

One of the merits of my theory of style is that it allows us to define and explain this intuitive distinction between individual and general style. On my view, the crucial difference is that whereas having an individual style necessarily involves the expression of personality in the implied author, belonging to a general style category has no such implications. Elsewhere[17] I have argued for this position in much greater detail than is either possible or appropriate here. If I am right, however, it follows that there can be works belonging to a general style category which possess the formal and expressive qualities characteristic of that style but which do not express any individual personality in the implied author. Hence these formal and expressive qualities, although qualities of general style, do not contribute to any individual style in the work just because they do not contribute to the expression of an individual personality in the implied author of the work.

(3) Finally, formal and expressive qualities such as "Latinate," "euphonious" and "dramatic" may be qualities that are present in works of individual style and which do contribute to the expression of personality in those works. It does not follow, however, that the implied author is a Latinate, euphonious or dramatic sort of fellow. These qualities in themselves do not express any particular trait in the implied author. Rather they can help to express many diverse traits, depending upon the artistic acts to which they contribute. In a similar way, Henry James' fondness for negatives does not in itself express any feature of "his" personality; it is the way the negatives are used in the performance of artistic acts, such as describing Strether's state of mind, which gives this feature of James' work its stylistic significance.

The quality of euphony, for example, may indeed contribute to individual style, but it does so by contributing to the expression of individual personality in a work. Consequently the contribution it makes is very different in different works. Both Swinburne's "Garden of Proserpine" and large passages of Milton's *Paradise Lost* can be described as euphonious, but the personalities expressed in the individual style of these two works are very different. In the Swinburne poem the gentle, musical sounds help to express the implied author's sense of world-weariness, melancholy and resignation,[18] whereas the famous Miltonic melody generally serves to help express the implied author's sense of the dignity and grandeur of his theme. To say that both works are in a "euphonious style" means simply that euphony is a formal quality of both works, which in both cases contributes to individual style. The way it contributes, however, is quite different in the two cases. Similarly it could be argued that both Jane Austen and Donne have *dramatic* styles, but clearly the dramatic qualities in each help to express quite different personalities and hence contribute quite differently to the styles of each.[19]

In summary then, the formal and expressive qualities I have been discussing are not always qualities of the individual style of a work: they may be present in works lacking any style at all or in works which belong to a general style category but do not have individual style. Moreover, even when such qualities contribute to the individual style of a work, they do so in very different ways. The "same" quality in two different works may contribute to the expression of quite different traits of mind and personality in the implied authors of those works.

There are two interesting corollaries of my discussion. First, it would seem to follow that no verbal element or formal or expressive quality in a work is always and inevitably an element or quality of individual style. Even such qualities as "euphonious" and "Latinate" do not contribute to individual style wherever they appear, and even when they do contribute to individual style, they do so in virtue of how they are used in the artistic acts in the work. Secondly, it would also seem to follow that *any* verbal element or formal or expressive quality in a work *can* be an element or quality of individual style, provided it contributes in the appropriate way to the expression of personality in the implied author.

In short, if my thesis is correct, then there is no "taxonomy" or checklist of style elements, that is, elements which contribute to individual style wherever they appear.[20] Euphony, Latinate diction, and the presence of many negatives are elements of individual style only if they are used in such a way as to contribute to the expression of traits of mind and personality in the implied author.

We cannot, therefore, identify the elements of individual style merely as the most striking or salient features of a work. On the one hand there are striking features which do not invariably contribute to individual style. I have argued that

euphony, for example, may be a striking feature of works which lack individual style. Again, it would be a striking feature of a work if all the proper names in it began with the letter "X," yet intuitively this would not be a feature of its *style* (although it could be if, for example, it were used to express the implied author's sense of fun).

On the other hand, moreover, there are many elements which are not particularly salient but which contribute to individual style. Thus a certain writer who has a formed individual style may have a preference for the indefinite article over the definite which contributes in a small way to the expression of her generalizing imagination and tendency to abstraction. Again, any careful, sensitive reader of *The Ambassadors* can tell that James tends to "interpolate" elements in his sentences, but we may not notice that the interpolations typically occur between verb or adjective and complement, or between auxiliary and main verb, and that they cluster towards the center of a sentence.[21] Yet it is non-salient elements such as these which contribute significantly to James' style, because they all help to express "James'" characteristic attitudes, interests and qualities of mind and personality.

IV   Some Problems Resolved

I have argued that if a literary work has an individual style, the artistic acts in the work are performed in such a way as to express qualities of mind, attitudes, personality traits, etc., which make up the individual personality of the implied author of the work. The verbal elements of (individual) style are those elements which contribute to the expression of this personality. There is no "checklist" of elements or qualities which inherently or intrinsically contribute to individual style, no matter where they appear.

So far I have merely tried to make my thesis seem reasonable and to forestall some possible objections to it. In this final section I should like to make some more positive remarks in its favor. The best reason for accepting my theory is that it answers an array of difficult questions surrounding the concept of style.

(1)   First, my theory explains why a correct description of a writer's style mentions some of its verbal characteristics but not others. On my view, what count as the elements of a style are precisely those verbal elements which contribute to the expression of the implied author's personality. In

Henry James, for example, the relevant verbal elements include the recurrent use of non-transitive verbs, abstract nouns, negatives and the word "that." These all help to contribute to the expression of "James'" personality. But we could, no doubt, if we searched for them, discover many recurrent elements in James' work which are not stylistically significant. Thus perhaps it would turn out that James had a penchant for nouns beginning with the letter "f" or that his sentences invariably had an even number of words in them. A description of James' style would not mention these elements, however, precisely because they do not contribute to the expression of the personality of the implied author. In short, many quite diverse and seemingly unrelated verbal elements belong to the same style in virtue of the fact that they all contribute to the expression of the same personality. It is only if the frequent use of nouns beginning with the letter "f" can be shown to contribute to this personality that this particular verbal characteristic would be an element of style.

(2) For similar reasons, my theory explains why it is that the same verbal element may have stylistic significance in one work or author and no stylistic significance, or a different significance, in another work or author. For the same stylistic element may play no expressive role in the one case and an important role in the other. Alternatively, it may simply play different expressive roles in the two cases. Suppose, for example, that two writers tend to use the indefinite article rather than the definite. In one writer, who has a formed individual style, this may contribute to the expression of her generalizing imagination and tendency to abstraction. In the other writer, it may be an accident and it may have no expressive effect in the work, or perhaps it indicates a lack of strength and precision in the style. In the first writer we have located the presence of a stylistic element; in the second writer the same element has no stylistic significance or a different one. If we were to view a person's style as consisting of a set of elements which we can check off on a checklist, then it would make no sense to say that a particular element is sometimes stylistic and sometimes not. But if we view style as a function of the literary personality expressed by a work in the way I have suggested, then the problem dissolves.

(3) It is commonly believed that if a writer or a work has an individual style, this implies that the various stylistic elements have a certain unity. Yet there are no intrinsic connections among the features of James' style, for example: why should negatives, abstract nouns and "elegant variation" go together to form a unified style? My theory explains in a clear way what stylistic unity amounts to: a style has a unity because it is the expression of the personality of the implied author. Just as we see the way a person performs the various actions of daily life as expressive of different facets of her personality, so we see the way in which a writer seems to perform the various artistic acts in a literary work as expressive of different facets of "her" personality. The many disparate elements of verbal style fit together only because they are being used to express the "same" personality: the writer uses the elements of verbal style to describe her characters, treat her theme, etc., thereby seeming to reveal a set of personality traits, qualities of mind, attitudes and so forth which "makes sense" out of (unifies) this multitude of artistic acts.

The question arises as to whether this set of "standing" traits forms a coherent personality. The concept of a "unified" or coherent personality is admittedly somewhat vague, since the most disparate and apparently inconsistent psychological traits seem capable of coexisting in normal, rational people.[22] All I need to insist on, however, is that if a work has an individual style then the different traits expressed by the various artistic acts in the work (portraying Jane Fairfax, characterizing Emma's treatment of her father, etc.) coexist in a way which is consistent with our knowledge of persons and human nature. Moreover, the same traits must be consistently expressed throughout a work. Thus the implied author of *Le Rouge et le Noir* both admires and despises the aristocratic world to which Julien Sorel aspires, but because he does so consistently and because the conflict in his attitudes is one which we recognize as possible in a basically rational person, his admiration and scorn are both part of the personality expressed by the style of the work.[23] If, however, a work expresses no individual personality at all or if the personality expressed is a confusion of different traits which do not fit together in an intelligible way, then it follows from my thesis that the work in question lacks individual style.[24]

(4) It used to be a commonplace of literary theory that the subject-matter of a text is *what* the writer writes about, whereas the style is *how* she writes about it. This distinction has recently been questioned by several writers, including Nelson Goodman, who argues that

some differences in style consist entirely of differences in what is said. Suppose one historian writes in terms of military conflicts, another in terms of social changes; or suppose one biographer stresses public careers, another personalities.[25]

The theory of style which I have outlined in this essay accounts for the intuition that sometimes features of subject-matter may be stylistic features and explains which features of subject-matter will count as stylistic and why. Briefly, a feature of subject-matter is of stylistic relevance just in case it is expressive of the implied author's personality. Thus it is reasonable to construe the subject-matter of *The Ambassadors* as the development of Strether's consciousness. In this case the choice of subject-matter is clearly of stylistic relevance. Again the differences in the histories and biographies envisioned by Goodman are clearly differences in the personalities of the implied authors of these works.

(5) My theory also has a satisfying explanation for the difference between what Goodman calls "style" and "signature." A "signature" is anything which identifies a work as being by a particular author, school, or whatever, such as an actual signature. A "signature," however, may have no stylistic significance. Goodman says:

Although a style is metaphorically a signature, a literal signature is no feature of style.[26]

It is true that a style, like a "signature," may *identify* a work or an author, but the way it performs the identification is quite different. A "signature" may have nothing to do with the qualities of the implied author expressed by a work. Perhaps it is an actual signature or perhaps some other convention is used: a writer might be uniquely identifiable by the particular Latin tag which appears at the head of all her books, regardless of their subject-matter or style (if any). A style, on the other hand, identifies a work or an author because it is an expression of a set of attitudes, qualities of mind, character traits and so on which are unique to the implied author of that work or *oeuvre*.

(6) Finally, as I have already remarked, one of the virtues of my theory is that it allows me to clarify the distinction between general and individual style.[27] If a work belongs to a general style category, then, although it may have formal and expressive qualities that are distinctive of that style, it may nevertheless remain "characterless": no personality "informs" the work. Alternatively, there may be personality traits expressed but they do not seem to belong to any particular individual. The work has an "anonymous" air about it, because the artistic acts are performed in a way which is common to a large number of different writers.[28] By contrast, as I have argued throughout this paper, the defining quality of an individual style is that it expresses a coherent set of attitudes, qualities of mind and so on which seem to belong to the individual writer of the work: a work which has an individual style expresses the personality of the implied author of that work.[29]

Notes

1 Ian Watt, "The First Paragraph of *The Ambassadors*: An Explication," reprinted in *Henry James*, ed. Tony Tanner (London: Macmillan, 1968), p. 301.

2 See Richard Wollheim, "Pictorial Style: Two Views," in *The Concept of Style*, ed. Berel Lang (Philadelphia: University of Pennsylvania Press, 1979), pp. 129–145. My chief debt in this paper is to Wollheim, whose remark that style has "psychological reality" provided its initial stimulus.

3 See especially Richard Wollheim, "Expression," in Royal Institute of Philosophy Lectures, Vol. I, 1966–67, *The Human Agent* (New York: St. Martin's Press, 1968), and *Art and its Objects* (2nd edition; Cambridge: Cambridge University Press, 1980), sections 15–19. See also Guy Sircello, *Mind and Art* (Princeton: Princeton University Press, 1972).

4 Sircello, *Mind and Art*, Chapter 1. I am not sure whether Sircello would approve of the use to which I put the concept of artistic acts.

5 See Frank Sibley, "Aesthetic Concepts," in *Philosophy Looks at the Arts*, ed. Joseph Margolis (New York: Scribner, 1962), and a large subsequent literature.

6 Watt, "The First Paragraph of *The Ambassadors*," p. 291.

7 Wayne Booth, *The Rhetoric of Fiction* (Chicago: University of Chicago Press, 1961), especially pp. 70–77. Kendall Walton has developed the related, but more general notion of an "apparent artist" in his paper "Points of View in Narrative and Depictive Representation," *Noûs* 10 (1976), pp. 49–61, and elsewhere. Walton's own theory of style, in which the

idea of the "apparent artist" plays an important role, is to be found in "Style and the Products and Processes of Art," in *The Concept of Style*, ed. Berel Lang (Philadelphia: University of Pennsylvania Press, 1979).

8   What "having a compassionate nature" means is a large question: presumably at the least it involves having certain beliefs and desires and being prone to certain kinds of behavior. For a discussion of compassion, see Lawrence Blum, "Compassion," in *Explaining Emotions*, ed. Amelie Rorty (Berkeley: University of California Press, 1980).

9   It is not appropriate for me to argue here for any general thesis about the correct way to interpret literary texts, but it is interesting to notice that my view that style is the expression of personality fits very nicely with a plausible theory of critical inter-pretation recently defended by Alexander Nehamas ("The Postulated Author: Critical Monism as a Regulative Ideal," *Critical Inquiry* 8 (Autumn, 1981), pp. 133–149. In his words,

> To interpret a text is to consider it as its author's production. Literary texts are produced by agents and must be understood as such. . . . And since texts are products of expressive actions, under-standing them is inseparably tied to understand-ing their agents.

Here Nehamas uses the word "author" to mean "implied author." His claim is that a text must be read as an expression of the attitudes and so on of the implied author. Of course it could turn out that Nehamas is wrong and the correct way to read liter-ary texts is as the expression of attitudes in the actual author. My thesis can accommodate either view.

10 Compare the way in which actors "adopt" the per-sonality which they express.

11 See Booth, *The Rhetoric of Fiction*, p. 265.

12 Compare *Tristram Shandy* which is written in Tristram's (the narrator's) style. The implied author seems to have a personality much like that of Tristram, but he is distinct from Tristram and appears from time to time to correct Tristram's opinions in helpful footnotes.

13 See, for example, *The Oxen of the Sun* episode.

14 Notice that plays can have individual style despite the fact that they contain many different "voices."

15 However, the implied author of the late fragment *The Watsons* may seem less mature than the implied author of *Persuasion*.

16 From now on I shall write as if the personality expressed by the style of a work were that of the implied author, because typically this is the case. However the implied author may sometimes have all his or her properties in common with the actual author. Moreover, as I have already noticed, in some cases the personality expressed is that of the narrator.

17 "General and Individual Style in Literature," *The Journal of Aesthetics and Art Criticism*, 43 (1984). I argue there that if a work belongs to a general style category, such as a school or period style, then it obeys certain rules and observes certain conventions, some of which undoubtedly foster certain kinds of formal and expressive properties. However, it is pos-sible to write works which belong to a general style category and succeed to some extent in achieving the formal and expressive goals of that category without thereby expressing an individual personality in the implied author.

18 There go the loves that wither,
    The old loves with wearier wings;
And all dead years draw thither,
    And all disastrous things; . . .

19 Sometimes a writer performs the artistic act of "expressing" some quality in the external world, as when she, for example, "expresses" the violence of a battle or the fragility of an elf. Again, however, it is not the violence or fragility themselves which con-tribute to style, but the way in which violence or fragility is "expressed" (in this sense) by the writer. Thus one woman may "express" the violence of a battle with gusto, thereby expressing "her" enjoy-ment of fast-moving action and enthusiasm for heroic exploits, whereas another may "express" the violence with cool detachment, thereby expressing "her" ironic awareness of human folly. For further discussion of this issue, see Guy Sircello, *Mind and Art*, Chapter 4, and my "Expressing the Way the World Is," *Journal of Aesthetic Education* 13 (1979), pp. 29–44.

20 Cf. Richard Wollheim, "Pictorial Style: Two Views." It is possible that there are taxonomies for *general* style categories, unlike individual style.

21 See Seymour Chatman, *The Later Style of Henry James* (Oxford: Blackwell, 1972), pp. 126–127. Chatman's book contains many more examples of non-salient (as well as salient) verbal features that are important to James' style. In his comparison between a successful parody of James' style (by Max Beerbohm) and a rather unsuccessful one (by W. H. D. Rouse), Chatman shows how Beerbohm incorpo-rates into his parody many features of James' style which were obviously not salient to Rouse.

22 See the work on emotions by Amelie Rorty, "Explaining Emotions" and Patricia Greenspan, "A Case of Mixed Feelings: Ambivalence and the Logic of Emotion," both in Rorty ed., *Explaining Emotions*.

23 Lee Brown brought this example to my attention.

24 If for example, *for no apparent reason*, an author describes a certain character with unqualified approval in chapters 1, 3 and 5 and with a certain kind of qualified disapproval in chapters 2, 4 and 6, then it might be that the implied author is schizo-phrenic or, more likely, simply a confused creation.

25 Nelson Goodman, "The Status of Style," *Critical Inquiry* 1 (1975), p. 801. Goodman's explanation for this fact is different from mine, however.

26 Goodman, "The Status of Style," p. 807.

27 See also my "General and Individual Style in Literature."

28 There are some general style categories such as the heroic epic, in which individual style is rarely found and might even be deemed inappropriate. The Homeric epics, however, do seem to contain passages that have individual style. It is interesting to note that the argument over the authorship of the *Iliad* is partly an argument about style and personality in the work. Those parts of the *Iliad* which have individual style provide a strong argument for scholars who wish to argue that there was one central author of the *Iliad* (call him "Homer") even though parts of it had been handed down by an oral tradition. By contrast, scholars who argue that there were a number of bards who contributed importantly to the creation of the *Iliad* point to the fact that there is no individual style to the *Iliad* as a whole. Interestingly, both sets of experts seem implicitly to grant the connection between individual style and an individual personality which is expressed in the style. For an introduction to the problem of multiple authorship in the *Iliad*, see E. R. Dodds, "Homer," in *The Language and Background of Homer*, ed. G. S. Kirk (Cambridge: Cambridge University Press, 1964), pp. 1–21.

29 Many people have helped to improve this paper. I am particularly indebted to Lee Brown, Ann Clark, John Martin, Francis Sparshott, Kendall Walton, Richard Wollheim and the editors and referees of *The Philosophical Review*. I am also grateful to Berel Lang whose NEH Seminar on the Concept of Style aroused my interest in this topic.

36

Literary Aesthetics and Literary Practice

Stein Haugom Olsen

I

The question 'What is literature?' is the starting-point of literary aesthetics. The question is not a request for information about what texts are literary works. It is asked by those who know literature and know the literary canon. Nor does the question merely ask for a definition of literature. The motivation for asking and the interest in possible answers can only be understood against a cultural background where literature figures as an important cultural value. What is asked for is an account of the characteristic features and functions of literature. It is expected that in explaining these, the account should also explain why it is worthwhile to single out certain texts as literary works. It must display those features which define and justify that interest which members of the culture take in its literature. This is the setting which gives the question its point and it should not be forgotten when an attempt is made to answer it.

Two different types of answer to this question are possible. In their traditional form these answers have one feature in common. They are atomistic. They answer the question 'What is literature?' with reference to the single literary work. The concept of literature is taken to cover a number of texts with some common property or properties. And these properties constitute their aesthetic nature

Stein Haugom Olsen, "Literary Aesthetics and Literary Practice," from Stein Haugom Olsen, *The End of Literary Theory* (Cambridge: Cambridge University Press, 1987), pp. 1–19. © by Cambridge University Press.[1]

and thus their aesthetic worth. The two types of answer, however, differ sharply in that one is reductive and the other non-reductive. To characterize this difference it is useful to introduce a distinction between a *textual feature* and an *aesthetic feature*. A textual feature is a feature of style, content, or structure. These are features possessed by all texts. All texts have phonological, syntactic, semantic and a minimum of rhetorical features. All texts have a content which can be described in various ways. And all texts structure their content in some way. Imprecise and vague as it is, this notion of textual feature will serve well enough as a contrast to the notion of an aesthetic feature. For aesthetic features constitute a text a literary work of art, and the question 'What is literature?' concerns the nature of a literary aesthetic feature.

A reductive answer to the question 'What is literature?' makes an attempt to determine what textual features are necessary and sufficient for classifying a text as a literary work. Traditionally, these features have been identified with reference to their relationship to human emotion (emotive theories: a literary work expresses, evokes, or defines emotions) or to 'reality' or 'the world' (theories of *mimesis*: a literary work mirrors reality, is a true representation of general nature, etc.). Recently, rhetorical theories have claimed to be able to identify the 'literarity' of a text without referring to anything outside the text. Semantic and structuralist theories insist upon the autonomy of the text and attempt to show that a literary work possesses characteristic features of style and structure which can be recognized as characteristic without reference to either the world or human emotion.

A non-reductive answer to the question 'What is literature?', on the other hand, would deny that those features which make a text a literary work of art (aesthetic features) can be defined as sets of textual features. It would deny, what is implied by reductive theories, that the notion of aesthetic feature is logically superfluous. Consequently, a non-reductive theory has to give an account of literary aesthetic features making it clear in what sense, since they are not to be defined as bundles of textual features, they can be said to be properties of literary works. While non-reductive theories have played an important part in general aesthetics, there has been little enthusiasm in literary aesthetics for any sort of non-reductive answer to the question 'What is literature?' Emotive theories and theories of *mimesis* have dominated literary aesthetics since Aristotle, and, together with rhetorical theories, dominate it today. There is good reason for this. The recognition of words and sentences, the raw material of literary works, requires construal and the exercise of the understanding in quite another way than does recognition of colours, lines, shapes, musical notes, harmonies, and musical themes. Construing the words and sentences of a text one determines their meaning and purpose. The textual features of style, content, and structure are then determined at the same time. Superficially, it seems quite plausible to see the appreciation of visual art and music as requiring the exercise of a particular kind of sensibility or taste which enables one to recognize aesthetic features as supervening on the perceptual qualities of the work. It is less plausible to see literary appreciation as involving the recognition of features supervening on the construed features of style, content, and structure. For it seems that appreciation of and discourse about literary works of art are appreciation of and discourse about style, content, and structure. Style, content, and structure are the subjects of literary criticism, and it is difficult to see what else it can be about.

II

It is, nevertheless, possible to make a case for a non-reductive analysis of literary aesthetic features. And it is possible to show that, rather than being a curiosity in the museum of literary theories, such an analysis is in tune with some important trends in modern philosophy and offers a more plausible and sophisticated account of literary aesthetic features than reductive theories. As a first step in

this account I shall outline a theory which I shall call the *supervenience-theory*. Several well-known philosophers have presented accounts of aesthetic features and aesthetic terms which come close to this theory, though they do not always agree with each other; some of them might take issue with the following sketch.[2] The supervenience-theory accounts for aesthetic features by construing them as supervenient on textual features. An aesthetic feature, the theory says, is identified by a reader, in a literary work, through an aesthetic judgement as what one may call a *constellation* of textual features. A constellation of textual features constitutes an aesthetic feature of a particular work. It is not identified with reference to 'the world' or to human emotion, nor does it stand out as a constellation identifiable independently without exercise of aesthetic judgement. Outside the literary work in which a constellation is identified, the textual features constituting it cannot be recognized as a constellation. Nor does it exist as a constellation in a particular literary work for just any reader, but only for those who are able and willing to exercise aesthetic judgement. The constellation of textual features exists only as the object of an aesthetic judgement. These textual features deserve to be referred to as a 'constellation' rather than as a mere 'collection' because the aesthetic judgement confers on them, taken together, a significance or a purposive coherence.

An example. Here is Shakespeare's sonnet 129:

The expense of spirit in a waste of shame
Is lust in action; and till action, lust
Is perjur'd, murderous, bloody, full of
    blame,
Savage, extreme, rude, cruel, not to
    trust;   4
Enjoy'd no sooner but despised straight;
Past reason hunted; and no sooner had,
Past reason hated, as a swallow'd bait
On purpose laid to make the taker
    mad, –   8
Mad in pursuit, and in possession so;
Had, having, and in quest to have,
    extreme;
A bliss in proof; and prov'd, a very woe;
Before, a joy propos'd; behind, a
    dream.   12
  All this the world well knows; yet none
    knows well
  To shun the heaven that leads men
    to this hell.

The sensitive reader will have noticed that the poem displays a symmetrical pattern of words with focus in the repetition of 'mad' at the end of line 8, beginning of line 9. 'Had' in line 6 balances 'Had' in line 10, 'extreme' in line 4 balances 'extreme' in line 10, 'Enjoy'd' in line 5 balances 'a joy' in line 12, and, perhaps, the antimetabole in line 2 balances the antimetabole in line 13. This pattern is a textual feature in the sense that the words pointed to are actually there in the text in positions which make it not unreasonable to say that they are placed symmetrically on each side of 'mad/ Mad' (though one may be in doubt about the position of the two occurrences of 'extreme'). It is also a textual feature in the stronger sense that it is an example of a conventional rhetorical device often used by Petrarch to mark the *volta* of his sonnets.[3] But it becomes an aesthetic feature only for the reader who succeeds in assigning the pattern a function in this particular poem. Knowledge that symmetrical patterns were used to emphasize the *volta* of petrarchan sonnets may ease the reader's identification of this particular pattern in 129 as a textual feature. It may spur him to search for a significance for the pattern in *this* sonnet. But the knowledge forms no part of the aesthetic judgement through which significance is conferred on this pattern in this poem. And it is *only* through the exercise of aesthetic judgement that the reader can determine the nature of this aesthetic feature, if such it is. In my own judgement this pattern is constituted by terms which define the rise, climax, and ebb of an emotional reaction of disgust. This emotional reaction accompanies the speaker's reflections on the experience of lust, its satisfaction, and the emotional consequences of this satisfaction. I shall leave it to the reader to exercise his own aesthetic judgement in exploring this suggestion. In an illustration of the supervenience-theory it is sufficient to note that the pattern is identified as an aesthetic feature through the reader's judgement concerning its function in the poem: he assigns it a purposive coherence. Its identity as an aesthetic feature is dependent upon an aesthetic judgement being made with regard to *this* poem about the connection between the different words in the pattern in their different positions.

III

According to the supervenience-theory, an aesthetic feature is irreducible in the sense that it is a *unique* constellation of textual features which can be described as a coherent pattern or *gestalt*, contributing, in the particular work of art, towards the overall artistic design or vision. This uniqueness is, so to speak, part of the logical make up of the concept of an aesthetic feature. 'There are no non-aesthetic features which serve in *any* circumstances as logically *sufficient conditions* for applying aesthetic terms,' says Frank Sibley,[4] and Strawson makes the same point more strongly. 'There can be no general descriptive criteria for aesthetic assessment,' he says.[5] And Strawson finds that this lack of general descriptive criteria makes the very notion of an aesthetic *property* problematic:

> there are no aesthetic merit-conferring *properties*, with non-evaluative names. When you draw attention to some feature on account of which terms of aesthetic evaluation may be bestowed, you draw attention, not to a property which different individual works of art may share, but to a part or aspect of an individual work of art.[6]

This problem, if a problem it is, goes deeper than Strawson seems to admit in this paragraph. For if there are no general descriptive criteria for aesthetic assessment, then it is not only the status of aesthetic features which is problematic, but also the nature of the aesthetic judgement itself. For how is it then possible to identify a collection of textual features as features 'on account of which terms of aesthetic evaluation may be bestowed'?

The explanation offered by the supervenience-theory of how aesthetic judgements are possible and meaningful builds on a general philosophical point made much of by those working in the Wittgensteinian tradition: there are many types of judgement to which it would be absurd to deny the epithet 'rational', but which are supported by arguments with structures other than, and with criteria of validity different from, those of the deductive/inductive arguments. These different *patterns of support* define different *types of judgement*, and differences in pattern of support constitute logical or grammatical differences between judgements.[7] So the fact that there are no general descriptive criteria for the application of aesthetic terms does not mean that aesthetic judgements are arbitrary or impossible to support. There is, the supervenience-theory claims, a characteristic pattern of support with its own peculiar logic which defines aesthetic judgement as a type. This pattern of support has two distinctive features. When an aesthetic judgement is made, there is an appeal to aesthetic sensibility:

> It is essential to making an aesthetic judgement that at some point we be prepared to say in its support: don't you see, don't you hear, don't you dig? The best critic will know the best points. Because if you do not see *something*, without explanation, then there is nothing further to discuss.[8]

To recognize what aesthetic judgements are all about, one has to possess at least the rudiments of aesthetic sensibility. Just like taste it can be cultivated and trained, and, as one develops aesthetic sensibility, one comes to see and appreciate what other aesthetically sensitive people see and appreciate. The second feature distinguishing the pattern of support characteristic of aesthetic judgement is what one might call its *directive* character. Aesthetic argument produces conviction by directing the addressee's perception and the interpretation of what he perceives. The goal of an aesthetic argument is to make the addressee see what the critic sees, to make him share the critic's aesthetic appreciation: '. . . we can say', says Arnold Isenberg, 'that it is a function of criticism to bring about communication at the level of the senses; that is, to induce a sameness of vision, of experienced content.'[9] Aesthetic argument is made up of a series of strategies to open up the work to the reader, to make him see a collection of textual features as a constellation of textual features constituting an aesthetic feature.

The proponents of the supervenience-theory tend to give the impression that the directive aspect of aesthetic argument and the appeal to aesthetic sensibility are equal partners in defining aesthetic judgement. There are, says Stanley Cavell, 'ways [of argument] that anyone who knows about such things will know how to pursue'.[10] And Frank Sibley gives a list of critical procedures employing such patterns of support as we conventionally accept as aesthetic argument.[11] The implication is that the directive aspect of the pattern of support can be identified without reference to aesthetic sensibility, thus constituting an independent element of aesthetic judgement. But this is not the case. According to the supervenience-theory, it is a necessary and sufficient condition for saying about somebody that he has identified an aesthetic feature that he is able to produce a successful directive

argument in support of it, thus bringing us around to his way of 'seeing' a set of textual features in a literary work. But this argument does not *constitute* the identification. The argument does not give meaning and content to the aesthetic perception. Rather, it is the other way around:

> the critic's *meaning* is 'filled in', 'rounded out', or 'completed' by the act of perception, which is performed not to judge the truth of his description but in a certain sense to *understand* it.[12]

If the logical relationship between the recognition of an aesthetic feature and the directive argument is such that the argument in no way defines the content of the recognition, then there are no constraints on the pattern of support which may be employed. No conventions and concepts defining a structure for the argument and criteria of validity can be specified. You travel any way you like as long as you get there. The appeal to aesthetic sensibility must thus be seen as logically prior to any directive argument, and the only criterion of validity for a directive argument is success in bringing about agreement in aesthetic perception.

IV

There is a conflict, then, in the supervenience-theory between the felt need for a characterization of the directive argument involving no reference to aesthetic sensibility and the insistence upon the basic role of aesthetic sensibility which, in principle, prohibits such an independent characterization. Such a characterization is nowhere attempted by the proponents of the theory while the central role of aesthetic sensibility is always acknowledged. The need for assuming the existence of aesthetic sensibility arises in the supervenience-theory because it wants to avoid reducing aesthetic features to textual features. It does this by postulating that the single reader possesses an aesthetic sensibility enabling him to recognize the aesthetic features of the work. The aesthetic sensibility is conceived with reference to the relationship between the single reader and the single work. The reader responds with his aesthetic sensibility when he is confronted with a particular literary work. So this notion of aesthetic sensibility is bound up with an atomistic view of literature.

There are strong practical and theoretical reasons for insisting that aesthetic judgement is defined, at least in part, by ways of argument with their own structure, standards and criteria of validity which can be characterized without reference to aesthetic sensibility. The practical reasons are glaringly obvious if one wants to view the supervenience-theory as a general aesthetic theory applicable also to literature. For literary aesthetic argument interrelates a number of concepts describing the textual features of a literary work in a *critical statement* and such statements *constitute* literary aesthetic judgement. So in literary aesthetic judgement the aesthetic argument usurps the place of aesthetic sensibility. The recognition in Shakespeare's sonnet 129 of the symmetrical pattern of words with focus in 'mad/Mad', as an aesthetic feature, takes place through the description of the function or significance of the pattern in the poem: 'It defines the rise, climax, and the ebb of an emotional reaction of disgust which accompanies the speaker's reflections on the nature of lust, its satisfaction, and the emotional consequences of this satisfaction.' The further support of this interpretative hypothesis will constitute a further articulation of the aesthetic feature which this interpreter sees. The argument is here constitutive of the recognition and articulation of the aesthetic feature. And this is a general point about literary aesthetic judgements: the imaginative reconstruction of the literary work, by help of a set of general concepts enabling the reader to refer to and interrelate the textual features of the work, constitutes his understanding and appreciation of the text as a literary work of art. Thus, in literary aesthetic argument, the aesthetic sensibility is pushed into the background. It is certainly true that some people are naturally more sensitive than others to the finer nuances of literary creation. But this sensibility is defined by their ability to construct a conceptual network which illuminates the work they speak about, not by guiding perception, but through ascribing significance to patterns of textual features. Every feature the reader 'sees' in a literary work is capable of this articulation in concepts, and if the description of aesthetic features can never be complete, this is because the reader's view of a work is always capable of development.

The theoretical reason for insisting on the independence of directive argument from aesthetic sensibility is as strong as the practical reasons. The central insight of the supervenience-theory is that while aesthetic features cannot be *defined* as a set of textual features, they are nevertheless recognized as a set of textual features in the particular literary work. The theory holds out the promise of a characterization of the peculiar nature of this recognition which makes it an aesthetic judgement. This characterization, it is claimed, will also justify the description of an aesthetic judgement as rational in spite of the fact that the judgement is not based on general descriptive criteria. However, if it is impossible to give an independent characterization of the logic of the directive argument, if the only characteristic feature of directive argument is that it is successful in producing agreement in aesthetic perception, then this promise remains unfulfilled. For then the aesthetic judgement must be understood simply as the exercise of aesthetic sensibility, guided or unguided. And it will then be meaningless to talk about a 'pattern' of support or aesthetic argument. To have explanatory power the supervenience-theory must admit the directive aspect of the pattern of support to be characterized by its own peculiar structure, standards of argument, and criteria of validity. But if this is admitted, then, as the example from Shakespeare's sonnet also illustrates, there is really no room for aesthetic sensibility in the definition of aesthetic judgement. For one then accepts that directive arguments are judged by other standards than success in bringing about agreement in aesthetic perception. And if there is disagreement on the level of aesthetic perception it must be settled by argument. Which means that the notion of agreement itself must ultimately be understood with reference to the evaluation of different aesthetic arguments.

The problem for the supervenience-theory is that its atomistic view of literature makes a general characterization of aesthetic argument impossible and so makes an assumption that aesthetic sensibility is the basis of aesthetic judgement unavoidable. If one takes as the point of departure for the analysis of aesthetic judgement the single reader's appreciation of the single work, and if one denies the possibility of analysing it as the application of general descriptive criteria, then nothing further can be said about the reader's aesthetic judgement than that, in making it, he is exercising his aesthetic sensibility. In themselves, instances of particular people exercising aesthetic judgement in connection with single works of art do not yield to analysis in general terms. Proponents of the supervenience-theory try to make this lack of generality and the pre-eminence of aesthetic sensibility in their analyses a virtue, by stressing that it is the essence of aesthetic experience that it is a *personal* experience of value:

> If we say that the *hope* of agreement motivates our engaging in these various patterns of support, then we must also say, what I take Kant to have seen, that even were agreement in fact to emerge, our judgements, so far as aesthetic, would remain as essentially subjective, in his sense, as they ever were. Otherwise, art and the criticism of art would not have their special importance nor elicit their own forms of distrust and of gratitude.[13]

However, if basing the explanation of aesthetic judgement on the relationship of the single reader to the particular work makes a general account of the logic of aesthetic argument impossible, then the focus of the supervenience-theory will have to be changed. Otherwise we shall soon be back to considering reductive theories.

V

Consider now a phenomenon completely different from a literary work: a transaction between two people which one may call a purchase. A purchase involves a transfer of goods (property, services, shares, foreign currencies, etc.) from one person to another in return for a transfer of money the other way. A purchase is different from theft, borrowing, bartering, accepting a prize, receiving a gift, or the restitution of an object. The difference consists in the fact that a purchase involves a payment in money for the goods received. Now, a payment in money has no characteristic qualities which can be seen, heard or smelt. A payment of ten pounds in notes and/or coins can have a number of different physical shapes. Then again it need not be paid in cash. One may pay by cheque, by credit-card, or giro, which all involve different physical objects, pieces of paper, bits of plastic, inky stamps and different procedures. One can even pay by computer transfer (soon there will be a terminal outside every bank and in a few years in every shop), which involves no physical objects whatsoever. So money is not defined by physical appearance or structure. Its distinctive features are defined by its function as a means of exchange inherently without value, but providing a measure of the comparative value

of goods, and by a background of concepts and conventions embodied in an agreement how this function is to be served. This agreement defines what a payment is and how it is measured. It both determines what actual physical forms a transfer of money can take and regulates the transfer. Such an agreement may be, as it has been, continually modified. It has been extended from covering gold and silver coins to covering notes, to cheques, to credit-cards, to computer transfer. Without this background agreement money would not exist, just as credit-cards could only be seen as plastic oblongs (if something like it had existed) until the agreement was modified to define and assign a use to them.

An economic system based on the circulation of money is a social practice or institution defined by a normative structure of concepts and conventions. The conventions which make up this normative structure not only regulate social behaviour but also create the possibility for identifying, and thus for engaging in, the behaviour which they regulate.[14] These *constitutive* conventions specify the characteristics of and label certain types of behaviour, objects, and events, and assign a function to these facts in relation to some purpose which the practice defines, thus constituting them institutional facts. The logical status of the constitutive conventions can be highlighted by comparing them with *summary* or *regulative* rules. These regulate behaviour which can be recognized and described without reference to these conventions. 'Never shake hands with your gloves on' would be such a convention. Handshakes and gloves can be recognized and described without any knowledge of this convention. An institution or practice is explained by pointing out the function which it serves or the purpose it has, by formulating the constitutive conventions and displaying the logical interrelationships between practice concepts themselves and between practice concepts and the descriptions of the brute facts which constitute the institutional behaviour, objects and events. The function or purpose of the institution is not necessarily identifiable independently of the practice. It may have been formulated and developed together with it. An economic system based on the circulation of money has the function that it increases the level of economic activity. And this economic activity cannot itself be described without referring to transactions involving money.

It may be reasonably suggested that literature is a social institution of the same kind as an economic system, defined by a normative structure which makes possible a literary practice. And that to give an account of literary aesthetic judgement, with reference to individual situations in which it is exercised, is like trying to give an account of money and its use with reference only to individual transactions without mentioning the framework of concepts and conventions which makes the transaction possible. Literature is obviously a social practice in the minimal sense that it involves a group of people among whom literary works are produced and read. The present suggestion is that it is a social practice in a stricter sense; i.e. a practice whose *existence* *depends* both on a background of concepts and conventions which create the possibility of identifying literary works and provide a framework for appreciation, and on people actually applying these concepts and conventions in their approach to literary works. If literature is such an institution then aesthetic judgement must be understood as defined by the practice and apart from the practice aesthetic judgements are impossible. And a literary work must then be seen as being offered to an audience by an author with the intention that it should be understood with reference to a shared background of concepts and conventions which must be employed to determine its aesthetic features. And a reader must be conceived of as a person who approaches the work with a set of expectations defined in terms of these concepts and conventions. Somebody who did not share this *institutional* *background* would not be able to identify aesthetic features in it because he did not know the concepts and conventions which define these features. And just as it is quite unnecessary to postulate that somebody who knows what a pound will buy has a monetary sensibility, it is unnecessary to postulate an aesthetic sensibility to explain how it is possible for people to identify aesthetic features. If literature is an institution defined by a normative structure, aesthetic features are no more subjective than judgements identifying sums of money.

VI

If literature is conceived as a social practice rather than as a collection of texts, then literary aesthetics must change its focus away from the relationship between the individual mind and the individual work to the social practice of which both the reader and the work are elements. An explanation of aesthetic judgement, aesthetic features, and aesthetic value must then be sought by attempting a description of the logical relationships between the concepts of literary practice and a formulation of the conventions which govern the practice and make the identification of aesthetic features possible. This explanation represents an internal viewpoint. It can only be given by somebody who shares in the practice and a full understanding of the explanation implies that one would be able to engage in the practice. For an explanation of the practice is really an articulation of the normative structure which defines it. Indeed, the very request for an explanation will involve practice concepts, and is, most likely, motivated by an urge to clarify a pattern of behaviour on which the culture confers special importance or which is construed as being of importance for the culture. The question 'What is literature?', as was pointed out in the first paragraph of this essay, is of the type which one should expect to be asked about a practice by the practitioners. It concerns a phenomenon we already know how to identify and how to approach, but about which we can formulate no general insights, nor can we justify the interest we take in it.

Furthermore, an explanation of aesthetic judgement in institutional terms is non-empirical. A reader is able to offer reasons why certain literary aesthetic judgements are better than others; reasons, that is, why an interpretation of an aspect or the whole of a work is unacceptable or inferior to another interpretation. For example, one may argue that it is wrong to see, in Dickens' *Our* *Mutual Friend*, a slow erosion of Noddy Boffin's amiable qualities as he is being corrupted by wealth,[15] because Boffin never sees himself as the possessor of wealth but only as the custodian of the wealth of others. This reason can be supported by further reasons. One may point to actual events and passages which show Boffin's attitude to his wealth: he does not make public Harmon's last will bequeathing him the Harmon fortune unconditionally, and immediately upon coming into possession of the fortune he offers Bella Wilfer, John Harmon's intended bride, a star role in the new Boffin household and he starts searching for an orphan who can take John Harmon's place. Still further support for these interpretative remarks could consist in pointing to Boffin acting the miser to bring out the gold in Bella. He does this for the young John Harmon just as he sifted the dust for old Harmon and turned that into gold. The institutional approach to literature would construe this type of argument as relying on certain conventions for what are illuminating literary judgements. These conventions must be shared by a reader for him not only to be able to evaluate literary judgements but to be able to understand them. If one does not share these conventions, the whole point of the reconstructive exercise which a literary judgement involves will pass one by. Consequently, the formulation of these conventions and the analysis of the concepts involved can be based on the theorist's own knowledge of the practice. In so far as he is unsure of his grasp of literary judgement, he can study other critics, inquire what judgements are well known and much respected, try to see why they are much respected, to learn what sort of commonsense considerations are used to support an argument, and so on. But his theory does not rest upon an empirical inquiry into what norms readers use as basis for their judgements concerning literary works. He trains himself as a reader and his theoretical venture consists in formulating the conventions which define and structure his possibilities of response. The institutional approach to literature thus rests on an assumption of a fundmental agreement concerning what literature is and what literary judgements are. The task of literary aesthetics is to display the nature of this agreement.

VII

There is an objection against construing literature as a social institution, which addresses itself to the assumption that there is a fundamental agreement concerning literature and literary judgements. It runs as follows. There is, in fact, no agreement on how to understand and evaluate any particular work. Not only are there endless critical disputes on famous questions of interpretation like the delay of Hamlet or the motivation of Lear, but any two critical interpretations of a work are in competition. It is the nature of critical debate that critics suggest their own and criticize other interpretations. This objection has two weaknesses. It overlooks the implications of the fact that there is agreement concerning the literary canon. There will at any time be a number of demarcation disputes concerning whether or not a text is a literary work, but this is a discussion which only makes sense if there is agreement about the existence of a canon. This agreement does not merely concern the fact that such and such texts should be classified as literary works. It is an agreement assigning

these texts a cultural value. These texts are grouped together because they repay a special type of attention. This is the justification for distinguishing certain texts as literary works. It gives the concept of literature its point. An explanation of this agreement will have to offer an account of the particular type of attention which literary works require and of the implicit assumption that a literary work is aimed at creating some sort of cultural value, as well as an account of what makes a text a suitable object of this kind of attention. A reductive explanation of this agreement would be unattractive because it would try to show that the agreement was based on the application of general descriptive criteria. It would have nothing to say about the special attention that literary works are accorded, nor about the value-judgement which constitutes part of the agreement concerning the literary canon.[16] Alternatively, one can argue along the lines of the supervenience-theory that the agreement rests on the exercise of aesthetic sensibility coupled with the employment of directive argument. But the supervenience-theory fails to give an account of either aesthetic sensibility or directive argument and, as was argued above, thus fails to explain how one identifies aesthetic features. In contrast to the reductive theories and the supervenience-theory, an institutional theory would aim at specifying the concepts and conventions which define the special attention texts, construed as literary works, are accorded. In doing this, it would also clarify the nature of the value-judgement involved in the agreement on the literary canon and specify how the reader, in interpretation, identifies such features as make the text a literary work and thus aesthetically valuable. So the type of agreement which, in fact, exists concerning the literary canon seems to require explanation in institutional terms.

The objection that there is no agreement in questions of understanding and evaluation of particular works also makes the mistake of assuming that *such* agreement is necessary for an institutional theory to be possible. It is not. The fact that critical disagreement and competition between arguments concerning interpretation and evaluation is in the nature of critical practice does not mean that it is impossible to distinguish between good and bad arguments and to give reasons why some arguments are better than others. All the institutional theory requires to get off the ground is an agreement on what is good and what is bad argument, an agreement on which literary judgements are worth preserving and which are not. And such an agreement is certainly in evidence in literary practice. For there exists, as a matter of fact, not only a canon of literature, but also a canon of criticism. It is possible to talk about 'The great critics of Shakespeare', and there is not much disagreement about who they are. And this criticism is kept in print, in cheap popular editions, just like the literary works themselves. This critical canon embodies standards for literary judgement. Some of these standards will be those relevant also to other intellectual exercises, such as clarity, consistency, coherence. But one important criterion must be labelled something like profundity or illumination.[17] Philip Collins, in a recent article in *The Times Literary Supplement*,[18] points out that the prison in Dickens' *Little Dorrit*, now considered by all its readers to be one of its central symbols, had not been mentioned in the critical literature before Edmund Wilson gave his lectures on 'Dickens: the Two Scrooges' in 1939 (later published in *The Wound and the Bow*). Wilson establishes the prison as the central symbol by making an imaginative reconstruction which consists in identifying prison analogies and references to imprisonment everywhere in the book. The result is a view of *Little Dorrit* as a highly unified and powerful novel. And the recognition of the prison as one of the symbols around which the novel is constructed with the consequent identification of a pervasive pattern of analogies and references to prisons was the basis for the revaluation of *Little Dorrit* as one of Dickens' masterpieces. Wilson's essay is coherent and clear, which it needs to be successfully to establish the pervasiveness of the idea of imprisonment and its function as an organizing principle in the novel. But it is the imaginative leap of seeing the prison as a central symbol and the idea of imprisonment as being expressed in a number of the novel's textual features which makes it great criticism. It is the paradigm of an illuminating judgement. It is important that it is realized that the conventions which the institutional view of literature assumes to be the constitutive conventions of the institution, and which underlie our recognition of Wilson's interpretation as illuminating, are *not standards of criticism*. The concept of criticism embraces all sorts of discourse about literary works. This discourse is made possible by judgements of interpretation and evaluation which constitute the reader's appreciation of a work, but much criticism is concerned with matters beyond

appreciation. Only in so far as criticism is relevant to appreciation is it possible to see the conventions of the institution as defining and regulating criticism. Criticism can be judged as illuminating in so far as it contains or inspires illuminating judgements, but the purpose of criticism is not necessarily to promote aesthetic appreciation.

VIII

There is thus no reason to dismiss the institutional approach without further consideration. And there are reasons to believe that literature does yield to explanation in institutional terms. First, the reader's response to a literary work seems to be correctly described as an *imaginative reconstruction* of its literary aesthetic features. The supervenience-theory seems to be correct in saying that to identify an aesthetic feature an aesthetic judgement is required. And this imaginative reconstruction has, as a matter of fact, a certain logical structure. Secondly, literary aesthetic judgements are formulated in a vocabulary with its own criteria of application and a hierarchical structure. This vocabulary is open. It is impossible to give a list of its terms. This is not merely because technical terms can be added to the vocabulary as the need arises. There is, indeed, a class of terms referring exclusively to textual features of all kinds and this part of the vocabulary is technical but open ended. It includes terms of rhetoric such as 'diction', 'metaphor', 'rhyme', 'rhythm', 'verse', and terms referring to aspects of content such as 'scene', 'character', 'plot', and to these terms can be added whatever technical terms may be required. But the vocabulary of literary aesthetic argument is open in a more radical way than this. For its terms are not technical terms, but terms which have an established use in other spheres of life. One describes Hamlet, prince of Denmark, using such terms as one would use to describe a real human being. One describes the conditions of the royal Danish court in the same terms as one would describe a real-life situation. One imputes motives, mental states, and emotions to characters and uses them to explain plot, and so on. In this there is a disanalogy between literature and institutions like the law, an economic system, or a game like chess. In these institutions the practice concepts have no non-institutional uses. When it is nevertheless possible to construe the vocabulary used to express literary aesthetic judgement as forming a part of a *literary* practice, this is because the vocabulary is subject to certain constraints on what terms one can use in the explanation of textual features; constraints which are the result of those conventions which govern the application of the vocabulary and give it coherence and structure. These conventions are different from those which normally govern the terms making up the vocabulary. The reader's imaginative reconstruction of the literary aesthetic features of a work is restricted by the possibilities of description provided by the vocabulary and his possibilities for supporting his reconstruction are defined by the conventions giving the vocabulary coherence and structure. So an example of a reader's imaginative reconstruction of a work is an example of the vocabulary in use.

The vocabulary can best be described as having four different levels. There is a level of *thematic* concepts:

Little Dorrit is seen to be about a problem which does not yield easily to time. It is about society in relation to the individual human will. This is certainly a matter general enough – general to the point of tautology, were it not for the bitterness with which the tautology is articulated, were it not for the specificity, and the subtlety, and the boldness with which the human will is anatomized.[19]

Thematic concepts embody concerns of universal interest in the culture. 'Devouring time', 'love', 'birth', 'youth', 'age', 'society', 'free will', 'predestination', 'morality', 'justice', 'mercy', 'order', 'chaos', etc., are all typical thematic concepts. As Trilling points out, such concepts are themselves vacuous. They are made interesting by the way they are 'anatomized', through the 'specificity' and 'subtlety' with which the artistic vision is built up. Thematic concepts constitute the highest level of the interpretative vocabulary. The lowest level is occupied by an open set of *descriptive* concepts:

The subject of *Little Dorrit* is borne in upon us by the informing symbol, or emblem, of the book, which is the prison. The story opens in a prison in Marseilles. It goes on to the Marshalsea, which in effect it never leaves. The second of the two parts of the novel begins in what we are urged to think

of as a sort of prison, the monastery of the Great St Bernard. The Circumlocution Office is the prison of the creative mind of England. Mr Merdle is shown habitually holding himself by the wrist, taking himself into custody, and in a score of ways the theme of incarceration is carried out, persons and classes being imprisoned by their notions of predestined fate or of religious duty, or by their occupations, their life-schemes, their ideas of themselves, their very habits of language.[20]

These descriptive terms refer to the textual features of content, structure and style. They are not strictly descriptive. They embody interpretative judgements concerning how these textual features are to be construed. In between the thematic and descriptive levels, there is a *redescriptive* level of terms which connect the thematic judgements with the descriptions, thus supporting the former by basing them on the latter:

[the prison's] connexion with the will is real, it is the practical instrument for the negation of man's will which the will of society has contrived.[21]

The terms of the redescriptive level are used in the formulation of reasons for accepting a thematic judgement. Finally, the vocabulary has a level consisting of *aesthetic* terms. These terms fall in three groups. There are terms referring to the coherence and unity of the work; terms referring to the inner articulation which it is possible to recognize in the work, for example complexity, tension, and balance; and there are terms referring to the quality of the thematic terms used to organize a work and the way in which these terms are 'anatomized', such as universality, sublimity, concreteness, and vividness. Literary appreciation is an attempt to see the work as possessing these aesthetic qualities.

The institutional theory permits an understanding of the connection between the different levels of the vocabulary, of the conventions determining which descriptions of textual features in a particular work are acceptable, which redescriptions and thematic terms are appropriate in the interpretation of a particular work. And it can offer an interpretation of the three types of literary aesthetic terms by linking them to the way in which, and to what extent, a text yields to interpretation governed by institutional conventions. If the reader does respond to a work with an imaginative reconstruction of its aesthetic qualities, and if the reader, in his reconstruction, employs such a vocabulary as has been sketched here, then some sort of institutional theory seems to be the only type of theory complex enough to throw some light on notions like literary aesthetic feature, literary aesthetic judgement and literary aesthetic value.

Notes

1 A version of this paper was read at a meeting of the British Society of Aesthetics in Edinburgh, 26 April 1980.

2 See, e.g., Stanley Cavell, 'Aesthetic Problems of Modern Philosophy', in Max Black ed., *Philosophy in America* (London 1965) and reprinted in Stanley Cavell, *Must We Mean What We Say? A Book of Essays* (Cambridge 1976); Stuart Hampshire, 'Logic and Appreciation', *World Review* (1952) and reprinted in W. Elton ed., *Aesthetics and Language* (Oxford 1954); Arnold Isenberg, 'Critical Communication', *The Philosophical Review*, 58 (1949) and reprinted in W. Elton ed., *ibid.*; Frank Sibley, 'Aesthetic Concepts', *The Philosophical Review*, 68 (1959) and reprinted in Cyril Barrett ed., *Collected Papers on Aesthetics* (Oxford 1965); 'Objectivity and Aesthetics', *Proceedings of the Aristotelian Society*, supp. vol. 42 (1968); P. F. Strawson, 'Aesthetic Appraisal and Works of Art', *Oxford Review*, 3 (1966) and reprinted in P. F. Strawson, *'Freedom and Resentment' and Other Essays* (London 1974). References to the articles by Cavell, Isenberg, Strawson and to 'Aesthetic Concepts' by Sibley are to the books in which they are reprinted. The supervenience theory is not usually developed with reference to literature, but it is held to have general application to all the arts and examples from literature are often used. Here it will be developed as a theory of literary aesthetic features.

3 This was pointed out to me by colleague Roy Tommy Eriksen. Try the example without thinking about the fact that it is a conventional rhetorical feature. The pattern then becomes invisible without an aesthetic judgement.

4 Frank Sibley, 'Aesthetic Concepts', p. 64.

5 Strawson, 'Aesthetic Appraisal and Works of Art', p. 186.

6 *Ibid.*, p. 186.

7 Cavell, 'Aesthetic Problems of Modern Philosophy', p. 93.

8 *Ibid.*, p. 93.

9 Isenberg, 'Critical Communication', pp. 137–8.

10 Cavell, 'Aesthetic Problems of Modern Philosophy', p. 92.

11 Sibley, 'Aesthetic Concepts', pp. 82–4.

12 Isenberg, 'Critical Communication', p. 137.

13 Cavell, 'Aesthetic Problems of Modern Philosophy,' p. 94.

14 For the idea of an institution or practice see H. L. A. Hart, *The Concept of Law* (Oxford 1961), ch. 5: 'Law as the Union of Primary and Secondary Rules'; John Rawls, 'Tow Concepts of Rules', *The Philosophical Review*, 64 (1955) and reprinted in Philippa Foot ed., *Theories of Ethics* (Oxford 1967); John Searle, *Speech Acts* (Cambridge 1969), pp. 33–42.

15 See Philip Hobsbaum, 'The Critics and Our Mutual Friend', *Essays in Criticism*, 13 (1963), pp. 234–5.

16 There are also epistemological reasons for rejecting reductive explanations in literary aesthetics. I have tried to spell out these reasons elsewhere. See *The Structure of Literary Understanding* (Cambridge, 1978), the first three chapters, and also 'What is Poetics?' and 'Defining a Literary Work' in S. H. Olsen, *The End of Literary Theory* (Cambridge 1987).

17 I have tried to suggest why certain types of literary judgement fail to illuminate the works they refer to in 'On Unilluminating Criticism', in *The End of Literary Theory*.

18 Philip Collins, '*Little Dorrit*: the Prison and the Critics', *The Times Literary Supplement*, 4021, 18 April 1980.

19 Lionel Trilling, Introduction, *Little Dorrit* (New Oxford Illustrated Dickens, Oxford, 1953), p. vi.

20 Trilling, Introduction, p. vi.

21 *Ibid.* p. vi.

37

The Death of the Author:
An Analytical Autopsy

Peter Lamarque

> The artist is the creator of beautiful things.
> To reveal art and conceal the artist is art's
> aim.
>
> **Oscar Wilde, The Picture of Dorian Gray**

> Honest criticism and sensitive appreciation
> are directed not upon the poet but upon the
> poetry.
>
> **T. S. Eliot, "Tradition and
> the Individual Talent"**

I

It is now over twenty years since Roland Barthes proclaimed the "death of the author," and the phrase, if not the fact, is well established in the literary critical community. Yet it remains far from clear what it means. I suspect that many Anglo-American aestheticians have tended, consciously or otherwise, to shrug off Barthes's formulation as a mere Gallic hyperbole for their own more sober "intentionalist fallacy" and thus have given the matter no further attention. In fact, as I will show, the significant doctrines underlying the "death of the author" are far removed from the convivial debate about intentions and have their sights set not just on the humble author but on the concept of literature itself and even the concept of meaning as well.

My aim is to identify and analyze the main theses in two papers that are the seminal points of reference for the relevant doctrines: Roland Barthes's "The Death of the Author" and Michel Foucault's "What is an Author?"[1] I will be asking what the theses mean and whether they are true. I will not be discussing in any detail the broader context of the papers either in relation to general currents of thought or with regard to other work by the two theorists. My interest is with the arguments, not the authors. I believe that the ideas as formulated in these essays – ideas about authorship, texts, writing, reading – are fundamental to the movement labeled poststructuralism yet are imprecisely expressed and often misunderstood. Submitting them to an analytical study will, I hope, be instructive not only to those skeptical of poststructuralism but also for those supporters who might be unclear about the precise implications.

I will focus on four main theses that strike me as prominent. These I will dub the Historicist Thesis, the Death Thesis, the Author Function Thesis, and the *Ecriture* Thesis. All are closely interwoven, and each has subcomponents that I will need to spell out. It is not my contention that Barthes and Foucault agree at every point – they clearly do not – but together they do present a case about authors and texts which has had a powerful influence on the development of a whole school of modern thought.

II

Barthes's own words provide a general characterization of the Historicist Thesis:

Peter Lamarque, "The Death of the Author: An Analytical Autopsy," *British Journal of Aesthetics*, 40: 4 (1990), pp. 319–31. Reprinted by permission of Oxford University Press.

The author is a modern figure, a product of our society. ("Death of the Author," p. 142)

Foucault speaks of the "coming into being of the notion of 'author'" at a specific "moment . . . in the history of ideas" ("What Is an Author?" p. 101). Both locate the birth of the author in postmedieval times, a manifestation of the rise of the individual from the Reformation through to the philosophical Enlightenment. I am less concerned with the historical details than with the status (and meaning) of the Historicist Thesis. The idea that written works acquired authors only at a specific time in history clearly needs some explanation. I suggest that at least three possible explanations, not mutually exclusive, can be offered and they will have a bearing on how to interpret the other theses in the overall argument. I am going to eliminate as uninteresting a merely lexicographical interpretation of the Historicist Thesis, that is, an interpretation that sees the thesis as about the word *author*. I take it that there could be authors prior to there being a word *author* just as there can be writers before the word *writer* and thoughts before the word *thoughts*. No doubt for some even this is controversial, but I do not believe that Barthes and Foucault had lexicography in mind in their defense of the Historicist Thesis.

The first (plausible) interpretation, then, is this:

A certain conception of a writer (writer-as-author) is modern.

For Foucault this conception is highly specific; in effect it is a legal and social conception of authorship. The author is seen as an owner of property, a producer of marketable goods, as having rights over those goods, and also responsibilities: "Texts, books, and discourses really began to have authors . . . to the extent that authors became subject to punishment," Foucault states (p. 108). In a similar vein, Barthes identifies the author with "capitalist ideology" (p. 143). I will call this interpretation of the Historicist Thesis the "social conception," the point being that at a determinate stage in history, according to the thesis, writers (of certain kinds of texts) came to acquire a new social status, along with a corresponding legal and cultural recognition.

Again, I will not debate the truth of this historical claim – I suspect the actual details would not stand up to close scrutiny – but only comment on its theoretical implications. For example, it entails a distinction between an unrestricted notion of writer-per-se (any person who writes) and a more restricted notion of writer-as-author, the latter conceived in social or ideological terms. That distinction is useful in showing that the mere act of writing (writing on the sand, jottings on an envelope) does not make an author. An author so designated is a more weighty figure with legal rights and social standing, a producer of texts deemed to have value. Significantly, the thesis on this interpretation is about social conventions and a class of persons engaged in particular acts: it is not about a persona, a fictional character, or a construct of the text. Being about the personal status of authors, it can offer no direct support, as we will see, for either the Author Function Thesis or the *Ecriture* Thesis, both of which conceive the author in impersonal terms.

The second interpretation of the Historicist Thesis I will call the "criticism conception":

A certain conception of criticism (author-based criticism) is modern.

Here the idea is that at a certain stage of history the focus of criticism turned to the personality of the author. Thus Barthes notes that "the image of literature to be found in ordinary culture is tyrannically centred on the author, his person, his life, his tastes, his passions, while criticism still consists for the most part in saying that Baudelaire's work is the failure of Baudelaire the man, Van Gogh's his madness, Tchaikovsky's his vice" (p. 143). This state of affairs arose, according to Barthes, only after the bourgeois revolution that gave prominence to the individual. We can leave it to historians to debate the historical development of author-based criticism. No doubt it is a matter of degree how much critical significance is given at different periods of history to an author's biographical background or personality. Although the author as person (writer, cause, origin, and so forth) is again evoked in this interpretation, it is nevertheless distinct from the "social conception." No direct implications about criticism follow from the fact that the author comes to be viewed as having rights over a text. Purely formalist criticism is compatible with a state of affairs where an author is accorded a secure legal and social identity.

The third interpretation is the most controversial but also the most interesting:

A certain conception of a text (the authored text) is modern.

This I will call the "text conception" of the Historicist Thesis. The idea is that at a certain point in history, (written) texts acquire significance in virtue of being "authored." "There was a time," Foucault writes, "when the texts which we today call 'literary' (narratives, stories, epics, tragedies, comedies) were accepted, put into circulation, and valorized without any question about the identity of their author" (p. 109). He contrasts this with the case of scientific discourses that, in the Middle Ages, owed their authority to a named provenance (Hippocrates, Pliny, or whomever). A radical change occurred, so Foucault claims, in the seventeenth and eighteenth centuries, when literary texts came to be viewed as essentially "authored," while scientific writing could carry authority even in anonymity.

These sweeping generalizations invite substantial qualification from the scrupulous historian of ideas. For our purposes, further clarification is in order. The text conception is itself open to different interpretations. At its simplest it is just the claim that at a specific point in history (perhaps a different point for different discourses) it became important that texts be attributed. A stronger claim is that this attribution actually changed the way texts were understood. That is, they could not be properly understood except as *by so-and-so*. The author attribution carried the meaning, perhaps as personal revelation, expression of belief, seal of authority, or whatever. Foucault probably has in mind at least this latter claim. But from the evidence of his Author Function Thesis, which we will look at later, he seems to want something stronger still for the text conception. The suggestion is that the personal aspects of author attribution disappear altogether. It is not actual causal origins that mark the difference between an authored and an unauthored text but rather certain (emergent) properties of the text itself. The authored text is viewed as the manifestation of a creative act but, importantly, what this yields or makes accessible is a distinctive kind of unity, integrity, meaning, interest, and value. And it is these qualities themselves, rather than their relation to some particular authorial performance, that are given prominence under this strengthened version of the Historicist Thesis.

Thus there is a slide in the text conception from the mere association of text and author to the much fuller conception of a text as a classifiable work of a certain kind fulfilling a purpose, expressing a meaning, and yielding a value. I suggest that the plausibility of the Historicist Thesis weakens as it progresses along this scale. In other words, the conception of certain pieces of writing as having meaning, unity, and value seems much less datable historically (was there ever a time when there was no such conception?) than the mere inclination to highlight author attribution.

III

Against this background we can now turn to the second substantive thesis, which I have called the Death Thesis. At its simplest, this merely claims:

The author is dead.

The meaning of the claim and assessment of its truth can be determined only relative to the Historicist Thesis, under its different interpretations. The underlying thought is this: if a certain conception (of an author, a text, and so on) has a definite historical beginning – if it arises under determinate historical conditions – then it can in principle come to an end when the historical conditions change.

One complication is that the Death Thesis can be read either as a statement of fact or as wishful thinking, that is, either as a description of the current state of affairs (we simply no longer *have* authors conceived in a certain way) or as a prescription for the future (we no longer *need* authors so conceived, we can now get by without them).[2] Both Barthes and Foucault seem to waver on the question of description and prescription. Barthes, for example, admits that "the sway of the Author remains powerful" (p. 143), yet in speaking of the "modern scriptor," in contrast with the Author (pp. 145, 146), he suggests that (modern) writing is no longer conceived as the product of an author. Similarly, Foucault tells us "we must locate the space left empty by the author's disappearance" (p. 105), the latter thus taken for granted, yet makes a prediction at the end of his essay that the author function, which is his own conception of the author, "will disappear," sometime in the future, "as our society changes" (p. 119).

To see what the Death Thesis amounts to, let us run briefly through the different permutations.

The writer-as-author is dead, or should be (deriving from the social conception of the Historicist Thesis).

Does the conception of writer-as-author, with a certain social and legal status, still obtain? Surely it does. Authors are still, in Foucault's words, "subject to punishment" (they can even be sentenced to death); there are copyright laws and blasphemy laws; authors can be sued for libel or plagiarism; they attract interest from biographers and gossips. Authors under this conception are certainly not dead. But should they be killed off? Should we try and rid ourselves of this conception? The question is political and moral, not philosophical. Should we promote a society where all writing is anonymous, where writers have no legal status and no obligations? Maybe. But the point is quite independent of any theoretical argument about *écriture* or the author function, for it is a point about the treatment of actual people in a political and legal system.

Author-based criticism is dead, or should be (deriving from the criticism conception of the Historicist Thesis).

Here we come closest to the Intentionalist Fallacy in that anti-intentionalists can be seen as advancing some such version of the Death Thesis. But note, first, that anti-intentionalists are not committed to a version based on the social conception of authorship, or indeed to the text conception. Also, second, they are committed only to the normative element (author-based criticism should be dead) not to the descriptive element (it is in fact dead).

Although there is certainly an overlap here between the anti-intentionalists and Barthes and Foucault, it seems to be the only point of contact. If the Death Thesis simply records and endorses the decline of crude author-based criticism, then it is of only modest theoretical interest. The debate continues about the proper role of authorial intention in literary criticism, but there does seem to be a general consensus that concentration on purely biographical factors – or the so-called personality of an author – is not integral to a serious critical discipline (the point goes back at least to T. S. Eliot in 1919). In fact, as we shall see, it is quite clear that Barthes and Foucault had something more substantial in their sights when they advanced the Death Thesis. Nevertheless, much of the credibil-

ity of the thesis undoubtedly trades off the more secure intuitions within the community of literary critics that pure author-based criticism is a legitimate target. It is thus important to identify the real Death Thesis as intended by Barthes and Foucault so that we do not find ourselves forced to assent through a mistaken interpretation.

The authored text is dead, or should be (deriving from the text conception of the Historicist Thesis).

Does the conception of the authored text still prevail, that is, the text conceived as having a determinate meaning, as the manifestation of a creative act? Certainly the qualities of unity, expressiveness, and creative imagination are still sought and valued in literary works; indeed, they are bound up with the very conception of literature. If possession of these is sufficient for something's being an authored text, then authored texts are not dead. Remember, though, that an authored text, on the strong interpretation, is defined independently of its relation to an actual author (or author-as-person). The meaning and unity of an authored text are explicable not in terms of some real act of creation, some determinate psychological origin, but only as a projection of these in the text itself. This is the import of the Author Function Thesis.

Foucault would accept that literary criticism still retains its conception of the authored text; in fact, he perceives this conception as the foundation of literary criticism. The Death Thesis, then, in this version, must be seen as a prescription, not a description. Foucault's project is to get rid of the authored text itself (along with its concomitant notions of meaning, interpretation, unity, expression, and value). The Author Function, which is the defining feature of an authored text, is, according to Foucault, "an ideological product" (p. 119), a repressive and restricting "principle of thrift in the proliferation of meaning" (p. 118). In effect, Foucault's death prescription is aimed at the very concept of a literary work that sustains the practice of literary criticism (it is also aimed, more broadly, at any class of work subject to similar interpretative and evaluative constraints). The prescription has little to do with the role or status of authors-as-persons.

Seen in this light, it is no defense against Foucault's attack to point out that the literary institution has long ceased to give prominence to an author's personality. That would be to give undue

[Marginal handwritten note: Author is very much alive]

weight to the weaker versions of the Death Thesis. There is no room for the complacent thought that Foucault is just another anti-intentionalist. On the other hand, Foucault cannot find support for his attack on the authored-text merely through an appeal to the inadequacy of crude author-based criticism. He has in effect pushed the debate beyond the author altogether.

IV

The Author Function Thesis is intended to provide further support for the strong version (the "authored-text is dead" version) of the Death Thesis. Although the notion is never explicitly defined by Foucault, the central idea is that the author function is a property of a discourse (or text) and amounts to something more than its just being written or produced by a person (of whatever status): "There are a certain number of discourses that are endowed with the 'author function,' while others are deprived of it" (p. 107).

We can identify a number of separate components of the thesis which help to clarify the notion of "author function." First is the distinctness claim:

(1)   The author function is distinct from the author-as-person (or writer).

Foucault makes it clear that the author function "does not refer purely and simply to a real individual" (p. 113). He complicates the exposition by often using the term interchangeably with "the author"; however, the term *author* itself is not intended as a direct designation of an individual. He says that "it would be . . . wrong to equate the author with the real writer" (p. 112), speaking of the author as "a certain functional principle" (p. 119).

What are the grounds for postulating an impersonal conception of an author as distinct from a personal conception? Foucault does not simply have in mind the literary critical notion of an "implied author," that is, a set of attitudes informing a work which might or might not be shared with the real author. For one thing, Foucault's author function is not a construct specific to individual works but may bind together a whole *oeuvre*; and whereas an implied author is, as it were, just one fictional character among others in a work, the

author function is more broadly conceived as determining the very nature of the work itself.[3]

One of the arguments that Foucault offers for the distinctness claim (1) – it is also his justification for describing the author as an "ideological product" (p. 119) – rests on a supposed discrepancy between the way we normally conceive the author as a person (a genius, a creator, one who proliferates meaning) and the way we conceive texts that have authors (i.e., as constrained in their meaning and confined in the uses to which they can be put). But this argument is unsatisfactory simply because there is no such discrepancy. To the extent that we conceive of an author as offering "an inexhaustible world of significations" (p. 118), as a proliferator of meaning, then we expect precisely the same of the work he or she creates.

It is more promising to read Foucault as proposing a semitechnical sense of the term *author*, one that conforms to the following principle:

(2)   "Having an author" is not a relational predicate (characterizing a relation between a work and a person) but a monadic predicate (characterizing a certain kind of work).

This principle signals the move from "X has an author" to "X is authored" or, more explicitly, from "X has Y as an author" (the relational predicate) to "X is Y-authored" (the monadic predicate). The author function becomes a property of a text or discourse, not a relation between a text and a person. We need to ask what the monadic predicate "being authored" or being "Y-authored" actually means in this special sense.

First, though, it might be helpful to offer a further elaboration of (2) in terms of paraphrase or reduction:

(3)   All relevant claims about the relation between an author-as-person and a text are reducible to claims about an authored text.

In this way the author disappears through a process comparable to ontological reduction by paraphrase. In place of, for example, "The work is a product of the author's creative act," we can substitute "The work is an authored text" and still retain the significant cognitive content of the former. Such a semantic maneuver is not intended to show that authors (as persons) are redundant. At best its aim is to show that *relative to critical discourse*, references to an author can be eliminated without loss of significant content. I take it that some such thesis underlies Foucault's statement that the "aspects of an individual which we designate as making him an author are only a projection, in more or less psychologizing terms, of the operations that we force texts to undergo, the connections that we make, the traits that we establish as pertinent, the continuities that we recognize, or the exclusions that we practice" (p. 110). Foucault is thinking of such aspects as an author's "design" and "creative power," as well as the meaning, unity, and expression with which the author informs the text. He believes, as we have seen, that these features can be attributed directly to an authored text without reference back to the author-as-person. This is the heart of the Author Function Thesis.

What support can be offered for propositions (2) and (3)? After all, they are not obviously true, and they depart from the more familiar meaning of "author." The main logical support that Foucault offers is an argument about authors' names. An author's name, he suggests, does not operate purely referentially; rather than picking out some individual person, it has, he says, a "classificatory function," it "serves to characterize a certain mode of being of discourse" (p. 107). I think he has something like the following in mind:

(4) (Some) author attributions (using an author's name) are nonextensional.

If we say that a play is by Shakespeare, we mean or connote more than just that the play was written by a particular man (Shakespeare). For one thing we assign a certain honorific quality to it (it is likely to be a play worthy of our attention); we also relate the play to a wider body of work – to *Hamlet*, *King Lear*, *Twelfth Night*, and so on. Being "by Shakespeare" signals not just an external relation but an internal characterization. We move from "X is a play by Shakespeare" to "X is a Shakespeare play" or even "X is Shakespearean." The latter formulations are nonextensional – or at least have non-extensional readings – in the sense that substitution of coreferential names is not always permissible (does not preserve truth); if Shakespeare turns out to be Bacon, it does not follow that the plays become Baconian, where that has its own distinctive connotations.

Let us suppose that stated like this the argument has some merit. Does it in fact support the Author

Function Thesis? Certainly it provides an illustration of the move from a relational predicate to a monadic predicate, in this case from "by Shakespeare" to "Shakespearean" Is this an instance of the move from "X has Y as an author" to "X is Y-authored"? Maybe. But what it shows is that we are not obliged to make the move. "X has Shakespeare as an author" has both a nonextensional, classificatory meaning *and* a fully extensional, relational meaning. In other words, the reference to Shakespeare the person still stands. By pointing, quite rightly, to the classificatory function of authors' names, Foucault mistakenly supposes that this in itself eliminates the referential function.

What about the move in (2) from "X has an author" to "X is authored"? This move is not directly supported by the argument from authors' names but hangs on a distinctive conception of an "authored text." This takes us back to the Historicist Thesis. Foucault, as we saw, has in mind not just the attribution of an author to a text, nor in the more sophisticated version of (4) a text classified through a nonextensional attribution, but rather a notion of an authored text conceived more broadly:

(5) An authored text is one that is subject to interpretation, constrained in its meaning, exhibiting unity and coherence, and located in a system of values.

It is precisely this notion he is attacking when he attacks the author function. But now we can begin to see how uncomfortably the pieces fit together for Foucault. The author as a person – with a personality, a biography, a legal status and social standing – has no role in (5). The reductive theses (2) and (3) see to that, as does the distinctness thesis (1). In effect, Foucault has recognized, in postulating the author function and the notion of an authored text, that the qualities in (5) are *institutionally based* qualities – part of the conception of literature – and not *individualistically based* – formulated in terms of individual psychological attitudes.[4] There is no need to see the constraints on interpretation, or the source of unity and coherence or the criteria of value, as directly attributable to an individual (the author-as-person).

If that is the point of the Author Function Thesis, then it has some force, albeit reiterating a position well-established in anti-intentionalist critical theory. But Foucault cannot have it both ways: he cannot distance the authored text from the author-as-person and at the same time mount his attack on the authored text on the grounds that it perpetuates the bourgeois ideology of the individual, that it elevates the author into a position of God-like power and authority, enshrined in law. It is as if Foucault has not fully assimilated the implications of his own Author Function Thesis; he speaks as if his main target is still the author-as-person behind and beyond the work, informing it with a secret and inner meaning. Perhaps the source of the problem is the misleading invocation of the author in "author function" and "authored text." Strictly speaking, authors have nothing to do with it; the authored text, so-called, at least in its most obvious manifestation, is a literary work, defined institutionally. Literary works have authors, of course; they are the product of a creative act (a real act from a real agent), but the constraints on interpretation and the determination of coherence and value are independent of the individual author's will. That is the lesson of the Death Thesis in its more plausible versions, and it should be the lesson of the Author Function Thesis.

V

Barthes's version of the author function is what he calls the "modern scriptor" who is "born simultaneously with the text" (p. 145). But Barthes bases his move from the relational author to the non-relational scriptor – his version of the Author Function Thesis – on a thesis about writing (*écriture*). The basic claim of what I have called the *Ecriture* Thesis is this (in Barthes's words):

> Writing is the destruction of every voice, of every point of origin. (p. 142)

The implication is that the very nature of writing makes the author (the author-as-person) redundant. What arguments does Barthes offer to support this thesis?

The first is an argument from narrative: "As soon as a fact is *narrated* no longer with a view to acting directly on reality but intransitively, that is to say, finally outside of any function other than that of the very practice of the symbol itself . . . the voice loses its origin" (p. 142). It is difficult to conceive of any act of narration which satisfies the condition of having no other function than the "practice of the symbol itself." Nearly all narration

has some further aim, indeed, the aim in some form or other to "act . . . directly on reality": be it to inform, entertain, persuade, instruct, or whatever. Narration is by definition an act, and no acts are truly gratuitous. Strictly speaking, the narrative argument collapses here.

Still, one might suppose, charitably, that certain kinds of fictional narrative come close to Barthes's specification: narratives where playfulness is paramount. It is a convention of some kinds of fiction that they draw attention to their own fictional status, that they point inward rather than outward, that they teasingly conceal their origin. But even if we grant that in these special cases attention focuses only on the "symbol itself," nothing here supports a general thesis about writing (or authors). For one thing, different kinds of conventions, often far removed from the tricks of fiction, govern written narratives (as with speech acts), and in many such cases narrative purpose (and thus the "voice of origin") is manifest. Also not all writing is in narrative form.

A second argument for the *Ecriture* Thesis rests on the characterization of writing as performative: "*Writing* can no longer designate an operation of recording, notation, representation, 'depiction' . . . ; rather, it designates . . . a performative . . . in which the enunciation has no other content . . . than the act by which it is uttered" (pp. 145–146). But the claim that writing has the status of a performative utterance, instead of supporting the *Ecriture* Thesis, in fact directly contradicts it. A performative utterance counts as an act – a promise, a marriage, a declaration of war – only under precisely specified contextual conditions; and one of those conditions, essential in each case, is the speaker's having appropriate intentions. Far from being the destruction of a "voice of origin" the successful performative relies crucially on the disposition and authority of the speaker. The analogy, then, is unfortunate, to say the least.

Clearly what impressed Barthes about the performative utterance is another feature: self-validation. If I say "I promise," I am not reporting some external fact but, under the right conditions, bringing a fact into existence. But even if we set aside the requirement of the speaker's authority and focus only on the feature of self-validation, the analogy with performatives is still inadequate. Once again Barthes is led to an unwarranted generalization about the nature of writing by taking as a paradigm a certain kind of fictive utterance, which creates its own facts or world, and ignoring more commonplace illocutionary purposes.

The third argument is about meaning. The thought is that writing per se, in contrast to the constrained authored text, does not yield any determinate meaning: "A text is not a line of words releasing a single 'theological' meaning (the 'message' of the Author-God) but a multi-dimensional space in which a variety of writings, none of them original, blend and clash" (p. 146). We find the same idea in Foucault, even though he voices some skepticism later on about *écriture*: "today's writing has freed itself from the dimension of expression," "it is an interplay of signs," it "unfolds like a game" (p. 102). How does this support the thesis that writing has destroyed the voice of origin? The argument seems to go something like this: determinate meaning is always the product of authorial imposition, where there is no determinate meaning there is no author, writing per se (*écriture*) has no determinate meaning (it is a mere play of signs), so writing per se shows the author to be redundant. The reasoning is bizarre. Its formal validity is suspect, and it also begs the question that there is such a thing as writing per se. *Ecriture* is in effect stipulated to be authorless, to be lacking in determinate meaning, to be free of interpretative constraints. But this very conception of *écriture* needs to be challenged.

The key is the idea of a "text." A "text," as Barthes conceives it, is a specific manifestation of *écriture*. It is to be contrasted with a "work": a work belongs in a genre, its meaning is constrained, it has an author, it is subject to classification. A text, Barthes tells us, is "always *paradoxical*"; it "practises the infinite deferment of the signified";[5] "it answers not to an interpretation, even a liberal one, but to an explosion, a dissemination" ("From Work to Text," p. 159); "it cannot be contained in a hier-archy, even in a simple division of genres" (p. 157); and "no vital 'respect' is due to the Text: it can be *broken*" (p. 161). This idea of a text as an explosion of unconstrained meaning, without origin and without purpose, is a theoretician's fiction. Perhaps we could, by abstraction, come to look at writing in this way, but it would be quite idle to do so. It would be like trying to hear a Mozart symphony as

a mere string of unstructured sounds. More impor-tant, though, it is no part of the concept of writing (or language) that it should be so viewed. Writing, like speech, or any language "performed," is inevitably and properly conceived as purposive. To use language as meaningful discourse is to perform speech acts; to understand discourse is, minimally, to grasp what speech acts are performed. In his view of *écriture* and of texts, Barthes tries to abstract language from the very function that gives it life.

An underlying assumption in both Barthes and Foucault is that there is intrinsic merit in what Foucault calls the "proliferation of meaning." Perhaps the fundamental objection to their com-bined program is that this assumption is unsup-ported and untenable. By prescribing the death of the author and by promoting the text over the work, both writers see themselves as liberating meaning from unnatural and undesirable restric-tions. They both assume that more is better. Part of the problem is that they are trapped by a gratuitous and inappropriate political vocabulary: "repression," "authority," "control." But deeper still they reveal a predilection for a peculiarly sterile form of literary criticism, exemplified perhaps by certain passages in William Empson's *Seven Types of Ambiguity* and pressed almost *ad absurdum* in Barthes's own *S/Z*, where the literary work is seen as a limitless and unrestricted source of connota-tion and allusion. What is objectionable is that they have set up this conception as a paradigm not only of criticism but, worse, of reading itself.

The critical community at large soon tired of the simplistic proliferation of meaning, and outside the literary institution, it never found a foothold. It is a nonstarter – pointless if not impossible – to conceive of scientific or historical or philosophical discourse as *écriture*. It is always more interesting, more demanding, and more rewarding for under-standing to consolidate meaning, to seek structure and coherence, to locate a work in a tradition or practice. This has nothing whatsoever to do with reinstating some bullying, authoritarian author. But, then, that figure was always just a fiction anyway.

Notes

1   I will be using the following editions: Roland Barthes, "The Death of the Author," in *Image-Music-Text*, essays selected by and trans. Stephen Heath (London, 1977); and Michel Foucault, "What Is an Author?" in *The Foucault Reader*, ed. Paul Rabinow (Harmondsworth, England, 1986).

2   A similar ambiguity lies in the origin of the Death Thesis, namely, Nietzsche's proclamation that "God is dead." Was Nietzsche describing a new human consciousness already in evidence, or was he heralding a radical break with the past?

3   I am guided here, indeed throughout this essay, by the useful discussion in Alexander Nehamas, "Writer, Text, Work, Author," in *Literature and the Question of Philosophy*, ed. Anthony J. Cascardi (Baltimore, 1987).

4   For a useful account of institutional qualities in the literary context, see Stein Haugom Olsen, "Literary Aesthetics and Literary Practice," in *The End of Literary Theory* (Cambridge, 1987).

5   Roland Barthes, "From Work to Text," in *Image-Music-Text*, p. 158.

Part IX

Music

Introduction to Part IX

In what might be called classical writings on aesthetics, music is curiously under-represented. Neither Hume nor Kant nor Hegel gave special attention to it. This relative neglect is evident also in the early years of analytical aesthetics, partly because primary focus was given to the nature of critical judgments or critical concepts without much reference to individual art forms, partly because the issues surrounding music seemed out of step with those arising from representational arts like painting and literature.

But if that was the situation then, matters could not be more different now. In the final three decades of the twentieth century the aesthetics of music came more and more to the fore and arguably at the start of the twenty-first century it occupies a central place. Exactly why this shift of interest occurred is hard to say. Certainly some prominent writings on the philosophy of music helped. Leonard Meyer's *Emotion and Meaning in Music* (1956) was widely regarded. Nelson Goodman had provocative things to say both about the ontology of music and its modes of denotation in *Languages of Art: An Approach to a Theory of Symbols* (1969). Peter Kivy was a major influence with a succession of books on musical aesthetics: *The Corded Shell* (1980), *Sound and Semblance* (1984), *Music Alone* (1990), and others. Malcolm Budd's *Music and the Emotions* (1985), a number of papers by Roger Scruton, culminating in the monumental *The Aesthetics of Music* (1997), and important contributions by Kendall Walton, Jerrold Levinson, Stephen Davies, among others, helped push music to the forefront of analytic aesthetics. But it wasn't only the prominence of these contributors that made the difference. There was also a discernible shift from the 1980s onwards toward dealing with individual art forms, rather than concentrating on features all art works putatively shared. And certain topics – like art and emotion, representation, and ontology – assumed special importance in this period and music raised distinctive, indeed pressing, questions on these counts.

So what issues are central to the analytic aesthetics of music? Three broad areas come immediately to mind:

- the nature of music or the kinds of existence pertaining to musical works;
- the appreciation of music or the kinds of experiences musical works afford;
- the values of music or the criteria under which musical works should be judged.

We have included a prominent debate on the nature of music – between Levinson and Kivy – in Part II, on Ontology. And we present some issues about musical value in the next section, Part X on Popular Art, which includes the debate between Bruce Baugh and Stephen Davies on criteria for valuing rock music in relation to "classical" music. In this section we highlight a number of important issues to do with the appreciation of music, notably what it is to understand music, whether music can be called "profound" (and what that might mean), and how music relates to the emotions. We hope that together these articles give a good account of the contribution of analytic aesthetics to the philosophy of music.

Scruton's essay "Understanding Music," clearly outlines his views on many aspects of music, which are later developed in *The Aesthetics of Music*.

445

"Music belongs uniquely to the intentional sphere, and not to the material realm," he argues, with the consequence that only a special kind of understanding – "intentional understanding" – is possible for it. Music is not susceptible to scientific explanation and in the end only a deeply metaphorical language is adequate for apprehending music. When we speak of "movement" in music or musical "space" we speak metaphorically and these metaphors are irreducible. Hearing a "tone" – and concomitantly harmony, rhythm, and melody – is distinct from hearing mere "sound," the former something only a rational being can achieve. Appreciating music is like seeing an aspect, a product of active imaginative experience.

Scruton denies that music is representational. Exactly what he means by artistic representation is spelled out in his essay "Photography and Representation," in Part VII. Peter Kivy too thinks that music does not represent, is not literally "about" anything, and this poses a problem for his – widely shared – intuition that some music is "profound." Yet surely to be profound is in some sense to address a profound *subject matter*. What makes the great tragedies profound is their treatment of profound human issues: death, evil, loss, weakness of will. But what could make pure instrumental music – like Beethoven's late quartets or Bach's *Well-Tempered Clavier* – profound? Kivy's subtle, if controversial, discussion in "The Profundity of Music" first sets up some highly plausible conditions for profundity then explores what aspects of music might satisfy them. He suggests that the subject matter of music we call profound might be music itself, the possibilities of musical sound, and "supreme musical craftsmanship" might be the required treatment that yields profundity. However promising the suggestion, though, it will only carry conviction if musical sound itself could be shown, independently, to be a profound subject matter (like that listed). Kivy admits it is not easy to justify that except in a circular fashion.

It has sometimes been thought that music's ability to express emotions is what gives it its enduring value – and indeed might account for its "profundity." Jenefer Robinson's essay here, "Expression and Arousal of Emotion in Music," is a subtly nuanced debate with other analytic philosophers, notably Peter Kivy, Kendall Walton, and Jerrold Levinson, on exactly what is involved in ascribing expressiveness to music. Robinson's particular interest is the relation between the emotions *expressed* in music and the emotions *aroused* by music. Kivy is known for his impassioned attack on "arousal theorists," those who explain the sadness, say, of music in terms of the arousing of sadness in an audience. Walton rejects simple arousal theories but explains expressiveness in terms of music's power to evoke *imaginative* emotional experiences. Levinson is somewhere between Walton and the arousalists, arguing that something *like* the emotion expressed is induced in an audience, with similar affective qualities, even if, again, occurring only at an imaginative level. Robinson carefully analyzes these positions, seeking the strongest points in each, and develops her own view that some emotional experiences are – and must be – aroused by expressive music, even if they are not always identical to the emotions expressed. Apart from its intrinsic interest in contributing to a well-established debate, Robinson's essay shows well the virtues of the analytical approach in pushing a debate forward by drawing on the strengths of previous arguments.

Further reading

Budd, Malcolm (1985). *Music and the Emotions* (London: Routledge).

Davies, Stephen (1994). *Musical Meaning and Expression* (Ithaca, NY: Cornell University Press).

DeBellis, Mark (1995). *Music and Conceptualization* (Cambridge: Cambridge University Press).

Goodman, Nelson (1969). *Languages of Art: An Approach to a Theory of Symbols* (Indianapolis: Bobbs-Merrill).

Kivy, Peter (1980). *The Corded Shell: Reflections on Musical Experience* (Princeton, NJ: Princeton University Press).

Kivy, Peter (1984). *Sound and Semblance: Reflections on Musical Representation* (Ithaca, NY: Cornell University Press).

Kivy, Peter (1990). *Music Alone: Philosophical Reflections on the Purely Musical Experience* (Ithaca, NY: Cornell University Press).

Kivy, Peter (1993). *The Fine Art of Repetition: Essays in the Philosophy of Music* (Cambridge: Cambridge University Press).

Levinson, Jerrold (1992). "Musical Profundity Misplaced," *Journal of Aesthetics and Art Criticism*, 50, pp. 58–60.

Levinson, Jerrold (1997). *Music in the Moment* (Ithaca, NY: Cornell University Press).

Meyer, Leonard (1956). *Emotion and Meaning in Music* (Chicago: Chicago University Press).

Robinson, Jenefer (ed.) (1997). *Music and Meaning* (Ithaca, NY: Cornell University Press).

Scruton, Roger (1997). *The Aesthetics of Music* (Oxford: Oxford University Press).

Walton, Kendall (1993). "Listening With Imagination," *Journal of Aesthetics and Art Criticism*, 52, pp. 47–61.

38

Understanding Music

Roger Scruton

Musik . . . Du Sprache, wo Sprachen enden.
Rilke

Words move, music moves, but only in time.
Eliot

Many music critics, and many critical listeners, feel impelled to ascribe content to certain works of music, and to describe this content in emotional, or at least mental, terms. At the same time music is an abstract, which is to say non-representational, art. It has (although some have doubted this) no narrative or descriptive powers, no way of referring to and presenting for our contemplation an object independent of itself.[1] So what do we mean when we ascribe a content to music? And how could we ever be justified? By shifting from terms like 'representation' and 'description' to the vocabulary of human expression, critics and philosophers have hoped to locate an idea of content that will be compatible with music's status as an abstract art. But terms like 'expression', 'expressive', and the like are far from clear: they also have implications that many would be reluctant to accept. Their use seems to imply that the meaning of music is to be found in some state of mind (for example an emotion) that is conveyed by it. But how is this possible, if music cannot describe things? Is not every

Roger Scruton, "Understanding Music," in Roger Scruton, *The Aesthetic Understanding* (London: Methuen, 1983), pp. 77–100. Reissued 1998 by St. Augustine's Press, South Bend, Ind. (pp. 88–115 their volume) and reproduced here by permission of St. Augustine's Press.

state of mind identified at least in part through its intentional object, and does that not imply that an expressive medium must also be capable of representation? To put it more trenchantly: if music has a content, how can that content be described? It was thus that Hanslick posed the problem, and despite subsequent studies, the problem remains roughly as he posed it.[2]

It is not surprising, therefore, that the discussion of expression has become dominant in musical aesthetics. But little clarity seems to me to have informed this discussion. This is largely because another, and more basic concept, has been overlooked: that of musical understanding. It is clearly wrong to think that one could explain meaning in language while saying nothing about understanding language: for the meaning of a sentence is what we understand when we understand it – it is the intentional object of a particular mental act. Likewise it must be wrong to attempt to give a theory of musical expression which cannot be rewritten as a theory of musical understanding. If music has a content, that content must be understood. This chapter explores the idea of musical understanding; at the end I return to the problem of expression, which by then should seem less intractable.

Many writers, pursuing a phantom of scientific knowledge, have overlooked – what in aesthetics you can overlook only by losing sight of the subject – that there is a kind of understanding that rests in appearance. I shall call this kind of understanding 'intentional'. A scientific understanding addresses itself to the world as material object, and seeks out the causal connections which underlie and explain appearances. But scientific explanation does not eliminate appearance: it only dispenses with it. An intentional understanding considers the world as intentional object (or, to use the Husserlian idiom, as *Lebenswelt*): it therefore uses the concepts through which we perceive the world, and makes no connections or observations that are not in some way already implicit in them.[3] When we look at the dispute between Goethe and Newton about colour, it is surely difficult to resist the conclusion that, while the first is attempting to describe appearances, the second is concerned to explain them. Helmholtz criticized Goethe, arguing that the poet, by confining himself to appearance, made it impossible to find the concepts with which appearance could be explained. At the same time, there is something to be learned from Goethe: we understand colours better after reading his account of them, for we are given a way in which to bring together and harmonize the descriptions which experience forces upon us.

Although there is a sense in which we always know how things appear to us, the study of appearance is appropriate when the concepts which inform it are outside the perceiver's grasp. Consider the curious art of bird-watching. I may know as much about the science of birds as a trained bird-watcher; and yet I perceive things differently from him. I need to relate my knowledge of the parts of birds, their flight, walk and plumage, to an experience. I have to see, for example, the rings of the plover, and its short rapid step, in the exclamatory way that can best be captured in the expression 'plover!'. Thus, because all our perception is informed by concepts, and those concepts in their turn determine our understanding and our practical reasoning, a critic or a philosopher can bring system to an appearance, by drawing out the implications of the concepts through which it is described. This description need not be one that the man who perceives with understanding can provide. But when he understands it, he will recognize it immediately as a description of the experience that is his.

Understanding music is a special case of intentional understanding. How we hear music clearly depends upon our intellectual capacities and education, upon concepts, analogies and expectations that we have inherited from a culture steeped in musical expression. Yet the understanding that we derive from this culture is manifest in our way of hearing, and not just in our way of thinking about music. I shall suggest that the ways of hearing *sound* that we consider to be ways of hearing *music*, are

based in concepts extended by metaphorical transference. The metaphors are deeply entrenched in our language: but they are metaphors nevertheless, and this means that the ability to hear music is dependent upon the capacity for metaphorical transfer (a capacity which belongs only to language-users). I will try to illustrate my meaning through a study of certain fundamental musical categories.

There are certain basic perceptions involved in hearing music, and these are crucial to understanding it. For example, there is the hearing of movement – as when one hears a melody, theme, or phrase, move from one note to another. There is the hearing of tones as opposed to the hearing of pitched sounds: the hearing of one tone as higher than another; the hearing of rhythm (as opposed to temporal sequence); the hearing of harmony, as opposed to aggregates of tones, and so on. All these experiences are basic, in that a person who did not have them would be deaf to music. And all other musical experiences depend upon them: for example, the hearing of melodies would be impossible without the hearing of musical movement, the hearing of counterpoint impossible without the hearing of harmony (else it would be simply the hearing of simultaneous strings of sound). And so on. It is plausible to suggest, therefore, that whatever character is possessed by these basic perceptions will be possessed also by the musical experiences that are built on them.

I have made various distinctions – between hearing a sound, and hearing a tone, hearing succession and hearing rhythm, hearing change of pitch and hearing movement, hearing agglomerated sounds and hearing harmony. The distinctions here lie *in* the experience (in its intentional object) and not in the material object perceived. But clearly they demand further analysis, especially given the fact that to take such distinctions seriously is to conclude that no speechless creature hears music, and that no birds sing.[4] What, for example, is the distinction between hearing a sound and hearing a tone? It would be tempting to take refuge in the analogy with language, to say that a tone, like a word, is a sound pregnant with meaning. My dog hears the sound 'walk' – which for him constitutes a signal, a trigger to excitement. But he does not hear the *word* 'walk', since he is deaf to its character as language. For him it is not what it is for me, the point of intersection of indefinitely many meaningful utterances. It has not, for him, the audible character of a semantic unit. Of course I may often hear words that I do not understand –

but to the extent that I hear them as words I hear them as filled with semantic and grammatical implications, even when I have only the haziest idea what those implications are.

Similarly, when I hear a tone, I hear a sound imbued with musical implications. What are these implications? It is tempting to assimilate the case to that of language, and to argue that the implications are semantic. But this misrepresents the phenomenon. The analogy with language is no more than an analogy, and to take it seriously as the basis for a musical aesthetic is to invite the greatest confusion. Common sense points us, rather, to the traditional triad: harmony, melody and rhythm. A tone has implications in these three dimensions, which correspond to three kinds of expectation that are aroused or thwarted in musical experience. A tone arouses 'vertical' and 'horizontal' expectations – the first being harmonic, the second melodic and rhythmic. To say that is not to elucidate the distinction between sound and tone. On the contrary, I shall argue that a proper description of musical expectations depends upon an account of that distinction. It must further be remembered that, in identifying the implications of a tone under these traditional categories, I have already incorporated some of the demands of a musical culture. There are musical traditions without melody in our sense (the Javanese), without rhythm in our sense (the Japanese Gagaku), without harmony (much of the music of Southern Asia). But in all these (with the possible, and highly curious, exception of the Gagaku) there are tones, and it is from the idea of a tone that I shall begin.

Tones, unlike sounds, seem to contain movement. This movement is exemplified in melodies, and can be traced through a 'musical space', which we describe in terms of 'high' and 'low'. It seems fairly clear that this description is metaphorical, and this fact has had an important part to play in the development of modern musical aesthetics.[5] The questions that I wish to consider, and which, I believe, have not been correctly considered, are these: can the metaphor be eliminated? If not, what does its persistence tell us about the character of musical experience?

It seems that, because of instrumental positions, the Greeks and the Chinese called those tones high which we call low, and vice versa. On the basis of such facts, Berlioz (to take a distinguished example) professed to find the whole description of music in spatial terms arbitrary and dispensable. This profession is consistent, but not wholly compatible, with the tone-painting exemplified in such works as *Harold in Italy* and the *Symphonie Fantastique*.[6] (It is *consistent* with the practice since the denial of a metaphor is always consistent with the facts, whether or not the facts also render it appropriate.) I doubt that it is possible to share Berlioz's opinion without also recognizing a conflict with musical experience. It is, of course, impossible to draw any conclusions from the example of Greek musical vocabulary, for this does not show us how the Greeks *heard* music. To imagine the spatial metaphor reversed is to imagine a thorough-going alteration of musical experience. If someone *heard* those sounds as high which we hear as low we might, I think, wish to deny that he heard the same *tones* as we do. For him the opening bars of *Rheingold* fall slowly from a great height; for us they rise from the depths of the universe. Is that not, musically speaking, the greatest difference imaginable? For us the solo violin in the 'Benedictus' of the *Missa Solemnis* soars like an angel above the swell of the chorus: for him it is like a murky serpent undulating in the deep.

Because the experience of 'height' and 'depth' is so irresistible, some have tried to argue that these terms are used *literally* of music, say, because they denote the position of the human larynx as it strains to encompass its range of sounds. This strange suggestion, which clearly confuses the cause of a description with its ground, has nevertheless won some favour among psychologists, and even among philosophers, of music.[7] But it is clear that it does nothing to capture the true significance of the spatial reference, and leaves the whole phenomenon of musical movement unexplained. Further examination shows, moreover, that, whether or not we accept as inevitable the designations of 'high' and 'low' in music, we must recognize that the idea of musical space, and of movement within that space, is a metaphor.

In discussing this topic, we need to know the point of saying, of some gradation, that it is, or is not, spatial. The answer seems to require examination of the difference between dimension and continuity. The colour spectrum is an example of gradation, and exhibits continuity: so too does the arithmetical continuum. We can speak of a greater or less distance between points on a continuum, and between any two points there is always a third. But neither the colour spectrum nor the arithmetical continuum is a dimension: they do not constitute frames within which we identify colours or numbers, but rather ordered aggregates of colours and numbers. The distinction here is difficult to draw. It was the attempt to draw it, I believe, which motivated much of Kant's concern with space, both in the pre-critical writings, and in the first *Critique*, and which fortified his belief (surprising in someone familiar with the Cartesian reduction of geometry) that arithmetic and geometry are wholly different sciences.

A dimension stands in a specific relation to the things that it contains. For example, an object is located *in* space; it *occupies* a certain position which might have been occupied by something else; it is also oriented in space. Now the place occupied by blue in the spectrum is not a 'space' that might have been occupied by red, say. Nor is blue oriented: it is indeed hard to know what would be meant by that. It is the feature of orientation that Kant particularly remarked on in his well-known essay on this subject.[8] Orientation is present whenever there is 'incongruity', of the kind displayed between an object and its mirror image. Kant tried to show that there is more to space than spatial relations between objects. He therefore produced an example of two universes which, while identical in all spatial relations, are not identical in their spatial properties. One consists of a left-hand glove, the other of a right-hand glove. These are asymmetrical mirror images, and are therefore incongruent; the one cannot be fitted into the space occupied by the other. This feature of orientation seemed to Kant to provide a reason for identifying space as existing independently of the objects which occupy it. The example has been generalized, for example by Wittgenstein, in *Tractatus* 6.36111, in order to suggest that incongruence can always be overcome by adding a further dimension through which the mirror image can be turned. In general, the Kantian feature of orientation is now considered to be one among several features which show dimension to be, not a metric, but a topological feature of space. It is the topological structure of space that conditions the possibility of movement in space, and secures the observed character of that movement.[9]

By Kant's criterion, the auditory 'spectrum' might seem to be a dimension: objects occurring within it possess orientation, as well as position. This is so, at least, provided we can consider a chord to be an 'object in auditory space'. For a chord can be the exact mirror of another, even though it is not possible to shift the one through musical space so as to coincide with the other – chords may make what seem to be 'incongruent counterparts', as in the following example:

Example 1

Here the first chord mirrors the second, but cannot be shifted through musical space ('transposed') so as to coincide with it. And just as perfectly symmetrical physical objects are congruent with their mirror images, so are perfectly symmetrical chords congruent with theirs:

Example 2

However, is it true that a chord is an 'object in auditory space'? Someone could easily doubt that the basic individuals in musical space (the 'place-occupiers') include chords. The first chord in ex. 1 is indeed the mirror of the second. But this means only that the distances between the component tones in the first (travelling 'upwards') are the same as the distances between the component tones in the second (travelling 'downwards'). So three points taken in one direction seem to provide the mirror image of three points taken in the other. But that is not enough. For by that criterion the ordered triple of numbers $(2, 5, 7)$ is a mirror of the ordered triple $(7, 9, 12)$: in which case there is orientation (and therefore dimension) in the mathematical continuum. But we have produced this orientation artificially, by arbitrarily composing objects in arithmetical 'space' out of individual numbers which, taken separately, possess no orientation at all. Such groupings of arithmetical objects cannot in themselves suffice to change the topological properties of the continuum. Likewise, there is only genuine orientation in the musical 'space' if a chord can be considered as a single musical object, spread over the 'area' which it 'occupies'. But what compels us to think so?

Of course, we *hear* a chord as a single musical object: but that is the result of our musical understanding. It is not a feature of the 'spatial' distribution of sounds. Hence, in order to construe musical 'space' as analogous to physical space, we have to construe it, not materially, but intentionally, in terms of that very capacity for musical understanding that we are trying to explain. It is a phenomenal fact about auditory space that it possesses the topological feature of orientation; but it

Roger Scruton

is not a fact about sound, construed independently of the musical experiences of which it is the (material) object.

Nevertheless, have we not admitted the existence of individuals in auditory space, when we speak of the tones out of which chords are composed? Again we find serious disanalogies with physical space. First, it seems that tones have no parts, and are therefore not divisible within the 'space' that they occupy: this already deprives them of orientation. Moreover, with certain rather peculiar exceptions, the basic individuals in physical space obey the law that no two individuals can be in the same space at the same time.[10] Do tones obey this law? The question is exceedingly difficult to answer, and the difficulty is that of identifying the basic individuals that occupy auditory space. Suppose a violin and a flute play in unison. Is the result one individual or two? It seems that our answer will depend on the musical context. If the unison occurs through the crossing of two lines of counterpoint, then what we hear is *two* tones; otherwise we hear only *one* tone, with a distinct timbre due to its being sounded on two instruments simultaneously. But to talk of tones is already to talk at the sophisticated level of musical phenomenology. If we wish to speak of what is indisputably and objectively true of the auditory world, we should refer only to sounds. Suppose, however, that we retreat to this point of comparative safety; we still find that the law of spatiality – that no two objects can be at the same place simultaneously – is repeatedly and unproblematically violated. The natural way of counting sounds (the way which corresponds to their physical nature) is in terms of their manner of production. So that the violin and flute in unison produce not one sound, but two.

That suggests that there is something odd in the idea that *sounds* have a spatial order (an order, that is, other than that conferred by the *physical* space in which they occur). Perhaps we should confine ourselves to the study of tones; whatever auditory space should turn out to be, it is tones that are to be its basic occupants. But what now of musical movement? It seems to follow that no individual in auditory space can be in two places at different times. We have no way to individuate tones except in terms of their uninterrupted continuity at a single pitch. Therefore no tone can move from one pitch to another, without becoming another tone. Hence no individual in auditory space actually moves. We cannot separate the individuals from the places that they occupy, not even in thought. So

there is no such thing, materially speaking, as musical movement.[11] (Unless of course, we mean to refer to the material transfer of sounds from place to place, as when a character walks singing across the stage in opera, or as in some of the orchestral extravaganzas of Stockhausen, in which orchestras 'hand' sounds to each other across the floor of a concert hall.)

Even if we do not accept that radical conclusion, we must concede that hearing movement in auditory space is very different from seeing or hearing movement in physical space. It does not involve an act of re-identification: it does not require the perception of the same thing at different places, and the consequent inference of a movement from one place to the other. Of course we can hear a melody, now at middle C, now transposed upwards an octave or a fifth. And that might seem to be an example of hearing the same thing at two different places. But this would only provide us with a model for the perception of musical movement if we could think of melodies as basic individuals, whose re-identification at different places gives rise to our concept of musical movement. But that is not so. A melody is itself a *kind* of musical movement, and it cannot therefore be an example of the individual whose changing position is supposed to provide us with our conception of how music moves.

The conclusion that we should draw is that, while we hear movement in music, this is a fact about our experience, which corresponds to no actual movement in the auditory world. Musical movement is, in Gurney's words, 'ideal movement'.[12] It might be tempting then to renounce altogether the idea that there is an auditory space, and that music moves within the confines of that space. We might say that 'movement' is simply a way of describing what is in fact nothing more than a process, which changes through time, but involves no movement through space. But if we take that extreme point of view, we end by reducing the experience of music to the experience of sound: the distinction between a sound and a tone has vanished. Sounds too belong to processes – indeed, they *are* processes, and can be combined sequentially, and heard in sequence, even when they are not heard as music. If we take away the metaphors of movement, of space, of chords as objects, of melodies as advancing and retreating, as moving up and down – if we take those metaphors away, nothing of music remains, but only sound.

It seems then that in our most basic apprehension of music there lies a complex system of metaphor, which is the true description of no material fact. And the metaphor cannot be eliminated from the description of music, because it is integral to the intentional object of musical experience. Take this metaphor away and you cease to describe the experience of music. But suppose it is objected that you cease to describe, not the experience of music, but only *that* experience of music (the experience constituted by the metaphorical transfer to which I have referred). What is the reply? Why do sounds have to be experienced as I have described them in order to be heard as *music*?

It is hard to find an irrebuttable answer to that question. However, it seems to me that much of its force can be dispelled by emphasizing just how *radically* different the experience of sounds would have to be for reference to space to be eliminated from its description – so different, in fact, that it might seem justifiable to say that we are no longer concerned with an experience of tones. It may be (though I doubt it) that we ought to regard the descriptions 'high' and 'low' as dispensable, replaceable, say, by 'left' and 'right' or by some non-metaphorical predicates defined purely over the set of sounds. But what would it be like to dispense altogether with the experience of space? My argument suggests that this would involve ceasing to hear orientation in music. In which case tones would no longer move towards or away from each other; no phrase would mirror another, no leaps would be larger or bolder than others. In short the experience of music would involve neither melody nor counterpoint as we presently know them. Musical movement would have disappeared, direction having been entirely replaced by succession. In which case, why should we continue to talk of music?[13]

An important corollary should here be mentioned. It has been well argued that our perceptual field has an intrinsic orientation, including a sense of 'up' and 'down' that cannot be intelligibly subtracted from the contents of perception.[14] And this sense of 'up' and 'down' is not a purely geometrical idea – it is, rather, an idea of human movement, made available to us by our own activity. It therefore depends upon our sense of what obstructs and furthers action. At a deep level, the sense of 'up' and 'down' is a sense of the human will. And it is not implausible to suggest that it is this sense of ourselves as agents – rather than any purely geometrical idea of space – which underlies our experience of musical movement, and prompts us to describe that movement in spatial terms. This

observation is perhaps obscure as yet; but below I make further remarks about rhythm which will serve to clarify it. Later I shall give philosophical grounds for thinking that it is indeed our experience of ourselves, rather than any scientific representation of the world, which both prompts and explains the metaphors which we apply to music.

If the description of music is so dependent upon metaphor, we might go on to conclude that music is not, strictly speaking, a part of the material world. By that I mean that any scientific description of the world of sound should not mention – as an independent fact of the matter – the phenomenon of music. For there is no explanatory function to be filled by the concept of music that will not equally be filled by the concept of organized sound: no scientific method need discriminate between these two (the extension of each concept in the material world being identical). Hence, by the axiom of simplicity, the concept which describes the material essence of what is heard (the concept of sound) is the only one that we need employ. If there is an additional *fact* of the matter, it is that we (beings of a certain kind) hear music. Music belongs uniquely to the intentional sphere, and not to the material realm. Any analysis of music must be an exercise in intentional rather than scientific understanding.

But, someone might object, that only shows that musical properties and relations are secondary, rather than primary properties, of the sounds that possess them. To think that they are therefore not part of the material world in some significant sense (some sense that does not merely reiterate the scientific realist's commitment to the explanatory priority of primary qualities) is to repeat a mistake at least as old as Berkeley. It is to think that because the sense of a term (e.g., 'red') is to be specified in terms of certain experiences involved in its application, its reference must therefore be intentional rather than material.

In a sense the objection is fair. It is true that the terms used to describe music *refer* to material sounds. But they refer to them under a description which no material sound can satisfy. Sounds do not move as music moves (so as to 'reach into the silence'). Nor are they organized in a spatial way (*pace*, for example, Strawson[15]), nor do they rise and fall. These are all metaphors, and one thing that distinguishes metaphors from scientific descriptions is that they are, when successful, false. The case is quite unlike that of secondary qualities for another reason. The ability to perceive a secondary quality is a sensory capacity, and depends only upon the power of sensory discrimination. Many animals may discriminate sensory qualities better than we do (bees, for example, may perceive a wider range of colours, birds a wider range of sounds, through the secondary qualities that make these features audible). This ability does not depend upon superior intellect, nor upon any other faculty that might be improved or impaired through education. It is this that leads us to think of the secondary qualities as really *inherent* in the objects that possess them. For no amount of education can persuade us to perceive, or dissuade us from perceiving them; all that is required for their perception is an apparatus of sensory discrimination. Musical qualities, however, are not, in that sense, secondary. They are more closely analogous to aspects – the man in the moon, the face in the cloud, the child in the picture – which are sometimes called 'tertiary' qualities, in order to emphasize the peculiar nature of their dependence upon our capacities to observe them. 'Tertiary' qualities are often thought not to be genuine qualities of the things which possess them: first, because of their 'supervenience',[16] secondly, because they are neither deductions from experience nor used in the explanation of experience; thirdly, because their perception requires peculiar capacities (such as imagination) which cannot be tied down to any 'sense', and which perhaps do not belong to speechless beings. It does not much matter for present purposes whether we take a 'realist' view of these qualities. What does matter is that we should recognize the peculiar dependence of our power to observe them upon our power of thought.

A consideration of aspects helps us to make sense of the metaphorical transfer that is integral to musical experience. It also enables us to incorporate into our account of musical understanding the essentials of harmonic and rhythmic perception. Consider the face in the cloud. You see the face in the cloud only when you also see that it is not there. To believe that there is a face in the cloud is not (in the relevant sense) to perceive it. It is to be the victim of an illusion, of a kind from which animals too may suffer. There is a transfer involved in seeing the face: the intentional object of experience must be described using a concept that is known not to apply to the material object of perception. This transfer is not unlike that which occurs in metaphor. This is one reason for thinking that the perception of aspects is confined

to beings with imagination – beings who can extend concepts beyond the field of their literal application.

The perception of an aspect is not, then, the acquisition of a peculiar false belief. For this reason, it remains partly, or perhaps wholly, within the control of the subject. He cannot choose what to believe, but he may often choose what to 'see'. The structure of this control is difficult to describe.[17] But its musical manifestations are readily identified. They illustrate the peculiar way in which the subject is active in the perception of music, however indifferent or hostile towards it he may be. By 'active' I mean something quite specific. According to the Kantian doctrine of the synthesis, and all the many philosophies which have issued from it, all perception has an active component. But in my sense not every perception is 'active'. To be 'active' a perception must exhibit that kind of conscious participation that is involved in the perception of an aspect: it must involve an engagement of attention, an interest in surface, a transference of concepts from sphere to sphere (as in metaphor); in the limiting case it may itself be a voluntary act.

All those features of 'activity' are exhibited in the perception of musical movement. The voluntary character of this perception provides one of the foundations for structural criticism of music. It is because I can ask someone to hear a movement as beginning in a certain place, as phrased in a certain way, and so on, that the activity of giving reasons in support of such analysis makes sense. Much of music criticism consists of the deliberate construction of an intentional object from the infinitely ambiguous instructions implicit in a sequence of sounds.

Rather than dwell further on musical movement, I wish now to consider rhythm, which is the dimension of musical experience that exhibits 'activity' most strikingly. An unusually complex example of rhythmic organization is presented by the first three bars of *Parsifal*:

Example 3

Only the eighth tone of this phrase falls on an accented beat, and the listener hears the accent there. All that precedes this tone is, in his hearing, held in rhythmic suspension. It is extremely difficult to describe this suspension. Its impact, however, is immediate, and is understood in the very first tone. Suppose the phrase had been written:

Example 4

Perhaps the orchestra would have produced an identical *sound* in response to the first written note. But the instructions for hearing it have (in a sense) been changed. The rhythmic character is now altered in the ears of the beholder. It may seem rather extraordinary that one can hear the difference between ex. 3 and ex. 4 from the first tone. But we must remind ourselves that the rhythmic character of the first tone is not a feature of the material world of sound; it belongs to the intentional world of musical perception. The active listener can set his mind to changing that character: he could decide to hear ex. 4 (or rather, what ex. 4 most naturally represents) in place of ex. 3. (What I wish to say here is of course extremely difficult to express, since the content of this decision is precisely what no mode of musical notation can determine.)

It might be objected that this hearing of rhythmic implications is nothing more than a perception of temporal pattern; one simply hears the tones and the spacing between them, and then fits them, as it were, into a temporal grid. But that fails to account for the difference between the two ways of hearing the first note in ex. 3 above; it also fails to take account of the phenomenon which we might (on the analogy with tone deafness) call 'rhythm deafness'. For it seems quite possible for someone to hear regularity in sound, and to fit sound into a temporal 'grid', while having no sense of rhythm. Our musical education leads us to hear rhythm in the click of a train along the tracks. Indeed, we hear this rhythm in all kinds of sounds, and sometimes, by an act of will, make the most obnoxious repetitions bearable (and in due course unbearable) by hearing them in syncopated forms. But this act of hearing rhythm seems to be something over and above the perception of time. Rhythm may not be perceived by all who perceive sound, and who gain through that perception knowledge of a temporal order. A striking illustration is provided by the cross-rhythms of classical music. Why do we hear this:

Example 5

and not this:

Example 6

There is no material differences between the sounds, but in the first case there are two rhythms, while in the second case, there is one. The answer is that the first contains two musical movements (albeit of the simplest kind), whereas the second contains only one. Thus our capacities for spatial and melodic perception in music guide our perception of the rhythm.

All this leads me to doubt that animals hear rhythm. Just as laughter is confined to rational beings, so too is dancing. (Only rational beings can be so perfectly without purpose.) Naturally, animals must hear temporal sequence, since this is part of perceiving. But can they hear a bar line, an off-beat, an anacrusis, a suspension, and the rest? Does the dove hear the subtle rhythm that we perceive in his call?

Example 7

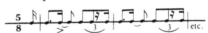

Surely it is not only quixotic to suggest it; it also makes the entire phenomenon mysterious. If he heard that rhythm, would he not be persuaded of the merits of another? What is there in his behaviour that requires explanation in such terms? Animal experience is accessible to us only because we can describe its material causes, and its material effects. Distinctions which exist purely in the intentional realm can be attributed to an animal only in so far as they are revealed in these material circumstances. But it seems impossible to envisage what a dove's behaviour would have to be like for us to attribute to him, not only the perception of organized sounds, but also the perception of rhythm.

In changing the example, I have also changed the emphasis. When referring to musical movement I was at pains to point out that the experience of music depends upon a metaphorical transfer. In

Roger Scruton

speaking of the rhythm of music, it could be argued, we are not speaking metaphorically; we are not transferring to music a term which has its proper application in some other sphere. Music is as central an example of rhythm, it might be said, as anything within our experience. Whether or not that is so is, however, not of the first importance. What matters is the nature of our perception of rhythm. In hearing rhythm we hear the music as *active*; it seems to be doing something (namely, dancing) which no sounds can do. When we hear a rhythm we hear sounds joining to and diverging from each other, exerting over one another peculiar 'fields of force', determining each other in a manner familiar from our knowledge of human movement. At the same time, we do not believe that any such thing is happening in the realm of sound: in a crucial sense, we are aware of the movement as *ours*. Hence, although we may not wish to describe the idea of rhythm as metaphorical, we must acknowledge that the perception of rhythm involves imaginative transfer of the kind involved in metaphor. We should not, therefore, be surprised that the peculiarly 'active' character of imaginative perception is also exemplified by the experience of rhythm. How we hear a rhythm is dependent upon our attention; it may be more or less voluntary, and more or less subject to imaginative activities of comparison and contrast. The experience bears the marks of imaginative endeavour, and cannot be assimilated to the perceptual capacities that we share with speechless beings.

Before proceeding to analyse the more complex instances of musical understanding, it is important to say something about the third fundamental category of musical experience, that of harmony. I remarked earlier upon the important intentional distinction between the perception of harmony and the perception of simultaneous tones. In the first case the tones are heard as *one* thing – a chord – in the second as several. The difference here is not that between discord and concord. I think it is normal to hear the following collection of tones, which opens the second section of Stravinsky's *Sacre du Printemps*, as a chord:

Example 8

Here it is almost impossible to hear the tones separately, and this is not because one hears a block of undifferentiated sound, as in certain of the 'chords' of Stockhausen. The peculiar character of Stravinsky's chord (in which a seventh of E flat is squeezed as it were into the interstices of an E major triad) is that it is heard as one musical entity, spread over the whole range of the bass voice, with no tone 'emerging' as the principal bearer of musical significance. By contrast, the following famous concord from the 'Hostias' of Berlioz's *Grande Messe des Morts*, sounded simultaneously on three flutes and eight trombones, is often not heard as a chord:

Example 9

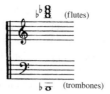

Once again it is quite easy to explain the effect: the extraordinary distance between the single bass note and the high minor triad, the agonizing difference of timbre, the absence of any intermediate parts (note how the effect disappears at once with the *pizzicato* octaves in the middle range that follow, and compare the similar example offered by the opening of Britten's first string quartet). But the explanation serves only to remind us that we can perceive consonance even where we do not perceive chords. Perhaps the best illustration of that truth is given by counterpoint, in which separate musical *movements* are heard as harmonizing, but in which at no point before the end does anything emerge that could be called a chord. One of the most important changes in the history of music is precisely that which occurred when the chord itself became a dominant musical unit, as it is in the symphonies of Beethoven, and as it remained until Schoenberg's *Pierrot Lunaire*. The Viennese school attempted to overthrow the dominance of chordal writing by overthrowing tonality: what it achieved, however, was not genuine counterpoint, but something wholly new.

One can envisage many explanations of the experience of concord. Since Helmholtz first opened this field to the methods of modern physics, the relations between sounds that had seemed so wondrous to the Pythagoreans have ceased to be puzzling. That we should distinguish concords and discords has become profoundly unsurprising; nor would it be surprising if birds and beasts distinguished them, and felt pleasure at the first and pain at the second. But the ability to make that kind of discrimination among sounds is not sufficient for the perception of harmony. The harmonic essence of musical dissonance lies not so much in the pattern of overtones that causes us to register it, as in the relations of tension, transition and resolution that it bears to surrounding chords. The following chord would be considered to be discordant, by anyone asked to classify it simply on the basis of its sound:

Example 10

But in the context of Chopin's Nocturne Op.27 No. 1, in C sharp minor, it is simply one of a harmonious sequence effecting a transition. Likewise, in a style like that of jazz, where accessory notes are often added to the chords, it is not normal to hear dissonance in discord: an all-pervading sweetness of harmony may be the more usual perception, so that sonorities considered highly dissonant in other contexts are felt to require no resolution. Here is how Art Tatum harmonizes the first bar of 'Aunt Hagar's Blues':

Example 11

From the first cluttered chord you feel the force of D flat major. The little gesture to the bass simply reinforces an existing sense of lazy consonance and delicious relaxation. Nevertheless that fairly standard jazz augmentation of a major chord would be an intolerable dissonance even in Wagner.

When considering such examples it is important to note that musical analysis often distinguishes

identical sounds. Depending on context, a chord may be given several conflicting descriptions. The chord in ex. 10 would be described as a diminished seventh over an A flat pedal, forming part of a sequence which steadily increases the tension in A flat major so that the music passes with a feeling of release into D flat. Had it occurred in a Schoenberg string quartet (which is a possibility), you could not have described the chord in that way. Likewise, it is only the peculiar expectations associated with jazz improvisation that enable us to describe the first chord of ex. 11 as a seventh chord of D flat with a flattened ninth. If those sounds were to occur in Berg (which is highly likely) we would again have to alter our description. This is, of course, not surprising. But it shows very clearly that the dynamic relations that we perceive when we hear music enter into the description of what we hear. In effect we are forced to determine the criteria of identity of chords differently from the criteria for the identity of the sounds that compose them. This surely must reinforce the view that harmony belongs not to the material world of sound, but to the intentional world of musical experience. Consider the many cases in which critics cannot decide which chord a composer is using. What, for example, is the last chord of Janáček's 'On an Overgrown Path' (first series)? No answer seems right, because you cannot say what key the piece has ended in – whether the triumphant E major of the melody, or the questioning C sharp minor of the owl's call. In Debussy's early song 'Recueillement', we find the following:

Example 12

What is the chord in the first bar? Surely, you would say, an open fifth on C sharp. But the effect of the second bar, according to one critic, causes even this first bar to be heard as a suspension over a dominant seventh in A major.[18] Here we see a harmony feeding back into the tones that precede it, and causing us to hear and so to describe them differently. You might say, parodying Frege, that only in the totality of a musical phrase do sounds determine harmony. In which case our perception of harmony is dependent upon our musical understanding as a whole. It cannot be separated from the understanding of movement, tension, and release. Moreover, what we experience in hearing harmony is something that has to be described in metaphorical terms. Chords are heard as 'spaced', 'open', 'filled', 'hollow' (to use the basic metaphors of musical experience): harmony is described in terms of geometrical relations between parts, in terms of the coming together and separating of movements, in terms of oppositions and agreements. Just as melody involves the metaphorical transference of ideas of 'movement', 'space', 'height' and 'depth', so does harmony involve the metaphorical transference of ideas of 'tension', 'relaxation', 'conflict' and 'resolution'. Although there is a material base to the perception of these things, there is more to perceiving them than perceiving their material base.

In exploring the three dimensions of musical perception we seem to have laid bare a realm of intentional understanding which is both active in the manner of imaginative experience, and also essentially dependent upon metaphor. My aim has been to specify, not sufficient, but necessary conditions of musical understanding, in the form of constraints upon the *experience* in which understanding rests. It remains to explore how those constraints limit the experience of musical content, and so determine the form which a theory of musical expression must take. The defender of the 'absolute' in music may not agree with such an explanation. But if I am right, then even Hanslick's description of music, as *tönend-bewegte Form*, contains a description (*bewegte*) that does not literally apply to it. So why not allow that music may also be 'melancholy', 'expressive', and 'passionate'? In addressing this question I shall confine myself to a few far from obvious remarks, in the hope that the reader will see a way forward which also promises a solution to the original problem.

One way of theorizing the metaphorical character in musical perception is in terms of 'projection'. Since the movement is not literally *in* the music, it must, we are inclined to think, have been put there by the listener. It results from an act of 'projection', whereby, to borrow Hume's famous simile, the mind 'spreads itself upon objects'.[19] To say this is relatively harmless, so long as we realize that we have said nothing. For the only truth of the matter is that sounds heard as musical movement do not move. The disposition to hear them as moving is inseparable from the experience of music, but that

does not mean that there is some act of 'projection' that transfers movement, as it were, to the auditory world.

Nevertheless, the language of 'projection' is useful. It presents a picture of how a theory of musical understanding might be extended from the primitive 'dimensions' that I have been discussing, to the more complex phenomena that interest the critic. According to the doctrine of projection we do not merely 'transfer a term' when we hear musical movement: we also transfer the movement. (As we might be thought to 'transfer' the face from our thought to the canvas in which we see it.) The temptation to speak in this way must eventually be resisted. But by giving way to it now, and then resisting it later, we will gain some insight into what can, and what cannot, be said by way of elucidating musical expression. So let us give way to it. Just as we transfer an experience of movement to music (which does not move), so do we transfer an experience of passion to music (which has no passions). We project into the music the inner life that is ours, and that is *how* we hear it there. This is not the same as hearing resemblances between music and feeling, any more than hearing musical movement is hearing structural relations on which the movement depends. The experience of transfer is *sui generis*. The emotion that is heard belongs purely to the intentional and not to the material realm. Such a theory would explain, for example, the enormous gap that exists between the material reality of the sounds that we hear, and the spiritual complexity of the emotions that we 'project' into them. There can be as large a gap as you like between an intentional object which is the construct of imagination, and the material object in which it is experienced. But the theory leaves unsolved the perennial difficulties surrounding the idea of musical 'content'.

In attempting to overcome those difficulties, it is useful to draw attention to another context in which 'understanding' occurs, and in which understanding has often been thought to involve 'projection': the context of human relations. It has often been said that, in order to understand the gesture, state of mind, or feeling of another, some kind of 'empathy' or '*Einfühlung*' is required, whereby I imaginatively project myself into his position and see the world through his eyes. Without that act of projection I know only his behaviour, not his mind. First in the field among theories of musical expression during the twentieth century were those that sought to extend the doctrine of *Einfühlung* from people to art.[20] In neither case is it correct: but in both cases it is illuminating.

The original picture offered by the proponents of *Einfühlung* was this: a state of mind has two aspects, that which is revealed in body and behaviour, and that which is 'subjective', captured by the contents of the subject's immediate awareness, but by nothing else. The essence of the mental state consists in the second aspect, and genuine knowledge of another's state of mind must involve knowledge of that aspect. However, that aspect is purely intentional: it is therefore the object only of immediate awareness and its nature is falsified by awareness of any other kind. To know it is also to know that you do not *discover* its nature: you know it only as 'given'. How then, can *I* know in *that* way, what is given to *you*? *Einfühlung* is invented as the faculty whereby I adopt, as it were, the vestiges of your outward expression, and so come to feel inwardly in myself the subjective awareness that is yours. I then re-create the intentional object of your awareness, and so know your state of mind in its inner essence. What I then know can be communicated only through the act of *Einfühlung*. I could not set out to describe the intentional structure of this state of mind and thereby make it available in its inner essence to you: nor could I make it available to you *simply* by acquainting you with its expression.

The claim is two-fold: that there is an objective and a subjective aspect to states of mind; and that there is a form of knowledge proper to each. These claims can each be interpreted in a misleading and in a harmless way. The misleading interpretation is the most usual, and goes as follows: there are properties of the mental which are perceivable only from the first person point of view. (This is the subjective aspect of the mental.) Those properties are knowable only by acquaintance. That way of putting the doctrine is misleading because of its commitment to a Cartesian view of the mind. The mind is represented as a subjective residue which is neither reducible to nor identical with any item in the physical world.

The harmless interpretation reads as follows. There are two modes of knowledge of the mental, which we could call, borrowing Russellian terminology, knowledge by description and knowledge by acquaintance. One is characteristic of my knowledge of your mind, the other characteristic of my knowledge of mine. The second is 'immediate' (based on nothing); hence it involves no recognition of features whereby I identify my mental state. Hence it does not involve the discovery of purely subjective properties of the mental. It is immediate knowledge of the very same thing that is known mediately and in the normal manner through the study of those physical processes which give evidence of the mental. There is a difference between being in pain and merely observing it. In the former case the pain features among the objects of immediate awareness. Even on this metaphysically harmless interpretation, however, there is an epistemological asymmetry between the first and the third person points of view. One can speak of someone not only as having theoretical knowledge of the characteristics of fear, say, but also as having another kind of knowledge associated with the 'immediate' perception about which nothing can be said. This second kind of knowledge is 'knowing what it's like'. It is an important part of the theory of imagination to show how such knowledge can be acquired by someone who does not *have* the mental state that is known. How can I know what your fear is like without feeling it? One answer is by *Einfühlung*. There is a kind of response to your face and gestures which makes available to me your first-person perspective on the mental state that I can otherwise know only by observation. I imagine what it is like to feel as you do. I then entertain your emotion within the field of my own point of view. There is nothing to be *said* about what I thereby come to know, for there is no new proposition that I know. But the experience may be of a peculiar importance, both as cementing the bond between us, and as helping me to see the force of the reasons that you offer for your action. Knowing your fear in *that* way I can see why you are compelled to flee. There is (or seems to be) a close connection between 'knowing what it's like' and the premises of practical reasoning.

'Knowledge by acquaintance' lies wholly outside the reach of any third-person perspective; it is a perspective on the mental that cannot be transcribed, a form of knowledge that contains no proposition known. If this is so, then there is no longer any paradox, either in the claim that you have to 'enter into' someone's state of mind in order to know it by acquaintance, or in the claim that what you thereby know is inexpressible.

Often *Einfühlung* has for object not a recognized emotion, but simply a facial expression, a gesture, or a frown. Such things often seem peculiarly significant, and, whether by an act of imitation, by the residue of such an act, or by whatever method (who knows, in fact, how it is done?), we 'enter into' them, and transform our observation of another's expression, into the imaginative knowledge of 'what it is like'. This might lead us to understand the place of his present state of mind in his projects and intentions. Thus *Einfühlung* may give us a picture of the complete elaboration of a state of mind which, from the third person point of view, is merely hinted at or roughly sketched.

Suppose however that someone is *not* feeling what I imaginatively feel in responding to his expression. He is feeling nothing, say, or something quite different. If he is a mimic or an actor, he may be intending to represent a character who is feeling exactly what I am prompted to 'know by acquaintance'. It is his intention that I should have just the kind of *Einfühlung* that I have. Here is a case where I might be tempted to say: behind that gesture, there is feeling. But of course I do not attribute the feeling to anyone, least of all to the actor before me. I have 'entered into' an absent state of mind. We could say, to return to the metaphor that we should now see how to eliminate, that I have 'projected' the feeling into the gesture that I see.

In the normal case, an actor will be representing a precise character in precise circumstances, suffering, no doubt, some identifiable emotion. The dramatic context will provide the thoughts through which the object of that feeling can be defined. My act of *Einfühlung* takes place against a background of knowledge by description, and so I need feel no hesitation in characterizing what is expressed. If someone says to me 'There is a quite definite emotion in these lines', then I may be able to reply to him with a description: 'It is a sentimental remorse over the murder of Desdemona'. But such descriptions, however complex and astute, never seem to give us what we are looking for. They never seem to capture what is known by the person who understands the play. We want to add; 'But of course, the important thing is the quite peculiar *shade* of remorse that is conveyed by the lines'. In answer to the question 'What shade?' the sensible critic then has recourse to ostension: '*That* shade!', and he points to the text. This way the critic also gives a reason for returning to the lines, for there is no other way of rehearsing what they tell you. At the same time it begins to look strange that we harbour the belief in an expressed 'content'. For, even in these dramatic examples, we are reluctant to identify the content independently of its form.

This problem has been discussed in aesthetics under many labels: the 'heresy of paraphrase', the 'inseparability of form and content', the contrast between 'intuition' and 'concept', or between 'expression' and 'description'. All these time-honoured phrases are ways of approaching, from rival theoretical standpoints, the area upon which our enquiry has now focused. In certain circumstances, observing a gesture of expression, we have the experience of *Einfühlung*, of knowing what it is like, whereby the gesture becomes, in imagination, our own. We then feel it, not from the observer's, but from the subject's point of view. This experience may occur, and may grant a sense of the completeness of its object, whether or not the context permits *description* of the object of the other's feeling; whether or not we believe that 'feeling' is the right term for what is known; and whether or not we even believe that there *is* another, into whose mental arena we have felt our way. It is as though we have been granted a first-person perspective on a world that we know is not ours. Neither is it anyone else's. It is a creation of the imagination, and retains the impersonality of the imaginative act. What we know from the first-person perspective can be known only from that perspective – which is not to say that it is mysterious. Or rather, it is mysterious only in the way that the first-person perspective is mysterious. (I believe that, when Schopenhauer referred our experience of music to the will, he was consciously invoking this idea of 'immediate' first-personal knowledge. The will is the inner essence of the mental, which can be known either directly, through its own activity, or else indirectly, through representation. Music is the only art that conveys that 'direct', immediate knowledge of the will that we gain through our own activity.[21])

We have now effectively eliminated all reference to 'projection'. That term stood proxy for the following ideas: a gesture can be treated as the sign or expression of a state of mind; it can also be imaginatively 'adopted' so as to enter into the first-person perspective of the observer. This adoption may occur even when the circumstances surrounding the gesture are so incomplete as to provide no description of its intentional object. There may be a sense of 'what it is like' from which all intentionality has been extruded. When I see a gesture from the first-person point of view then I do not only see it as an expression; I grasp the completeness of the state of mind that is intimated through it. That is all that should be meant by saying that I 'project' my feeling into the gesture. And only in context will my perspective on the gesture also contain some intimation of its object.

It remains to fit those observations into our earlier account of musical understanding. In dramatic use, or in the context of a song, the circumstances that surround the musical gesture give us some intimation of its intentionality. We can then say something about *what* is expressed. But this context is not normally present, and even when it is, it will not provide the 'inner meaning' of what we hear. Normally we hear musical gestures as we might see a man gesticulating to an unseen audience, perhaps guessing at the objects of his feeling, perhaps remaining entirely ignorant of them. Even in such circumstances, we may enter into gestures and see them from 'within'. For we may see them as containing spirit, character, and an outlook on the world. Just as we see spirit, life and activity in gestures, so do we hear movement, life and activity in music. And sometimes we enter into that movement as we do into the movement of an imaginary being: a first-person perspective on that movement is opened to us, and for a moment it is ours. Then comes, in addition to the recognition of expression, the sense of being acquainted with a whole state of mind, which cannot be independently described, except perhaps in lame and unformed gestures.

That is only a sketch, and of course it falls far short of giving a full account of musical understanding. In particular it leaves the *critical* question – the question, when is it right to hear music in terms of some 'content' – unanswered. But perhaps that is a merit; for it seems to me a singular defect of those theories of musical meaning which proceed by giving conditions for the application of emotion terms to music that they solve the critical question too *easily*.[22] They enable us to say what a passage expresses, only by reducing the experience of expression to a recognitional capacity, and so removing its importance. It becomes impossible to say why it *matters* that emotions should be heard in music, why this should be a part of musical understanding. To show why it matters is also to show why criticism is hard. And that is as it should be.

I have given necessary, but not sufficient, conditions for musical understanding. I hope, however, that I have given some indication of how a theory of musical understanding in terms of entrenched metaphor may be extended to account for the more puzzling features of musical expression: its importance, its ineffability, and the 'immediacy' which Schopenhauer regarded as so important. Understanding music involves the active creation of an intentional world, in which inert sounds are transfigured into movements, harmonies, rhythms – metaphorical gestures in a metaphorical space. And into these metaphorical gestures a metaphorical soul is breathed by the sympathetic listener. At a certain point, he has the experience of a first-person perspective on gestures that are no-one's. This can be as much a part of understanding what he hears as is the hearing of a melody. For it is no more than a continuation of the imaginative activity which is involved in hearing music: the activity of transfiguring sound into figurative space, so that 'you are the music while the music lasts'.

Notes

1 See 'Representation in Music' in my *The Aesthetic Understanding* (London, 1983).

2 See 'The Nature of Musical Expression'. in *The Aesthetic Understanding*.

3 In this chapter and in 'Photography and Representation', in *The Aesthetic Understanding*, I assume familiarity with the concepts of intentionality, and intentional object. For some indication as to how analytical philosophy must treat these concepts, see my 'Intensional and Intentional Objects', *Proceedings of the Aristotelian Society* (1970–1), pp. 187–207. For further remarks on 'intentional understanding' and the *Lebenswelt*, see 'Emotion and Culture' in *The Aesthetic Understanding*.

4 See my *Art and Imagination* (London, 1974), chapter 12; *The Aesthetics of Architecture* (London, 1979), chapter 4.

5 See, for example, D. N. Ferguson, *Music as Metaphor* (Minneapolis, 1960); Carl Stumpf, *Tonpsychologie*, 2 vols. (Leipzig, 1883), I; and the extremely suggestive, though indecisive, discussion in V. Zuckerkandl, *Sound and Symbol*, trans. W. R. Trask, 2 vols. (London, 1956; Princeton, 1973).

6 See A. Wellek, *Musikpsychologie und Musikästhetik* (Frankfurt, 1963), p. 299.

7 See C. C. Pratt, *The Meaning of Music* (London, 1933).

8 I. Kant, 'Concerning the Ultimate Foundations of the Differentiation of Regions in Space' (1768), in *Selected pre-Critical Writings*, trans. G. B. Kerferd and D. E. Walford (Manchester, 1968).

9 See further, Bas C. Van Fraasen, *An Introduction to the Philosophy of Space and Time* (New York, 1970), pp. 134–8.

10　The exceptions to this law, discussed in a lecture by Saul Kripke, are independently puzzling. For example, the case of a plant and its stem raises special questions about identity through time which are not, I think, raised by inorganic things.

11　Cf. Zuckerkandl, pp. 82–3.

12　Edmund Gurney, *The Power of Sound* (London, 1880).

13　Thus I uphold a thesis argued for very differently by both Zuckerkandl and Ferguson. On the importance of 'direction' in the experience of music, see *The Power of Sound*, pp. 139–40. Gurney notes the complete absence of this feature from the experience of the colour spectrum. (I am grateful to Malcolm Budd for drawing my attention to this passage.)

14　The locus classicus (drawing on many of the arguments of earlier phenomenologists) is M. Merleau-Ponty, *The Phenomenology of Perception*, trans. Colin Smith (London and Atlantic Highlands, NJ, 1962). Of more immediate relevance to the above remarks are thoughts contained in Charles Taylor, 'The Validity of Transcendental Arguments', *Proceedings of the Aristotelian Society* (1978–9), p. 154. See also the discussion in Gareth Evans, *Varieties of Reference* (Oxford, 1982), p. 155ff.

15　P. F. Strawson, *Individuals* (London, 1959), chapter 2.

16　That is, for every instance of a tertiary quality, there are instances of secondary qualities on which it depends, such that, to remove the secondary qualities is to remove the tertiary qualities. But not vice versa.

17　On this point, and all the points in the preceding paragraph, see my *Art and Imagination*, part II.

18　Robin Holloway, *Debussy and Wagner* (London, 1979), p. 44.

19　For theories along these lines, see Ernst Maumann, *Untersuchungen zur Psychologie und Ästhetik der Rythmus* (Leipzig, 1894); Ernst Kurth, *Musikpsychologie* (Berlin, 1931); W. V. Bingham, *Studies in Melody* (Baltimore, 1910).

20　See for example, T. Lipps, 'Das Wesen der musikalischen Konsonanz und Dissonanz', in Lipps, *Psychologische Studien* (Leipzig, 1905).

21　See *The World as Will and Representation*, trans. E. F. J. Payne, 2 vols. (Colorado, 1958), I, 2, section 52, and II, chapter 39.

22　For example, the theories, largely of eighteenth-century provenance, seemingly endorsed by Peter Kivy in *The Corded Shell* (Princeton, 1980).

39

The Profundity of Music

Peter Kivy

Certain works of the instrumental repertoire are considered to be somehow "profound" musical works: Beethoven's late quartets, Bach's *Well-Tempered Clavier*, works like that. But does that belief in their profundity make sense?

The reason for the question is this. If I were to say that Goethe's *Faust* is a profound work of art where Oscar Wilde's *Importance of Being Earnest* is not, it is clear what I would mean. The former deals with deep philosophical and moral matters whereas the latter is a clever, frothy comedy of manners with no depth at all, meant to amuse and to be enjoyed. This is not to say that *The Importance of Being Earnest* is an imperfect work. Nor need I be saying, necessarily, that it is a lesser work of art. It *is*, of course. But it is possible for one work to be more profound than another yet less perfect and, perhaps, not as good. However, and this is the crucial point, we are clear that what makes one literary work more profound than another must be, at least, that it is about more profound matters.

Of course, being about something profound is not, by itself, sufficient for our ascribing profundity to a literary work. For profound subjects can be botched as well as beautiful, bungled as well as splendidly brought off. So we will surely have to add that for a literary work to be profound, it must not only have a profound subject but must treat it in a way adequate to that profundity. We may say, then,

Peter Kivy, "The Profundity of Music," in Peter Kivy, *Music Alone: Philosophical Reflections on the Purely Musical Experience* (Ithaca, NY: Cornell University Press, 1990), pp. 245–55. Used by permission of the publisher, Cornell University Press.

that for a work to be profound it must fulfill at least three conditions: it must be able to be "about" (that is, it must possess the possibility of a subject matter); it must be about something profound (which is to say, something of abiding interest or importance to human beings); it must treat its profound subject matter in some exemplary way or other adequate to that subject matter (function, in other words, at some acceptably high aesthetic level).

That being the case, the difficulty I am having with musical profundity is obvious. Music alone isn't about anything. Hence one musical composition cannot be more profound than another in virtue of being about a more profound subject. And indeed, if being a profound work of art requires being about a profound subject, it looks as if music cannot be profound at all, and when we call Bach's *Well-Tempered Clavier* "profound" we are just talking nonsense.

Now because the version of musical purism I espouse does countenance expressive properties, there appears to be an easy way out of this dilemma. It seems plausible for me to argue that music is profound in virtue of being expressive of the darker, which is to say "serious," emotions. Thus the somber seriousness of Brahms's first and fourth symphonies warrants their being considered more profound works than (say) his two serenades for orchestra, expressive as *they* are of the lighter end of the emotive spectrum.

Perhaps there is something to this suggestion in that it may correspond to the way many laypeople perceive and talk about instrumental music. I think such people do tend to perceive and to describe music expressive of the serious emotions as deeper,

Peter Kivy

more profound, than music expressive of the cheerful or frivolous ones. And I think we can easily see why this is the case. There is obviously a connection between dark emotions and profound subjects. "Serious" literature, tragedy in particular, deals with death, crime and punishment, the problem of evil, human loss, sorrow and discontent, the human condition, freedom of will, human weakness – the whole litany of human complaints. These are the subjects we find profound and difficult, and the literature that deals with them we find profound (and difficult) on that account.

But although this may be an adequate account of what music the layperson tends to perceive and describe as profound, and perhaps even productive of a sound psychological explanation of why he or she does tend to perceive music expressive of the serious emotions as more profound than music expressive of the frivolous and cheerful ones, it hardly provides a *justification* for doing so. For if, as I argue, music alone is a quasi-syntactical structure of sounds, with no sense or reference, that happens to have as some of its properties expressive ones, there seems absolutely no reason for believing that a structure with serious expressive properties is any more profound than a structure with frivolous or happy ones. Perhaps profundity arises as a result of a work's concerning, being about, serious emotions. But as, on my view, music expressive of serious emotions is not about them, that it is expressive of them is no grounds at all for ascribing profundity to it.

I have suggested that laypeople tend to ascribe profundity to music expressive of the serious emotions and that there is no real justification for so doing. A logical next step would be to inquire what kind of music the musically learned tend to describe as profound and whether their ascriptions of profundity are any more justifiable than the layperson's. I begin this inquiry with an example.

In his book on J. S. Bach, Albert Schweitzer gives the following description of the now blind composer's last days and of his last musical composition.

He appears to have passed his last days wholly in a darkened room. When he felt death drawing nigh, he dictated to Altnikol [his son-in-law] a chorale fantasia on the melody "Wenn wir in höchsten Nöten sind," but told him to head it with the beginning of the hymn "Vor deinen Thron

tret ich allhier," that is sung to the same melody. . . .

In the dark chamber, with the shades of death already falling round him, the master made this work, that is unique even among his creations. The contrapuntal art that it reveals is so perfect that no description can give any idea of it. Each segment of the melody is treated in a fugue, in which the inversion of the subject figures each time as the counter-subject. Moreover the flow of the parts is so easy that after the second line we are no longer conscious of the art, but are wholly enthralled by the spirit that finds voice in these G major harmonies. The tumult of the world no longer penetrated through the curtained windows. The harmonies of the spheres were already echoing round the dying master. So there is no sorrow in the music; the tranquil quavers move along on the other side of human passion; over the whole thing gleams the word "Transfiguration."[1]

I think it requires no argument to convince the reader that Schweitzer thought Bach's last composition "profound," although the word does not occur in the passage. And it seems obvious too that the profundity has something to do, to his mind, with the "contrapuntal art . . . so perfect that no description can give any idea of it," manifested, in particular, in the fact that we have "a fugue, in which the inversion of the subject figures each time as the counter-subject." What can we make of this?

Counterpoint itself, since time out of mind, has been associated in the thinking of musicians with the profound and the serious. And in the modern musical era, composers of instrumental music have continually turned and returned to "learned" counterpoint, always in the interest of "deepening" their style. Is the association of counterpoint with profundity merely a psychological association, like the layperson's association of profundity with the serious emotions? Or is there a real connection, as there is between profundity in literature and profound subjects? That is to say, is there some rational justification for thinking that contrapuntal music is profound in virtue of being contrapuntal? I do not mean to suggest that contrapuntal music might be the only profound music. But if we can discover just what it is about counterpoint that so frequently elicits the judgment "profound," perhaps – if indeed that judgment is rationally justified – we may be able to generalize from that to all profound music properly so-called. Let us see, then, where this strategy may lead.

The *New Harvard Dictionary of Music* defines "counterpoint" as "[t]he combination of two or more melodic lines," and continues: "its nature is indissolubly linked to the nature of melody. A melody must have coherence; its tones follow one another in a musically sensible way, and this is true for melodies combined contrapuntally no less than for those that are not."[2] The challenge of counterpoint, therefore, is, most simply stated, to juggle successfully a complex function of two variables: the number of melodies combined together, and the intrinsic, melodic interest of each of those melodies. An additional parameter that has become inseparable from the art of counterpoint is what might be termed the principle of "melodic economy," which is to say, the use of as little melodic material as possible, commensurate with intrinsic melodic interest. This principle expresses itself in all of the familiar contrapuntal artifices that composers have indulged in throughout the centuries: combining a melody with itself (canon or imitation), combining it with itself in larger or smaller note values (augmentation and diminution), combining it with its mirror image (inversion), combining it with itself, back to front (crab). I call it the principle of melodic economy because, in all of the above-mentioned relationships, the trick is to combine a melody not with a different melody but with itself or some recognizable version thereof. This is particularly plain in the Bach chorale prelude that Schweitzer so admires for its use of the theme's inversion for the countersubject each time. And Bach's feat here is all the more remarkable, all the more difficult, because the theme he is using, that is, the chorale melody "Wenn wir in höchsten Nöten sind," preexists his use of it, thus putting an added constraint on the composer, since he is not free to invent any theme he likes that can go with its own inversion but has to do it with a theme already given. That theme he can, indeed, meddle with to a certain extent, but not beyond the point where it would become unrecognizable.

In the modern era, in which the institution of instrumental music as we know it came into being and flourished, this juggling act has come to represent perhaps the preeminent symbol of musical craftsmanship and learning, venerable with age and almost mystical in significance for the musician. Certainly it has come to be associated with the notion of profundity. But what makes that associ-ation more than psychological or sociological? Certainly, that contrapuntal music is difficult to write and venerable with age does not alone speak for its profundity.

Let me return to Bach's last composition: the chorale prelude on "Wenn wir in höchsten Nöten sind." In it each phrase of the melody is treated as a fugue theme, with the counter-subject always an inversion of the subject. Because the chorale melody preexisted the composition of his work, it seems entirely appropriate to describe what Bach did as *discovering* that the chorale melody could be treated in this way.[3] That is to say, Bach discovered that (with suitable tinkering) each phrase of the chorale could be accompanied with its mirror inversion. The chorale was there. Bach discovered and revealed to us through his chorale prelude that it contained this "potential" (if you will) within. Bach's contrapuntal art here is the "art of the possible": an art of discovery, of revelation.

Now this, of course, is a special case. But might we not generalize from it to counterpoint as a whole? What we find so mysteriously fascinating about contrapuntal music, I want to suggest, is that it seems to us to reveal in some deep sense the very possibilities of musical sound itself. Whether we start with preexistent material, as Bach did in his chorale prelude, or start from scratch, by devising our own fugue subject and then putting it through its paces, it is tempting to describe the process here, more perhaps than in any other kind of music, as the "discovery of possibilities." The contrapuntist seems to us as an explorer: he or she discovers what sound can do, reveals the possibilities of a theme: with what it can be combined and how. If melody appears to us as the most basic music – a melody, after all, is a complete musical composition – then counterpoint, whose "nature is indissolubly linked to the nature of melody," is the ultimate musical art, for it pursues to the outer limits the ultimate possibilities of melody, in terms of melody's possible combinations with itself. If melody is for us the simplest complete entity in the musical universe, then the contrapuntist, not the "tunesmith," is the ultimate "melodist" and, in so being, the Columbus and the Newton of our musical universe.

It appears now that we really do have a leg up on the problem of musical profundity. Recall that the first condition for a work's being "profound" is that it be able to have a subject matter, that it be able to be about something. And recall, further, that music alone, being without subject matter, being about nothing, posed a seemingly insuperable problem in that regard. But now we have found that one kind of music, contrapuntal music, seems, perhaps more frequently and consistently than any other, to be thought "profound" by the musically learned. We have found too that here we are more strongly tempted than anywhere else in music to think of composition as a discovery of possibilities and music hence to be about these possibilities, about the possibilities of musical sound or, in words we have previously used, about music itself. We have, then, a subject matter for just that kind of music which is most frequently associated in the mind of the musician with the musically profound. And the rest follows directly.

Our second condition for the profundity of a literary work was that it be about a profound subject: a subject of abiding interest or importance to human beings. That condition can immediately be seen to be fulfilled by contrapuntal music, for it is a matter of observable fact that instrumental music is of abiding interest and importance to a significant number of human beings. And as the subject matter of counterpoint is the possibilities of musical sound – that is, music – it is a subject matter *eo ipso* of abiding interest and importance to the same significant number of human beings.

It is clear, of course, that we would not call all contrapuntal music "profound." But that coincides completely with our third condition for profundity, namely, that the profound subject matter be treated in an exemplary way, a way appropriate to the subject matter's profundity. We find Bach's counterpoint matchlessly worked out, that of his lesser contemporaries clumsily or pedantically or inadequately worked out. That is why we find Bach's works profound, his contemporaries' trivial. The subject matter of his contemporaries' fugues and canons is as profound as the subject matter of Bach's, for it is the same subject matter. But Bach was a match for it, and they were not.

To sum up, then, we find that contrapuntal music tends to be called "profound" by the musically learned and that there seems to be some rational justification for their doing so. The justification is that such music seems to fulfill the three requirements for the profundity of (for example) literary works. We are tempted to say that this music is about something, namely, the possibilities of musical sound itself; what it is about is of abiding interest and importance to many of us; and at least some of this music is matchlessly executed – executed with aesthetic distinction. The problem is that contrapuntal music is not the only kind of

music the musically learned tend to call profound. And if it is the only kind of music that there *seems* to be any rational justification for calling profound, I think that would cast grave doubt on whether there is in fact any real justification for it. I myself would rather give up the notion that any music is profound than accept the notion that only contrapuntal music is. Surely I find the fugues of Bach profound, but so also Brahms's symphonies. And it would seem to me naked prejudice or dogmatism to give up the latter judgment while holding on to the former. Here I think we need to insist on all or nothing. Perhaps we can have it all.

I suggested, when I began this discussion of counterpoint, that we might find in it that which elicits the judgment of profundity; that something, moreover, might be the very thing we find profound in other kinds of music as well. I think we are now in a position to determine what that something is and to generalize it for all music within the tradition with which we are concerned.

I said that in the modern era counterpoint became the preeminent symbol of musical *craftsmanship*. That, I think, is the key. Supreme musical craftsmanship is, I believe, the common denominator between counterpoint and other instances of musical profundity. Where music is great, and where its greatness is seen as the result, *significantly*, of its consummate craftsmanship, it elicits the judgment "profound" from the musically learned.

But the crucial point is that although counterpoint may be the ultimate musical craftsmanship, perhaps the one most admired by the learned, it is not the only one. Craftsmanship is a relative notion. Every major style or idiom will have a concept of craftsmanship defined relative to it. The classical style, for example – and an important example it is – provides another preeminent symbol of musical craftsmanship. The style that came of age, many would say, in Haydn's String Quartets, Op. 33, and reached various climaxes of perfection in the mature works of Haydn, Mozart, and Beethoven, provides us with another concept of craftsmanship in music, one devolving on its notably "syntactic" character.

What justification, though, is there for attributing profundity to musical craftsmanship? Well, it is the same justification, generalized, that we have in the special case of counterpoint. Craftsmanship in music is the exploration of musical possibilities within some given set of stylistic parameters. What I am suggesting here is that if anything tempts us to refer to music as being about itself, it is musical craftsmanship in general and, in particular, counterpoint, its most prestigious special case.

But how, it is fair to ask, do we know when musical craftsmanship is to be singled out as an element in a composition important enough to warrant our calling the music profound? The most obvious answer is that when the craftsmanship obtrudes, when it presses itself forcefully enough upon our musical attention, we then are motivated and (perhaps) licensed to judge the music importantly craftsmanlike and hence profound, at least to a degree. But this obvious answer must be resisted, for the obvious reason that, at least in one sense, the obtrusion of musical craftsmanship is not only not a sign of musical profundity but, quite to the contrary, a form of musical ineptitude (at least when measured against the highest standards of musical achievement). The musical craftsmanship and learning of Mendelssohn's youthful string symphonies is truly prodigious. Their counterpoint and classical techniques of symphonic exposition and development stick out all over the place. But, to appropriate Alfred Einstein's fine phrase, these youthful works still "smell of the lamp."[4] Their craftsmanship and learning have not yet been integrated into the composer's distinctive style. The same might be said of Haydn's String Quartets, Op. 20; marvelous and satisfying as the fugal finales are, they are not yet part of the classical style as are, for example, the fugal finales of Mozart's G-Major Quartet, K. 387, and "Jupiter" Symphony. Haydn had not yet achieved the integration and perfection of craftsmanship that Einstein called "that 'second naïveté' for which only a few masters in all the arts were predestined."[5] It is this same mastery of the craft, making the difficult seem transparent, which Schweitzer recognized in Bach's last composition, when he wrote that "the flow of the parts is so easy that after the second line we are no longer conscious of the art."

Thus to a certain extent, it is just when the craftsmanship does not obtrude that we want to call the musical work profound. The craftsmanship must be there, and it must demand our attention as a primary factor in our musical experience of the work. But craftsmanship must be supremely well brought off for us to call a work possessing it profound on that account, and supremely well brought off craftsmanship is just the kind that is so well integrated into the musical work – and into the composer's personal style – that "we are no longer conscious of the art. . . ."

Nor is this inconsistent with our intuitions about the profound in the literary arts. A novelist may deal with a profound subject matter and may, indeed, have original and important things to say about it. But if the subject matter, regardless of how profound and informative it might be, fails to be treated in a novelistically successful way, fails to become "literature," we will not see the work as a profound novel, although we may see it, perhaps, as a profound contribution to its subject. The dialogues of Plato are profound literary as well as philosophical works; those of Bishop Berkeley, for all of their philosophical profundity, fail to achieve literary profundity for just the reason cited above. The characters are wooden, and the philosophy sticks out, when the works are viewed as literature.

We are now in a position to ask whether this proffered analysis of profundity in music fulfills the conditions laid down previously for success. And on first reflection it does seem to do so. The first condition, it will be recalled, is that a work be about something. In the case of profound musical works, that condition is fulfilled, in the present analysis, in that such works are profound in virtue of their consummate craftsmanship, which, we are tempted to say, makes them "about" music itself: "about" the possibilities of musical sound.

The second enabling condition for profundity is that the work be about something profound, have a profound subject matter. And as musical sound appears to be, for many people, of abiding interest and supreme importance, that condition too seems to be satisfied by at least some musical works.

Finally, we said that the subject matter of a profound work must not only be profound but be treated in a way adequate to that profundity: must be treated in some artistically supreme and exemplary way. And that condition seems, indeed, to be embodied in Einstein's requirement that supreme musical craftsmanship not "smell of the lamp" but achieve the transparency of what he calls the "second naïveté" and in Schweitzer's observation that in such supreme musical craftsmanship as Bach's "we are no longer conscious of the art."

It would *seem*, then, that we do now have adequate rational justification for the ascription of profundity to some musical works, and that justification does seem to apply just where we want it to: to just those works which, in fact, musical experts and connoisseurs tend to call "profound" or its equivalent. But I underscore "seem" because the reader is likely to detect some sleight of hand here;

and I think there are at least two reasons to be somewhat uncomfortable with this rather facile exercise.

One problem rests with the second condition for profundity: that the subject matter of a profound work be a profound subject matter. For we slipped rather easily – too easily, as it turns out – from "of abiding interest and importance" to "profound." The second condition is too weak if it takes as a sufficient condition for something's being a profound subject merely that it is of very great interest, even of great concern, to a large number of people. It omits a vital normative component. For profundity to obtain, we seem to require that something be not just of great concern but *worthy* of great concern, in some suitably strong sense of "worthy" (to be discussed in a moment). I dare say far more people are vitally concerned with and interested in the subject of baseball than are in the subject of determinism and freedom of the will or the problem of evil. Yet with all due respect to the national pastime, it is a *pastime*; we would hardly take it to be a more profound subject than human freedom – or a subject with pretensions to profundity at all – just because it commands great and intense interest among us, indeed greater and more intense interest, overall, than the alternative subject.

Now I say a suitably strong sense of "worthy" because there are, it would seem, subjects of abiding interest and concern to human beings, and justifiably so, that do not merit or receive the judgment "profound." Certainly, to take an example, proper nutrition is a subject of abiding interest and concern to human beings, and surely it is worthy of such abiding interest and concern. Yet we would hardly want to say that nutrition is a profound subject matter or works about nutrition, no matter how well brought off, profound works.[6]

Why is the nature of the universe (say) a profound subject and nutrition not? Not because nutrition is of no importance to us: it *is* of importance and worthy of our concern. And not, I think, because it is of "practical" rather than "theoretical" significance. For I dare say there are environmental issues, obviously "practical," that we would surely want to call "profound." I would think those practical issues which we call profound are just those which go to the moral heart of the human condition. A life without "Nature" in something like the form we now know it in does not measure up to our moral ideal of the good life for human beings; and environmental issues addressing that

concern are, therefore, "profound." A life without proper vitamin supplements is not on that account morally bankrupt, desirable as proper nutrition might be; and if the study of nutrition goes no further – in particular, does not touch the vital center of our moral and metaphysical concerns – it surely is worthy of interest and concern but not profoundly so.

We have a pretty good idea about why such questions as freedom of the will and the problem of evil are of great concern to us. Knowing why makes clear to us why we feel justified in thinking of these as profound subjects of interest, whereas the collection and contemplation of baseball cards, no matter how intense and widespread the interest, would fail to be seen as anything but trivial pursuits. The problem is that we – at least *I* – have no clear idea at all about why serious, well-educated, adult human beings should find pure musical sound of *such* abiding interest that we are moved to call the subject "profound." And without such understanding, I cannot see that we have any real rational justification for doing so. That is to say, I cannot see that we have, to paraphrase Bentham, any reason for thinking that music is better than pushpin or more worthy of our vital and enduring interest. I believe that it is, and my belief is intense, but the strength of my belief hardly counts as an argument.

Furthermore, it is not altogether clear whether the general strategy of construing musical sound as the subject of profound musical works is free of a vicious circularity?[7] For, it might be argued, the question whether musical sound is a profound subject matter cannot be answered without first answering the question whether there are any profound musical works. If musical sound just is the class of musical works, then for it to be a profound subject matter it must, one might insist, contain at least some profound musical works. Thus there being some profound musical works would be a necessary condition for musical sounds being a profound subject matter, and the circle would be closed. There are profound musical works only if musical sound is a profound subject matter; musical sound is a profound subject matter only if there are profound musical works.

The question of circularity, then, turns on the question whether it makes sense to think of musical sound as a profound subject matter independently of its containing profound musical works. And an answer, one way or the other, seems to me to be difficult to make out. If one can prise apart the question whether musical sound is a profound subject matter from the question whether there are profound musical works, then the project of understanding profound musical works as being profound (in part) in virtue of having a profound subject matter (namely, musical sound itself), although in an unsatisfactory state, may be so merely because it is temporarily incomplete, awaiting assurance that it fulfills the strengthened normative requirement of profundity. If one cannot so prise them apart, then the project is hopelessly compromised by the fatal logical flaw of circularity.

Which of these alternatives is correct I do not presently know. But even if it is the more favorable one, I must end here on a note of mystery and puzzlement. Those of us who cultivate a taste for the instrumental music of the West seem to find certain examples of it so enormously compelling and of such enduring interest that "profound" forces itself upon us as the only (and fully) appropriate term to describe them. Yet there seems to be no rational justification for our doing so. For even if the works we describe as profound have a subject matter, and that is debatable, the only subject matter they can plausibly be thought to have, namely, musical sound itself, does not bear, at least on the face of it, any obvious mark of profundity, as do such subject matters as freedom of the will or the problem of evil, love and marriage or crime and punishment, and so forth: the subjects of "profound" literary works.

Now in saying that I have so far failed to find any rational justification for calling musical works profound, I do not want to be misunderstood as denying that I have rational grounds for thinking certain musical works great works of art. I am not using the word "profound" as synonymous with the word "great" or any other word like it. I think all but not only profound musical works are great musical works. And I think we do have rational grounds for thinking some musical works great and some greater than others. These are just the usual grounds for evaluations that abound in the music-critical literature. But I take the word "profound" as not simply a portmanteau evaluative epithet. I have taken it, when applied to music, as having the same implications as it would have when applied to literature or philosophy. In other words, I have taken it seriously. And in spite of the fact that there seems to me to be substantial agreement among enthusiasts about which musical works deserve the description "profound," I fail to see any rational justification for their deserving it. Yet, for certain works, I can find no other word as appropriate. Yes: the *Well-Tempered Clavier* and the late Beethoven quartets are great works of art. So also are Mozart's divertimenti for winds. But the former are something else, they are profound, and there's an end on it.

I find myself at present, then, unable to refrain from thinking that some musical works are profound yet unable, as well, to provide any rational grounds for my thinking it. So if you ask me, now, what my justification is for thinking the *Well-Tempered Clavier* profound, the only response that comes readily to mind is that notorious misquotation: "Play it again, Sam."

Notes

1   Albert Schweitzer, *J. S. Bach*, trans. Ernest Newman (New York, 1950), I:223–224.
2   Mark De Voto, "Counterpoint," *The New Harvard Dictionary of Music*, ed. Don Randel (Cambridge, Mass., 1986), p. 205.
3   In suggesting the possibility of musical composition as discovery, I spin out a suggestion that I have made in a rather different context twice before: "Platonism in Music: A Kind of Defense," *Grazer Philosophische Studien* 19 (1983), and "Platonism in Music: Another Kind of Defense," *American Philosophical Quarterly* 24 (1987).
4   Alfred Einstein, *Mozart: His Character, His Work* (New York, 1951), p. 155.
5   Ibid., p. 156.
6   I owe this objection, as well as the accompanying example, to Christopher Peacocke.
7   I am grateful to Christopher Peacocke and Kendall Walton for pressing me on this point.

40

The Expression and Arousal of Emotion in Music

Jenefer M. Robinson

I

This essay is about the relation between the expression and the arousal of emotion by music. I am assuming that music frequently *expresses* emotional qualities and qualities of human personality such as sadness, nobility, aggressiveness, tenderness, and serenity. I am also assuming that music frequently *affects* us emotionally: it evokes or arouses emotions in us. My question is whether there is any connection between these two facts, whether, in particular, music ever expresses emotion *by virtue of* arousing emotion. Of course, what it means to say that music expresses emotion is a contentious issue and I shall not be directly addressing it here, although what I say will have implications for any theory of musical expression. Nor will I be examining all the possible contexts in which music can be said to arouse emotion. My focus in this essay will be narrower. The question I shall try to answer is this: Are the grounds on which we attribute the expression of emotion to music ever to be identified with the arousal of that same emotion in listeners?

II

According to some theories of musical expression, the grounds on which we attribute expressive qualities to music have nothing to do with the arousal

Jenefer M. Robinson, "The Expression and Arousal of Emotion in Music," *Journal of Aesthetics and Art Criticism*, 52: 1 (Winter 1994), pp. 13–22. Reprinted by permission of Blackwell Publishing Ltd.

of emotion in the audience. According to Peter Kivy's account in *The Corded Shell*, a musical element such as a melody, a rhythm, or a chord expresses a feeling not because it arouses that feeling in anyone but for two quite different reasons. (1) It has the same "contour" as expressive human behavior of some kind and thus is "heard as expressive of something or other because heard as appropriate to the expression of something or other" (for example, the "weeping" figure of grief in Arianna's lament from Monteverdi's *Arianna*) or it contributes in a particular context to the forming of such an expressive contour (as the diminished triad in a suitable context can contribute to a *restless* quality in the music, although all by itself it does not express anything). (2) The musical element is expressive by virtue of some custom or convention, which originated in connection with some expressive contour. The minor triad, for example, is "sad" by convention, although it may have started life as part of some expressive contour.[1]

There are many examples of musical expression for which Kivy's argument is convincing. Thus it does seem to be true that Arianna's lament mirrors the passionate speaking voice expressing grief, that Schubert's "Gretchen am Spinnrad" mirrors Gretchen's monotonous, leaden gestures at the spinning wheel and her correspondingly dejected, leaden heart, and that the "Pleni sunt coeli" from Bach's B Minor Mass maps "bodily motion and gesture . . . of tremendous expansiveness, vigor, violent motion," thus mirroring the exuberance of "'leaping' joy."[2] At the same time, as Renée Cox, among others, has pointed out,[3] virtually all the musical examples in Kivy's book are examples of music with a text, and it is relatively uncontroversial that a text can specify a particular feeling or object which is characterized by the music. Moreover, when we look closely at Kivy's examples of particular emotions said to be expressed by music we find mainly varieties of joy, sorrow, and restlessness. The vast majority of musical examples in *The Corded Shell* can be characterized as expressions of either positive or negative emotion (joy or sorrow) of various sorts.[4] Thus although what Kivy says seems to be true as far as it goes, it does not go very far, and leaves a great deal of expressiveness in music unexplained.

Kivy holds that music can express particular emotional states such as sorrow and joy, restlessness and serenity. Susanne Langer, while agreeing that emotional qualities are to be found in the *music*, rather than in the *listener*, follows Hanslick in arguing that since only the dynamic qualities of anything (including emotional states) can be expressed by music, no particular emotions can be expressed by music, but only the felt quality of our emotional life and its dynamic development:

[There] are certain aspects of the so-called "inner life" – physical or mental – which have formal properties similar to those of music – patterns of motion and rest, of tension and release, of agreement and disagreement, preparation, fulfillment, excitation, sudden change, etc.[5]

[Music] reveals the rationale of feelings, the rhythm and pattern of their rise and decline and intertwining, to our minds . . . .[6]

In contrast to Kivy's view that the words of a text supply the "fine shadings" to otherwise only grossly expressive musical meanings, Langer holds that musical meanings are inherently rich and significant yet cannot be linked to any particular words. Langer's theory emphasizes the development of structures of feeling throughout a lengthy piece of music, which Kivy ignores, but she in turn ignores the expression of particular emotional qualities which Kivy emphasizes. Both theorists have insightful things to say about musical expression but neither tells the whole story.

III

A very different view of musical expression is presented by Kendall Walton in a paper called "What

is Abstract About the Art of Music?" Walton proposes that one important way in which music is expressive is by virtue of the fact that in listening to music we imagine ourselves introspecting, being aware of, our own feelings. As he puts it, we imagine "of our actual introspective awareness of auditory sensations" that "it is an experience of being aware of our states of mind."[7] Thus the expressiveness of music has to do with its power to *evoke* certain imaginative emotional experiences. Moreover, Walton says that if this is right, then:

music probably can be said to "portray particulars" in the sense that figurative paintings do, rather than simply properties or concepts. Presumably the listener imagines experiencing and identifying *particular* stabs of pain, *particular* feelings of ecstasy, *particular* sensations of well-being, etc., as in viewing a painting one imagines seeing particular things.[8]

However, whereas one perceives the psychological states of other people, as in figurative paintings, one "introspects one's *own* psychological states."[9]

There are at least two problems I see with Walton's account. (1) First, suppose someone denies that this is what she does when listening to expressive music; we should be able to *explain* to her why this is what she should be doing. What reason is there why we should imagine our awareness of auditory sensations – experienced sequences of musical tones – to be an experience of our feelings and other inner states? True, there are similarities between the two: the experience of auditory sensations is an introspectible state, and so is awareness of our feelings. True, part of what we are aware of in these auditory sensations is, as Langer points out, their ebb and flow, and our feelings too have ebb and flow. But beyond these points of resemblance there seems to be little explanation *why* we should be inclined to imagine our awareness of musical sounds to be an awareness of our feelings. Imagination requires some guidance if it is not to be merely free association: I can imagine the tree at the end of the garden to be a witch because it has a witch-like appearance, but it is unclear what it would mean for me to imagine the snowdrop at my feet to be a witch if there is nothing about the snowdrop to set off my imagination. Similarly, in order for me to imagine my awareness of musical sounds to be awareness of my feelings, something in the musical sounds must guide my imagination. However, if the only points of resemblance between feelings and sounds is introspectibility and ebb and flow, then I would suggest that this is insufficient to ground an imaginative identification between the two. There are, moreover, striking *differences* between the two which would seem to preclude any such imaginative identification. In particular, whereas our feelings clearly rise up inside us (as we say), musical sounds as clearly rise up at a distance from us: even when listening to music over good earphones – when the music is experienced with peculiar immediacy – we still experience the auditory sensations as coming from an external source, such as trombones and the like. That is why although we can perhaps imagine these sounds as feelings welling up inside the *composer*, or perhaps in some *character* described by the music, it is not obvious to me that we can imagine them as feelings welling up inside ourselves.

(2)   There is a second problem related to this one. I am willing to grant that there are indeed movements in music which it is appropriate to call "stabbing" or "surging." According to Walton, however, the music induces me to imagine myself feeling a particular ecstatic surge or stab of pain. He says that the music *portrays* these particulars (it picks them out or refers to them). A number of questions need to be distinguished here. (1) Can the stab be identified as a stab of feeling rather than the stab of a dagger or some other kind of stab? (2) If the stab is a stab of feeling, can it be identified as a stab of pain rather than some other feeling such as excitement or jealousy? (3) If the stab is indeed a stab of pain, can it be identified as a stab of pain which I imagine myself experiencing rather than a stab of pain attributed to someone else, such as Othello or the composer? If the music *portrays* my imagined stab of pain, as Walton suggests, then the music must be able to distinguish my imagined stab of pain from all these other possible alternatives. Can music do this? Can music portray this particular stab of pain and no other?

If the music were accompanied by an appropriate verbal text, then perhaps it could. As we listen to the music we hear in it particular tones, rhythms, harmonic modulations, phrases, melodies, counterpoint sections, etc., etc. We might also hear particular movements that we characterize as "stabbing" or "surging." Given a particular accompanying text, we might then be able to identify the stabbing as the stabbing of Mercutio rather than a stab of pain. With a different text, we might be able

to identify the stabbing as Othello's stabbing pains of jealousy rather than his stabbing pains of remorse. And so on. However, in the absence of a text, Walton suggests no good reasons for identifying the stabbing in the music (1) with a stab of feeling (rather than some other kind of stab), (2) with a stab of pain (rather than some other kind of feeling), or (3) with my imagined stab of pain (rather than yours or Othello's real or imagined pain). Walton claims earlier in his paper that musical characterization is inherently *general*. It would seem to follow that without the specification of a particular context we cannot specify that the stab is even a stab of emotion, let alone the stab of a particular emotion, let alone an *imagined* stab of *my* particular emotion. However, Walton gives us no guidance as to how a particular context could be specified. In short, although we can hear a stabbing movement in a piece of music, Walton does not show us how to tell from the music alone – without any accompanying text – what, if any, particular stabbing is occurring.

IV

Although Walton's theory does not identify musical expression with the straightforward arousal of feelings, he does try to explain expression in terms of the arousal of *imaginary* feelings. I am not actually feeling a stab of pain as I listen to the stabbing music; I am *imagining* experiencing a stab of pain, so it would seem that the pain is an imaginary feeling. In his paper "Music and Negative Emotions," Jerrold Levinson makes a similar point. Levinson's paper deals with the problem of why people enjoy music when it evokes negative emotions such as sadness in them. While the paper does not develop a theory of musical expression, it does make certain assumptions about what often happens when people listen to music which we would characterize as sad. In particular, he assumes that it is a normal response for people to have a sadness-reaction to music.

When a person has a "deep emotional response" to music, this is "generally in virtue of the *recognition* of emotions expressed in music," but recognition then leads to a kind of empathic identification: we "end up feeling as, in imagination, the music does."[10] Such empathic emotional responses to music consist in "something very like experience of the emotion expressed in the music"[11] but not *exactly* like it. In both cases the physiological and affective components of emotion are present and in both cases there is cognitive content, but the "empathic" response lacks *determinate* cognitive content:

> When one hears sad music, begins to feel sad, and imagines that one is actually sad, one must, according to the logic of the concept, be imagining that there is an object for one's sadness and that one maintains certain evaluative beliefs (or attitudes) regarding it. The point, though, is that this latter imagining generally remains indeterminate.[12]

I feel sad but my sadness has no determinate object; it is directed only to "some featureless object posited vaguely by my imagination."[13] Levinson illustrates his view with various kinds of negative emotion: "intense grief, unrequited passion, sobbing melancholy, tragic resolve, and angry despair."[14] Suppose, for example, that the music evokes in me an empathic response of unrequited passion. On Levinson's view, this means that I recognize unrequited passion in the music, I imagine that I am experiencing unrequited passion, and I actually experience the physiological and affective components of unrequited passion. My imagined unrequited passion has a cognitive content which is "etiolated by comparison to that of real-life emotion",[15] however, since I am not really suffering the pangs of unrequited passion, and in particular there is no special person for whom I am languishing.

I am sympathetic to some of Levinson's assumptions: I think he is right to stress that the detection of emotional qualities in music has something to do with the arousal of emotion by music, and I think he is right also to stress the role of the imagination in the appreciation of emotional qualities in music. However, the theory as it stands will not do. First of all, it is far from clear that every emotional state has identifiable physiological and affective components. For example, real-life unrequited passion might on different occasions be accompanied by a great variety of inner feelings (love, grief, longing, jealousy, wretchedness, despair, self-contempt, etc., etc.). For another thing, the particular feelings I experience on a given occasion of unrequited passion may be just the same as I have felt on occasions of angry despair or intense grief. The truth of the matter is that there may be very little difference between the affective and physiological

components of very different emotions: I may feel the same mixture of grief and rage when I am jealous or when I am grieving (without jealousy); I may have very similar feelings whether angrily despairing, tragically resolving, or suffering from the pangs of unrequited passion. The difference between these emotions lies not so much in their affective and physiological components as in their cognitive content. The chief difference between unrequited passion, tragic resolve, and angry despair is how I view or conceive of the situation.

But now we come to a second set of difficulties. Levinson argues that I can recognize unrequited passion (say) in the "emotion-laden gestures embodied in musical movement"[16] and by virtue of this recognition respond empathically with feelings of unrequited passion of my own, since I identify with the music or perhaps "with the person whom we imagine owns the emotions or emotional gestures we hear in the music."[17] However, he fails to tell us how we detect or empathically feel the unrequited passion in the music. Although we all have some idea of what *sad* music is like, I suggest that it is much less clear what a piece of music is like in which we can recognize, and hence empathize with, unrequited passion (always assuming, of course, that there is no accompanying verbal text to help us out). If I am right and there are no distinctive affective or physiological components of unrequited passion, then the obvious way to clarify the nature of music in which we can detect unrequited passion would be to specify its cognitive content. Now, Levinson claims that the cognitive content of an emotional response to music is normally "etiolated." This could mean simply that my imagined feelings of unrequited passion are not directed to any particular individual. While it is a little odd to say that one can feel unrequited passion for someone I know not whom, we can perhaps make sense of this suggestion since on Levinson's view the unrequited passion I feel empathically belongs to the music itself or to someone whom we imagine feels unrequited passion, so that we merely empathize with this imagined person's unrequited passion.

Even if we grant, however, that there need be no specific object for the unrequited passion I detect in the music and empathize with, it would seem that there must be some identifiable cognitive content, however etiolated, which is detectable in the music in order to justify the attribution of this particular emotion. I would suggest that if my response is to count as a response of unrequited passion rather than some other emotion, then I must imagine that there is someone whom I care about deeply, that this person does not care deeply about me, and that I care deeply that this person does not care deeply about me (or something of this sort). It is a serious problem for Levinson's account that he does not tell us how such conceptions can be embodied in music and hence how we can either recognize or empathize with the corresponding emotion. We find the same problem with tragic resolve and angry despair: we cannot clearly distinguish these emotional responses by their affective and physiological components alone, but only by their cognitive content. However, Levinson gives us no clue as to how their cognitive content can be recognized in or induced by music.

In a later paper, "Hope in *The Hebrides*," Levinson claims that perhaps it is possible for music to express "higher" emotional states, and that in addition to the affective and physiological components of an emotion, music might even be able to convey part, at least, of its cognitive content. He points out that emotions are normally intentional but that music can convey a general "sense of intentionality (aboutness)."[18] He also notes that just as ordinary extra-musical emotions are often individuated by their context of occurrence, it might perhaps be the case that *musical* context can play a similar role for emotions in music. When he illustrates his thesis by reference to the emotional state of hope, which he claims to be able to distinguish in Mendelssohn's *Hebrides* overture, he remarks that "perhaps some of the pure conceptual content of hope – its favorable assessment of future in relation to present"[19] – can be suggested by the position of the hopeful passage in its musical context. Levinson does not develop this idea very far, however, and what he does say along these lines is very tentative. Certainly he gives us no clue as to how the three marks of unrequited passion that I distinguished above could be adequately conveyed by music.[20]

V

Recently Levinson's view has been criticized by Peter Kivy on the grounds that the expression of emotion in music is entirely independent of the arousal of that emotion. Kivy argues that to have one's emotions aroused by a piece of music – in particular, to be moved by a piece of music – is quite distinct from perceiving a particular emo-

tional quality in that piece. Music that is sad or expresses sadness is music with a sad expressive contour or music that is sad by convention, not music that arouses or evokes sadness. Levinson argues that a "deep emotional response" to sad music consists in the arousal of a kind of imaginative but cognitively truncated sadness. Kivy rightly attacks this claim, arguing on the one hand that sad music may or may not make me feel anything, depending on how great the music is (the "yards and yards of mournful music" written by Telemann[21] may fail to make me feel anything much at all), and on the other hand that there are important emotions aroused by music which are full-blown, ordinary, real-life emotions, not "truncated" or "imaginary" in any sense. He illustrates his point by reference to a performance of Josquin's "Ave verum virginitas" which, he says, *moves* him deeply.

When listening to the "Ave verum virginitas" I may simply be moved by "the sheer beauty of the sound as it unfolds in its ebb and flow."[22] If my sophistication increases, however, I may also be moved by "the incomparable beauty and craftsmanship of Josquin's counterpoint"[23] and by the fact that despite its seeming effortlessness, the music is written in a particularly difficult canonic form, "a canon at the fifth, with the voices only one beat apart."[24] This, then, is the cognitive component of the emotion aroused by the music, my being moved by the music. It is not a truncated emotion in any way. It is a genuine emotional experience, arising out of my perception of the music and its qualities. Furthermore, this emotion might be directed at emotional, expressive qualities in the music, such as sadness, but it does not follow that the emotion *aroused* by the music is the emotion *detected in* the music. Part of what I may be moved by in a piece of music may be its sadness, but I can be moved by joyful, by energetic, and by serene music just as well, as well as by music which does not have any marked emotional character. The expressive qualities, if any, which I detect in the music are entirely independent of the emotions I feel as I listen to the music.

Now, Kivy is certainly right to claim that when I am moved by a piece of music, my emotion may be independent of the emotional qualities, if any, that the music happens to have. When I appreciate a piece of music I may indeed be moved in the way Kivy describes. On the other hand, Kivy has not succeeded in showing that the expression of emotion by a piece of music is always and entirely unconnected to the arousal of emotion. Kivy makes this claim based on an analysis of just one emotion, "being moved," and it may well be true that we can be equally moved by music with different emotional qualities, as well as by music which has no marked emotional qualities. However, I believe that music arouses other feelings as well and that some of these may indeed be connected to the expressive qualities that music has. Furthermore, I think Kivy is wrong to insist that *all* the feelings aroused by music have to have a complex cognitive component as in his example from Josquin. It may be true that being moved by music involves complex evaluative judgments, but being moved is not the only emotional or feeling response which music can arouse.

Let me summarize the results of my discussion so far. Walton argues that expressive music evokes the imaginative experience of the emotion expressed: more precisely, music expressive of sadness, say, induces the listener to imagine herself experiencing sad feelings. Levinson similarly claims that sad music has the power to evoke a kind of truncated sadness-response: the listener feels certain symptoms of sadness, has an "indeterminate" idea that there is something or other to be sad about and imagines that she in fact feels sad. Both writers find a connection between the presence of an emotional quality in music and the arousal of that emotion in the listener's imagination. I have urged, however, that neither Walton nor Levinson has shown *how* complex feelings such as unrequited passion, stabs of pain, or even sadness can be aroused by music whether in fact or in imagination. Furthermore, Kivy is clearly right to hold that to have a deep emotional response to music is not necessarily to mirror the feelings that the music expresses.

At the same time, however, I believe that Walton and Levinson are right to stress the connection between the expression and the arousal of emotion in music, and that Kivy is quite wrong to think that his analysis of the one emotion "being moved" demonstrates that no such connection exists. In what remains of this paper I will try to sketch a more adequate account of what this connection really is.

VI

None of the writers I have discussed in this essay has focused on the way in which music can *directly* affect our feelings. For both Walton and Levinson the arousal of feeling is imaginative and it relies on a good deal of cognitive activity on the part of the listener. For Kivy the emotion of being moved is a real emotion, not an imagined one, but it too relies on cognitive activity, such as recognizing the clever part-writing, etc. However, some music has the power to affect our feelings without much, if any cognitive mediation. In particular, music can induce physiological changes and a certain quality of inner feeling (what Levinson calls respectively the "phenomenological" and "sensational" aspects of the "affective" component in emotion).[25] Music can make me feel tense or relaxed; it can disturb, unsettle, and startle me; it can calm me down or excite me; it can get me tapping my foot, singing along, or dancing; it can maybe lift my spirits and mellow me out.

Emotions vary in degree – and perhaps in kind – of cognitive content. At one end of the scale there is the startle response, which is an innate response, found in human neonates as well as throughout the phylogenetic scale. At the other end of the scale there is unrequited passion which, by contrast, is found only in humans with their highly developed cultural norms. What I want to suggest is that in addition to the sophisticated emotions of appreciation, which Kivy identifies as "being moved" by certain perceived aspects of the music, there are more primitive emotions aroused by music, perhaps requiring less developed cognitive mediation. There are, after all, moments in music which make us jump or startle us. Similarly, the perception of certain rhythms may be enough – without any further cognitive mediation – to evoke tension or relaxation, excitement or calm. If the melodic and harmonic elements in a piece of music affect our emotions, this would seem to require familiarity with the stylistic norms of the piece, but no further cognitions need be required in order for us to feel soothed, unsettled, surprised, or excited by developments in the music. Certainly we need not notice that we are listening to a canon at the fifth in order for that canon to soothe us.

We have seen that to feel unrequited passion necessarily involves a certain fairly complicated conception of one's situation. By contrast, to feel disturbed or calm does not require having a conception of one's situation in this way. Music can make me feel disturbed or calm just by perceiving it (listening to it). The feeling is a result of a perception and to this extent it has "cognitive content," but it is not the full-blown cognitive content required for tragic resolve, angry despair or unrequited passion. The sense of relaxation we feel at the end of "Tristan und Isolde," for example, is the result of the long-awaited resolution, after over four hours of constant modulation without resolution. The feeling is the result of a perception, but we may not even be aware why we feel as we do: the effect of the constantly shifting harmonic pattern affects us "directly" without conscious cognitive mediation (except, of course, what is required by our understanding of Wagner's style). There is some psychological evidence (from Berlyne and others) that people seek high levels of arousal in order to have them drop afterwards: "excitement and complex, conflicting information are sought because of the 'arousal jag.'"[26] The effect of the final Tristan chord may be partly accounted for in these terms.

Now, the feelings evoked "directly" by music explain some of the cases of musical expressiveness that the contour theory finds hard to deal with. Music that disturbs and unsettles us is disturbing, unsettling music. Modulations that surprise us are surprising. Melodies that soothe us are soothing. Furthermore, unexpected harmonic shifts excite us and are exciting; protracted stay in a harmonic area distant from the home key makes us uneasy and produces uneasy music; the return to the home key after a protracted stay in a distant harmonic area relaxes the tension in us and produces relaxing music. And so on. In short, as against Kivy's position, it seems to me that the expression of a feeling by music can sometimes be explained straightforwardly in terms of the arousal of that feeling. However, the feelings aroused "directly" by music are not stabs of pain or feelings of unrequited passion, but more "primitive" feelings of tension, relaxation, surprise, and so on. These feelings do, therefore, in a sense have an "etiolated" cognitive content, in the way that Levinson specifies in "Music and Negative Emotions," but it is not an etiolated, imaginary version of an emotion which normally has a complex cognitive content (such as unrequited passion), but rather a feeling such as surprise, which by its nature just has – or can have – a relatively simple cognitive content.

VII

Even more interesting, however, is the way in which the simple feelings "directly" aroused by music can contribute to the imaginative expression of more complex emotions such as those discussed

by Levinson. When we listen to a piece of music in a relatively familiar style, a succession of feelings is aroused in us: in a pattern typical of Classical sonata form, we may first be made to feel relaxed, then jolted into uncertainty, then made to feel uneasy for a prolonged period before experiencing relief and final release of tension. Now, something that most philosophical theorists of musical expression have either ignored or underemphasized is the fact that the musical expression of complex emotions is not a function of a few isolated measures here and there, as in Kivy's examples in *The Corded Shell*; rather it is very often a function of the large-scale formal structures of the piece as a whole.[27] We cannot understand the expression of complex emotions in music apart from the continuous development of the music itself. None of the philosophical writers I have discussed has fully appreciated this point. Langer has indeed stressed the importance of large-scale movements of ebbing and flowing, tension and relaxation in musical expression, but she denies that any particular emotions can thereby be expressed. Levinson suggests at times that we need to look at the total musical context before we can say what particular emotions are being expressed, but he does not explore this idea very far. In order to explain how particular cognitively complex emotions can be expressed musically, we need to look at the overall structure of a piece and at the feelings aroused by the piece as it develops in time.

In his celebrated book, *Emotion and Meaning in Music*, Leonard Meyer showed how the formal structure of works in the Classical and Romantic styles could be analyzed in terms of the emotional *responses* of the practiced listener: his was a kind of "Reader-Response" or rather "Listener-Response" theory of musical structure.[28] In order to understand a piece of music, on this view, the listener has to have her feelings aroused in a certain way. If we are experienced in the style of the piece, then we have certain expectations about the way the music will develop; in a meaningful piece of music these expectations will be either frustrated or satisfied in unexpected ways. As we listen new expectations are constantly being aroused and we are just as constantly being *surprised* by novel developments, *relieved* by delayed resolutions, made *tense* by the delays, etc., etc. In short, understanding musical structure, according to Meyer, is not just a matter of detached analysis; rather, it is impossible without the arousal of feeling in the listener.

Now, just as the formal structure of a piece of music can be understood in terms of the arousal of such feelings as uncertainty, uneasiness, relaxation, tension, relief, etc., so too can we understand the expressiveness of that piece of music in terms of the arousal of those and similar feelings. After all, as Anthony Newcomb has put it: "Formal and expressive interpretations are in fact two complementary ways of understanding the same phenomena."[29] Emotional expressiveness in music frequently corresponds to or mirrors its formal structure. The "direct" arousal of cognitively "simple" emotions such as being made surprised, disturbed, satisfied, relaxed, etc. is a clue not only to the formal structure of a musical piece, as Meyer showed, but also to its structure of emotional expressiveness. If a piece of music is heard as successively disturbing and reassuring, or as meandering uncertainly before moving forward confidently, or as full of obstacles which are with difficulty overcome, this is at least in part because of the way the music makes us feel. Disturbing passages disturb us; reassuring ones reassure. Passages that meander uncertainly make us feel uneasy: it is not clear where the music is going. Passages that move forward confidently make us feel satisfied: we know what is happening and seem to be able to predict what will happen next. Passages that are full of obstacles make us feel tense and when the obstacles are overcome, we feel relieved. It is important to notice that the feeling *expressed* is not always the feeling *aroused*: an uncertain, diffident passage may make me uneasy; a confident passage may make me feel reassured or relaxed.[30]

Now, of course we are still a long way from showing how unrequited passion can be expressed by a piece of music, but we can perhaps begin to see how the development of a complex piece of music can mirror the development of a complex emotional experience, and how we can become aware of both the formal development and the corresponding emotional development by means of the relatively "simple" feelings that are *aroused* in the listener as she follows that development. As I listen to a piece which expresses serenity tinged with doubt, I myself do not have to feel serenity tinged with doubt, but the feelings I do experience, such as relaxation or reassurance, interspersed with uneasiness, alert me to the nature of the overall emotional expressiveness in the piece of music as a whole. Consider, for example, a piece of music in sonata form in which the two chief themes in their

initial formulation are respectively lively and ponderous (we can suppose that the contour theory accounts for these characterizations). Now, suppose that the initially lively theme (in the major) gets gradually but relentlessly overwhelmed by the ponderous (minor) theme in such a way that the first theme is never allowed to return to its initial lively formulation but gets increasingly distorted, becomes darker and is finally heard in a truncated form in the same minor key as the ponderous theme. Such music might well make me feel increasingly nervous and tense, even disturbed, as it develops. On the view I am suggesting, the emotional experience aroused by the music is essential to the detection of the emotional expressiveness in the music itself. At the same time, the emotions aroused in me are not the emotions expressed by the music. *I* feel nervous, tense, and disturbed; the *music* expresses cheerful confidence turned to despair, or something of this sort.[31] If this account is correct, then it shows that Kivy is wrong to suppose that expressiveness in music is just a matter of contour and convention, even if some expressive passages in music can be explained in such terms.[32] In my example, it is not enough to spot the respective lively and ponderous contours of the initial statements of the two themes; the expressiveness of the piece as a whole can only be grasped if the listener's feelings are aroused in such a way that they provide a clue to both the formal and the expressive structure of the piece as it develops through time.

VIII

We can now see that Levinson and Walton are right to insist on a connection between the arousal and expression of emotion in music. However, neither of them has succeeded in showing how music can actually arouse, even in imagination, the complex emotional states that music sometimes expresses. In my example, I did not myself have to feel cheerful confidence turning to despair in order to detect that emotion in the music. The feelings I felt, which were evoked "directly" by the music, were less cognitively complicated, such as unease, tension, and disturbance. At the same time, we can see why Levinson is tempted to say that we empathize imaginatively with the feelings expressed by the music, for in order to detect these feelings in the music I am myself emotionally involved in listening to the music: I feel genuine feelings of unease, disturbance, and so on. Moreover, if I imagine that the themes are themselves characters in a kind of musical drama, then perhaps I can empathize with the fate of the lively theme, feeling sorrow and pity for it as I might for a character in a drama, and maybe I can even feel anger and frustration at the ponderous theme.[33]

Walton wants to say that I imagine of my introspective awareness of auditory sensations that they are an experience of particular states of my own psyche, such as particular stabs of pain. Again we can see why Walton is tempted by this idea, since on the one hand the music does arouse feelings in me, although not usually the ones expressed, and on the other hand I may perhaps imagine that the feelings expressed by the music do belong to me. However, I think this view is more problematic than Levinson's. In my example, must I imagine of both themes that they are an experience of my own emotions? In this case my imagination must take both sides in the conflict as it were. Why cannot I identify entirely with the suffering lively theme, or even – gloatingly – entirely with the powerfully

insistent ponderous theme? Why, more fundamentally, should I imagine these musical events as belonging to my own psyche at all? When I watch a performance of *King Lear* I do not imagine the drama to be taking place inside my own head; it seems to me that the same is just as true of the *King Lear* overture.

In this essay I have tried to confine my attention to the question of how the expression of emotion by music is related to the arousal of emotion in the listener. Obviously I have left many questions unanswered. In particular, I have given only a skeletal account of how music can express cognitively complex emotions such as the "cheerful confidence turning to despair" of my example. I have not attempted to show how cognitive content can get expressed by music nor whether particular emotions such as unrequited passion can be so expressed. What I *have* tried to do, however, is to indicate how such analyses might proceed. And the point I have urged above all is that any such analysis must begin with the emotions that are aroused by the music in the listener.

Notes

1 Peter Kivy, *The Corded Shell* (Princeton: Princeton University Press, 1980), p. 83.

2 Kivy, *The Corded Shell*, p. 54.

3 Renée Cox, "Varieties of Musical Expressionism," in George Dickie, et al., eds., *Aesthetics: A Critical Anthology*, 2nd ed. (New York: St. Martin's, 1989), pp. 614–625.

4 Anthony Newcomb has made this point effectively in "Sound and Feeling," *Critical Inquiry* 10 (1984): 614–643.

5 Susanne Langer, *Philosophy in a New Key*, 3rd ed. (Cambridge, Mass.: Harvard University Press, 1957), p. 228.

6 Langer, *Philosophy in a New Key*, p. 238.

7 Kendall Walton, "What is Abstract About the Art of Music?," *The Journal of Aesthetics and Art Criticism* 46 (1988): 359.

8 Walton, "What is Abstract About the Art of Music?" p. 359.

9 Walton, "What is Abstract About the Art of Music?" p. 360.

10 Jerrold Levinson, "Music and Negative Emotions," *Pacific Philosophical Quarterly* 63 (1982): 336.

11 Levinson, "Music and Negative Emotions," p. 336.

12 Levinson, "Music and Negative Emotions," p. 337.

13 Levinson, "Music and Negative Emotions," p. 337.

14 Levinson, "Music and Negative Emotions," p. 327.

15 Levinson, "Music and Negative Emotions," p. 337.

16 Levinson, "Music and Negative Emotions," p. 336.

17 Levinson, "Music and Negative Emotions," p. 336.

18 Jerrold Levinson, "Hope in *The Hebrides*," in his *Music, Art, & Metaphysics* (Ithaca: Cornell University Press, 1990), p. 355.

19 Levinson, "Hope in *The Hebrides*," p. 373.

20 This paper receives more detailed attention in Gregory Karl and Jenefer Robinson, "Shostakovich's Tenth Symphony and the Musical Expression of Cognitively Complex Emotions," *Journal of Aesthetics and Art Criticism*, 53 (1995): 401–415.

21 Peter Kivy, *Music Alone* (Ithaca: Cornell University Press, 1990), p. 162. This chapter of Kivy's book, "How Music Moves," is a later version of a paper of that title first published in *What is Music?: An Introduction to the Philosophy of Music*, ed. Philip Alperson (New York: Haven Publications, 1987; Pennsylvania State University Press, 1994).

22 Kivy, *Music Alone*, p. 159.

23 Kivy, *Music Alone*, pp. 159–160.

24 Kivy, *Music Alone*, p. 160.

25 Levinson, "Music and Negative Emotions," p. 332.

26 Nico Frijda, *The Emotions* (Cambridge: Cambridge University Press, 1986), p. 346.

27 This point has been stressed by Newcomb, "Sound and Feeling," and by Gregory Karl, "Music as Plot:

A Study in Cyclic Forms," Ph.D. dissertation, University of Cincinnati, 1993.

28 Leonard Meyer, *Emotion and Meaning in Music* (Chicago: University of Chicago Press, 1956).

29 Newcomb, "Sound and Feeling," p. 636.

30 In his comments on an earlier version of my paper at the American Society for Aesthetics Annual Meeting, New York, 1989, Kendall Walton defends his own view by claiming that when music "actually startles, or excites, or soothes us 'we' may imagine these feelings to be components of other more complex emotions."

31 In "Shostakovich's Tenth Symphony and the Musical Expression of Cognitively Complex Emotions," Gregory Karl and I attempt to show in detail how a particular passage in Shostakovich's Tenth expresses the cognitively complex emotion of hopefulness.

32 Nothing I have said, moreover, is meant as an objection to Kivy's claim that we may be moved, awed, delighted, etc., by music and that these emotions of appreciation, as I have called them, have or can have a highly sophisticated cognitive content.

33 This idea that musical expression can be explained in terms of a "drama" in which musical "characters" take part has been suggested by Fred Maus, "Music as Drama," *Music Theory Spectrum* 10 (1988), and by Marion Guck, "Cognitive Alchemy: Transmuting Theoretical Vices into Analytical Virtues," unpublished manuscript.

Part X

Popular Art

Introduction to Part X

One consequence of the universal literacy achieved in many European countries toward the end of the nineteenth century was a democratization of culture. The new and vast literate public possessed no formed standards of taste and was ready to accept any reading material that had some sort of "human interest." The democratization of culture led to the democratization of taste. Says Walter Allen in his book *The English Novel*: "The provision of reading matter for a semi-literate public became the concern of a vast industry which set its own standards, standards which had nothing to do with literary and artistic standards as normally understood" (*The English Novel*, Harmondsworth: Penguin Books, 1958, p. 260). This "vast industry" worked on the principle "give the public what it wants" and its aims were primarily commercial. A similar development took place in music, and the new medium of film was premised on the appeal to large audiences so as to cover its costs and make profits for its investors.

Neither the new mass audience nor the producers of popular fiction, popular music, and film claimed the status of art for their products. There was no artistic measure of success. The new audience simply did not care for such a standard, nor did the industry that produced the products. Indeed, for the majority of the new literate audience, human interest stories were equally sought in a new kind of newspaper (what today is called the tabloid) that sprang into existence in the 1890s. Again, for these newspapers as for popular fiction, the primary measure of success was the number of copies sold. However, popular fiction and popular music not only shared some obvious features with products that historically had been recognized as works of art in these media, but they also bore similar names. Popular music was still *music* (rather than mere sound) and popular fiction was also referred to as the popular *novel*. Both the actual resemblance between the products and the similarity in their names invited the application of the term "popular art" to these products. Once this step is taken it looks as if there are two kinds of art, "high" or serious art and popular art, and it becomes a problem how the two are connected in the way in which they are appreciated and evaluated. It also opens the way for those seeking cultural prestige for their taste for or production of popular music or fiction or film, to claim that these "popular arts" are really as artistically and/or aesthetically valuable as "high" art. The aesthetics of popular art consequently tends to take the form of attempts to legitimize the individual arts in question.

There are two courses open for those who want to legitimize aesthetically a popular art form. One is to insist that popular art is not really different from "high" art and that the distinction is the product of social, economic, and political factors obtaining in a certain historical period. According to this line, no special problem arises concerning the appreciation and evaluation of popular art for all the explanatory work is carried by these external factors. It does face a serious challenge, though, in how to produce a plausible general theory of artistic value and modes of artistic appreciation applicable across the board.

An alternative line is to insist that popular art is appreciated and evaluated in accordance with standards other than those that apply in the case of high art, but that these standards are nevertheless aesthetic and/or artistic standards. This is the course taken by Bruce Baugh in his article "Prolegomena to Any Aesthetics of Rock Music," where he argues that rock music has "standards of its own, which uniquely apply to it." However, to establish an alternative aesthetics for popular art is a difficult undertaking. In Baugh's case he has to establish aesthetically significant differences between rock and classical music, and this, as Stephen Davies points out in "Rock versus Classical Music," he succeeds in doing only by relying on "questionable distinctions between music's formal and nonformal elements and between the kind of musicianship involved in performing the two kinds of music." More generally, the problem with alternative standards is that their aesthetic credentials become progressively weaker as they increasingly diverge from the standards associated with "high" art.

There is a further, somewhat different, approach to the aesthetics of popular art. This largely bypasses the question of aesthetic legitimacy and goes on to address questions of ontology, of comprehension, of form and content, etc. that arise in connection with a form of popular art. This is what Noël Carroll does in "The Power of Movies" where he attempts to explain the widespread and intense engagement that movies give rise to by reference to those features that make them generally accessible to broad, untutored audiences and those that enable movies to depict situations with a high degree of clarity. It is, Carroll argues, the fact that movies are made up of pictorial representations that makes them so accessible. For pictorial representations are recognizable by people from all cultural backgrounds without any tutoring in how to "read" pictures. The clarity is achieved through variable framing and what Carroll calls an erotetic narration, i.e. a narration that asks questions and answers them to the full satisfaction of the audience.

Carroll's analysis of movies makes reference to such traditional aesthetic features as pictorial representation, the techniques of presentation, and narrative form. However, the question still arises whether the purpose to which these features contribute – widespread and intense engagement – is an aesthetic one. Whatever intrinsic interest this question might have in itself, it returns us squarely to the key issue of why in the first place we should want to claim that "a popular pastime" like the movies constitutes an art form. (The term "popular pastime" comes from David Bordwell, who writes: "The 1910s initiated the effort of intellectuals to legitimize this popular pastime as what has been called 'the seventh art'" ["Film Theory," in Michael Kelly (ed.), *Encyclopedia of Aesthetics*, Vol. 2, Oxford University Press, 1998, p. 197]).

Further reading

Carroll, Noël (1996). *Theorizing the Moving Image* (Cambridge: Cambridge University Press).

Carroll, Noël (1998). *A Philosophy of Mass Art* (Oxford: Oxford University Press).

Cohen, Ted (1999). "High and Low Art, and High and Low Audiences," *Journal of Aesthetics and Art Criticism*, 57, pp. 137–43.

Currie, Gregory (1995). *Image and Mind: Film, Philosophy, and Cognitive Science* (Cambridge: Cambridge University Press).

Gracyk, T. (1996). *Rhythm and Noise: An Aesthetics of Rock* (Durham, NC: Duke University Press).

Novitz, David (1992). "High and Popular Art: the Place of Art in Society," chapter 2, *The Boundaries of Art* (Philadelphia: Temple University Press), pp. 20–41.

Shusterman, Richard (1991). "Form and Funk: The Aesthetic Challenge of Popular Arts," *British Journal of Aesthetics*, 31, 203–13.

Shusterman, Richard (1992). *Pragmatist Aesthetics: Living Beauty, Rethinking Art* (Oxford: Blackwell) chapters 7 and 8.

41

The Power of Movies

Noël Carroll

For much of its history, film theory has been obsessed with various notions of realism. In what has come to be called classical film theory, i.e., film theory until 1965, the writings of André Bazin evince the extreme form of this obsession. Bazin held that the film image was an objective representation of the past, a veritable slice of reality.[1] In addition to this view of the ontology of film, Bazin also advanced the psychological corollary that spectators somehow regard the images on screen as identical with their referents. Contemporary film theorists reject Bazin's metaphysics concerning the nature of the film image; influenced by semiotics, such theorists deny there is any literal sense to be made of the idea that film is some kind of natural mirror onto reality. Yet contemporary film theorists do hold onto a portion of the realist approach, notably its psychological presuppositions. That is, contemporary theorists, while rejecting the notion that film is a slice of reality, nevertheless agree that in its standard uses, film imparts a *realistic effect* to its viewers. This effect, a psychological effect, is described by various formulas, including the notions that film gives the impression of reality narrating itself; film causes an illusion of reality; or film appears natural.[2]

Surely, contemporary theorists are correct in forsaking the extravagances of Bazin's ontology of film, the great influence of his theory notwithstanding. However, contemporary film theory's psychologizing of the realist approach, in terms of realist effects, is not very persuasive. For it requires attributing rather bizarre and frankly dubious mental states to spectators. Spectators are said to be under the illusion that the film image is its referent; or we are thought to believe that the film image is reality narrating itself; or that the film image is somehow natural. Some of these imputed psychological effects – for example, "reality narrating itself" – sound downright incoherent. But all of these variations on the realistic effect are suspect because they attribute to spectators states of belief that would preclude our characteristic forms of response to, and appreciation of, cinema. For, were we spectators ever to mistake the representations before us for the referents those images portray, we could not sit by comfortably, inactively, and appreciatively while buffaloes stampede toward us, while lovers reveal their deepest longings to each other, and while children are tortured.[3]

The realist approach to film theory, either as an ontological thesis or in its more contemporary, psychologized variations, is a dead end. However, the questions that motivated the realist answers may well be worth asking. That is, what is it that the various realist approaches in film theory are designed to explain, and is it worth explaining? At least two candidates seem key here. Realism, especially as a psychological effect, is supposed to play a role in explaining the way in which film disseminates ideology, according to contemporary film theorists. Second, the attribution of realism is meant to explain the power of movies, to explain

Noël Carroll, "The Power of Movies," *Daedalus*, 114:4 (Fall 1985), pp. 79–103. Reprinted by permission of *Daedalus*, Journal of the American Academy of Arts and Sciences, from the issue entitled "The Moving Image."

why the moving picture, including narrative TV, is *the* dominant art form of the twentieth century.

Certainly, "How does cinema promote ideology?" and "What makes movies powerful?" are good questions. The purpose of this paper is to attempt to answer the second question, without resorting to the invocation of realism.[4] We shall try to explain what makes motion pictures our dominant mass art, one that is so widespread, internationally pervasive, and accessible across boundaries of class and culture. We shall furthermore attempt to explain what makes the response to movies *so intense for so many*, especially when compared to art forms such as opera and theater.

The hypothesis of realism was meant to deal with such questions by suggesting that since films appear to be slices of reality, they are widely accessible insofar as everyone is familiar with reality. But the reference to reality here won't give us much help with the intensity of our response to movies, because in large measure we conceive of the special intensity of movies exactly in contrast to our more diffuse responses to quotidian reality. Another way to put this, of course, is to point out that since our response to reality is so often lackluster, claiming that a film appears to be a slice of reality promises no explanation of our extraordinarily intense response to films. So another explanation, one not reliant upon realism, must be found to account for the power of movies.

To begin an account of the power of movies, some characterization of the phenomenon in question is relevant. First, the word "movies," as used here, does not refer to film or cinema at large – that is, to a body of cultural productions that includes, not only commercial, narrative films, but also industrial documentaries, medical training films, ballistics tests, experimental films, modernist art films, propaganda films, and so on. Rather, "movies" refers to popular mass-media films, the products of what might be called Hollywood International – films made in what has been dubbed the "classical style," whether they be American, Italian, or Chinese, and whether they be made for the screen or for TV. Movies, in this sense, are a genre, not the whole, of cinema. It is about this genre's power that my paper is concerned. Why speak of the power of a genre of cinema rather than of the power of the medium? Well, the answer to that is simply that the medium of cinema is not, in and of itself, powerful; it is not the medium of cinema that has gripped such widespread audiences

so intensely. Instead, it is the adaptation of the medium to the purposes of Hollywood International. When people speak of the power of the medium, they are, I believe, talking about the power of this particular genre or style. For it is the movies, and not modernist masterpieces or medical instruction films, that have captivated the twentieth-century popular imagination. It is the power of movies about which researchers are really curious.

To speak of movies rather than film or cinema deliberately eschews essentialism. Posing the problem in an essentialist idiom – i.e., what makes the *medium* of cinema powerful – would pervert the question. For neither the medium nor every style of film found in it is accessible to or intensely engaging of mass, popular audiences. Thus, plumbing the essence of the medium, if there is such a thing, would not provide the information we seek. Instead of comparing the medium of film to other media such as theater or literature, then, this paper will focus on the *genre of movies* in order to determine just what features of the stylistic choices of Hollywood International enable it to evoke a level of widespread, intensive engagement that is, ex hypothesis, unrivaled by other media. Indeed, this way of stating the project is not quite accurate; for it is not the case that the genre of movies is really to be contrasted with other media, but rather that movies will be contrasted with other *genres* within other media. We want to know what features of movies like *Red River*, *Psycho*, and *Blue Thunder* make them more appealing and more intensely engaging for mass audiences than, for example, plays like *King Lear* and *Hurlyburly*, ballets like *Giselle*, and novels like *Middlemarch*. My anti-essentialism amounts to a refusal to answer questions about the power of movies in terms of the specificity of the medium of cinema. It may seem that proclaiming this variety of anti-essentialism at this late date is so much redundant arm-waving. But I'm not sure. The influence of Christian Metz's essay, "The Imaginary Signifier," which proceeds methodologically in an essentialist manner, trying to isolate and analyze a cinema-specific feature of the medium which he identifies as a special sort of play of presence and absence, testifies to the persistent appeal of the essentialist approach.[5]

The power of movies comprises two factors: widespread engagement and intense engagement. This paper will attempt to explain the former in terms of those features of movies that make them highly accessible to broad audiences. It will also try to explain the intensity of movies by examining those features that enable movies to depict a very high degree of clarity. In a nutshell, its thesis is that the power of movies resides in their easily graspable clarity for mass audiences.

We can begin to understand the general popularity of the movie genre by considering those features that make it generally accessible to mass, untutored audiences. A good place to start this investigation is with the image projected by the single-shot – a close-up of the hero's face, or a long-view of Castle Dracula. These images are, for the most part, representational, but, more important, they are *pictorial* representations. They refer to their referents by way of *picturing*, by displaying or manifesting a delimited range of resemblances to their referents. By recognizing these similarities, the spectator comes to know what the picture depicts, whether a man, a horse, a house, and so on.

Given that the typical movie image is a pictorial representation, what has this to do with accessibility? Well, a picture is a very special sort of symbol. Psychological evidence strongly supports the contention that we learn to recognize what a picture stands for as soon as we have become able to recognize the objects, or kinds of objects, that serve as the models for that picture. Picture recognition is not a skill acquired over and above object recognition. Whatever features or cues we come to employ in object recognition, we also mobilize to recognize what pictures depict. A child raised without pictorial representations will, after being shown a couple of pictures, be able to identify the referent of any picture of an object with which he or she is familiar.[6] The rapid development of this picture-recognition capacity contrasts strongly with the acquisition of a symbol system such as language. Upon mastering a couple of words, the child is nowhere near mastering the entire language. Similarly, when an adult is exposed to one or two representational *pictures* in an alien pictorial idiom, say a Westerner confronting a Japanese image in the floating-point-of-view style, he will be able to identify the referent of any picture in that format after studying one or two representations of that sort for a few moments. But no Westerner, upon learning one or two linguistic symbols of the Japanese language, could go on to identify the reference of all, or even merely a few more, Japanese words. Moreover, historically the Japanese were eminently able to catch on to and replicate the Western system of perspectival picturing by examining a selection of book illustrations; but they could never have acquired any European language by learning the meanings of just a few words or phrases.[7]

Pictorial representations thus differ radically from linguistic representations. The speed with which the former is mastered suggests that it does not require special learning, above the realization, perhaps, that flat surfaces are being used to stand for three-dimensional objects. Rather, the capacity to recognize what a picture depicts emerges in tandem with the capacity to recognize the kind of object that serves as the model of the picture. The reciprocal relation between picture recognition and object recognition, of course, explains how it is possible for us, having acquired detailed visual information from pictures, to recognize objects and places we have never encountered in real life. And, of course, the fact that pictorial recognition does not require any special learning process would also explain how movies, whose basic constituent symbols are pictures, are immediately accessible to *untutored* audiences in every corner of the world. These audiences do not need any special training to deal with the basic images in movies, for the capacity to recognize what these images are about has evolved part and parcel with the viewer's capacity to recognize objects and events.

The technology of film could be adapted in such a way that the basic images of a film genre or film style were not pictorial representations. One could imagine a motion picture industry of changing abstract forms, after the fashion of Hans Richter's *Rhythmus 21*, or one of spectacles of color, such as Stan Brakhage's *Text of Light*. But that was not the road taken by the movies. Movies became a worldwide phenomenon – and a lucrative industry – precisely because in their exploitation of pictorial recognition – as opposed to symbol systems that require mastery of processes such as reading, decoding, or deciphering in order to be understood – they rely on a biological capability that is nurtured in humans as they learn to identify the objects and events in their environment.

The basic images in movies are not simply pictorial representations; they are, standardly, *moving* pictorial representations. But just as an audience need not go through a process of learning to "read" pictures, neither is its perception of movie "movement" learned. Rather, it is a function of the way stroboscopic or beta phenomena affect the brain's organization of congruous input presented in specifiable sequences to different points on the retina. Of course, following a movie involves much more than the capacity to recognize what its moving images represent. But we should not overlook the crucial role that the relative ease of comprehending the basic symbols of movies plays in making movies readily accessible.

The remarks thus far are apt to displease the majority of cinema researchers. For the contention that pictures (and, by extension, moving pictures) work by looking like their referents in those pertinent respects to which our perceptual system is keyed, goes against the contemporary received wisdom that pictures, like any other symbol, are matters of codes and conventions. Undoubtedly, some reader will recall an anthropology class in which he was told that certain non-Western peoples were unable to understand pictures shown to them by missionaries and other field workers. However, this evidence has never been entirely decisive. Complaints about the fidelity of the photographs involved have been raised, along with the more serious objection that what the subjects failed to understand, and then only initially, was the practice of using flat surfaces to portray three-dimensional objects.[8] Once they got the hang of that, they had no trouble in recognizing what hitherto unseen pictures referred to – assuming they were familiar with the kinds of objects displayed in the pictures.[9] Also, on the non-conventionalist side of the scale, we must weight the psychological evidence of the child's acquisition of pictorial recognition, the easy cross-cultural dissemination of pictorial practices, and the zoological evidence that certain animals have the capacity for pictorial recognition,[10] against exotic anecdotes that are meant to demonstrate that the practices of picturing are cultural conventions that must be learned in the fashion of a language. We can consider our own cases. We all recall our own language acquisition, and we know how to go about helping youngsters to learn to speak and to read. But who remembers undergoing a similar process in regard to pictures, and what techniques would we employ to teach a youngster pictorial literacy? Yes, we may show a child a few pictures and say the name of the object portrayed. But very shortly the child just sees what the picture is of; the child doesn't "read" the picture or decode it or go through some process of inference. And from a meager set of samples, the child can proceed to identify the subjects of a plethora of pictures, because there is a continuum between apprehending pictorial representations and perceiving the world that does not depend upon learning anything like the conventional, arbitrary correlations of a vocabulary, or the combinatory principles of a grammar.

There is undoubtedly a temptation to think that picture recognition involves some process of decoding or inference because of the contemporary influence of the computational metaphor of the mind. We think that computers supply us with powerful insight into how the mind works. And if we were to build a computer to simulate pictorial recognition, it would require a complex information-processing system. But it does not follow that if computers employ complex information-processing systems in pictorial recognition, then humans must likewise possess such systems. It may rather be that our neurophysiology is so constructed that when stimulated by certain pictorial arrays, we see what the picture is of. John Searle notes that balance is controlled by the fluids in our inner ear. Were a robot to be built, balance would probably be governed by some complex computational program. But, for us, balance is a matter governed by our fleshy hardware.[11] A similar case might be made that biology – rather than information processing – may have a great deal to tell us about the workings of object recognition and picture recognition. And to the extent that pictorial representation is a matter of the way in which humans are made, a practice rooted in pictorial representation – such as the movies – will be widely and easily accessible to all humans made that way.

Many contemporary semiotically inclined film theorists resist approaching pictorial representation in the movies in the preceding fashion. Their resistance rests on a confusion, or rather a conflation, on their part of the ideas of code, convention, and culture; terms that in film studies are treated as equivalent. If something is coded or conventional, then it is regarded as a cultural production. This seems fair enough. But it is more problematic to presume, as film researchers do, the opposite; that if something is a cultural product, then it is an example of coded or conventional phenomena. Thus, if pictorial representations, including moving, pictorial representations, are cultural productions, which they certainly are, then they must be conventional. The difficulty here lies in the assumption that everything that is cultural is necessarily conventional.

Consider plows. They are cultural productions. They were produced by certain agricultural civilizations that had culturally specific needs not shared, for example, by hunter-gatherers. Is the design of a plow a matter of convention? Recall, here, that for semiotic film theorists, arbitrariness is a key defining feature of a convention. That is, a group creates a convention – like driving on the right side of the road – when there are a number of alternative ways of dealing with the situation *and* when the choice between these alternatives is arbitrary, a matter of fiat. But the adoption of the design of the plow could not have been reached by fiat. The plow had a purpose – digging furrows – and its effectiveness had to be accommodated to the structure of nature. It would have to be heavy enough and sharp enough to cut into the earth, and it had to be adapted to the capacities of its human users – it had to be steerable and pullable by creatures like us with two arms and limited strength. A device such as a plow had to be discovered; it could not be brought into existence by consensus. We could not have elected pogo-sticks to do the work of plows. The plow was a cultural *invention*, not a cultural *convention*. It was adopted because it worked, because it met a cultural need by accommodating features of nature and biology.

The point of introducing the concept of a *cultural invention* here is, of course, to block the facile identification of the cultural and the conventional. Applied to the sort of pictorial representations found in movies, this concept suggests that pictorial representations may be cultural inventions, inventions that, given the way people are built, cause spectators who are untrained in any system of conventions to recognize what pictures stand for. The structure of such images is not determinable by a mere decision. Given the constraints of the human perceptual apparatus, we cannot decree that anything *looks like* anything else, though we may decree that anything can *stand for* anything else. It seems cogent to suppose that this limitation is in large measure attributable to human biology. And insofar as movies are constituted of a mode of representation connected to biological features of the human organism, they will be generally more accessible than genres in other media, such as the novel, that presuppose the mastery of learned conventions such as specific natural languages. Also, if the recognition of movie images is more analogous to a reflex than it is to a process like reading, then following a movie may turn out to be less taxing, less a matter of active effort, than reading. Perhaps this can be confirmed by recalling how much easier it is to follow a movie when one is fatigued than it is to read a novel.

The claim has so far been made that a crucial element in the power of movies is the fact that movies usually rely, in terms of their basic imagery, on pictorial representations that allow masses of untutored spectators easy access to the fundamental symbols in the system, due to the way humans are constructed. But is this not just a reversion to the kind of realist explanation we began by dismissing? Not at all. The Bazinian claims that the spectator somehow takes the film image to be identical with its referent, while contemporary film theorists hold that the typical film image imparts the illusion of reality, transparency, or naturalness. This paper, though, has not invoked any of these realist, psychological effects, nor anything like them. It has instead claimed that the untutored spectator recognizes what the film image represents without reference to a code; it has *not* claimed that the spectator takes the pictorial representation to be, in any sense, its referent. Man's perceptual capacities evolve in such a way that his capacity for pictorial recognition comes, almost naturally, with his capacity for object recognition, and part of that capacity is the ability to differentiate pictures from their referents. Thus, we are not talking about a realist, psychological effect – the taking of a representation for its referent – but only about the capacity of movies to exploit generic, recognitional abilities. Another way to see the difference between this approach and that of the realists is to note how often their accounts of the power of movies emphasize the importance of the fact that movies are photographic, whereas in the account offered here the important technology for explaining the accessibility of movies is the non-cinema-specific technology of pictorial representation.

If up to this point anything can be said to have been demonstrated, then, admittedly, it must also be conceded that we are a good distance away from a full account of the power of movies. We have explained why movies are more accessible than genres like novels. But what features of movies account for their presumably superior accessibility and intensity in comparison with media and genres like drama, ballet, and opera, in which recognition of what the representations refer to is, like movies, typically not mediated by learned processes of decoding, reading, or inference? What standard features of movies differentiate them from the standard features of the presentation of plays, for example, in a way that makes typical movies more accessible than typical theatrical performances? Our hypothesis is that due to certain devices developed early in the evolution of movies, the typical movie is, all things being equal, easier to follow than the typical play, i.e., theatrical performances as have so far been commonly encountered. This caveat is added because there is no reason to believe that theatrical devices that would be functionally equivalent to the movie devices about to be discussed could not be invented, thus changing the relative accessibility of typical movies and typical plays. Our anti-essentialist bias, however, demands that we not compare the eternal essence of the film medium with its putative theatrical counterpart, but rather the state of the art of movies with the state of the art of theatrical production.

Movies are said to be more accessible than plays. What does this mean? We have asserted that movies are easier to follow than plays. What is it that is distinctive about the way in which spectators follow movies? With the typical movie, given certain of its characteristic devices, notably variable framing, the movie viewer is generally in a position where he or she is attending to exactly what is significant in the action-array or spectacle on screen. Another way of getting at this point is to say that the filmmaker in the movie genre has far more potential control over the spectator's attention than does the theatrical director. The consequence of this is that the movie spectator is always looking where he or she should be looking, always attending to the right details and thereby comprehending, nearly effortlessly, the ongoing action precisely in the way it is meant to be understood. Due to various devices, such as variable framing, movies are easier to follow and, therefore, more accessible than theatrical productions because movies are more perspicuous cognitively. The element of cognitive clarity afforded by movies may well account, too, for the widespread intensity of engagement that movies elicit.

Of course, movies and standard theatrical productions share many of the same devices for directing the audience's attention. Both in the medium-long shot and on the proscenium stage, the audience's attention can be guided by: the central positioning of an important character; movement in stasis; stasis in movement; characters' eyelines; light colors on dark fields; dark colors on light fields; sound, notably dialogue; spotlighting and variable illumination of the array; placement of important objects or characters along arresting diagonals; economy of set details; makeup and costume; commentary; gestures; and so on. But movies appear to have further devices and perhaps more effective devices for directing attention than does theater as it is presently practiced. The variability of focus in film, for example, is a more reliable means of making sure that the audience is looking where the spectator "ought" to be looking than is theatrical lighting. Even more important is the use in movies of variable framing. Through cutting and camera movement, the filmmaker can rest assured that the spectator is perceiving exactly what she should be perceiving at the precise moment she should be perceiving it. When the camera comes in for a close-up, for example, there is no possibility that the spectator can be distracted by some detail stage-left. Everything extraneous to the story at that point is deleted. Nor does the spectator have to find the significant details; it is delivered to her. The viewer also gets as close or as far-off a view of the significant objects of the story – be they heroines, butcher knives, mobs, fortresses, or planets – as is useful for her to have a concrete sense of what is going on. Whereas in a theater the eye constantly tracks the action – often at a felt distance, often amidst a vaulting space – in movies much of that work is done by shifting camera positions, which at the same time also assures that the average viewer has not gotten lost in the space but is looking precisely at that which she is supposed to see. Movies are therefore easier to follow than typical stage productions, because the shifting camera positions make it practically impossible for the movie viewer *not* to be attending where she is meant to attend.

Variable framing in film is achieved by moving the camera closer or farther away from the objects being filmed. Cutting and camera movement are the two major processes for shifting framing: in the former, the actual process of the camera's change of position is not included in the shot; we jump from medium-range views, to close views, to far-off views with the traversal of the space between excised; in camera movement, as the name suggests, the passage of the camera from a long view to a close view is recorded within the shot. Reframing can also be achieved optically through devices such as zooming-in and changing lenses. These mechanical means for changing the framing of an on-screen object or event give rise to three formal devices for directing the movie audience's attention: indexing, bracketing, and scaling. Indexing occurs when a camera is moved toward an object. The motion toward the object functions ostensively, like the gesture of pointing. It indicates that the viewer ought to be looking in the direction the camera is moving, if the camera's movement is being recorded, or in the direction toward which the camera is aimed or pointing, if we have been presented with the shot via a cut.

When a camera is moved toward an array, it screens out everything beyond the frame. To move a camera toward an object either by cutting or camera movement generally has the force of indicating that what is important at this moment is what is on screen, what is in the perimeter of the frame. That which is not inside the frame has been *bracketed*, excluded. It should not, and in fact it literally cannot, at the moment it is bracketed, be attended to. At the same time, bracketing has an inclusionary dimension, indicating that what is inside the frame or bracket is important. A standard camera position will mobilize both the exclusionary and inclusionary dimensions of the bracket to control attention, though the relative degree may vary as to whether a given bracketing is more important for what it excludes, rather than what it includes, and vice-versa.

There is also a standard deviation from this use of bracketing. Often the important element of a scene is placed outside the frame so that it is not visible onscreen, e.g., the child-killer in the early part of Fritz Lang's *M*. Such scenes derive a great deal of their expressive power just because they subvert the standard function of bracketing.

As the camera is moved forward, it not only indexes and places brackets around the objects in front of it; it also changes their scale. Whether by cutting or camera movement, as the camera nears the gun on the table, the gun simultaneously appears larger and occupies more screen space. When the camera is pulled away from the table, the gun occupies less screen space. This capacity to change the scale of objects through camera positioning – a process called "scaling" – can be exploited for expressive or magical effects. Scaling is also a lever for directing attention. Enlarging the screen size of an object generally has the force of stating that this object, or gestalt of objects, is the important item to attend to at this moment in the movie.

Scaling, bracketing, and indexing are three different ways of directing the movie spectator's attention through camera positioning. In general, a standard camera positioning, whether executed by cutting or camera movement, will employ all three of these means. But one can easily think of scenes

in which the bracket is reoriented, but the scaling stays effectively the same, for example, a lateral pan as a character walks toward the edge of the frame. Likewise, a camera movement might be important for what it indexes rather than for whatever changes occur in the bracketing or the scaling: there are moving shots in the early Italian film *Cabiria*, for example, where the camera nudges a few feet forward in a spectacle scene in order to point the viewer's eye in a certain direction, though neither the bracket nor the scale of the objects in the scene are changed appreciably. Both the swamp scene and the trolley-car scene in *Sunrise* are artistically important for the way in which they call attention to the bracket, rather than for their scaling or indexing. However, bracketing, scaling, and indexing can be employed in tandem, and when they are, they afford very powerful means by which the movie-maker controls the audience's attention. We suddenly see a close-up of a gun, indexed, scaled, and bracketed as the important object in the scene, and then the bracket is changed – we see a medium shot in which the gun is being pointed at the heroine by the villain, telling us that now the important thing about the gun is its role within this newly framed context or gestalt. The constant reframing of the action that is endemic to movies enables the spectator to follow the action perfectly, and, so to say, automatically.

Adaptations of stage technology, of course, could probably establish theatrical means that would be functionally equivalent to the scaling, bracketing, and indexing functions of movies. Magnifying mirrors might be used to enlarge stage details at appropriate moments; the leg curtains could be motorized to constantly reframe the action; and indexing might be approximated by use of revolving stages that rotate the important characters and actions toward the audience. If these devices were not too distracting in and of themselves, they might provide the theater director with attentional levers that are functionally equivalent to scaling, bracketing, and indexing. However, these devices are not customary in theater as we presently know it, and our project here is to contrast movies as they are with theater as it currently is.

Of course, *films* can be made without variable framing; but *movies* rely on variable framing to automatize the spectator's attention. Also, variable framing is not unique to movies; other film genres employ it. Yet it is key to why movies are accessible; as we have noted, it contributes to the intensity of engagement movies promote. Through variable framing, the director assures that the spectator is attending where and when she should. The action and its details unfold in such a way that every element that is relevant is displayed at a distance that makes it eminently recognizable and in a sequence that is intelligible. Ideally, variable framing allows us to see just what we need to see at changing distances and at cadences that render the action perspicuous. The action is analytically broken down into its most salient elements, distilled, that is, in a way that makes it extremely legible. This kind of clarity, which is bequeathed to the audience automatically by variable framing, contrasts strongly with the depiction of action in theatrical representations. There, the depiction is not analytic but a matter of physical enactment, generally occurring in something approximating real time, and presented at a fixed distance to each viewer. Of course, theatrical action is abstracted, simplified, for the sake of legibility, often employing emblematic gestures. It is clearer, that is, than the actions we encounter in everyday life. But theatrical action is not as clear and analytically distinct as movie action as portrayed by variable framing. Movie action, given the way it can be organized through camera positioning, is also far more intelligible than the unstaged events we witness in everyday life. This is an important feature that helps account for the way in which movies grip us.

Our experience of actions and events in movies differs radically from our normal experiences; movie actions and events are so organized, so automatically intelligible, and so clear. The arresting thing about movies, *contra* realist theories, is not that they create the illusion of reality, but that they reorganize and construct, through variable framing, actions and events with an economy, legibility, and coherence that are not only automatically available, but which surpass, in terms of their immediately perceptible basic structure, naturally encountered actions and events. Movie actions evince visible order and identity to a degree not found in everyday experience. This quality of uncluttered clarity gratifies the mind's quest for order, thereby intensifying our engagement with the screen.

So far, our speculations about the sources of the power of movies have been restricted to what would have classically been considered the medium's "cinematic features": pictorial representation and variable framing. This, of course, does not reflect a belief that these elements are uniquely cinematic, but only that they are features that help

account for movies' power, the capacity to engender what appears to be an unprecedentedly widespread and intense level of engagement. There is another core defining feature of what we are calling movies that needs to be treated: this is that they are fictional narratives. The question naturally arises to what degree this fact about movies can help explain their power.

The fact that movies tend to be narrative, concerned primarily with depictions of human actions, immediately suggests one of the reasons they are accessible. For narrative is, in all probability, our most pervasive and familiar means of explaining human action. If you ask me why George is watering the tulips, I may answer that George intends to have, or wants, a beautiful garden, and that he believes that he can't have a beautiful garden unless he waters the tulips. So I say he undertakes to water the tulips. You might ask me how he formed the desire to have a beautiful garden. I may refer to either his belief that this is a means to being a good citizen or his guilt about never caring for his father's garden, or both if his action is overdetermined. If you ask, where did he get the notion that the garden would not be beautiful unless he watered it, I say he read it in a book called *Beautiful Gardens* on May 17, 1953. Now if we tried to sum up this somewhat banal explanation of George's action, a narrative would probably be the likeliest, though not the only, means of organizing our information: George, racked with guilt feelings about his father's tulips and convinced that a beautiful garden is a means to the coveted ideal of good citizenship, decided to have a beautiful garden; and when he read, on May 17, 1953, that such gardens could not be had without watering the tulips, he went out and watered the tulips (on May 18). We might add that he continued to do so happily ever after. Insofar as this sort of narrative is one of the most common forms of human explanation, and insofar as much movie narration belongs to this category, movies will be familiar and accessible. Moreover, the explanatory quality of such narration will also contribute to the clarity of movies.

Of course, the logical relations that subtend this sort of narrative, at crucial points, remind one, and are parasitic upon, those of practical inference. If I am George, for example, I reason thusly: I want a beautiful garden; I do not believe I can secure a beautiful garden unless I water the tulips; therefore, I proceed to water the tulips. What makes narratives of the sort that I told above explanatory is that they, at nodal moments, reflect processes of practical reasoning. Practical reasoning is part of everyone's life. And the actions of others are intelligible to me when I can see them as consequences of the sort of practical reasoning I employ. Insofar as movie narratives depict the human actions of characters in forms that are reflective of the logic of practical inference, the movies will be widely accessible, since practical inference is a generic form of human decision-making.

Undoubtedly, this discussion of narrative may be too broad and too abstract to be of much use to the film analyst. In all probability nothing of great interest would be gained in film studies by showing that a series of scenes reflected a series of practical inferences on the part of characters. Rather, the film scholar will be interested in an analysis of the characteristic forms of plotting found in movies; she will want these described more specifically than they were in the preceding discussion. And she will want to know what it is about these forms, if anything, that contributes to the power of movies.

In a paper on film suspense,[12] I attempted to identify what I think is the most basic form of movie plotting, and I would like to take advantage of those speculations now. My position owes a great deal to the Soviet filmmaker and theoretician V. I. Pudovkin.[13] Pudovkin, like his teacher, L. Kuleshov, studied American movies, contrasting them with Russian films in order to discern what made the American films of the twenties more effective on popular audiences than were comparable Russian films. Pudovkin and Kuleshov undertook this investigation, of course, in order to calculate the best means for creating a new Soviet cinema for the masses. The theories of filmmaking they produced were meant to instruct other filmmakers in technique and praxis. As is well known, Pudovkin and Kuleshov tended to become very prescriptive in these matters, a tendency for which they have been duly chastised ever since. But whatever their dogmatism, we should not overlook the fact that beneath their debatable prescriptions about the way films should be made, they often had valuable insights into the way in which popular films, especially Hollywood movies, were actually constructed. What Pudovkin has to say about movie narration is a case in point.

A story film will portray a sequence of scenes or events, some appearing earlier, some later. A practical problem that confronts the filmmaker is the way in which these scenes are to be connected, i.e., what sort of relation the earlier scenes should bear to the later ones. Pudovkin recommends – as a primary, though not exclusive, solution – that earlier scenes be related to later scenes as questions are to answers. If a giant shark appears offshore, unbeknownst to the local authorities, and begins to ravage lonely swimmers, this scene or series of scenes (or this event or series of events) raises the question of whether the shark will ever be detected. This question is likely to be answered in some later scene when someone figures out why all those swimmers are missing. At that point, when it is learnt that the shark is very, very powerful and nasty to boot, the question arises about whether it can be destroyed or driven away. The ensuing events in the film serve to answer that question. Or, if some atomic bombs are skyjacked in the opening scenes, this generates questions about who stole them and for what purposes. Once the generally nefarious purposes of the hijacking are established, the question arises concerning whether these treacherous intents can be thwarted. Or, for a slightly more complicated scenario, shortly after a jumbo jet takes off, we learn that the entire crew has just died from food poisoning while also learning that the couple in first class is estranged. These scenes raise the questions of whether the plane will crash and whether the couple in first class will be reconciled by their common ordeal. Maybe we also ask whether the alcoholic priest in *Coach* will find God again. It is the function of the later scenes in the film to answer these questions.

Of course, the narrative organization of Hollywood films is far more complex than these examples suggest, and I have tried to develop this subject with more precision elsewhere.[14] For present purposes, let us say that, as is suggested by the writings of Pudovkin, the core narrative structures of Hollywood-type films – the movies discussed in this paper – involve generating questions that ensuing scenes answer. Not all narrative films employ this approach. Often, modernist films generate questions – e.g., did I meet her at Marienbad before? – without supplying any answers. Or, I might chronicle my day at the beach: first I had a hot dog, then I put on suntan lotion, then I swam, then I went home. Surely we can conceive of a home movie like this, where none of the early scenes raised any questions, and where none of the later ones supplied any answers. Thus, to narrate by generating questions internal to the film that subsequent scenes answer is a distinctive form of narration. Admittedly, this is not a form unique to films or movies, for it is also exploited in mystery novels, adventure stories, Harlequin romances,

Marvel comics, and so on. Nevertheless, it is the most characteristic narrative approach in movies.

How can this be proven? The best suggestion one can make here is to embrace the question/answer model of movie narration – what I call the *erotetic* model of narrative – and then turn on your TV, watch old movies and new ones, TV adventure series and romances, domestic films and foreign popular films. Ask yourself why the later scenes in the films make sense in the context of the earlier scenes. My prediction is that you will be surprised by the extent to which later scenes are answering questions raised earlier, or are at least providing information that will contribute to such answers. In adopting the hypothesis that the narrative structure of a randomly selected movie is fundamentally a system of internally generated questions that the movie goes on to answer, you will find that you have hold of a relationship that enables you to explain what makes certain scenes especially key: they either raise questions or answer them, or perform related functions including sustaining questions already raised, or incompletely answering a previous question, or answering one question but then introducing a new one.

Apart from the confirmation of the hypothesis afforded by this confrontation with empirical data, further support for the question/answer model might be gained by using it, not to analyze, but to develop movie scenarios. For when certain complexities and qualifications are added to the model of the erotetic narrative, it is a very serviceable guide for producing stories that strike one as typically "movieish," especially in their economy. Partial confirmation of the question/answer model is its capacity to direct the simulation of movie scenarios.

If the model of the erotetic narrative captures the characteristic narrative form of movies, then perhaps we can note certain features of this model of narration which will shed light on the power of movies. A movie scene or a series of depicted events make certain questions salient. An orphan wanders the street, importuning adults needfully. Will the orphan find a surrogate parent? This could be answered in the next scene, or it could take the entire film to answer. However, by characterizing the function of this scene as that of saliently posing a question, we have put ourselves in a position to account for one of the most notable features of audience responses to linear narrative movies, that is, expectation. Given the erotetic model, we can say what it is that audiences expect: they expect

answers to the questions that earlier events have made salient – will the shark be stopped; will the jumbo jet crash? If it is a general feature of our cognitive make-up that, all things being equal, we not only want but expect answers to questions that have assertively been put before us, this helps explain our widespread, intense engagement with movies. Even if the question is as insignificant to us as whether the suburban adolescent in *Risky Business* will be found out by his parents, our curiosity keeps us riveted to the screen until it is satisfied.

Though space does not allow for a full elaboration of the matter, important distinctions can be made among the different types of questions that animate the erotetic movie narrative. One such distinction can be drawn between micro-questions and macro-questions. A scene or an event may raise a question that is immediately answered in the succeeding scene or by the succeeding event, or by a scene or event temporally proximate to the questioning scene. For example, some burglars trigger an alarm. This raises the question of whether the authorities will hear it. Next, there is a scene of two policemen reading magazines in their squad car; they look up and switch on their siren, raising the question of whether they will arrive at the scene of the crime on time, and so on. Such localized networks of questions and answers are "micro" in nature. They connect two individual scenes or a limited series of scenes and sequences. But movies are also generally animated by macro-questions, ones for which we await answers throughout most of the film, and which may be thought of as organizing the bulk of significant action in the movie – indeed, the micro-questions are generally hierarchically subordinate to the macro-questions. For an example of a macro-question, consider *Wargames*; at a certain point most of the action is devoted to answering the question of whether nuclear destruction can be averted. Of course, movies often have more than one macro-question. *Into the Night* asks both whether the romantic leads can escape the Middle Eastern villains *and* whether this couple will become lovers. Both macro-questions are answered by means of roughly the same sequences of action, and the micro-questions and answers that structure those sequences tend, finally, to dovetail with the answers to these presiding macro-questions. What is called "closure" in movies can be explained as that moment when all the saliently posed and sustained questions that the movie has raised have been answered.

A successful erotetic narrative tells you, literally, everything you want to know about the action being depicted, i.e., it answers every question, or virtually every question, that it has chosen to pose saliently. (I say "virtually" in order to accommodate endings such as that in the original *Invasion of the Body Snatchers*, where the audience is left with one last pregnant question.) But even countenancing these cases, an erotetic movie narrative has an extraordinary degree of neatness and intellectually appealing compactness. It answers all the questions that it assertively presents to the audience, and the largest portion of its actions is organized by a small number of macro-questions, with little remainder. The flow of action approaches an ideal of uncluttered clarity. This clarity contrasts vividly with the quality of the fragments of actions and events we typically observe in everyday life. Unlike those in real life, the actions observed in movies have a level of intelligibility, due to the role they play in the erotetic narrative's system of questions and answers. Because of the question/answer structure, the audience is left with the impression that it has learned everything important to know concerning the action depicted. How is this achieved? By assertively introducing a selected set of pressing questions and then answering them – by controlling expectation by the manner in which questions are posed. This imbues the film with an aura of clarity while also affording an intense satisfaction concerning our cognitive expectations and our propensity for intelligibility.

The clarity imparted by the erotetic narrative in movies is, of course, reinforced by other clarity-producing methods, such as directing audience attention through the single shot or variable framing. These devices are the filmmaker's means of visual narration. They enable him to raise questions *visually*: the question "Will Jones be shot?" can be "asked" by focusing on a close-up of a gun. At the same time, the visual depiction of an action can either sustain or answer a question. "Will Eli Wallach die by hanging?" can be sustained by showing him teetering on a chair with a noose around his neck, or answered by showing us Clint Eastwood severing the rope in an act of superhuman marksmanship. Of course, many of the pressing questions that drive movies forward are not primarily set forth visually but are stated explicitly in the dialogue, or are already implied in the scripting of the action. Nevertheless, the devices of visual narration, if not the original source of the questions, help make those questions salient.

The visual devices of movies were earlier described in terms of the type of clarity they afforded the audience, of how they enable the audience to see all that it is relevant for them to see at the appropriate distance and in the appropriate sequence. At the same time, another sort of clarity has been attributed to the erotetic narrative as a primary ground of the power of movies. How do these two "clarities" relate to each other? Well, generally in movies, devices such as scaling, bracketing, and indexing will be employed so that the first item or the first gestalt of items that the audience is led to attend to in a given shot is the item or gestalt that is most relevant to the progress of the narrative – to the posing, sustaining, or answering of those questions the movie elects to answer. The importance of variable framing for movies is the potential it affords for assuring that the audience attends to everything that is *relevant*, and that it does so automatically, so to speak. "Relevance" is here determined by the narrative, or, more specifically, the questions and answers that drive the narrative, which in turn are saliently posed and answered in important ways by means of variable framing.

In order for this account to be adequate, certain qualifications need to be acknowledged. While generally processes such as variable framing are coordinated with the narrative for the purpose of emphasizing the first item, or gestalt of items, seen by the audience, there are standard deviations to this principle. These deviations are often employed in thrillers for shock effect: the important subject, say, the killer, is hidden in the shot in such a way that the audience only comes to see him belatedly (but unavoidably). In terms of our account, these deviations are not destructive counterexamples, because they still illustrate how the flow of narration is kept under strict control and the audience in rapt attention.

Standard movies also often contain much material that is digressive from the point of view of the erotetic narrative, for example, a melodic interlude from the heroine by the campfire in a Western. While this paper cannot fully develop a theory of such digressions, it will suggest that the most important digressions typically found in movies are a function of the sub-genres the movies in question belong to (one could go on to explain those digressions by analyzing the sub-genres they most frequently appear in and, perhaps, proceed to analyze the power of those sub-genres).

We began by addressing the issue of the power of movies, which was understood as a question concerning the ways in which movies have engaged the widespread, intense response of untutored audiences throughout the century. We have dealt with the issue of the widespread response to movies by pointing to those features of movies that make them particularly accessible. We have also dealt with our intense engagement with movies in terms of the impression of coherence they impart, i.e., their easily grasped, indeed, their almost unavoidable, clarity. The accessibility of movies is at least attributable to their use of pictorial representation, variable framing, and narrative, the latter being the most pervasive form of explaining human actions. Their clarity is at least a function of variable framing in coordination with the erotetic narrative, especially where erotetic narration and variable framing are coordinated by the principle that the first item or gestalt of items the audience apprehends be that which, out of alternative framings, is most important to the narration. In short, this thesis holds that the power of movies – their capacity to evoke unrivaled widespread and intense response – is, first and foremost, at least a result of their deployment of pictorial representation, variable framing, and the erotetic narrative.

It will undoubtedly be noted that in this attempt to account for the power of movies, we have restricted our purview to features in movies which address the *cognitive* faculties of the audience. This is absolutely central to the argument. For only by focusing on cognitive capacities, especially ones as deeply embedded as pictorial representation, practical reason, and the drive to get answers to our questions, will we be in the best position to find the features of movies that account for their phenomenally *widespread* effectiveness; since cognitive capacities, at the level discussed, seem the most plausible candidate for what mass-movie audiences have *in common*. That is, the question of the power of movies involves explaining how peoples of different cultures, societies, nations, races, creed, educational backgrounds, age groups, and sexes can find movies easily accessible and gripping. Thus, the power of movies must be connected to some fairly generic features of human organisms to account for their power *across* class, cultural, and educational boundaries. The structures of perception and cognition are primary examples of fairly generic features of humans. Consequently, it seems that if we can suggest the ways in which movies are designed to engage and excite cognitive and perceptual structures, we will have our best initial approximation of their *generic* power.

Some qualifications, of course, are in order. First, we are not claiming that people do not respond intensely to forms other than movies; indeed, some people respond more intensely to other art forms than they do to movies. There are opera buffs and balletomanes, after all. But this is compatible with the claim we are examining, that there is something special about the widespread and intense, though not necessarily universal, response that movies have been observed to command.

Next, we are not denying that there may be levers beyond those we have discussed that also figure in the account of the power of movies. Marketing structures, including advertising, are important elements, as well as factors such as the transportability and reproducibility of movies. Research in these areas should not be abandoned. However, considerations along these lines do not obviate the present sort of speculation, since there must still be something about the product, so marketed, that sustains interest.

Pictorial representations, variable framing, erotetic narration, and the interrelation of these elements in the ways proposed will, at the very least, be constituents of any account of the power of movies. This paper does not pretend to have offered a *complete* account of why movies are powerful – its modesty is signaled by the hedge "at the very least." Perhaps movies employ other clarifying features, such as music, that require analysis. Furthermore, apart from the question of why movies are powerful, we may wish to pursue different, but related, questions about why certain movies or groups of movies are powerful for certain groups of people; how do movies, or at least certain varieties of movies, engage particular classes, nations, genders, and so on. Theoretical interest in these questions would undoubtedly lead to a focus on elements of structure and content that have not been addressed here, since we have been concerned with the *generic* power of movies, not the power of movies for specific times, locales, sexes, and interest groups. However, nothing we have said suggests an objection in principle to these more specific questions, which questions, of course, will, in all probability, lead to speculation about aspects of audiences over and above their cognitive faculties. Social conditioning and affective psychology, *appropriately historicized*, must be introduced to explain the power of given movies for target groups. Sociology, anthropology, and certain forms of psychoanalysis are likely to be useful in such investigations. We can therefore continue to examine the power of movies by asking about the power of certain movies for historically specific audiences. However, if we wish to explain the power of movies for the world community, then pictorial representation, variable framing, and the erotetic narrative will be key elements in our account because of the ways in which they address common cognitive and perceptual capacities.

Notes

1 See André Bazin, *What is Cinema?* (Berkeley: University of California Press, 1971), especially vol. I.

2 For an example of an author who employs these approaches, see John Ellis, *Visible Fictions: Cinema, TV, Video* (London: Routledge and Kegan Paul, 1982).

3 For detailed criticism of the Bazinian approach see "Concerning Photographic and Cinematic Representation," in my *Theorizing the Moving Image* (Cambridge: Cambridge University Press, 1996). For extensive criticism of contemporary attributions of realistic psychological effects to viewers, see my "Address to the Heathen," *October*, no. 23, 1982, and my "A Reply to Heath," *October*, no. 27, 1983.

4 The question of film's ideological operation is also a good one, which I take up in *Philosophy of Mass Art* (Oxford: Oxford University Press, 1998), Ch. 6.

5 This essay is in Christian Metz's *The Imaginary Signifier* (Bloomington: University of Indiana Press, 1982). I criticize Metz's approach in a review of this book in the *Journal of Aesthetics and Art Criticism*, Winter 1984.

6 J. E. Hochberg and V. Brooks, "Pictorial Recognition as an Unlearned Ability," *American Journal of Psychology*, no. 75, 1962, pp. 624–628.

7 Ichitaro Hondo, "History of Japanese Painting," in *Painting 14–19th Centuries: Pageant of Japanese Art* (Tokyo: Tokyo National Museum, 1957), vol. II, pp. 54–55.

8 J. B. Deregowski, E. S. Muldrow, and W. F. Muldrow, "Pictorial Recognition in a Remote Ethopian Population," *Perception*, no. 1, 1972, pp. 417–425.

9 John M. Kennedy, *A Psychology of Picture Perception* (San Francisco: Jossey-Bass, 1974), p. 79.

10 K. J. Hayes and C. Hayes, "Picture Perception in a Home-Raised Chimpanzee," *Journal of Comparative and Physiological Psychology*, no. 46, 1953, pp. 470–474.

11 John Searle, *Minds, Brains and Science* (Cambridge: Harvard University Press, 1984), pp. 51–52.

12 Noël Carroll, "Toward a Theory of Film Suspense," in *Persistence of Vision: The Journal of the Film Faculty of the City University of New York*, no. 1, 1984.

13 V. I. Pudovkin, *Film Technique and Film Acting* (New York: Grove Press, 1960).

14 Carroll, "Toward a Theory of Film Suspense," op. cit.

42

Prolegomena to Any Aesthetics of Rock Music

Bruce Baugh

Can there be an aesthetics of rock music? My question is not: Can traditional ways of interpreting and evaluating music be applied to rock music, for clearly they can, with very mixed results. My question is rather: Does rock music have standards of its own, which uniquely apply to it, or that apply to it in an especially appropriate way? My hunch is that rock music has such standards, that they are implicitly observed by knowledgeable performers and listeners, and that these standards reflect the distinctiveness of rock as a musical genre. Rock music involves a set of practices and a history quite different from those of the European concert hall tradition upon which traditional musical aesthetics have been based. That being so, any attempt to evaluate or understand rock music using traditional aesthetics of music is bound to result in a misunderstanding. It is not that rock music is more modern, since there are many modernist composers in the European tradition, their modernity being precisely a function of their relation to that tradition, which they aim to radicalize and subvert.[1] The difference between rock and "serious" music is that rock belongs to a different tradition, with different concerns and aims. In this paper, I will try to get at the nature of those differences, and in so doing, if only in a negative way, the route that an aesthetics of rock music might take. I will initially make the contrast between rock and European concert music as strong and sharp as

Bruce Baugh, "Prolegomena to Any Aesthetics of Rock Music," *Journal of Aesthetics and Art Criticism*, 51: 1 (Winter 1993), pp. 23–9. Reprinted by permission of Blackwell Publishing Ltd.

possible, which will lead to some one-sided and simplistic distinctions between the two genres. Nevertheless, even when the distinctions are properly qualified and nuanced, I think the difference remains real and substantial.

If I were to indicate this difference in a preliminary way, I would say that traditional musical aesthetics is concerned with form and composition, whereas rock is concerned with the *matter* of music. Even this way of putting things is misleading, since the form/matter distinction is itself part of traditional aesthetics. But leaving aside the inappropriateness of the term, by "matter" I mean the way music feels to the listener, or the way that it affects the listener's body.

One important material aspect of rock music is the way an individual tone sounds when played or sung in a certain way. Making a tone sound a certain way is a large part of the art of rock music performance, something rock inherits from the performance-oriented traditions from which it springs, particularly the blues. This is obvious in the case of the voice, which is why in rock, as in blues and most jazz, it is the singer and not the song which is important. But it also true in the case of the electric guitar, an instrument which takes on the expressive function of the voice in much of rock music. The emphasis on the very sound of a musical note as a vehicle of musical expression was summed up in guitarist Eric Clapton's statement that his ideal is to play a single note with such feeling and intensity that it would cause listeners to weep (and not, cynics please note, because the music is painfully loud, but because it is painfully beautiful.)

The materiality of tone, or more accurately, of the performance of tones, is only one important material element of rock music. Two others are loudness and rhythm. Both of these are also more properly felt by the body than judged by the mind, at least as far as rock music is concerned, and the proper use of both is crucial to the success of a rock music performance, a success which is judged by the feelings the music produces in the listener's body. The fact that rock music aims at arousing and expressing feeling has often been held against it, as if arousing feeling were somehow "cheap," or unworthy of true musical beauty. But the alternative is to look at the material properties of rock music, or those properties correlative to the bodily feelings it arouses, as the key to rock's own criteria of musical excellence. These material or "visceral" properties of rock are registered in the body core, in the gut, and in the muscles and sinews of the arms and legs, rather than in any intellectual faculty of judgment, which is why traditional aesthetics of music either neglects them or derides them as having no musical value.

Classical aesthetics of music explicitly excludes questions concerning how music feels or sounds, and the emotional reactions music provokes, from considerations of musical beauty. This exclusion is argued for in Kant's *Critique of Judgment*, and follows from Kant's definition of "the beautiful" as that which is an object of a judgment claiming universal validity.[2] What pleases me because of the sensations it produces in me, says Kant, is merely agreeable. I call something beautiful, by contrast, when I claim that anyone should find its form, or the arrangement of its parts, intrinsically pleasing, not because of the sensations the form arouses or because of its usefulness, but because the form is inherently suitable to being perceived, and so leads to a harmonious free play of the imagination and the understanding. Pleasures and pains based on mere sensation (*Empfindung*), which constitute the "material" part of a perception (*Vorstellung*), are interested and purely subjective. The idiosyncratic responses sensory stimuli produce in me because of my particular dispositions and physical constitution cannot be the basis for a judgment that claims to be valid for all perceiving subjects, since "in these matters, each person rightly consults his own feeling alone," and these feelings will differ from person to person (Kant, p. 132). The elements of a work of art that produce sensations, then, such as tones or colors, may add charm to the work or provoke emotions, but they add nothing to beauty.

When someone speaks, improperly, of a beautiful musical note, this is "the matter of delight passed off for the form" (Kant, pp. 65–66).

Kant does allow (in section 14) that certain tones and colors may be intrinsically beautiful when they are "pure": that is, when they are considered not in their immediacy as mere sensations, but reflectively, as having a determinate form in virtue of the measurable frequency of vibrations of light or air, or the ratio of one frequency to another in the case of juxtaposed tones or colors. Even here, however, the beauty belongs to the *form* of the tone or color (its frequency or ratio), and not to its merely felt or subjective *matter* (see sections 51–52). In any case, too much attention to the individual notes is a dangerous distraction from the proper object of aesthetic regard, compositional form. "The matter of sensation . . . is not essential. Here the aim is merely enjoyment, which . . . renders the soul dull" and the mind dissatisfied (Kant, p. 191). This is a moral fault, and not just an aesthetic one. The hearer who seeks pleasurable or exciting sensations in music forms judgments concerning musical worth that are conditioned by his body and his senses (Kant, p. 132), since they are based on passively experienced pleasures and pains (Kant, p. 149). Such judgments of musical beauty are heteronomous: free, active, judging reason is subordinated to the passive body's involuntary reactions. The beauty of fine art, on the other hand, is not based on sensations, but on the mind's free and autonomous judgment of the suitability of a form for perception (section 44). Consequently music, since so much of its appeal depends on the actual sensations it produces in the listener rather than on composition alone, "has the lowest place among the fine arts" (Kant, p. 195).

Kant, notoriously, was no music lover. Everyone is familiar with his complaint that music lacks urbanity because "it scatters its influence abroad to an uncalled for extent . . . and . . . becomes obtrusive," a remark that contains a grain of truth, especially in an age of powerful stereo systems and "boom boxes," but which does not indicate much appreciation for music. Yet although Kant himself was insensitive to musical beauty, others more sensitive took up his preoccupation with beauty of form in their aesthetics of music. So Hanslick, who knew music well, made every note of the musical scale "pure" in Kant's sense of having determinate form, in that each note is "a tone of determinate measurable pitch,"[3] inherently related to every other tone in virtue of the ratios between the pitches, which determine their relation on the scale (Hanslick, p. 95). By making notes "pure" in this way, Hanslick partially rescued musical notes from the disreputable position of being merely the cause of conditioned, subjective sensations and pleasures, which could form the basis only of impure and heteronomous aesthetic judgments. This, though, was only a first step in Hanslick's project of elevating music from the position of lowest of the fine arts to the highest and most formal art of all. "Music is unique among the arts," wrote Hanslick, "because its form is its content and . . . its content is its form" (Hanslick, p. 94). In music, unlike painting or literature, there can be no content apart from the form itself, no subject matter independent of the composition or organization of the work. Musical beauty, then, is entirely based on form, that is, on tonal relationships (Hanslick, p. xxiii), and not on any feelings or emotions aroused or expressed by the music (Hanslick, p. 95). By making the matter of music (musical tones) formal, and by making form identical with content, Hanslick made the art Kant regarded as the basest and most material into the highest and most formal.

Of course, the story doesn't stop with Hanslick. The preoccupation with musical form continues on into twentieth century aesthetics, notably in Adorno's philosophy of music, but in a more everyday way, formal concerns predominate in music criticism in general, from journalism to academia.[4]

The obvious rejoinder to this characterization of traditional aesthetics is that it is not *exclusively* formal, but takes into account non-formal or material elements as well. The timbre of a voice or instrument is clearly of great importance to European concert music; if they weren't, top caliber *bel canto* sopranos and Stradivarius violins wouldn't command so much respect and such high prices. Music criticism also takes performance aspects of music into account. But timbre and performance are usually secondary, and are often discussed in terms of the "faithfulness" or "adequacy" of the performance/interpretation to the composition performed or to the composer's "intentions." One justification for playing music on period instruments and in period style is that this better captures what the composition was trying to express, not simply that it sounds better or is more pleasant to listen to. In that case, performance and the notes' sounds are judged in terms of what the composition requires. In classical aesthetics of music, matter is at the service of form, and is always judged in relation to form. Even though traditional aesthetics is not exclusively formal, formal considerations predominate.

When this preoccupation with form and composition is brought to bear on rock music, the chief result is confusion. Usually, rock music is dismissed as insignificant on account of the simplicity of its forms, a simplicity which is real, and not a misperception by those unfamiliar with the genre. Alternatively, more "liberal" critics will try to find significant form where there is very little form at all, and at the expense of neglecting what is really at stake in rock music. This liberal tolerance is a worse mistake than conservative intolerance. In the first place, it is highly condescending to suppose that rock music has value only when it approximates the compositional forms of baroque or romantic music. The Beatles, in particular, were victims of this patronizing attitude. Is "Penny Lane" a better rock song than "Strawberry Fields" because the former contains flourishes of Baroque trumpet and the latter doesn't?[5] Does knowing that "She's Leaving Home" ends on an Aeolian cadence add to our appreciation of it *as a rock song?*[6] I don't think so. Yet for a time, in the late 1960s and early 1970s, critics fawned over complicated works by Yes or Genesis because traditional aesthetics of music could find something to say about their form, never noticing that criteria appropriate to the music of Handel or Boulez might be inappropriate when applied to rock music, and have very little to do with the informal standards of practice and evaluation employed by people who actually perform or listen to rock music on a regular basis.

To the extent that some rock musicians took this sort of criticism seriously, the results were disastrous, producing the embarrassing, pretentious and – in the final analysis – very silly excesses of "art rock." To the extent art rock succeeded, it did so because it was rock, not because it was "art." This was especially noticeable in the case of the mercifully short-lived sub-genre, the "rock opera." The Who's *Tommy*[7] was a good rock opera because it had good rock music and was done tongue-in-cheek (hence its "Underture"), but other attempts were merely bombastic, neither rock nor opera. Rock's borrowings from "classical" music had similar results. Combining a soulful rhythm and blues vocal with a Baroque organ line worked in Procul Harem's "Whiter Shade of Pale,"[8] but in other instances the incorporation of "classical music" (usually this meant a string section) led to rather slight pop songs collapsing under the weight of extraneous instrumentation.[9]

So what standards are appropriate to rock music? I think that the basic principles of an aesthetics of rock can be derived from turning Kantian or formalist aesthetics on its head. Where Kant prized the free and autonomous judgment of reason, and so found beauty in form rather than matter, an aesthetics of rock judges the beauty of music by its effects on the body, and so is primarily concerned with the "matter" of music. That makes beauty in rock music to some extent a subjective and personal matter; to the extent that you evaluate a piece on the basis of the way it happens to affect you, you cannot demand that others who are affected differently agree with your assessment. But that does not mean that rock's standards are purely and simply an individual matter of taste. There are certain properties a piece of rock music must have in order to be good, although knowledgeable listeners may disagree concerning whether a given piece of music actually has those properties. In every case, these properties are material rather than formal, and they are based on performance-based standards of evaluation, rather than compositional ones.

The most *obvious* material property of rock is rhythm. Rock music, from its origins in blues and country and folk traditions, is for dancing. It's got a back-beat, you can't lose it. In dance, the connection between the music and the body of the listener is immediate, felt and enacted rather than thought. A bad rock song is one that tries and fails to inspire the body to dance. Good rhythm cannot be achieved through simple formulas; the sign of a bad rock band is that the beat is not quite right, even though the correct time signature and tempo are being observed. A song with beat and rhythm is one that is performed well, not well composed, and this emphasis on performance is one rock shares with other forms of popular music. It is less a matter of tempo than of *timing*, of knowing whether to play on the beat, or slightly ahead of it or behind it, and this is one of those "knacks" that Plato would have refused the status of truly scientific knowledge: it cannot be captured or explained by any stateable principle. It is not accessible to reason.

It might be a bit unfair to claim rhythm and timing as distinctive elements of rock music, since rhythm, beat and timing are important considerations in traditional aesthetics, and are capable of formalization in musical notation. Some classical music is based on traditional European dance forms; some music is written expressly for dance, such as ballet; some music is structured primarily around rhythm, rather than tonal sequences. All these forms of music, then, have a prominent relation to the body because of their connection to dance.

Yet the relation is not the same as in the case of rock music. In the first place, the forms of dance that found their way into classical music were already highly formalized versions of what were (perhaps) once folk dances. Whatever their origins, the courtly dances to which Beethoven and Mozart provided the accompaniment were appreciated for their formal qualities (precision and intricacy of movement, order and geometry of patterns), not for their somatic or visceral aspects. On the contrary, in courtly dance, matter and the body are subject to form and the intellect. This was never more true than in Romantic ballet, where the chief effect of the dance consists of the illusion that highly strenuous and athletic movements are effortless, and that the bodies of the dancers are weightless. Here the body is used to negate the body: in ballet, the materiality of the body itself becomes pure form. This is less true of modern music, such as Stravinsky's, but even in this case the music and its performance are regulated by formal structures to which the musicians and dancers must accommodate their motions. In contrast, the effect of the music on the body is of prime importance for rock music and its antecedents (blues, jazz), so that the music is regulated by the dancers: musicians will vary beat, rhythm and tempo until it feels good to dance to. Rock music has no correct tempo, beat or rhythm independent of its effects on the body of the listener or dancer, which is why when non-rock musicians play rock, it often sounds "flat" and feels "dead": it is not that the musicians are playing the wrong tempo, notes or beat, but only that no standard score captures the subtleties or timing and rhythm that a good rock musician can feel. Feeling is the criterion of correctness here, probably because the dance forms on which rock is based do not deny the body's physicality, but emphasize it: feet stomp, bodies gyrate, bodily masses are propelled by masses of sound with insistent and compelling rhythms.

But beat is not the only thing, or the most important. There is a significant body of highly regarded rock music which has no swing, and which you can't dance to because you are not *meant* to dance to it. From the mid-1960s onward, rock music broke out of the rigid confines of verse/chorus/verse in $^{4}/_{4}$ time. But the significance of this change is not that it made rock more interesting formally. The importance of the change lay rather in the way it called into question some of the boundaries rock set for itself, and opened up new possibilities for expression through the matter of music, through elements other than rhythm. Let me briefly summarize the history of how this transition took place.

In rock music, the voice had always been the main vehicle of expression, and the factor that could make or break a song. One need only compare a Fats Domino original with its pallid Pat Boone "cover" to see that the expressivity of the voice itself, rather than the composition, makes a rock song good. As in blues, it is the performance that counts, and standards of evaluation are based on standards of performance. In this sense, rock music reverses the priorities of European concert hall music, and questions of "faithfulness" to the music rarely arise. The only question is whether the performance/interpretation is convincing, not whether it is "faithful" to some (usually non-existent) score. No one got too upset when Joe Cocker performed the Beatles' "With a Little Help From My Friends" in a way that was not in the least suggested by the original recording. In fact, the originality of Cocker's interpretation was counted a virtue by most. Listeners to European concert hall music are not nearly so tolerant in this regard: they will accept some deviation from the original score, but within limits established by the score itself, rather than by the effectiveness of the performance. Few discerning rock listeners liked Deodato's pop version of Richard Strauss' *Also Sprach Zarathustra*, but they disliked it because it was inane, not because it was a misinterpretation and a "sacrilege." Again, it is a matter of degree, but there is a heavier emphasis on performance, rather than composition, in rock music.

These performance elements of rock music are not easily accounted for by traditional aesthetics. The performance standards for rock vocalists have little to do with the virtuosity of an opera singer or with an ability to hit the note indicated in the composition at the time indicated. Some of the best rock vocalists, from Muddy Waters to Elvis to Lennon to Joplin, are technically quite bad singers. The standards have to do with the amount of feeling conveyed, and with the nuances of feeling expressed. On the other hand, it is not the vocalist

who can sing the longest and loudest who is best, either, heavy-metal notwithstanding. A good rock vocalist can insinuate meaning with a growl or a whisper. This does constitute a virtuosity of sort, but one that connects directly with the body, provoking a visceral response which may be complicated and hard to describe, but easy to recognize for those who have experienced it. Still, what the body recognizes may not lend itself to notation or formalization, and it is unlikely that a more adequate form of notation could capture these "material" qualities.

In the 1960s, the modes of expression that had been uniquely associated with the voice were taken up, with various degrees of success, by the instruments themselves, especially by the guitar. I will mention only two fairly striking examples, Cream's performance of the blues song "Spoonful" at the Fillmore Auditorium in 1968,[10] and Jimi Hendrix's "Machine Gun," recorded in concert on New Year's Day, 1970.[11] Neither of these songs, as performed, have much in the way of musical structure, and they do not swing.[12] But they do allow Clapton, with Cream, and Hendrix to explore different ways an electric guitar can sound. Both guitarists have been guilty of virtuosity for its own sake on many occasions, but in these performances, their playing goes beyond mere show-boating. Clapton's playing ranges from droning sitar-like passages to bursts of tightly clustered notes; Hendrix's use of feedback in the central passage *is* the anguish the music conveys, rather than the bald symbolism of his Woodstock performance of "The Star Spangled Banner."[13] In both cases, the guitarists have dropped their "see what I can do with a guitar" pose in favor of "hear what I can say with a guitar." And in both cases, it is a matter of how the tones are played, not the tones themselves, that makes the music successful.

In instances like these, rock achieves the expressivity through musical instruments more closely associated with jazz or blues, a use of the guitar far removed from its earlier uses as either a rhythm instrument or a bit of instrumental "filler" between choruses. On the other hand, neither Clapton nor Hendrix, nor any other good rock instrumentalist, takes an intellectualized approach to music. Both play with an intensity that still connects directly with the body, and like good rock singers, both are often not that good technically; they take chances and they make mistakes. Which is why they are unpredictable and exciting in a way that flawless musicians are not. Even when they hit the wrong notes, they do so in interesting and even exciting ways, creating a tension that can add to musical expression. When they hit the right notes, it is not because the notes are right that makes them great guitarists, but the way the notes sound, and the "timing" of the notes.

Part of the intensity of rock performance has to do with an aspect of rock that is often held against it: the sheer volume or loudness of the music. Loudness, in good rock music, is also a vehicle of expression. Obviously, very loud music has an effect on the body, and not just on the ears; you can feel it vibrate in your chest cavity. This can, of course, become simply exhausting and overwhelming, but used properly, it can add to expressivity. The best rock performances, such as the ones discussed here, make extensive use of dynamics, much as a good blues singer does. And just as the blues sometimes must be shouted or hollered to convey the right emotion, so some passages of rock music must be played loud in order to have the proper effect. Bad rock musicians, like any bad musician, take a mechanical or rule-based approach to dynamics and sonority, resulting in derivative and simplistic music. But loudness can be good, if used wisely.[14]

Rhythm, the expressivity of the notes themselves, loudness: These are three material, bodily elements of rock music that would, I submit, con-stitute its essence, and might form the basis for a genuine aesthetics of rock. Adorno called for the emancipation of dissonance; an aesthetics of rock requires an emancipation of the body, an emancipation of heteronomy. Such an emancipation is also required for the many forms of music centered on the voice and on dance, rather than on compositions and the mind's free judgment of formal beauty. In fact, preoccupation with formal beauty is appropriate to only a very small fragment of the world's music.

I realize that this brief account of rock music leaves out of consideration the question of what makes a good rock *song*, which raises a whole different set of questions, ones where issues of compositional form are clearly relevant, and which would have to deal with the vexed question of the relation of words to music.[15] But my concern here has been with what the knowledgeable listener finds important in rock music, which is almost always performance rather than composition, and the "matter" of the notes rather than the form of the whole. Whatever form the aesthetics of rock will take, it will not be the Kantian one that underlies conventional musical aesthetics. If these *prolegomena* do nothing more than avert the misunderstandings that arise when formalist aesthetics over-reaches its proper domain in being applied to rock music, they will have done enough.

Notes

1 See Theodor W. Adorno, *Philosophy of Modern Music*, trans. Anne G. Mitchell and Wesley V. Blomster (New York: Continuum, 1985).

2 Immanuel Kant, *Critique of Judgement*, trans. James Creed Meredith (Oxford: Clarendon Press, 1978); further references given parenthetically in the text.

3 Eduard Hanslick, *On the Musically Beautiful*, trans. Geoffrey Payzant (Indianapolis: Hackett, 1986), p. 71; further references given parenthetically in the text.

4 In addition to Adorno's *Philosophy of Modern Music*, see his *In Search of Wagner*, translated by Rodney Livingstone (London: New Left Books, 1981), which deals at length with the formal qualities of Wagner's superficially formless music (form as repetition of gestures and *motifs*; harmony, color and sonority as elements in composition, etc.). As did Hanslick, Adorno makes even the apparently *material* aspects of music into formal elements of composition.

5 Released as the "A-side" and "B-side" respectively of a "single" in 1967; later included in *Magical Mystery Tour*, EMI/Capitol, 1967.

6 On the Beatles, *Sgt. Pepper's Lonely Hearts Club Band*, EMI/Capitol, 1967.

7 Decca, 1969.

8 Released as a single by A&M records in 1968.

9 This was the problem with most of Procul Harem's music, at least on their first three albums. In the Beatles' "A Day in the Life" (on *Sgt Pepper's*), strings were used in an unorthodox and interesting way. In less capable hands, the same technique had awful results; cf. the Buckingham's "Susan" (1967), a song that has mercifully faded into obscurity, where the string passages bear no plausible relation to the song, but are there simply because "A Day in the Life" received critical praise. Rock music does not get any worse than this.

10 On Cream, *Wheels of Fire*, Polydor/Atco, 1968.

11 On Jimi Hendrix, *Band of Gypsies*, Reprise/Capitol, 1970.

Bruce Baugh

12 "Spoonful" is based on a descending progression from G to E; all the rest is variation, the point being that the improvised variations are what count here.

13 On *Woodstock*, Warner-Cotillion, 1970.

14 The clearest illustration of stupid and derivative rock is the movie, *Spinal Tap*. Unfortunately, the heavy-metal music portrayed there is actually far more laughable than the parody.

15 To my mind, the best essay on this subject remains Robert Christegau's "Rock Lyrics Are Poetry (Maybe)," in *The Age of Rock: Sounds of the American Cultural Revolution*, ed. Jonathan Eisen (New York: Random House, 1969), pp. 230–243.

43

Rock versus Classical Music

Stephen Davies

In this paper I consider the issue whether rock and classical music require different criteria for their appreciation and evaluation. I address this issue through a consideration of Bruce Baugh's "Prolegomena to Any Aesthetics of Rock Music."[1] I consider Baugh's position because it represents a widely held viewpoint. Versions of it are held by unreflective rock fans and professional commentators on the rock scene alike. Ideas central to Baugh's positive account of rock music – for instance, that it has a nonrational, Dionysian appeal that depends on its power and rhythm – are presented by a wide range of rock's defenders, from proto-rock-journalist Richard Meltzer to musicologists Susan McClary and Robert Walser to rock critic and historian Robert Palmer, as well as by its critics, for example, Allan Bloom.[2] Nevertheless, I think that this position is mistaken. I suggest that, at the level of generality presupposed by classifications as broad as "classical" and "rock," it is not distinctive aesthetics that separate these types.

I The Arguments

Baugh asks: "Does rock music have standards of its own, which uniquely apply to it, or that apply to it in an especially appropriate way?" (p. 498). He believes the answer to be "yes" and notes that

Stephen Davies, "Rock versus Classical Music," *Journal of Aesthetics and Art Criticism*, 57: 2 (Spring 1999), pp. 193–204. Reprinted by permission of Blackwell Publishing Ltd.

any attempt to evaluate or understand rock music using traditional aesthetics of music is bound to result in a misunderstanding. . . . Rock belongs to a different tradition, with different concerns and aims. . . . Traditional musical aesthetics is concerned with form and composition, whereas rock is concerned with the *matter* of music. . . . By "matter" I mean the way music feels to the listener, or the way it affects the listener's body. (p. 498)

Baugh makes no attempt to define what he means by "rock" or "classical" music. The rock songs he names are confined largely to the 1960s and 1970s. As regards classical music, he mentions a number of composers, but refers to only a few works or performers. Obviously there are gray areas. How should we class rock operas, or the efforts of the Boston Pops? Despite these worries, I will accept, as does James O. Young,[3] Baugh's critic, that our precritical groupings of the relevant musical types coincide well enough to make the dialogue possible.

Baugh's argument can be summarized as follows: Classical works are appreciated primarily for their forms, and the focus of attention in this music falls more on the work than the performance. The performer is subservient to the score she follows. By contrast, in rock music the performance is the object of attention and it is enjoyed and valued for its nonformal properties. The musicians usually have no score to direct them, and the sonic effects at which they aim are not ones that could be notated easily. Of importance among the nonformal properties central to rock are the "material features of sound," especially rhythm, the expressivity of notes, and volume. These affect the listener's body directly and are appreciated nonintellectually. They produce a response that is visceral or somatic. It is the aim of rock music to elicit this reaction, whereas classical music does not have this effect or purpose.

Young responds by arguing that nonformal features are no less present in classical than rock music. Classical music often is expressive of emotion. Sheer beauty of tone is important and loudness sometimes is of expressive significance. Moreover, classical music also affects the listener's body, eliciting foot-tapping, head-nodding, air-conducting, and (in private, if not in the concert chamber) dancing. While classical performers usually follow a score, considerable freedom in the score's interpretation is tolerated; also, some classical works, such as those with a figured bass, require the performer to improvise. Because classical performers can adopt a more earthy, primitive technique when the music calls for it, Young decides that classical music encompasses all the features presented by Baugh as distinctive of rock, and more besides. He concludes:

> Each of the standards of excellence in rock music performance which Baugh identifies applies as well to performances of classical music. . . . This is not to say that no difference exists between rock and classical music. For better or worse, however, rock music has to be judged by the standards which have always been used to judge music.[4]

In his reply to Young's criticisms, Baugh argues that the techniques of performance for rock are not merely primitive versions of those used in classical music.[5] A different kind of virtuosity is required, which is why good classical musicians cannot usually transfer their skills to the successful performance of rock music. Moreover, the rock player's techniques are untrained and natural, rather than mechanical and polished. He suggests, in addition, that classical music long has lost its connection with the listener's emotional or bodily response:

> A tradition is an ongoing, developing thing, and the classical tradition has . . . become more formalist in its standards of composi-

tion and performance and more intellectualist in its approach to listening. . . . If feeling and formalism once vied with each other . . . , the battle is long since over, and the formalists won.[6]

As to Young's conclusion, Baugh approaches it in a fashion that is perhaps surprising. He might have insisted that his goal was to identify features that are distinctive of, if not always exclusive to, rock music. Instead, and somewhat disingenuously, he writes: "the main aim of my essay was to establish the limits of formalist criticism when it comes to music."[7] He closes by turning Young's conclusion on its head.

> Perhaps Young is right that what is truly valuable in classical *performances* is also a matter of feeling rather than form. But in that case, in classical music, as in rock, formal complexity can never make up for an absence of expressive qualities, and for better or for worse, classical music would have to be judged by the same performance-based standards used to judge rock music.[8]

Whereas Young intimates that rock will fare badly in the comparison with classical music according to the criteria of evaluation that apply to all music, Baugh implies the reverse. If its performance is overly intellectual, and rule governed, as Baugh often intimates, classical music will be revealed as sterile and unappealing when nonformal criteria of evaluation come into play.

Some good points are made on both sides of this exchange. Young does well to emphasize how limited is Baugh's view of the role of the performer and of the place of expressiveness in classical music. Baugh is correct to insist that rock players harness distinctive skills in the pursuit of goals different from those that concern the classical performer. Nevertheless, my overall impression is that the arguments miss each other. This occurs despite the fact that Young seems to accept the parameters set up by Baugh. Their differences might have been more clearly articulated had those parameters been examined. Baugh's argument relies on questionable distinctions between music's formal and nonformal elements and between the kinds of musicianship involved in performing the two kinds of music.

II Formalism and Expressiveness

Baugh believes that the interest in classical music is exclusively formal, and he cites Kant, Hanslick, and Adorno in support of the claim. "Classical aesthetics of music explicitly excludes questions concerning how music feels or sounds, and the emotional reactions music provokes, from consideration of musical beauty" (p. 499). Formalist issues continue to predominate in music criticism in general, from journalism to academia (p. 499). Against all this, Young observes that composers and musicians have always regarded classical music as including the expression and arousal of emotions.[9] (He could have added, of course, that many philosophers of music in the twentieth century have taken the analysis of music's expressive powers as their prime topic.) He argues that nonformal properties are often of more interest than formal elements in classical music.

For my part, I am more inclined to question the viability of the distinction on which Baugh founds his argument. I cannot imagine how one could listen to music without concerning oneself with form, with the structuring of sound. Music is patterned sound, and one can hear the music in the noise it makes only by detecting its pattern.[10] At the micro-level, much music is organized in terms of tonalities or modalities, harmonic combinations, meter, and so on. At the mid-level, there are units such as melodies. At the macrolevel, there are chunks, some of which repeat or vary previously introduced material. Unless one can hear a tune – hear when it begins and ends, when it is repeated – one cannot locate the music that is there. This way of listening is not any more "intellectual" than is hearing a sentence in one's mother tongue with understanding. In both cases, a great deal of enculturation lies behind the process, but that process is "natural" to the extent that it is our effortless way of hearing music and language as such. The perceptual experience that would require thought and special effort is that of hearing one's native music or language merely as strings of unrelated sounds.

As music, rock is no less formal than any other kind. Typically, it is tonal (though the third and seventh degrees of the scale can be inflected, as in the scale used in blues). It employs the meter of common time and a persistent back-beat. It uses familiar harmonic patterns. It contains melodies. It is sectioned according to strophic or other repetitive structures. Baugh allows as much, but he sug-

gests that art rock was a disaster when it attempted to make its forms the focus of interest (p. 25).[11] When rock succeeds, it does so not in virtue of its formal interest but, rather, by using the "materiality" of sound to generate nonformal properties. With classical music, by contrast, the listener's attention should be directed to the form, and nonformal properties are of secondary importance only. "In classical aesthetics of music, matter is at the service of form, and is always judged in relation to form" (p. 500).

It might be said that form is one thing and expressiveness quite another. The two are distinct, certainly, but they operate in such intimate proximity that a rigid distinction between the formal and nonformal properties of music is easily undermined. The expressive character of music often depends on its structure, and we might understand a piece's form as much in terms of its expressive progress as in terms of textbook models. Micro, medium, and macro patterns of organization affect the piece's expressive character. Imagine two musical sections: a slow, dragging part (X) and an upbeat, lively one (Y). The expressive mood of the piece obviously is affected in part by how these are ordered – for example, as XY, YX, XYX, YXY, and so on.[12] Take the twelve-bar pattern of blues as an example. The micro-form usually is of an XXY type. In the final four measures, the pace of harmonic change is doubled. When this is coupled with an appropriate melodic and rhythmic intensification, the resulting impression is one of compression, of centripetal collapse, which lends a special inexorability and power in the drive to the tonic that resolves the tension and closes the section. It is these "formal" elements, as much as any others, that create the expressive effect of the singer's being over-burdened and crushed by sadness.

In addition, it is not possible to distinguish the formal from the nonformal by arguing that perception of the former is intellectual where that of the latter is not. Emotions have a large cognitive component. And one needs to perceive and understand lots of things about music in order to be able to recognize expressiveness in it (and to respond to what one hears with appropriate emotions). So practical is the knowledge involved that its role is not always apparent to the absorbed listener. But as soon as she is presented with music ordered according to conventions very different from those with which she is at home, its expressive character is rendered opaque. I suspect that most Western listeners can make little of the "nonformal" properties of Japanese *gagaku* or Chinese opera when they encounter such music for the first time.

Baugh implies that those who listen to classical music attend in an intellectual way to its form, whereas rock music engages the listener's feelings and thereby engenders a noncognitive response. I believe that he mischaracterizes the person who listens to classical music. While that person's experience must be informed by a knowledge of the relevant conventions, practices, and idioms, it need not be intellectual in the sense of requiring an internal commentary that refers to technical notions.[13] And while some pieces, such as Bach's fugues, do invite attention specifically to the details of their structure, many others are to be understood and appreciated in terms of their expressive or lyrical character.

In general, I doubt that a distinction can be drawn between formal and nonformal properties that will be such as to show that a person might listen in terms of the one without an awareness of the other. And I doubt that there is any basis for distinguishing the person who listens to rock music from the one who listens to classical music on the grounds that the former's interest is in nonformal properties that are appreciated noncognitively, whereas the latter's concern focuses on forms that are recognized in a self-consciously intellectual fashion. If the discussion is about a person who *listens* to the music she appreciates, Baugh's contrast between rock and classical music is unconvincing.

One way of breathing life back into the distinction between formal and nonformal musical properties is by arguing that the person who appreciates rock does *not* listen to it, though she is affected, nonetheless, by what she hears. In effect, this is how Baugh develops his argument. While he sometimes writes as if what is important to rock music is its engagement with the audience's emotions, more often he characterizes the crucial response as yet more primitive than this. He insists that rock affects the *body* and that the reaction that it provokes is somatic, visceral, in the gut. The three features he mentions as constituting rock's "essence" (p. 28) are such because of their capacity to provoke this response.

> The materiality of tone, or more accurately, of the performance of tones, is only one important material element of rock music.

Two others are loudness and rhythm. Both of these are also more properly felt by the body than judged by the mind . . . and the proper use of both is crucial to the success of a rock music performance, a success which is judged by the feelings the music produces in the listener's body. . . . These material or "visceral" properties of rock are registered in the body core, in the gut, and in the muscles and sinews of the arms and legs, rather than in any intellectual faculty of judgment. (p. 499)

> Obviously, very loud music has an effect on the body, and not just on the ears; you can feel it vibrate in your chest cavity. (p. 503)

As he describes it, the rock audience's response is not based on their listening to the music as such, but is a physiological reaction to the noise it makes.

Baugh is inclined to take the argument further by suggesting that, because of the way it affects the body, rock music falls in a tradition in which music is for dancing, not listening, to. "A bad rock song is one that tries and fails to inspire the body to dance" (p. 501). He allows that there is a significant body of rock music that one is not meant to dance to. Nevertheless, he maintains that rock remains in touch with its historical roots in dance music, as classical music does not. The dance types from which classical music arose were appreciated for their formal qualities, "not for their somatic or visceral aspects. On the contrary, in courtly dance, matter and the body are subject to form and the intellect. This was never more true than in Romantic ballet" (p. 501). In response to Young's objection that those who danced to the music of Mozart and Haydn were not in the least concerned with the music's form,[14] Baugh replies:

> The fact that at one time the music was played and listened to with dance in mind does not mean that it is still played and listened to that way. . . . In the second place, even in the eighteenth century, dance was a highly formal affair: minuets and waltzes observe strict formal patterns. . . . Rock dancing can include a lot of fancy footwork and intricate movements, but not often according to a set pattern, and sometimes there is no formal pattern at all.[15]

I am unconvinced by the claim that rock music is always more intimately connected to dance than is classical music. Is it the case that baroque dance suites or contemporary minimalist works – not to mention Bartók's music for the ballet *The Miraculous Mandarin* or Stravinsky's for *The Rite of Spring* – are less kinetically impelling than rock ballads such as "The Rose," or "Yesterday"? Is "A Day in the Life" more "in touch" with the dance tradition to which it is heir than is Beethoven's Seventh Symphony? I doubt that most people feel irresistibly impelled to dance to rock music heard on the radio. Rock music, like other kinds, is very frequently used as a background accompaniment to other activities. Anyway, does no one ever dance to Mozart in the privacy of her home? Of course, rock music that is written to be danced to is danced to when it is played at dances, but this is how people respond to dance music at dances, and it is how they always have done. It is worth recalling that dancing is a socially sophisticated, self-conscious, and deliberate reaction to music. Low-level motor and physiological responses triggered by music might impel the listener to dance, but this is by no means inevitable. Whether the primitive response finds expression in this way depends on the social context and personal inclination of the listener.

Baugh's more interesting and basic point, I think, is the one about the way that music affects the body. Particular timbres or discords can turn the listener's blood cold and make his skin-hairs stand on end. Certain tones, intervals, cadences, or sudden changes in dynamics, tempo, or rhythm can cause the listener to catch breath, or to exhale. Sometimes it is only when he does so that he realizes how responsive to the music his pattern of breathing has become. And above all, music's regularities and its cross-patterns are echoed kinesthetically by both the performer and the listener, who twitch, tap, contract, flex, twist, jerk, tense, sway, and stretch as they react bodily to the music. Music moves us, quite literally, and often we are unaware of the small motions we make in response to it.

It seems to me that, when Baugh writes of a somatic, visceral, body-core reaction to rock music, it is the response just described above that he is referring to. His main claims are these: Rock music engages the listener's body by provoking such a response. It does so mainly in terms of timbral quality, loudness, and rhythm. This reaction is unthinking and noncognitive; it does not require listening as such. Classical music does not have as its main aim the stimulation of an equivalent response.

I would reply with two points. All music, classical as much as other kinds, produces a visceral response in those who are familiar with, and who enjoy, its style and idiom. This reaction usually is unselfconscious but it is not thereby noncognitive. Because the response is to the multi-stranded pattern of tensions and relaxations that propel the music forward and bring it to a close, the listener must have internalized aspects of the style's "grammar," so that she has expectations that can be confirmed, delayed, or defeated by the music's course. (Music that is entirely unfamiliar and unpredictable makes one feel consistently uncomfortable or indifferent, whereas the response I have been describing reflects the articulation of the music.) Accordingly, while the listener need not attend to the music to the exclusion of all other actions and thoughts, at least she must register its features and hear them as such if it is to affect her body. Despite Baugh's emphasis on the nonintellectual character of the rock audience's response, there is no reason to doubt that the followers of rock attain an appropriate awareness of the music presented to them. The rock listener might not be aware of her awareness of relevant features, but the same goes equally for the person who listens to classical music. The second point is this: While timbral quality, rhythm, and loudness all can contribute to evoking a visceral reaction, so too can many other musical elements. These other elements are significant in rock music, as much as classical. Baugh underestimates the extent to which the visceral response he describes depends not only on the musical features he highlights, but also on a song's melodic and harmonic shape, its words, its overall structure, and so on.

Baugh may be correct in thinking that some rock music takes as its prime goal the arousal of a physiological response. I suspect, however, that this truth cannot easily be generalized into one about the fundamental difference between rock and classical music. As I have already indicated, there are many classical works that are no less direct in their appeal to the listener's body. In the past, innovations in all kinds of music have been consistently condemned as lascivious and morally corrupting for this very reason. Meanwhile, many types of rock music invite attention more to their lyrics, their melodies, their expressiveness, or their self-conscious playing with the conventions of the genre than to the "materiality" of their sounds.

Stephen Davies

III Works, Performances, and Notations

Baugh maintains that, for classical music, the object of attention is the work, whereas for rock music it is the performance. In rock, it is the singer (or the electric guitar), not the song, that is important (p. 498). This difference is "a matter of degree," he allows (p. 502), as he surely must. Few people think all rock songs are equally good and it is similarly plain in the case of classical music that certain singers and performers are lauded, whereas no one would turn out to hear me sing opera.[16]

Baugh often makes his point by suggesting that musical notations are not adequate to capture the nuances of rock performance, whereas performances of classical music are governed by faithfulness to the composer's score. He writes: "no standard score captures the subtleties or timing and rhythm that a good rock musician can feel" (p. 501). In rock music,

> questions of "faithfulness" to the music rarely arise. The only question is whether the performance/interpretation is convincing, not whether it is "faithful" to some (usually non-existent) score. No one got too upset when Joe Cocker performed the Beatles' "With a Little Help from my Friends" in a way that was not in the least suggested by the original recording. . . . What the body recognizes may not lend itself to notation or formalization, and it is unlikely that a more adequate form of notation could capture these "material" qualities. (p. 502)

And again: "Classical music and technique do lend themselves to formalization, and to a certain extent a classical musician's performance, however bravura or subtle or nuanced, is still going to be judged by the score."[17]

Baugh takes his position further with the suggestion that playing the right notes is far less important in rock than in classical music.

> Neither Clapton nor Hendrix, nor any good rock instrumentalist, takes an intellectualized approach to music. Both play with an intensity that still connects directly with the body, and . . . both are often not that good technically; they take chances and they make mistakes. Which is why they are unpre-

dictable and exciting in a way that flawless musicians are not. Even when they hit the wrong notes, they do so in interesting and even exciting ways, creating a tension that can add to musical expression. When they hit the right notes, it is not because the notes are right that makes them great guitarists, but the way the notes sound, and the "timing" of the notes. (pp. 502–3)

By contrast with those who listen to classical music,

> rock listeners are willing to concede a fair number of wrong and roughly rendered notes, as long as the tones are played in a way that engages the ear and the body. Rock listeners also prefer a performance where the beat is staggered to one where it is even, playing around the beat to playing on the beat, and playing that is emotionally engaging to the sort of technically accomplished and polished performances at which some classical (and rock) musicians excel.[18]

Implicit in these remarks is a view about the kinds of musicianship required by rock and classical music. I will return to that topic presently, but here wish to take up the claims about notation. I regard their introduction as a red herring.

The absence of a notation is no barrier to the preservation of a performance or interpretation in all its subtle detail. Some rock groups can duplicate their recordings in live performance. For that matter, other groups sometimes can sound, down to the smallest detail, uncannily like the original recordings made by others. (Young rock players often learn their trade by trying as hard as they can to sound just like those they emulate.) Also, the absence of a notational system need not be a barrier to the faithful preservation over decades or longer of complex, extended works. This is apparent in the gamelan music of Central Java and the early church traditions of Gregorian and Ambrosian chant, for instance. In sum, there is no direct connection between the absence of notation and the performer's freedom in rendering the given music.

On the other hand, no notation specifies every aspect of performance. As instructions issued to performers, scores underdetermine many of the concrete details of an accurate performance.[19] Interpretive niceties always remain the prerogative of the performer who works from a notation. The difference between an adequate and a great classical performance often depends on fine distinctions in shades of timbre, attack and decay, phrasing and rhythmic articulation, balance between parts, pitch wobbles. These are not notated; neither could they be achieved by a formulaic approach to the score's rendition.

Also, it should be recalled that notations must be interpreted in conjunction with the performance practices they assume. Baugh writes of rock music: "Good rhythm cannot be achieved through simple formulas. . . . It is a less a matter of tempo than of *timing*, of knowing whether to play on the beat, or slightly ahead of it or behind it. . . . It cannot be captured or explained by any stateable principle" (p. 501). Though he takes himself to be characterizing a distinctive feature of rock performance, it seems to me that he might as well be talking here of the performance of classical music.[20] For instance, in the Viennese waltz the second beat of the measure should be "early." This is not apparent in the notation if it is read literally and naively, but of course the notation should not be read this way and is not so interpreted by a musician at home with the appropriate performance tradition. Notations of rock music, when read by those who know what to do with them, are no less adequate to the subtleties of the performance practice than is an equivalent notation of a classical piece.

I hazard that Baugh should be discussing ontology rather than notation. Though he does not mention the nature of musical works, what he seems to have in mind is that the rock musician has more freedom than her classical counterpart because of differences in the types of works they play.

Some musical pieces are thick with constitutive properties, while others are thinner. Any attempt to instance the piece should aim to reproduce its constitutive properties. If the work is thick, much of the performance is specified, though countless other details remain to be added by the performer in realizing the work. Accurate interpretations will differ in many respects, but also will possess much that is common. If the piece is thin, more of the performance's details are interpretive and fewer are work–constitutive. Inevitably, where pieces are very thin, performers are valued above composers and the focus of attention is more on the performance than the work.[21] Jazz standards are examples of thin works. For these, the piece might consist only of a melody and basic chord sequence. Many, but not all, classical works are thick. For

them, the work is likely to be as interesting as its performance.

If a piece is specified by a notation, it is often apparent whether it is thick or thin. For thick works, lots of details are indicated and the performance practice treats these as work-determinative.[22] For thin pieces, many of the details of performance are not specified and there may be instructions indicating that the performer is to improvise within given parameters or stylistic constraints. If a piece is communicated, instead, via a model instance, as is the case in oral traditions, that instance will be thick with properties. Which of these belong to the work and which to the particular interpretation is evident only against the background practice in the treatment of relevant pieces. The piece might be thick or thin. Which it is, is governed by standards accepted within the appropriate performance tradition as determining what counts for accuracy in performances.

As a song, the Beatles' "With a Little Help from my Friends" is rather thin in work-constitutive properties. Joe Cocker's recorded versions are in a different style and feature an introduction and coda, along with a great deal of elaboration, that are not present in the Beatles' recording, but, in the main section, the words, the melody, and the basic harmonic structure preserve what is constitutive of this song. It is appropriate that "no one got too upset" by Cocker's version, since, in my view, it instanced the song he purported to be performing. This does not show that questions of "faithfulness" to the music never arise in cases of this kind. It reveals, instead, that rock songs are ontologically of the thin variety.[23]

In light of the above, I find it difficult to follow Baugh's claim that wrong notes do not matter in rock music, as they do in classical music. If he means that we are not concerned that Hendrix departs from Dylan's recording of "All Along the Watchtower" because we are more interested in what Hendrix does with the song than with his mimicking the original recording, then of course he is correct. But that does not show that what we value are "wrong" notes, because it does not show that the notes are wrong. Alternatively, if he thinks that, within passages improvised as part of the song's rendition, notes that are stylistically inappropriate are welcomed, I am skeptical. When the guitarist's hand slips, the result might sometimes be interesting, but this happy accident surely is the exception rather than the rule. Bum notes are just that, and rock musicians try as hard as any others to avoid those notes or chords that are deemed clangers within the style they adopt.[24] Finally, Baugh's point could be that rock audiences tolerate wrong notes because they recognize the pressures of live performance. They sometimes esteem a performance for its enterprise and verve, despite its containing wrong notes. This last claim applies as readily to performances of classical as to those of rock music, however. Schnabel's recorded performances of Beethoven's piano sonatas contain many wrong notes, while being respected as great interpretations.

So far I have criticized Baugh for the way in which he sets up the point he intends to make. He presents what should be a claim about ontological types – namely, that rock songs are ontologically thinner than most classical works – as one about the role of notations and about the kind of musicianship that is involved in executing them. But even if he makes his point poorly, is he not correct, after all, to insist that rock music differs from classical in allowing more freedom to the performer, and that, as a result, performances rather than songs are properly of more interest to the rock aficionado? Though he unduly denigrates the creative contribution made by the performer of classical music, along with the audience's interest in this, is he not fundamentally correct in his insistence that the appreciation of rock music is more performance-based than is so for classical music?

What one makes of this question will depend on what one takes the primary text of rock to be. If it is the song, Baugh may be right after all. But are songs the only musical works on view in rock music? There is reason to think not.

Theodore A. Gracyk has argued that what distinguishes rock, construed as a broad musical type, is that the primary work is the recording.[25] One could say that there are two works here, the song and the recording. Or, alternatively, one might maintain that one work, the recording, manifests (without thereby instancing) another, the song. But, however one counts the number of works that are on display, Gracyk is insistent that, in rock music, the piece on which the focus falls is the recording. His argument is plausible, though I cannot review its details here. Suppose that he is correct in his analysis. What are its implications for Baugh's position?

If the primary works in rock are recordings, then these works are very thick with properties. Every aspect of the sound captured by the recording technology is constitutive of the work. A piece of this kind is not for performing, it is for play-back, though performing might be involved in its initial creation.[26] On this account, rock will be quite distinct from classical music, which remains mainly for performance, though performances can be transmitted by recordings. While the classical tradition accepts electronic works within its purview, these form a minority, rather than the mainstream. The primary works in rock music will be ontologically very different from most classical works, then, and this will be because rock pieces depend essentially on the electronic medium for their creation and dissemination.

Baugh argues that, in rock as distinct from classical music, performances rather than works are the focus of aesthetic attention. He writes of rock as if it always involves live performance. To pick just one instance, he says: "The effect of the music on the body is of prime importance for rock music and its antecedents (blues, jazz), so that the music is regulated by the dancers: musicians will vary beat, rhythm and tempo until it feels good to dance to" (p. 501). He does not acknowledge the fact that rock is much more often presented as, and transmitted via, recordings, and that its effects on the body, when heard through speakers or headphones, is very different from those when it is heard live. If Gracyk is correct about the nature of rock, Baugh must be importantly mistaken. It could still be true that rock emphasizes the "material aspects of sound" more than classical music does, but it could not be that this is a function of the manner of live performance, which is a claim that Baugh makes central to his argument. Moreover, our interest in rock would primarily be an interest in works (that is, recordings), not in performances.

IV Musicianship

Earlier I observed that Baugh regards classical and rock musicianship as differing. He argues that these types of music require different techniques of performance, so that it is inappropriate to view rock as employing a crude version of classical technique. I believe that he is right in this observation. Many of the claims he makes in arguing for it strike me as dubious, however. In particular, he is wrong to equate classical technique with mechanical, heartless efficiency, and also mistaken in characterizing musicianship in rock music as "natural" and "innate."

I have already quoted passages in which Baugh implies that technique in classical performance is mainly a matter of following a score with automatic, literal-minded precision and with only a cursory nod toward expressiveness and the like. That attitude is present when he writes: "The performance standards for rock vocalists have little to do with the virtuosity of an opera singer or with an ability to hit the note indicated in the composition at the time indicated" (p. 502). Though he describes great rock singers and guitarists (p. 502) as lacking in technique, obviously he means that they lack the kind of technique that is appropriate for classical music, and that their music is the more exciting and powerful for this. Rock music has its own, different standards of virtuosity – "a virtuosity . . . that connects directly with the body, provoking a visceral response" (p. 502). He develops his position this way:

> The standards of rock music are not formalizable into a science but are a knack or an art that is learned by practice. . . . The techniques necessary for good rock music can sometimes be mastered through a simple combination of exposure to the idiom and raw, inborn talent. . . . The acquisition of "proper" technique serves only to obscure and distort a technique that has been acquired "naturally," which is to say, by a combination of innate gifts and lucky circumstances. . . . They are often not the sorts of techniques that could be formalized in such a way as to be taught. . . . The difference between formalizable and non-formalizable technique comes from the different traditions behind rock and classical music.[27]

As regards what passes for virtuosity and musicianship in classical music, I think Baugh is simply uninformed. He implies that the ideal classical performance would be one that might be generated on a synthesizer, and nothing could be further from the truth; nothing is denigrated more in classical music than a performance that is judged to be mechanical and "unmusical." As I have already indicated, classical music depends for its successful performance on inflections and articulations that are controlled by the performer, even if she is following the score as she plays. Raw musical talent might be a matter of "natural" or "innate" potential and there might be aspects of musicianship that

cannot be taught, except perhaps by example. But if this is true, this truth applies as much to classical as to rock performers. In either case, the realization of innate potential is likely to depend on hours of practice. I suspect that there are as many rock musicians who are inseparable from their guitars and who practice constantly as there are violinists who are similar.[28] It is not so that the performance techniques are more formalizable in the one kind of music than the other. In both, many basic aspects of playing can be taught, while others, ones that distinguish gifted masters from those who are merely competent, cannot easily be acquired solely by training and practice.

There is a further respect in which the techniques of rock music might be regarded as "natural" by contrast with those of classical music; namely, in the sense of "natural" that is opposed to "artificial" or "contrived." (Baugh does not make the claim explicitly, but it is heard often enough.) It might be thought that, unlike rock musicians, classical musicians need years of training, since they must master sound production of a kind that is inherently unnatural.

My interest in and exposure to non-Western musics makes me very skeptical of claims of this sort. The singing in classical opera is highly stylized, I accept, but the same is true in Chinese folk music or Australian aboriginal song-cycles. What sounds natural depends on the conventions of performance practice that have been absorbed by the listener. For instance, in the recent African-American popular repertoire (and in much white rock besides), the tessitura for male singers is consistently and spectacularly high. Baritones and basses are as common among males in this group as they are in others, I assume, but one would gain no inkling of this from listening to the most popular male vocalists. Also, when rock appeared in Britain, singers adopted an American accent. Later, the first use of a Liverpudlian inflection was regarded as gimmicky, but soon was accepted (and copied). If rock singers sound natural, they do so only in relation to the mutable norms established for such music. Further, rock music has its standard riffs and expressive protocols, as it must, given that it displays a recognizable style.

The musicianship of rock performers is not to be distinguished from other kinds in terms of its naturalness. The difference is better described with reference to the sonic ideals to which the performers aspire; that is, it is a matter of differences in musical styles and idioms. Generalizing wildly, rock prefers "dirty" timbres and "bent" pitches more often than classical music does. Also, there are techniques that are distinctive to the instruments associated with rock music, for instance, that of creating special timbral qualities on the electric guitar through the exploitation of volume and feedback. I take it that these are the kinds of things Baugh has in mind when he claims that rock concerns itself with the "materiality" of sound, though I do not find his terminology especially appealing because I see these as arbitrary aspects of style that are not more musically elemental or engaging than the many alternatives promoted in other musical idiolects. I agree, though, that achieving the sonic ideals of rock in a convincing fashion requires virtuosity, because I think that almost all musical styles make demands on the performer.

There is a hint in Baugh's paper that he would take the argument a step further. He mentions that Eric Clapton and Jimi Hendrix "have been guilty of virtuosity for its own sake on many occasions" (p. 502). It may be that he thinks classical music values virtuosity for its own sake in a fashion that rock does (or should) not.[29] In rock music, virtuosity should be the means to other ends, such as expressiveness. But again, this indicates how limited is Baugh's view of the classical tradition. Some types of classical music – in particular, the concerto – feature the instrumentalist's mastery of her medium, but even in this music "mere" virtuosity is condemned. Most kinds of classical music call for virtuosity not in order to highlight it but to achieve other effects, such as expressive ones, that depend upon it.

So far I have been agreeing with Baugh that rock music involves a kind of virtuosity, the standards of which differ from those of classical music, though I have suggested that this is a function both of the particular sonic goals at which the performers aim and of the different kinds of instruments they play. I conclude this part of the discussion by registering a caveat that draws attention, as I did before, to the crucial role of recording technology in the production of rock music.

Increasingly, rock musicians make extensive use of sampling and of synthesizers, not only in their recordings but in live performance. This inevitably raises doubts about their musicianship. Even if the players themselves lay down the material that later is sampled, we all know that their efforts can be modified and reconstructed in the editing process, so that what one hears is by no means transparent

to what was done. Studio manipulation, rather than musicianship, might be what is on display, even in the case of "live" performance.

It could be suggested that the move to knobs-on, rather than hands-on, sound generation leads to a new kind of musicianship and virtuosity.[30] Many rock musicians take an active role in the studio methods that lead to their recordings or to the electronic material that is incorporated into their performances. Even if this idea is accepted, it offers little support for Baugh's approach to the distinction between rock and classical music, with its emphasis on the idea that rock is performance based in a fashion that allows for a mutual interaction between the performer and the audience.

V   Is there a Distinctive Aesthetics of Rock Music?

Does rock music require a different aesthetics from that appropriate to classical music? What you answer might depend on the level at which you take the question to be pitched. If you take it as low level, as asking if we attend to different features in appreciating and evaluating rock and classical music, the answer might be "yes." If you take it as high level, as asking if the principles of evaluation and appreciation are radically different for these two kinds of music, the answer might be "no."

Considered at the low level, our aesthetic interests tend to be specific to genres, periods, and styles. In considering a particular work, we attend to subtle differences in relevant properties. In works of another genre, period, or style, those properties might not be aesthetically appropriate or important, and it is others that are relevant. (Compare listening to baroque pedagogical fugues and romantic opera, or Schubert's songs and Bruckner's symphonies.) The aesthetics of different genres, periods, and styles vary to the extent that the properties relevant to an aesthetic interest in, and evaluation of, their member works differ.

Considered at a higher level, an aesthetic interest does not vary from genre to genre. Many aesthetically important properties – such as narrational, representational, and expressive ones, or others such as unity in diversity – are common to many genres, periods, or styles (though they might depend on low-level features that differ according to the particular work's type). Moreover, in all genres, periods, or styles, our concern is with what Kendall Walton has called "variable" properties.[31] That is, we focus on a subset of the work's properties (those that are most likely to be varied) and consider what is done with these in the given work. Viewed at an abstract level, we concentrate on the same thing, on the set of variable properties, even if the members of this set vary between genres, periods, or styles.

Baugh aims his question at the low level, presumably, for it is here that it most obviously makes sense to maintain that rock and classical music require different aesthetics. But at that level, the relevant distinctions are those of genre, period, and style, which is a much more fine-grained level of categorization than the one he considers. Rock, as a broad classification, encompasses many genres and styles – pop, art, progressive, alternative, and experimental; blues, metal, punk, techno, ballads, rock and roll, rhythm and blues, industrial, reggae, grunge, hip-hop, and so on. It seems to me that the appreciation of blues requires a different aesthetics from hip-hop, for instance. And while expressive tone, loudness, and rhythm might be crucial for heavy metal, it is far from obvious that they are similarly important in songs such as "She's Leaving Home" and "Strawberry Fields," which are among the examples of rock offered by Baugh. Similarly, classical music covers many kinds –

sonata, concerto, quartet, symphony, madrigal, Lieder, mass, overture, ballet, opera. It also has distinctive styles or periods – late-nineteenth-century romantic symphonies are quite distinct from late-eighteenth-century classical symphonies, and seria, buffa, Singspiel, grand, and verismo are very different kinds of operas. At the low level, each of these requires its own aesthetics.

In this connection, it is striking to note that the features listed by Baugh as distinguishing rock from classical music have, in the past, been identified explicitly as marking crucial differences between certain types of classical music. In about 1600, its concentration on new, rough timbres, rhythmic vitality, and loudness was thought to separate the newly emerging operatic style from other music of the day. Early in the twentieth century, Stravinsky's ballets were distinguished from their predecessors in virtue of the centrality they accorded to these same features.

I think that properties as specific as the ones Baugh points to fail to capture a difference between rock and classical music construed as broad kinds, for they apply only to much more fine-grained types. And if there are differences between the broad categories, I suspect they are rather trivial. At the relevant level of generality, I doubt that one will find contrasts deep or distinctive enough to provide the basis for an aesthetics.

Notes

1 Bruce Baugh, "Prolegomena to Any Aesthetics of Rock Music," *The Journal of Aesthetics and Art Criticism* 51 (1993): 23–29. In subsequent references, page numbers given in parentheses are to the reprinted article in this volume.

2 See Richard Meltzer, *The Aesthetics of Rock Music* (New York: Something Else Press, 1970); Susan McClary and Robert Walser, "Start Making Sense! Musicology Wrestles with Rock," in *On Record: Rock, Pop, and the Written Word*, eds. Simon Frith et al. (London: Routledge, 1990); Robert Palmer, *Rock and Roll: An Unruly History* (New York: Harmony Books, 1995); and Allan Bloom, *The Closing of the American Mind* (New York: Simon and Schuster, 1987).

3 James O. Young, "Between Rock and a Harp Place," *The Journal of Aesthetics and Art Criticism* 53 (1995): 78–81.

4 Ibid., p. 81.

5 Bruce Baugh, "Music for the Young at Heart," *The Journal of Aesthetics and Art Criticism* 53 (1995): 81–83.

6 Ibid., p. 82.

7 Ibid., p. 81. Baugh goes on to interpret Young's conclusion to the effect that rock must be evaluated by the standards that apply to all music as suggesting that rock "can appropriately be assessed by formalist criteria" (p. 81). Presumably Baugh takes Young to be saying that all music must be assessed in both formalist and nonformalist terms, whereas a more charitable reading would have Young claiming that the evaluation of music is sometimes one, sometimes the other, and, where appropriate, both.

8 Ibid., p. 83.

9 Young, pp. 78–79.

10 Some music might not be patterned – for instance, John Cage's 4'33", or works all aspects of which are generated by chance procedures. But, though these pose a challenge for what I say, that can provide no comfort for Baugh's position.

11 Baugh seems to think that form in rock is so highly standardized that it is not a worthwhile object of aesthetic attention. Ted Gracyk has suggested to me that Baugh's dismissal of art rock ignores the fact

that, in this genre, basic forms sometimes are treated as jumping-off points for extended improvisations by groups such as Pink Floyd and King Crimson. That is, Baugh does not appreciate that the *lack* of formal restraint in this music provides for a different listening experience from that afforded by most rock music.

12 Moreover, in some cases, it can be the expressive character of the material that provides the key to an appreciation of details of its formal structure, or so Gregory Karl and Jenefer Robinson have argued in "Shostakovich's Tenth Symphony and the Musical Expression of Cognitively Complex Emotions," *The Journal of Aesthetic and Art Criticism* 53 (1995): 401–415.

13 See chapter 6, "Understanding Music," in my *Musical Meaning and Expression* (Cornell University Press, 1994).

14 Young, p. 80.

15 Baugh, "Music for the Young at Heart," p. 82.

16 One could argue that rock performance usually is a theatrical event in which the personalities, dress, actions, and make-up of the performers are crucial elements, whereas, in the performance of *instrumental* classical music, such cross-media displays are suppressed. Whatever we should make of this idea, it is not one to which Baugh appeals and neither will it separate rock from classical opera and ballet.

17 Baugh, "Music for the Young at Heart," p. 82. There are "notationists" in fields such as rock, jazz, and flamenco, though. Frank Zappa scored "The Grand Wazoo" of 1972 and from the early 1980s most of his pieces were notated. Some others who do not use notations require the band to memorize their parts and do not allow deviations from their instructions. One such was Captain Beefheart.

18 Baugh, "Music for the Young at Heart," p. 82.

19 For further discussion, see my "Authenticity in Musical Performance," *The British Journal of Aesthetics* 27 (1987): 39–50.

20 An anonymous referee makes these claims: Rock music is much more locked-in rhythmically than classical music. Orchestras and chamber groups are notoriously imprecise and take great liberties with the pulse. The importance of the drum set and the ongoing, always present rhythmic template beneath all of rock music is its signature and most defining feature.

21 See my "Authenticity in Musical Performance" and also "The Ontology of Musical Works and the Authenticity of their Performance," *Noûs* 25 (1991): 21–41.

22 Scores can contain notational elements that serve as interpretational recommendations without being work-determinative. I take this to be the case in eighteenth-century scores that mark dynamics,

phrasings, and fingerings, and that write out cadenzas and decorations. Unless properly interpreted, such notations could give the impression that the work is thicker than in fact it is.

23 Alternatively, we could regard Cocker's version as a transcription of the Beatles' song. In that case, it is pertinent to observe, as Young does (p. 80), that classical composers often have produced variations on others' themes and transcriptions of others' pieces, many of which depart radically from the original. So there would be nothing here distinctive to rock music.

24 Allan Beever tells me Eric Clapton said that playing wrong notes ruined concerts for him.

25 Theodore Gracyk, *Rhythm and Noise: An Aesthetics of Rock Music* (Duke University Press, 1996). I should add that Gracyk does not completely neglect the role of live performance in rock.

26 An illustrative analogy can be drawn here with movies. A movie is not for acting, but for screening, though acting might go into its creation as a work.

27 Baugh, "Music for the Young at Heart," p. 82.

28 In *Running with the Devil: Power, Gender, and Madness in Heavy Metal Music* (Wesleyan University Press, 1993), Robert Walser devotes a chapter to the connections between classical music and heavy metal. He records classical influences on the guitar techniques used by performers of heavy metal (pp. 63–75) and notes that both kinds of music esteem similar kinds of virtuosity (pp. 76–102). He quotes vocalist Robert Halford as saying: "I don't think that playing heavy metal is that far removed from classical music. To do either, you have to spend many years developing your style and your art. . . . It's very much a matter of dedication" (p. 106).

29 I think that there are respects in which rock virtuosity is not very different from the classical variety. Some rock musicians – Zappa, Clapton, and Van Halen – make manifestly difficult-to-play music sound fluent and they are respected and admired for doing so, as well as for whatever else they achieve. Baugh, as quoted previously, holds that Clapton and Hendrix are poor in techniques and, anyway, that virtuosity is never admired for its own sake in rock music. I believe he is wrong on both counts.

30 Theodore A. Gracyk makes the point in "Listening to Music: Performances and Recordings," *The Journal of Aesthetics and Art Criticism* 55 (1997): 139–150. As he recognizes, it applies also, though in a slightly different way, to recordings of classical music. Classical musicians exploit the advantages of recording technology, but they are expected to be able to play live the works they record.

31 Kendall Walton, "Categories of Art," *Philosophical Review* 79 (1970): 334–367.

Part XI

Aesthetics of Nature

Introduction to Part XI

Since the end of the eighteenth century when the theory of beauty became a theory of the aesthetic, philosophers have had an increasing tendency to explain the aesthetic in terms of art. Hegel considered the main task of aesthetics to reside in the study of the various forms of art and of the spiritual content peculiar to each. Much of recent aesthetics has been similarly focused on artistic problems, and it is still fairly standard to approach aesthetics through the study of art. Certainly in the early years of the analytic tradition, "Aesthetics" was often used synonymously with "Philosophy of Art." Ronald Hepburn's "Contemporary Aesthetics and the Neglect of Natural Beauty" (below), published in 1966, did much to change this perspective. The article re-opened the field of the aesthetics of nature and set the agenda for what later developed as "environmental aesthetics." Hepburn focuses on ways in which the aesthetic appreciation of nature is different from the appreciation of works of art, nature offering its own distinctive and valuable aesthetic experiences. Aesthetic experience of nature is not an experience of an *object* but of what Allen Carlson (in the article reprinted here) calls an "environment" of which man experiences himself as being a part. This environment challenges all his senses and envelops him. Secondly, unlike a work of art, which is "framed," the environment provides no frames and offers no formally complete objects intended for appreciation. The observer is challenged to provide his own focus for appreciation and to include or exclude any aspect that the environment offers for observation. Thirdly, nature offers scope for the play of the imagination with its many-faceted and complex "designs." Consequently, it has a function similar

to that of a work of art, but the function is served in a way that is distinctive to nature.

Hepburn not only makes a distinction between the aesthetic appreciation of nature and the appreciation of works of art, but suggests that one's training in appreciating artworks may get in the way of the aesthetic appreciation of nature because it will lead one to look for the wrong things in nature. This point is developed further by Allen Carlson, who in "Appreciation and the Natural Environment" introduced the concept of "environmental aesthetics." Carlson distinguishes between three models for the appreciation of nature. Two of these he dismisses as unsuitable: the object model which isolates the object under appreciation from its natural environment, and the scenery or landscape model which takes the object of appreciation as being a prospect of a landscape. These are both models derived, according to Carlson, from the appreciation of artworks and cannot be used as models for the aesthetic appreciation of nature. Instead he favors the environmental model, which refines the distinctive features attributed by Hepburn to the aesthetic experience of nature. However, Carlson also adds an important element to his model in pointing out that the spectator does not look at his environment with an innocent eye: his perception is conditioned by the conceptual schemes available to him for describing the natural environment as well as by his beliefs about it. Consequently, the question arises whether the observer has sufficient knowledge to experience the environment "truly" as the environment it is. Carlson argues that commonsense knowledge coupled with relevant scientific knowledge is essential to set the appropriate boundaries (to provide foci) for the appreciation of the natural environment and to appreciate it appropriately, and that this knowledge plays a role similar to that played in art appreciation by knowledge of artistic traditions and styles.

Because of its insistence that nature be understood as an enveloping environment, environmental aesthetics rejects as aesthetically inappropriate or even pernicious the appreciation of natural objects in isolation from their natural environment and, as a consequence of this, also the appreciation of scenery or landscapes. However, there are two serious conceptual problems in the way environmental aesthetics develops its thesis. It is not clear that the notion of "natural environment" captures what seems to be one central element in the notion of "nature" as it is traditionally used in discourse about the aesthetic appreciation of nature. That is, it seems to be quite natural to speak about appreciating aesthetically natural objects and landscapes. Secondly, if nature is understood as an enveloping environment challenging all man's senses and involving a multifaceted experience, it is not clear how the aesthetic appreciation of the natural environment can be differentiated from other forms of appreciation of the natural environment. It does seem to be necessary to distinguish between experiences of the natural environment that are just generally positive, pleasant, enjoyable, gratifying, rich, intense, etc. (the kind of total experience one has cross-country skiing on a sunny day through the woods with the cold air of a light breeze against one's face, etc.) and an aesthetic experience of nature.

A conceptual analysis of the notions of "nature" and "aesthetic appreciation" is undertaken by Malcolm Budd in "The Aesthetic Appreciation of Nature," who points out that "nature exhibits a remarkable variety of different kinds of things" and that what is important in the aesthetic appreciation of these things is that they should be appreciated *as being natural*. He also provides an analysis of the concept of aesthetic appreciation that is "neutral about the relative importance or priority of art and nature within the field of the aesthetic." On Budd's account it is quite possible to appreciate aesthetically a natural object (as natural) in isolation from its natural environment. Budd's account also realigns the aesthetic appreciation of nature with appreciation of art and provides a concept of aesthetic appreciation that makes meaningful a distinction between aesthetic and other forms of appreciation of nature.

Further reading

Berleant, Arnold (1992). *The Aesthetics of Environment* (Philadelphia: Temple University Press).

Berleant, Arnold and Carlson, Allen (eds.). (1998). *Special Issue: Environmental Aesthetics, Journal of Aesthetics and Art Criticism* 56, 139–47.

Carlson, Allen (2000). *Aesthetics and the Environment. The Appreciation of Nature, Art, and Architecture* (London: Routledge).

Crawford, Don (1983). "Nature and Art: Some Dialectical Relationships," *Journal of Aesthetics and Art Criticism* 42, 49–58.

Hepburn, Ronald (1996). "Landscape and the Metaphysical Imagination," *Environmental Values* 5, 191–204.

Kemal, Salim and Gaskell, Ivan (eds.) (1993). *Landscape, Natural Beauty and the Arts* (Cambridge: Cambridge University Press).

Parsons, Glenn (2002). "Nature Appreciation, Science, and Positive Aesthetics," *British Journal of Aesthetics* 42, 279–95.

Stecker, Robert (1997). "The Correct and the Appropriate in the Aesthetic Appreciation of Nature," *British Journal of Aesthetics* 37, 393–402.

44

Contemporary Aesthetics and the Neglect of Natural Beauty

R. W. Hepburn

Open an eighteenth-century work on aesthetics, and the odds are that it will contain a substantial treatment of the beautiful, the sublime, the picturesque in nature.[1] Its treatment of art may be secondary and derivative, not its primary concern. Although the nineteenth century could not be said to repeat these same emphases, they certainly reappear in some impressive places, in Ruskin's *Modern Painters*, for instance – a work that might have been entitled, no less accurately, 'How to look at nature and enjoy it aesthetically.' In our own day, however, writings on aesthetics attend almost exclusively to the arts and very rarely indeed to natural beauty, or only in the most perfunctory manner. Aesthetics is even *defined* by some mid-twentieth-century writers as 'the philosophy of art', 'the philosophy of criticism', analysis of the language and concepts used in describing and appraising art-objects. Two much-quoted anthologies of aesthetics (Elton's in Britain, Vivas and Krieger's in America) contain not a single study of natural beauty.[2]

Why has this curious shift come about? For part of the answer we have to look not to philosophers' theories but to some general shifts in aesthetic taste itself. This is a legitimate procedure, since, despite the difference of logical level between them, judgements of taste and the theorizings of aesthetics exert unmistakable influences upon one another. Relevant facts, then, are these: that – for all the cult of the

R. W. Hepburn, "Contemporary Aesthetics and the Neglect of Natural Beauty," in Bernard Williams and Alan Montefiore (eds.), *British Analytical Philosophy* (London: Routledge & Kegan Paul, 1966), pp. 285–310. Reprinted by permission of the publisher, Routledge.

open air, the caravans, camps and excursions in the family car – serious aesthetic concern with nature is today rather a rare phenomenon. If we regard the Wordsworthian vision as the great peak in the recent history of the subject, then we have to say that the ground declined very sharply indeed from that extraordinary summit, and that today we survey it from far below. In one direction it quickly declined to the deeps of the romantics' own 'dejection' experiences, and in another to the forced ecstasies and hypocrisies of a fashionable and trivialized nature-cult. At its most deeply felt the Wordsworthian experience brought a rekindling of religious imagination for some who found it no longer sustained by the traditional dogmas. But a still more radical loss of religious confidence came to undermine the undogmatic Wordsworthian experience itself.

The vanishing of the sense that nature is man's 'educator', that its beauties communicate more or less specific morally ennobling messages, this is only one aspect of the general (and much anatomized) disappearance of a rationalist faith in nature's thorough-going intelligibility and in its ultimate endorsement of human visions and aspirations. The characteristic image of contemporary man, as we all know, is that of a 'stranger', encompassed by a nature which is indifferent, unmeaning and 'absurd'.

The work of the sciences, too, has tended to increase bewilderment and loss of nerve over the aesthetic interpretation of nature. Microscope and telescope have added vastly to our perceptual data; the forms of the ordinary landscape, ordinarily interpreted, are shown up as only a selection from countless different scales.

It is not surprising that (with a few exceptions) the artists themselves have turned from imitation and representation to the sheer creation of new objects, rewarding to contemplate in their own right. If they are expressive of more than purely formal relationships, then that 'more' tends to be not the alien external landscape but the inner landscape of the human psyche.

On the theoretical level, there are other and distinctive reasons for the neglect of natural beauty in aesthetics itself, especially in an aesthetics that seeks to make itself increasingly rigorous. One such reason is that if we are aiming at an entirely general account of aesthetic excellence, this account cannot make essential reference to experience of (or imitation of) nature; since there are arts like music which are devoid of any such reference. Some writers have been impressed by the fact that certain crucial features of aesthetic experience are quite unobtainable in nature – a landscape does not minutely control the spectator's response to it as does a successful work of art; it is an unframed ordinary object, in contrast to the framed, 'esoteric', 'illusory' or 'virtual' character of the art-object. And so the artefact is taken as the aesthetic object *par excellence*, and the proper focus of study.

Although it is now very much in eclipse, the last widely accepted unified aesthetic system was the expression theory. No single new system has taken its place; and some of its influences are still with us. The expression theory is a *communication-theory*: it must represent aesthetic experience of nature either as communication from the Author of Nature, which it rarely does, or else (rather awkwardly) as the discovery that nature's shapes and colours can with luck serve as expressive vehicles of human feeling, although never constructed for that end.[3] The theory most readily copes with artefacts, not natural objects; with successful interpersonal communication, not the contemplation of sheer entities *as* entities. Although some very recent aesthetic analyses provide instruments that could be used to redress the lopsidedness of these emphases, they have not yet been applied extensively to this task.[4]

We may note, finally, that linguistic or conceptual analysts have been understandably tempted to apply their techniques first and foremost to the arguments, counter-arguments and manifestoes lying to hand in the writings of critics of the arts. In the case of natural beauty, however, such a polemical critical literature scarcely exists. The philosopher must first work out his own detailed and systematic account of the aesthetic enjoyment of nature. And this he has so far been slow, or reluctant, to do.

Having outlined the situation, the neglect of the study of natural beauty, I now want to argue that the neglect is a very bad thing: bad, because aesthetics is thereby steered off from examining an important and richly complex set of relevant data; and bad because when a set of human experiences is ignored in a theory relevant to them, they tend to be rendered less readily available as experiences. If we cannot find sensible-sounding language in which to describe them – language of a piece with the rest of our aesthetic – the experiences are felt, in an embarrassed way, as off-the-map; and, since off the map, seldom visited. This result is specially unfortunate, if for other reasons the experiences are already hard to achieve – in some of their varieties at least. What, then, can contemporary aesthetics say on the topic of natural beauty?

In a one-chapter study like this the whole problem (or tangle of problems) cannot be teased out minutely. There must be drastic selecting among possible themes. I have tried in what follows to strike a reasonable compromise. On the one hand, the reader needs some surveying of the philosophical situation, some indicating of the main patterns of current argument and opinion; and on the other hand (knowing how much emphasis is put upon minute logical analysis in British philosophy), he must be provided with some samples of that – brief and tentative though they will have to be. This essay has begun with some very general remarks indeed: it will move gradually towards discussing more specific and limited issues, and its last topic of all will be its most highly particularized one. These various topics are not so intimately related as to be links in a single chain of argument. But the later discussions make frequent and essential reference back to points made earlier. I call this in one sense a compromise (in that neither the survey nor the analysis is more than a sketch); but in another sense it tries to exhibit what are always legitimate, indeed necessary, tasks for the writer on aesthetics. He is ill-advised to do *nothing but* general surveying, or his work would be too loosely and remotely related to the particularities of actual aesthetic experiences. But a mono-maniacal concern with analysis alone can be equally unfortunate. It may prevent even an intelligent choosing of cruces for the analysis itself, and make it impossible to see the bearing of the analyses upon the inquiry as a whole, far less upon the related fields of ethics and the philosophy of mind.

If I am right that systematic description is one main lack in the treatment of our subject, my first obligation may well be to supply some account of the varieties of aesthetic experience of nature. But their variety is immense, and mere cataloguing would be tedious. I shall suggest, therefore, two principles of selection that may throw together some samples interesting in themselves and useful for our subsequent arguments.

First, we have already remarked that art-objects have a number of general characteristics not shared by objects in nature. It would be useful if we could show (and I think we can) that the absence of certain of these features is not merely negative or privative in its effect, but can contribute positively and valuably to the aesthetic experience of nature. A good specimen is the degree to which the spectator can be involved in the natural aesthetic situation itself. On occasion, he may confront natural objects as a static, disengaged observer; but far more typically the objects envelop him on all sides. In a forest, trees surround him; he is ringed by hills, or he stands in the midst of a plain. If there is movement in the scene, the spectator may himself be in motion, and his motion may be an important element in his aesthetic experience. Think, for instance, of a glider-pilot, delighting in a sense of buoyancy, in the balancing of the air-currents that hold him aloft. This sort of involvement is well expressed by Barbara Hepworth:

> What a different shape and 'being' one becomes lying on the sand with the sea almost above from when standing against the wind on a sheer high cliff with seabirds circling patterns below one. (Hepworth, Ch. 4)

We have not only a mutual involvement of spectator and object, but also a reflexive effect by which the spectator experiences *himself* in an unusual and vivid way; and this difference is not merely noted, but dwelt upon aesthetically. The effect is not unknown to art, especially architecture. But it is both more intensely realized and pervasive in nature-experience – for we are *in* nature and a part *of* nature; we do not stand over against it as over against a painting on a wall.

If this study were on a larger scale, we should have to analyse in detail the various senses of 'detachment' and 'involvement' that are relevant

here. This would prove a more slippery investigation than in the case of art-appreciation; but a rewarding one. Some sort of detachment there certainly is, in the sense that I am not *using* nature, manipulating it or calculating how to manipulate it. But I am both actor and spectator, ingredient in the landscape and lingering upon the sensations of being thus ingredient, rejoicing in their multifariousness, playing actively with nature, and letting nature, as it were, play with me and my sense of myself.

My second specimen is very similar, though, I think, worth listing separately. Though by no means all art-objects have frames or pedestals, they share a common character in being *set apart* from their environment, and set apart in a distinctive way. We might use the words 'frame' and 'framed' in an extended sense, to cover not only the physical boundaries of pictures but all the various devices employed in the different arts to prevent the art-object being mistaken for a natural object or for an artefact without aesthetic interest. Our list of frames, in this wide sense, would include the division between stage-area and audience-area in the theatre, the concert-convention that the only aesthetically relevant sounds are those made by the performers, the layout of a page in a book of poems, where typography and spacing set the poem apart from titles, page-numbers, critical apparatus and footnotes. Such devices are best thought of as aids to the recognition of the formal *completeness* of the art-objects themselves, their ability to sustain aesthetic interest, an interest that is not crucially dependent upon the relationships between the object and its general environment. Certainly, its environment may enhance or weaken its effect; and we may even see parts of the environment in a new way as a result of contemplating an art-object. But this does not affect the central point, that these works of art are first and foremost bounded objects, that their aesthetic characteristics are determined by their internal structure, the interplay of their elements.

In contrast, natural objects are 'frameless'. This is in some ways a disadvantage aesthetically; but there are some remarkable compensating advantages. Whatever lies beyond the frame of an art-object cannot normally become part of the aesthetic experience relevant to it. A chance train-whistle cannot be integrated into the music of a string quartet; it merely interferes with its appreciation. But where there is no frame, and where nature is our aesthetic object, a sound or a visible intrusion from beyond the original boundaries of our attention can challenge us to integrate it in our overall experience, to modify that experience so as to make room for it. This, of course, *need* not occur; we may shut it out by effort of will, if it seems quite unassimilable. At any rate, our creativity is challenged, set a task; and when things go well with us, we experience a sudden expansion of imagination that can be memorable in its own right.

> And, when there came a pause
> Of silence such as baffled his best skill:
> Then sometimes, in that silence, while
>   he hung
> Listening, a gentle shock of mild surprise
> Has carried far into his heart the voice
> Of mountain-torrents;
>   Wordsworth, *There Was a Boy*

If the absence of 'frame' precludes full determinateness and stability in the natural aesthetic object, it at least offers in return such unpredictable perceptual surprises; and their mere possibility imparts to the contemplation of nature a sense of adventurous openness.[5]

Something more definite can be said on the determinate and indeterminate in this connection. In, say, a painting, the frame ensures that each element of the work is determined in its perceived qualities (including emotional qualities) by a limited and definite context. Colour modifies colour and form modifies form; yet the frame supplies a boundary to all relevant modifies, and, thus, any given colour or shape can be seen, in a successful painting, to have a determinate, contextually controlled character. Obviously, this is one kind of determinateness that cannot be achieved with natural objects; and that for several reasons. To consider only one of them: the aesthetic impact made upon us by, say, a tree, is part-determined by the context we include in our view of it. A tree growing on a steep hill-slope, bent far over by the winds, may strike us as tenacious, grim, strained. But from a greater distance, when the view includes numerous similar trees on the hillside, the striking thing may be a delightful, stippled, patterned slope, with quite different emotional quality – quixotic or cheery.[6] So with any aesthetic quality in nature; it is always provisional, correctible by reference to a different, perhaps wider context, or to a narrower one realized in greater detail. 'An idyllic scene? But you haven't noticed that advancing, though still distant, thundercloud. Now you

have noticed it, and the whole scene takes on a new, threatened, ominous look.' In positive terms this provisional and elusive character of aesthetic qualities in nature creates a restlessness, an alertness, a search for ever new standpoints, and for more comprehensive gestalts. Of this restlessness and of this search I shall, very shortly, have more to say.

My last point on the present topic is this. We can distinguish, in a rough and ready way, between the particular aesthetic impact of an object, whether natural or artefact, and certain general 'background' experiences, that are common to a great many aesthetic situations and are of aesthetic value in themselves. With an art-object, there is the exhilarating activity of coming to grasp its intelligibility as a perceptual whole. We find built-in guides to interpretation, and contextual controls for our response. We are aware of these features as having been expressly put there by its creator. Now I think that we can locate a nearly parallel but interestingly different background experience when our object is not an artefact but a natural one. Again, it is a kind of exhilaration, in this case a delight in the fact that the forms of the natural world *offer scope* for the exercise of the imagination, that leaf pattern chimes with vein or pattern, cloud form with mountain form and mountain form with human form. On a theistic view this begets a distinctive sort of wonderment at the 'artistry' of God. On a naturalistic view it can beget at least no less wonderment at this uncontrived adaptation. Indeed, when nature is pronounced to be 'beautiful' – not in the narrower sense of that word, which contrasts 'beautiful' with 'picturesque' or 'comic', but in the wide sense equivalent to 'aesthetically excellent' – an important part of our meaning is just this, that nature's forms do provide this scope for imaginative play. For that is surely not analytically true; it might have been otherwise.

I have been arguing that certain important differences between natural objects and art-objects should not be seen as entailing the aesthetic unimportance of the former, that (on the contrary) several of these differences furnish grounds for distinctive and valuable types of aesthetic experience of nature. These are types of experience that art cannot provide to the same extent as nature, and which in some cases it cannot provide at all.

Supposing that a person's aesthetic education fails to reckon with these differences, supposing it instils in him the attitudes, the tactics of approach, the expectations proper to the appreciation of artworks only, we may be sure that such a person will either pay very little aesthetic heed to natural objects, or else will heed them in the wrong way. He will look – and of course look in vain – for what can be found and enjoyed only in art. Furthermore, one cannot be at all certain that he will seriously ask himself whether there might be other tactics, other attitudes and expectations more proper and more fruitful for the aesthetic appreciation of nature. My sampling of these 'differences', therefore, is not a merely introductory exercise in distinction-making. It has the polemical purpose of showing that unless these distinctions are reckoned with both in aesthetic education and theorizing, one can neither intelligently pursue nor adequately comprehend experience of natural beauty, save only in its most rudimentary forms.

So much for the listing of neglects and omissions. I want now to turn to something more constructive, and to take as a starting-point certain recurrent and *prima facie* attractive ways in which natural beauty has in fact been attended to and described, both in the past and present. I say 'as starting-point', because I do not plan to examine in detail specific philosophical theories that have incorporated them. Rather, we shall take note of those approaches, the characteristic vocabulary that goes with them, and inquire how far (if at all) they point to an aesthetic of natural beauty that could be viable today.

Accounts of natural beauty sometimes focus upon the contemplating of single natural objects in their individuality and uniqueness (for an example – Pepita Haezrahi's analysis of the aesthetic contemplation of a single falling leaf in (Haezrahi, Ch. 2). Other writers, with greater metaphysical daring – or rashness – speak of the enjoyment of natural beauty as tending towards an ideal of 'oneness with nature' or as leading to the disclosure of 'unity' in nature. The formulations vary greatly and substantially among themselves; but the vocabulary of unity, oneness as the key aesthetic principle, is the recurrent theme. (On this point see terminal Note, p. 532).

There are strong influences in contemporary British philosophy that prompt one to have the fullest sympathy with a particularist approach to natural beauty – as the contemplation of individual objects with their aesthetically interesting perceptual qualities; and to have very little sympathy for the more grandiose, speculative and quasi-mystical language of 'oneness with or in nature'. Yet it seems to me that we do not have here one good and one bad aesthetic approach, the first sane and the second absurd. Rather, we have two poles or well-separated landmarks between which lies a range of aesthetic possibilities; and in the mapping of this range those landmarks will play a valuable, perhaps a necessary role.

We must begin by bluntly denying the universal need for unity, unity of form, quality, structure or of anything else. We can take aesthetic pleasure in sheer plurality, in the stars of the night sky, in a birdsong without beginning, middle or end.[7]

And yet to make unity, in some sense, one's key concept need not be simply wrong-headed or obscurantist. Nor do we have to say, rather limply, that there are two distinct and unrelated types of aesthetic excellence, one that contemplates individual uniqueness and the other – no better or worse – that aims at some grand synthesis. I want to argue that there are certain incompletenesses in the experience of the isolated particular, that produce a *nisus* towards the other pole, the pole of unity. Accuracy, however, will require us to deny that there is a single type of unification or union; there are several notions to be distinguished within the ideal, and the relations between them are quite complex.

One such direction of development we have already noted; namely, the *nisus* towards more and more comprehensive or adequate survey of the context that determines the perceived qualities of a natural object or scene. Our motives are, in part, the desire for a certain integrity or 'truth' in our aesthetic experience of nature; and of this more shortly. In part also we are prompted by our awareness that in all aesthetic experience it is contextual complexity that, more than any other single factor, makes possible the minute discrimination of emotional qualities; and such discrimination is accorded high aesthetic value. It is largely the pursuit of such value that moves us to accept what I called 'the challenge to integrate' – to take notice of and to accept as aesthetically relevant some shape or sound that initially lies outside the limit of our attention. 'Challenge' was not, I think, an over-dramatic word to use. For we can contrast the stereotyped experiences of the aesthetically apathetic and unadventurous person with the richly and subtly diversified experiences of the aesthetically courageous person. His courage consists in his refusal to heed only those features of a natural object or scene that most readily come together in a familiar pattern or which yield a comfortingly generalized emotional quality. It also involves taking the repeated risk of drawing a blank, of finding oneself unable to hold the various elements together as a single object of contemplation, or to elicit any significant aesthetic experience from them at all.

The expansion of context may be a spatial expansion, but it does not have to be spatial. What else can it be? When we contemplate a natural object, we may see it not as sand-dune or rock but simply as a coloured shape. If this is difficult, we can look at the world upside down, with our head between our legs. But although an aesthetic view of an object will strive to shake free from conventional and deadening conceptualizings, that is not to say that *all* interpretings, all 'seeings as . . .' are lapses to the non-aesthetic. We ought not to accept a dichotomy of 'pure aesthetic contemplation' – 'impure admixture of associations'. Suppose I am walking over a wide expanse of sand and mud. The quality of the scene is perhaps that of wild, glad emptiness. But suppose that I bring to bear upon the scene my knowledge that this is a tidal basin, the tide being out. The realization is not aesthetically irrelevant. I see myself now as virtually walking on what is for half the day sea-bed. The wild glad emptiness may be tempered by a disturbing weirdness.

This sort of experience can readily be related to the movement we were examining, the movement towards more complex and comprehensive synopses. In addition to spatial extension (or sometimes instead of it), we may aim at enriching the interpretative element, taking this not as theoretical 'knowledge about' the object or scene, but as helping to determine the aesthetic impact it makes upon us. 'Unity' here plays a purely 'regulative' role. Nature is not a 'given whole', nor indeed is knowledge about it. But in any case, there are practical, psychological limits to the expansion process; a degree of complexity is reached, beyond which there will be no increase in discrimination of perceptual or emotional qualities: rather the reverse.

A second movement away from contemplation of uninterpreted particulars is sometimes known as the 'humanizing' or the 'spiritualizing' of nature. I shall merely note its existence and relevance here, for there have been a good many accounts of it in the history of aesthetics. Coleridge said that 'Art is . . . the power of humanizing nature, of infusing the thoughts and passions of man into every thing which is the object of his contemplation' (Coleridge, Vol. II). And Hegel, that the aim of art is 'to strip the outer world of its stubborn foreignness' (Hegel, Introduction). What is here said about art is no less true of aesthetic experience of nature itself. Imaginative activity is working for a *rapprochement* between the spectator and his aesthetic object: unity is again a regulative notion, a symbol of the unattainable complete transmutation of brute external nature into a mirror of the mind.

By developing and qualifying the 'humanization' ideal we can come to see yet a third aspect of the *nisus* towards unity. A person who contemplates natural objects aesthetically may sometimes find that their emotional quality is describable in the vocabulary of ordinary human moods and feelings – melancholy, exuberance, placidity. In many cases, however, he will find that they are not at all accurately describable in such terms. A particular emotional quality can be roughly *analogous* to some nameable human emotion, desolation for instance; but the precise quality of desolation revealed in some waste or desert in nature may be quite distinctive in timbre and intensity. To put this another way: one may go to nature to find shapes and sounds that can be taken as the embodiment of human emotion, and in so far as this occurs, nature is felt to be humanized. But instead of nature being humanized, the reverse may happen. Aesthetic experience of nature may be experience of a range of emotion that the human scene, by itself, untutored and unsupplemented, could not evoke. To extend the scope of these remarks, recall once again our quotation from Barbara Hepworth. To be 'one' with nature in that sense was to realize vividly one's place in the landscape, as a form among its forms. And this is not to have nature's 'foreignness' or otherness overcome, but in contrast, to allow that otherness free play in the modifying of one's everyday sense of one's own being.

In this domain, again, we need not confine ourselves to the contemplating of naked, uninterpreted particulars. In a leaf-pattern I may 'see' also blood-vessel patterns, or the patterns of branching, forked lightning: or all of these. In a spiral nebula pattern I may see the pattern of swirling waters or whirling dust. I may be aware of a network of affinities, of analogous forms, that spans the inorganic or the organic world, or both. My experience has a quality of *multum in parvo*.[8] This is not necessarily a 'humanizing' of nature; it may be more like a 'naturizing' of the human observer. If, with Mr Eliot, one sees 'The dance along the artery/The circulation of the lymph' as 'figured in the drift of stars', something of the aesthetic qualities of the latter (as we perceive them) may come to be transferred to the former. Supposing that by this kind of aesthetic experience nature is felt to lose some of its 'foreignness', that may be because we have ourselves become foreign to our everyday, unexamined notion of ourselves, and not through any assimilation of nature's forms to pre-existent notions, images or perceptions.

A fourth class of approaches to the ideals of 'unity' is itself rather heterogeneous; but we can characterize its members as follows. They are, once again, concerned less with the specific content of particular aesthetic experiences than with what we have called the 'background' quality of emotions and attitudes, common to a great many individual experiences. In their case the background is a sense of reconciliation, suspension of conflict, and of being in that sense at one with the aesthetic object. This particular sort of 'at-one-ness' could hardly be present in art-experience, since it requires that the aesthetic object should be at the same time the natural environment or some part of it. This is the same environment from which we wrest our food, from which we have to protect ourselves in order to live, which refuses to sustain our individual lives beyond a limited term, and to which we are finally 'united' in a manner far different from those envisaged in the aesthetic ideals of 'unity': 'Rolled round in earth's diurnal course / With rocks and stones and trees.' To attain, and sustain, the relevant detachment from such an environment in order to savour it aesthetically is in itself a fair achievement, an achievement which suffuses the aesthetic experiences themselves with that sense of reconciliation. A cease-fire has been negotiated in our struggle with nature.

There is immense variety in the ways in which this can manifest itself in individual experience. The objects of nature may look to us as if their *raison d'etre* were precisely that we should celebrate their beauty. As Rilke put it: 'Everything beckons to us to perceive it.' Or, the dominant stance may be that of benediction: the Ancient Mariner 'blesses' the watersnakes at his moment of reconciliation.

The fourth type of unity-ideal is notably different from our first three specimens. The first three quest after unity in the particular aesthetic perception itself: the attainment of complex unified synopses, the grasping of webs of affinities and so on. The fourth, however, could arise in the contemplation of what is itself quite *un*-unified in the

above senses, the night sky again, or a mass of hills with no detectable pattern to unite them. It is more strictly a concomitant, or a by-product of an aesthetic experience that we are already enjoying, an experience in which there may have been no synoptic grasping of patterns, relating of forms or any other sort of unifying.

I suspect that someone who tried to construct a comprehensive aesthetic theory with 'unity' as its sole key concept would obtain his comprehensiveness only by equivocating or punning over the meaning of the key expression, only by sliding and slithering from one of its many senses to another. When one sense is not applicable, another may well be. The fourth sense in particular can be relevant to vivid aesthetic experience of any natural object or collection of objects whatever.

So much the worse, we may conclude, for such a theory *qua* monolithic. But to say that is not to imply that our study has yielded only negative results. This is only one of several areas in aesthetics where we have to resist the temptation to work with a single supreme concept and must replace it by a *cluster* of related key concepts. Yet, in searching out the relevant key-concepts, the displaced pseudo-concept may yet be a useful guide – as it is in the present case. We should be ill-advised, however, to take this cluster of unity-concepts as by itself adequate for all explanatory purposes. Our analysis started with the stark contemplation of the uninterpreted, unrelated natural object in all its particularity and individual distinctness. This was not a mere starting-point, to be left behind in our pursuit of the 'unities'. On the contrary, aesthetic experience remains tethered to that concern with the particular, even if on a long rope. The rope is there, although the development and vitality of that experience demand that it be stretched to the full. The pull of the rope is felt, when the expanding and complicating of our synopses reaches the point beyond which we shall have not more but less fine discrimination of perceptual quality. It is felt again, when we risk the blurring and negating of natural forms as we really perceive them, in an anxious attempt to limit our experience of nature to the savouring of stereotyped and well-domesticated emotional qualities. It is even relevant to our fourth type of unity-ideal: for the sense of reconciliation is not an independent and autonomous aesthetic experience, but hangs entirely upon the occurrence of particular experiences of particular aesthetically interesting natural objects.

Up to this point my aim has been chiefly to describe some varieties of aesthetic experience of nature. From these we may make the following inferences. (i) Although some important features of art-experience are unattainable in nature, that by no means entitles the aesthetician to confine his studies to art; for even these points of apparent privation can yield types of aesthetic experience that are well worth analysis. (ii) Accounts of natural beauty that take 'unity' as their central concept are often metaphysically extravagant, and are chronically unperceptive of ambiguities in their claims. Nevertheless, a cautious aesthetician would be unwise to let this extravagance deflect him from patiently teasing out the numerous and important strands of experience that originally prompted these accounts.

I turn now to a second main topic. Although recent aesthetics has been little concerned with natural beauty as such, yet in the course of its analysis of *art*-experience, it has frequently made comparisons between our aesthetic approach to art-objects and to objects in nature. It has made these comparisons at crucial points in argument, and in several different sorts of context. But what has not been asked – or adequately answered – is whether the comparing has been fairly done; whether, in particular, the account of nature-experience, given or presupposed, is an adequate or a distorted account. Our discussion of some 'varieties' may have furnished us with useful data.

A substantial part of recent aesthetics has been the criticism of the expression theory of art. Right at the centre of this criticism is the denial that we need concern ourselves with discovering the intention or the actual feelings or intuitions of the artist, when we try to appreciate or to appraise his artefact. The expression theory saw the artefact as the middle link in a communication from artist to spectator; the critics of the theory see the artefact first and foremost as an object with certain properties, properties which are, or should be, aesthetically interesting, worth contemplating, and which in their totality control and guide the spectator's response. This change of emphasis chimes in well with the desire for a 'scientific' criticism (the properties are *there* in the artefact, the object), and with the anti-psychologistic mood of current British and American philosophy (the work of art is not an 'imaginary' one: and we are not probing behind it to its creator's states of soul).

Clearly this is an aesthetic approach that reduces the gulf between art-object and natural object.

Both are to be approached primarily as individual, self-contained entities, exciting to contemplate by virtue of the objective properties they can be seen to possess.[9] But, let us ask, how far can we accept this comparison? Critics of the critics have pointed out some deficiencies. They have insisted, for instance, upon the irreducible relevance of linguistic, social and cultural context to the interpretation of a poem. The identical words might constitute *two* poems, not one, if we read them in two different contexts.[10] We could extend this criticism as follows. Suppose we have two perceptually identical objects, one an artefact and the other natural. They might be a 'carved stone' of Arp and a naturally smoothed stone; a carving in wood and a piece of fallen timber. Or they might be identical in pattern, though not in material; for example, a rock face with a particular texture and markings, and an abstract expressionist painting with the same texture and the same markings. If we made the most of the *rapprochement*, we should have to say that we had in each of these cases essentially *one* aesthetic object. (Although numerically two, the pair would be no more aesthetically different from one another than two engravings from the same block.) Yet this would be a misleading conclusion. If we knew them for what they are – as artefact or natural object – we should certainly attend differently to them, and respond differently to them. As we look at the rock face in nature, we may realize imaginatively the geological pressures and turmoils that produced its pattern. The realizing of these need not be a piece of extra-aesthetic reflection: it may determine for us how we see and respond to the object itself. If we interpreted and responded to the abstract painting in the same way (assuming, of course, that it is a thoroughgoing abstract and not the representation of a rock face!), our interpretation would this time be merely whimsical, no more controlled or stabilized than a seeing of faces in the fire.[11] If we arbitrarily restricted aesthetic experience both of nature and art to the contemplating of uninterpreted shapes and patterns, we could, of course, have the *rapprochement*. But we have seen good reason for refusing so to restrict it in the case of nature-experience, whatever be the case with art.

Take another example. Through the eye-piece of a telescope I see the spiral nebula in Andromeda. I look next at an abstract painting in a circular frame that contains the identical visual pattern. My responses are not alike, even if each is indisputably aesthetic. My awareness that the first shapes are of enormous and remote masses of matter in motion imparts to my response a strangeness and solemnity that are not generated by the pattern alone. The abstract pattern may indeed impress by reminding me of various wheeling and swirling patterns in nature. But there is a difference between taking the pattern as that sort of reminder, and, on the other hand, brooding on this impressive instantiation of it in the nebula. Furthermore, a point already made about the emotive 'background' to aesthetic experience is relevant here again. Where we confront what we know to be a human artefact – say a painting – we have no special shock of surprise at the mere discovery that there are patterns here which delight perception; we know that they have been put there, though certainly we may be astonished at their particular aesthetic excellences. With a natural object, however, such surprise can figure importantly in our overall response, a surprise that is probably the greater the more remote the object from our everyday environment.

A more lighthearted but helpful way of bringing out these points is to suppose ourselves confronted by a small object, which, for all we know, may be natural or may be an artefact. We are set the task of regarding it aesthetically. I suppose that we might cast upon it an uneasy and embarrassed eye. How shall we approach it? Shall we, for instance, see in its smoothness the slow mindless grinding of centuries of tides, or the swifter and mindful operations of the sculptor's tools? Certainly, we can enjoy something of its purely formal qualities on either reckoning; but even the savouring of these is affected by non-formal factors that diverge according to the judgement we make about its origin.

To sum up this argument. On the rebound from a view of art as expression, as language, and the work of art as the medium of communication between artist and spectator, some recent aesthetics has been urging that the artefact is, first and foremost, an object among objects. The study of art is primarily the study of such objects, their observable qualities, their organization. This swing from intention to object has been healthful on the whole, delivering aesthetics and criticism from a great deal of misdirected labour. But it has countered the paradoxes of expressionism with paradoxes, or illuminating exaggerations, of its own. Differences between object and object need to be reaffirmed: indiscernibly different poems or carvings become discernibly different when we reckon with their aesthetically relevant cultural contexts; and the

contextual controls that determine how we contemplate an object in nature are different from those that shape our experience of art. In other words, we have here a central current issue in aesthetics that cannot be properly tackled without a full-scale discussion of natural beauty.

That, however, is not the only current issue about which the same can be said. It can be said also (and this introduces our final topic) about the analysis of such expressions as 'true', 'false', 'profound', 'shallow', 'superficial', as terms of aesthetic appraisal. These have been studied in their application to art-objects, but scarcely at all in connection with nature.[12] It might indeed be contested whether they have *any* meaningful use in the latter connection. I should readily admit that ordinary language can give very little help here; but I am equally sure that a use or uses can be *given* to these expressions in that context, and that such uses would be closely related to the more familiar uses in talk about art. But would this not constitute a merely arbitrary and pointless extension of a vocabulary useful only in art-criticism? Not really: it would rather be to give comprehensiveness to a set of discriminations important throughout aesthetic experience, but which has tended, for various understandable reasons, to be worked out in detail only with respect to art.

Where then, in the aesthetic experience of nature, is there any room for talking of 'truth', 'depth', 'triviality'? We can best approach an answer by way of some analysis of an expression which we have used once or twice already but not explained. It is a sense of the word 'realize'. Here are some examples of the use. 'I had long *known* that the earth was not flat, but I had never before *realized* its curvature till I watched that ship disappear on the horizon.' 'I had seen from the map that this was a deserted moor, but not till I stood in the middle of it did I realize its desolation.' Here 'realize' involves making, or becoming, vivid to perception, or to the imagination. If I suddenly realize the height of a cumulo-nimbus cloud I am not simply *taking note* of the height, but imagining myself climbing into the cloud in an aeroplane or falling through it, or I am superimposing upon it an image of a mountain of known vastness, or . . . or . . . Auxiliary imagings may likewise attend my realizing of the earth's curvature, the image of my arms stretched out, fingers reaching round the sphere; and the realization of loneliness may involve imagining myself shouting but being unheard, needing help but getting none. In some senses, to realize something is simply to 'know' or 'understand', where 'know' and 'understand' are analysable in dispositional terms. But our present sense of 'realize' has an essential episodic component: it is a coming-to-be-aware, a 'clock-able' experience. In the aesthetic setting that interests us, it is an experience accompanying and arising out of perceptions – perceptions upon which we dwell and linger: I am gazing at the cumulo–nimbus cloud, when I realize its height. We do not discard, or pass beyond, the experience, as if we were judging the height of the cloud in flight-navigation, or the loneliness of the moor in planning a murder. Realizing, in our sense, is not estimating or calculating. When I am told that the moon is a solid spherical body, 200,000 miles from the earth, I may go outside and look up at it and try, in the aesthetically relevant sense, to realize its solidity and its distance. Reference to perception can again be made obvious. We could not seriously ask ourselves 'Am I, in fact, accurately realizing its distance at 200,000 miles, or am I mistakenly imagining it as 190,000?' Such discriminations cannot be made perceptually: they can only be calculated.

Though we have no room to multiply examples, it should be obvious that this sort of realizing is one of our chief activities in the aesthetic experiencing of nature. It has been central in earlier illustrations, the contemplation of the rock face, the spiral nebula, the ocean-smoothed stone.

But my suggestion that realizing is 'episodic', occurrent, may properly be challenged. Suppose that I am realizing the utter loneliness of the moor, when suddenly I discover that behind sundry bits of cover are a great many soldiers taking part in a field-exercise. Could I, without illogic, maintain that I had been realizing what was not in fact the case? Hardly. 'Realize' contains a built-in reference to truth. It may have episodic components, but it cannot be exhaustively analysed in that way. I cannot be said to have realized the strength and hardness of a tall tree-trunk, if, when I then approach it, it crumbles rotten at a touch. But surely I was doing *something*: my experience did occur; and nothing that subsequently occurs can alter it.

Now, this experience was, of course, the aesthetic contemplation of apparent properties. That they turn out not to be also actual properties may disturb the spectator, or it may not. For some people aesthetic experience is interested not at all

in actuality – only in looks, seemings: indifference to truth may be part of their definition of the aesthetic. If the soldiers appear or the tree crumbles, the aesthetic value of the prior experiences is (to those people) not in the least affected.

But it is possible to take a rather different view. One could agree that a large range of aesthetic experience is not concerned about truth; but yet attach a peculiar importance to the range that is. I am not sure that the gulf between this and the contrasted view is wholly bridgeable by argument; but some reflections can be offered along the following lines.

If we want our aesthetic experiences to be repeatable and to have stability, we shall try to ensure that new information or subsequent experimentation will not reveal the 'seemings' as illusions, will not make a mock, as it were, of our first experience. If I know that the tree is rotten, I shall not be able again to savour its seeming-strength. I could, no doubt, savour its 'deceptively strong appearance'; but that would be a quite different experience from the first, and one that accepted and integrated the truth about the tree's actual rottenness.

Suppose the outline of our cumulo–nimbus cloud resembles that of a basket of washing, and we amuse ourselves in dwelling upon this resemblance. Suppose that on another occasion we dwell, not upon such freakish (or in Coleridge's sense 'fanciful') aspects, but try instead to realize the inner turbulence of the cloud, the winds sweeping up within and around it, determining its structure and visible form. Should we not be ready to say that this latter experience was less superficial or contrived than the other, that it was truer to nature, and for that reason more worth having? Or, compare again the realizing of the pressures, thrustings and great age of the rock before us, with merely chuckling over the likeness of its markings to a funny face. If there can be a passage, in art, from easy beauty to difficult and more serious beauty, there can also be such passage in aesthetic contemplation of nature.

If there were not a strong *nisus* in that direction, how could we account for the sense of bewilderment people express over how to bring their aesthetic view of nature into accord with the discoveries of recent science? Because of these discoveries (as Sir Kenneth Clark puts it), 'the snug, sensible nature which we can see with our own eyes has ceased to satisfy our imaginations'.[13]

If the aesthetic enjoyment of nature were no more than the contemplation of particular shapes and colours and movements, these discoveries could not possibly disturb it. But they do: they set the imagination a task in 'realizing'.

An objector may still insist that reference to truth (whether in nature or art) is aesthetically irrelevant. To him the only relevant factors are the savouring of perceptual qualities and formal organization. Can anything be said in reply to his claim? The formalist might at least be reminded that a major element in his own enjoyment is the synoptic grasping of complexities. A particular colour-patch may be seen as part of an object, as modifying the colour of adjacent patches, and as contributing to the total perceived pattern – all simultaneously. One could argue that reference to truth – the striving to 'realize' – should be taken as adding one more level of complexity, a further challenge to our powers of synopsis, and that for the *exclusion* of it no good reason could be given.

But a more searching anxiety might be expressed, in these terms. Sometimes, indeed, such realizings may enhance an aesthetic experience, but may they not on other occasions destroy it? If, for example, you see the full moon rising behind the silhouetted branches of winter trees, you may judge that the scene is more beautiful if you think of the moon simply as a silvery flat disc at no great distance from the trees on the skyline. Why should you have your enjoyment spoiled by someone who tells you that you ought to be realizing the moon's actual shape, size and distance? Why indeed? There may be cases where I have to choose between, on the one hand, an aesthetic experience available only if I inhibit my realizing, and, on the other hand, a different aesthetic experience, available if I do some realizing. In our example, the first experience is of beauty (in the narrow sense), and we could not count on the alternative experience being also one of beauty, in the same sense. It might, of course, be still aesthetically exciting, that is, of beauty in the wider sense, the commoner sense in aesthetics. But, the objector might still press, there is no guaranteeing even this latter possibility for *all* cases where we attempt to realize the nature of the objects contemplated. And this is exactly the difficulty we feel with regard to the bearing of present-day science on our vision of the natural world. Sometimes our attempts at realizing fail altogether, as with some versions of cosmologies and cosmogonies; or if they do succeed, they may be aes-

thetically bleak and unrewarding. Compromises, the balancing of one aesthetic requirement against another, are frequent enough, and may well be inevitable. One may say in a particular case – "This is the nearest I can come to making imaginatively vivid what I know about that object. My realizing is still not quite adequate to my knowledge; but if I were to go any farther in that direction I should lose touch altogether with the sights, sounds and movements of the visible world, seen from the human point of view. And that would impoverish, not enrich my total aesthetic experience.' What we should be feeling, (need I say?), is the tug of that rope – the rope that tethers aesthetic experience to the perception of the particular object and its perceived individuality.

To be able to say anything more confident about this problem, one would need to hold a metaphysical and religious view of nature and science, which denied that the imaginative assimilating of scientific knowledge could ultimately lead to aesthetic impoverishment. Probably Christian theism is one such view; and Goethe's philosophy of nature seems to have been another. These possibilities we can only take note of in this essay, without being able to explore them.

We may recall at the same time, and in conclusion, that the 'unitary' accounts of natural beauty have, historically, been closely allied with various sorts of pantheism and nature-mysticism. I have argued that there are, in fact, not one but several unity-ideals; that it is most unlikely that any single aesthetic experience can fully and simultaneously realize them all; and I believe that with certain of them the notion of full realization makes dubious sense. Nevertheless, it does not follow that the idea of their ever more intense and comprehensive realization is without value, nor that the link with nature-mystical experiences must be severed.[14]

Although I can only hazard this suggestion in the most tentative way, I suspect that no more materials are required than those with which we are already furnished, in order to render available certain limited varieties of mystical experience, and logically to map them. Those materials provide us, not with affirmations about a transcendent being or realm but with a *focus imaginarius*, that can play a regulative and practical role in the aesthetic contemplation of nature. It sees that contemplation as grounded, first and last, in particular perceptions, but as reaching out so as to relate the forms of the objects perceived to the pervasive and basic forms of nature; relating it also to the observer's own stance and setting, as himself one item in nature – a nature with whose forces he feels in harmony through the very success of this contemplative activity itself.

But even if something of the intensity and momentousness of mystical experience can be reached along such lines, this would be – for all I have said or shall say – a mysticism without a God. And surely the absence of belief in transcendence would make this quite different from a mysticism that admits it and centres upon it. Different, indeed, in the quality of available experience and in expectations aroused both for the here-and-now and the here-after; but not so radically different as to make 'mysticism' a misnomer for the former. Belief in a transcendent being means that, for the believer, the 'focus' is not imaginary but actual – in God; and it is doubtless psychologically easier to work towards a goal one believes to be fully realizable than towards a focus one believes, or suspects, to be imaginary. Rather similarly, in ethics a student may exercise a check to his practical moral confidence, when he discovers that 'oughts' cannot be grounded in 'is's'. Yet it is seldom that he indulges for this reason in a permanent moral sulk. Perhaps, if I am right, it is no more reasonable to indulge gratuitously in a nature-mystical sulk. But I begin to moralize: a sign that this paper has come to its proper end.

Note to p. 525

(a)   Graham Hough's *Image and Experience* (1960) contains some suggestive reflections stemming from his discussion of Ruskin and Roger Fry.

> By intense contemplation of . . . experiences of form and space we become conscious of the unity between ourselves and the natural world. (Hough, p. 175)

> It is Ruskin's special distinction to show . . . how the experience of the senses can lead directly to that unified apprehension of nature, and of ourselves as a part of nature, which can fairly constantly be recognized, under various mythological disguises, not only as that which gives value to aesthetic experience but also as one of the major consolations of philosophy. (Hough, p. 176)

(b)   We have quoted Barbara Hepworth on the mutual involvement of the spectator and natural aesthetic object, the changes in the sense of one's own being, according to one's position in the landscape. She goes on, in the same autobiographical sketch, to call this a 'transmutation of essential unity with land and seascape, which derives from all the sensibilities . . .'

(c)   The nature-mystical interpretation of the experience of unity-with-nature is briefly stated by Evelyn Underhill in her *Mysticism*. In moments of intense love for the natural world, 'hints of a marvellous truth, a unity whose note is ineffable peace, shine in created things' (Underhill, p. 87).

W. T. Stace, listing the common characteristics of 'extrovertive mysticism' (to which nature-mysticism belongs), includes the following. 'The One is . . . perceived through the physical senses, in or through the multiplicity of objects.' Also: 'The One is apprehended more concretely as being an inner subjectivity in all things, described variously as life, or consciousness, or a living Presence.' He adds: 'There are underground connections between the mystical and the aesthetic . . . which are at present obscure and unexplained' (Stace, pp. 79, 81).

(d)   On Coleridge, see Willey, Ch. 1 generally, especially Sects. III and IV. Coleridge wrote:

> The groundwork . . . of all true philosophy is the full apprehension of the difference between the contemplation of reason, namely that intuition of things which arises when we possess ourselves as one with the whole . . . and that which presents itself when . . . we think of ourselves as separated beings, and place nature in antithesis to the mind, as object to subject, thing to thought, death to life. (*The Friend*, Bohn Ed., p. 366; quoted Willey, pp. 29 f.)

Coleridge's statement has, of course, a much wider application than the topic of natural beauty; but he certainly applied it there.

(e)   See also Wordsworth, *The Prelude*, Bk. VI, lines 624–40, and *Tintern Abbey*, lines 88–102.

If this were primarily a historical study, we should have had to trace systematically the development of those conceptions (nature – mystical, Platonic, romantic, etc., etc.) that are behind the vocabulary of 'unity with nature'. What we are asking here, however, is how far these ideas could be of help to someone trying to make sense of natural aesthetic experience at the present time.

Thus these brief quotations and references, culled from a fairly wide field, may suffice to show at least the existence of the tendencies with which we shall be chiefly concerned.

Notes

1 By 'nature' I shall mean all objects that are not human artefacts. This will of course include living creatures. I can afford to ignore for the purpose of this study the many possible disputes over natural objects that have received a marked, though limited, transformation at man's hands.

2 Elton; Vivas and Krieger. Compare also Osborne, which likewise confines its investigation to art-experience. Beardsley is sub-titled *Problems in the Philosophy of Criticism*.

Osborne defines beauty as the 'characteristic and peculiar excellence of works of art'. Beardsley's opening sentence reads: 'There would be no problems of aesthetics, in the sense in which I propose to mark out this field of study, if no one ever talked about works of art.'

3 For Croce's view, see Croce, Part I, Ch. 13.

4 I am thinking, for example, of the recent insistence that even the art-object is primarily *object*, that it must not be approached simply as a clue to its creator's states of mind. See Beardsley *passim*, especially the earlier sections. I discuss some aspects of this 'anti-intentionalism' later in this paper.

(It should be mentioned that Beardsley's book contains an exceptionally rich bibliography of recent English and American writing in aesthetics. A reader who follows up the references given in his notes and discussions (appended to each chapter of the book) is given a very full survey of current argument and opinion.)

5 Unrestricted generalizations in aesthetics are usually precarious in proportion to their attractiveness. I have taken care not to set out the above contrast between 'framed' and 'unframed' as a contrast between *all* art-objects and *all* natural objects considered aesthetically; for not every art-object has a frame, even in the extended sense I have used above. Works of architecture, for instance, are like natural objects, in that we can set no limits to the viewpoints from which they can properly be regarded, nor can we decree where the aesthetically relevant context of

a building ends. A church or castle, seen from several miles away, may dominate, and determine how we see a whole landscape. The contrast between framed and frameless can none the less be made for very many types of aesthetic object – far enough at least to justify the general points made in the text.

6 On emotional qualities I have written elsewhere. (Hepburn)

7 Compare Montefiore (2).

8 See Kepes *passim*, on such analogies and affinities among natural forms.

9 This account is highly general and schematic. I have said nothing about the basic differences among the arts themselves, which make the 'aesthetic object' in (say) music so unlike that in literature or that again in architecture. My account as it stands is most immediately relevant to the visual arts, especially sculpture; but what is said about overall trends and emphases has extension beyond those.

10 H. S. Eveling argues (Eveling) that we should have a clash of competing criteria in such a situation. We should want to say 'same words, same poem': but, knowing how differently we shall interpret the words, according to the context in which we read them, we also want to say, 'one set of words but two poems'.

11 It is a weakness of some abstract painting that it sacrifices almost all the devices by which the spectator's response can be controlled and given determinateness. In the case of natural objects one is free to rely upon 'controls' external to the object – as in the present example. But even if the artist makes his artefacts very like natural objects, our knowledge that they are in fact artificial and 'framed' prevents us relying, in their case, upon such external controls.

12 On art, see Hospers.

13 Clark, p. 150. Sir Kenneth Clark is writing of art and artists, but his points are no less relevant to a contemplation of nature that never passes into the constructing of art-objects.

14 See Hough, p. 174 *seq*.

References

Beardsley, M. C. *Aesthetics* (New York: Harcourt Brace, 1958).

Clark, K. *Landscape into Art* (London: Murray, 1949; London: Pelican Books, 1956).

Coleridge, S. T. *Biographia Literaria* (London: Fenner, 1817).

Croce, B. *Estetica come scienza dell' espressione e linguistica general* (Milan: 1902; English tr.: *Aesthetic as*

Science of Expression and General Linguistic by D. Ainslie; London: Macmillan, 1922).

Elton, W. (ed.). *Aesthetics and Language* (Oxford: Blackwell, 1954).

Eveling, H. S. 'Composition and Criticism.' *Proceedings of the Aristotelian Society*, LIX (1959), pp. 213–32.

Hegel, G. W. F. *Ästhetik* (Berlin: Aufbau-Verlag, 1955; English tr. (*The Philosophy of Fine Art*) by F. P. S. Osmaston; London: Bell, 1920).

Hepburn, R. W. 'Emotions and Emotional Qualities.' *British Journal of Aesthetics*, I (1961), pp. 255–65.

Hepworth, B. *Carvings and Drawings* (London: Lund Humphries, 1952).

Hospers, J. *Meaning and Truth in the Arts* (Chapel Hill: University of North Carolina Press, 1946).

Hough, G. *Image and Experience* (London: Duckworth, 1960).

Kepes, G. *The New Landscape in Art and Science* (Chicago: Theobald, 1956).

Montefiore, A. C. *A Modern Introduction to Moral Philosophy* (London: Routledge, 1958).

Montefiore, A. C. Review of 'The Meaning and Purpose of Art.' *Mind*, LXVIII (1959), pp. 563–4.

Osborne, H. *The Theory of Beauty* (London: Routledge, 1952).

Stace, W. T. *Mysticism and Philosophy* (London: Macmillan, 1960).

Underhill, E. *Mysticism* (London: Methuen, 4th ed., 1912).

Vivas, E., and Krieger, M. (eds.). *The Problems of Aesthetics* (New York: Rinehart, 1953).

Willey, B. *Nineteenth Century Studies* (Cambridge: Cambridge University Press, 1949).

45

Appreciation and the Natural Environment

Allen Carlson

I

With art objects there is a straightforward sense in which we know both what and how to aesthetically appreciate. We know *what* to appreciate in that, first, we can distinguish a work and its parts from that which is not it nor a part of it. And, second, we can distinguish its aesthetically relevant aspects from its aspects without such relevance. We know that we are to appreciate the sound of the piano in the concert hall and not the coughing which interrupts it; we know that we are to appreciate that a painting is graceful, but not that it happens to hang in the Louvre. In a similar vein, we know *how* to appreciate in that we know what "acts of aspection" to perform in regard to different works. Ziff says:

> . . . to contemplate a painting is to perform one act of aspection; to scan it is to perform another; to study, observe, survey, inspect, examine, scrutinise, etc., are still other acts of aspection. . . . I survey a Tintoretto, while I scan an H. Bosch. Thus I step back to look at the Tintoretto, up to look at the Bosch. Different actions are involved. Do you drink brandy in the way you drink beer?[1]

It is clear that we have such knowledge of what and how to aesthetically appreciate. It is, I believe,

Allen Carlson, "Appreciation and the Natural Environment," *Journal of Aesthetics and Art Criticism*, 37 (1979), pp. 267–76. Reprinted by permission of Blackwell Publishing Ltd.

also clear what the grounds are for this knowledge. Works of art are our own creations; it is for this reason that we know what is and what is not a part of a work, which of its aspects are of aesthetic significance, and how to appreciate them. We have made them for the purpose of aesthetic appreciation; in order for them to fulfill this purpose this knowledge must be accessible. In making an object we know what we make and thus its parts and its purpose. Hence in knowing what we make we know what to do with that which we make. In the more general cases the point is clear enough: In creating a painting, we know that what we make is a painting. In knowing this we know that it ends at its frame, that its colors are aesthetically important, but where it hangs is not, and that we are to look at it rather than, say, listen to it. All this is involved in what it is to be a painting. Moreover, this point holds for more particular cases as well. Works of different particular types have different kinds of boundaries, have different foci of aesthetic significance, and perhaps most important demand different acts of aspection. In knowing the type we know what and how to appreciate. Ziff again:

> Generally speaking, a different act of aspection is performed in connection with works belonging to different schools of art, which is why the classification of style is of the essence. Venetian paintings lend themselves to an act of aspection involving attention to balanced masses: contours are of no importance, for they are scarcely to be found. The Florentine school demands attention to contours, the linear style predominates. Look

for light in a Claude, for color in a Bonnard, for contoured volume in a Signorelli.[2]

I take the above to be essentially beyond serious dispute, except as to the details of the complete account. If it were not the case, our complementary institutions of art and of the aesthetic appreciation of art would not be as they are. We would not have the artworld which we do. But the subject of this paper is not art nor the artworld. Rather: it is the aesthetic appreciation of nature. The question I wish to investigate is the question of what and how to aesthetically appreciate in respect to natural environment. It is of interest since the account which is implicit in the above remarks and which I believe to be the correct account for art cannot be applied to the natural environment without at least some modification. Thus initially the questions of what and how to appreciate in respect to nature appear to be open questions.

II

In this section I consider some paradigms of aesthetic appreciation which *prima facie* seem applicable as models for the appreciation of the natural environment. In this I follow tradition to some extent in that these paradigms are ones which have been offered as or assumed to be appropriate models for the appreciation of nature. However, I think we will discover that these models are not as promising as they may initially appear to be.

The first such paradigm I call the object model. In the artworld non-representational sculpture best fits this model of appreciation. When we appreciate such sculpture we appreciate it as the actual physical object which it is. The qualities to be aesthetically appreciated are the sensuous and design qualities of the actual object and perhaps certain abstract expressive qualities. The sculpture need not represent anything external to itself; it need not lead the appreciator beyond itself: it may be a self-contained aesthetic unit. Consider a Brancusi sculpture, for example, the famous *Bird In Space* (1919). It has no representational connections with the rest of reality and no relational connections with its immediate surroundings and yet it has significant aesthetic qualities. It glistens, has balance and grace, and expresses flight itself.

Clearly it is possible to aesthetically appreciate an object of nature in the way indicated by this model. For example, we may appreciate a rock or a piece of driftwood in the same way as we appreciate a Brancusi sculpture: we actually or contemplatively remove the object from its surroundings and dwell on its sensuous and design qualities and its possible expressive qualities. Moreover, there are considerations which support the plausibility of this model for appreciation of the natural environment. First, natural objects are in fact often appreciated in precisely this way: mantel pieces are littered with pieces of rock and driftwood. Second, the model fits well with one feature of natural objects: such objects, like the Brancusi sculpture, do not have representational ties to the rest of reality. Third and most important, the model involves an accepted, traditional aesthetic approach. As Sparshott notes, "When one talks of the aesthetic this or that, one is usually thinking of it as entering into a subject/object relation."[3]

In spite of these considerations, however, I think there are aspects of the object model which make it inappropriate for nature. Santayana, in discussing the aesthetic appreciation of nature (which he calls the love of nature) notes that certain problems arise because the natural landscape has "indeterminate form." He then observes that although the landscape contains many objects which have determinate forms, "if the attention is directed specifically to them, we have no longer what, by a curious limitation of the word, is called the love of nature."[4] I think this limitation is not as curious as Santayana seems to think it is. The limitation marks the distinction between appreciating nature and appreciating the objects of nature. The importance of this distinction is seen by realizing the difficulty of appreciating nature by means of the object model. For example, on one understanding of the object model, the objects of nature when so appreciated become "ready-mades" or "found art." The artworld grants "artistic enfranchisement" to a piece of driftwood just as it has to Duchamp's urinal or to the real Brillo cartons discussed by Danto.[5] If this magic is successful the result is art. Questions of what and how to aesthetically appreciate are answered, of course, but in respect to art rather than nature; the appreciation of nature is lost in the shuffle. Appreciating sculpture which was once driftwood is no closer to appreciating nature than is appreciating a totem pole which was once a tree or a purse which was once a sow's ear. In all such cases the conversion from nature to art (or artifact) is complete; only the means of conversion are different.

There is, however, another understanding of how the object model applies to the objects of nature. On this understanding natural objects are simply (actually or contemplatively) removed from their surroundings, but they do not become art, they remain natural objects. Here we do not appreciate the objects *qua* art objects, but rather *qua* natural objects. We do not consider the rock on our mantel a ready-made sculpture, we consider it only an aesthetically pleasing rock. In such a case, as the example of non-representational sculpture suggests, our appreciation is limited to the sensuous and design qualities of the natural object and perhaps a few abstract expressive qualities: Our rock has a wonderfully smooth and gracefully curved surface and expresses solidity.

The above suggests that, even when it does not require natural objects to be seen as art objects, the object model imposes a certain limitation on our appreciation of natural objects. The limitation is the result of the removal of the object from its surroundings which the object model requires in order even to begin to provide answers to questions of what and how to appreciate. But in requiring such a removal the object model becomes problematic. The object model is most appropriate for those art objects which are self-contained aesthetic units. These objects are such that neither the environment of their creation nor the environment of their display are aesthetically relevant: the removal of a self-contained art object from its environment of creation will not vary its aesthetic qualities and the environment of display of such an object should not affect its aesthetic qualities. However, natural objects possess what we might call an organic unity with their environment of creation: such objects are a part of and have developed out of the elements of their environments by means of the forces at work within those environments. Thus the environments of creation are aesthetically relevant to natural objects. And for this reason the environments of display are equally relevant in virtue of the fact that these environments will be either the same as or different from the environments of creation. In either case the aesthetic qualities of natural objects will be affected. Consider again our rock: on the mantel it may seem wonderfully smooth and gracefully curved and expressive of solidity, but in its environment of creation it will have more and different aesthetic qualities – qualities which are the product of the relationship between it and its environment. It is here expressive of the particular forces which shaped and con-

tinue to shape it and displays for aesthetic appreciation its place in and its relation to its environment. Moreover, depending upon its place in that environment it may not express many of those qualities, for example, solidity, which it appears to express when on the mantel.

I conclude that the object model, even without changing nature into art, faces a problem as a paradigm for the aesthetic appreciation of nature. The problem is a dilemma: either we remove the object from its environment or we leave it where it is. If the object is removed, the model applies to the object and suggests answers to the questions of what and how to appreciate. But the result is the appreciation of a comparatively limited set of aesthetic qualities. On the other hand if the object is not removed, the model seemingly does not constitute an adequate model for a very large part of the appreciation which is possible. Thus it makes little headway with the what and how questions. In either case the object model does not provide a successful paradigm for the aesthetic appreciation of nature. It appears after all not a very "curious limitation" that when our attention is directed specifically toward the objects in the environment it is not called the love of nature.

The second paradigm for the aesthetic appreciation of nature I call the scenery or landscape model. In the artworld this model of appreciation is illustrated by landscape painting; in fact the model probably owes its existence to this art form. In one of its favored senses "landscape" means a prospect – usually a grandiose prospect – seen from a specific standpoint and distance; a landscape painting is traditionally a representation of such a prospect.[6] When aesthetically appreciating landscape paintings (or any representative paintings, for that matter) the emphasis is not on the actual object (the painting) nor on the object represented (the actual prospect); rather it is on the representation of the object and its represented features. Thus in landscape painting the appreciative emphasis is on those qualities which play an essential role in representing a prospect: visual qualities related to coloration and overall design. These are the qualities which are traditionally significant in landscape painting and which are the focus of the landscape model of appreciation. We thus have a model of appreciation which encourages perceiving and appreciating nature as if it were a landscape painting, as a grandiose prospect seen from a specific standpoint and distance. It is a model which centers attention on those aesthetic qualities of color and design which are seen and seen at a distance.

It is quite evident that the scenery or landscape model has been historically significant in our aesthetic appreciation of nature.[7] For example, this model was evident in the eighteenth and nineteenth centuries in the use of the "Claude-glass," a small, tinted, convex mirror with which tourists viewed the landscape. Thomas West's popular guidebook to the Lake District (first published in 1778) says of the glass:

... where the objects are great and near, it removes them to a due distance, and shews them in the soft colours of nature, and most regular perspective the eye can perceive, art teach, or science demonstrate ... to the glass is reserved the finished picture, in highest colouring, and just perspective.[8]

In a somewhat similar fashion, the modern tourist reveals his preference for this model of appreciation by frequenting "scenic viewpoints" where the actual space between the tourist and the prescribed "view" often constitutes "a due distance" which aids the impression of "soft colours of nature, and the most regular perspective the eye can perceive, art teach, or science demonstrate." And the "regularity" of the perspective is often enhanced by the positioning of the viewpoint itself. Moreover, the modern tourist also desires "the finished picture, in highest colouring, and just perspective"; whether this be the "scene" framed and balanced in his camera's viewfinder, the result of this in the form of a kodachrome slide, and/or the "artistically" composed postcard and calendar reproductions of the "scene" which often attract more appreciation than that which they "reproduce." R. Rees has described the situation as follows:

... the taste has been for a view, for scenery, not for landscape in the original Dutch – and present geographical – meaning of the term, which denotes our ordinary, everyday surroundings. The average modern sightseer, unlike many of the Romantic poets and painters who were accomplished naturalists, is interested *not* in natural forms and processes, but in a prospect.[9]

It is clear that in addition to being historically important, the landscape model, like the object

model, gives us at least initial guidelines as to what and how to appreciate in regard to nature. We appreciate the natural environment as if it were a landscape painting. The model requires dividing the environment into scenes or blocks of scenery, each of which is to be viewed from a particular point by a viewer who is separated by the appropriate spatial (and emotional?) distance. A drive through the country is not unlike a walk through a gallery of landscape paintings. When seen in this light, this model of appreciation causes a certain uneasiness in a number of thinkers. Some, such as ecologist Paul Shepard, seemingly believe this kind of appreciation of the natural environment so misguided that they entertain doubts about the wisdom of *any* aesthetic approach to nature.[10] Others find the model to be ethically suspect. For example, after pointing out that the modern sightseer is interested only in a prospect, Rees concludes:

In this respect the Romantic Movement was a mixed blessing. In certain phases of its development it stimulated the movement for the protection of nature, but in its picturesque phase it simply confirmed our anthropocentrism by suggesting that nature exists to please as well as to serve us. Our ethics, if the word can be used to describe our attitudes and behaviour toward the environment, have lagged behind our aesthetics. It is an unfortunate lapse which allows us to abuse our local environments and venerate the Alps and the Rockies.[11]

What has not been as generally noted, however, is that this model of appreciation is suspect not only on ethical grounds, but also on aesthetic grounds. The model requires us to view the environment as if it were a static representation which is essentially "two dimensional." It requires the reduction of the environment to a scene or view. But what must be kept in mind is that the environment is not a scene, not a representation, not static, and not two dimensional. The point is that the model requires the appreciation of the environment not as what it is and with the qualities it has, but rather as something which it is not and with qualities it does not have. The model is in fact inappropriate to the actual nature of the object of appreciation. Consequently it not only, as the object model, unduly limits our appreciation – in this case to visual qualities related to coloration and overall design, it also misleads it. Hepburn puts this point in a general way:

> Supposing that a person's aesthetic educa-tion . . . instills in him the attitudes, the tactics of approach, the expectations proper to the appreciation of art works only, such a person will either pay very little aesthetic heed to natural objects or else heed them in the wrong way. He will look – and of course look in vain – for what can be found and enjoyed only in art.[12]

III

I conclude that the landscape model, as the object model, is inadequate as a paradigm for the aesthetic appreciation of nature. However, the reason for its inadequacy is instructive. The landscape model is inadequate because it is inappropriate to the nature of the natural environment. Perhaps to see what and how to appreciate in respect to the natural environment, we must consider the nature of that environment more carefully. In this regard there are two rather obvious points which I wish to emphasize. The first is that the natural environ-ment is an environment; the second is that it is natural.

When we conceptualize the natural environment as "nature" I think we are tempted to think of it as an object. When we conceptualize it as "landscape" we are certainly led to thinking of it as scenery. Consequently perhaps the concept of the "natural environment" is somewhat preferable. At least it makes explicit that it is an environment which is under consideration. The object model and the lanscape model each in its own way fail to take account of this. But what is involved in taking this into account? Here I wish initially to follow up some remarks made by Sparshott. He suggests that to consider something environmentally is primar-ily to consider it in regard to the relation of "self to setting," rather than "subject to object" or "trav-eler to scene."[13] An environment is the setting in which we exist as a "sentient part"; it is our surroundings. Sparshott points out that as our surroundings, our setting, the environment is that which we take for granted, that which we hardly notice – it is necessarily unobtrusive. If any one part of it becomes obtrusive, it is in danger of being seen as an object or a scene, not as our environ-ment. As Sparshott says, "When a man starts

talking about 'environmental values' we usually take him to be talking about aesthetic values of a background sort."[14]

The aesthetic values of the environment being primarily background values has obvious ramifica-tions for the questions of what and how to appre-ciate. In regard to what to appreciate this suggests the answer "everything," for in an essentially unob-trusive setting there seems little basis for including and excluding. I will return to this shortly. In regard to how to appreciate, the answer suggested is in terms of all those ways in which we normally are aware of and experience our surroundings. Sparshott notes that "if environmental aspects are background aspects, eye and ear lose part of their privilege" and goes on to mention smell, touch, and taste, and even warmth and coolness, barometric pressure and humidity as possibly relevant.[15] This points in the right direction, but as Sparshott also notes, it seems to involve a difficulty: that "the concept of the aesthetic tugs in a different direc-tion" – the direction of the subject/object relation involving primarily the visual scrutiny of an aes-thetic object.[16] However, I do not think this diffi-culty need be as serious as Sparshott seems to think. I suspect the apparent tension here is not due to the concept of the aesthetic being necessar-ily tied to the subject/object relation or to the visual, but rather is due to its being antithetical to the appreciation of anything only as unobtrusive background. To confirm this we need to consider the concept of the aesthetic as it is elaborated by John Dewey in *Art as Experience*.[17] Dewey's concept is such that anything which is aesthetically appreciated must be obtrusive, it must be fore-ground, but it need not be an object and it need not be seen (or only seen). Moreover, to assume that that which is aesthetically appreciated need be an object or only seen is to confine aesthetic appreci-ation to either the object model or the landscape model, which, as we have noted, impose unaccept-able limitations on the aesthetic appreciation of the natural environment.

I suggest then that the beginning of an answer to the question of *how* to aesthetically appreciate an environment is something like the following: We must experience our background setting in all those ways in which we normally experience it, by sight, smell, touch, and whatever. However, we must experience it not as unobtrusive background, but as obtrusive foreground! What is involved in such an "act of aspection" is not completely clear. Dewey gives us an idea in remarks such as:

Allen Carlson

To grasp the sources of esthetic experience it is . . . necessary to have recourse to animal life below the human scale. . . . The live animal is fully present, all there, in all of its actions: in its wary glances, its sharp sniffing, its abrupt cocking of ears. All senses are equally on the *qui vive*.[18]

And perhaps the following description by Yi-Fu Tuan gives some further indication:

An adult must learn to be yielding and careless like a child if he were to enjoy nature polymorphously. He needs to slip into old clothes so that he could feel free to stretch out on the hay beside the brook and bathe in a meld of physical sensations: the smell of the hay and of horse dung; the warmth of the ground, its hard and soft contours; the warmth of the sun tempered by breeze; the tickling of an ant making its way up the calf of his leg; the play of shifting leaf shadows on his face; the sound of water over the pebbles and boulders, the sound of cicadas and distant traffic. Such an environment might break all the formal rules of euphony and aesthetics, substituting confusion for order, and yet be wholly satisfying.[19]

Tuan's account as to how to appreciate fits well with our earlier answer to the question of what to appreciate, viz. everything. This answer, of course, will not do. We cannot appreciate everything; there must be limits and emphasis in our aesthetic appreciation of nature as there are in our appreciation of art. Without such limits and emphases our experience of the natural environment would be *only* "a meld of physical sensations" without any meaning or significance. It would be a Jamesian "blooming buzzing confusion" which truly substituted "confusion for order" and which, I suspect contra to Tuan, would not be wholly satisfying. Such experience would be too far removed from our aesthetic appreciation of art to merit the label "aesthetic" or even the label "appreciation." Consider again the case of art. In this case, as noted in Section I, the boundaries and foci of aesthetic significance of works of art are a function of the type of art in question, e.g., paintings end at their frames and their colors are significant. Moreover, I suggested that our knowledge of such matters is due to art works being our creations. Here it is relevant to

note the second point which I wish to emphasize about natural environments: they are natural. The natural environment is not a work of art. As such it has no boundaries or foci of aesthetic significance which are given as a result of our creation nor of which we have knowledge because of our involvement in such creation.

The fact that nature is natural – not our creation – does not mean, however, that we must be without knowledge of it. Natural objects are such that we can discover things about them which are independent of any involvement by us in their creation. Thus although we have not created nature, we yet know a great deal about it. This knowledge, essentially common sense/scientific knowledge, seems to me the only viable candidate for playing the role in regard to the appreciation of nature which our knowledge of types of art, artistic traditions, and the like plays in regard to the appreciation of art. Consider the aesthetic appreciation of an environment such as that described by Tuan. We experience the environment as obtrusive foreground – the smell of the hay and of the horse dung, the feel of the ant, the sound of the cicadas and of the distant traffic all force themselves upon us. We experience a "meld of sensations" but, as noted, if our state is to be aesthetic appreciation rather than just the having of raw experience, the meld cannot be simply a "blooming buzzing confusion." Rather it must be what Dewey called a consummatory experience: one in which knowledge and intelligence transform raw experience by making it determinate, harmonious, and meaningful. For example, in order for there to be aesthetic appreciation we must recognize the smell of the hay and that of the horse dung and perhaps distinguish between them; we must feel the ant at least as an insect rather than as, say, a twitch. Such recognizing and distinguishing results in certain aspects of the obtrusive foreground becoming foci of aesthetic significance. Moreover, they are natural foci appropriate to the particular natural environment we are appreciating. Likewise our knowledge of the environment may yield certain appropriate boundaries or limits to the experience. For example, since we are aesthetically appreciating a certain kind of environment, the sound of cicadas may be appreciated as a proper part of the setting, while the sound of the distant traffic is excluded much as we ignore the coughing in the concert hall.

What I am suggesting is that the question of *what* to aesthetically appreciate in the natural environment is to be answered in a way analogous to the similar question about art. The difference is that in the case of the natural environment the relevant knowledge is the common sense/scientific knowledge which we have discovered about the environment in question. This knowledge gives us the appropriate foci of aesthetic significance and the appropriate boundaries of the setting so that our experience becomes one of aesthetic appreciation. If to aesthetically appreciate art we must have knowledge of artistic traditions and styles within those traditions, to aesthetically appreciate nature we must have knowledge of the different environments of nature and of the systems and elements within those environments. In the way in which the art critic and the art historian are well equipped to aesthetically appreciate art, the naturalist and the ecologist are well equipped to aesthetically appreciate nature.[20]

The point I have now made about what to appreciate in nature also has ramifications for how to appreciate nature. When discussing the nature of an environment, I suggested that Tuan's description seems to indicate a general act of aspection appropriate for any environment. However, since natural environments differ in type it seems that within this general act of aspection there might be differences which should be noted. To aesthetically appreciate an environment we experience our surroundings as obtrusive foreground allowing our knowledge of that environment to select certain foci of aesthetic significance and perhaps exclude others, thereby limiting the experience. But certainly there are also different kinds of appropriate acts of aspection which can likewise be selected by our knowledge of environments. Ziff tells us to look for contours in the Florentine school and for color in a Bonnard, to survey a Tintoretto and to scan a Bosch. Consider different natural environments. It seems that we must survey a prairie environment, looking at the subtle contours of the land, feeling the wind blowing across the open space, and smelling the mix of prairie grasses and flowers. But such an act of aspection has little place in a dense forest environment. Here we must examine and scrutinize, inspecting the detail of the forest floor, listening carefully for the sounds of birds and smelling carefully for the scent of spruce and pine. Likewise, the description of environmental appreciation given by Tuan, in addition to being a model for environmental acts of aspection in general, is also a description of the act of aspec-

tion appropriate for a particular kind of environment – one perhaps best described as pastoral. Different natural environments require different acts of aspection; and as in the case of what to appreciate, our knowledge of the environment in question indicates how to appreciate, that is, indicates the appropriate act of aspection.

The model I am thus presenting for the aesthetic appreciation of nature might be termed the environmental model. It involves recognizing that nature is an environment and thus a setting within which we exist and which we normally experience with our complete range of senses as our unobtrusive background. But our experience being aesthetic requires unobtrusive background to be experienced as obtrusive foreground. The result is the experience of a "blooming, buzzing confusion" which in order to be appreciated must be tempered by the knowledge which we have discovered about the natural environment so experienced. Our knowledge of the nature of the particular environments yields the appropriate boundaries of appreciation, the particular foci of aesthetic significance, and the relevant act or acts of aspection for that type of environment. We thus have a model which begins to give answers to the questions of what and how to appreciate in respect to the natural environment and which seems to do so with due regard for the nature of that environment. And this is important not only for aesthetic but also for moral and ecological reasons.

IV

In this paper I have attempted to open discussion on the questions of what and how to aesthetically appreciate in regard to nature. In doing so I have argued that two traditional approaches, each of which more or less assimilates the appreciation of nature to the appreciation of certain art forms, leave much to be desired. However, the approach which I have suggested, the environmental model, yet follows closely the general structure of our aesthetic appreciation of art. This approach does not depend on an assimilation of natural objects to art objects or of landscapes to scenery, but rather on an application of the general structure of aesthetic appreciation of art to something which is not art. What is important is to recognize that nature is an environment and is natural, and to make that recognition central to our aesthetic appreciation.

Allen Carlson

Thereby we will aesthetically appreciate nature for what it is and for the qualities it has. And we will avoid being the person described by Hepburn who "will either pay very little aesthetic heed to natural objects or else heed them in the wrong way," who "will look – and of course look in vain – for what can be found and enjoyed only in art."[21]

Notes

1 Paul Ziff, "Reasons in Art Criticism," *Philosophy and Education*, ed., I. Scheffler (Boston, 1958). Reprinted in *Art and Philosophy*, ed., W. E. Kennick (New York, 1964), p. 620.

2 Ibid. Ziff is mainly concerned with the way in which knowledge of types yields different acts of aspection. For an elaboration of this point and its ramifications concerning what is and is not aesthetically significant in a work, see K. Walton, "Categories of Art," *Philosophical Review* (1970), 334–67. How our knowledge of art (and the artworld) yields the boundaries between art and the rest of reality is interestingly discussed in A. Danto, "The Artistic Enfranchisement of Real Objects: the Artworld," *Journal of Philosophy* (1964), 571–84.

3 F. E. Sparshott, "Figuring the Ground: Notes on Some Theoretical Problems of the Aesthetic Environment," *Journal of Aesthetic Education* (1972), 13.

4 George Santayana, *The Sense of Beauty* (New York, 1961), p. 100.

5 Danto, op. cit., p. 579.

6 This favored sense of "landscape" is brought out by Yi-Fu Tuan. See *Topophilia: A Study of Environmental Perception, Attitudes, and Values* (Englewood Cliffs, 1974), pp. 132–33, or "Man and Nature: An Eclectic Reading," *Landscape*, Vol. 15 (1966), 30.

7 For a good, brief discussion of this point, see R. Rees, "The Scenery Cult: Changing Landscape Tastes over Three Centuries," *Landscape*, Vol. 19 (1975). Note the following remarks by E. H. Gombrich in "The Renaissance Theory of Art and the Rise of Landscape," *Norm and Form: Studies in the Art of the Renaissance* (London, 1971), pp. 117–18: ". . . I believe that the idea of natural beauty as an inspiration of art . . . is, to say the least, a very dangerous oversimplification. Perhaps it even reverses the actual process by which man discovers the beauty of nature. We call a scenery 'picturesque' . . . if it reminds us of paintings we have seen. . . . Similarly, so it seems, the discovery of Alpine scenery does not precede but follows the spread of prints and paintings with mountain panoramas."

8 Thomas West, *Guide to the Lakes* (London: 1778) as quoted in J. T. Ogden, "From Spatial to Aesthetic Distance in the Eighteenth Century," *Journal of the History of Ideas*, Vol. XXXV (1974), 66–67.

9 R. Rees, "The Taste for Mountain Scenery," *History Today*, Vol. XXV (1975), 312.

10 Paul Shepard, *The Tender Carnivore and the Sacred Game* (New York, 1973), pp. 147–48. Shepard made this position more explicit at a lecture at Athabasca University, Edmonton, Alberta, November 16, 1974.

11 Rees, "Mountain Scenery," op. cit., p. 312. Ethical worries are also expressed by Tuan, *Topophilia*, op. cit., Chapter 8, and R. A. Smith and C. M. Smith, "Aesthetics and Environmental Education," *Journal of Aesthetic Education* (1970), 131–32. Smith and Smith put the point as follows: "Perhaps there is a special form of arrogance in experiencing nature strictly in the categories of art, for the attitude involved here implies an acceptance, though perhaps only momentarily, of the notion that natural elements have been arranged for the sake of the man's aesthetic pleasure. It is possible that this is what Kant had in mind when he said that in the appreciation of natural beauty one ought not assume that nature has fashioned its forms for our delight and that, instead, 'it is we who receive nature with favour, and not nature that does us a favour.'"

12 R. W. Hepburn, "Aesthetic Appreciation of Nature," *Aesthetics and the Modern World*, ed. H. Osborne (London, 1968), p. 53. Hepburn implicitly argues that our aesthetic appreciation of nature is enhanced by our "realizing" that an object is what it is and has the qualities which it has. See pp. 60–65.

13 Sparshott, op. cit., pp. 12–13. Sparshott also considers other possible relations which are not directly relevant here. Moreover, I suspect he considers the "traveler to scene" relation to be more significant than I do.

14 Ibid., pp. 17–18.

15 Ibid., p. 21.

16 Ibid., pp. 13–14, p. 21.

17 John Dewey, *Art as Experience* (New York, 1958), especially Chapters I–III.

18 Ibid., pp. 18–19.

19 Tuan, *Topophilia*, op. cit., p. 96.

20 I have in mind here individuals such as John Muir and Aldo Leopold. See, for example, Leopold's *A Sand County Almanac* (1949).

21 Hepburn, op. cit., p. 53.

46

The Aesthetic Appreciation of Nature

Malcolm Budd

Die liebe Erde allüberall
Blüht auf im Lenz und grünt aufs neu!
Allüberall und ewig blauen licht die Fernen!
(Gustav Mahler, Das Lied von der Erde)

I

What is it to appreciate nature aesthetically? Is there such a thing as the aesthetic appreciation of nature? These questions refer on the one hand to an object and on the other to a type of appreciation: the object is nature and the type is aesthetic. So an illuminating response must do two things: it must provide both a delimitation of the field of nature and an account of what constitutes the aesthetic appreciation of items in that field. Although the first element of such a response appears to be independent of the second,[1] it is clear that the second must be informed by the first, for the aesthetic appreciation of nature, as I understand the idea, is the aesthetic appreciation of nature *as nature*.[2] It follows that in my understanding of the notion, not every aesthetic experience available from a natural object is an instance of the aesthetic appreciation of nature. The aesthetic appreciation of nature is not co-extensive with the set of aesthetic responses to natural objects or to aspects of what is found in nature. Rather, an aesthetic response to something natural constitutes aesthetic appreciation of nature only if the response is a

Malcolm Budd, "The Aesthetic Appreciation of Nature," *British Journal of Aesthetics*, 36 (1996), pp. 207–22. Reprinted by permission of Oxford University Press.

response to nature *as* nature, and what this requires is that it must be integral to the rewarding (or displeasing) character of the experience offered by nature that its object is experienced *as* natural. Hence, if some expanse of an attractive shade of colour presented by an outcrop of ochre delights, but not *as* a natural colour or *as* the colour of a natural object, or a pattern in a snow flake delights, but not *as* naturally produced, or the iridescent colours of a hummingbird delight, but not *as* the appearance of its wings, although the experience is aesthetic and provided by nature, it is not an instance of the aesthetic appreciation of nature. Furthermore, the aesthetic appreciation of nature, as I understand the idea, requires not only that nature is appreciated as nature but that this appreciation does not essentially involve perceiving or imagining nature as a work of art.[3] One kind of appreciation that the aesthetic appreciation of nature is opposed to is artistic appreciation, so that the appreciation of nature as art is different from the aesthetic appreciation of nature. Accordingly, if an observer adopts towards nature an attitude appropriate to a work of art, regarding it *as if it were* such a work, the resulting experience, although aesthetic and directed at nature, falls outside the aesthetic appreciation of nature.[4] Of course, it is possible to appreciate nature *as looking like a beautiful picture of nature* – nature as picturesque – although the occasions when this would be a natural thing to do are rare, since, except perhaps for landscape, nature does not in general strike us as looking like a picture – as it might when the prevailing conditions of illumination greatly weaken the impression of the third dimension –

and other occasions would require the adoption of a peculiar attitude to the world, one that it does not invite. But this possibility is beside the point, for to appreciate nature as looking like a picture is not to appreciate nature *as nature*. In sum: the aesthetic appreciation of nature, as I understand the idea, is identical with the aesthetic appreciation not of that which is nature, but of nature *as nature and not as art*.

II

There are difficulties in arriving at a satisfactory understanding of the idea of nature as it figures in the aesthetic appreciation of nature. How should this idea be understood?[5]

In one sense, everything is part of nature, for there is a sense in which nature is just the totality of everything that is the case. But this all-inclusive sense does not distinguish nature from anything else, and what is needed is a distinction within nature, when nature is understood in this all-embracing sense as 'the world'.

Natural objects are often contrasted with man-made objects, even in the case of artefacts that are made out of natural objects merely by modifying them. But the distinction between what is man-made[6] and what is not will divide the world into the natural and the non-natural only if the idea of art or skill is built into the idea of making, and perhaps not even then. For human beings make other human beings, usually by natural means, not by art or skill, and the human body remains a natural object no matter how it may be clothed, or shaped or coloured by human design.[7] So what is natural should be opposed not to what is man-made but to what is artificial (a product of human artifice).

What does nature consist of? Well, there are natural *substances* (gold, water), natural *species* (animals, insects, trees, shrubs, plants), natural *objects* (icebergs, mountains, volcanoes, planets, moons), natural *forces* (gravity, magnetism), natural *appearances* (the sky, sunrise and sunset, a rainbow, shadows), natural *phenomena* (rivers, wind, rain, snow, clouds), natural *products* of living things (birdsong, beaver dams, birds' nests, spiders' webs, faeces, the smell of a rose), and so on. But in one sense, nature consists of individual natural things standing in relations to one another. These things are instances of natural kinds – natural species and natural 'substances' – and they interact through the operation of natural forces. So in nature there are,

on the one hand, individual spatio-temporal items, and on the other, the types that they instantiate and the forces under the influence of which they affect one another.

Is the aesthetic appreciation of nature confined to individuals (and individuals as related to one another) or does it extend to kinds? In fact, this disjunction does not exhaust the possibilities. Schopenhauer held neither of these positions but maintained, instead, that the aesthetic appreciation of nature – of the beauty of individual natural objects – is essentially the appreciation of natural kinds (understood as atemporal items), which are made manifest to us in the perception of individual instances of those kinds: we appreciate, not individual natural items, nor natural kinds *as realized in the specific forms of individuals*, but natural kinds themselves, made available to us through the medium of the individuals we perceive. But he embraced this view in a peculiar form: natural kinds, although non-spatial and atemporal, are essentially perceptible items, object for a subject, 'representations'; in the aesthetic appreciation of nature we have an especially vivid and compelling perceptual awareness of the inner essential nature of the natural kind an individual exemplifies; and each natural kind is beautiful.[8] It follows from Schopenhauer's position – and he explicitly drew this conclusion[9] – that from the aesthetic point of view it is immaterial which instance of a natural kind is being contemplated: differences among instances are aesthetically irrelevant, since the upshot of aesthetic contemplation is always the same, namely, awareness of the natural kind itself, the proper object of aesthetic contemplation. Although Schopenhauer's train of thought is not compelling, it suggests a significant difference between the aesthetic appreciation of nature and the appreciation of art: whereas two exactly similar objects of the same natural kind, two indistinguishable melons or ladybirds or sea trout, for example, must have the same aesthetic value in themselves, two exactly similar works of art, as has often been pointed out, might differ in artistic meaning with a resulting difference in artistic value.[10]

Much of terrestrial nature has not remained in its natural condition, but has been subjected to human interference. Wild animals have been domesticated, new strains of plant developed by selective breeding, species native to one area have been transplanted to other parts of the world, rivers have been dammed, land reclaimed from the sea, hillsides terraced, seas polluted, forests felled, and so on indefinitely. In some cases, humanity's influence is detectable without specialist knowledge, being manifest in the result, at least in the short term; but often this is not so. In any case, much of our natural environment displays, for better or worse, the influence of humanity, having been shaped, to a greater or lesser extent, and in a variety of ways, by human purposes, so that little of the world's landscape is in a natural condition. Accordingly, our aesthetic experience of the natural world is often *mixed* – a mixture of the aesthetic appreciation of nature as nature with an additional element, of a variable nature, based on human design or purpose or activity.[11]

A scene can consist entirely of natural objects yet be constructed or planned, wholly or in part, by humanity. Accordingly, the portion of the world a spectator is appreciating, a landscape, say, might contain only natural things but include traces of humanity, in the form of orchards, fields of wheat, or pastures on which cows have been put to graze, for example. But it might contain both natural and non-natural objects, houses and bridges, for instance. In both cases, the presence and character of the non-natural element might or might not be determined by aesthetic considerations; and if partly determined by aesthetic considerations, this might be in the light of the appearance of the non-natural element from the point of view a spectator happens to occupy or the path she is following, or not so. But although a natural item is often not in its natural state or natural location or habitat, or has arisen only through human contrivance or as an intended or unintended result of human activity, or is in a scene composed of natural objects but which has not been naturally produced, or is adjacent to or surrounded by non-natural items, or has been positioned where it is, not by nature, but by humanity, this does not prevent it from being appreciated aesthetically as natural and does not mean that its appreciation must be mixed. For whether an item is natural is not the same as whether other aspects of the scene or other properties of the item are natural, and it is possible, with more or less difficulty in particular cases, to focus one's interest only on what is natural. Whether what you are confronted by is (entirely) natural[12] is one thing; what it is about the situation you are appreciating is another. At a zoo you cannot appreciate an animal in its natural environment. But it does not follow that your appreciation must be of a caged animal – an animal as caged. Rather, you can ignore its surroundings and appreciate the animal itself (within the limits imposed by its captive state). In looking at a fountain, you are not looking at a natural state of affairs. Nevertheless, you can appreciate some of the perceptible properties of water, a natural substance, in particular its liquidity, mobility and the way in which it catches the light. All that follows from the fact that much of our natural environment displays the influence of humanity and that we are usually confronted by scenes that in various ways involve artifice is that the aesthetic appreciation of nature, if it is to be *pure*, must abstract from any design imposed on nature, especially a design imposed for artistic or aesthetic effect.[13]

III

But if the aesthetic appreciation of nature is the aesthetic appreciation of nature *as* nature, what is meant by a 'response to nature *as* nature'? There are two obvious possibilities, which I shall call the internal and external conceptions, the first given by a strong and the other by a weak reading of the phrase, the external conception being entirely unproblematic. The weak reading understands the idea in a merely negative fashion: a response to nature as nature is just a response to nature *not* as whatever is opposed to nature – as art (or artefact), for example (so that there is no intended meaning or function to be understood).[14] The strong reading requires more: a response to nature as nature is a response to nature, not merely 'not as art (or artefact)', but 'in virtue of being natural'. Accordingly, in the case of an aesthetic response to a natural item, its being natural constitutes an element of one's appreciation, i.e. of what one appreciates, so that it grounds and enhances, diminishes or otherwise transforms the experience. In other words: on the one hand, 'as natural' might mean 'not as designed by humanity (or another intelligent species)', so that certain possible aspects of an item – the item's being an artefact, in particular a work of art, and any characteristic of the item that being a work of art or another kind of artefact are necessary conditions of – are to be deemed *irrelevant* to its appreciation; on the other hand, 'as natural' might be understood to imply that the appreciation must be *based* on the item's being natural, in which case a replica that mimics the item's appearance, experienced as being non-natural, would not do just as well.

The requirement imposed by the strong reading might induce scepticism about the possibility of the aesthetic appreciation of nature.[15] How could an aesthetic response be founded on the fact that its object is natural? How could the fact that an item is natural be integral to, or integrated into, an aesthetic response to it? The answer is, in outline, simple. For it is a general truth that we are delighted or otherwise moved by states of affairs, processes, and so on *under certain concepts or descriptions*;[16] the descriptions under which we experience something properly affect the nature of our response to it; accordingly, the fact that we experience something as natural might be integral to the emotion we feel towards it, so that if this emotion is a component of an aesthetic response to the object, this response is based on the object's being part of nature.

Consider, for example, the aesthetic appreciation of birdsong. What is the object of delight – what do we delight in – when we take an aesthetic delight in birdsong *as birdsong*? As with all other instances of the aesthetic appreciation of nature untouched by human hands, the appreciation of birdsong is free from a certain constraint of understanding, namely the understanding of its meaning *as art*. This is not to say that if you delight in listening to the songs of birds, your delight is aesthetic only if you hear the sounds merely as patterns of sounds. On the contrary, you hear the sounds as *products of (unaided) bodily actions*, of 'voices', or 'whistles', or 'warbles'. But you do not hear them *as intentionally determined by artistic considerations*. You delight in the seemingly endless and effortless variety of a song thrush's song – variations in pitch, timbre, dynamics, rhythm and vocal attack, for example – but not as the product of artistry and not as a construction guided by consideration of its effectiveness as art. The song consists of a series of rhythmic phrases, the various segments differing from one another in the number of similar phrases that form the segment and in the nature of the constituent phrases, which vary in the number, duration, timbre, pitch and loudness of the sounds that compose them. These phrases succeed one another but never seem to reach a final goal, a final ending; instead, they continue for an indefinite time in a way that does not appear to be meaningful overall. In other words, you hear the song as an unpredictable, apparently random mélange of phrases. Now the aesthetic listener is not absolutely required to ignore the actual function of the bird's singing, which is to affirm its territory and,

perhaps, to attract a mate. It might even be possible to appreciate the song not just as 'music' but as especially well suited to its seductive function, although it is hard to see that any such sense of appropriateness by one of us could be securely based in an awareness of what it is like to be a female song thrush.[17] But such a possibility aside, the song of a thrush is heard as being attractive to listen to, in its own right, in abstraction from its function of seducing the opposite sex. The object of aesthetic delight is the sounds *as issuing 'naturally' from a living, sentient creature*, more specifically, a bird.[18]

With this illustration in mind, we can return to and fill in the outline answer to the sceptical doubt. In one sense, what you experience when you experience an item under one description is not the same as what you experience if you experience that item under another, incompatible, description. In other words, your experience of an item is sensitive to what you experience it as, so that an experience of it under one description has a different phenomenology from that of an experience under an incompatible description. Furthermore, the description under which you experience something constrains the qualities that such an item can manifest to you, that is, that it can display as an item of the kind that falls under that description; and so qualities of an item available under one description might not be available under another description. It follows that there is no difficulty in the idea of a response to nature being a response to it *as* nature. Hence, scepticism about the idea of the aesthetic appreciation of nature must be focused specifically on the possibility of an *aesthetic* response to nature as nature. But how easy or difficult it is for nature, or a particular natural item, to meet the requirement imposed by the internal conception turns on the idea of the aesthetic, more specifically, the idea of an aesthetic response to something. It is therefore necessary to clarify the idea of an aesthetic response.

IV

What makes a response *aesthetic*? Is it the intrinsic nature of the response or the nature of the features to which it is a response? What constitutes aesthetic, as opposed to non-aesthetic, appreciation? What is necessary, and what is sufficient, for a response to something to be an aesthetic response to that item? Many attempts have been made to capture the notion of what is aesthetic, concentrating on the idea of aesthetic judgement, or the idea of aesthetic properties, or the idea of aesthetic experience, pleasure or emotion, or some other aspect of the aesthetic. Perhaps the aesthetic should be elucidated in terms of the judgement that lies at the heart of an aesthetic response, the judgement that the response is founded upon; or in terms of the property or properties (Beauty, Sublimity, Gracefulness) it is a response to; or in terms of the property it 'projects' upon its object ('Beauty' construed as a projective property); or in terms of some other aspect of its phenomenology, its hedonic or affective character, for example; or in terms of a reaction, positive, negative or one of indifference, to certain kinds of property, e.g. immediately perceptible qualities, manifest to the person who has no non-perceptual knowledge of the object, or, instead, the object's 'form', in either case the reaction being to the object's appearance, not to what it actually is; or in terms of a response caused and sustained by a specific kind of attitude ('the aesthetic attitude') adopted towards an object; or in terms of a distinctive kind of value, 'aesthetic value'; or in terms of some combination of these suggestions.[19] But such attempts do not command assent, if they are seen as attempts to capture some commonly and pre-theoretically recognized notion of the aesthetic. And it is unhelpful merely to be told that the idea of the aesthetic, as commonly understood, lacks an essence, covering an indeterminate set of heterogeneous responses.

It is true that the idea of the aesthetic, both in everyday speech and philosophy, is too indefinite and multivalent to merit close attention. The best that can be hoped for, therefore, is an account that captures what, once articulated, appears to be central to at least one familiar conception of the idea; that is neutral about the relative importance or priority of art and nature within the field of the aesthetic; and that chimes with our own experience of nature, art and other objects of aesthetic interest. An attractive conception of the aesthetic along these lines represents a response as being aesthetic insofar as the response is directed at the experienced properties of an item,[20] the nature and arrangement of its elements or the interrelationships among its parts or aspects, and which involves a felt positive or negative reaction to the item, considered in itself, rather than as satisfying a pre-existing desire for the existence of something of that kind,[21] so that what governs the response is whether the object is intrinsically rewarding or dis-

pleasing to experience in itself. Such a conception applies to nature and art; it allows for the aesthetic appreciation of sport, juggling, circus acts, furniture, clothes, wine, motor cars, machines and tools of all kinds, and much else; it does not discriminate against certain kinds of perceptible property in favour of one privileged kind; and it does not restrict aesthetic experience to a small class of categories (such as experiences of the beautiful and the sublime).[22] For the present purpose it does not matter if this conception is thought not to exhaust the nature of an aesthetic response, or to be inferior to some alternative conception, as long as the satisfaction of the condition it articulates is considered sufficient for a response reasonably to be deemed aesthetic.

V

We now have an understanding of the idea of (the internal conception of) a response to nature *as* nature, and also the idea of an *aesthetic* response. If we marry these two ideas we have the idea of an aesthetic response to nature as nature. What this comes to is, in effect, the idea of a response to a natural item, grounded on its naturalness – on its being a part of nature or on its being a specific kind of natural item – focused on its elements or aspects as structured or interrelated in the item, the item being experienced as intrinsically rewarding, unrewarding or displeasing, the hedonic character of the reaction being 'disinterested'. So the question is whether – and, if so, how – nature, or a particular natural item, can be the intentional object of such a response. In what way, if any, can the fact that something is natural, or a certain kind of natural thing, ground an aesthetic response to it?

How the very naturalness of an object – the mere fact that the object is natural, not its being a natural thing of a certain kind – can properly ground an aesthetic response to it is severely limited,[23] for what is common to all natural items in virtue of being natural is only a negative, not a positive, characteristic: they must not be the products of human skill or design. This leaves only such a possibility as marvelling at the fact that something as beautiful, attractive or remarkable as *this* – a rainbow or the exquisite fan-shaped leaf of a ginkgo, for example – is a product of nature. So if the idea of the aesthetic appreciation of nature as nature (on the internal conception) is coherent and the aesthetic appreciation of nature can have a more substantial foundation than the mere naturalness of its object, there must be aspects or properties that a natural item can possess in virtue of which it can be appreciated aesthetically *as* natural. What kinds of feature might these be?

Now nature exhibits a remarkable variety of very different kinds of things – living and non-living, sentient and non-sentient, animal and non-animal, and so on – and the aesthetic appreciation of nature ranges over everything in nature,[24] often in more than one way, involving either a single perceptual mode or a combination, focusing on a single natural object, at rest or in motion, at a moment or over time, or a product of a natural object, or a complex of natural items, or a natural process, or an appearance or impression (perhaps a changing one, as when mist slowly clears or the sun rises or sets). It would therefore be exceptionally daunting and probably fruitless to attempt an exhaustive account of the kinds of aspects in virtue of which natural items can be appreciated aesthetically *as* natural. But the principle that would underlie such an attempt is clear. The crucial question is, what qualities capable of aesthetic appreciation – in themselves or in virtue of their contribution to an overall aesthetic effect or structure – might be possessed by an item in virtue of being natural or in virtue of being a certain kind of natural item? So what is required is the identification of characteristics that are capable of figuring in aesthetic appreciation, whether this is positive or negative, and that accrue to an item only in virtue of its being a natural item of a certain kind.

It is easy to indicate examples of such characteristics. For instance, there are qualities that can accrue to something only because it is a form of life. A living thing has a history of a distinctive kind, a life of growth and decline, nourished by its environment, at the mercy of the elements, perhaps responding to or anticipating changes in the seasons, its external appearance being determined by natural processes and structures within it; and this enables its condition at a certain time to be seen as a stage in or phase of its development, wherein it is flourishing or wilting, in a state of need or decay, and as contrasting with earlier or later conditions. Thus the fact that a natural item is a tree allows its form to be seen as determined by its internal nature, its age, its habitat and the friendly or hostile forces of nature, and its condition at any time of the year to be seen as deter-

mined by the cycle of the seasons. This enables the aesthetic observer to delight not only in the visual appearance of its blossoms, say, but in what they indicate, and to experience the flowering of the tree as a manifestation and beautiful expression of the resurgence of life triggered by the arrival of spring; or to marvel at the way in which the tree, restricted by its intrinsic nature, has adjusted to the constraints imposed on it by its location, its environment and the climate. Again, there are many kinds of quality that accrue to an item only in virtue of its being a sentient thing, capable of locomotion. For example, only sentient creatures can be seen as looking at or otherwise perceiving the world, and in particular as being aware of the presence of another creature, and so as exploring, hunting, diving, disputing a territory or engaging in courtship rituals; and there are styles of movement that are specific to sentient creatures, as with the graceful movements of a gazelle, and styles of movement that only sentient creatures of a certain kind are capable of, as with the various forms of the flight of birds. These open the possibility of a distinctive kind of aesthetic delight – at the cavorting of an otter or a school of dolphins at play or the exploratory behaviour of a fox cub, for instance. Furthermore, the parts of both sentient and non-sentient living things, animals and plants, for example, have natural functions and a sentient creature has a style of life determined by its nature. In each kind of case, there is a possible source of aesthetic delight focused on the idea of suitability: the parts of these living things can be seen as manifestly or strikingly suitable to discharging their functions, especially in the given environment and climate, and the creature can be seen as perfectly suited to its style of life.[25]

As these examples show, there is not inherent difficulty in the concept of the aesthetic appreciation of nature: whichever conception of a response to nature as nature is preferred, the idea of the aesthetic appreciation of nature as nature is coherent and it is possible for the aesthetic appreciation of nature to be solidly founded on characteristics that accrue to items in virtue of their being natural items of certain kinds.

VI

A further clarification of the idea of the aesthetic appreciation of nature is achieved by the resolution of a number of interlinked issues about the identification of natural things, ignorance of their nature, mistakes about them, and the relevance of 'scientific' understanding. What kind of understanding of nature does a correct and full aesthetic appreciation of it require? Do we need the knowledge of the natural scientist – the naturalist, the geologist, the biologist and the ecologist?[26] Does experiencing something with scientific understanding of it deepen or enhance the aesthetic appreciation of it? Does it matter aesthetically whether you correctly experience something as being a certain type of natural phenomenon or of natural kind K? Does it matter whether you misexperience something as being of a certain natural kind?[27] Does it matter whether you are not mistaken about, but ignorant of, the natural kind you are appreciating?[28]

Clearly, the mere ability to identify things as being of certain types on the basis of their appearance, to classify them (either under 'everyday' or 'technical' categories), to give names to them – to clouds, for example – does not thereby endow the subject with an enhanced appreciation of nature, although it may be the result of or encourage or facilitate a heightened or finer or richer awareness of natural features.[29] But there are cases where knowledge of the nature of a phenomenon – not merely the ability to identify that type – can transform one's aesthetic experience of nature. People have thicker or thinner conceptions of the nature of the phenomena which they see or otherwise perceive under concepts of those phenomena: children have exceptionally thin conceptions, adults have conceptions of greater and varying thickness. The thicker the conception, the greater the material available to transform the subject's aesthetic experience of nature. It follows that people can recruit to their perceptions of natural phenomena different levels of understanding, superficial or deep. If you have the right kind of understanding of nature, you can recruit to your perceptual experience of nature relevant thoughts, emotions and images unavailable to those who lack that understanding – as when you see a 'shooting star' *as* the glow of a meteor burning in the earth's atmosphere, or a gigantic crater *as* having been produced by the impact of a meteorite, or a canyon *as* having been cut by a swift-flowing river, or a mountain *as* a massive block of rock thrust up by enormous pressures beneath the earth's surface, or – an extreme case – the Himalayas *as* the product of a collision between the Indian subcontinent and the main bulk of Asia, or obsidian *as* a coal-black volcanic glass composed of fast-cooled lava, or stalactites, stalagmites and helictites *as* formed by minerals deposited by dripping water, or broomrape *as* a parasite that feeds on other plants. And the transformation your experience undergoes when relevant knowledge is enlisted carries with it the possibility of varieties of aesthetic appreciation of nature and species of aesthetic emotional responses otherwise unavailable.[30] If when looking at a cloud you identify its type as cumulonimbus, your aesthetic experience is not thereby transformed. But if, in virtue of additional knowledge, you see the anvil top and ragged base of a cumulonimbus as a *thundercloud*, your impression of the cloud might change, for you might now have a sense of *power* in the cloud and see it *as* shaped by powerful forces at work in it; and this sense of power will inform your experience and change the nature of your aesthetic response. Or consider the experience of looking at the Milky Way. As a child, you might experience it just as a white streak with a somewhat milky appearance running across the night sky. You might then come to see it as being the appearance of an exceptional congregation of stars in that region of the night sky, but possess no greater understanding of it. Finally, when you realize the truth about what you are seeing and why you are seeing it, your experience can assume quite a different nature: you now experience the Milky Way as the view into the heart of our galaxy, and by the use of your imagination you 'see' yourself as located on a small planet of a minor star on one of the spiralling arms near the edge of the galaxy into whose heart you are looking. A correct understanding of what is visible in the night sky thus makes possible a transformation of your experience from a condition in which you are struck by a milky path running across the sky to one in which your position in the universe – your position and that of everyone else you care about – is manifest to you in a manner that encourages an awareness of the minute stage on which the history of humanity unfolds, the peripheral status of what happens on the earth even in our own galaxy, the awesome immensity of the multitude of stars that compose that galaxy, and the realization that you are forever isolated from whatever civilizations, perhaps countlessly many, are present elsewhere in space and that you must remain ignorant of their different natures and histories, no matter how fascinating these might be. Such thoughts, harnessed to your perceptual experience, constitute an important change in your perspective, and are likely to produce one of those peculiar combinations of mental states that have been called experiences of the sublime[31] – in this case a feeling of wonder combined with an experience of vulnerability woven together with a sense of the relative insignificance of your individual self, a mental state with both a positive and a negative side, a duality that has often been thought of as the hallmark of an experience of the sublime.

But this is not to say that knowledge of the nature of a phenomenon always endows the subject with the ability to transform her perception of the world and facilitate an enhancement of aesthetic appreciation. Many of us know the explanation of rainbows, but not so many of us know the explanation of supernumerary bows. In either case, it seems that possession of the explanation does not make possible an aesthetic experience of its object that is otherwise unavailable. Most of us know that water is H_2O, but this knowledge does not enable an enhanced aesthetic appreciation of water, in dew, mist, rain, snow, rivers or waterfalls, for example. For knowledge of the nature of a natural phenomenon to be able to effect a transformation of the subject's aesthetic experience of it, the knowledge must be such that it can permeate or inform the perception of the phenomenon, so that what the subject sees it *as* is different from how it is seen by someone who lacks the requisite knowledge. We do not see water or copper differently from one who is ignorant of their nature: we do not see water as H_2O or copper as possessing atomic number 29, for the knowledge we bring to our perception is not such as to integrate with the perception in such a manner as to generate a new perceptual-cum-imaginative content of experience.

If you misexperience an item as being of natural kind K through misperception, then of course your aesthetic appreciation of it is malfounded. But to misexperience an item as being of a certain natural kind is not of any aesthetic significance if, first there is no error in perception, and, second, the mistake is merely a matter of getting the *name* wrong, as when I can see a flower perfectly clearly, mistakenly take it to be an orchid (when in fact it is a fritillary) and have no further knowledge of or belief about either kind. Suppose, however, that you do have some relevant knowledge of two natural kinds and you misidentify the natural kind to which an item belongs, the mistake not being founded on misperception. In such a case, the item will usually possess many aspects that you can respond to aesthetically without error *as* aspects of a natural thing, although you are mistaken about what kind of thing it is.[32] But if you aesthetically appreciate a natural object *as* an instance of natural kind K, and it is not of kind K, then your appreciation is, in that respect, malfounded, and an awareness of your mistake undermines *that* aspect of your appreciation. For it is no longer available to you with respect to that object and you must reject as mistaken the enjoyment or excitement you felt that arose from this misapprehension. Furthermore, your misidentification might in any case result in aesthetic deprivation, for the correct identification of the type of natural object before you might enable an additional element of aesthetic appreciation of nature as nature: perceiving the thing under its true kind might allow not only the appreciation of all that the mistaken identification allows that is not malfounded, but something aesthetically valuable in addition.

Notes

1 But in fact the relevant understanding of the concept of nature cannot be determined by putting aesthetic considerations entirely to one side: the desired distinction between the natural and the non-natural can be drawn only by bearing in mind the purpose for which it is required.

2 Of course, this is not the only way of understanding the idea of the aesthetic appreciation of nature, which might instead be understood to mean no more than the aesthetic appreciation of anything that is available in nature for aesthetic appreciation – any *natural* thing or phenomenon that is susceptible of aesthetic appreciation. But just as artistic appreciation is the appreciation of art *as* art, so the aesthetic appreciation of nature should be understood to demand the appreciation of nature *as* nature. It will be clear that my conception of the aesthetic appreciation of nature requires that one appreciates nature *under a concept*, so that on Kant's understanding of the experience of finding something 'freely' beautiful, the aesthetic appreciation of nature is impossible – a conclusion profoundly unsympathetic to Kant, given the special claim he makes for it. See note 14.

3 It follows that those who have assigned primacy to the aesthetic appreciation of art will find it hard to accommodate the aesthetic appreciation of nature *as nature*. The account of the aesthetic that I later offer

assigns priority neither to the appreciation of art nor to the appreciation of nature. Of course, art can be imposed on nature, in which case aesthetic appreciation will combine the aesthetic appreciation of art with the aesthetic appreciation of nature as nature. See note 10.

4 Those who have regarded nature as an artefact of God and have delighted aesthetically in it *as* such a creation, so that their appreciation is permeated by the idea of it as the creation of God, appreciate nature as an artefact, but not thereby as a work of art (unless it is God's revealed intention that it should be so regarded). The aesthetic appreciation of nature might well be understood to require that nature is not seen as an artefact, which would appear to rule that the aesthetic appreciation of nature as an artefact of God falls outside the aesthetic appreciation of nature as nature; but an artefact is normally something made from what is present in nature, and the creation of nature *ex nihilo*, rather than from pre-existing natural things, might well be thought, in virtue of its exceptional character, to fall outside the requirement. Nevertheless, the aesthetic appreciation of nature as an artefact of God conceives of nature as being designed, and inasmuch as God's design is read into nature its appreciation differs in a crucial respect from the aesthetic appreciation of nature as nature.

5 In a different context Hume wrote: 'our answer to this question depends upon the definition of the word, Nature, than which there is none more ambiguous and equivocal'. (David Hume, *A Treatise of Human Nature*, Book III, Part I, §II).

6 'Man-made' is here understood not only in a gender-free sense, but as including anything made by another, non-human, intelligent species as a result of a decision to do so, if there should be such a species in the universe.

7 But insofar as it is a human artefact (usually a self-artefact), it is a natural item stamped with human activity, even if not 'aestheticized' by human design. In one sense, what makes a human body a natural object – whether it has been produced naturally or by artificial means – is the fact that its principle of growth as it endures through time is a matter of nature, not human contrivance: as with certain other kinds of natural objects, trees, for example, the pattern of growth of human bodies is inherent in them.

8 Arthur Schopenhauer, *The World as Will and Representation*, trans. E. F. J. Payne (New York: Dover Publications, 1969), vol. 1, §41, and 'On the Metaphysics of the Beautiful and Aesthetics', §212, in *Parerga and Paralipomena*, vol. 2, trans E. F. J. Payne (Oxford: Clarendon Press, 1974). Schopenhauer's thoughts about the aesthetic appeal of natural ensembles of natural objects, rather than the aesthetic contemplation of an individual natural thing,

reveal his difficulty in accommodating the insights yielded by his own aesthetic experience within the general framework of his metaphysics and aesthetics.

9 Arthur Schopenhauer, *The World as Will and Representation*, vol. 1 §41.

10 See Kendall L. Walton, 'Categories of Art', *The Philosophical Review*, LXXIX (1970), and Arthur C. Danto, *The Transfiguration of the Commonplace* (London: Harvard University Press, 1983).

11 From an aesthetic point of view, the imposition of art on the natural world, or making a portion of nature into a work of art, as with garden design or the art of landscape, the aesthetic appreciation of which requires two forms of aesthetic appreciation to function hand in hand, is of special interest. There are significant differences between the appeal of 'wild' nature and any form of domesticated nature or nature stamped with human design, and within the second class there are further differences, especially between those instances subjected to art and those not so subjected.

12 If to be completely natural a scene must lack all signs of humanity, there cannot be people in it. If all that needs to be missing are signs of human artifice, then, since human bodies are natural objects, but *clothed* human bodies are not, although the scene cannot contain clothed human bodies it can contain naked human bodies – so long as they do not indicate artifice. (But perhaps the manifest possibility of human artifice, as indicated by the presence of human bodies, might be thought to detract from the naturalness of the scene, thus avoiding this curious result.)

13 A beholder might not be aware that a landscape has been in some ways designed by humanity and might delight in it as nature's handiwork. In such a case, although the delight in the way in which the elements of the landscape relate to one another is aesthetic delight in what is taken to be nature as nature, it is malfounded: it is not delight in what actually is natural as being natural.

14 In fact, taking nature to be opposed to art (or artefactuality), the external conception can assume two forms, the non-artistic and the anti-artistic. The non-artistic construes 'as nature' to mean only 'not in virtue of being a work of art'. An example of the non-artistic response would be this: an observer comes across an object, does not know, and is indifferent to, whether it is a natural object or a work of art, yet finds its appearance beautiful (whatever the status of the object might be). The anti-artistic construes 'as nature' to mean '*in virtue* of lacking the distinctive properties of works of art'. In this case, the observer is not indifferent to whether the object appreciated is a work of nature or of art; on the contrary, the observer's response is founded on the thought that the object is not art.

15 Kant insisted that you experience an object as being 'freely', as opposed to 'dependently', beautiful only if your pleasure in perceiving it is founded on nothing other than, as I shall put it, the analogue content of your perception of an object's intrinsic nature, and then only on the perceived 'form' of the object, so that any other concepts under which you perceive it play no essential role in generating and maintaining the pleasure. He also held that the aesthetic appreciation of natural beauty is, paradigmatically, a matter of free beauty. This conjunction of views implies that there is no such thing as the aesthetic appreciation of nature as beautiful, in the internal sense. The moral is that experiencing an item *under a concept* has a much greater significance in aesthetic experience than is credited to it by Kant's aesthetic theory.

16 To experience O under description 'D' is for it to seem to you in your experience that O is D: this is how your experience represents O.

17 We cannot even reasonably conclude how in the most fundamental sense it sounds to a song thrush on the basis of how it sounds to us. For example, a song thrush might hear additional sounds in the song, sounds too high for us to hear.

18 But is this quite right? To appreciate it fully does one need to appreciate it as the song of *a bird*, specifically? And, if so, as the song of a particular kind of bird, a blackbird, for example? Most of us acquire, at best, the concept of a certain type of bird and, perhaps, an idea of the look of a bird of that type, or an ability to recognize such a bird by sight. Aesthetic appreciation of a bird's song appears to be the same before and after you learn which type of bird it is, or whether you know it's a song thrush, say, and how a song thrush looks, at rest or in flight.

19 Leaving aside his misbegotten notion of an 'aesthetic idea', Kant operated with an exceptionally clear and minimal conception of the aesthetic: a judgement is aesthetic if and only if it is one whose 'determining ground' cannot be other than 'subjective', that is, a feeling of pleasure or displeasure (see Immanuel Kant, *Critique of Aesthetic Judgement*, §1). And he distinguished three positive types (although there are more): the judgement that an item is pleasant, the judgement that an item is beautiful, and the judgement that an item is sublime. (In fact, Kant maintained that we speak improperly in predicating sublimity of a natural item: the natural item is only the occasion of our becoming conscious of our superiority to nature in being moral agents, the experience of which is properly called 'sublime'.) In what follows, I am not rejecting this conception but offering a rather more substantial conception of the aesthetic – or, at least, of an aesthetic response. Jerrold Levinson presents a superior conception of aesthetic pleasure in his 'pleasure, aesthetic', in David Cooper (ed.), *A Companion to Aesthetics*

(Oxford: Blackwell, 1992); Kendall Walton presents a superior conception of aesthetic value (and also aesthetic pleasure) in 'How Marvelous! Toward a Theory of Aesthetic Value', *The Journal of Aesthetics and Art Criticism*, vol. 51 no. 3 (Summer 1993).

20 'An item' includes not just physical objects or combinations of objects, or types, but also appearances, events, processes and any other kind of thing that is susceptible of aesthetic appreciation. 'Experienced properties' is to be understood in an all-embracing sense, covering not only immediately perceptible properties, but also relational, representational, symbolic and emotional properties, and including the type or kind of thing the item is experienced as being.

21 This means that aesthetic pleasure is 'disinterested' in Kant's sense (see op. cit., §2).

22 Traditionally, the aesthetic appreciation of nature was often thought of as consisting of two (positive) kinds: the aesthetic experience of the beautiful and the aesthetic experience of the sublime. How comprehensive this typology is, and in particular whether it is exhaustive of the possibilities, depends on how these two kinds of experience are characterized. It will not be exhaustive unless the beautiful covers all purely positive possible aesthetic responses to nature, and the sublime all positive responses with an admixture of negative emotion.

23 Compare and contrast the difficulty in seeing how the mere fact that an item is a work of art – rather than some specific property it possesses in virtue of being, not nature, but a work of art – could ground an aesthetic response to the item *as* a work art.

24 The aesthetic appreciation of nature is often restricted to the 'macroscopic'. But there is no good reason for excluding microscopic entities or the appearances of natural items (snowflakes, for example) when seen, not with the naked eye, but under a microscope. There is no relevant difference between unaided perception, perception by means of a microscope and many other forms of aided perception – perception of distant objects by optical telescopes, for example.

25 'It is evident, that one considerable source of *beauty* in all animals is the advantage which they reap from the particular structure of their limbs and members, suitably to the particular manner of life, to which they are by nature destined' (David Hume, *An Enquiry Concerning The Principles of Morals*, Section VI, Part II). The well-known opening lines of Hopkins' *The Windhover*, which seek to capture a falcon's manner of flight and an observer's emotional response to the enviable ability that enables the falcon to flourish in the element in which it must live, provide a vivid illustration:

I caught this morning morning's minion, king- / dom of daylight's dauphin, dapple-dawn-drawn Falcon, in his riding / Of the rolling level underneath him steady air, and striding / High there, how he rung upon the rein of a wimpling wing / In his ecstasy! then off, off forth on swing, / As a skate's heel sweeps smooth on a bow-bend: the hurl and gliding / Rebuffed the big wind. My heart in hiding / Stirred for a bird, – the achieve of, the mastery of the thing!

26　As Allen Carlson has argued: see, for example, 'Appreciation and the Natural Environment', *Journal of Aesthetics and Art Criticism*, vol. 37 (1979), reprinted in Alex Neill and Aaron Ridley (eds), *Arguing about Art* (London: McGraw-Hill, 1995).

27　The question concerns the misidentification of the natural kind to which the object belongs, not the misidentification of a natural object as a work of art or vice versa. This other question (along with much else, especially significant differences between the aesthetic appreciation of nature and artistic appreciation, about which I have said nothing in this paper) is well dealt with in R. W. Hepburn's seminal essay 'Contemporary Aesthetics and the Neglect of Natural Beauty', in B. Williams and A. Montefiore (eds), *British Analytical Philosophy* (London: Routledge and Kegan Paul, 1966), reprinted in Hepburn's *'Wonder' and Other Essays* (Edinburgh: Edinburgh University Press, 1984). There are further kinds of misunderstanding of the natural world that affect the aesthetic appreciation of nature, but these are also not my concern here.

28　Ignorance about the natural kind you are appreciating can be more or less extreme: you might see a flower but not *as* a flower, only as a coloured three-dimensional natural object of some kind jutting from the earth: or you might see an arum lily as a flower of some kind, but one that you do not recognize.

29　But unless you see O as being of natural kind K, you cannot experience it as being, or not being, an especially beautiful specimen of *that kind*.

30　The transformation of perception effected by knowledge of the nature of an object of aesthetic appreciation will by no means always result in an intensification of aesthetic delight. On the contrary, it can diminish or erase it, as might happen when a plant is seen as poisonous; or the beautiful appearance of a turquoise sea anemone might recede or disappear when its protuberances are seen as tentacles with the power to paralyse small prey and its greenish centre is seen as its mouth.

31　Kant disallowed such thoughts to enter into the experience of the sublime in nature, but his reason for doing so is not compelling (see Immanuel Kant, *Critique of Aesthetic Judgement*, 'General Remark upon the Exposition of Aesthetic Reflective Judgements').

32　As Noël Carroll has emphasized, and has illustrated with someone's taking a whale to be a fish, rather than a mammal: see his 'On Being Moved by Nature: Between Religion and Natural History', in Salim Kemal and Ivan Gaskell (eds), *Landscape, Natural Beauty and the Arts* (Cambridge: Cambridge University Press, 1993), reprinted in Alex Neill and Aaron Ridley (eds), *Arguing about Art* (London: McGraw-Hill, 1995).

Index